BK 296.61 S368S
SABBATAI SEVI; THE MYSTICAL MESSIAH, 1626-1
/SCHOL
1973 11.00 FV
418120 3001
St. Louis Community College

D0152882
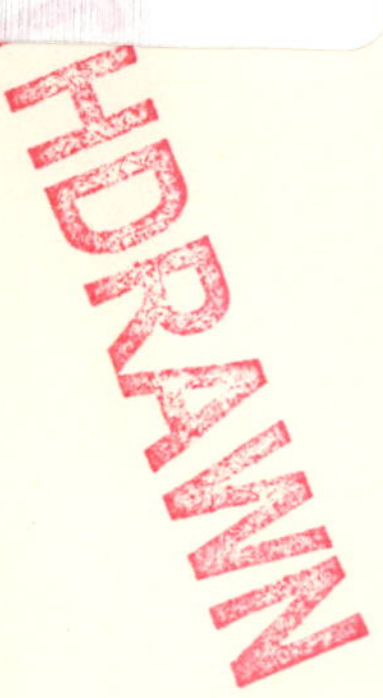
HDRAWN

EV

BOLLINGEN SERIES XCIII

True Portrait of Sabbatai Ṣevi, sketched by an eyewitness in Smyrna, 1666. From Thomas Coenen, *Ydele Verwachtinge der Joden . . .* (Amsterdam, 1669)

GERSHOM SCHOLEM

SABBATAI ṢEVI

The Mystical Messiah

1626–1676

BOLLINGEN SERIES XCIII

PRINCETON UNIVERSITY PRESS

THIS IS THE NINETY-THIRD
IN A SERIES OF WORKS
SPONSORED BY BOLLINGEN FOUNDATION

A revised and augmented translation of the Hebrew edition: *Shabbatai Ṣevi veha-tenuᶜah ha-shabbethaʾith bi-yemei ḥayyav* (Sabbatai Ṣevi and the Sabbatian Movement during His Lifetime), published by Am Oved, Tel Aviv, Israel, 1957.

ISBN 0-691-01809-x (paperback edn.)
ISBN 0-691-09916-2 (hardcover edn.)

Library of Congress catalogue card no. 75-166389
Printed in the United States of America

First PRINCETON/BOLLINGEN PAPERBACK printing, 1975
Second hardcover printing, with corrections, 1975

TO MY WIFE FANIA

in remembrance of all those years

of common purpose

Paradox is a characteristic of truth. What communis opinio *has of truth is surely no more than an elementary deposit of generalizing partial understanding, related to truth even as sulphurous fumes are to lightning.*

—From the correspondence of Count Paul Yorck von Wartenburg and Wilhelm Dilthey

True Portrait of Nathan of Gaza, sketched by an eyewitness in Smyrna, 1667. From Thomas Coenen, *Ydele Verwachtinge der Joden* . . . (Amsterdam, 1669)

PREFACE

I

A DETAILED HISTORY of the Sabbatian movement, the most important messianic movement in Judaism since the destruction of the Second Temple, has long been badly lacking in Jewish historiography. When, thirty-five years ago, I published my Hebrew essay "Redemption through Sin," now available in English in my book *The Messianic Idea in Judaism,* my aim was to establish a basis for understanding the ideas which determined the character of the movement as it developed after the apostasy of Sabbatai Ṣevi, and particularly after his death. But direct contact with the sources has made me realize that historians have never done justice to this great and tragic chapter in Jewish history, either because they lacked the knowledge or because they lacked even the wish for knowledge. In my innocence I assumed that we at least had adequate factual information about the messianic outburst until the apostasy of the messiah, about the life of Sabbatai Ṣevi, and about the development of the movement before it reached its crisis. All that I needed to do, so I thought, was to provide the accurate historical perspective which was so noticeably absent from the existing literature. But it became clear that even this expectation was much too optimistic. As I became more deeply involved with the sources, I became convinced not only that important and vital sources had escaped the eyes of previous scholars, but that even those sources which had been used were often not correctly interpreted.

I myself was surprised by the wealth of unknown material that I uncovered which shed new light on all phases of Sabbatai Ṣevi's career, and it soon became apparent that the entire picture of the movement's history had to be reconstructed from the start. Since then I have published a series of sources and studies relevant to the subject. Moreover, others have followed suit and have undertaken research in this neglected field. As a result of all this spadework a comprehensive and lively picture of the entire Sabbatian movement began slowly to emerge.

The present work is a synthesis that offers a comprehensive history of the movement up to the deaths of Sabbatai Ṣevi and of his prophet, Nathan of Gaza, and I hope that I will be able to complete at a later time a sequel covering the history of Sabbatianism in its various forms after the death of Sabbatai Ṣevi—its conflicts, its metamorphoses, and its reverberations.

In this book I hope to prove that those sources which historians have tended to regard with particular contempt are the very sources which can make an essential contribution to an understanding of the period. What I have in mind are the documents of kabbalistic literature and the theological writings of the followers of Sabbatai Ṣevi. This literature has not been considered worthy of the attention of "enlightened" Jews (among whom one is inclined, of course, to include historians). Most of the heretical literature of the Sabbatians was destroyed during the persecution of the sectarians in the eighteenth century, and it has been virtually unknown that important parts of it survived. Half-articulated mutterings about mystical secrets, symbols, and images, all rooted in the world of esoterica and in the abstruse speculations of the kabbalists, became transformed, in my eyes, into invaluable keys to an understanding of important historical processes and into matters worthy of profound analysis and serious discussion. Sources and documents of this kind, which formerly found no place in historical literature, receive as much attention in the present book as do other archival documents, manuscripts, and broadsheets of all kinds, among which I have also found much new information. Often one type of source sheds light on another. Only by combining and analyzing all kinds of sources in the light of historical criticism can one gain a true picture of the age.

I have written this book on the basis of a particular dialectical view of Jewish history and the forces acting within it. But from the start more than just this view has been at work, guiding my presentation—the view itself is the outcome of a constantly renewed immersion in the sources themselves. I have not hesitated to change the opinions I expressed in earlier publications on specific points when renewed consideration of the sources required a new interpretation of the documents or of the historical processes reflected in them. I do not hold to the opinion of those (and there are indeed many of them) who view the events of Jewish history from a fixed dogmatic standpoint and who know exactly whether some phenomenon or another is "Jewish" or not. Nor am I a follower of that school which proceeds on the assumption that there is a well-defined and unvarying "essence" of Judaism, especially not where the evaluation of historical events is concerned. The internal censorship of the past, particularly by rabbinical tradition, has tended to play down or to conceal many developments whose fundamentally Jewish character the contemporary historian has no reason to deny. We are frequently as surprised by the level of vitality inherent in these developments as we are by their boldness and radicalism of thought. The last two generations have had their eyes opened and have been able to perceive the spark of Jewish life and the constructive aspirations even in phenomena which Orthodox Jewish tradition has denounced with full force.

One of the remarkable features of research on Sabbatianism is the tendency to minimize the scope of the movement and to distort its meaning. Although such a stance is understandable among Orthodox Jews, what is surprising is that it has also been adopted, without further reflection, by scholars whose basic historical approach is far removed from the traditionalists. Critical faculties which are so alert when dealing with other weighty issues seem almost to slumber and to become blinded when it comes to the Sabbatian movement and its transformations. The reason for this obtuseness is obviously the rationalist outlook, which narrows the historical perspective and prevents an unbiased understanding of phenomena such as the mystical movement in Judaism. If the narrowing of vision was destructive and caused distortions, misapprehensions, and general indifference even in the field of kabbalah and Hasidism, then one should not wonder at its having had an even more adverse effect on assessments of the Sabbatian movement. The lack of objectivity among scholars was brought about both by the sheer irrationality, so to speak, of the events they were studying and by their moral condemnation of the consequences of the movement and of many of its leaders. This rationalist perversion of sound judgment is especially visible in the chapters on Sabbatianism in the books of Heinrich Graetz, David Kahana, and Shlomoh Rosanes. For all the debt we owe to these pioneers in Sabbatian research, we cannot avoid recognizing that much of their argument is faulty and does not stand up to a critical review. The picture that will unfold in the chapters that follow differs fundamentally from theirs both in general and in detail. Even when, by good fortune, a writer of imagination and psychological insight approached the history of Sabbatai Ṣevi, his knowledge of the sources was extremely limited and he filled the vacuum created by the lack of historical content with rather nebulous psychological fiction. Josef Kastein's *The Messiah of Izmir* (1931), written along these lines, was hitherto the only volume on the subject published in the twentieth century.

I have tried to learn from my predecessors while evading their pitfalls and their partisanship. This book was not written for the sake of an apology nor as a condemnation but in order to elucidate all aspects of the very complex phenomenon known as Sabbatianism. No doubt, it would also be possible to write on this subject from a metaphysical and theological, a-historical point of view. This book however, was not written as a treatise on theology but as a contribution to an understanding of the history of the Jewish people. Insofar as theology is discussed—and a great deal of theology, for that matter—it is done in pursuit of historical insight. A movement which shook the House of Israel to its very foundations and has revealed not only the vitality of the Jewish people but also the deep, dangerous, and destructive dialectics inherent in the messianic idea cannot be understood without considering questions that reach down to fundamentals. I admit that in such discussions much depends on the basic outlook of the historian with regard to what he considers the constitutive elements of the historical process. Perhaps it is permissible at this point to say, with all due caution, that Jewish historiography has generally chosen to ignore the fact that the Jewish people have paid a very high price for the messianic idea. If this book may be regarded as a small contribution to considering a big question: What price messianism?— a question which touches upon the very essence of our being and survival—then I hope that any reader who studies it from this point of view will obtain some reward. Anyone who can appreciate the gravity of this problem will also understand why I have refrained from expressing opinions or drawing conclusions with respect to any contemporary issues bound to arise out of the subject matter with which this book deals.

II

Since the publication of this book in Hebrew, in 1957, and not unconnected with it, a considerable number of hitherto unknown sources have come to light. They supplied an important body of new information which enabled me to correct earlier statements and to present entirely new details, some of them highly significant. The most impressive of these documents were contained in the collection of manuscripts that until 1924 had formed a part of the archives of the Sabbatian sect of the Dönmeh in Salonika, which had embraced Islam following Sabbatai Ṣevi's example and had kept its identity distinct throughout the ages. The archives had been inaccessible to outsiders and were generally thought to have been lost, especially after the great fire of 1917. This fire was known to have destroyed at least part of them. Only after the appearance of my book in Hebrew did it transpire that, at the time of the exchange of populations between Greece and Turkey in 1925, a group of Dönmeh departing for Turkey had handed over some particularly valuable manuscripts to the late rabbi Saul Amarillo in Salonika, who, taking a lively interest in the history of Salonika Jewry, kept the treasure but allowed no rumor about it to reach the scholarly world. It survived the period of the Nazi occupation of Greece, concealed in Athens. Mr. Abraham Albert Amarillo, a son of the owner, settled in Israel and, after the publication of my book, remembered the hidden papers and, in 1960, transferred them as a precious gift to the Ben-Zvi Institute for the History of Oriental Jewish Communities, affiliated with the Hebrew University in Jerusalem. They contain, among others, autograph letters written by outstanding figures of the movement, chronicles that no one had dreamed existed, and confirm in a striking manner the new insight into Sabbatai Ṣevi's character and psychology advanced in the present book.

All the new sources have been taken into account in preparing the English edition, which therefore is no mere translation from the Hebrew but embodies the results of the latest research.

The credit for the English version is due to Dr. R. J. Zwi Werblowsky, Professor of Comparative Religion at the Hebrew University in Jerusalem, who—over several years—invested much time and work in its preparation. Literary Hebrew is notoriously difficult to translate into English. The original edition of the present work was addressed to Hebrew readers—which, in the nature of things, also means, in the main, Jewish readers. Hence, the author could assume familiarity with certain ideas, concepts, traditions, institutions, rituals, liturgical practices, historical events, and names. In the case of the English reader such familiarity could not be taken for granted, and therefore translating meant not only rewriting the Hebrew, to do justice to the spirit of the English language, but also occasionally paraphrasing, enlarging, or adding explanatory remarks. Werblowsky's virtuosity in this respect and his deep familiarity with the subject enabled him to carry out this decidedly difficult task. I wish to express my gratitude and obligation to Professor Werblowsky, without whose assistance this book could not have attained the degree of readability which I hope will recommend it to the reader.

Some documents which are composed in a flowery rabbinical style have been condensed to make their content clear without the rhetorical ornament that could not well bear literal translation. Sometimes, when the subject matter was too technical and hinged on the minute analysis of words and phrases in Hebrew documents, the argument was merely summarized and the more expert reader referred to the fuller discussion in the original edition. Biblical quotations are rendered according to the Authorized Version or that of the Jewish Publication Society of America, except in those not infrequent cases where the context necessitated another translation. Biblical verses were often interpreted in a playful or a mystical manner in Hebrew literature, and it would be misleading to translate them according to their literal meaning wherever it was necessary to establish the connection with the kabbalistic or theological exegesis which it was meant to serve.

The whole English manuscript, from beginning to end, has again been revised and in many places enlarged by me. My grateful thanks are also due to Miss Lisa McGaw who copy-edited the final manuscript and shared—together with Professor Werblowsky—the main burden of proofreading. I cannot conclude these remarks without deep thanks to the Bollingen Foundation, which for years took great interest in the preparation of this work, and without mentioning the friendship and sympathy with which Mr. John D. Barrett, its president, has accompanied the progress of this book through all its tribulations to its final stage. My thanks go equally to Mr. William McGuire who, as associate editor of the Bollingen Series, generously gave his invaluable advice in many matters pertaining to its publication.

I wish to acknowledge the help that libraries and archives have extended to me. Among the institutions that agreed to the use and publication of their material I feel especially indebted to the Jewish National and University Library, Jerusalem; the Ben-Zvi Institute, Jerusalem; the Library of the Schocken Institute, Jerusalem; the British Museum, London; the Public Record Office, London; the Bodleian Library, Oxford; the Bibliotheca Rosenthaliana in the University Library, Amsterdam; the Library (*Eṣ Ḥayyim*) of the Portuguese Jewish Community, Amsterdam; the University Library, Cracow; the Jewish Theological Seminary, New York; the Library of Columbia University, New York; the Library of the Hebrew Union College, Cincinnati; the Zentralbibliothek, Zurich; the State Archive, Oslo. Many of these institutions have given me exceedingly liberal assistance during my work there. Last but not least, Mr. Zalman Shazar, now President of the State of Israel, permitted me to quote extensively from a Yiddish manuscript source in his possession, the *Beshraybung fun Shabsai Ẓvi,* written 1717/18 by Leyb b. Ozer, the notary of the Ashkenazic community in Amsterdam.

Jerusalem, September 1971 GERSHOM SCHOLEM

TABLE OF CONTENTS

2

THE BEGINNINGS OF SABBATAI ṢEVI (1626–1664) 103

3

THE BEGINNINGS OF THE MOVEMENT IN PALESTINE (1665) 199

4

THE MOVEMENT UP TO SABBATAI'S IMPRISONMENT IN GALLIPOLI (1665–1666) 327

5

THE MOVEMENT IN EUROPE (1666) 461

LIST OF PLATES

TABLE OF TRANSLITERATION

A measure of consistency in the transliteration of Hebrew has been aimed at, but absolute uniformity proved unfeasible. As a rule the system given here has been followed. For names and terms with a more or less established English spelling (e.g., kabbalah, Cordovero) the latter has been used instead of the philologically more accurate transcription. An outstanding example of the resulting inconsistency is the spelling of the name *Ṣevi*, although as a rule every Hebrew [בּ] is transcribed as *b* (e.g., *Ṣiṣath Nobel Ṣevi*). Biblical names are generally given in the form used in the Authorized Version. Modern Hebrew names or titles of books are given in the form in which they usually appear in print.

א	ᵓ	מ	m
ב בּ	b	נ	n
ג	g	ס	s
ד	d	ע	ᶜ
ה	h	פּ	p
ו	w	פ	f
ז	z	צ	ṣ
ח	ḥ	ק	q
ט	t	ר	r
י	y	שׁ	sh
כּ	k	שׂ	s
כ	kh	תּ	t
ל	l	ת	th

SABBATAI ṢEVI

THE MYSTICAL MESSIAH

1

THE BACKGROUND OF THE SABBATIAN MOVEMENT

I

A SURVEY of Jewish history during the period immediately preceding the outbreak of Sabbatian messianism would unduly surpass the limits of the present study. Nonetheless there are problems that cannot go unmentioned if we are to understand the generation that gave birth to this messianic movement. Many factors were involved in producing the events described in the following pages. An analysis of their relative importance is all the more urgent as historians have reached no unanimity in answering the great initial question: What exactly were the decisive factors that brought about the messianic outbreak?

The usual, somewhat simplistic explanation posits a direct historical connection between the Sabbatian movement and certain other events of the same period. According to this view, the messianic outbreak was a direct consequence of the terrible catastrophe that had overtaken Polish Jewry in 1648–49 (see below, pp. 88–93) and had shaken the very foundations of the great Jewish community in Poland. The destruction had, in fact, surpassed anything known of earlier persecutions in other countries. This explanation was plausible enough as long as it could be maintained—as, indeed, it has been until now—

that Sabbatianism as a popular movement started as far back as 1648, when Sabbatai Ṣevi came forward for the first time with messianic claims. It was supposed that Sabbatai's followers conducted a propaganda campaign, converting more and more believers until the movement reached its climax in 1666. Though it will be argued in what follows that there is no foundation whatever for this view, at the outset we may duly take note of one grimly concrete historical fact: there had been a major disaster, and soon afterward there was a messianic outbreak. The real significance of the former for an understanding of the genesis of the latter will become clearer as our story unfolds.

Even on its own premises the aforementioned explanation accounts for only half the facts—and the lesser half, for that matter. The weightiest argument against overestimating the causative role of the massacres of 1648 follows from a consideration of the difference between the Sabbatian outbreak and previous messianic movements. This difference lies in the extension, in space and time, of Sabbatianism. All earlier messianic movements, from Bar Kokhba, who led the Jewish revolt against Rome in 132–35 C.E., onward, were limited to a certain area. Somewhere a prophet, or possibly a messiah himself, arose proclaiming that the end of days was at hand and launched a movement limited to a province or a country. Never before had there been a movement that swept the whole House of Israel. It would seem unwise to try and explain this wide extension by factors that were operative in one area only, whatever their weight and significance there. Our caution will increase when we consider the fact that the Sabbatian movement did not originate in Poland but in Palestine. If the massacres of 1648 were in any sense its principal cause, why did the messiah not arise within Polish Jewry? And if there was such a messiah, why did he fail to rouse the masses, and why did he sink into oblivion? The Sabbatian movement spread wherever Jews lived—from the Yemen, Persia, and Kurdistan to Poland, Holland, Italy, and Morocco. There is no reason for assuming that Moroccan Jewry was particularly affected by the massacres of 1648, of which they probably had heard very little anyway. It is also a remarkable fact that Polish Jews were not particularly conspicuous among the main propagandists of the movement.

Of even greater relevance to our argument is the collapse of earlier messianic movements as a result of disappointment. Initial reports turned out to be untrue, the messiah disappeared or was killed, and the movement petered out. This was the usual course of things; but for some contemporary chroniclers or letter writers not even an echo of many of these movements would have reached us. Occasionally traditions about such an outbreak would linger in popular memory, but after a generation or two everything would be forgotten. The Sabbatian movement is the great exception to this rule: not only did history belie its message, but the disillusionment was so exceptionally cruel that normally it should have been the last nail to the movement's coffin. The messiah had apostatized and publicly betrayed his mission. If the movement did not die out there and then but survived the seemingly fatal crisis, persisting for generations in various forms and metamorphoses, then its roots must have lain deeper than in local circumstances and conditions. Indeed, they must have reached down to the layer of common heritage on which the attitudes of seventeenth-century Jewry as a whole were founded. The massacres of 1648 no doubt contributed their share, but as an historical factor they lack the dimension of depth within which alone the Sabbatian movement becomes intelligible. We must, therefore, look for other factors of wider and more fundamental validity.

The quest for other specific conditions, common to Poland as well as other Jewish communities, is not likely to be more successful. In some countries the situation was actually or potentially one of persecution, and the message of redemption could reasonably be expected to find ready ears. Persia, the Yemen, and Morocco are instances of this kind. However, the movement did not manifest any lesser momentum in those Jewish centers that enjoyed peace and prosperity. If these communities too were haunted by a sense of catastrophe, it did not stem from their immediate experience but from deeper and less specific causes.

For the same reason we must view with grave doubts all attempts at an easy sociological or economic explanation of the Sabbatian success, all the more so as there is no possibility at all of describing the movement in terms of an eruption of social or class tensions within Jewry. As regards the economic situation, one is struck by the similarity of responses to the messianic tidings in ruined and pauperized communities, such as Poland, and in the most prosperous and flourishing centers. The Jewries of Constantinople, Salonika, Leghorn, Amsterdam, and Hamburg, whose star had for some time been in the ascendant, were in the vanguard of Sabbatian enthusiasm. Christian contemporaries more than once voiced their angry surprise at the privileges and freedoms enjoyed by the Jews of Salonika, Leghorn, and Amsterdam. Yet these Jews threw all economic considerations to the winds and, as far as we can ascertain, gave way to unbridled messianic enthusiasm. Our knowledge of the last-named communities and of their attitudes during the messianic outbreak is good. Turkish Jewry was safely established and had not yet passed its prime. Palestinian Jewry was, as usual, sunk in the depths of misery, but its misery has no bearing on our evaluation of the position of the Jews in the rest of the expanding Ottoman Empire in which anti-Jewish persecutions were extremely rare and ran counter to the considered policy of its rulers. Here, in the empire, by far the great majority of Spanish Jews, the main bearers of the Sabbatian movement, had settled. The amazing rise of the communities of Amsterdam and Hamburg is well known. Yet the members of these communities, descendants of marranos, reacted no differently from their brethren in Morocco who smarted under almost continuous oppression and persecution.

The question of internal social relations is far more delicate and obscure and requires very careful examination. Whatever the legitimacy of generalizations about the attitudes of particular communities to Sabbatianism, we ought still to ask what were the personal and social differences in the attitudes of the rich and the poor, of the ruling class and the masses. The problem is much confused by the subsequent arguments of both Sabbatian believers and opponents. In the years of the great disillusionment following Sabbatai's apostasy, the opponents again raised their heads and contended that the "rabble" had forced the unwilling rabbis and sages to comply or, at least, to keep quiet. Conversely we find the Sabbatians themselves accusing the rabbis and the rich, that is, the social elite, of opposing the movement.[1] The suspicion that the response to the Sabbatian message was conditioned by social factors thus appears to be confirmed by both sides and supported by such diverse witnesses as Jacob Sasportas and Joseph ha-Levi on the one hand, and Abraham Miguel Cardozo on

1. Abraham Miguel Cardozo, in a Spanish letter addressed to his brother (MS. Oxford 2481, fol. 4b), argues that opposition from the leading classes was necessary in order that the truth about the messiah should appear doubtful and belief in him be an act of faith. Cardozo's argument seems to reflect the state of affairs *after* Sabbatai's apostasy. Also, the prophet Nathan began to accuse the "rich misers" after the apostasy; see below, ch. 7.

the other. This unanimity, however, is misleading, and the measure of truth that it contains is less than appears at first sight. We are dealing here with an explanation after the fact, useful to both sides, though for opposite reasons. It provided an easy way out to the leaders of the Jewish communities—particularly if they were anti-Sabbatians—who could now exculpate themselves and their colleagues by claiming that their unwilling co-operation had been extorted under pressure from the "mob." The Sabbatians, on the other hand, who wanted an explanation for the failure of the movement, could easily agree with their opponents and point to them as the scapegoats whose lack of true faith had led to the messianic debacle.

None of these explanations is borne out, however, by the documents composed during the high tide of the movement. True enough, the opposition to Sabbatai Ṣevi included rich merchants, lay leaders, and rabbis, that is, members of the ruling class. There is nothing surprising in this. The theologians were faced with grave religious and intellectual difficulties by the personality and behavior of the "messiah"; their doubts could easily turn to opposition. The rich had something to lose by the new order which the messiah was supposed to inaugurate. The "small man" was more easily drawn into the emotional vortex generated by the messianic proclamation; he had neither reason nor strength to resist. All the more surprising is the real proportion of believers and unbelievers within the ruling classes. All later statements notwithstanding, the majority of the ruling class was in the camp of the believers, and the prominent and active part played by many of them is attested by all reliable documents. No doubt there was also pressure from below, yet most of the communal leaders did not wait for this pressure; as a matter of fact, they did not require it in order to be spurred into action. The essential correctness of this picture is not impugned in the least by the "revised version" of events that was put forward afterward by a kind of self-imposed censorship. As a matter of fact, this picture is supported by some later writers who had long ago given up all their former hopes and wrote without special pleading, but just spoke their minds. Their reports tend to confirm the earlier documents. The movement knew no class distinctions. It embraced the millionaires of Amsterdam who, much as Abraham Pereira, offered their whole fortunes to the messiah, as well as the poorest beggars in forlorn corners of the Diaspora. Social stratification cannot account for the actual alignment of forces, which contradicts all expectations based on social instinct or interest alone. Very possibly there were economic reasons for the hesitancy of some of the rich, and we can easily appreciate the tendency of some of them to hold fast to the status quo. But what about the majority who acted against their ostensible interests? The messianic awakening clearly transcended all classes, insofar as we are at all entitled to apply this term to Jewish society, where the social mobility of individuals and the frequency of sudden changes of fortune were hardly conducive to the consolidation of "classes."

It should be possible, no doubt, to draw a picture of Jewish social life in the middle of the seventeenth century that would bring out its inner tensions. Exploitation of authority or of connections with gentile rulers for private or clique interests, graft, and even occasional corruption in the direction of communal affairs, the helplessness of the small artisan and shopkeeper—all these are facts which social historians have had no difficulty in establishing wherever sufficient documentary evidence has survived. Even if there is much exaggeration in the fulminations and criticisms of preachers and moralists, the substance of their charges is amply confirmed[2] by the documentary material that has been preserved in archives. No doubt the specific social conditions in any given community and the relations obtaining between individuals and groups duly influenced the responses to the messianic movement. The strained personal relations between the rabbis of Smyrna at the time of Sabbatai's revelation in 1665 present one such instance among many which we shall come across. Local conditions certainly shaped and colored the movement in many places; yet, without wishing to minimize their significance, we must also beware of overestimating their role as a general factor explaining the

2. Complaints about grinding the poor and abuse of power by the rich were made practically everywhere. At about the same time that the famous preacher Berakhya Berakh pilloried the social abuses in Polish Jewry, Moses Judah Abbas in Turkey wrote his poems, one of which (dedicated to Abraham Yakhini) is a bitter indictment of the shamelessness and injustice with which the poor are robbed. The poem was written before the Sabbatian outbreak, and Abraham Yakhini, who played an important part in the movement, had nothing to do with the incidents to which it refers. The poem, published by M. Wallenstein in the *JSS*, I (1956), 165–71, provides valuable testimony of the social tensions and abuses in a Turkish (or possibly Egyptian) community under a "patrician" regime.

phenomenon as a whole. If there was one general factor underlying the patent unity of the Sabbatian movement everywhere, then this factor was essentially religious in character and as such obeyed its own autonomous laws, even if today these are often obscured behind smokescreens of sociological verbiage. The interrelations and interaction of religion and society should not make us forget that ultimately the two are not identical. It was this religious factor that set up the peculiar spiritual tension out of which Sabbatian messianism could be born, manifesting itself as an historical force throughout Israel, and not merely in one of the many branches of the Diaspora. Religious factors are not isolated entities and they never operate in a vacuum. Impinging on the social situation, the religious factor caused the various groups, the leading classes in particular, to join the messianic movement. As it happens, we are in a position to identify and name this religious factor. It was none other than Lurianic kabbalism, that is, that form of kabbalah which had developed at Safed, in the Galilee, during the sixteenth century and which dominated Jewish religiosity in the seventeenth century.

The powerful kabbalistic movement that issued from Safed and quickly spread over the Jewish world is an excellent and perhaps unique example of the reciprocity between center and periphery in Jewish history. Safed, which had never before possessed any special status or significance, became a major center of Judaism in the sixteenth century as a result of a steady flow of immigrants from the Diaspora.[3] The principal founders of the new center were Spanish exiles, but they were soon joined by enthusiasts from other communities, until Safed became a kind of miniature distillation of the whole Jewish Diaspora. The creative genius of the Galilean center drew its strength from the Diaspora, and it was thither that its influence radiated back, transforming Jewish spirituality everywhere. The doctrines developed in the schools of Safed apparently embodied some fundamental and universal Jewish quality that transcended all local variations, some kind of quintessential historical experience of Jewry in exile, for otherwise they would hardly have succeeded in opening up a new dimension to the traditional universe of Jewish religiosity.

3. See S. Schechter's essay "Safed in the 16th Century," in *SJ*, 2nd series (1908), pp. 202–328.

As the kabbalistic movement, highly charged with messianic tension, spread from Safed and conquered the Diaspora, it also laid the foundations for the future discharge of this tension. Here we may have part of the answer to our initial question. The kabbalism of the age was the spiritual heritage common to all Jewish communities; it had provided them with an interpretation of history and with a fund of ideas and practices without which the Sabbatian movement is unthinkable.

II

Before, however, defining more precisely the specific contribution of Lurianic kabbalism to the spiritual climate of the seventeenth century, a few words are in order about the nature and function of the messianic idea in Jewish history. It cannot be our task to discuss the origin of the messianic idea and its impact on Judaism during the decisive periods of its formation. Our immediate and more limited aim is an understanding of the messianic idea as it affected medieval Judaism, existing as it did in conditions of exile.[4] To this end we must distinguish two main tendencies in which the messianic longing of generations had crystallized. These were the popular-mythological and the philosophical-rationalist traditions. They existed side by side. They often converged and even merged. Nevertheless, we are entitled to treat them as basically distinct.

What, we may ask, did the messianic idea imply for the simple Jew whose hopes were nourished, in addition to the biblical prophecies, by a number of popular and well-known legends and apocalyptic midrashim?[5] Traditional popular messianism was characterized by catastrophe and utopianism, and both elements play an important role in the dynamics of the messianic faith. Both have their roots in biblical prophecy, the one in the vision of the end of days (as in Isaiah), the other in the notion of a day of the Lord (as in Amos). In the system of values as well as in the practical life of the ordinary

4. The ideas in this section have been elaborated by the author in an essay, "The Messianic Idea in Judaism," published in a collection of essays, *The Messianic Idea in Judaism and Other Essays in Jewish Spirituality* (New York: Schocken Press, 1971), pp. 1–36.

5. Apocalyptic texts and midrashim from the end of the Talmudic period to the late Middle Ages have been collected and edited by J. Even-Shemuʾel, *Midreshey Geʾullah*, 2nd edn. (Jerusalem, 1954).

medieval Jew, these two tendencies fulfilled different functions, with regard to both his surrounding environment and his own universe of rabbinic tradition.

Messianic legend indulges in uninhibited fantasies about the catastrophic aspects of redemption. Partly drawing on old mythologies, partly creating a popular mythology of its own, it paints a picture of violent upheaval, wars, plague, famine, a general defection from God and His Law, license, and heresy. There is no continuity between the present and the messianic era; the latter is not the fruit of previous developments, let alone of a gradual evolution. Far from being the result of historical process, redemption arises on the ruins of history, which collapses amid the "birth pangs" of the messianic age. The bitter experience of many generations that had tasted the heavy yoke of alien rule, oppression, and humiliation was not likely to mitigate the violence of this type of eschatology, whose roots go back to the apocalyptic literature of the period of the Second Temple. It has been one of the strangest errors of the modern *Wissenschaft des Judentums* to deny the continuity of Jewish apocalypticism. The endeavors of leading scholars to dissociate apocalyptic from rabbinic Judaism and to associate it exclusively with Christianity have contributed much to the modern falsification of Jewish history and to the concealment of some of its most dynamic forces, both constructive and destructive. The continued existence of popular apocalyptic literature and the history of the many messianic movements during the Middle Ages sufficiently dispose of such wishful rewriting of the past. As a matter of fact Jewish experience during the thousand years following the destruction of the Temple could only intensify the catastrophic traits of the eschatological picture, whose basic outline had been drawn in a famous Talmudic passage.[6] Redemption meant a revolution in history. Apocalyptic imagination supplied the details in which comfort and horror had an equal share and in which a persecuted and downtrodden people settled many a bitter account with its torturers. The apocalyptic war was described in all its stages. Israel too, though ultimately led through all tribulations to national restoration, would have to bear its share of suffering in the final cataclysm. The figure of the messiah of the House of Joseph, who would fall at the gates of Jerusalem fighting against the gentiles, constituted a new mythological

6. B. Sanhedrin 97 f.; also the last mishnah of the Tractate Sotah.

trait whose function it was to differentiate between the messiah of catastrophe and that of utopia.

The utopian aspect of traditional eschatology fulfilled a special function in the world of the medieval Jew, for it implied much more than merely the hope of a quiet life of moral perfection and human freedom. It contained all the qualities of a golden age, including miraculous manifestations and a radical transformation of the natural order. To express these hopes and ideas, there were detailed descriptions of the future Jerusalem as well as of the ideal contemplative life: the rabbinic scholars would devote themselves to the study of the law and would enjoy revelations of the mysteries of the Torah in the academy of the messiah. But messianic utopia also harbored explosive elements. Its overt intention was, no doubt, the perfection and completion of the rule of traditional religious law (halakhah) and its extension to those spheres of life to which it could not be applied in conditions of exile. Hence also the rabbinic term "halakhah of the messianic age." Yet messianic utopia also contained forces that tended to undermine its very intentions. In the closed world of narrowly circumscribed Jewish existence, messianic utopia represented the possibility of something radically and wonderfully different. It opened vistas which traditional halakhah had tended to cover up. The tendency had manifested itself more than once in clear symptoms of antinomianism in some medieval messianic movements.[7] As long as the messianic hope existed in the abstract, real for the imagination only, the gap between traditional law and "messianic law" was relatively easy to bridge: the latter was simply the application of traditional law to life in the messianic age. Popular piety undoubtedly took this view for granted. But whenever messianic hopes assumed actuality, the tension with regard to rabbinic tradition became manifest. There seems to be an intrinsic connection between active messianism and the courage for religious innovation. Messianic movements would often produce individuals with sufficient charismatic authority to challenge the established authority of rabbinic Judaism. Attempts to realize the messianic dream inevitably brought out, that is, manifested and strengthened, this hidden tension.

Rabbinic authority and messianic authority could not but

7. Cf. Jacob Mann, "Messianic Movements at the Time of the First Crusade" (Hebrew), *ha-Tequfah,* XXIII (1925), 243–61 (particularly p. 251), and XXIV (1928), 335–58.

clash. No doubt many a pious and faithful soul lived in blithe unawareness of the dangerous tensions implicit in every assertion of messianism. On the other hand, we may assume that there were always some individuals who realized the truth and who were attracted by the revolutionary aspects of the notion of a "renewed Torah" in the messianic age. There is, admittedly, not much evidence of this in popular eschatological literature, which obviously passed a thorough editorial censorship before attaining the form in which it has come down to us. The tension does, however, break through in rather extreme form in the eschatology of a kabbalistic book, the *Raᶜya Mehemna* (*Faithful Shepherd*).[8] The author of this part of the Zohar, evidently a capable if somewhat embittered Talmudic scholar, expresses in telling symbolic images what he, and probably some others as well, thought about the possible meaning of the law of the Lord in a messianic world. Very possibly the author of the *Raᶜya Mehemna* does not voice the opinions of his fellow kabbalists in this respect, and his speculations are not representative of any definite social tendency or movement (though I, for one, have some doubts on this score). Indeed, it appears that this extraordinary text did not exert any noticeable influence for a considerable time after its composition. Nevertheless, it is evident that the author expresses not merely his own views but also those of certain other individuals less articulate than himself. Like other kabbalists, he distinguished between the revealed and the hidden aspects of the Torah, but unlike them he was led by this distinction to extreme conclusions. The Torah manifests itself under two aspects: that of the "Tree of Life" and that of the "Tree of the Knowledge of Good and Evil." The latter aspect is characteristic of the period of exile. As the Tree of Knowledge comprises good *and* evil, so the Torah deriving from it comprises permission and prohibition, pure and impure; in other words, it is the law of the Bible and of rabbinic tradition. In the age of redemption, however, the Torah will manifest itself under the aspect of the Tree of Life, and all previous distinctions will pass away. The positive manifestation of the Torah as the Tree of Life is thus accompanied by the abrogation of all those laws and rules whose authority and validity obtain unconditionally during the present era of exile. The pure

8. See Y. F. Baer, "The Historical Background of the *Raᶜya Mehemna*" (Hebrew), *Zion*, V (1939–40), 1–44.

essence of the Torah will be revealed and its outer shell cast off. The remarkable thing about this conception is its clear consciousness of possible contradictions and of a revaluation of values within the one absolutely valid Torah which, for the kabbalist, was nothing less than the manifestation of God's holy name.

The popular mythological versions of eschatology combined literary and legendary traditions with the grim experience of exile. Apocryphal legends easily found their way into the hearts of men where they satisfied secret needs and longings by their descriptions of messianic catastrophe and utopia. They established themselves not only in the mind of the masses but even in the writings of leading rabbinic authorities, as is apparent from the eighth chapter ("On Redemption") of Saadia Gaon's *Book of Beliefs and Opinions*.[9] Others viewed the rank growth of apocalyptic imagination with undisguised misgivings and endeavored to minimize its influence. There is an unmistakable tone of hostility in their references to the doctrine of an apocalyptic catastrophe, and they may well have been aware of the explosive charge inherent in the messianic idea as such. Utopianism not only arouses hopes and expectations; it also threatens existing traditional patterns. Once the longing for a new world and for the tree of life seizes the hearts, who knows what may come next? Every utopia that is more than an abstract formula has a revolutionary sting. It hardly occasions surprise that Maimonides, the most extreme representative of the antiapocalyptic tendency, rejected all those myths that lived in the hearts of the believing masses, whom he contemptuously referred to as the "rabble." Against the luxurious and rank growth of legend from which the "rabble" derived hope and comfort, Maimonides formulated an eschatological doctrine from which utopian elements were as far as possible excluded. As the hallowed character of tradition did not permit him to suppress them completely, he resorted to careful sifting. The utterances of the early teachers on the subject were declared to be theologically not authoritative; details concerning redemption could be known only after the event. This antiapocalyptic bias found its definite expression in Maimonides' well-known formulations in chapters eleven and twelve of "Laws of Kingship" in book fourteen of his great code *Mishneh Torah:*

Do not think that the messiah will have to work signs and miracles or perform any spectacular deeds or resurrect the dead and the

9. English translation under this title by S. Rosenblatt (New Haven, 1948).

like. . . . But this is the truth of the matter: the Torah with all its laws and ordinances is everlastingly valid and nothing will be added to it or taken away from it. When a king arises out of the House of David who diligently studies the law and, like his ancestor David, assiduously performs good works according to the written and the oral law, and who compels all Israel to walk therein . . . and who will fight the battles of the Lord, then it may be presumed that he is the messiah. If he proves successful and succeeds in rebuilding the Temple and in gathering in all the exiles, then it is certain that he is the messiah. He will reform the world so that all shall serve the Lord. . . . And do not think that in the days of the messiah there will be any departure from the normal course of things or any change in the cosmic order. That which is prophesied in the Book of Isaiah [11:6]—"the wolf also shall dwell with the lamb and the leopard shall lie down with the kid"—is merely a parable and a figure of speech . . . and the same holds for similar prophecies concerning the messiah. They are all parables, though only in the days of the messianic king will people understand the precise meaning and intention of the parables. . . . There is none that now knows how these things shall come to pass, . . . for even scholars have no [clear] traditions on this matter but merely the interpretation of Scripture; therefore, there is much difference of opinion among them. In any case, neither the sequence of events nor their details are articles of faith. One should make it a rule not to occupy oneself with legends and midrashim on the subject . . . as they are conducive neither to the fear nor to the love of God. . . . Sages and prophets longed for the messianic age not in order that they should dominate the world and rule over the gentiles . . . but solely in order to be free to devote themselves to the Torah and divine wisdom without oppression and hindrance, so as to merit eternal life. . . . The sole occupation of the world will be to know the Lord. Therefore [the children of] Israel shall all be great scholars; they shall know hidden things and attain to the knowledge of God as far as is within human reach.

The quotation from Maimonides illustrates the difficulties of formulating a messianic and thus essentially utopian doctrine while at the same time trying to eliminate its utopian elements. The attempt could hardly be expected to succeed, and the compromise is clearly discernible in Maimonides' wording. What Maimonides did succeed in doing was to suppress completely the apocalyptic moment. There is no hint of a cataclysmic end of history, no catastrophe, not even miracles. The reader might also think that the historical process initiated by the appearance of the messianic king would lead, by a gradual and continuous transition, to the ideal state of things, that is, to the perfect contemplative life—Maimonides' version of utopia. Maimonides very skillfully concealed the dangerous dialectics inherent in messianism, and the carefully chosen words with which he emphasizes the conservative function of the messiah in safeguarding the Torah and traditional law tell their own story. Maimonides was well aware of the messianic movements that had agitated previous generations as well as his own. His *Epistle to the Jews of Yemen*[10] shows that he entertained no illusions as to the dangers which such movements harbored for traditional religion. In a way the struggle of Maimonides and his followers against the "beliefs of the rabble" was also inspired by utopian ideal, albeit an aristocratic utopia in which philosophic mysteries had taken the place of historic dynamism. His antiapocalyptic utterances, designed to abolish messianism as a historic force, were subsequently invoked by all who opposed messianic actualization and by all who distrusted the messianic idea as a motive force in social life. The authority of the "Great Eagle" (as Maimonides was called) was considerable, but it could not conceal the essential weakness of his eschatology. The two classical writers on the subject of messianism, Don Isaac Abravanel, writing soon after the expulsion from Spain at the end of the fifteenth century and R. Loew of Prague, writing at the end of the sixteenth century, both retreated from Maimonides' extreme position. Living through times of dire misery and persecution, they could not afford to ignore the apocalyptic tradition and its message of catastrophe. Each reintroduces in his own manner those elements that Maimonides had sought to eradicate. It is only fair to add that both authors were also at pains to safeguard the continuity of the historical process culminating in redemption. Both preserve a large measure of common sense, expressing itself in allegorical interpretations of eschatological legends. Yet the fact that they both felt constrained to readmit apocalypse and popular mythology is sufficient proof of the strength of these elements in their times. The eschatological writings of Abravanel and R. Loew exerted a profound influence on later generations, and even adherents of the Sab-

10. Written by Maimonides in 1172 to counter the messianic preaching of a false prophet who agitated Yemenite Jewry.

batian movement would quote them in support of their contentions. In a way, the two main tendencies of Jewish eschatology had merged in the writings of these two authors, with the result that everyone could find in them whatever best suited his temper.

III

The contribution of the kabbalah to the religious revival that followed upon the expulsion from Spain can be adequately appreciated only by paying attention to its novel attitude toward the messianic tradition. In its earlier stages kabbalism had shown little interest in messianism. The early kabbalists drew on old gnostic traditions and on philosophical ideas that lent themselves to a mystical and symbolic view of the world. These ideas, together with the inner experiences of contemplative mystics for whom "adhesion" or "cleaving" to God (*debequth*) was the final goal on the ladder of spiritual ascent, shaped contemplative kabbalism with its twofold aim of grasping the mysteries of the Godhead and of the Torah, on the one hand, and of teaching elect souls the way of total *debequth,* on the other. The kabbalists were conservative in outlook, and they shared the hopes and views of traditional religion. Their own peculiar spiritual impulse had no specifically messianic quality. Their ideal of the contemplative life in communion with God did not require a messianic world for its realization; it was quite compatible with life in exile. Like other mystical movements, kabbalism began as a way of spiritual renewal for individuals or groups of individuals (which, of course, did not prevent it from becoming a social force). Redemption, that is, redemption of the soul, was a private, individual matter and therefore independent of the sphere of national redemption with which traditional messianism was concerned.

Kabbalistic doctrine developed apart from eschatology because in its original setting it concentrated less on the end of the world than on the primordial beginning of creation. For this is what the kabbalistic conception of the Godhead, as enshrined in the doctrine of *sefiroth,* really amounts to. The hidden God, known in kabbalistic terminology as *En-Sof* (the Infinite) is far removed from everything created; he is unrevealed, nonmanifest, and unknown. Only the emanation of his power, operating in the creation of both the higher and the nether worlds, transforms *En-Sof* into the Creator-God. The different stages of emanation manifest the hidden potencies and attributes by which God acts and which are all essentially one in the unity of God, even "as the flame is bound to the coal." Ten such stages, known as *sefiroth,* constitute the inner life of the Godhead; in them He becomes manifest as a personal God. Though inaccessible to immediate comprehension or contemplation, they can be apprehended through the structure of all being—from the beginning of creation in the supernal worlds down to the last and lowest creature. The mystical contemplation of the universe reveals its symbolic character. Creation does not exist for its own sake but for the sake of pointing to the divine emanation that shines through it. The inner meaning of creation, as well as the Law and the commandments, is revealed to the kabbalist through an understanding of the mysteries of mystical symbolism. "All proceeds from the One and returns to the One." In other words, even as the whole chain of being proceeded, link by link, from the manifestation of the Creator in His *sefiroth,* so everything would return in the end to its original source.

The kabbalist, however, jumps this cosmic rhythm and takes a short cut. By means of proper contemplative concentration, particularly during prayer or when performing a religious act, the human will cleaves to the divine will and to the world of the *sefiroth.* Here we have a real ascent of the soul, not of the actual kind as in the concrete ecstatic experience of a heavenly journey,[11] but in a purely spiritual process produced by meditation. The mystic who in his contemplative ascent attains the point of communion with the source of all being has by that act reached the end of the path to his individual redemption. Kabbalistic contemplation is a kind of individual anticipation of eschatological messianism. The kabbalists were aware that the historical and public character of traditional messianic belief precluded any identification or confusion of the latter with their own mystical ideal of an individual, contemplative ascent. They consequently had no reason for tampering with traditional messianism, though they did not hesitate to interpret it in their manner as an event within the inner life of the Godhead. Their interpretation presupposes the new meaning with which the author of the Zohar had invested the old concept of the "exile of the Shekhinah," based on the Talmudic saying that wher-

11. Such as practiced by earlier Jewish mystics; see *Major Trends,* ch. 2.

ever Israel is exiled, the Shekhinah goes with it.[12] For the Talmud, Shekhinah simply meant the presence of God. Not so for the kabbalists for whom Shekhinah served as a technical term for the tenth and last *sefirah*, while the term "the Holy One Blessed Be He" (the usual rabbinic idiom for God) referred to the sixth *sefirah*, otherwise known as *Tif'ereth*. During the present period of exile, the Shekhinah, or "bride," was separated and exiled from her "husband," the Holy One Blessed Be He. The disjunction of these two aspects of the Godhead signifies that in the present state of things the unity of the divine attributes is not complete. Only with the advent of messianic redemption will the perfect unity of the divine *sefiroth* be permanently re-established. Then, to use the symbolic language of the kabbalists, the Shekhinah will be restored to perpetual union with her husband.

In its eschatological teaching the main part of the Zohar continues the apocalyptic and utopian tradition against which Maimonides had so sternly warned. In spite of some changes of detail as compared with earlier apocalyptic midrashim, the attitude is fundamentally the same: the messianic events are all of a supernatural character. Mention has already been made of the utopian conception of the "messianic Torah" to be found in the later parts of the Zohar, the *Ra'ya Mehemna* and the *Tiqquney Zohar*. A very special and novel feature of some trends in Spanish kabbalism was the emphasis on the close connection between the approach of redemption and the increasing knowledge of kabbalistic mysteries. In the days of exile, minds have been beclouded and are unfit to receive esoteric lore; but now, with the end of time approaching, the mysteries of the kabbalah are increasingly revealed. This doctrine provided a justification for the boldness of the kabbalists' speculative innovations, and it was invoked as such by the authors of the Zohar and by many others. Yet it never led to a thorough reinterpretation of eschatological ideas. The creative originality of the early kabbalists spent itself exclusively on the mysteries of creation and the mysteries of the "divine chariot," that is, on mystical cosmology and the doctrine of the *sefiroth*. No messianic

12. On the concept of Shekhinah and its kabbalistic development, see Scholem, "Schechina, das passiv-weibliche Moment in der Gottheit," in *Von der mystischen Gestalt der Gottheit* (Zurich, 1962), pp. 135–91.

movements of any consequence arose among kabbalists, and the few instances of individuals claiming angelic revelations or actual prophecy evoked no serious response. The agitations around the prophet of Ávila in Castile (1295), or of Abraham Abulafia at about the same time, did not lead to any widespread messianic unrest. Apocalyptic messianism and kabbalah remained distinct spheres of religious life.

The expulsion from Spain (1492) wrought a radical change also in this respect. The traumatic upheaval, which so profoundly altered the situation of a large part of the nation, inevitably called forth corresponding reactions in the specifically religious sphere. The exiles proceeded to their new abodes and created a new Diaspora which, as a matter of fact, soon flourished, at least in parts. Yet even after Sephardic Jewry had ostensibly recovered from the shock, many minds still continued to search for the meaning of the catastrophe that had overtaken them. The first generation of Spanish exiles responded to the events with a wave of apocalyptic agitation. The Spanish disaster was the beginning of the "messianic birth pangs."[13] The eschatological perspective soon embraced other contemporaneous events, among which the fall of Constantinople in 1453 was no doubt the most dramatic and one that could easily assume symbolic significance as the overture to the wars of Gog and Magog. Apocalypse flourished not only in its conventional form—as, for example, in the writings of Don Isaac Abravanel—but also in a specifically kabbalistic guise. In the same years in which Abravanel wrote his book *Yeshuʿoth Meshiḥo* (*Deliverance of His Anointed*), an anonymous kabbalist composed the commentary *Kaf ha-Qetoreth* (*The Spoonful of Incense*),[14] which interpreted Psalms as songs of war for the great apocalyptic struggle. Messianic movements developed around the public activity of kabbalists such as Asher Lemmlein in northern Italy[15] and the marrano Solomon

13. R. Joseph Sheʾaltiel b. Moses ha-Kohen added in the margin of a MS. of the book *Peliʾah* (MS. Vatican 187): "I think that the afflictions visited on the Jews in all the Christian kingdoms between the years 5250–55 [1490–95] . . . are the messianic birth pangs." These lines were written on the Island of Rhodes in 1495.

14. Extant in a Paris MS. (Bibliothèque Nationale, No. 845).

15. Lemmlein's kabbalistic background is proved by his replies to R. Moses Ḥefeṣ of Salonika; see A. Marx in *RÉJ*, LXI (1911), 135–38.

Molkho in whose writings apocalyptic and speculative kabbalah had fused.

Eschatological tension abated after the failure of the messianic prophecies for the year 1530. The intensive messianic propaganda conducted by the kabbalists of Jerusalem in particular[16] ended in a complete fiasco. Nevertheless messianism had penetrated the heart of kabbalism, and it continued to influence kabbalistic development in diverse ways. The creation of the new spiritual center of Jewry in Safed was itself a decisive positive response to the expulsion. The movement of spiritual and moral reform that spread from Safed sprang from the innermost heart of Judaism. Nourished by the living experience and memory of exile at its very worst, the movement aimed at "fulfilling" this exile and thereby preparing redemption. Apocalypse disappeared or, at least, went underground and was transformed in the process. Ascetic piety reigned supreme in Safed. At first the religious ideal of a mystical elite only, asceticism now allied itself to an individual and public morality based on the new kabbalism; it struck deep roots in the collective consciousness. According to certain eschatological texts the messiah was due to make his first appearance in Galilee, and it is not impossible that this and similar expectations contributed to the establishment of the community of saints in Safed, which numbered more inspired enthusiasts and devout seekers of mystical salvation than any other city. Though the messiah did not come from Safed, there were many who heard the wing-beats of approaching redemption in the kabbalistic teaching that went forth from there. Even the purely halakhic achievements of the great Talmudic scholars of Safed were largely inspired by the new messianic kabbalah. R. Joseph Karo deliberately ignored kabbalism in his great rabbinic code *Shulḥan ᶜArukh*, yet there is little doubt as to the secret eschatological motives of its composition. Unsuccessful attempts have been made to deny Karo's authorship of the mystical diary *Maggid Mesharim* (*Preacher of Righteousness*) in which the writer describes the regular manifestations of a celestial mentor, or *maggid*, who was none other than the Mishnah herself.[17] We may take this mani-

16. Cf. my two articles on R. Abraham b. Eliezer ha-Levi in *Kiryath Sepher*, II (1925) and VII (1931).

17. On Karo as a mystic, see R. J. Z. Werblowsky, *Joseph Karo, Lawyer and Mystic* (Oxford, 1962).

festation as an indication of the essentially conservative character of Safed kabbalism and of its firm anchorage in rabbinic tradition. The personified Mishnah, that is, the oral law, represented nothing less than historic Judaism as a whole. Only by virtue of its conservative character and its patent continuity with rabbinic tradition could the new kabbalism gain popular appeal and even succeed in carrying on its wings—or perhaps hidden under its wings—some startling novel ideas.

In Safed, where all the arteries of Jewish spiritual life converged, kabbalism became a social and historical force. The process by which kabbalah established its supremacy over the religious consciousness of those who were themselves no kabbalists calls for some explanation. Though it is true that the kabbalists at last emerged from their solitary esotericism and began to seek ways of influencing the masses, yet their spectacular success remains something of an historical problem. Both philosophy and kabbalah were aristocratic disciplines, appealing primarily to an intellectual and spiritual elite. How and why did the kabbalists succeed—where the philosophers had failed—in decisively shaping the religious consciousness of the Jewish people? The actual triumph of kabbalism in the sixteenth century is a fact beyond dispute. It is only the interpretation of this fact which is at issue. Rationalist historians, such as Graetz and others, have offered an engagingly simple explanation: persecution and suffering had dimmed the light of reason and paved the way for an eruption of mystical obscurantism. It is hardly necessary to expend many words over an "explanation" whose bias is so obvious. The real answer to the question should be positive, not negative in character. Kabbalism triumphed because it provided a valid answer to the great problems of the time. To a generation for which the facts of exile and the precariousness of existence in it had become a most pressing and cruel problem, kabbalism could give an answer unparalleled in breadth and in depth of vision. The kabbalistic answer illuminated the significance of exile and redemption and accounted for the unique historical situation of Israel within the wider, in fact cosmic, context of creation itself.

The kabbalistic appeal to the public, unheard of before the expulsion from Spain, is in evidence soon afterward. There was, of course, much hostility and opposition on the part of those "who jeer at and scoff at the students of kabbalistic books, and who greatly insult and revile them . . . and whenever they hear of the kabbalah, of a prophet, or visionary, they [mockingly] enquire of each other 'what hath this madman spoken unto thee.'"[18] On the other hand Joseph Yabeṣ (or Jabez), a typical representative of orthodox public opinion after the expulsion, complains of the inordinate popular success of kabbalism. His complaints were echoed by later moralists who were alarmed at the growing attraction of kabbalistic lore for the masses, namely, for people without previous rabbinic training. "There are today many ignorant people, smitten with the blindness of pride, who believe that they have attained the hidden mysteries of the Torah without ever having savored [rabbinic] learning or tasted good works."[19] Yabeṣ and his like continue the line of conservative theological thinking which passes from Judah ha-Levi's *Kuzari* through Naḥmanides, Jonah of Gerona, Solomon b. Adreth, and Ḥasdai Crescas. His attitude toward kabbalah (whose mysteries "one should not contemplate" in an age of ignorance), like that toward the philosophy of Maimonides, is one of extreme reserve.[20] Yet in spite of his public exhibition of reserve, we find Joseph Yabeṣ, when in Mantua, entreating a fellow exile from Spain, Judah Ḥayyat, to compose a treatise on the principles of kabbalah.[21]

Of course, nobody at that time would have explicitly suggested that kabbalism should supersede the study of traditional nonesoteric teaching. Nevertheless the intensive propaganda for kabbalistic studies did not fail to produce its results. A sixteenth-century kabbalist has left us a valuable testimony of the general feeling prevalent at the time:

I have found it written that the heavenly decree prohibiting the study of kabbalah in public was valid only until the end of the year 250 [1490 C.E.]. Thereafter it [the generation living at that time] would be called the last

18. ʾ*Ohel Moʿed* (MS. Cambridge Add. 673¹, fol. 13a). This work, a kind of introduction to the kabbalah, was probably written at the beginning of the 16th century.

19. Joseph Yabeṣ (Jabez), ʾ*Or ha-Ḥayyim*, fol. 4a.

20. Very characteristic of this critical attitude is the *bon mot* Yabeṣ quotes from a "certain great thinker" (perhaps Don Isaac Abravanel) who was wont to conclude his lectures on Maimonides' *Guide* with the words: "This is the teaching of our Master Moses [Maimonides], but not of Moses our Master [*scil.* the biblical Moses]" (*ibid.*, fol. 21a).

21. See Judah Ḥayyat's introduction to his commentary *Minḥath Yehudah* on *Maʿarekheth haʾElohuth* (Mantua, 1558), fol. 3a.

generation [before the final redemption]. The decree was abrogated and permission was granted to study the Zohar. From the year 300 [1540 C.E., the beginning of the kabbalistic movement in Safed] onward it will be accounted an act of special merit to both old and young to study [kabbalah] in public, as it is stated in the *Raᶜya Mehemna*.[22] And since the messianic king will appear through the merits [of this study] and through none other, it behooves us not to be remiss.[23]

The principle that the study of kabbalah was itself a factor in hastening the advent of redemption became established as a generally accepted doctrine and represents a significant development of the notion, already mentioned before, that at the end of days the mysteries of kabbalism would be revealed anew. Henceforth kabbalistic esotericism and messianic eschatology were intertwined and acted in combination.

IV

The attempts of the sixteenth-century kabbalists—and those of Safed in particular—to codify or at least formulate their doctrines present themselves under a double aspect. On the one hand, they continue the old traditions of pre-expulsion Spanish kabbalism; on the other hand, they testify to a mystical revival whose speculative originality is evident in the teachings of the more inspired masters. The ideas which they produced differ widely even on fundamental issues, and to lump them all together would be doing them less than justice. There were masters whose teaching developed by way of commentary on earlier, classical texts; others were more systematic thinkers who used earlier authorities merely as pegs on which to hang their own speculations. Some were essentially speculative types; others derived their ideas from visions and from contemplative insights attained through mystical meditation.

By and large the older generation of kabbalists seems to have been of a predominantly speculative cast of mind. Their teaching endeavored to clothe the mystical symbols of kabbalah with a conceptual garb. This holds true of Solomon Alkabeṣ, of the author of *Pardes Rimmonim* and *ᵓElimah*, Moses Cordovero (1522–70), and of Sheftel Horovitz, the author of *Shefaᶜ Tal*. But with the younger

22. Referring probably to the statement (Zohar III, 124b) that through the merits of the book Zohar the children of Israel would be redeemed from exile.

23. Quoted by Abraham Azulay of Hebron in the introduction to his commentary on the Zohar, entitled *ᵓOr ha-Ḥammah* (Jerusalem, 1879).

generation the symbolic element and the concomitant tendency to think in mythological images came to the fore. The tension between the speculative and the mythological tendencies and their mutual attraction and repulsion have to a large extent determined the history of kabbalism.[24] If it is true that the great achievement of the kabbalists was their creation of genuine symbols, then the presence of mythical elements need occasion no surprise, for mythology inevitably appears wherever reality is apprehended in symbolic forms. The kabbalists not only produced symbolic images of the historical realities surrounding them, but they also endowed their images with the vitality of genuine myth. Symbols are produced and nourished by historical and social experience. Those of the kabbalah, pregnant with myth from the very beginning, immediately appealed to the unsophisticated masses, whose "popular religion" had always had room for mythology and, for that reason, had always incurred the displeasure of the philosophical theologians. The inner world which the kabbalists discovered in their symbolic forms did not have a function primarily in terms of a social ideology of any kind. But once kabbalism came to perform a social function, it did so by providing an ideology for popular religion. It was able to perform this function in spite of its fundamentally aristocratic character, because its symbols, reflecting as they did the historical experience of the group, provided the faith of the masses with a theoretical justification. The powerful momentum which kabbalism developed in Safed derived more from its social, that is, ideological, function than from the profundity of its mystical vision—however great and significant the latter may have been for the kabbalists themselves.

The above holds true more particularly for the kabbalistic doctrines of the great "Lion" of Safed, Isaac Luria Ashkenazi (1534–72). When Luria died in the prime of his life, his teachings had not yet spread, though his reputation as a holy man of God was high.[25] Of the different kabbalistic systems developed in Safed,

24. Cf. Is. Tishby, "On Concrete (Mythological) and Abstract Thinking in the Kabbalah" (Hebrew), in *ᶜAley ᶜAyin*, "S. Schocken Jubilee Volume" (Jerusalem, 1952), pp. 147–55 (hereafter cited as *Schocken Volume*).

25. Many semihistorical and semilegendary traditions about Luria's life have been preserved, particularly in the epistles of Solomon Dresnitz, written in Safed between 1603–9 and printed for the first time in 1629. They were subsequently reprinted many times under the title *Shibḥey ha-ᵓAri* (*Praises of the Lion*).

Cordovero's was the first to make a wide impact. Cordovero had been Luria's teacher and died two years before him. His writings spread together with the movement that issued from Safed and dominated kabbalistic thinking for about half a century. Lurianic teaching, whose originality and novelty set it apart from all other kabbalistic systems, was known only to a small circle of elect in Safed, Jerusalem, and Damascus. Originating in Luria's visions and meditations, his teaching was revealed orally to his disciples in Safed but was never published. When two of Luria's disciples, Ḥayyim Vital and Joseph ibn Tᵓbul,[26] committed this oral teaching to paper, they jealously guarded their notes and did not permit them to circulate. Not until the end of the sixteenth century did copies of parts of Vital's writings begin to circulate in Palestine and outside it, much against Vital's wish. Vital, an extraordinary personality, spent most of his long life (1534–1620) concealing his master's teaching from his contemporaries who, he thought, were not yet worthy of receiving it. By that time, however, a complete description of Luria's teaching, composed by another pupil, had reached Europe in manuscript copies. This was the book *Kanfey Yonah* (*Wings of a Dove*) by R. Moses Jonah.

Meanwhile Luria's doctrine underwent further developments at the hands of Vital and those other kabbalists who studied Vital's or Ibn Tᵓbul's papers. By the time Lurianic teaching became known, at first in manuscript, but after 1630 also in print, the original doctrines had suffered additions and revisions. It was this mixture of authentic tradition and later accretions which henceforth circulated under the designation "the writings of the Sacred Lion," namely, the Lurianic writings. The ground had been well prepared for Luria by earlier kabbalists. During the three decades following Vital's death, the new Lurianic kabbalah conquered Judaism and superseded all earlier systems, particularly in those circles that were the real bearers of the religious revival. Lurianism was considered the final and ultimate revelation of kabbalistic truth. The hidden processes in the divine world of the *sefiroth* which it described were felt by adherents of the system to refer to far deeper levels of the divine realm than were dealt with in the kabbalah of Cordovero and others. When Luria was questioned about

26. On Joseph ibn Tᵓbul, whom historians have overlooked completely, see my article in *Zion*, V (1939–40), 149–60.

the relationship between his own revelations and earlier teaching, Cordovero's in particular, he replied that the latter described the "world of confusion or disorder";[27] whereas he had come to reveal the structure of the "world of *tiqqun*, or harmony." As the influence of the religious revival radiating from Safed become more and more specifically Lurianic, it impressed its characteristic traits on Jewish religion everywhere. The ritual, liturgical, and other practical innovations of the Safed kabbalists became public property with a distinctively Lurianic slant. By 1650, only one generation after the actual dissemination of Lurianism had begun, the system had established an almost unchallenged supremacy. In fact, Lurianic kabbalism was the one well-articulated and generally accepted form of Jewish theology at the time.

One of the most active agents in disseminating Lurianic ideas was Israel Sarug, who appeared in Italy toward the end of the sixteenth century posing as Luria's disciple, which he certainly was not, or which he was, at best, in a metaphorical sense only.[28] In Italy, where he had established schools for kabbalistic studies, as well as in other European countries, Sarug actively propagated the new doctrine in a version of his own making. His missionary zeal stands in strange contrast to Vital's retiring disposition. Sarug's seed fell on fertile ground in Italy and he succeeded in attracting some of the leading scholars, more particularly those with imagination and feeling, such as Menaḥem Azaryah Fano (1548–1620) and Aaron Berakhya Modena (died 1639). The writings of the Italian (that is, Sarug's) school reached other European countries at about the same time as those of the Palestinian (that is, Vital's) school. In due course both traditions merged, and the new composite version was accepted even by the Palestinian kabbalists as the authentic and authoritative form of Luria's teaching.

The contrast between Sarug's propagandistic activity and Vital's seclusion gains interest when we consider Vital's autobiographical notes, which he himself put together in book form some time between

27. For these and related concepts of Lurianic kabbalism, see *Major Trends,* p. 265.

28. See G. Scholem, "Was R. Israel Sarug a Disciple of Luria?" (Hebrew), *Zion* V (1939–40), 214–41. The possibility should be considered, however, that Sarug had known Luria from the latter's days in Egypt before Luria came to Safed. There is now some evidence that Sarug lived in Egypt at that time.

1610–12. This *Book of Visions,* as it was called, is one of the most curious and revealing documents we possess, for very few authors have revealed their most intimate thoughts and feelings with such disconcerting candor.[29] It appears that Vital not only believed Luria to have been worthy of messiahship but actually saw himself destined for a messianic career. For more than forty years he entertained messianic expectations for himself and collected testimonies and hints to that effect from the dreams and visions of others. Yet he would never move as much as a finger to implement any of his expectations, and he even refused to propagate his master's doctrines, replete with messianic tension as they were. For all we know, there may have been many such "hidden messiahs" at the time who, unlike Vital, left no autobiographical notes. Sarug, on the other hand, who had no messianic pretensions himself, devoted all his life to the dissemination of the Lurianic doctrine—a doctrine more likely than any other to increase messianic tension among the people.

Many of the tenets of Lurianism were undoubtedly new in the sense that they had been unknown to earlier kabbalists, in spite of the exegetical skill with which the Lurianic writers read their views into the Zohar. But the decisive innovation, that which held the secret of the Lurianic appeal to the age, was the transposition of the central concepts of exile and redemption from the historical to a cosmic and even divine plane. The eschatological vision of redemption from oppression by the gentiles widened in scope to include not only the whole of creation but even the divine realm. Exile and redemption are the two poles of the axis around which the Lurianic system revolves; viewed in a dimension of depth, they now stand out as numinous symbols of a spiritual reality of which historical exile and redemption are merely the concrete expression. Luria himself developed his system without any "ideological" intentions. He merely revealed what in his opinion was the mystical reality of momentous processes in the sphere of the "supernal lights." But once developed, his system provided what may be described as a new myth of Judaism. The realistic character of Luria's mythical symbols enabled them to fulfill an ideological function of immediate historic bearing.

The character of Lurianic symbolism presents a special problem.

29. The full text of the *Sefer ha-Ḥezyonoth* (*Book of Visions*) has been published by A. Z. Aeshcoly (Jerusalem, 1954), from Vital's autograph preserved in Leghorn. Earlier editions were incomplete.

The accusation of anthropomorphism directed against the kabbalists is an old one. Their manner of speaking in a material fashion about things spiritual was often held to fall little short of actual blasphemy, yet it merely exemplified the essential paradox of all symbolism. Symbols express in human speech that which is properly inexpressible. Hence they are always material and anthropomorphic, even though the mystic may regard them as mere crutches to aid his frail human understanding. The kabbalists, whose mystical thinking strained after expression in symbolic forms, endeavored to evade responsibility for their symbols by the frequent use of qualifying phrases such as "so to speak," "as if," "as it were," and the like. These reservations were supposed to minimize the real significance of the symbols employed. The kabbalists used the most outrageous material and even physical and sexual imagery but immediately qualified their statements by adding the solemn warning, "Cursed be the man that makes any graven or molten image," that is, who attributes reality to symbolic expressions.[30] From their higher theological vantage point the kabbalists might argue that the material interpretation of their symbols was a misunderstanding, yet it was precisely this creative misunderstanding that determined the public significance of kabbalistic symbolism. He was a bold man indeed who undertook to draw the line between understanding and misunderstanding in such matters. The inescapable dialectic of symbolism is central to a proper appreciation of the historical and social function of kabbalism, even as it underlies most of the discussions between kabbalists and their opponents.

Lurianism is mythological in the precise meaning of the term. It tells the story of divine acts and events, and it accounts for the mystery of the world by an inner, mystical process which, taking place within the Godhead, ultimately produced also the "outer," material creation. According to the kabbalists everything external is merely a symbol or intimation of an inner reality that actually determines the external reality which we perceive. The main concepts of Lurianism all refer to the mystery of the Godhead, but on each and every level they also point to a corresponding aspect in the manifest cosmos.

Lurianic kabbalism provided the background of the Sabbatian movement. To attempt a concise survey of its essential features and

30. Cf. the characteristic warning at the beginning of the most deliberately anthropomorphic section of the Zohar, the *Idra Rabbah* (Zohar III, 127b).

their underlying mythology is to risk error and court misunderstanding. Nevertheless, the risk must be taken if we want to clear the way to a satisfactory understanding of the roots and the subsequent development of Sabbatianism. Let us glance, therefore, briefly at the basic notions which contain, *in nuce,* as it were, the whole of Lurianic kabbalah. These are the notions of "retraction," the "breaking of the vessels," "restoration" (or *tiqqun*), and the "raising of the sparks."

The doctrine of retraction is based on a simple if somewhat crudely naturalistic assumption. How is it possible for the world to exist at all if there is nothing besides *En-Sof,* the infinite Deity that is all and fills all? If *En-Sof* or "the light of *En-Sof*" is all in all, how can there be anything that is not *En-Sof?* Luria's answer is deceptively simple and significantly different from that which earlier kabbalists would have given. Others would have replied to the question by a statement of their doctrine of emanation: God projects His creative power outside Himself. From His hidden essence, namely, from the brilliance radiating from His essence, He emanates the *sefiroth,* or divine lights. These *sefiroth* are the stages in which God manifests Himself in His different attributes; they contain the archetypes of all that exists. As the stream of the divine emanation proceeds, it becomes progressively less spiritual and refined, more material and coarse; thus all the worlds come into being by the descent of the divine power from the hidden Root of Roots. Our own material world is merely the last and outermost shell of this—to use the phrase of the Zohar—"garment of the Deity." The higher levels of being, even the divine *sefiroth* themselves, are garments only, clothing the hidden light of *En-Sof* to which they are related as the body is to the soul. The *sefiroth* are the soul of the lower orders of being, whereas *En-Sof,* the Creator, is their "soul of souls." The process of creation, as seen by the early kabbalists unfolds in progressive stages of a gradually coarsening, that is, materializing, "light." It is essentially a one-way process, from God to the world and man.

For the kabbalists of Safed things were not quite so simple and straightforward. Even before Luria the theory of emanation had become much more complicated. On every level and at every stage of emanation we find not only the "straight," "direct light" of the primary ray of emanation, but also its reverse, the "reflected light," which, instead of proceeding further downward, longs to return to its original supernal source. There is thus a double action in every *sefirah:* It "filters" the light which it receives from above and passes it on to the next lower order, but, like a mirror, it also reflects back some of it. The total structure of the divine World of Emanation, as well as every single part of it, is thus constituted by the simultaneous activity of the "direct light" and the "reflected light." This dialectical understanding of the procession of emanation introduced an element of tension into the systems of Cordovero and Alkabeṣ. Luria added paradox to dialectic when he formulated his doctrine of *ṣimṣum,* or "retraction" or "withdrawal." According to this doctrine, the first act of the Creator was not His revelation of Himself to something outside. Far from being a procession outward, or a "going out," of His hidden self, the first step was, rather, a withdrawal or retreat. God withdrew "from Himself into Himself," and by this act, abandoning a region within Himself to emptiness, He made room for the worlds to be. At some point within the light of *En-Sof,* the divine essence, or "light," departed; by withdrawing into the depth of *En-Sof* all around, it left an empty space in the middle. In relation to the infinite *En-Sof* this space was no more than an infinitesimal point, but in relation to creation it was the whole of cosmic space. God could manifest Himself only because He had first withdrawn, or "contracted," Himself.

In Lurianic writings, the space in which all processes of emanation and creation were subsequently to take place is termed *tehiru.* The term is taken from the Zohar where, however, it means the exact opposite:[31] It refers to the splendor or brilliance that from eternity enveloped *En-Sof.* In the Lurianic system this splendor departed as a result of the divine *ṣimṣum,* and this withdrawal produced the vacuum of the *tehiru.* Only a faint vestige or residue of the divine fullness and light, the *reshimu,* remained in the primordial vacuum thus created. Although the kabbalists used spatial concepts to describe the divine cosmos from the *tehiru* downward, they nevertheless endeavored to strip their terminology of its plain meaning by interpreting the *tehiru* and the emanation as purely spiritual processes. Spatial categories become applicable only at the very last stage of the process of emanation, that is, in our material cosmos. No doubt the use of spatial concepts had introduced an alarmingly anthropomorphic qual-

31. Zohar I, 15a: "In the beginning [Gen. 1:1] when the will of the King began to take effect, he engraved signs into the heavenly brilliance [that surrounded him]."

ity into kabbalistic symbolism, and there is indeed no better illustration of the paradox of symbolism than Luria's doctrine of retraction. The kabbalists went on unabashed, neutralizing their daring utterances by a qualifying "as it were" or "so to speak." With the aid of this formal reservation they attenuated their symbols in appearance but saved them in reality. All original kabbalistic thinkers, from the author of the Zohar in the thirteenth century to the great Hasidic *ṣaddiqim* of the eighteenth, availed themselves of this approved method of taking the sting out of their sometimes shocking symbolism.

The idea of *ṣimṣum* is related to the concept of a reflected light. In the primordial, infinite light of the divine essence all the forces, lights, and attributes destined to be made manifest later—including also the opposing forces of Mercy and Stern Judgment—were already present, albeit in an undifferentiated state and in "indistinct unity." Within *En-Sof,* Mercy and Stern Judgment are, of course, merely the hidden or potential roots of the corresponding forces that become manifest and "existent" in the world. The root of divine Judgment, or Sternness (in Hebrew, *din*), was not, therefore, recognizable as such; it was dissolved in the infinite abyss of the divine essence like a grain of salt in the ocean. However, by condensing and crystallizing, as it were, at one point, the concentrated power of the "roots of *din*" caused a corresponding withdrawal of the other lights[32] within *En-Sof.* This withdrawal, or regression, which all Safed kabbalists considered to be a function of the principle of limitation or negation—and hence of *din*—partakes of the nature of the reflected light. There is no unanimity among the Lurianists regarding the momentous question of priority. Did the "roots of divine Stern Judgment" bring about the *ṣimṣum,* or was it the latter that caused the "roots of *din*" to appear? The balance of probability is in favor of the former version, which was then intentionally mitigated so as to obscure the daring suggestion that the whole process of *ṣimṣum* and emanation was set in motion in order to eliminate the forces of *din,* like a sort of waste product, from the essence of the Godhead. The whole process would thus have to be conceived as a kind of divine catharsis. Echoes of this doctrine

32. *Din* (lit., "law," "ruling," "judgment") in kabbalistic terminology signifies the divine principle of Stern Justice, hence punishment and destruction—and ultimately the source of evil. On the whole problem, see *Major Trends,* Index s. vv. *Din,* "Evil." The opposite principle is that of Mercy, or Love. The "other lights" are the roots of love and compassion.

can be discovered in later Sabbatian theology and particularly in Nathan of Gaza's doctrine of the "thought-some light" and the "thought-less light."

The kabbalists did not explicitly say that the act of *ṣimṣum* was a divine type and prefiguration of the exile, though the analogy seems obvious. God, instead of revealing Himself, "banishes" and withdraws Himself into the hidden seclusion of His essence. Yet it is surely no accident that the doctrine of *ṣimṣum,* the first inklings of which appeared among the kabbalists of Gerona in the thirteenth century, struck root and blossomed only at a later period, when the problem of exile had become central to religious consciousness.

Into the *tehiru,* the empty space left by the retreating light of *En-Sof,* God sends a ray of His creative light. This ray illuminates the primordial space of creation and acts on the residual light (*reshimu*) within it. It is also the principle of organization which sets the cosmic process in motion according to the structural order of the ten *sefiroth.* Retraction and emanation are thus the two principles through which God reveals Himself as Creator. At every stage of the process of emanation the two principles act and react upon each other, for what is required in order to produce the next stage of being is not merely a further extension of the emanation but, in the first place, another retraction which must provide the possibility of further existence. All existence presupposes a dialectical, twofold movement; nothing comes into being by a simple one-way action. Everything subsists by the combination of retraction and emanation. The rhythm of the living God, like that of organic forms including man, can be described as a double process of inhaling and exhaling. The analogy with organic life suggested itself quite naturally to the Jewish mystics, who viewed God primarily as "living," that is, as a kind of perfect organism whose unity is neither motionless nor static. The vitality of God reveals itself in the organic analogy. In fact, God is the supernal root and origin of all the organic patterns that are manifest in the lower world. The double rhythm of regression and egression is at the root of everything that exists.

Within the primordial space—partly a symbol, partly a concrete reality—the structures of the emanation, that is, the *sefiroth,* begin to delineate themselves next, each revealing a particular aspect of the world of divine lights. The self-manifestations of God to His creatures are really the manifestation of His light in primordial space, for the absolute *En-Sof,* as distinct from primordial space, is beyond thought and comprehension. The supreme manifestation produced by the first ray of light, that is, by the "straight line" penetrating the primordial space, is called the Primordial Man (*Adam Qadmon*). From this being, which is none other than the mode of existence of the supernal lights in the *tehiru,* or primordial space, various lights were bursting forth in a manner that led to that central and decisive event which forms the very heart of Lurianism, and which is described in symbolic terms as the "breaking of the vessels," or the "death of the kings."

In order to grasp the significance of these terms it is necessary to explain briefly the meaning of the Hebrew word translated here as "vessel." The Hebrew *keli* can mean an instrument or tool used by an artisan for a definite purpose, as well as a container or vessel, which contains but also limits that which is inside it. The former meaning was in the minds of the earlier kabbalists when they spoke of *sefiroth* as "vessels," that is, tools used by the Emanator God in the process of creation. But soon the second meaning asserted itself, particularly since the *sefiroth*—unlike ordinary tools—were not distinct from the essence of the artisan that used them. On the contrary, they were "one with Him." The question whether the *sefiroth* were divine substance or merely divine tools was finally resolved in Safed by a definition which largely determined the later Lurianic use of the term: the *sefiroth* are vessels in which the substance of *En-Sof* extends itself and through which it acts. Every *sefirah* can therefore be viewed under the double aspect of substance and vessel, its specific and individual character being due to its quality as vessel, whereas the divine substance is always and unalterably the same and hence supraindividual. The similes by which the kabbalists endeavored to explain how the one and unchangeable divine substance could, in fact, manifest itself in diverse forms generally emphasized the "vessel" aspect, although the other meaning of *keli*—"tool"—was not surrendered. Moses Cordovero summed up the classic solution:[33]

There is no change and division in the Emanator such as would justify the statement that in the ten *sefiroth* He is divided in parts. Division and change do not apply to Him, but [only] to the external *sefiroth* [that are His vessels]. We may make this more plausible to the under-

33. *Pardes Rimmonim,* bk. IV, ch. 4.

standing of the thoughtful student by means of a suitable comparison, to wit, of water in communicating vessels of different colors, such as white, red, green, and so forth. As the water spreads through the vessels, it appears to be colored with the hues of the vessels, although it is essentially one and the same. . . . Even so is it with the *sefiroth:* The vessels are the *sefiroth* . . . whereas the light of the Emanator, which is their essence . . . is the water which by itself has no color whatever.

Luria employed the term "vessels" in a similar sense. The first lights to appear within the Primordial Man were so subtle and spiritual that they could hardly be described as vessels at all. Even the lights that burst forth from his ears, nose, and mouth coalesced in a totality that knew as yet no differentiation between *sefiroth* such as would require distinct vessels. The direct and the reflected lights were perfectly balanced. However, the lights bursting forth from the eyes of Primordial Man emanated in atomized or "punctiform"[34] separation and consequently had to be caught and preserved in special bowls, or vessels, consisting of stronger and more resistant lights. These vessels were supposed to perform a double function. On the one hand, they were to provide a shell or clothing for the divine essence which they contained, in accordance with the kabbalistic principle that no spiritual reality can subsist, as it were, "naked": that which has no "clothing" cannot become manifest. On the other hand, the vessels also served the purpose of purging the "hard" lights of Stern Judgment of the "dross" which they contained. The latter had to be precipitated and then eliminated from the sphere of the divine emanation.

When these lights finally emanated, their impact proved too much for their vessels, which could not contain them and collapsed. Most of the liberated light reascended to its supernal source, but some sparks (according to Luria, two hundred and eighty-eight) remained stuck to the fragments of the shattered vessels. These fragments, together with the sparks of divine light that adhered to them, "fell" into the primordial space. There they produced in due course the forces of the *qelippah,*[35] which are known in kabbalistic terminology

34. The curious Lurianic terminology of "punctiform" vs. collected, viz., coalescing lights, etc., is based on an untranslatable pun on the Hebrew text of Gen. 30:39.

35. Lit., "husk" or "shell." In kabbalistic terminology the realm of the "shells" is that of evil and the demonic powers.

as "the other side." Luria discovered an allusion to his doctrine of the breaking of the vessels in the Zohar's interpretation[36] of Genesis 36:31: "and these are the kings that reigned in the land of Edom before there ruled any king of the children of Israel." The seven kings of Edom signify the forces of Stern Judgment untempered by Mercy; they "died" because the world is maintained only through the balance and harmony of these two principles. These "kings," that is, structures of the untempered forces of *din,* are identical, according to the Zohar, with the primordial worlds which an ancient midrash[37] said were created and destroyed before the creation of our present cosmos. The death of the kings of Edom, that is, of the sphere of untempered *din,* thus preceded the establishment of a balanced and harmonious cosmos, called the realm of the "Patriarch Israel"—not, to be sure, the physical Jacob, but his spiritual, celestial archetype.

The breaking of the vessels introduced a dramatic element into the mystery of the Godhead. In the kabbalistic view, the lights that burst forth from the Primordial Man belonged to the sphere of the divine; they were part of the Godhead. The breaking of the vessels was thus an event that took place within the Deity itself. Its repercussions are manifest in every single detail of Lurianic cosmology. But for the breaking of the vessels, everything would have occupied its rightful and appointed place. Now everything is out of joint. Even the *sefiroth,* whose vessels should have received the supernal influx of light and passed it on—according to the laws of emanation—to the lower orders of being, no longer are where they ought to be. Henceforth everything is imperfect and deficient, in a way "broken" or "fallen." That which should have occupied its appointed and appropriate place has moved somewhere else. However, this situation of not being where one ought to be, namely, of being removed from one's rightful place, is what is meant by the term "exile." In fact, since the breaking of the vessels, exile is the fundamental and exclusive—albeit hidden—mode of all existence. In Lurianism the historical notion of exile had become a cosmic symbol.

Luria himself described the breaking of the vessels as a process obeying certain very definite laws. By pointing out the natural causal-

36. Particularly in the *Idra Rabbah* (Zohar III, 127b–145a).

37. Gen. Rabbah IX, 2. Commenting on Eccles. 3:11 ("He has made everything beautiful in its time"), R. Abbahu (a 3rd-century teacher) said: "God made many worlds and destroyed them until he made the present universe."

ity, as it were, of the event, Luria did not mean to minimize its catastrophic character. Hence arises the crucial question why such a catastrophe should have occurred at all. Luria's disciples were at some pains to account for the breaking. Ultimately all their explanations hinge on the implied necessity of eliminating the *qelippah* from the sphere of holiness, that is, of precipitating the latent germs of evil into real existence and separate identity. Some kabbalists maintained that the breaking was not just an unfortunate accident, but a carefully planned occurrence designed to provide man with the freedom of choice between good and evil. Other kabbalists felt that the ultimate purpose of the breaking of the vessels had to be defined with reference to God Himself and not to man. Once the Godhead was conceived in analogy with a living organism, it was but one step to the notion of this organism eliminating and ejecting the condensed dross of Stern Judgment, whose ultimate roots were sunk deep in the hidden recesses of *En-Sof*. The whole process of emanation thus serves not only the purpose of creation but also that of purging the divine light of its "impurities."

It is immaterial for our present purpose which of the two explanations represents Luria's original view.[38] What matters is that both accounts appear in Lurianic literature. The laws inherent in the divine organism demanded the breaking: "Know therefore that the supernal space is like a field, and the ten points [that is, *sefiroth*] are sown in it. And even as the grains [of seed] grow each according to its virtue, so also these points grow each according to its virtue; and as the grains do not attain to growth and perfection if they remain in their original manner of being—for only in their decomposition is their growth—so it is also with these points. . . . Only by their breaking could the divine configurations [*parṣufim*] be perfected."[39] Another kabbalist gave the simile of the grain of wheat a slightly different

38. Cf. Is. Tishby's analysis in *The Doctrine of Evil and the "Qelippah" in Luria's Kabbalah* (Hebrew) (Jerusalem, 1942), particularly pp. 39–61. Tishby shows that Luria's original and radical mythological conception of a divine catharsis was later mitigated and obscured by Vital.

39. Menaḥem Azaryah Fano "On the *tehiru*" (printed at the beginning of his *Yonath ᵓElem*), and Joseph Solomon del Medigo of Crete, *Taᶜalumoth Ḥokhmah* (1629), fol. 85a. The text is quoted as early as 1625 in Isaiah Horovitz's commentary on the prayer book (*Shaᶜar ha-Shamayim*, Amsterdam, 1717, fol. 56c). Naphtali b. Jacob Bacharach, *ᶜEmeq ha-Melekh*, fol. 24b, reproduces the same text without indicating the source.

twist. The lower seven *sefiroth* are said to constitute the "world of confusion" or "disorder" (*tohu*),[40] for although they are rooted in "absolute whiteness," that is, in the undifferentiated pure spirituality of the highest *sefirah,* yet they contain the beginnings of the differentiation of "colors," that is, of different qualities and attributes, in the vessels. This world of disorder "had to fall from the high summit to the depth of the pit so as to be smashed and dashed to pieces, like the wheat which is separated into flour and bran by grinding. Moreover by their fall the unclean forces are separated from holiness."[41] Vital himself is very cautious in expressing himself on the subject, but he suggests that the breaking resulted from a lack of harmony in the supernal worlds. The various *sefiroth* were not yet constituted and structured as an organic whole or *parṣuf* ("configuration," lit., "countenance"), such as, for example, the human figure. "At the beginning of the process of emanation, the ten *sefiroth* were not ordered one beneath the other so that one would receive [the supernal influx] from the other, neither were they organized in 'configurations.' Each contained all the others, but in this totality each was confused and commingled with all the others without order and system. That is why the seven kings died."[42]

The lights of the ideally integrated and perfect order could become manifest only after the breaking. According to Luria these lights burst forth from the forehead of the Primordial Man in order to restore the disturbed harmony, or—to be more exact—to produce that harmony which could not be attained without a prior breaking. Since the occurrence of this "fortunate fall," the lights of the forehead are arranged in complicated structures called *parṣufim*, each of which manifests a distinctive aspect of the Godhead and its creative power. The divine emanation henceforth exists as a sphere of being, distinct from the Primordial Man; its five configurations (*parṣufim*)[43] express the mystery of the Godhead as it is mystically revealed in the Torah. From this sphere, called the world of

40. The Hebrew word in Gen. 1:2 generally rendered "without form."

41. In an epistle written by the kabbalist Elchanan (of Kremsier in Moravia), printed in Moses b. Solomon's commentary *Yo᾿el Moshe* on Menaḥem Azaryah Fano's *ᶜAsarah Ma᾿amaroth* (Amsterdam, 1649), fol. 87a.

42. Vital, *Shaᶜar Ma᾿amarey RSHBY* (Jerusalem, 1898), fol. 58a.

43. For a brief account of the doctrine of the five *parṣufim,* see *Major Trends,* pp. 269–71.

ʾaṣiluth ("emanation"), the great chain of being descends to the lower worlds of *beriʾah*, *yeṣirah*, and *ʿasiyyah*, which are no longer of the essence of the divine emanation but, rather, "garments," enveloping and clothing the inner soul of things which is none other than the divine power ruling them.

Tiqqun, meaning "mending," "restoration," or "reintegration," is the process by which the ideal order is restored, but the lights of the divine emanation are incapable of bringing it about by themselves. It is true that some of the fallen *sefiroth* were raised up again to a certain level. Generally speaking, however, they could not be restored to the mode of being which they were originally meant to realize but which, as a matter of fact, they had never realized. God in His wisdom allotted this task to man, who thus has to play a major part in the great drama of restitution and *tiqqun*. Adam's original function was conceived by Luria somewhat like this: In the beginning the mode of being of all the four worlds[44] was of a high spiritual order. In fact, all the worlds that issued from the highest "world of emanation" (*ʾaṣiluth*), including even the lowest "world of making" (*ʿasiyyah*), were essentially spiritual. Also the "configuration" of man as manifest in each of these worlds in gradually descending—that is, in increasingly material—configurations of light was a spiritual form reflecting the specific nature of each world. Hence, the configurations appear as "Adam of *beriʾah*," "Adam of *ʿasiyyah*," and so on. However, as a result of its sudden descent or fall after the breaking of the vessels, the world of *ʿasiyyah* no longer occupies its proper place but is situated in dangerous proximity to the *qelippah*, the "shell" and sphere of evil. The original state of the world of *ʿasiyyah* was one of pure being, and even its "matter," or body, was not of the grossly material kind. When Adam, the first man, was created, the process of *tiqqun* of the supernal lights and configurations had almost achieved its end. Almost everything had been "restored" to its proper place, and Adam, the last link in a holy and spiritual chain of being, merely had to administer the last and final touches of *tiqqun*. He was eminently qualified for his task, since his pure and spiritual essence contained within itself all the supernal configurations with which

44. On the "Four Worlds" of the kabbalistic cosmos (*ʾasiluth*, *beriʾah*, *yeṣirah*, *ʿasiyyah;* abbreviated *ʾABYʿA*), cf. *Major Trends*, p. 272, and more fully in *Tarbiz*, III (1932), 33–64.

it stood in a relation of reciprocity. The parts of his body reflected the supernal parts (that is, lights), and every limb of his would affect the corresponding limb of what might be described as the supernal-cosmic *anthropos*. By a mystico-spiritual effort through which he would have attached his whole being to its supernal root, Adam might have accomplished the *tiqqun* and restored all things to their rightful place. This act required a free choice and decision, perfect communion with God, and a definite separation of good from evil, of "flour from bran," the last remnants of which still intermingled in the world of *ᶜasiyyah*.

Had Adam fulfilled his mission, the sphere of holiness would have been purged of the last residue of dross; the *qelippah* would have sunk below the world of *ᶜasiyyah* and would have remained impotent, cut off from the source of true being, and the whole cosmos would have achieved a state of eternal communion with the divine light. The divine influx would have streamed down and back again without let or hindrance, and the soul of the divine emanation would have illuminated from within all the levels of creation to the point of obliterating the separation between the Creator and His creation. The cosmic exile would have come to an end, with Adam acting as the redeemer who restored the world to its unity. The historical process would have ended, even before it had begun, with the establishment of utopia.

Alas, Adam failed. Instead of joining that which needed joining and separating that which needed separation, he tore asunder that which was joined. Expressed in a kabbalistic metaphor inspired by the account of the fall in Genesis 2, Adam "separated the fruit from the tree" and thereby "destroyed the plantations."[45] His intentions were good, but the result was disastrous. Adam's communion with the higher spheres was interrupted, and instead he became attached to the lower worlds and to the evil forces of the "other side." The sin of the historical Adam repeats and re-enacts on the anthropological and psychological levels the havoc wrought by the breaking of the vessels on the ontological plane of the Primordial Adam. The worlds that had begun to rise and to move to

45. "Destroyed the plantations," an expression taken from the Talmudic account of the "Four who entered Paradise" (B. Ḥagigah 14b), is the standard kabbalistic metaphor for "wrong," i.e., disruptive and destructive mystical contemplation.

their ideal positions when Adam entered the Garden of Eden again "fell" when he was driven out, precisely as the vessels of the "world of disorder" had fallen at the primordial catastrophe. But this time they sank even more deeply, for the whole world of *ʿasiyyah* with its constituent ten *sefiroth* descended into the realm of the *qelippah*, and good and evil were again inextricably mixed. Henceforth all beings in the world of *ʿasiyyah*, including man, were clothed in gross matter and in physical bodies deriving from the *qelippah*, instead of in the original subtle and refined matter, namely, in spiritual bodies. Adam's great mission, but now incomparably more difficult and complicated, was laid upon his descendants.

The matter does not end there, however. Through Adam's sin the fate of the divine Shekhinah, imprisoned in the scattered fragments of the broken vessels, is now also shared by "sparks" of human souls: both are prisoners of the *qelippah*. Before the fall, Adam's soul, which contained all other human souls, filled the whole world of *ʿasiyyah*. Luria taught that the soul consisted of six hundred and thirteen parts, precisely as—according to traditional rabbinic anatomy—the human body. Each part is a total configuration or *Gestalt*, that can again be subdivided into six hundred and thirteen parts or "roots." Each of these roots—one might almost call them "soul-limbs"—constitutes a so-called major root or great soul, which subdivides into a number of minor roots or sparks. Every such spark is an individual holy soul.[46] If Adam had fulfilled his mission, all these souls and sparks would have abided within his frame. Being part of him, they would have participated with him in the great work of redemption and would have attained to the consequent eternal bliss. Adam's sin undid all this. Some of the more exalted souls refused to be associated with Adam (that is, with his supersoul) in his sin and left him, ascending to higher spheres. These souls are known as the "supernal splendor" and will not return to this world until the messianic age. Other souls, though associated with the original sin, managed to remain within Adam. Most soul-roots and soul-sparks, however, fell outside the frame of Adam into the realm of the *qelippah*, where they invigorated the Satanic Anti-Adam, who corresponds, on the evil side, to the Primordial Adam of the holy sphere. Adam's stature was drastically reduced and became grossly material.

46. The idea that all human souls were contained in Adam goes back to the Midrash (cf. *Tanḥumah, Ki Thissa*ʾ 12).

Redemptive restitution (*tiqqun*) therefore involves two things: the gathering of the divine sparks that had fallen, together with the fragments of the broken vessels, into the realm of *qelippoth,* as well as the ingathering of the holy souls imprisoned in the "shells" and subserving the Anti-Adam of Belial since Adam's sin. Both processes of *tiqqun* are subsumed under the symbol of the "raising of the sparks." This symbol expresses the true meaning and mystery of the history of mankind, and of Israel in particular. The gentile nations have abandoned the task entrusted to Adam. In fact, their souls actually stem from the *qelippah* and not from the realm of holiness, although, like all things of the *qelippah,* they also harbor some fallen holy sparks waiting to be raised and restored. Since Adam's fall there were a few propitious occasions on which the *tiqqun* could have been achieved, all the fallen sparks raised, and the good finally separated from evil. But none of these opportunities was realized. With the revelation of the Torah on Mount Sinai the world was about to be fully restored, but the sin of the golden calf threw everything back into chaos again. Thereafter the Law was given in order to prepare the *tiqqun* by way of the commandments: each of the six hundred and thirteen commandments of the Law restores one of the six hundred and thirteen parts of the *corpus mysticum* of the Primordial Adam.

The restitution of the human essence to its full spiritual stature is a complicated and protracted process. In every generation a few souls escape from the *qelippah* and enter the cycle of purification and *tiqqun,* migrating from one body to another throughout the four kingdoms of nature until their *tiqqun* is complete. The combination of the traditional view of nature with the Lurianic doctrine of the breaking of the vessels is succinctly formulated by Israel Sarug:

Traces of the divine light adhered to the fragments [of the broken vessels] like sparks or drops. This may be compared to a vessel full of oil; if it breaks and the oil is spilt, some of the liquid will stick to the fragments in the form of drops. Likewise in our case, some of the sparks of light remained. . . . And when the fragments descended to the bottom of the [fourth and last] world of *ʿasiyyah*, they there produced the four elements—fire, air, water, and earth—which in their turn produced the four degrees of mineral, vegetable, animal, and human forms. When all these became completely materialized, some of the drops still remained within the elements. Therefore it should be the aim of every Jew to raise these drops from where they are [imprisoned] in this world and to elevate them to holiness by the power of his soul.[47]

The human soul consists of different lights or aspects which together constitute the "individual spark" of each man. Of particular importance in this connection is the division of the soul into *nefesh, ruaḥ,* and *neshamah* ("soul," "spirit," and "supersoul"). This division recurs in every single spark. The three kinds of soul are ordered in an ascending hierarchy, so that a man realizes his *ruaḥ* only after he has perfected his *nefesh,* and so on, and each exhibits the complete structure of six hundred and thirteen spiritual "limbs." Two further levels, *ḥayyah* and *yeḥidah,* are attained by a few elect souls only, for they are illuminated by the light of the highest configurations of the divine emanation. Thus *yeḥidah,* whose light is that of the highest *parṣuf* (known as the Ancient Holy One), was bestowed only on Abraham and King David—according to some writers not even on them, as it was to be the exclusive distinction of the messianic king. The theory of the five levels of the soul makes use of the five different terms with which, according to a midrashic saying,[48] the soul can be described. But unlike the midrash, for whom these five terms are synonymous, the kabbalist correlates every term with a different aspect of the soul. Man's task is the perfection of his individual spark on all levels; but all its levels or aspects are not necessarily joined simultaneously in one life. The *tiqqun* may thus have to be realized laboriously and piecemeal in the course of numerous lives and transmigrations. The kabbalists took great pains to discover the root of their souls, as only such knowledge would enable a man to restore his soul to its supernal root or would tell him what precisely he was still lacking for the completion of his *tiqqun.* The first calling of Nathan of Gaza, Sabbatai Ṣevi's prophet, was to reveal to penitents and inquirers the root of their souls and to give to each individual instructions for his *tiqqun.* The great Italian kabbalist and poet Moses Zacuto, a contemporary of Sabbatai Ṣevi, provided the exemplary formulation of this doctrine when he wrote:[49] "It behooves every man to inquire diligently

47. Joseph Solomon del Medigo of Crete, *Nobeloth Ḥokhmah* (1631), fol. 175b, and Israel Sarug, *Limmudey ʾAṣiluth* (falsely ascribed to Vital) (Munkacs, 1897), fol. 4d.

48. Gen. Rabbah XIV, 9.

49. In his commentary on Zohar I, 78a; printed in Shalom b. Moses Busaglo's *Miqdash Melekh* (Amsterdam, 1750), fol. 132a.

and to know the root of his soul, so as to be able to perfect it and to restore it to its origin, which is the essence of its being. The more a man perfects himself, the closer he comes to his self."

The laws of transmigration are no less complicated than those of the *tiqqun* of the supernal *parṣufim,* and a full account of them is unnecessary here. One point, however, should be mentioned in passing, as it proved to be of considerable importance in the moral theology of the kabbalists: there is an inner bond, a kind of sympathy of souls, linking all sparks deriving from the same root,[50] and they—and they only—can help one another and influence one another for their mutual *tiqqun.*

The exile of the "lower," terrestrial Congregation of Israel in the world of history is thus merely a reflection of the exile of the supernal Israel, that is, the Shekhinah. Israel's state is symbolic of the state of creation as a whole. It is the Jew who holds in his hands the key to the *tiqqun* of the world, consisting of the progressive separation of good from evil by the performance of the commandments of the Torah. *Tiqqun* is thus an essentially spiritual activity directed at the inner side of the cosmos. But once it will have achieved its end, then this hidden, spiritual perfection will also become manifest outwardly, since outward reality is always symbolic of inner reality. In exile, spiritual activity and mystical concentration (*kawwanah*) affect the inner strata of the cosmos only, "but the [outer] worlds in general are not elevated until the advent of the messiah, when they will all rise by themselves. At present the only exaltation of the worlds is in their inner aspect. . . . In the present period of exile we can raise—even on the Sabbath—the inner side of the worlds only, but not their outside. For if the outer reality were elevated too, then we could behold with our eyes the exaltation of all the worlds on the Sabbath."[51] Once the last trace of holiness is extracted from the *qelippah* so that no divine sparks are left in it, the world of *tiqqun* will become manifest. This is the meaning of redemption.

The Lurianic doctrine of the exile of the Shekhinah and of the meaning of redemption has received its clearest formulation by Vital:

50. On this subject, as well as on the kabbalistic doctrines of the soul and transmigration generally, see G. Scholem, "Seelenwanderung und Sympathie der Seelen," in *Von der mystischen Gestalt der Gottheit,* ch. 4.

51. Ḥayyim Vital, "Shaᶜar ha-Tefillah," ch. 6 *Peri ᶜEṣ Ḥayyim* (Dubrovna, 1804), fol. 7c.

Know that through Adam's sin all souls fell into the depths of the *qelippoth,* which are the remnants of the impurity and the dross that were separated from holiness at the death of the kings of Edom. These *qelippoth* are called the "degrees of death," whereas holiness is [called] the "living God and everlasting King." Therefore they [the *qelippoth*] pursue the holiness that is called "life" in order to draw from it life and sustenance; for as long as they contain some holiness, they feed on it and live, but when there is no holiness at all in them they must die. Therefore they are at pains to search out [and capture] holiness and to cause man's holy soul to sin . . . like one who exerts himself in the pursuit of the food necessary for his sustenance, "and none despises the thief that steals to fill his hungry soul." And behold, when the Temple was destroyed the Shekhinah went into exile among the *qelippoth,* because the souls that had been exiled there no longer had sufficient strength—as a result of their sins—to free themselves. Therefore the Shekhinah . . . descended among them in order to gather in the soul-sparks, . . . to sift them [from the *qelippoth*], to raise them to the sphere of holiness, and to renew them and bring them down again into this world in human bodies. Thus you may understand the mystery of the exile of the Shekhinah. Since the destruction of the Temple this is the work of God, until He shall have ended His work of gathering all the souls that have fallen into the *qelippoth* of the Anti-Adam of Belial and mingled with him from his head to his feet. Until He has finished gathering in even those [last and lowest souls] that have fallen to the feet [of this Adam of the *qelippah*], the messiah cannot come, neither can Israel be redeemed. . . . However, the Shekhinah can gather them only by means of the good works and prayers of the nether worlds according to the mystery of the verse [Ps. 68:35], "Give ye strength to God."[52] The liberation of souls and sparks is proportionate to the good works done by Israel in this world. . . . Only when all souls have left [the realm of the *qelippoth*] can the Shekhinah too depart from there. Then the vitality of the *qelippoth* will depart and they will die and "all evil will vanish like smoke." This is the mystery of [Isa. 25:8], "Death will be swallowed up in victory," which means that the *qelippoth* that are called "death" will be swallowed up in one instant because

52. The prayers from the nether worlds are those of the historical Israel. A kabbalistic interpretation of the verse from Psalms is that Israel, by its good works and mystical *kawwanoth,* gives strength to God (viz., to His Shekhinah) and increases His power in the struggle for *tiqqun.*

of the departure of the divine Shekhinah and all soul-sparks from among them. . . . But the Shekhinah [now] goes into exile among the *qelippoth* only because of the souls [that have to be redeemed from there].[53]

V

This, in brief, is the basic outline of Lurianic mythology. In order to appreciate the myth we must understand its double function as an interpretation *of* history and as a factor *in* Jewish history. The assumption underlying this historical myth is that evil, namely, the *qelippah* or "other side," is no figment of the imagination but a powerful reality. The kabbalists sought the roots of this mighty force in some hidden divine drama, which they proceeded to describe in very realistic terms. Evil, they taught, arose as the result of a process whose dynamics were rooted deeply within the Deity. The conception is sufficiently daring to account for subsequent attempts to conceal or obscure at least some of its more dangerous aspects and implications. In a way the kabbalist doctrine implied that there had been no defect, let alone disaster and catastrophe, in the divine process, but, rather, an organic unfolding of certain fixed laws inherent in the creative activity of God. However, as Lurianic ideas were mediated to the masses by the popular preachers and moralists of the sixteenth and seventeenth centuries, the more dramatic and spectacular aspects of the mystery inevitably tended to become increasingly emphasized. In the popular mind, the history of the world was essentially the drama of God seeking to perfect His true image and "configuration" and of man seeking to promote this aim by means of good works. An explicit statement to this effect will be sought in vain in kabbalistic literature, yet this is clearly the view that underlies the whole Lurianic system.

The historical significance of these ideas is evident. They provided an immediate answer to the most pressing question of the time—Israel's existence in exile. The kabbalistic symbols assured the Jew that his sufferings affected not him alone but contained a profound mystery. Rooted in the very nature of creation, they symbolized the process by which the cosmos struggled to purge itself of the *qelippah*. Israel's bitter experience was only a symbol—albeit a painfully con-

53. Vital, *Shaʿar ha-Gilgulim* (Jerusalem, 1912), fol. 16b, §15.

crete one—of a struggle in the heart of creation. The Jews' very existence was profoundly symbolic, both in its present suffering and in its future redemption. By his works the Jew healed the sickness of the world and reunited the scattered fragments. In fact, he alone could bring about this unification. In the words of a leading kabbalist,[54] "the supernal *tiqqun* can be performed by man only, for he alone is made in the divine image and comprises [within himself] the higher and the lower orders." The kabbalists were not content with the general statement that good works promoted the *tiqqun,* but they showed in considerable detail precisely how each commandment was related to the mystical cosmos, in what part of the "supernal configurations" it was rooted, and how its spiritual essence acted on the "lights" from which it was derived.

Exile, therefore, had its reason, and this reason was rooted in the nature of creation. There is something startlingly novel about this kabbalistic explanation which regarded exile not merely as a test of our faith or a punishment for our sins, but first and foremost as a mission. The purpose of this mission was to raise the scattered, holy sparks and to liberate the divine light and the holy souls from the realm of the *qelippah,* represented on the terrestrial and historical plane by tyranny and oppression.

When the kings fell, some fell into the mineral realm; and because they were seven in number there are also seven kinds of metals. Minerals grow because they contain sparks of holiness. Others fell into the vegetable realm; therefore, there are seven kinds of trees. Others again fell among the seventy nations. And because Egypt is "the nakedness of the land" and the place to which the *qelippoth* principally adhere, many sparks got entangled there and Israel too was enslaved there; even the Shekhinah was exiled with it in order to raise the sparks that were there. . . . When Israel went out of Egypt, all holiness was selected [that is, completely purged] from there. For that reason Israel has been condemned to bondage among the seventy nations, so that it might extract the holy sparks that have fallen among them. Our sages have taught that if a single Jew is taken prisoner by a nation, this is sufficient and is accounted as if the whole of Israel had been in bondage there . . . for the purpose of raising all [the sparks] that had fallen

54. Isaiah Horovitz, *Sheney Luḥoth ha-Berith* (Amsterdam, 1698), fol. 189a.

among that particular nation. Therefore it was necessary that Israel be scattered to the four winds in order to raise everything.[55]

This view represents a profound change in the traditional significance of exile and redemption. Its novel conception of a redemptive mission was very different from that of nineteenth-century "reform" Judaism. Israel's task, according to the kabbalists, was not to be a light to the nations but, on the contrary, to extract from them the very last sparks of holiness and life. The process of *tiqqun,* though essentially constructive, is thus not without destructive aspects in terms of the power usurped by the *qelippoth* and their historical representatives, the gentiles. Some kabbalists, notably in Italy, held that the *qelippah* too would be transformed and restored at the end of days, but the authentic doctrine of Luria and his disciples seems to have predicted the utter disintegration, collapse, and death of the *qelippah* once the completed *tiqqun* deprived it of the source of its vitality. As the divine *parṣuf,* or "countenance," is restored in the world, that of the *qelippah* vanishes. Even more revolutionary than the idea of a mission is the abandonment of the traditional catastrophic conception of messianism. Redemption does not come suddenly but appears as the logical and necessary fruition of Jewish history. Israel's labors of *tiqqun* are, by definition, of a messianic character. Final redemption is therefore no longer dissociated from the historical process that preceded it: "The redemption of Israel takes place by degrees, one purifying after another, one refining after another."[56] The messianic king, far from bringing about the *tiqqun,* is himself brought about by it: he appears after the *tiqqun* has been achieved. The cosmic redemption of the raising of the sparks merges with the national redemption of Israel, and the symbol of the "ingathering of the exiles" comprises both.[57]

The extent to which the eschatological ideas of the Safed kabbalists were removed from those of earlier rabbinic Haggadah is convincingly illustrated by the following example. In Genesis Rabbah XII,

55. Vital, *Sefer ha-Liqqutim* (Jerusalem, 1913), fol. 89a.

56. Samuel Vital's formulation (*Meqor Ḥayyim,* Leghorn, 1791, fol. 7a) with regard to the exodus from Egypt. But Israel's exile in Egypt is the prototype of all subsequent exiles and sufferings.

57. Cf. Tishby, *The Doctrine of Evil and the "Qelippah,"* p. 137. All traditional prayers for the ingathering of the dispersed were interpreted by the kabbalists in both senses.

6, R. Berakhya is reported to say: "although all things were created in the fullness of their being [in a state of perfection], by Adam's sin they were corrupted and they shall not be restored to their perfection until the messiah comes." R. Berakhya clearly regarded the general restoration to perfection as contingent on the coming of the redeemer. The exact opposite is implied by a text written in Palestine or Egypt by a leading kabbalist of the generation before Luria. Discussing the doctrine of metempsychosis, Meir ibn Gabbay writes: "Everything was tainted and hence requires purifying and refining . . . , for the spirit of uncleanness has spread over the world and all orders have been corrupted . . . , pure and impure have mingled, and the abomination has been introduced by the sinners into the sanctuary. . . . Therefore purifying and refining is required to restore everything to its pristine state; for the sweet must be extracted from the bitter that has possessed it as by robbery, and the sweet will eject the bitter [that had penetrated it], so that all will be perfected. But until everything is perfected it is impossible that the messianic king come."[58] These two texts illustrate the profound change in the conception of the messiah's function. The purification and *tiqqun* of souls is not, in Ibn Gabbay's conception, a utopian event dependent on supernatural intervention; rather, it is the outcome of a long process of purification taking place *in* the world. The *tiqqun* which, according to the old Haggadah, must await the arrival of the messiah is now required to take place beforehand, for without it "it is impossible that the messianic king come." Understandably enough the kabbalists themselves wavered between the two conceptions. Ibn Gabbay, after emphatically declaring the *tiqqun* of all souls to be a precondition for the advent of the redeemer, concludes his next chapter, on the restoration of all things by the messiah, with these words:

And this is the *tiqqun* of the world and the restoration of all things to their pristine state, as they were before Adam sinned. For then all the worlds were perfectly balanced and co-ordinated, and the Great Name [that is, God] was in perfect union with his glorious Shekhinah.

58. Meir ibn Gabbay, *ᶜAbodath ha-Qodesh* (Venice, 1566), pt. II, ch. 37. Ibn Gabbay's source is the responsa in a letter which Joseph al-Castili (a Spanish kabbalist writing a few years before the expulsion) sent to his disciple Judah Ḥayyat. See G. Scholem in *Tarbiz*, XXIV (1954–55), 181.

But by Adam's sin the unity was disrupted, the buildings destroyed, and the world corrupted, so that the innermost things were turned out and the outward things [the *qelippoth*] penetrated inside and the spirit of uncleanness spread over the world, as a result of which humankind sinned further, hewed down the beautiful plantations, and sundered the holy union. . . . But with the coming of the messianic king all will be repaired . . . , for the curtain that separates and prevents [the union of all things with God] will be removed, and then the purpose of creation will be fulfilled.[59]

Ibn Gabbay's apparently contradictory statements are really complementary. Clearly the kabbalists had no intention of divesting the traditional image of the messianic world of its utopian traits. Their point was merely that this world could only come into being after the prior completion of the *tiqqun* by man. The purification of souls is not an event that happens in the last stages of history, immediately preceding the final redemption, but it is a process coextensive with history as such. Nothing of the sort was known to the ancient Haggadah, for even where it spoke of a gradual manifestation of salvation, the reference was obviously to stages of the eschatological denouement, as in the well-known conversation of R. Ḥiyya: "R. Ḥiyya and R. Simon ben Ḥalafta walked at sunrise in the valley of ᵓArbela and beheld the light of dawn breaking through. Said R. Ḥiyya to R. Simon: Thus is the redemption of Israel. R. Simon answered: This is what Scripture says, 'When I sit in darkness, God is a light unto me.' At first it [the redemption] comes little by little, then it breaks through, then it increases and multiplies, and finally it spreads everywhere."[60]

Lurianic kabbalah went much further. Only after the termination of all "selections" and purifications and the return of all the lights to their pristine state could the messiah come at all. His advent is the sign that Israel has fulfilled its mission: It has traversed the "valley of tears" and gathered on its way "through the nations the roses of holy souls which were scattered among the thorns."[61] The Talmud

59. Ibn Gabbay, *ibid.*, end of ch. 38.

60. P. Berakhoth I, 2; Midrash Tehillim XXII, 13.

61. Vital, *Shaᶜar ha-Pesuqim* (Jerusalem, 1912), fol. 20c; cf. also fol. 45a. Only if the messiah came "speedily" (i.e., before the "appointed time"), some of the necessary *tiqqunim* might still be incompleted; cf. Tishby, *The Doctrine of Evil and the "Qelippah,"* p. 137.

had said that no converts would be accepted in the messianic era. Ḥayyim Vital explained that there would be no converts because no more holy souls would be left among the gentiles, since, by definition, the messiah could come only after the last spark of holiness had been extracted from them. No doubt here we have Luria's real view, although Lurianic literature offers other and more moderate formulations. "For the kings [that died at the breaking of the vessels] will not be finally selected until the days of the messiah, for then only will they be completely purified and all dross will pass away. . . . The good in them will be united with the holiness that is selected daily and by degrees in the course of time and, with the arrival of the messiah, their selection will be accomplished."[62] In the messianic era the process that began with the breaking of the vessels will be completed. The process is continuous, though the advent of redemption is not necessarily dependent on its prior completion. In any case it is true to say that most kabbalistic texts emphasize the redemptive task laid upon Israel in exile. The messianic king merely puts his seal to the bill of freedom which Israel has written itself by its redemptive labors.

The Lurianic system functioned on the assumption that the *tiqqun* had reached its final stages and that salvation was at hand. The assumption is patent in the imagery used to describe the restoration of the stature of the first Adam. All the lights that had fallen from Adam's limbs and mingled with the limbs of the Adam of Belial were already restored to their proper stations in Adam's frame, and the *tiqqun* had, in fact, proceeded as far down as the heels of the Adam of Belial. It was now only a matter of extracting the last sparks, but this part of the task proved to be the most difficult. The commixture of the sparks of the heel with elements of Stern Judgment, that is, with the potential roots of evil, was so great that the restoration of these sparks to their supernal root required special efforts. The peculiar nature of the souls, that is, sparks, originating in the heels also explains why the present age is rife with insolence. The Talmudic saying, "Before the advent of the Messiah, insolence will increase," was interpreted as hinting at these heels, whose *tiqqun* had to precede the arrival of the redeemer. The final stages of *tiqqun* are thus the hardest of all, and it is in connection with them that the Lurianic writings have preserved many of the catastrophic traits of apocalyptic

62. Vital, *ᶜEṣ Ḥayyim*, XIX, 3.

Haggadah. However, even into this obdurate generation consisting largely of the last remaining souls of the "world of confusion" and the *qelippah,* a few superior souls descended from the "world of *tiqqun*" to assist this last generation in overcoming the sufferings of the final persecutions. These brought the message of *tiqqun* and revealed the divine mysteries enshrined in the new kabbalah.

In this scheme of things much, if not everything, depends on the pious mystics, for only they know the proper "intentions" and meditations and hence can raise ever so many sparks of holiness in one single act of devotion. "If we were perfectly pious and repentant, we would be able to liberate all the good souls from the *qelippah* in one instant, and then the messiah would appear immediately."[63] Now, although we are not worthy, at least we know the rules of mystical meditation during prayer, for the positions of the spiritual worlds are continually changing, and there are appropriate mystical "intentions" for every hour. Every mystical "intention," or *kawwanah,* draws light to the corresponding supernal configurations and raises sparks from the broken vessels. Similarly every religious commandment contains a whole world of inner significances. Yet in spite of this mystical reinterpretation of ritual acts and prayers, the traditional corpus of religious practice did not satisfy the appetite of the Safed kabbalists for redemptive acts of *tiqqun,* and they added new rites and customs as the spirit moved them. Traditional practice, and especially the liturgical calendar, left ample scope for expansion and creation. The kabbalists discovered in every day a specific and individual mystery, which they marked by appropriate rituals and devotions. The conquest of the Diaspora by the new kabbalism, and particularly by its Lurianic version, was accompanied by the spread of a multitude of ritual and devotional innovations. Some of these were glorious mystical celebrations, others were penitential and mournful exercises. Some were complete rituals, others mere trifling details. All were characterized by a messianic tension that necessarily created its own symbols. In Safed the celebration of the Sabbath took on a new character and the kabbalists there invented new penitential seasons, such as the Minor Day

63. Judah Pochawitzer, *Kebod Ḥakhamim* (1695), fol. 10a, quoting Vital's *Shaᶜar ha-Gilgulim.* The wording in the printed edn. of the *Shaᶜar ha-Gilgulim* (Jerusalem, 1912), fol. 16b, is slightly different.

of Atonement, preceding each New Moon, and new times of lamentations, such as the regular midnight devotions.[64]

But not only by means of the speculative writings of its great thinkers did the new kabbalism conquer Jewry. No doubt the so-called Lurianic writings such as Vital's *Tree of Life* (in many different versions) and the works of Israel Sarug and Menaḥem Azaryah Fano, were diligently copied and studied long before they saw print. But together with these theoretical and systematic writings another, no less influential, kind of literature spread from Safed and conquered hearts: the ascetic and moralistic writings of members of the pious brotherhoods, such as the *Beginning of Wisdom* by Elijah de Vidas, the *Book of the Devout* by Eliezer Azikri, and such practical manuals as *The Daily Order* by Moses ibn Makhir. The mounting enthusiasm for ascetic devotions flowed from a double source, for not only was this kind of intense piety the proper attitude for those living during the eve of redemption, but it was also able, by its inherent mystical power, to shorten the painful period of transition, traditionally known as the "birth pangs" of the messianic age. The war against the forces of evil, the mystical promotion of the holy union of God and His Shekhinah, and the ascetic exercise of tasting to the dregs the bitter cup of exile—all became weapons in the kabbalists' battle for hastening the "end." According to a Talmudic saying[65] the son of David would appear only in a generation that was "either wholly sinful or wholly righteous." The Safed kabbalists would not for a moment entertain the idea of the messiah appearing to a sinful generation. Instead they strove to render their generation wholly righteous.

The immense popularity gained by the doctrine of metempsychosis as a result of kabbalistic propaganda no doubt also mirrors some of the deepest emotions of the age. The transmigrations of souls through the four kingdoms of nature provided an added note of agony to exile, which now appeared to be exile of the soul as well as of the body. In fact, even the Torah suffers exile, for "since the day that the Temple was destroyed and the Torah burned, its mysteries and secrets have been delivered up to the demons. And this is called

64. On the ritual innovations of the Safed kabbalists, see G. Scholem, "Tradition and New Creation in the Ritual of the Kabbalists" in *On the Kabbalah and Its Symbolism* (New York, 1965), 118–57.

65. B. Sanhedrin 98a.

the exile of the Torah."[66] This may be an allusion to the Christian exegesis of the Bible.

The most surprising feature of this system, with its characteristic eschatological tension, is the feebleness of its image of the messiah. Lurianic kabbalism hinges on the idea of redemption. It expected the primarily mystical reality of a redeemed cosmos to translate itself ultimately into outward reality and to become manifest. But in this process the messiah himself plays a pale and insignificant role. Except for the highly developed and firmly established tradition of the messiah, perhaps the kabbalists would have dispensed with him altogether. Their imaginative originality, greatly in evidence when a subject is close to their hearts, fails them completely where the messiah is concerned. Where he is mentioned at all, it is in the standard and somewhat hackneyed phrases of the traditional texts. By transferring to Israel, the historical nation, much of the redemptive task formerly considered as the messiah's, many of his distinctive personal traits, as drawn in apocalyptic literature, were now obliterated. On the other hand, the kabbalists left the traditional descriptions of the messianic woes and of subsequent redemption much as they found them. Two strands, therefore, coexisted side by side in kabbalistic eschatology: the old apocalyptic tradition, not yet transformed in the crucible of mystical reinterpretation, and the new kabbalistic conception of *tiqqun*. Both strands played their part in the Sabbatian movement, each in a different social milieu. The masses continued to cling to the conceptions of ancient apocalyptic legend, as is evident from the course of events as well as from the type of messianic propaganda which they conducted. The spiritual elite, on the other hand, tended to interpret everything in terms of the doctrine of *tiqqun*, ultimately eliminating, thereby, all popular elements from their eschatology.

The two strands are clearly distinct in Lurianic literature. In fact very little is said about the concrete, historical woes and "birth pangs" of the messianic age, and even less about the personality of the messiah. Vital's views are of special interest in this connection, since he raises the problem of the self-recognition of the messiah, which subsequently assumed paramount importance in Sabbatian thought, as it had earlier in Christianity.

66. Vital, *Sha^c^ar ha-Kawwanoth* (Jerusalem, 1873), fol. 58a, and *Sefer ha-Gilgulim* (Frankfurt, 1684), fol. 34a.

The messiah will certainly be a righteous man, born of a man and a woman, and he will grow in righteousness until the end of days, acquiring a holy *nefesh, ruaḥ,* and *neshamah.* Then on the day appointed as the end, his *neshamah* of *neshamah* [the highest soul-light called *yeḥidah*], which was preserved in Paradise, will be given to this righteous man and he will become the Redeemer. . . . This is the meaning of what is written [in the Zohar] "and he will awake in Galilee"; as if beforehand he was sleeping he will awake with the infusion of the *neshamah* of *neshamah,* receive more prophetic power, and arise from his sleep . . . and then he will recognize himself as the messiah. His messiahship had not been known [to him] before, but now it will be revealed [to him]. Others, however, will not recognize him. . . . Even as Moses ascended to heaven in body and soul and remained there for forty days, so also this messiah, while remaining unknown to others and known only to himself . . . will be hidden away body and soul in the manner of [Moses, of whom Scripture says] "and Moses entered into the cloud." Then he will be raised up to heaven even as Moses ascended to heaven, and thereafter the messiah will reveal himself fully and all Israel will recognize him and gather around him.[67]

In this instructive passage Vital does not link the messiah's self-recognition with the problem of the messiah of the House of Joseph, a problem mentioned only rarely by Luria's disciples, probably because of their messianic interpretation of Luria's personality. In the *Raᶜya Mehemna* section of the Zohar certain mystical thoughts are propounded concerning the souls of the two messiahs—of the House of David and of the House of Joseph—the roots of their souls, and their destiny at the end of time. But these ideas are shrouded in mystery so that it is difficult to clarify them, except for their principal motif that the two messiahs are somehow connected with Moses and will reveal themselves together with him in the final generation.

In the same context the *Raᶜya Mehemna* also makes a brief reference to Isaiah 53. In the Tannaitic period the "suffering servant" passages had occasionally been interpreted as referring to the messiah, but later Haggadists as well as the medieval commen-

67. Vital, as quoted by Abraham Azulay in his commentary on the Zohar entitled *ᶜOr ha-Ḥammah,* on the Zohar II, 7b. The quotation was used by the author of the spurious (pseudo-Vital) *ʾArbaᶜ Meʾoth Sheqel Kesef* (Korzec, 1804), fol. 78b.

tators preferred different interpretations. In order to undermine Christian exegesis, which identified the suffering servant with Christ, he was interpreted as a figure of Moses, or of Israel, or of the pious in general. In Jewish-Christian disputations the Jewish spokesmen always denied that the passages referred to the messiah. In contrast to this exegetical policy, some late midrashim, particularly the impressive eschatological sections in the *Pesiqta Rabbathi*, maintained the Tannaitic tradition of a messianic understanding of the servant chapters. A new impetus was given to this tradition by the Portuguese marrano Solomon Molkho. Molkho, writing some thirty years after the Spanish expulsion, introduced into his writings the traditional Christian typology, which saw in Job a type of the messiah. In his homily "On the Messiah and Job," Isaiah 53 is unreservedly made to refer to the messiah, albeit with a pointedly anti-Christian polemical turn. The Safed kabbalists did not adopt this messianic interpretation of the servant chapters, and Ḥayyim Vital still explains that Isaiah 53 refers to Moses or to the righteous in general.[68] However, Moses Alsheikh, one of Vital's teachers, popularized the messianic interpretation of the chapter by his widely read commentary on the Prophets, *Marʾoth ha-Ṣobeʾoth* (*The Looking Glass*).

In fact, even Vital occasionally resorted to the messianic interpretation of the figure of the suffering servant, associating it with the person of his master, Isaac Luria. One of Vital's last disciples, Hayyim ha-Kohen of Aleppo, enlarging on the messianic significance of Isaiah 53, thus comments on the expression "a man of pains and acquainted with disease."[69] "I received the interpretation of this from my master, the divine kabbalist [R. Ḥayyim Vital] of blessed memory. The Redeemer of Israel will be marked by two signs: He will be a man of pains and acquainted with disease. The meaning of 'man of pains' is that he will always be suffering, and also that he will always and permanently suffer from a specific disease. That is [the meaning of] 'acquainted with disease,' which was the case with his [Vital's] master,

68. Vital, *Sefer ha-Liqqutim*, fols. 55d, 83b.

69. Isa. 53:7, in the translation of the Jewish Publication Society of America. This translation renders the literal meaning underlying Vital's exegesis as against the better known A.V. rendering "a man of sorrows and acquainted with grief."

Isaac Luria of blessed memory."[70] The idea that the messiah suffers from a chronic disease is of interest in appreciating subsequent Sabbatian developments. Vital was convinced of the messianic character of his master, Luria, and, like other kabbalists, he seems to have regarded the year 1575 as the appointed date of the "end." Had the generation been worthy, Luria would no doubt have revealed himself that year as the messiah. Because the generation did not prove worthy, the "Holy Ark was hidden" and Luria died in the prime of life, three years before the time appointed for redemption. His disciples realized only afterward that he had been the messiah of the House of Joseph. Vital reports that "once, as we went to the tombs of Shemayah and Abtalyon[71] to pray, my master urgently and repeatedly entreated us to recite the words [from the Eighteen Benedictions] 'and the throne of thy servant David' with the special intention that the messiah of the House of Joseph should live and not die. . . . At the time we did not understand his words, but God knows the hidden things, and his end was accounted for by his beginning, for my pious master died because of the multitude of our sins."[72]

Not all writers were careful to distinguish between the victorious hero, the messiah of the House of David, and the hero who falls in battle, the messiah of the House of Joseph. Different views could be taken of Haggadic statements or scriptural hints concerning the sufferings of the messiah, and there was no agreement as to which exactly was intended. The messianic Haggadah embodied in the Talmud (B. Sanhedrin 97–98) makes no mention of the messiah of the House of Joseph. The description of the messiah as "the leper of the House of R. Judah the Prince" (B. Sanhedrin 98b) or the legend describing him as sitting at the gates of Rome clearly refers to the messiah of

70. Ḥayyim ha-Kohen, *Torath Ḥakham* (Venice, 1654), fol. 17d. Ḥayyim ha-Kohen's book was published a few years before the Sabbatian outbreak, and its remarks on Isa. 53 and on the messianic suffering were much quoted by Sabbatian writers.

71. Two Palestinian teachers (1st century B.C.E.) whose tombs were venerated near Safed.

72. Vital, "Shaᶜar ha-ᶜAmidah," *Peri ᶜEṣ Ḥayyim*, ch. 19. In the original source (on which Shlomel Dresnitz drew for his account in *Shibḥey ha-ᵓAri*), the story is told in a more solemn style. Vital himself omits any reference to Luria's messianic character in his *Shaᶜar ha-Kawwanoth*, but his son, Samuel Vital, writes (*Shaᶜar ha-Gilgulim*, fol. 42b) that if Israel had repented, his father (Ḥayyim Vital) would have become the messiah of the House of Joseph.

the House of David. Unlike Christianity, Judaism could not draw on the concrete experience of a messianic personality in shaping its image of the messiah. Consequently the image remained indefinite and vague. The fact that Sabbatai Ṣevi fitted Vital's definition so uncannily well is one of the curious accidents of history.

The Talmudic statement that God had intended to make King Hezekiah the messiah indicated to the kabbalists that God sent a spark of the messiah-soul into this world in every generation. Its function is "to redeem [Israel] if they repent, or to preserve the world in evil times, as in the generation of the great [Hadrianic] persecution, or else to enlighten the world in the period of exile through His Torah."[73] One of the most widely read kabbalistic books in the time of Sabbatai Ṣevi states: "After the land has been paid its Sabbaths,[74] God waits for Israel to repent so as to redeem it. In every generation he creates one perfectly righteous man, worthy—like Moses—on whom Shekhinah rests, provided that also his generation merits it. . . . He will redeem Israel, but everything depends on the transmigration of the souls and their purification. It is in the hands of God whether to prolong or to hasten the creation of souls. This is the mystery [expressed in the Talmudic saying] 'the son of David will not come until all souls contained in the *guf* ["body" or "frame"] of the first Adam are exhausted.' Until this day we are waiting for God . . . to create him [the Messiah] again, enlighten our eyes with His Torah, and take the Land of Israel out of the hand of Ishmael."[75] The disciples of Luria also discovered a hint in the *Tiqquney Zohar* to the effect that "the messiah of the House of Joseph is reborn in every generation. If there is a sufficient number of righteous men in his generation to save him from death [by their merits, then all is well], but if there is no one to save him, then he must die. However, by the repeated deaths he suffers in every generation, he atones for himself so that

73. Nathan Shapira of Jerusalem, *Tub ha-ᵓAreṣ* (Venice, 1655), fol. 38a, quoting a Lurianic homily on Ps. 15:1: "Lord who shall sojourn in thy tabernacle." I have found no such homily in the known writings of Luria and Vital.

74. I.e., the claims of the Holy Land for atonement (cf. Lev. 26:34–35) have been satisfied. Now the only remaining impediment to redemption was Israel's sinfulness.

75. *ᶜEmeq ha-Melekh*, fol. 33a. I have inverted the order of the two parts of the quotation.

he need not die at the hands of the wicked Armilus,[76] but may die every time by a divine kiss."[77]

The idea that a spark of the messiah-soul is present in a number of righteous, namely, "messianic," men throughout the generations is fairly general in the writings of the Safed kabbalists. All agree, however, that the highest part of the soul, *yeḥidah*, comes to him only after the consummation of the general *tiqqun* and is not subject to metempsychosis. In fact, nobody except the actual messiah ever arrives at it.[78] On the other hand, the Safed school preserved a tradition going back to the early Spanish kabbalists and known since Moses de Leon, according to which the messiah is a reincarnation of Adam and of King David. The three Hebrew consonants forming the word "ADaM" can be read as an acrostic made up of the initials of the names Adam, David, Messiah. The earliest kabbalists, such as the author of the *Bahir*, believed that the messiah was not subject to metempsychosis; his soul, when it finally descended, would be quite new. The Lurianic system combined the two contradictory traditions. The messiah's *nefesh*, *ruaḥ*, and *neshamah*, or possibly sparks deriving from their root, were subject to metempsychosis and had to be saved from the *qelippah*, much as the souls of the patriarchs and other saints. Yet the highest part of the messiah's soul, the *yeḥidah*, by virtue of which he acquires his full messianic nature, is conferred on him only at the consummation of the general *tiqqun*. Then it will descend on him from the "supernal splendor," that is, the realm of the souls that never participated in Adam's fall but departed from him before he sinned and ascended to their supernal source in the sphere of *ʾaṣiluth*.

At this point, it may be mentioned that even the idea of the messiah having in himself by necessity something of the "evil side" was not entirely foreign to orthodox kabbalism. It is attested to by R. Moses Galanté (about 1580), one of Moses Cordovero's outstanding disciples. He says: "It is known that in all our doings we give some part to the *qelippah,* the power of evil, in order to prevent it from accusing us [in the courts of heaven]. . . . And therefore, there

76. The Antichrist of Jewish apocalyptic legend.

77. Nathan Shapira in his addenda to Vital, "*Shaʿar ha-ʿAmidah,*" *Peri ʿEṣ Ḥayyim*, ch. 19.

78. Vital, *Sefer ha-Gilgulim*, ch. 19.

has to be something of the power of the *qelippah* in him, so that if the forces of the *qelippah* see that its own power is in this thing [that is, in messianic redemption], they do not come forth as accusers, and do ye understand [this mystery]."[79]

We have described, so far, some of the characteristic features of the Lurianic conception of the messiah. We can now turn to what seems to be a novel conception of the woes, or "birth pangs," of the messianic age. Needless to say, the traditional ideas on the subject remained firmly established in Safed. Thus Moses Cordovero writes that "the sufferings of Israel will increase to the utmost, and they [the people of Israel] will be so distressed that they shall say to the mountains 'cover us,' and to the hills 'fall upon us.' . . . And the reason for this is that the Shekhinah will judge her house [Israel] so as to purify it for redemption. . . . And whoever makes his neck stiff and repents not will be lost, and whoever puts his neck into the yoke of penitence, gladly accepting all tribulations, will be purified and found worthy. . . . [Israel] will pass through one refining after the other, until it will be [like] pure unalloyed silver; and this dispensation will occur with the utmost sternness of Judgment."[80] Vital's description, however, is more differentiated and clearly distinguishes between those who have to pass through the trials and woes of the advent and those who have not. Kabbalists, we are told, belong to the second category:

Those who have adorned themselves with the mystery of good works and have practiced the doing of their commandments and have prayed in cleanliness and purity in the way of mystery [that is, in a mystical manner], will no doubt share in the shining of the Tree of Life, because they were on the side of the soul of *ʾaṣiluth*, and they need not be tried at the time of redemption. For the trial is only for those who are concerned with the mystery of the interpretations of Torah from the side of the Tree of Knowledge of Good and Evil, because their souls stem from the side of *beriʾah*, *yeṣirah* and *ʿasiyyah* where "the evildoers go about" [that is, where they are surrounded by the power of the *qelippah*], and they have to be tried in order to show whether they will adhere to good or to evil. But they who are from the side of the Tree of Life [that is, the kabbalists]

79. From *collectanea* which one of Galanté's pupils assembled in Safed (ca. 1590), MS. Halberstam 348 (now in Jews' College, London), fol. 2b.

80. Cordovero, *ʾElimah Rabbathi* (1881), p. 91.

. . . will not suffer from the trials of exile at the end of days as will ordinary sinners.[81]

The woes and tribulations of the messianic advent are conceived literally enough, but kabbalists, whose religious understanding is of a spiritual, nonliteral kind, will be spared the messianic suffering in its literal sense. The view that kabbalists were beyond apocalyptic catastrophe is eloquent testimony to a sense of superiority that undoubtedly acted as a powerful factor in the propagation of kabbalistic doctrines.

The kabbalists in Safed had developed this feeling of superiority before Luria's arrival. This is indeed what one would expect in a community of saints and inspired ecstatics, and the history of religions provides many analogies. This superior attitude found a particularly extreme expression in the writings of a poor and humble yet high-flying kabbalist, R. Solomon Turiel, who composed his *Homily on the Redemption*[82] some time between 1560 and 1570, probably in Safed. Developing some of the statements in the *Raᶜya Mehemna* concerning the Tree of Life and the Tree of Knowledge, Solomon Turiel declared that the messiah would rule exclusively over those concerned with the Tree of Knowledge of Good and Evil, that is, the interpreters, the masters of the body of Torah, the Talmudists. To them the messiah would appear "meek and sitting upon an ass." It was different with the kabbalists who applied themselves to the Torah according to the Tree of Life, that is, spiritually, and not corporeally. By their mystical practice they had joined the two trees and therefore did not need a messiah at all. They will dwell in Paradise "and their messiah will be Moses," not the son of David to whom they cannot be subject since they are superior to him. Moreover, those who dwell in the Holy Land at the end of time (in Turiel's view, his own time) and study the kabbalah will be exalted to a particularly high degree and will hear the law directly from God's mouth, "like children at school" from their teacher. The Talmudic saying that there was no difference between the present age and the "world to come" except for Israel's subjection to the gentiles referred only to the literal in-

81. Nathan Shapira of Jerusalem, *Tub ha-ᵓAreṣ*, fol. 36a, quoting from a MS. of Ḥayyim Vital.

82. I have published Solomon Turiel's extraordinary homily in *Sefunoth*, I (1956), 62–79.

terpreters, who would merely exchange their subjection to the gentiles for subjection to the messiah, whereas the spiritual elite would be translated to a different sphere of being altogether.

We have already had occasion to remark that two kinds of eschatology, the mystical and the apocalyptic, existed side by side in the sixteenth century. The kabbalists in Safed remained unaware of the possibility of a clash between the two views. They emphasized the spiritual aspects of redemption more than its external trappings, yet the latter were not obliterated but were interpreted as symbols of a spiritual process of transformation. It never occurred to them that a chasm might open between the symbol and the reality symbolized. When the kabbalists shifted the center of gravity of their messianism from the outside world to an inner, spiritual realm, they did not sense what they were doing. They thought that the national redemption of Israel, which they conceived as the outward symbol of a profounder cosmic change, would of necessity follow all those mystical processes in which they were primarily interested. In a world of homiletical and allegorical interpretations there are no incompatibilities and contradictions. According to an old rabbinic adage, "Scripture has seventy faces," that is, a multiplicity of equally valid aspects and interpretations. The distinction between the literal and the mystical significance of religious symbols concealed the fact that in the guise of mystical symbolism a fundamentally new conception had established itself. As long as the messianic idea had not been tested in the crucible of historical experience, the different conceptions could coexist and eschatological propaganda could draw on them all. But in the hour of trial, the dialectical contradictions became manifest. Until Sabbatai's appearance, in fact until his apostasy, the paradox remained unrecognized. The political messianism of the masses and the mystical messianism of the kabbalists appeared to form an integral complex of ideas. Even within the Sabbatian movement, where the two strands appeared one after the other, everything seemed at first perfectly straight. Political messianism quite naturally took the lead, until by dint of historical failures and disappointments it was gradually displaced by a new version of purely mystical messianism.

The messianic mood that prevailed in Safed had found its faithful and most systematic expression in Lurianic kabbalism. There were, however, also other, no less extreme expressions of the messianic spirit, connecting in their own ways the doctrine of the transmigration of soul-sparks with eschatological speculations. One such text, composed in 1552–53 by an anonymous author, probably a member of the kabbalistic circle in Safed, may serve as an example. In some manuscripts, as well as in the printed editions of parts of this book, the authorship is attributed to Abraham ha-Levi Berukhim, one of the most striking figures in the community of the devout in Safed who greatly influenced its ascetic and devotional practices.[83] The attribution is still uncertain, and no trace of Cordoverian, let alone of Lurianic, kabbalah can be discovered in the voluminous work. But we definitely know that the *Gali Razaya*ᵓ (*Revealed Mysteries*) circulated widely in the early seventeenth century and in the years preceding the rise of the Sabbatian movement. Extracts from it appeared in many kabbalistic anthologies and provided subject matter for kabbalistic preachers.[84]

The author frequently discusses a problem that seems to have held a particular fascination for him. Why did so many biblical heroes, Israel's ideal saints, love "strange women" and contract alliances that were, strictly speaking, forbidden? The cases of Judah and Tamar, Joseph and the wife of Potiphar, Moses and Zipporah, Samson and Delilah, Boaz and Ruth, Joshua and Rahab (whom Joshua married in rabbinic legend), and others suggest a mysterious relationship between Israel's saints and heroes and the "other side" that requires some explanation. The mystery—a very curious piece of kabbalistic psychoanalysis, so to speak—discovered by the author is this: "Whenever God wants to raise a king or hero to wreak vengeance on the heathen, it is necessary that there be some kind of relationship or rapport between the gentile nations and the Jewish king, so that Scripture should be fulfilled [Isa. 49:17]: 'Thy destroyers and they that make thee waste shall go forth from thee' . . . , for whoever is born in order to humble the

83. The writings of the Safed kabbalists recount many details of Berukhim's ascetic life. He had come from Morocco to Safed, where his soul was held to be a spark from that of the prophet Jeremiah. He once beheld the Shekhinah in the guise of a mourning woman as he was performing his devotions at the Wailing Wall in Jerusalem.

84. On the *Gali Razaya*ᵓ see my remarks in *Kiryath Sepher*, II (1925), 119–24, to which much more could be added. About a third of the work was printed in Mohilev in 1812. A complete text is preserved in MS. Oxford 1820. Numerous extracts are quoted in some 17th-century kabbalistic anthologies (e.g., *Yalqut Ḥadash* and *Yalqut ha-Re*ᵓ*ubeni*).

foes of Israel must have some measure of communion with the 'left side.'"[85] This principle is a contingency of the nature of the world itself. Throughout the cosmos there exists a dichotomy between male and female worlds, and the process of *tiqqun* is the effort to reunite them. The feminine is under the dominion of the "other side," and this situation has far-reaching effects on the economy of the cosmos, since it results in what amounts to a cosmic law: namely, "that all offspring of the 'pure side' have a part in the 'impure side,' through the females . . ."; ". . . all females belong to the 'left side,'"[86] and the "left side," as we know, is the source of the *qelippah*. This law is operative on all levels, from the exiled Shekhinah that has fallen under the sway of the *qelippah* and must be purified, to the soul of man whose transmigrations take place according to the causality of purification. In this process the "strange women," who are the daughters of the pious heathen, play an important part, for they provide the necessary point of contact between the great souls of Israel and the "other side." Our author explains:[87] "Know for sure that the 'other side' has been permitted to contract marriages between some of its women and the heroes and saints of Israel. The souls of these women are descended from the pious gentiles, and the pious gentiles thereby acquire a share in the world to come because [in this way] they mingle with Israel. Therefore, whenever the 'other side' sends its impure forces to oppress Israel by destroying its religion, it is necessary that an Israelite king or hero, who has some contact with the 'impure side' through the daughter of a strange god [a gentile woman], step out against them." Inner Jewish history consequently unfolds according to the nature of the hidden ties binding Israel's heroes to the "other side," ties not altogether negative. No decisive action takes place in which the protagonist's situation is not characterized by a fundamental ambiguity acquired either through birth (as the case of David, descended from Ruth the Moabite) or through marriage. More than a hundred years before the Sabbatian movement we find a philosophy of history based on a mystical psychology exhibiting striking similarities to some of the doctrines of later Sabbatians. The similarities are even more surprising if we consider the fact that the *Gali Razaya*ʾ did not constitute a direct source of Sabbatian speculations. The differences between the two

85. *Gali Razaya*ʾ, 1812, fol. 23a.

86. *Ibid.*, fol. 6d. 87. *Ibid.*, fol. 29.

systems are obvious. However daring the doctrine of *tiqqun* and of the raising of the sparks from the *qelippah*, our author did not link it with active preparations for the coming of the messiah. He was careful not to apply to the future the theory which he had so successfully used to explain the past. Thus he saved his messiah from an unduly close and compromising relationship with the "other side."

Nevertheless, our author connects the idea of the raising of the souls of the "daughters of strange gods" with the familiar motif of the "holy deceit," a concept that we meet again in different form in Lurianic literature through which it exercised considerable influence on Sabbatian thought. Samael, the prince of the "other side," is aware of the proximity of holiness to the female principle of the "left side." He also knows that he is entitled to demand permission of the celestial court to bring into this world some of the female souls under his sway. Therefore, as soon as he learns that a great soul is about to descend to a leader of Israel not yet born, he claims his due. On receiving permission from the celestial court, Samael prepares to send an impure soul from the "outer [thoroughly evil] power" of darkness to seduce the leader of Israel and frustrate his mission. At the last minute, however, a soul from the "inner [essentially holy] power" of darkness, that is, one of the souls of the pious gentiles, is substituted for the impure soul and enters the newborn child. Samael, rejoicing in his supposed victory, remains unaware of the substitution, which actually promotes the process of purification, since *tiqqun* is only possible by liberating the female aspect of holiness from the sway of the "other side."

The Lurianic system has some similar notions, but it does not limit the fall into the "other side" to the feminine alone. All kinds of holy souls from the most diverse roots, including sparks of saints and perfectly righteous men, fell into the *qelippah,* which now holds them fast and yields them only with great difficulty, in obedience to the divine law of *tiqqun*. The more holy a soul, the greater the difficulty of extracting it from the clutches of the "other side." The birth of holy souls necessitates the pretense of some visible or hidden blemish. "Sometimes the higher and more exalted souls remain in the depths of the *qelippoth* and cannot leave unless assisted by special merits. . . . Sometimes when a man commits a sin in this world, and the *qelippoth* try to destroy him and to lead him astray, they draw down on him, from his own root, a soul that has been sunk in the deep mire of the *qelippoth*. This [soul] they bring out [from the *qelippoth*] and infuse . . . into the man who has sinned, so as to make him sin even more. Sometimes it happens that this soul which they have made to descend on the sinner is a great soul . . . but [because they have linked it to the person of a sinner] the *qelippoth* believe that it is lost forever and will never regain its original [holy] state. But God helps it, and it shakes off the *qelippoth*, showing its strength and holiness and even helping the man [that is, the sinner to whom it has been joined] to turn to good."[88] Vital expressly states that "when a soul is exceedingly great [holy], it is impossible to save it from the *qelippah* except by ruse and cunning." Vital's soul was, on his own evidence, of this kind. "In my case too, the evil powers did not mind the matter [of my soul coming into this world] because they thought that I was already lost; but God snatched me from them. . . . They thought it would be to their advantage [to use me for their purposes], but I became their enemy."[89] A disastrous miscalculation indeed! The *qelippah* lets go a "great soul" in the hope that on account of its origin—particularly when its birth was due to a sinful union—it would work more evil, sinning and causing others to sin. Samael relies on the old Talmudic rule that the greater a man, the greater also his temptation to sin, but his hope is disappointed. The soul which he has let go overpowers all evil, even that inherent in its own origin, and performs mighty acts of *tiqqun*. In this way Luria accounted for the otherwise shocking origins of Abraham, for example, who was conceived by a menstruating, that is, impure woman; or David, whose conception involves another objectionable detail.[90] In fact, God devised all sorts of devices at the time of their conception in order to deceive the *qelippah* and make it yield its prisoners. In this manner the concept of the holy fraud, which so enthralled Vital, was turned into a cornerstone of Sabbatian doctrine from the start. Vital, as we have seen, who thought himself a potential messiah yet pictured at length the rising of his soul from the depths of the *qelippah*, unwittingly furnished the doctrine of Nathan of Gaza with its image of the messiah's soul. At the same time it is difficult

88. Vital, *Sha^car ha-Gilgulim*, fol. 28a (*Haqdamah* 27). 89. *Ibid.*, fol. 65a.

90. Cf. Vital, *Sha^car ha-Pesuqim*, fol. 52c (on Abraham), and *Sha^car ha-Gilgulim*, fol. 62a (on David). For David see also the references in *SS* (Hebrew version of *Sabbatai Ṣevi*), I, p. 50, n. 3; L. Ginzberg, *The Legends of the Jews*, IV, p. 82.

to escape wondering about the prefiguration of some very modern psychoanalytical ideas in these paradoxical theses of kabbalistic psychology.

We have sketched the profound change that Lurianic messianism had wrought to the idea of redemption. In the last resort evolution had taken the place of revolution in the eschatological scheme. No doubt traditional notions of apocalyptic catastrophe still lingered in the new understanding of the final annihilation of the *qelippoth*, but ultimately the conception of a causally determined and continuous progress toward redemption was by far the more important element. We also noted the significant analogy between the Lurianic notion of a causally governed process of *tiqqun* and the ideas of the author of the *Gali Razaya*ᵓ. A somewhat different, though no less interesting, parallelism can be found in the view of Luria and of R. Judah Loew of Prague, one of his outstanding contemporaries. In the thought of R. Loew, kabbalah and philosophy intermingle, and both are submerged by a stream of homiletic eloquence. His prolixity tends to hide his profundity.[91] In his work on eschatology, *Neṣaḥ Yisraᵓel* (*Glory of Israel*, 1599), the figure of the redeemer dwindles into insignificance beside the subject of redemption itself. Combining breadth with profundity, R. Loew endeavored to construct a theological system around the themes of exile and redemption. There is a surprising similarity between his system, built on philosophical premises, and the Lurianic doctrines, whose presuppositions are essentially gnostic.

For R. Loew, too, exile and redemption form part of a system of cosmic law. Exile is a disturbance of the natural order of history, and every disturbance requires to be set right again. "The exile of Israel and the destruction of our Temple are an [anomalous] exception to the order of the universe, and it is known that whatever is a deviation from the order of the universe and an exception, has only temporary existence." He goes on to explain that "time actualizes everything intended to become actual in the world, because everything depends on time. And because everything depends on the time process, everything becomes actual at the proper time."[92] Redemption, which is the perfection of being and the final actualization of all things,

91. On R. Loew (Liva) see Ben Zion Bokser, *From the World of the Cabbalah: the Philosophy of R. Judah Loew of Prague* (New York, 1954).

92. *Neṣaḥ Yisraᵓel*, chs. 24 and 27.

must therefore take place at the end of days. Like every perfect thing in the world, redemption conforms to the Aristotelian rule that nonexistence precedes existence. Existence "comes into being little by little" and not all at once. The same applies to the unity of the redeemed world, which R. Loew regards as the final goal of history. Until the advent of the messiah the world cannot attain its true unity, for this would contradict the basic law of all being, which requires everything to develop step by step toward its perfection and the actualization of unity.[93] In accordance with these laws, R. Loew assumes that there can be no direct continuity between exile and redemption. An intermediary period, that is, the "birth pangs" of the messianic age, is a logical necessity. "Before the messiah manifests himself, the weeding out of being in the world will take place, for every new being is the ruin of the being preceding it and only then [with the ruin of the old] will the new being begin." He continues: "It appears that there will be a ruin of the old being in the world that changes different things; and just as there shall be change from the ruin of the old being, so will there be a difference in the world because of the new that has come into it; as every ruin is change so every being is change in the world—and this is called the birth pangs of the messiah. . . . Thus when a new reality will be actualized, it will be the age of the messiah, the actualization of the new being—and that will be truly different. In this manner, the pangs of the messiah will appear, just as with a woman in labor, because of the new being and creation entering the world."[94] The catastrophic character of redemption is still preserved in this account, but it is no longer due to a miraculous intervention from above. The final catastrophe is sufficiently accounted for by the laws of development toward actual perfection immanent in the nature of things. On this point the similarity between the views of R. Loew and the parallel notions of Lurianic kabbalism is quite close.

VI

Our preceding analysis has yielded some kind of answer to our initial question whether, at the time of the Sabbatian movement, any religious and national factor embraced with equal relevance the whole of Israel transcending geographical and class boundaries. We have

93. *Ibid.*, chs. 22–23. 94. *Ibid.*, chs. 35 (end) and 36.

emphasized that the importance of economic and local factors, though of limited effect, is not to be neglected. In the period under discussion, the spectacular rise to economic prosperity of certain Jewish groups was matched by the pauperization of the Jewish masses in such important centers as Poland. The net result of these developments was a perpetuation of the Jew's sense of basic instability. The feeling of uncertainty had become general and deep-seated, and in this respect at least, there was no difference between the experience of the rich and the poor. On the contrary, the wealthy members of the community were exposed to all sorts of misfortunes, such as extortions, arbitrary and sudden financial demands of rulers, economic fluctuations, and the adverse effects of political events. The seventeenth century saw no improvement over earlier centuries in this respect. The fears and anxieties of a prosperous Jew in Smyrna or Shiraz were not much different from those of his brethren in Venice, Lvov, or Amsterdam. This basic instability largely prevented the crystallization of essential differences in the social psychology of various communities of the Diaspora. We need not be surprised, therefore, that writings expressive of the eschatological mood of the age were eagerly read throughout the Jewish world.

In this social and psychological context, the religious revival in Safed, and Lurianic kabbalism in particular, fulfilled an ideological function that went far beyond the religious consciousness of its originators. Their depth of vision evidently embraced the needs and problems of a very wide public. It would surely be a grave misrepresentation were we to describe Lurianism, by itself and in isolation, as an active historical factor. But in the context of Jewish existence in the Diaspora, the gnostic myth of the kabbalist mystics could become a national myth of great dynamic power. Whatever the transformations in which Lurianic doctrine reached the masses, they all contributed toward the same result. Wherever Lurianism came, it produced messianic tension; and everywhere there were smaller or larger groups responding to it. Often, as in Italy and Turkey, these groups were organized as fraternities of devout and pious men desirous of adopting the devotions and ascetic exercises propagated from Safed. Elsewhere they existed more loosely, without an organizational framework. Finally, the real centers from which Lurianic messianism radiated into Jewry were the schools and the disciples of the kabbalistic enthusiasts, and more especially the popular preachers.

Many preachers proclaimed the kabbalist gospel unembellished. Others avoided the technical terminology of Lurianism and preferred to spread its tenets in a language that would be meaningful to the uninitiated. Characteristic of the latter group and of their earnest desire to communicate kabbalistic ideas to the masses are works such as *Geburoth ʾAdonay* (*Mighty Deeds of the Lord*, 1582) by R. Loew of Prague, and *Beyth Moʿed* (*Meetinghouse*, 1605) by R. Menaḥem b. Moses Rava of Padua. R. Isaiah Horovitz, on the other hand, gathered together all the strands of revealed and esoteric tradition in his *Two Tablets of the Law* (*Sheney Luḥoth ha-Berith*, 1620–30, abbreviated to *SHeLaH*), weaving from them an all-inclusive fabric of Jewish life. Yet the mystical perspective determined his view throughout the whole voluminous work, and the light of kabbalism suffuses every subject it touches. Its objectives, both to guide the reader to a saintly life in the manner of the kabbalah and to clarify theoretical Jewish learning, are mixed together.

Lurianic kabbalism first spread from Palestine to Europe orally and through manuscripts; in 1630–60 Lurianic works begin to appear in print. Among the works printed in this period are Isaiah Horovitz's *SHeLaH;* the writings of Joseph Solomon del Medigo of Crete, *Thaʿalumoth Ḥokhmah* (*Hidden Wisdom*) and *Nobeloth Ḥokhmah* (*Fruits of Wisdom*); *Yonath Elem* by Menaḥem Azaryah Fano; *Megalleh ʿAmuqoth* (*Revealer of Deep Things*) by Nathan Shapira of Cracow; the kabbalistic commentaries on Karo's rabbinic code *Shulhan ʿArukh* by Vital's disciple Ḥayyim ha-Kohen of Aleppo; and the writings of Nathan Shapira of Jerusalem and of Abraham Herrera.[95] These writings represent a small, though perhaps the most representative and influential, selection of Lurianic literature. Of all authors, Naphtali b. Jacob Bacharach of Frankfort-on-Main went furthest in his uninhibited revelation of the Lurianic mysteries. His *ʿEmeq ha-Melekh* (*Valley of the King*, or less literally, *Mystical*

95. Herrera was a former Spanish marrano who studied Lurianic kabbalah with Israel Sarug. He was the only kabbalist to write in Spanish. His works were translated into Hebrew by R. Isaac Aboab, who later became one of the leading Sabbatian believers in Amsterdam. Two of his translations, *Beth ʾElohim* ("The House of God") and *Shaʿar ha-Shamayim* ("The Gate of Heaven") were printed in Amsterdam in 1655. The second one was then translated into Latin in Christian Knorr von Rosenroth's *Kabbala Denudata* (Sulzbach, 1684) and widely read by Christian scholars.

Depths of the King, 1648) gives a full and detailed account of Luria's system based on Israel Sarug's interpretation of it, and the author does not miss an opportunity to stress the messianic function of the doctrine.

This intense literary activity was no peradventure. Toward the end of the seventeenth century the kabbalist Moses Prager wrote that

> Since the year 335 [1575] the souls from the world of *tiqqun* shone forth, and the Emanator [God] granted him [Isaac Luria] permission to open the supernal sources and channels with the mysteries of Torah; and he [Luria] expressly told us that at the present time esoteric knowledge has become like that which was formerly exoteric knowledge. Although Luria's disciples discretely concealed his teaching from the years 335–390 [1575–1630], which is the mystery of pure oil.[96] . . . The year 390 contains the mystery of drawing the pure oil down on the head of the kingdom of the House of David which is the perpetual union of *Zeᶜir ᵓAnpin* with his consort,[97] the mystery of redemption and freedom, the shining forth of the souls from the world of *tiqqun* according to the degree attained by these souls in the year 390, as is known to us [kabbalists]. From 390 onward we are in duty bound, every one of us, to achieve the *tiqqun* of our souls in their aspects of *nefesh*, *ruaḥ*, and *neshamah*, and to accomplish, together with our own *tiqqun*, that of the whole world . . . [and] to refine and purify the holy sparks by the study of the Zohar and the *Tiqquney Zohar* according to their Lurianic interpretation.[98]

The author of these lines was no Sabbatian believer. His testimony is particularly valuable because it proves that the belief that

96. The numerical value of the Hebrew word for "oil" is 390.

97. That is to say that in that year, the divine *parṣuf*, or "configuration," *Zeᶜir ᶜAnpin* (the Holy One Blessed Be He) is reunited with his consort, the "configuration" of the Shekhinah.

98. Moses Graf of Prague, *Vayyaqhel Moshe* (Dessau, 1699), fol. 58d; cf. also fol. 8c on the year 1575 as the beginning of the period of *tiqqun*. The year 1575 was considered a messianic year by many kabbalists; e.g., by the leading Italian kabbalist Mordecai Dato, who devoted a special work to this subject (*Migdal David*, MS. Oxford 2515) and the anonymous author of *ᶜAbodath ha-Qodesh* (Brit. Mus. 1074). David Tamar, "The Messianic Expectations for 1575 in Italy" (in Hebrew), *Sefunoth*, II (1958), 61–88, has studied these messianic stirrings. The Yemenite traveler al-Dahari, who visited Safed in 1567, reports messianic expectations for the year 1575; cf. the extract from his *Sefer ha-Musar*, published in *Ohel David*, the Catalogue of MSS. in the Sassoon Library, col. 1026.

Lurianic teaching functioned as a means "to draw down the messiah" was current in kabbalistic circles even before Sabbatai's appearance.[99] With the spread of Lurianism "the Shekhinah began to cast off her dark and black garments from the world of destruction and to clothe herself in royal robes from the sparks of the world of *tiqqun*."[100]

This same mood is exhibited to an even greater degree in Bacharach's *ᶜEmeq ha-Melekh*, written shortly before the great Polish massacres of 1648. The author repeatedly impresses upon his readers that Luria had actually been the messiah of the House of Joseph "and that in his days the heaviness of the yoke of the *qelippoth* of Edom [Christianity] and Ishmael [Islam] had been somewhat lightened, for we did not suffer the yoke of exile, persecution, and tribulation as before his time and that of his father, who was also a very saintly man. His merits were like a shield to his generation, and for some years afterward the *qelippoth* were mitigated and there were benevolent kings in Edom and Ishmael. His distinguished disciple R. Ḥayyim [Vital] lived after his death, . . . but afterward the persecutions of Israel began to increase, and we have none to comfort us. Disaster follows upon disaster, wars abound, and plague, sword, and hunger have come upon Israel because there is none who preaches repentance [as a preparation] for the coming of the messiah."[101] According to the author, "the tribulations of the sparks of the Ten Martyrs[102] in Poland" began after Vital's death in 1620 "because they [the Jews] did not repent while the sun, that is, the light of Luria's teaching, still shone. . . . A partition of iron now separates Israel from their Father in heaven. . . . Therefore those holy sparks must now sacrifice their lives for the sanctification of the Name in order to remove the partition. . . . Also, in my native country, Germany, many holy congregations have been destroyed through the multitude of our sins, by sword, plague, and famine in those evil wars. Lo, the soul grieves at the

99. Jacob Ṣemaḥ, writing in 1643, complains that there were no public lectures on Lurianic kabbalah similar to those on Talmudic subjects (Introduction to *Qol be-Ramah,* published by G. Scholem in *Kiryath Sepher,* XXVI [1950], 194).

100. Moses Graf, *op. cit.,* fol. 8c.

101. *ᶜEmeq ha-Melekh,* fol. 116a; see also fol. 33a–b.

102. The Ten Martyrs of ancient Jewish legend suffered during the Hadrianic persecution, but the kabbalists saw sparks of their souls reincarnated and undergoing martyrdom in every great persecution.

hearing of the ear."[103] ᶜ*Emeq ha-Melekh* was already in print by 1648, and it is unlikely that the allusion to the Polish martyrs, whose souls contained sparks of R. Akiba and his companions, the celebrated Ten Martyrs of Jewish legend, refers to the Chmielnicki massacres of 1648, which did not actually begin until the summer of that year. It is more likely that the author was thinking of the massacre of 1637 in Cracow or of similar events. The allusion to "those evil wars" clearly refers to the Thirty Years' War, in the course of which a great part of Germany was destroyed and its Jewish communities suffered heavily.

Two moods vie with each other in this voluminous book. One is a mood of joyful exaltation at the revelation of the Lurianic mysteries and the laws of the world of *tiqqun,* which the author helped make known so as to enable his contemporaries to repent and become worthy of the redemption that already "stands behind our wall." The other is a feeling of bitterness at the agonizing severity of the "pangs of redemption." Even more than by external tribulations and persecutions, this bitterness was nourished by the evils manifest in Jewish society. Dissatisfaction and social criticism were rankling in the breasts of the kabbalists who saw themselves standing on the threshold of redemption, and they did not hesitate to give poignant expression to their feelings. Two examples must suffice here.

The author of ᶜ*Emeq ha-Melekh* repeatedly and approvingly quotes the diatribes of the *Tiqquney Zohar*, included by mistake in the main text of the Zohar (I, 25a), in which the five classes of men constituting the "mixed multitude"[104] are enumerated with biting sarcasm. They are called Amalekites, Giants, Mighty Men, Refaim, and ᶜAnakim, and according to the author, they infested his own generation. Upon them he pours his wrath, applying all the invective of the Zohar. The specific objects of his indignation are the wealthy leaders of the community, the proud elders who exploit their position of power. Their days are like feasts, while they remain insensitive to the sorrow and anguish of the Shekhinah. Dishonest and corrupt, they are not satisfied with their present position but "desire to be heads of academies and judges, in that they see that

103. ᶜ*Emeq ha-Melekh,* fol. 141c.

104. The Egyptian rabble that joined the children of Israel in their exodus; cf. Exod. 12:38. The kabbalists considered them the ancestors of all the inferior souls in Israel.

justice is not done to their enemies nor anything that displeases them or might harm them or their relatives, even when it concerns the Law of the Torah; and the rabbis and judges are not strong enough to make the Law of the Torah prevail . . . because the earth is filled with violence." They lord it over the poor who are like the dust of the earth, and if they "do some good works, such as building synagogues and houses of study, it is for ulterior motives and in order to satisfy their pride; it goes without saying that they rob in the matter of taxation,[105] and pervert judgment for their own benefit." They despise scholars and even

> to this day oppress the students of Torah with staffs and cruelty, whereas they evade the yoke, though they pretend to bear the burden of taxation as [already denounced] in the *Raᶜya Mehemna*, until the Lord's anointed will come and pour on us a spirit from high to comfort us. . . . Then Scripture will be fulfilled, "they stood at the nether part of the mount," and God will overturn the mountains like a cask, saying to them: if you accept the [authority of] the scholars as an ox takes upon himself the yoke and an ass his burden, then all will be well. But if not, then your grave will be in exile[106] and Scripture will be fulfilled, "and to the land of Israel you shall not come," and the messiah will not deliver them at the ingathering of our exiles. . . . The prophet also calls them "foolish shepherds," and at the end of days God will judge these shepherds who vainly lord it over the community and who put their money to usury. It is they who have devoured Jacob, and whoever is capable of protesting against them and does not do so will have to render account. . . . Moses our teacher will himself come to avenge the honor of the Torah on every one of them, and the day to come shall burn them up.[107]

Even more violent criticism of the rich is voiced by R. Nathan Shapira. He expresses the general mood of the kabbalists of Jerusa-

105. I.e., they shift the burden of taxes unfairly on the poor.

106. The passage echoes the rabbinic account of the giving of the Law. The midrash (B. Sabbath 88a) interprets Exod. 19:17 "and they stood at the nether part of the mount" as meaning "and they stood *underneath* the mountain," and elaborates: "God lifted the mountain and held it over the heads of the people like an [inverted] cask, and said, 'If you accept the Law, all is well, if not, this will be your grave.' "

107. *ᶜEmeq ha-Melekh*, fols. 67d, ff., 107b.

lem who carried the flag of Lurianism in the seventeenth century and edited most of the so-called Lurianic writings. In the years preceding the Sabbatian movement, this group played approximately the same role in Jewish life that the kabbalists of Safed had played in the sixteenth century. The author of *ᶜEmeq ha-Melekh* wrote of them: "But for the prayer of the men of Jerusalem, who pray at the Wailing Wall with weeping and supplication, and who are all great ascetics and saints, the world would—Heaven forfend—no longer exist; and concerning them it is written, 'and on mount Zion there shall be deliverance,' meaning the Jews that live there and devote themselves to the life of the world to come."[108]

Nathan Shapira had come from Cracow to Palestine, where he lived till the end of his life when he was sent by the community of Jerusalem to gather charities in Italy. In his writings, social criticism of the wealthy mingles with the more specific grievances of the poor, small, and "spiritual" community of Jerusalem against Diaspora Jewry sitting at the fleshpots and not coming to Palestine. Nathan Shapira's *Tub ha-ᵓAreṣ* (*The Goodness of the Land*), written in praise of the Holy Land, is based on the Zohar and Lurianic doctrines and was published in Venice only ten years before the Sabbatian outbreak. This is what it has to say on the eschatological relations of Palestinian and Diaspora Jewry:

> Know that we possess a tradition that on the day when the messiah comes to Palestine for the ingathering of the exiles there will be seven thousand Jews [in Palestine]. On this day the dead in Palestine will arise and the walls of fire will depart from Jerusalem. . . . On this day the dead in Palestine will resume their former lives and will become new spiritual creations. And the seven thousand that were alive there [when the messiah arrived] will become a new creation, that is, a spiritual body like Adam's body before the fall and like the body of Moses, and they will fly in the air like eagles—all this in the sight of the returning exiles. When the returning exiles see that their [Palestinian] brethren have become a new creation and are flying in the air toward the lower Paradise where they will study the Law from the mouth of God, then their heart will fill with sorrow and dismay and they will complain to the messianic king, saying, "Are we not Jews like the others? And

108. *Ibid.*, fol. 116c.

why have they become spiritual beings and we not?" Then the messiah will answer them, "It is known to all that God dispenses justice measure for measure. Those of the Diaspora who endeavored to come to Palestine to receive a pure soul, who spared neither money nor efforts and came by sea and by land and were not afraid of being drowned in the sea or captured by cruel masters [pirates]: because they were concerned primarily for their spirits and their souls and not for their bodies and money, therefore they were turned into spirits—measure for measure. You, however, who could have come to Palestine like them, but failed to come because of your cupidity, having made a principal concern of your wealth and your bodies, while considering your souls and spirits a lesser concern: you shall remain corporeal—measure for measure. As for the money that you coveted, behold God shall give you riches. . . . However they that were not concerned with their bodies and their possessions but only with their spirits, God shall make of them a new creation and lead them into Paradise.[109]

These brave words of a man sent from the Holy Land to gather money from Diaspora Jews stand out for their sharp formulation of differing emotions and their connecting of social differences with those of place and spirit—differences between "Zionists" and "men of the dispersion," to use contemporary conceptions that spring to mind. The quotation betrays the same kind of sense of superiority already evinced in Solomon Turiel's *Homily on the Redemption.* Nathan Shapira attributes the closing sentences of his diatribe to Vital. Though not altogether impossible, the attribution does not seem very probable. The sentences are more likely to have been written by one of the poor but inspired ascetics who had come to Palestine from the Diaspora, rather than by a native who had spent most of his last thirty years outside it. But whoever the author, his message, like that of the *ᶜEmeq ha-Melekh*, shows that messianic utopia had struck deep roots in the historical consciousness of the kabbalists. Their utopia included, but also far surpassed, the purely social and revolutionary attitude against the ruling classes in Jewish society. Indeed, it filled the whole of Jewish life and practice with messianic content. Once this particular conception of the essence

109. *Tub ha-ᵓAreṣ*, fol. 37a. His source was, no doubt, Abraham Azulay's *Ḥesed Leᵓ Abraham*, ch. *ᶜeyn ha-ᵓareṣ*, §22, but this book was published only thirty years later.

and meaning of Jewish existence had established itself, it was only natural that the accumulated tension sought release after a generation or two.

Even orthodox Lurianism, though emphasizing the complexity and slow progress of the process of *tiqqun,* admitted, as we have seen, the possibility of bringing about the end and redemption with one stroke, that is, by one powerful and concentrated act of meditation (*kawwanah*)—provided that the generation was worthy. This idea was only marginal to the Lurianic system, and its source lay in popular legend rather than in speculative kabbalah. But it appealed to a number of kabbalists, and some even thought that by an act of "practical kabbalah," that is, by the use of holy names and kabbalistic (magical) formulas, it would be possible to force the end. As a matter of fact, practical kabbalah as a whole forms no organic part of Lurianism, and modern writers have caused much confusion by their misleading terminology which describes Lurianism as "practical kabbalah," as if kabbalism before Safed had been purely theoretical. Actually, the kabbalists themselves call all teaching concerning God and creation "theoretical" or "speculative," whereas "practical" kabbalah is synonymous with magic, which, of course, existed long before kabbalah proper. The special use of divine mysteries to produce supernatural changes in the world is called "practical kabbalah." Generally speaking Lurianism was far removed from this aspect of kabbalah, which nevertheless loomed large in the consciousness of the age. A few years before Sabbatai's appearance, Solomon Navarro of Casale in Italy, a member of the kabbalist circle in Jerusalem, wrote "The Fearful History of Rabbi Joseph della Reyna," a story, half folk tale and half kabbalistic legend, based on an earlier account of an actual attempt of a Spanish kabbalist around 1470 to bring on the messiah by methods of practical kabbalah. Through severe mortifications and the use of magical formulas, he succeeded in conjuring Samael, the devil, and binding him in iron chains. He would almost have succeeded had he not thoughtlessly granted Samael's request to sustain him in captivity with incense, his normal food; by virtue of this incense he would remain bound and fettered forever. Unfortunately R. Joseph forgot not only that Samael was the father of lies and merely proposed a stratagem to free himself, but also that the burning of incense—except to God alone—was tantamount to idolatry. As soon as Samael smelled the incense he regained his former strength and broke his fetters. R. Joseph's ill-fated attempt only served to prolong exile for many more years.[110]

Solomon Navarro rewrote the tale dramatically, injecting into it something of the story of Faust. He transferred the action to Safed just as other writers afterward set the tale in Hebron. Navarro had the hero sell himself to the devil after his first failure: "He despised the world to come and made a covenant with Lilith, the queen of demons. He delivered himself to her and she became his wife." He used the holy names he knew for evil purposes,[111] and finally threw himself into the sea near Sidon. Messianism had become a magical enterprise. By conjuring up Satan and binding him, one could break his power and bring the messiah. This is nothing but a mythological simplification of the struggle with the *qelippoth*. The fact that the new version of the legend of Joseph della Reyna was written in the kabbalistic circles in Jerusalem shows that popular mythological motives had lost none of their attraction even under the sway of Lurianism. The story was very popular in the period after Sabbatai's apostasy and may well have served as an appropriate symbol for the movement which, as many felt, had *almost* succeeded but had failed at the last moment. The man who proposed to bring redemption had delivered himself up to evil. To complete the analogy, Solomon Navarro, the author of the story, went to Morocco together with R. Elisha Ashkenazi, the father of Sabbatai's prophet Nathan of Gaza, to gather charity for the communities of Palestine. But R. Elisha "lost

110. For the original version of the story by Abraham b. Eliezer ha-Levi, see G. Scholem, "The Story of R. Joseph della Reyna," *Zion* (annual), V (1939–40), 123–30. For a later version see Z. Shazar (Rubashov) in *ʾEder ha-Yaqar*, "S. A. Horodezky Jubilee Volume" (Tel Aviv, 1947), pp. 97–118; cf. also J. Dan in *Sefunoth*, VI (1962), 313–26. Joseph della Reyna was an historical personality and probably died as a professing Jew. Magical traditions in his name and that of his son, Isaac della Reyna, are quoted in some kabbalistic MSS. Texts written by him were discovered by M. Benayahu in a MS. of the Sassoon Collection.

111. R. Judah al-Buttaini, who lived in Jerusalem in the first half of the 16th century, expressly warned in his *Sullam ha-ʿAliyyah* ("The Ladder of Ascent," a kabbalistic manual dealing with holy names and letter combinations necessary for the practice of mystical contemplation) that it was absolutely forbidden to use kabbalistic formulas "even to bring about the advent of the messiah, although this is the most important and urgent thing for all the worlds," unless there was definite evidence "that it was God's desire and wish" to work in this way. Judah al-Buttaini was a contemporary and friend of Abraham ha-Levi, the author of the first version of the story of della Reyna. (*Kiryath Sepher*, XXII [1946], 170.)

all the money he had collected, because his companion, the scholar and kabbalist Solomon Navarro, fell in love with a gentile woman when he came to Reggio in Italy, married her, and apostatized from his religion."[112] When Navarro apostatized as an old man in 1664, there lived in the same city of Reggio his fellow kabbalist from Jerusalem, R. Nathan Shapira, who died a few years later, at the height of the Sabbatian movement, as a pious Jew.

VII

By the middle of the seventeenth century the movement emanating from Safed, and Lurianism in particular, had spread to all parts of the Diaspora. The impact was strongest in Italy and Poland, and the latter merits detailed consideration. Simone Luzzatto, an Italian scholar who was no lover of kabbalah and did his best to minimize its significance, summed up the situation when he wrote in 1638, "Jews are not bound to accept their [the kabbalists'] teaching, though it is gladly received by many of this nation, especially in the eastern countries and in Poland."[113] Luzzatto adroitly omitted mention of his own country, yet we know that Polish kabbalism was nourished by Italian influences no less than by Palestinian. Those among the Polish kabbalists who could not go to the Holy Land proceeded to Italy in order to study under the masters there. The two chief propagandists of kabbalism in Poland in the second half of the sixteenth century were Mattathias Delacrot of Cracow and Mordecai Yaffe of Lublin. Their commentaries on the classical writings of the early Spanish authors show them to be faithful disciples of the Italian kabbalists. Delacrot's commentary on Joseph Gikatila's *Sha*ᶜ*arey* ᵓ*Orah* (*Gates of Light*) and Mordecai's commentary on Menaḥem Recanati's *Commentary on the Pentateuch* were the first products of Polish kabbalism to be printed at the time. The large number of kabbalistic works that flowed from the printing presses in Cracow and Lublin since the

112. Sasportas, *Ṣiṣath Nobel Ṣevi,* p. 136. In his autobiographical account (quoted by Bartolocci, *Bibliotheca magna rabbinica,* IV [1693], 526), Navarro states that his Jewish wife, who had come with him from Jerusalem, had been baptized two months after him, in August 1664. Either Navarro told a lie, or else Sasportas tried to blacken the apostate even more.

113. Simone Luzzatto, *Discorso circa il stato de gli Hebrei . . .* (Venice, 1638), fol. 80 a and b. A similar statement was made in 1624 by the kabbalist Aaron Berakhya Modena in his ᵓ*Ashmoreth ha-Boqer* (Mantua, 1624), fol. 247b.

end of the sixteenth century proves that there was a genuine demand for this kind of literature. Popular interest in kabbalism was so lively that as early as 1570 R. Moses Isserles felt prompted to protest emphatically against the enthusiasm of the "ignorant crowd" for kabbalistic lore:

Many of the unlettered crowd jump at kabbalistic studies, for they are a lust to the eyes, especially the teachings of the later masters who expounded their doctrines clearly and in detail. And especially now that kabbalistic books such as the Zohar, Recanati, and [Gikatila's] *Shaᶜarey ᵓOrah* are available in print every reader can indulge in their study believing that he has penetrated their meaning; whereas in reality it is impossible to understand these things unless they are expounded orally by a master. Not only scholars try to study it, but even ordinary householders, who cannot discern between their right hand and their left hand and who walk in darkness unable to explain [even] a portion of the Pentateuch or a chapter of the same with Rashi's commentary, rush to the study of kabbalah. . . . A single coin in a box causes a noisy rattle, and anyone who has merely sniffed a little [kabbalah] preens himself on it and discourses on it in public—but he will have to render account [at the day of judgment].

A generation later R. Samuel Edeles warns against "those who spend their time—even in their youth—with kabbalistic studies," and adds that "it behooves us to protest against those who discourse on it [kabbalah] in public."[114]

The protests of Isserles and Edeles do not seem to have been very effective, and kabbalism, abetted by some of the leading rabbis, struck deep roots in Poland. The first edition of Cordovero's *Pardes Rimmonim* (*Garden of Pomegranates*) was printed in Cracow in 1592. The scholars in the community—the successors of Isserles—devoutly studied this work, and the illustrious Talmudist R. Joel Sirkes wrote a commentary on it.[115] Cordovero's system maintained itself among Polish kabbalists even after the advent of Lurianism, and the common view that Lurianism conquered Poland immediately after Isaac Luria's death is demonstrably false. The legends about Israel

114. Isserles, *Torath ha-ᶜOlah*, pt. III, ch. 4; Edeles, Novellae to B. Ḥagigah 13a.

115. MS. Oxford 1805[1]. S. A. Horodezky, *Three Hundred Years of Polish Jewry* (Hebrew) (Tel Aviv, 1946), p. 85, quotes a responsum written ca. 1617 in which Sirkes advises that a physician in Amsterdam who had spoken mockingly of the kabbalah be excommunicated.

Sarug's activity in Poland and his visit to Solomon Luria (died 1574) in order to teach him Lurianic kabbalah have no historical foundation.[116] Until the end of the sixteenth century only faint echoes of the new, Lurianic teachings had penetrated to Poland. Now and then an emissary from the Holy Land would bring a few leaves from some of Luria's or Vital's writings, but never a complete work or a systematic doctrinal statement that would be likely to exert theoretical or social influence. Sarug visited Poland after 1600, some thirty years or more after Luria's death. He stayed for some time and made a considerable impression on the Polish rabbis to whom he revealed the mysteries of the transmigrations and roots of their souls, as he had done in Italy.[117] At about the same time the writings of Menaḥem Azaryah Fano and of other kabbalists of the Italian circle began to arrive in Poland, some of which were already attributed to Luria. Simultaneously, important parts of Vital's writings began to circulate, and the Polish kabbalists accepted both types of literature as equally authentic Lurianic doctrine. There is no doubt that in the first half of the seventeenth century, Poland, and more particularly its southern parts Galicia, Podolia, and Volhynia, was the scene of a considerable kabbalistic revival.[118]

Polish kabbalism was not conspicuous for speculative original-

116. The legendary character of the story is proved by an analysis of the earliest extant version; see *Kiryath Sepher,* V (1929), 161.

117. The quotation from Sarug by Abraham Ḥayyoth (Chajes) in *Holekh Thamim* (1634), fol. 55a (by a misprint in the pagination, actually fol. 54a), is nowhere to be found in Sarug's writings. Clearly Ḥayyoth had heard the statement from Sarug himself during the latter's visit to Poland. Later legend then antedated the visit by one generation. Sarug's visit is corroborated by a family tradition referred to in passing by Abraham Segal Heller. In the introduction to his edition of the *Yalqut Shimᶜoni*, Heller mentions that R. Israel Sarug, "one of Luria's most eminent disciples, said of my grandfather R. P[inḥas] ha-Levi Horovitz that his soul was [a reincarnation of] that of the holy tanna R. Pinḥas b. Yaʾir." Pinḥas Horovitz, a brother-in-law of Moses Isserles, died in Cracow in 1618, and there is no reason to doubt the tradition preserved in his family.

118. It was a Hungarian Jew, Judah Kohen of Buda, who printed the first Lurianic work in Poland: *Tiqquney Shabbath* (Cracow, n.d., probably between 1609–12). In his introduction, printed in the 1st edn. only, the editor recounts that the rabbis of Cracow, while encouraging him to publish the book, also prevailed upon him to omit all theoretical expositions of Lurianic kabbalah, and to limit the kabbalistic material in his liturgical manual to brief hints, devotional instructions, and the like. The first genuinely Lurianic work written and published in Poland is *Ziz Saday* (Lublin, 1634) by Judah b. Moses Aaron Samuel of Lublin.

ity. Its distinctive character was due to certain other features. There was, at first, an almost complete merging—perhaps confusion would be more accurate—of elements deriving from Cordovero's and Luria's kabbalah respectively. Certain kabbalists regarded such confusion as sinful, since it was not permissible to harmonize the different kabbalahs and treat them as one system.[119] Yet this was precisely what the Polish kabbalists were doing with great enthusiasm. Everything was grist to their mill, the classical tradition of Spanish kabbalism as well as the teachings of the German Hasidim. This syncretistic tendency is illustrated by the writings of two of the leading Polish kabbalists of that time, Aryeh Leyb Pryluk and Nathan Shapira, chief rabbi of Cracow (died 1633).[120] The latter is of special interest in this connection. Shapira was a leading Talmudic authority whose contemporaries, it was said, marveled at the breadth and depth of his wisdom. He would preach every Sabbath "words sweeter than honey and the honeycomb, great principles [of faith] derived from the Zohar and from other kabbalistic works."[121] His homiletical method can be studied in his *Megalleh ᶜAmuqoth* (*Revealer of Deep Things*),[122] which was renowned for many generations, but which can hardly be described as a Lurianic work in the strict sense. Shapira constructs his exegeses of Pentateuchal passages—especially Deuteronomy 3:23, for which he offers 252 different interpretations—not by means of a methodic application of a theoretical system; rather, he is content with "explaining" a text by offering a number of interpretations or homilies, based on various and at times contradictory kabbalistic "principles" drawn from the most diverse sources.[123] He is not

119. Moses Zacuto, *Letters* (Leghorn, 1790), fol. 5a, strongly criticized another Italian kabbalist, Solomon Rocca, for confusing different schools of kabbalism (Cordovero's, Luria's, etc.) in his commentary on the prayer book *Kawwanath Shelomoh* (1670).

120. Not to be confused with the kabbalist Nathan Shapira of Jerusalem, who also lived in Cracow before coming to Palestine.

121. Berakhya Berakh (Nathan Shapira's disciple), in the introduction to *Zeraᶜ Berakh* (Cracow, 1646).

122. Pt. I, on the Prayer of Moses (Deut. 3), was printed in Cracow, 1637; pt. II, on other portions of the Pentateuch, in Lvov, 1795.

123. Including Eleazar of Worms, *Sodey Razaya*, and Ḥayyim Vital, *Sefer ha-Kawwanoth* (Venice, 1620). Vital's work, an anthology based on the author's own writings, was the only authentic Vital in print at the time.

even aware of the incompatibility of the elements he combines. The absence of a purely theoretical interest and the preponderance of homily results in a blurring of the specific qualities of the different systems. All systems and traditions are equally valuable and open the gates to an understanding of the profoundest mysteries. This is hardly the orthodox Lurianic attitude. The procedure of Shapira, who in a work now lost presented one thousand explanations of the letter *aleph* in the first word of Leviticus, is perhaps best understood as an echo of the peculiar method of Talmudic study evolved in his country. His varied interpretations of the "Prayer of Moses" bear a striking resemblance, from a formal point of view, to the dialectical method known as *pilpul* applied to a Talmudic legal text. Another characteristic feature of Polish kabbalistic literature is the prominence of *gematria*, the system of calculating the numerical values of words and letters in exegesis and interpretation. Of course the Polish kabbalists were not the first to combine ideas into a half-homiletical and half-speculative train of thought by juggling with numbers. The method of *gematria* had been developed and employed by the early German Hasidim, and again by Menaḥem Azaryah Fano, particularly in his version of Moses Jonah's *Kanfey Yonah* (*Wings of a Dove*), which became one of the principal sources of the then current Lurianic kabbalism. Yet there is a world of difference between the relatively simple and rather unexciting use of *gematria* by these earlier writers and the surprising, and at times fantastic, numerical constructions in *Megalleh ᶜAmuqoth*, whose author has rightly been described as "drunk with numbers."[124]

An even more striking feature of the writings of the great Polish kabbalists is the strong preoccupation with the doctrine of the *qelippah* and the "other side," the dark and demonic aspect of the world. Here, as in other matters, their originality did not lie in the formulation of basic ideas. The notions of the *qelippah,* of its power in the world, and of the necessity of fighting it were inherited from the Zohar and—more recently—from Lurianic kabbalah. But a unique fascination with the sphere of evil, and a markedly personalistic conception of it, were typical of Polish kabbalism. Nowhere else do we find kab-

124. The mathematician Y. Ginzburg, in his excellent article on Nathan Shapira in *ha-Tequfah,* XXV (1929), 488 97, says that "he thought in numbers as we think in words" (p. 497).

balists so indifferent to the theoretical aspects and doctrinal details of the mystery of the Godhead. Of the whole gamut of Lurianic teaching concerning retraction, the breaking of the vessels, and restoration, only those elements that stressed man's personal struggle with distinct and, as it were, individual *qelippoth* became actually and vitally meaningful. But the mystical task of annihilating particular *qelippoth* presupposes an exact knowledge of the nature and name of the *qelippah* concerned. The result was an extraordinary growth of weird and bewildering demonology for which, in our time, I know of no better illustration than that displayed in Isaac Bashevis Singer's stories. The demonic side of the world cast its shadow on all the manifestations of human life in a manner unparalleled in other kabbalistic traditions. The reader of the literature of seventeenth-century Polish kabbalism is confronted with legions of *qelippoth* erupting from a strange mythological universe that cannot be found in earlier texts.

The most remarkable figure in this respect was R. Samson b. Pesaḥ of Ostropol, who died a martyr's death at the head of his congregation in Polonnoye in the Ukraine during the 1648 massacres. R. Samson is as yet an unsolved riddle. In his own lifetime he was considered one of the greatest kabbalists of his country, and the fame of his kabbalistic eminence persisted for many generations after his death. It was rumored that he had been the messiah of the House of Joseph, killed in the "messianic woes." Like other outstanding kabbalists (Joseph Karo, for instance), he was reported to have had a *maggid,* that is, a celestial, angelic mentor who appeared to him every day to teach him kabbalistic mysteries. Maggidic revelations, by the prophet Elijah or other heavenly visitants, occasionally provided the sanction for novel and daring speculations. The appeal to celestial revelation took the place of the more usual appeal to ancient oral tradition. From the psychological point of view these *maggidim* were products of the unconscious levels of the psyche, crystallizing on the conscious level of the kabbalists' minds into psychic entities. *Maggidim,* holy angels, or the souls of departed saints speaking either *to* the kabbalist or *through* his mouth (often in a voice different from his usual one) had their counterparts on the "other side" in the dibbuks, demons, or evil souls that possessed some unhappy or mentally sick creature. R. Samson's contemporaries knew that his *maggid* had warned him of the impending massacres, and that at the *maggid*'s behest Samson had repeatedly preached in the synagogue and exhorted the people to repent. Indeed "there had been great repentance in all congregations, but it was of no avail because the [divine] decree had already been sealed. And when the enemies came and besieged the city, the kabbalist [R. Samson] went into the synagogue accompanied by three hundred members of his congregation, all of them great scholars and all of them dressed in their shrouds and wrapped in their prayer mantles. There they remained in prayer until the enemies entered the city, and all were killed in the synagogue on holy ground."[125]

R. Samson has been regarded as the chief propagandist of Lurianic kabbalism in Poland. However, his extant kabbalistic utterances present a serious riddle, since they show no point of contact with the teachings of the Lurianic school.[126] Their chief concern is with the names of the forces of the "other side" and with the knowledge of the holy powers likely to overcome and annihilate them. This new and at times extremely artificial mythological tissue is constructed by combining letters and juggling numbers. Beyond this demonology there is no trace of a consistent understanding of the mystery of the Godhead or of the mystical cosmos.[127] Our contention that this kabbalah is quite independent of Lurianism may appear strange in the light of R. Samson's many references to the "Lurianic writings." In point of fact, however, almost all these quotations—whether purporting to come from Luria himself or from other "Lurianic" sources—are

125. Nathan Hanover, *Yewen Meṣulah*, fol. 6; cf. also Gurland, *le-Qoroth ha-Gezeroth ᶜal Yisraᵓel*, fasc. 2 (1888), pp. 19, 25.

126. Nathan Hanover writes that R. Samson "composed a commentary on the Zohar according to the kabbalah of Isaac Luria, but it was never printed." This commentary (*Maḥaneh Dan*) is repeatedly quoted in the extant fragments of R. Samson's writings, but shows no trace of genuine Lurianism.

127. The Polish kabbalists quote a messianic interpretation of Isa. 24:16 by R. Samson (e.g., Eliezer Fishel of Stryzov, *Midrash la-Perushim* [Zolkiev, 1800], fol. 57c). A similar homiletic interpretation of this verse as a messianic prophecy is given by Nathan Shapira of Jerusalem, in *Tub ha-ᵓAreṣ*, fol. 38, and in *Torath Nathan* (Lvov, 1894), fol. 20a. As these interpretations hinge on the words "Glory [Hebrew, *Ṣevi*] to the righteous" [i.e., to the messiah], it is not surprising that they were picked up later and exploited by the followers of Sabbatai Ṣevi. Originally, of course, no reference to the name Ṣevi was intended, Tishby's contention to the contrary notwithstanding (cf. his *Paths of Faith and Heresy* (Hebrew, 1966, p. 285). Shapiro quotes his remarks in the name of R. Abraham Ḥizquni, who died before the Sabbatian movement started.

spurious and nowhere occur in the original texts. Very often their tenor is in sharp contradiction to the general character of Luria's authentic teaching.

We are dealing here, in all probability, with a pseudepigraphal literature whose character suggests that it was composed neither in Palestine nor in Italy, but in Poland. Its purpose should be obvious. Hiding behind the names of nonexistent books or behind the vague designation "the Lurianic writings" (whose actual scope and contents were as yet unknown), the Polish kabbalists could express the inventions and musings of their hearts, and the emotions—or rather, fears—animating their lives. Luria's name was freely used because the Lurianic legend as well as the popular hagiography *Shibḥey ha-ʾARI* was widely known by that time, whereas Lurianic theories were still unknown to the majority of kabbalists. But if the authentic Lurianic writings were unobtainable because of the embargo put on them by the Palestinian rabbis, who considered the very air of all other countries as impure, substitutes could easily be produced locally by freely adding to the few Lurianic tracts that had reached Poland. These additions represent the original contribution of the Polish kabbalists. By ascribing their ideas to earlier authorities, they concealed the true measure of their originality, and their specific contribution was drowned in the great sea of the so-called Lurianic kabbalah. At this point one cannot help wondering about the relation of the pseudepigraphical quotations throughout R. Samson's writings to his *maggid*. For all we know these citations themselves are part of the same psychic activity that had its climax in the appearance of the *maggid*. In that case we would have to say that the main source of the new doctrine of the *qelippah*, the *Sefer Qarnayim* (*Book of Horns*), written under the name of R. Aaron Kardina,[128] was written by R. Samson himself, who also composed the commentary *Dan Yadin* to it. Samson's authorship of the main text seems to have been suspected at an early date. Eliezer Fishel of Stryzov, an

128. The *Sepher Qarnayim* with the commentary *Dan Yadin* was printed by R. Samson's nephew in Zolkiev, 1709. The book shows no relation whatever, either in language or content, to Aaron b. Baruch's *ʾIggereth ha-Teʿamim*, although R. Samson clearly wished to convey the impression that both works were written by the same author. One cannot help suspecting that "R Aaron of Kardina" is a purely fictitious personality.

eighteenth-century commentator on the book, protested[129] the "common rumors" to the effect that R. Samson had "written the main text of the *Sefer Qarnayim* and then 'showed the riches of his glorious kingdom' [that is, his great learning] in his commentary *Dan Yadin* of which he made 'a gold frame for its borders.'" All these writings, text and commentary, are equally far removed from the spiritual atmosphere of Vital's *ᶜEṣ Ḥayyim* (*Tree of Life*) and from the writings of the Italian school of Israel Sarug and his disciples. How much of their strange demonology reflects Jewish folk beliefs in the Ukraine and Volhynia—of which we know very little—and how much is the author's personal contribution[130] remains an open question.

One conclusion emerges clearly. Polish kabbalism in its golden age, that is, in the early seventeenth century, consists of Lurianic ideas grafted onto a stock of new and original conceptions evolved by the Polish kabbalists themselves. The popular and almost folkloristic character of many of these undoubtedly contributed to their wide reception and distinguishes them sharply from the closely knit systems of Cordovero, Luria, and Sarug. It was largely because of its unsystematic character and its homiletical presentation that for a long time Polish kabbalism failed to influence kabbalistic theory. The Sabbatian movement led in Poland to sporadic efforts to deal with the basic notions of kabbalism in a systematic way, but the thoroughly Sabbatian character of these attempts is evident. Yet there can be no doubt of the amazing popularity of kabbalistic studies in Poland. In 1660, about a hundred years after Moses Isserles' fulminations against the popular study of kabbalah, R. Jacob b. Moses Temerles, a kabbalist who had taught in Volhynia for many decades, commented as follows on the spread of the teachings of Cordovero and Luria: "They [the kabbalistic mysteries] have spread to all sides, . . . they are known in the

129. In the introduction to his commentary *Parashath Eliᶜezer*, printed together with the *Sepher Qarnayim* in Zytomir, 1805.

130. R. Samson applied the Christian symbol of the Holy Virgin to the Shekhinah. His polemical, anti-Christian intention appears clearly when he concludes his discussion of the subject with the words: "and understand this [matter from my brief hints], as it cannot be fully explained because of the danger"—the danger threatening, of course, from Christians if they should hear of this Jewish blasphemy; see *Dan Yadin* on *Sepher Qarnayim*, ch. XII (commentary on Isa. 50:1).

gates, . . . and the earth is full of knowledge. Verily, all, great and small, are knowledgeable in the mysteries of the Lord. This is my comfort in my affliction: to behold the great desire and longing of our contemporaries for this hidden wisdom, and all—people and priests, small and great—desire to be admitted to the mystery of the Lord and live by it. Surely this signifies that our salvation is soon to come."[131] R. Moses Isserles, in his time, had endeavored[132] to harmonize the rationalist tradition of Jewish philosophy with the doctrines of kabbalah, and to emphasize their basic identity. But times had changed and kabbalism no longer sought the protection of philosophy. The terrible catastrophe of 1648 merely strengthened this tendency.

Kabbalistic ideas, particularly mystical messianism, became regular features of the message of the great Polish preachers. Indeed, the popular sermon contributed to the spread of kabbalah among a wider public no less than the prayer books and the devotional moralistic manuals. The most celebrated preacher in the years immediately preceding and following 1648, R. Berakhya Berakh, still exercised some restraint in his sermons, although he did not hesitate to propagate certain kabbalistic doctrines (metempsychosis in particular) in his writings. His homilies, published under the title *Zera^c Berakh* (*Blessed Seed*), contain striking differences, in this respect, between the first part, which appeared before the great massacre, and the second part, which came out in 1662. Whereas the first part expresses appreciation of the homilies of R. Nathan Shapira (the author's teacher), which are built "upon the principles of kabbalah, publicly proclaimed," there is a complete about-face in the second part. It is true that R. Berakhya holds the dialecticians and Talmudic casuists responsible for the terrible visitation, yet at the same time he criticizes the public interest in kabbalah in a manner which provides an instructive complement to the enthusiastic effusions of Jacob Temerles. R. Berakhya writes:

I have seen a scandalous thing in the matter of kabbalistic studies . . . , for the very name *kabbalah* ["tradition"] indicates that it was transmitted

131. Jacob Temerles, in his approbation for a prayer book according to the kabbalistic rite, which his disciple Ḥayyim Buchner intended to publish from a Palestinian MS. The prayer book was never published, but Temerles' approbation was printed by Buchner as an introduction to his *ᵓOr Ḥadash* (Amsterdam, 1672–75).

132. In his *Torath ha-ᶜOlah* (*The Law of the Burnt Offering*) (Prague, 1569).

> individually and that it must not be revealed [publicly]. . . . But now there have appeared presumptuous men who abuse the crown [of heavenly wisdom], turning it into a spade with which to feed themselves. They write books on kabbalistic subjects, obtain permission to print them, and then hawk them around to "divide [that is, distribute] them in Jacob." . . . They reveal hidden and secret things to great and small, and even mingle the inventions of their hearts with [authentic] kabbalistic teachings, until it becomes impossible to distinguish between the words of the kabbalist masters and their own additions. . . . Thus they speak grievous things against God [by revealing] that which He has hidden. But even if they contented themselves with merely copying faithfully the words of the kabbalist masters, their sin would be too great to bear, for they make public this wisdom and turn it into common talk, all the more so as they stretch out their hands against the Sanctuary. I know that the rabbis of old kept aloof from this science because they feared it might have been adulterated by unqualified persons, as indeed we now see it has been . . . . May the sages of our generation forgive me if I say that they are responsible for this abuse, because they grant approbations and licenses for printing [these books], commending, justifying, and extolling them to heaven, whereby they make themselves like false witnesses on behalf of liars.[133]

This burst of anger was probably occasioned by the publication of Naphtali Bacharach's *ᶜEmeq ha-Melekh*, which had provoked the criticism and wrath of other kabbalists too. R. Ḥayyim ha-Kohen of Aleppo, the guardian of the pure and undefiled Vital tradition, even hinted that Bacharach had corrupted by his additions—many of which actually derive from Israel Sarug and his school—the true Lurianic teaching.[134]

Berakhya Berakh's protest is an eloquent witness to the effectiveness of kabbalistic propaganda in his time; but eloquent as it was, it seems to have been singularly ineffective—even with regard to himself. For after his angry denunciations, it comes as something of a surprise to learn that some of his homilies are based on Zoharic teachings and on quotations from writings of his master, Nathan Shapira. Berakh, toward the end of his career, became an ardent follower of

133. "Introduction," *Zeraᶜ Berakh*, pt. II (Amsterdam, 1662).

134. Ḥayyim ha-Kohen, at the end of the introduction to *Meqor Ḥayyim* (Amsterdam, 1665); cf. G. Scholem in *Zion*, V (1939–40), 235.

Sabbatai Ṣevi and wrote an enthusiastic account of his pilgrimage to the messiah in Gallipoli. The writings of other Polish preachers, many of whom migrated to Germany and Holland, are permeated with kabbalism—albeit of a very special brand, combining elements peculiar to the Polish heritage with those deriving from Safed kabbalism, whose writings had by then spread everywhere.[135]

The catastrophe of 1648, and the subsequent disturbances and massacres that continued until 1655, fell as a stunning blow upon Polish Jewry. It was one of the tragic ironies of history that 1648, the year of wrath, had been the focus of the most enthusiastic hopes for redemption. After all the messianic dates mentioned in the Zohar and other early sources had passed, the kabbalists seized upon a passage in the Zohar that, though it did not refer to the advent of the messiah (which, according to the Zohar passsages, was due soon after 1300), promised the final resurrection of the dead for the year 1648: "In the year 408 [1648] of the sixth millennium they that lie in the dust will arise. . . . Scripture refers to them as the 'sons of Heth'[136] because they will wake in the year 408. As it is written [Lev. 25:13]: 'In this year of jubilee ye shall return every man unto his possession'—at the end of *this*[137] year ye shall return every man to his possession, that is, to his soul which is his [true] possession and inheritance."[138] The passage was later interpreted beyond its plain sense, and some kabbalists of Safed, Italy, and Poland proclaimed the year 408 as the ultimate and final date of redemption. This view was also shared by Moses Cordovero, who answers the question of why people were so insensitive to the approaching redemption: "And if you say, 'We see not our signs' [Ps. 74:9], do not wonder at this . . . , for our sins have caused it, and especially those among us who have desecrated the name of God [by converting to Christianity] in the [recent] persecutions. Though not delaying the date of redemption, they have

135. The writings of Aaron Samuel Kaidanover (*Tif'ereth Shemu'el*) and Bezalel of Kobryn (*'Amudeyha Shib'ah* and *Qorban Shabbath*) are examples of this kind of literature. It is in the circle of kabbalistic preachers in Poland that we may have to look for the origins of the *Midrash Peli'ah*, literally the "amazing" (because paradoxical and apparently nonsensical) midrash; see *SS*, I, 69–70, n. 3.

136. The numerical value of the Hebrew letters of the word *Ḥeth* is 408.

137. Numerical value in Hebrew 5408.

138. Zohar I, 139b. The passage is found in the earliest MS. of the Zohar, and there is no reason for suspecting it—with Graetz—of being a later interpolation.

hidden it so that its light is invisible until the appointed time. But none of these things will be later than the year 408, and some will occur earlier, such as the resurrection [of the dead] in the Holy Land, which will precede the resurrection outside Palestine by forty years. And [even] redemption may take place earlier if God so wills."[139]

Other interesting details concerning the sequence of messianic events are provided by Naphtali Bacharach from whom we have already learned that in every generation a saint lives worthy to be the messiah and that his revelation depends on the process of transmigration and the selection of souls. Thus we are told in the *ᶜEmeq ha-Melekh*[140] that "to this day we wait for God the Lord; and He will show us light [cf. Ps. 118:27], will pour out on us His holy spirit from above, and create him [the messiah] anew. He will enlighten our eyes with His Law, take the Land of Israel away from Ishmael, for it is written concerning him [Ishmael] 'I will multiply him exceedingly, I will make him a great nation' [Gen. 17:20; 21:18]. The numerical value of [the Hebrew word] 'I will make him' is 407, signifying that until the year 407 [1647] he will be a great nation, but then he will have consumed the merits acquired through his circumcision [cf. Gen. 17:23 ff.] . . . and in the year 408 the messiah will take the kingdom away from him. And although it is stated [in the Zohar] that this is the date of the resurrection, this constitutes no objection, since owing to our sins the years have passed [without the messiah having come, so that his advent will now have to coincide with the resurrection]. . . . 'In *this* year of jubilee ye shall return every man unto his possession—that is, the year 408, a time of grace and one of those dates of the end counted from the day that the king of Ishmael captured Constantinople—and this is the mystery of [Ps. 132:14] '*this*[141] is my rest forever.' " In the year 408 "the lights of freedom and of the jubilee" will appear and "utterly rout the hosts of impurity, and the sons of unrighteousness will no longer afflict Israel as before."[142] Then every Israelite will know his family and his tribe, and the mysteries of the Torah will no longer be hidden. The "fountains of salvation," which are none other than the Torah of the messiah,

139. See *ᵓOr ha-Ḥammah* on Zohar II, 10a, for an abbreviated quotation of Cordovero's statement.

140. Fol. 33b; cf. also 68a, 79a.

141. Numerical value 408.

142. *ᶜEmeq ha-Melekh*, fol. 123c.

will be revealed; they are the "mysteries which the Ancient of Days[143] has concealed, which He has decreed should not be revealed until the advent of the redeemer . . . who will save us from the plagues of the dark of blindness and the curtains that separate us [from the higher worlds]." Once the mysteries of the Ancient of Days are revealed, their "illumination will be manifest below. . . . Therefore it was ordained that neither the mysteries nor the [supernal] worlds should be revealed before the fullness of the 'acceptable time,' . . . Because of this many were punished who studied the mysteries proudly and contemptuously, not with desire and yearning and great longing, with weeping and fasting and great fear [as did Ḥayyim Vital when he studied under Isaac Luria]. . . . And unlike the scholars of the present age [who pride themselves on a knowledge which they do not possess] . . . [a teacher] should withhold the mysteries of the Torah from people, even if they are among the great ones of the earth, unless he recognizes that he [the disciple] eagerly drinks in the mystical teaching with weeping and a mighty longing, for we cannot recognize the degrees [of perfection] of the few exalted souls."[144]

However, the "acceptable time" appointed for salvation turned out to be one of disaster. R. Nathan Shapira, who died fifteen years before the Chmielnicki revolt, had pointed out a similar paradox with regard to the massacres of the first Crusade. For also "the year 4856 [1096] was an 'acceptable time' and one of the [possible] dates appointed for the end, as indicated by the verse [Lev. 25:24] 'ye shall grant a redemption for the land.'[145] Therefore there were great persecutions at that time in Germany and France in order to arouse [the people] to repentance; but because they did not repent they were not redeemed."[146] The idea that a propitious messianic moment may turn into a time of disaster already occurs in kabbalistic writings composed after the expulsion from Spain. The authors quoted earlier prophecies, such

143. One of the highest and most hidden "configurations" of the divine emanation.

144. ᶜ*Emeq ha-Melekh*, fol. 126a.

145. The numerical value in Hebrew of "ye shall grant" is 857.

146. Berakhya Berakh (*Zera*ᶜ *Berakh*, pt. II) quoting Nathan Shapira. The passage is reproduced by Judah Loeb Pochawitzer of Pinsk, *Qeneh Ḥokhmah* (Frankfurt/Oder, 1681), fol. 2c.

as from the fourteenth-century book *Peli'ah*, to the effect that redemption would come in the year 5250 (1490), as indicated in Job 38:7, "when the morning stars sang together."[147] Instead, the year *beron* [1492] brought the expulsion.

The kabbalists who lived through the massacres of 1648 discovered an apt symbol of this paradoxical transformation of the date of redemption in a frequently recurring Zoharic motif. The Zohar[148] distinguishes between the Aramaic form *qeṣ ha-yamin* and the Hebrew form *qeṣ ha-yamim* ("the end of days"). The Aramaic, which occurs in Daniel 12:13, can also be rendered "the end of the right hand," referring to the end of days that is ushered in under the dispensation of God's "right" hand, that is, his attribute of Mercy. The other dispensation, that of the end according to the left hand, symbolizes the activity of the powers of evil and of the attribute of Stern Judgment; it is indicated by the expression *miqqeṣ yamim,* which opens so many biblical stories of misfortune and distress—beginning with the account of the murder of Abel in Genesis 4:3. In the Zohar this symbolic pun has no historical or temporal significance, but that is precisely what the Polish kabbalists found in it. Here was a fitting symbol of what had happened. The end according to the right hand had turned into an end according to the left hand; the forces of impurity had grown powerful and had caused terrible calamities. "The end of days is called 'this,' whose numerical value is 408 [1648]. Therefore it was indeed a fitting time for redemption, but because of our many sins—so I was told—the end of *ha-yamin* had to give way to the end of *ha-yamim,* and thus there came 'the end of all flesh.' "[149] One of the martyrs of 1648, R. Yeḥiel Michal of Nemirov, was quoted as saying that the massacre planned by Haman, which did not take place because of Israel's repentance, had merely been postponed to the year 1648, and that this was hinted at in the Book of Esther.[150] On the other hand, it was believed that the terrible sufferings had hastened the advent of redemption: they were, in fact, the messianic

147. The numerical value of Hebrew *ron* ("sang") is 250.

148. E.g., I, 54a, 62b, 210b; cf. also *Midrash Tehillim* on Ps. 137. On the distinction between a "right" and a "left" end of days, see also Abraham bar Ḥiyya, *Megillath ha-Megalleh* (1924), p. 110.

149. R. Israel Yaffe of Shklov (b. 1640), *Tif'ereth Yisra'el* (Frankfurt/Oder, 1774), fol. 36a.

150. *Idem, 'Or Yisra'el* (Frankfurt/Oder, 1802), fol. 122c.

woes. "By the sufferings of the martyrs of that time the souls have been sifted from the *qelippah* and have become 'souls of redemption.' Also redemption has been brought nearer."[151] Expounding Jeremiah 30:7, a leading rabbinic authority calculated by means of *gematria* that the phrase "it is a time of trouble unto Jacob" referred to 1648, "but out of it [that is, as a direct result of the sufferings], he shall be saved."[152]

The feeling that the "birth pangs" of the messianic age had begun with the massacres is expressed in many accounts of the events. The name of the enemy himself was interpreted as an acrostic of the Hebrew sentence "the 'birth pangs' of the messiah are coming into the world." In fact, the numerical value of the Hebrew words for "the messianic woes" equaled 408.[153] "Not only did the resurrection of the dead [predicted by the Zohar for that year] fail to take place, but on the contrary tens of thousands were killed and were not buried, and the dogs ate their flesh. . . . But although the resurrection did not take place, yet the messianic woes have begun."[154] R. Sabbatai Horovitz, the son of the famous author of the *SHeLaH,* lamented in his dirge:

In the year 408 of the sixth millennium
I had hoped in my heart to go out free,
But [instead] they have taken crafty counsel to destroy Thy people.[155]

Similar ideas were expressed by the Italian rabbis. R. Judah ᶜAsahᵓel de Buono wrote in 1652 that the tribulations "which were wreathed and came up upon our neck [cf. Lam. 1:14] at different times and in different ways at the four corners of the earth . . . are the harbingers of our messiah that bring tidings of redemption from our exile."[156]

The agitation following the massacres and miseries of 1648 did not subside for some time. Renewed persecutions during the Swedish-Russian war (1655–56) intensified the feelings of crisis. In 1674 a well-known preacher, R. Isaac the Reprover (a brother-in-law of R. Sam-

151. *Ibid.* 152. *Ibid.*

153. ḤMYL (the usual Hebrew abbreviation of Chmielnicki) = *Ḥebley Mashiaḥ Yaboᵓu la-ᶜOlam*; cf. Gurland, *op. cit.*, pt. II, p. 27.

154. Gurland, *ibid.;* also pt. I, p. 12. 155. *Ibid.*, pt. III, p. 19.

156. *RÉJ*, vol. XXV p. 212. The letter was written in connection with a mission to ransom prisoners of the pogroms of 1648.

son of Ostropol), summed up the experience of his generation: "The difference between the [ordinary] woes of exile and the messianic woes is this, that the former 'put a space between drove and drove' [that is, are intermittent; cf. Gen. 32:17], whereas the messianic woes are unremitting. Indeed since the year 1648 until this day we have not had rest."[157] After the appearance of Sabbatai Ṣevi, R. Jacob b. Solomon of Lobsenz discovered another reference to the troubles of 1648 and 1656 in Zechariah 6:12, "Behold, a man whose name is the Branch (*Ṣemaḥ*), and he shall grow up out of his place." By means of a play on the Hebrew letters the verse could be interpreted as a prophecy of the advent of Sabbatai Ṣevi, growing up out of the tribulations of those years.[158] Other preachers attempted to explain away the plain meaning of the kabbalistic prophecies after the bitter disillusionment. They argued that these prophecies referred to a revival of "prayer, penitence, and charity," as the numerical value of the corresponding Hebrew terms equaled 408. Therefore, "408" indicated not a particular year but a revival of prayer and repentance.[159] However, such preaching could not blunt the acute awareness of crisis and of the increased pressure of "the yoke of exile" felt by the Jews of Poland and Germany in the years preceding the appearance of Sabbatai Ṣevi.[160] The analysis and description of the various strands and elements that contributed to the tremendous messianic tension of those years, seem to leave but one riddle: Why did the messiah not come out of Polish or German Jewry?

VIII

Concluding our inquiry into the background of the Sabbatian movement, let us return once more from a different angle to the subject of the revolutionary aspects of apocalyptic messianism. We have briefly

157. Isaac Mokhiaḥ in his introduction to *Shibrey Luḥoth* (Lublin, 1680) by his uncle, R. Michal of Nemirov.

158. *Shem Yaᶜakob* (Frankfurt/Oder, 1716), fol. 26d.

159. Cf. e.g., *ᵓOr Ḥadash*, fol. 52a, quoting R. Phoebus of Vienna, and R. Heshel of Cracow, *Ḥanukath ha-Bayith* (Piotrkov, 1900), p. 44.

160. R. Nathan Shapira of Jerusalem, preaching in Reggio (Italy) shortly before 1664, explained that the more northern parts of the Diaspora would have "a harder exile to bear, such as [the Jews in] Poland and Russia, may the Lord have mercy on them." This is quoted from Shapira's sermon in a handwritten Catalogue of the MSS. that were (before 1903) in the collection of R. Isaac Alter in Warsaw, MS. n. 45, fol. 238.

discussed the manifestations of a revolutionary tendency in Jewish eschatology prior to the Sabbatian movement and its struggle with an opposite tendency that wished to rid messianism of utopian and revolutionary qualities. It may be useful at this point to glance at some similar conflicts in Christianity. A consideration of analogous Christian struggles may contribute to our understanding of the Sabbatian explosion and its aftermath. Indeed, some writers have assumed—on what seem to me insufficient grounds—a causal connection between the Sabbatian movement and certain millenarian movements in the contemporaneous Christian world. But even if no such connection existed, the apparently similar manifestations of the *Zeitgeist* merit closer examination.

Official Christianity—both Catholic and Protestant—traditionally described the messianic hopes of Judaism somewhat disparagingly as material and carnal compared to its own more spiritual conception. The Jews, on the other hand, tended to pride themselves on this alleged shortcoming. They saw no spiritual progress in a messianic conception that admittedly abdicated from the sphere of history and denied that redemption was a public act, manifest on this earth in soul *and* body. They prided themselves on their refusal to betray their ideal, and distrusted a spirituality whose redemption was not realized on earth as in heaven. In reality, however, even the Christian world harbored trends that would not renounce the historical realization of messianic utopia. Although such trends were condemned by the official spokesmen of Christianity and stigmatized as "Jewish" or "Judaizing," their influence and significance were far from negligible.

These unorthodox tendencies were, of course, rooted in the historical beginnings of Christianity and in Jesus' message of the imminent coming of the kingdom of Heaven. The precise significance of this message posed problems for the first generation of Christians as it does for modern scholarship, which again has taken up the problem of eschatology, so long obscured and played down by official theology. One of the main results of modern research has been a return, at times somewhat shamefaced and surreptitious, to the originally rejected "Judaizing" conceptions. Did the message of Jesus relate to a particular dimension of human existence now redeemed, or did the proclamation of the imminent coming of the kingdom of Heaven, or of its presence within or among us, have any bearing on the historical world? There is no need here to go into exegetical detail with regard to the ambiguous and contradictory statements in the Gospels and in the Epistles of Paul. The subject has been discussed in one of the most exciting works of historical scholarship, Albert Schweitzer's *The Quest of the Historical Jesus.* According to Schweitzer the apocalyptic messianism of Jesus was thoroughly Jewish, and all attempts to expurgate from it the utopian vision of a heavenly kingdom on earth are mistaken. For our present purpose these messianic beliefs are of interest because of their role in subsequent Christian history, where they appear under two headings: the "Second Coming" and the "millennium."

The very early church lived in the certainty of the Second Coming. If at his first coming Jesus had been the suffering servant, even unto death, he would appear at the Second Coming (*parousia, adventus*) as victor and as judge of the world. Descriptions of the Second Coming were modeled on Daniel 7:13–14: "behold, one like the Son of man came with the clouds of heaven, and came to the Ancient of days . . . . And there was given him dominion, and glory, and a kingdom, that all people, nations, and languages, should serve him: his dominion is an everlasting dominion which shall not pass away, and his kingdom that which shall not be destroyed." The question was whether this prediction indicated an earthly appearance with earthly characteristics, as assumed by Jewish eschatology, or whether it discarded all political, historical, and earthly elements. The New Testament writers themselves were sharply divided. Acts, the Epistles of Paul, and particularly the first three Gospels represent the "Jewish" view, whereas the author of the Fourth Gospel provided the earliest formulation of the opposite doctrine. The most thoroughgoing statement of the *parousia* as an earthly appearance of the messiah is to be found in the Revelation ascribed to John. This last book of the New Testament had gone a long way from the original and simple beliefs of the first apostles who, according to Acts 1:6, could still ask the resurrected Christ, "Lord, wilt thou at this time restore again the kingdom to Israel?" Although the kingdom of Israel no longer interested the author of Revelation, its metamorphosis into the dominion of the messiah and his saints loomed large in his eschatological vision. Revelation, charged as it is with intense hatred of the rulers of the earth and of the whore of Babylon, that is, the Roman Empire, became one of the most revolutionary books in literature. Composed during the persecutions under the emperor Domitian, the book meant to encourage and strengthen the Christian martyrs. The feverish visions of its author were in accord with Jewish apocalyptic tradition—with Christian elements added—and far removed from anything that could fairly be called "Christian love." They proved an unfailing source of inspiration to all revolutionary dreamers under the rule of the Christian church. The prophecies concerning the last war, a development of Ezekiel's prophecy of the war of Gog and Magog, and the appearance of the Antichrist (who, no doubt, originally signified the Roman persecutors of the church) applied remarkably well to whoever was in power or against whomever the commentators on Revelation wished to revolt. The course taken by interpretations of Revelation forms one of the most important chapters in the history of messianic utopianism.[161] The book acquired dangerously explosive force when extreme sects and reform movements declared that the Antichrist was none other than the pope and that the whore of Babylon was Catholic Rome and the Catholic Church.

In the eschatology of Revelation, the vision of the millennium—evidently derivative from Daniel's vision concerning the fourth beast—plays an important part. Daniel had spoken of the downfall of the beast, when "the Ancient of days came, and judgment was given to the saints of the most High; and the time came that his saints possessed the kingdom" (Dan. 7:22). The author of Revelation first gives a symbolic description of the final war, at the end of which Satan would be bound for a thousand years in the bottomless pit, and then continues: "And I saw thrones, and they sat upon them, and judgment was given unto them: and I saw the souls of them that were beheaded for the witness of Jesus, and for the word of God, and which had not worshipped the beast, neither his image . . . and they lived and reigned with Christ a thousand years" (Rev. 20:4). The vision refers to a messianic millennium, conceived as a period of transition between the victory of the messiah and the last judgment, before which Satan would again "be loosed out of his prison" for a little while. The Second Coming is crowned by the establishment

161. On the history of Christian apocalypse and the interpretation of Revelation, see the comprehensive survey of L. E. Froom, *The Prophetic Faith of Our Fathers,* 4 vols. (Washington, 1950–54). The author was an Adventist theologian, and thus in the line of succession of Christian chiliasm. See also Walter Nigg, *Das ewige Reich* (Zurich, 1944), and Norman Cohn, *The Pursuit of the Millennium* (London, 1957).

on earth of the kingdom of the saints who will rule together with the messiah in a period in which Satan has no power. The affinity of this expectation with the traditional Jewish conception of the messianic age is evident.

Revelation 19–22 proved a major stumbling block in the history of the Christian church. At first these chapters were interpreted as referring to the establishment of the kingdom of Heaven on earth, and they were even combined with the restoration of Israel after its conversion to Christ as spoken of by Paul in Romans. But from the third Christian century onward the tendency gained ground to discard this literal interpretation and not to count the millennium of the heavenly kingdom from the future appearance of Jesus but from the time of his first revelation.[162] For some time controversy, born of the profound and bitter disappointment over the delay of the Parousia, raged between "Judaizers" and "Spiritualists" concerning the interpretation of Revelation. "The whole history of 'Christianity' down to the present day, that is to say, the real inner history of it, is based on the delay of the Parousia, the non-occurrence of the Parousia, the abandonment of eschatology, the progress and completion of the 'de-eschatologizing' of religion which has been connected therewith."[163] As the church attained a dominating position, her leaders grew more sensitive to the revolutionary implications and the utopian dangers of Revelation; they consequently threw all their weight in the balance to overcome millenarian tendencies that were now judged heretical. Tertullian, the most prominent defender of the literal interpretation among the early fathers, could still maintain against Marcion that "we confess and believe that a kingdom on earth has been promised to us . . . in the heavenly Jerusalem that will descend on earth for a thousand years after the resurrection," arguing that it was "just and worthy of God that his servants should rejoice in the place [on earth] where they suffered torments for his sake."[164] It is this same feeling which made the medieval rabbis quote Psalm 90:15, "Make us glad according to the days wherein thou hast afflicted us, and the years wherein we have seen evil," and argue that the messianic era ought to be equal in length to the period of suffering and exile. But

162. Cf. H. Bietenhard, *Das tausendjährige Reich* (Bern, 1944).

163. A. Schweitzer, *The Quest of the Historical Jesus* (New York, 1957), p. 360. See also J. Klausner, *From Jesus to Paul* (Boston, 1961), pp. 539 ff.

164. Tertullian, *Adversus Marcionem* III, 24.

such views and arguments were fast becoming unpopular with the leading Christian theologians, who dubbed the belief in an earthly messianism and in the kingdom of saints "chiliasm," and its adherents "chiliasts" (from the Greek *chilias,* "1,000"). The ancient struggle between the heritage of Greek thought—which never inclined to apocalypse—and that of Judaism reached a new climax inside the Christian church in the chiliast controversy. The theological spokesmen of the "Greek" mentality denounced chiliasm as a "Jewish heresy" and argued that a kingdom limited in time was devoid of religious value. Chiliasm was officially condemned at the Council of Ephesus (431 C.E.) as "error and illusion." But the official rejection of chiliasm could not prevent chiliastic tradition from surviving among individuals as well as in diverse groups and sects. The decisive point about chiliasm is, of course, not the number 1,000 but its tenacious insistence on a literal understanding of the messianic prophecies. Christian chiliasm, like popular Jewish apocalypse, preserved both the catastrophic and the utopian aspects of messianic eschatology. In due course other hopes and ideas, the products of diverse combinations of religious, political, and social factors, crystallized round these messianic beliefs. The ecclesiastical authorities were well aware of the revolutionary character of such hopes and expectations, and they opposed them accordingly. Official opposition, however, kept chiliastic tendencies down, but also contributed to increasing their latent force and influence, particularly in times of crisis.

Chiliasm underwent many changes and developments. It assumed one of its most significant and interesting forms in the teachings of the Calabrian abbot Joachim of Floris (died 1202). For Joachim, and for his many followers in the late Middle Ages, the vision of the angel "having the everlasting gospel to preach unto them that dwell on the earth, and to every nation, and kindred, and tongue, and people" (Rev. 14:6) held the secret to a new conception of history, which is divided into three periods reflecting the three persons of the Trinity. The hidden nature of the Deity becomes fully manifest in the succession of historical periods. The first period, from Abraham to Jesus, is the age of the Father and of the rule of the Law. The second period, beginning with the birth of Jesus, is the age of the Son of man and of the rule of the church and her ordinances. The third period, whose inception Joachim awaited in the middle of the thirteenth century, would be the age of the Holy Ghost, in which the spirit alone would rule. All outward forms and mores would disappear, and the mystical meaning of the gospel would become manifest. The explosive charge of Joachimite teaching became apparent when enthusiasts and radical reformers turned the notion of an "everlasting gospel" into the watchword of a new revelation, to be found in the writings of Joachim and others. An anarchist conception of the freedom of the children of God could appeal to the authority of a gospel that had done away with all outward forms and laws. These tendencies crystallized in the more radical sections of the Franciscan Order, and the struggle of the Catholic Church to suppress them constitutes one of the most dramatic episodes in the religious history of the Middle Ages. Joachim's followers called themselves *spirituales,* and as "men of the spirit" they sharply criticized the faults and corruption of the church "according to the flesh." Their criticism illustrates the vitality of the utopian ideal, which survived even in an atmosphere in which the original "materialist" notion of an earthly, millennial kingdom had long ceased to play any role.[165] At the same time the more naïve and popular forms of chiliasm continued to exist. In the Hussite movement, and more especially in its radical Taborite wing, chiliastic longings for perfection on this earth assumed the character of a social revolution for the first time.[166] The Taborites in the first half of the fifteenth century were the first Christian sect to preach communist doctrines by appealing to the ideal communism of the early church in Jerusalem as described in Acts.

In the general agitation that set in with the Reformation at the beginning of the sixteenth century, chiliasm proved its inspirational as well as destructive power. Messianic chiliasm assumed revolutionary form in three major historical movements. It was the motive force actuating Thomas Münzer, the spiritual leader of the German peasant revolt in 1525, who has been aptly described as the "theologian of revolution."[167] It was also the source of perpetual conflicts in the

165. On the Joachimite movement and the *spirituales,* see E. Benz, *Ecclesia Spiritualis* (1934), and J. Huck, *Joachim von Floris und die joachitische Literatur* (1938).

166. On the persistence of this element in subsequent Taborite history, cf. W. Nigg, *op. cit.,* pp. 184–96.

167. Ernst Bloch, *Thomas Münzer als Theologe der Revolution* (1921). Written after the Bolshevik Revolution, this study, an expressionist rehash of Karl Kautsky's work, is a propagandistic work, advocating a synthesis of chiliastic religion and modern political communism.

Anabaptist sect, whose influence during the first decades of the Reformation was immense. The tug-of-war between the moderates and the radicals ended with one of the most celebrated episodes in the history of political messianism. In 1534 the messianic activism of an extremist Dutch group led to the proclamation of the kingdom of Zion and the establishment of a reign of apocalyptic terror in Münster in Westphalia. The failure of this messianic revolution put a damper on chiliastic propaganda for a long time to come,[168] and actually promoted the development of a mystical, chiliast "underground" movement around the Dutchman David Joris (died 1556), reminiscent in some ways of the Sabbatian underground after the apostasy of Sabbatai Ṣevi. In the person of David Joris the fever pitch of Anabaptist chiliasm produced a messiah who—unlike Sabbatai Ṣevi—was also the prophet, theologian, and apostle of the movement.[169] To be sure, the impact of the Anabaptist messiah not even remotely approximated that of the Sabbatian movement. Nevertheless, enough has been said to show the impossibility of understanding the religious history of early Protestantism without reference to the prolonged and violent controversies between chiliasts and their opponents. (The same could be said of the Greek Orthodox Church in Russia.) We must not be surprised to find the chiliasts of the sixteenth century sharing the fate of their predecessors in the Catholic Church a thousand years earlier. Luther's part in quelling the peasant revolt is well known. The Augsburg Confession of 1530, the chief Lutheran creed, drawn up by Philipp Melanchthon, explicitly condemns the chiliastic belief in the rule of the saints of the Most High on this earth as a "Jewish doctrine." We happen to know from a letter written by Melanchthon only a week before the composition of the Augsburg Confession, that Solomon Molkho's apocalyptic and military propaganda, which created such a profound stir in Jewry, had come to his notice and had greatly irritated him.[170] The insertion of an explicit condemnation

168. Cf. the sympathetic account of these millenarian groups by Rufus M. Jones, *Studies in Mystical Religion* (London, 1909), pp. 369–427, with the hostile description of R. A. Knox, *Enthusiasm* (London, 1950), pp. 71–175.

169. On David Joris, see Gottfried Arnold, *Unpartheyische Kirchen und Ketzer-Historien,* (1740), I, 876–99, 1313–1500; Nippold, "Leben, Sekte und Lehre des David Joris," in *Zeitschrift für historische Theologie, 1863–64;* Roland Bainton, *David Joris* (Leipzig, 1937).

170. Bietenhard, *op. cit.,* p. 112. Molkho's name is not mentioned in the letter, whose historical context and significance therefore escaped Bietenhard. The date, however, can leave no doubt as to the circumstances referred to.

of Jewish chiliasm into the most authoritative statement of the Lutheran faith may well be a reaction to Molkho's messianic agitation.

It was, however, in the Puritan movement in England, and in similar movements on the continent—especially the Bohemian Brethren—that chiliasm asserted its greatest vitality as an historical force. During the great struggle in seventeenth-century England the extreme chiliastic groups enjoyed mounting influence and success, and for some time the Fifth Monarchy Men[171] had control of Parliament. Even after Cromwell had clashed with them in 1653 and dissolved the "Parliament of Saints," their views continued to exert considerable influence. Quakerism was born in Fifth Monarchy circles, and in its beginnings exhibited all the characteristic symptoms—later obscured—of a thoroughly chiliastic movement. In 1656, only a few years before the great Sabbatian awakening, James Nayler, a simple peasant, entered Bristol amid shouts of Hosanna as the king of Israel, the Sun of Righteousness, the head of the prophets and the first-born of God.[172] Personal visionary experience and biblical prophecy combined to inspire the chiliast prophets and leaders with their particular brand of political utopianism. Chiliast sectarians were among the first to defend in public the rights of the Jews and to proclaim the restoration of the kingdom of Israel an essential part of millenarian fulfillment. Some, such as Johann Amos Comenius, the revered leader of a group of Bohemian Brethren living in Holland, and Peter Serrarius succeeded in establishing contact with local Jewish scholars.

Nevertheless, chiliast influence on the Sabbatian movement should not be exaggerated, as has been done by some Jewish scholars. The messianic awakening was nourished from internal sources. Only a small minority of the Jewish people lived at the time in Protestant countries where chiliasm can be said to have been a significant factor in public affairs. In fact, only the Jews of northern Germany and Holland could possibly have felt such influence. Whether the expectations for 1666 of chiliast circles in Russia which later became a factor in the split between the Orthodox Church of Moscow and the schismatics (*raskolniki*) could have been known, let alone influential, among Jews in Russia (of which there were few) is more than doubtful. The handful of marrano Jews in London can hardly be considered a significant historical factor. There is no evidence that contempo-

171. "Fifth" Monarchy because the kingdom of the saints would succeed the four kingdoms of the four beasts of the Book of Daniel.

172. Cf. Emilia Fogelklou, *James Nayler, the Rebel Saint* (London, 1931).

raneous Christian chiliasm played a part in preparing Jewish hearts for the advent of the redeemer. Nor is there any evidence to confirm the hypothesis of Graetz and others that the messianic dreams of the young Sabbatai Ṣevi were inspired by the chiliast beliefs of English and Dutch merchants in Smyrna. The opposite seems to be true. Some chiliast circles expected the Second Coming in the year 1666, basing their calculations on the "number of the beast" given in Revelation 13:18 as 666. Just as the kabbalists focused their speculations on the year 408 [1648] mentioned in the Zohar, so the Christian computers of the end of days held fast to their messianic number and interpreted it as signifying the year 1666 when the beast would be subdued and the rule of the saints established. It will be shown later that these computations had no influence whatever on the Sabbatian outbreak of 1665; the synchronism is accidental. But even the mere analogy, as seen against the background of a similar religious climate, is instructive. The millenarian movements sufficiently illustrate the revolutionary possibilities inherent in precisely those forms of messianism which the church had always suspected of being influenced by Jewish conceptions. These revolutionary tendencies expressed themselves in Christian history at least as much as in Judaism, where for many generations rabbinic authority exercised a sufficiently firm control. The Sabbatian explosion was no less significant for Judaism than the analogous chiliast movements had been for Christianity. In fact, Judaism was affected far more profoundly. The more deeply the messianic hope was rooted in the Jewish soul, the more serious and far-reaching the effects of the outburst were bound to be.

2

THE BEGINNINGS OF SABBATAI ṢEVI (1626–1664)

I

To UNDERSTAND the personality of Sabbatai Ṣevi, we must begin by asking: Who was this man who initiated the messianic movement that bears his name? What sort of a person was he? What did he do? What was his role in the movement? By endeavoring to answer these questions, we may perhaps see more clearly the nature and sequence of the events connected with him, and the causes that led to the outbreak and the spectacular spread of the mighty messianic awakening.

At first I believed that the biography of Sabbatai Ṣevi had been exhausted by historians. Little, or so it seemed, was left to be done, except for kabbalistic specialists who could still elucidate the theoretical aspects of the Sabbatian movement, perhaps with more sympathetic understanding than historians had been willing to accord it. But I quickly discovered that I was mistaken, for even with regard to the bare historical and biographical facts, not to mention the ideology of the movement, we remain far from knowing the whole truth, and stand in need of more information. It seems to me that the sources, both old and new, uncovered during the last four decades can increase our understanding of Sabbatai Ṣevi's personality far beyond the hopes of earlier scholars. Many details, particularly of his early life, still remain obscure. But it appears possible now to paint a more satisfactory picture of Sabbatai Ṣevi, even without resorting to the method of reconstruction of many earlier novelists and dramatists who imaginatively filled in the gaps where the sources failed them.

Sabbatai Ṣevi was born in Smyrna on the Ninth of Ab—the day commemorating the destruction of the First and Second Temples—in the year 5386 (August, 1626). Children born on a Sabbath were frequently called Sabbatai, and the Ninth of Ab of that year did, in fact, fall on a Sabbath. The name Sabbatai thus confirms the accuracy of an otherwise suspect date, for the Ninth of Ab is also a "theological" date and fits rather too nicely the ancient rabbinic tradition that the date of the destruction of the Second Temple was to be the birth date of the messiah. It is likely that the day and the year are both correct; and if Sabbatai was really born on the Ninth of Ab that fell on a Sabbath, then 5386 (1626) must be the year of his birth and neither 5384 nor 5385, mentioned in three old sources, is a possible alternative. A letter written from Constantinople in November, 1666, states that Sabbatai was born in 1625, but at the same time asserts that he was given the name Sabbatai because he was born on a Sabbath.[1] Similarly Leyb b. Ozer, in the original Yiddish manuscript of his recollections of Sabbatai Ṣevi, written in Amsterdam in the early eighteenth century, at first notes the year (5)384 but then corrects the number 4 to 5; later, he assumes the former date, since he writes that in 5408 (1648) Sabbatai Ṣevi was twenty-four years old.[2]

1. *Relation de la veritable Imposture du faux Messie des Juifs, nommé Sabbatay Sevi* (hereafter cited as *Relation*), p. 12. The pamphlet, which was written by a Catholic clergyman (Jacob Becherand?) who was in Constantinople in 1666, and printed at Avignon in the spring of 1667, is the hitherto unrecognized source of the Dutch account *Beschryvinge van Leven en Bedryf . . . van den gepretendeerten Joodsen Messias* (Haarlem, 1667). The Dutch pamphlet, which is referred to by Graetz and others as a "Letter from Galata," is merely a condensed version of the French original. For another contemporary account by an Italian Jesuit, see S. Simonsohn, "A Christian Report from Constantinople regarding Shabbethai Sevi (1666)," in *JJS,* XII (1961), 33–58.

2. The original Yiddish MS., *Beshreybung von Shabsai Tzvi*, of these memoirs is now in the possession of Zalman Shazar, president of the State of Israel. It was

Other sources, particularly the *Vision of R. Abraham,* an apocalypse composed by Nathan of Gaza at the beginning of the messianic awakening in 1665, give the date as 5386 (1626): "Behold, a son has been born to Mordecai Ṣevi in the year 5386."[3] We may safely assume that Nathan got his information from Sabbatai Ṣevi himself. On the other hand, a tradition that Sabbatai was born in 5385 seems to have been current in some circles that disseminated Sabbatian propaganda in the early days of the movement. We possess a document purporting to be "the text of a letter sent from Safed to the city of Lunel in the year 5385," but which is, in fact, nothing but the revised version of a much earlier messianic propaganda letter, composed sometime between 1525–30. In a later version it reports that a man, about twenty-eight years old, had come to Safed in the year 5385. His name was David—a clear reminder of the sixteenth-century messianic adventurer, David Reubeni—and in addition to his tales about the lost Ten Tribes (taken from another, much earlier source) he announced the birth of the messiah, son of David. Although no mention is made of Sabbatai Ṣevi, there is little doubt that the letter was rewritten in Sabbatian circles and embodies a separate tradition regarding the year of his birth.[4] If he was born on any other Sabbath and not on the Ninth of Ab, then 1625 may well be the correct year. In that case Sabbatai Ṣevi would himself have transferred his birthday to the "theologically" desirable date and consequently changed the year from 385 to 386. Among Sabbatians the accepted date was, of course, that given by Sabbatai Ṣevi himself and fixed

---

formerly in the collection of R. Carmoly (died 1876) who presumably bought it from the author's family (Rosenkranz). Thus also the Hebrew version of Leyb b. Ozer's account (in Jacob Emden's *Torath ha-Qena᾿oth* [Lemberg, 1870], p. 4). Thomas Coenen (in *Ydele verwachtinge der Joden* [Amsterdam, 1669]) makes no mention of the year of birth, but reports (p. 8) that at the time of his first marriage Sabbatai was twenty-two or twenty-four years old. Coenen's chronology suggests that the marriage took place before the first messianic manifestation in 1648; hence, both 1624 and 1626 would be possible dates. Coenen's information on this point is not confirmed by other sources.

3. Sasportas, *Ṣiṣath Nobel Ṣevi,* published from MS. by Dr. Z. Schwarz, ed. by Isaiah Tishby (Jerusalem, 1953), p. 158. Kahana's date (21 Adar 384) is due to his reliance on late and corrupt MSS. of the Sabbatian festival calendar (see *SS,* I, p. 84, n. 3).

4. I discovered the letter in a MS. of *To*ᶜ*ey Ruaḥ* in New York, and described it in *Zion,* VII (1942), 172–73.

by him during the high tide of the movement as a special feast, "The Nativity of our King and Messiah." Leyb b. Ozer reports, apparently on the authority of his relative Abraham Kokesh of Vilna, who saw Sabbatai Ṣevi on the Ninth of Ab 5426 (1666), that Sabbatai had then said he was "forty years old on this day, as it was hinted in Scripture [Ps. 95:10], 'forty years long was I grieved with this generation, and said, It is a people that do err in their heart' "; moreover, he had shown him many allusions in Scripture and in kabbalistic texts to his age and to his revelation at the age of forty. It is evident, therefore, that the traditional date 1626 goes back to Sabbatai Ṣevi himself.

The family had lived in Greece until his father, Mordecai Ṣevi, moved to Smyrna, which was developing into a major center of Levantine trade. His place of origin in Morea, in Greece, is nowhere specified, but taking Morea in its narrower sense, that is, the Peloponnese, we may assume the family to have come from Patras, the largest Jewish community in the Peloponnese. In fact we do find a member of the family, Samuel Ṣevi, mentioned as a witness at a wedding in Patras in the year 1614.[5] The name Ṣevi is unknown among Sephardim, either as a personal or as a family name, and it is likely that both the name and the family are of Ashkenazi origin. Emanuel Frances tells us that Sabbatai "belonged to an Ashkenazi family [originating in Germany] that came to live there" (in Smyrna).[6] This detail would be of considerable interest if it could be corroborated; but hitherto no reference to it in other sources has been found, and Emanuel Frances' account is not very reliable and contains many inaccuracies. Many of the Jews living in Greece were not descended from the Spanish exiles, and even if the Ṣevi family was not Sephardi, this does not necessarily imply that it was Ashkenazi. There is only one other relevant piece of evidence on the subject. In the account of envoys from Poland, who visited Sabbatai in 1666, we are told (see below, p. 624) that he rebuked one of them in German (or Yiddish) by saying *schweig* ("keep quiet").[7] However, it should not be inferred that he knew more than a few words of German, and the emphasis on this one word is, perhaps, an indication that the rest of this memorable conversation was conducted in another language.

5. *Mishpat Ṣedeq* (responsa of R. Meir Melammed), pt. I, no. 68. I owe the reference to the late Dr. Alfred Freimann.

6. *Ṣevi Muddaḥ,* p. 134.

7. David Kahana, *History of the Kabbalists, Sabbatians, and Hasidim* (Hebrew) (Tel Aviv, 1925), I, 95.

In any case there is no clear evidence here that Sabbatai was familiar with either German or Yiddish. One of the earliest letters about him, written in December, 1665, mentions that he knew "several languages."[8] Yet because we know from reliable sources that before 1666 he had no command of Turkish, the question arises what these "several languages" were and whether German was one of them. Of course, knowledge of German does not necessarily imply Ashkenazi descent, particularly since his Polish wife was of Ashkenazi stock, and in the year that had passed since their marriage, he could easily have learned some German from her. On the other hand, his third wife had spent a few years in Italy, and if she had learned Italian, the most widely spoken language in the Levant, she could easily have changed from it to Spanish.

At the time when friction developed between the followers and the opponents of Sabbatai Ṣevi, the latter spread libels about his descent: "His father would sell himself for a pair of shoes, and his mother would prostitute herself to get her food";[9] but even Sasportas, with all his unwillingness to allow Sabbatai one redeeming feature, admits that these were just slanderous lies without any foundation. In 1665, several Christians who had made inquiries about his father were told that in Morea and during his early days in Smyrna he had been a poulterer and egg-dealer but later became a broker and agent for some English merchants in Smyrna.[10] As a result of the war between Turkey and Venice, which obstructed the sea route to Constantinople, Smyrna became an important center for trade with Europe, and the insignificant Jewish community there rose to prosperity in the years 1625–30.[11] Traders from Italy, Holland, France, and England settled there, and almost all employed Jewish agents who knew the languages

8. M. Balaban, *Sabataizm w Polsce* (Warsaw, 1935), p. 38.

9. Sasportas, p. 92.

10. *Relation,* p. 5, "vendeur de volaille dans la Morée"; Coenen, *Ydele verwachtinge,* p. 5; Paul Rycaut gives this information as "spoken to an English Merchant" ("History of Sabatai Sevi," in *The History of the Turkish Empire from 1623–1677* [London, 1680], p. 201. J. Nehama, *Histoire des Israélites de Salonique,* V (Salonika, 1959), 100, quotes some similar traditions about Sabbatai's father from a Greek work about dervishes (Vladimir Mirmiroglou, *Hoi Derbissa* [Athens, 1940], p. 330), which I have been unable to examine. He reports that the father was popular with the Turks, who used to call him Kara Mentesh, a diminutive of Mordecai (in modern Ladino, Mantash).

11. Cf. de la Croix, *Mémoire* . . . (Paris, 1684), II, 261, on the political background of the economic prosperity of the Jews of Smyrna.

of East and West and who could act for them in establishing local contacts. The Jews' economic situation improved rapidly, and Mordecai Ṣevi succeeded in his business and became fairly well-to-do. It is thus possible that the knowledge of languages, which was part of his father's business, came quite naturally to Sabbatai Ṣevi while still at home.

Sabbatai was the second of Mordecai Ṣevi's three sons.[12] Both his elder brother Elijah and the younger Joseph followed their father's profession and became commercial agents. According to our reports they were both prosperous, particularly Elijah Ṣevi, whose wealth is mentioned in a number of independent sources. At the outbreak of the messianic movement both brothers lived in Smyrna and were esteemed members of their community; both joined the party of "believers," and Elijah Ṣevi was of some consequence in it. Although he had forsaken his religion in the footsteps of his brother, Elijah subsequently returned to the fold and died as a Jew.[13] No sisters are mentioned in our sources, though a Swedish traveler, Michael Eneman, who visited Smyrna in 1712, implies that Sabbatai did have a sister; according to his report, the only surviving member of Sabbatai's family at the time of his visit was Sabbatai's sister's son (*sein Neffe*), Samuel Penina. The name should probably read Peña and is that of a wealthy Smyrna family.[14]

12. According to the French *Relation* (p. 13), Sabbatai was the eldest son, but Coenen and Baruch of Arezzo (in A. Freimann [ed.], *Inyeney Shabbatai Ṣevi,* p. 45; this collection of documents and sources regarding Sabbatai Ṣevi, published in Berlin, 1913, is cited hereafter as Freimann) assert the contrary. Solomon Katz, in his letter of 1672 (Freimann, p. 65) reports that he had spoken with the messiah's brother, "the learned and very wealthy rabbi, who is Our Lord's senior by a few years. He told me about the life of his brother—whose majesty be exalted—from his youth to this day, and I wrote down everything." Unfortunately this biography seems to be lost.

13. Some time after 1684 the two brothers were involved in a lawsuit on which the legal opinion of R. Solomon b. Benjamin ha-Levi was sought (responsa *Leb Shelomoh,* no. 57). From 1667 to Sabbatai's death, Elijah seems to have resided in Adrianople. There are several testimonies to his "conversion" to Islam in 1671, as will be seen in ch. 8.

14. Eneman (quoted in H. J. Schoeps's anthology *Jüdische Geisteswelt* [Darmstadt, 1953], p. 187) was also told that Peña, one of the wealthiest and most learned Jews in town, was later condemned to the galleys. Coenen (see below, ch. 4) mentions Peña's father or uncle among the opponents of Sabbatai who subsequently became fervent believers. On the other hand, it seems that Eneman's information was incomplete. In the same year, 1712, Benjamin Isaac

We do not know the exact dates of the founding of the various synagogues in Smyrna, each of which was the center of a particular congregation in accordance with the organizational pattern of Turkish Jewry. Mention is made in the sixties and seventies of the seventeenth century of the congregations Neveh Shalom, Pinto, Bakis, and Portugal. Some of these synagogues had *yeshiboth* attached to them, places of retreat for Talmudic studies, established by wealthy members; for example, the Portuguese congregation founded a *yeshibah* in 1657.[15] Unfortunately, we do not know to which congregation Mordecai Ṣevi belonged.

Sabbatai's parents died before the movement began. The tombstones of his father and his uncle (Isaac Ṣevi) still existed at the time of World War I; both died in the same year (Shebat and Nisan, 5423 = 1663), and both were referred to with the honorifics "aged, wise, and esteemed."[16] From another source we learn that Sabbatai's father suffered greatly from gout in his last years.[17] The name of his mother's family is unknown. Her first name was Clara and is mentioned in a poem written by Sabbatian sectarians (Dönmeh) in Salonika that has only recently come to light.[18] She died some years before 1666,[19] and her memory seems to have held the attention of Sabbatai and his followers.[20] The son's emotional ties to his mother

---

Ṣevi, a wealthy Smyrna merchant, contributed money for the publication of the book *Shebet Mussar* by R. Elijah Cohen Ittamari. There were, then, other living male members of the Ṣevi family. He may have been a grandson of Sabbatai's uncle Isaac Ṣevi.

15. *Baʿey Ḥayyey* (responsa of R. Ḥayyim Benveniste), pt. II, no. 34. Benveniste was the leading rabbinic authority in Smyrna, and his four volumes of responsa contain important material on the development of the Jewish community there.

16. Abraham Galanté, *Nouveaux documents sur Sabbatai Ṣevi* (Istanbul, 1935), p. 71.

17. Paul Rycaut, the English consul in Smyrna, who had a firsthand knowledge of people and events, speaks of him as "decrepid in his body and full of the gout and other infirmities" (*op. cit.,* p. 201). Similarly, John Evelyn, *The History of the three late famous Impostors . . .* (London, 1669), p. 34.

18. Dönmeh hymn, published by M. Attias in *Studies and Reports of the Ben-Zvi Institute,* no. 2 (1957), p. 14.

19. *Relation,* p. 12.

20. A letter written in the autumn of 1665 but preserved only in a Polish translation actually asserts that on his return to Smyrna "Sabbatai Ṣevi resuscitated his mother who had died twenty years earlier" (Balaban, *op. cit.,* p. 39).

appear in the fact that while imprisoned in Gallipoli, he wrote to the Jews of Smyrna that the merit of visiting her grave and placing one's hand on it was equal to a pilgrimage to the Temple in Jerusalem.[21] The prophet Nathan did, in fact, act on Sabbatai's recommendation before leaving Smyrna in 1667.

There is little reliable information on Sabbatai's studies and religious training. He seems to have passed through all the stages of a traditional Jewish education and to have been encouraged to concentrate on his rabbinic studies when he showed signs of talent. Some childhood reminiscences are preserved by the prophet Nathan in the Sabbatian apocalypse the *Vision of R. Abraham:* "Let the man called Isaac be remembered for the good; by him he was taught the ways of serving God, and from the age of five or six he made himself *like an ox bearing a yoke and an ass bearing a burden* to serve God."[22] The italicized phrase occurs in the Talmud (ᶜAbodah Zarah 6b) and also in the midrash *Tanna debey Eliyahu*, in a saying connected with the messiah.[23] The words of praise do not refer to Isaac Luria as one might be tempted to think, but to Sabbatai's first teacher. Moses Pinheiro (died in Leghorn, 1689),[24] a friend of Sabbatai's youth, explicitly states that the visionary's blessing was addressed to "Rabbi Isaac, who for six years labored with AMIRAH[25] in the spiritual life, and AMIRAH first studied with him."[26] Moses Pinheiro was in a position to know, and his statement may help us to identify Sabbatai's first teacher. From what we know of the rabbis of Smyrna it seems probable that the

21. Coenen, *op. cit.*, p. 55. After his pilgrimage to the tomb, Nathan also drank from a well nearby (*ibid.*, p. 137). Leyb b. Ozer's account (Emden, p. 25) draws on Coenen.

22. *Be*ᶜ*Iqvoth Mashiaḥ*, ed. G. Scholem (Jerusalem, 1943), p. 60; Sasportas, p. 159. See also below, ch. 3.

23. *Seder* ᵓ*Eliyahu Rabba*ᵓ (edn. Friedmann), p. 8; cf. also Abraham Yakhini's sermon preached on 14 Tammuz 426 (1666) and quoted by Abraham Danon, *Études Sabbatiennes* (Paris, 1910), p. 40.

24. The year of his death is now known from the chronicle of Abraham Khalfon of Tripoli, MS. Ben-Zvi Institute, Jerusalem, who (in 1815) testifies to having seen his tombstone.

25. The initials of the Hebrew words for "Our Lord and King, his Majesty be exalted," and the customary designation for Sabbatai Ṣevi by his followers.

26. Freimann, p. 95. I have corrected the corrupt printed text in accordance with the original New York MS.

reference is to Isaac di Alba,[27] later a member of the rabbinic court at Smyrna and co-signatory of a letter sent out by this court after Sabbatai's apostasy, containing a biographical account of his strange and immoral behavior as a youth.[28] Di Alba died in 1681. R. Isaac Silveira, who died toward the end of 1681, can hardly qualify as Sabbatai's teacher, since he is mentioned in our sources as a colleague and disciple who studied kabbalah with him in 1650.

The first six years of Sabbatai Ṣevi's training were thus spent under the supervision of a master who taught him "matters pertaining to piety" and the ways of serving God. Thereafter he continued his studies under the most illustrious rabbi of Smyrna at the time, Joseph Eskapha, the author of *Rosh Yosef* and a recognized halakhist. Sasportas, in his account of Sabbatai's first clash with Eskapha, describes him as Sabbatai's principal teacher, and there is no reason to doubt this information. We may infer that Sabbatai received a thorough religious and Talmudic training and that he fully mastered the sources of rabbinic culture. Even after he had become a controversial personality no one ever thought of denying his competence as a Talmudic scholar. Thomas Coenen, the Protestant minister serving the Dutch congregation in Smyrna, tells us (no doubt on the authority of Sabbatai Ṣevi's family) that he received the title *ḥakham,* the Sephardi honorific for a rabbi, when still an adolescent.[29] This may perhaps be taken to mean that he was ordained a rabbi by Joseph Eskapha or by members of his court. According to the testimony of Leyb b. Ozer, the notary of the Ashkenazi community of Amsterdam who collected reminiscences concerning Sabbatai Ṣevi, Sabbatai was eighteen years old when he was ordained *ḥakham.* Indeed, his opponents would call him a fool or madman but never an ignoramus. His followers later told many tales illustrating his knowledge of the law and his quick-wittedness. Moses Pinheiro, who studied Talmudic casuistics with him, reported that there was "none like him."[30] The value of such testimony should not be overrated, although it certainly points

27. Thus S. Rosanes, *History of the Jews of Turkey and the Levant, Part IV, from 1640–1730* (Hebrew) (Sophia, 1933–34), p. 406 and Tishby (note to Sasportas, p. 159).

28. Unfortunately the letter is lost, but its general tenor can be guessed from Cardozo's reply to it; cf. "An Epistle of Abraham Miguel Cardozo to the Rabbis of Smyrna," *Zion,* XIX (1954), 4.

29. Coenen, *op. cit.,* p. 6.

30. Freimann, p. 95.

to a core of truth. Sabbatai liked to provoke discussions on points of law and halakhah, and even many years after his apostasy, he would gather with companions in Adrianople and would berate them for not starting an argument with him whenever he appeared to infringe the law.[31]

So far we have relied on the evidence in the *Vision of R. Abraham* for determining the sequence of Sabbatai Ṣevi's studies. There are, however, strong reasons for inverting that sequence. It hardly seems probable that the study of "matters pertaining to piety" and the strict discipline of the ascetic life of a Hasid should precede the normal study of law, nor that a child five or six years old should devote himself to their practice. Perhaps Moses Pinheiro's statement should be understood to refer to the period when, having finished his traditional course of studies under Joseph Eskapha, Sabbatai turned to the ascetic life and began his career as a Hasid, while the account in the apocalypse may be confused, perhaps deliberately.

There are two other independent sources describing Sabbatai's adolescent development. Coenen reports that Sabbatai left the *yeshibah* at the age of fifteen, having finished his studies with spectacular success. Thereafter he lived a life of abstinence and solitude, studying by himself. Two references, however, to his youth have been preserved in letters sent to Yemen in the early days of the movement; in these it is explicitly stated that from the year 1642 onward "he began to accept discipline, to renounce all pleasures because of their sinfulness, and to reject the frivolous one [the evil inclination in man] who turns us to frivolity."[32] This account of the beginnings of his ascetic life agrees with the testimony that a R. Isaac "for six years labored with him in the spiritual life" and may well give us the correct sequence. For even if Sabbatai studied by himself, it is probable that in matters of the ascetic life, which, according to general consensus, require expert guidance, R. Isaac acted as his first director. At any rate the year 1642 is in harmony with Coenen's dates, for if Sabbatai was born on the Ninth of Ab, 1626, he would be fifteen years old in 1642. This chronology is con-

31. Cf. my article in *Schocken Volume* and the story quoted there (p. 165) from MS. Kaufman 255.

32. The author of the Sabbatian apocalypse *Gey Ḥizzayon* (written in Sanaᶜ, the capital of Yemen, in 1666), knew and quoted this account; see *Qobeṣ ᶜal Yad*, IV, New Series (1946), 116.

firmed by an extraordinary story told toward the end of the *Vision of R. Abraham:* "When he [Sabbatai] was six years old a flame appeared in a dream and caused a burn on his penis; and dreams would frighten him but he never told anyone. And the sons of whoredom [the demons] accosted him so as to cause him to stumble and they beat him, but he would not hearken unto them. They were the sons of Naᶜamah, the scourges of the children of man, who would always pursue him so as to lead him astray."

Although all this is said to have happened at the age of six, it is fairly obvious that the account can hardly reflect the emotional and sexual experiences of a six-year-old. The vision or dream of a flame descending and injuring his sexual organ does, however, express what may have happened to a sixteen-year-old. The reference to the injury is evidently an allusion to Sabbatai's refusal to consummate any of his different marriages, for when the apocalypse was written Sabbatai was already married to his third wife, whom he had not yet touched.[33] From an early age he is said to have been tortured by nightmarish dreams, whose sexual character is beyond doubt. The account clearly describes severe sexual temptations within the conventional kabbalistic imagery of demonic activity. He is accosted by "the sons of whoredom" who are "the scourges of the children of man." The latter is the Zohar's technical term for those demons born of masturbation, when Naᶜamah, the queen of demons, seduces men by lascivious fantasies.[34] This terminology is current in all kabbalistic and in many moralistic writings, and its meaning in the context of the apocalypse is evident. Contrary to what is stated there, it must be assumed that the story, which was probably told to Nathan by Sabbatai himself, refers to real temptations which he experienced in his adolescence when he set out upon the ascetic path—temptations that particularly beset those who embark on the spiritual and ascetic life.

When Sabbatai began a life of solitude, which spiritual manuals declared to be indispensable to "piety" and communion with

33. The story of the burn should not be confused with the testimony of Moses Pinheiro and Bejamin Rejwan that Sabbatai had a wart on his left arm (see Sasportas, p. 94, and *Schocken Volume,* pp. 166–67). According to the Zohar II, 73b, King David had a similar wart or "sign" on his right arm, and the similarity gave rise to mystical speculations among the Sabbatian believers.

34. Cf. Zohar I, 54b; III, 76b.

God, he continued his rabbinic studies. To these he added, after some time, study of kabbalah. We do not know exactly when this occurred; perhaps he turned to kabbalah after he was ordained. About that time too his family began to prosper and his elder brother became very wealthy. Sabbatai seems to have been supported by his family and to have enjoyed material independence; at any rate, he never served as a rabbi, nor is there any mention of his ever doing anything for a livelihood. Probably he began to study kabbalah when he was about eighteen or twenty years old. This is in no way remarkable. Moses Cordovero had already stated in his *ᵓOr Neᶜerab*[35] that the appropriate age for commencing the study of the Zohar was "when man reached half the years of understanding."[36] The comparatively late "prohibition" against the study of kabbalah before the age of forty was never recognized by the Sephardim; an authority of such standing as Cordovero (who wrote his kabbalistic *magnum opus* at the age of twenty-six) mentions the prohibition only in order to reject it emphatically. It appears that the ban was enacted as a result of the Sabbatian movement, and even so it is doubtful that it ever had any practical significance. At all times, even after the great ban of 1757, a large number of people devoted themselves from their youth to kabbalistic study, and the practical significance of the prohibition should not be overestimated.

Another important detail that has aroused considerable surprise has been preserved by the Dutchman Coenen and by Sabbatai's friend Moses Pinheiro, both residents of Smyrna. According to their reports Sabbatai studied kabbalah by himself, without teacher and mentor and, at first, even without colleagues. According to Leyb b. Ozer, Sabbatai "lived in his father's house during those years, secluded and closeted in a special room and completely given over to his studies, so that in a short time he became proficient in kabbalistic learning."[37] The source for this information is not clear; it is not mentioned by either Coenen or Pinheiro. Unfortunately, Leyb's ideas of kabbalah are of the popular and legendary kind so that little is to be gained from him concerning Sabbatai's training. Moses Pinheiro, however,

35. *ᵓOr Neᶜerab*, III, 1.

36. According to the *Mishnah ᵓAboth* (V, 24), forty is the age of understanding; hence, "half the years of understanding" means the age of twenty.

37. Emden, p. 3.

was a knowledgeable kabbalist himself, and weight must be given to his testimony. The fact that his account was written when he lived in Leghorn, some years after Sabbatai's apostasy, in no way detracts from its historical accuracy; on the contrary, it still faithfully reflects the spiritual atmosphere in which the young Sabbatai Ṣevi lived, and its content is sufficiently surprising to deserve to be quoted at length:

> In the science of truth [kabbalah] he [Sabbatai] never studied any other books but the Zohar and the book *Qanah*. Whenever R. Moses Pinheiro, who had studied much, raised objections and answered them, he [Sabbatai] ridiculed these dialectical exercises. . . . He learned everything from himself, for he was one of the four to arrive at the knowledge of their Creator by themselves, as it is stated in the midrash; these are Abraham, Hezekiah, Job, and the messiah.[38] He also said that he attained to it [to his doctrine of the Mystery of the Godhead] because he always prayed with great concentration (*kawwanah*) and always meditated on the plain meaning of the words, like one praying before his King. At times he would recoil at the thought of saying such things of *En-Sof,* but he worked much to know the truth until he attained his great insights. He never practiced any [of the standard kabbalistic] meditations, except as indicated above. But R. Moses Pinheiro, who studied with him once before the Day of Atonement, could not desist from these [Lurianic] meditations to which he was accustomed, until the Devil put strange [that is, impure] thoughts into his heart; whereupon he resolutely said to himself: "Am I greater than he [Sabbatai Ṣevi]? After all, he is exceedingly great in Talmudic learning, in piety [that is, ascetic life] and wisdom [that is, kabbalah], and yet he does not practice these meditations, so why should I?" So he persevered in no longer meditating, except in the aforementioned manner.[39]

I shall return to Sabbatai's special mystical doctrines of the Mystery of the Godhead, to which Pinheiro alludes. Our present concern is with the account of Sabbatai's attitude to kabbalistic literature and to the doctrine of meditative concentration on the words of prayer. Pinheiro's account, which we have no reason to doubt, and which probably refers to Sabbatai's early beginnings, is truly illuminating. In the years 1644–48, when Sabbatai began his kabbalistic studies,

38. *Numbers Rabbah,* XIV, 2.

39. Freimann, p. 95 (text corrected in accordance with MS. in the Jewish Theological Seminary, New York).

Lurianic kabbalism was in the ascendant and practically all students of kabbalah immersed themselves in the writings—printed and in manuscript—of the Safed mystics. The spirit that blew from Safed quickly dominated the kabbalistic public, and the chief desire of all students of mysticism was to drink from the fountains of wisdom that poured forth from the writings of the sages of Safed. Not so Sabbatai Ṣevi. Pinheiro does not tell us what we would have expected to hear: how Sabbatai immersed himself in Lurianic kabbalism or in the writings of Cordovero, how he surpassed all his fellow students in his understanding of the mighty and complicated drama on which Lurianic kabbalah is based. Sabbatai may have devoted himself to these studies after parting with Pinheiro in the early fifties of the seventeenth century, but during the first and decisive years of his development they played no role. His reading was restricted to the five volumes of the Zohar and the two volumes of the *Qanah*. The latter, in particular, is of considerable importance.

The book *Qanah* is a voluminous work on the "meaning of the commandments," of the same type as the kabbalistic commentary on Genesis 1–6 known as the book *Peli᾿ah* and written by the same author. The two books were not yet printed in Sabbatai's days and only the Hasidim, toward the end of the eighteenth century, dared to publish them. But manuscript copies circulated freely and were available to every student of kabbalah. These writings exerted considerable influence, although the Safed kabbalists disagreed about their authority and value. Moses Cordovero advised students not to use them, attacked some of their doctrines, and actually declared that they were of a late date, in spite of their disguise as productions of the Talmudic period. But they were esteemed by Luria's circle, which upheld their early date, as appears from Luria's own words quoted by Vital in the introduction to *ᶜEṣ Ḥayyim*. Very possibly the extreme kabbalistic views of these books and their characteristic way of focusing the whole of Judaism on its mystical core attracted the Lurianists. The *Peli᾿ah* and *Qanah*, which were written by an anonymous Spanish kabbalist in the fourteenth century,[40] are a curious combination of mystical devo-

40. The fantastic theories of A. Marcus (*Der Chassidismus* [1901], pp. 244–61), according to whom the two books *Peli᾿ah* and *Qanah* were written by R. Avigdor Kara of Prague, have no foundation whatever. The author was a Spanish kabbalist of the mid-14th century.

tion and reverence for Talmudic halakhah and of half-veiled but occasionally very radical criticism of halakhic methods and precepts. The author clearly wished to preserve the world of halakhah, but only by showing that a purely interpretive or "literal" Judaism simply cannot exist, and that there was no autonomous sphere of Talmudic and legal reasoning. The literal, exegetical understanding of the Talmud breaks down in the dialectic of its own immanent criticism and can only be saved by virtue of its inherent mystery. The only possible interpretation of Torah and Talmud is mystical interpretation. We need not assume with Graetz that the author was a decided anti-Talmudist hiding his deadly critique under a cloak of kabbalistic piety. The book contains enough explosive material even if we do not credit the author with conscious antinomian intent. Very possibly the seed sown by the study of the *Peliʾah* and *Qanah*[41] yielded fruit in its season, when visions of exaltation and greatness swept Sabbatai into their vortex. But for the time being Sabbatai remained a young *ḥakham* seeking God by the practice of solitude and ascetic piety.

Although, as we have seen, Sabbatai did not study the kabbalistic systems of the Safed school, there are indications that he was profoundly influenced by their moralistic and ascetic writings, such as *Reshith Ḥokhmah, Sefer Ḥaredim,* and *SHeLaH.* Thus Coenen and others tell us of Sabbatai's habit of taking frequent ritual baths. He would go to the seashore near Smyrna—not necessarily to the communal bath or *miqvah*—a few times a week. This new stress on ritual immersion seems to have originated in Safed and was propagated from there by the kabbalistic moralists. It is a common error to regard these ascetic practices as evidence of Luria's influence, for, as a matter of fact, popular piety (or "practical kabbalah," as the misleading terminology of modern historians has labeled it) received its inspiration from Moses Cordovero, the master of "theoretical" kabbalah, and his disciples, rather than from Luria. If Sabbatai Ṣevi indulged in mortifications, fasts, and baptisms it was not in obedience to Luria's teaching but in conformity with a practice that was already well established before Luria arrived in Safed.

41. The *Qanah,* which is concerned with the meaning of the commandments, was printed in Porick, 1786, and in Cracow, 1894. On the two books see Yitzhak Baer, *A History of the Jews in Christian Spain,* pt. I (1961), pp. 369–373, and S. A. Horodezky in *ha-Tequfah,* X (1921), 283–329.

More than anything, the fact that Sabbatai abstained from special meditations at prayer shows his aloofness from, or even opposition to, Lurianic kabbalah. Such "intentions" are the pivot of Lurianic practice, but Sabbatai does not care for them. Instead he "concentrates on the words," that is, simply speaks them with heartfelt devotion and with intellectual concentration on their exact sense, "like one speaking to a king," careful not to attach hidden meaning to his words. It thus appears that the major part of the new kabbalah, the whole world of *kawwanoth,* or "contemplative intentions"—in practice, meditative exercises—had no place in Sabbatai's spiritual life. His prayer is simple on principle. He did not confide anything to Pinheiro concerning the seductions of the "sons of whoredom," who "always pursued him so as to lead him astray." But Pinheiro himself wrestled with a very similar difficulty, the well-known and disturbing "strange thoughts" at prayer—particularly at contemplative prayer—without suspecting that Sabbatai encountered the same temptations in his own way.

Here then is something that sets Sabbatai Ṣevi apart from his kabbalistic contemporaries. He is at home in the writings of the "ancients" (that is, in what was considered in his time to be ancient literature), but eschews the kabbalah of the later masters, seeking his own key to the Zohar. He certainly is not representative of the new forces that moved kabbalistic thought; if he functioned as a kind of transformer of these forces, he did so unconsciously and unwittingly. He was carried along, like so many others, by the waves of the great awakening associated with Lurianism, but they did not strike any original or personal chords in his heart. In what we know of his later ways and kabbalistic speculations there is little of specifically Lurianic kabbalism, though its influence is not totally absent. Certainly Lurianic kabbalah played no part at all in Sabbatai's first messianic awakening. For a considerable time his language remained that of the Zohar, whose symbols always remained more alive to him than the new symbolism of Lurianic kabbalah. The same non-Lurianic mentality is apparent again in a document dating from his last days. The remarkable fact that this young rabbi became the messiah of a world steeped in Lurianic kabbalism may serve as a lesson in the need for caution, for clearly the course of the movement was determined by the public climate more than by the personality or the inner life of the young kabbalist Sabbatai Ṣevi.

What was the "Mystery of the Godhead" that Sabbatai discovered in reading these early kabbalistic texts? The answer to this question is not made easier by the fact that there are quite different traditions among Sabbatai's disciples, some of them going back to the years after his apostasy. His thought may well have developed and deepened with the years. As a matter of fact the final and more complicated version of the mystery (so far as its details are known at all) does not correspond to the original and apparently much simpler formulation which a number of his disciples claim to have heard from his own lips in his youth in Smyrna. To establish the original views of the young Sabbatai Ṣevi, we cannot even make use of the one and only kabbalistic text that has come down to us from him. For even if the few pages of the short tract called *The Mystery of Faith* are genuine and authentic—we shall return to the subject in the last chapter—they were dictated to a follower when he lived as an exile in Dulcigno, in Albania. It is clearly inadmissible to identify this later theory with his first speculations, particularly as there are indications of a steady development of his thought. Nevertheless, the starting point of his ideas needs to be examined for clarification and definition.

Like many other students of kabbalah, Sabbatai could not but feel disturbed by a problem that of necessity arose from his reading of the Zohar and similar writings. A recurrent theme in these texts is the distinction between the first emanator, the hidden God, called *En-Sof*, shrouded in the mystery of his hidden recesses, and the emanation, that is, the sphere of the ten *sefiroth* and the divine attributes. Who is the God of Israel whom we address in prayer and whose commandments we obey? Reference has already been made to an important testimony concerning the youthful Sabbatai's perplexities in this matter, and we have seen how he shrank from attributing to *En-Sof* all the divine names and attributes by which the God of Israel is called in prayer. Did not the kabbalistic texts explicitly state that *En-Sof* had no attributes whatsoever, that it was even beyond will and thought, and that it was absolutely inaccessible and hidden? However, in the course of his reading Sabbatai discovered that the Zohar specified the term "The Holy One Blessed Be He," and the name of the Godhead, the Tetragrammaton, as symbols of one particular *sefirah: Tif'ereth.* According to the Zohar and the later kabbalists, this *sefirah* concentrates within itself the active force of the Godhead. The first three *sefiroth* (*Kether*, *Ḥokhmah*, and *Binah*) do not manifest themselves by direct activity in the world below. But the lower seven, the so-called *sefiroth* of construction, are the forces that build the manifest and visible universe; their structure constitutes the hidden work of creation. These seven *sefiroth* expressed themselves in the seven days of creation; they are the seven primeval days and as such are not measurable in time. They are composed of six *sefiroth* called the "six directions," plus the last *sefirah* that receives the power and influx of them all. The six active *sefiroth* (*Ḥesed*, *Din*, *Raḥamim*, *Neṣaḥ*, *Hod*, *Yesod*) each reveals a different aspect of the creative, self-manifesting power of God. At the same time they are all contained in the central *sefirah* (*Raḥamim*, or *Tif'ereth*). By correlating a different divine name with every *sefirah*, the kabbalists indicate that any divine name is the symbolic expression of a specific aspect of the divine force in a particular *sefirah*. All kabbalistic writings agree that the divine name correlated with *Tif'ereth* is YHWH; in this *sefirah* God expresses Himself as the God of Israel and reveals Himself in His characteristic and ineffable name.

So far the symbolism of the Zohar differs little from that taught, for example, by Naḥmanides (ca. 1250) in his commentary on the Pentateuch. It was this symbolism that so greatly impressed the young Sabbatai in his search for God. The hidden Mystery of the Godhead was the realization that the God, who revealed Himself to Israel in His Torah, was not the inaccessible and utterly transcendent *En-Sof*, but that particular aspect of His power which is manifest in *Tif'ereth*. The first formulations of the "mystery," which were quoted later by Sabbatai's disciples in Smyrna, do not say very much more than this; and as this symbolism was a commonplace among kabbalists, one may rightly wonder what Sabbatai's original contribution to it was. When Abraham Cardozo passed through Leghorn in 1675, he had long discussions with Pinheiro on the precise meaning of this doctrine. Pinheiro reports that in 1650 Sabbatai revealed to him that the Mystery of the Godhead was nothing but the sixth *sefirah*, *Tif'ereth*, the "attribute of mercy and the name YHWH." Perhaps Sabbatai really did not, at first, draw any other conclusions from this conception, and what he "revealed" to his friends was precisely what all kabbalists, including authors of such unimpeachable orthodoxy as Naḥmanides, Baḥya b. Asher, and Menaḥem Recanati had taught before him. This is how Cardozo seems to have understood the traditions of the first disciples, for according to him "AMIRAH was then a mere youth and had only just begun to enter into the mystery of the Godhead, and as he adhered to the kabbalistic system of these sages he seized on the *sefirah Tif᾿ereth.* This is also what he revealed to the disciples in 1650, and when they advanced objections from the Talmud,[42] he met their objections with great sagacity and finally said to them: 'The Lord will grant wisdom.'"[43] The fact that the later formulations are much profounder suggests that Cardozo's assumption may be correct and that Sabbatai's thought developed as time went on. But we must not exclude the possibility that there was a profounder layer in his teaching from the very beginning.

This, at least, is certain: Those who received the Mystery of the Godhead from Sabbatai in later years heard it with a shift of accent which, however slight, made all the difference. Sabbatai revealed to them that "the Tetragrammaton is our God and that He is superior to the whole emanation; He is also signified by the letter W of the Tetragrammaton YHWH and is called the husband of the Shekhinah."[44] Similar extant formulations of the "Mystery" no doubt express Sabbatai's thinking as it had crystallized beginning with 1666. But again it is not impossible that even in his first period he had already arrived at the idea that it was not the *sefirah* (that is, emanation) itself that was called the "God of Israel" but something superior to the emanation that merely manifested and clothed itself in the particular *sefirah* from which it borrowed its names and symbols.

The decisive feature of this conception of the "Mystery" is the distinction between the *En-Sof,* or unmanifested Root of Roots, and the divine Self called YHWH, which is *above* the sefirotic emanations, though it manifests itself *in* one of them. The latent implication of

42. I.e., the objection that it was inconceivable that the Creator and God of Israel was no more than one *sefirah,* or attribute, among others.

43. See *Derush ha-Kethab* in A. H. Weiss, *Beth ha-Midrash* (1865), p. 67, and Pinheiro's account of Sabbatai's confidences to his friends (Freimann, p. 95).

44. *Raza᾿ de-Razin* (MS. Jewish Theological Seminary of America, Deinard 153, fol. 3a). The text contains a long and thorough discussion of the various traditions regarding the "Mystery of the Godhead."

this paradox came to light only in later years and is not explicitly referred to in the testimonies regarding the early period. It amounts to transferring the supervision of providence from the hidden substance (*En-Sof,* or whatever we choose to call it) to the "God of Israel." We cannot decide, in the light of our present knowledge, whether at this early stage Sabbatai intended this doctrine, for which there is no analogy in traditional Jewish thought—including that of the kabbalists—but which became notorious in the Sabbatian movement a generation or two later. What we know for certain is that Sabbatai's mystical thinking developed in a definitely gnostic direction. The symbol YHWH no longer signified one *sefirah* among others, but a substance that derives from the highest and utterly hidden Root and that, together with the Shekhinah, remains above the whole structure of *sefiroth.* There is a good reason for dating this development to a period when Sabbatai had come into contact with Lurianic kabbalism. He could have found support for his conception that there were substances distinct from *En-Sof* and yet above the *sefiroth* and attributes in the Lurianic doctrine of *parṣufim,* or "configurations," which similarly places an entity called the "most primordial man of all," or simply the "Primordial Man" (*Adam Qadmon*), above the world of emanation (of *sefiroth*). Although Sabbatai never accepted the propositions of Lurianism as they are formulated in the kabbalistic writings of the school, it is quite possible that they stimulated him to a more novel and daring formulation of his own Mystery of the Godhead.[45]

All our sources up to 1666 speak of the *sefirah Tif᾿ereth* (or of its hidden core?) as the God of Sabbatai Ṣevi's "faith." As late as that year his prophet Nathan, writing in the *Treatise on the Dragons* of Sabbatai's suffering and persecution at the hands of the *qelippoth* and the forces of evil, specified that during his depressions "they [the *qelippoth*] would show him that they had dominion and

45. The expression "Mystery of the Godhead" is no Sabbatian innovation and occurs in much earlier kabbalistic texts, e.g., in the ancient commentary on the book *Temunah* (edn. Lvov [1894], fol. 7b) and literally hundreds of times in R. Joseph Taytatsak, *Mal᾿akh ha-Meshib* (MS. Brit. Mus., Margoliouth 766). It is used in texts that were available in print in Sabbatai's time, e.g., Meir ibn Gabbay's *ᶜAbodath ha-Qodesh* (Venice, 1560), and Judah Khalas' *Sefer ha-Musar.* The latter (edn. Mantua, fol. 56b) speaks of "the Mystery of Redemption which is the beginning of the Mystery of the Godhead." For another example of pre-Sabbatian use of the term, cf. Abraham Yakhini's letter to the Dutch scholar Warner (MS. Leiden, Warner 71).

that their power was equal to that of [the object of] *his faith, which is Tif'ereth.*" At a later date Sabbatai was reported to say that certain combinations of the letters comprising the names YHWH and Shadday, engraved on two of his rings represented "the name of the God of my faith."[46]

Sabbatai Ṣevi acquired the reputation of an inspired man among his fellow citizens in Smyrna, and before long a number of young scholars of his age collected around him. They studied with him both Talmudic and mystical lore; like him they took ritual baths in the sea, and they accompanied him in the fields outside the city where they devoted themselves to the mysteries of the Torah.[47] These excursions were not ordinary country walks but, probably, an imitation of similar practices by groups of kabbalists in sixteenth-century Safed. The practice is described in Moses Cordovero's *'Or Ne'erab*, a guidebook for beginners in kabbalah. There we are told "what I and others have experienced on our wanderings, when we wandered through the fields with the kabbalist R. Solomon Alkabeṣ[48] and discussed verses from the Pentateuch, all of a sudden [that is, spontaneously] and without conscious thinking new insights came to us that cannot be believed unless one has seen or experienced it a number of times."[49] These peregrinations were undertaken with the express purpose of stimulating the powers of intuition to operate spontaneously and without preparation. The author of the Yiddish memoirs, expanding Coenen's account, writes that Sabbatai and his friends used to sit in his father's house, clad in *tallith* and *tefillin* (phylacteries) and would interrupt their studies only two or three times a week, when they would leave the town, bathe in the sea, fast all day, and apply themselves to kabbalah—probably according to the aforementioned method.

There is nothing unusual about this picture, fairly normal in its time, of a young scholar applying himself to the exoteric and in particular to the esoteric study of Torah. The only deviation from the

46. Cf. my article in *Schocken Volume,* p. 165. Israel Ḥazzan of Kastoria reports that Sabbatai Ṣevi had ordered these rings to be made for him in Gaza.

47. Coenen, *op. cit.,* p. 7.

48. Cordovero's teacher and brother-in-law.

49. *'Or Ne'erab*, III, 2. The inspirations thus received during the years 1548–51 were recorded by Cordovero in his *Sefer ha-Gerushim* (Venice, 1600 or 1601). See also R. J. Z. Werblowsky, *Joseph Karo* (1962), pp. 50–54.

norm was Sabbatai's exclusive study of the early kabbalists to the neglect of the doctrine of "intentions," or meditation in prayer. Here was a young scholar, neither inferior nor greatly superior to his colleagues, without literary ambition and perhaps also without literary talent. There is not one book that he has written, no treatise, not even a responsum or Talmudic novellae. Judging from his later development, he was probably never capable of a sustained and organized creative intellectual effort (see also below, p. 158). Not one Talmudic discourse of the conventional type has been transmitted in his name by members of his inner circle, many of whom were outstanding scholars.

At the age of twenty, according to Coenen[50] at twenty-two, he married his first wife and soon the singularity of his behavior expressed itself in marriage as well. He did not approach his wife and preferred to divorce her a few months later, after his father-in-law had complained to the rabbinic court. Soon afterward he married another woman, "of a highly respected family in Smyrna" (in Coenen's words), but his behavior was in no way different. The marriage was nominal and ended in divorce.[51] The names of his wives are still unknown.[52] Coenen reports that the local populace accounted for Sabbatai's behavior by reference to his excessive purity and saintliness. On the other hand, Leyb b. Ozer noted rumors that Sabbatai had declared that the Holy Spirit had revealed to him only after the wedding that this woman was not his predestined mate. Both explanations are plausible as far as they go, but ultimately the whole chapter of Sabbatai Ṣevi's married life has to be seen in the light of a new turn in the development of his personality. A change had overtaken his

50. Coenen, *op. cit.,* p. 8; Leyb b. Ozer in Emden, p. 3. Rycaut says (*op. cit.,* pp. 201–2) that the marriage took place in Salonika, after Sabbatai's expulsion from Smyrna, but this is surely a mistake.

51. Many exaggerated stories of Sabbatai's married life circulated in Constantinople during the high tide of the movement. The author of *Relation* was told, by way of proof of Sabbatai's exceeding holiness, that he had lived three, viz., five years with his first wife and second wife respectively, without ever approaching them (*Relation,* p. 10). These stories can be dismissed in the light of Coenen's more sober reports.

52. The names and details supplied by the anonymous author of *Me'ora'oth Ṣevi* (Kopust, 1814), and many subsequent edns. are purely fictitious. The book is, in fact, the first Hebrew novel about Sabbatai, and utterly devoid of historical value. It has misled several historians, who used it, at least partly, as an historical source.

emotional life and the first symptoms of illness were beginning to appear.

II

There is no doubt that Sabbatai Ṣevi was a sick man, and it is worthwhile to try and understand the nature of his illness. His contemporaries speak of him as a madman, a lunatic, or a fool, and even his followers admitted that his behavior, at least from puberty onward, provided ample reason for these appellations. Needless to add that such epithets, when used by opponents in polemical writings, are not to be overvalued. In matters of religion and faith, who has not been dubbed "mad," "foolish," or "wicked" by his enemies? More than a grain of salt should be taken with the words of R. Joseph ha-Levi of Leghorn who wrote to one of the "believers" in Egypt that Sabbatai Ṣevi "was known as a fool and madman all his life," or with similar statements, occurring with remarkable frequency in the documents quoted by Sasportas in his *Ṣiṣath Nobel Ṣevi*. Epithets of this sort are, perhaps, no more than the natural expression of wrath and anger which Sabbatai's appearance provoked in those who denied his mission. The statements of his opponents must be assessed even more critically if we remember that none of them ever spoke to Sabbatai or knew him. It is a strange fact that of the "unbelievers" who did know him none troubled to write down his report. In the circumstances it is not surprising that historians and writers who described Sabbatai as a mental case often erred in their theories. Some have spoken of pathological hysteria, others of paranoia. Because none could adduce definite proof,[53] and because their information derives from secondary and antagonistic sources, it would be easy to dismiss their theories as mere guess-work. However, the picture has changed completely with the discovery of the original Sabbatian sources. These preserve the memoirs of members of Sabbatai's closest entourage and thus enable us to re-examine critically the core of truth contained in the polemical writings of his opponents.

53. Of earlier writers on the subject, S. A. Trivus (in the Russian monthly *Voschod,* no. 7 [1900]), came closest to the truth in his description of Sabbatai's pathological states (*ibid.,* pp. 99–100). But the diagnosis he suggests (that Sabbatai suffered some kind of degenerative-hallucinatory paranoia) seems to me off the mark though taken up lately by Baruch Kurzweil in a review of the Hebrew edition of the present work (published first in 1957 and reprinted in his book *Be-maʾabhaq ʿal ʿarkhey ha-yahaduth* [Tel Aviv, 1970], especially pp. 119–122).

The sources suggest with almost absolute certainty that Sabbatai suffered from a manic-depressive psychosis, possibly combined with some paranoid traits—a constitutional disease, perhaps not a mental illness at all in the ordinary sense, though psychiatrists generally consider it as such. It is characterized by a more or less fixed pattern of psychophysical behavior from which the patient does not deviate once it has emerged. The manic-depressive type develops with puberty, and the characteristic pathological phenomena generally appear between the ages of fifteen and twenty-five and not during infancy. Thereafter, typical pathological states alternate, sometimes in regular rhythms, sometimes (as in Sabbatai's case) at unpredictable intervals. The violence and intervals of these "ups and downs" are indicative of the severity of the illness. The "ups" consist of states of excessive mental exaltation, joyful enthusiasm and feelings of sublime happiness to the point of ecstasy, and the certainty of inspiration from above. The person so affected sees a new and glorious world and himself as a reborn creature on top of it; he cogitates the most astounding and original thoughts and may even see visions. Then there are the "downs": periods of dejection and melancholia, utter passivity and lack of initiative, agony of mind and a feeling of being persecuted from without and—worse—even from within. (That this persecution is felt only during the depressive state differentiates it from the same feeling present in paranoia.) The soul swings between these extremes, although between the moments of exaltation and depression there are relatively "normal" periods in which the patient behaves like any other human being. Remedies for this constitutional disease were as unknown in former days as they are today. In one important respect the disease is different from most other mental illnesses: it leaves the total personality intact and, in particular, does not affect the intellectual powers. Most mental diseases (such as schizophrenia, which in many ways resembles manic-depressive disturbances) lead to a disintegration of the personality and their general development is, as a rule, destructive. They dissolve the wholeness and unity of the personality, destroying also the intellectual capacities, until the character of the patient changes and he remains a ruin of his former self. It is different with the manic-depressive psychosis which, though certainly introducing dangerous oscillations into the mental life of the sufferer, does not loosen the bonds of reason. If the patient is intelligent or gifted in any particular respect, these capacities will not be affected; after an attack—which may last for days or weeks or even longer—has passed, he returns to a normal state. There is no progressive degeneration or general collapse of the intellectual or emotional powers.[54]

It is precisely this typical pattern that began to emerge as Sabbatai Ṣevi approached his twentieth year, and it fully manifested itself when he was twenty-two. There are many circumstantial testimonies corroborating the cyclical rhythm of his psychic life right to his last days, and the medical description of the disease finds startling confirmation in the accounts of Sabbatai's contemporaries and particularly in those of his entourage. The sources that mention Sabbatai's peculiarities contain many details indicating that the first pathological symptoms appeared as he approached his twentieth birthday. Coenen reports that according to Sabbatai's fellow citizens of Smyrna, certain manic states began to manifest themselves in the period before his marriage. "He would quote Isaiah 14:14, 'I will ascend above the heights of the clouds; I will be like the most high' . . . , and once it happened that he recited this verse with such ecstasy that he imagined himself to be floating in the air. Once, when he asked his friends whether they had seen him levitate and they truthfully answered, 'No,' he retorted: 'You were not worthy to behold this glorious sight because you were not purified like me.' "[55] The experience of levitation is a well-known characteristic of ecstatic experiences. According to Coenen it occurred to Sabbatai a number of times before his first messianic self-revelation. Shortly afterward he revealed to the members of his circle who shared his studies and ascetic exercises that great things might be expected from him. One hint was added to another until, at last, he revealed himself as the messiah son of David.

Before quoting some of the testimonies bearing on Sabbatai's alternating moods of exaltation and depression, it may not be out of place to draw attention to another fact, which is of considerable importance for an understanding of both the man Sabbatai Ṣevi and the reactions of his fellow citizens to his messianic claims. In his moments of exaltation, a manic personality may perform extraordinary acts.

54. Practically all textbooks of psychiatry which I consulted give similar descriptions of the manic-depressive psychosis; cf., e.g., J. Lange, *Handbuch der Geisteskrankheiten,* VI (1928), 93, and practicing psychiatrists have confirmed the diagnosis offered here.

55. Coenen, *op. cit.,* p. 9.

He may reveal himself a genius and produce the most original ideas while "inspired." On the other hand, he may also do the strangest things and actually behave like a fool, or develop idiosyncrasies of a paranoid character. Everything depends on the specific "content" of his mania and on his talent and ability. By itself the diagnosis of a manic-depressive psychosis does not tell us anything about the content or value of the patient's thoughts and actions. These may vary from one individual to another, and the only general rule is that all manic experiences have *some* specific content which, as in Sabbatai's case, may have some sort of consistency.

Whenever manic enthusiasm swept the young Sabbatai to the dizzy heights of euphoric exaltation and to the vision of himself as the messiah, another apparently contradictory phenomenon presented itself. The young rabbi, whose conscious life was devoted to ascetic piety and who mortified himself for six days each week, would transgress the law and act in a manner that seemed strangely incompatible with his normal behavior. These outbreaks, which occurred in his moments of exaltation, constituted what Sabbatians later called his "strange [or paradoxical] acts." This highly significant and ambiguous term, *maᶜasim zarim*, has a double meaning in Sabbatian tradition. It refers to actions which in themselves were not prohibited by either biblical or rabbinic law, but were merely bizarre, strange and amazing, bordering perhaps on the absurd and foolish; but it also refers to actual transgressions, both light and serious, of Jewish religious law. Either type of action, however, represents something utterly unexpected from a man leading a life of piety and holiness and would be unlikely to win him approval, let alone admiration. Sabbatai Ṣevi felt himself subject to a superior and mysterious impulse that drove him to act in a thoroughly irrational way, flouting the commandments of the Torah and offending its dignity. These actions no doubt expressed a hidden and unconscious opposition to traditional religious law, at first in a relatively harmless, later in a more violent form. They amount to what in an otherwise rather passive personality could be called an attitude of aggression. We can now understand the significance of the talk about "madness" and "folly" in otherwise very reliable traditions. Those near to Sabbatai would discuss these phenomena, in substance, though not in modern psychiatric language, in their epistles and tracts addressed to initiates. This is also the reason why the same facts did not come to the knowledge of the wider Jewish public.

One of the first documents describing the personality of Sabbatai after the inception of the messianic awakening of 1665 already refers to his "illness." In those early days, the theological terminology subsequently used to disguise the pathological facts had not yet gained currency, and we find them, therefore, plainly stated by Samuel Gandoor, one of the "court kabbalists" of the *nagid* Raphael Joseph Chelebi in Egypt, the civilian or lay representative of Egyptian Jewry before the government. Gandoor was sent to Gaza from Cairo in order to observe the prophet Nathan at close range and became Nathan's ardent follower and companion on his travels for fifteen years. His testimony is perfectly reliable: "It is said of him [Sabbatai Ṣevi] that for fifteen years he has been afflicted in the following manner: he suffers anxieties that leave him constantly depressed and do not even permit him to read, without his being able to say what is the nature of this pain that has come upon him. Thus he suffers until the anxiety departs from him, when he returns with great joy to his studies. For many years he has suffered from this illness and no doctor has found a remedy for it, but it is the sufferings [inflicted] by Heaven."[56] The same letter contains a description of an incident during the *Shabu*ᶜ*oth* vigil of 1665 when "R. Sabbatai Ṣevi was suddenly overcome by anxiety [that is, depression] and he remained in his house, like a man sick with worry [in a state of melancholia], for he could not even go to read [the liturgy of the *Shabu*ᶜ*oth* vigil] with R. Abraham Nathan, as is the custom [of that night]."[57]

It is noteworthy that no mention is made in this account of the manic phases of the illness. The general tenor of this description of melancholic gloom, depression, and anxiety, as well as the use of the word "illness," suggests that the account ultimately goes back either to Sabbatai himself or to someone who knew him well during those years. The description corroborates the statement in psychiatric textbooks that although the depression is keenly felt by the patient and considered by him an acute illness, no such consciousness of disease

56. The letter was published by A. M. Haberman, *Qobeṣ* ᶜ*al Yad*, III, New Series, no. 2 (Jerusalem, 1940), p. 209.

57. *Ibid.*, p. 208.

exists with regard to his manic euphoria.[58] The exuberant and even ecstatic exaltation is not recognized by the patient as part of his illness, least of all during the manic state itself.

However, if the manic phases are not mentioned in Gandoor's letter, they are in many other documents—albeit with a difference. For after the beginning of the mass movement in 1666, the believers no longer spoke of an "illness." This term disappears. In their view both phases of the disease were divine dispensations for which they employed theological terms, traditional ones as well as new coinages, corresponding exactly to the modern terms "depression" and "mania." The new vocabulary such as used by the prophet Nathan, Baruch b. Gerson of Arezzo, Abraham Yakhini, Mattathias Bloch Ashkenazi, Jacob Najara, and Israel Ḥazzan of Kastoria, speaks of periods of "illumination" and of the "hiding of the face" respectively. The anguish of the melancholic sufferings, which all specialists agree are extremely severe though they have no physiological basis, is explained by Nathan in theological terms when in the summer 1665 he writes about "the severe afflictions, too immense to be conceived, which R. Sabbatai Ṣevi suffered on behalf of the Jewish nation."[59] In his *Treatise on the Dragons* (1666), Nathan pointed to the analogy between Sabbatai and Job, the prototype of the messianic king: "All the sufferings of Job really refer to him [Sabbatai] who has suffered many great afflictions by all kinds of *qelippoth*." The reference is clearly not to voluntary fasts and mortifications, as has been erroneously thought.[60] The same text continues even more explicitly: "By his labors he [Sabbatai] liberated the whole root [of the messiah's soul, sunk in the *qelippoth*]; yet even after he had redeemed the whole root, God tempted him with great temptations. Many times when he stood in the height of heaven, he fell again into the depth of the great abyss where the serpents tempted him, saying, 'Where is thy God . . . ?' This is a thing which reason can hardly bear, yet he remained steadfast in his faith. Also apart from this he suffered other

58. Lange, *loc. cit.,* "für die Manie fehlt jedes Krankheitsbewusstsein."

59. Sasportas, p. 9. The reference is obviously to Sabbatai's anguished depressions—as described also in Nathan's *Treatise on the Dragons*—and not to ascetic mortifications which are never described in kabbalistic literature as "unbearable afflictions." But Sasportas misunderstood the plain meaning of the sentence.

60. *Treatise on the Dragons*, in G. Scholem (ed.), *Be ᶜIqvoth Mashiaḥ*, p. 17.

severe and bitter afflictions in all his limbs; and when he was thus tempted, his name was Job."[61]

Nathan's account describes the psychical experiences of the "fall" into melancholia. The same text contains another important passage that renders in symbolic language all aspects of Sabbatai's illness:

> We have described all these matters in order to proclaim the greatness of Our Lord,[62] may his majesty be exalted, how he annihilated the power of the serpent, whose roots are deep and mighty and who always tempted him. And as he labored to extract great holiness from among the *qelippoth,* they would attach themselves to him whenever his illumination[63] was taken away, and then they would show him that they too had dominion. . . . But when the illumination came over him, he again conquered him [the great dragon]. . . . For I have already explained that Scripture calls him [the messiah] Job, because he had sunk deep into the *qelippoth* in the days of darkness which are the days of his anguish. But when the illumination came over him, in the days of calm and rejoicing . . . then he was in the state of which it is said [of Job] "and eschewed evil"; for then he emerged from the realm of the *qelippoth* where he had sunk in the days of darkness.[64]

One point, which Nathan stresses again later, emerges quite clearly. Sabbatai's illness was not a matter of a single, unique transition from illumination to depression; the change was a regular, recurring phenomenon. The days of "anguish" and depression regularly alternate with days of rejoicing and illumination, according to a scheme which is a strange mixture of mythology and psychology. The content, too, of the temptations of the *qelippoth* are indicated in the text. What was said at first, in the *Vision of R. Abraham,* about the "sons of whoredom" is now repeated on a considerably deeper level about the serpents of the great abyss, with the difference that we are now explicitly told that these seductions or allurements pursued him only

61. *Ibid.,* p. 21. The doctrine is repeated by the Sabbatian prophet Mattathias Bloch in his Epistle to Kurdistan; see *Zion,* VII (1942), 194.

62. A standard Sabbatian designation for the messiah Sabbatai Ṣevi.

63. The term *ha'arah* ("illumination") was not invented by Nathan; it occurs in earlier kabbalistic texts; cf. the early 17th-century *Seder Na'eh* (MS. Oxford, Neubauer 1913), a manual of contemplative practice "to purify the soul and to illuminate it, and to increase its power and illumination [*ha'arah*]."

64. *Treatise on the Dragons,* p. 39.

when "God's face was hid from him." It appears that psychic experiences, which were fairly normal in Sabbatai's life before the outbreak of his illness, subsequently underwent a process of differentiation in accordance with the characteristic rhythm of exaltation and depression.

In some testimonies, Sabbatai's state of illumination also exhibited other characteristic features of near ecstasy. Thus Israel Ḥazzan tells us that those who had the good fortune of seeing Sabbatai during the days of his illumination in Adrianople, "such as his faithful servants," know that at the time his face was "like the face of Moses which was like the face of the sun."[65] In other words, Sabbatai's face was burning like fire. This is confirmed by other witnesses who saw him during his illumination in the fortress of Gallipoli, for example, some envoys from Poland who left an account of their encounter with Sabbatai. Leyb b. Ozer is even more circumstantial: "I talked to people who had eaten and drunk with him and who had been with him in the fortress where he was imprisoned but who were not of his party. They told me that there is no comparison to his majesty; his face was like that of an angel of the Lord and all the time his cheeks were red. They also testified that whenever he was singing songs of praise to God, as he would do several times every day, it was impossible to look into his face, for it was like looking into a fire. Many worthy people who had visited him have testified to this, and although they opposed him, yet they confirmed that this was the truth; for this reason also many believed in him."[66]

There is good evidence of Sabbatai's alternating states of illumination and dejection during the high tide of the movement in 1666. Baruch of Arezzo reports that the envoys from Poland "saw his face shining with a great light, like the face of our teacher Moses, for at the time he had a great illumination." But then Baruch continues, speaking of the period after the apostasy, "when Our Lord was in Adrianople . . . the great illumination that had been upon him in the fortress of Gallipoli [and which had been succeeded by a period of melancholy] returned to him; thereafter he was for some time in

65. See *Schocken Volume,* p. 162.

66. MS. Shazar, fol. 32b. The printed version too, though much shorter, preserves the Talmudic simile: Sabbatai's face shone "like the face of the sun" (Emden, p. 12).

a state of alienation [from God] but after a while it [the illumination] came back to him and this went on until he was hidden from us."[67] Similar references to alternating illuminations and "alienations," and to fits of melancholia accompanied by great mental anguish and suffering are frequent in the writings of the believers, both before and after the apostasy. The prophet Nathan, Jacob Najara, and Israel Ḥazzan explicitly state that his "strange acts" were performed during moments of illumination. This agrees with the psychiatric considerations already adduced. About 1673 Nathan writes in a letter that "at the times when God lets His light shine upon him [Sabbatai], he does some exceedingly strange things in the sight of all." Nathan's disciple Israel Ḥazzan, reporting events after the apostasy, tells "that our master Nathan warned us: 'Keep as far away as possible from AMIRAH when he is in a state of illumination, for at such moments he wants to persuade all those in his presence to embrace Islam!'" This sort of thing thus happened during illuminations only and not in his normal hours.[68]

In 1670 Nathan wrote in his *Book of the Creation*[69] that Sabbatai "at times stood on the highest step, at other times he was in the extremes of abject misery." A believer from Volhynia who visited Sabbatai in Adrianople in 1672, R. Solomon Kohen, or Katz, "saw him in a great illumination for a full week." Of Sabbatai's behavior during this period he reports in his letter: "He did not have any regular sleep, only dozed occasionally, and his face was like a shining mirror and like the sun going forth in its might."[70] Abraham Yakhini refers to the same alternations of mood when he writes in his *Wawey ha^{c}Amudim:* "When the messianic king comes, he will not reveal himself by [bringing complete] redemption, but he will appear first in all manner of pain and suffering, as our very eyes have seen it with Our Lord in whom there is at some times darkness and at others light."[71] Obviously the psychological import of such hints was understandable only to those who knew Sabbatai

67. Freimann, pp. 53 and 64. 68. *Schocken Volume,* p. 163.

69. MS. Berlin, State Library Or. 8°3077, fol. 6a.

70. Freimann, p. 65. For the full text of the letter, see below, ch. 8, pp. 843–45.

71. Yakhini's autograph, MS. Oxford 2761, fol. 57d. The original text of the translated passage is in Aramaic; see also fol. 100a. The text was written a few years after Sabbatai's death, in 1681–82.

Ṣevi; to all others they must have remained mysteries and symbolical figures of speech and, therefore, went unnoticed.

The evidence shows that these fluctuations of mood continued until Sabbatai's death. A particularly valuable testimony to that effect is contained in a letter of the prophet Nathan discovered in Salonika. Writing in 1675 to the rabbis of Kastoria where he lived, Nathan tells, in very meaningful images, of his abortive attempt to visit Sabbatai at his place of deportation in Albania. Samuel Primo had arrived before him "and he stood yet before the Lord. But when he went there he found him [Sabbatai] in [the state of] the mystery of *bar nafle* [lit., "the fallen one"]. I remained in Durazzo for fifteen days and sent a messenger to ask for permission [to visit Sabbatai] but he refused. So I was compelled to come here to Berat and wait until his great light would shine again."[72] The Talmudic byname of the messiah, *bar nafley* (B. Sanhedrin 96b), is interpreted by Nathan as a symbol of the moods of depression, alienation, and "fallenness" during which Sabbatai would not see anybody.

There is thus ample evidence that the acute alternations of Sabbatai's mental states were known to those nearest him. It would be a matter of some importance if our conclusions were to be confirmed by Sabbatai Ṣevi himself. Although to our present knowledge Sabbatai wrote no books or tracts (see below, p. 158), a few authentic words of his are extant as he spoke them to others or put them in writing in the few letters that have survived. Others, again, have been preserved in the notes of his closest and most faithful followers, who claim to have copied them from his own handwriting. The testimonies from all three sources corroborate one another.

Johann Heinrich Hottinger, a Christian contemporary of Sabbatai and an amateur historian, preserved among his papers a Latin translation of a letter of Sabbatai's which he had obtained from Amsterdam in the summer of 1666. The letter was clearly written at the beginning of Sabbatai's residence in Gallipoli, and it brings the believers the good tidings of "a great illumination" that had come upon him, apparently after a period of depression that followed immediately upon his arrest. The change seems to have occurred on the

72. Nathan's letter was published by Michael Molho in the *RÉJ,* CIV (1938), 120. For the correct date and historical context of the letter, see below, ch. 8, p. 900.

Sabbath, May 22, 1666, and the message, whose style confirms its genuineness, mentions both his sufferings (*afflictio mea*) and the great light (*splendor*) that filled his soul since that Sabbath. "And the Lord saw my great affliction [or sickness] and covered me with great joy and comfort, by which I understood . . . that the expected time for the hope of Israel is very near. . . . My soul, whose trouble and anguish were great, has now been filled with light and leaps with joy."[73] Israel Ḥazzan saw notes which Sabbatai "had written down with his own hand during the great illumination"[74] in Adrianople (1671), the same phase about which we have the detailed chronicle of Jacob Najara. Sabbatai's same notes also made mention of periods of darkness ("the Lord my God shall lighten my darkness"). I regard this as a reference to the real darkness that descended on his soul from time to time, rather than a figure of speech hinting at his apostasy. Abraham Yakhini writes in a similar vein in 1681, a few years after Sabbatai's death: "The times of Our Lord the true messiah [Sabbatai Ṣevi] were diverse, at times [he was] in an exalted illumination, at others in darkness, as is well known to the faithful. Therefore David said [Ps. 31:15], 'My times are in thy hand.' "[75] Perhaps the most important point in this testimony of one so close to Sabbatai is the admission that the "changes of his times," that is, the alternation of moods, were well known to the intimate circle of Sabbatai Ṣevi's faithful.

Moreover, we also have Sabbatai's own precious testimony. When he passed through Aleppo in 1665 he became very friendly with the rabbi of this important Jewish community, to whom he confided many personal details. R. Solomon Laniado became a fervent believer in Sabbatai Ṣevi and persevered in his faith for many years after the apostasy. In the summer of 1669 he wrote a letter to two rabbis in Kurdistan in which he related some of the details that Sabbatai had told him. The letter[76] is extremely revealing in spite of the obscure language of the believers in which it is written. The text is corrupt

73. Hottinger Collection, Zentral-Bibliothek Zurich, vol. XXX, fol. 347a.

74. Israel Ḥazzan, "Commentary on the Psalms" (MS. Kaufman 255 [Budapest], fol. 32b). The date of this illumination is ascertained by the chronicle published in *Sefunoth,* V (1961), 254.

75. *Wawey ha-ᶜAmudim*, MS. Oxford 2761, fol. 114c.

76. I discovered the letter in a New York MS., and published it in *Zion,* VII (1942), 190–91.

in one or two places only, and the story which it tells must have imprinted itself deeply on the writer's mind, though, of course, we cannot be sure of the accuracy of all the details.

> When he [Sabbatai Ṣevi] passed through Aleppo, he told us his personal experiences: how in the year 1648 the Spirit of God descended upon him one night while he was walking at about two hours distance from the city in solitary meditation, until he heard the voice of God speaking to him, "Thou art the savior of Israel, the messiah, the son of David, the anointed of the God of Jacob, and thou art destined to redeem Israel, to gather it from the four corners of the earth to Jerusalem. . . ." From that moment on he was clothed with the Holy Spirit and with a great illumination; he pronounced the [ineffable] name of God and performed all sorts of strange actions as seemed fit to him by reason of the mystical *tiqqun* intended by them. Those who saw him did not understand his actions, and in their eyes he was like a fool. Repeatedly he was flogged by our teachers in Palestine for his many deeds[77] which appeared repugnant to reason, until he retired, away from men, to the wilderness. Every time he appeared again he had grown mightier, seeing what no mouth can utter, though at other times he suffered great anguish. Sometimes he beheld the splendor of the Shekhinah, and sometimes God tried him with severe temptations, all of which he withstood, until in 1665,[78] when he was in Egypt, God tried him with a very great temptation but he—praise be to God—withstood it. But afterward he adjured God with a mighty oath and with many prayers and supplications not to tempt him again and since the day that he made this adjuration, the Holy Spirit has forsaken him and so has his illumination, and he became like an ordinary man. He also repented all of his "strange acts," since he could no longer understand their [mystical] significance which he had understood when he originally performed them.[79]

77. I.e., he was sentenced to the statutory punishment of "thirty-nine stripes" by the rabbinic court for what is perhaps—by a slight emendation of the text—"his evil deeds."

78. By a slight emendation of the text, which has 1668.

79. The same psychological feature is stressed by the prophet Nathan in a letter written in 1672, after a long meeting with Sabbatai in the previous year. He reports, as something well known to the members of the inner circle, that when the illumination leaves him, "all his actions during this time seem to him like a dream and he has completely forgotten the valid reasons for those doings." (See *Sefunoth,* V [1961], 264.) The description of Sabbatai's activities during this long period of illumination in 1671, which has been published in *Sefunoth,* V (1961), 254–61, is one of the most detailed we possess.

Here we have Sabbatai's own account of his states of illumination and inspiration, on the one hand, and the "great anguish"[80] and temptations of the *qelippoth,* on the other. We are told again that the "strange acts" that gave him the reputation of a fool were performed while in a state of illumination and under the impulsion of a hidden force that convinced him that they were "fit" to do for some mystical reason. We also learn that in his normal moods, after the illumination had departed and he was like "an ordinary man," he himself could no longer understand the meaning of his actions, "repugnant to reason" and offensive as they were. He then regretted his actions, for he was, after all, a pious ascetic whose one desire was to walk in the ways of saintliness whenever this superior power did not take possession of him and force on him such strange behavior. If Gandoor, as we have seen, stresses the periods of depression (which he recognized as an illness), Laniado stresses the illuminations. Their joint testimony yields a complete picture, the essential correctness of which is borne out by all that we know of Sabbatai's private life.

We are now in a position to appreciate the references to Sabbatai's madness, or folly. Tobias Rofe Ashkenazi, who had collected many traditions concerning Sabbatai Ṣevi in Turkey, writes: "In spite of his knowledge and learning, he always used to do childish things. It was said that a spirit of foolishness possessed him occasionally, and then he behaved like a fool so that people used to talk about him and call him a fool."[81] We know from our evidence that he acted the "fool" only in his manic periods of illumination.

Abraham Cuenque[82] of Hebron, who recounts Sabbatai's doings in Smyrna in the style of a true believer, does not hide the important differences between Sabbatai's behavior and that of the other pious young men, "so that some people voiced their disapproval, calling him a fool from beginning to end. . . . He would retire to the mountains or caves without his brothers or family knowing his whereabouts; at other times he would withdraw to a miserable little room where he locked himself in and from which he emerged only occasionally. . . . His brothers were grieved by his behavior and were greatly

80. The same words were used by Samuel Gandoor in the letter quoted above, p. 129.

81. Tobias Ashkenazi, *Maᶜaseh Tobiah*, I, 6, also quoted in Emden, p. 45.

82. The name, commonly transliterated as Conque, derives from the Spanish town Cuenca. The Cuenque family was still flourishing in Jerusalem in the 20th century.

ashamed but could not prevail upon him to change his ways. . . . Being wealthy, *they felt disgraced by his behavior;* they upbraided him but to no avail."[83] The epithet "fool" seems to have accompanied Sabbatai for many years and to have left an impression on him but, as happens often with such terms of abuse, he turned it into a title of honor for himself. Israel Ḥazzan of Kastoria claimed to have seen a handwritten note of Sabbatai that began with the words, "Thus speaketh the utter fool."[84] He who appeared in the eyes of the world as an utter fool was in his own eyes the holiest of saints!

III

All this may explain to some extent the absence of any reactions to Sabbatai's first proclamation of himself as the messiah. We should think of him as a young scholar gifted in some ways and desirous of leading a saintly life. Suddenly he begins to manifest symptoms of illness, is sunk in melancholy, hides from his family in a dark little room, and behaves in a childish and foolish way. He is evidently persecuted and possessed by demons, and in the eyes of the world even his behavior during his periods of manic exaltation is evidently due to demonic influence. He does strange, irregular, and paradoxical things. At times he openly transgresses the Law in the belief that this was what he ought to do. He cannot explain or adequately communicate himself to others. On the contrary, his illogical and occasionally ungodly behavior bars every genuine contact. Then the year 1648 arrives, which had been mentioned in the Zohar as the year of the resurrection, and which was widely believed to be the date of the potential, if not of the actual, redemption (see p. 92). Instead, there is confusion and bewilderment: They had "looked for righteousness, but behold a cry."

The cry went up from the whole House of Israel at the horrors of the Cossack insurrection that had broken out in Poland and Russia and that became known in Jewish history as the Chmielnicki mas-

83. A. Cuenque's memoirs, in Emden, pp. 34–35.

84. MS. Kaufmann 255, fol. 79b; see *Schocken Volume*, p. 168. Additional testimony has come to light in the Sabbatian notebook of R. Abraham Rovigo, MS. Ben-Zevi Institute (bequest of Dr. Isaiah Sonne), fol. 42b: "The messiah is called a fool when the [light of the] *sefirah Tif'ereth* departs from him, and this was also said of Job who is the [archetype of the] messiah [Job 34:35]: Job speaketh without knowledge [that is, like a fool]. And this is why he [Sabbatai Ṣevi] used to perform strange actions which looked like sheer folly."

sacres. Jewish blood was shed like water, and refugees began to arrive as far south as Turkey, where the stream of horrifying tales was widely echoed. Sabbatai Ṣevi, torn between the extreme moods of exaltation and melancholia, must have been impressed both by the messianic expectations and by the shattering news, though we cannot tell which of the two affected him most. In any event the date given for his first messianic revelation seems to be authentic and based on reliable tradition. The agitation that swept Jewry as a result of the atrocities and Sabbatai's inner excitement during the euphoria of his illumination coalesced. One day he heard the voice that proclaimed his mission: "Thou art the savior of Israel. . . . I swear by my right hand and by the strength of my arm, that thou art the true redeemer, and there is none that redeemeth besides thee."[85] In the eyes of the world, however, Sabbatai was merely a young man possessed by a spirit of folly, if not by an evil spirit. Nobody would listen to him or to his visions, in which the patriarchs Abraham, Isaac, and Jacob told him that he was destined to be the future messiah. There is no proof that anybody took him seriously at the time, and the view of historians to the contrary is based either on a misunderstanding of the original sources or on fantasy.[86] Sabbatai Ṣevi was considered to be ill or to be possessed by an evil spirit; if he provoked any reaction at all, it was pity rather than excitement or faith.

There is some information concerning Sabbatai's first revelation of himself. Coenen says that at first he revealed his messiahship to his associates and family only; later, when he proclaimed it in public, various factions arose. But no trace of such factions seems to have remained, and even at the high tide of the movement nobody ever came forward to say that he had believed in Sabbatai as early as 1648. We must therefore ask ourselves whether Sabbatai did, in fact, publicly claim the role of messiah. Elsewhere Coenen reports a detail that actually implies the contrary, for he tells us that after 1648 a very pleasant and fragrant odor exuded from Sabbatai's body. (This fact is also mentioned in Sabbatian sources; the believers later maintained that it was the smell of the Garden of Eden.) The matter caused some gossip, and people found fault with the use of perfumes

85. Sabbatai's words as given in Laniado's letter, see above, p. 136.

86. Tishby's renewed attempt to maintain that there were indeed some circles who adhered to Sabbatai's messianic claims before 1665 is not substantiated by any authenticated fact, in his review of *SS* in *Tarbiz* XXVIII (1959), 123–33. The texts do not say what he makes them say.

by a rabbi. Finally a Smyrna physician, Dr. Baruch,[87] reproved Sabbatai, who thereupon took him home and stripped himself so that the physician could smell the odor. Sabbatai then told him of the vision of the patriarchs, who had anointed him with oil, and commanded him not to reveal this mystery to anyone until the proper time. The doctor did, in fact, keep quiet and revealed his story only eighteen years later, at the height of the movement.

The incident of the anointing was reported by another witness too, and again on the authority of Sabbatai Ṣevi. This time the testimony comes not from Smyrna but from Leghorn, where Moses Pinheiro, a friend of Sabbatai's youth, was interrogated about his early reminiscences. Among other things he remembered Sabbatai telling him of "a voice calling out three times, night after night, 'Do not touch my anointed Sabbatai Ṣevi,' and at the third time he was visited by the patriarchs who anointed him."[88] This witness suggests that the story of the anointing by the patriarchs was no late invention but formed part of the original account of Sabbatai's vision as known to his intimate circle. It is the details only and the scriptural quotations that vary in the independent accounts of Laniado, Coenen, and Pinheiro.

No doubt this vision, or rather, emotional upheaval, made an overwhelming impression on Sabbatai. Traces of it are preserved in Sabbatian tradition, which kept a record of the decisive dates in Sab-

87. Coenen, *op. cit.*, p. 93, spells "Doctor Barut," but this may be a printer's error. He is probably identical with the physician who later played a prominent role in the Sabbatian movement, and in whose house Nathan was hiding after the apostasy, in 1667. He was said to be a marrano from Portugal. Sasportas confused him with another well-known Sabbatian physician, the Spanish marrano Abraham Cardozo. "Doctor Barut" may have renounced Sabbatianism at a later date, for "the well-known physician from Smyrna called Doctor Carun [?]" is said to have reported to Moses b. Ḥabib an attempt by Sabbatai's wife to seduce his son ("Testimony given before the rabbinic court in Jerusalem," allegedly by Moses b. Ḥabib and printed—without date or signatures—in Emden, p. 53). According to M. Benayahu, *Studies in Mysticism and Religion in Honor of G. Scholem* (1968), pp. 35–40, the author of this testimony (which was given around 1700–17) was not the chief rabbi of Jerusalem of that name but the Salonikan scholar Moses b. Isaac b. Ḥabib who spent some time in Jerusalem after the death of his namesake. This would explain the many difficulties which the authorship of the Jerusalem rabbi would involve. Doctor Barut's, or Carun's, real name is still an unsolved problem. Regarding the odor exuding from Sabbatai's body, see also Sasportas, pp. 4, 95.

88. Sasportas, p. 94.

batai's life and later turned them into religious feasts. The festival calendar was arranged by Sabbatai's closest associates and may be presumed to preserve significant historical dates.[89] The calendar states that on the Twenty-first of Sivan, Sabbatai was "anointed by the prophet Elijah."[90] Sabbatian tradition thus substituted Elijah for the patriarchs, and it seems probable that Sabbatai himself later altered the story when he told it to the faithful. In the recently discovered Sabbatian hymns we find special hymns for this festival, which has been celebrated without interruption by the Dönmeh in Salonika.[91] One hymn expressly mentions the day and the year by playing on two Hebrew words whose numerical values are 408 (1648) and 21.[92] Another hymn for the same day reads:

> Truly[93] God is good to Israel
> This is the day on which AMIRAH was anointed . . .
> Every man returned unto his possession[94] . . .
> On the day of the anointing,
> The Shekhinah found relief.[95]

89. They were mostly celebrated as days of remembrance but not as festivals in the proper sense. R. Abraham Miranda of Salonika, the compiler of MS. Ben-Zevi Institute 2262, says in a marginal note to his copy of the festival calendar (p. 38) that its indications (saying of the Hallel prayer, festival meals, etc.) were no longer practiced among those rabbis who still believed in Sabbatai Ṣevi in the preceding generation (about 1700–50). The only exception was the 15th and 16th of Kislev, which were observed as a fast and a feast. Miranda, whose information is generally reliable and even excellent, does not speak of the practice of the Dönmeh apostates but of the "outstanding rabbis," *geʾoney ʿolam*, who were secretly adhering to the "faith." There is good reason to assume that his information came from R. Meir Biqayam in Smyrna and Biqayam's teacher R. Jacob Vilna in Jerusalem.

90. Thus all versions of the festival calendar, including the earliest (MS. Adler 493).

91. The list of dates obtained by A. Danon, *op. cit.*, p. 13, is correct, but Danon misunderstood the nature of the event referred to, and thought that Elijah stood for the prophet Nathan. In the later lists (see Galanté, *op. cit.*, p. 47) the date was corrupted to 24 Sivan.

92. M. Attias, G. Scholem, and I. Ben-Zvi, *Sabbatian Hymns* (1948), p. 77. These hymns were composed between 1680–1800 in the Sabbatian (Dönmeh) sect.

93. Numerical value, 21.

94. Cf. Lev. 25:13, and above, ch. 1, p. 89.

95. *Ibid.*, p. 92; cf. also p. 177, where no. 192 should be emended to read "in 408 Elijah anointed the Redeemer, the messianic King, with the oil of gladness." 21 Sivan 5408 fell on June 11, 1648.

Israel Ḥazzan likewise refers to a period "after the anointing of AMIRAH, but before his kingdom was made manifest and known throughout the world." Elsewhere Israel Ḥazzan mentions 1658 as the year of the anointing, but this is probably due to a confusion of two events taking place on very similar dates.[96]

A detail which Coenen heard from Sabbatai's brothers seems to connect the anointing with the characteristic brightness of Sabbatai's face during his ecstasies: "After being anointed messiah by the patriarchs, his face was exceedingly bright and shining, like the face of Moses after the giving of the Law" (Exod. 34:35).[97]

There is no evidence that Sabbatai experienced messianic dreams when not in a state of manic exaltation, and there is not the slightest proof that he made any messianic claims in public. As a matter of fact, such a claim is reported once only. Sasportas, writing about 1669, tells that "some twenty years ago, he [Sabbatai] opened his mouth, saying, 'I am the messiah' and uttering the Ineffable Name of God, so that the great rabbi Joseph Eskapha, who was his principal teacher, rebuked and outlawed him, and announced 'whoever strikes him down first deserves well, for he will lead Israel into sin and make a new religion.' He also wrote to Constantinople about this matter."[98]

Unfortunately we do not possess the first letters written against Sabbatai Ṣevi. Sasportas' details are not always reliable, particularly as he was fond of rewriting earlier accounts and statements in the light of subsequent developments. What Sabbatai definitely did do in public—and apparently more than once—was to pronounce the holy name of God; all the rest, and particularly the messianic proclamations, are probably later additions. The incident was told by Sabbatai to Laniado and is mentioned in all other accounts of Sabbatai's beginnings. There is no evidence of any other demonstration of a messianic character, and even the messianic import of this incident is open to interpretation. The Mishnah (Sanhedrin xi, 1) declares that "he who pronounces the Name with its proper letters" has no share in the world to come, but there is nowhere the slightest hint that the messiah was supposed to pronounce the Ineffable Name. Indeed, the subject is never mentioned in rabbinic sayings about the messianic era.[99] Another Talmudic passage, however, states that in the world

96. See *Schocken Volume,* p. 163, and below, p. 868.

97. Coenen, *op. cit.,* p. 94. 98. Sasportas, p. 4.

99. Coenen was wrong on this point, since he did not know the original

to come the divine name would be pronounced exactly as it is written (B. Pesaḥim 50a). It was probably this Talmudic statement that inspired Sabbatai Ṣevi. He felt himself standing on the threshold of the messianic era which, though strictly speaking was not identical with the world to come, often merged with it in popular eschatology. His provocative demonstration, performed most probably when reciting the blessing before reading the Law in the synagogue, certainly did not stake a definite messianic claim. We do not possess, for the time being, a single text written before 1648 and suggesting that the messiah would begin his career by pronouncing the Ineffable Name. Sabbatai's action merely implied that the new age was at hand, and that he did not distinguish clearly between the world to come and the messianic era; it was a proclamation of imminent redemption and not of the messiah's person. The messianic declaration quoted by Sasportas is either a literary embellishment or it preserves a secret communication of Sabbatai Ṣevi to his followers, which Sasportas wrongly converted into a public proclamation.[100]

We may conclude that Sabbatai's first public appearance ended in some sort of scandal, which, no doubt, greatly incensed the rabbis and provided a fair amount of gossip, but which was of no further consequence. It is surely significant that the subsequent persecution of Sabbatai—of which we have several reliable reports—did not result in his expulsion or banishment until three years later, contrary to Sasportas' account, which seems to suggest that he was "outlawed" in 1648, immediately after his first "strange actions," and that "he and his friends who supported him were besieged and harassed until he went away, driven out and exiled to Salonika."[101] Without regard for chronological sequence, Sasportas compresses the history of several years into one sentence. We know from an unimpeachable source that in 1650 Sabbatai and his friends were still in Smyrna, studying kabbalah without hindrance. Many years later Abraham Miguel Cardozo, who, twenty-five years afterward, had lived in Smyrna and who knew Sabbatai's circle well, wrote a letter in which he tells how Sabbatai had pondered the problem of *En-Sof* and its relation to the *sefiroth,* how he had tried to find an answer to the question of who

---

rabbinic sayings on the subject, but only the interpretations propounded by the Sabbatian believers in Smyrna in 1666.

100. Sasportas, p. 149. 101. *Ibid.,* p. 4.

was the true God, and how he had arrived at the Mystery of the Godhead, which played such a prominent role in Sabbatian theology. For our present purpose, the fact that Cardozo mentions the names of some of the young scholars who studied together with Sabbatai in 1650 is important. Cardozo had spoken to them personally[102] and learned that Moses Pinheiro had received the Mystery of the Godhead from Sabbatai in Smyrna, in 1650, and so had the rabbis Barzillay, Moses Calameri, Silveira, and some others. He writes: "And when I came to Smyrna [in 1675] I heard [this mystery of] their faith from their own mouth." Cardozo later mentions two other scholars who claimed to have heard the mystery from Sabbatai Ṣevi "three or four times," but there is no proof that these two, Moses ha-Kohen and David Algazi, belonged to the original circle of 1650. Very possibly they were among those who heard the mystery only after the apostasy.

The names and the kabbalistic interests of these early friends and disciples are significant. They show that they were mainly concerned with Sabbatai's Mystery of the Godhead, and not with belief in his messiahship, and that Sasportas' account of the persecution of Sabbatai's associates is grossly exaggerated. Only Moses Pinheiro left Smyrna, for all we know for private reasons and not because he was "exiled and banished." At the time many Jews moved to Leghorn, where the dukes of Tuscany had granted them liberal privileges, and the Pinheiro family may have been among them. Others of the circle remained in Smyrna and became esteemed rabbis. *Ḥakham* Silveira is none other than R. Isaac Silveira who died toward the end of 1681 (11 Ḥeshvan 5442) and is described on his epitaph as the "pious and humble,"[103] an honorific generally reserved to men of outstanding saintliness. Moses Calameri is otherwise unknown; perhaps the spelling is corrupt and we should read Calamidi or Galamidi—the name of a well-known family in Constantinople. A certain "pious and humble R. Isaac Calomiti"—almost certainly the same as Calamidi—died in Smyrna in 1683. Of R. Abraham Barzillay we know that R. Ḥayyim Benveniste addressed a responsum to him in 1660.[104] His son was

102. A. Cardozo, "Epistle to Samuel de Paz in Leghorn," in A. H. Weiss, *Beth ha-Midrash* (Vienna, 1865), p. 64. I have corrected the text according to MS. Adler 1653.

103. Freimann, p. 142.

104. *Baᶜey Ḥayyey* (responsa by R. Ḥayyim Benveniste), pt. I, no. 122.

involved in a lawsuit with the two brothers of Sabbatai Ṣevi in the years 1684–90, when he is already referred to as deceased.[105]

Barzillay's name is connected in Sabbatian tradition with an important event in Sabbatai's life. Coenen tells us that as early as 1665 there was talk of a miracle said to have happened to Sabbatai about 1648–50 when he was almost drowned in a whirlpool while bathing in the sea.[106] The incident is mentioned in the festival calendar of the Sabbatians and subsequently became one of their most important feasts called "Purim." Later Sabbatians no longer knew the exact nature of the festival, but the oldest manuscript of the festival calendar states "16 Kislev—the day when he rose from the sea and was saved; it is like the day of Purim."[107] The hymns for the day interpret the event as a symbol of the rising of the messiah's soul from the depth of the abyss. Some of the allusions in the hymns are still obscure.[108] One hymn states that he was drowned in the sea, but that he rose from the abyss and beheld the "crooked serpent,"[109] that his clothes were stolen, and that the sea took on the color of blood. Barzillay is mentioned in this context:

His disciple Barzillay was strong, till evening he cried.
He brought new clothes from his home, and rejoiced with the son of David.[110]

105. Cf. my remarks in *Sabbatian Hymns,* p. 22.

106. Coenen, *op. cit.,* pp. 94, 141. The miracle occurred in the *Xiose Zee,* i.e., the Sea of Chios.

107. MS. Adler 493. The historical explanation is omitted in the other versions, leaving only the word "Purim." I first proposed the correct explanation in my notes to *Sabbatian Hymns,* pp. 136, 217. Miranda's calendar (cf. above, n. 89) explains the event but omits the comparison with Purim.

108. E.g., "A dog fought with him and caused him great pain, but he killed and mounted him," or the story of the stolen clothes. Coenen (*op. cit.,* pp. 94–95) tells of a wolf attacking Sabbatai and then miraculously submitting to him. This may refer to some real event.

109. A mystical symbol of the whirlpool that threatened to swallow him? Sabbatai's encounter with the demon (dog and serpent) in the sea near Smyrna has an interesting analogy in Jesus' fight with the serpent in the waters of the Jordan. The incident is referred to in oriental hymns and possibly goes back to the motif of the fight of the king's son (the redeemer?) with the dragon of the sea as described in the "Hymn of the Pearl" in the Syriac *Acts of Thomas;* cf. A. Adam, *Die Psalmen des Thomas und das Perlenlied* (Berlin, 1959), p. 74.

110. *Sabbatian Hymns,* pp. 136, 217.

To commemorate the event, the Sabbatians instituted a fast on the day preceding their Purim, which, of course, corresponds to the fast of Esther. It is the most important fast in their calendar, and in the prayer recited at the beginning of the fast it is recalled that it was instituted by "*Ḥakham* Barzillay, the disciple of Our Lord."[111] It would appear, therefore, that Barzillay was either present at the event or otherwise connected with it; in any event, he seems to have accompanied Sabbatai to the beach.

Sabbatai did not discover his Mystery of the Godhead at once in his manic illuminations. It is more probable that the idea that the true God of his faith was the *sefirah Tif'ereth*, or the supernal principle within the *sefirah*, emerged slowly and as a result of prolonged searching. In this connection it is of interest to note that the author of the Yemenite apocalypse *Gey Ḥizzayon* (*Valley of Vision*) seems to have had access to letters containing biographical information and reporting some mystical event for the year 1650. From 1642, so we are told, the messiah began "to accept discipline," rising seven rungs on the mystical ladder, corresponding to the seven *sefiroth* from *Malkhuth* to *Gedullah*. During those years he was "manifest and hidden"—a phrase applied in the midrash *Pesiqta Rabbathi* to the messiah, but also applicable, as we have seen, to the person of Sabbatai Ṣevi. After seven years of mystical preparation and ascent "God laid his hand upon him," but the House of Israel was visited with severe tribulations and persecutions, "from the year [1648] of 'proclaiming liberty to them' in which the good one [the messiah] began to receive peace. Two years later he rose to the mystical level of his mother, but all his people were in mourning." In the year of liberty, that is, of disappointed hope and the Chmielnicki massacres, the messiah "received peace," that is, the illuminations that came upon him at intervals. Two years later, in 1650, he rose yet another step, to "his mother." In the symbolic language of kabbalism this can only mean that he rose to the *sefirah Binah*, which is also called the Supernal Mother. These hints, gathered no doubt from letters containing detailed biographical information, can perhaps be interpreted as allusions to the spiritual knowledge at which Sabbatai had arrived. He had risen to the stage of *Binah* ("Under-

111. *Ibid.*, p. 22. The explanations offered by A. Danon, *op. cit.*, p. 54, should be corrected accordingly. Danon was not aware of the origin and meaning of the fast.

standing"), and had "understood" the Mystery of the Godhead, but Israel was in mourning over the unabating atrocities in Poland.

So much, at least, is clear: no public outcry followed immediately on Sabbatai's provocative actions. He was known as a sick man, and his strange behavior was of little consequence, particularly as it manifested itself only when the spirit was upon him. At all other times he endeavored to lead a life of ascetic piety, indulging in fasts and ritual baths, studying the Law, and struggling with himself. Nobody could foresee that these "strange actions" were the harbingers of something far more serious. Without method or deliberate purpose, Sabbatai's actions established a pattern of positive experience that went beyond the recognized limits of historical Judaism. Even at a later period the transgressions, which formed so characteristic a part of his behavior, did not become a "normal" pattern. Their significance was purely symbolic. They were indicative of some special, exalted condition of the soul. "Transgressions" by ordinary, traditional standards, these actions, such as uttering the Ineffable Name, were positive commandments to Sabbatai and acts of *tiqqun,* which he performed at a superior, divine behest. This much he confided to Laniado, and he certainly heard in the voice that roused him to act not Satan the tempter but a divine calling. The very possibility of such a positive evaluation points to the presence of latent antinomian tendencies. The paradox of "doing a good deed by sinning" (as the Talmudic phrase goes) began to manifest itself in Sabbatai's behavior, although, for the time being, his activities remained a purely personal matter. The antinomian "commandment" did not commit anyone else, and Sabbatai himself was unable to explain the paradox to others. Yet this paradox proved to be his one distinct and dangerous contribution to the movement that bore his name. Once he became invested—for reasons that were not the product of his own activity—with supreme religious authority, the paradoxical pattern of his behavior determined the pattern of the movement's theology. The inner law of the Sabbatian movement sprang from the depth of its founder's torn personality, though he himself lacked the intellectual power to formulate it. To Sabbatai, these strange acts remained mere mystical improvisations, whose profound and holy mystery he could neither fully grasp nor explain. He, and probably his friends as well, accounted for the acute anguish during his periods of melancholia, and for the well-known hypochondriac sufferings that came in its wake, as a mysterious passion in which the suffering messiah atoned for his own sins or (according to some of the sources already quoted) for those of Israel.

We do not know what brought about the intensification of the action against him. All witnesses agree that he used to utter the Ineffable Name frequently, but it is improbable that this should suddenly have inflamed the rabbis after their having countenanced it for many years, perhaps out of consideration for his illness. Israel Ḥazzan, Sabbatai's faithful disciple in later days, interpreted Psalm 21:3, "For thou preventest him with the blessings of goodness," with reference to this habit: "This shows that Our Lord, before his kingdom became manifest, used to pronounce the holy name when reciting the blessing during his illuminations. . . . This is the meaning of 'thou preventest'—thou preventest [= anticipate] his fame by 'blessings of goodness,' that is, by his blessings in which he uttered the divine name."[112] No other "strange actions" are attested during this early period, and reliable reports are available only from 1653 onward. Paul Rycaut later heard in Smyrna, where he served as British consul, that Sabbatai's "religious innovations" had caused a scandal in the synagogue. Only the poet Emanuel Frances of Leghorn, a foe of the movement, goes beyond generalities and gives a detailed account of such an incident. Frances wrote "The Story of Sabbatai Ṣevi" in 1667, drawing on letters and written reports that arrived in Leghorn. In this cursory account of not more than three pages, one incident stands out by its greater detail. We know that after the apostasy, the rabbis of Smyrna dispatched letters to the rabbinates of other cities in which they expatiated on Sabbatai's many "evil deeds." It is not impossible that similar letters had been disseminated earlier by the "unbelievers" with whom Frances was in close contact, or that Frances saw such a letter before he composed "The Story" as an appendix to his collection of satirical poems *Ṣevi Muddaḥ* (*Chased Roe*), an obvious pun ("roe" = *Ṣevi*). According to Frances' story (which we cannot verify), Sabbatai once assembled his friends for an attempt to make the sun stand still at midday. After the appropriate preparations and purifications, they went out into the fields early one morning, "and they went up the mountains and Sabbatai cried to the sun with a mighty voice to stand still, and so did his disciples, until they were ashamed." When R. Joseph Eskapha and the elders of Smyrna heard

112. *Schocken Volume,* p. 162.

of this affair, they summoned Sabbatai, who refused to appear. Thereupon they threatened excommunication, but he "returned the ban" with the impudent message "that his little finger was bigger than his [Eskapha's] loins[113] and that he excommunicated him and his associates [that is, Eskapha and the members of the rabbinic court]." When it was suggested killing Sabbatai, R. Eskapha objected and advised "castigating him, so that he should not return to his foolish ways, and banishing him from the city."[114] This advice was followed.

The story shows that its authors believed Sabbatai to have engaged in more than theoretical kabbalah. According to Frances, he discoursed every day with his associates on the Mystery of the Chariot "of his own invention" (perhaps an allusion to Sabbatai's Mystery of the Godhead) but also engaged in practical kabbalah, that is, in the study of the holy names by which miracles can be worked. Sasportas evidently held the same belief when he wrote that Sabbatai "devoted himself to both the holy and the unclean [demonic] names."[115] These reports cannot simply be dismissed as polemical inventions, since they are supported by Sabbatai's statement to Laniado concerning his great exorcism of the Holy Spirit in 1665. He was, then, something of a magician, too.

Whatever it was, something must have happened that caused the rabbis of Smyrna to lose their temper, to forget about Sabbatai's illness and unstable moods, and to resort to persecution. The fact of his persecution by the rabbis seems to be established beyond doubt by testimonies from both sides, though the details are far from clear and no original documents on the subject have survived. Sasportas reports that not only Joseph Eskapha, but also R. Aaron Lapapa, author of the collection of responsa *Beney Aharon* and one of the foremost scholars of Smyrna and all Turkey, "opposed Sabbatai Ṣevi" from the beginning. R. Joseph ha-Levi of Leghorn tells how Sabbatai "proclaimed himself a prophet"—he does not say messiah—"and the whole congregation persecuted him. He and his friends were thoroughly beaten, and banished from the district."[116] Ha-Levi's report

113. Cf. I Kings 12:10.

114. On the matter of killing Sabbatai, Frances' account plainly contradicts the testimony of Coenen and others; the "castigating" may refer to the floggings (thirty-nine stripes) that Sabbatai had to endure.

115. Sasportas, p. 4.

116. *Ibid.*, pp. 208, 256. On the first persecutions see also p. 302.

probably goes back to gossip current in Leghorn about Moses Pinheiro, who had come from Smyrna and settled there. Sasportas claims to have heard of the excommunication soon after it happened from "truthful reporters who had been there at the time when R. Eskapha outlawed him . . . saying 'this one will entice you to serve the Baals.' "[117] The "truthful reporters," identified at the beginning of Sasportas' book, were one person, Yedidyah b. Isaac Gabbay, the owner of the Jewish printing house in Smyrna, who later moved his business to Leghorn. But therefore Sasportas can hardly have heard of the events at the time of their occurrence. He probably heard these details in the fifties, on the occasion of a well-documented journey of the old printer to Amsterdam sometime before 1659. Gabbay, who started printing in Leghorn toward the end of 1649, possibly returned to Smyrna on one of his journeys, where he witnessed some of the events (Sabbatai certainly did not leave the city before 1650). Coenen mentions the persecutions without giving exact dates. The "Grand Rabbi Eskapha" is said to have advised the secret killing of Sabbatai, but since nobody wanted to lay hands on him, it was decided to banish Sabbatai from the city.[118] In 1665 Nathan writes[119] that Sabbatai "suffered exile for eighteen years, hunted from pillar to post, and many a time his blood was declared free for all." Very possibly his banishment was precipitated by an increase in the violence of his disease leading him to more serious transgressions of the Law.

When exactly did Sabbatai leave Smyrna? A history of Sabbatai Ṣevi that appeared in a Dutch chronicle of 1666 refers to his expulsion from Smyrna of "fifteen years ago." This would put the date at 1651. The report in the chronicle was taken from the letter of a Dutch merchant in Smyrna, written in the beginning of April, 1666, and published soon afterward in a German translation.[120] In a letter writ-

117. *Ibid.*, p. 313.

118. Coenen, *op. cit.*, p. 10. Leyb b. Ozer's account draws on Coenen, but adds legendary embellishments, e.g., that Sabbatai formally notified the rabbinic court of his messianic dignity (Emden, p. 4). Leyb's date of Sabbatai's banishment (1648 or 1649) is wrong in any case. Rycaut, *op. cit.*, p. 201, says that Sabbatai "was by the censure of the Kockhams . . . banished from the city."

119. In his letter to Raphael Joseph.

120. The letter appeared first in the *Hollandtze Merkurius* of January, 1666, p. 2. The German version appeared in Martin Meyer, *Diarium Europaeum,* XVI (1668), 509, whence it was reprinted in the *Theatrum Europaeum,* X (1703), 438. Both the *Hollandtze Merkurius* and the *Diarium* were unknown

ten by the French Jesuit in Constantinople, the expulsion is dated as late as 1654.[121] We may thus put the probable date some time between 1651 and 1654.

We possess, moreover, an interesting piece of information about this period that may throw some light on the beginning of Sabbatai's wanderings. According to the Amsterdam memorialist Leyb b. Ozer, Sabbatai is said to have engaged, in the spring of 1653, a servant, who accompanied him on all his travels till the time of Sabbatai's apostasy. If this report is correct, we may presume that he needed a servant to attend to him on his travels and not in his voluntary seclusion in his father's house or on his solitary walks in the fields outside Smyrna. As the son of a wealthy and respected family, Sabbatai could permit himself this amenity. Unfortunately the trustworthiness of this particular detail is open to serious doubt in spite of its apparently authoritative source—the servant himself. Yeḥiel, the servant, had long conversations with Leyb b. Ozer, the notary of the Ashkenazi community in Amsterdam and author of the *Account of Sabbatai Ṣevi,* who writes: "This servant told me many stories and details about Sabbatai Ṣevi. But since for many of these I depend on his word alone—they may be either true or false—I preferred not to recount them here. . . . But everything that I have told so far has been vouched for by this servant or valet."[122] Here the critical historian finds himself on the horns of an uncomfortable dilemma. Either Yeḥiel is responsible for all the chronological inaccuracies and bad mistakes in Leyb's "account," in which case he was certainly a liar and his testimony has no value, or else the inaccuracies are not his fault. In the latter case we must conclude that Leyb was evidently incapable of assimilating the details with which he was supplied by the best-qualified informant possible.

Leyb's account of Sabbatai's travels in the "dark years" until

---

to Graetz and other writers who held the *Theatrum Europaeum* to be the original source of the report. For some unknown reason the Dutch version does not reveal the source of its information.

121. *Relation,* p. 13.

122. The original Yiddish text in Z. Rubashov-Shazar's article "Sabbatai Ṣevi's Servant," *Tarbiz* V (1934), 351. Shazar's attempts at identifying the servant Yeḥiel with R. Yeḥiel b. Ṣevi of Kavela are vitiated by his erroneous assumptions regarding the existence of a Sabbatian movement prior to 1665; cf. *SS,* I, 121, n. 1.

1665 is undeniably the worst and most unreliable of all, and can be refuted at almost every point. Some of his inaccuracies are enormous by any standards, such as the length of thirteen years or more attributed to Sabbatai's stay in Jerusalem, or the mention of a third visit to Egypt after a prolonged sojourn in Jerusalem. Was the servant so ignorant of the simplest facts and so confused about his chronology? Or did he give an accurate and true account, and Leyb b. Ozer, lacking all critical sense of reality, confused everything and then presented his garbled version as the servant's testimony? The gravest doubts must arise as to the value of the whole memoir which, nevertheless, often reveals sound historical and psychological insight. There is no easy way out of this dilemma, which is further complicated by a statement of Abraham Cuenque of Hebron. Cuenque, who knew the Sabbatian traditions well and who had met Sabbatai in Hebron, stated that Sabbatai Ṣevi "came to Jerusalem *without servants and attendants*. He lived alone in one room, fasting throughout the week and on Sabbath eve buying Sabbath provisions himself."[123] If Cuenque's account is correct, then why did Sabbatai need a servant? Pending the discovery of further documents, our attitude to Yeḥiel's story of his thirteen years of service with Sabbatai Ṣevi must be marked by extreme caution. Perhaps he invented all of it and never served Sabbatai at all—which is to say that Leyb b. Ozer fell victim to a mountebank. Perhaps he became Sabbatai's servant only when the messiah began to live in royal state at the height of the messianic movement. Afterward, when Yeḥiel wandered about reminiscing, he may well have added to his story years and facts about which he really knew nothing, such as Sabbatai's stays in Jerusalem and Cairo. The date 1653 is thus uncertain too, and we must remain content for the time being with the little that we positively know: sometime between 1651 and 1654 Sabbatai was compelled to leave his birthplace and go into exile.

IV

Before we follow Sabbatai on his peregrinations, it may be useful to dispose of a serious misconception that has been the subject of many unfounded hypotheses and to clear the way for a proper understanding

123. Emden, p. 35. Cuenque's testimony, which contradicts Yeḥiel's account, has been overlooked by Shazar.

of events. Some authors have put forward the hypothesis that Sabbatai's messianic ambitions, as well as the timing of the great awakening in 1666, owed much to Christian stimuli. Graetz[124] surmised that Sabbatai's father, Mordecai Ṣevi, had heard from the English merchants, whose agent he was, all sorts of rumors about the impending restoration of Israel to their land in the apocalyptic year of redemption 1666. Mordecai Ṣevi would report these rumors at home and create in his house a messianic atmosphere whose origin was ultimately non-Jewish. The imagination of one modern novelist has actually supplied the details of the discussion between Mordecai Ṣevi and a Puritan Englishman concerning the date and the preparatory stages of the redemption of Israel.[125] Both, so we are told, agreed on all points except for the date: Mordecai Ṣevi (who has meanwhile been turned into a kabbalist) expected the redemption in 1648, while the Christian insisted on 1666 as the year foretold in Revelation. Thus the messianic seed was sown in young Sabbatai's heart. When his expectations for 1648 were miserably disappointed, he pinned his hopes—perhaps unconsciously—on the year 1666 as the next messianic date. A Christian factor was thus operative in the movement from its very inception.

There is not the slightest historical justification for any of these fond inventions. Sabbatai Ṣevi needed no Christians to be impressed with the probability of 1666 being a messianic year. He had much closer stimuli in this direction from his immediate religious tradition and upbringing. There is not a shred of evidence to show that Mordecai Ṣevi's employers were millenarians, and we may positively assert that they could not have mentioned 1666 as a messianic year. The propaganda for this date made its appearance in Dutch and English literature in the fifties only, that is, after Sabbatai had left Smyrna. There had, of course, been a few medieval writers who had interpreted the "number of the beast," 666, in Revelation 13:18[126] as a prophecy of the coming of Antichrist in the year 1666,[127] but

124. Graetz, *Geschichte der Juden,* X, 434–35. His view was adopted by D. Kahana, *Toledoth ha-Mequbbalim* (1913), pt. I, p. 59, and others.

125. Joseph Kastein, *The Messiah of Ismir Sabbatai Zevi* (1931). The book is a psychological novel rather than a history of Sabbatai Ṣevi.

126. Cf. Paulus Cassel, *Die Offenbarung S. Johannis und das Tier* (1889). He quotes many interpretations of the passage.

127. Thus the German monk Heinrich of Hessen, writing in 1388; see Lynn Thorndike, *A History of Magic,* V, 505.

these isolated views were not widely known. Shortly before 1666, some Protestant chiliasts remembered the date and began to propagate the view that the "fifth kingdom" would begin in that year. They also connected with that date their hopes for a restoration of the Jews to Palestine and their conversion to Christianity. It was mainly in the fifties that the year 1666 gained in importance in the Latin writings of a few chiliastically inclined theologians, such as, for example, Coccejus and Comenius who, in their turn, influenced other Dutch, English, and German authors.[128] There is, however, no causal connection between this type of literature and the history of Sabbatai's development, although the synchronicity of the tracts of Peter Serrarius and others, published in 1665, with the happenings in the Jewish world, is certainly worthy of attention. Parallelism and synchronicity are no rare phenomena in history, but as an explanation of Sabbatai's development they are useless. Discussions between Jews and their Christian neighbors concerning the expectation of the messiah or the Second Coming probably took place in Europe at all periods. We should not overrate their influence on the immanent development of eschatological traditions in rabbinic and kabbalistic Judaism.

As has been shown before, it is very doubtful whether Sabbatai's messianic self-revelation in 1648 was more than a secret communication to a few friends and companions, and in any event the claim was made intermittently only, without continuity or permanence. Sabbatai's public utterance of the Ineffable Name cannot, as we have seen, be construed as a formal proclamation of his messiahship. If he ever made an unequivocal public claim, it must have left little or no impression. Were it not for the major events of some eighteen years later, no echo of Sabbatai's activities in 1648 would ever have come to our ears. As it is, there are good reasons to inquire whether there were other messianic stirrings, during that period, which have fallen into oblivion. Some such forgotten testimonies seem to have survived, curiously enough, in Christian sources.

In 1654 a former rabbinic student who, after his conversion, called himself Paul Jesaja published in London a missionary tract entitled *A Vindication of the Christians' Messias*. According to this author a false messiah had appeared in Bohemia some time about

128. Cf., e.g., the chapter on Paul Felgenhauer and his circle, in H. J. Schoeps, *Philosemitismus im Barock* (1952), pp. 18–53.

1650 and won many followers until he was exposed as an impostor.[129] This report agrees so well with what we would expect in the wake of the Chmielnicki massacres, that there is no reason to dismiss it as fantasy merely because of the lack of confirmation from Jewish sources. On the other hand, there is sufficient evidence to show that the imagination of Christian contemporaries could by itself be productive of Jewish messiahs. There is on record a particularly striking example which, moreover, played a role in the dissemination of the news about the Sabbatian movement among Christians. In 1642 a small tract circulated in Germany, which a Protestant minister later quoted in full in his book against the Sabbatian movement, arguing that fantastic reports about the appearance of messiahs were no novelty and had actually occurred within living memory.[130] The description is completely imaginary, and exhibits the characteristic contemporary style of wonderfully strange news reports:

> The ambassador residing in Constantinople writes from there that a new messiah was born to a Turkish Jewess in Ossa. He has conquered not only mighty cities and fortresses such as Aleppo, Alexandria, and Filandia [?], but even Popistel [?], the kingdom of Egypt, and the provinces of lower Syria. To Don Sebe, the king of Persia, he merely sent his sword, signifying to him thereby that he should lay down his kingdom and deliver it of his free will, otherwise to expect his sword. Likewise he sent a similar sword to the Turkish emperor in Constantinople, signifying to him that he should deliver up Jerusalem and Damascus. He says that all the kingdoms are his because he is of the seed of the kings of Judah, and therefore his dominion is deservedly due to him. They also say that the sultan was greatly perturbed by this and proposes to move his residence from Constantinople to Mecca. He calls himself Jesus Eli-Messias, the God of heaven and earth, pretending that he created all and that without him no man can attain to eternal life. He was born in the year 1624, on the twenty-fourth of September, in the village

129. I have not been able to see a copy of Paul Jesaja's tract and rely on the account in Johann F. De Le Roi, *Die evangelische Christenheit und die Juden* (1884), I, 187.

130. Michael Buchenroeder, *Eilende Messias Juden-Post* (Nurenberg, 1666), fol. B iii. The "newsletter" was printed in full by Buchenroeder from a copy found among the papers of a schoolmaster in his neighborhood and entitled *Extract-Schreiben aus Augspurg vom 24 Sept. anno 1642*. No further copies of the original news letter have so far come to light.

of Ossa, near Basiliske. His mother is called Gamaritta, a beautiful woman but not of noble descent. On his eighth day, when he was circumcised according to the manner of the Jews, he began to speak and to give mighty signs, saying that he was the son of God, God, and the true messiah. On the day of his birth mighty signs and wonders occurred. The sun became dark in the middle of the day; at about the eighth hour, a mighty voice was heard at a hundred miles distance calling out, "Repent ye sons of men, for today the messiah was born," and many fiery dragons and devils were seen in the air. The birth of this Antichrist is truly to be marveled at, for after a few months he had grown to the stature of a youth of twenty-four or twenty-five. His father is unknown. His neck is thick-set, his head pointed, his face like that of a Turk, his brow wrinkled, his eyes terrible, his ears long, his genital organ big, and his teeth sharp. Many who saw him and refused to bow to him, fell down and died on the spot. The Lord Chamberlain [*Hoffmarschall*] in Jerusalem, Mr. Sebastian Maches, dispatched twenty-four of his best horsemen to find out the truth of these rumors. They reported that he raised the dead and healed the sick by his look, provided they adored him and believed in him. . . . When he appears in public, he is surrounded by a blue cloud and another cloud is under his feet. At times the sun surrounds him, and then his face shines with a great brightness so that nobody standing in front of him or near him remains alive. He wants to subdue the whole world and says that all kings are his servants and would be subdued by his weapons. He is a furious hater of men, and in Alexandria, Aleppo, and Egypt alone he killed a few hundred people who refused to believe in him or accord him divine honors. But to those who believe in him and accord him divine honors, he promises kingdoms and distinctions, and then commands them to put his mark on their foreheads.

He has twelve apostles, whom he calls prophets, and they preach that only in his name is eternal life. They also perform great miracles, like the Antichrist himself. Among themselves they condemn the state of matrimony and practice community of women, though he himself has about four hundred wives and seven hundred virgins. More than fifty thousand Jews from all parts of the world have already joined him, and he has provided them with weapons. According to the intelligence of My Lord the Ambassador, he is already reported to have conquered Damascus and killed all the inhabitants that refused to believe in him. An old man of seventy-five from Jerusalen, who happened to be in Damascus, was skinned, and his flesh smeared with honey and exposed to the sun until he was eaten by flies and other vermin. Let all Christians take this to their hearts and repent, as it is evident that the end of all flesh is not far away, and that he is the Antichrist prophesied by Daniel, John, and Paul in their epistles. Here ends the tale.

In this weird description we find the Antichrist of Revelation combined with fantastic popular ideas about the Jewish messiah. The similarities with certain details in the Christian pamphlets of 1665–66 about the Sabbatian movement are as patent as they are surprising. Apparently the two popular traditions were confused in the later pamphlets, since even the name of the Jewish messiah reappears in the first Christian reports about Sabbatai Ṣevi, where Jesus Eli-Messias has become Joshua El Kam, or Helkam (see below, p. 558).

All early sources are agreed that after his banishment from Smyrna, Sabbatai proceeded to Salonika,[131] which was then the largest Jewish community in the Turkish Empire and an important center of rabbinic and kabbalistic learning. None of his friends and associates accompanied him into exile, and none seems to have remained in communication with him. If Sabbatai came to Salonika as an outcast or excommunicate, this is not discernible in our sources. Leyb b. Ozer reports that he was kindly received—nothing was known, in Salonika, of his strange actions—and that he soon found disciples and friends. Abraham Cuenque's information that Sabbatai refused to accept financial help from his brothers is probably incorrect. We may assume that the brothers supported him liberally during his wanderings and that he remained in Salonika for some time, behaving like any other rabbinic scholar.

131. The original report in the *Hollandtze Merkurius* mentions Constantinople first, but it merely lists the cities where Sabbatai had been and does not pretend to give his itinerary. The version in the *Theatrum Europaeum* can be ignored. Rosanes (IV, pp. 411–12) maintains that Sabbatai went to Constantinople first, and appeals to de la Croix, who actually suggests the opposite. The anonymous French priest, who was one of the first to make investigations on the spot, writes (*Relation,* p. 13), "il alla premièrement à Tessalonique." De la Croix, after saying that Sabbatai was ordered to present himself at the rabbinic court in Constantinople, then begins a new paragraph with the words, "In order to escape these quarrels, Sabbatai decided to go to Salonika." Sasportas, too, says that Sabbatai went to Salonika after his expulsion from Smyrna (*Ṣiṣath Nobel Ṣevi,* p. 4), though the second part of his sentence is obscure.

A general remark about Sabbatai's personality and the impression it made on others needs to be inserted here. Sabbatai was undoubtedly a well-educated and competent, though in no way outstanding, scholar. His intellectual capacities were well developed but by no means extraordinary. He was not intellectually creative or original, and he was completely devoid of literary talent. Until his last years he never wrote any kabbalistic papers or treatises, and the only piece of kabbalistic writing of which a copy has been preserved is the short glosses on the margins of his copy of the Mantua edition of the book *Tiqquney Zohar* (1558). They do not amount to much.[132] His emotional life, however, was intense and stormy. He had a gift for music and loved music and song. He would often sing to himself, and whenever he chanced upon a Spanish love song whose tune caught his fancy he would convert it into a mystical song of divine love, somewhat in the manner of such famous Hasidic *ṣaddiqim* of later days as R. Isaac of Kalov and the descendants of R. Israel the Maggid of Koznice, who "redeemed" exalted tunes from their "exile" among the Hungarian and Slav peasants, restoring them to the sphere of holiness. But even apart from his musical gifts, Sabbatai must have possessed a very real personal charm. This is attested by all witnesses. The Christian writers who lived in Turkey speak of his wonderful power in gaining the hearts of men, and many of them, particularly some chroniclers, were frankly puzzled by its most striking manifestation: the evident liking for him which the sultan evinced for at least six years after his apostasy. There was an air of nobility about his dealings with people, and a very winning kindness. Leyb b. Ozer has preserved some echoes of the profound impression made by his dignified demeanor toward both rich and poor during the mass pilgrimages in 1666. The same man who would deliver himself to unbridled emotionalism during his illuminations could deport himself at other times with skill and superior tact. The one authentic picture of Sabbatai which we possess does not lack an expression of quiet nobility. We need not marvel, therefore, that this personal magnetism was in evi-

132. The notes were copied in MS. Ben-Zvi Institute 2262, pp. 209–15: "glosses on the book *Tikkunim* by AMIRAH." They contain on p. 213 a remark on Isaac Luria whose name he found to be equivalent to the number 455 "which is the sum-total of all the powers of rigor [*din*] as *I have written in another place.*" The MS. derives from the Dönmeh archives. Sabbatai's copy of the book was probably kept in Salonika, along with some other records of his.

dence during his wanderings in exile and later. In spite of his charm, however, Sabbatai did not succeed in establishing around himself a permanent circle of obedient followers and companions, obviously because of his psychopathological traits.

The Sabbatians in Salonika preserved many memories of Sabbatai's stay in their city, though it is likely that these were confused later with reminiscences of the period following his apostasy when, if we can rely on Tobias Rofe, he again lived for a while in Salonika. Some of these traditions definitely go back to Sabbatai's first sojourn there. He prayed in the synagogue of Qehal Shalom ("Congregation of Peace"), and as late as the nineteen-twenties there were people in Salonika who could point out the ḥouse of R. Joseph Florentin where Sabbatai had stayed.[133] He also made friends with other young scholars. But before long his periods of exaltation, accompanied by "strange actions," returned. There are two versions of what actually happened. According to de la Croix, Sabbatai resumed his habit of pronouncing the divine name, justifying his action by vague hints at private mystical reasons; he did not, however, voice messianic pretensions. He did do something which throws a great deal of light on his "strange actions." Having invited the most prominent rabbis to a banquet, he erected a bridal canopy, had a Torah scroll brought in, and performed the marriage ceremony between himself and the Torah. The deeply shocked rabbis would not be reassured by his mystical explanation that every lover of the Torah could be considered her bridegroom or husband, and that this mystery had already been adumbrated in the Book of Proverbs. "Instead of attributing this action to his great holiness, they accused him of madness. And as they were afraid that these and similar innovations might have dangerous consequences, they forced him to leave the city."[134]

The story bears the mark of authenticity and clearly brings out the characteristic features of Sabbatai's later "strange actions": his fondness for bizarre and singular ceremonials and for the invention of ritual with a hidden, personal symbolism. Actions of this kind do not constitute, strictly speaking, transgressions of the Law. They were

133. See J. M. Molho in *Reshumoth,* V (1930), 537. This particular Salonika tradition, unlike many others, seems to be authentic—but it confused the names of Joseph Filosoff (later Sabbatai's father-in-law) and Solomon Florentin.

134. De la Croix, *op. cit.,* p. 267.

the paradoxical and odd behavior of a "queer" person, who seemed to consider his grotesque demonstrations as the performance of some exalted and mysterious commandment. This kind of behavior was to be repeated more than once, and we may well understand the reaction of the rabbis: they considered him mad. The essential correctness of the report about the mystical marriage is confirmed by Sabbatai's letters, which he occasionally signed "the bridegroom coming out of his chamber, the husband of the dearly beloved Torah, who is the most beauteous and lovely lady."[135] These words, written in 1666, show that a ceremony like that reported from Salonika must have been deeply engraved in Sabbatai's heart. He describes the Torah, almost as a matter of course, as "the beauteous and lovely" bride, and himself as the bridegroom who stood under the bridal canopy with her and became her husband. The signature of the letter and the account of the French diplomat complement, and vouch for, each other.

Leyb b. Ozer's version is more conventional, in keeping with his messianic formulation. The scandal in Salonika is said to have been a repetition of that in Smyrna, which, of course, casts serious doubt on the correctness of Leyb's account. Sabbatai "returned to his evil ways and resumed his former habit of uttering the divine name." To those who protested he replied that as messiah he was entitled to do so. For his reply he was banished by the rabbis, who served him with a court order demanding he leave the city immediately.[136] Thereafter Sabbatai wandered through the cities of Greece, visiting Athens, the communities of the Peloponnese,[137] and probably also the original home of his family, Patras. His rovings continued until 1658, when he arrived in Constantinople. His stay there lasted about eight months[138] and ended with a public scandal. We are relatively well informed about this period, since de la Croix's informant, a former Sabbatian believer, had been closely associated with Sabbatai Ṣevi. His

135. Freimann, p. 56.

136. Emden, p. 4. Leyb b. Ozer seems to have copied Coenen's account, which he misunderstood. Coenen merely says that Sabbatai behaved in Salonika as in Smyrna, and with the same results. Leyb took this in a literal sense and simply duplicated the events.

137. Coenen, *op. cit.*, p. 10; *Relation*, p. 13.

138. *Relation*, p. 13. The date is confirmed by de la Croix, who says that the great fire in Constantinople (1660) occurred in the year after Sabbatai's expulsion from the city.

information contains much valuable local tradition and is essentially reliable. Sabbatai, it appears, arrived in Constantinople well provided with means,[139] was well received by the scholars, and generally moved in better circles. Again he underwent periods of depression and illumination, and he acquired some notoriety by his "strange actions" which, however, were attributed at first to mere folly. As time went on his behavior became more bizarre and provocative. One day he bought a very large fish, dressed it up like a baby, and put it into a cradle. "The rabbis who heard of this incident were much amazed and saddened at the mental derangement [*bouleversement de la cervelle*] of such a scholar." However, it was not the incident of the fish that led to his later persecution by the rabbis. For the time being, Sabbatai's queerness was simply attributed to mental illness. He himself explained his last performance in terms of astrological symbolism. The redemption of Israel—which appears to have occupied him at the time—would take place under the sign of Pisces. The idea can be found in earlier Jewish tradition, but for Sabbatai the cradle evidently symbolized the slow growth toward the fullness of Israel's redemption;[140] the fish in the cradle served as a grotesque illustration of rabbinic sayings to that effect. When the rabbis realized "that some new sect, which might confuse minds, was fermenting in his brain, they did not act like the rabbis of Salonika who expelled him, but dispatched an officer of the rabbinic court who gave him forty stripes, and forbade his company to all Jews on pain of a penalty"; that is, they excommunicated him.[141] The whipping is also mentioned in Sabbatai's account to Laniado, though there seems to be some confusion in the extant version, where Sabbatai is said to have been flogged "several times."[142] Perhaps the original text referred in a general way to the several floggings which Sabbatai had received during his wanderings on the order of local rabbinates for his "strange actions."

139. De la Croix, *op. cit.*, p. 268: "il parut en bon equipage." The author of *Relation* reports that Sabbatai devoted himself exclusively to his studies; apparently he could afford it.

140. Cf. above, p. 48. The advent of the messiah under the sign of Pisces is mentioned in Isaac Abravanel's commentary on Daniel, *Maᶜayney ha-Yeshuᶜah* (Amsterdam, 1647), fol. 86b.

141. De la Croix, *op. cit.*, p. 268.

142. There are further corruptions in the text as given in *Toᶜey Ruah;* see *SS*, I, p. 129, n. 4.

De la Croix does not explain whether the fear of a "new sect" was due solely to the incident with the fish, or whether there had been other, more flagrant offenses against tradition. The latter suspicion is confirmed by a Sabbatian source. A supplement to the apocalypse of the *Vision of R. Abraham* prophesies a violent antinomian outbreak for the year 1658. The prophecy obviously refers to past events, in spite of the future tense adopted by its author. It predicts that "In the year 1658 he [the messiah] will celebrate the three festivals of pilgrimage in one week, so as to atone for all the sins ever committed by Israel during festival times. Then God will give him a new law and new commandments to repair all the worlds. In the year 1658 he shall bless 'Him who permits that which is forbidden.'" This is one of our most important testimonies, coming as it does from Sabbatai's immediate entourage[143]—probably from Nathan. Since Sabbatai was in Constantinople in the year 1658, the strange act of celebrating the three pilgrim festivals all in one week must have occurred there. This was strong stuff indeed and far more provocative than the incident with the fish, which could, if necessary, be dismissed as a puerile and harmless folly. This time resolute punitive action was required of the rabbinic court. The provocation displayed some of the most characteristic features of Sabbatai's strange behavior pattern, for throughout his career he exhibited a predilection for shifting dates, changing fixed times, and moving Sabbaths and holy days to other days. The celebration of the festivals in one week was merely the first installment in a long series of similar ceremonies reported by the most diverse sources. Half a year before his death, he again celebrated the feasts of Tabernacles and Pentecost in one week, in his place of exile, Dulcigno.

But this was not all. According to the *Vision of R. Abraham*, Sabbatai was also vouchsafed, in the same year, "a new law and new commandments." The old law was abrogated, and new rituals were revealed that would bring mystical perfection to all the worlds. Their character was defined in the blasphemous benediction which Sabbatai used here for the first time and which henceforth accompanied the Sabbatian movement through all its strange meta-

143. The prophecy is found in the Sabbatian documents from Damascus and Kurdistan, quoted in *Toᶜey Ruaḥ;* see G. Scholem in *Zion*, VII (1942), 182; it is also mentioned in copies of the vision in Dönmeh MSS. that have come to light recently.

morphoses. The essence of the new law, apparently valid for Sabbatai only, is to be found in the sanctification of transgressions and their elevation to the level of positive religious precepts requiring a formal ritual blessing. But even for Sabbatai the new law did not impose itself at all times; it was valid during moments of illumination only, that is, when in a state of contact with the supernal light, when transgressions and sins did not become mere neutral, indifferent categories, but solemn ritual ceremonies. Ideas that had been incubating in Sabbatai's storm-tossed soul since his first reading of the *Peliʾah* and *Qanah* now broke forth in full-blown antinomian extremism. The "loosening of them that are bound [*ʾasurim*]" of the traditional prayer formula, becomes, in a far-reaching pun, the "loosening of all bonds [*ʾissurim*]" of religious obligation and prohibition. Until now Sabbatai's actions had been blind and haphazard; now they acquired the paradoxical character of holy deeds through sinning. We cannot be sure whether the Sabbatian formulation of this principle was not influenced by subsequent events in 1666. But essentially the doctrine was no invention after the event, for which, as a matter of fact, the believers had no need. Most probably Sabbatai himself confessed his inner experiences to Nathan.

Sabbatian tradition has preserved many more hints concerning certain decisive events in Sabbatai's life during that year. The historical core of these traditions is sufficiently explained by the foregoing. Israel Ḥazzan of Kastoria mentions a report to the effect that Sabbatai was anointed (again?) in "the year 5418 [1658], the numerical value of which is indicated in the verse [Job 38:8], 'when he had issued out of the womb'—which mystically refers to his issuing out of the holy Torah, which he had studied already in his mother's womb."[144] The correctness of the numeral value of the Hebrew letters proves that there is no error in the date. The report agrees well with what we know of the "new law" and the blessing of the "loosening of prohibitions." In 1658 Sabbatai "issued out" of the authority of the law that he had studied in his youth. Henceforth he was beyond the authority of rabbinic Judaism, and subject to a higher law. God had "hid" from him the "true Law," that is, rabbinic law. This exodus from the law of his youth was probably marked by spectacular performances, which Israel Ḥazzan does not mention but which, as we

144. *Schocken Volume,* p. 163.

have seen, are reported or "prophesied" in the *Vision of R. Abraham.* Illuminations of an antinomian character, such as experienced by Sabbatai Ṣevi, are by no means rare in the history of religious mysticism. The famous Sufi mystic al-Junayd (died 911)—to quote but one example—declared that "God brings upon those that love him a kind of sudden and supernatural madness, in which a man may speak and act against the directions of religion, without his being responsible for his actions and without God caring to make them accord with the religion which He has revealed from heaven."[145] There is no need to belabor the similarity between Sabbatai's "strange actions" and al-Junayd's description.

Immediately after the account of Sabbatai's exodus from the "holy law" in 1658, Israel Ḥazzan refers to another event which may belong to the same year. "And I set bars and doors against him [cf. Job 38:10]—this refers to the prison in which he was imprisoned; 'and said hitherto shalt thou come but no further' [Job 38:11]—because this imprisonment was the end of his sufferings."[146] The reference is, perhaps, to Sabbatai's confinement in the fortress of Gallipoli in 1666. Abraham Cardozo, however, mentions in one of his letters[147] that Sabbatai was imprisoned twice. It is difficult to avoid the impression that Sabbatian tradition knew of a second imprisonment.[148] If this is correct, the tradition must refer to something that occurred prior, and not subsequent, to 1666, since Sabbatai's final exile to Albania is never described as "arrest" or "imprisonment" in Sabbatian writings, and can therefore be disregarded for our purpose. It is obvious that the expression is meant to be taken literally and not as an allegory. Perhaps we may venture the surmise that the rabbis of Constantinople considered thirty-nine stripes insufficient punishment for his blasphemous benediction and imprisoned him.

Sabbatai's behavior in 1658 is described in a somewhat different terminology in parallel traditions which appear, for the first time, in the writings of Nathan. There it is stated[149] that the "exaltation of the Shekhinah from her exile" began in 1658. On the basis of independent computations, Nathan had originally determined the year 1657

145. L. Massignon, *La Passion d'Al-Hallaj,* I (1922), 36.

146. MS. Kaufmann 155, fol. 74a.

147. MS. Hamburg, 312.

148. Cf. *Zion,* XIX (1954), 12.

149. In the Sabbatian notebook in the library of Columbia University, New York, fol. 9b.

as the date of the Shekhinah's "rising from the dust."[150] There was no difficulty in combining the two dates, so as to make Nathan's a priori calculations fit events in Sabbatai's life. The former date had merely to be interpreted as "following on 1657," that is, 1658. The tradition of the Dönmeh in Salonika distinguished between two stages of Sabbatai's early activity: In the year 408 (1648) "he *began* to lift up the Shekhinah,"[151] whereas in 418[152] (1658) "he uplifted the Shekhinah." The first phase of the messiah's ministry, beginning in 1648, resulted in the exaltation of the Shekhinah in 1658, as calculated by Nathan. The raising of the Shekhinah, her exaltation, and the revelation of a new, supernal law, seem to be somehow related. The exaltation of the Shekhinah was, perhaps, also given outward expression by the abolition of the midnight service of mourning for the Shekhinah, called the Service of Rachel, instituted in the sixteenth century by the kabbalists of Safed. Although explicit evidence for the abolition of this nocturnal liturgy exists only from 1665, there are confused traditions to the effect that "it has been handed down that the Service of Rachel is not to be recited as from 1657."[153] There is no way of telling whether these traditions refer to a distinct event in Sabbatai's life prior to 1665; but at any rate, the decisive importance of the year 1658 as the beginning of some kind of new dispensation can be established beyond doubt.

The phrase "a new law" has a distinctly messianic flavor. Based on Isaiah 51:4, "for law shall proceed from me," the subject is mentioned in later rabbinic legend in connection with the messiah, but there the reference was to the revelation of a new understanding of the old law, whose hidden reasons the messiah would disclose.[154] Even if we assume the theological formula of the "new law" to have been

150. Nathan's *Treatise on the Dragons*, p. 15, and Cardozo's letter *Magen Abraham*, in *Qobeṣ ᶜal Yad*, XII (1938), 130. This letter is largely based on Nathan's writings which were then available to Cardozo.

151. See *Sabbatian Hymns*, p. 177.

152. Thus the correct reading of the date in *Sabbatian Hymns*, p. 77. Attias (*ibid.*) mistranslated 5408 and I accepted his reading and translation in the first (Hebrew) edition of the present work. I am indebted for the correction to Mrs. R. Shatz.

153. I have examined these traditions in detail in *Zion*, XIII–XIV (1949), 60–62.

154. A detailed discussion of this concept is to be found in William D. Davies, *The Torah in the Messianic Age* (Philadelphia, 1952).

coined by Nathan in 1665, after his recognition of the messiah, we are still left with Sabbatai's "strange actions" and with his shocking benediction of the year 1658. For all we know the doctrine of the "new law" may be Sabbatai's invention. Its antinomian character once again raises the problem of possible Christian influences. The revelation by the messiah of a new meaning to the Law is one thing; the revelation to him of a new law is quite another. The kabbalistic commandments in another cosmic aeon or world cycle had no messianic reference whatever. It was only in Christianity that the messiah had revealed new commandments—or so, at least, it seemed to Jews who had heard Christian arguments about the Law of Moses being superseded since the advent of the messiah by the laws and customs of the church. Until his arrival in Constantinople, Sabbatai's non-Jewish environment in Smyrna, Salonika, and the cities of Greece had been predominantly Greek-Orthodox, and Christian influences cannot a priori be excluded. The basis of Sabbatai's antinomianism and his revaluation of sin as a holy act were definitely not Christian; they welled up from hidden impulses in his soul. In his normal periods Sabbatai remained faithful to traditional Jewish practice. There was an obvious and widening discrepancy between the practice of religion and the mortifications of the pious ascetic in his ordinary life, and his bewilderingly strange behavior when the spirit was upon him. One thing, however, is certain. Nobody ever mistook these "strange actions" for signs of a messianic calling. They deviated too much from the expected behavior of the messiah, who, far from abolishing the Law and the commandments, was supposed to restore them to their full glory. It is not surprising, therefore, that Sabbatai's messianic pretensions made no impression whatever.

A great deal has been written about the circle of Sabbatai's first followers who, it is said, accepted him as their messiah in those early years. Special mention is usually made in this connection of Abraham Yakhini, one of the best-known preachers in Constantinople.[155] As a result of a misunderstanding due to a slight confusion in one of Sasportas' letters (see p. 229), the purely imaginary "fact" has been

155. Sasportas, p. 160, writes that Yakhini was generally recognized as a great scholar "and a mighty preacher, equaled by none in Constantinople." Hezekiah Roman (see p. 169, n. 163) indicates the same. David Kahana's account of Yakhini, *Toledoth ha-Mequbbalim,* pt. I, p. 61, as well as the purely imaginary details supplied by Rosanes (IV, p. 11) do not require serious rebuttal.

established that Yakhini was one of Sabbatai's earliest followers in Constantinople, and that it was he who actually composed the notorious "ancient scroll" in which "R. Abraham the Pious, a contemporary of R. Judah the Pious" (twelfth century) prophesied the messiahship of Sabbatai Ṣevi. Further evidence was found in the fact that as a professional "calligrapher" and copyist of Hebrew manuscripts for Christian scholars in Holland, Yakhini could easily have forged an "ancient scroll." The one flaw in this theory is that we definitely know the scroll to have been written in the spring of 1665 in Gaza. There is not a shred of evidence to show that Yakhini believed in Sabbatai at that early date, let alone that he conspired to lead Jewry astray. These fantastic constructions, which misled even Graetz, are exploded by more recent findings and by the publication of the complete version of Sasportas' correspondence, *Ṣiṣath Nobel Ṣevi.*

Yakhini, who later became an ardent believer in Sabbatai Ṣevi and one of his most active supporters, deserves some closer attention. Born in Constantinople in 1615,[156] he studied under Joseph Mitrani (died 1639), the chief rabbi of that city. Later he became a preacher in his native city and in a sermon preached in 1652, he could say of himself that for twenty years he had forsaken the ways of the world because of his love of the Torah.[157] He also wrote halakhic works, which include the lost *Tosefeth Merubbah*—the first commentary ever to be written on the Toseftha.[158] His main activity, however, was as preacher, poet, and kabbalist. We also possess a poem which the poet Judah Abbas, who used to present members of the community with laudatory poems, sent to Yakhini one Passover Eve.[159] Yakhini was an enthusiastic follower of Lurianic kabbalah, and his "forsaking the ways of the world" did not fail to yield results. He had mystical dreams of which he kept a record, and some of which (from the years

156. Yakhini, autograph of *Razi Li* (and not of the book *Raziel* as erroneously printed in the Catalogue) MS. Adler 2360 in the Jewish Theological Seminary of New York, fol. 20a, refers to Constantinople as "my native city." Fol. 193a mentions the name of his father, Elijah, and that his grandfather was called Shemaryah Yakhini.

157. Danon, *op. cit.*, p. 30. Danon's date of Yakhini's birth (1611) is due to a misunderstanding of his source. The dates given in *Meʾoraʿoth Ṣevi* are sheer invention.

158. See S. Liebermann, Introduction, *Tosefta ki-fshutah, Seder Zeraʿim* (1955), p. 14.

159. MS. Oxford, Neubauer 2580, fol. 49.

1652–63) have been preserved.[160] His dreams are extremely revealing, and should be of considerable interest to psychologists. Few rabbis ever committed similar dreams to writing.

Once, in 1652, he dreamed that a camel was pursuing him from one room to another. Though he locked the door with a complicated lock, the camel burst the lock and pursued him further until, at last, he found himself in a room at the seaside. He was no longer afraid of the camel. Then a beautiful maiden came forth, embraced and kissed him, and adjured him not to forget her, as he was to marry a queen. This queen was, at present, covered by the moon, and the moon covered by the sun, so that the queen whom he was to marry would emerge from between the two. He swore the desired oath, "and I thought that I also had intercourse with her." Thereupon another maiden appeared, and afterward the sun and the moon and between them his destined queen, shining as the sun, "and from fear and terror I awoke." Yakhini marvels at this extraordinary dream and adds "by the life of Torah, I have not withheld anything." In another dream of equally erotic character, he saw the Mishnah addressing and reproving him—rather like the *maggid* of R. Joseph Karo—in the guise of an old man. When he had confessed his sins to the old man, who represented both the Torah and the Mishnah, the latter suddenly changed into a beautiful maiden, "and I took her in my arms . . . embracing and kissing her violently. I then arose in great fear, my hair standing on end, trembling and weeping over this great vision—God understands the way of it, and he knows the interpretation of it."[161] These dreams are characteristic of the seductions with which the sexual instinct in man accosts those who want to sanctify themselves. The dreamer's fear and trembling at the sight of the Torah changing into a maiden, and at the confusion of the spheres of holiness and sensuality, are understandable enough.

His enthusiasm found vent in poetry. In 1655 he published a small volume entitled *Hod Malkhuth* ("Glory of the Kingdom") "that I have swaddled and brought forth, I, the little one, Abraham Yakhini,[162] for the sake of the blessed God . . . here in Constanti-

160. In a MS. containing many of his homilies and novellae. The MS. used by Danon, *op. cit.*, pp. 29–47, has disappeared since.

161. Danon, *op. cit.*, p. 43. See also the dream from the year 1663.

162. Yakhini's usual way of signing his writings and letters. The same signature occurs on a book from Yakhini's library (*Meqor Ḥayyim* by Ḥayyim Kohen

nople."[163] The only one of Yakhini's many writings to be printed, it is an imitation of the Psalms, written in biblical style and composed of bits and pieces of scriptural verses. The contents seem simple enough: words of praise and supplication, and exhortations to remember "the day of visitation, when God shall visit redemption on Mount Zion. Then the mighty will praise Thee, they will proclaim hidden things, wonders that have not been heard before." But for the author's intimations, nobody would suspect profounder meaning in his poetry. But Yakhini expressly states in his introduction that "in every word written in this book, in the development of its themes and in its details, I have alluded to the precious sayings, both known and hidden, of our sages . . . and it contains the proper intentions (*kawwanoth*) for the purpose of giving thanks to His Name, for He is praised at all times by all creatures." Unfortunately, the book does not provide a key for understanding the mystical allusions woven into its text.

It would not be surprising in the least if Sabbatai, soon after his arrival in Constantinople in 1658, made the acquaintance of Abraham Yakhini and discoursed on kabbalah with him. But it is a long way from acquaintanceship to influence, let alone to Yakhini's acceptance of Sabbatai's ideas and messianic claims. There is conclusive evidence to show that until 1665 Yakhini kept aloof from Sabbatai's ways. His spiritual world was that of Lurianic kabbalism in its most orthodox form. When the Polish kabbalist Ṣevi Tuchführer of Cracow passed through Constantinople, Yakhini gave him an approbation for his book *Naḥalath Aboth,* a commentary on the Sayings of the Fathers, printed in Venice in 1660. In the approbation Yakhini applauds the author's method of interpreting his text according to the traditional four methods (the literal, the homiletical, the allegorical, and the mystical), but also severely takes him to task for basing the mystical interpretations on Cordovero's system. That chapter had better be omitted

---

of Aleppo, a kabbalistic commentary on the *Shulhan ᶜArukh* [Constantinople, 1650]) in my possession.

163. The book contains 36 leaves 8°. The author, in his introduction, announces his intention of publishing before long his book *ᵓEshel Abraham* on the Pentateuch. Fol. 2 has an approbation and introductory poem by R. Hezekiah Roman, who was also known as a poet (cf. Pinsker, *Liqqutey Qadmoniyoth*, p. 137). Danon, *op. cit.*, printed another letter by Yakhini, but its artificial and allusive style prevented any understanding of it. Yakhini's *Hod Malkhuth* is extremely rare, and only three or four copies are known.

altogether, he says, "since from the day that the man of God, the great Isaac Luria, appeared to us, whoever studies in his school or his writings gives a bill of divorcement to the kabbalistic systems of all other masters who did not know his [Luria's] ways and paths. Not that I would deprecate, God forbid, the worth of these holy rabbis . . . , for they attained to the mystical insight which their generation was worthy of receiving . . . [but now] their writings no longer correspond to the true intent of mystical wisdom. Then why should a scholar [such as you] concern himself with these dubious matters. . . . Therefore he who seeks wisdom should study [exclusively] the writings of Luria and of his disciples."

The same outlook is expressed in Yakhini's *Little Tract on the Basic Principles of the* [*Kabbalistic*] *Science*, a kind of Lurianic introduction to the study of the Zohar, preserved in manuscript at the National Library in Jerusalem.[164] The treatise is not dated, but its substance is fully confirmed by the book *Razi Li*, of which we possess Yakhini's autograph.[165] The latter is a large work, containing various notes on kabbalistic matters, without order or trace of literary editing. The earliest note dates from 1658, the latest entry[166] is from the summer of 1663. There is not a single reference to Sabbatai as the messiah or to Sabbatai's other kabbalistic doctrines in these intimate notes. Instead we have lengthy and hairsplitting disquisitions on kabbalistic technicalities and on the Lurianic doctrines of configurations, intentions, divine names, and so forth. There is no trace of the messianic and eschatological speculations that fill Yakhini's writings after 1666, and a comparison of *Razi Li* with the later *Wawey ha-ᶜAmudim* is enough to show the tremendous change which the faith in an actual, specific messiah had wrought in the kabbalist preacher. If, as is probable, Yakhini met Sabbatai in 1658, he cannot have been greatly impressed by him. Yakhini's world, at that time, was far removed from, not to say incompatible with, Sabbatai's. Sabbatai, as we know, rejected Lurianic kabbal-

164. MS. Jerusalem 1161 8°, fol. 155a–157b. The MS. is no autograph but an early 18th-century copy.

165. MS. Adler 2360. References to *Razi Li* occur also in the MS. used by Danon. According to Catalogue Adler, Sabbatai Ṣevi's name occurs on p. 312 of the MS., but I could not find it there. I studied the MS. in 1957 and it deserves closer analysis; it contains also dreams, homilies, and other disquisitions.

166. Toward the end of the volume, fol. 358a.

ism in practice, though theoretically admitting its truth, "for it caused him confusion and no advancement in his pursuit of the knowledge of the Lord." Abraham Cardozo, from whom this last quotation is taken, not only had a vital interest in that particular point, but also possessed reliable information on the subject.[167]

We have learned from the testimony of Moses Pinheiro that at the time of his association with Sabbatai in Smyrna, Sabbatai studied only the early kabbalists. Did he take up the study of Lurianic kabbalah at a later period? What were Sabbatai's kabbalistic pursuits in Constantinople? De la Croix records two details that may throw light on these questions. According to his report, Sabbatai was befriended by a kabbalist named Elijah Carcassoni,[168] who did not obey the rabbinic sanction threatening excommunication, but studied "practical kabbalah" with Sabbatai. Although de la Croix's account contains more legend than fact, it is possible that Elijah Carcassoni was a "practical kabbalist," that is, "a master of the Name," who exorcised evil spirits, and that in his company Sabbatai began to use holy names. Tobias Rofe too had heard that Sabbatai "was versed in practical kabbalah and the incantation of spirits."[169] The rumor is probably true, for, as we know, exorcisms and the like were practiced not only by the lower sort of "masters of the Name," but also by prominent kabbalists, such as Ḥayyim Vital and his son Samuel. Contemporary manuscripts contain lengthy and detailed instructions how to exorcise evil spirits that have entered and possessed a living person and split his psychic unity, and leading kabbalists would collect these instructions in their writings.[170]

De la Croix's second item of information is even more interesting and can, moreover, be verified. In 1658 an emissary from Jerusalem, said to be a well-known preacher and kabbalist, arrived in Constanti-

167. Cardozo's letter to Samuel de Paz (MS. Adler 1653, fol. 4a).

168. Thus the correct spelling of the name, though de la Croix spells it "Carcadchioné." Elijah Carcassoni is mentioned as a kabbalist in Yakhini's autobiographical notes (autograph of *Razi Li,* MS. Adler 2360, fol. 225a). The name Caracachon, or Carcassoni, is otherwise known from various historical documents. A certain David Carcassoni came to Venice in 1651 to collect money from the ransom of Jewish prisoners from Poland and Russia; see *RÉJ,* XXV, 206–16.

169. *Ma^casey Tobiah,* fol. 26, and Emden, p. 45.

170. As was done, e.g., by R. Moses Zacuto in his *Shoreshey ha-Shemoth,* of which a number of MSS. are extant.

nople and studied together with Sabbatai and Carcassoni. His name is given by de la Croix as David Capio,[171] and we may infer with almost absolute certainty that the reference is to R. David Ḥabillo, whose presence in Constantinople is mentioned at the beginning of Yakhini's notes in *Razi Li*.[172] Ḥabillo seems to have visited Constantinople a number of times in his capacity as collector of charities for the Holy City, for one of Yakhini's manuscripts contains a sermon which he had preached in the presence of Ḥabillo, apparently before 1653.[173] Ḥabillo was a famous kabbalist, frequently quoted by other kabbalistic writers, and the author of kabbalistic works (extant in manuscript) including a commentary on the book *Yeṣirah*.[174] A disciple of the leading Lurianic kabbalist Benjamin ha-Levi, Ḥabillo was completely immersed in Lurianism. According to local tradition in Jerusalem,[175] he had a heavenly mentor (*maggid*). This shows that he enjoyed the reputation of an inspired religious personality to whom special revelations would be vouchsafed. When we learn that this prominent Lurianic kabbalist had personal relations with Sabbatai and even taught him mystical lore, we may safely presume that he initiated him into the Lurianic kabbalah which Sabbatai had, perhaps, not known before. De la Croix renders the name "Ḥabillo" phonetically as "Capio," as he heard it from his Jewish informant. A similar rendition of the same name appears in a Sabbatian Hebrew document.[176] Many Sephardi Jews pronounced names ending in "illo" without the "ll," for example, Amario (particularly in Salonika) for Amarillo, Kario for Karillo, and so on. Also "b" and "p" were often interchanged. De la Croix probably heard Ḥabillo pronounced as

171. De la Croix, *op. cit.*, p. 270.

172. The entry (fol. 41a) must have been made before 1660, as another entry, one hundred pages later, is explicitly dated in that year.

173. Danon, *op. cit.*, p. 30, who quoted Yakhini's note from the MS. in his possession, did not realize that "the great rabbi, the King David" referred to R. David Ḥabillo, and tried to identify the *chef spirituel David* among the rabbis of Constantinople.

174. See G. Scholem in *Zion*, XIII–XIV (1949), 61, and A. Yaᶜari, *Sheluḥey ᵓEreṣ Yisraᵓel* (Jerusalem, 1950), p. 287.

175. Preserved by H. Y. D. Azulay in his biographical dictionary *Shem ha-Gedolim*.

176. Letter from Smyrna, written by an anonymous Sabbatian believer ca. 1705 (MS. Oxford 2211); see G. Scholem in *Zion* (annual), III (1929), 178.

"Habio," or "*Kh*apio," and thus arrived at the form "Capio," behind which nobody suspected the famous kabbalist and emissary from Jerusalem, who was visiting Smyrna and Constantinople at the time.[177] The French diplomat has recorded a significant historical fact, whose value is not diminished by the largely imaginary character of the details with which he embellishes his story. The speeches and discussions attributed to Sabbatai, Nathan, and others are hardly more than a romanticized literary setting, yet the names as well as the basic outline of events seem to go back to authentic local tradition, and stand the test of historical criticism. Perhaps the ban of excommunication was lifted after some time, since, according to de la Croix, Ḥabillo's association with Sabbatai was no secret. David Ḥabillo was a pious ascetic, and his habits and general behavior were probably very similar to Sabbatai's as long as the latter's normal self was not upset by periods of illumination.

David Ḥabillo may have evinced a genuine understanding of the spiritual struggles of his young friend and disciple. In a very daring and revealing saying Ḥabillo once declared that there were two kinds of Satans, one the "Satan of holiness," who was mystically indicated by the four-headed letter *shin* (ש)[178] of the *tefillin*.[179] This remarkable dictum seems to suggest that not all "satanic" actions were necessarily evil or infernal. It would not be surprising if Ḥabillo did not outrightly reject Sabbatai Ṣevi, whose strange actions may have appeared to him as inspired by the "Satan of holiness."

177. After his death there was litigation between his son and heir, Judah Ḥabillo, and the Jerusalem community. The documents (collected in Ḥayyim Benveniste's responsa *Baᶜey Ḥayyey*, *Ḥoshen Mishpat*, I, no. 136) show that at the time of his death David Ḥabillo possessed the exclusive right to collect charities for Jerusalem in Smyrna for a period of three years. The representative of the Jerusalem community in this trial (in 1662) was Samuel Primo, who later became one of the most important members of Sabbatai's circle.

178. As distinct from the normal, three-headed letter *shin*. The small leather case (frontlet) worn on the forehead has both a three-headed and a four-headed *shin* impressed upon it. Ḥabillo's identification of the "fourth head of the shin" with the "Satan of holiness" provides an interesting illustration of C. G. Jung's interpretation of the quaternity symbol. According to Jung, the fourth represents the Satan or an analogous entity, whereas three (or the Trinity) is an incomplete and one-sided symbol of divine wholeness.

179. Quoted by R. Elijah Kohen of Smyrna, *ᵓEzor ᵓEliyahu* (Salonika, 1846), fol. 3b.

De la Croix says that the rabbinate of Constantinople compelled Sabbatai to leave the city, and that he set out for Smyrna in the company of Ḥabillo. In the following year, 1660,[180] the great fire occurred, in which the Jews of the capital suffered heavily. Sabbatai is said to have been pleased about it, "not because of the insults he had suffered in Constantinople, but because he saw in it the finger of God, calling his people to repentance."[181] David Ḥabillo spent the last years of his life in Smyrna and died there on the Ninth of Ab, 5421 (1661).[182] There was no other emissary from Jerusalem in Smyrna in those years; the title and rights of the Jerusalem emissary were conferred exclusively on Ḥabillo, as is clear from a discussion of the terms of the appointment in a collection of rabbinic responsa. De la Croix's account agrees so well with what we know of Ḥabillo's biography that we may safely identify the emissary David Capio with R. David Ḥabillo.

Sabbatai's return to his native city after an exile of five years does not seem to have caused any sensation or stir. Perhaps the ban had been forgotten, or its duration limited from the start. Possibly the fact that Sabbatai returned under the wings, as it were, of a kabbalist and scholar of such unquestioned authority as Ḥabillo did not fail to make an impression. The emissaries from Jerusalem, all of them men of Talmudic learning, were generally considered supreme spiritual authorities by Sephardi Jewry; if Ḥabillo told them to leave Sabbatai in peace, they would probably have obeyed. Joseph Eskapha, the first chief rabbi of Smyrna, who had expelled Sabbatai from the city, was by then old, and the memory of the earlier persecutions may have faded. Eskapha died in early 1662, toward the end of Sabbatai's second stay in Smyrna.

Information concerning Sabbatai's activities in those years is vague and obscure, though Sabbatian tradition, as represented by Abraham Cuenque, seems to have preserved a few facts overlaid with legend. Cuenque tells us that when Sabbatai later came to Palestine, he came from Smyrna (not from his wanderings in exile); this seems to indicate that at least some reliable information was available to

180. Hebrew date 420, which happens to be the numerical value of the word *ᶜashan* ("smoke"), under which designation the fire was remembered by the Jews of the capital.

181. De la Croix, *op. cit.,* pp. 272–73.

182. According to his epitaph in Smyrna; see Freimann, p. 141.

him. De la Croix says that Sabbatai remained in Smyrna for about three years, and left in 1662. The date is confirmed by an independent source.[183] Cuenque's report that "at times he [Sabbatai] would hide himself in a miserable room in Smyrna" and only rarely show himself clearly refers to this time and evidently alludes to Sabbatai's periods of melancholia. "Trustworthy people" had told Cuenque that they had seen Sabbatai in this room, "wallowing in the dust and his bed turned upside down." All this sounds credible enough, even though Cuenque's informants added that they had also seen two angels holding Sabbatai, comforting him, and drawing him up, and saying, "Shake off your dust, arise, and return, O Jerusalem." The business of extracting a core of fact from what may be later legend is a dubious and difficult one; so we pass on to more solid evidence. A valuable detail is provided by the prophet Nathan, who writes in 1666 that Sabbatai "had to spend seven years in the prison of the *qelippah,* during which time he suffered very great afflictions, as it is said in the *Pesiqta* [*Rabbathi*] on the chapter 'Arise, shine' [Isa. 60:1]."[184] Nathan does not specify which seven years; he may refer either to the period of Sabbatai's youth 1642–48, which ended with the first messianic outburst, or to the years of wandering and exile in Greece and Constantinople, which ended with the revelation of the "new law" in 1658. In any event we learn that the demons not only persecuted and afflicted Sabbatai, but actually overpowered him in his states of melancholia, for which the expression "prison of the *qelippah*" would seem a suitable description.

Restless and without peace of mind, Sabbatai wandered about in quest of a cure for his troubled soul. At home his brothers felt disgraced by his "strange actions" which "were a burden and a scandal to them." According to Cuenque the brothers suggested that Sabbatai go to Palestine, and Sabbatai left "by himself, and with nothing but his garment," refusing to take money from his family. The exact op-

183. Leyb b. Ozer's account of the period 1653—62 is based on the "testimony" of the servant and altogether useless. The servant claimed to have accompanied Sabbatai to Jerusalem, where Sabbatai stayed thirteen or fourteen years, until his visit to Egypt where he married for the third time. The sojourn in Constantinople as well as the return to Smyrna are ignored in this more than dubious testimony. The account in Solomon Joseph Carpi's *ᵓEleh Toledoth Pereṣ* ("The History of Sabbatai Ṣevi from an ancient MS.," ed. by Brüll [1879], p. 14)—further cited as Carpi—is equally confused and worthless.

184. *Be ᶜIqvoth Mashiaḥ*, p. 47.

posite is told by de la Croix: Sabbatai decided to go to Palestine, and his brothers amply provided him with money and other necessities because they believed that it was through his merits that they had prospered.[185] The subsequent history of Sabbatai's stay in Jerusalem seems to support de la Croix's version of the departure from Smyrna.[186]

The date of Sabbatai's journey to Jerusalem is established by an eyewitness report. R. Ḥayyim Segré, who lived in northern Italy and was a fervent "believer," collected information of Sabbatai Ṣevi and the prophet Nathan from other believers who came to Italy in the seventies and eighties of the seventeenth century. Much of it is a curious mixture of fact and fiction,[187] but among other things Segré records that he had heard from R. Solomon b. Moses de Bossal of Rhodes, that "three years before AMIRAH revealed himself, that is, in the year 422 [1662], he passed through Rhodes on his way from Smyrna to Jerusalem. He stayed at his father's [de Bossal's father, the rabbi of Rhodes] house for one month, and studied with him the book Zohar." De Bossal had much to tell about Sabbatai's miracles and prophecies, "and swore an oath to the truth of his report."[188] Though we cannot attach much historical value to the Sabbatian legends, and must make allowance for the habit of the "believers" to support their stories by oaths, we may accept the authenticity of at least the skeleton of de Bossal's report.[189] According to our evidence,

185. De la Croix, *op. cit.*, p. 273; Emden, p. 35.

186. At this point de la Croix's reliability ceases and his account of the years 1662–65, made up of fictitious letters and of information from third or fourth hand, reads like a novel rather than a history. Evidently, he had no reliable witness for this time and—like so many modern writers on the subject—made up for his lack of evidence by using imagination. Nevertheless, de la Croix preserves an occasional authentic detail regarding the events in Smyrna and Constantinople. His value as an historical source increases again as he comes to the events in Constantinople in 1666. He also seems to have collected very precise information regarding the emissaries from Jerusalem and the terms of their letters of appointment. (See pp. 273–74 of his book.)

187. MS. Günzburg 517, which also gives Segré's name. Freimann, who printed a very corrupt text of this collection of informations (pp. 93–98), attributed it to R. Benjamin Kohen of Reggio.

188. Freimann, p. 97.

189. Solomon de Bossal was a Sabbatian believer and may well have put many *vaticinia post eventum* into the messiah's mouth. Some of his stories, however, reflect the characteristic peculiarities of Sabbatai's imagination. Thus Sabbatai is said to have told a dream which prophesied that he would redeem

then, Sabbatai passed through Rhodes in 1662. According to Rycaut he also passed through Tripoli in Syria.

V

Sabbatai Ṣevi did not proceed straight to Jerusalem, but spent some time in Egypt where he was friendly with the rabbis and leaders of the Egyptian community. He also made the acquaintance of Raphael Joseph,[190] who occupied a position of special importance and great distinction among Egyptian Jews. He was called the *chelebi* (Turkish, "lord") which, in this case, was not a complimentary title of esteem or courtesy, but a title of office, corresponding to the earlier and traditional *nagid*. The *nagid* was the head of Egyptian Jewry and their civil representative to the government; the office had been held, among others, by Maimonides and his descendants. From the chronicle *Dibrey Yosef* by Joseph Sambari, a contemporary of Raphael Joseph and a good authority on Egyptian Jewry, we learn that the title *nagid* had been abolished in the sixteenth century and the holder of the

---

Israel, but that prior to that event he would go to Palestine, retreat for one year to the cave of R. Simon bar Yoḥay, and reveal himself after three years. Perhaps Sabbatai really toyed for some time with the idea of retreating to the cave of R. Simon b. Yoḥay near Meron. It is worthy of note that de Bossal, unlike other believers, did not credit the messiah with prophecies concerning his future apostasy. He also received many personal prophecies from Sabbatai, which, de Bossal assures us, all came true. Solomon de Bossal, who was in Constantinople in 1682 (Freimann, p. 97 line 21, has 422, but the correct MS. reading is 442), may well have been in Salonika in 1683, the year of the mass apostasy of the Sabbatians in Salonika. Rosanes, *op. cit.*, p. 116, quotes a responsum from ca. 1683 by R. Moses b. Jacob Salton, or Shilton (*Beney Moshe*, no. 58) concerning "a son of the Rabbi Moses de Bossal, who apostatized." If this responsum refers to Solomon de Bossal (and not to a brother of his), it may explain his presence in Italy in the eighties. Return from Islam to Judaism being a capital offense in Turkey, many of the repentant Sabbatian apostates fled to Italy.

190. The second name "Joseph" appears to be a patronymic or family name, as it was also used by Raphael's brothers. In the original Hebrew edn. of the present work (I, p. 143), I expressed doubts as to the correctness of Rosanes' statement that the name of the family was Bar Hin. Since then all doubt has been removed by M. Benayahu (*H. Y. D. Azulay*, 1959, p. 295), who has shown that no such name ever existed, and that Bar Hin is a misreading. Benayahu, pp. 295–98, has collected all available information about R. Joseph.

office was henceforth styled *chelebi*.[191] The *chelebi* was the Egyptian viceroy's treasurer, master of the mint and controller of all banking activities; often he was also tax farmer and collector—an office which did not necessarily increase the popularity of its holder. In contemporary letters Raphael Joseph is called *ṣaraf bashi,* which is the Turkish designation of his position as head of the Egyptian treasury. He resided in Cairo, but his influence extended to Alexandria and to the business connected with its port. Raphael Joseph became *chelebi* in 1662, the year of Sabbatai's arrival in Egypt. His generosity and his penchant for extreme ascetic piety were well known. Sambari, who spent a few months in his house, tells that "he raised the standard of the Law to observe and to keep it, and there was no king like him before him who turned to the Lord with all his heart and with all his soul and with all his might. All his days were spent in fasting, and at night, when the members of his household would eat sumptuously, he would eat pulse. At midnight he arose and studied the Law in holiness and purity, for he immersed himself in a ritual bath and flogged himself; he also wore sackcloth on his body. And the whole nation was obedient to him, so that in his days every man of Israel lived under his vine. . . . And I, the unworthy author [of this chronicle] was one of his servants; I ate his fruit and drank his water. . . ."[192] In 1666 a rabbi from Leghorn wrote that "fifty ordained rabbis were eating at his table." Raphael Joseph was representative of the wealthy and ascetic Jewish lay leader—a type fairly frequent in Jewish history, before and after him. His ascetic inclinations and his support of kabbalists generally probably made for bonds of sympathy between him and Sabbatai, who, as we have seen, normally practiced the same system of mortifications.

About two years after Sabbatai's first arrival in Cairo, Raphael Joseph brought to his court a kabbalist of rare eminence: Samuel Vital, the son of Luria's principal disciple Ḥayyim Vital. Samuel Vital (b. 1598) acted as guardian of his father's writings, which expounded Luria's doctrine pure and undefiled. For many years Samuel had lived in Damascus, where he arranged and edited his father's papers, adamantly refusing permission for them to be copied. Gifted scholars

191. Rosanes, *op. cit.,* pp. 497–98. Raphael Joseph was the last *chelebi,* and after his murder in 1669 no successor was appointed (Sambari).

192. MS. in the library of the Alliance Israélite Universelle, Paris, fol. 95. The passage is missing in the text printed by Neubauer, but appears in *Me'ora'-oth 'Olam* (used by Graetz).

trained themselves to memorize whatever they learned whenever they were permitted to look at the precious manuscripts; then they hurried home and wrote down what they recalled. In this way the first collections of "Lurianic writings" were formed, as that by R. Jacob Ṣemaḥ. Samuel Vital was still in Damascus in the summer of 1663,[193] and Sabbatai did not, therefore, meet him at that time. But he almost certainly met the historian Sambari at Raphael Joseph's court. Sambari could have given us a firsthand description of Sabbatai; in fact, he did, and it is one of the ill-fated vicissitudes of Jewish historiography that the precious pages have been torn out of the only two extant manuscripts of his chronicle. At the bottom of one page the introductory sentence of what was evidently a sort of history of the messiah Sabbatai Ṣevi has remained: "And now we shall report matters of controversy, strife, and discord which befell in the market places and streets."[194] The rest of the account has fallen victim to the censorship of later anti-Sabbatian zealots. By a stroke of luck, Sabbatai had encountered a Jewish scholar with a genuine interest in history who, unlike his contemporary fellow historian David Conforti, did not wish to suppress the whole affair. To our misfortune others repaired this "omission" of Sambari by removing the crucial leaves from his manuscripts.

The importance of Sambari's testimony would have been of the first order, for the reports of other witnesses—none of whom was on the scene himself—are confused and conflicting. Sabbatai visited Egypt twice, but the distant chroniclers and writers of memoirs never distinguished between events taking place during his first and his second visits. Particularly with regard to the date of Sabbatai's third marriage (see p. 191), confusion and contradiction in the sources impede our understanding of his messianic biography. Sabbatai seems to have stayed in Egypt for a few months,[195] and to have arrived in Palestine in the summer of 1662. We have no details about his journey from Cairo to Jerusalem. The accounts of his passage through Gaza, his encounter there with his future prophet Nathan, and their joint in-

193. A responsum, written in that year in Damascus, is found in the collection of his responsa (MS. Oxford 832) *Be᾽er Mayim Ḥayyim*, no. 54; cf. also *Beḥinoth*, no. 8 (1955), p. 88.

194. MS. Paris, referred to above, n. 192.

195. A sojourn of "two years in Cairo" for his first visit (*Relation*, p. 13) is chronologically impossible. The author confused the two visits.

trigue are purely fictitious, since Nathan did not yet live in Gaza at that time.[196]

VI

In Jerusalem, where Sabbatai stayed for about one year,[197] his behavior exhibited the usual combination of ascetic saintliness and shockingly strange actions. The dignity and charm of his personality aroused genuine sympathy and appreciation. No more telling evidence of this can be required than the fact that about one year later Sabbatai was requested to visit Egypt as a special emissary to collect money for the community of Jerusalem and its charitable institutions. One can hardly imagine the elders of Jerusalem charging a man they despised with such an honorable and public mission or choosing a man whose orthodoxy was not above suspicion, even according to their exacting standards. On the other hand, there can be no doubt that Sabbatai's strange actions provoked not only consternation, but also punitive measures. Sabbatai himself told Laniado that on more than one occasion he had received "stripes" at the hands of "our masters in Palestine" for his actions which, even if not always and necessarily transgressions in the technical sense, were sufficiently unconventional and "unreasonable" to provoke hostile reaction. He seems to have been a laughingstock to some people, for when the first anti-Sabbatian letters circulated at the beginning of the messianic movement, the writers referred to him as the R. Sabbatai Ṣevi "who was a general object of derision."[198] There is no mention of persecution or opposition in

196. The ultimate source of this error is Coenen, who did not know of Sabbatai's second visit to Egypt. He therefore believed that the events which took place in Gaza "two or three years ago," i.e., in 1665 (since Coenen wrote in 1667), occurred before Sabbatai came to Jerusalem. Leyb b. Ozer (Emden, p. 4) reproduced this error and embellished it with additional legendary details: Sabbatai had been hiding for a few weeks in Nathan's house before continuing his journey to Jerusalem, etc. Later authors added to the confusion.

197. The duration of Sabbatai's stay in Jerusalem is unduly lengthened to two years by Tobias Ashkenazi, *Ma^casey Tobiah* (Emden, p. 45). A letter from Gaza, written 1665, states explicitly that he had spent the two preceding years in Cairo, which would have him arriving there in 1663. The same information is given, from reports current in Constantinople, in *Relation*, p. 13, and in the Italian letter, published by S. Simonsohn, *JJS*, XII (1961), 40. This letter was written in December 1666.

198. "Del quel si facevano burla," according to an Italian letter, written in Skoplje (Üsküb, in Macedonia) in December 1665 and drawing on reports from Jerusalem and Aleppo; see *Zion,* X (1945), 63.

connection with messianic claims and the like, only of mockery and derision. It was certainly not Sabbatai's ascetic piety that provoked the scoffers. The small Jewish community in Jerusalem harbored a good number of ascetic saints whose behavior was in no way different from Sabbatai's in his normal periods. That which was really peculiar and irregular in Sabbatai's behavior was considered as folly; the appropriate reaction was pity and derision, not public indignation or hatred.

The Jewish community of Jerusalem numbered at the time two to three hundred families. They lived poorly in the narrow lanes of the Jewish quarter in the Old City.[199] There were many scholars among them, though hardly any outstanding luminaries. The report that there were only three scholars of standing in Jerusalem[200] is a gross understatement, for we know of many rabbis at the time of Sabbatai's arrival—such as Moses Galanté, Samuel Garmizan, Jacob Ḥagiz, Abraham ibn Ḥananiah—and also possess their writings. Jacob Ḥagiz presided over a small academy endowed by a rich Livornese family and raised many disciples. In the words of his son Moses Ḥagiz, "since his arrival in the Holy City [some time between 1650–60] the population has greatly increased, and eminent scholars have come there."[201] The causal connection between his father's arrival in Jerusalem and the subsequent influx of prominent scholars may be no more than a tribute of Moses Ḥagiz' imagination to the

199. According to Uriel Heydt the Turkish archives show that in the year 1690 head-tax was paid by a hundred and eighty-two Jews, mostly householders, in Jerusalem. Rabbis did not pay head-taxes. Raphael Mordecai Malkhi wrote in the same year that "today there are about three hundred householders in Jerusalem," i.e., about one thousand souls; cf. the quarterly *Jerusalem,* IV (1952), 177. The numbers were probably not much different in Sabbatai's days. Other, and less reliable, sources have smaller estimates. Buchenroeder (*Eilende Messias Juden-Post,* 1666) mentions a report by the geographer Johannes Boterus (late 16th century) to the effect that there were few Jewish houses in Jerusalem "because they believe that before the advent of the messiah a great fire would descend from heaven and destroy the city and its surroundings, in order to cleanse it from the defilement of the abominations of the gentiles. That is the reason why so few Jews go to Jerusalem." This detail is not mentioned in any other source.

200. Thus in the "Testimony given before the Rabbinic Court" (in Jerusalem?) by Moses [b. Isaac] b. Ḥabib from Salonika during his visit to Jerusalem (Emden, p. 53), cf. M. Benayahu's article quoted in n. 87.

201. Moses Ḥagiz, *Mishnath Ḥakhamim,* no. 624.

revered memory of his father, yet it is a fact that there was a busy coming and going of scholars during those years. Altogether the picture painted by Moses Ḥagiz is more reliable than the contrary report given on the authority of Moses b. Ḥabib of Salonika (who, unlike his namesake with whom he has been confounded, was not one of the disciples of Jacob Ḥagiz). It is strange that this report omits the names of three eminent scholars and substitutes that of R. Saul Saḥwin, who was so little known that until quite recently his existence has been questioned and the name accounted for by a corruption from S[amuel] Garmizan.[202] The later testimony ascribed to Moses [b. Isaac] b. Ḥabib is therefore suspect, and credence should rather be given to Abraham Cuenque's statement in his memoirs of Sabbatai Ṣevi to the effect that there were "many and great scholars" in Jerusalem.[203]

The kabbalists in Jerusalem are of particular interest to our inquiry. They were the true and authoritative representatives of Lurianic kabbalism after the decline of Safed at the beginning of the seventeenth century. A generation earlier Jerusalem had sheltered some leading kabbalists who gave the Lurianic system its authoritative literary expression and canonized the tradition of Ḥayyim Vital. The alternative version of Lurianism, as developed in Italy by the school of Israel Sarug, was not very popular with the Jerusalem circle, which flourished between 1620–60. It is true that the influence of Sarug's writings was felt also in Palestine after their appearance in print, and especially after the publication of Naphtali Bacharach's *ᶜEmeq ha-Melekh* in 1648,[204] yet the main concern of Jerusalem kabbalists was with the writings of Ḥayyim Vital. Though they could not copy the final autograph version which Samuel Vital jealously guarded in Damascus, they had at their disposal a number of volumes containing writings by Ḥayyim Vital, as well as by his colleagues and disciples, which had been copied before Vital's death in 1620. Benjamin ha-Levi (the teacher of David Ḥabillo), Jacob Ḥayyim Ṣemaḥ (a former marrano from Portugal), and Meir Kohen Poppers had prepared in Jerusalem the three different versions of the "Lurianic writings" which subsequently circulated in many manuscripts. Their reputation was

202. M. Benayahu found the signatures of both Samuel Garmizan and Saul Sahwin (or Sahin) on a document of 1662.

203. Emden, p. 35.

204. Cf. D. Tamar's note in *Zion,* XIX (1954), 173.

great, and their opinion of a younger fellow kabbalist would certainly have carried much weight. However, Meir Poppers died in the winter of 1662,[205] a few months before Sabbatai's arrival in Jerusalem. Benjamin ha-Levi had returned to Safed after many years of wandering. There is no chronological objection to his having met Sabbatai in Egypt, though in that case we would have to assume that he stayed there for several years, and there is no evidence for this assumption.[206] Only the old kabbalist Jacob Ṣemaḥ—he was seventy-five or more[207]—was still living in Jerusalem. We do not know what he thought about the young rabbi from Smyrna—unless he was a member of the rabbinic court that sentenced Sabbatai to "stripes" for his strange actions. The example of David Ḥabillo shows that even a strict Lurianist could appreciate Sabbatai and sympathize with him. We cannot, therefore, argue what Jacob Ṣemaḥ's attitude to Sabbatai might have been on kabbalistic grounds alone. On the other hand, it is beyond doubt that Sabbatai could never have fitted into the messianic conceptions of Lurianism to which Ṣemaḥ adhered with all his soul. This impossibility is fully confirmed by Ṣemaḥ's attitude in 1665, when events came to a head.

We know very little about Sabbatai's stay in Jerusalem before his first public "revelation." Coenen heard a story that Sabbatai had been miraculously cured of blindness after all medical efforts had failed.[208] This is probably a garbled reminiscence of one of Sabbatai's severe fits of depression during which, as we know, he was unable to read. Abraham Cuenque, too, gives us a few concrete and authentic facts, in spite of the legendary light that suffuses all his memoirs and reports. At the time, Cuenque was fifteen years old and lived in Hebron, yet he may have heard a good deal about

205. According to one tradition he died as late as 1664, having finished the MS. of his book *Mathoq Ha᾿Or* (MS. Isaac Alter, no. 170, see above, ch. 1, n. 160, about this collection) in Jerusalem on Rosh Ḥodesh Shebat, 424 (winter, 1664). In that case he may have met Sabbatai in Jerusalem.

206. Chronological and other considerations too vitiate A. Yaᶜari's attempt to identify Benjamin ha-Levi as the author of *Ḥemdath Yamim;* cf. A. Yaᶜari, *Taᶜalumath Sefer* (1954), p. 57, and G. Scholem in *Beḥinoth*, no. 8 (1955), pp. 88–89.

207. See my article on Jacob Ṣemaḥ in *Kiryath Sepher,* XXVI (1950), 185–88.

208. Coenen, *op. cit.,* p. 94.

Sabbatai, whose eccentric behavior must have excited attention and comment. The strange rabbi from Smyrna undoubtedly became the subject of conversation in the small communities of Jerusalem and Hebron. At first Sabbatai used to attend the Talmudic academy daily and study with the other scholars after the morning prayer. After a few months he bought the house of a Sephardi Jew (or built himself a house on his grounds).[209] Cuenque gives the name of the landlord as Kufia or Cupia. Considering the badly corrupt spelling of names in Emden's *Torath ha-Qenaʾoth*, we may hazard two suggestions: (1) Kufia is very similar to Capio. Capio is mentioned by de la Croix where, as we have seen, it probably stands for Ḥabillo. Sabbatai may have taken over the house of David Ḥabillo, which was vacant after his son Judah Ḥabillo had left Jerusalem as a result of a serious quarrel with the community about funds collected by his father. The persecution of the son started soon after the father's death in 1661; in 1663 we already find him as rabbi of Chios.[210] This explanation of the name Kufia seems to me to be the correct one. (2) A family by the name of Kufio or Capio, as distinct from Ḥabillo, may have existed in Jerusalem, and a scholar like Cuenque would probably not have been guilty of the same confusion as the Christian writer de la Croix. A certain Raphael Capio is mentioned as residing in Jerusalem a few years before Sabbatai's arrival.[211]

209. Emden, p. 35. Here Cuenque contradicts his earlier statement that Sabbatai had refused to accept money from his family, viz., had given it to the poor.

210. The documents relating to the suit of the Jerusalem community vs. Judah Ḥabillo are collected in Ḥayyim Benveniste's responsa (see above, n. 177). Benveniste gave judgment in favor of Ḥabillo, but advised him to arrive at a compromise with the representatives of Jerusalem, so as to clear the memory of his father of even "the doubt of theft." The emissaries were sometimes subject to suspicions of embezzlement and malpractice.

211. A number of MS. copies of Ḥayyim Vital's *Peri ʿEs Ḥayyim* (MS. Munich 331; MS. Jews' College, London [Neubauer no. 76]; MS. Goldschmidt, formerly in Hamburg) contain an account by Raphael Capio of his flight to Damascus when the plague ravaged Jerusalem in 1652 or 1653. During his stay in Damascus (Rosh Ḥodesh Iyyar, 1653, to Rosh Ḥodesh Iyyar, 1654) he tried in vain to obtain Samuel Vital's permission to copy his father's autograph of *ʾEs Ḥayyim*. Finally he trained himself to memorize that which he read. He returned to Jerusalem in 1654, and it is not impossible that Sabbatai's house was in his courtyard. The name Capio is also found in Italy; the well-known poetess Sarah

In this house Sabbatai set aside one room in which he enclosed or cloistered himself, fasting from one Sabbath to the next. "It was his habit to cease taking food after the fourth Sabbath meal." In other words, he ate the three statutory Sabbath meals, performed the *habdalah* ceremony at the conclusion of the Sabbath, and took the fourth meal known as "Accompanying the Queen [Sabbath]," that is, at the "Banquet of David the messianic king,"[212] and then began his fast. He also practiced other rules of piety, such as doing all the shopping for the Sabbath himself, exerting himself so much "that the perspiration of his body soaked his clothes." Setting apart a "room for solitude" in one's house is recommended as a laudable practice by contemporary ascetic and moralistic manuals.[213] Occasionally Sabbatai would leave his house and spend a few days in utter solitude in the mountains and caves of the Judean desert where, as he told Laniado in Aleppo, he would hear voices from the graves.[214] Altogether he led the life of a pious ascetic and hermit, seeking nothing but the presence of God.

In Jerusalem he made the acquaintance of a number of people who were subsequently to become the most active members and apostles of his messianic movement. Some of them were notable scholars, such as David Yiṣḥaki of Salonika, Samuel Primo of Brussa, and Judah Sharaf; others, such as Sabbatai Raphael of Mistra in Greece, were downright scamps. In 1667 Sabbatai Raphael told Sasportas that when he came to Jerusalem in 1663, at the age of twenty, he had heard that "Sabbatai Ṣevi was in the Holy Land and studied with a few disciples, though he was not yet called messiah. He [Sabbatai Raphael] went to him and became a member of his circle."[215] This is the only testimony definitely asserting the existence of a circle

---

Capio, also known as Sara Copia Sullam (see Geiger's *Jüdische Zeitschrift*, III [1869], 179–82), was a member of the family.

212. The latter designation occurs in the liturgical and devotional manual *Ḥemdath Yamin* by an anonymous Sabbatian author.

213. Elijah de Vidas, "Shaᶜar ha-Qedushah," ch. 6, *Reshith Ḥokhmah* (Munkacz, n.d.), 140d–141a. The "solitary retreat" is also frequently mentioned in 18th-century Hasidic literature.

214. Cuenque reports the same. An echo of the same tradition is preserved by the Greek monk Meletios, who knew that Sabbatai "and his companions" retired to the caves "around Palestine" (Galanté, *op. cit.*, p. 108).

215. Sasportas, p. 271.

or group around Sabbatai Ṣevi in Jerusalem, but as Sabbatai Raphael's mendacity appears in practically everything he said, it is of little value, and no conclusions can be based on it. S. Raphael does not say that, at the time, any claim to being the messiah was made by Sabbatai.

The troubles of the Jewish community of Jerusalem were many and frequent, but among the principal causes of its distress were the recurrent extortions of the Turkish governors and pashas. A misfortune of this kind befell the community during the year of Sabbatai's residence in 1663. The sum demanded this time was so high that the elders could not raise it, and many prominent scholars had to flee. Toward the end of the winter of 1663–64 we find a number of them in Ramleh, among them Judah Sharaf (who apparently proceeded to Egypt), Samuel Garmizan (who later returned to Jerusalem), and Abraham ibn Ḥananiah.[216] Sabbatai either remained in the city, or else left it, as he had done on previous occasions, to wander through the countryside and pray at the graves of holy rabbis. If a document from which Y. M. Toledano copied a letter addressed by Sabbatai Ṣevi to Judah Sharaf and the "Lord" Raphael (the *chelebi* Raphael Joseph in Cairo) is authentic and correct, we would have valuable evidence of his presence in Safed in 1664.[217] Unfortunately the text presented by Toledano is a jumbled collection of incoherent and fragmentary sentences which make no sense, but are sufficient to raise serious doubts whether the letter was really written in 1664 and not in 1665, after Sabbatai had left Jerusalem and formally proclaimed himself messiah. He then passed through Safed on his way to Aleppo and Smyrna.

A stay in Safed is not, in itself, improbable. The town had suffered a spectacular decline as a result of continual warfare between the local rulers and the pasha of Damascus, who represented the central government. The Jewish community had dwindled so much that documents speak of its "destruction." Many scholars had left and set-

216. See M. Benayahu, *Kiryath Sepher,* XXI (1945), 313. The chronology suggests that Moses Ḥagiz's story (Emden, p. 36) on Nathan's kabbalistic studies in Gaza from a book that he had stolen from R. Abraham ibn Ḥananiah, is a legend that was current in Jerusalem when Ḥagiz was a young man.

217. See Y. M. Toledano, *Sarid u-Falit,* no. 1 (1945), p. 21. An examination of the entire document (whose genuineness I see no reason to doubt) may throw considerable light on Sabbatai's biography, but it is impossible to arrive at any safe conclusions on the basis of the obscure extracts cited by Toledano.

tled in other parts of Palestine or in Egypt. Some of them returned later, and their numbers were increased by former inhabitants of Tiberias who settled in Safed after the destruction of their city about 1660.[218] In any event it is certain that a Jewish community existed in Safed in the years 1664–67, and that pilgrims to the tombs of the saints in the vicinity were sure to find co-religionists and friends.

The extortionist demand made in 1663 prompted the community to dispatch an emissary to Egypt in order to raise the necessary funds. Their choice fell on Sabbatai Ṣevi, whose friendly relations with the *chelebi* Raphael Joseph on the occasion of his previous stay in Cairo were well known.[219] Sabbatai's financial independence may have been another point in his favor, quite apart from his reputation for ascetic piety, which was sure to recommend him to the similarly inclined head of Egyptian Jewry. Sabbatai accepted the mission and probably left for Egypt toward the end of 1663. Before leaving, he paid a visit to Hebron where he prayed in the cave of Machpelah, the burial place of the patriarchs. There the young Abraham Cuenque saw him for the first and only time in his life, but the memory of this meeting remained engraved in his heart. Many years later he described this visit in his memoirs, and the account, in spite of seeming exaggeration and inaccuracies of detail, is trustworthy. "I did not take my eyes off him from the moment of his arrival, both when he said the afternoon prayer with us in the synagogue, and when he recited the evening prayer in the cave of Machpelah, together with the crowd that had accompanied him." Cuenque then goes on to tell of the "supernatural" tears that Sabbatai shed during his prayer, and adds "most of the night I kept near the house at which he stayed,[220] observing his behavior. The other citizens spent a sleepless night too, watching him through the windows. He strode up and down in the house, which

218. See M. Benayahu in *ʾEreṣ Yisraʾel*, III (1954), 245–46.

219. The correspondent of the *Hollandtze Merkurius,* too, knew that in Cairo Sabbatai had been very friendly with "the head of the city and the chief publican." Cuenque reports the same but inverts the names, writing "the Lord Joseph Raphael" for Raphael Joseph.

220. According to Cuenque's account, as printed by Emden, Sabbatai lodged with "the outstanding sage, the noble R. Aaron Abin of blessed memory, for it was his express wish to stay with that sage." The reading is certainly corrupt, and the name should read Aaron Arḥa, who was the grandson of one of Luria's disciples and the son of the well-known kabbalist Eliezer ibn Arḥa. All three lived in Hebron.

was illuminated at his command with many candles. All night he recited psalms with a mighty voice, 'the voice of joy and the voice of gladness,' a most agreeable and pleasing voice, until the light of morning dawned and we went to attend morning service. I testify that his demeanor was awe-inspiring, different in every respect from that of other men, and my eyes were not satisfied with seeing him. After the morning prayer he traveled alone to some place six miles away, accompanied only by one Jew on foot.[221] While he was among us, he neither ate nor drank, nor did he sleep at all. He left, as he had come, fasting, and my eyes have not seen him since then."

The account is valuable for its explicit statements as well as for its implicit suggestions, whose full significance becomes apparent in the light of what we already know about Sabbatai Ṣevi. What Cuenque really describes is Sabbatai in a typical state of manic illumination, and the psychological truth of his account greatly strengthens its general reliability. Some of the details are confirmed by other sources describing Sabbatai's behavior during his illuminations. At such moments he lived in a state of emotional high tension; he required no sleep;[222] he walked up and down singing Psalms with near-ecstatic enthusiasm and in a sweet voice. The last habit is also described in a document which Cuenque could not have known, that is, the letter written by the emissaries from Poland who visited Sabbatai about two years later in Gallipoli. The details of the two accounts agree to a remarkable extent and carry the mark of truthfulness. The impression made by Sabbatai's chanting of psalms is also attested by Israel Ḥazzan for the period of his residence in Adrianople.[223] Abraham Kokesh of Vilna told his relative Leyb b. Ozer of his visit to Sabbatai: "When Sabbatai Ṣevi chanted psalms, as he would do frequently, it was impossible to look into his face, for it was like looking into fire. This has been attested by many others, and even by his opponents."[224]

221. A guide, or the valet Yeḥiel? Cuenque says that Sabbatai came to Jerusalem without a servant, but he also describes his arrival in Hebron on horseback with "a man preceding him on foot."

222. R. Solomon Katz in a letter of 1672 testified to the same detail.

223. See *Schocken Volume,* p. 165, and particularly p. 169. When he was arrested in 1672, Sabbatai was chanting psalms (de la Croix, *op. cit.,* p. 383).

224. See Leyb b. Ozer's *Beshreybung* (MS. Shazar, fol. 54b; also fol. 32b). Abraham Kokesh's wife was a second cousin of Leyb. Sabbatai's opponent Nehemiah Kohen told the author "that when Sabbatai sang psalms, it was impossible to look into his face" (*ibid.,* fol. 55b).

On his way to the cadi's house after his arrest in Smyrna, he chanted psalms in the street.[225] The sweetness of his singing was one of his most outstanding qualities, and exercised a powerful attraction on others. Music aroused him and filled him with enthusiasm. During the great illumination in Gallipoli, musicians were in attendance who played to him day and night, and all his life he used "to sing melodies and romances."[226] His musicality is also referred to by Nathan, who gave it a mystical interpretation.[227]

Being satisfied with the essential veracity of Cuenque's information, we may also give weight to facts which he passed over in silence or alluded to in vague and general terms. Cuenque does not specify the nature of the "awe-inspiring" (or "frightening") behavior, "different from that of other men," which he beheld that night, but perhaps we are not far wrong in surmising that he witnessed some of Sabbatai's "strange actions." Did Sabbatai also commit definite transgressions on that occasion? Cuenque, who was a believer, would certainly not reveal to outsiders what he had seen. In any case he seems to have been profoundly impressed by the amazing and "frightening" things which he had beheld as a young man without fully understanding them. After the rise of the movement, he probably reinterpreted what he had seen as a supreme messianic mystery.

Cuenque's remarks on Sabbatai's outward appearance are confirmed by writers who saw him two or three years after his visit to Hebron. Sabbatai was tall of stature, "his face [was] very bright, inclining to swarthiness, his countenance beautiful and majestic, a black, round beard framed his face, and [he was] dressed in royal robes; he was very stout and corpulent." Making allowance for Cuenque's exaggerations, we find the essential elements of his description recurring in reports that cannot be dismissed as the inventions of Christian news writers. "Stout and corpulent" agrees with the description given by Coenen, who saw him two years later: "corpulent and fat." An-

225. Coenen, *op. cit.*, pp. 28–29.

226. Coenen, *op. cit.*, p. 35, on Sabbatai's youth in Smyrna. Israel Ḥazzan (MS. Kaufmann, see *Schocken Volume*, p. 165) protests against the "fools" who mistook Sabbatai's mystical love lyrics for erotic songs. Sabbatai once sang such an erotic romance in the synagogue of Smyrna, at what was one of the most dramatic moments of his life; see below, p. 401.

227. In his *Treatise on the Dragons* (*BeᶜIqvoth Mashiaḥ*, p. 15). See also Moses Ḥagiz's comment on Cuenque's report (Emden, p. 35) and *Relation*, p. 37 ("chants melodieux").

other Dutch report from Smyrna says that Sabbatai was "corpulent, but otherwise of beautiful bodily appearance."[228] Witnesses who had seen him in Gallipoli told Leyb b. Ozer that in spite of his mortifications he was "corpulent,"[229] healthy, and strong. Abraham Kokesh even claimed to have seen him pulling out a medium-sized tree in the garden of the fortress of Gallipoli.[230] Cuenque's description of Sabbatai's bright complexion has its parallel in the description of Leyb b. Ozer, who had heard that "his countenance was beautiful and that there was almost none like him" and that "his cheeks were red all the time."[231] The latter phrase suggests that the description refers to Sabbatai's appearance during his manic enthusiasm and illumination, for during his periods of depression nobody was admitted into his presence. The peculiar form of Sabbatai's round beard is described by Israel Ḥazzan of Kastoria: "the hairs of his beard stood in one equal row from his upper jaw to his chin, not one hair protruded beyond the others."[232] All these characteristics—the healthy appearance, corpulence, and round beard—are in evidence in the one authentic picture of Sabbatai Ṣevi that we possess (see frontispiece A). It was drawn, according to Coenen, by a Christian who saw Sabbatai in Smyrna toward the end of 1665, and who immediately went home to do the portrait. The picture was inserted on a special sheet at the beginning of Coenen's book, but seems to have circulated also separately in an enlarged format before the publication of Coenen's *Ydele Verwachtinge* in 1669. All other pictures of Sabbatai, particularly those printed with the tracts and prayer books of 1666, are either imaginary or imitations of the portrait reproduced by Coenen.[233]

228. Coenen, *op. cit.,* p. 90, and the news letter in the *Hollandtze Merkurius,* January, 1666, p. 2; "dicklyvig van postuyr, dan wel geproportioneert van lichaem."

229. Emden, p. 3.

230. Leyb b. Ozer, *Beshreybung* (MS. Shazar, fol. 54).

231. *Ibid.,* fol. 32b.

232. *Schocken Volume,* p. 166. The details occur in a lengthy story about an astrologer who converted to Judaism and who possessed an astrological book from which he read a description of the bodily signs of the messiah to the Sabbatian group in Adrianople. Nathan then recognized all the signs in Sabbatai.

233. The picture in J. B. de Rocoles, *Les Imposteurs Insignes, ou Histoires de plusieurs Hommes de Néant* (Amsterdam, 1683), is a bad copy from Coenen, in which the characteristic and individual features have disappeared. Joshua Levinsohn reprinted de Rocoles' picture as a true "portrait of Sabbatai Ṣevi" in S. P. Rabino-

From Hebron, Sabbatai continued his journey to Egypt where he arrived early in 1664, if not—as is more probable—in the fall of 1663. On his way he passed through Gaza without, however, meeting Nathan, who had settled there in the meantime.[234] Sabbatai stayed in Cairo for nearly two years, and it was during that period that, on March 31, 1664, his strange marriage to Sarah, the "messiah's consort," took place.[235]

---

witz (ed.), *Keneseth Yisra'el*, III (1898), 554. The portraits in the anonymous French *Relation* (1667) and in de Rie, *Wonderlyke Leevens-Loop van Sabbatai-Zevi* (Leiden, 1739)—the latter picture being reproduced in Joseph Kastein, *Sabbatai Zewi: Der Messias von Izmir* (Berlin, 1930)—are purely imaginary. Judging from certain similarities between them, they seem to be based on a common original, probably in some pamphlet that appeared toward the end of 1665. A description of Sabbatai corresponding exactly to the two pictures (thick moustache, very thin beard) occurs in a Polish "news letter" of December, 1665; see M. Balaban, *Sabataizm w Polsce*, p. 38. The news letter is most probably a translation from a Dutch or a German source, and its description of Sabbatai is obviously imaginary, as it is contradicted by all firsthand testimonies. The portraits appearing as frontispieces in the prayer books printed in Amsterdam in 1665–66 merely depict a royal figure seated on a throne. For another imaginary picture of Sabbatai as commander of an army, see below. Isaiah Sonne has put forward the hypothesis that the figure of a (bearded?) bareheaded man riding a lion on the title page of a halakhic book printed in Venice in 1665 represents a fictitious portrait of Sabbatai Ṣevi; see *Sefunoth*, III–IV (1960), 68–69. Similar claims have been made for some other books from the same printing press in 1665, giving a messianic *gematria* (*mashiaḥ nagid*) amounting to 425 [1665]. I doubt this very much, because the precise dates (June and early July) exclude the possibility that news of the messiah's "coronation" could have reached Venice at this time. It is a pity that Bernard Lazare, the great French and Jewish author and a man of considerable insight, has never executed his intention to write an essay "reflections à propos of a portrait of Sabbatai Ṣevi."

234. Sabbatai's passage through Gaza is mentioned by Cuenque (Emden, p. 36). A Sabbatian letter (Haberman, p. 208) written not long after the event reports that when Sabbatai returned from Egypt, Nathan asked his pardon for having failed to pay homage to him during his first passage through Gaza. This sufficiently disposes of the fictitious accounts and legends put forward by Sabbatian believers as well as by imaginative historians.

235. The date of the marriage has been a moot question (cf. above, p. 179, and *SS*, I, p. 145, n. 1) until the recent publication of an important and trustworthy document bearing on the subject (document no. 5 in A. Amarillo, "Sabbatian Documents from the Collection of Saul Amarillo," *Sefunoth,* V [1961], 256). Sabbatai's marriage took place on 5 Nisan 5424. This disposes of my surmises and speculations in the original Hebrew edn. of the present

This messianic marriage is a baffling paradox by any standards, for Sarah's story is indeed amazing. Although it is almost impossible to separate fact from fiction, there can be no doubt that the girl's life had been—to say the least—extraordinary. But whatever the facts, they were soon smothered by fantastic accretions. The nature of her influence on, and the measure of her significance for, Sabbatai's messianic career will always remain matters of conjecture and speculation. Her enigmatic history and role provided ideal subject matter for the imagination of authors of historical novels and dramas. In fact, romance is in evidence even among her contemporaries. Emanuel Frances reports (or invents) a rumor to the effect that Sabbatai had never made messianic claims until incited by her "to set himself as king over Israel."[236] This is clearly an exaggeration, since there is no evidence that Sarah ever took any initiative in the movement. As a rule she merely followed the example of her husband, even to the extent of sending letters to her friends and signing them with the symbolic name that Nathan had bestowed upon the messiah's wife: "the Lady Queen Rebekah."[237] Her real name, as appears in all sources, was Sarah.[238]

Sasportas had known her as a child or young girl, when she came to Amsterdam in 1655;[239] "a girl devoid of intelligence, who in her madness said that she would marry the messianic king. Everybody laughed at her, and she betook herself to Leghorn. . . . But as she

---

work. The document states that on the seventh anniversary of the marriage, 5 Nisan 5471, Sabbatai divorced his wife before the cadi of Adrianople. This document proves that Cuenque's and Coenen's reports, according to which the marriage had taken place during Sabbatai's second stay in Egypt, were basically correct.

236. "The Story of Sabbatai Ṣevi," in *Ṣevi Muddaḥ,* p. 133.

237. Sasportas, p. 4. She thus usurped the title of the messiah's consort which Nathan had reserved for "Rebekah, the daughter of Moses"; cf. below, p. 274.

238. Only de la Croix erroneously gives her name as Miriam. The reports and letters concerning her which he quotes (pp. 277–86) are pure fiction, and devoid of historical value. The short version of Sasportas (in Emden) as well as Coenen and Leyb b. Ozer do not mention her name, which is given by Cuenque (Emden, p. 36) and in Moses b. Ḥabib's deposition (*ibid.*, p. 59). The author of *Meʾoraʿoth Ṣevi* took the name from Emden.

239. Sasportas says "about fourteen years ago." The year can be determined on the basis of Tishby's convincing discussion regarding the date of composition of the first pages of *Ṣiṣath Nobel Ṣevi.*

continued to say these foolish things and was, moreover, beautiful, this was reported to Sabbatai, who was in Egypt with Raphael Joseph."[240] This chronology recommends itself by its inherent probability: letters from Leghorn arrive in Egypt, telling of a beautiful maiden who does "strange things" and announces herself as the bride of the messiah. The news comes to the ears of Sabbatai Ṣevi, and strikes responsive chords in his sensitive imagination. Might it not be that she really is his predestined mate? For the first time in his life, flesh and blood seemed to respond to his heart's most secret dreams and wishes. It is not altogether improbable that, in Sasportas' words, "he sent for her and married her." It is, of course, equally possible that Sarah chanced to come to Egypt in the course of her wanderings, and that her being sent for by Sabbatai is a later embellishment of the story. The marriage took place in the spring of 1664,[241] most probably at the house of Raphael Joseph.

The story of her childhood is strange and fascinating enough, though it seems that she herself had already woven a web of legend around herself. In 1671 a book appeared by a former Jew who, before his conversion in 1669, had been a preacher or schoolmaster in his birthplace, Cleve, in northwestern Germany. The author, Jacob Ragstatt, a son of R. David Weill, tells how many years earlier he had seen the girl as he set out with his father for "Hanau"[242]—probably on his way to Frankfurt where he intended to study at the rabbinic school. He had also met her brother, who had been a tobacco sorter in Amsterdam until the appearance of Sabbatai Ṣevi. The brother passed through Cleve in 1666, on his way to Constantinople, where he expected Sabbatai to confer a dukedom upon him. After Sabbatai's apostasy the brother returned to Amsterdam, ashamed and disgraced, to become a tobacco sorter again.[243] This brother, Samuel b. Meir, is mentioned as a resident of Amsterdam in Leyb b. Ozer's account, where we are also told that he was popularly nicknamed "Samuel Messiah."[244] Leyb b. Ozer, Baruch of Arezzo, and Jacob

240. Sasportas, p. 5.   241. See above, n. 235.

242. Graetz, *op. cit.*, p. 440, mistranslated his Latin source. *Hanovia* near Frankfort is not Hannover but Hanau. The latter name is correctly given in the German version appended to J. Ragstatt-de Weile's *Theatrum Lucidum*.

243. German version, p. 59.

244. Emden, p. 5. The nickname occurs in the Yiddish original only (MS. Shazar, fol. 16b).

Ragstatt de Weile present different versions of the amazing stories told of the girl in Germany, Holland, and Italy. These stories were evidently the joint product of her own fantasies and of the imaginations of the Sabbatian believers. Since, in their present form, they could not have circulated before 1666, it is impossible to ascertain what measure of truth they contain.[245] It appears that she and her

245. The four accounts which we possess all agree that Sarah grew up as a Christian. In spite of the many fantastic details, the accounts show certain similarities and points of contact. Sarah probably changed her story wherever she went.

In Ragstatt's version the orphaned girl was adopted by a Polish nobleman. When she had reached womanhood, her father's spirit appeared to her, told her that she was Jewish, and commanded her to return to her ancestral religion. Her stepfather died and the family wanted her to marry, but she was miraculously transported through the air to Persia, where her father had fled from the Chmielnicki massacres. In Persia she was shown her father's tomb, and was miraculously transported to "Asia" and deposited in a Jewish cemetery, where an angel gave her a "coat of skin" (*pergamentum*) inscribed with divine names. Ragstatt says that this coat of skin was widely held to have been Adam's garment. The angel also revealed to her that she would be a queen and the messiah's wife (later this became "Sabbatai Ṣevi's wife").

Leyb b. Ozer (Emden, p. 5, and MS. Shazar, fols. 16ff.) had heard from "reliable reporters and rabbis, and also from my late father," who had seen and known the girl and heard her own story, that from the age of six she lived in a Polish nunnery. When she was sixteen, her dead father (who had been a rabbi in a Polish community) appeared to her, spirited her through the window of her cell, and deposited her in the Jewish cemetery of a distant town. There she was found, dressed in nothing but a shirt. Her father had also commanded her to wander from one city to another until she found the messiah, who would marry her. She was finally sent on to Amsterdam, whither her brother Samuel had fled from Poland. Many witnesses claimed to have seen the marks which the father's fingernails left in the girl's body as he transported her through the air.

Baruch of Arezzo recounts the version current in Italy—probably the one Sarah had told when she lived in Leghorn: she had been forcibly baptized and was thereafter brought up by a Polish noblewoman who wanted to marry her to her son. On the day before the wedding, her father, who had died two years earlier, appeared to her and gave her a "garment of skin" inscribed: "She will be the messiah's wife." Thus attired, she went to the Jewish cemetery, where she was found and sent from one city to the next, until she came to Leghorn, where she stayed for some years, and to Egypt.

De la Croix's account (*op. cit.*, pp. 277–81), presented in the form of an "Epistle of the German Rabbis to the Rabbis of Leghorn," shows the presence of the same basic motifs in the stories current in Constantinople in 1670: Sarah was forcibly abducted from the house of her stepfather (who was a famous

brother were orphaned in the Chmielnicki massacres of 1648. The children subsequently came to Amsterdam, and Sarah later drifted to Italy and apparently spent some years in Mantua and Leghorn. If report is true, her behavior too was "strange" and far from saintly. All sources record rumors about her licentious life. Rabbi Joseph ha-Levi wrote letters to Sasportas and others—it is true, only after the apostasy—in which he declared that in Leghorn she had prostituted herself to everybody.[246] Emanuel Frances, who lived in Leghorn at the time and knew that she had been a maidservant in the house of David Jessurun, called her a "witch" and composed a satirical poem on her "whoredoms."[247]

Coenen reports similar rumors from Smyrna: "She was a maidservant in a charitable institution [or beggars' hospice] in Mantua, which housed all sorts of people and which she did not leave without damage to her reputation; I refrain on purpose from enlarging on the subject. Later she traveled through the country without any company except those she met on the road, and so she went from place

---

rabbi) and brought to a Polish nobleman who wanted to convert her. At night her father's spirit appeared and brought her back to her stepfather, who scolded her for her absence. Again the dead father intervened and demanded that she be sent away to a less dangerous environment. On her travels she was accompanied by two elderly matrons. This last detail seems to indicate early attempts to counteract rumors of Sarah's licentiousness by providing her with two chaperones. De la Croix himself never knew about these rumors. In addition to Ragstatt's version I should like to quote the description of Sarah's heavenly coat as given to Johannes Braun "by the circumcised [in Holland] who flatter themselves quite nicely about the new messiah." I translate the passage from Braun's Latin work *Bigdei Kehunna, De vestitutu sacerdotum Hebraeorum* (Amsterdam, 1698), p. 69: "All the world, I suppose, knows the tasteless tale which the Jews, who believe any story, still relate as true history. A few years ago, the wife of that new impostor, Sabbathi Zebi, got the coat of skins that Eve made almost six thousand years ago. Embroidered with many names of saints and patriarchs and adorned with letters of gold, it was by a stupendous miracle lowered down from heaven in a field to which she was led naked by the spirit of her father who had been a Jew while she herself only knew she was born a Christian. Whether that heavenly garment was kept undamaged in a chest by the new bride of the new messiah . . . and to what use it has been put today, I own I do not know." Dr. Chimen Abramsky (London) has kindly drawn my attention to Braun's book.

246. Sasportas, p. 5; also p. 197, on the "harlotries of the adulterous Ashkenazi woman . . . as is well known in Leghorn."

247. *Ṣevi Muddaḥ,* pp. 126–27.

to place."[248] Rycaut writes more or less the same things.[249] The most outspoken statement comes from an anonymous French correspondent, who not only says that her reputation as a harlot preceded her to the East, but also that Sabbatai married her precisely for that reason, so as to imitate or fulfill the words of the prophet Hosea (1:2), "take unto thee a wife of whoredoms."[250] This testimony is of considerable psychological interest, and agrees with what we have come to expect of Sabbatai's manner of thinking. He may easily have discovered in her (past or present) behavior one of those "strange actions" of *tiqqun* of which he was so fond himself. There is, in fact, a late and unconfirmed tradition to the effect that Sarah indulged in immoral behavior even at the height of her career in Smyrna, and that her husband approved of these "acts of *tiqqun*," but the information is late and of doubtful veracity.[251]

Another tradition, apparently designed to counteract the slanderous rumors, maintains the exact opposite and emphasizes that Sabbatai married a virgin. Coenen reports that when Sabbatai came to Smyrna in the autumn of 1665 he is said to have had marital intercourse with his wife for the first time, and the believers burst into demonstrations of joy on being shown proof of her virginity.[252] It is not impossible that the whole scene was staged, in accordance with the provisions of Deuteronomy 22:15–30 concerning contested virginity, in order to stop the malicious *lèse majesté* against "Queen Sarah." It is worthy of note that Nathan does not mention the matter at all clearly, nor does he refer Hosea 1 to Sabbatai, although it is precisely from him that we should have expected this kind of typological interpretation. There are some obscure hints in the *Treatise on the Dragons*[253] regarding the union which the messiah would perform before his revelation "in the mystery of Jacob and Rachel" and which would have to be

248. Coenen, *op. cit.*, p. 11.

249. "By the way [he] picked up (!) a Ligornese lady whom he made his third wife" (Rycaut, *op. cit.*, p. 202).

250. "Elle a porté jusqu'au Levant la reputation publique de femme perdue (*Relation*, p. 14); also, p. 10: "la dernière femme de S. avoit à la verité esté une coureuse dans sa jeunesse."

251. See Emden, p. 53, for Sarah's attempt to seduce the son of the Sabbatian physician, Doctor Carun, and Sabbatai's reaction (cf. also above, n. 87). But the testimony, allegedly by R. Moses b. Ḥabib, is suspect.

252. Coenen, *op. cit.*, p. 15, who is also the source of Leyb b. Ozer. Coenen does not conceal his doubts and attributes the rumor to the "foolish crowd."

253. *Be^cIqvoth Mashiaḥ*, pp. 41–43.

preceded or accompanied by a similar "union" in the sphere of evil (the *qelippah*) that was contained in the mystery of holiness. All this is said to be mystically indicated by Scripture as the mystery of "the way of a man with a maid" (Prov. 30:19) and the mystery of "the way of an adulterous woman" (Prov. 30:20). It is difficult, in this context, to determine what are kabbalistic metaphors for processes in the "spiritual worlds," and what are veiled references to real situations, if any, in Sabbatai's life. Because the *Treatise* was composed before the apostasy, the reference cannot be to the concubines that Sabbatai took later, and one wonders what was Nathan's occasion for his long excursus on the "mystery of the concubines . . . corresponding to Bilhah and Zilpah."[254] There is, as yet, no clear answer to the problem, though it is not unlikely that Nathan on purpose kept his utterances concerning the messiah's wife as dark as possible, and from later evidence (see ch. 7) it is clear that he disliked her.

Frances says that Sarah was known in Leghorn for her "witchcraft," by which he probably means fortunetelling. A tradition about her activity as a fortuneteller has been preserved by Italian Sabbatians. Baruch of Arezzo was told by R. Isaac ha-Levi Vali (or Valle, died 1680) of Sarah's reputation as a fortuneteller; Vali himself had consulted her in order to learn "the root of his soul" and other matters—"and she answered all his questions." When her landlady said to him in her presence: "Does your reverence know what this girl says? That she will be the messiah's wife?" Sarah remained silent. There are, therefore, at least some common elements in what believers and unbelievers told of her. If Sarah's own story about her forced conversion as a child and her upbringing in a Polish convent is true, it could have a bearing on the history of Sabbatai Ṣevi.

When Sabbatai left Palestine for Egypt, he was riding the crest of his manic wave. This much we know from Cuenque's account of his behavior in Hebron (see above, pp. 187–88). If this mood lasted throughout his first few months in Cairo, it would account for the provocative paradox of the messianic marriage. But sooner or later the "illumination" would pass, and Sabbatai would find himself, once again, either in the throes of anguished depression, or else in a state

254. Nathan's lucubrations on the subject are indebted to Vital's exposition in *ᶜEs Ḥayyim* ("Shaᶜar ha-Qelippoth," ch. 2). Since even the details are borrowed from traditional Lurianic kabbalah, it may seem unnecessary to look for corresponding events in Sabbatai's life, were it not for the fact that throughout the *Treatise* biographical and kabbalistic elements intermingle.

of normalcy in which his ordinary self was unable to comprehend the mysterious impulses and actions which it exhibited at other times. Some time during his stay in Egypt, Sabbatai meant to put a stop, once and for all, to the absurdities of his behavior which gained him nothing but hostility and derision. Whatever the messianic implications of his manic actions, he did not think of proclaiming himself as the messiah of Israel; much less did he leave Palestine for Egypt with the preconceived plan of launching a movement. In fact, since 1648 he had neither devised nor attempted to execute any such scheme. He struggled with himself and with the demons that possessed his soul, and his one desire was to rid himself of those troublesome mental states that were to him, no doubt, an unbearable affliction. He had but one wish: to be a rabbi or, as the parlance of the Sephardim would have it, a *ḥakham,* among others. Our source for this part of Sabbatai's spiritual biography is his confession to Solomon Laniado in Aleppo (summer, 1665), the essential reliability of which we have no reason to doubt. Sabbatai had studied "practical kabbalah" and had learned the (magical) use of divine names. One day he performed a great exorcism, as a result of which his "illumination" departed from him. The modern historian with his psychological bias may suspect it to have been the other way around: after the natural termination of a phase of illuminate intoxication with its feeling of exaltation, Sabbatai's normal self reasserted itself, together with the desire to make this state of normalcy a permanent one. As a "practical kabbalist" Sabbatai performed the exorcism and became, in his own words to Laniado, "like one of the people," regretting his strange actions, now utterly incomprehensible to him. Alas, it was a vain hope that he entertained, and psychological laws are not changed by either exorcisms or supplications. Nevertheless, it appears that in 1664–65 Sabbatai enjoyed a fairly long period of normalcy. He successfully discharged his mission and collected between three and four thousand lion's thalers for the poor of Jerusalem. This was a considerable sum, equivalent to about one thousand gold ducats or more, since at that time the value of the *Löwenthaler* ("lion's thaler") was fairly high.[255]

255. A letter sent from Smyrna to Holland in the spring of 1666 mentions the sum of "4 thousand lion's [thalers]." There were fluctuations in the value of the *real,* or lion's dollar (thaler), and in later times it fell considerably. In Sabbatai's time, however, four *reales* would have been worth one gold ducat. (I owe this information to the late Prof. L. A. Mayer.)

3

THE BEGINNINGS OF THE MOVEMENT IN PALESTINE (1665)

I

SABBATAI arrived in Jerusalem in the late summer of 1662 and left again for Egypt toward the end of 1663. One of the most illustrious rabbinic scholars in Jerusalem at the time was R. Jacob Ḥagiz (1620–74), author of a commentary on the Mishnah (*ʿEṣ Ḥayyim*) and of other works. He stood at the head of a Talmudic college (*Hesger*, that is, "close" or "cloister" in Sephardi idiom), which a wealthy family in Leghorn, de Vega, had endowed; and there he studied and raised many disciples, among whom were such well-known scholars and rabbis as R. Joseph Almosnino, subsequently rabbi of Belgrade in Serbia, and R. Moses ibn Ḥabib of Jerusalem. One of Joseph Almosnino's contemporaries at the college was a young student of Ashkenazi origin, whose father had come to Jerusalem from Poland or Germany. His name was Abraham Nathan b. Elisha Ḥayyim Ashkenazi, and he was to become famous as Nathan, the prophet of Gaza, or simply—at least among the anti-Sabbatians after the debacle—as Nathan of Gaza.[1] His father, Elisha Ḥayyim b. Jacob, was surnamed Ashkenazi after settling in Jerusalem where almost the whole community was Sephardi; the son too is referred to in some of the earlier documents and letters as Nathan Ashkenazi. The father spent many years traveling as an emissary of the Jewish community of Jerusalem; he visited Poland, Germany, Italy, and (repeatedly) Morocco,[2] and was everywhere received with great respect. His activities on behalf of the Sabbatian movement did not in the least detract from—and perhaps even increased—his prestige with the Moroccan rabbis. He died in Meknes, Morocco, in the year 1673.[3] The Palestinian emissaries used to take advantage of their sojourns abroad to print their own works or those of others, and Elisha too was instrumental in publishing and spreading kabbalistic manuscripts, which he brought from the Holy Land. He published the second part of the mystical diary *Maggid Mesharim* by the author

1. The appellation "Nathan of Gaza" was first used by Sabbatian believers (cf. R. Mahallallel Halleluyah of Ancona's poem, composed in 1666 in honor of "our master Rabbi Nathan Ghazzathi [of Gaza]," *HUCA*, VII [1930], 512). After Sabbatai's apostasy the appellation was adopted by the opponents, who also dropped the usual honorifics ("rabbi," etc.) which they had used earlier (cf. the letters written by R. Joseph ha-Levi of Leghorn before the apostasy), whereas the Sabbatians discarded it. Sasportas and Emden popularized this form of the name, which was subsequently mistaken for a family name, and bibliographies and catalogues even ascribed books to "Nathan Ghazzathi." Some Sabbatian documents and prayer books of the period 1665–66, as well as Abraham Cuenque, still have Nathan Ashkenazi (in Spanish texts: Natan Esqenasi), but as a rule the Sabbatian believers referred to him either as MOHARAN (abbreviation of the Hebrew for "our master, the rabbi Nathan"), or as the "Holy Lamp" (the title of R. Simon bar Yoḥay in the Zohar). Christian sources often wrote Nathan Levi, and their mistake was taken over by some historians. The form Nathan Levi is an amalgamation of the names of the two chief protagonists Nathan Ashkenazi and Sabbatai Ṣevi. The latter name being unfamiliar to Christians, it was automatically "corrected" to Levi.

2. See A. Yaᶜari, *Sheluḥey ᵓEreṣ Yisraᵓel*, pp. 147, 281–82. Sasportas repeatedly mentions that he met Elisha when he was rabbi of Salé in Morocco, i.e., in the late forties and at any rate before 1651. R. Joseph Azobib, writing in 1665 from Alexandria to R. Moses Tardiola of Jerusalem in Tripoli, mentions that Nathan, "the son-in-law of Samuel Lissabona is, if I am not mistaken, the son of the rabbi Elisha" (see *Zion*, VI [1941], 86). Evidently "the rabbi Elisha" was a well-known personality.

3. See G. Scholem, *Kitvey Yad be-Kabbalah*, p. 104, and Yaᶜari, *op. cit.*, p. 157, who also mentions another son of Elisha, about whom nothing is known.

of the *Shulhan ᶜArukh*, R. Joseph Karo (Venice, 1649), as well as Abraham Galanté's important commentary on the Zohar on Genesis, entitled *Zohorey Ḥammah* (Venice, 1649–50).[4] Also on his mission to Morocco he carried with him manuscripts of works by the kabbalists of Safed.[5] His son Nathan remained in Jerusalem where he studied under Jacob Ḥagiz, whose son R. Moses Ḥagiz—a violent and relentless opponent of the Sabbatians—later admitted that Nathan Ashkenazi had been one of his father's foremost disciples.[6] Nathan was born in Jerusalem, probably about 1643–44,[7] and spent most of his life up to 1664 with his master, Ḥagiz, at the college. He seems to have been an extremely gifted student, of quick apprehension and a brilliant intellect. His talents, as displayed in his writings, are noteworthy for their rare combination of intellectual power and capacity for profound thinking with imagination and strong emotional sensitivity (even excitability). Sabbatai Ṣevi lived in Jerusalem at the time that Nathan was coming to manhood, and the two may well have met in the streets and lanes of the Old City, although there is no evidence that they actually knew each other.[8] Sabbatai was, after all, twice Nathan's age and, moreover, would not visit the *yeshibah* of R. Jacob Ḥagiz, but, rather, would shut himself up in his house or else go on solitary pilgrimages to the wilderness and to the tombs of the saints near Jerusalem. All this, however, merely increases the likelihood of Nathan's knowing about Sabbatai. The strange ascetic and kabbalist rabbi, perse-

4. See Moses Zacuto's approbation to that work; also the introduction to pt. II of the *Maggid Mesharim* (Venice). The dates of printing of these two works were uncertain. My preference for the date 1649 (see *SS*, p. 164, n. 1) has since been conclusively justified (see Werblowsky, *Joseph Karo,* p. 25, n. 5).

5. The MS. of Abraham Galanté's commentary *Yareaḥ Yaqar* on the Zohar on Exodus, in the National Library in Jerusalem, is a copy made from the MS. which Elisha brought to Meknes in 1672.

6. Emden, p. 36.

7. At the height of the movement he was said to be twenty-two years old. Coenen gives the same age for April, 1667. Nathan's autobiographical letter states that he began to study kabbalah at the age of twenty. Chronologically this must have been in 1664, and the date of birth would therefore be 1644. Baruch of Arezzo's information that Nathan was twenty-two years old in 1665 (Freimann, p. 46) may be a mistake.

8. Cuenque too says that he never met Sabbatai in Jerusalem, although he repeatedly visited there from Hebron.

cuted because demonic powers impelled him to do bizarre and at times even forbidden things, and leading a saintly life until the spirit of madness came upon him, must surely have been the talk of the small city, and particularly of its synagogues and rabbinic schools. It was rumored that at times he held himself to be the messiah-elect, and the rumor would arouse ridicule with some and pity with others. His pleasant deportment, his dignified countenance, and his lovely voice were common knowledge. The occasional glimpses of the ḥakham Sabbatai Ṣevi, as well as the rumors and legends circulating about him, may well have left a mark in some profound albeit unconscious layer of the young scholar's impressionable soul. A strange seed had fallen in a particularly fertile soil where, in due course, it would bring forth its fruit. To change our metaphor: a spark had been lighted in Nathan's imagination; it smoldered in obscurity as long as he stayed in Jerusalem, but leapt into a mighty flame after he moved to Gaza and began to devote himself to kabbalistic studies.

At the age of nineteen or twenty, Nathan was married in the manner customary for brilliant students in the rabbinic schools all over the world. Samuel Lissabona, a wealthy Jew from Damascus who had settled in Gaza,[9] asked Jacob Ḥagiz, the head of the *yeshibah* in Jerusalem, to recommend a groom for his daughter, who was "perfect in beauty, although with a defect in one eye."[10] He promised, in accordance with the custom at the time, to provide for his son-in-law and to enable him to devote himself to study. Ḥagiz selected his best student and Nathan went to live with his wife's family in Gaza. The rabbi of the small Jewish community there was Jacob Najara, a grandson of the kabbalist poet Israel Najara, who had settled in Gaza toward the end of his life.[11] Nathan's marriage must have taken

9. According to Cuenque (Emden, p. 36) in order to escape the heavy taxes in Damascus, and because the "king" (obviously the Turkish official; Sabbatian documents of 1666 similarly refer to a "king" or "pasha" of Gaza) of Gaza took a benevolent attitude toward the Jews.

10. Thus Cuenque, whose account here does not inspire confidence. Nathan is said to have been a beggar who was supported by the Sephardi congregation. But surely the Ashkenazi congregation would have looked after the family of the distinguished rabbi whom they had sent abroad as their emissary (see Sasportas, pp. 34, 136). Sasportas says that Nathan was cared for by his master, Jacob Ḥagiz.

11. Rosanes, *op. cit.*, IV, p. 357. Jacob Najara succeeded his father Moses Najara (d. 1660) as rabbi of Gaza.

place before the end of 1663,[12] for he already lived in Gaza when Sabbatai passed through on his way to Egypt.

Having reached the age of twenty and being a married man, Nathan took up the study of the kabbalah. In this he followed the Sephardi custom (followed, as we have seen, also by Sabbatai Ṣevi) and the rules laid down by the kabbalists of Safed in the middle of the sixteenth century. In Jerusalem he had neglected kabbalistic studies, and possibly for that reason had formed no conscious impressions and views regarding Sabbatai Ṣevi. We have, however, some information concerning kabbalistic sources based on mystical inspiration or revelation that were known to the youthful Nathan. There exists a manuscript containing among other things revelations which came in dreams to the Safed kabbalist Eliezer Azikri—one of the shining lights of Moses Cordovero's school at the end of the sixteenth century. This manuscript had come into the hands of Nathan's father, and Nathan himself jotted down a number of marginal comments, just before his own awakening took place. He signs himself as "I, Nathan Ashkenazi."[13] This proves an early involvement in mystical studies. As soon as Nathan began to delve into the depths of kabbalah,[14] he experienced an awakening that had the violence of an explosion. Nathan more than once refers to the experience, and actually describes it in a letter written about 1673, which he wrote in order to

12. Letters written in Gaza in 1665 mention the birth of Nathan's son in the summer of that year (see Haberman, *Qobeṣ ᶜal Yad* [hereafter referred to as Haberman], III, New Series, p. 20). Baruch of Arezzo too mentions Nathan's marriage in Gaza and the name of his father-in-law, but much in his account (Freimann, p. 46) is legendary and impossible, e.g., the information that Nathan had a number of children in 1665.

13. The MS. (in the Jewish Theological Seminary of N.Y.) contains also information about the activities of Nathan's father (communication from M. Benayahu); Nathan had, therefore, firsthand knowledge of rabbinic revelations other than those of Joseph Karo, mentioned above. Another earlier source of similar character, the revelations of R. Joseph Taitatsak written in Spain shortly before 1492—the author later settled in Salonika—was, at least in some parts, in the possession of Nathan's father, but we have no direct proof that this MS. was equally known to the son. A copy made from Elisha Ashkenazi's MS. will be published in my study of Taitatsak's revelations in *Sefunoth,* XI.

14. The extraordinary rapidity with which Nathan mastered the difficult and abstruse kabbalistic subject matter is surprising but not unique. Of Elijah, the Gaon of Vilna (18th century) it is reported that at the age of nine he learned Vital's *ᶜEṣ Ḥayyim*, within six months! See the article of J. Dienstag, "The Preface to Elijah of Vilna's commentary on *ᵓOraḥ Ḥayyim*, by His Sons," in *Talpioth*, IV (1949), 262.

defend himself against certain charges brought against him after Sabbatai's apostasy. The account of his prophetic awakening, which deserves to rank as a precious *document humain,* appears by way of introduction to a lengthy mystical disquisition on the subject of the messiah and the mystical necessity of his apostasy:

These things [I write] to make known unto you in faithfulness the certainty of the words of truth, the great cause and reason of the tidings which I have announced to the assembly of the congregation of Israel concerning our deliverance and the redemption of our souls. Whosoever knoweth me can truthfully testify that from my childhood unto this day not the slightest fault [of sin] could be found with me. I observed the Law in poverty, and meditated on it day and night. I never followed after the lusts of the flesh, but always added new mortifications and forms of penance with all my strength, nor did I ever derive any worldly benefit from my message. Praise be to God that there are many faithful witnesses to testify to this and to much more. I studied the Torah in purity until I was twenty years of age, and I performed the great *tiqqun* which Isaac Luria prescribes for everyone who has committed great sins. Although, praise be to God, I have not advertently committed any sins, nevertheless I performed it in case my soul be sullied from an earlier transmigration. When I had attained the age of twenty, I began to study the book Zohar and some of the Lurianic writings. [According to the Talmud] he who wants to purify himself receives the aid of Heaven; and thus He sent me some of His holy angels and blessed spirits who revealed to me many of the mysteries of the Torah. In that same year, my force having been stimulated by the visions of the angels and the blessed souls, I was undergoing a prolonged fast[15] in the week before the feast of Purim. Having locked myself in a separate room in holiness and purity, and reciting the penitential prayers of the morning service with many tears, the spirit came over me, my hair stood on end and my knees shook and I beheld the *merkabah,*[16] and I saw visions of God all day long and all night, and I was vouchsafed true prophecy like any other prophet, as the voice spoke to me and began with the words: "Thus speaks the Lord." And with the utmost clarity my heart perceived toward whom my prophecy was directed [that

15. Called *hafsaqah.* It lasts for several days and is only interrupted by a light meal in the evening.

16. The sphere of the divine *sefiroth.*

is, toward Sabbatai Ṣevi], even as Maimonides has stated that the prophets perceived in their hearts the correct interpretation of their prophecy so that they could not doubt its meaning.[17] Until this day I never yet had so great a vision, but it remained hidden in my heart until the redeemer revealed himself in Gaza and proclaimed himself the messiah; only then did the angel permit me to proclaim what I had seen. I recognized that he was [the] true [messiah] by the signs which Isaac Luria had taught, for he [Luria] has revealed profound mysteries in the Torah and not one thing faileth of all that he has taught. And also the angel that revealed himself to me in a waking vision was a truthful one, and he revealed to me awesome mysteries.[18]

When Nathan came to Leghorn in 1668, some years before writing this letter, he recounted further details of this period of his life to Moses Pinheiro. For many years he had "applied himself diligently to Talmudic casuistry," and he knew most of the Talmud by heart. Making due allowance for an element of hyperbole in this account, it remains an intellectual feat.[19] Nathan described to Pinheiro his first prophetic experiences, when he was visited by blessed souls from the beyond who desired to initiate him into the secrets of kabbalah: "He used to see [says Pinheiro] a sight like unto a pillar of fire that spoke to him, and sometimes he would see a sight like unto a human face. He would always know the nature [the degree of spiritual perfection, or possibly the identity] of the soul that spoke to him, but he would never speak of it, so as not to appear presumptuous." He studied the Lurianic writings by himself, that is, under angelic tuition and without a human master. In due course he was told to expect a "great light," and once, "as he was attired in his *tallith*[20] and *tefillin*[21] all his senses were extinguished, though his eyes

17. This is a quotation from Maimonides' *Mishneh Torah, Hilkhoth Yessodey ha-Torah,* VII, 3.

18. When I first published this text, with some omissions, in *Major Trends* (1st edn. [1941], p. 410) I dated it as being from 1667, but the complete text of the whole letter discovered by me in one of the Amarillo MSS. in the Ben-Zvi Institute, Jerusalem, disproved my assumption. The complete text was published by me in *Qobeṣ ᶜal Yad*, VI, New Series (1966), pp. 419–56.

19. Even Moses Ḥagiz admits (Emden, p. 36) that his father had ordained Nathan, "who knew the Talmud thoroughly."

20. Prayer mantle, worn every day at morning prayer.

21. The so-called "phylacteries," worn at morning prayer on weekdays. Pious ascetics would wear *tallith* and *tefillin* all day.

remained open and his reason was more lucid than ever. And he beheld all the stages [of creation], and the *merkabah,* and the countenance of AMIRAH."[22] In this vision, which lasted for twenty-four hours, everything appeared to Nathan in a supernal light not of this world, but the primordial "light of the seven days of Creation" by which a man can behold the whole cosmos "according to its order, first the heavens, and then ascending higher in the scale of being."[23]

The psychological authenticity of these autobiographical accounts is as convincing as it is decisive. Here, at last, we have the simple truth, which had escaped both historians and novelists, about the awakening of Nathan's messianic prophecy. Whatever had been lodged in the depths of his conscious or unconscious mind now came to the fore in a tremendous emotional upheaval. As his ecstasy progressed, he beheld the mysteries of creation—which he was to expound later in his *Book of Creation* (*Sefer ha-Beri᾽ah*)—and the sphere of the *merkabah.* Suddenly he saw the image of Sabbatai Ṣevi engraved on the *merkabah*, even as the image of the patriarch Jacob was engraved, according to a well-known rabbinic legend, on the Throne of Glory, and his mouth uttered the prophecy: "Thus saith the Lord, behold your savior cometh, Sabbatai Ṣevi is his name. He shall cry, yea, roar, he shall prevail against his enemies."[24] This, then, was the precise wording of the aforementioned "true prophecy," which he was not permitted to make

22. MS. New York. Freimann (p. 35) garbled the text to the point of utter incomprehensibility.

23. Further interesting details as to the nature of his prophetic experience are given by Nathan in an (unfortunately) fragmentary letter, which I discovered in the library of the Jewish Theological Seminary in New York (MS. Adler 494, p. 7); The prophetic word first manifests itself in the form of letters appearing in relief; out of these letters arises an angel who announced the divine message. For the full text see G. Scholem in *᾽Ereṣ Yisra᾽el*, IV (1956), 191–92. We learn from this letter that Nathan's dogmatic statements on the nature of prophecy (in *Zemir ᾽Ariṣim*, MS. Brit. Mus., Margoliouth 856, fol. 72a; ". . . the prophet . . . beheld the creation of letters by the divine lights, and when they prophesied the letters materialized and produced an angel. . . . [and the angelic] speech reached the prophet who prophesied. . . .") were based on personal experience. Echoes of this experience are preserved in the accounts of Cuenque and Baruch of Arezzo (Freimann, p. 47), though both writers add legendary material and confuse dates.

24. Isa. 42:13. The prophecy (either in his version or in similar ones) occurs in several sources, e.g., Nathan's letter to Amsterdam (Sasportas, p. 138) and in Cuenque's otherwise legendary account of the event (Emden, p. 37).

known until after the beginning of the messianic movement in the summer of 1665. The ecstatic experience, which took place some time between the end of February and early March, 1665,[25] opened two apparently distinct vistas: visions of cosmogony and the *merkabah*, on the one hand, and messianic visions of redemption, on the other. The speculative and imaginative originality of Nathan's mind showed itself in the manner in which these two spheres were made to interpenetrate and elucidate each other.

The crucial point of this vision, as far as the history of Sabbatai Ṣevi is concerned, is the fact that for the first time someone else had recognized him, in an ecstatic vision, as the messiah. In vain have historians tried to discover Sabbatai's early followers. They never existed. Even his old friends and disciples were converted to faith in his messiahship only by Nathan's gospel. At long last the eccentric kabbalist ascetic had made an impression on somebody—and Nathan was indeed somebody. He enjoyed a well-deserved reputation. He combined in his personality, traits and qualities that only rarely meet in one individual, and for that reason alone he would merit a place in the history of religions. By virtue of his visionary power, intellectual capacities, and untiring energy he became the precursor and harbinger of the messiah, as well as the ideological and theological exponent of the Sabbatian faith. Borrowing a metaphor from an earlier but in many ways analogous messianic movement, Nathan was at once the John the Baptist and the Paul of the new messiah. The progress of Nathan's charismatic life is important for an understanding of his personality. For although he continued to receive illuminations and to hear voices, only on that one occasion did he consider himself a prophet in the full sense. His first experience was the source of his gospel. All subsequent graces were but interpretations. Last but not least, Nathan's character was very different from that of Sabbatai Ṣevi. We shall look in vain for any of the prophet's outstanding qualities in the messiah: tireless activity, unwavering perseverance without manic-depressive ups and downs, originality of theological thought, and considerable literary ability. Sabbatai's fumbling attempts in theology, for example, his "Mystery of the Godhead," are pale

25. Also Baruch of Arezzo says that the vision took place "shortly before Purim, 425" (Freimann, p. 46). But the Günzburg MS. 517 (in Moscow), fol. 99a, which contains Nathan's letter, gives the week after Purim as the date of the vision, which would fix it at the middle of March.

shadows when compared to the systematic audacity that made Nathan the first great theologian of heretical kabbalism. With all the charm, dignity, and attractiveness of the "man of sorrows . . . smitten of God and afflicted," Sabbatai lacked strength of character. For seventeen years he had never taken an active initiative except for temporary outbursts, which he often seemed to regret afterward. Even in his moments of manic exaltation he did not really "act," and the flurry of provocative gestures spent itself without producing permanent effects. At the height of the movement he remained passive, and his activity exhausted itself in increasingly bizarre and "strange" acts. The two men complemented each other in a remarkable fashion, and without that combination the Sabbatian movement would never have developed. Sabbatai was a poor leader. Devoid of will power and without a program of action, he was a victim of his illness and illusions. But his paradoxical personality inspired Nathan and provided him with the impetus for his actions and ideas. It is idle to speculate what might have become of the brilliant young scholar had he never met Sabbatai Ṣevi. It is certain that only the encounter of the two gave birth to the Sabbatian movement. The hidden, revolutionary tendencies of his generation crystallized in Nathan Ashkenazi. He functioned as a kind of "transformer"—concentrating in his person, articulating, and transmitting the historical forces at work. In the eyes of Nathan, the curious, ascetic sinner and saint, who occasionally dreamed of a messianic calling but who lacked the strength to believe in himself consistently, assumed the quality of an ultimate symbol. By making himself the herald and standard-bearer of the messiah, Nathan gave the crucial impetus to the formation of the Sabbatian movement.

Nathan's account of his kabbalistic studies and of the revelations he had experienced sounds reasonable and convincing. The way in which later anti-Sabbatian legend garbled the historical facts can be learned from Moses Ḥagiz, who writes:

I have seen a letter written by my father of blessed memory, wherein he commanded his disciple Nathan, on pain of excommunication(?), to tell him whence he had got that knowledge. Nathan replied that [he had learned all this] from a book of practical kabbalah which he had stolen from the rabbi Abraham Ḥananiah, when the latter had fled to Gaza on account of the plague. There he fell ill, and commanded that he be carried to the city of the tombs of his ancestors, that is, the valley of Hebron; and while he was busy with his departure, he [Nathan] stole from him the book with which he [then] practiced his magic, and hence the event.[26]

This is obviously a hostile legend, in spite of the appeal to an alleged correspondence between the master and his disciple. R. Abraham Ḥananiah did not flee in 1662 from a (legendary) plague, but in 1663 from the extortions of the Turkish governor of Jerusalem. He fled to Ramleh and not to Gaza. Even if he came to Gaza some time during that year (1662–63), Nathan was not yet there.[27] The reference to studies of "practical kabbalah" rather than Lurianic doctrine is characteristic of the way popular legend treated all things kabbalistic. On the other hand, there may well be a core of truth in Ḥagiz's impossible story. Abraham Ḥananiah may have been in Gaza at a later date, after Nathan had settled there. Study by way of "revelations," or illuminations, is a well-attested phenomenon in kabbalistic literature. Many kabbalists received visits of celestial mentors (angels or holy souls) called *maggidim*, who would convey to them heavenly wisdom. Psychologically, *maggidim* can be described as elements of the mystic's unconscious, crystallizing and coming to life, and behaving in an autonomous fashion as if they were independent agents with an identity of their own.[28] We do not know whether Nathan had meant from the beginning to study by himself, or whether he did so because he found no master in Gaza who would initiate him into

26. Emden, p. 36 (text corrected according to the 1st edn., Altona, fol. 18a, since the 2nd edn. contains many errors).

27. A. Yaᶜari (*op. cit.*, p. 410) accepted the fantasies of Ḥagiz as historical facts and added further errors. Ḥagiz only said that R. Abraham fell ill in Gaza and wanted to be carried to Hebron to die there. As a matter of fact, he died neither in Gaza nor in Hebron, but in Jerusalem. There is no evidence that he resided in Hebron, and Ḥagiz's chronology is impossible anyway. Nathan settled in Gaza after his marriage, at the end of 1663 or beginning of 1664. Yaᶜari was misled by Frumkin, *Toledoth Ḥakhmey Yerushalayim*, II, p. 30.

28. Heavenly visitants and *maggidim* are frequently mentioned in postexpulsion kabbalistic writings, and are systematically discussed by Cordovero and Vital. Some kabbalistic texts were composed under maggidic inspiration, e.g., the *Sefer ha-Meshib* (see G. Scholem, *Kitvey Yad be-Kabbalah,* pp. 86–89) and Joseph Karo's *Maggid Mesharim*. On the whole subject, see Werblowsky, *Joseph Karo,* pp. 75–83, 265–66, 283 ff.

kabbalistic teaching. It is a reasonable assumption that Nathan used some book of "practical kabbalah," that is, one of the ascetic-mystical manuals emanating from the schools of Abraham Abulafia (thirteenth century) and Joseph ibn Ṣayyaḥ (sixteenth century), and containing divine names, mystical formulas, and combinations of letters designed to aid the student in his meditations and in his contemplative *ascensus*. These kabbalistic techniques were purely meditative and involved no activity beyond mental concentration. It may thus be possible to harmonize Moses Ḥagiz's confused memories (written down many years after the event), regarding some correspondence on the subject between Nathan and his teacher, with Nathan's own story. Manuscript copies of Abulafia's writings and similar works were circulating among kabbalists at the time, no less than copies of the "revelations" vouchsafed to masters such as Karo and Joseph Taitatsak. If Nathan studied these "practical" manuals in conjunction with the Zohar, the result would depend solely on his psychological disposition. The reaction to techniques of meditation can be very quick and sudden, and it should occasion no surprise if after a short time *maggidim* began to appear to Nathan and guide him to the depths of Lurianic doctrine.

Judging from Nathan's early kabbalistic writings, it appears that he studied Lurianic kabbalism not only in the canonical version of Ḥayyim Vital, but also according to the very different version taught in the school of Israel Sarug.[29] Nathan's kabbalistic key concepts and terms can be found in the works of Menaḥem Azaryah Fano and in Naphtali Bacharach's *ʿEmeq ha-Melekh*, the publication of which a few years earlier had greatly irritated Vital's disciples, who objected to the appearance of "unauthorized" traditions. It was precisely the "Lurianic" kabbalah stemming from Sarug which fathered the kabbalistic doctrines of Sabbatian theology. Since Nathan studied by himself and without the guidance of expert masters, he may have been unaware, at the time, that the details of the doctrine of *tehiru*, which fascinated him so powerfully and which he was later to reinterpret so thoroughly, formed the subject of sharp controversies among the kabbalistic pundits.

29. See G. Scholem, "Was Israel Sarug a disciple of Luria?" (in Hebrew), *Zion*, VIII (1940), 214–43. S. A. Horodezky's criticism of this article (*Torath ha-Qabbalah shel ha-ʾAri* [1947], pp. 79–81) has failed to disprove any of its facts or contentions; cf. also above, ch. 1, p. 25.

During his great ecstasy that lasted for a whole day, Nathan learned "awesome mysteries" from the "angel of the Covenant." Some of these mysteries he mentioned in his letter of 1673–74, and we have no grounds for dismissing his testimony, which is of considerable importance for our understanding of the earliest stages of his thinking. The angel had told him that "now was the time of the last end meant by Scripture [Isa. 63:4], 'for the day of vengeance is in my heart.' " The "last end" refers to the final and definite end which will supervene at the predestined date independent of Israel's merits, according to the rabbinic explanation of Isaiah 60:2: "I the Lord will hasten it in its time—if they have merits, I shall hasten it; if not, then it will have to bide its predestined time." Penitence was not, therefore, a *conditio sine qua non* of redemption, though it would alleviate the sufferings and tribulations of the messianic woes. The angel had confirmed to Nathan "that even if, God forbid, all Israel were sinners, they could not delay the advent of redemption by their sins, as our Sages have said.[30]

Even more significant for the subsequent development of Sabbatianism is another message of the angel: "Moreover I was told that Israel ought to believe [in the messiah] without any sign or miracle. And whoever does not believe, it is evident that his soul contains an admixture of evil from the generations that rebelled against the kingdom of Heaven and against the kindgom of David."[31] This important passage explicitly poses the problem of faith which, in all its variety of shades and nuances, played a central role in Nathan's teaching. For the historian of religion there is also the intriguing question of the Christian overtones of this concept of faith. Were these overtones present from the very beginning, owing to Christian influences of one kind or another on Sabbatai and/or Nathan, or were they added later, possibly during the first meetings of the two, to the original and traditional signification of the term? A distinctly Christian flavor in Nathan's use of the term "faith" is beyond doubt in many instances; for example, in the long letter to Raphael Joseph (summer, 1665) where it is stated that man is saved by his faith in the messiah and not by

30. The reference is to B. Sanhedrin 98a: "The son of David will come only in a generation that is either completely righteous, or completely wicked." See also above, p. 51.

31. Text in *Zion*, III (1938), 228.

good works or other merits. On the other hand, the association between faith and redemption is attested also in genuine Jewish traditions untainted by foreign influences. An old Tannaitic midrash, the *Mekhilta*, states that "the dispersed will be redeemed for the sake of faith only," though, of course, faith *never* means, in the old rabbinic sources, faith in the redeemer. The connection was elaborated in homiletical style in the twenty-ninth chapter of R. Loew of Prague's *Neṣaḥ Yisraʾel*, probably the most authoritative book summing up the rabbinic doctrine of redemption as it had developed by the sixteenth century. Nathan quotes from R. Loew's work in the letters that he composed after Sabbatai's apostasy; he may well have read it before the great prophecy came to him in 1665. The doctrine that the messiah need not prove himself by supernatural signs and miracles but would be recognized by other criteria had the authority of the same rabbinic tradition with which the Sabbatian movement later clashed so violently. Maimonides had ruled in his code, *Mishneh Torah*, *Teshubah* xi; "Do not conceive the idea that the messiah would have to perform signs." Indeed, "the children of Israel did not believe in our master Moses because of the signs which he wrought, for he that believes because of miracles will of necessity feel doubt whether he [the prophet] did not work [the miracle] by means of magic and sorcery" [*Mishneh Torah*, *Yesodey ha-Torah* viii, 1]. Already in his *Epistle concerning the Resurrection* Maimonides had expressed similar ideas and stated that no signs were required of the messiah.[32] Nathan's exhortation that "one should believe in him without a sign" does not, therefore, constitute a radical innovation. The conclusion of the sentence, however, which ascribes unbelief to a depravity of the soul, seems to introduce a novel idea. Faith now appears as a special merit, peculiar to the souls of the saints. The shift of emphasis may seem but slight, yet it constitutes a turning point even if Nathan was not conscious, at the time, of all its implications.

The immediate results of Nathan's vision were other than literary in character. The young scholar, who had become first a kabbalistic student and then a visionary prophet, was now turned into another man. He began to act as spiritual director for those who sought the *tiqqun,* the "reformation" of their souls. In this he followed in the

32. *Qobeṣ Iggeroth ha-Rambam,* II, 9b.

footsteps of Isaac Luria, who was said by his disciples to have read people's secret sins from their faces and to have prescribed their *tiqqun* accordingly. At a later period the same ministry was again exercised by the more illuminate and charismatic among the leaders and saints of the Hasidic movement. Nathan became a "prophet"—not in the technical sense of a messenger entrusted with the word of God but, rather, in the popular usage of the term. He was the charismatic man of God, who could read a man's innermost heart. In short, "the spirit of the Lord moved him, and he whispered their sins into the ears of some people" and prescribed the appropriate *tiqqun*.[33] The oldest and most reliable records have preserved accounts of Nathan's first public appearance in this capacity. In an atmosphere saturated with Lurianic kabbalism, such things could not but make a profound impression.[34] Nathan was visited by penitents seeking the *tiqqun* of their souls, and—if we may judge from similar events in 1666—he imposed on them heavy and prolonged fasts, and other mortifications. He himself practiced the same austerities.

Reports from Gaza concerning the apparition of the man of God may have reached Egypt as early as spring, 1665. Raphael Joseph immediately decided to find out more about the matter, and dispatched several emissaries to investigate on the spot. We know of at least three emissaries that came to Gaza in 1665, but there were probably many more. The first, anonymous, visitor confirmed that Nathan imposed penances on the whole congregation of Gaza, that everybody obeyed his ascetic instructions in fear and trembling, and that "he was worthy of being called a man of God." The next visitor was R. Samuel Gandoor, who came to find out whether Nathan owed his success to the use of magical formulas or whether he was truly filled with the spirit of God.[35] Gandoor, who seems to have been a

33. The speed with which Sabbatian legend succeeded in changing the chronology of events appears from one of the letters published by Haberman (p. 207): Nathan discovered the "Book" (i.e., the *Vision of R. Abraham*) and *thereafter* was moved by the spirit of prophecy. Gandoor's letter (*ibid.*) gives the opposite—and correct—sequence of events.

34. See Baruch of Arezzo (Freimann, p. 46). Cuenque reports Palestinian tradition: "The inhabitants of Gaza noticed a change in his deportment. He began to preach repentance, and gave proof of the indwelling of the Holy Spirit by telling people their secret sins and the like." See also *Zion,* X (1945), 58.

35. The main source for our knowledge of the events in Gaza is the letters published by Haberman, pp. 207 ff.

member of Raphael Joseph's circle of scholars, completely succumbed to Nathan's power of fascination. He became Nathan's confidant, and his companion on most of his travels.[36] Two other Egyptian emissaries, Raphael Joseph's brother Ḥayyim (or possibly Ḥananiah) Joseph,[37] and Judah Sharaf, one of the most distinguished rabbis of Jerusalem and Egypt, arrived in Gaza when the messianic movement was already well under way.

Gandoor's enthusiastic report came to the ears, and possibly even to the eyes, of Sabbatai Ṣevi, who was still in Egypt on his mission on behalf of the community of Jerusalem.[38] At first nobody seems to have mentioned Sabbatai's name in connection with the excitement about the appearance of the prophet. This important fact has been obscured by the cloud of legends which soon surrounded the events and which effectively upset their chronological order. The actual course of events is told in a letter from Egypt: "When [the Rabbi Sabbatai Ṣevi] heard of the letter from the aforementioned R. Samuel [Gandoor], he abandoned his mission and repaired to Gaza in order to find a *tiqqun* and peace for his soul. But when R. Abraham Nathan beheld him, he fell to the ground before him, and asked his forgiveness for not having done homage to him when he had passed through [Gaza] on his way to Egypt. He also announced to him that he was a very exalted soul."[39] The ring of truth in this account admits of no doubt, and we can easily gauge its real significance. Sabbatai came to Gaza neither in accordance with a secret plan hatched years before, nor because he was on his way home after having achieved his mission. Least of all did he come as a messiah, although the wags of Jerusalem, so Moses Ḥagiz tells us,[40] later punned: "He went a *shaliah* ('emissary') and returned a *mashiaḥ* ('messiah')." In reality

36. Gandoor appeared in the company of Nathan as late as the end of the seventies (see the Sabbatian notebook in the library of Columbia University; also the text in *Toᶜey Ruaḥ* as published in *Zion*, VII [1942], 180). He subsequently returned to Egypt (probably after 1680), where he lived as a highly respected rabbi. In 1704 he signed an approbation of a work by R. Joseph b. Elijah Ḥazzan, *ᶜEyn Yehosef*. There is no indication that he ever gave up his Sabbatian belief.

37. Frances (*Ṣevi Muddaḥ*, p. 134) calls him Ḥayyim. Ḥananiah is suggested by the form *Hannie* in the English version (in *Several New Letters concerning the Jews* [1666], p. 1) of a letter he wrote to his brother Raphael Joseph.

38. The chronology is established by the report in a letter written in Egypt in the second half of 1665 (Haberman, p. 208).

39. *Ibid.* 40. Emden, p. 36.

he went in quest of "a *tiqqun* and peace for his soul." The kind of peace he sought for his soul should be clear by now. Sabbatai did not come as a messiah to his prophet, but, rather, as a sick man to the doctor of souls, who knew the hidden roots of every soul and who could prescribe to each its appropriate *tiqqun*. Sabbatai had been troubled by his emotional oscillations and unaccountable actions. He was afraid of new waves of dejection and euphoric illumination, and, as was mentioned before, sometime in late 1664 or early 1665 he had performed the great exorcism. Now, like the Hasidic devout of a later generation, he besought the doctor of souls to cure him. But the cure was a surprise. Nathan announced to him that his was a soul of a very high order which needed no *tiqqun;* he was, in fact, the messiah. The accounts according to which Nathan publicly welcomed Sabbatai with a messianic proclamation[41] are clearly contradicted by Nathan's own story in the letter quoted above. Nathan spoke to Sabbatai under four eyes, and probably disclosed to him the contents of his vision. Sabbatai, who had come to Gaza with a different purpose and who was not, at the moment, in a state of illumination, demurred. The refusal is attested by Laniado's account of Sabbatai's autobiographical confession. Laniado's story may not be accurate in all respects, as imagination quickly added fiction to fact,[42] yet it contains many authentic details. We are told that Sabbatai's exorcism and the departure of the Holy Spirit from him occurred at the same time as Nathan's vision. Even if we do not accept the statement that the two events took place "on the very same day," they may well have occurred at about the same time, that is, toward the end of the winter of 1665—some weeks before Sabbatai's marriage to Sarah by the end of March. Sabbatai Ṣevi also told Laniado that when Nathan addressed him as the messiah, "he laughed at him and said, 'I had it [the messianic vocation], but have sent it away.' "[43] Sabbatai's

41. Cuenque (Emden, p. 37).

42. The transition from history to legend took place with extraordinary rapidity in what are practically eyewitness accounts. Already the earliest documents confuse dates and chronologies, and abound in legendary accounts of miracles. A letter written in Gaza early in July, 1665 (it was received in Aleppo on July 20), and purporting to give an account of the events of the preceding four months, is one of our first witnesses to this process of legendary transformation. See G. Scholem, "A New Document Relating to the Beginning of the Sabbatian Movement" (Hebrew) in *Kiryath Sepher,* XXXIII (1958), 532–40.

43. *Zion,* VII (1942), 191.

refusal is also mentioned in other documents, where it is presented as mere dissimulation.[44] But this view is a rationalistic induction from events that in reality followed very different laws, and which unfolded in accordance with the peculiar psychological dynamics of the *dramatis personae*. There was no carefully laid plot and Sabbatai did not dissimulate; yet we can also understand the perplexity of the unbelievers as they tried to account for what had happened in terms intelligible to them. Sasportas suggests[45] that Sabbatai had tricked Nathan by using some magic formula whereby "he showed him a phantom, or made him hear a voice which declared that he was the messiah." This theory, that Sabbatai had *de facto* hypnotized Nathan, seemed reasonable enough to Sasportas, though he himself later added an alternative explanation to the effect that there had been a prearranged plot. Neither explanation is supported by the evidence.

These events took place in the spring of 1665. Sabbatai and Nathan spent the following weeks together in intimate converse, Nathan trying to prove the truth of his prophecy and to convince Sabbatai of his messianic mission. Together they betook themselves to Jerusalem and Hebron, visiting the tombs of the patriarchs and saints, but "their [mystical] intent was unknown" to the world.[46] We do not know whether their pilgrimage also took them to Safed, but wherever they went—the same source informs us—Nathan "taught the people knowledge," that is, preached repentance, told men their innermost secrets and gave them their *tiqqun*. During their joint travels (a few weeks at the utmost), they would retire together and open their hearts to each other in intimate talks that were in fact a prolonged spiritual struggle between Nathan and Sabbatai. Nathan would listen to Sabbatai's story of his life, illness, and afflictions, of his dreams and persecutions, and he would fit all these details into the picture of the Godhead and

44. *Relation*, p. 15, and particularly pp. 7–8: "Sabatay Seuy arriue quelques jours apres a Gaza. Nathan Benjamin ne manque pas de l'accueillir auev toute sorte de respect, & luy defere comme a son superieur son maistre & son tout, & veut luy persuader en dépit qu'il en ait, qu'il est en effet le Messie. Sabatay s'en excuse & professe ingenument qu'il n'y a en luy aucune de ces qualitez éclatantes qui doiuent estre les Appanages d'vn employ si auguste." An echo of Sabbatai's refusal is also preserved, albeit in legendary transformation, by Baruch of Arezzo (Freimann, p. 47). According to the letter from Gaza (see above, n. 42) Sabbatai reacted to the messianic welcome in a negative way. He saw in it a meaningless dream (*ibid.*, p. 534).

45. Sasportas, pp. 3–4. 46. Haberman, p. 208.

the cosmos which he had formed as a result of his apocalyptic vision. It was, perhaps, during these conversations that Nathan imbibed some of the curiously "Christian" elements of his theological terminology. Where and when could the young scholar, who had spent all his years studying rabbinic casuistry at the college of R. Jacob Ḥagiz in Jerusalem, pick up this strange vocabulary? No doubt there were many Christian institutions—particularly monasteries—in Jerusalem, but it is difficult to imagine the channels by which their influence could have reached Nathan. Sabbatai, on the other hand, may well have heard the history of Jesus during his wanderings, and may even have meditated on the possibility of a mysterious connection between Jesus and himself. Some of his later actions leave no doubt that they were modeled on examples from the Gospels. The "faith" that animated him during his "strange actions" may easily have acquired the character of a distinct spiritual value independent of any actions. His innate urge to provoke amazement would have full scope in the telling of his story to a sympathetic and fascinated listener. His autobiographical confession would find a ready echo in the inflammable imagination of a man who also heard celestial voices and held intercourse with blessed spirits but who, unlike Sabbatai, possessed the intellectual vigor to deduce the consequences from his visions. The more Nathan learned about Sabbatai's personality, the more he was fascinated by it, but still Sabbatai would not surrender. This was not the cure for which his soul had been yearning.

Shortly before Pentecost, 1665, they returned to Gaza.[47] Sabbatai, who had enjoyed a prolonged respite from his mania and completed his peregrination with Nathan without arousing astonishment or attention, again fell prey to his periodic sickness. On the eve of Pentecost he had one of his "unaccountable" fits of melancholia, "and he was like a sick man filled with anxiety, because he was unable to attend the reading" of the watch-night liturgy on the eve of Shabuᶜoth together with Nathan. (Sabbatai apparently stayed at the house of the rabbi, Jacob b. Moses Najara.)[48] In Sabbatai's absence, and while the assembled scholars were chanting hymns, Nathan fell into a swoon during which

47. The statement in the letter from Gaza (see above, n. 42) that Sabbatai arrived in Gaza three days after Pentecost (*ibid.*, p. 534) is obviously wrong.

48. Baruch of Arezzo (Freimann, pp. 46–47), whose circumstantial details concerning the reception tendered to Sabbatai at his arrival in Gaza are purely legendary.

he uttered individual exhortations to those present to repent of their sins. Finally a voice was heard, saying, "Heed ye Nathan my beloved,[49] to do according to his word. Heed ye Sabbatai Ṣevi, my beloved. For if ye knew the praise of Rabbi Hamnuna the Ancient,[50] 'and the man Moses was very meek.'"[51] The voice repeated this three times. The assembled rabbis did not understand the reference to Sabbatai Ṣevi and inquired of Nathan, after he had recovered from his trance, the meaning of his prophecy. And now Nathan came forward, for the first time, with a public messianic declaration: Sabbatai Ṣevi is worthy to be king over Israel. The events of the Shabuᶜoth vigil later gave rise to a variety of legendary accounts, in some of which Sabbatai is said to have been present at the occasion.[52] But the essential facts seem fairly clear, and their likelihood is increased by their striking resemblance to many well-known and well-attested "*maggidic*" phenomena, that is, cases of voices proceeding from the lips of kabbalist rabbis in an unconscious, or trance-like, state. Solomon Alkabeṣ' description of a similar manifestation—also in the night of Pentecost—when the voice spoke through the mouth of R. Joseph Karo in the presence of many brethren, provides a perfect analogy to the case of Nathan.[53] Among those

49. We have now the account of Mahallallel Halleluyah of Ancona about what Nathan told him in 1668. Nathan said that it was on this occasion that Sabbatai changed his name from Abraham Nathan to Benjamin Nathan, as he was consistently called in later sources. He said that this was because Nathan represented the tribe of Benjamin among the Twelve Tribes, whose souls were mystically present on this night; cf. the Hebrew report published be me in the Harry Wolfson Anniversary Volume (1965), Hebrew section, p. 234. It is difficult to say whether this was a lapse in Nathan's memory or a conscious misleading of his partner. See below, n. 69, on the election of the Twelve Tribes. The change of names is reminiscent of the account in the Gospels, according to which Jesus changed the name of the apostle from Levi to Matthew.

50. One of the mystical heroes of the Zohar; here evidently a symbolic reference to Sabbatai, perhaps a reference to Zohar III, 47b.

51. Num. 12:3, a reference to Sabbatai's refusal to assume the messianic office?

52. E.g., Sasportas (p. 16), whose informants no longer knew whether the event took place on Pentecost, 1665, or on the festival of Sukkoth four months later. More legendary confusion in Frances, *Ṣevi Muddaḥ,* p. 134.

53. Alkabeṣ' epistle was first printed in Isaiah Horovitz's *SHeLaH* (1648), and later added, by way of introduction, to edns. of Karo's *Maggid Mesharim;* see H. L. Gordon, *The Maggid of Karo* (1949), pp. 104–11, and Werblowsky, *Joseph Karo,* pp. 19–21.

present at the vigil in Gaza was R. Meir b. Ḥiyya Rofe, a well-known scholar and head of the *yeshibah* at Hebron which had been founded by Abraham Pereira, the merchant-prince from Amsterdam.[54] Rofe became one of the most enthusiastic rabbinic supporters of Sabbatai. His account of the brethren's enthusiastic singing, and of Nathan's ecstatic dance during which he gradually stripped himself of his clothing until he fell into a swoon, is realistic and convincing.[55]

Sabbatai recovered from his attack of melancholia and visited Nathan, who reasserted and confirmed his earlier prophecies. Meanwhile a strong bond of interaction and reciprocal influence had developed between the two men, and Nathan's persuasive prophecy began to take root in Sabbatai's anguished soul. Something had begun to move in Sabbatai, though it is difficult to be precise about it. We do know, however, from Laniado's memoirs, how things appeared to Sabbatai himself three months later. Nathan, so Sabbatai told Laniado, had fainted and "a voice went forth from his mouth, saying [Hos. 6:2], 'After two days he will revive us, in the third day he will raise us up and we shall live in his sight'—and this was all."[56] Sabbatai may well have begun to ponder the meaning of this verse, and perhaps he even thought of the Christian interpretation according to which it referred to the resurrection of the messiah.[57] But he "understood that the letter *n* in the [two Hebrew] words *yeḥayyenu* ('he

54. On Pereira's *yeshibah* in Hebron, see A. Yaᶜari in the Hebrew quarterly *Yerushalayim*, IV (1952), 185–202.

55. Meir Rofe was in Leghorn in the years 1674–78, and Baruch of Arezzo may have obtained some of his information from him; e.g., he correctly reports (Freimann, p. 47) that Sabbatai was not present at the *Shabuᶜoth* vigil. A number (24) of autograph letters of Sabbatian content by Rofe are preserved in the British Museum (Or. 9165) and were published by Is. Tishby in *Sefunoth*, III–IV (1960), 71–130. It is curious that Baruch of Arezzo should have mistaken Rofe's family name (originally del Medico?) for a professional title and described him as a physician. The incident which he reports surely does not prove much: Nathan had swooned in his prophetic ecstasy, and R. Meir "felt his pulse as physicians do, and said that there was no life in him. Thereupon they covered his face, as one does with the dead, but soon afterward a low voice was heard, whereupon they removed the veil, and behold a voice came out of his mouth but his lips did not move."

56. *Zion*, VII (1942), 191.

57. Against the plain meaning of the text, where the object of the verb "revive" is in the first-person plural.

will revive us') and *yeqimenu* ('he will raise us up') was dotted . . . ,[58] for *n* indicates *nistar* ('hidden, absent' [the grammatical term for 'third person']), meaning that God would revive *him* and raise *him* up. Not as the plain sense would have it, that the speakers—in the first-person plural—would be revived, but . . . the verse means a third-person singular, and this singular individual would be revived. Thus did Our Lord understand [this verse], and then he went away without another word."[59] Sabbatai's understanding of the verse seems to indicate that some echoes of Christian exegesis had lodged themselves in his breast. In fact, "on the third day after the prophet Nathan's utterance, the illumination and the holy spirit returned to Our Lord with redoubled power, and his spirit revived . . . , for since the aforementioned exorcism his spirit had been [as] dead within him. But now on the third day after Nathan's prophecy, his spirit was renewed and Our Lord had [new] strength."

The significance of this testimony is evident. With the renewed manic onrush,[60] everything erupted that had remained hidden and repressed in Sabbatai's heart during the preceding months. At long last he was no longer alone, a pitiful object of derision. With the far-famed man of God at his side, his messianic dream could express itself with redoubled strength. The seed sown in the preceding weeks by Nathan's arguments and persuasive insistence had germinated and waited for the right moment to blossom and bear fruit. One result of this unconscious process was increased faith and confidence in himself. At last Sabbatai announced himself, during prayer, by his favorite biblical title, as the "anointed of the God of Jacob," *Meshiaḥ ʾElohey Yaʿaqob.*

According to Laniado these events took place between the Fourteenth and Seventeenth of Sivan, 425 (May 28–31, 1665). The beginning of the Sabbatian movement could thus be formally dated on May 31, 1665, the day of Sabbatai's first proclamation of himself as the messiah. The date is, in fact, commemorated in the Sabbatian festival calendar. A manuscript from the late seventeenth century states "the Seventeenth of Sivan, the day on which AMIRAH's king-

58. I.e., had a *dagesh forte,* the grammatical sign indicating duplication of a consonant. In the Masoretic text the *N* in the two words has no *dagesh.*

59. *Zion,* VII, *loc. cit.* Accordingly, Sabbatai would have been there.

60. The return of Sabbatai's illumination is also mentioned in the letter from Gaza to Aleppo (see above, n. 42), p. 534, albeit given a date about one week later.

dom began to grow in Gaza." In another manuscript of about the same time, the date Seventeen was corrupted to Fifteen which, in its turn, later became Fourteen[61] (although the latter date perhaps refers to the beginning of the three-day period Fourteen-Seventeen Sivan). In any event the description of Sabbatai's messianic proclamation as "the beginning of the growth of the kingdom" seems a fair evaluation of the events.

There is, however, a serious difficulty, suggesting that two different dates and events may have been confused in these accounts. Laniado makes no mention at all of the messianic self-proclamation and of the "growth of the kingdom." His story relates the regeneration of Sabbatai's spirit and his renewed illumination as if this was all that had happened at the time. On the other hand, the Seventeenth of Tammuz is entered in the aforementioned festival calendar as "the first day of the illumination and the regeneration of the spirit and the light of AMIRAH"[62]—which seems to refer to the same events attributed earlier to the Seventeenth of Sivan. It is highly improbable, though not impossible, that two so very similar events should have taken place[63] within four weeks of one another. In two letters written in 1666 Sabbatai refers to the Seventeenth of Tammuz as "the day of the regeneration of my spirit and my light."[64] The significance of the date for Sabbatai is connected with his abrogation of the fast of the Seventeenth of Tammuz, and his proclamation of the day as a holiday.[65] A hint in the same direction may, perhaps, be gleaned from Laniado, who reports that after the return of his illumination, Sab-

61. 17 Sivan: The New York MS. from which Freimann (p. 95) printed the list of Sabbatian festivals; 15 Sivan: MS. Adler 493, which, however, omits the important words "in Gaza"; 14 Sivan: Emden, p. 75 (where the whole "etiology" is omitted and only the word *ṣemaḥ* ["growth" or "branch"] remains) and the festival calendar of the Dönmeh, who no longer knew the meaning of the festival (see Galanté, p. 47).

62. Thus two good 17th-century MSS. The corruptions in the later MSS. (e.g., *horatho*, "his conception," for *haʾaratho*, "his illumination") have misled many writers; see above, ch. 2, n. 3.

63. Thus Tishby (note to Sasportas, p. 78), who suggests that 17 Tammuz refers to some occurrence in 1666, and not to 1665 and the events recounted by Laniado.

64. Sasportas, pp. 78, 130. The latter text refers to 23 or 24 Tammuz as "the eighth day since the revival of my spirit and my soul on 17 Tammuz."

65. Assuming that he was still in Gaza on 17 Tammuz, which is very doubtful; see below, pp. 236–37. The way in which the date ("the Seventeenth day") is written in Hebrew also permits the reading "festival day."

batai suggested that twelve men go with him to Jerusalem to make a sacrifice on the site of the Temple. In a letter written in July, 1665, from Gaza, it is said, however, that he took "about forty men with him" to Jerusalem, and the writers testify to having participated in this "wonderous journey," full of awesome and miraculous signs and happenings.[66] The association of the events of the Seventeenth with the Temple seems to point to the fast of the Seventeenth of Tammuz on which the fall of Jerusalem is traditionally commemorated. With the evidence available at present, there can be no certainty on this point. Perhaps everything happened on the Seventeenth of Sivan (as Laniado's memoir has it), or else events that took place partly on the Seventeenth of Sivan and partly on the Seventeenth of Tammuz were telescoped by Laniado on the former date. From letters written in Egypt we learn that after Nathan's prophecy of Pentecost, 1665, the rabbis of Gaza and Jerusalem[67] rendered special honor to Sabbatai, who "went forth like a king in the city of Gaza, mounted on a horse with a man walking in front of him, but no one knew his intention in this."[68] Although Laniado does not mention the incident, it appears that Sabbatai did, in fact, proclaim himself in the streets of Gaza as the king of Israel before he went up to Jerusalem.

Laniado's account of what befell on the day of the "regeneration of the spirit and the light" resembles other descriptions of Sabbatai's manic phases, and its details appear to be substantially true, even if they cannot all be confirmed. Sabbatai bore himself with majesty: he "was higher than any of the people" and his face was shining with a great radiance. The whole congregation assembled in the synagogue, where they spent many hours while Sabbatai's countenance shone radiantly so that all stood in fear and trembling. Also the usual pattern of "strange actions" reasserted itself, as always, for during the same assembly in the synagogue, Sabbatai chose twelve of the rabbinic scholars of Gaza to represent the twelve tribes.[69] The analogy

66. *Kiryath Sepher,* XXXIII (1958), 534.

67. Cf. the letter from Gaza to Aleppo (ibid.): "and in Jerusalem all bowed down before him."

68. Haberman, p. 208.

69. The election of the Twelve Tribes is also mentioned by Nathan (letter to Aleppo from the end of 1666; see Coenen, p. 101) and by the "History of Sabbatai Ṣevi" published by N. Brüll from an ancient MS. (Vilna, 1879, p. 14). The Italian author (probably R. Samson Bacchi, see below, p. 376) ap-

with the Gospel account of the choice of the apostles comes to mind, though, of course, the idea of a symbolic representation of Israel by twelve disciples or adherents may well have struck Sabbatai spontaneously and without outside influence, much as it did in the case of Jesus. Sabbatai next commanded the priestly blessing to be recited at the afternoon prayer—not only by the priests but also by three nonpriestly Israelites. Henceforth the habit of decreeing fanciful changes in the liturgy and in religious custom, and of making all sorts of bizarre appointments persisted throughout his career. But when he was in a state of illumination no one thought of disobeying him.

II

The great messianic awakening began on the Seventeenth of Sivan. A prophet as well as a king had arisen in Israel, but the people accepted their king only because the prophet had confirmed his kingship. It is this particular combination which accounts for the impetus of the initial events.

During their peregrinations in the Holy Land, and in their conversations in Gaza, Sabbatai and Nathan had discussed two of their most crucial problems. Sabbatai had explained to Nathan his right to transgress the Law, and even to command others to do so, by way of special dispensation. In a later letter, Nathan reports that on more than one occasion Sabbatai had quoted to him Jeremiah 31:35 in support of his privilege: "If those ordinances depart from before me, saith the Lord, then the seed of Israel also shall cease from being a nation before me forever." "Forever," Sabbatai explained, meant that these ordinances would not depart, but that they might depart temporarily![70] Clearly the problem of justifying his "strange actions" exercised him greatly, but he was unable to arrive at a more original answer than the traditional Talmudic

---

parently saw documents confirming Laniado's account, for he reports that "according to what I heard, and [also] saw in written documents" Sabbatai began his evil ways in Gaza, when he appointed twelve men and called them the Twelve Tribes." According to a letter in the Hottinger Collection in Zürich (vol. XXX, fol. 349b), believers in Constantinople expected Nathan to arrive in the summer of 1666 "accompanied by twelve rabbis." See also n. 49, above.

70. From a letter by Nathan, published in *Qobeṣ ͑al Yad*, VI, New Series, pt. 2 (1966), p. 433. As the letter was written about 1673–74, it may refer to later conversations, but there is nothing to exclude the possibility of such talks having taken place between them when they were together in Palestine.

concept of a special dispensation to meet the requirements of the moment (*hora'ath sha'ah*). He never approached even remotely the profound insights and formulations ultimately provided by his prophet. During the weeks of intimate converse he had revealed to Nathan his innermost thoughts on the other great subject that exercised his mind: his "Mystery of the Godhead." He was aware of a very special and intimate relationship between himself and the "God of his Faith," and already at this early date there seems to have been an element of self-deification, or identification with some divine principle, in his understanding of his messianic character. Very possibly the ecstatic experiences in his manic states, perhaps also some vague echoes of Christian doctrines, played their part in producing this identification and in coloring his experience.

In addition to Nathan's aforementioned letter, written about eight years after the events described in it, we possess a most extraordinary testimony concerning the spiritual relationship between the two at that time. Shortly before the proclamation of Sabbatai as king of Israel, an event occurred in Gaza which yielded the first of what was to be a long series of messianic pseudepigrapha. This species of Sabbatian literature was initiated one day in the spring of 1665, apparently sometime between Sabbatai's return to Gaza and the "Growth of the Kingdom" at the end of May (cf. p. 225, n. 75), when Nathan "discovered" a leaf from an allegedly ancient apocalypse. The language and symbolic imagery leave no doubt that it was composed by Nathan himself. Some sentences are written in partly rhymed prose. The document purports to recount the vision of a certain R. Abraham, "a great sage who lived in the days of R. Judah the Pious [fl. ca. 1200, in Germany] . . . and who lived as a recluse for forty years, eating his food in [ritual] purity and never seeing any man. Every New Moon he would come to the synagogue, and then a curtain would be spread between him and the congregation so that he should not see anybody, and he expounded the mysteries of the Torah. After forty years he beheld this vision," which merits to be quoted in full:[71]

And I, Abraham, after having been shut up for forty years grieving over the power of the great dragon that lieth in the midst of his rivers,

71. I translate from the text established by me in *Be'Iqvoth Mashiaḥ*, pp. 59–61; cf. also the text in Sasportas, pp. 157–60.

[wondering] how long it shall be to the end of these wonders [cf. Dan. 12:6], when behold the voice of my beloved knocketh[72] [saying], "Behold a son will be born to Mordecai Ṣevi in the year 5386 [1626] and he will be called Sabbatai Ṣevi. He will subdue the great dragon, and take away the strength of the piercing serpent and the strength of the crooked serpent, and he will be the true messiah. He will go forth to the war without hands [that is, without weapons], [until the time of the end]. His kingdom will be forevermore and there is no redeemer for Israel besides him. Stand upon thy feet and hear the power of this man, although he be poor and lean. [He is] my beloved, like the apple of my eye and my very heart . . . [there follow some untranslatable kabbalistic puns which imply a reference to Moses, the first redeemer] and he shall sit on my throne, 'for the hand [is] on the throne of the Lord'" [cf. Exod. 17:6].

And I was still wondering at this vision, and behold a man stood before me, his appearance was like that of polished brass from the appearance of his loins even downward, and he had the brightness of fire round about. And from the appearance of his loins even upward like bdellium and like the body of heaven in its clearness. He called with might: "Loose the knots [of the demonic powers] and make war [against them], and prepare a refuge[73] for there is no provision." And a deep sleep fell on me, and lo, a horror of great darkness in all the land of Egypt. And there came a ferret and a chameleon[74] and brought forth a great light, "the light of the hiding of his power." And behold there was a man, his size was one square cubit, his beard a cubit long and his *membrum virile* a cubit and a span.[75] He held a hammer in his hand and tore up a great mountain of ten times sixscore thousand. And the man went up the mountain, and there was a pit that went

72. The expression, taken from the Song of Songs, was apparently first used by Joseph Karo and subsequently by other writers, to describe the charismatic phenomenon of "automatic speech," viz., the voice of a heavenly *maggid*.

73. Or a "boat (*ᵓarbaᵓ*), perhaps suggesting Noah's ark. Tishby (note to Sasportas, p. 158) prefers the reading *ᵓarkaᵓ;* the sentence seems to be intentionally obscure.

74. Cf. Lev. 11:30. MS. Adler 494 adds "and a lizard"; the unclean animals are evidently symbolic representatives of the *qelippah*.

75. Based on the denigrating description of Pharaoh given in the Talmud (B. Moᶜed Qatan 18a). In Nathan's paradoxical symbolism the messiah is the true Pharaoh; see below, p. 296.

down to the bottom of the mountain and he fell in.[76] And he [the man resembling polished brass] said unto me: "Do not grieve [over the fall of the messiah], for thou shalt see the power of this man." But I could no longer restrain my grief, and I fell into a deep sleep and saw no more vision for a month until the awesome man came again and said unto me: "My son, how great is thy strength, since I reveal unto you things that are unknown even unto the angels.[77] And now write the vision and conceal it in an earthen vessel, that it may continue many days. Know that the man of which I have spoken shall strive hard to know the faith of Heaven,[78] and Habakkuk prophesied concerning him, 'the just shall live by his faith.'"[79] Because for a long season Israel will serve "without the true God,"[89] but he shall restore the crown to its pristine glory. His contemporaries shall rise against him with reproaches and blasphemies—they are the "mixed multitude" [cf. Exod. 12:38], the sons of Lilith, the "caul above the liver,"[81] the leaders and rabbis of the generation. He will do wondrous and awesome things,[82] and he will give himself up to martyrdom to perform the will of his Creator.

Let him be well remembered, the man called Isaac, by whom he will be taught the ways of serving God (cf. above, p. 110). From the age of five to six he will make himself like unto an ox bearing the yoke and an ass bearing a burden to serve the Lord. When he is six the Shekhinah, which has revealed herself to us, will appear to him in a dream as a flame, and cause a burn on his private parts. Then dreams shall sorely trouble him, but he shall not tell anybody. And the sons of whoredom[83] will accost him so as to cause him to stumble, and they will smite him but he will not hearken unto them. They are the sons of Naᶜamah, the scourges of the children of men, who will always pursue him so as to lead him astray.

76. An obvious reference to Sabbatai's ups and downs, his moods of exaltation and his "falls" into the abyss and prison house of the *qelippoth*.

77. Cf. Mark 13:32, "no one knows, not even the angels in heaven."

78. A reference to Sabbatai's "Mystery of the Godhead."

79. Hab. 2:4. The initials of the Hebrew words form the word *ṣevi*.

80. II Chron. 15:3, a favorite verse with Sabbatian authors.

81. Expression based on Lev. 3:4. The description of the wicked and reprobate leaders is taken from the Zohar (*Raᶜya Mehemna* and *Tiqqunin*); see above, p. 11, and Zohar III, 124b.

82. A reference to Sabbatai's "strange actions."

83. Demons born of nocturnal pollutions; see Zohar III, 67b ff. and above, p. 113.

Two conclusions may be drawn from this text. Its author had read, and been impressed by, the visions of Solomon Molkho.[84] In his apocalypse he described the life and adventures of Sabbatai Ṣevi, as he then understood them, in a symbolic language heavily indebted to Molkho's imagery, and in a manner which combined his own apocalyptic vision and the biographical information obtained from and about Sabbatai. In the second place, it is evident that the figure of the messiah has been refashioned in a thoroughly kabbalistic mold. There is, as yet, no explicit contradiction to the traditional messianic image, but the messiah of the *Vision* was clearly made to fit not so much the ancient legends as a concrete, personal experience. The apocalypse is an attempt to explain the mystery as well as the actual personality of a concrete messiah. The redeemer will not appear at the head of an army to fight the messianic war; he will come "without hands" and without military strength. His real war will be against the demonic powers of the *qelippah,* and it will be waged essentially on the "inner," spiritual levels of the cosmos, although it might eventually manifest itself on the material level as well. The messiah struggles in the depths of his soul to extract the sparks of the divine light from the embrace of the *qelippah*. Hence also the mystery of his suffering. He will subdue Pharaoh, the great dragon; but he is also himself the true Pharaoh and the "holy serpent." He is locked in combat with the very principle that is his own metaphysical source, subduing it, but at times also subdued by it and falling into its bottomless abyss. His ultimate messianic task consists, apparently, not merely in the defeat and annihilation of the power of evil, but in raising it up to the sphere of holiness, that is, in the *tiqqun* of the *qelippah*. The "wondrous and awesome" things which, according to the apocalypse, the messiah had to do (and which, in fact, he had already done), were the "strange actions" by which transgressions were sanctified, and the *qelippah* transformed and hallowed at its very root; they symbolize the transformation of values inherent in the messianic task. The messiah of the *Vision* is no pale and abstract figure as that of Lurianic kabbalah, but definite and personal. It is drawn from life—and a very peculiar and paradoxical life at that. The author of the apocalypse merely interpreted the contradictory features of his

84. This was already noticed by D. Kahana, *Toledoth ha-Mequbbalim,* vol. I, p. 71.

concrete experience of the messiah in terms of the metaphysical essence of the messianic mission.

This short text makes no mention at all of the general process of *tiqqun* in which everybody is supposed to participate. Perhaps Nathan simply took it for granted, though in his later writings he would refer to the subject more explicitly. But at present everything was overshadowed by the new insight into the nature of redemption, which had probably come to him in his great vision. It is evident from the apocalypse that its author not only knew Sabbatai's inner life and the "faith" that had been revealed to him by the "God of his Faith," but was also aware of the rabbis' attitude toward him. There is great bitterness in Nathan's words. He adopts the extreme language of the *Raʿya Mehemna* in the Zohar, but with a significant difference. The Zoharic writer had used the typological expressions "mixed multitude" and "sons of Lilith" to designate the leaders and the rich in his generation, possibly also the scholars who clung to exoteric traditional teaching and rejected kabbalistic esotericism. In this apocalypse the terminology acquires a new signification. It is they who deny the messiah and who persecute him on account of his "awesome actions" whose hidden light they cannot comprehend, that are the "mixed multitude." There is a striking analogy between the "sons of Lilith" of this apocalypse, and the "children of Satan," namely, the leaders of the Jews who rejected the messiah, in the Fourth Gospel. Also in the eyes of Nathan the "leaders and rabbis of the generation" are the "mixed multitude." This suggests that the violence and acerbity which characterize subsequent polemics between Sabbatian believers and "infidels" are more than a result of developments in 1666. They are rooted in the contempt which the founders of the movement, true *spirituales*, felt from the very beginning for the carnal rabble that could not comprehend the spiritual light. Nathan's resentment probably echoes the bitterness of Sabbatai's feelings as he told the story of his life. Nathan's indignation can hardly have been due to any experiences of his own. He had performed no "strange actions"; he merely interpreted someone else's. As he found the key to their understanding, new worlds opened before his eyes; yet he steadfastly refused to apply to himself that which he advanced as a valid explanation for the messiah's behavior. He remained a meticulously observant Jew and no complaints were ever voiced against him on that score, however numerous and grave the accusations leveled against him in other respects.[85] The prophet interpreted the messiah's actions; he did not imitate them.

We have argued that Nathan's authorship of the apocalypse is borne out by the internal evidence. Further proof of our contention is provided by the conflicting accounts of its discovery. All these accounts can be traced back either to Nathan or to his friends, and they all agree on one essential point: the apocalypse was found by Nathan and by nobody else. The legend which ascribed the apocalypse to Abraham Yakhini has been ably disposed of by S. Rosanes.[86] We now also know how the mistake arose; it was born from a confusion in the memory of Sasportas, who failed to check his story against the documents in his archive.[87] Thence the Yakhini legend passed, via Jacob Emden, into all subsequent literature.

Sasportas never realized the importance of the apocalypse; in fact, he lacked the background knowledge for understanding it. He either did not know about the oscillations of Sabbatai's mood, or—if he did—he paid no attention to them. He was a rabbinic judge and not a psychologist. If Sabbatai was guilty of wicked deeds it mattered little why he did them. Folly and madness are no justification, and hence Sasportas paid little attention to details to which we would attach major importance. His comment on the apocalypse was: "A

85. De la Croix says that Nathan was persecuted by the rabbis of Jerusalem (p. 289; also p. 293: they decided to kill him, but revoked their decision after the discovery of the *Vision of R. Abraham*), but all his details are pure legend. Either de la Croix hopelessly confused some authentic information he may have had, or else he drew on legendary reports received in Constantinople. In any event he attributed the persecution to Nathan's activity as a "false prophet" who might endanger the Jewish community, and not to any transgressions of the Law.

86. Rosanes, *op. cit.,* IV, pp. 411, 437. Rosanes could not explain the origin of this fantastic theory, and the puzzle was only solved with Tishby's publication of the complete text of Sasportas' *Ṣiṣath Nobel Ṣevi.*

87. Sasportas (p. 207) quotes a letter from Adrianople according to which Sabbatai publicly cursed Nathan, because the latter had deceived him with the faked *Vision.* He also cursed Yakhini because of "his lies and falsehoods." When Sasportas edited his account (p. 157), he failed to look once more at the letter (reproduced correctly on p. 207) in his archive, and relied on his memory. As a result of this neglect he attributed to Yakhini what his source had explicitly said of Nathan, and Yakhini started on his literary career as the main villain of the piece, from Emden (p. 38) and the anonymous *Me᾽ora῾oth Ṣevi* to J. Kastein's *The Messiah of Izmir.*

best version simply says that the book was revealed from Heaven to be nonsense mingled with heresy." Elsewhere he dismisses the *Vision* as "tales wherewith to frighten children."

Accounts of the discovery of the mysterious leaf, as well as of the book from which it was allegedly taken, are conflicting.[88] The

88. I have discussed the different versions in *Be^cIqvoth Mashiaḥ*, pp. 54–56: (1) According to R. Hosea Nantawa of Alexandria, Nathan found the prophecy in a volume of the "Greater Wisdom of Solomon" (Sasportas, p. 157). (2) Nathan told Pinheiro that he was commanded [by the prophet Elijah?] to go to a certain place and find a book (Freimann, p. 95). (3) An early letter from Egypt (Haberman, p. 207) connects the discovery of the *Vision* with the beginning of Nathan's prophecy: Elijah appeared to Nathan and commanded him to search for a book in a certain spot in the synagogue of Gaza. Digging at the prescribed spot, Nathan discovered a cave in which he found the book, which he took home and read, whereupon he began to prophesy. (4) The Sabbatian apostle Mattathias Bloch Ashkenazi quotes from the "Book of Abraham which he [Nathan] found in the cave of the prophet Samuel," i.e., in the vicinity of Jerusalem and not in Gaza. (Incidentally, the passage quoted by Mattathias Bloch does not occur in our text of the *Vision* but in the commentary on it; see *Zion*, VII [1942], 193). A strange story about a visit of Sabbatai and his companions to the tomb of Samuel is told in the "Testimony" of Moses [b. Isaac] b. Ḥabib (Emden, p. 53); (5) de la Croix, p. 293, tells a confused story according to which Sabbatai, accompanied by a number of unbelieving rabbis, visited some ancient sepulchers, one of which was opened on his orders. There he dug and found an earthen vessel, which contained a book written on parchment and saying "a son is born unto Mordecai Ṣevi, and he is the messiah of Israel." (6) Cuenque's story is altogether different; Nathan told Sabbatai that Elijah had given him a book that contained the history of the world from Sabbatai to the end of the sixth millennium. Sabbatai commanded him to bring the book, from which he then tore the first page (which he permitted to be read and copied). The rest of the book he ordered to be buried in the cemetery (Emden, p. 38). References to the hiding of the book occur in several other sources, e.g., MS. Halberstamm 40, which was written in Jerusalem toward the end of the 17th century (i.e., in spatial and temporal proximity to Cuenque!). The New York MS. printed by Freimann (p. 99) also quotes from a holy book revealed to Nathan, who "did not show it to anyone but his father. To his companions he permitted to copy this [part only] and not more. . . . And the holy R. Nathan possesses two other books which were revealed to him from heaven." This text was written in the summer of 1667, since the copy opens with the words "On Wednesday, the 7th of Tammuz, a letter written in Ofen [i.e., Buda] on the 1st of Tammuz arrived here [in Italy]." The 7th of Tammuz fell on a Wednesday in the years 1667 and 1670, but we know that Elisha Ashkenazi was in Buda only in the summer of 1667. The letter from Adrianople printed by Sasportas (p. 207) alleges that Sabbatai had stated after his apostasy that Nathan had found an ancient MS. concerning the messianic redemption from which he erased the messiah's name and substituted that of Sabbatai. But the testimony is hardly credible.

best version simply says that the book was revealed from Heaven to Nathan, who then copied from it. All the other versions are literary elaborations and embellishments of the first. Nathan writes in his letter of 1673–74: "A handwritten book was revealed to me, and therein were the name of the Redeemer and that of his father, as well as the year of his birth. And many things were written there which he would do, but it was obscure and mysterious and so I hid it until the appointed time."[89] This testimony suggests that Nathan may have written actual "prophecies" concerning the messiah, but suppressed them and merely produced the apocalypse, which was really a prophecy from the event. We know that Nathan wrote more than one apocalypse. His father declared in 1667 that two other books had been revealed to his son from Heaven.[90] There is no way of telling whether he wrote these works in full consciousness as mystical pseudepigrapha, or in states of ecstasy wherein he felt himself to be the copyist rather than the author. There are many psychological stages of transition between downright forgery, and composition in a state of ecstasy or trance. Nathan's behavior as well as his theological writings suggest that he genuinely believed in the revealed character of his messages and doctrines, and support the assumption that he was not in a state of ordinary consciousness when he composed his heavenly revelations.[91] Fortunately we possess another document which is of considerable relevance to this question. Some time in 1666, but at any rate before Sabbatai's apostasy, Nathan wrote a commentary in which the apocalypse is interpreted word for word in the most uninspiring kabbalistic fashion. Very often the meaning of the text is twisted into its exact opposite.[92] The commentary is far-fetched, and devoid of the poetic ardor and imagery that characterize the *Vision;* in fact, it is conscious composition at its most artificial. But in the last analysis the problem of Nathan's mental states when writing

89. *Zion,* III (1938), 229; also the Sabbatian notebook, Columbia University, fol. 18b. See also the preceding note regarding the hiding of parts of the *Vision.*

90. Cf. the letter from Buda, quoted at the end of n. 88.

91. Cuenque's statement that the scroll was written "in an ancient script and on paper that was worn out with age" (Emden, p. 38) belongs to the legendary part of his story.

92. E.g., the interpretation of the ascent of the mountain and of the fall into the pit. I have published the extant part of the commentary in *BeᶜIqvoth Mashiaḥ,* pp. 61–65.

is of no importance. The fact remains that the *Vision* is a literary forgery, though we may prefer to call it a "pseudepigraph" in order to avoid the moral opprobrium attached to the former term. Pseudepigraphy is a well-recognized category in the history of religious literature, and at all times there were authors who produced works allegedly written or inspired by ancient worthies. There is no reason to single out the Sabbatian movement for moral disapproval in a matter with which Jewish literature too is more than familiar. Practically all apocalyptic midrashim are pseudepigrapha of this kind. Certain psychological factors also may have been operative in causing the visionaries to prefer the anonymity of a literary disguise to the public assertion of individual property rights over their revelations. In fact, there were readers who understood this situation perfectly well, without detriment to their faith in the apocalypse. Joseph Almosnino, the rabbi of Belgrade, and a friend and former fellow student of Nathan in the college of R. Jacob Ḥagiz, copied in his own handwriting "a prayer sent from Gaza by the kabbalist Nathan Benjamin,"[93] followed immediately by "the vision which the aforementioned kabbalist has beheld." Almosnino evidently realized that Nathan was identical with R. Abraham the Recluse—without detriment to his religious acceptance of the text.

Almosnino was right, for the apocalypse does hint obliquely at its author's name which, in full, was Abraham Nathan. This form of the name appears in the early letters concerning the Sabbatian movement written from Egypt, as well as in Nathan's own signatures until the summer of 1665 when, in obedience to Sabbatai Ṣevi, he changed his name to Nathan Benjamin or Benjamin Nathan.[94] An element of probably unconscious or half-conscious projection seems to be present in the apocalypse: Abraham Nathan sees himself in the role of a twelfth-century R. Abraham, who beholds in a vision what he himself had learned only a short while ago, partly in a prophetic experience and partly in conversation with Sabbatai Ṣevi. The accounts[95] according to which Nathan's awakening occurred after the discovery of the apocalypse are hardly credible, whereas Nathan's version is both psychologically and chronologically convincing. Writing the apocalypse under the impulsion of his prophetic experience and

93. MS. Oxford, Neubauer, 1777.

94. Baruch of Arezzo (Freimann, p. 58). See also n. 49.

95. E.g., in the letters from Egypt, published by Haberman.

the vision of the *merkabah,* he drew on fresh and intimate knowledge, rather than on distant memories and impressions. The details of Sabbatai's sexual temptations are hardly of the kind which Sabbatai would have confided to an unknown youth in Jerusalem. Nathan's visionary dialogues with the angelic beings re-echo his conversations with Sabbatai and the latter's candid confessions. The apocalypse is the product of Nathan's struggle with a messiah who refused the mission laid upon him by his prophet. From the end of 1665 onward the text of the apocalypse was frequently included in letters to Europe and became widely known.

III

Sabbatai Ṣevi revealed himself as the messiah in May, 1665. The proclamation sparked off a chain reaction, and events followed in quick succession. The first developments took place, naturally enough, in Palestine, and our attention must return once more to the disconcerting personality of the middle-aged rabbi whom the prophet had announced to "be worthy of being king over Israel." We already know that he had entered on a new phase of manic illumination, more acute, and indeed frenzied, than ever before. The reason is not far to seek. For the first time he was surrounded by believers and supporters, and "in the multitude of people is the king's honor." Samuel Gandoor, who spoke to Sabbatai in Gaza and whose weighty testimony regarding Sabbatai's illness has already been quoted at length, describes the messiah's appearance during those weeks with a believer's enthusiasm: "Blessed is he who beheld the countenance of the rabbi Sabbatai Ṣevi, like unto the awesome appearance of an angel of God, [excelling] all the rabbis in [his knowledge of] the Talmud and kabbalah, in majesty, virtue, and saintliness."[96] Gandoor emphasizes the virtue and saintliness of Sabbatai's behavior, although we know that in his fits of euphoria the saintly ascetic was apt to do the most surprising things. As a matter of fact, Sabbatai did revert, before long, to his "strange actions," this time with unprecedented vehemence. His exaltation knew no bounds.

His consciousness of a very special nearness to God expressed itself in a symbolic act of which Nathan's disciple Israel Ḥazzan of Kastoria has left us a detailed account. While still in Gaza, Sabbatai

96. Haberman, p. 209. All quotations in this chapter are from this source, unless indicated otherwise.

had made himself three rings, which he always wore on his fingers. One ring was engraved with the full kabbalistic spelling of the Tetragrammaton יוד הי ויו הי, the numerical value of which is seventy-two; the second with the full kabbalistic spelling of the name Shadday; while the third ring had no inscription.[97] This important testimony permits two conclusions.

Sabbatai Ṣevi busied himself with inventing mystical allusions to himself by way of *gematria* (numerology). The numerical value of the full spelling of the divine name Shadday (Shin, Daleth, Yod) is 814, which also happens to be the numerical value of the name Sabbatai Ṣevi. This *gematria* appears frequently in later Sabbatian writings, and it was evidently invented by Sabbatai himself. There are many testimonies, direct and indirect, confirming Sabbatai's addiction to *gematria*. Leyb b. Ozer reports that Sabbatai frequently asserted that his name was indicated in ancient books "in a kabbalistic manner," that is, probably in *gematria*. Aryeh Leyb Ziwitover, a scholar who visited the Italian Sabbatians a few years after the messiah's apostasy, reported to them a number of such allusions by *gematria* in a manner which suggests that he had heard them from Sabbatai himself.[98] Israel Ḥazzan's testimony is even more explicit. He tells us that on his first visit to Sabbatai Ṣevi in Adrianople (1667) he saw a manuscript of such *gematria*s which "he had written concerning himself."[99] This fanciful search of mystical allusions in which he could give full rein to his feverish imagination is in keeping with what we know of Sabbatai's character, and he may well have indulged in it even before his revelation as the messiah. Some of the *gematria*s current in Sabbatian literature were no doubt invented by Sabbatai himself, and there were many more allusions to him than the divine name Shadday. In fact, the first word of the Bible contained a messianic prophecy, since the letters of the Hebrew word for "in the beginning," בראשית, contain the letters that make up the word "sabbatai," שבתאי. The second verse of Genesis was even more fascinating. An old rabbinic source comments on the verse, "And the earth was without form and void . . . and the spirit of God moved upon the waters," in these words: "this is the spirit of the Messiah." Sab-

97. See *Schocken Volume*, p. 165.

98. *Ibid.*, p. 164 (from MS. 8° 1466 in the Jewish National Library, Jerusalem).

99. *Ibid.*

batai discovered that the numerical value of the Hebrew words for "God moved" was equal to that of his name. The verse thus mystically signified "and the spirit of Sabbatai Ṣevi was upon the waters." He also computed the numerical value of the Hebrew words for "the true Messiah," which equaled that of his name. (This *gematria* is already alluded to in the *Vision of R. Abraham.*) Poor as these fancies are as a spiritual or mental effort, they served as a considerable imaginative stimulus. Nathan took them over from Sabbatai and made them part and parcel of his doctrinal system.

Moreover, we learn from these rings that Sabbatai genuinely sought to establish a connection between himself and the names of God. In fact, he was the mystical fullness and manifestation of the name Shadday, which appeared on his second ring. Shadday was the name of the "God of his Faith" and, as he explained to Israel Ḥazzan in Adrianople, "there is no division, distinction, or separation whatever between me and Him—these were his holy words." Sabbatai's awareness of a relation of particular intimacy with his father in Heaven, is reminiscent of similar utterances of Jesus as reported in the Gospels. For the time being, all this was merely hinted at, but it was only a short step from there to such public and audacious expressions of his faith as his later signatures to his letters: "the firstborn" of the Lord, or even "I am the Lord your God Sabbatai Ṣevi." R. Moses Galanté, one of the most prominent rabbis in Jerusalem and for some time a follower of Nathan (he actually accepted the latter's invitation to join him in Gaza), later confessed to his disciples that he had not opposed Sabbatai until the receipt, by the believers in Jerusalem, of the first letters with the offensive signature. His testimony, incidentally, proves that these letters were not written during the Gaza period of the movement, that is, in the summer of 1665. As will be shown, Galanté was more of a follower of Sabbatai than he later cared to admit.

The most intriguing of the three rings mentioned by Israel Ḥazzan is, undoubtedly, the third. If it had no inscription, was there, perhaps, an image engraved on it? Rings of this kind were usually signet rings, and we should therefore expect an engraving which might serve as a seal. We do know that Sabbatai signed his letters with the figure of a crooked serpent after his name. The meaning of the symbol is obvious: it is the "holy serpent," the numerical value of which was equal to that of the Hebrew word *mashiaḥ* ("messiah"). Sabbatai signed his letter to the famous Polish rabbi, David ha-Levi,[100] in this fashion,[101] and the sign still appears in a recently discovered probably autograph letter of Sabbatai of the year 1676.[102] In the same year "Sabbatai Ṣevi made a serpent of silver and put it upon a pole," which seems to mean that he used the sign of a serpent as his seal on the letter quoted in our source.[103] It is tempting to surmise that such a serpent was engraved on the third ring. However that may be, it is certain that Sabbatai never used the symbol of the *ouroboros,* the circular serpent biting its own tail, which is one of the best-known symbols of the unity and eternal renewal of life: in my beginning is my end, and in my end is my beginning. It would no doubt be interesting to know that Sabbatai had used this rich symbol, pregnant with profound psychological associations,[104] of which he might have been aware through references to it in the Zohar.[105] But Sabbatai's signature was a crooked, not a circular, serpent (approximately like this: §). If our surmise concerning the three rings is correct, then they would express Sabbatai's consciousness of identity with the "God of his Faith" as well as his awareness of being the messianic "holy serpent."

Sabbatai did not rest content for long with minor deviations—however bizarre—from normal behavior. While the prophet was busy preaching repentance and imposing heavy fasts and mortifications on penitents coming to him for their *tiqqun,* the fast of the Seventeenth of Tammuz, 1665, approached. The prophet saw signs that "the exaltation of the rabbi Sabbatai Ṣevi as the Anointed of the God of Jacob" was about to begin. Sabbatai too felt the movement of the spirit and he abolished the fast.[106] His word was obeyed in

100. Author of the commentary *Turey Zahab* on part *Oraḥ Ḥayyim* of Karo's *Shulḥan ᶜArukh.*

101. Sasportas, p. 78.

102. Documents from the Saul Amarillo Collection, in *Sefunoth,* V (1961), 249; see Pl. XII.

103. Z. Rubashov-Shazar, in the annual *Zion,* VI (1934), 56. The words quoted here are missing from the copy of this letter in Baruch of Arezzo's memoir (Freimann, p. 68).

104. Cf. the chapter on the *ouroboros* in Erich Neumann, *The Origins and History of Consciousness* (New York, 1955).

105. Zohar II, 176b, 179a; III, 205b.

106. This account follows the traditional assumption that Sabbatai remained in Gaza until after the 17th of Tammuz. But this chronology is not

Gaza, and instead of the liturgy of the fast "the Great Hallel [the festival psalms, 113–118] was recited, and there was rejoicing in the gardens." The letter from Egypt which reports this incident adds that the prophet confirmed the innovation because he was confident that this day would mark the beginning of the ingathering of the exiles. The abolishment in Gaza of a hallowed and strictly observed religious custom by messianic authority is confirmed by other sources.[107] The letter which was sent from Gaza to Aleppo early in July, 1665, ends with the glad tidings "and the Seventeenth of Tammuz was made a festival day of feasting and rejoicing in honor of the Shekhinah, for thus had it been revealed."[108] The English consul in Smyrna knew that Nathan had sent letters to the Jewish communities, advising them of the abolition of the fast, "forbidding all the fasts of the Jews at Jerusalem; and declaring that the bridegroom being come, nothing but joy and triumph ought to dwell in their habitations, writing to all the assemblies of the Jews to persuade them to the same belief."[109] Rycaut's style suggests that he actually quotes from some such letter, which someone may have translated for him. These letters are our first evidence that Nathan had begun to take active steps to spread the good news to the Diaspora. The absence of any messianic propaganda in the early summer of 1665 has always been a puzzle. Until then no news of what had happened in Gaza seems to have reached the more distant communities, and Sabbatai's name probably remained unknown in the neighboring countries until midsummer.[110]

---

certain at all, in view of the fact that Sabbatai arrived in Aleppo on the 8th of Ab (letter from Aleppo, *Kiryath Sepher,* XXXIII [1958], 534), i.e., less than three weeks later, part of which was spent in Jerusalem. The letter from Gaza, incorporated in the letter from Aleppo, suggests that Sabbatai's summons to his followers, "Let us arise and go up to Jerusalem," was uttered very shortly after the messianic proclamation. It is possible, therefore, that he arrived in Jerusalem toward the end of Sivan or beginning of Tammuz. In that case the fast was abolished by Nathan and not by Sabbatai, who at that time was no longer in Gaza (and perhaps not even in Palestine). The letter from Gaza suggests that Sabbatai's fit of illumination was particularly intense, but also relatively short.

107. See Rycaut, p. 202, and Coenen, p. 11. The letters from Egypt leave no doubt that this happened in 1665 (and not in 1666, as Graetz thought).

108. *Kiryath Sepher,* XXXIII (1958), 534.

109. Rycaut, p. 202.

110. Why no news of the incipient movement reached Europe during the summer is still something of a mystery.

We now know, at any rate, that letters were written to Egypt, to Aleppo,[111] and to the messiah's native city, Smyrna. But this is about all the evidence that news of the messianic awakening had spread beyond Palestine. Nathan was still completely absorbed in a paroxysm of visionary fever; his missionary activity consisted of calls to repentance so that Israel might be spared the messianic woes. The abolition of the fast, however, precipitated the crisis. It sounded the alarm for the rabbis of Jerusalem, who considered themselves the guardians of Israel's tradition.

There can be no doubt about the reaction of Palestinian Jewry to the news from Gaza. The majority in Gaza and Hebron[112] joined the camp of the believers.[113] As a matter of fact it was during these first weeks of the movement that the word "believers" made its appearance as a technical term by which the followers of Sabbatai Ṣevi referred to themselves. The modern term "Sabbatians" never occurs in original sources and documents. Later expressions such as "Shebsel," "Shebselach," "Shabse Ṣevinikes," etc. were names of abuse invented by their opponents in the early eighteenth century. The Sabbatians never called themselves anything but "believers." Some of the prophet's utterances during those weeks have been preserved in Samuel Gandoor's letters. He is said to have declared that he had not come to provide a *tiqqun* for the souls of men, although he would not refuse it if approached by penitents desirous of atoning for their sins. This particular charisma of his was merely a by-product of his apostolic mission. His message was that "Sabbatai Ṣevi was worthy of being the messiah." To the question why he did not punish the unbelievers, he would reply that this was "to test Israel to [see whether they would] believe without any sign or miracle," and that it was concerning the believers that Scripture [Jer. 3:14] had prophesied, "and I will take you, one of a city and two of a family." A most revealing answer indeed! In his original vision Nathan had been told that Israel *ought to* believe in the messiah even without signs; he was not told

111. The letter from Gaza to Aleppo arrived on the 7th of Ab, July 20 (*Kiryath Sepher,* XXXIII [1958], 532) and was, therefore, written toward the end of Tammuz, in early July, 1665.

112. The histories of the two Jewish communities were always closely related, probably by reason of family ties no less than of geographical proximity.

113. Cf. Haberman, p. 209, and the letter of Shalom b. Joseph, a former schoolteacher from Amsterdam (Sasportas, p. 142).

that they would, in fact, believe, and hence his prediction is pessimistic in the extreme. Only a chosen few will believe, and their faith will be accounted for them as a special merit. A few months later, when the messianic awakening had snowballed to a powerful mass movement, the biblical phrase was used in the opposite sense, and the mass of believers contemptuously referred to the few infidels as "one of a city and two of a family." Safed seems to have had a fair number of believers, but there is no precise information on the situation there in the early summer of 1665.

In Jerusalem, however, things were different. Reports regarding the number of Sabbatai's followers in the city are, admittedly, conflicting, yet it is possible that the numbers given are all equally correct. The number of believers may well have increased after Sabbatai had left the city, and more particularly after the news of the great awakening in the Diaspora had reached Palestine; this might also account for the existence of a Sabbatian center in Jerusalem even after the apostasy. One fact, however, is beyond dispute: the majority of rabbis opposed the "faith," and refused to acknowledge the messiahship of Sabbatai and the prophecy of Nathan. They knew Sabbatai, who had lived among them, and they were not the kind to wax enthusiastic about a paradoxical saintliness that expressed itself in the abolition of laws and in the abrogation of biblical and rabbinic ordinances.[114] They were thoroughly conservative, as befits the guardians of rabbinic tradition. The messiah's credentials would have to be very different from those offered by Sabbatai Ṣevi. They had previously sentenced him to disciplinary flogging for his "strange" behavior, and there was no reason at all why they should now think differently. The oldest sources know nothing about Nathan having accompanied Sabbatai to Jerusalem, but if he did so, the rabbis may have heard him expounding his doctrine of the messiah as we know it from the *Treatise on the Dragons*. If so, they were certainly shocked rather than edified by Nathan's audacious justification of the messiah's behavior. Rumors would have reached them that Sabbatai was applying to himself the names of God; he had even declared that the prayer "It is our duty to praise the Lord of all" referred to him, since it contained the phrase "to establish the world in the kingdom of the Almighty (Shad-

114. But cf. p. 250. If Sabbatai passed through Jerusalem before the 17th of Tammuz, then the abolition of the fast in Gaza cannot have been a factor in the rabbinic opposition to him.

day)."[115] These surely were no kabbalistic mysteries but blasphemies. And now Sabbatai himself appeared in Jerusalem. The pun with which his arrival was greeted—"He went away a *shaliaḥ* ["emissary"] and came back a *mashiaḥ* ["messiah"]—has already been quoted. His visit to Jerusalem was accompanied by characteristically "strange actions." In Gaza he had appointed twelve rabbis who were to accompany him to the site of the Temple (occupied by the Muslim sanctuary *Ḥaram esh-Sharif,* the so-called Mosque of Omar), where he was to perform a sacrifice. This symbolic action was probably intended to mark the beginning of the rebuilding of the Temple. Preparations were apparently made with a certain amount of publicity. Sabbatai's fondness for making appointments and bestowing titles again asserted itself, and Rabbi Najara of Gaza, who was not of priestly descent, was appointed high priest.[116] Sabbatai later told Laniado that when news of the preparations reached the rabbis of Jerusalem, they rent their clothes in mourning over the blasphemy and in fear of the dire consequences for the community which such an entry into a Muslim holy place would provoke. They sent a message to Sabbatai: "Why do you want to deliver Israel to death and why do you destroy the Lord's inheritance?" Sabbatai abandoned his plan but "smote his hands and cried: Woe! It was so near, and now it has been put far off" because of the interference of the rabbis.[117]

Whatever the measure of truth in Laniado's story, it is certain that Sabbatai did go up to Jerusalem accompanied by some followers. We may safely disregard the legendary account of the journey, which we owe, no doubt, to enthusiastic participants who left out the more realistic and sobering details. According to the letter from Gaza, Sabbatai took about forty men and traveled with royal pomp and circumstance over fearful and terrifying roads "which even a bird

115. Shadday = Sabbatai Ṣevi by *gematria.*

116. In addition to his appointment as high priest, Najara was also made representative of the tribe of Reuben. As late as 1672 he still signed his name Reuben Jacob Najara (during a visit to Morocco; see Freimann, p. 98).

117. Laniado's letter (*Zion,* VII [1942], 192). The detail agrees with a curious fact concerning Jacob Najara, who inscribed his name (with some others from Gaza) on the tomb of Aaron, the first high priest, where he seems to have performed a mystical *tiqqun.* The late I. Ben-Zvi was the first to point out the connection between the pilgrimage to Aaron's tomb and Najara's appointment as high priest by the messiah (*Zion,* VIII [1943], 156–57). The problem of the resumption of sacrifices was actually discussed by several halakhic authorities at a previous period.

would not fly over," and many mighty miracles were wrought on the way.[118] For some mysterious reason not all the companions could enter the Holy City, where everyone paid homage to the messiah.[119] In reality Sabbatai found himself in trouble soon after his arrival in Jerusalem. Sabbatian sources mention quarrels about the funds entrusted to him. One report says that he was accused of withholding some of the money he had collected in Egypt. According to another and rather improbable version, the rabbis of Jerusalem were furious because he had distributed the money to the poor and the widows, without paying to them and to the local institutions their shares. The Egyptian letters report that two charges were brought against him before "the judge of the city," namely the Turkish cadi: "that he wanted to rule, and that he had embezzled some of the money of his mission." The report suggests that the rabbis may have tried to get rid of Sabbatai by denouncing him as a rebel to the Turkish authorities. If this is true, then it remains unexplained why the attempt failed. Sabbatai was acquitted by the cadi, and the acquittal is described in the Sabbatian letters as a great miracle. Sabbatai also demanded permission "to ride on horseback through the city, although [Muslim] custom strictly forbade a Jew to ride a horse," and his request was granted. Seven times he rode around the city, showing himself to the public "on his horse, and clothed in a green mantle in accordance with his mystical intentions."[120] The green mantle worn by Sabbatai during this symbolic circuit is reminiscent of a messianic movement in Baghdad in the first half of the twelfth century, where believers in the message "attired themselves in green."[121] The choice

118. For the date of the journey to Jerusalem, see p. 237. Probably it took place in the middle of June, 1665.

119. *Kiryath Sepher,* XXXIII (1958), 534.

120. See Haberman, pp. 208–9; the letter of December, 1665, published by G. Scholem in *Zion,* X (1945), 63 (which also mentions the green cloak or possibly headgear); Sasportas, p. 17; Baruch of Arezzo (Freimann, p. 48). According to the French *Relation* (p. 8), Sabbatai visited the cities of Palestine unaccompanied by his prophet. The distribution to the poor of the 4,000 grossos (i.e., reales) which he had collected in Egypt is reported by the Dutch correspondent of the *Hollandtze Merkurius.* The other Christian writers in Smyrna and Constantinople, as well as Leyb b. Ozer, had not heard of the denunciation and the proceedings before the cadi.

121. See Jacob Mann, in *Ha-Tequfah,* XXIV (1928), 346. Cf. also S. Goitein's article on "The Scroll of Obadiah the Proselyte," in *Ha-Arets* of December 9, 1955.

of color is not explained, although Muslim influence may be assumed. In Muslim tradition green is the symbolic color of Paradise; the green robe would thus signify the robe of Paradise, and the garment of the new age.

But there were more dramatic incidents than the proceedings before the cadi. Sabbatai was still in a state of illumination, and his inspired behavior inevitably created a major scandal. Abraham Cuenque, a devout Sabbatian believer, reports (no doubt on the authority of local Palestinian traditions) that "Sabbatai Ṣevi, accompanied by many followers, proceeded via Ramleh to Jerusalem; and in Jerusalem he did many things that were passing strange and incomprehensible to all who beheld them."[122] Cuenque carefully omits details, but the Dutch correspondent from Smyrna informed his readers that the rabbis of Jerusalem wanted to kill Sabbatai because he had blasphemed God and His Law.[123] What was the outrage referred to? The clue seems to be provided by Moses [b. Isaac] b. Ḥabib, who reports a detail, which, in the light of our other knowledge, is eminently credible. According to Moses b. Ḥabib, it was a well-known fact among the scholars in Jerusalem and Hebron[124] that even "before his apostasy" Sabbatai had caused ten Israelites to eat *ḥeleb,* "fat of the kidney," and had actually "recited a benediction over this ritually forbidden fat: 'Blessed art Thou, O Lord, who permittest that which is forbidden.' I also heard from a very pious scholar that he had done likewise, but had then repented of it."[125] The wording of the benediction is confirmed by another source too (see above, p. 162) and the consumption of prohibited fat is known to us from the subsequent history of the movement as a Sabbatian ritual. The significance of the act is evident. The consumption of certain kinds of animal fat (*ḥeleb*) is strictly prohibited by the Torah, and is punishable by "excision"; in biblical language, "that soul shall be cut off from among his people." Of the thirty-six transgressions listed in the Talmud as incurring this punishment, the majority are sexual offenses, and incest in particular. The eating of fat is not, in itself, an act

122. Emden, p. 38.

123. *Hollandtze Merkurius,* January, 1666. The Dutch word *lastering* may refer to blasphemous actions as well as to verbal utterances.

124. Hebron was the home town of Abraham Cuenque, whose vague hints in the same direction have already been mentioned.

125. Emden, p. 53.

that would yield special pleasure or gratification, and the transgression of this particular prohibition should therefore, rather, be interpreted in a symbolic sense. It was, in fact, a demonstration of antinomian, revolutionary messianism, in keeping with the tenor of the accompanying benediction (which, we remember, also symbolized the "new law and new commandments" revealed to Sabbatai Ṣevi in 1658). If anything of the kind really happened in Jerusalem, then the violent reaction of the rabbis should occasion no surprise. Sabbatai had raised the standard of rebellion against the hallowed traditions of the Law, and abrogated its prohibitions—including, by implication, those against incest and fornication. The symbolic overtones of his breaking the taboo on *ḥeleb* must have been obvious to anyone. To make things worse, Sabbatai demanded that others do likewise. There is no reason for doubting Moses b. Ḥabib's testimony regarding a rabbi of his acquaintance who had allowed himself to be seduced in the atmosphere of enthusiasm, but who repented afterward. The relevance of the testimony may be impugned on the grounds that it makes no mention of the date and place of the event. But on the other hand, the explicit statement that the story was a tradition of the rabbis of Jerusalem and Hebron[126] suggests that the event took place in Palestine and not in Salonika or Constantinople. At the same time it should be emphasized that there is no evidence of debauchery during Sabbatai's fits of manic enthusiasm at that period. All allegations of immoral excesses date from a later period, and more particularly from the period after his apostasy.

Cuenque's story, though it had passed the filter of Sabbatian legend before being written down twenty-five years after the event, is confirmed by letters from the Orient (including Palestine) which were received in Amsterdam as early as December, 1665. In these letters the writers, Sabbatian believers, reported that Sabbatai had been "banished and expelled by the rabbis of Jerusalem because of unusual actions which they could not understand."[127] Curiously

126. Many of the rabbis in Hebron remained faithful believers even after Sabbatai's apostasy.

127. The letters are no longer extant, but their substance is contained in Christian news reports (probably written in Latin or German) sent from Amsterdam to certain Polish noblemen. The Polish text was published by Balaban, *Sabataizm w Polsce*, p. 40. The letters, like other early reports, confuse Nathan and Sabbatai Ṣevi, but it is obvious that the account refers to the latter.

enough, this particular scandal did not come to the ears of Sasportas. All he knew was that Sabbatai had "conducted himself with royal pomp" in Gaza and Jerusalem and that the rabbis of Jerusalem did not believe in him.[128] For some unknown reason he could obtain no information about the events in Jerusalem from the anti-Sabbatian rabbis in Egypt, who did not reply to his queries. He did see letters written by "believers," but he ignored their contents.

The rabbis in Jerusalem were apparently divided over the "faith." There was no doubt that the appearance of the prophet had wrought a great awakening of piety, moved many hearts, and even neutralized to some extent the disconcerting impression made by the messiah. The prophet had been examined by rabbinic scholars who had to admit that the spirit was truly upon him. The conclusion was inescapable: if Nathan was a true prophet, then his prophecy *ipso facto* established the position of the messiah and some, possibly kabbalistic, explanation had to be found for the latter's unbecoming and questionable behavior. The messianic decision really hinged on the credit accorded to the prophet, and some rabbis became his followers at least at the beginning. R. Abraham b. Samuel Gedaliah, a highly esteemed scholar and the author of learned rabbinic works,[129] who had served abroad as emissary of the community of Jerusalem, persevered in his belief for a whole year. In 1666 he still signed, together with R. Jacob Najara, letters to the Diaspora confirming the prophetic dignity of Nathan. With other rabbis he had gone to Gaza, and accompanied the prophet on his pilgrimages to Jabne and Lydda[130] where they prayed at the tombs of the ancient sages that Nathan, guided by the Holy Spirit, pointed out to them[131] (precisely as Isaac Luria

128. Sasportas, pp. 21, 46.

129. See Frumkin, *Toledoth Ḥakhmey Yerushalayim*, pt. II, pp. 33–34; Is. Tishby in *Kiryath Sepher*, XXV (1949), 113–14. He is quoted by Elijah Kohen of Smyrna, *Mizbeaḥ ᵓEliyahu* (1867), fol. 122c. He died in 1672; an elegy on his death by R. S. Graziano is mentioned in *RÉJ*, IV (1882), 118.

130. Important centers of rabbinic learning in the first centuries of our era.

131. Letter from Egypt (Haberman, p. 210); letter from Skoplje (drawing on letters from Palestine) dated December 11, 1665 (*Zion*, X [1945], 64); Cuenque (Emden, p. 38). The similarity with Luria's habit of discovering tombs and obtaining inspiration from the spirits of the saints buried there is brought out clearly in all the accounts. A very detailed and highly colored account of the discovery of the tomb of R. Eliezer b. Hyrkanos was later given by Samuel Gandoor to Shemaya de Mayo, the rabbi of Kastoria. Gandoor was one of the party accom-

had done a century before him). R. David Yiṣḥaki of Jerusalem became a fervent believer, and persevered in his faith for many years;[132] his son, R. Abraham Yiṣḥaki later became one of the most prominent opponents of the movement. One of the letters written from Gaza to Egypt by (probably) Ḥayyim Joseph,[133] the brother of the *chelebi* Raphael Joseph, reports that Nathan had "invited some rabbis from Jerusalem for the sake of the *tiqqun* of their souls, among them the rabbis Primo and Galanté. They repaired thither at his behest, likewise also a Sephardi of the Kuta family, and the beadle of the brotherhood, who for a time had been in Egypt, for he [Nathan] had assured them that they were all superior souls." The genuineness of this report is evident, though the identity of the Sephardi of the Kuta, or Guta,[134] family is not clear. R. Nathan Guta, who was in Jerusalem at the time, confesses in a responsum that although he never believed in Sabbatai, he yet did not dare to speak out. Possibly the reference

---

panying Nathan on that trip. The account is preserved in *Maᶜaseh Ṣaddiqim* by Abraham Kalfon composed in Tripoli 1815, MS. Ben-Zvi Institute, §132.

132. See Sasportas, p. 187, and G. Scholem, *Zion,* VI (1941), 87–88, XIII/XIV (1948), 59–62. Born in Salonika, he went to Palestine where he became the son-in-law of the famous kabbalist Abraham Azulay of Hebron. He died in Jerusalem and probably knew Sabbatai in the years 1662–63.

133. The letters from Egypt published by Haberman are based, up to p. 210, line 10, on reports from Samuel Gandoor. The authorship of the continuation (p. 210, line 11–p. 211, line 8) can be established by the following considerations: (*a*) Emanuel Frances (*Ṣevi Muddaḥ,* p. 134) mentions that the *chelebi* had sent his brother Ḥayyim Joseph to Gaza. A letter by Ḥayyim Joseph (or extracts from it) appeared in English translation in *Several New Letters concerning the Jews,* p. 1. (*b*) This letter, which was written toward the end of 1665, reports the same legend about R. Israel Benjamin of Jerusalem (see below, pp. 263–65) as the letter from Gaza in Haberman, p. 210, bottom. It seems reasonable to assume that both letters are from the pen of the same correspondent. The news reports from Gaza were passed on by the *chelebi* to Italy. In fact the English letter concludes with the information: "Wrote from the Treasurer of all Egypt to his Brother here [i.e., in Leghorn] concerning the Prophesie relating to the Jews. Leghorn January 25, 1666." We know from other sources that one of the *chelebi*'s brothers, Solomon Joseph, was in Leghorn in 1665–66. Baruch of Arezzo, who also tells the legend of R. Israel Benjamin (Freimann, p. 46), surely did not take it from the English pamphlet but, rather, from a copy of the letters sent from Cairo to Leghorn and Venice.

134. See M. Benayahu, *Asaf Jubilee Volume* (1953), p. 116, who has shown, on the basis of the spelling in other documents, that the names Kuta and Guta are identical.

is not to this well-known rabbi, but to some unknown member of his family. Samuel Primo and his friend Mattathias Bloch Ashkenazi[135]—both eminent rabbinic scholars and confirmed kabbalists—wholeheartedly embraced the faith. Primo later left Gaza, possibly with a whole group of believers from Palestine, to join Sabbatai in Smyrna and Gallipoli, where he became his secretary. Moses Galanté was one of the leading Talmudic scholars in Jerusalem and the father-in-law of Jacob Ḥagiz (possibly only after 1666). He died in 1689 as *Rishon le-Zion,* meaning, the "First in Zion," a traditional title of the Sephardi chief rabbi of the Holy Land, and his memory was greatly revered by the Palestinian rabbis. Galanté must have known Sabbatai from his first sojourn in Jerusalem. If he went to Gaza at Nathan's bidding and remained there, he may have missed the scandal in Jerusalem. He certainly took no part in the proceedings of excommunication, of which his son-in-law was one of the initiators. His grandson Moses Ḥagiz writes: "I heard my grandfather, the celebrated R. Moses Galanté of blessed memory, quoting a remark which my father of blessed memory [R. Jacob Ḥagiz] used to make in jest: 'Behold a messiah who is afraid of my ban of excommunication.'"[136] Moses Ḥagiz hardly knew his father, who died when the boy was five years old, and was brought up by his maternal grandfather. Galanté's words seem to imply that his son-in-law had had a part in

135. His full name is given on the title page of his *Kelal Qatan* (Constantinople, 1665) as "Mattathias, also known as Lieberman . . . the son of R. Wolf Reich Feiwels of the Bloch family from Cracow"; see A. Yaᶜari, "Who Was the Sabbatian Prophet Mattathias Bloch?" in *Kiryath Sepher*, XXXVI (1961), 525–34. He was thus descended from a very well-known family in Cracow. As Yaᶜari has shown, "Lieberman" is the Germano-Jewish equivalent of "Mattathias." His father's name "Wolf" accounts for the usual signature "Mattathias ben Benjamin Zeʾeb Ashkenazi Bloch." The aforementioned *Kelal Katan* (of which very few copies are extant) is an extract from his larger work *Kelal Gadol*. It is a homily on Deut. 32, which Bloch preached in Jassy in Rumania, in the autumn of 1660 (Yaᶜari, p. 529)—or should it be 1665?—on his way to Palestine. He also wrote a kabbalistic work (Yaᶜari, *ibid.*). Bloch had studied in Cracow in the school of R. Menaḥem Mendel Krochmal (a disciple of R. Heshel of Cracow), author of the responsa *Ṣemaḥ Ṣedeq*, who died in Nikolsburg in 1661. R. Mattathias was a survivor of the great massacres 1648–55, as appears from his rhymed ethical will to his sons and disciples (Yaᶜari, pp. 531–32). The chronology seems to indicate that he met Sabbatai Ṣevi neither in 1668 (as stated by Yaᶜari, p. 534), nor in 1663 (as I thought, see *SS*, p. 155), but in 1665, before Sabbatai's departure from Jerusalem.

136. Moses Ḥagiz's annotation to Cuenque (Emden, p. 38).

the excommunication of Sabbatai, but that he himself had not. The deposition of Moses ibn Ḥabib[137] preserves a testimony that is relevant to the issue. In this deposition, R. Abraham Yiṣḥaki—a witness who is hardly suspect of Sabbatian sympathies—is quoted as reporting Galanté's own words to the effect that he had neither despised Sabbatai nor believed in him, but that he had turned against him after having seen letters which Sabbatai had written to Jerusalem and signed "I am the Lord your God Sabbatai Ṣevi."[138] Since then (that is, probably since 1666), "I am cursing him every day." This testimony should be taken with more than a grain of salt, and it clearly represents an attempt to whitewash Galanté and to minimize his involvement with the Sabbatian movement; but whether Galanté himself or his brother-in-law Moses b. Solomon b. Ḥabib, was responsible for this, there is no way of telling. For we possess definite evidence[139] that, for some time, Galanté was an active follower of Sabbatai, and actually one of the prophets who prophesied in Aleppo at the great outpouring of the spirit there on September 19, 1665 (see below, p. 257). As a matter of fact Galanté was traveling abroad, as an emissary of the Jerusalem community, in 1666, during the heyday of the Sabbatian movement. Later this period in his career was removed from the record by making it appear that he had been in Jerusalem all the time. At any rate, he was there in part of June and in July, 1665, and left only "shortly" before he came to Aleppo.

137. Emden, p. 53. The deposition, which contains much important and authentic information together with confused and semilegendary material, has been shown by M. Benayahu as coming from Moses b. Isaac b. Ḥabib from Salonika and not from Moses b. Solomon b. Ḥabib, who died in Jerusalem in 1696 and was the brother-in-law of Moses Galanté, see ch. 2, n. 87.

138. *Ibid.* The details about Sabbatai's letters and Galanté's reaction to them may well come from Moses b. Ḥabib. We know that Sabbatai signed letters in this fashion also in 1666. Another detail in the deposition may contain a valuable core of truth, in spite of its patently legendary presentation. Sabbatai and his companions are said to have visited the tomb of the prophet Samuel, where, after some riotous behavior, Sabbatai struck the grave with a stick. Thereby he "took away" Samuel's prophecy, which he transferred to "a certain licentious and profligate fellow Samuel Lazabani." Considering Sabbatai's fondness for this kind of ceremonial (see below, p. 393), it is not impossible that some such ceremony took place, and that Sabbatai appointed Nathan's father-in-law, Samuel Lissabona, to the dignity of "Prophet Samuel."

139. MS. formerly in the library of the Jewish Community of Vienna 141, no. 8, a photostat of which is in my possession.

Sabbatai was put into the ban, in spite of the enthusiastic belief of some rabbis and the hesitation of others. We know the names of four of the rabbis who took a leading part in the proceedings: R. Abraham Amigo, at the time apparently at the head of the Jerusalem rabbinate;[140] R. Jacob Ṣemaḥ, the leading kabbalist in the city and an acknowledged authority on Lurianic kabbalah; R. Samuel Garmizan (or Garmizano);[141] and R. Jacob Ḥagiz, Nathan's principal teacher. One of the Sabbatian letters to Egypt contains the purely imaginary, but nonetheless instructive, information that the rabbis of Jerusalem "had decided to go and ask pardon of A. N. [Abraham Nathan] and S. Ṣ. [Sabbatai Ṣevi] before he proceeded to Smyrna." Who precisely craved the messiah's pardon? The extant manuscript copies of the letters show two readings. One version[142] has: "the members of the 'close' in Jerusalem"; the other[143] reads: "the kabbalist rabbis of Jerusalem" (the two readings are very similar in Hebrew). All texts agree that "their chief opposed the 'faith.'" Historically both versions point to the truth, though textually the former reading seems to be more correct.[144] *Hesger* ("close"

140. See Frumkin, *Toledoth Ḥakhmey Yerushalayim,* pt. II, pp. 54–55. H. Y. D. Azulay saw letters which the rabbis of Constantinople had sent "with great reverence" to Amigo. When the rabbinate of Constantinople made official inquiries regarding Nathan from the rabbinic court in Jerusalem, they addressed their letter to Amigo (Sasportas, p. 123).

141. Amigo, Ṣemaḥ, and Garmizan appear to have been the three members of the court who signed the ban of excommunication. The three names are given in Moses [b. Isaac] b. Ḥabib's deposition (Emden, p. 53), but the third name is spelled Samuel ibn Sahn. Freimann (note to the supplements to Frumkin's *Toledoth Ḥakhmey Yerushalayim*, pt. II, p. 17) suspected a copyist's or printer's error, but the existence of a R. Saul ibn Ṣaḥwin or Ṣaḥin in Jerusalem has been established by recently discovered documents (see above, ch. 2, n. 202). On the other hand, we also know that Samuel Garmizan was a militant anti-Sabbatian (M. Benayahu discovered, in a MS. in the Badhab Collection, now in the National Library, Jerusalem, a work by Garmizan, *ᵓImrey Noᶜam,* which contains a reference to a sermon preached in 1666 against Sabbatai Ṣevi), and it seems more likely that Moses b. Ḥabib's reference is to him and not to Saul Ṣaḥwin.

142. MS. Schocken (published by Haberman), and MS. Brit. Mus., Margoliouth 1077, reads: *Ḥakhmey ha-Hesger.*

143. MS. Columbia University, New York, reads: *Ḥakhmey ha-Sod.*

144. A copyist's corruption of the unfamiliar *hesger* to the more familiar *ha-sod* is more probable than the converse. The expression *ḥakhmey ha-sod* is most unlikely in the 17th century, when kabbalists were referred to as *ḥakhmey ha-Kabbalah.*

or "cloister") is a technical term denoting a privately maintained retreat for rabbinic studies; it corresponds precisely to its Yiddish counterpart *klaus* (from *clausura*). The college *Beth Ya^c^akob* founded by the rich de Vega family of Leghorn was, indeed, known as *hesger*,[145] and Jacob Ḥagiz was its principal, or "chief." Abraham Amigo seems to have been the president of the rabbinic court. But also the opposition of the "chief" kabbalist, the octogenarian Jacob Ṣemaḥ, is a well-established fact. An Armenian poem on Sabbatai Ṣevi, composed soon after his apostasy in Constantinople and preserving many important details, tells of Sabbatai's failure in Jerusalem because of an "old scholar and physician from Portugal"—none other than Jacob Ṣemaḥ—who preached against him and forced him to leave the city.[146]

Moses Ḥagiz's memory served him right, and the detail about Sabbatai's excommunication is no mere rumor, as might, perhaps, be suspected after reading the report of de la Croix or the French *Relation*.[147] Coenen was told in Smyrna that the rabbis of Jerusalem had not believed in Sabbatai, but had expelled and excommunicated him, and sent a full report of his doings to Constantinople. Thereupon the rabbis of the capital dispatched a letter, signed by R. Yomtob (b. Ḥananiah) b. Yaqar, to their colleagues in Smyrna. R. Yomtob b. Yaqar had added a postscript after his signature: "The man who spreads these innovations is a heretic, and whoever kills him will be accounted as one who has saved many souls, and the hand that strikes him down without delay will be blessed in the eyes of God and man."[148] It appears from the sequel of Coenen's account that R. Ḥayyim Benveniste of Smyrna did, in fact, receive this letter. The

145. On the "cloister" in Jerusalem, see the important documents published by M. Benayahu in *HUCA*, XXI (1946), Hebrew section, 1–28.

146. See Galanté, p. 84, and G. Scholem in *Kiryath Sepher,* XXVI (1950), 185–88. According to his own testimony, Ṣemaḥ was born in Viano de Caminha, a well-known marrano center in Portugal. He was then in his seventies.

147. De la Croix, p. 288; *Relation,* p. 14. The anonymous French author knew that Sabbatai was expelled from Jerusalem, but attributes the quarrel with the rabbis to Sabbatai's refusal to return once more to Egypt as a collector of charities.

148. Coenen, p. 12. The details of the account show that Coenen either saw the letter from Constantinople (including a copy of the Jerusalem ban of excommunication), or else received a very precise and reliable report of its contents. Coenen knew enough Hebrew to understand at least the main outlines of the document.

conclusion seems warranted that Sabbatai was excommunicated not on account of his messianic pretensions—the prophet Nathan continued to live in Palestine without tangible molestation until after the apostasy—but because of certain provocative actions and "innovations" which were considered blasphemous violations of the Law. The news letter in the Dutch journal suggests the same. In fact, Sabbatai's manner of tampering with the Law, and even more his provocative benediction over the permitting of all things forbidden while transgressing a major prohibition, would have brought down a ban of excommunication on anyone's head in those days. The abolition of the fast of the Seventeenth of Tammuz for all believers would by itself suffice to provoke rabbinic reprisals, all the more so as it had been preceded by the discontinuation of another traditional custom. Since with the advent of the messiah the redemption of Israel had begun, and the Shekhinah was no longer in exile, the midnight liturgy of mourning and lamentation over the "exile of the Shekhinah" could be allowed to lapse. During his first weeks in Gaza, Sabbatai had changed the ritual of the "midnight devotions," instituted by the Safed kabbalists, and had substituted for its first, rather melancholic part (known as *tiqqun Rachel*) a new liturgy, consisting probably of hymns of comfort and joy. The new liturgy was forwarded to Raphael Joseph in Egypt and to other friends.[149]

Alternative accounts of the motives underlying the rabbinic opposition to Sabbatai in Jerusalem are less plausible. Emanuel Frances attributes the hostility of the rabbis to Sabbatai's messianic pretensions and to their fear of the Turkish authorities. According to his version of the story, the community of Jerusalem[150] had written to Gaza, with

149. Cf. Nathan's *Treatise on the Dragons* (in *Beᶜ Iqvoth Mashiaḥ*, p. 15); "Since the year 417 [1657], the holiness of the [cosmic] Sabbath has begun, and the Shekhinah has risen from her exile. . . . Therefore we must no longer perform the [midnight] devotion and weep over the exile of the Shekhinah as we were wont to do, but [we should perform] the devotion instituted by AMIRAH *as you well know*" (italics added, G.S.).

150. The printed text (*Ṣevi Muddaḥ*, p. 134) says "Gaza," but this is an obvious error. A few lines further down Frances explicitly states that "the whole community" of Gaza were believers, and that they enticed the *chelebi's* brother, Ḥayyim Joseph, to believe in Sabbatai and Nathan. See also the end of the sentence, *ibid.*, ". . . the rabbis of Jerusalem." Perhaps the word "Gaza" in Frances' text is no error, and merely the preposition "to" has dropped out: "Also [to] the community in Gaza [they] sent a letter. . . ."

the advice to "separate yourselves from the tents of these madmen, lest both we and you be found sinning against the king [that is, the sultan], but neither Sabbatai nor Nathan would listen to the voice of the rabbis of Jerusalem." The Jerusalem rabbinate are also said to have written to the congregations in Egypt "to stand for their life and to put away the madness of the people which incline to Sabbatai Ṣevi. But the congregations would not hearken to the voice of the rabbis of Jerusalem." The excommunication is not mentioned at all—only attempts to warn and caution. Though unconfirmed from other sources, it is not unlikely that some such warnings were sent to Nathan and Sabbatai at the beginning of their messianic activities; yet it remains unexplained why so implacable an opponent as Frances remained unaware of the radical measures taken against Sabbatai: his excommunication and banishment from Jerusalem. Perhaps there is some confusion in his account, and the letter of warning to the congregations in Egypt was merely a duplicate of the report sent by the Jerusalem rabbinate to Constantinople.

IV

Sabbatai's opponents were powerful enough to expell him from Jerusalem; they could not stop the growth of the movement. The presence of an accredited "true" prophet, whose messages—unlike the actions of the messiah—were comprehensible to everyone, outweighed the rabbinic ban of excommunication. The prophet displayed remarkable spiritual power. On the one hand, he appealed to the traditional longing for redemption, successfully directing it into channels that were immediately meaningful to the public: penitence and mortification. On the other hand, he succeeded in explaining to selected individuals—including, we dare say, Sabbatai Ṣevi himself—the mystical significance of the strange and repellent aspects of the messiah's personality. These explanations did not reach a wider public. They were reserved for a small elite of kabbalist initiates, and exercised a considerable fascination on scholars living in the peculiar mental climate of Lurianism. Nathan, in fact, succeeded in splitting the kabbalist camp, since not all kabbalists would follow Jacob Ṣemaḥ in his denial of any possibility of bridging between the Lurianic tradition (to whose literary crystallization he had contributed so much) and Nathan's message. Others were attracted to Nathan's doctrine that the messiah's behavior, strange as it might appear, was essentially a *tiqqun* of profound mystical significance. The absence of a more sharply delineated messiah-image from kabbalistic tradition now avenged itself. The enthusiasts could argue that in matters messianic the most unexpected was really the most natural.

More decisive, however, than the esoteric doctrines that were evolved and crystallized during the following months in Nathan's letters and homilies, was the explosive force of the messianic message as such. It appealed to the people as a whole, stirred up hidden longings, and triggered a mighty emotional upheaval. Sabbatai's absence from the Palestinian stage during those months was a decisive factor in the subsequent development of events. The main impetus came from the prophet and the circle of believers around him in the Holy Land. The prophecy of imminent redemption filled their hearts, while the tragic, disconcerting and, indeed, somewhat disturbing person of the messiah was not at hand. It is a remarkable fact: the mighty wave of penitence and messianic fervor was unrelated to whatever Sabbatai did or did not do in the months following his expulsion from Jerusalem; it gushed forth from Gaza and was strengthened by the developments there, or—to be more precise—by the fast-spreading legends about what was going on in Gaza. The sudden and almost explosive surge of miracle stories is of considerable interest in more than one respect. The more the concrete figure of the messiah recedes and becomes blurred, the better the climate for the rank growth of a messianic legend which substituted for Sabbatai's actual deeds fantastic accounts of performances far more marvelous and, moreover, far less offensive to religious sentiment. The messiah functioned as a slogan or image rather than as a living personality. Unencumbered by his actual presence, the movement developed rapidly by following the lines of popular apocalyptic tradition. An unprecedented atmosphere spread over Palestine. Until Tammuz [June–July], 1665, no miracles are reported. Nathan's prophecy had explicitly stated that Israel would have to believe in the messiah without signs and wonders, and hence nobody felt the need, during the first weeks, to credit Sabbatai with miracles. But Nathan's stern doctrine was one thing, the demands of popular belief were another. Curiously enough, the manifest and irreconcilable opposition between the two tendencies was hardly noticed, and certainly not disturbing. From Sabbatai's departure in midsummer to about the end of 1665, an unreal and legendary atmosphere characterizes all reports emanating from Palestine. Yet these reports, which reached Europe, stimulated the great awakening. Particularly noteworthy in these reports is the small part played by Sabbatai; the stage is occupied by Nathan and the miracles taking place in his surroundings.

The ban against Sabbatai played no role at all in the subsequent development. It was as if it never existed. It seems strange that a sentence of excommunication from the Holy City, signed by no less an authority than Jacob Ṣemaḥ, whose name was widely known in kabbalistic circles, should have carried so little weight; but perhaps historians have tended to overrate the influence of the Jerusalem rabbinate in those days. Its authority would evaporate in a serious clash of interests, or be swept away by a wave of enthusiasm. Another factor, too, has to be taken into consideration. Not all kabbalists shared the extremely conservative attitude of Jacob Ṣemaḥ, whose numerous writings bespeak a somewhat rigid and narrow adherence to Vital's system, rather than bold and original thought. The teachings of Luria and Vital harbored very different possibilities as well. Indeed, for many kabbalists the tremendous gnostic drama of redemption, which is the essence of Lurianism, was no mere booklore but a deeply felt experience whose inner tension would find its natural and adequate discharge in actual messianism. It would be these kabbalists who everywhere embraced the good news from Gaza.

Since Sabbatai's departure from Gaza, he and Nathan followed two different lines of activity, though to speak of activity in connection with Sabbatai is, perhaps, something of a misnomer. His performance consisted mostly in his mere presence and appearance, and in the impression made by his strange character and his noble and engaging bearing. He probably also carried letters from Nathan, whose energetic activity was more than metaphorical. Sabbatai might "manifest" or "conceal" his messianic glory in accordance with the rhythm of his sick soul, but even during his longest periods of what was kabbalistically termed the "hiding of the face" (periods of eclipse), his prophet would be indefatigably at work.

Sabbatai left Jerusalem in Tammuz, arriving in Aleppo on the Eighth of Ab (July 20, 1665).[151] He seems to have said very little about the circumstances of his departure in his autobiographical account to Solomon Laniado, the rabbi of the community, unless it

151. Letter from Aleppo, *Kiryath Sepher,* XXXIII (1958), 534.

is to the latter's discretion that we owe the rather vague statement "that there had been much strife between him [Sabbatai] and the people of Jerusalem." Sabbatai therefore "left Jerusalem and cursed them. But on his way he saw a group of Jews going to Jerusalem, and he was seized with pity for them. So he sent them his pardon, and turned his curse into a blessing." Sabbatian legend promptly seized upon this detail and completely inverted it; in the letters from Palestine to Egypt it is said that the rabbis of Jerusalem had decided to ask Sabbatai's pardon before he left for Smyrna. He passed through Safed and Damascus[152] on his way to Aleppo, and his arrival produced remarkable charismatic effects everywhere. Men and women—subsequently also children—would be filled with enthusiasm, fall to the ground, and stammer prophecies. At first this phenomenon was restricted to places where Sabbatai's actual presence had converted messianic longing into mass ecstasy. But soon the wave of prophecy spread to countries which had never seen Sabbatai and never would see him. We shall have to examine the phenomenon in greater detail. For the present it suffices to point out that the prophetic outbreak seems to be connected with Sabbatai's journey. The mass prophecy in Smyrna began in the second or third week of December, 1665, yet prophetic manifestations in Safed, Damascus, and Aleppo are reported in letters that were written earlier. As early as the middle of November it was known in Egypt that ten prophets and ten prophetesses had arisen in Safed "and prophesied great things."[153] In Safed, Sabbatai almost certainly met the aged kabbalist Benjamin ha-Levi, no less celebrated an authority on Lurianic kabbalah than Jacob Ṣemaḥ. Ha-Levi became a fervent believer, and later wrote letters to his friends in Italy "on the subject of our redemption by our king Sabbatai Ṣevi."[154] The precise dates of Sabbatai's movements are unknown, and so are the names of his companions, if any. Perhaps he traveled alone.[155]

152. Letters from Damascus concerning Sabbatai are referred to in a letter from Skoplje of December 11, 1665; see *Zion,* X (1945), 63.

153. See the document dated the 18th of Kislev, 426, published by Cassuto in *Vessillo Israelitico,* LV (1907), 330. This is, incidentally, the first reliable reference to Safed in the annals of the Sabbatian movement. Safed was just being resettled after a long period of decline; see above, p. 186.

154. These letters are referred to by him in a later letter (Freimann, p. 59), written after Sabbatai's apostasy. A. Yaᶜari (*Beḥinoth,* no. 9 [1956], p. 78) doubts the authenticity of the letter, without valid reason.

155. De la Croix (p. 288) says that the rabbis of Jerusalem gave "Sabbatai,

Sabbatai was received in Aleppo with great honor. As late as 1668 the rabbi of the city still remembered that "he came here, to Aleppo, and the land was resplendent with his glory."[156] We have firsthand knowledge about Sabbatai's demeanor in Aleppo in the letter written by Laniado and another rabbi, Nissim b. Mordecai Dayyan, on February 22, 1666, the original of which is extant. They tell that at first he did not make any messianic claim and "did not reveal anything" about himself. He asked to be treated as just any other rabbi, and ordered the precentor to call him up to the reading of the Torah in synagogue not as the messianic king—as which he surely was announced by letters from Gaza—but with the familiar appellative for a rabbi: "the distinguished *ḥakham*." In private, however, he was much less restrained, and his autobiographical tale made a profound impression on Laniado and the other rabbis, who repeated—and thereby preserved—this extremely valuable memoir in the letters which they later wrote in support of the movement and its chief protagonists.[157] The faith and the enthusiasm of the people of Aleppo knew no bounds, and found expression in many incidents that were immediately reported to Egypt and to Constantinople. A

---

his wife and servants" three days to leave the city. Servants are mentioned in the plural, but de la Croix's details are not very reliable. The problem of Sabbatai's valet has been discussed above, pp. 151 f. An interesting and possibly authentic detail is mentioned by de la Croix, who reports that the rabbis attempted to impose silence on Nathan. His messianic preaching was bound to endanger the Jewish people, and if he was really sent by God, his message would be vindicated anyhow (p. 289). If de la Croix's information is correct, it may perhaps, be linked with the testimony of Moses Ḥagiz (Emden, p. 36) regarding an exchange of letters between his father and Nathan. Perhaps Jacob Ḥagiz, at the instance of the rabbinic court, attempted to influence Nathan. The accounts in some of the earlier pamphlets regarding Nathan's persecution by the rabbis (and their subsequent apologies) seem to be based on confusion with the persecution of Sabbatai, and no conclusions can be drawn from them; see also below, p. 264.

156. Laniado's letter, *Zion,* VII (1942), p. 192.

157. In the original (Hebrew) edn. of this work (*SS*, p. 208, n. 2), I mourned the loss, during the Second World War, of MS. Epstein (Vienna), which contained what appeared to be another letter of Laniado concerning Sabbatai Ṣevi (see A. Z. Schwarz, *Die hebräischen Handschriften in Oesterreich,* I [1931]. Since then the MS. of this specific letter has turned up and reached the Jewish National Library in Jerusalem; see the article in *Kiryath Sepher,* XXIII (1958), p. 534.

detailed summary of one such letter, written in October or November, 1665, has been preserved for us by the French diplomat de la Croix.[158] Nathan, we are told, had written to Aleppo and warned the community not to do as the people of Jerusalem, who had driven away their king and brought upon themselves the curse of God. They should, rather, honor him and beg him to stay with them, for in his presence there would be great blessing for them. Blessings flowed in great abundance, as the letters from Aleppo testify, though the particular charisma of prophecy began to manifest itself only on the Day of Atonement, September 19, about six weeks after Sabbatai's departure.[159] "There are today in Aleppo twenty prophets, among them Rabbi Galanté and master Aaron Isaiah ha-Kohen, and four prophetesses."[160] Another letter gives the names of six prophets.[161] The identity of "Rabbi Galanté" is proved by another letter sent to one

158. De la Croix, pp. 289–92. The details given in this particular letter can be checked against the information contained in another letter from Aleppo, a partial copy of which (made in Skoplje) was forwarded to Italy (see G. Scholem, in *Zion,* X [1945], 63–64). There is even external evidence showing that this letter is genuine and not one of the author's belletristic fictions. All the fictitious letters are printed by de la Croix in italics (i.e., as "letters"), whereas this particular letter appears as part of the text. Perhaps de la Croix was not so much reproducing a letter as summarizing several letters from Aleppo. The legendary atmosphere of the reports seems to reflect the revivalist mood in Aleppo, and not to be due to de la Croix's editing.

159. Letter from Aleppo, *Kiryath Sepher,* XXXIII (1958), 534. Sabbatai left Aleppo for Smyrna on *Rosh Ḥodesh* Ellul (August 12, 1665).

160. *Zion,* X (1945), 64; see also above, n. 157. The aforementioned MS. Epstein, formerly in the library of the Jewish Community in Vienna, also contained other documents giving information on the movement in Aleppo. These were a letter from Abraham Kohen to his son (MS. 141 in A. Z. Schwarz Catalogue, n. 7) and a letter from Shem Tob b. Samuel Kohen to Constantinople (*ibid.,* no 8), quoted further on.

161. Freimann, p. 49: Isaiah Kohen, Moses Galanté, Daniel Pinto, the wife of Yomtob Laniado, the wife of R. Nissim Mizraḥi, the daughter of R. Abraham Simḥon (thus according to MS. Cambridge, and not Abraham Tammamun as in Freimann). Daniel Pinto was a rabbi in Aleppo where he died 1681. Ḥayyim Joseph's letter to his brother mentions twenty prophets and twenty prophetesses in Aleppo. Christian pamphlets and news letters subsequently increased the numbers. The author of "A New Letter concerning the Jews" of February 26, 1666 (see also in C. Roth, *Anglo-Jewish Letters,* p. 71), reported that from Smyrna Sabbatai "will go straight on to Constantinople, and that in the company of 400 prophets sent to him from Aleppo." This, of course, is fanciful.

of the notables of Constantinople by one Shem Tob Kohen from Aleppo, elaborating the information about the prophets: "We have today in this city twenty prophets and four prophetesses, several of whom are well known and two of them are from among the rabbis, the distinguished R. Moses Galanté, long may he live, who left Palestine as an emissary only a short time ago, and R. Isaiah ha-Kohen, whose fame and pious devotion have long been known to us . . . and also the distinguished R. Solomon Laniado about whom they say that he is [a reincarnation of] Solomon the king, and a *spiritus familiaris* has revealed himself to him, and even the prophet Elijah, of blessed memory."[162] The famous Jerusalemite rabbi was, then, swept away by the general excitement and became a Sabbatian prophet and devotee, something which later tradition tended to forget. Reports received in Leghorn toward the end of 1665 said that even illiterate women had uttered mystic combinations of numbers and letters (*gematria*); one woman had "prophesied" on the verse [Exod. 23:21], "for my name is in him," that the divine name Shadday spelled out in full equaled Sabbatai Ṣevi—evidently an echo of Sabbatai's favorite *gematria*, which was discussed everywhere and by all, also in the hearing of women and children.[163]

De la Croix summarizes the contents of a letter from Aleppo, which his Jewish acquaintance, a former Sabbatian believer, had probably shown him:

> Henceforth the gates of rejoicing were opened, and the days had come when God would fulfill what He had promised through His prophets. The messiah dwelt among them, and thus they depended no longer on Nathan's letters, for they saw with their own eyes and heard with their own ears, and signs were wrought to them. They entreated him to stay with them for at least two months, but he refused as he was in a hurry to get to Smyrna before the appointed time was fulfilled. As they would not let him go without retinue, they provided him with guides who, on their return, told the most marvelous things. Every night they were joined by a host of people who would accompany them, but disappear again at dawn. He always traveled with his *tallith* drawn over his head. When they remonstrated with him that he was endangering his life and theirs by thus showing that he was a Jew, as they might be killed by brigands [who would take them for rich Jewish merchants],

162. MS. Epstein, no. 8. 163. Sasportas, p. 73.

he interrupted them and assured them that it was not of his own will but by command from above that he acted thus. . . . At the end of their letter they added that since they believed in the prophecy of Nathan, they had decided to cease all business, to put on sackcloth and ashes, and to devote themselves to penitence, charity, and prayer so as to be worthy to behold the fulfillment of the prophecy. They also established a fund for the poor, to enable them to give all their time to prayer.[164] Finally they called on their friends [in Constantinople] to follow their example and not that of the people in Jerusalem, who had driven out their king. Already they had felt the abundance of grace, and their wives and children had begun to prophesy. Some of them had fallen to the ground at the sound of the *shofar*[165] and remained lying there, cold, and without pulse or movement, and a wonderful voice come out of their open mouths, articulating Hebrew words which they themselves did not understand, and in the end they exclaimed "Sabbatai Ṣevi our redeemer and holy one."[166]

According to other rumors, the prophet Elijah had appeared in the synagogue of Aleppo, dressed in white with a belt made of black copper.[167] In brief, "the people of Aleppo were like the generation of Hezekiah,"[168] worthy of the advent of the messiah.[169]

These enthusiastic reports from Aleppo must have been received

164. Another letter from Aleppo tells the same story with legendary improvements: the rich established a charity chest, and distributed money to enable the poor to study and pray. When after some time more money was needed, they opened the chest and found it full of coins, as if nothing had ever ever been taken from it (*Zion,* X [1945], 64).

165. The ram's horn, blown on the New Year festival and at the end of the Day of Atonement. De la Croix says "au son des instruments," but it is difficult to see the connection between musical instruments and the outbreak of mass prophecy. I assume that the original Hebrew letter said *shofar,* and that de la Croix's Jewish informant translated "musical instrument." The reference to the *shofar* would agree well with the statement in the letter from Aleppo that the prophecy began on the Day of Atonement.

166. De la Croix, pp. 290–92.

167. *Ibid.,* p. 295. Elijah's appearance in the synagogue is mentioned also at the end of Shem Tob Kohen's letter.

168. According to a rabbinic saying, King Hezekiah was worthy of being the messiah.

169. Letter from Skoplje, *Zion,* X (1945), 64. The text published by Cassuto in *Vessillo Israelitico* (LV [1907], 329) mentions other marvelous events: ten Jews had appeared in the mosque of Smyrna, killed the guard, and ordered the Turks "to pray."

in the various congregations in Turkey not long after the arrival of the letter of the Jerusalem rabbinate with the news of Sabbatai's excommunication. The contrast between the two communications would be enough to split any community into opposing camps, but the sober admonitions from Jerusalem were, inevitably, the less effective. There were not only the glowing reports from Aleppo with their description of Sabbatai's majestic bearing—unmarred, this time, by any "strange actions"—but also a stream of letters from Gaza (and Palestine generally) which made the Jerusalem rabbis appear as blind and deaf to the signs of redemption that were visible everywhere. The combination and convergence of the different reports, with their mixture of facts and legend, were a major factor in bringing about the great awakening in Turkey, and particularly in Constantinople, even before the messianic tidings had reached Europe.

The three months following Sabbatai's departure from Aleppo (August 12, 1665) are a blank in his biography. We know, of course, that he arrived in Smyrna early in September, 1665,[170] but there he remained quiet for two or three months and did not manifest himself as messiah until December. The psychological reason for Sabbatai's passivity and his failure to play the messianic role may well have been a spell first of depression and then of normalcy following upon the manic "illuminate" phase in Aleppo. During these same three months, Nathan and his associates in Gaza were engaged in feverish activity, and it is to them that we must turn now.

Our sources[171] do not permit a reliable reconstruction of the chronology of events in Gaza. After Sabbatai's departure, great multi-

170. Some sources suggest a later date. Coenen (p. 13) says that on the 4th of Tebeth [December 6, 1665] it was "about two months since his return"; similarly the letter dated December 7, 1665 in *Several New Letters concerning the Jews,* p. 6. On the other hand, the emissary from Casale (in Solomon Carpi, *Toledoth Pereṣ,* ed. Bruell, p. 14) as well as a letter from Smyrna dated April, 1666 (and quoted in the *Hollandtze Merkurius,* 1666, p. 3), state that Sabbatai arrived in the month of Ellul (September). He is said to have hastened his departure from Aleppo because he wanted to arrive before the New Year festival. The earlier date is now confirmed by the letter from Aleppo: if he left the city on *Rosh Ḥodesh* Ellul, he could easily have arrived in Smyrna early in September; see G. Scholem in *Kiryath Sepher,* XXXIII (1958), 540. De la Croix's chronology (p. 300), according to which Sabbatai arrived in Smyrna in March, 1665, and remained incognito for six months is impossible.

171. These are (*a*) Cuenque's memoirs, (*b*) letters written between September–November 1665, (*c*) letters based on copies of (*b*).

tudes began to seek out the prophet and ask him for a *tiqqun*. They came in groups from all the cities of Palestine, and Nathan would speak words of comfort, and preach to them on the imminent redemption in the spirit of the "new kabbalah" that was gradually taking shape in his mind. The atmosphere prevailing in Gaza is faithfully reflected in Cuenque's memoir, though the events appear somewhat transfigured, in retrospect, in the dazzling light of the author's profound experience:

Everybody went to the prophet in Gaza, and when the turn of Hebron came, I went with the whole holy congregation. When I stood before Nathan the prophet all my bones shook, although I had known him before, for his countenance was completely changed. The radiance of his face was like that of a burning torch, the color of his beard was like gold, and his mouth which [formerly] would not utter even the most ordinary things, now spoke words that made the listeners tremble. His tongue speaks great things . . . and the ear can hardly take in that which comes out of his mouth with a wonderful eloquence. And verily, every moment he tells new things, the like of which have not been heard since the day that the Law was given on Mount Sinai.[172]

Cuenque's description of the prophet's outward appearance raises some questions. Jacob Emden, who incorporates into his edition of Cuenque's memoirs interjections and comments ridiculing the author's Sabbatian faith, here observes that this detail was a plain lie, since Nathan had no beard, "as can be seen from the portrait that was drawn at the time and afterward printed." But as a matter of fact we have two portraits of Nathan, one from Gaza (which Emden did not know), and another from Smyrna. The latter was drawn when Nathan passed through the city in the spring of 1667, and was reproduced in Coenen's book (see frontispiece B). The former picture was drawn by a sailor who had seen Nathan in Gaza on Sunday, July 26, 1665, and gives the impression of being a fair likeness of its subject rather than sheer invention.[173] It shows Nathan with

172. Emden, pp. 38–39.

173. The portrait appeared on the title page of the first German pamphlet reporting on the Sabbatian movement and publishing a selection of (partly genuine and partly fictitious) letters. The caption reads: *Warhaffte Abbildung dess Neyen Jüdischen Propheten Nathan. So von etlichen Seefahrern gesehen und von denen Mitgesellen einen abgezeichnet worden. Anno 1665, den 26 Juli.* Nathan's head and cheeks are covered by his prayer mantle, but the beard

a mustache and a short beard framing his face. Nathan appears slightly plumper than in the Smyrna portrait, of which Coenen said that it was a fairly accurate representation. The similarity between the two pictures is evident. Did Nathan shave his beard during his escape after Sabbatai's apostasy? The detail about the reddish color of Nathan's beard strengthens the reliability of Cuenque's testimony, for the "golden color" of hair and beard would be more likely to be found among Ashkenazi than among Sephardi Jews.

The burden of Nathan's preaching was, as we have seen, a call to repentance and prayer. The first community to heed his call was Gaza, but the message soon spread to other Palestinian congregations. Even in Jerusalem there were many who responded to the prophet's message in spite of Sabbatai's disconcerting behavior and his condemnation by the rabbinic court. No doubt the believers somewhat exaggerated when they wrote to Egypt that "the majority of the inhabitants of Jerusalem believe and repent,"[174] but there must have been a good many who did; and perhaps the numbers fluctuated. A traveler writing from Jerusalem to Leghorn in 1666 strongly understated the numbers when he reported that only "one among a thousand" believed in Sabbatai Ṣevi.[175] There are no such uncertainties with regard to the situation in Gaza, Hebron, and Safed. Cuenque's statement that "the people slept in the streets and bazaars because the houses and courtyards could not contain" the multitudes is confirmed by a letter from Gaza written toward the end of September, 1665: "at the afternoon prayer there were two hundred and twenty penitents who were fasting for two days and nights, not to speak of those who fasted even longer, and the women and children who fasted single days only."[176]

---

is clearly recognizable. Very probably the publishers of the pamphlet first had this picture, and then added to it (in the manner of other Christian news letters) the fictitious "Letter from the Jews of Jerusalem to the Jewish Community in Europe" and other legendary letters concerning the Ten Tribes. The similarity of the two pictures should dispel any natural suspicions regarding the genuineness of the portrait allegedly drawn in Gaza. The description in the French *Relation* (p. 6) seems to be that of an imaginary scarecrow: thin, ugly ("la mine affreuse"), pale as death, his eyes bleary and squinting, bald and "contre-fait."

174. Haberman, p. 209. 175. Sasportas, p. 142.

176. *Ibid.*, see also Cuenque: "No business is transacted, and all—boys and old men, young men and virgins, pregnant women and such as have just given birth—are fasting from Sunday to Friday without suffering any harm."

The movement exhibited even in its initial stages the characteristic combination of severe penitence and exuberant rejoicing. Each group, after finishing the penances imposed by the prophet, celebrated a festival with great rejoicing, banquets, and dancing. Cuenque's description of the proceedings at Gaza, though written many years later, is strikingly similar to the account given by other writers of the subsequent revivals in the Diaspora, which Cuenque never witnessed, having remained in Gaza and Hebron all that time. His account of those blessed days ends with the words:

> Let no one think that such a thing, or anything remotely like it, has ever happened before. It was like the revelation at Sinai of which Moses used superlative language, saying, "Did ever people hear the voice of God speaking out of the midst of the fire." . . . Even so I shall use superlative language and say that it was supernatural that Israel should do such things in their exile, in the midst of the nations . . . in the kingdom of Ishmael [that is, Turkey] and particularly in the kingdom of Barbary [that is, Morocco], and none turning against them to cut off their name, [for evidently] the fear of the Jews had fallen upon the nations.[177]

The messianic awakening expressed itself in other ways, too. The traditional prayer for the rulers of the land, recited in the synagogues every Sabbath, was altered in Palestine and Sabbatai's name substituted for that of the sultan.[178] The prayer was now offered for the king of Israel, the "sultan Sabbatai Ṣevi," and a new time-reckoning was introduced. By 1666 these innovations spread to the Jewish communities outside Palestine. Letters from Jerusalem and Gaza were dated by the year "of the kingship of Our Lord and King."[179] The new time-reckoning may be related to a tradition mentioned in several sources according to which the "Jubilee Year" had begun;[180] that is, the world had entered upon a new era marked by the kingdom of the messiah. The name by which Sabbatai was to become known among his followers through-

177. Emden, p. 39.

178. This detail, mentioned by de la Croix (p. 28) and doubted by Graetz, is confirmed by the early letters from Egypt (Haberman, p. 209).

179. Haberman, *ibid.*

180. Letter from Alexandria, published by G. Scholem, *Zion,* VI (1941), 86. The idea seems to reflect the teachings of Nathan in his letter of September, 1665, to Raphael Joseph, to be discussed below.

out the history of the movement came into use during that time in Gaza. AMIRAH (the initials of the Hebrew words for "Our Lord and King, his majesty to be exalted") also suggests the Arabic word *ʾamir* ("emir"). The khalif's title was "Emir of the Believers," and the current Arabic expression and its phonetic association may have caught the fancy of those who invented the title AMIRAH. During the first year, however, high-sounding titles like that mentioned above, and more modest apellations such as "the rabbi Sabbatai Ṣevi" were still used indiscriminately. Even after he had revealed himself as the messiah, his disciples continued to call him the rabbi Sabbatai Ṣevi. Jesus too continued to be addressed as "rabbi," even after he had revealed himself to his disciples as the messiah of Israel.

Among the scholars who came from Jerusalem to see and possibly to test Nathan was R. Israel Benjamin the Second, grandson of the great kabbalist R. Benjamin, who had been one of the first editors of the Lurianic writings. Legendary accounts of his conversion appear in Sabbatian pamphlets and letters, but what appears to be a reasonably credible version of the story is told in letters from Egypt which probably drew on Ḥayyim Joseph's reports from Gaza. Nathan had been to Jerusalem and Hebron,[181] and returned with Israel Benjamin to whom he had revealed that his soul was that of the murderer of the prophet Zechariah.[182] Zechariah had been killed in the Temple at Jerusalem[183] and his death had engaged the attention of ancient Jewish legend.[184] R. Israel Benjamin "repaired to the graveyards in

181. On R. Benjamin the First and his grandson, see Frumkin, *Toledoth Ḥakhmey Yerushalayim*, pt. II, pp. 28, 62. Benjamin the Second went abroad in the winter or spring of 1666 on behalf of the community of Jerusalem (or perhaps on behalf of the Sabbatian group there?) and was taken prisoner in Malta; see M. Benayahu in *Scritti in memoria di Sally Mayer* (1956), pp. 35–36. The visit to Hebron is confirmed by Cuenque, p. 40.

182. Freimann, p. 46. The MS. reading "a *gilgul* (i.e., metensomatosis) of [the murderer of] Zechariah" is surely defective.

183. Jesus too had taken up this motif in his diatribe against the scribes and the Pharisees, who would kill and crucify their prophets, "and some of you will scourge in your synagogues and persecute from town to town . . that upon you come all the righteous blood shed on earth, from the blood of innocent Abel to the blood of Zechariah the son of Berachiah whom you murdered between the sanctuary and the altar" (Matt. 23:34–35).

184. *Lamentations Rabbathi*, *Pethiḥah* 23. Rabbinic legend connected the verse "and they shall look upon me whom they have pierced" (Zech. 12:10)

Jerusalem. There he found an old man—it is said that he was the prophet Zechariah—who carried vessels [that is, a ewer and a basin] for the washing of the hands, and a towel. He took the vessels and poured water over his hands, saying, 'Oh pardon thy people Israel,' and the old man washed his hands and replied, 'And the blood shall be forgiven them,'[185] and thereby the sin was forgiven."[186] There is, so far, no evidence to show that a homiletic or legendary association between the death of Zechariah, the son of Ido, and Israel's exile existed prior to the Sabbatian movement.[187] Perhaps Israel Benjamin's visionary experience should be interpreted as a symbolic expression of the end of Israel's exile: the sins that had originally caused exile

---

with the murder of Zechariah the son of Jehoiada the priest, in the Temple (II Chron. 24:20–21); see B. Gittin 57b and the Targum to Lam. 2:20. See also S. Blank, "The Death of Zechariah" in *HUCA,* XII–XIII (1937–38), 327–46. Jewish legend, however, does not assume any relation between the murder of Zechariah and Israel's exile, or the destruction of the second Temple, as was accepted in Christian tradition. Prof. David Flusser drew my attention to a passage in the medieval book *Yosippon,* a Hebrew adaptation from Josephus using also Christian sources. In chapters 75 and 80 of this book the murder of Zechariah is told in a context which suggests that the medieval author was aware of this connection, known to him through one of his Christian sources, namely Hegesippus.

185. Cf. Deut. 21:6–9. According to rabbinic legend, the earth refused to cover the blood of the murdered prophet.

186. Haberman, p. 210; Freimann, p. 46. The letters written in the middle of September (see *Hollandtze Merkurius,* January, 1666, p. 3, footnote; *God's Love to His People Israel,* p. 3 (reprinted by Wilenski in Zion, XVII [1952], 170); the German pamphlet *Wahrhaffte Abbildung,* etc., already introduce some changes into the story: Nathan is said to have been present at the mysterious encounter in the sepulcher, and R. Jacob Ḥagiz ("R. Gagas" or "Gogas") is substituted for R. Israel Benjamin. The substitution was evidently meant to provide a legendary atonement for the "murderous" persecution of the messiah by Ḥagiz and the rabbis of Jerusalem. The English letter explicitly states that R. Gagas afterward "made penitence in sackcloth and ashes, for having ever opposed him [Sabbatai]" (Wilenski, p. 170). See also Sasportas, p. 15, and the letters in Balaban, p. 41.

187. The association is explicitly stated and elaborated in the anonymous *Beʾer ha-Golah* (ed. Brüll, with introduction by S. Sachs [Mainz, 1879], p. 89), but the character, origin, and date of this work are obscure. Brüll and Sachs believed that the work contained references to the period after Sabbatai's apostasy, but their arguments are not convincing. If the work was composed after 1665, the reference to Zechariah is evidently due to the popular and widespread legend concerning the meeting in the sepulcher.

were now forgiven. The prophet who was killed by order of the king in the court of the House of the Lord was, perhaps, also understood as a "type" of the new prophet or messiah. According to a Talmudic adage the rabbis are kings, but the rabbis of Jerusalem had excommunicated and proscribed the messiah. It is not surprising, therefore, that the story was soon transferred from R. Israel Benjamin to R. Jacob Ḥagiz who had, in fact, persecuted the messiah and repudiated his prophet. The legend developed and spread at an amazing speed; its plastic substance lay ready in the souls of men, merely waiting to be shaped into concrete symbols.

The story of R. Israel Benjamin, based, most probably, on an actual or visionary experience of some kind, marks the transition to the realm of imaginative legend, which, as has been remarked earlier, soon dominated the mental climate in Palestine. The sway of imagination was strongly in evidence in the letters sent to Egypt and elsewhere and which, by the autumn of 1665, had assumed the character of regular messianic propaganda in which fiction far outweighed the facts: the prophet was "encompassed with a Fiery Cloud" and the voice of an angel was heard from the cloud.[188] The prophet had either discovered[189] or was about to discover the ashes of the red heifer, which had been hidden away until the last days,[190] in order to purify Israel.[191] At the anointing of Sabbatai by the

188. *Several New Letters concerning the Jews,* p. 2 (also in C. Roth, *Anglo-Jewish Letters,* p. 73); a confused version of the same legends in Balaban, p. 40. Sasportas (p. 15) draws on letters from Egypt that had arrived in Hamburg toward the end of 1665 and which, in their turn, were probably based on reports from Ḥayyim Joseph; exactly the same legends occur in a letter (*Several New Letters*, Wilenski, p. 164) said to be by "Hannie Joseph."

189. Sasportas, p. 15.

190. The discovery of the ashes of the red heifer, prophesied by Nathan to take place after a year and some months (see below, p. 273), was advanced to the more immediate future (December, 1665) in *Several New Letters* (Wilenski, p. 171): on "the Third of December (called by the [Jews] Chanuke [i.e., Hanukkah] a Feast-day, for to remember the Prophanation of the Temple, in the days of the Maccabees) an Altar should be erected unto the Lord, in which the King should offer, and fire come down to consume the Sacrifice; and that against that time, the ashes of the RED COW (without which, the King could not offer) should be found." The same wording also in the German pamphlet *Wahrhaffte Abbildung.*

191. Cf. Num., ch. 19. Without prior ritual cleansing, the sacrificial service in the Temple could not be resumed.

prophet—a purely imaginary event which, however, was associated by the believers with the Shabuᶜoth vigil at Gaza—the assembled multitude beheld drops of oil descending from his head to his beard, although no human hand had poured oil on him.[192] The most sensational item, however, appearing in all accounts dating from the end of that first period, is the report that all Christian churches had sunk into the earth. Sasportas quotes letters to the effect that at the prophet's command "great stones had fallen from heaven on the house of worship of the gentiles. Some say that it collapsed completely, others say only partly."[193] The reference may be either to the Church of the Sepulcher or to the Dome of the Rock (or even to the Mosque of Omar). On the Twenty-fifth of Kislev there would be a great darkness among the gentiles; "there should fall great Hailstones, Fire, and Brimstone," in sundry places in Palestine "which should destroy many houses of Idolaters [that is, churches], but among the Jews there should be clear light, without any hurt or disturbance."[194] "At Aleppo the great Turkish church sank down into the earth, and was swallowed up; even as the church at Jerusalem of the Franciscan monks."[195] One letter specified that "the foundations of the houses in Jerusalem had been raised, whereas the foundations of the churches had sunk a few cubits, as everyone could behold."[196]

The letters from Egypt carried the news as far as Yemen, where it was further embellished: "The sky will be overcast with clouds, and the earth with a thick mist that will surround Mount Zion and the messiah, together with Elijah and Michael. Mount Zion will be

192. Balaban, p. 39; also Sasportas, p. 16.

193. Sasportas, p. 20. As Sasportas wrote these lines in December, 1665, the letters on which they are based must have been dispatched in October or possibly even in September.

194. *Several New Letters* (Wilenski, p. 165).

195. *Several New Letters,* p. 4; also in Roth, *Anglo-Jewish Letters,* p. 73. Cf. also the reference to the "two high places that were swallowed up," in the reports from Amsterdam quoted in the Italian pamphlet published by G. Scholem, *Zion,* X (1945), 66.

196. Balaban, p. 39; see also the testimony of R. Lemmel, an emissary from Jerusalem, given in Venice in the winter of 1666 (Sasportas, p. 122): Nathan had prophesied that 102 stones from the sanctuary of the gentiles in Jerusalem would fall down, "and the falling of the stones was actually seen on this very day."

covered by clouds for three months, and when they disperse slowly after three months, the houses will have fallen down and the Western Wall[197] will have been raised very high and also its foundations [will be higher by] three cubits. A blazing fire will surround Zion and Hebron lest any gentile or uncircumcised enter. . . . Askelon and Ekron will disappear by sinking into the earth."[198]

The accounts of the imminent destruction of mosques and churches take up a motif that had been in evidence in earlier messianic movements too. Asher Lemmlein had made similar prophecies in Istria in 1501.[199] There is no need to assume a direct literary dependence of the Sabbatian authors on earlier texts. Traditions and motifs of this kind are not uncommon, and they would find expression whenever apocalyptic events were expected. The anti-Sabbatian poet-pamphleteer Emanuel Frances mocked and lamented

> Is't true? no more on Zion hill
> their heathen temples stand?
> Alas, they are abiding still
> and aliens possess our land.[200]

V

In the months that followed Sabbatai's departure, first from Gaza and then from Palestine, Nathan was in a state of high elation. Though he had no more prophetic experiences in the narrow, technical sense of the term (indicated by the opening phrase "thus saith the Lord"), yet he continued to receive revelations of *maggidim* and to hear heavenly voices. His mind was absorbed in a world of visions and of unbounded enthusiam, and the ardor of his utterances bears out the genuineness of his feelings of exaltation. At the same time he also felt impelled to act, and his activity exhibits his peculiar combination of imagination and practical efficiency. Whether some of this

197. The remaining outer wall of Herod's Temple in Jerusalem, often referred to as the "Wailing Wall."

198. The Yemenite apocalypse *Gey Ḥizzayon* (*Qobeṣ ᶜal Yad*, IV, New Series [1946], 125).

199. Lemmlein's prophecy as reported by Johannes Pfefferkorn (discovered by Graetz, see vol. IX, 4th edn. [1907], p. 507).

200. *Ṣevi Muddaḥ,* p. 123; Frances adds in an explanatory note that reports had been received in Italy to the effect that all houses of idolaters had suddenly been destroyed.

activity may have its source in the letters that no doubt were exchanged between the prophet and the messiah, we have no means of knowing. Their correspondence is lost. But we already know the nature of Nathan's special charismatic gift: by establishing a psychical rapport with those in his presence, or by other mental responses, he could read people's consciences. The phenomenon is so well known in the history of religions that no one would want to dismiss it as legendary and "impossible." The fact that so far no satisfactory psychological explanation of this kind of phenomenon has been advanced does not make it any the less real. The facts are well attested, and it makes little difference whether we refer them to the Holy Spirit, to telepathy, or to some other concept of paranormal psychology. The spirit that moved Nathan created a very special atmosphere around him. Let him protest as much as he will against the popular hunger for miracles, the faithful, who recognized in his capacity to read men's thoughts the manifest workings of the Holy Spirit, needed no further encouragement to credit him with other fond inventions of their hearts. The contradiction between the prophet's theory—pure faith without signs—and the practice of his followers who beheld miracles on all sides was natural and all but inevitable. Nathan himself contributed to this atmosphere by creating a new messianic legend out of his visionary insights. His theoretical and speculative activity also increased in intensity in the months that followed his meeting with Sabbatai, and the contents of his revelations combined in his fertile mind with his kabbalistic theorizing. We can now appreciate the significance of Cuenque's reference to kabbalistic discourses and new doctrines pouring forth continually from Nathan's mouth. The "words, the like of which have not been heard since the revelation at Sinai," were Nathan's novel interpretations of the kabbalistic doctrines of the cosmos and of creation.

On September 5, 1665, Nathan heard a "voice in the Celestial Academy, proclaiming that the messiah, the son of David, would become manifest to the world in a year and some months," namely, according to a slightly different version of the same account, that "the kingdom of the messiah, the son of David, would become manifest."[201] This and other visionary experiences are set forth in Nathan's

201. The date of the revelation was specified by Nathan in his testimony to the rabbinic court in Ipsola (Emden, p. 50). The heavenly message is frequently mentioned in letters from the years 1666–67. The relevant material was

long letter to Raphael Joseph—one of the most precious documents in our possession. The letter was probably written in September, 1665, soon after the heavenly proclamation just mentioned. An anthology of the letters written from Gaza to Egypt attests that a lively correspondence was carried on between Nathan and the circle of Raphael Joseph in Egypt, for "every day the lord Raphael Joseph would write to the aforementioned Rabbi [Nathan] to inquire of him whatever he desired to know. . . . and every day the posts went out and returned from the one to the other."[202] The *chelebi* begged the prophet for a cure for his weaknesses, particularly his choleric temper; his genuine devotion to the cause of the faithful is confirmed by Nathan's replies. Sasportas suggests, probably rightly, that the *chelebi* played the role of a Maecenas and trustee to the brotherhood of believers, and particularly to those who made the pilgrimage to Gaza. "He would provide food to all the people in Gaza that were with Nathan, and everyone that came from afar would leave his moneybag with him and then proceed to Gaza."[203]

Nathan's long letter consists of two parts,—the one kabbalistic and doctrinal, dealing particularly with devotions and special intentions (*kawwanoth*) at prayer, the other apocalyptic, describing the stages of the process of redemption. Its extraordinary significance resides in its combination of mystico-kabbalistic and popular elements. Nathan merged Lurianic messianism with the legendary messianism of earlier generations, drawing far-reaching conclusions from the one and adding more imaginative elements to the other. The document deserves closer analysis, for it began to circulate in all Jewish communities immediately after the first news of the messianic awakening

---

collected by Wirszubski in *Zion,* III (1938), 217–19; cf. in particular Nathan's autobiographical letter, *ibid.,* pp. 217, 227. This letter, however, was actually written several years later, 1673–74. Later Sabbatian writers confused Nathan's initial prophetic experience and vision of the *merkabah* (spring, 1665) with the celestial proclamation of September 5, and dated the event Sunday, 25th of Ellul (Baruch of Arezzo, in Freimann, p. 47). As a matter of fact the 25th of Ellul, 1665, fell on a Sabbath and not on a Sunday. Also the Sabbatian festival calendar states "on 25 Ellul the proclamation was made in the Celestial Academy." The proclamation was made, of course, by an angelic herald; hence also Nathan's insistence on the distinction between his first, strictly "prophetic" experience, and the subsequent revelations.

202. Haberman, p. 210.

203. Sasportas, p. 6.

had reached Europe in October, 1665. The letter was read in Smyrna and Constantinople as well as in Yemen, Italy, Germany, and Holland. It served as a kind of "order of the day" for the believers, and provided an outline of the messianic program. Although the actual course of events differed almost wholly from Nathan's apocalyptic schedule, yet it is important to realize what kind of immediate future the faithful themselves expected. The publicity given to the letter, and the fact that it was considered by many of its readers as a semiofficial statement of the aims of the movement, give added significance to the novel ideas and tendencies expressed in it, which henceforth formed an integral part of Sabbatian history.

Surprisingly enough, the combination of the diverse messianic elements and motifs is, as yet, purely external. The two parts of the letter do not form a systematic whole, and it is at one point only—albeit an important one—that they converge toward an organic unity. The following translation of the letter is based on the best critical text established so far.[204]

Holy to praise and mighty in deeds, the exalted prince, the master and rabbi [Raphael Joseph], may his light shine . . .

[i] This is to notify you that I received your letter and rejoiced, for thanks be to God that you believe this faith which is as bright as the sun and beyond any doubt, and there is no uncertainty in it. This is the faith through which Israel will inherit and merit the "inheritance" of the Lord, which is the mystery of the Jubilee Year that will become manifest at this time, and the "rest" [cf. Deut. 12:9] which is the mystery of the manifestation of the Holy Ancient One within the configuration of *Zeᶜir ᵓAnpin*[205] in the year 1670. Therefore I instruct you to concentrate your "intention" [meditation] when praying or reading on the Cause of All Causes, and also to state this intention explicitly when reading or praying [see below, p. 279]. When you utter the word *ᵓeḥad* ("one") of the *Shemaᶜ*

204. Tishby's excellent critical text (Sasportas, pp. 7–12) supersedes all other versions, though occasionally and in some minor details I have preferred their readings. The letter "To Our Brethren, the Children of Israel" in Leyb b. Ozer's story (Emden, p. 5) never existed, but is a précis of the letter under discussion. The variations are due to Leyb's uninhibitedly imaginative paraphrase, and not to his use of a variant text (as Tishby thought). Sasportas punctuates his text with sarcastic, and often very instructive, interjections. I have divided the letter into numbered paragraphs so as to facilitate understanding of its structure and of the arrangement of its subject matter.

205. See Scholem, *Major Trends*, pp. 270–71.

prayer [Deut. 6:4 "Hear, O Israel, YHWH our God, YHWH is one"], you should meditate that He is the absolute one, the absolute being and the absolute end, that from Him all the worlds emanate, and that you offer your whole self (*nefesh-ruaḥ-neshamah*) to martyrdom for His holy name to unite the [aspects of] WH and YH [of the Tetragrammaton YHWH]. You should also meditate on the combinations of the letters of the divine names YHWH, ᵓHYH and ᵓDNY,[206] so that the illumination of the Cause of All Causes may become manifest in them from WH to YH, and from YH to WH. Do not meditate on any particular *sefirah*. At night do not meditate on the combinations of names, but solely on the aforementioned name.[207] In our days all things will be purified with God's help, the [mystical] lights will spread, and [the *sefirah*] *Malkhuth* [that is, the Shekhinah] will be [restored to the mystical state symbolized as] "the crown of her husband." The holy name YHWH will then be read as a double YHYH,[208] and Scripture will be fulfilled [Zech. 14:9] "in that day YHWH shall be one and His name one." For the WH of the Tetragrammaton will be in complete union with YH, and they will nevermore be separated.[209]

[ii] Know for certain that at the present time there are no more sparks of the Shekhinah left in the demonic realm.[210] All the worlds are now in the mystical phase of the letter L of ṢLM (the divine "image") which was [hitherto mystically anticipated] on the eve of the Sabbath.[211] Hence we must no longer perform actions of *tiqqun*, but merely adorn the bride [that is, the Shekhinah] and make her face the bridegroom. . . . All these things require lengthy explanations, and time does not permit me to disclose them. But what I want to say is this: the meditations (*kawwanoth*) which the great master Isaac Luria had revealed are no

206. The reference is to the traditional kabbalistic method of combining the letters to form more complicated names of God.

207. Sasportas interjects with a sneer: "He [Nathan] copied from Luria's writings . . . but misunderstood it."

208. The metamorphosis of the letter *W* of the Tetragrammaton to a *Y* is mentioned in earlier kabbalistic texts; cf. the kabbalistic lexicon *Qoheleth Yaᶜaqob* by R. Jacob Jolles (Lvov, 1870), s.v. *yiheyeh*.

209. In the time of exile the two halves of the divine name are separated. In the messianic age they will be united forever, representing the divine unity.

210. According to Lurianic doctrine the Messiah will come only after the last spark of holiness has been extracted from the realm of the *qelippoth*; see above, pp. 48–49.

211. Ḥayyim Vital in his *kawwanoth* for the Sabbath eve.

longer applicable in our days, since all the worlds are now [on a] different [mystical level], and it [that is, the meditation of the Lurianic devotions today] would be like performing actions appropriate to a weekday on a Sabbath. Beware lest you perform any of the Lurianic *kawwanoth* or read [Lurianic] devotions, homilies, or writings, since they are obscure and no living man understood his words except R. Ḥayyim Vital of blessed memory. He followed the rabbi Luria's system for some years, but thereafter attained greater insight than Isaac Luria himself. He might have been the messiah [see above, p. 26] if the merits of his generation had been sufficient, and if there had not been so many contrary forces caused by sin.[212]

[iii] At the present time, too, there are opposing forces, but they are merely harming themselves. They cannot oppose [the progress of the messiah] because now it is surely [the preordained time of] the last end. Do not ask how our generation has merited this. For because of the great and infinite sufferings—more than any mind can comprehend—which the rabbi Sabbatai Ṣevi has suffered, it is in his power to do as he pleases with the Israelite nation, to declare them righteous or —God forfend—guilty. He can justify the greatest sinner, and even if he be [as sinful] as Jesus[213] he may justify him. And whoever entertains any doubts about him, though he be the most righteous man in the world, he [that is, the messiah] may punish him with great afflictions. In short, you must take it for absolutely certain that Israel will have no life unless they believe all these things without a sign or miracle. It is by a divine dispensation that they who are worthy in this generation have been allowed to see the beginning of redemption. Do not mind them that do not believe, even if it was your dearest friend.

[iv] And now I shall disclose the course of events. A year and a few months from today, he [Sabbatai] will take the dominion from the Turkish king without war,[214] for by [the power of] the hymns and praises which he shall utter, all nations shall submit to his rule. He will take the Turkish

212. Nathan had probably heard of R. Jacob Abulafia's strong opposition to Vital (see the complete text of Vital's autobiographical *Sefer ha-Ḥezyonoth*, Jerusalem, 1954).

213. Here many MSS. are illegible; see Sasportas, p. 9, and Tishby's note, *ad loc.*

214. Cf. above, p. 225 (*Vision of R. Abraham*): "He will go forth to war without hands."

king alone to the countries which he will conquer, and all the kings shall be tributary unto him, but only the Turkish king will be his servant. There will be no slaughter among the uncircumcised [that is, Christians], except in the German lands [see below, p. 287]. The ingathering of the exiles will not yet take place at that time, though the Jews shall have great honor, each in his place. Also the Temple will not yet be rebuilt, but the aforementioned rabbi [Sabbatai Ṣevi] will discover the exact site of the altar as well as the ashes of the red heifer, and he will perform sacrifices. This will continue for four or five years. Thereafter the aforementioned rabbi will proceed to the river Sambatyon, leaving his kingdom in the charge of the Turkish king [who would act as the messiah's viceroy or Great Vizier] and charging him [especially] with regard to the Jews. But after three months he [that is, the Grand Turk] will be seduced by his councillors and will rebel. Then there will be a great tribulation [the messianic woes] and Scripture shall be fulfilled [Zech. 13:9]: "and I will try them as gold is tried, and I will refine them as silver is refined," and none will be saved from these tribulations except those dwelling in this place [that is, Gaza] which is the ruler's residence, even as Hebron was unto David. The name [of the city] expresses its nature,[215] for its name is [in Hebrew] ᶜ*Azzah* ("the strong one"), and with the advent of redemption, strength [that is, the *sefirah Geburah*] will spread and the people [of Gaza] will act in this strength. King Solomon [in his time] wished to do the same, as it is written [II Chron. 9:20], "silver was accounted nothing in the days of Solomon,"[216] but he did not succeed, for the time had not yet come. In our time, however, this will be fulfilled in the dominion of Gaza, which means "the strength of the Lord." At the end of this period the signs foretold in the Zohar[217] will come to pass, and they will continue until the next sabbatical year [that is, 1672]. This is the meaning of the Talmudic saying, "In the seventh year the son of David will come."[218] The seventh year, that is the Sabbath, signifying King Sabbatai. At that time the aforementioned rabbi will return from the river Sambatyon, together with his predestined mate, the daughter of Moses. It will be

215. Sasportas adds in an angry parenthesis that the word can also mean "impertinence."

216. Silver, which is white, is a kabbalistic symbol of mercy (the *sefirah Ḥesed*); gold, which is red, symbolizes judgment and the *sefirah Geburah.*

217. In the long and circumstantial eschatological description, Zohar II, 8 ff.

218. Cf. B. Megillah 17b.

known that today it was fifteen years since Moses was resuscitated[219] and that [today] the aforementioned rabbi's predestined wife, whose name is Rebekah, was thirteen years old. His present wife will be the handmaid, and the wife which he will marry shall be the mistress; but as long as he is [still] outside Jerusalem, the handmaid is mistress. However, this can be explained by word of mouth only.[220] In the same year he will return from the river Sambatyon, mounted on a celestial lion; his bridle will be a seven-headed serpent[221] and "fire out of his mouth devoured." At this sight all the nations and all the kings shall bow before him to the ground. On that day the ingathering of the dispersed shall take place, and he shall behold the sanctuary all ready built descending from above.[222] There will be seven thousand Jews in Palestine at that time, and on that day there will be the resurrection of the dead that have died in Palestine.[223] Those that are not worthy [to rise at the first resurrection] will be cast out from the Holy Land. The [general] resurrection outside the Holy Land will take place forty years later.

Behold these are some of his ways. You should have perfect faith

219. This translation suggested by Tishby is borne out by the reading in Nathan's letter of 1673–74, *Qobeṣ ʿal Yad,* VI, p. 448. He could, therefore, have married a wife from one of the lost tribes and have a young daughter.

220. The meaning may be either that the kabbalistic symbolism of "Rebekah, the daughter of Moses" must be explained orally, or that the veiled criticism of Sabbatai's present wife had better not be elaborated in writing. I am aware of no other "mystical" reference to Sabbatai's wife Sarah in Nathan's writings.

221. A combination of several Talmudic and Zoharic symbols. The "celestial lion" occurs as a symbolic expression in B. Ḥullin 59b. A seven-headed dragon is mentioned in B. Qiddushin 29b, and a seven-headed serpent in *Zohar Ḥadash,* fol. 45d. King Nebuchadnezzar rode a lion, and in his hands he held, as a bridle, a serpent (B. Sabbath 150a). Cf. also the "great red dragon with seven heads" in Rev. 12:3. In this symbolism the messiah masters the forces of the *qelippah,* and raises them to the realm of holiness by making them subservient to the latter.

222. A traditional conception in Jewish legend. Unlike the earlier sanctuaries, which were built by men, the third Temple would descend from heaven; cf. B. Sukkah, 41a, Zohar I, 114a (*Midrash ha-Neʿelam*).

223. Tishby has shown that this part of Nathan's account, including the number of seven thousand Jews in Palestine on the day of resurrection, is based on a text by Ḥayyim Vital, quoted in Nathan Shapira Yerushalmi's *Tub ha-ʾAreṣ* (Venice, 1665), fol. 37. The latter work was published a few years before Nathan began his kabbalistic studies. At the time the author was traveling in Italy as an emissary of Jerusalem; his book was probably widely read in Palestine.

in them, for I know that you fear God, and out of love I have therefore informed you of all this. May your peace prosper and not decrease, according to your desire and the desire of him that seeketh your peace and that of all who are steadfast in the faith. Abraham Nathan.[224]

The importance of this document and the light which it throws on the mind of the prophet of Gaza are evident. Let us examine some of its most salient features.

Nathan subscribed to the kabbalistic view that at the time of redemption the supernal lights of the hidden *sefiroth* and configurations would become manifest on earth. This process could be described in various terms: as the "Mystery of the Jubilee," that is, of the *sefirah Binah*, whose eschatological significance is described in the Zohar, or as the manifestation of the "Holy Ancient One" in *Ze*ᶜ*ir* ᵓ*Anpin*, which is the Lurianic symbol (borrowed from the Zohar) for that manifestation of the divine will and grace which subdues all forces of severity. The Holy Ancient One is the name of the highest of the divine configurations; it corresponds to the first *sefirah*, *Kether*, and the supernal "Will," and hence is inaccessible to created beings. In due course, however (according to Nathan, in four or five years' time), the light of the Holy Ancient One would become manifest even on earth. But this traditional Lurianic idea was now given a special twist that remained characteristic of Sabbatian belief. Ḥayyim Vital had taught that the innermost aspects of the configuration of ᶜ*Atiqa* (that is, in Nathan's terminology, the light of the Holy Ancient One) would become manifest at the time of redemption;[225] he had never said that they would be made manifest by the messiah. Nathan held, as we know from other letters which he wrote shortly before and after the long letter to Raphael Joseph, that Sabbatai Ṣevi would bring this new light. This is a significant innovation. The light of the Holy Ancient One will not shine forth of itself in *Ze*ᶜ*ir* ᵓ*Anpin*, but will "become manifest through our messiah Sabbatai Ṣevi, whose name equals [by *gematria*] that of Shadday." To be more precise, "the manifestation of the [hidden] light of the name Shadday will take place through the messianic king. Through him the light of the Holy

224. The signature shows that at the time Nathan had not yet changed his name to Benjamin Nathan in his writings; see above, p. 232.

225. *Sha*ᶜ*ar ha-Kawwanoth* (edn. Jerusalem, fol. 19c). There exists a letter of R. Moses Zacuto to R. Samson Bacchi on this subject.

Ancient One will be manifest in *Ze*ᶜ*ir* ᵓ*Anpin*, and thereby the souls of the present generation will find their *tiqqun*."[226] The notion that such illumination from above may come in lieu of our earthly efforts, that is, strict observance of the Law, penitence, mortification, and mystical devotions, to achieve the *tiqqun* can already be found in Lurianic literature. The light coming from above would cause the Shekhinah to "face" her bridegroom, and would awaken in her all those forces that are necessary for her union with the higher configuration, and that had to be stimulated hitherto by human action. Nathan follows the Lurianic pattern in his account of the state of the Shekhinah in the premessianic period. With the process of *tiqqun* drawing to its conclusion, some change would inevitably occur in the structure of the mystical cosmos, and the partitions that prevented the supernal lights from manifesting themselves would vanish. This Lurianic assumption is presupposed by everything Nathan says in his letter, which—we should remind ourselves—was not addressed to an average pious and esteemed Jew but to the *chelebi*, who was a kabbalist himself and a student of the Lurianic writings. During Sabbatai's first stay at his court in Cairo, Raphael Joseph had invited Samuel Vital from Damascus. Samuel Vital, now sixty-six years old, was no less a believer than his host and, far from rejecting the messages from Gaza, he actually supervised the spiritual exercises held at Raphael Joseph's court by order of the prophet: "and he supervised the penitential exercises, including ritual immersions, prolonged fasts and flagellations, right from the beginning."[227] When he arrived from Damascus in 1664, he brought his father's manuscripts, including the "Eight Gates" of the Lurianic encyclopedia ᶜ*Eṣ Ḥayyim*, and his other books. He was certainly entitled to be regarded as the legitimate heir and representative of the Lurianic tradition. The fact that he, too, had joined the movement no doubt provided a counterpoise to the hostility of the other leading kabbalist, R. Jacob Ṣemaḥ. Samuel Vital does not seem to have uttered a single word of protest against Nathan's radical departures from traditional Lurianic doctrine and devotional practice.

226. Nathan in his "Penitential Devotions" (MSS. Coronel and Halberstamm); see Tishby, "Nathan of Gaza's Penitential Devotions," *Tarbiz,* XV (1944), 164–65.

227. Raphael Supino's letter from Leghorn (Sasportas, p. 73).

The state of the world before the *tiqqun* is essentially different from that after its achievement. At present all our acts and meditative intentions aim at the *tiqqun*, for they are meant to produce a spiritual effect on the innermost levels of reality, and to restore the divine sparks and essences to their rightful place. In fact, the Lurianic system of meditation appears as a highly developed technique for speeding up the otherwise slow and long process of *tiqqun*. By correlating the words of the daily liturgy with the dynamic movements and the corresponding rising toward God and falling earthward of the mystical worlds, Lurianism taught its adepts to inject new strength into them, and to lift them out of the depths into which they had fallen at the "breaking of the vessels." The proper *kawwanah* establishes a hidden harmony between the meditating kabbalist and the cosmos. Now, however, that redemption had been proclaimed, everything was different. The method of prayer without mystical meditations, which Sabbatai had adopted in his youth, now should become the norm for all believers. What had been Sabbatai's private method (see above, pp. 115, 118)—a deviation from, rather than an application of, Lurianic kabbalah—was turned by Nathan into a doctrine which he developed logically from Lurianic premises: if the cosmic *tiqqun* was achieved, and if no sparks of the Shekhinah were left in the realm of the "shells," then the present structure and order of the mystical cosmos corresponded to the "new law" of redemption. The classic Lurianic devotions had lost their purpose, and hence their relevance. There was no longer anything to be "restored," and hence the traditional *kawwanoth* could not be aimed at anything. All that remained to be done was to "adorn the bride" and to beautify the Shekhinah; there was no more need to raise her from the dust of exile, since she was already risen. A wave of Nathan's hand, and the complex theosophical "apparatus" of Lurianic devotions vanished. Of course, the ultimate state of perfection was not yet achieved. The Sabbath-day of the cosmos had not yet dawned, but at least the eve of the Sabbath had arrived. Until now the state of the world could be compared to the days of the week; now it was like unto the eve of the Sabbath with its distinct character and prayers. The purpose of every prayer was to lift the Shekhinah from her low position at the bottom of the divine pleroma, to her rightful and exalted place. At present she was still below the *sefirah Tif'ereth*, known by the symbolic name the Holy One Blessed Be He, but soon she would rise not only to the level of *Tifʾereth* (the "husband of the Shekhinah") but even to the very highest *sefirah*, *Kether* ("crown"). Kabbalists referred to this process as the Shekhinah's "ascent by which she was mystically raised to a realm where she would be the crown of her husband." This ascent would no longer be brought about by human action, performed in the lower world and radiating its spiritual effects to the higher worlds, but by an act of supernal grace in which the Ancient One would manifest his light and let it stream downward. The Lurianic devotions, having fulfilled their mystical role in the hidden history of the cosmos, had now become not only obsolete but almost positively sinful. Practicing them was "like unto doing weekday labors on the Sabbath," a dubious and perhaps even forbidden activity. Their place would be taken by different and much simpler devotions, as befitted the cosmic "Sabbath eve." No particular *sefirah* or divine configuration should be meditated on; instead, the two halves YH and WH of the divine name should be united with the intention that the divine names contained therein should manifest the light of the "Cause of All Causes." The latter term, of course, was not Nathan's invention; it occurred in philosophical literature as well as in the *Tiqquney Zohar.*[228] But Nathan invested it with a new and very specific meaning. His Cause of All Causes seems to be none other than the Holy Ancient One whose light would become manifest at the time of redemption. As the Most Hidden of All, whose effects are manifest in the supernal worlds of *ʿaṣiluth* and *beriʾah*, it stands at the head of the chain of causes and emanations, corresponding to the "supernal *anthropos*"[229] of kabbalistic literature. But it is also possible that Nathan's terminology refers to the hidden *Ḛn-Sof* itself, and not to its manifestation in the Holy Ancient One. In that case Nathan's teaching that no *sefirah* or divine configuration should be intended in prayer, but only the primordial Godhead itself, would be a truly revolutionary innovation in devotional practice, since the kabbalists had always insisted that *En-Sof* could never be directly intended in meditation. However, this latter and extreme interpretation does not seem to

228. In the well-known "Prayer of Elijah" at the beginning of the *Tiqqunin* (fol. 17a).

229. The *ʾadam qadmon ʿelyon*, the source of the "straight line" of divine light that produced the cosmos.

be supported by the general tenor of Nathan's letter or by the terminology of his other writings.[230] In any event, the instructions to Raphael Joseph were meant to be taken seriously, and expressions such as "May it be thy will, O Cause of All Causes" recur consistently in all the prayers and penitential devotions composed by Nathan.[231]

Yet, surprisingly enough, the apparent radicalism of Nathan's demand not to meditate on any particular *sefirah* is not borne out by his prayers and devotional exercises. These compositions abound with divine names and their combinations, as well as with references to the particular *sefiroth* to which they are supposed to correspond. In the earlier letters from Gaza to Egypt explicit mention is made of particular *sefiroth* in connection with the devotions for the penitential fasts prescribed by Nathan.[232] Either Nathan exaggerated in his letter, or his instruction referred to the opening formula but not to the subsequent details of prayer. Nathan's predilection for extreme statements appears elsewhere in the letter. He not only abolishes the classical Lurianic meditations in prayer, but even disapproves of the study of Luria's "homilies and writings, since they are obscure." And this disapproval of Luria's, that is, Vital's, writings was addressed to the very man who had just gone to considerable trouble to acquire them, for Raphael Joseph had only recently brought Samuel Vital to his court. Nathan's implicit criticism of Luria is very curious indeed. No other kabbalistic writer had ever bestowed such excessive praise on Ḥayyim Vital at the expense of the great master Luria. After all, Luria was supposed to have received his knowledge from the prophet Elijah, whereas Vital had learned everything from Luria. Yet Nathan asserts in his letter—which Samuel Vital certainly read—that Ḥayyim Vital was a greater kabbalist than Luria. Sasportas' angry comment, "He hath testified falsely against the rabbi [Luria]," is understandable

230. The latter interpretation was proposed by Tishby in his note to Sasportas, p. 8. I prefer the former interpretation. Later Sabbatian theology did not identify *En-Sof* with the "Cause of All Causes" (= the Holy Ancient One), and Nathan's prayers often refer to the "Light [of *En-Sof*] in the Cause of All Causes."

231. See also Tishby, *Tarbiz,* XV (1944), 166. In general, Nathan's prayers follow the traditional kabbalistic patterns (*le-shem yihud,* etc.), but it is precisely the changes which he introduced that are revealing and significant.

232. Cf. Gandoor's letter in Haberman, p. 210.

enough. Perhaps Nathan uttered his criticism of Luria in a fit of enthusiasm, for he certainly was not guided by it in his actual practice, and his kabbalistic writings bespeak a thorough and profound knowledge of Lurianic literature, both what had been published and what was in manuscript. Another factor may have contributed to Nathan's critical attitude: Lurianic kabbalism was to manifest itself at present in a different form, appropriate to the *kairos,* and hence Nathan's writings would have to take the place of the earlier versions of Lurianic teaching. There was nothing particularly shocking about this suggestion, since the prophet of Gaza was a reincarnation of Isaac Luria. This view was certainly current among Nathan's disciples in Salonika;[233] perhaps it had already been put forward during the early stages of the movement in Palestine. Nathan's vague hints on the subject, as well as his refusal to name the blessed spirits that communicated the Lurianic mysteries to him, "lest he appear to pride himself," begin to make sense once we assume that he believed himself to be taught by Luria. The Lurianic teachings had been appropriate and useful in their own time, but now they had to be reinterpreted in terms of a kabbalah newly revealed to fit the new *aion.* Clearly the proper vehicle of this new revelation would be a man whose soul was a spark of Luria's. There is, in fact, indirect evidence suggesting that Nathan believed himself already at this early stage to be the *gilgul* (reincarnation) of Luria. One of the early Gaza letters reports that Nathan had prophesied "that the rabbi Luria would appear soon to teach and elucidate his *kawwanoth.* When he was asked whether it [that is, Luria's reappearance] would be by way of *gilgul,* he did not reply."[234] The most natural explanation of this prophecy seems to be that Nathan hinted at an imminent revelation of the true and appropriate devotions. One being asked whether Luria's soul would transmigrate for that purpose, Nathan made no reply because he believed that Luria had, in fact, already returned, though he would not divulge the true nature of his soul "lest he appear to pride himself." The continuation of the letter leaves us in no doubt as to how Nathan's silence was interpreted: "and they [Nathan's interlocutors] believe that the rabbi Nathan will soon bring his [Luria's] words, which Heaven has not permitted until now."

233. See the Sabbatian list of transmigrations, published by G. Scholem in *Zion,* VI (1941), 127.

234. Haberman, p. 211.

Unlike Sabbatai Ṣevi, Nathan did not reject the Lurianic doctrine of *tiqqun;* he merely held it to have become obsolete. As a result of Israel's religious acts and the messiah's struggle against the demonic powers, the last sparks of divine light had been liberated from their captivity in the realm of the "shells." Nathan's formulation exhibits his usual radicalism and bespeaks an acute apocalyptic expectation. The forces of evil cannot subsist for long after the light of holiness has been withdrawn from them, and they must inevitably collapse. But the forces of evil are not only the demonic powers of the kabbalistic realm of the "shells"; they are also present in the rule of tyranny on earth, in the profane history of the world, and in Israel's exile among "Edom" and "Ishmael." The destruction of the dominion of the gentiles and the collapse of the "demonic powers" are therefore closely related. Lurianic messianism and Nathan's apocalyptic vision could coalesce at this point. Hence also the precise dating of messianic events in the second part of the letter. As from the year 418 (1657–58), the Shekhinah was being raised up; now, with the year 426 (1665–66) approaching, this process had been completed and the Shekhinah (the "crown of her husband") was, at last, in full and complete union, "face to face," with her husband. The dissolution of the kingdom of oppression and the end of the external, visible exile were merely a matter of "one year and some months." Nathan does not attempt to explain how the realm of the *qelippah* could subsist after the departure of the last sparks of holiness, let alone whence it would draw the strength to revolt against the dominion of holiness as stated in the prophecy. The inconsistency further illustrates the way in which the different trends of eschatological thought combined in Nathan's mind. The Haggadic tradition of an apocalyptic catastrophe was too much alive to be simply discarded, though its details could be changed. It held its own even in an eschatological system in which it had no logical place. Perhaps Nathan too was not quite immune to the fascination of the old legendary apocalyptic. With a little less extremism and a little more caution, he could easily have allowed some holy "sparks" to remain behind in the realm of the *qelippah,* thus accounting for the final revolt of the Grand Turk—the equivalent of the war of Armilus, or the Antichrist, of earlier legends. But Nathan apparently did not care to provide for this escape, though later, when the great crisis came, he fell back on this explanation. Meanwhile, only the most radical formulations satisfied his ardent faith. Impervious to logical inconsistencies, his mind absorbed the most diverse elements of messianic tradition, both exoteric and esoteric, and merged them in his eschatological vision.

A further point in the letter merits closer attention, since it presents more than just a variation of an older, traditional motif. This is Nathan's emphatic stress on pure "faith" as a religious value. This notion of faith as independent of, and indeed outweighing, all outward religious acts and symbols is distinctly Christian in character. Some hints of this theology of faith were already contained in the *Vision of R. Abraham,* and particularly in its exegesis of Habakkuk 2:4, "and the just shall live by his faith." But the real significance of this faith becomes fully explicit in the letter to Raphael Joseph. Faith is no longer the messiah's relationship to the "God of his Faith," but the relationship of Israel to its messiah.

The analogy is striking indeed. The type of pure faith, without signs or miracles, that Nathan demands, is the same as that extolled in the Gospels ("Blessed are they that have not seen, and yet have believed," John 20:29) and so greatly admired by some historians of Christianity (for example, Rénan) as the acme of religious achievement. According to Nathan, "Israel has no life unless it believes all these things without sign or miracle." The unbelievers were unable to arrest the process of redemption, and were merely hurting themselves. This principle has been consistently upheld by Nathan in all his later letters and treatises, and became a part of the heritage of the Sabbatian movement as a whole. At this point, however, another motif enters Nathan's thought: the messiah himself justifies those who believe in him and condemns those who disbelieve. "And he that entertains doubts, though he be the most pious man in the world, he [that is, the messiah] may punish him with great afflictions." The latter part of the sentence appears, at first sight, to mitigate the harshness of Nathan's doctrine: salvation is not impossible for the unbelievers, though dire punishment will be visited upon them. But this note of moderation is absent from Nathan's other writings, which place extreme emphasis on the saving power of faith. Samuel Gandoor, writing from Gaza in the autumn of 1665, quotes the following statement of Nathan's *sola fides* doctrine: "Let the lying lips be put to silence that speak grievous things against the righteous [Ps. 31:18]; and he that does not believe in him [that is, in Sabbatai Ṣevi] has no part or inheritance with Israel, neither in this world nor in the world to come, even though he have *misvoth* and good works, and he shall not behold the comforting of Zion."[235] The unbelievers, who observe the Law but deny the messiah, are no true Israelites at all but souls of the "mixed multitude," and shall have no share in the world to come.

Whence this radical and almost sacramental conception of faith? Perhaps the overwhelming character of Nathan's profound messianic experience is sufficient as a psychological explanation. Perhaps Christian influences, too, should be taken into account, although it is difficult to imagine how Christian doctrines could have come to Nathan's knowledge. The young scholar at the *yeshibah* of R. Jacob Ḥagiz would hardly have held converse with the Christian monks in Jerusalem. Did Sabbatai Ṣevi pick up some information regarding christological beliefs during his wanderings? There is, as yet, no certain answer to these questions; perhaps it is even unnecessary to look for specific Christian influences where the respective situations are so similar. Early Sabbatianism and the early church went similar ways in accordance with the same psychological laws. But however that may be, the fact remains that at the very beginning of the movement, pure faith, independent of the observance of the Law, was proclaimed as the supreme religious value which secured salvation and eternal life for the believers. We should note in passing that this proclamation did not provoke the reaction one would have expected if some of today's clichés regarding the "essence" of Judaism and of Christianity were correct. As a matter of fact they are not, and most modern generalizations on the subject of Jewish *versus* Christian religiosity are more than doubtful. There is no way of telling a priori what beliefs are possible or impossible within the framework of Judaism. Certainly no serious historian would accept the specious argument that the criteria of "Jewish" belief were clear and evident until the kabbalah beclouded and confused the minds. The "Jewishness" in the religiosity of any particular period is not measured by dogmatic criteria that are unrelated to actual historical circumstances, but solely by what sincere Jews do, in fact, believe, or—at least—consider to be legitimate possibilities. There was no general and immediate rabbinic outcry against the Sabbatian definition of the "holy faith" (as it was called

235. Haberman, p. 209. The same radicalism (as against the more moderate formulation in the letter to Raphael Joseph) is apparent in a quotation occurring in R. Joseph Azubib's letter to R. Moses Tardiola; see *Zion*, VI (1941), 87.

as early as 1666). Many rabbis adopted the "faith," and there were few who opposed it only on grounds of principle. Extreme caution should, therefore, be exercised before pronouncing on the "Jewish" (namely, "un-Jewish") character of spiritual phenomena in Jewish history. This remark may not find favor with dogmatists of Judaism, but it will serve as a guideline in the inquiry with which the present book is concerned.

However, the Christian character of Nathan's religious terminology becomes more and more pronounced in the years 1666–67, and it becomes increasingly difficult to account for it solely by the immanent development of the two movements. Statements such as "Blessed is he that believeth in the faith which giveth life to its adherents in this world and in the world to come"[236] and Nathan's almost technical language in his exegesis of Habakkuk 2:4 ("He whose soul is justified [sic!] by faith shall live")[237] strongly suggest that more is involved than spontaneously analogous development.

Nathan's second tenet is no less surprising. The messiah has authority to do with the Israelite nation as he pleases, by virtue of his unspeakable sufferings on their behalf. He may justify the greatest sinner. Two distinct motifs seem to be combined in this doctrine: (1) The messiah justifies the believers through their faith in him, even though they have no good works. This would correspond to the Christian doctrine of the messiah as the savior of the soul.[238] (2) The messiah can save sinners of past generations, even Jesus himself. The adverb "even" in this context is tantamount to saying "especially" Jesus. This would indicate that Nathan was much exercised by the problem of earlier messiahs. The interest in this problem may have been suggested to him by Sabbatai. There are indications that Sabbatai, once he came to regard himself as the messiah, was fascinated by the problem of his relationship to such earlier messianic figures as Jesus and Bar Kokhba. Some of Nathan's later theories seem to have been evolved as answers to such doubts. In letters written toward the end of 1665, the prophet declared that Bar Kokhba's soul had been re-

236. Letter of Nathan, written in March, 1667 (Sasportas, p. 201). Sasportas comments (*ibid.*, p. 202): "This is the faith of the Christians."

237. Wirszubski (*Zion*, III [1938], 225) pointed out that the passive form reflects Christian terminology (*per fidem justificata*). The sentence quoted was written about 1673–74.

238. Through faith (Luther), or by arbitrary election (Calvin).

incarnated in Sabbatai Ṣevi.[239] The idea is further developed in the *Treatise on the Dragons,* where Nathan explains that the numerical value of *Koziba*[240] is equal to that of the letters used in a particular kabbalistic method of spelling the divine name.[241] The association was certainly not invented by Nathan, since Ḥayyim Vital had already taught that a spark of the soul of the Davidic messiah was lodged in Bar Kokhba's soul.[242] According to a Talmudic legend, Bar Kokhba was killed at the behest of the sages, but popular tradition did not subscribe to the rabbinic disparagement of Bar Kokhba's memory. He remained a kind of hero-saint, and kabbalists such as Vital rehabilitated the messianic dignity of his soul. Such rehabilitation was hardly possible in the case of Jesus, who had become the supreme symbol of a religion that for more than a thousand years had caused the greatest hardship and suffering to the Jewish people; hence Nathan posited a different kind of relationship between him and the true messiah. According to Nathan's kabbalistic messiology, the messiah's soul is engulfed by the *qelippoth* until the time of its manifestation. The holy root of the messianic soul is surrounded by a particular "shell" (namely, demonic power), which is none other than Jesus. The latter is thus intimately related to the soul of the messiah, though not in its aspect of holiness. As the shell appears before the core of the fruit, even so the soul of the messianic *qelippah* (that is, Jesus), appeared first in this world "to entice Israel and lead it astray," as the Talmud put it. Yet there is some strange relation of identity between the messiah and Jesus, for the great mystery of the messiah's "root" is precisely in the paradox that the absolutely good grows from the absolutely evil, disengaging and liberating itself from its matrix in the process of its emergence. "And finally he [that is, the messiah] will restore [to holiness] his *qelippah* which is Jesus Christ."[243] The Talmud tells some grim details about the punishment meted out in hell to Jesus; but for Nathan it was a certainty, not merely a possibility, that he would ultimately be saved by the messiah. The idea that

239. Sasportas, p. 156. Nathan's letter is no longer extant, but parts of it were quoted by R. Hosea Nantawa of Alexandria.

240. Bar Kokhba's name as given in the Talmud. Documents recently discovered near the Dead Sea prove that this was Bar Kokhba's real name.

241. See *Beᶜlqvoth Mashiaḥ*, p. 45.

242. *Sefer ha-Liqqutim* (Jerusalem, 1913), fol. 23c.

243. *Beᶜlqvoth Mashiaḥ*, p. 43; cf. also below, p. 306.

the *qelippah* would not simply be annihilated, but would be saved and raised to holiness was already formulated in Nathan's first apocalypse. Now, however, it was restated in exemplary radicalism. One has to realize the significance—for seventeenth-century Jewish minds—of the doctrine of an eschatological restoration of Jesus to his people and to his "holy root" in order to grasp the full extent of Nathan's boldness. Nathan's vision of Sabbatai redeeming the soul of Jesus is an exact analogy, nay, anticipation, of the later Hasidic legend according to which Israel Ba^cal Shem attempted to save the soul of Sabbatai Ṣevi. There is something impressive about the messianic *élan* of Nathan's refusal to acknowledge that the "lost souls" of Jewish history were irrevocably lost. This idea of Nathan's was—actually or implicitly—only part of an even more radical conception: nothing and nobody is irrevocably lost, and everything will ultimately be saved and reinstated in holiness. The "redemption of Jesus" was, perhaps, merely the first symbolic expression of a doctrine that was as yet inarticulate, but which Nathan developed and formulated more clearly in subsequent years. If Jesus was capable of salvation, then there was also hope for the unbelieving rabbis who rejected the true messiah Sabbatai Ṣevi.

Nathan's critics, however, interpreted his doctrine differently. The notion of the salvation of Jesus, whose soul, according to Talmudic tradition, was forever condemned, was particularly offensive to R. Jacob Sasportas, who commented: "May boiling liquid be poured into his [Nathan's] mouth. God forbid that because of their belief in Sabbatai Ṣevi, Jesus and his like should have greater merit than a believer in God, in His Law and in His prophets." R. Joseph ha-Levi in Leghorn described Nathan's doctrine as "sheer heresy,"[244] adding, "Has it ever been heard in Israel that a man can reward or punish souls according to his pleasure? Does he wish to implant in us the faith of the misbelievers who say that their Jesus saves and justifies souls? How is it possible that one who has knowledge of the Law as well as good works should forfeit his hope because he would not believe in the messiah without a sign or miracle?" The critics, it is true, used language as strong as this only after Sabbatai's apostasy, when it was safe to do so. Yet we may assume that this is how they had always felt on this issue, even if they may have hesitated to express

244. See Sasportas, pp. 9, 195, 311. The sentence quoted is from p. 195.

themselves in such strong terms. The radical formula of the condemnation of the righteous and justification of the sinner was bound to provoke their hostility. But there were many others, particularly in the oriental communities, who were hardly irritated by what must have seemed to them mere hyperbole. The idea of the salvation of Jesus did not per se offend them.

The second part of the letter abounds with popular motifs and seems to address itself mainly to the imagination of ordinary folk. There was nothing military about Nathan's fantasies. Sabbatai Ṣevi would not have to fight, at any rate at the beginning of his career. Everything would be achieved by means of hymns, in the singing of which Sabbatai excelled more than in feats of arms. This idea, too, was not new. Earlier books of a highly apocalyptic character[245] had explained that the psalms were really the battle songs of the eschatological war. The weapons with which Israel would fight were the words of the psalms and the power inherent in them. Nathan predicted decisive events for the year 1667, and his timetable is not devoid of interest. The important years, it appears, were 1665, when the messiah revealed himself, and 1667, when he would begin to reign. In that year all kings would become tributary to him, and Israel would live in peace and honor in their usual dwelling places in the Diaspora. The apocalyptic year 1666, to which many writers have attached such exaggerated importance as the decisive year in Sabbatai's (or his friends') messianic program, in fact plays no role at all in Nathan's prophecy, except as a period of preparation and repentance. The great events were scheduled to take place partly before, partly after 1666. Equally interesting is the fact that Nathan took no account at all of the desire of the masses to leave the Diaspora and to repair at once to the Holy Land. Though himself born and bred in Jerusalem, the prophet encouraged nothing of the sort. The time for the ingathering of the exiles had not yet come. Meanwhile there would be no vengeance on the gentiles, and only the Polish massacres of 1648 and the following years would be avenged. This, at least, seems to be the meaning of the prediction of slaughter among the uncircumcised "in the German lands" (*beʾareṣoth ʾashkenaz*) only. The "German lands" should probably be taken in the wider sense of certain lands of

245. E.g., *Kaf ha-Qetoreth,* composed shortly after the expulsion from Spain; cf. above, p. 18.

Ashkenazi Jewry, that is, Poland and Russia.[246] Elsewhere Nathan is more specific. In 1668 he declared in Ancona that the messiah would wreak vengeance only on the "cities of Poland"[247] for the Jewish blood shed there. There is indeed, another version of his letter, written in 1666, where he said as much.[248] Sabbatai's assumption of kingship would be the only miracle so far. The other miracles would begin with Sabbatai's journey to the lost Ten Tribes, whom he would bring back from beyond the legendary river Sambatyon. The Ten Tribes did not, as yet, play a major part in Nathan's imagination, and the contrast between his brief remarks in the letter and the luxurious growth of legends on the subject immediately afterward is very striking indeed. Popular imagination responded to this particular detail and seized on it with a suddenness and enthusiasm unforeseen by the prophet, who still lived in an imaginary world of his own. The messianic woes would begin after 1672. In this time of tribulation for Jacob, the only safe refuge would be Gaza, the "strength of the Lord," the new metropolis of the Holy Land. The most obvious reason for Gaza's new status seems to be the fact that the city was the scene of the revelation of the messiah and his prophet. Soon, however, believers looked for other explanations. The author of the Yemenite apocalypse writes rather soberly: "Why from Gaza? Because Gaza never produced either scholar or prophet, therefore the destroyer of Rome will go forth from there."[249] The most fanciful interpretations of the name Gaza were rife during the height of the messianic enthusiasm. One interpretation of Psalm 21—a great favorite in

246. Sasportas' Sephardic blood boiled at such discrimination. Was Ashkenazic blood more precious than Sephardic? The biblical prophecies of vengeance on the persecutors of Israel did not distinguish between Sephardim and Ashkenazim. Evidently Nathan wanted to beguile the Ashkenazi communities who had suffered so much only recently and entice them to the Sabbatian faith. Sasportas may have been a good polemicist, but here he shows himself a very poor psychologist.

247. And not *ᵓAshkenazi* in general; see the text in *H. A. Wolfson Jubilee Volume*, Hebrew part (1965), p. 231.

248. See ch. 5, n. 326.

249. *Qobeṣ ᶜal Yad*, IV, New Series (1946), 125. Raphael Supino thought that the merits of the mystic bard and rabbi of Gaza, Israel Najara, whose hymns and prayers dealt with the theme of redemption, were another contributing factor (Sasportas, p. 71).

the Sabbatian hymnal—said: "The king shall rejoice in Thy strength, O Lord; and in thy salvation how greatly shall he rejoice. 'In Thy strength' [Hebrew, *be*ᶜ*ozzekha*], that is, 'in Gaza' [Hebrew, *be*ᶜ*azzah*]. 'Shall rejoice' consists [in Hebrew] of the same letters as [the Hebrew word for] 'messiah.' 'And in Thy salvation' has the same numerical value as the name Sabbatai Ṣevi."[250] This sample of Sabbatian exegesis occurs in a letter written in Egypt in the winter 1665–66, but it surely originated in Gaza.

Next there would follow all the miraculous events mentioned in the apocalyptic legends of the midrash and the Zohar. To these Nathan added the strange detail of Sabbatai's marriage to Rebekah, the daughter of Moses. The implication seems to be that the Ashkenazi wife whom the messiah had married in Egypt was not, after all, his foreordained mate; in due course she would be degraded to the position of a mere handmaid or concubine. Is this merely the free play of Nathan's imagination, or a veiled criticism of Sabbatai's wife, whose premarital behavior had given rise to unedifying rumors? The whole fantastic incident is further surrounded by mystery, as it "can be explained by word of mouth only." On his return with the "children of Moses" and the Ten Tribes (who are not explicitly mentioned, but obviously implied), he would find in Palestine only seven thousand righteous and saints, who had remained steadfast in the period of tribulation in the reign of Armilus, namely, his substitute. In the same year the ingathering of the exiles would begin. Nathan distinguishes somewhat surprisingly between the prosperity of the Jews in the Diaspora, who maintain themselves in spite of all adversities, and the bitter fate visited on the Jews of Palestine. The messiah's final manifestation is portrayed in thoroughly mythical terms, and as these differed from the popular myths of traditional literature, Sasportas dismissed them contemptuously as "old wives' tales."[251]

The singularly fantastic character of the letter, whose predictions were so soon belied by the course of events, astonished not only the infidels. Under the pressure of the actual developments, even a leading rabbi of the Sabbatian party would pronounce the letter a fabrication, forged by the "opponents and scoffers" in order to discredit the movement. In 1669 R. Jacob ibn Saᶜadun of Salé

250. Haberman, p. 212.
251. Sasportas, p. 197.

in Morocco described the letter as "vain dreams," and declared that "this cursed voice has never been heard in our land [that is, in Morocco], in none of the writings that came from the east and from the west."[252] The letter, which had achieved such wide notoriety by the end of 1665 had, apparently, never come into the hands of Saᶜadun, or else had been completely forgotten by him. At any rate it was possible, three years later, to represent it as a forgery. The opinion voiced in complete seriousness by Saᶜadun had already been expressed ironically by Sasportas at the very beginning of the Sabbatian controversy. Writing in January, 1666, to a believer in Amsterdam, Sasportas ironically affirmed that the letter was surely not by Nathan himself. In the summer of the same year he repeated the same gimmick in his letters to Aaron Sarphati and Raphael Sufino, pretending that the letter was an obvious forgery.[253]

VI

Nathan's letter says nothing about Sabbatai's actual, concrete personality, with the exception of one brief and somewhat vague hint: Sabbatai had received his unique power of justifying and condemning through the unspeakable agonies which he had suffered "on behalf of the Israelite nation." For the rest, we are given information about the future acts of the messiah and doctrinal instruction about the new status of Lurianic kabbalah. Sabbatai's character and personality seem to be of no interest; the prophet's endorsement of his mission was deemed sufficient. This absence of more personal elements is characteristic of yet another type of literature which Nathan produced at the same time, and which was of considerable significance for the development and success of the movement. These were his penitential tracts.

Nathan had predicted an interval of "one year and some months" between the messiah's first manifestation in Gaza and his departure from Palestine (which would not be attended by any "messianic" phenomena), on the one hand, and the onset of the actual messianic events, on the other, for example, his taking the crown from the Grand Turk and his conquest of all the kingdoms by singing psalms and hymns. What would the messiah do in the interval? At first Nathan gave no reply to this question, though as time went on, his reticence

252. *Ibid.*, p. 327.
253. *Ibid.*, pp. 37, 70, 139.

was swept away by his enthusiasm, and he began to feel that events might move more rapidly than allowed for in his first revelation. However that may be, the messiah's self-revelation was not intended as a prelude to the immediate accomplishment of a concrete mission or of any spectacular acts during the years 1665–67. The interval was meant to provide Israel with a chance to acquire the specific merit of "faith," and to repent, so as to be saved from the great tribulations of the messianic woes. The call to repentance was the obverse side of Nathan's apocalyptic prophecy. The proclamation of the messiah's advent and the recognition of his identity led quite naturally, to a mighty call to the House of Israel to repent. At about the same time that he wrote the letter to Raphael Joseph, Nathan also dispatched, to the same person as well as to others, his first penitential tracts and instructions. These penitential exercises and devotions were first arranged by Nathan, and subsequently much revised and elaborated by the kabbalistic circle in Gaza and by the kabbalists at the court of the *chelebi* Raphael Joseph. A letter written by a member of the *chelebi*'s circle (which was, no doubt, a center of messianic propaganda) states: "And in recent letters sent by him [Nathan?] in the first third of the month Ḥeshvan [beginning of October, 1665], it is said that he very much urges repentance, for events would be [moving] rapidly. And whoever has not put on the breastplate of repentance[254] as behooves him, will suffer tribulations. He also sent penitential lessons for the day and for the night, as well as devotions for the reparation of sins."[255]

This literature enjoyed a wide circulation. The devotions it enjoined were of two kinds: penitential lessons for the masses, and penitential exercises and acts of reparation mainly for kabbalists. The latter consisted of special kabbalistic devotions and prayers, more particularly for fast days: but although not intended for popular use, "their influence reached wider circles."[256] The penitential lessons, or readings, on the other hand, were mainly selec-

254. Cf. Isa. 59:17; Eph. 6:14–17; I Thess. 5:8.

255. Haberman, p. 211.

256. Tishby, in his important study on this second type of penitential tracts, in *Tarbiz,* XV (1944), 161–80. Tishby's analysis, to which my account is indebted, is based on a close study of two MSS.; other MSS. (particularly in the Günzburg Collection, Moscow) still await examination (reprinted in Tishby's *Paths of Faith and Heresy* [Hebrew, 1964], pp. 30–51).

tions from the Bible and the Mishnah, on the pattern of the earlier *tiqqunim* composed by the kabbalists of Safed and Italy for various special occasions, for example, the New Moon, and the vigil of *Shabu*ᶜ*oth*, *Hosha*ᶜ*na Rabbah* (the "Great Hosanna," the seventh day of the Feast of Tabernacles), and the seventh night of Passover. These little anthologies of biblical and rabbinic passages were meant for the ordinary man; their kabbalistic character showed only indirectly in the principles underlying the selection of texts, and in the extracts from the Zohar appended to the *tiqqun*. Nathan's readings were of the same type. Verses from the weekly portions of the Pentateuch and from other books of the Bible, and a selection of psalms, were arranged to form "penitential readings" for congregational recitation, both after midnight[257] and after the morning service. Many editions of these liturgies[258] were printed during the year 1666 and they played an important part in the messianic awakening. In some editions and manuscript copies it is explicitly stated that they were composed by Nathan[259] or that they had been sent from the Holy Land.[260]

The more strictly kabbalistic exercises and devotions for the reparation of sins were printed only much later (Smyrna, 1732), in a very rare and heavily purged edition, but full manuscript versions have been preserved. They are long lists of detailed instructions for fasts and the like, rather than liturgical texts. Thus "the order of undertaking a great fast of six days and nights (that is, the whole week, from Saturaday evening to Friday evening)" contains detailed instructions and prayers for the beginning of the fast on Saturday evening, the special prayers for each day, the devotions and meditations for each particular prayer, and finally the great confession of sins with its detailed enumeration of transgressions. The confession, too, is couched in prayer form ("May it be thy will, O Cause of All Causes"). The specifically kabbalistic character appears in the

257. The mystic intention of the "lesson for every night" was the adorning of the Supernal Bride (i.e., the Shekhinah) now returning to her Husband.

258. A complete list is still an urgent bibliographical desideratum. A tentative list is given below, pp. 936–39.

259. See the title page of the Spanish edn. in the library of the Hebrew Union College in Cincinnati reproduced here, plate IV.

260. E.g., the title page of the edn. printed in Constantinople in autumn, 1665.

enumeration of the particular combinations of divine names which the sinner has blemished, and in his prayer for the reparation of the injury. "And he should say [this confession] with devotion and humility, and it is desirable that he shed tears and wipe them across his forehead."[261] Such a six-day fast accompanied by the proper meditations and devotions is equal, so we are told, to nine hundred and sixteen ordinary fasts! The devotional intensity of the mortification equals the enormous number of days. Even so, one "great fast" is not sufficient, for although forgiveness may have been obtained for previous sins, new ones may have been committed since then, "for there is not a just man upon earth that sinneth not." The prophet therefore "sent this further devotion for two days and two nights" as well as a similar devotion for three days and three nights. He also provided "orders of fasts" for thirty-six hours as well as for the *Shobabim Tat* period. The latter term is an acrostic, formed by the initial letters of the names of the eight weekly portions of the Pentateuch (Exod. 1–30) read during the winter months. Lurianic kabbalists believed that fasting during these weeks was particularly efficacious in retrieving the "backsliding children," that is, the spirits dwelling in the drops of semen which a man had lost through masturbation or in wet dreams, and which provided "bodies" for demons and evil spirits. The Lurianic identification of the backsliding children (the expression is taken from Jer. 3:14) and the somewhat punning application of the Hebrew word for "backsliding" (*shobabim*) clearly caused the choice of this particular period of the year for the penitential exercise.[262] The new *tiqqun* would restore these "fallen sparks" to the sphere of holiness. Although the prophet had already announced in his letter that there were no more divine sparks imprisoned in the *qelippah,* he had not said that no sparks of human souls were left there. The sparks of the divine light and those of individual human souls are different things. The latter still had to be saved by human effort, in accordance with Lurianic principles.

The penitential devotions illustrate the abiding influence of Lurianic kabbalism on the prophet of Gaza. Even the smallest details can be traced back to Luria's devotions; there are no specifically Sab-

261. See Tishby, *Tarbiz,* XV (1944), 162.

262. For an account of the kabbalistic mythology and rituals connected with this subject, see G. Scholem, *On the Kabbalah and Its Symbolism* (New York, 1965), pp. 154–57.

batian modifications or additions. Nathan took his material from the penitential classics of the Lurianic school,[263] combining them in ways that suited his purpose and occasionally making some additions of his own. The "great confession," for example, is not found in this form in any known Lurianic text, although all its elements are traditional.[264]

Of particular interest in this respect is Nathan's adaptation of the statutory daily *ᶜAmidah* prayer, the prayer consisting of eighteen benedictions. Nathan simply inserted into his prayer the "devotions for the *ᶜAmidah*" found in the writings of Vital, and recommended it as "a prayer conveying special grace[265] which one should say with great devotion." For kabbalist readers these new devotions could easily form a bridge from their traditional life of prayer to Nathan's new theology. Here are excerpts from four of the eighteen benedictions of the *ᶜAmidah*, the standard opening sentence using the plural, but the mystical additions for the penitent changing into the singular:

O look upon our affliction and plead our cause; make haste to redeem us with a perfect redemption for the sake of Thy Name, and may I too be found worthy to behold redemption and so see the king [that is, the Messiah] in his beauty [cf. Isa. 33:17]. Redeem all the sparks of holiness [originating] from my [soul-] root, and from the root of my root, and from the ultimate root of the roots of my root, which are now in the [realm of the] *qelippoth*. May they be conceived in the womb of the holy [*sefirah*] *Malkhuth,* and do not turn unto their evil deeds, for the "other side" [that is, the demons and *qelippoth*] has enticed them to separate themselves from under the wings of Thy Shekhinah. For Thou, O God, art a merciful King and Redeemer. . . .

Heal us, O Lord, and we shall be healed; save us and we shall be saved, for Thou art our praise. Grant healing and cure for all our diseases and the diseases of our soul . . . heal us with a healing of the soul and a healing of the body, and may my soul be free from dross and blemish . . . heal me from all plagues and sorrows that are in my body and soul. If my soul needs a bath of purification, let Michael the great

263. E.g., Menaḥem Azaryah Fano's *Kanfey Yonah*, Ḥayyim Vital's *Shaᶜar ha-Yiḥudim*, Abraham Ṣahalon's *Marpe le-nephesh*, etc.

264. Tishby, *Tarbiz, loc. cit.*, pp. 167–71.

265. This is the meaning of the Hebrew term *Tefillath Nedavah.*

prince, who offers sacrifices on the altar of the heavenly Jerusalem, dip her into the fiery stream [cf. Dan. 7:10]. . . .

Sound the great horn for our freedom, raise the banner to gather our exiles, and gather us speedily from the four corners of the earth to our land. May all drops of semen that I have emitted [by accidental or deliberate pollution], whether in the present or in former transmigrations, whether willingly or unwillingly, whether intentionally or unintentionally . . . return to their holy source in the holiness of Thy Name. Blessed art Thou, O Lord, Who wilt gather the exiles of Thy people Israel.

O dwell in the midst of Jerusalem Thy city as Thou hast spoken, and speedily set up the throne of Thy servant David therein. Grant us a redemption without the sadness and the sorrow of seeing the messiah of the House of Joseph, who hath begun to comfort us and to raise our banner above the nations, slain in our sight. For then all the gentiles will arise to cut off our name, and the name of Israel will be remembered no more. Remember that we have no good works on which to rely in order to be saved from the messianic woes, but Thou hast not created Thy world in vain [cf. Isa. 45:18].[266]

The last benediction adheres to traditional patterns to the extent of mentioning the messiah of the House of Joseph without even asking whether he had already appeared before Sabbatai Ṣevi, or whether he would appear only later, during the imminent messianic tribulations. Evidently Nathan had simply taken over the wording of the earlier Lurianic devotions for this prayer.

On the other hand, Nathan's *tiqqunum* also contain allusions to Sabbatai Ṣevi and additions reflecting his messianic and kabbalistic doctrines. Some of the extant manuscripts omit Sabbatai's name, but in several others it occurs in enlarged letters.[267] But Sabbatian literature—and more especially the penitential devotions—abound with allusions of the *gematria*-type, one of the more conspicuous being the Hebrew word for "in thy salvation," the numerical value of which is equal to that of Sabbatai Ṣevi. Since the word occurs frequently in the psalms and in the prayer book, there was ample scope for messianic allusions. The text of the *ᶜAmidah* prayer has "O cause the branch of Thy servant David speedily to flourish, and let his horn be exalted by thy salvation"

266. Full text in Tishby, *Tarbiz, loc. cit.*, pp. 179–80.
267. See Tishby in *Sefunoth,* III–IV (1960), 82.

to which Nathan added the instruction: "When saying 'by thy salvation' meditate on the numerical value of this word, which is equal to that of the divine name Shadday and to that of Our Lord, the King and Messiah Sabbatai Ṣevi." Similarly in the prayer, "On thee I have cast my burden, sustain me and grant me to behold the face of Thine anointed. Let us exult and rejoice *in thy salvation*," the last word is written in conspicuously large letters.[268] In my discussion of Nathan's reference, in his letter to Raphael Joseph, to the manifestation of the light of the Holy Ancient One, I mentioned that this doctrine was expressed more explicitly in the penitential devotions. According to Nathan, the manifestation of the light of the Holy Ancient One was related to the manifestation of another light—that of the name Shadday, "which will become manifest in the name of the messiah whose name has the same numerical value," The messiah is the true Shadday, because he robbed (Hebrew, *shadad*) the *qelippoth* of their power.

We have seen that Nathan posited a special relationship between Sabbatai's soul and the realm of the *qelippoth*, and that he regarded Jesus as the *qelippah*, or "husk," of the messiah's soul. Nathan's fondness of ringing the changes on the theme of the messiah's paradoxical relation to the sphere of the *qelippah* shows in the symbolism of the *Vision of R. Abraham*, in his penitential devotions, and in his writings composed after 1666. The procedure is always the same: by means of kabbalistic exegeses, Sabbatai's name or the word "messiah" is brought into relation with the symbols of the "other side," which the messiah conquers. The messiah himself is symbolized by Pharaoh, "the great dragon that lieth in the midst of his rivers (cf. Ezek. 29:3)." In this bold image Pharaoh, the prince of the realm of evil, also functions as a symbol of the holiness that conquers and annihilates the *qelippah*.[269] But the messiah is not only Pharaoh. He is also King Ahasuerus, for the numerical value of that name (in the defective spelling) equals that of Sabbatai Ṣevi. The providential salvation of

268. Cf. also above, p. 289, for an example of Sabbatian exegesis of Ps. 21.

269. The kabbalists found a further analogy between the title of Pharaoh for the king of Egypt, and the name Asmodai, king of the demons: the numerical values of both names are equal (see G. Scholem, *Tarbiz*, XIX [1948], 160). Some kabbalists assumed that Asmodai was indeed the title of the king of demons, not the proper name of one of them.

Israel, as told in the Book of Esther, would be wrought once more by the messianic king, the "Ahasuerus of Holiness." Some of these paradoxes were probably added in the course of later revisions of the penitential tracts, in the second half of 1666. But they were certainly formulated before Sabbatai's apostasy, which is nowhere hinted at. Similarly the messiah's personality and character are never made the subject of meditations and expositions in early documents. Apparently these themes were not considered fit for literary treatment; they were discussed in a small esoteric circle, and set forth in kabbalistic homilies whose symbolism obfuscated the underlying psychological and personal realities. Nathan's first apocalypse had stated his views regarding the soul of the messiah in striking symbolic images, but almost a year passed before he developed these ideas at greater length. Nevertheless, a discussion of this particular doctrine becomes necessary at this point, since Nathan's teaching was characterized by a strong and intimate continuity, even where it changed. The basic elements of his doctrine regarding the connection between the messiah's redemptive function and the mystery of creation are no later developments; they form part of his original intuition as crystallized in his great vision in the winter of 1665. Although the final literary formulation is of a later date, the terminological and stylistic similarities between the *Treatise on the Dragons* and Nathan's earlier writings, particularly the apocalypse, admit of no doubt that we are entitled to view his thinking and experience during the period 1665–66 as a unity.

VII

The *Treatise on the Dragons* is only one in a series of kabbalistic tracts in which Nathan expounded his new messianic doctrine. These tracts are lost, but they are referred to in the one surviving *Treatise.*[270] They were probably composed at the request of the *chelebi* Raphael Joseph, who desired more information concerning the prophet's vision and teaching and who, as a close acquaintance of Sabbatai, wished to be enlightened as to the significance of the messiah's strange character and the nature of his own soul.[271] The original epistolary form still shows at the end of Nathan's tract, which purports to be a commentary on a passage in the Zohar.

270. Ed. G. Scholem, *Be^cIqvoth Mashiaḥ*, pp. 9–52.

271. Toward the end of the *Treatise* (p. 51) Nathan addresses the recipient and informs him of the root of his soul.

The obscure Zoharic text [ii, 34a–35b] with its luxuriant mythological symbolism, had given rise to many commentaries by the Safed kabbalists. The commentators all agreed that the mysterious passage dealt with the nature, power, and roots of the *qelippah.* One of Luria's principal disciples, Joseph ibn Tᵓbul, wrote a special tract on this passage, entitled—in some manuscripts—*Treatise on the Dragons.* Nathan possibly took his title from some such manuscript,[272] but that is where the similarity ends.

Nathan's tract presents the transition from Lurianic kabbalism to a completely new and original type of speculation. Hence also its outstanding importance for any attempt at understanding the spiritual development of Sabbatianism. The two characteristic features of Sabbatian kabbalism are clearly present here: (1) the reinterpretation of traditional Lurianic doctrines in terms of the new faith in Sabbatai's messianic calling, a reinterpretation which inevitably at times completely distorted the original meaning; (2) the central role assigned to the messiah. These innovations involved the introduction of other new elements into the kabbalistic system. Prima facie the pattern of thought of the *Treatise* is Lurianic; it contains no obvious heresies and most of its statement can be referred back to the classical Lurianic texts. Even where no such points of contact exist, Nathan's utterances do not go beyond the bounds of possibilities inherent in the traditional teaching. He shows himself thoroughly familiar not only with Vital's writings and the intricacies of the doctrine of divine configurations (*parṣufim*), but also with the rival traditions of Luria's other disciples, whether genuine or pretended, such as Joseph ibn Tᵓbul and Israel Sarug. Nathan was evidently aware of the existence of different "schools" or tendencies within the Lurianic kabbalah, as well as of the fact that it contained later additions (for example, by Israel Sarug). For Nathan these differences served as proof of the existence of different levels of reference in esoteric teaching. There was one

272. MS. Badhab 160 (National Library, Jerusalem) is a late copy of a "Treatise on the Dragons by Isaac Luria"; R. Isaac Medina of Aleppo quotes from this "Treatise on the Dragons" (which he attributed to Ḥayyim Vital) in his *Nefesh Dawid* (Constantinople, 1736), fol. 4a, 13b. R. Meir Poppers, in his commentary on the Zohar (MS. Mousaioff 35) refers to a "*Mystery of the Dragon* which we found among the papers of R. Joseph ibn Tᵓbul. . . . but I did not copy it, since it appears to be not by the Master [i.e., Luria or Vital]." See also G. Scholem in *Zion,* V (1940), 154–60. The present evidence about ibn Tᵓbul's treatise had then escaped my notice.

supernal sphere in the divine lights concerning which Vital had said nothing at all, and it was this sphere of lights "above the primordial Adam Qadmon" which Nathan undertook to explain. R. Israel Sarug had already "said a few things" with regard to these mysteries, but Nathan felt entitled to expatiate on them at greater length. His arguments and terminology leave no doubt that he had studied the writings of both schools,[273] though his main tenets constitute a new departure in kabbalistic thinking. He must have been aware of his originality, as he warns the recipient of the *Treatise* that "although it may, at first sight, appear to contradict your kabbalah, yet both are equally true."[274]

The obscure and involved technicalities of Nathan's "Lurianic" discussions contrast strikingly with the plastic distinctness of the new Sabbatian elements. The starting point of the Lurianic system, the doctrine of *ṣimṣum*, or retraction, has been outlined in an earlier chapter (see above, pp. 28–31). The primordial space that came into being as a result of the divine retraction was called *tehiru*[275] in the terminology of Luria and Sarug (the latter got the term from Ibn Tᵓbul). The *tehiru* was still full of traces (*reshimu*, "imprint") of the supernal light, since the divine light could not withdraw itself without leaving vestiges of its presence. The *reshimu* of the light of *En-Sof*, though not identical with *En-Sof*, is a tremendous power. According to Luria it is a holy power, although the roots of the forces of rigor (*din*)—which would then produce the *qelippoth*—were intermingled with it (or, according to another version, manifested themselves in it). It is precisely with regard to the crucial question of the ultimate origin of evil and the *qelippah* that the versions of the Lurianic schools differ most. Vital did everything to obscure his master's daring conception of creation as a cathartic act in which *En-Sof* purged itself of the latent *din* inherent in it. This doctrine was successfully concealed in Vital's

273. His discussion of the *tehiru* reflects Sarug's teachings. Apparently he had also read the writings of Menaḥem Azaryah Fano and Bacharach's *ᶜEmeq ha-Melekh,* as well as Nathan Shapira's *Megalleh ᶜAmuqoth* (1637) and the writings of the other Nathan Shapira Yerushalmi. Considering the fact that Nathan began his kabbalistic studies in the second half of 1664, his mental ability must have been truly astounding.

274. *Beᶜlqvoth Mashiaḥ*, p. 17.

275. Originally a Zoharic term meaning "splendor"; it is the Aramaic form of Hebrew *zohar*.

exposition in *ᶜEs Ḥayyim,* though Luria's authentic sayings and their exposition by Ibn Tᵓbul preserve the original character of Luria's mythical insight:[276] the "straight line" proceeding from the light substance of *En-Sof* entered the *tehiru,* and, under the impulsion of the new light, the residual lights (*reshimu*) that had remained in the *tehiru* after the retraction rearranged and re-formed themselves in such manner that at the end of the process the divine pleroma could eject the rudimentary, latent *qelippoth* present in it. In this way the mystical cosmos would be accomplished and perfected. In this view of the process of creation, there is no room for the soul of the messiah. None of the kabbalists who took the Lurianic doctrine of creation for what it was, that is, a doctrine of divine *katharsis* in which *En-Sof* purged itself of the roots of the *qelippoth* hidden in the depth of its being, ever thought of ascribing any function in this process to the messiah's soul.

Nathan evidently seized on the account of the "roots of *din*" within the *tehiru,* which he had found in the Lurianic texts that had been rejected by Vital. He adopted their ideas, but gave them a new twist. He acknowledged that the *tehiru* was the "empty space" (in Vital's terminology) which *En-Sof* had produced in its center by "retracting" its light substance. The *tehiru,* in fact, was the stage on which the subsequent drama of creation, fall, and restoration was to be enacted. However, for Nathan the *tehiru* was also more than that. It was the symbol of all the forces indifferent, or even hostile, to the emergence of a *kosmos.* The *reshimu,* that is, the residual light in the *tehiru,* contains the forces of darkness, the roots of the *qelippoth,* the primordial inertia resisting creation. Nathan was to call this unproductive, and even destructive, light the "thought-less light."

The question of how all this was possible is not yet—at this point—systematically discussed in the *Treatise.* Nathan formulated his answer in writings which he composed after Sabbatai's apostasy. There are, however, sufficient indications in the penitential exercises to suggest that he had already—much earlier—developed the main outline of his answer. There are two kinds of light: the "thought-some light"[277] and the "thought-less light." According to Nathan it is un-

276. For a fuller analysis of this problem, see Tishby, *The Problem of Evil and the "Qelippah" in Lurianic Kabbalah* (Jerusalem, 1942), pp. 21–28.

277. The term *ᵓOr ha-Maḥashabah* occurs in MS. Jerusalem 8° 159 of Nathan's penitential devotions (see Tishby in the article quoted in n. 256); the doctrine was therefore evolved before Sabbatai's apostasy.

thinkable that the infinite light of *En-Sof* should contain only such lights as were focused (and, as it were, limited) on the purpose of creation, for this would be tantamount to saying that the act of creation exhausted the contents of *En-Sof*. Hence another force or principle must be present in *En-Sof:* the thought-less light, that is, a light devoid of any thought or "idea" that would be prefigurative or constitutive of a cosmos. The thought-some light had withdrawn in the act of retraction in order to penetrate again into the *tehiru* and there to build the cosmos. After the retraction, and until the "shining forth of the straight line" (that is, the penetration of the thought-some light), the *tehiru* contained residual lights only, most of which were thought-less lights, resisting, by their very nature, the coming into being of the cosmos. Essentially a principle of inertia, the thought-less light tends to passivity and immobility; but in its resistance to all creative change and process it becomes, from the point of view of the creative purpose, a positively hostile and destructive power. The forces of destruction and the *qelippah* are thus rooted in certain lights within *En-Sof* itself. These lights in the *tehiru* are called *golem,* that is, "unformed" or "undifferentiated." When the light substance of *En-Sof* entered the *tehiru* in a straight line, the divine forms crystallized, and even the *qelippoth* and *dinim* deriving from the thought-less light found their appropriate, positive place in the emergent structures. However, not the whole *tehiru* was affected by the irruption of the ray of light from *En-Sof*. The "straight line" penetrated only the upper half of the primordial space (which should be pictured as a sphere), and there built the world of its "thought"; it did not reach the lower half, described by Nathan as "the deep of the great abyss." The great work of cosmic *tiqqun,* which Israel has to accomplish through the strength of the Law and the divine commandments, relates to the upper part of the *tehiru* only. The lower part persists in its unformed and chaotic condition (*golem*), dominated by the *qelippah* until the advent of the messiah, who alone can perfect it. As a matter of fact, the thought-less lights too built worlds unto themselves, to wit the demonic worlds of the *qelippah,* whose sole intent is to destroy the worlds of the thought-some light. These demonic forces manifest themselves in Samael and his hosts; they are the "serpents" dwelling in the "hole of the great abyss."[278] In the context of this doctrine, the

278. "Serpents" as symbols of the forces of the "evil side" occur in Lurianic texts; cf. *Maḥbereth ha-Qodesh* (Korzec, 1783), fol. 56a.

Zoharic designation of the sphere of evil as the "other side" takes on a startlingly novel meaning. It refers to the "other side" of *En-Sof* itself, that is, to that half of it which resists the process of differentiation and organization, and which, by its very resistance to the dramatic process of creation, becomes actually Satanic. The *tehiru* and the "straight line" are thus conceived as two opposing principles, comparable to the duality of matter and form. Both derive from the same divine light, and creation is a dialectical movement taking place between these two aspects of *En-Sof.*

The messiah's role in the *tiqqun* of the *qelippah* follows from his special position in this kabbalistic universe. Since the primordial act of retraction, the messiah's soul was sunk deep in the realm of the *qelippoth,* that is, in the lower half of the *tehiru.* How it got there is another problem. Nathan held that the *reshimu* consisted not only of thought-less lights, but also of other light-sparks, namely, "souls" that had originated in the thought-some light; or perhaps these souls were now in the *reshimu,* because the *qelippah,* a true parasite, had snatched them in order to draw its life from them. Nathan advances both explanations in his writings. In any event, the root of the messiah's soul is sunk deep in the lower *tehiru.* In bondage to the *qelippoth* since the beginning of the world, the messiah is struggling, amid great suffering and anguish, to free himself from their embrace and to "redeem" them. But the *qelippoth* hold him fast, seeking to possess him and prevent him from fulfilling his messianic task.

At this point, however, Nathan's argument gets involved in two conflicting motifs, and although the matter is of some importance for an understanding of the texture of his thought, there is no indication in his writings as to how he resolved the contradiction. We must briefly recall here the analysis given in Chapter I of the Lurianic doctrine of soul-roots. The doctrine assumed that the souls coming into this world were all contained in the First Man. The prelapsarian Adam was a spiritual substance. He was one great soul. The various limbs of his mystical body corresponded to the roots of all the human souls, and each of these roots reflected a light from the supernal worlds and the configurations of their *sefiroth*—more particularly from the "world of *beri᾿ah*" and the "world of *yeṣirah.*" There were also superior and hidden souls from the "world of *᾿aṣiluth*" that had never been in the mystical body of the First Adam; these would come into this world only at the end of days. Thus whenever, in Lurianic writings, soul-roots are related to the anatomy of the mystical Adam (for example, his head, trunk, or feet), the reference is to souls of a lower order. In the Lurianic scheme, souls are more imperfect the lower their *locus standi* in the body of the mystical Adam. The souls that fell with Adam and were scattered require "restoration" (*tiqqun*) in the infinitely varied ways of metempsychosis. The hardest of all to save are the souls whose roots are below, at the heels of the First Adam, and which, after the first sin, fell as low as the heels of the Satanic counterfigure to Adam, called "Adam of Belial." Souls of this order are characterized by the presence of "severe judgment," that is, the power of *din* in excessive strength; their *tiqqun* will be accomplished only after most other souls have been "restored," that is to say, shortly before redemption. Not before then will they enter this world, to be launched on their course of transmigration and *tiqqun*. This, according to the Lurianists, was the meaning of the Mishnah (*Sotah* ix, 15): "With the footprints [lit., heels] of the messiah [as one of the signs which herald his advent] insolence shall increase." In the souls deriving from the mystical heels of the "Adam of Belial," insolence and the power of *din* will assert themselves. These souls will enter the world only toward the advent of redemption, and their *tiqqun*, which is exceedingly difficult, can be accomplished only in the sufferings and pangs of the messianic woes. Nathan adopted this Lurianic scheme, as is evident from his prophecy regarding the events to be expected from 1667 on. Similarly in the *Treatise on the Dragons* he states that in the period 1665–71 "the souls originating in the skin of the heel will begin to descend . . . for they are the worst souls of all." As a matter of fact, some souls of this order had already begun to enter this world after 1575, "and these souls will attain the most wonderful wisdom, for they are of the messiah's generation, that is, of the same root as he [!]. Even as the merits of Moses benefited his contemporaries and all their descendants, so it will be with the souls of the messiah's generation."[279]

The messiah's soul, it appears, is of an inferior order and not,

279. *BeᶜIqvoth Mashiaḥ*, pp. 45–46. The remark about the year 1575 is taken from Bacharach's *ᶜEmeq ha-Melekh*, fol. 33a; see also above, p. 69.

originally and essentially, of a holy and exalted nature. It has to struggle hard to achieve its *tiqqun,* and it acquires its unparalleled holiness through heroic effort. In this respect the Sabbatian myth differs conspicuously from the classical gnostic myths according to which the fallen soul is of exalted origin and princely nature. The contradiction in Nathan's conception is obvious. On the one hand, the messiah's soul, as well as the souls of his contemporaries born into the world at the advent of the messianic age, never formed part of the body of the mystical Adam. On the other hand, the very designation "souls of the messianic advent" is explained by kabbalistic etymology as meaning "souls from the heel [of Adam]," and Nathan in fact suggests in his writings that this is where the souls of his contemporaries came from. But we are also told that the messiah's soul did not descend into the *qelippoth* as a result of the fall; it was sunk there from the very beginning. The messiah is the true ADaM (that is, Adam, David, Messiah), though his soul was never actually part of the First Man, and consequently also never implicated in the fall. At the same time, his mission is precisely the redemption of the "souls from the heel" with whom he is said to share a common root and nature.

The doctrine of the inferior order of the messiah's soul is certainly not Lurianic. On the contrary, Luria held that the messiah would receive the most exalted kind of soul (*neshamah* of *neshamah*) from the supernal splendor of the First Adam, being the only man ever to possess a soul of the rank of *yeḥidah* of the *sefirah Kether.*[280] Luria's and Nathan's ideas on this point are not irreconcilable, since it can be argued that the supereminence of the messiah's soul was not original and essential, but the outcome of its messianic evolution. There is nothing in Nathan's system to preclude such a development of the messiah's soul from the lowest level to the most perfect and exalted light. On the contrary, such a view would accord well with the emphasis on the effort and unending struggle that are the messiah's lot.

Did Nathan go further and teach that the messiah's soul was not only of a low order but actually belonged to the *qelippah?* The recurring description of the messiah's soul as "sunk" in the *qelippah* seems to suggest the contrary. To be sure, such a profoundly fascinating and paradoxical idea would be anything but incompatible with

280. See, e.g., *Sefer ha-Gilgulim,* ch. 19, and Vital's *Liqqutey Torah* on Gen. 5:22.

Nathan's thinking as we know it: before "restoring" and perfecting the *tehiru* and the cosmos as a whole, the messiah would first redeem himself by transforming his essence, which was of the *qelippah,* into the substance of holiness. His soul originated indeed in the *qelippah,* but purified and refined itself until its absolute evil became absolute good. Was this, perhaps the source both of his power to redeem the world and of his messianic authority? This interpretation was, in fact, proposed by Ch. Wirszubski, who argued[281] that in Nathan's view the messiah's soul "was generated from the same *tehiru* which also produced the serpent." But Nathan never uses such wording. He says that the soul of the messiah came into being, and was then placed in the *tehiru.* There is no explicit suggestion that it was also of the same substance. "Know that the soul of the messianic king exists in the lower *golem* [that is, the *tehiru*]. For even as the primordial serpent came into being in the *tehiru,* so also the soul of the messianic king was created and came into being by the will of *En-Sof.* It existed before the creation of the world, and abides in the great abyss." Elsewhere it is said to abide *above* the abyss and not *in* it.[282] The messiah's soul was never affected by the entry of the "straight line" into the *tehiru.* The exact significance of the statement that the messiah's soul "came into being by the will of *En-Sof*" is debatable. It may mean that his soul came into being within *En-Sof* and was then placed in the *tehiru*—the messiah over against the serpent. But in that case it could hardly be described as of an inferior order, since all manifestations of the will of *En-Sof* are of its "thought-some light." Moreover, an analysis of Nathan's terminology does not tend to confirm this interpretation. The expression "the will of *En-Sof*" occurs frequently in his writings in connection with actions that take place in the *tehiru* by the will of *En-Sof.* Maybe Nathan really thought, as Wirszubski suggests, that the messiah and the serpent, though locked in mortal combat, were of the same substance, but then he would also have to explain how the messiah succeeded in purging himself of his essence and overcoming the inferiority of his root. No such explanation is given, whereas there is much to lend support to the view that the

281. In his excellent analysis of "Nathan of Gaza's Sabbatian Theology," *Keneseth,* vol. VIII (1944), pp. 210–46, a pioneer study of Nathan's kabbalistic thinking, particularly after Sabbatai's apostasy.

282. The *Treatise on the Mystery of the Messianic King* reads "in the abyss," but other texts (see *Be^cIqvoth Mashiaḥ,* p. 105) have "above the abyss."

root of the messiah's soul was in the sphere of holiness of the "supernal configurations." His soul is "sunk" *in* the *qelippah,* but is not *of* it. Ultimately the answer to our problem hinges on the precise significance of the word "inferior." One passage in the *Treatise on the Dragons* seems to support Wirszubski's thesis that "inferior root" signifies a root from the very substance of the *qelippah.* Expounding Job 1:8, Nathan declares that Job was described as one who "departed from evil" because he symbolizes the messianic king who made [the *qelippah*] depart from evil and raised it to a higher level as 'a perfect and an upright man, one that feareth God and departeth from evil,' for *his own root is the absolute evil*[283] which is his *qelippah,* namely, Jesus whom he will ultimately redeem." By a very slight emendation, the Hebrew text of the italicized passage can be made to read "for his own root is [sunk] *in* absolute evil," that is, under the sway of evil but not consubstantial with it. The reference to the "inferior root" would mean only that the messiah's soul was not of a high order, and that its origin was in the heels of the mystical body of the First Adam,[284] that is, in the lowest part of the sphere of holiness.

Nathan defines the dignity of the messiah's soul as follows: "the root of the messianic king [of the House of David] is in the [*sefirah*] *Yesod* of [the configuration called] 'Father,' whereas that of the messiah of the House of Ephraim is in the [*sefirah*] *Yesod* of [the configuration called] 'Mother.'"[285] This definition is taken from the Lurianic writings, where it is said that the soul of Moses was a spark from the *sefirah Yesod* of the configuration 'Father'[286] as manifest in the world of *beri*ʾ*ah.* But according to Nathan, whatever is said of Moses can be applied to Sabbatai Ṣevi, since the Hebrew letters composing the name Moses can be read "Ṣevi" by inversion of the alphabet. According to Ḥayyim Vital the *sefirah* "*Yesod* of the Father" was symbolically identical with Mordecai; hence also its redemptive quality.[287] Sabbatai's disciples, and perhaps also Sabbatai himself, held Mordecai to be a spark from the

283. *Be*ᶜ*Iqvoth Mashiaḥ,* p. 43 (reading, with MS. Halberstamm, *ha-ra*ᶜ *ha-gamur;* MS. Brit. Mus. 856 *ra*ᶜ *ha-gamur);* cf. above, p. 285.

284. *Be*ᶜ*Iqvoth Mashiaḥ,* p. 50.

285. *Ibid.,* p. 20.

286. ᶜ*Es Ḥayyim, Sha*ᶜ*ar ha-Kelalim,* chs. 10 and 11, and elsewhere.

287. *Maḥbereth ha-Qodesh,* fol. 58b, 63a. (This book, ascribed to Vital, is in fact the second part of Nathan Shapira's *Me*ʾ*oroth Nathan.*)

messiah's soul.[288] By taking up these motifs, Nathan contradicted everything he had said about the messiah's "inferior root." Vital certainly never meant to ascribe an inferior dignity to the messiah when he equated him with Moses and Mordecai. On the contrary, he defined the mystical process by which the messiah's soul came into being in such a way as to leave no doubt that its source was higher than even the configuration 'Father'; it was in the highest of the five Lurianic *parṣufim*, or configurations, the one known as the long-Suffering (that is, merciful) One, *ᵓArikh ᵓAnpin*. The "holy union" of the latter with his consort is never mentioned in the Lurianic accounts of creation, whereas the *hieroi gamoi* of the four lower configurations ("Father," "Mother," and the "Impatient One" and his consort, the Shekhinah) loom large as the motor powers that set the creative process in motion. "For the *sefirah Yesod* [symbolically, the phallus] of the Long-Suffering One never acted in the creation of the world [by way of union with his consort, but exclusively by way of union] with himself, for only at the end of days will he unite himself with his consort. But when the time comes for the world to be renewed by his simple will, then the union of the Long-Suffering One with his consort will take place, and it will produce the mystery of the soul of the Davidic messiah who is in the mystery of *yehidah* [the highest type of soul], and then there shall be permanence and establishment and dominion."[289]

The inferiority of the messiah's soul and its origin in the highest of the divine configurations are incompatible. It seems futile to attempt to resolve the contradiction, as Nathan himself probably never arrived at a consistent account of the matter. I do not believe that Nathan ever completely identified the root of the messiah's soul with the *qelippah*. The tenor of the *Treatise on the Dragons* points in the opposite direction. From the beginning of time the holy serpent dwells together with the evil primordial serpent, struggling with it but not consubstantial with it. It was the "will of *En-Sof*" that planted in the depth of the Great Abyss an element that would ultimately overcome it and "redeem" the chaotic, unformed matter, and thereby

288. Israel Ḥazzan (MS. Kaufmann 255, fol. 99b): "Mordecai was a spark of AMIRAH." The reason was, of course, the redemptive role of Mordecai in the scroll of Esther.

289. Vital, as quoted in David Ḥazzan's *Qoheleth ben David* (Salonika, 1748), fol. 18d.

accomplish the *tiqqun* of the cosmos, including the worlds of the *qelippah.*

The notion that the messiah's soul was enmeshed in the *qelippah* also occurs in Lurianic literature. Nathan combines it with the idea of the "holy ruse," which he found in Vital's writings and which has been discussed in the first chapter. At times the *qelippoth*—by what turns out to be a serious miscalculation on their part—release a particularly holy soul from their clutches.[290] In this way, according to Vital, the souls of Abraham and David came into the world. From this idea it was but one step to a similar conception of the peripaties of the messiah's soul, and its applicability to Sabbatai Ṣevi was particularly striking. Ḥayyim Vital had spoken of the terrible struggle against their evil inclination (*yeṣer*) in which these choice souls were engaged. Such souls were prone to melancholy, "for of necessity such a person is always sad and anxious without any reason." King David's soul was of this kind. Vital here anticipates the pattern of Nathan's psychological theories regarding the soul of the messiah. The ups and downs of Sabbatai's emotional life have a metaphysical foundation: they are the consequence of what may be termed his biographical prehistory in the *tehiru.* Since the beginning of time the redeemer dwelt in the great deep, together with the serpents that tormented him and tried to entice him to betray his faith. The chief of the serpents and ruler of the abyss was Pharaoh, the "great dragon" who held the "holy serpent" in his power until the latter would overcome him at the end of days.[291] The similarity of their apellations—both are "serpents"—was due to the fact "that the *qelippah* ('shell') takes its name from the holiness that serves as its shell." In proffering this explanation, Nathan seems to imply a clear distinction between the holiness of the messiah's root and the *qelippah* which serves as its husk or wrapping. As long as the messiah's soul was held in bondage by Pharaoh, it was called Job. (According to rabbinic legend, Job was originally one of Pharaoh's servants.) But at the victorious end of his struggle, the messiah will go forth from the "prison of the *qelip-*

290. Vital, *Shaᶜar ha-Gilgulim*, fol. 28; see above, pp. 63–64.

291. The term "holy serpent" occurs in the *Tiqquney Zohar* (edn. Jerusalem, 1948), fol. 43a. The *gematria* messiah = serpent (namely, 358), and the idea that the serpent-messiah would destroy the evil serpent are expressed as early as the 13th century by R. Isaac Kohen of Soria in Spain, in a text published by G. Scholem, *Maddaᶜey ha-Yahaduth*, II (1926), 273.

poth," which he will subdue, and Job, the man of sorrows and suffering, shall become the Pharaoh who will tear (Hebrew, *paraᶜ*—a verb which also serves as a technical term, denoting the uncovering of the *glans penis* at circumcision) the "prepuce" off the *qelippah.* Then the messiah will himself be the "great dragon," the "piercing serpent," and the "crooked serpent" (cf. Isa. 27:1).

Nathan elaborates the typological allegory of Job as a symbol of the messiah at considerable length. Fairly common in Christian literature, this allegory was introduced by Solomon Molkho, the former maranno, into Jewish homiletics. By the time Nathan came to develop it in his own way, it had already been current for over a century.[292]

The sufferings reported of Job really refer to him [Sabbatai], who suffered the most dreadful torments at the hands of diverse *qelippoth* . . . in great temptations. Thereby he extracted all the holiness from them, and he repaired the *qelippoth* themselves. For the *qelippoth* are called *golem*, that is, a formless mass. For that reason it is said [Gen. 1:2], "and the earth was without form (*tohu*) and void"—for there is building [that is, structure, *kosmos*] and there is formless mass (*tohu*) which is the *qelippoth* and which will be perfected by him [the messiah]. This is similar to the mystery of the *tehiru*. . . . Scripture says concerning him, "and the spirit of God moved upon the waters," and the rabbis explained, "this is the spirit of the messiah." The numerical value of "God moved" is equal to that of his name [Sabbatai Ṣevi], for his soul was in the depth of the great abyss. Darkness, clouds, and thick darkness were round about him, and when he issued as if out of the womb, thick darkness was a swaddling-band for him. . . . And if you inquire why the abyss exists in this world, the reason is that every time God works a great miracle, he extracts [the precious] elements from the mystery of the *tehiru*. God's wonderful creations are produced out of this formless mass. . . . The messiah too has extracted from it [many sparks of holiness] . . . and he will [finally] sift the *tehiru* so that Scripture shall be fulfilled [Isa. 27:1]: "the Lord with his sore and

292. Solomon Molkho (*Sefer ha-Mefoʾar*) introduced many Christian typological allegories into Jewish homiletics. He also mentions (1884, p. 33) the Messiah-Job allegory, although in general he interprets Job as a symbol of the suffering Jewish people. Tishby (*Kiryath Sepher*, XXI [1944–45], 16) suggests that Nathan's imagery may have been influenced by the homilies of Vital's disciple Ḥayyim Kohen of Aleppo (*Torath Ḥakham*, Venice, 1654), but the latter too was undoubtedly inspired by Solomon Molkho, whose writings enjoyed wide circulation.

great and strong sword shall punish Leviathan the piercing serpent" and his consort "the crooked serpent." . . . The explanation of the matter is this: the aforementioned soul [of the messiah], which was sunk among the *qelippoth*, sent forth sparks in every generation. If they [the generation] had been worthy, and the spark in question had exerted himself in the service of the Lord, then it might have become the messiah and have extracted the whole root of his [holy] soul from the *qelippoth*. Also AMIRAH originally came forth from the *qelippoth* as a spark of this root, but by his efforts he extracted the whole root. Therefore, after he had extracted the whole root [and become the messiah], God led him into great temptations. Many times, after he had scaled the heights of Heaven, he fell into the depth of the Great Abyss, and there the serpents would seduce him, saying to him with convincing proofs and in a manner which practical reason cannot withstand: "Where is thy God?" Yet he persevered in his faith. Apart from this he also suffered great and bitter afflictions in all his limbs. During the periods of these temptations he is called "Job" and the "servant of Pharaoh," for "Pharaoh" is the messiah's true name, which is derived from the word *phara*ᵓ . . . in the mystery of the complete uncovering of the foreskin of the *qelippah* by the messiah. When he accomplishes this he will no longer be called Job but will be called Pharaoh. Behold the power of this great serpent, [which it exercises] because it is the *qelippah* of the holy serpent. Therefore Scripture says [Exod. 4:3], "and Moses fled from before it.'"[293]

This passage is clearly meant to account for Sabbatai's actual personality, and for his changing moods and behavior. In an earlier chapter another extract from the same text has been quoted (see above, pp. 130–31), describing Sabbatai's periods of illumination, peace and gladness, on the one hand, and his persecution by the *qelippoth* in the days of darkness and anguish, on the other. Even after having extricated itself from the realm of the *qelippoth,* this greatest and holiest of souls was still, at times, subject to them, persecuted by them, and liable to sink back into their power. This terrible and incessant struggle raises the messiah even above Abraham. Abraham's soul, after extricating itself from the *qelippah,* remained free. The messiah, however, would have to continue his struggle until the manifestation of his kingdom and the beginning of his public ministry, as set forth in Nathan's letter.

293. *Be*ᶜ*Iqvoth Mashiaḥ*, pp. 17–21.

In Nathan's doctrine of the messiah's soul, kabbalistic and metaphysical motifs merge with psychological and biographical elements. The prehistory of the messiah's soul in the *tehiru* provides the key for an understanding of the mysterious and disconcerting personality of the man Sabbatai Ṣevi. His strange behavior, far from belying his messianic dignity, actually confirmed it. No ordinary soul, let alone that of a pious ascetic, would ever seek expression in such "strange actions." Clearly these were "hidden acts of *tiqqun*." The messiah still continued his warfare against the *qelippah,* and he alone who had struggled free from the depth of the abyss knew by what paradoxical ways this realm of darkness, impervious to the power of Torah, could be subdued. Nathan was to expound all this more fully in his subsequent writings.

Nathan's imagery is borrowed largely from the Zohar and the Lurianic writings. But the way these images are combined, the structure of the new system, and the emphasis on the mission of the "holy serpent" together form a pattern that may well be described as a genuinely gnostic myth. Lurianic kabbalism, too, had its markedly gnostic features,[294] but its powerful—and typically Jewish—messianic vision followed traditional lines: the war of holiness and the *qelippah* took place in the life of every individual Jew. Nathan, on the other hand, introduced a new dualistic element and a new conception of the redeemer. The two innovations are interdependent, for the existence of the Great Abyss, that is, the formless *golem* resistent and impervious to Israel's religious labors of *tiqqun,* requires a redeemer endowed with a special character and charged with a special mission. Images that had crystallized once before in a heretical Jewish myth—it was from such a myth that, in my opinion, gnosticism originally started—now rose again in the soul of a young scholar from the academy of R. Jacob Ḥagiz. The new gnostic myth was composed of elements which, taken by themselves and in isolation, were perfectly within the bounds of kabbalistic tradition. But this fact merely throws into relief the peculiar psychological dynamics of the new system and its remarkable explosive force. A slight, almost imperceptible shift of emphasis would be sufficient to transform this kabbalistic doctrine into heresy. This is precisely what happened after Sabbatai's apostasy. Yet

294. See G. Scholem, *Major Trends,* pp. 260, 279, and Is. Tishby, "Gnostic Doctrines in Sixteenth-Century Jewish Mysticism," *JJS,* VI (1955), 146–52.

it would be a mistake to believe that the characteristic features of Sabbatian theology developed only after the apostasy and as a result of it. Nathan's original conceptions lead, in a straight and continuous line, from the mystical interpretation of Sabbatai's unbalanced and paradoxical personality to the even more paradoxical doctrine of the mysteriously tragic mission of the apostate messiah.

The central symbol of the first- and second-century gnostic sect known as Ophites, or Naassenes, suddenly reappeared in mystical Judaism, but this time we need not look for either Persian or Egyptian influences. It sprang to life from the sources of Lurianic kabbalism pure and undefiled. There are no indications of foreign influence on the structure of Nathan's mythological system, except for the emphasis placed on "faith" as an absolute value, which may well be indebted to Christian doctrines, possibly absorbed by Sabbatai himself. The apostasy did not produce any major changes in Nathan's system; it merely made explicit some of the motifs implicit in his earlier writings with their paradoxical and near-heretical doctrines concerning the redeemer, his personality, and his connection with the mysteries of creation and of the divine pleroma. The product of both prophetic vision and intellectual elaboration, Nathan's concepts and symbols proved ideal instruments for dealing with the scandal of an apostate messiah. The mystical significance of this event could easily be explained in terms of Nathan's original teachings. There is nothing intrinsically heretical about the notion that the Christian messiah was the "husk," or *qelippah,* of the true messiah, and that this "messiah of the *qelippah*" would ultimately be redeemed by the true messiah of Israel. As a matter of fact, nowhere in Nathan's writings is there a trace of even the faintest sympathy for Christianity in general or for Jesus in particular. The theological interest in Jesus was probably due to Sabbatai himself, who was given to meditations on previous messianic figures. On the other hand, it seems that Nathan's carefully guarded hints about the messiah's strange actions and transgressions of the Law as the *tiqqun* of the Great Abyss were already well on the way to heresy.

No doubt Nathan evolved other original ideas, or at least systematically developed the confused hints which he may have heard from Sabbatai Ṣevi. Among these is the theory concerning the succession of the supernal configurations (*parṣufim*) in the government of the lower worlds. The theory has obvious affinities with the doctrine of world-cycles as expounded in the thirteenth-century *Sefer ha-Temunah*.[295] Nathan knew this doctrine, widely discussed in kabbalistic literature, and used it as a starting point for his own speculations, though he believed that the author of the *Temunah* had misunderstood it. According to the original doctrine, which was emphatically rejected by Moses Cordovero and Isaac Luria, each *sefirah* governs one world-cycle (*shemittah*) in the succession of created world ages or *aions*. In Nathan's version, our world is successively governed by the *parṣufim* of Lurianic kabbalism. The present dispensation is that of *Zeᶜir ᵓAnpin*, also referred to by the designation "the Holy One Blessed Be He," and it governs our world for the first six thousand years—each millennium corresponding to one of God's own days—or at least up to the beginning of the sixth millennium, in which we are actually living. But when *Zeᶜir ᵓAnpin*, that is, the dispensation of the six cosmic "weekdays," is raised to the mystery of the Sabbath, then the government will pass to the higher configurations called Father and Mother, "and concerning this rise [of the worlds] AMIRAH used to sing a most holy song in the vernacular."[296] Nathan does not name the song, but we may safely assume that he referred to Sabbatai's favorite song, the Spanish erotic *romance* "Meliselda, the Emperor's Daughter," to which Sabbatai used to give all sorts of mystical interpretations. It consequently acquired great sanctity in the eyes of the Sabbatian believers, who sang it at their meetings, as is proved by its inclusion in the hymn book of the Dönmeh in Salonika.[297] But if the future name of the Holy One Blessed Be He will be "Sabbath," as the government of the world passes from the configuration *Zeᶜir ᵓAnpin* (that is, the "weekdays") to that of Father and Mother, then the messiah too—so Nathan concludes—"will be exalted to a very high degree, both in body and in soul. His body will be pure and shining like sapphire stone[298] . . . and he will ascend to the

295. See Scholem, *Major Trends*, pp. 178–79 and *Les origines de la Kabbale* (1965), pp. 480–504; cf. *Ursprung und Anfänge der Kabbala* (1962), pp. 407–19.

296. *Beᶜlqvoth Mashiaḥ*, p. 15.

297. M. Attias, *Romancero Sefaradi* (Jerusalem, 1956), p. 84, see also below, p. 401.

298. Nathan here quotes Exod. 24:10, which he interprets as a kabbalistic allusion (by *gematria*) to Sabbatai.

highest world, than which there is no higher. And concerning this occultation, Scripture says, 'So Job died at the age of an hundred and forty years,' . . . using the expression 'death,' which means 'occultation.'"

Here Nathan introduces a motif that subsequently was to play an important role in Sabbatian theology—the notion that in the world to come, that is, after the resurrection, the purified and glorified bodies of the righteous would ascend to ever higher spheres. The doctrine was clearly enunciated by Naḥmanides, one of the greatest figures of the early Spanish kabbalah, in his tract *On Retribution* (*Shaᶜar ha-Gemul*).[299] But Nathan's version of it carries a special overtone, and his formulation of the idea of the messiah's ascent to a supernal world "than which there is no higher," is strongly reminiscent of the Christian doctrine of the messiah's transfiguration, when he appeared to his disciples on Mount Tabor, and of his ascension into Heaven to sit at the right hand of the Father. Nathan claimed in one of his later writings[300] that the doctrine of occultation was revealed by Sabbatai himself, and his testimony confirms the impression gained previously from our analysis of other Sabbatian notions that it was indeed Sabbatai who mediated Christian influences to Nathan. In itself, the doctrine of occultation could also point to Shiᶜite Muslim influence. In the theology of the more radical Shiᶜite groups the doctrine of the occultation of the imam was widely accepted. But in the historical context of Sabbatai's biography before his apostasy, such Shiᶜite influence would seem highly improbable. The messiah—according to Sabbatai's and Nathan's teaching—will, then, not die, but will be translated to higher worlds. The idea would agree well with what we know of Sabbatai's illuminations and the concomitant psychological experiences of exaltation and ascensions to the celestial lights. It is not impossible that conversations with Christians suggested to Sabbatai the very congenial idea of the messiah's transfiguration.

There is, in all this, no definite implication of an incarnation of the divine in the messiah, although there are the seeds of what might, ultimately, produce such a doctrine. For the time being, however, Nathan refrained from explicitly describing Sabbatai's ascension to the supernal lights as a deification or apotheosis, though

299. See Scholem, *Les origines de la Kabbale,* pp. 325, 408.
300. See *Beᶜlqvoth Mashiaḥ*, p. 124, and *Zion*, VI (1941), 183.

he can hardly have meant anything else. From the lowest depth of the *qelippoth*, the messiah would be exalted, by the processes of purification and *tiqqun*, to the highest degrees of *ʾaṣiluth*. One is reminded here of Joseph b. Shalom ha-Ashkenazi of Barcelona,[301] who taught that all things, from the *sefirah Kether* down to the last stone on earth, were subject to a continuous process of change and transformation (*din beney ḥalof*)[302]; what appears at one time as inanimate may, in due course, assume animate or angelic form, and even the light-form of the *sefiroth*. Yet the similarity is more apparent than real. The Spanish kabbalist enunciated a general, cosmic law of transformation, whereas Nathan practically repudiates this doctrine by limiting the process to the messiah alone. On the other hand, Nathan's remarks on the messiah's transfiguration seem to foreshadow certain allusions that begin to appear in his writings of 1666. The messiah, we are told, would be called by the names of the Godhead—and here we may remember the earlier equation of the divine name Shadday with the name Sabbatai Ṣevi. These, surely, are the first stirrings of the more extreme, later doctrines.

In his early kabbalistic writings Nathan also attempted to interpret Sabbatai's "Mystery of the Godhead." The Mystery means that the Godhead which we address in prayer ("the God of his faith") is the *sefirah Tifʾereth*. This interpretation permits us to understand Sabbatai's ascent to an "exalted degree" as an expression of his very special relationship to the supernal lights, but not yet as presenting him as an incarnation of such divine lights. Nathan expounded these ideas not in the *Treatise on the Dragons*, but in an earlier exposition of "the Faith of Our Lord," a very short tract on "Jonah's Ship."[303] Jonah's ship had been interpreted in the *Tiqquney Zohar* as an allegory of the body (the ship) and the soul (Jonah). The principal limbs of the body are the pilots of the ship, which signifies the bodily garment of the soul. In the *Tiqquney Zohar* the allegory has no messianic implication whatever. The great wind which swept the sea on which Jonah was voyaging is allegorized thus: "When the limbs of the body are moved by this wind [= spirit] in accordance with the commandments of the Torah,

301. Author of a commentary, wrongly ascribed to Abraham b. David, on the Book *Yeṣirah*. He wrote in the early fourteenth century.

302. A term taken from Prov. 31:8.

303. *BeʿIqvoth Mashiaḥ*, p. 39.

then the ship too will be moved in the direction that man desires," that is, his worldly wishes too shall be fulfilled. Nathan turns the Zoharic passage into a messianic proclamation, calling upon all believers to give themselves wholly to the messianic labor "so that our brethren may go forth from their exile." The text of the manifesto was sent to different countries with the instruction "to recite it every morning and evening."[304] In his kabbalistic commentary on the passage, the prophet explains why the "Cause of All Causes" was not identical with the God of revealed religion, and why the divine name EHEYEH—("I am"), which is correlated to the "Cause of All Causes"—may be pronounced, whereas the Tetragrammaton YHWH—which is correlated to the *sefirah Tif'ereth*, that is, the "God of his Faith"—may not:

I shall tell you a parable. This is like unto a great king who appointed another vice-king under him. All the king's orders are executed through him, and whoever wants to make a request has to make it through him [that is, the vice-regent] and he brings it before the king. Now it is certain that whoever asks anything of anyone else, even if he be greater than [the vice-regent], offends the king. The application [of this parable] is this: the Tetragrammaton, which is the choicest of all [divine] names and which must not be pronounced, generally signifies [the *sefirah*] *Tif'ereth*, whereas the name EHEYEH, which signifies [the highest *sefirah*] *Kether* may—strangely enough—be pronounced. The explanation is this. Know that the supernal [world of] Emanation [that is, the *sefiroth* of the Godhead] is like unto the great sea. The water at the shore is the same as that in the middle of the sea, and all are one. Even so it is with His Emanation. For though we speak of His [distinct] *sefiroth*, yet they are parts of Him, and we receive the influx of that [divine] light which is nearest to us and which is [the tenth *sefirah*] *Malkhuth*, the Gate of the King. When we stimulate and unite the supernal lights so that they may be joined together, they are like waves of the sea beating against one another until they reach the supernal source. If there is no wind blowing over the sea, the waves abate and the sea ceases from her raging. Thus all depends on the wind. It is the same with the divine Emanation. *Tif'ereth* is the wind, and unless we ask the wind to agitate the waves of the sea—which are the *sefiroth*—and to cause [the divine influx] to descend, how can we expect our meat and food? Therefore we must pray to the wind to agitate the waves, each

304. *Ibid.*, pp. 67–68. Several MSS. of this proclamation are extant.

sefirah beating against the other, until [the movement reaches] *En-Sof*, and then the influx will descend upon us through *Malkhuth.* Therefore [the wind] is called YHWH, for this is the name which the Cause of All Causes gave to the wind which is in *Tif'ereth*, so that we should ask everything of it, and it [the wind] would ask it from on high. To ask anything from any other *sefirah* would be against the will of the Cause of All Causes, and an offense to the king. *Our Lord the king* [Sabbatai Ṣevi] *greatly labored concerning this faith* until he caused the king which is *Tif'ereth* to sit on his throne.[305] Therefore the prophet Habakkuk prophesied concerning him: "the just shall live by his faith," of which the initial letters [in Hebrew] form the word "ṣevi." After he [that is, the messiah] had enthroned the king, he was greatly exalted, even so that he alone was granted permission to address the Holy Ancient One.[306] Wherefore it was said concerning him [Prov. 28:20]: "a man of faith [shall abound with blessing]." For at first he had the faith of *Tif'ereth;* but the mystery of the faith [Hebrew root, *'mn*] is "sucking" [the divine blessing], as is indicated by the word "nurse" [also *'mn* in Hebrew], and therefore [at first] *Tif'ereth* was a nursing, or foster, father unto him. But then he was exalted, and the Holy Ancient One became his nursing father. Therefore the "man of faith"—*'ish 'emunoth*, the numerical value of which is 814, equal to that of Sabbatai Ṣevi—prays to Him [to the Holy Ancient One]. This is the mystical intention of the "Faith of Our Lord," which [namely, this creed] should be recited twice daily, in the morning and in the evening.[307]

So far Nathan's interpretation of the "Mystery of the Godhead" was still fairly simple. It lacked, as yet, the later complications as well as the additional detail about the messiah's ascension to, and absorption into, the mystery of the Holy Ancient One. Sabbatai is merely said to have received permission to pray to the

305. The *Treatise on the Dragons* begins with the words: "And now I announce unto you that Our Lord and King Sabbatai Ṣevi has caused the King to sit on His throne" (*ibid.*, p. 14).

306. *ʿAttiqa kaddisha*, i.e., the Supernal King, symbolized by the *sefirah Kether* and by the name *'Eheyeh.*

307. This refers to the Treatise on Jonah's Ship. The text as presented here is taken from MS. Schwager and Fraenkel (list 11, no. 142) now in the Jewish Theological Seminary of America, where it is entitled "The Mystery of the Faith of Our Lord, from R. Nathan." Freimann's text (p. 93) leaves out most of it, and what is printed is hopelessly corrupt and utterly incomprehensible, although the MS. is perfectly legible and clear.

Holy Ancient One alone and not to any other, that is, lower, *sefirah*, not even to *Tifʾereth*, although the latter was the "God of his Faith." Evidently what is said here about the Holy Ancient One corresponds to the statements about the Cause of all Causes in some of the texts that have already been analyzed. Even before his exaltation, the messiah was in communion with the light of the Holy Ancient One and "sucked" from this source. Nathan's doctrine of the *parṣufim* now becomes intelligible: the light of the Holy Ancient One will manifest itself in the configuration *Zeʿir ʾAnpin* —which is none other than the "God of Israel"—through the messiah; and by the influx of this light all the souls of the messiah's generation will accomplish their own *tiqqun*. But if the messiah draws, that is, "sucks," his light-sustenance from his "nurse," the Holy Ancient One, it is hardly surprising that ultimately he would also ascend to these supernal lights and disappear in them.

The doctrine of Sabbatai's ascension and transfiguration is the focal point of a very remarkable eschatology. Job died at the age of one hundred and forty years. And since "today [that is, in the summer of 1666] AMIRAH is forty years old," he would clearly continue in this life for another hundred years, during which his body would become progressively spiritualized until it disappeared in his final occultation. Then "there will be a great weeping in the world, such as has been never before since the foundation of the world, and rivers of tears will run down from their eyes, but then the mystery of the beauty of the Lord shall become manifest."[308] The "beauty of the Lord" [Ps. 90:17] is none other than eternal blessedness and the beatific vision, concerning which the psalmist had prayed [Ps. 90:16]: "Let thy work appear unto thy servants." The weeping over the redeemer's occultation will open men's eyes to see the hidden works of the Lord, and the manifestation of this beauty will continue for the remaining four hundred and seventy-four years after the messiah's transfiguration, until the end of the sixth millennium. These remaining years would correspond to the eve of the cosmic Sabbath. Thereafter, in the seventh millennium, which is the mystery of the world to come, all things will be raised to the supreme degree of "Sabbath."

Once embarked on eschatological speculations, Nathan could not help arriving at other extreme conclusions, which subsequently assumed enormous importance in the history of Sabbatian theology.

308. *BeʿIqvoth Mashiaḥ*, p. 16.

Nathan began with interpreting Sabbatai's special status and explaining his "strange actions" as the messianic way of restoring the *qelippoth* to holiness, but the panorama of his eschatological vision soon widened. At a very early stage—and certainly before Sabbatai's apostasy—he had linked the problem of the Law and the commandments to the doctrine of the "new law" that had been revealed to the messiah, and concerning which the latter had pronounced, in 1658, the blasphemous benediction "that permittest things forbidden." Here too, as in other instances, Nathan's ideas were not invented *ex nihilo,* though he imbued them with a pungency and a sense of actuality that was absent from the similar speculations of earlier mystics. The Safed kabbalists had talked about the "spiritual" character of the Law as well as about the peculiar nature of the souls of the era preceding the messiah's advent. But the two subjects were treated as completely distinct and were never linked as in Nathan's *Treatise on the Dragons.* A closer analysis is necessary if we want to understand the significance of Nathan's new departure and the perilously explosive quality of his combination of the two doctrines.

All kabbalists were agreed that the Torah, being the supreme expression of the hidden divine power, was essentially nonmaterial. The Torah is the law of the cosmos, and if the latter had preserved its original spiritual character, the Torah, too, would never have been "materialized," even as Adam's body would not have become material. The mystery of the supernal Torah is that of the "Tree of Life"; its commandments are essentially and basically spiritual lights, shining forth in various combinations in the pure spirituality of the Torah. It is difficult to imagine kabbalists more devoted to the traditional Law than Moses Cordovero and his school. Yet this is what his disciple Elijah de Vidas quotes him as saying: "Every commandment is, in the higher world, a supernal light united to the Tree of Life. But as a result of Adam's sin, and again of the sin of the golden calf, the Torah and the commandments materialized, and hence men must now perform material [that is, practical] commandments, such as wearing a four-cornered garment with fringes, or *tefillin* made of leather and the like—and my master has treated this subject on many occasions."[309] The implications of this doctrine are obvious. In the messianic age, with the *tiqqun* accom-

309. *Reshith Ḥokhmah* (ed. Munkacs), fol. 17a. Cordovero expounded these ideas in his *Shiᶜur Qomah.* De Vidas' classical work was first published in Venice in 1579.

plished and the effects of sin undone, all things will be restored to their pristine spirituality, and the traditional type of "material" practice and observance of the commandments will automatically pass away. This conclusion was already hinted at in the *Raᶜya Mehemna* in the Zohar (see above, pp. 11–12). It was expressed again with great clarity, though without the acute spiritualist extremism of the *Raᶜya Mehemna*, by Abraham Azulay of Hebron in his work *Ḥesed le-Abraham*, which was composed when Sabbatai Ṣevi was a child. Azulay's work, based mainly on the writings of Cordovero, contains the following statement:

This is [the mystery of] the innovations of the Torah which God will introduce in the [eschatological] future. For although the Torah is immutable, yet originally [when revealed on Mount Sinai] it was presented in this material form [solely] for the sake of the material world [in which we exist since Adam's fall]. But in the [eschatological] future men will divest themselves of their material bodies and ascend . . . to the mystery of the [spiritual] body which Adam possessed before the fall. Then they will understand the secret meaning of the Torah, as that which is hidden will become manifest. After the sixth millennium they will attain to even higher degrees [of spirituality], and they will understand the mystery of the Torah in its most hidden essence, . . . which will then become manifest to those who seek it. This is the basic principle: the Torah was clothed in a material clothing, exactly like man. As man will rise, in the future, from his material clothing to a spiritual one, so will the Torah rise above her material clothing and be perceived on increasingly spiritual levels. This clothing will last until the time of the resurrection. Then they [that is, men] will be [completely] pure, and they will understand the Torah according to its innermost clothing. . . . But in the sabbatical year [that is, the seventh millennium] they will rise to an exceedingly high degree, and so will the Torah. For even as men divest themselves of their bodies, so will the Torah divest itself of its material [aspects], and its hidden countenance will shine, and the righteous will contemplate it [in its spiritual essence]. Yet the Torah is one and the same in the beginning and forever, and it will never change.[310]

The study of the Torah and the observance of its commandments will ultimately become a purely spiritual contemplation, since no practical performance is possible after the Torah has divested itself of its

310. *Hesed le-ᶜAbraham* (*ᶜEyn ha-Qoreᵓ* xi).

material clothing. Nobody would consider this eschatological doctrine as antinomian in character. Yet the process of our restoration to a spiritual state need only be accelerated, and the realization of the eschatological—and inevitably antinomian—possibilities of the eternal and immutable Torah becomes perilously imminent.

Nathan took this step in his *Treatise on the Dragons,* in which the old symbols and figures of speech suddenly assumed new meanings and new life. The *Vision of R. Abraham* had merely said that the messiah would "restore the crown to its pristine glory, but his contemporaries will rise against him and blaspheme." The two halves of the sentence appear to be without inner connection, and the Talmudic figure of speech about restoring the crown to its pristine glory does not seem to go beyond its surface meaning. But when viewed in the light of the *Treatise on the Dragons* and of Nathan's even more extreme later writings, this apparently harmless sentence assumes a different complexion. For when Nathan explicitly states that the messiah had "restored the crown to its pristine glory in the mystery of the Tree of Life,"[311] then it is obvious that we are dealing with more than a mere figure of speech. Even if we do not attribute to the symbol of the Tree of Life the full significance which it has in Nathan's other writings, the quotation from de Vidas' *Reshith Ḥokhmah* leaves no doubt that the restoration of the Torah to the mystery of the Tree of Life can only mean its restoration to the original state of pure spirituality. The "pristine glory" is none other than the mystery of the Tree of Life to which the Torah had been united before its materialization, when—according to the Zohar—it still existed in spiritual unity without the opposites of permission and prohibition, pure and impure. These opposites derive from the Tree of the Knowledge of Good and Evil. The new Torah revealed to Sabbatai Ṣevi is thus the original, supernal Torah of the Tree of Life. And since its manifestation implies the abolition of the norms of permitted and forbidden, pure and impure, it is not surprising that "his contemporaries will rise against him and blaspheme."

From his doctrine of the messianic Torah, Nathan drew a peculiar conclusion with regard to the messiah's contemporaries, whose souls, we remember, were said to stem from the same "root" as the messiah's soul. As a matter of fact, Nathan's view is some-

311. *Be^cIqvoth Mashiaḥ,* p. 50.

thing of a puzzle. There would be no difficulty about the view that exalted souls from the world of *ʾaṣiluth*, untainted by original sin, would understand the Torah in its most spiritual aspect, that is, in its *ʾaṣiluth* character. There is nothing paradoxical about Nathan's statement, in one of his later writings,[312] that when Israel received the Law at Mount Sinai, they were united to the Tree of Life. At that moment "they obtained a soul from the world of *ʾaṣiluth*, and hence their Torah was devoid of obligations, prohibitions and permissions." Only afterward, as a result of the sin with the golden calf, did the Torah materialize again into the form of practical commandments. However, we have seen that it is not this kind of superior *ʾaṣiluth* soul that is discussed in the *Treatise on the Dragons*. On the contrary, Nathan makes it quite plain that he was talking of inferior souls from the "heels" of the First Adam. It is true that, unlike Vital, he does not insist on the obdurate impudence and hardness of these souls, and on the near-impossibility of perfecting them; yet he is very emphatic about the great labor required of the messiah in order to purify and redeem them. Here now is the puzzling paradox: Nathan applies to these inferior souls the statements of the earlier kabbalists regarding the superior souls that would enter this world, after the general resurrection, from the sphere of *ʾaṣiluth*. By doing so, Nathan undermines the continued relevance of the practical commandments. If there is still room, at the dawn of the messianic age, for practical observance, the sole reason is the incidental fact that among the souls of the "period of advent" there are some that belong to other roots and cycles of metempsychosis. These "irregular" souls still require the active performance of practical commandments in order to accomplish their *tiqqun*. But all the other souls of this age, stemming as they do from the same root as the messiah, may substitute contemplative study of the spiritual Torah for material performance. The contemplative ideal of the study of Torah takes the place of the practical ideal of the performance of the commandments. Nathan explains that at the present time "most bodies are in the mystery of souls of whom no action is required." They are souls who realized at once all their constituent parts (*nefesh*, *ruaḥ*, and *neshamah*), and most of them were actually "new souls,"[313] that is, such as had

312. *Zemir ʿAriṣim*, *ibid.*, p. 93.

313. See Is. Tishby in *Tarbiz,* XV (1944), 166.

Nathan leading his people from Exile to the Holy Land, after (3) anointing of the new king Sabbatai and (4) the capture of Mecca. (6) At the head of the army, the general Josua Helkam. Also depicted are (2) the Tables of the Law being dug up and (5) Mohammed's corpse being thrown out of the mosque. Fictitious etching from a German broadsheet: *Warhafftes Conterfey . . . des Jüdisch-vermeinten Wunder-Propheten Nathan Levi . . .* (probably Augsburg, 1666)

never before passed through bodies; hence they had no sins from earlier human incarnations to atone for. The purpose of their descent into this world was not the performance of specific actions but, rather, the contemplative study of Torah "until everything is renewed by AMIRAH. All these souls are called the offspring of a levirate marriage, because they are the offspring of the union of [the mystical principles called] Jacob and Rachel. . . .[314] Nevertheless, it behooves us to perform the practical commandments [even] at this time, since perforce some sparks of 'old' are mingled [among the 'new' souls of the messianic advent], and for their sake it is necessary to observe the practical commandments."[315] As a matter of fact, very special efforts should be made for their proper observance, for during the present *shemittah*, that is, the seven years 1665–72, people will be "impregnated" by countless souls that still need one or the other specific performance of a commandment in order to attain their full stature and *tiqqun*. But these souls are not representative of the age. "Most of our generation, in this period of advent, are of the messiah's root and are almost perfected. Nothing remains for them to do except [to neutralize] the forces of severe judgment which they have strengthened by their sins," and for this purpose Nathan's penitential exercises were sufficient.[316] It may be an exaggeration to describe this doctrine as downright heretical and antinomian.[317] In fact, the doctrine, as we have seen, allowed for considerations that not only acted as a barrier against full-fledged antinomianism, but actually served as a stimulus for intensified devotional practice. Nevertheless, there is no denying that it comes uncomfortably near to antinomian heresy. The Torah of the Tree of Life had appeared on the horizon, and a more radical change was evidently expected to take place after Sabbatai's return from his expedition to the river Sambatyon. The study of the Torah of messianic freedom would then take the place of the traditional

314. The association of the union of Jacob and Rachel with the levirate marriage is obscure. In the Zohar III, 216b, Job is described as the offspring of a levirate marriage, and his sufferings explained as atonement for the reincarnated soul of his mother's first (and childless) husband. In Nathan's symbolic system everything said of Job could be applied to the messiah.

315. *Be^cIqvoth Mashiaḥ*, pp. 51–52.

316. *Ibid.*

317. As is done by Tishby (*Kiryath Sepher,* XXI [1944–45], 14–15).

type of study of Torah, which Nathan still recommended for the immediate present. This was potential antinomianism, and it exercised a powerful fascination on the prophet. Nathan extended the sphere of application of the "new Torah" to all the souls contemporaneous with the messiah, but at the price of a radical departure from Lurianic teaching on the subject. The novel combination of traditional and disparate elements represents Nathan's main contribution to this particular subject, and reveals the apocalyptic fire burning in him. We should not be surprised at the radicalism of the *Treatise on the Dragons*, as compared with Nathan's more moderate formulations in the writings composed after Sabbatai's apostasy. His apocalyptic mood, geared to the feverish expectation of an imminent realization, erupted with inspired violence during the initial period; after the apostasy, when the events had belied his prophecies, the fires burned more quietly, and tortuous explanations had to take the place of high-flown expectations.

Our brief survey of Nathan's early writings, from the *Vision of R. Abraham* to the *Treatise on the Dragons,* should be sufficient to show their profound originality. But his views were not widely known. We may doubt whether even the more discerning kabbalists who read his tracts really fathomed all their far-reaching implications, particularly as Nathan's literary technique consisted in concealing more than he revealed. He would utter a strikingly radical proposition, but immediately obscure its import by surrounding it with a smoke-screen of conventional kabbalistic mysteries, *gematria,* combinations of letters, and the like. These contribute nothing at all to the development of his basic ideas, though they create the desired impression of a close connection between the new revelations and the traditional Lurianic doctrines. The modern, critical reader has little difficulty in separating the different strands, but this is precisely what the seventeenth-century kabbalists were incapable of doing. To them Nathan's speculations could not but appear as legitimate elaborations of Lurianic teaching. In 1666 Nathan's bold doctrines played no major role. They were not even singled out for systematic attack by the opponents of the movement during its first phase, who may not have seen them at all. Their original function seems to have been to provide a clue to an understanding of the "mystery" of Sabbatai Ṣevi to his immediate entourage—and possibly to the messiah himself. For the time being, the seed sown in Nathan's early writings remained hidden, though it was not long before it blossomed forth and bore its fruit in the dramatic development of the movement.

Meanwhile, old and new elements merged. Some manuscripts containing the earlier version of Nathan's penitential exercises also preserve a hymn that the prophet had composed in honor of the messiah.[318] Only a few stanzas have survived, but their initial letters (A, B, R) suggest that it was an acrostic poem giving the author's name. Since we know from later acrostic compositions the form of the name generally used by the prophet ("I, Abraham Nathan Benjamin, the son of Elisha Ḥayyim"), we may assume the hymn to have been fairly long. Nathan's lyrical effusion marks the beginning of a long history of Sabbatian religious poetry and hymnology. Most of these hymns were later concealed or destroyed, and only a few have come to our knowledge. Judging from the extant stanzas, Nathan's hymn praised the power and glory of the messiah who subdued the primordial serpent that was wound around man's heel. In fact, this lost hymn seems to have been a poetic version of the doctrines of the *Treatise on the Dragons*.

318. The hymn was published by Pereṣ Smolenskin in *Ha-Shaḥar*, 1873 (by way of supplement to the 1st edn. of D. Kahana's ᵓ*Eben ha-Tho*ᶜ*im*, p. 88), and again in D. Kahana, *Toledoth*, p. 72, and in the original (Hebrew) edn. of the present work (vol. I, p. 261). The MS. copies of Nathan's penitential tracts that were made after Sabbatai's apostasy, omit the hymn.

4

THE MOVEMENT UP TO SABBATAI'S IMPRISONMENT IN GALLIPOLI (1665–1666)

I

THE MESSIANIC AWAKENING originated in Palestine, but it was not until after Sabbatai's departure from the Holy Land, and in the wake of the manifestations of mass enthusiasm produced by his passage through Smyrna, that the movement began to spread further. By the end of the summer of 1665, the messianic tidings had as yet had little effect on the public; perhaps the news had been too vague to produce definite responses. The Egyptian kabbalists—who are our earliest source of information on the movement—were too amazed at first to believe the reports; their first reaction, as we have seen, was to dispatch emissaries to Gaza to investigate. Until the messianic announcement was confirmed—that is, until Nathan's prophetic status was authenticated—they were in no hurry to pass the good news on even to those countries and communities with whom they were in close contact, for example, the Yemen, North West Africa, and Italy. All this changed in September, 1665. Enthusiastic letters from Aleppo began to arrive in Constantinople, contradicting the earlier reports concerning Sabbatai's excommunication that had come from Jerusalem at about the same time. From Egypt, and possibly also directly from Palestine, there came glad tidings as well as calls to repent. It was probably in this way that the messianic tidings spread, rather than by formal proclamations from Gaza such as the alleged letter quoted by Emanuel Frances:[1] "Know ye, our brethren, the House of Jacob, that God has visited his people and has sent us a redeemer and savior, our king Sabbatai Ṣevi, who has been anointed by the prophet Nathan according to the word of the Lord. And now, by decree of our king [and?] prophet, call a fast and a solemn assembly, turn from your evil ways, gather yourselves together and come to worship before your king." Proclamations of this kind were probably never issued, and Frances either presents his own summary of the messianic reports, or freely paraphrases a letter from Palestine. The summons to come and worship before Sabbatai Ṣevi casts grave suspicions on the text, since Sabbatai had left Palestine before any such call could possibly have been made. There is no indication that Sabbatai's followers indulged in this kind of exhortation as early as June, 1665.

Actually our records of definite messianic propaganda begin with the middle of September, 1665. The earliest letters of which Sasportas obtained knowledge were written toward the end of September. Sasportas does not reproduce the text of these letters, in accordance with his customary avoidance of verbatim quotations from pro-Sabbatian documents emanating from Palestine and Egypt, but his allusions are clear enough. The letters must have traveled some two months, as they arrived in Hamburg, where Sasportas had just taken up residence, on November 30.[2] The letters "in praise of Sabbatai Ṣevi and Nathan of Gaza" preserved by Emanuel Frances, were written in Gaza and Egypt not later than November 29;[3] the greater part was probably written much earlier, and the whole collection was arranged on or before that date and then dispatched from Egypt in its present form. The report published by U. Cassuto[4] was written in Egypt on November 26. Ḥayyim Joseph's letter to his brother the *chelebi* was written the day before, and was published in an English

1. *Ṣevi Muddaḥ,* p. 134.

2. Sasportas, p. 1.

3. Haberman, p. 207. The collection published by Haberman was attached by Frances to his *Ṣevi Muddaḥ*.

4. *Vessillo Israelitico,* LV (1907), 330.

translation in one of the first pamphlets to spread the news of the messianic awakening in the Christian world. There were, however, earlier reports. The first German pamphlet on the movement[5] mentions a letter from Alexandria written on September 14, 1665, as well as "letters from Jerusalem, Hebron, and Gaza that have arrived by way of Venice and Leghorn."[6] A letter written on September 24 by Joseph b. Nehorai Azobib (of Algiers?) to his friend Moses Tardiola of Jerusalem has been preserved in its entirety.[7] The writer, who was in Alexandria at the time, apprised his friend, who was traveling in Tripolitania on behalf of the community of Jerusalem, of the glad tidings. Tardiola was esteemed as a rabbinic scholar by Sasportas also, who had met him during an earlier visit to Morocco on behalf of Jerusalem. Azobib's letter appears to be a reply to earlier queries by Tardiola regarding certain vague and confused rumors that he had heard. Azobib's reply not only mentions the prophet of Gaza, the messiah Sabbatai Ṣevi, and the rebuilding of the Temple "in five years' time," but also conveys the enthusiasm that was prevalent during those weeks: "even if I wrote to you for two weeks, day and night, I could not report a thousandth part of the new things continually revealed by the prophet, all uttering speech concerning our redemption." In Alexandria there was "a great repentance such as has never been before, for over a third of the community have put on sackcloth." Azobib describes the fasts of adults and children at considerable length, and exhorts his correspondent to think of the public good and to preach repentance, that is, to spread the Sabbatian message in Tripoli. The letter affords us a glimpse of the kind of reports that reached Tripoli at that early stage. Abraham Miguel Cardozo, living there at the time as physician to the bey of Tripoli, heard the message and became one of its prophets.

The early history of the movement's spread raises a difficult problem. There is abundant evidence of the Sabbatians' zealous activity; their letters, too, testify to their enthusiasm and ardor. All the more surprising is the initial silence of the opponents. The rabbinic court

5. *Wahrhaffte Abbildung,* on the last page but one.

6. Thus also the English pamphlet *God's Love to His People Israel,* reprinted by Wilenski in *Zion,* XVII (1952), 170: from there (or from a similar source) the report was quoted in the French news letters published by Aeshcoly, *Dinaburg Jubilee Volume,* p. 222.

7. Published in *Zion,* VII (1942), 86–87; cf. also Sasportas, p. 55.

of Jerusalem had formally notified the rabbis of Constantinople and Smyrna of Sabbatai's excommunication. The letters from Jerusalem had been duly received. Similar letters were, perhaps, also sent to Egypt, where the excommunicate had only recently tarried as official emissary of Jerusalem. Yet nobody seems to have bothered to copy these documents and pass them on to Europe. It is a curious fact that in spite of the brisk correspondence between Europe and the Orient stimulated by the messianic news, neither the writ of excommunication nor any similar official document ever came to the attention of the anti-Sabbatian "infidels" in Amsterdam, Venice, and Hamburg. It is perfectly understandable that Sasportas, writing with a distinct anti-Sabbatian bias, would suppress letters and reports favorable to the movement and its leaders. But it is inconceivable that he should have concealed the kind of document he wanted most: a condemnation of Sabbatai Ṣevi by the rabbis of Jerusalem. In this case the *argumentum ex silentio* is decisive, and the conclusion is inescapable that neither Sasportas nor his friends (who would surely have been glad to provide him with copies) had ever seen this or any similar document. Sasportas argued and speculated at length about the credibility of the conflicting rumors: Had the Jerusalem rabbinate excommunicated Sabbatai? Had they repented of their excommunication? Without documentary evidence, Sasportas was condemned to conjectures and guesswork. But the question remains: Why did the rabbis concerned keep silent? Were they, perhaps, forced to keep silent? As regards the rabbis of Constantinople and Egypt we may safely assume that they kept quiet for reasons that will appear later. But the silence of the Jerusalem rabbinate remains a puzzle. It is not impossible that the very influential Egyptian circle of enthusiastic believers—the *chelebi* Raphael Joseph and the kabbalists at his court—suppressed all hostile documents because "it is the glory of God to conceal a thing" (Prov. 25:2), not least out of respect for the rabbis of Jerusalem who had offended the messiah. But even though the possibility of such censorship cannot be completely ruled out, it cannot solve the riddle. Shalom b. Joseph, a former schoolteacher from Amsterdam who happened to be in Egypt in or about September, 1665, reported that the majority of the Egyptian rabbis were uncertain about the truth of the message and about their faith in Sabbatai Ṣevi. His testimony suggests that in Egypt, as elsewhere, the believers were organized in a definite and active circle (for example, that of the *chelebi* Raphael Joseph), and that this elite of believers would draw supporters from among the mass of ordinary people. But then there were also the many rabbis "who doubted this faith"—and they can hardly be suspected of abetting, let alone taking part in, the suppression of the official communication from Jerusalem. If the believers put out rumors to the effect that the Jerusalem rabbinate had repented of the excommunication, the doubters would hardly have allowed this falsehood to go unchallenged. The striking contrast between the silence of the party most immediately concerned, that is, the rabbinic court which had condemned Sabbatai, on the one hand, and the eloquent propaganda of the believers, on the other, is apparent more than once throughout the first and fateful year of the movement, but its reason is still unknown.

The messianic tidings seem to have spread very fast in the oriental communities, but no details are known. Precise dates, however, are available for the progress of the good news in Europe. The earliest evidence discovered so far is a Hebrew ditty, composed by an anonymous rhymer in Italy, on October 5, 1665. The poem celebrates the advent of the messiah, and ends:

O God, let Sabbatai be with Thy glory filled
Thy sanctuary raise up again and build.[8]

The fact that the author added to his composition a note giving the precise date, may be taken as an indication that he wrote the poem under the impact of the messianic reports that had arrived that same day or the day before. But for the time being this early testimony is unique. The more detailed reports and letters of which we have knowledge did not begin to arrive in Italy until toward the end of October and the beginning of November. If the authors of the letters written in Alexandria on September 14 sent copies also to Italy and the winds were favorable, these copies may have arrived in Leghorn or Venice by October 5. The first reports, however, did not create a mass movement.

8. MS. Jerusalem 8° 1466, fol. 123a, and again fol. 322a. The volume contains many letters and poems from the circle of R. Moses Zacuto, some of them bearing on the Sabbatian movement.

II

The short poem by the anonymous Italian believer contains a brief but very significant allusion. The poet knows that the messiah, about to "appear in the majesty of his beauty," would "subdue all the kingdoms of Persia." The mention of Persia introduces a motif which not only predominated in the earliest reports that spread among European Jewry, but also drew the attention of the Christian world. "Persia" clearly refers to the lost Ten Tribes and their reappearance somewhere between the Persian and Arabian deserts or the Sahara. The question arises whether these rumors developed independently of the first reports from Gaza, or whether they arose spontaneously in the Orient, immediately on receipt of the messianic tidings.

An analysis of the extant references to the reappearance of the lost tribes suggests that these reports did not arise independently of one another. The conclusion is inescapable that at the bottom of the many and diverse rumors was an original report concerning a leader, messiah, or prophet who had arisen in Israel. The early rumors and reports were evidently still unaware of any specific events in Palestine; everything is vague, and legendary figures appear instead of concrete *dramatis personae.* Yet the details, taken together, suggest a definite, albeit hidden, connection. There is a *prima facie* case for suspecting Christian writers of having invented some of these reports by way of embellishment of the news of a messianic revival among the Jews. A careful examination of their letters and pamphlets, however, shows that this suspicion is unfounded: rumors about the lost tribes were afoot even before Christian writers had heard about the Jewish messianic movement. The subject is, in fact, far more complicated. The earliest, albeit vague and hazy, reports that reached some oriental and North African communities had already passed through a "filter" of popular legend, which had removed all concrete and specific details and added instead a good many imaginary elements. This process was not necessarily due to conscious manipulation or censorship. It would certainly be wrong to represent these reports as emanating from Europe and then awakening an echo in the oriental Jewish communities. The news progressed in the opposite direction. After the first vague reports about tribes in the East had reached Europe toward the end of the summer of 1665, they were taken up and further embellished by Christian writers with millenarian inclinations.

According to letters which circulated in November and December, 1665, the sons of Reuben and Gad, or, according to another version, Reuben, Gad, and half the tribe of Manasseh, were marching on Gaza. These letters, which originated in Jewish circles, clearly represent the literary condensation of earlier rumors which, at first, had not mentioned Palestine but merely spoke of events in faraway countries and the abodes of legendary Jews such as the Sahara, or Habor in the Arabian desert.

Similar rumors coming from Salé in Morocco (the former residence of Jacob Sasportas), reached Europe in September, 1665. At the time nothing had been heard there about Sabbatai and Nathan, and the impression made subsequently by the coincidence and parallelism of the reports was, therefore, all the greater. This was particularly true of the man who was more active than anyone else in spreading the first news both of the lost tribes and of Sabbatai Ṣevi among his Christian co-religionists, the Dutch scholar Peter Serrarius (1580–1669).[9] Serrarius, a leading Dutch chiliast of Walloon stock, entertained close relationships with Protestant millenarian circles all over Europe. In these circles expectation of the millennium prophesied in the Revelation of St. John was widespread. The Second Coming would usher in the kingdom of Christ and his saints, and this Fifth Monarchy would triumphantly supersede the secular "four kingdoms" of the Book of Daniel. The "Jewish" character of these millenarian doctrines has already been commented upon (see above, p. 98). In fact, the first to evolve such doctrines were precisely those Jewish Christians who would not renounce Jewish apocalyptic even after they had accepted Jesus as their messiah. It was not without reason that chiliasm was denounced in orthodox quarters as a "Judaizing" heresy. Many chiliasts, particularly in the seventeenth century, were sympathetic to the Jews, and some of them were genuine philo-Semites. While expecting the conversion of the Jews, they also had visions of Israel's glory in the new kingdom. Serrarius, who was a friend of Manasseh b. Israel, wrote in defense of the Jews and acted in their interests. When, in the fifties, an emissary of the Jewish community in Jerusalem, the kabbalist Nathan Shapira, arrived in Amsterdam, Serrarius helped him to obtain alms for the Holy City from Christian

9. See *Nieuw Nederlandsch Biographisch Woordenboek,* X (1937), 911–13. His original name was Pierre Serrurier.

sympathizers as well as from the Jews.[10] At the time he also translated an English book into Dutch on the future *Glory and Salvation of Israel,*[11] and during 1662–65 he wrote a number of millenarian tracts in which he discussed the conversion of the Jews to faith in the true messiah. He also engaged in a voluminous and sensational controversy with an orthodox Calvinist opponent of millenarianism. In his writings Serrarius showed himself to be one of those who "compute the end"; at any rate he agreed that the mysterious "number of the beast," 666, referred to the year 1666 as the year of the conversion and redemption of the Jews (see above, p. 102).

Serrarius' millenarian beliefs account for his keen interest in everything regarding the Jews and the resurrection of their "dry bones" (a favorite expression with him). Every rumor concerning the Jews was sure to find its way to him, and his many Jewish friends in Amsterdam would certainly keep him informed of all major and minor events in the Jewish world. Serrarius proved to be an interested and eager collector and retailer of messianic news. From the end of 1665 to his death in 1669 his sympathies were with the Sabbatian party, even after the majority of believers had found their way back from the first flush of enthusiasm to traditional Judaism. His personal integrity is beyond suspicion. In a letter on the beginnings of the Sabbatian movement, he mentions that as early as September, 1665, he had been questioned by English correspondents about the appearance of Israelite tribes in the Arabian desert; the report said that the Jews were encamped before Mecca, awaiting the arrival of the main body of the army of the Ten Tribes that had appeared in Morocco. This report refers us back once more to the letters from Salé in Morocco which purported to convey the accounts of Jewish eyewitnesses[12] that

10. See C. Roth, *Miscellanies [of the] JHSE,* II (London, 1935), 100–4.

11. Henry Jesse, *De Heerlickheydt en Heyl van Jehuda en Israel* (Amsterdam, 5602). The year is fictitious, and the translation was apparently published in 1653; cf. Wolff, *Bibliotheca Hebraica,* vol. IV, p. 501. The translator's name is given in initials, but the identity of P[eter] S[errarius] is beyond doubt.

12. Serrarius' tract *God's Love to His People Israel* was printed early in 1666 (reprinted by Wilenski in *Zion,* XVII [1952], 169–72), and is based on a letter written in autumn, 1665. Internal contradictions, probably due to misprints of certain dates, make it impossible to date the letter more accurately. Wilenski (*loc. cit.,* p. 158) realized the identity of the author of the pamphlet "P. Secarius," but ignored the Sabbatian connections and interests of Serrarius, as well as the fact that many of the letters sent from Amsterdam to Christian

had arrived from the desert and the interior Maghreb (a designation covering the whole of North Africa from Tripoli to Fez).

The correctness of the date of the questions addressed to Serrarius from England is confirmed by a Latin letter from Johannes Duraeus (1596–1680), which fortunately has been preserved. Duraeus, in his time a well-known English theologian, was living in exile in Bern, from where he carried on a friendly and intimate correspondence with Serrarius. Writing on October 28, 1665, he reports: "Mr. Serrarius, in letters from Amsterdam of September 15 and October 1, tells marvelous news of the Ten Tribes of Israel. . . . They have already made their appearance at the borders of Arabia, conquered Mecca, where the tomb of Mohammed is, and other cities, and put to death all the inhabitants except the Jews. In my next letter, God willing, I shall let you have a copy of the account which he sent me. It is a most marvelous story, which he holds to be true as it is confirmed by many testimonies. . . . If the reports should prove to be true, then manifestly the face of the earth will soon be renewed."[13] Copies of a few of these letters have been preserved in the archives of a contemporary Swiss theologian who was interested in the movement (see below, p. 344). In any event there can be no doubt that reports of this kind were actually received in September, 1665, at the latest.

As early as the autumn of 1665 a pamphlet entitled *The Restauration of the Jews, or true Relation of their Progress and Proceedings in order to the regaining of their ancient Kingdom, being the substance of several letters from Antwerp, Leghorn, Florence* was published in London.[14] The pamphlet consists of various letters, one of which (written in Antwerp in the middle of October) reports at great length on the writer's discussions with a leading Christian chiliast, perhaps none other than Serrarius himself. Another letter summarizes the contents of reports from Leghorn and Tunis, while a third gives an abstract of other letters from Florence, Leghorn, and Amsterdam. The characteristic editing of these news letters suggests that they

correspondents were either written or inspired by him. Also "the good Christian friend, who lives here in Amsterdam in friendship with the rabbis," and who was the Polish correspondent's authority regarding the prophet of Gaza (Balaban, p. 42), was surely none other than Serrarius.

13. Hottinger Collection (Zurich), vol. XXX, fol. 360; for the Latin text, see *SS,* p. 269, n. 1.

14. The pamphlet was reprinted by Wilenski, *loc. cit.,* pp. 160–64.

emanated from Amsterdam and that the writer was a millenarian enthusiast rather than a journalist inventing an amusing canard, as was often the case in contemporary news letters. The letters may well be Serrarius' summaries of the news received by the Jews of Amsterdam from the Near East. The important thing about the pamphlet is the absence of any reference to the events in Gaza; the one possible reference is so vague that it may well refer to something else. One letter makes mention of recent reports from Jerusalem, announcing good news, though the writers had no permission to be more specific ("and from Jerusalem came this week [!] to our Jews, that there was good news; but what, they durst not express"). This interesting detail is corroborated by other letters, written from Jerusalem in autumn, 1665 (see below, p. 499). One suspects that the correspondent in Jerusalem meant to hint at recent or imminent events in his immediate surroundings as early as the end of June or the beginning of July, 1665—which, of course, would be an oblique hint to the events described in the previous chapter. There is no allusion to the Ten Tribes in this particular letter, although they form the main subject of the pamphlet. Serrarius evidently interpreted the report—the true meaning of which was of necessity unknown to him at the time—in the light of his own chiliast preoccupation with the lost tribes. Only later did concrete reports about the messiah and his prophet begin to arrive, and the first appearance of the legend of the returning tribes was thus uncontaminated by Sabbatian messianism. If this interpretation is correct then it is not impossible that the two sets of reports were independent of each other in their origins no less than in the minds of their recipients in Amsterdam. Sasportas, too, clearly distinguishes between the two types of reports. As early as 1665, when he was still residing in London as rabbi of the nascent Sephardi community, he had heard rumors to the effect that "multitudes of Israel had come by way of the desert to Mecca, the burial place of the prophet of the Muslims, which they had despoiled. When the Grand Turk marched against them with a mighty army they wrought vengeance on him and also laid siege to the great city called Mocca. These rumors were accepted even by Christians in England, and 'the voice waxed stronger.' Some said that [these Israelite armies] were the sons of Jonadab b. Rechab who had preceded the Ten Tribes."[15]

15. Sasportas, p. 14. Mocca may be a misspelling for Mecca. In the com-

The dates of the Christian letters require careful examination, and the possibility cannot be ruled out, in spite of our previous considerations to the contrary, that these reports were not entirely independent of the messianic events in Palestine. On the other hand, it does happen not infrequently that legends suddenly spring to life after a long period of dormancy when the cultural climate is especially favorable to them. There was a persistent popular legendary tradition about the lost tribes. In times of eschatological propaganda (for example, the years before 1648) and millenarist expectation, such reports, combining half-true accounts of Jews in far-away countries with uninhibited imaginings, would naturally proliferate.

A perfect example is furnished by the apocalyptic propaganda of R. Abraham b. Eliezer ha-Levi and his circle in Jerusalem during the years 1517–28. Their letters, sent from Jerusalem to correspondents and supporters in Italy, abound in information regarding the lost tribes and the "children of Moses."[16] In this instance the interest in the lost tribes manifested itself before the appearance of a concrete messianic figure; it was precipitated by the eschatological mood of the period. A very similar mood prevailed in Jewry during the expansion of Lurianic kabbalism and in Sabbatai's youth. An otherwise unknown emissary R. Baruch Gad, who had left Jerusalem for Persia in 1641, told, on his return, a strange story of his adventures on the way. Despoiled by robbers, he had wandered for many days through the desert until he met "a mighty warrior, extremely tall, and holding a spear in his hand," who wanted to kill him. The forbidding warrior turned out to be one Malkiel of the tribe of Naphtali. He did not grant Baruch's request to take him to the abode of the lost tribes and the children of Moses, but at least agreed to deliver them a letter in which Baruch described the tribulations that the Jews of Jerusalem suffered at the hands of the gentiles. Malkiel miraculously covered a three months' distance in three days, and returned to Baruch with a reply, signed by King Aḥitub b. Azaryah, the *nasi* (prince) Jehozadak b. Uzza, and the elder Uriel b. Abisaf. The letter, parts of which will

plete text of the broadsheet whose upper half is reproduced in plate I, it is explained that no. 4 in the illustration denotes Mecca "conquered by the Jewish army."

16. See the sources collected *Qobeṣ ᶜal Yad*, IV (Berlin, 1888), and my notes on R. Abraham ha-Levi in *Kiryath Sepher*, II and VIII.

be quoted later, was addressed to "our brethren, the children of Israel of the tribes of Judah and Benjamin." It contained words of encouragement and reassurance for the Jews of the Diaspora, and an account of the freedom enjoyed by the Ten Tribes. "And do not ask why we wage no war against the nations [to liberate you], for you should know that we, the tribe of the children of Moses, cannot cross the river [Sambatyon] until the end be, when the Lord will say to the prisoners 'Go forth,' and to them that are in darkness, 'Show yourselves' [cf. Isa. 49:9] . . . and you, O holy people, trust in the Lord evermore."

This message of comfort and messianic assurance was clearly based on older sources, such as the early medieval "Tale of Eldad the Danite," though adapted to the needs and to the style of a later generation. The letter seems to have made a great impression on the rabbis of Jerusalem, possibly because of its unstinting praise of the Holy City. Judging from their own testimony, they evidently believed in the genuineness of the letter. When R. Nathan Shapira was sent to Italy, in the middle of the seventeenth century, to collect alms for the Holy City, he equipped himself with a certified copy of the "Letter of the Children of Moses." In the interest of his mission, the rabbis of Jerusalem complied. They made and duly certified a copy, which contained at least "part of the original text, for we could not copy the whole as these are very secret things" which must not be divulged to the public. In 1657 another certified copy, signed by such distinguished rabbis as Jacob Ṣemaḥ and Nathan Guta (subsequently an opponent of Sabbatai Ṣevi), was sent to Nathan Shapira, who was then in Reggio (Emilia). There is no reason to doubt the authenticity of the signatures.[17] The contents of the letter throws much light on the sort of rumors about the lost tribes that were current in Sabbatai Ṣevi's day, and on their messianic associations.

A very similar rumor was started in 1644, when a marrano by the name of Aaron ha-Levi, formerly Antonio de Montezinos, ap-

17. The literature on the subject is listed in A. Yaᶜari's article on Baruch Gad, *Sinai*, VI (1940), 170–77. The signatures of the rabbis of Jerusalem were also certified by a Catholic priest (July 31, 1657), possibly in order to enhance the propagandistic value of the epistle. The bibliographer H. Y. D. Azulay saw the document in the archives of the Jewish community in Reggio, and testified that he recognized most of the signatures. Nothing is known of Baruch Gad, or of the circumstances of the composition of the "Letter of the Children of Moses."

peared before Manasseh b. Israel and declared under oath that in Ecuador he had met members of the tribe of Reuben, which had come to America even before the Red Indians. He also claimed to have heard rumors concerning the presence of the tribes of Ephraim and Manasseh on certain islands. Manasseh b. Israel quoted this testimony in his book *The Hope of Israel*,[18] in which he attempted to synthesize all that was known about the lost tribes and to systematize the various accounts within the framework of a messianic scheme that included their imminent reappearance and the end of Israel's exile. Manasseh's work was widely read by Jews and gentiles alike, and did much to bring the debate concerning the lost tribes to the notice of a wider Christian public. As a matter of fact, Manasseh's messianic scheme also served to bolster an immediate political program, namely, his demand for the readmission of the Jews to England. Prior to the advent of the messiah, the prophecy in Deuteronomy 28:64 had to be fulfilled: "And the Lord shall scatter thee among all people, from the one end of the earth even unto the other." In medieval Hebrew[19] the words *qeṣeh ha-ʾareṣ* ("the end of the earth") served as the standard Hebrew term for "England," of which it was a literal translation (*Angle-terre*). The residence of the Jews at "the end of the earth" can then be seen as a prerequisite for the advent of the messiah.[20]

Speculations of this kind incurred favor in chiliast circles. The copious literature on the subject created an almost pro-Jewish climate of opinion, and some Christian circles in western Europe expected the imminent repentance of Israel and their acceptance of Jesus, their return to the Holy Land under the rule of a visibly manifest messianic king, and the assembly, in the Holy Mount, of them that "were ready to perish in the land of Assyria, and the outcasts in the land of Egypt." Of course only a small minority entertained such views, and there was much oral and literary polemic against them, particularly in England and Holland. But the sectarian minority, though small, was quite active and exerted some influence. The rumors of 1665 concern-

18. *Miqveh Yisraʾel*, Amsterdam, 1650.

19. The usage is attested from Abraham ibn Ezra (1098–1164) to Isaac Abravanel (1437–1508).

20. See C. Roth, *A History of the Jews in England* (1941), p. 155, and *id.* in *Transactions of the Jewish Historical Society of England*, XI (1929), 113–14.

ing the lost tribes must have attracted their attention and prepared them to see the finger of God in the subsequent events.

It is impossible to detect any logical development and progression in the reports concerning the lost tribes. The different versions appeared at about the same time. A report from Tunis said that this year's (1665) caravan to Mecca would not leave, as the city was besieged by the children of Israel.[21] From Salé in Morocco it was reported early in August that

The tidings of the 15. of *July,* concerning the March of our Brethren, the *Ten Tribes* of *Israel,* is now from several places confirmed to Us, all *Things* being so full of wonder, that for some few days we could scarcely believe, or give credit to it, from the City of *Sus,* otherwise called *Santa-Crew.* But now We have certain Information, that they are on the side of the Desert, and move from several places to the said Desert Goth of *Morocco,* being not far from *Cape de Ver,* but more within the Land. And they appear daily more and more in great Multitudes, having suddenly and unexpectedly manifested themselves, covering a vast *Tract* of Ground, and consisting of about eight thousand Companies or *Troops,* each of which containing from one hundred to a thousand Men. They who went thither to see and enquire who they were, found them to be Strangers, and an unknown People, whose Language they understood not, onely some few of their Commanders speak *Hebrew.* Their Arms are swords, Bows, Arrows, and Lances, each Man being well armed therewith, but no Guns at all. They have for their Chief Leader, or Captain, a *Holy Man* who understandeth all Languages, and marcheth before them, doing miracles. These, with several of their Actions, were all related to me by a Convert Rabby, who has been discoursing amongst them and hath affirmed it by an Oath, upon the *Book of the Law.* But in Confirmation of all which, here are now arrived several Gentlemen of good repute and Credit, who relate, passing by the places above-mentioned, That they understood the same *Things,* which the *Rabby* and others, who had seen them before, had related, and many Things more: amongst the rest, that this unknown People were come from the Mountainous Countreys in the Wilderness, and were advanced as far as *Mechanas.* There is a certain Jew in the city

21. MS. Zurich; the French letter by Serrarius (see text, p. 346, n. 29); Wilenski, p. 162. The date (June 1) is given in MS. Zurich.

of *Sus,* who hath testified and declared, that he hath seen the People called *Israelites,* and going amongst them, discoursed with many of their Commanders in *Hebrew,* but understood not the Language of the great Multitude: yet withall heard of other *Jews* that several of them spake the *Holy Tongue;* and that whosoever goeth to contend with this People in Battel, are presently vanquished, and slain. They have already possest themselves of several Places and Cities, putting all the Inhabitants to the Sword, the *Jews* onely excepted. They are a People of a middle stature, their Bodies comely,[22] their Complexions fair: This Party saw no Woman amongst them, nor any other Arms, besides those above-mentioned; their Horses are many, their Attire blew, and their *Tents* black. From the aforesaid City of *Sus,* the whole Host of them might be plainly and distinctly viewed the whole Week, and might see their Fires and Smoak ascending; but on the Sabbath, neither of both could be discerned throughout the whole Camp, or Host. Several of them being got up on a very high Sand, the Mountain where they are employed to dig is very deep in the said Sand, where they expect to find a *Brass-Tamber,* that is, a *Trumpet,* with the which they are to sound 3 times, and then all Nations are to be gathered into One Universal Church. Their Leader is of an extraordinary discerning Spirit, and as soon as he sees a man, he knows his Mind, and what is in his Heart. [And when the Jew who reported these news saw that his Brethren doubted his words, he swore a solemn oath on the Book of the Law that he had told the pure truth, and that God punish him if his report were false. And I, the writer of this letter, have heard this report from the people in whose presence the aforesaid Jew swore his solemn oath, and I believe that it is true, although the matter seemeth very strange and requireth caution].[23]

22. The German versions says *von voller Proportion;* the French version *d'un bon embompoint.*

23. *Last Letters to the London Merchants . . . concerning the Restauration of the Jews* (London, 1665), pp. 4–6. Another English text is in the broadsheet *The Congregating of the Dispersed Jews,* printed in the year 1666. Other versions of the letter are extant in German (in the pamphlet *Wahrhaffte Abbildung*) and in French (Aeschcoly, pp. 221–22). The several versions complement one another. The passages given in brackets are lacking in the English version and have been translated from Aeshcoly's French text. The Latin translation published by M. Dercsényi in the *Goldziher Memorial Volume* (Budapest, 1948), pp. 399–411, is a free and extremely faulty version based on the German text.

The writer was evidently a Christian; yet the letter does seem to have been sent from Morocco. The real problem posed by the letter is its date of composition, since its description of the commander of the Jews combines the features of Sabbatai Ṣevi and of Nathan in a most surprising manner: he has Sabbatai's stature, obesity, and complexion as well as Nathan's gift of discernment of spirits. This may be sheer accident; it may also be the first echo of reports from Jerusalem or Gaza that had somehow reached Salé before becoming known elsewhere. The latter hypothesis seems to be supported by the fact that other early reports reaching Europe confused the two leading personalities, and identified Sabbatai and Nathan as one. The author of this letter knows neither messiah nor prophet, but only a commander or captain of the Jewish army who is, of course, also a holy man. The shift of emphasis is interesting. Unfortunately, we do not have the exact wording of the original report of July 15, 1665, which is merely hinted at in this letter. Neither do we have the letter of early June, from Tunis, mentioned in Serrarius' letter quoted below. Although no certainty is possible in this matter, we may perhaps assume that we are not dealing with two utterly different and unconnected events but, rather, with a translation of the actual messianic happenings into the imaginative language of popular legend. The legend must also have been current in the same or a similar form in the communities of Morocco.

There is, in fact, one document which appears to confirm our last suggestion. Among the Latin translations of several letters written at the beginning of the Sabbatian movement and preserved in the Czartoryski Museum in Cracow,[24] the letter from Salé mentioned above is immediately followed by the "copy of a letter sent in August from Jerusalem to Algiers." If this or a similar letter bringing news of events in Jerusalem really arrived in Algiers, and possibly also in Morocco, then we would have sufficient explanation both of the existence of rumors about the lost tribes and of the combination of these

24. Muzeum Czartoryskich, MS. 1656, fol. 489; cf. Balaban, p. 38. The late Prof. Sofia Amaizanóva of Cracow kindly transcribed the whole text, which, on examination, appears to be essentially the same as that in the letter from Jerusalem in the German pamphlet. The date (August 6, 1665) is erroneous. In the German pamphlet it occurs on a special title page ("Substance of a Letter from Salé in Barbary, the 6th day of August, 1665") and clearly refers to the first letter only and not to the other two.

rumors with the events of early summer in Jerusalem. There is no evidence that this happened, however. The second letter was not written in August but only toward the end of 1665, since it reports, with much legendary exaggeration, Nathan's activities during Hanukkah,
426 (end of November and early December, 1665). As a source for an analysis of the earliest reports, the letter is useless.

The reports emanating from Salé in September, 1665, were combined with similar information spread at about the same time by the Jews of Egypt. Letters from Egypt referring to the appearance of the lost tribes in Arabia had been received in Amsterdam as early as September. Allowing an interval of about two months for news to travel from Egypt to Amsterdam, the rumors must have been afoot in the Orient early in July. This would agree with the date of the first messianic excitement in Egypt, which set in immediately after the receipt of the first reports from Gaza.

The Egyptian Jews preferred the Arabian desert, which was nearest to them, and peopled it with the army of the Ten Tribes. When the reports from Arabia and Morocco merged, the "Arabian" army became the vanguard of an even larger Jewish army advancing from Africa. Other motifs, too, were transferred from one scene to the other; for example, the mighty captain of the host was moved from the African to the Arabian desert. Suddenly letters began to circulate in Italy, reporting such circumstantial details as the siege (that is, conquest) of Mecca, the immense number of the advancing armies, as well as their miraculous powers. The Turks were unable to fight them, "their own swords and muskets turning against themselves" and striking them down. The numbers of the host grew with every report, from tens of thousands to three hundred thousand to millions. Several reports, evidently deriving from the same source, give the exact number as one million one hundred thousand soldiers.[25]

Some of the extant reports are in Hebrew, but by far the greater part is known only from tracts printed in European languages or from quotations in letters which Jews as well as Christians wrote to their friends. Probably some of the earliest tracts and pamphlets are still buried in libraries and archives; even so, the details told in the known and available documents are sufficient to illustrate the atmosphere

25. The same number is also mentioned in connection with the tribes of Reuben and Gad advancing from Persia.

prevailing at the time. No reference is made, in the earlier reports, to events in Palestine, and there is no suggestion that the tribes in their rapid advance would converge on the Holy Land. For the time being, the action took place in far-away deserts, and was known only from reports given "on oath" by travelers arriving in Egypt. Unfortunately, there is no way of knowing the identity of the correspondents whose letters were so assiduously translated and spread throughout Europe by Serrarius. It is evident that Serrarius did not invent these letters; they and others like them were actually received from diverse quarters. The Hebrew letters written in Egypt in December, 1665, and found among the papers of Emanuel Frances, provide a good example of what the originals of Serrarius' letters must have been like.

Serrarius was of Walloon origin, apparently from Antwerp, and wrote some of his letters in French. A copy of his letter to Duraeus came into the hands of the Swiss scholar Hottinger, who kept it in his archives:[26]

I shall inform you of what seems to be incredible. The city of Mecca, the seat of the Mohammedan superstition, is now besieged by a people calling themselves the children of Israel and saying that they were merely the vanguard of the army of their brethren who were following them. The news, which arrived here from Leghorn three weeks ago, was sent by a Jew who says that he heard it from a Jew who had come from Alexandria in Egypt. He told that the bashaw of Alexandria accom-

26. Style and contents of the letter leave no doubt that it was written by Serrarius. His visit to North Holland is also mentioned in another (anonymous) letter by the same author, printed in the pamphlet *A New Letter concerning the Jews,* pp. 5–6. The identity of the writer is established by a reference, in the last-mentioned letter, to "our friend in Barn, which is in Switzerland," i.e., Duraeus; the letter is probably one of those referred to by Duraeus in his Latin letter of October 28. The French text is very close to the English version (Wilenski, p. 162), printed under the misleading superscription "The Substance of a letter from Legorn." The biblical terminology is the same as that found in Serrarius' other letters; most probably he was also the—evidently chiliast—informant who defended the messianic reports against the objections of the writer of the "Letter from Antwerp" (Wilenski, pp. 160–62). Wilenski's contention (p. 159) that the rumors concerning the appearance of the Israelite tribes in Arabia and Morocco originated among Christians influenced by the writings of Manasseh b. Israel, is not borne out by the sources. The rumors emanated from Jewish circles, and were not invented by Christians in Amsterdam or London.

panied by a king of Arabia, having made up a caravan of sixty thousand men, marched toward Mecca, and being but one day's journey thence, sent out a troop to take notice of the situation and the approaches of the city, from which he learned that the city was besieged and partly conquered by unknown people who called themselves Israelites. Thereupon the said bashaw with his army, and the said Arabs, resolved to march on and to attack these people, which they did, shooting at them with their muskets and arrows. But they were soon seized by a panic and terror, and cried out: "Who can fight these people. It seems that our arrows return back upon our selves!" So the Turks and the Arabs returned to their places, but to revenge themselves upon the Israelites they imposed on all the Jews in Egypt and Alexandria and Arabia a tax of five reales [lion's dollars] per head, instead of one real which they used to pay hitherto. The Jews dispatched ten learned men to Mecca to discover the truth of all this. When coming to them, these ten Jews found that they spoke Hebrew and that they were their brethren indeed, wherefore six of them remained there while the other four returned to Alexandria and brought the news to their brethren the Jews.[27] All this was confirmed by three letters from Leghorn. From Tunis it was reported on the first of June that the caravan which used to go every year to Mecca would not depart this year, because they had heard that the town was besieged by the Israelites. And yesterevening a Jew, Doctor Brecamera[28] visited me in order to tell me that the same news had also arrived from England by a boat coming from Alexandria, so that he was now satisfied of the truth of the reports from Leghorn.

Hence there will take place a general foregathering and assembly of all the nations of the world in one pasture which shall be in Zion, and there all contentions shall cease.

We have here in North Holland a person of good repute who secures us with a good conscience that God has revealed to him by living voice that next year Babylon shall fall at the beginning of the year, and that in the middle of the night there shall be wrought a judgment at which

27. So far the French text is substantially identical with the English version; the continuation (found only in MS. Zurich) agrees well with the chiliast mood of the authority so "well informed of the proceedings of the Israelites" with whom the writer from Antwerp had talked in Amsterdam.

28. The late Prof. Cecil Roth, in a written communication, identified him with Isaac de Rocamora from Avignon, a well-known physician living in Amsterdam. This is Dr. Isaac de Rocomora (died 1684), a friend of Manasseh b. Israel; cf. about him, Cecil Roth, *A Life of Manasseh ben Israel* (Philadelphia, 1934), pp. 120–22.

the whole world shall be afraid. All public worship will cease until the year 1672 because of that consternation, but that afterward a universal worship shall be raised up among all the peoples of the world.[29]

29. The French text (MS. Zurich, Hottinger Collection, vol. 30, fol. 346 a/b) reads: Extrait d'une lettre escrite d'Amsterdam. Touchant les particularités de la prise et siège de Meccha. Je m'en vay vous reciter ce qui semble estre incroyable, c'est que la ville de Meccha le siège de la superstition Mahumetane est à presant assiegée par un peuple, qui se disent les enfans d'Israel, estans seulement les avant-troupes de tous le corps de leur frères qui suivent: les nouvelles nous vinirent (!) il y a 3 sepmaines de Livorne escrites par un Juif qui disoit avoir entendu cela d'un Juif venu d'Alexandrie en Egypte; qui raconta que le Bassa d'Alexandrie accompagné d'un Roy des Arabes, compose d'une caravane de quelque 60 mill. hommes, s'estoit acheminé vers Mecca; mais qu'estant arrivé à une journée pres de la ville il y envoya un avant-troupe pour connoistre l'estat et les avenues de la ville, d'iceux il apprit que la ville estoit assiegée et prise en partie par des gens incognus, qui se disoient Israelites. sur ce le dit Bassa avec le gros de son armée et les dits Arabes prindrent la resolution de poursuivre leur chemin et d'attaquer ces gens comme ils firent, tirans sur eux musquets et flesches; mais tost apres furent saisis d'une frayeur et espouvantement et dirent entre eux; qui pourroit combatre contre ces gens, il semble que nos flesches retournent sur nous. Ainsi ces Turcs et Arabes retournerent chéz eux, et pour se revenger contre les Israelites ils imposerent sur tous les Juifs en Egypte et Alexandrie et Arabie une contribution de 5 Rsd. teste pour teste, au lieu d'une qu'ils souloyent donner. ces Juifs deputerent d'entre eux 10 hommes scavans vers Meccha pour scavoir la verité de tout ceci, ces dix hommes Juifs revenans parmi eux, trouverent qu'ils parloyent Hébreu, et que vrayement ils estoyent leur frères, donc les six demeurerent là, mais les 4 restans retournerent en Alexandrie et apporterent ces nouvelles à leur frères les Juifs. ceci nous est confirmé de Livorne par trois postes. Et de Tunis est escrit aussi du l. de Juin, que leur caravane, qui souloit aller tous les ans vers Meccha n'iroit cette année ci: à cause qu'ils avoyent appris que la ville estoit [f. 346v] assiegée par les Israëlites. Et hier au soir me vint trouver Doctr Brecamera Juif pour me dire que les mesmes nouvelles estoient aussi d'Angleterre par un navire venu d'Alexandrie tellement que lui témoigna qu'il estoit assuré de la verité du rapport venu de Livorne.

Voila d'on nous viendra un ralliement et rassemblage universel de tous les peuples du Monde et une seule bergeoie qui sera en Sion. C'est icy que se termineront tous les disputes.

Nous avons ici en Nort Hollande un persoñage de bon renom qui nous assure de bone (!) conscience que Dieu luy a revelé par vive voix, que l'añée prochaine Babylon la grande doit tomber, et ce du commencement de l'Añée, ez qu'au milieu de la nuit il arrivera un tel jugement, que tout le monde sera effrayé, et tout culte divin public cessera à cause de cette consternation jusqu'à l'an 1672, mais qu'a [près] sera dressé un culte universel parmi tous peuples du Monde.

The origin of the "letters from Leghorn" can be traced. The account, received in Amsterdam, of the news brought to Leghorn by a boat from Alexandria, came from the pen of Raphael Supino, a distinguished rabbinic scholar in Leghorn, the companion of Manasseh b. Israel on the latter's mission to London, and a friend of Sasportas. In the English pamphlet the name is wrongly spelled Rapheck Supi,[30] but there can be no doubt as to who is meant. Supino believed the earliest rumors about the lost tribes (which actually preceded the more concrete reports about Sabbatai Ṣevi) as eagerly as he later embraced the Sabbatian faith.

The earliest letters contented themselves with the siege of Mecca, which, however, soon became, in increasingly fantastic reports, the conquest and total destruction of the Muslim sanctuary. These later reports spread through Europe from Vienna, where the correspondents could draw on information received from the Balkans. There it was known that the Jewish commander came from Aden in South Arabia. Some letters gave his name as "Jeroboam." He had risen against the Turks and defeated them with a mighty army, consisting partly of Arabs and partly of Jews, and a whole province, including seventy mighty cities, had been ceded to him. Pamphlets printed in Amsterdam (but of which apparently no copy has survived) announced that eighty ships had sailed from India to Palestine, "and some say that one million and one hundred thousand Jews were on their way, on sea and on land. The sultan is said to have offered Alexandria and Tunis to the Jewish and Arab [!] conquerors of Mecca on condition that they give up Mecca, but they have demanded the entire Holy Land."[31] Also from Tartary—according to Manasseh b. Israel the

30. Wilenski, p. 163: ". . . a letter from *Alsasia Dipasi* and *Rapheck Supi.*" Dipasi is probably de Paz; the reference may well be to Samuel de Paz of Leghorn, subsequently a leading Sabbatian believer in the city.

31. Thus a letter written to Italy from Vienna in December, 1665 (text published by Scholem in *Zion,* X [1945], 60–61), and Italian letters drawing on "reports from Constantinople, Venice, Mantua and other places, as well as printed pamphlets" (*ibid.,* p. 60). Some of these pamphlets are lost, but the letter from Aberdeen, printed in London toward the end of 1665 and reprinted by C. Roth, *Anglo-Jewish Letters,* pp. 72–74, reflects the prevailing atmosphere. Roth, however, wrongly held the letter to be written by a Jew and addressed to Benjamin ha-Levi, the beadle of the first synagogue in London; actually it was written by Peter Serrarius (see above, n. 26) and addressed to a Christian chiliast who must have been an acquaintance of Duraeus. Similar

dwelling place of some of the lost tribes—a great multitude was marching on Jerusalem. Soon the early reports of the approach of a Jewish army from Persia began to merge with other popular eschatological ideas. Serrarius, who quotes some of these reports, claimed to derive his information from letters exchanged by various diplomats. Several pamphlets also contain quotations alledgedly taken from diplomatic correspondence.

Reports from the Orient regarding the movement of the lost tribes arrived in England, and quickly spread among chiliast circles where they begat more rumors. An instructive example is provided by the letter from Aberdeen in Scotland, published by Robert Boulter. Boulter took a great interest in the imminent redemption of Israel, and printed a number of pamphlets during the early days of the Sabbatian movement. The letter from Aberdeen reports that

> on the 23 instant [that is, October], by the foulness of the weather and storms, put into this place a Ship, from whence she came we cannot tell, but our Professor of the Tongues and Languages having notice thereof, went down unto them, but could not understand them; he supposes they spoke broken *Hebrew,* and by a letter they had in High-Dutch, they found them bound for *Amsterdam,* and to have correspondence with their Brethren (the *Jews*) there; which Letter further relates, That there is Sixteen hundred thousand of them together in *Arabia,* and that there came into *Europe* Sixty Thousand more; as likewise, that they have had Encounters with the *Turks,* and slain great numbers of them; none are able to stand up against them: They give Liberty of Conscience to all, except the Turks, endeavouring the utter Ruine and Extirpation of them: As for their Ship, the Sails thereof are white branched Sattin, and all their Ropes are Silk of the same colour; and in the Sails was this Inscription in fair Red Characters THESE ARE OF THE TEN TRIBES OF ISRAEL, which was to

---

reports also appeared in Perdou de Subligny's *Muse de la Cour,* a rhymed journal read in French court circles (cf. N. Szabolcsi in *Semitic Studies in Memory of Immanuel Löw* [1947], p. 185). According to this journal, the prince of the Jews, on being insulted by the Arabs, sacked Mecca. Coenen (p. 131) was probably drawing on Italian pamphlets when he wrote that the Duke of Tuscany and the Duke of Piedmont had received news of the movement of the tribes in Arabia and informed their Jewish subjects (in Florence and Turin respectively) of the matter; an army of 800,000 was said to be approaching from the deserts of Arabia.

discover them to be *Jews:* Their Food on board was only Rice and Honey: As for their Habit (or Clothing) it is of black and blew. It seems they have sent to all remarkable places in the World to their Brethren, to give them notice of their proceedings, to the end they may come unto, and joyn with them: I suppose you have not been ignorant of the Letters from several parts, the noise of them being communicated to most parts of Christendom.[32]

The letter contains many points of interest. There is, first, the explicit reference to earlier reports on the same subject. The reference may be to the letters from Salé and Egypt, or possibly to some earlier printed pamphlets that are lost. Those engaged in spreading the news did not fail to embellish it with details of topical interest by way of a contribution to contemporary discussion. "Liberty of Conscience" was a major issue at the time, and a political slogan with the Protestant sects in England. It was undoubtedly reassuring to be able to attribute the same ideal to the tribes of Israel. The anti-Turkish feeling, too, is not genuinely Jewish. The Jewish masses living under Muslim rule certainly did not harbor excessively warm pro-Turkish sentiments, yet it is evident that the particular note of hostility sounded by the letter from Aberdeen carries a different undertone. The "utter ruin and extirpation" of the Turks—and Turks in this context is usually synonymous with Muslims in general—was a Christian chiliast rather than a Jewish ideal. At any rate, the originally Jewish reports acquired a new coloring as they passed through Christian hands. Even the legend of the Flying Dutchman was adapted in Scotland and incorporated into the new tidings.

Although these rumors were spread both orally and in writing, they failed to produce a messianic echo among the Jews. The earliest extant pamphlets were all printed after the receipt of the more authentic reports concerning the appearance, in Palestine, of the prophet and the messiah. The letter from Aberdeen was probably printed in November, 1665, when news about Sabbatai Ṣevi was already known in Italy. A short time later the news also reached London.

32. *A New Letter from Aberdeen in Scotland, sent to a Person of Quality, wherein is a more full Account of the Proceedings of the Jews than has hitherto been published. by R.R.* Roth published the letter under the erroneous superscription "R.R. of Aberdeen"; the initials refer to the compiler in London who collected and edited the various pamphlets, and not to the letter writer in Aberdeen.

There is no evidence to show that the legends of the approaching desert armies of the lost tribes originated in Gaza. On the contrary, the popular quality of their military enthusiasm stood in marked contrast to the mentality of Sabbatai Ṣevi and Nathan, both of whom expected redemption to be worked through the singing of hymns rather than through military exploits and feats of arms. Actually there is something very realistic about the imaginary tales spun in Egypt and Morocco. The holy man walking at the head of the Jewish host is described as a military commander; his men are well armed, albeit with archaic and essentially magical weapons. But the Jews do not really fight, since the shots fired at them return like boomerangs against the Turks. Popular imagination cast the leading figure for the role it required. The prophet of Gaza had announced (see above, pp. 273, 287) that there would be no massacre of Christians except in Germany and Poland. Popular imagination immediately seized upon this prophecy as providing the most natural objective of the Jewish army. As early as the beginning of 1666 it was rumored in Casale in Italy that the army that had conquered Mecca "now intends to march against the Germans and the Poles that had so much persecuted the Jews, and that they would have no pity or compassion on them."[33] According to other reports, the sons of Jonathan b. Rechab[34] were preceding the rest of the Ten Tribes, but the origin of this particular detail is hardly Jewish. The Jews spoke of the "Sons of Moses," but never of the "Sons of Rechab," whereas Christian legend continued for some time to develop the version of the Rechabites as an ideal people beyond the river Sambatyon, also spelled Sabatyon.[35]

The legendary news reports purporting to come from Persia had the same warlike character. We do not know the origin of the intelligence that inspired the Italian author of the ditty referred to above (p. 331), but in December, 1665, reports from Vienna specified that the Israelite tribes were approaching from Persia. A letter written on December 18, 1665, from Vienna to Italy states that the postmaster of Flanders had received letters from distant lands, that is, from Persia,

33. See "Notes from Italy," *Zion,* X (1945), 60. Cf. also the reference above (ch. 1, n. 160) to a sermon preached some time between 1660–65 by the kabbalist R. Nathan Shapira of Jerusalem.

34. According to Sasportas (p. 14) and Emden (p. 6a), the pamphlets spoke of the Sons of Rechab and not of the Sons of Moses.

35. Cf. F. Nau, *Fils de Jonadab, fils de Réchab* (Paris, 1899).

via Wallachia. (The alleged pedigree of the letters bringing the marvelous news is not the least interesting part of them.) According to these reports from Persia, the country had been occupied by an unknown army without the use of arms, and solely by the will of God.[36] In February, 1666, a long letter of this kind, coming from Vienna and allegedly based on information received from Persia in October, 1665, was printed in London.[37] It is based on the assumption—also shared by Manasseh b. Israel—that the majority of the Ten Tribes had so far lived in the farthest parts of Tartary in Central Asia. Now, however, God had sent a prophet to assemble them and lead them to Palestine. The role attributed to the prophet suggests that the story originated after the first reports of the appearance of a prophet in Gaza had spread to the Near East. The story more or less corresponds to that told in the letter to Italy, with the addition of a detailed and circumstantial account of how the invaders had obtained permission from the Persian king to pass through his country on their way to Jerusalem and to take all the Jews with them. The Christian writer entertains the most fantastic notions regarding the Jews of Persia: their numbers are immense, and they are extremely rich and strong. However, they renounced everything at the behest of the emissaries of the tribes and of the king of Persia. At present they were in the Caspian mountains (that is, the Caucasus), and their journey was attended by mighty signs and miracles. The letter seems to have been written in Vienna under the impact of the first rumors.

Originating in Morocco and Egypt, these imaginative news reports reached the European and Asian Diaspora, as well as the Holy Land. Toward the end of 1665, the Palestinian believers began to include legendary information of this kind in their letters, thereby

36. See "Notes from Italy," *Zion,* X (1945), 61.

37. "A Brief Relation of several Remarkable Passages of the Jewes in their Journey out of Persia and Tartaria towards Jerusalem . . . in a letter written by Dom. Mareschalk Lira (?), from Vienna, to the Elector Palatine: very lately sent into England. Printed in the second Month, and hoped-for Year of Israels Restoration, 1666." A copy of this pamphlet, which supplements the other early reports regarding the ten tribes, is in the Mocatta Library, University College, London. The journey of the tribes from Tartary is also referred to by Serrarius, who had heard on November 2 from Brussels "that the Governour there, Don Cassel de Rodrigo, had received a Letter from Rome, from the Spanish Ambassador there, That they had received Tydings of an exceeding numerous people. . . . [and] that . . . a new Prophet and King was risen" (Wilenski, p. 172).

heightening the effect of eschatological urgency. Instead of the relatively distant future [1672] originally envisaged by Nathan (see above, p. 273), the current year was mentioned as the date of the arrival of the advance guard of the tribes. Very definite and precise prophecies regarding the arrival of the "Sons of Moses" or the "Sons of Reuben and Gad" were attributed to Nathan. The Sons of Reuben were to appear first, as befits the firstborn, on the Tenth or (according to others) Twentieth of Shebat (January 16, 1666).[38] A letter written in Usküb [Skoplje, Yugoslavia] in Macedonia on December 11, 1665, reported that the Sons of Moses had already arrived. The Hebrew letters dispatched from Egypt toward the end of November, 1665, were more careful: "as for the rumors from Mecca, there is no further news, though some Turks coming from there said that they had seen great multitudes of people, and that their [that is, the Muslim] governor was afraid of speaking to them because they were so many. But some of the Turks who had tried to speak to them said that they could not understand their language."[39]

By and large it appears that popular and mystical elements had already merged to some extent in the earliest letters that were sent to Europe. The fervent imagination of the believers, oblivious to the prophet's explicit warnings, beheld miracles everywhere. Or did Nathan, perhaps carried away by the enthusiasm of his followers, in fact utter the prophecies attributed to him? Bearing in mind the legendary tales of Nathan's miracles, one inclines to a negative answer. The evidence suggests that Nathan never modified his initial disapproval of the eagerness for miracles. His "miraculous" performances consisted in imparting mystical teachings, either in the form of personal guidance to penitents for the *tiqqun* of their soul-roots, or in doctrinal expositions of kabbalistic mysteries. His mystical insights were no doubt considered as inspired, but they were never regarded as signs or miracles in the usual sense. There must have been times when

38. The date 10 Shebat is given in a report from the end of November, 1665, published by U. Cassuto in *Vessillo Israelitico,* LV (1907), 329; 20 Shebat is given in the English pamphlet printed toward the end of 1665 (C. Roth, *Anglo-Jewish Letters,* p. 73), which also mentions Reuben's privilege of primogeniture. The idea that the tribe of Reuben would be the first to conquer Palestine occurs in earlier texts, e.g., Zohar I, 253b (the correct reading of the passage is quoted in *Libnath ha-sappir* [Jerusalem, 1914], fol. 76c).

39. Haberman, p. 212. The wording implies that letters received previously had reported the siege of Mecca, etc.

Nathan expected redemption to take place sooner than originally predicted in his letter to the *chelebi,* and he probably believed that Israel, by the intensity of its devotion and penitence, could advance the messianic hour. But all this is no argument in favor of the genuineness of the alleged prophecies, which appear for the first time in Ḥayyim Joseph's letter to his brother the *chelebi* in Cairo. Ḥayyim Joseph had been sent by his brother to Gaza, where he stayed for some time. His accounts are wrapped in clouds of legend. Nathan is said to have made repeated attempts to board a ship in Jaffa in order to join Sabbatai Ṣevi in Smyrna. Three times a violent storm prevented his voyage, until Nathan desisted. Thereupon an angel appeared to him in a pillar of fire, and commanded him to remain in Gaza, as redemption was at hand. "And when the prophet passed through the mountains of the wilderness, there appeared unto him the prophet Jehu, the son of Hanani [cf. I Kings 16:1], who confirmed the message of the angel . . . and that part of their tribe[s?] would all of a sudden appear in Gaza." The prophecy was repeated twice by the copyist (that is, the *chelebi* Raphael Joseph in Cairo) in his additions to his brother's letter. According to the second version R. Israel Benjamin of Jerusalem had accompanied the prophet into the wilderness where Jehu b. Hanani had appeared to them and announced that in two months' time two emissaries of the Sons of Moses would arrive from beyond the river Sambatyon.[40] The difference between the two accounts—two emissaries expected in Gaza, on the one hand, and an army of millions marching through Persia, Arabia, and Morocco, on the other—is blurred in the miraculous atmosphere in which the authors of these news reports were moving. Although the former version seems to be a secondary rationalization, the idea of emissaries from the lost tribes kept haunting the prophet and the messiah to the end.

40. From Leghorn, Raphael Supino wrote to Sasportas that he was expecting the arrival of the tribes (Sasportas, p. 74). Emanuel Frances, in a note to his poems, explained that Nathan "had prophesied regarding the tribes of Gad and Reuben, that they would conquer Palestine this year, and that there would be three days of darkness in Constantinople for the gentiles, but unto all the children of Israel will be light in their habitations" (*Ṣevi Muddaḥ,* p. 106). Frances evidently drew on letters which explicitly ascribed prophecies of this kind to Nathan, e.g., Raphael Joseph's letter to his brother in Leghorn (in *Several New Letters concerning the Jews,* London, January, 1666; reprinted by Wilenski, pp. 165–66).

The news of the approach of the lost tribes gave birth to further miracles. Writing from Amsterdam to Poland, one correspondent concluded his report with the information that "the Red Sea had dried up, even as in the days of their fathers." This report, originating in northwestern Europe, incidentally illustrates the independence of the imaginative faculty from geographical factors.[41]

III

Information on the development of the movement in Palestine is scarce, particularly from autumn, 1665, through winter, 1666. The mood of mystical enthusiasm and exaltation appears to have persisted among the believers. The prophet continued to compose kabbalistic tracts and homilies unfolding the meaning of his first great vision, and to advise penitent inquirers on the proper ways of perfecting their souls. He probably also kept up his correspondence with Sabbatai Ṣevi and members of his entourage.

Early in the summer of 1665,[42] R. Shalom b. Joseph, who had been a teacher at the *Talmud Torah* of the Sephardi congregation in Amsterdam for about forty years, left his city for Palestine. He was a scholar and a pious ascetic, and intended to spend his last years in the Holy City. On his way to Palestine he passed through Leghorn, where he met R. Elisha Ashkenazi, Nathan's father. Elisha too was on his way home, after extensive travels on behalf of the Jerusalem community,[43] and R. Shalom joined him. At about the same time, in the fall of 1665, the first reports of Nathan's prophecy arrived in Leghorn. The two traveled to Egypt where the prophet's father was received with royal honors. Upon a recommendation from Elisha, R. Shalom visited the prophet in Gaza and requested him "to consent to answer certain questions that he wished to ask. . . . The prophet replied that he was too busy at present, but that at some other time he would gladly fulfill his wish." We do not know what questions R. Shalom had meant to ask, or what Nathan finally told him. In

41. Balaban, pp. 41–42. The Polish correspondent had Ḥayyim Joseph's letter before him, but added freely from his own imagination.

42. According to one source (see *Zion*, X [1945], 66) he left on *Lag ba-ᶜOmer*, the thirty-third day after Passover.

43. Sasportas (p. 136) gives two conflicting versions of Elisha's travels: "he came . . . from Barbary" (i.e., North West Africa), but is said immediately afterward to have been in Hamburg and to have passed through Germany and Poland "until he arrived in Leghorn."

Warhafftige Abildung.

JOSVÆ HELCAMS, Welchen der Jüden neü entstandner Prophet NATHAN LEVI zum Obristen General uber die so genandte 10 Stäme Israelis erwehlet dessen Conturfey die See, fahrenden von Gaza, auf Constantinopel, und ferners an andre örter Versendet haben.

Fictitious portrait of Josua Helkam, whom the prophet Nathan is said to have appointed as supreme commander over the Ten Tribes of Israel. Broadsheet: *Warhafftige Abildung* [sic] *Josuae Helcams* . . . (in folio; early 1666)

any event, R. Shalom wrote to Amsterdam in December, 1665, that Nathan "is possessed of exceeding wisdom, and all scholars are coming from afar to hear his wisdom, and all agree that he speaks by the Holy Spirit." It is true, R. Shalom admits, that most of the Egyptian rabbis were still doubtful, but "in Gaza there is exceeding joy every day. Lights are kindled in the synagogue, and [special] hymns are recited. All are confident that as the messiah has gone to Constantinople, the Turkish king would set the royal crown upon his head, not by might nor by power."[44]

The "hymns" referred to in Shalom's letter were undoubtedly songs and liturgical compositions on the subject of the messianic redemption. Gaza witnessed a revival of the poetry of the sixteenth-century "mystic bard" Israel Najara, a former rabbi of that community. A hitherto unknown fact was now revealed—probably by Nathan, who, as we have seen, was an expert at discoveries of this kind: Israel Najara's soul had been a spark of that of King David. The diagnosis not only accounted for Najara's poetic gifts, but also explained why his hymns had a messianic content. Ḥayyim Vital, who knew not only Najara's hymns but also some of his weaknesses—including excessive drink—did not rate his soul among the most exalted. Other kabbalists too, for example, Menaḥem de Lonzano, were extremely reticent in their praise of Najara. But now one of Najara's hymns was circulated from Gaza to the Diaspora, together with the official pedigree of his soul, which was now attributed to the authority of Luria himself.

> Upon thy suffering people let
> Thy kingdom's glory shine.
> For long before kings ruled on earth
> The kingdom e'er was thine.

The hymn was considered a prophecy foretelling Sabbatai Ṣevi's coming. It was sent to Amsterdam and elsewhere, and in due course became a kind of signature which believers used for over a century.

44. Cf. the two accounts (both based on R. Shalom's letter) in Sasportas, pp. 136–37, and Haberman, p. 212. They traveled from Egypt to Gaza by land and not by sea, and the *chelebi* provided a mounted guard of honor. He also "gave to R. Elisha 411 grossos [i.e., reales], which equals the numerical value of the name Elisha." From this it would appear that R. Shalom went to Gaza together with Nathan's father.

Authors with Sabbatian sympathies would copy it in their notebooks, and print it in their tracts and books.[45]

R. Shalom seems to have met the prophet also on subsequent occasions, for his letters contained instructions for penitential exercises and devotions designed for the perfection of the souls of individual members of the Sephardi congregation in Amsterdam. He had obtained these instructions from Nathan, possibly at the request of his Amsterdam correspondents. To souls originating in "the heels of the messiah" (see above, p. 303), Nathan imposed fasts and immersion baths. Sasportas' criticism[46] that these mortifications were "more than the body could endure" seems to be due to a misunderstanding. If Nathan imposed a penance of one thousand four hundred and fifty fasts, he clearly did not intend that number of days but, rather, that the penitent should fast the "great periods" of six days each (see above, p. 292). This penance, if accompanied by the proper devotions, would be accounted as equivalent to so many thousand fasts. Even so, the penance was a hard one. Nathan, moreover, did not restrict his ministry as a diagnostician of "soul-roots" to believers only. As we shall see later, this habit of his led to frequent altercations.

R. Shalom b. Joseph ultimately settled in Jerusalem from where he wrote letters—unfortunately, all lost[47]—informing his friends of

45. The poem was sent to R. Yaʾir Ḥayyim Bacharach, in a letter from Amsterdam (ca. 1665–66) dealing "with the aforementioned affair," i.e., Sabbatai Ṣevi. The letter makes mention for the first time of the spark of King David's soul; the circle around Nathan added the further unhistorical and chronologically impossible detail about Luria's relationship to Najara (Najara was a child or a very young man when Luria died; about the wide use of the hymn in Sabbatian circles, see Scholem, in *Goldziher Memorial Volume,* p. 42, and in *Beḥinoth,* no. 8 [1955], p. 85).

46. Sasportas, p. 137.

47. What may be a fragment of Shalom's first letter to Amsterdam is preserved, by way of a quotation, at the end of the German pamphlet *Wahrhaffte Abbildung* and in Serrarius' letter of December, 1665 (in *God's Love to His People Israel,* Wilenski, p. 171). Both pamphlets quote a few lines purporting to be "a Copy of a Letter brought from Jerusalem to Alcaire, by one of the said Rabbies. Translated out of the Hebrew thus: I let you know, that on this day, there is in the City of Gaza, a Learned man, Just, Upright and True, and a very Humble one, which (as it appears), the Holy Ghost is upon him. He doth wondrous things, and can discover the secrets of mens hearts, having heard it, I went myself, and two Rabbies more with me to him, where he shewed [in books?] and told us wondrous things. Blessed be God, that has vouchsafed this grace to me [us], to let me [us] see what our Fore-fathers have

the state of messianic affairs in Palestine. He appears to have believed in Nathan's prophecy, for he wrote to his children that they should sell all their property and make haste to come to Jerusalem, since "we have a king and a prophet."[48] He also visited Hebron, at the time an important Sabbatian center, and in a letter to Amsterdam

---

not seen." These lines seem to be a direct translation from a Hebrew original, and sound definitely authentic, unlike the rest of the letter with its garbled and imaginary account of the anointing, by Nathan, of the "King of Judea, a certain Batchelor, named Rabbi-Sabothas Levi, a young man of Exemplary life." The letter was certainly not addressed to Cairo, where Nathan's prophecy had been known from the very beginning, nor was it written by one of the rabbis who had witnessed the appearance of the prophet Zechariah. The fragment seems to be taken from a letter that was actually sent from Jerusalem (via Cairo) to Amsterdam. There is nothing to contradict the assumption that it was written by R. Shalom. Serrarius could easily have obtained a copy from his Jewish friends, exactly as did the Polish correspondent who quoted the letter early in 1666 (see following note). The original Hebrew of the last sentence of the afore-quoted passage can be found almost verbatim in one of Sasportas' earliest letters to his friends in Morocco (Sasportas, p. 328; see also *ibid.*, p. 351). A very similar wording also in R. Aaron Sarphati's letter of December, 1665 (Sasportas, p. 26).

48. Quotations from his letter are preserved in two texts: (*a*) The news letter from Amsterdam to members of the Polish nobility (the "subscribers" to that particular private newspaper, as was customary at that period). The letter, which contains much important information, was published by Balaban (p. 42). It is said to be by a certain R. Szalem, and to have been sent from Cairo. R. Shalom may have returned to Cairo for some reason, or the letter may have been copied in Cairo, but it was undoubtedly written in Palestine (see preceding note). The full text in Balaban leaves no doubt that R. Szalem is none other than R. Shalom b. Joseph of Amsterdam. (*b*) The quotation in the Polish letter permits the identification of a passage in the *Diarium Europaeum* (XVI [1668], 514) erroneously attributed there to a letter by R. Solomon of Hebron to "his son and brother-in-law" in Constantinople. The German editor probably confused different things and substituted Constantinople for Amsterdam. R. "Solomon" is quoted as having computed the messianic end for the month Kislev of that year, and as urging his family to join him before the house which he had prepared for them would be occupied by the crowds which would arrive soon. R. Shalom may actually have written his letter during a visit to Hebron. The report in the *Diarium Europaeum* (1668), was reprinted thirty-five years later, without mention of the source, in the *Theatrum Europaeum* (1703), which Graetz and others held to be the primary source. The real state of affairs was pointed out by Moritz Stern in *Magazin für die Wissenschaft des Judentums* (1888, p. 101), but his correction was ignored by later writers.

(1666) reported on certain events there.[49] It is possible that this lost letter may have contained an eyewitness report of Nathan's visit to Hebron in the winter of 1665–66, of which, at present, we have only Abraham Cuenque's account: "In those days Nathan arrived in Hebron, accompanied by more than three hundred Jews. He came to Hebron to perform his devotions at the Cave of Machpelah and to undergo [the penance of] immersions in snow. For there is no snow in Gaza owing to its warm climate, whereas Hebron has snow most years, and the snow remains on the ground for a few days because of the cold air. . . . About a hundred Jews, with the prophet at their head, went out to the fields and performed the immersions by rolling [naked] in the snow according to [ascetic] custom. The Muslims beheld it every day."[50]

The center of Sabbatian fervor in Hebron was the *yeshibah* founded by the pious millionaire Abraham Pereira of Amsterdam and headed by R. Meir b. Ḥiyya Rofe. The scholars of the *yeshibah* had embraced the "faith" soon after the first messianic manifestations in the spring of 1665. As early as autumn, 1665, Meir Rofe, "the rabbinic professor of the Synagogue which he [that is, Pereira] supported by his donations,"[51] wrote to their benefactor in Amsterdam to thank him for his generosity and to inform him "that henceforth they no longer required his gifts, but that they wished that he would come and join them to behold the beauty of the Lord." But we must not hastily conclude that all the rabbis in Hebron believed in Nathan. Cuenque admits that the most prominent of them all, "esteemed among us as the greatest in our generation, [our] father in learning, R. Ḥayyim Abulafia" had listened to everything, but had "said with his holy mouth that he did not believe it, though he would act as all the others, so as not 'to separate himself from the congregation.' " Ḥayyim Abulafia was the second son of Jacob Abulafia, rabbi of Damascus and antagonist of Ḥayyim Vital. A well-known rabbinic authority,[52] he examined Nathan's rabbinic knowledge, and Nathan

49. A copy of the letter—now lost—of "R. Shalom of Hebron" was sent by friends in Amsterdam to R. Yaʾir Ḥayyim Bacharach, and was included in his "Collectanea on the affair of Sabbatai Ṣevi"; see A. H. Weiss, *Beth ha-Midrash* (1865), p. 92. 50. Emden, p. 40.

51. The Polish correspondent (Balaban, p. 42).

52. The rabbis of Constantinople selected him for the rabbinic commission of inquiry which was to examine Nathan in Gaza (Sasportas, p. 124). Rosanes (IV, p. 316) was misled by a corrupt reading in Baruch of Arezzo's account (Freimann, p. 48) and confused Ḥayyim Abulafia with Ḥagiz.

explained to Abulafia the burden of his great vision and the mystery of Sabbatai Ṣevi "from beginning to end." The details of Cuenque's account of the meeting are incapable of verification and may well be legendary, but the conclusion bears the mark of authenticity. After the prophet's departure, the rabbis of Hebron went to Abulafia to hear whether he had changed his mind on the subject of Sabbatai Ṣevi. Abulafia told them that although conceding Nathan's eminence as a rabbinic scholar, "yet I persist in my opinion. I do not believe that the messiah will come in this way. According to our tradition this is not the way. I shall not oppose them [publicly], but the convictions in my heart have not changed."[53] The ambiguity of the attitude adopted by Abulafia and by many others contributed much to the spread of the movement. There must have been many prominent rabbis who could not bring themselves to "believe" and who uttered their doubts and misgivings. They were disturbed by the obvious deviations from traditional eschatology, which knew of no "holy sinner" as redeemer, and Nathan's disquisitions on the mystery of the person of the messiah could not alleviate their uneasiness. Yet they would hesitate to interfere with the popular enthusiasm, which expressed itself in intensified piety and penitence. They kept their doubts to themselves, waiting to see how matters went.[54]

Cuenque's account suggests that Nathan went to some trouble to persuade prominent rabbis to embrace the "faith." We know that Nathan immediately gained followers in Jerusalem, and that he tried to attract R. Israel Benjamin and other rabbis to his side (see above, p. 263). He may well have had some partial success. When R. Jacob

53. Emden, p. 41.

54. R. Ḥayyim Abulafia of Hebron is probably not identical with his namesake who accompanied Nathan on his voyage from Palestine to Smyrna, where he received the deputation from Italy (Coenen, p. 135). Cuenque states that four rabbis from Hebron accompanied Nathan at the behest of Sabbatai Ṣevi, much to the regret of Ḥayyim Abulafia who said: "Do not go! and if you fear the king's [that is, Sabbatai's] anger, I shall defend you." Ḥayyim Abulafia was thus clearly not among the four who were invited. If he had changed his mind and converted to the faith (as did Nathan's companion Ḥayyim Abulafia, who remained a believer even after the apostasy), Cuenque would surely have mentioned the fact. Abulafia's subsequent change of residence from Hebron to Jerusalem may be connected with the fact that most of his colleagues in Hebron persevered in the faith even after Sabbatai's apostasy. He died in Jerusalem in or about 1684. It was in Abulafia's house that the well-known Sabbatian emissary Nehemiah Ḥayyon claimed to have grown up.

Najara sent out propaganda letters signed by "the rabbis of Gaza and its environment," R. Abraham Gedaliah of Jerusalem added his signature (or a separate letter) to authenticate, on his part, Nathan's prophecy and Sabbatai's messianic mission. The signatures were duly attested and certified by a rabbinic court. Sasportas possessed a copy of this letter, which was probably written in September, 1665, but deliberately omitted to reproduce it.[55] However, the text of another, much shorter letter, written at about the same time and brought to Italy early in 1666 by an emissary from Jerusalem, has been preserved by Sasportas. Of all the letters in the emissary's mailbag, only a brief note, written by "R. Israel Isserles, the son of the scholar R. Samson" to R. Solomon Ḥay Saraval in Venice, contains some vague allusions to the messianic events in Palestine. The author of this note, of whom Saraval says that he was "an old man of great learning, venerable, and of an illustrious family, the son of saintly ancestors," assures his correspondent that he was "ready to go forth with the army of prayer, praying for your peace and prosperity . . . to God who 'standeth behind our wall' [cf. Song of Songs 2:5], the holy Wailing Wall, which is the Gate of Heaven for our prayers. May we soon merit speedily to behold the glory of our might and our sanctuary, the place where our fathers prayed. For we have [beheld] many good signs . . . *which must not be committed to paper,* and everything [now] depends on [our] perfect repentance."[56]

Unfortunately, Saraval communicated only an abbreviated version of the letter which he had received, so that some of its allusions remain obscure. Yet the writer's faith in the import of the "signs" and the great penitential revival of the summer of 1665 is evident. His reticence about divulging any specific facts or names (for example, those of the messiah and his prophet) brings to mind the letter from Jerusalem mentioned in Serrarius' first tract: "that there was good

55. Sasportas (p. 22) refers to this letter in his reply of early December, 1665. The letter seems to have arrived in Amsterdam first, and its testimony is invoked by R. Isaac Aboab in his early letters to Sasportas. Sasportas mentions the letter again on p. 46 (together with an epistle of R. Jacob Najara) and on p. 82: "The teaching of R. Gedaliah and his colleagues has no authority in the face of [the divergent opinion of] greater scholars." The phrasing implies that the R. Gedaliah letter was also signed by several of "his colleagues"; but Sasportas evidently preferred "the teaching" of R. Jacob Ḥagiz (whose commentary on the Mishnah he knew) and the infidels.

56. Sasportas, p. 122.

news; but what, they durst not express." Other letters, written in July, 1665, in September, and even later, exhibit the same secretiveness. One of the first Egyptian letters reports (from Gaza?): "They write of the many things wrought by R. Abraham Nathan, but they must not be exposed [?] because people would not understand them at once and make a mockery [of them] and thus bring great evil upon themselves and upon Israel. For this reason they did not want to write down everything."[57]

The discretion displayed in the Sabbatian reports, and in the letters from Jerusalem in particular, may well have been due to the believers' fear of their opponents. The hostility of the rabbis in Jerusalem had not diminished, and those who joined the movement were certainly a minority. One incident in particular brought tempers to the boiling point. Letters from Sabbatai Ṣevi to his believers (possibly to the aforementioned R. Abraham Gedaliah) arrived in Jerusalem,[58] bearing the messiah's signature "I am the Lord your God, Sabbatai Ṣevi." Henceforth Sabbatai used this form to express his superior status and divine nature. The signature provoked a storm of indignation in Jerusalem. Moses Galanté said later he had been profoundly shocked.[59] Samuel Garmizan—who had been a member of the court that had excommunicated Sabbatai—preached a sermon before a "great multitude," in which he "explained that every man should know his worth and not wax proud . . . let alone make himself God." That this is not an anti-Christian, but an anti-Sabbatian, sermon is shown by the quotations of biblical verses and phrases containing the word *ṣevi*.[60] But these protests did not reach the Diaspora, and the silence of the "infidel" rabbis in Palestine remains something of a mystery.

Garmizan's sermon shows that the leaders of the opposition in

57. Haberman, p. 211.

58. From Aleppo or Smyrna?

59. Cf. Galanté's statement, quoted in the deposition of Moses b. Ḥabib: "At first I did not condemn Sabbatai Ṣevi; but [having seen his signature] I now curse him every day" (Emden, p. 53). But, as we have seen, this statement must be taken with a grain of salt; cf. above, p. 247.

60. The sermon, extant in MS. (*ʾImrey Noʿam*, sermons by R. Samuel Garmizan, MS. Badhab 32 in the Hebrew University Library), was not accessible to me, and I relied on the Catalogue of the Badhab Collection, prepared by M. Benayahu, which quotes a superscription, "a sermon which I preached in Jerusalem in the year 426" [1665–66].

Jerusalem had not changed their minds. When the Constantinople rabbinate wished to examine the authenticity of Nathan's prophetic mission, they appointed a committee of four Palestinian rabbis, all of them unbelievers, to conduct the inquiry. But for all we know, not one of them ever sent in his reply. While the letters of the believers circulated everywhere and thus "confirmed" the messianic tidings—from Jerusalem alone a considerable number of such letters were received in the Diaspora during 1666—the opponents wrapped themselves in silence. It is very unlikely that they did so for the same reasons as R. Ḥayyim Abulafia. For one thing, Abulafia's opposition was far more moderate; he had not been a party to Sabbatai's excommunication. Were they afraid of provoking the enthusiastic masses? When R. Asher Lemmel, an (apparently Ashkenazi) emissary from Jerusalem arrived in Italy in January, 1666, he carried a bag full of letters written by private individuals as well as by the leaders of the community. The several private and official communications were written in October and November, 1665, but with the sole exception of the note by Israel Isserles to Saraval, which was mentioned above, not one "as much as even mentioned those [messianic] matters."[61] This surely looks like a conspiracy of silence, and already Sasportas suspected as much. Admittedly the silence of R. Moses Tardiola cannot be used as evidence for such a conspiracy, for when Sasportas wrote to him for detailed information early in December, 1665,[62] he did not know that his correspondent was away from Jerusalem on some private or public business. On the other hand, Sasportas' remark that not one of the letters sent from Jerusalem at about the same time as Nathan's letter to Raphael Joseph (that is, September or October, 1665) "as much as mentions the name of the messiah or of the prophet"[63] is surely significant. If the Palestinian rabbis had attached any importance to the matter, Sasportas argues reasonably enough, they would have announced the glad tidings in an unmistakable manner, "in biggest letters" as he says. As early as the end of 1665, Sasportas knew that "the rabbis of Jerusalem utterly deny him [namely, Nathan and his prophecy],"[64] though he does not quote a single letter

61. Sasportas, p. 122; see also *Zion,* X (1945), 59.

62. The date is mentioned by Sasportas (p. 149), in a letter written a year later.

63. Sasportas, p. 84.

64. Sasportas (p. 42), in a letter of January, 1666, which was obviously

in support of this statement. Sasportas probably relied for his facts on the admission of the believers themselves, who in their letters never made a secret of the unremitting hostility of the Jerusalem rabbinate. Their testimony on this point is surely trustworthy. Perhaps the rabbis of Jerusalem had resolved never to refer to Sabbatai in writing and to ignore the whole matter; we know that the rabbis of Constantinople adopted a similar policy after Sabbatai's apostasy. Perhaps they were alarmed at the increasing excitement in Palestine and abroad; and with a view to the mounting tension between the two camps they may have decided on silence as the lesser evil. In any event, not a single document emanating from their side has come down to us. On more than one occasion the rabbis of Constantinople and Venice wrote to Jerusalem for information and guidance, but there is no reference anywhere to a reply from there. The rabbinate of Jerusalem was as good as nonexistent in this fateful year—not the least amazing fact in an amazing year! The wisdom of their decision may be questioned. Their eloquent silence did not save the nation from splitting into two camps, and it is more than doubtful whether the historian should count it to their credit. Events moved swiftly without the rabbis of Jerusalem taking any part in them.

R. Shalom b. Joseph, accompanied by R. Meir Rofe, visited the prophet once more—perhaps during the latter's pilgrimage to Hebron. Both testified in their letters to Amsterdam "that they had asked him for a sign or a miracle regarding his prophecy, but he refused, saying that he was not permitted to perform one. They should, rather, wait until they saw the fulfillment of everything. And R. Shalom greatly marveled at his [Nathan's] courage and his trust in the fulfillment of his prophecies." Nathan, it seems, was wont to send brief missives to the communities in the Diaspora. He also entrusted R. Shalom with such a message, which may probably be taken as fairly representative of Nathan's pastoral letters. Addressing the "holy congregation of Amsterdam, their leaders and sages, their judges, elders and officers with all the men of Israel, may God preserve them," Nathan writes: "Behold we were told that your heart was awakened to return unto the Lord your God to bring forth heavenly fruit. May it be God's will that repentance infuse the work of your hands. 'Strengthen

based either on private information received in 1665, or on letters from Sabbatian believers which made mention of "opposing forces" in Egypt and Jerusalem (e.g., Nathan's letter to Raphael Joseph, quoted *ibid.;* cf. above, p. 272).

ye the weak hands and confirm the feeble knees' [Isa. 35:3], for thus saith the Lord, behold thy savior cometh, his name is Sabbatai Ṣevi, 'he shall go forth as a mighty man, he shall stir up jealousy like a man of war; he shall cry, yea roar; he shall prevail against his enemies' [Isa. 42:13]. I pray that your eyes may behold the king in his beauty [Isa. 33:17]. From Nathan Benjamin."[65] Henceforth the prophet signed all his letters with the new name that Sabbatai had given him.[66] This symbolic change of name was perhaps a deliberate imitation rather than a fortuitous repetition of the act by which Jesus changed Simon's name to Peter. In the autumn of 1665, the believers also began to refer to Nathan by the mystical title[67] "the holy lamp." In the same way as AMIRAH came to stand for Sabbatai Ṣevi, so the expression "the holy lamp" came to signify Nathan in subsequent Sabbatian literature.[68]

Reference has already been made to Nathan's lack of interest in martial dreams. As we have seen, popular legend stepped in at this point, and assigned to the lost tribes all the military functions which Nathan's messianic prophecies had neglected. Nathan displayed his supreme apocalyptic confidence also in another matter of the utmost practical importance: the alms collected in the Diaspora to maintain the poverty-stricken Jewish community in Palestine, where little business could be transacted. R. Meir Rofe's letter to his patron in Amsterdam (see above, p. 358) was by no means exceptional. Early in 1666 it was rumored in Amsterdam that Nathan had urged the leading rabbi of Palestine: "Let not one more penny from the Diaspora come here: there will be sufficient treasures to distribute among all the tribes."[69] Perhaps Nathan uttered these words in a discussion with an unbelieving rabbi; perhaps, as Sasportas suggests, he wished to stop the transfer of charity

65. Sasportas, p. 138.

66. "R. Nathan, whom Our Lord called Benjamin" (Baruch of Arezzo, in Freimann, p. 58). R. Samuel Gandoor's first letter to Egypt states that Nathan "is worthy to be called by a new name, as one of the sons of the prophets" (Haberman, p. 207).

67. *Buṣina qaddisha,* the title applied in the Zohar to R. Simon bar Yoḥay.

68. The rabbis of Constantinople already use this title in their official letter, proposing a commission of inquiry to examine the prophet (Sasportas, pp. 123–24). Sasportas confirms (p. 125), that the title was in general use among the believers, for whom Nathan was a true prophet.

69. See "Notes from Italy," *Zion,* X (1945), 66.

funds to Palestine, by way of reprisal or threat against the infidels. Writing from Leghorn, Raphael Supino informed his friend Sasportas that the prophet had ordered that "no money from the Diaspora should enter Palestine,"[70] and in December 1665, Sasportas reports that the prophet had practically tried to starve his opponents by demanding that no more alms should be sent to the Holy Land.[71] Nathan was confident that hidden treasures would be discovered in Palestine in the wake of other miraculous discoveries (for example, those of the exact site of the altar and of the ashes of the red heifer required for ritual purification). He probably got this particular idea from *Tub ha-ʾAreṣ* by Nathan Shapira Yerushalmi. In this book, which had been published only ten years previously and which had influenced many of Nathan's ideas, we read (fol. 37c): "As for the underground treasures, the earth will form subterranean passageways so that all the royal treasures can be [miraculously] moved to Palestine, as it is written [Deut. 33:19, 'for they shall suck . . .] of the treasures hid in the sand.' Everything will be revealed in Palestine to the messianic king, and he will distribute them among the returning exiles, to each man his share, and they shall be filled with great riches." In Nathan Shapira's work the prediction forms part of a diatribe against the Jews of the Diaspora who were "concerned with their bodies and their money."[72] The prophet of Gaza applied it to the immediate situation. The inevitable results of this attitude formed the subject of discussions as early as December, 1665. Sasportas foresaw the distress of the poor in the Holy Land "since their king [that is, Sabbatai Ṣevi] had condemned them to death" by failing to provide for their needs and himself leaving the country.[73] Sabbatai's journey to Smyrna had indeed been mentioned in the earliest letter received at the time, but the accusation that he had doomed the poor to starvation while he was traveling in state in Turkey is almost certainly due to Sasportas' erroneous assumption that the refusal of foreign mammon by Nathan and Meir Rofe had been ordered by Sabbatai. Sasportas returned to the subject once more after Sabbatai's apostasy. Congratulating himself on his foresight, he reports "that many people had ceased to contribute their annual charity for the poor in Pales-

70. Sasportas, pp. 6, 74. 71. *Ibid.*, p. 20.

72. Cf. the analysis of Nathan Shapira's social criticism, above, pp. 73–74.

73. *Ibid.*, p. 23.

tine . . . , saying that 'since you have the messiah with you, you do not need our assistance.' Moreover they knew [that people in Jerusalem did not believe in] these vanities and that they held the messiah in no account. Wherefore the great mass, who were fanatic believers in this false faith, considered all Jerusalemites as infidels who denied the prophet and the messiah [and hence would no longer send alms to Jerusalem]."[74] The correctness of this account has yet to be proved, since the extant sources make no mention of such a vengeful mood among the believers in Amsterdam and elsewhere. Though it is not impossible that here and there arguments of this kind were advanced, Sasportas' account seems grossly exaggerated. Nobody would have argued that "the messiah is with you in Palestine" when it was well known that Sabbatai was in Turkey. We know of several emissaries from Palestine who were active in collecting alms in Italy, Germany, and Morocco in the autumn of 1665, and as our knowledge of them is purely accidental, we may assume that there were many more of whom we have no information. One wonders how these emissaries reconciled the patent contradiction between Nathan's taboo on foreign mammon, and their efforts to collect funds for relieving the actual misery. Perhaps Nathan, like the author of *Tub ha-ᵓAreṣ*, was referring to a more distant future, though Meir Rofe, in his first enthusiasm, seems to have understood the injunction differently. By informing us, in another context, that the *chelebi* Raphael Joseph provided for the needs of all the people in Gaza, Sasportas as much as demolishes his own story. There is no reason at all to assume that the believers who went to Palestine left their money behind. On the contrary, the extant accounts of their preparations for the voyage (for example, converting property to money, etc.) suggest the opposite. Sasportas' statement that the *chelebi* enriched himself by appropriating the money which the believers, in obedience to Nathan's injunction, entrusted to him before proceeding to the Holy Land, is sheer calumny. As a matter of fact most of Sasportas' information regarding the *chelebi* is incorrect and based on malicious hearsay (for example, the statement that Raphael Joseph followed Sabbatai into apostasy).[75]

74. *Ibid.*, p. 303.

75. *Ibid.*, p. 6. Sasportas' statements are contradicted by Sambari's chronicle, written by a man on the scene.

No doubt the great penitential awakening, stimulated and encouraged by Nathan, brought normal business to a standstill. Jerusalem had never been much given to trade and commerce, but the Jews of Gaza (including Nathan's father-in-law) were mostly traders. Cuenque's description of the devotional and penitential atmosphere in Gaza is confirmed and supplemented by a letter written toward the end of 1665, most probably in Egypt but almost certainly based on information from Gaza. The prophet and the king (that is, the messiah) were about to go to Constantinople, where they would ask the Grand Turk for the restitution of Judea; the prophet had predicted that the Grand Turk would himself put the crown on the messiah's head. "In the Interim, this is true already: That the Bashaw of Jerusalem,[76] and the Bashaw of Gaza, have kissed the hands of the Prophet; and the Confluence of People from all sides (both Jews, Turks, and Christians)[77] is so great, and the Vertues which are seen among them are so eminent, that all Neighbouring Nations do tremble at it. . . . all [are] plying nothing but Devotion, Penitence and Alms-giving; abstaining not only from all Vanity, but from Merchandizing and Trading; and especially from Exchange (which Natan[78] terms to be meer Usury) yea, such largeness of heart there is among them at Jerusalem:[79] that for One penny, may now be bought what was wont to cost Tenpence." Money-changing was one of the most widely practiced Jewish professions, particularly in Palestine. Nathan's condemnation of it, together with his ideas concerning alms from abroad, constitute a characteristic feature of what may be called his messianic economics. Nathan's attitude bespeaks an apocalyptic revolt. His rejection of certain very common features of Jewish life (for example, living on charity, money-changing, petty trading) expresses an unconscious rebellion against a traditional pattern of existence, though, of course, we must not interpret Nathan in anachronistic, modern terms,

76. Thus the more legendary account of Serrarius. The German version has only the pasha of Gaza.

77. Thus Serrarius. The German version does not mention Christians.

78. The English text (reprinted by Wilenski, p. 171) reads *Nature,* which is an obvious misprint. The German version reads: *enthalten sich aller Eitelkeiten und besonders des Kaufhandels und Wechsels welchen Natan für Wucher hält.*

79. The words "at Jerusalem" occur in Serrarius' text only. The German version is superior.

or attribute to him a desire for the "normalization" of Jewish life in the sense in which the modern Jewish national movement understood it. Nathan's concept of "normalization" was essentially messianic. In a redeemed and perfected age, the Holy Land would yield sufficient treasures to render trade and all that goes with it superfluous. The penitential awakening inevitably suspended routine economic activities, and the shift of interest was echoed in some of the earliest news reports. A letter from Leghorn to the East India Company (in London?) reported[80] that "the Jews of Alexandria write to their correspondents here, to send them no more business. They will have no further thoughts of it, but of higher matters."

In Safed, too, the movement gathered strength during the autumn of 1665. The reports about the utter destruction, in 1662, of the Jewish settlement there seem greatly exaggerated, and the conclusions based on them[81] are false. By the end of November, 1665, it was known in Cairo that immediately at the beginning of the mass movement ten prophets and ten prophetesses had arisen in Safed.[82] Perhaps Sabbatai and Nathan had visited the city during their joint travels in the spring of 1665. It may have been on that occasion, or during his passage through Safed in the summer, that Sabbatai wrote the letter to R. Judah Sharaf discussed in an earlier chapter (see above, p. 186). The enthusiasm of the people of Safed—or at least of an important group there—was a fact, and no mere invention of the Sabbatian propaganda machine. Early in the summer, several letters from Safed, enjoining adherence to the growing movement of

80. Toward the end of the tract *God's Love to His People Israel* (Wilenski, p. 172).

81. E.g., the statement (Rosanes, vol IV, p. 362) "no wonder that Safed took no part in the Sabbatian movement." Rosanes' account of the destruction of the Safed community is based on a misunderstanding of his sources; the community declined in numbers, but continued to exist (see M. Benayahu in *ʾEreṣ Yisraʾel*, III [1954], 244–48). A very lively account of the Jewish community is given by the French trader d'Arvieux who visited Safed in 1660. D'Arvieux realized the religious factor which enabled the community to survive, i.e., the fact that they believed "that the Messiah who will be born in Galilee, will make Safed the capital of his new kingdom on earth. Those who will be there at the time of his advent—both the quick and the dead—may expect from him special graces." In the circle of Nathan, Gaza had no doubt taken the place of Safed. If Nathan was a reincarnation of Isaac Luria (for this Sabbatian view see above, p. 280), then the association Safed-Gaza would be even more obvious.

82. Cassuto in *Vessillo Israelitico* LV, (1907), 329.

penitence and "faith," had been received in Amsterdam. Judging from the quotations in a Yiddish poem on Sabbatai Ṣevi by the Amsterdam schoolmaster Jacob Taussig,[83] the letters must have expressed the most sanguine enthusiasm. "Our brethren from Safed wrote . . . that we should prepare ourselves to offer the statutory sacrifices [in the rebuilt Temple] still in this year." All later editions of Nathan's devotional exercises contain certain changes and additions, printed under the significant heading: "Behold [Rabbi Nathan's] *Seder ha-Tiqqun* has just arrived here in a letter from Safed [!], and as we found that in two or three places it deviates from the earlier version as printed in this booklet . . . therefore we decided to print [these changes] in an appendix, and let the reader choose [which version he prefers for his devotions]."[84] The same booklet also refers to a "copy of a devotional manual (*tiqqun*) which arrived here from Safed."[85] In the editions printed after July, 1666, R. Solomon Oliveira added the following sentence to his original introduction: "And now behold a new thing which came to us from Safed, and I gave myself no rest until I had laid it before you."

Who were these enthusiastic followers of Nathan, who made it their business to disseminate his devotional exercises in their letters? A major part in this propagandistic effort was probably played by the aged kabbalist Benjamin ha-Levi of Safed. He had returned to spend his last ten years in his native city, after having traveled in Italy (1656–59) to collect alms for the Holy Land. He was greatly esteemed in kabbalistic circles, and during his travels he had occasion to establish personal connections with them. Forty years earlier, he had been one of the first editors of the writings of Ḥayyim Vital. His adherence to the messianic "faith" must have greatly impressed his many admirers. In 1666 he and his son Solomon wrote to their friends in Mantua "at great length concerning our redemption by

83. M. Weinreich, *Bilder fun der Jiddisher Literaturgeshichte,* Vilna (1928), p. 244.

84. The *tiqqun* was published by Joseph Attias in the year 426 [1665–66]; in one edn. (a copy of which is in the University Library of Amsterdam), fol. 82 is followed by four leaves bearing the aforementioned superscription.

85. The same edn., fol. 3b. Several other edns. printed at the end of the summer of 1666 introduce certain additions and changes with the words "From Safed."

our king Sabbatai Ṣevi."[86] While in Italy, R. Benjamin had been active in spreading the Lurianic liturgical devotions for special occasions.[87] These were later given their definite form by Benjamin's disciple, Moses Zacuto of Venice. There is reason to believe that R. Benjamin exhibited the same zeal in spreading Nathan's "revised devotions," particularly as their tendency and general character were well within the Lurianic tradition. R. Benjamin persevered in his faith even after the messiah's apostasy,[88] and after he himself had been forced to leave Palestine once more. It appears that R. Gabriel Esperança was chief rabbi of Safed at the time. His name was one of the four proposed by the Constantinople rabbinate for the committee that should examine Nathan's prophetic claims;[89] this suggests that he was not considered a committed believer.

There is no reliable information on the attitude of the Turkish authorities. The cadi of Jerusalem had refused to intervene in the dispute between Sabbatai and the rabbis. The accounts of the behavior of the other Turkish officials in Jerusalem and Gaza are pure legend: the pasha of Gaza had kissed the prophet's hands, and Nathan miraculously saved him from death by a poisoned shirt.[90] The report that the gentiles, too, had noticed the commotion in Gaza is no doubt

86. Baruch of Arezzo (Freimann, p. 59). The letter was written after Sabbatai's apostasy; there is no reason at all for doubting its authenticity (as is done by A. Yaᶜari, *Taᶜalumath Sefer*, p. 60, and *Beḥinoth* 9 [1956], p. 78).

87. Such as the midnight devotion known as *tiqqun ḥaṣoth,* and the penitential fasts for the winter weeks known as *shobabim thath.* The latter expression is formed by the initials of the first eight pentateuchal portions (*Shemoth* to *Theṣawweh*) of Exodus, but the term *shobabim* ("backsliding, wayward") also signifies, in kabbalistic idiom, the demons ("wayward children," cf. Jer. 3:14, 22) generated by masturbation. To atone for this sin, one of the gravest known to kabbalist morals, the series of winter fasts and penitential prayers had been instituted. See also, ch. 3, n. 262.

88. See *Beḥinoth*, IX (1956), 80, where I published an account of the meeting of R. Benjamin ha-Levi and the prophet Nathan (from MS. Adler 383, in the Jewish Theological Seminary of America). I deliberately refrain from bringing the famous work *Ḥemdath Yamim*, erroneously attributed by A. Yaᶜari (*Taᶜalumath Sefer*, 1954) to Benjamin ha-Levi, into the discussion. *Contra* Yaᶜari, see my arguments in *Beḥinoth*, XIII (1955), 79–95; IX (1956), 71–84; and Is. Tishby's penetrating analysis in *Tarbiz*, XXIV (1954–55), 441–55, and XXV (1955–56), pp. 66–92, 202–30. See also below, ch. 8, n. 80.

89. Sasportas, p. 124.

90. *Ibid.*, pp. 16–17. As a matter of fact, there was no office such as a pasha of Gaza. The writer may have meant the local Turkish official.

correct, though the reasons for their passive tolerance are still obscure. The believers, however, were quick to inform their correspondents that many Turks had come to pay homage to the prophet.[91]

IV

The character of the movement in the places through which Sabbatai passed in the autumn of 1665 differed widely from that which it assumed in those regions that depended for their knowledge on letters and hearsay. Far away from metropolitan Turkey, the messiah's personality played a very minor role in the consciousness of the masses. There is a peculiar, and at times possibly intentional, vagueness about the personal references to him. It was clearly advisable to avoid details that might perplex people, and at a distance it was not too difficult to soft-pedal Sabbatai's "strange actions" by a pious reference to certain "great mysteries that must not be divulged," or to omit or garble awkward facts. In the absence of the presumed messiah, popular imagination and credulity reigned supreme.

In Smyrna, however, once popular enthusiasm had been aroused, things took a different turn. Whereas our knowledge of Sabbatai's share in the events in Gaza and Jerusalem had to be laboriously pieced together, there is abundant information about his stay in Smyrna. We are in a position to follow almost every step of his during some of the stormiest days of the movement. In Smyrna, moreover, Sabbatai was alone, without his prophet. To the extent that he can be said to have acted at all, he did so by himself and at the bidding of his inner promptings. Nathan, it is true, continued to send letters and kabbalistic homilies, but he no longer exerted the same kind of personal, direct influence as before. Standing alone, and finding himself acknowledged by others, Sabbatai may also have gained in self-confidence. He stayed in Smyrna for about four months, but the period of his activity was short, about three weeks, and the most spectacular events took place within half that time. But the intensity and public character of the proceedings, as well as the uproar which they caused, assured them the widest possible echo. Gaza, after all, was a small and somewhat remote place, and nobody except the parties directly

91. Thus the letters from Jerusalem and Aleppo, mentioned in the letter from Üsküb of December 11, 1665. The original letters must therefore have been written not later than the end of October, 1665.

involved could possibly know exactly what had happened. Smyrna was different. A populous and important commercial center, whose Jewish community numbered several thousand souls, it also harbored a merchant colony of European Christians. Trade was largely dominated by the English and the Dutch, but there were also Italians and Frenchmen, some of whom were keen and knowledgeable observers. The whole action took place, as it were, on a stage, and the spectators could watch even the indoor scenes.

One of the shrewdest observers was Thomas Coenen, the Protestant minister sent out in 1662 by the Levant Trade Company in The Hague, as chaplain to the Dutch merchant community in Smyrna. Coenen had a fair knowledge of Jews and Judaism, and he was sufficiently interested in them not to miss the opportunity of closely observing the "madness of the Jews" and of following the development of their extraordinary mass enthusiasm. That which he did not know, he tried to learn from reliable informants. As a Christian minister he obviously had no access to the inner circle of believers, yet he would diligently collect information from all his acquaintances, Jews and gentiles alike. His letters to the directors of the company in Holland are a prime source for the history of the movement; they are conveniently collected, in an edited form, in Coenen's book, which was begun immediately after Sabbatai's apostasy and was finished in the summer of 1667. The great number of informants and sources on which Coenen drew inevitably introduced some contradictions into his account, but the essential facts can easily be discovered.

Sabbatai arrived in his native city in the late summer, just before the Jewish New Year, 426.[92] For about two to three months he "kept himself in private" which, of course, does not mean that nothing at all happened or that no news was sent abroad. Letters from Egypt reported in December, 1665, that "he had safely arrived in Smyrna . . . and the whole congregation, and his family in particular, were rejoicing greatly."[93] This piece of information was apparently reported to Egypt by a sympathizer of the movement, who was in contact with the family; there are no grounds for disregarding this earliest, albeit limited, evidence of the incipient awakening in Smyrna. Sabbatai's brothers must surely have been aware of what had been

92. See above, p. 259; Sabbatai had left Aleppo on August 12, 1665.

93. Haberman, p. 212. I have corrected some of Haberman's readings according to the superior text of MSS. Brit. Mus. and Columbia.

happening before his arrival, particularly as it was bound to affect their status. Whatever their original attitude—whether they believed in their brother's messianic calling or whether they felt disgraced by his madness—there seems little doubt that they now received him with open arms. Since the arrival of the good tidings from Gaza, at the latest, his family had rallied round him. Baruch of Arezzo's story[94] seems highly improbable: Sabbatai's brother Elijah persisted in his unbelief and said that it were better that Sabbatai die rather than that all the Jewish communities in Turkey perish. He actually tried to kill Sabbatai with his sword, "but Our Lord merely looked at him, so that he was seized by a trembling and fell down like dead and could not do anything." The letter to Egypt, mentioned earlier, with the report of the warm reception accorded to Sabbatai proves the purely legendary character of Baruch's account.

On the other hand, the great rejoicing of "the whole congregation" (referred to in the same letter) seems more doubtful, and certainly cannot be accepted without confirmation from other sources.[95] According to one account, Sabbatai remained outside the city, waiting for an appropriate occasion to make his entry, but the story contradicts all we know of Sabbatai's temperament. Rational planning and calculations were utterly alien to him, no matter what hostile writers were saying to the contrary after the apostasy. People in Smyrna were surely aware that a messianic campaign had been launched. If the news was known in other cities, then it must also have reached the messiah's home town, his family, his former fellow students and early companions, with many of whom he had probably remained in contact. His arrival must have precipitated a mood of expectation and tension. The townsmen would probably visit him and inquire concerning the rumors they had heard. Sabbatai would tell them, exactly as he had told the rabbi of Aleppo, what had happened in Palestine. Meanwhile, letters would arrive addressed to the "Anointed of the God of Jacob or the King of Israel, and he would secretly show these letters to his friends, so that they might make it public." Though this may be

94. Freimann, p. 48. Sabbatai's brother Elijah Ṣevi is always referred to in Sabbatian sources with the rabbinic honorific, though he had not received formal rabbinic training and ordination.

95. De la Croix's romantic account of the beginning of the movement in Smyrna is sheer fantasy and has misled later writers (e.g., Kastein). Leyb b. Ozer, who freely changes Coenen's chronology, is equally unreliable.

true, it is very unlikely that the people of Smyrna heard of the messianic awakening only through these letters.

In any event, nothing spectacular happened until Hanukkah (December, 1665). There was no agitation against Sabbatai, and even the rabbis who had denounced him in 1648 took no active steps against him. Evidently the report that for the first two months Sabbatai "kept himself in private" is correct, and the accounts of violent commotion and agitation in the city during three months—like the accounts of the "Sabbatian movement" in the years 1648–65—are merely the fond inventions of historians. By the end of September, 1665, the rabbis of Smyrna had probably received the letter signed by twenty-five rabbis of Constantinople, informing them that the Jerusalem rabbinate had excommunicated Sabbatai a few weeks earlier. The letter also contained the declaration of R. Yomtob b. Ḥananiah ibn Yaqar to the effect that it was a meritorious act to bring about Sabbatai's death as soon as possible. Yet nothing was undertaken against Sabbatai for many weeks. Perhaps the rabbis of Smyrna had decided to wait and to watch a while, although it is equally possible that events followed in a different sequence. If the rabbis of Constantinople advised their colleagues in Smyrna to do away with Sabbatai, then they must have been aware of his arrival there as well as of his doings. This is all the more probable in the light of the messianic fever that had seized the capital. In that case their letter would have been written much later, in November, and not immediately after the arrival of the report from Jerusalem. R. Ḥayyim Benveniste would hardly have kept the letter from Constantinople a secret for such a long period, particularly as his colleagues were men of outstanding eminence in the rabbinic world: Aaron Lapapa, Solomon Algazi, and Benjamin Melammed. They were all on the side of the unbelievers until the great crisis: then their ways parted.

In December, 1665, Dutch merchants as well as Sabbatian believers reported to their correspondents in Amsterdam that "King Sabbathai Levi [*sic*] doth now publickly shew himself abroad and professeth himself to be King of the Jews. For hitherto, for a time he lay incognito, until by signs and many wonders he had demonstrated he did act in the name of God, and not in his own." The letters also mention some of the signs and wonders that had been wrought.[96]

96. All these letters, Jewish as well as Christian, seem to have arrived between February 20 and 25, 1666; both types of letters are mentioned in the

The Christian informants explained their previous silence on the exciting events by the fact that Sabbatai had "kept himself so long in private" because of the unbelief of the Jews in Smyrna and Constantinople; now, however, "he is come forth from his private withdrawing" and it was known that he would soon proceed to Constantinople.[97] The first letters from Smyrna that arrived in Hamburg, full as they are of miraculous tales,[98] similarly state that Sabbatai had at first kept himself in private. Like Moses the first redeemer, the last redeemer too would reveal himself only after a previous incognito.[99]

Confirmation is provided by the two most authoritative extant sources regarding Sabbatai's sojourn in Smyrna. One is Coenen's book, written in the winter of 1666–67 with its detailed account of events in Smyrna.[100] The other report was known to Jewish writers

---

same English tract. The English letter from which the preceding quotation was taken is dated February 26; see also the following note. Sasportas (p. 85) too had heard that Sabbatai kept himself incognito for a while, before revealing himself as the Lord's anointed.

97. *A New Letter concerning the Jews* (London, 1666) pp. 5–6, reprinted in C. Roth, *Anglo-Jewish Letters,* p. 71. The phrase "our Merchants at Smyrna" refers to the Dutch author's fellow Christians, and not to the Jewish merchants, who are referred to as "our Jews." The author of the letter is undoubtedly Peter Serrarius who, as we know, was in correspondence with the English chiliasts. The writer mentions his visit to a man of God in North Holland (see above, p. 344) and misspells Sabbatai's name in the same way as Serrarius ("Sabbatai Levi"; cf. Wilenski, p. 171). The letters of Serrarius to members of the chiliast circle in England are explicitly mentioned by one of them, Thomas Chappell, in a letter preserved at the Public Record Office, London. In the abbreviated version of Chappell's letter, published in the Calendar of State Papers 1665–1666 (Domestic Affairs), p. 526 (1666, vol XII) Serrarius' name is omitted.

98. Sabbatai is said to have killed by the word of his mouth a band of robbers that had attacked his caravan. According to another version the brigands humbled themselves before him (Sasportas, pp. 16, 85).

99. Sasportas, p. 85. For Moses, cf. *Pesiqta Rabbathi* XV, fol. 73b.

100. Coenen, pp. 13–45, 63–74. De la Croix's account of Sabbatai's residence in Smyrna can be disregarded, since it not only confuses the chronology of the actual facts, but also abounds in sheer inventions of the imagination. (De la Croix's favorite method of presenting his story is by way of fictitious letters, allegedly written by the *dramatis personae*). The many inaccuracies and dramatic embellishments must be ascribed to de la Croix's story-telling talent; his Jewish informant proves himself reliable in so many details that he can hardly be credited with the wholesale invention of imaginary details. Nevertheless, a core of truth can occasionally be detected in the plethora of wild exaggerations.

in Italy from the seventies on, and was used both by believers (for example, Baruch of Arezzo) and by unbelievers (such as Solomon Carpi in the eighteenth century). The nature of this second source can be determined almost with certainty. The report was written by one of the three emissaries of the Jewish community in Casale (Italy), who arrived in Smyrna after Sabbatai's apostasy and stayed for a few months, until the spring of 1667. The author was a believer who had lost his faith after the apostasy; almost certainly he was Samson Bacchi, the rabbi of Casale.[101] The two accounts, written at about the same time and reflecting local traditions concerning the events of the previous year, are in essential agreement with each other, some minor discrepancies notwithstanding.[102] Their reliability is borne out

---

Thus although Sabbatai is said to have sojourned in Smyrna for a full six months before revealing himself as the messiah on the New Year's festival, 5426 (a date for which there is no confirmation from any source), de la Croix does emphasize (p. 303) that he lived incognito (*vivant privément*) "as if he was not in town at all." The detail that Sabbatai forbade his followers (i.e., perhaps his intimate friends and former companions) to address him as the messiah until he would formally permit them to do so may possibly be true and, moreover, agrees with his behavior during his stay in Aleppo. On the other hand, the stories (pp. 304–6) of the public reading of Nathan's letters to Sabbatai in Ellul, 5425 (September, 1665), and of Sabbatai's prohibition of all fasts until the end of 5425, as well as the details regarding the messenger who allegedly brought letters from Gaza, are sheer invention. Some of the events described by de la Croix did, in fact, happen, but only later, in January, 1666.

101. Carpi's *History of Sabbatai Ṣevi, from an old Manuscript* (Vilna, 1879), p. 20: "These are the words of the reverend emissaries of the city of Casale." This sentence, by Carpi, concludes a quotation from a report, but there is no clear indication in the text where the quotation begins. The text published by N. Bruell is composed of several fragments, but a stylistic analysis suggests that p. 13 (end) to p. 18, line 4, contains material from the same source from which p. 19, line 9, to p. 20 is derived. Thus the author uses the singular form when reporting information which he alone had heard (e.g., p. 17), whereas he describes the experiences of the whole deputation in the plural. Of the three emissaries R. Ḥayyim Segrè remained a steadfast believer. The other member of the delegation subsequently lived in Mantua. Hence the report from Smyrna was written by R. Samson Bacchi.

102. A close examination of the two accounts reveals no chronological discrepancies, although some writers claimed to have discovered such. Graetz, who ignored Samson Bacchi's report, erroneously assumed that Coenen's account followed the exact sequence of events, and hence arrived at a chronology which differs by one week from Bacchi's. The correctness of Bacchi's chronology is confirmed in a crucial detail by another rabbinic document. Rosanes rightly felt that the chronology in Carpi's *History of Sabbatai Ṣevi* (he did not realize

by various documents, particularly by Hebrew, Dutch, and other letters sent from Smyrna to Europe at the time the events described were taking place. Unfortunately, the dates and original text of the Hebrew letters have not been preserved and we know their contents only from references and quotations.[103] However, another document

---

that the latter was based on Bacchi's report) was correct, but his discussion of the alleged contradictions is vitiated by the fact that here, as elsewhere, he quotes from books which he never saw. His habit of secondhand quotations renders a discussion of his sources a futile and exasperating task. Thus Rosanes never saw Coenen's book, a great rarity, but quoted Graetz's incorrect deductions from Coenen as the latter's own statements. Coenen mentions very few definite dates, but those which he does mention flatly contradict Graetz's chronology. E.g., Coenen's definite statement that on 9 Tebeth Ḥayyim Peña's daughters prophesied and Peña acknowledged the messiah, entails that Sabbatai's outbreak of violence against Peña cannot have taken place on 11 Tebeth. A close examination of Coenen's story shows that he followed no strict chronological order. His account (pp. 14–17) begins with the happenings of 6–8 Tebeth (possibly a small mistake, as he should have begun with 4 Tebeth), and then continues (pp. 17–39)—*without mentioning any dates*—with a relation of the events that took place before his starting date of 6 Tebeth (i.e., the controversies about Nathan's letter, the councils of the rabbis, the attack of Ḥayyim Peña, the invasion of the Portuguese Synagogue and the dismissal of R. Aaron Lapapa, Sabbatai's visit to the cadi—which, perhaps, took place later—etc.). Coenen nowhere says that these events took place after 8 Tebeth. Graetz's mistake is understandable enough, but a careful reading of Coenen suggests that he interrupted his chronological account on p. 17 in order to say something about Nathan's prophecies as they had developed "meanwhile" which surely does not mean on 8 Tebeth, the date mentioned in the preceding paragraph. (Another example of Coenen's habit of shifting from later to earlier events is provided in pp. 63–74, where more details are told of Sabbatai's stay in Smyrna, in utter disregard of the chronological context). On p. 39 Coenen returns to where he had left off on p. 17, and gives an account of the mass prophecy, again mentioning a precise date (9 Tebeth), which is no doubt correct. It should be noted that Coenen got his facts from Jewish informants, and therefore dates events by the Jewish and not by the Christian calendar. Once the structure of Coenen's account is understood, the alleged contradictions vanish, and only very minor discrepancies remain. It should not be forgotten that Coenen composed his account in the form of letters, sent to the directors of his company in the summer of 1667; the editing and publication of the letters as a book was not supervised by Coenen.

103. Sasportas (pp. 61, 85–86), and the English pamphlets printed at the beginning of 1666. The substance of a letter from Smyrna, written early in April, 1666, is reported in the Dutch chronicle *Hollandtze Merkurius* for January, 1666 (actually printed much later), and again in the *Diarium Europaeum*, vol. XVI, pp. 509–12 (printed in 1668).

of decisive importance, written in 1667 by undoubtedly well-informed people, specifies the exact date of one of the principal events.

Although Coenen and the rabbi of Casale usually supplement each other's information, both fail to mention a detail which is of considerable importance for our understanding of the public background of the rapidly gathering messianic storm. Their omission, incidentally, may serve as a warning not to underestimate certain personal factors which the sources occasionally fail to emphasize sufficiently. Fortunately, the missing background information is provided by two complementary rabbinic documents, which reveal that from April, 1665, to the time of Sabbatai's appearance, a serious conflict was smoldering between the two leading rabbis of Smyrna. In due course one side tried to exploit the Sabbatian agitation against the other. Although this purely local quarrel is of no significance for the history of the movement as a whole, it suggests that in other communities, too, internal frictions and tensions may have played some part.

R. Joseph Eskapha was the undisputed rabbinic authority of Smyrna, and his status corresponded to that of a chief rabbi. But the question of his succession gave rise to conflicts even before his death. Smyrna counted among its rabbis R. Ḥayyim Benveniste, author of *Keneseth ha-Gedolah* and one of the most renowned rabbinic scholars of his time, but some rich members of the community took exception to him (or possibly to his rulings in the rabbinic court?). They pressed for a division of the chief rabbi's functions, and an agreement was signed in the court of R. Joseph Eskapha to the effect that after his decease two rabbinic chief justices would be appointed. Rabbi Eskapha died toward the end of 1661, and Ḥayyim Benveniste was appointed chief *dayyan* with jurisdiction in matters of marriage, divorce, and ritual law. It proved more difficult to find a candidate for the office of chief *dayyan* for civil cases, since no foreign rabbi would come to Smyrna to accept a divided jurisdiction. A few years passed before the elders of Smyrna found a suitable and willing candidate in R. Aaron Lapapa of Magnesia in Asia Minor. Lapapa and his family arrived in Smyrna in the spring of 1665, and he soon took up his office which, considering the commercial importance of the city, was regarded by many as superior to Benveniste's. The latter, indeed, had signed not only the original agreement providing for two chief justices, but also the formal letter of invitation delivered to Lapapa by the elders of Smyrna who had come to wait upon him in Magnesia. But the signature had been given unwillingly, and Benveniste felt that he was really entitled to the undivided office of chief rabbi. He declared in the presence of his supporters that his assent had been extorted under moral duress, and that the elders who had desired his appointment had been forced to agree to the double arrangement. Though personally he held Lapapa in great esteem, yet he felt that the elders of the community had dealt dishonestly with him.[104]

The relations between the two chief rabbis were therefore tense, albeit outwardly correct. Coenen's Jewish informants, partisans of Lapapa as it appears from the context, were careful not to breathe a word about the conflict between the two rabbinic leaders, and hence the background of Lapapa's dismissal is missing from Coenen's account of the matter. The report of the rabbi of Casale exhibits a similar lacuna, which, however, may be a deliberate and later mutila-

104. These facts emerge clearly from the joint evidence of two documents: (*a*) a MS. rabbinical responsum from the year 427 (1666–67) which was in the possession of R. Abraham Palache of Smyrna, and was printed by him in his *Abraham ᵓAzkir* (from where S. Bernfeld reprinted it in his collection of documents relating to Sabbatai Ṣevi, *Qobeṣ ᶜal Yad*, XV [Berlin, 1899], 1–11); (*b*) a responsum addressed in the year 428 (1668) by Benveniste to his friend R. Daniel b. Samuel, and printed in Benveniste's *Baᶜey Ḥayyey*, III, no. 172. The responsum mentions no names, and hence its autobiographical character was overlooked by both Bernfeld and Rosanes. H. Y. D. Azulay states in his biographical dictionary (*Shem ha-Gedolim*, s.v. Ḥayyim Benveniste), that Benveniste had written at length about the affair in his work *Keneseth ha-Gedolah*, but "it has been omitted in print, for reasons of reverence." Azulay also refers to the responsa of R. Moses Benveniste, *Peney Moshe* (ad *Ḥoshen Mishpat*), nos. 2 and 31. Benveniste writes with much feeling and bitterness, and is evidently trying to clear himself of accusations brought against him in connection with his support of Sabbatai Ṣevi and his treatment of Lapapa. Benveniste charges the leaders of the community with unfair dealing and actual deceit, and indicates that he had hinted to Lapapa not to accept the invitation on which he, Benveniste, appeared as a co-signatory. The other responsum is equally apologetic, but in a different direction: after Sabbatai's apostasy the author deeply regretted his support of Benveniste, and tried to have Lapapa reinstated. Bernfeld's suggestion that the responsum was written by R. Jacob Palache can be ruled out, since the latter is known to have persevered in the faith after the apostasy, and was actually suspected of having himself apostatized. The author must have been a prominent rabbi in Smyrna, since he confesses that his influence had caused many others to support Benveniste, and he expresses great sorrow over his share in the deposition of Lapapa. Further research into the writings of the rabbis of Smyrna may, perhaps, help to establish the identity of the writer.

tion due to rabbinic self-censorship.[105] Nevertheless, the whole picture can be pieced together from the several sources, whose details are not only chronologically consistent but also supplement one another. The fragmentary account of the rabbi of Casale omits some of the events that took place after Sabbatai's public revelation of himself, and which are mentioned by Coenen; conversely R. Samson Bacchi preserves many interesting details that are invaluable for an understanding of the psychological background of the great awakening, and which are lacking in Coenen's account.

The Dutch merchants had reported in their letter (see above, p. 375) that Sabbatai had kept himself in seclusion "by reason of the Incredulity of the Jews." The explanation is open to doubt; it is possible that the opposite may be true and the attitude of the public changed as a result of a spurt of activity on the part of Sabbatai. Once the spirit was upon him, he acted under the sole impulsion of his soul, and with utter disregard to what others thought about him. The usual complaints about Sabbatai's madness, repeated by Coenen (and his sources), hardly confirm the rationalist explanation proferred by the Dutch letter. The leaders of the community evinced no greater faith in Sabbatai when he began his public ministry than at the time when "he lay incognito." As a matter of fact their attitude changed not before but during the days of Sabbatai's activity. Taking into consideration the oscillations of Sabbatai's mental condition, it seems probable that after his arrival in Smyrna he entered upon a period of melancholia. This would account for his life of "private withdrawing." After the fit of depression had passed, Sabbatai would remain for a while in a state of normalcy, during which he lacked the active energy and initiative of his manic states. He was passive, waiting for the next "great illuminations." The reports of Sabbatai's private discussions with visitors are therefore credible enough. For the time being Sabbatai was not raving but arguing quietly—not because he was still busy planning his "strategy" with arrant cunning, but simply because he was not in a psychological state to act. He was essentially a passive personality, and it required the illumination of his manic mood to goad him into action.

105. Carpi (p. 15, bottom): "R. Aaron was a salaried chief rabbi [. . .]. In brief, Sabbatai intrigued until R. Aaron was deposed." Something—probably an account of the conflict between the two rabbis—seems to have been excised before the sentence beginning "In brief."

On the other hand, the report of the Christian merchants seems to reflect genuinely the atmosphere in Smyrna and Constantinople. An obscure excitement and a tense expectation were gradually building up around Sabbatai Ṣevi. Perhaps his presence in the city and his restrained behavior prevented premature outbursts. There were many who openly criticized the messianic agitation and who, no doubt, remembered Sabbatai's youth and his "mad behavior," in spite of the fact that since his return to Smyrna he had not caused any similar troubles. In Constantinople, however, the impact of the message was instantaneous and violent. Sabbatai had not been to the capital since 1658, but when the prophetic messages and the messianic tidings arrived, the excitement was greater than in Smyrna. Letters came pouring in from Aleppo, Gaza, and Egypt, and no doubt also the text of Nathan's letter to the *chelebi* Raphael Joseph was received in Constantinople by October, 1665. The letter from the rabbinate of Jerusalem must have arrived at about the same time. (Letters from Jerusalem to Constantinople took between one and two months to arrive, depending upon the sea winds.) The rabbis of the capital were no doubt bewildered by the conflicting reports. There were, on the one hand, the ban of excommunication by the rabbinate of Jerusalem, which described Sabbatai as a heretic and a tempter of Israel, and, on the other, Nathan's prayers and penitential exercises which released a torrent of ascetic piety. Probably some of Nathan's kabbalistic lucubrations on the mystery of the person of the messiah also reached the capital. Hearts and minds were divided on the issue. Some of the local scholars, roused to enthusiasm by the news of the revival of prophecy in Israel, accepted Nathan's ministry without waiting for further signs, and became fervent "believers";[106] R. Abraham Yakhini was one of them. Yakhini had not seen Sabbatai since the latter had left Constantinople in the company of R. David Ḥabillo, whom Yakhini revered so greatly that he referred to him as the "king" David (see above, p. 172). According to his own testimony, this orthodox kabbalist hitherto completely immersed in Lurianic doctrine and practice of *tiqqun,* now underwent a spiritual upheaval and was swept

106. De la Croix (p. 292) reports that immediately after receipt of the first messianic news, the two opposing camps were dubbed "infidels" (*kophrim*) and "believers" (*ma'aminim*) respectively. The terminology was probably taken over from letters arriving from Gaza and Aleppo.

away by the messianic excitement. We do not know exactly how the bond between the two was renewed: whether Sabbatai had written to Yakhini, demanding recognition and inviting him into his presence, or whether Yakhini proceeded to Smyrna on his own initiative after learning, in November, 1666, that Sabbatai had returned thither. In any event Yakhini was in Smyrna "during those blessed days of the year 426," and he was a member of the inner circle of followers whom Sabbatai appointed "kings of Israel" in December, 1666.[107] The awakening in Constantinople preceded that in Smyrna and was independent of it. Delacroix's information on this point is confirmed by a letter from Üsküb in Macedonia, dated December 11, 1665. No details of the events in Smyrna (which had begun during that week) could possibly have been known in Macedonia at that date. In fact, the letter makes no mention at all of Smyrna, although it speaks of prophetic manifestations in Aleppo and, more particularly, in Constantinople.[108] The letter also refers to reports that a number of people had set out from Constantinople and Smyrna to go to Jerusalem. This rumor makes sense only if the messiah was not yet known to be in Smyrna; it probably originated in Constantinople not later than November or early December. Even if we assume the detail about departures for Palestine to be an exaggeration, it is obvious that some reports concerning events in Palestine and Aleppo had come through to Constantinople by October, 1665, and had made a profound impression.

The report concerning the appearance of "one prophet" in Constantinople can be verified, and evidently refers to the prophet Moses Suriel.[109] The sources mentioning him all bear witness to his inspired utterance, and his case seems to be typical of what happened to many others during that year. The tidings of the restoration of prophecy unlocked hidden sources in many souls that hitherto had been like

107. I had wondered for some time how Sabbatai could appoint Yakhini as one of the first kings (see Coenen, p. 45), unless he knew him to be one of the principal believers. The puzzle was solved by a careful reading of Yakhini's letter of 1673 to Nathan, which revealed that Yakhini took a personal part in the events at Smyrna described there: See *RÉJ,* XXVI (1893), 215.

108. See *Zion,* X (1945), 64: *"In Constantina vi e anco profeta."*

109. Other sources spell his name Sarviel or Sarraval; see n. 248.

"dry wood," but "from the year 426 [1665–66] they were paved with love."[110] The gift of prophecy was infectious. Once the fountains of this particular charisma began to flow, everyone—the foolish and the wise, women and children—could prophesy, although, to be sure, certain superior graces such as the discernment of spirits or the gift of revealing kabbalistic mysteries ("the Torah of the messiah") were bestowed on a few elect only. However, the excitement generated in Constantinople by the letters from Aleppo and Gaza not only inspired a prophet. It also alarmed the rabbis and lay leaders, whose first reaction was to try and prevent the further spread of the disturbing rumors and to prohibit all public discussion of a subject that was more than delicate in the capital of the empire and under the very eyes of the Grand Turk and his viziers.[111] Perhaps this was the reason why the rabbis of Constantinople delayed so much dispatching their letter, advising Sabbatai's removal, to Ḥayyim Benveniste. By now the letter was too late, even though the mass movement in Smyrna had not yet begun.

The earliest mention of growing agitation in Smyrna occurs in a letter to England,[112] written by a Christian informant and dated December 7, 1665: "Here is a Jew in Town, who came about two Months since from *Jerusalem,* and gives out publickly, That the Messiah is come, and hath got to his Party a great many of the *Jews.* And not only in this place, but at *Constantinople,* and many other places through which he hath passed. And God alone knows whether he may be a means of the Conversion of that stiff-necked Generation." Perhaps the date should read December 17, since all our sources agree that it was then that the great revival swept Smyrna. On the other hand, the reading of the printed text is supported by the significant fact that the letter nowhere indicates that the Jew from Jerusalem had proclaimed himself *as* messiah. He had merely talked *about* the messiah without identifying him, and the author actually suggests that

110. The wording (based on a pun from the Song of Songs 3:10) is borrowed from a text referring to Heshel Ṣoref; see G. Scholem, *Cat. Cod. Cabbal. Hebr.* (Jerusalem, 1930), p. 239.

111. De la Croix (p. 292) reports an attempt to prohibit all public discussion of the messianic tidings, and there is no reason to doubt the correctness of his information.

112. *Several New Letters concerning the Jews,* p. 6.

he may have been a precursor sent by Providence to bring about the conversion of the Jews. It seems, therefore, that there was much excitement and agitation as early as the first week of December, but that Sabbatai was not yet publicly spoken of as the messiah.

R. Samson Bacchi of Casale says that Sabbatai arrived in Smyrna in September, 1665, "and there he remained silent until December. He would go to the synagogue early in the morning and recite [before the beginning of the morning service] the devotional prayers according to the Sephardi rite, with an agreeable voice that greatly pleased those who heard him. He also gave alms to the poor very liberally, fed them, and performed similar acts [of devotion and charity]." Coenen too had heard that Sabbatai slept little, rose at midnight to perform his ritual immersions in the sea, and was among the first in the synagogue every morning.[113] The reports sound authentic. So far there had been nothing odd about Sabbatai's behavior, and his ascetic piety would certainly win him popular sympathy. He (or his rich brothers) gave alms to the poor, and when the great crisis broke out "everyone that was in distress . . . and everyone that was discontented gathered themselves unto him."[114] His behavior was that of a pious rabbi who led the prayers of the community with a pleasing voice. Suddenly, early in December, all this changed and the familiar symptoms of illumination reappeared. As a matter of fact, two distinct events coincided during the critical week. On one of the first days of the Hanukkah festival—possibly on the first day, but certainly on a weekday[115]—

113. Coenen, p. 14.

114. Cf. I Sam. 22:2 (on David). The suggestion that the rich brothers distributed alms to win sympathizers for Sabbatai is made by the correspondent whose letter of April, 1666, provided the material for the report in the *Hollandtze Merkurius* for January, 1666 (p. 3). According to Leyb b. Ozer, the brothers were also able to prove Sabbatai's messiahship from kabbalistic books, but Leyb's story is made up of too many exaggerations and popular legends (not to speak of his fondness for "kabbalistic" embellishments) to be trustworthy.

115. The dates given in the two accounts using Samson Bacchi's report differ and are probably both corrupt. "Thursday, the third day of Hanukkah" (Baruch of Arezzo) is impossible, since the third day of the festival fell on a Sabbath; it was the first and the eighth days which fell on a Thursday, December 3 or 10, 1665. Carpi, too, specifies the "third day of Hanukkah," but the emphasis of the story on Sabbatai's festive dress and "royal apparel" suggests that the extraordinary demonstration took place on a weekday.

Sabbatai appeared in the synagogue "in royal apparel,[116] and intoned prayers and hymns, making a great rejoicing on that day."[117] Baruch of Arezzo reports that Sabbatai "began to intone melodiously the morning psalms, so that all the congregants marveled at his melodious singing."[118] The description is psychologically true to type. Sabbatai was evidently entering on another period of manic euphoria and, as usual during his prolonged ecstasies, he would startle everyone with his impressively paradoxical behavior. Another, completely independent, event coincided with Sabbatai's ecstatic illumination, for all reliable sources agree that a delegation from Aleppo arrived in the week of Hanukkah. They came to pay homage to the messiah, either at their own initiative or on behalf of their community. They had probably left Aleppo soon after Sabbatai's departure, but went to Gaza first in order to behold the prophet with their eyes. From Gaza they returned home and thence proceeded to Smyrna. The delegation was composed of two rabbis, Moses Galanté [from Jerusalem] and Daniel Pinto, and two laymen, possibly elders of the congregation.

The embassy was honorably received, and even Coenen, whose information on this point is confused and contradictory,[119] admits that the people, who had already heard of the prophet of Gaza, treated them with great honor. Evidently Nathan's messianic tidings, and possibly also some of his writings, were already known in Smyrna, al-

116. De la Croix, too (p. 306), mentions Sabbatai's royal costume, specifying that in public he wore a robe made of "white satin." But these white robes were the usual Sabbath apparel of the kabbalists, and if Sabbatai donned them on a Sabbath this could not possibly have provoked surprise or comment. According to very reliable testimony, he wore red robes when receiving delegations in Gallipoli, and expounded the significance of the color in homilies on Isa. 63:2: "wherefore art thou red in thine apparel." The red color fits with Nathan's doctrine of the predominance of the *sefirah Geburah* (judgment, red) rather than *Ḥesed* (mercy, white) in the messianic era. Either de la Croix's information is wrong or Sabbatai subsequently changed his colors.

117. Carpi, pp. 14–15.

118. Freimann, p. 48.

119. Coenen (p. 13) contradicts himself when saying that the Jews of Smyrna knew of Nathan and believed his prophetic message, but were ignorant of the person to whom his messianic prophecy referred. When the emissaries from Aleppo asked to be taken to the "Anointed of the God of Jacob," the reply is said to have been, "Whom do you mean?" In spite of the absence of precise dates, Coenen's account shows that Nathan's letters were known in Smyrna, and had been examined by the rabbis before Hanukkah.

though nobody had so far ever seen a person who had actually been in the prophet's city. Two of the emissaries, Galanté and Pinto, were themselves prophets.[120] The rabbi of Casale carefully avoids calling Galanté a prophet, and merely says that he "truly testified that he [Sabbatai] surely was the messiah." In the context such testimony can only mean the witness of the Holy Spirit speaking through him.

It is only natural to suspect that the arrival of the delegation at this moment was not fortuitous, and that Sabbatai had been apprised of their coming. But there is no compelling reason to assume a causal connection between Sabbatai's possible knowledge of the impending visit, on the one hand, and the onset of another manic phase. Sabbatai's states of illumination were neither faked nor induced by artificial means, and the manic-depressive rhythm is generally held to be independent of outside factors. Whatever the relation of the two facts, their combination produced a tempestuous outbreak of messianic mass hysteria. Even on the (highly improbable) view that the first waves of a confused and still inarticulate enthusiasm had swept the city as early as November, after the receipt of Nathan's letters, it would remain true that only Sabbatai's illuminative initiative, together with the witness of the freshly arrived delegation, fanned the smoldering fire into a mighty flame. A very similar combination of events had precipitated the messianic manifestation in Gaza.

120. See above, pp. 256–57. The date of their arrival in Smyrna can be determined almost with certainty. Coenen's date, 4 Tebeth, must be wrong, as that day was a Sabbath. Friday, 3 Tebeth, seems more probable, and this date is also suggested by the statement of R. Samson Bacchi (Carpi, p. 15; Freimann, p. 48) that "on the sixth day the rabbi Galanté came thither, who supported him [Sabbatai] and testified concerning him." The "sixth day" may refer either to the sixth day of the week, Friday, or to the sixth day of the Hanukkah festival. If Sabbatai's outburst occurred on the first day of Hanukkah (Thursday), then the arrival of the delegation on the next day (Friday, December 4, 1665, the second day of Hanukkah), would certainly have increased the messianic excitement. But it is equally possible that the delegation from Aleppo did not arrive until the following week, December 11, 1665. Before long the story was changed. The correspondent of the *Hollandtze Merkurius,* writing from Smyrna in April, 1666, says that the delegation came from Jerusalem in order to present the apologies of the rabbis there for their ignominious treatment of the messiah. His report thus, quite rightly, identifies R. Moses Galanté with the famous rabbi from Jerusalem. The Dutch report states that the delegation arrived two or three days after Sabbatai's arrival in Smyrna, i.e., in September, instead of connecting it with the public messianic outburst in December.

Our diagnosis of a renewed manic outbreak may be questioned. After all, Sabbatai was given to ecstatic singing of hymns, and all sources agree that his voice and person exercised a genuine fascination on these occasions. However, what seems to be decisive evidence is provided by a Sabbatian document that can hardly be suspected of maligning its hero, which tells us that, during the week of Hanukkah, Sabbatai "began to do things that seemed strange: he pronounced the Ineffable Name [of God], ate [forbidden] fats, and did other things against the Lord and His Law, even pressing others to do likewise."[121] This behavior is characteristic of Sabbatai's states of illumination. We know, from Sabbatai's own testimony as well as from that of his closest associates, that he acted in this way during his moments of exaltation only, and at no other time. The two details singled out by Baruch of Arezzo faithfully reflect the two aspects of Sabbatai's doctrine of the "world of *tiqqun*." That which had been separated was now united. Hence also the letters YH and WH, which had been separated during the exile of the Shekhinah were brought together again, and the divine name could—in fact, should—be articulated in its complete unity. The significance of the symbolic consumption of forbidden fat has been discussed in an earlier chapter (see above, p. 242). The transgression of this prohibition, for which the Pentateuch prescribes the penalty of *kareth,* symbolizes the return of the Law to its essence of pure spirituality, and the consequent abolition of all prohibitions. Even actions hitherto punishable by "cutting off" would no longer cut a soul off from its supernal root; on the contrary, they would strengthen the bond of mystical unity. Everything Moses b. Ḥabib, a sworn enemy of the movement, had said about Sabbatai's behavior, is now confirmed by an enthusiastic believer: Sabbatai sinned in public and caused others to sin for mystico-kabbalistic reasons. The obscure reference to "other things" may be a euphemistic allusion to sexual libertinism. Moses b. Isaac b. Ḥabib had mentioned the testimony of a former believer, a physician, regarding the adulterous behavior of Sabbatai's wife Sarah.[122]

121. Baruch of Arezzo (Freimann, p. 48).

122. Emden, p. 53: Sabbatai himself persuaded the doctor's son to enter his wife's room. When—like Joseph—he fled outside, Sabbatai complained that "if he had done her will, he would have performed a great *tiqqun*." A careful study of the document proved that Rosanes (IV, p. 403) was wrong in dismissing the "deposition" of Ḥabib as a forgery. His argument that Emden got the document

There can be no doubt but a fit of manic exaltation took possession of Sabbatai during the week of Hanukkah and pushed him to his subsequent provocative actions. Baruch of Arezzo's brief indications provide the key for a better psychological understanding of Coenen's detailed and circumstantial account. Coenen neglected this aspect of Sabbatai's personality and hence missed the significance of his "strange actions." Coenen's invaluable account is the fullest we possess of any period in Sabbatai's life, except Jacob Najara's chronicle on a later period of illumination in Adrianople. He, and some of the other chroniclers previously mentioned, reported not only single events whose correct interpretation remains uncertain, but a series of events and actions exhibiting the messiah's behavior and activity during several days. This continuity makes for the extraordinary importance of Coenen's account, since the many and full details add up to a convincing confirmation of our analysis of Sabbatai's character. Coenen well brings out the fantastic streak in Sabbatai's behavior which caused the cry of madness to be raised against him. To think of Sabbatai as acting in accordance with a carefully prepared long-term scheme, and to read Coenen's evidence in the light of this assumption, is to misunderstand everything. No carefully hatched plot, but the eruption of irrational forces determined Sabbatai's behavior. The combination of his illumination with the presence of a crowd of fascinated and deeply moved believers set up a vicious circle. The messiah's feverish exaltation and the mass ecstasy of a sizable portion of the public reinforced each other.

Coenen more than any other writer spotlights the peculiar pathological qualities of Sabbatai's character, and very clearly brings out the contradiction between his predilection for solemn rituals, gravely celebrated with royal pomp, on the one hand, and, on the other, a tendency toward sudden emotional outbursts of a libertine will that has let go all restraints. We have seen earlier instances of solemn and ritualized transgression of the Law, including the blasphemous benediction "Blessed is He Who hath permitted things forbidden," and have pointed out that this cultic sinning was not the whole story.

---

from Rabbi Ḥayyim Jonah whose whole family "are known to be Sephardim," while the Hebrew spelling of foreign words in the text was characteristically Ashkenazi (Rosanes, vol. IV, p. 403) involves a curious error. Ḥayyim Jonah Teʾomim was a Polish rabbi and *pukkah* Ashkenazi. The contents of the document stands the test of historical criticism, see above, ch. 2, n. 87.

Sabbatai's ritualistic longings were not satisfied by brief antinomian outbursts. They also sought expression in the invention of new cultic procedures in which the sublime and the ridiculous were curiously mingled. The secret satisfaction of transgressing the Law was merely one factor among others. Sabbatai seemed to derive a particular pleasure from the invention of new rituals. However grotesque and pathetic these may have been, there was nothing positively forbidden about them, and yet they, more than anything else, seemed to satisfy his growing appetite for the sublime. Coenen's account provides eloquent testimony: strange acts followed one another in rapid succession. Every such act intensified the mass hysteria which, in its turn, swept Sabbatai into its vortex, driving him into an even more frenzied ecstasy, until the whole force of his illuminate mania became fully manifest. Sabbatai had been through similar experiences before, particularly in Gaza, where for the first time he had felt the infectious presence of believers. But whereas our information regarding these occurrences is fragmentary, the historian is fortunate in that in Smyrna Sabbatai found a chronicler who carefully preserved every single detail. Coenen's account of the events in Smyrna may be taken as illustrative of Sabbatai's psychology and behavior in general, and its details agree well with the information provided by the other sources, just as its psychology is confirmed by Jacob Najara's chronicle, written five years later.

V

As people began to talk, even before Hanukkah, about Sabbatai Ṣevi, profound differences of opinion emerged. One section of the Jewish community immediately leaned to his side; no doubt Nathan's letters and the fantastic reports from Egypt had contributed their share. The rabbis of Smyrna, however, were less sanguine. They carefully studied the text of Nathan's letter to Raphael Joseph. The process of redemption seemed to be conceived very differently in the traditional rabbinic texts, and Nathan's exegesis of Scripture was disconcerting also. In spite of his skillful adaptation of tradition and legend, there was no real continuity. The allusions to Sabbatai's divine or near-divine nature were most alarming. R. Solomon Algazi, an ascetic kabbalist and member of the rabbinic council, had a very sensitive ear for such things. Only five years earlier he had published his work *Me'ullefeth Sappirim*,[123] an anthology of the Zohar, translated into Hebrew and "divided according to their subject-matter into thirty sections, to be studied one section every day of the month" and printed "at the request of members of the holy confraternity who support the students of the Talmudic academy of the Pinto congregation in Smyrna." In his opposition to Sabbatai's claims he voiced the attitude of many orthodox kabbalists whose mystical theology had not prepared them for a messiah who would raise himself above the Law and whose manifestation would deviate from the patterns of traditional eschatology. These kabbalists made no attempt to conceal their misgivings, and their followers openly declared that the writings of the prophet of Gaza sufficiently proved that it was not God who had spoken through him. In fact, his "words were suspect," which probably means suspect of being inspired by the powers of darkness.

Meanwhile, the enthusiasm of the believers was mounting steadily. The good news had opened up a fountain of joy and elation in their lives, and the violence of the awakening raised to danger pitch the tension that was developing between parts of the Jewish population. Believers and infidels talked different languages. The eyes of the believers beheld a new world, and the messianic tidings were accepted literally and uncritically. Whatever seemed inexplicable, either in the prophet's letters or in the messiah's behavior, was taken to be a mystery passing human understanding. They were ready to believe even without signs and miracles. The act of faith in Sabbatai Ṣevi, or the new SHADDAY, had transformed their world into one huge miracle where everything was possible. The mass movement which surged forward at the beginning of Hanukkah soon gave birth to all the miracles which Nathan's theory had dismissed as superfluous, but which popular religious psychology required.

Reports sent to Amsterdam stated as early as December, 1665, that Sabbatai Ṣevi had confirmed his mission by miracles. He had predicted the sudden death of certain people, as well as a day of

123. "Overlaid with sapphires"; cf. Song of Songs 5:14. The work was printed only once (Constantinople, 1660), and the later Smyrna edns., listed by the bibliographers, never existed. The wrong information given in the bibliographies misled both me (*Bibliographia Kabbalistica* [1927], 204) and Z. Rubashov (*Tarbiz*, V, [1934], 352–53), who connected the work with the Sabbatian propaganda preceding 1665.

darkness and the fall of "great Hail-stones, Fire and Brimstone." (According to other informants this prophecy of Sabbatai's concerned future events in Palestine and was communicated to Nathan in Gaza before Hanukkah.) Sabbatai also "commanded a Fire to be made in a publick place, in the presence of many beholders; as well as of Christians, as of Turks, and Jews; and entered into the fire twice or thrice, without any hurt to his Garments, or to an hair of his head."[124]

A study of the social composition of the warring factions in Smyrna shows that there were no clear-cut social demarcations. No doubt a large proportion of the rabbis and the more prominent laymen kept aloof as "infidels." The common people very largely joined the camp of the believers. They had no intellectual inhibitions or theological misgivings; but their ears had heard the glad tidings, and their eyes had beheld "the new light that shone on Zion." It was not only the knowledge that elsewhere, too, many eminent men had acclaimed the messiah which impressed the people of Smyrna, but above all the fascination radiating from Sabbatai's enigmatic personality and from the strange mixture of solemn dignity and unrestrained license which it exhibited. After his ecstatic outburst in the synagogue, Sabbatai's friends began to talk openly of his messianic calling, and hundreds of people would flock to him and accompany him wherever he went. This "bodyguard" was composed of the poorest and lowest in town. Coenen's sarcasm when describing their professional background is revealing on this point. They were "fishermen, vendors of eggs and poultry, oarsmen in the port, and servants, and more of this sort of noblemen, even the richest of whom had nothing to lose."[125] But Coenen's own account as well as the other sources show that this was far from being the whole story. From the beginning there were among the believers many burghers and elders, wealthy merchants and brokers as well as rabbinic scholars. Sabbatai's former fellow students, who had erstwhile received from him the "Mystery of the Godhead," would now be reminded of bygone days; perhaps much that had seemed strange then, now appeared differently in the light of Nathan's oracles regarding the struggle of the holy serpent against the primordial serpent. One of Sabbatai's early colleagues, R. Isaac

124. *A New Letter,* etc., p. 5, reprinted in C. Roth *Anglo-Jewish Letters,* p. 71.

125. Coenen, p. 35.

Silveira, is explicitly mentioned as a believer, and the revered memory of R. Abraham Barzilai in Sabbatian tradition is sufficient evidence that he too was not indifferent to the great awakening. The same picture emerges wherever the social composition of the movement can be analyzed in detail, which, unfortunately, is all too rarely the case. The leading group, that is, the scholars and lay leaders, was divided within itself. The motives determining the attitude of the wealthier merchant class were varied and complex: rational inhibitions such as always oppose messianic enthusiasm, genuine orthodoxy, and—no doubt—all those covert calculations of profit and loss when it came to leaving everything and going to the Holy Land, familiar to every student of "Zionist" movements. Considerations and obstacles of this kind played little or no part with the artisans and the poor. Chroniclers writing after Sabbatai's apostasy tended to emphasize the part played by the lowest class, suggesting that it was mob pressure that turned the scales in favor of the believers. There is little difference, in this respect, between Sasportas writing in Hamburg, his correspondents in Italy and Austria, and observers in Turkey. "The frenzied rabble," "the miserable beggars," "the poorest of the land," and like expressions recur frequently in contemporary reports. Perhaps the most withering social definition was given by the emissary from Casale who wrote that "everyone who was in distress and trouble, and all vain and light persons followed him."[126] This is true enough, but it is not the whole truth, and the somewhat one-sided presentation of the facts is contradicted by ample evidence. The eminent rabbi from Casale—as, indeed, many of his colleagues—evidently wished to minimize the rabbis' share in the movement, and to clear the scholars by throwing the blame, after the fact, on that inarticulate class which did not write books or pamphlets. The orthodox rabbis in particular tended to obscure, or at least to minimize, the importance of the genuinely religious motives which operated in the different strata of society, and which caused adherence to the messianic movement long before actual social pressure began to make itself felt. After the debacle, the sociological explanation was no doubt very convenient, but its partiality and exaggeration should be balanced by certain statements, made without apologetic intent, by Sabbatian writers. As a matter of fact the groups of believers were composed of all classes, and no social pressure was needed for their formation. However, once these groups had come

126. Carpi, p. 15.

into being, they undoubtedly exerted pressure on the unbelievers. Subsequent events showed that this pressure should not be underrated.

When Sabbatai learned that the rabbis had held consultations regarding him he was furious. According to Coenen[127] he reacted by proclaiming a day of public prayer. The believers spent the day in the synagogue, where Sabbatai displayed the demeanor characteristic of his illuminate fits, and indulged his taste for majestic ceremonial. He changed the order of the service, and ascended the steps of the Ark against which he knocked seven times with his staff. At the reading of the Torah he commanded the Ineffable Name to be pronounced. The entry into the synagogue too had been accompanied by unusual pomp and circumstance. Sabbatai was preceded by a great silver bowl filled with candies, and followed by two men carrying vases of flowers. The rest of the procession was brought up by a trusted believer, a rabbi, who carried Sabbatai's comb in its case. The messiah was accompanied by two rabbis who held the hem of his robe. In his hand he always carried a silver-plated fan—probably none other than the "royal scepter" mentioned in several letters. With this fan, to which reference is made in various sources,[128] he used to touch the heads of his believers, who considered this a sign of grace. The messiah was probably imitating King Ahasuerus, who held out his scepter to those whom he wished to show favor (Esther 4:11). The flowers and candies were interpreted by the believers—probably correctly—as symbols of the sacrifices to be offered when the messiah would have rebuilt the Temple.[129] The emissary from Casale reports that on the occasion of Sabbatai's solemn assumption of kingship, such candies were distributed.

This style, which Sabbatai now adopted for all his public appear-

127. Coenen, p. 26. Coenen gives no date and his account does not exclude the possibility that it refers to Sabbatai's solemn appearance in the synagogue at the beginning of Hanukkah, rather than to a distinct performance. If the phrase "day of public prayer" signifies a fast, this would have been in conflict with the liturgical regulations for Hanukkah. The earliest date for a fast would have been Friday, 3 Tebeth (December 11), the first day after Hanukkah. On the other hand, we must not forget Sabbatai's penchant for high-handed and surprising liturgical innovations. There is, of course, no need to understand Coenen's phrase as implying a fast.

128. De la Croix; the French *Relation,* p. 38 (where Sabbatai is said to have used the fan to hide his laughter at his foolish believers); Coenen, p. 15.

129. Coenen, p. 26.

ances, agreed well with his natural taste for dignified deportment toward others. Some sources mention that carpets were spread out before him in the streets, lest he soil his feet. This obvious imitation of the custom of Turkish rulers[130] may serve as an indication of the audacity of Sabbatai's behavior. The knocking against the Holy Ark too, so Coenen informs us, was a recurrent ritual, though the significance of the symbolic gesture remains obscure. Did the messiah, like a second Moses, wish to strike the wall of the Ark so as to bring forth the living waters of the "new law"? Or did he mean to rebel against the old, "carnal" law, and to set himself up as supreme authority? Perhaps the significance of this act of ecstatic impudence was not clear even to himself. He certainly acted without restraint, giving free rein to his impulses. In the words of an anonymous rabbi from Smyrna, Sabbatai believed that as the anointed of the God of Jacob "he could do whatever his heart desired."[131]

During the week of Hanukkah, the local rabbis seem to have held a number of deliberations. For the time being the leading scholars were still united in their opposition, though the breach between the two chief rabbis had already prepared the ground for a major schism. Benveniste was the most uncompromising in his hostility. In an assembly of rabbis he read the letter of the Constantinople rabbinate and proposed to follow their advice. Sabbatai had given sufficient proof, during the week, of his utter disregard both of the injunctions of Scripture and of the oral tradition of the sages. Benveniste's colleagues agreed, but when it came to taking practical action it appeared that nobody was prepared to strike at Sabbatai. The rabbinic deliberations ended without any result except that of inflaming factional passions even more.[132] Feeling between the two parties was running high, and the

130. Coenen, p. 34; de la Croix, p. 307; the Armenian source quoted by Galanté, p. 97 (which describes Sabbatai's royal ceremonial in detail).

131. Bernfeld, p. 7.

132. Coenen gives no dates, but his account (pp. 26–27) suggests that of the two rabbinic deliberations referred to, the one took place before the Sabbath on which the synagogue was occupied (4 Tebeth), and the other on the following Sunday. There were probably more such rabbinic consultations. Coenen's information on this point was secondhand, and hence his chronology and details are somewhat confused. Surely the letter from the rabbinate in Smyrna was read at the first consultation, and not—or at least not in the circumstances described by Coenen—at the meeting after the Sabbath, by which time Benveniste and Lapapa had irrevocably parted company. On the other hand, much of Coenen's information is substantially correct. Coenen states that the rabbis met at the house of

rumors about the intentions of the rabbis only added fuel to the flame. Did the rabbis mean to vent their anger on the Lord's anointed? Very well then, the Sabbatians would vent their anger on the rabbis first! Sabbatai seems to have agreed with his enthusiastic supporters that this kind of opposition was intolerable. The prevailing mood was described thus by Leyb b. Ozer's informants:[133] "The believers greatly hated the nonbelievers. And although they were afraid to speak up, yet since they [the nonbelievers] would not go with them and visit Sabbatai Ṣevi, they [the believers] hated them with a greater hatred than that of Midian and Moab, and they would fain have drunk their blood." The essential correctness of this account is illustrated by the incident with Ḥayyim Peña,[134] one of the wealthiest Jewish merchants in Smyrna and an ardent supporter of R. Ḥayyim Benveniste. Like most unbelievers in Smyrna, Peña was a member of the Portuguese Synagogue which was, as a matter of fact, considered the "headquarters" of the unbelieving party. On Friday, December 11, 1665, the crowd, incensed by a sharp exchange between Peña and some believers, tried to break into his house and stone him. There was a tumult, but as the Sabbath began with sunset—which, during the winter months, is very early in the afternoon—the crowd dispersed before anything serious developed.[135] Sabbatai's reaction, however, was

---

"Juda Murtia," evidently none other than R. Judah Murcia, to whom Benveniste addressed a responsum in 1671 (*Ba*ᶜ*ey Ḥayyey*, IV, no. 68). We learn from the responsum that in 1662 Murcia had married in Constantinople a wealthy woman, and that he lived in a richly appointed house. It was in his house that Lapapa subsequently went into hiding (Coenen, p. 39). The correct spelling of the name is Murcia, after the Spanish town of that name. The misprint or error in Coenen's book led to further corruption of the spelling by Emden (p. 28), and tempted Rosanes (vol. IV, p. 419) to the unwarranted "emendation" Judah Morteiro. There is no reason at all for accepting Bernfeld's view (p. 4) that the account of the rabbis' meetings is fictitious.

133. Emden, p. 7.

134. He defrayed the costs of publication of pt. I of Benveniste's work *Keneseth ha-Gedolah* (Leghorn, 1657); cf. Graetz, p. 445. See also above, p. 108, for the possibility that he or his brother Jacob Peña was Sabbatai's brother-in-law.

135. Leyb b. Ozer's story (Emden, p. 7), is a somewhat free elaboration of Coenen's account. Sabbatai is said to have himself led the attack against Peña, who had barricaded himself in his house and hid under a barrel. The messiah's party was about to smash the doors, when to Peña's "good luck someone arrived and said that the Sabbath service had begun at the synagogue," whereupon the attackers left.

more violent, and on the following morning he provoked the great scandal that inaugurated his rule over the Jewish community in Smyrna. The details of what actually happened on that memorable Sabbath, December 12, 1665 (*Vayyiqra,* Fourth of Tebeth, 5426), can be pieced together from the accounts in the various sources. The emissary from Casale, though he gathered his information a year or more after the event, has left us one of the most circumstantial accounts of those momentous three or four days:[136]

> On the Sabbath day, in his synagogue which is called[137] ——, he took a long time reciting the morning psalms and hymns [that is, the first part of the morning service], which they did not even finish, neither did they recite the *Shema*ᶜ. After they had spent a long time over the morning hymns, he [Sabbatai Ṣevi] proceeded to the Portuguese Synagogue,[138] accompanied by everyone who was in distress and trouble and all vain and light persons. The members of the Portuguese congregation did not believe in him, and as they were greatly afraid that the embittered crowd might strike at them, they locked the doors of the synagogue. Thereupon in his wrath he asked for an ax and began to smash the doors on the Sabbath. When they [in the synagogue] beheld this, they opened the doors and he entered the synagogue just as they were reciting the *Nishmath* [hymn]. He interrupted their prayer and began to preach a

136. Carpi, pp. 15–17.

137. *Ibid.,* p. 16: "Which is called Galanté"; in Baruch of Arezzo's shorter version of the same account (Freimann, p. 48): "which is called Algazi." Synagogues were often called by the names of the families which had founded or which supported them (e.g., the Pinto Synagogue in Smyrna), but the Galantés were not among the leading families in the city. The error may be due to the fact that R. Moses Galanté is mentioned a few lines earlier. "Algazi" may refer to the synagogue which R. Solomon Algazi used to attend, but Coenen explicitly states that on that particular Sabbath, Rabbi Algazi was present at the Portuguese Synagogue.

138. Peña's name is given by Coenen, but does not appear in Samson Bacchi's account, which appears to be a carefully revised version of the events. Bacchi presents the members of the Portuguese Synagogue as unbelievers all. This oversimplified picture is not corroborated by any other source. Letters from Smyrna written in 1666 suggest not so much that the majority of members were unbelievers, but that the majority of unbelievers were members of this particular synagogue; cf. The explanatory note of Emanuel Frances (p. 110): "Sabbatai . . . commanded to kill all his opponents, most of which were in the Portuguese Synagogue."

blasphemous sermon,[139] continuing with more hymns and prayers until the [prescribed] time for the statutory morning prayer had elapsed. Then he announced: "Today you are exempt from the duty of prayer,"[140] and took a printed copy of the Pentateuch from his bag, declaring that it was holier than the Torah scroll.[141] He read the pentateuchal lesson, calling his elder brother [Elijah] first as [if he were] a priest and making him king of Turkey. His second brother he appointed emperor of Rome. He called none of the many priests and Levites present in the synagogue to the reading of the Torah, but he called many [other] men and even women to whom he distributed kingdoms, and he forced all of them to pronounce the Ineffable Name. The next day the rabbis met in council and summoned him to explain why he had thus trespassed the Law. He replied angrily that he knew what he was doing, and immediately went to the cadi (which is the title of the judge of the city), to whom he spoke and whom he gave a valuable gift. The cadi thereupon sent for the rabbis, who feared for their lives and hid in their houses.

In [these?] days two of the rabbis in Smyrna, R. Aaron [Lapapa] and R. Ḥayyim [Benveniste] consulted together. R. Aaron was the salaried chief rabbi.[142] In brief, as a result of Sabbatai Ṣevi's intrigues he was dismissed, and R. Ḥayyim appointed to his office. Henceforth R. Ḥayyim acknowledged and honored him, and succeeded in making many of the people do likewise. He honored him [Sabbatai] like a king, but the other rabbis feared for their lives and kept silence.

On the following Monday there was a great rejoicing as the Scroll of the Law was taken from the Ark, and he sang all kinds of songs—also Christian songs in the vernacular—saying that there was a [kabbalistic] mystery hidden in these impure songs. He also declared "this day is my Sabbath day." At night he held a banquet and the people went to kiss his feet. To all of them he distributed money and candies, and he forced all, Jews and gentiles alike, to utter the Ineffable Name. One gentile admitted to me[143] that at Sabbatai's importunate demand he

139. This detail, reported at length by Coenen and others, is omitted by the fervent believer Baruch of Arezzo.

140. The same is also reported by Emanuel and Jacob Frances.

141. Frances (*ibid.*): "he read the pentateuchal lesson from a printed Bible," against rabbinic law.

142. Here Bacchi's original account must have said something about the strained relations between the two chief rabbis, see above, pp. 378–79.

143. I.e., to the author, R. Samson Bacchi.

had three times uttered the Ineffable Name. Even the Turks were talking about the affair, though no miracle was ever seen, not even a natural sign. But many unlettered men and women experienced all manner of convulsion and prophesied—though not one of their prophecies ever came true—and exclaimed, "Sabbatai Ṣevi is the king of Israel!" and the like.

This account gives the main outline of the events, but omits a number of major and minor details preserved by Coenen, and mentioned in letters sent as early as December, 1665, from Smyrna to Europe. What really happened was this: On the Sabbath morning Ḥayyim Peña went, as usual, to the Portuguese Synagogue. Sabbatai Ṣevi, offended by Peña's remarks, interrupted his own prayers and sent a message to the elders, demanding that the "infidel" be ejected from the synagogue. (Possibly he remembered having himself once been the victim of such a forcible ejection, when many years ago he had been called to the Torah and had pronounced the Ineffable Name.) The elders, who had no reproach to make to one of the most esteemed members of the congregation, refused. Thereupon Sabbatai marched to the synagogue at the head of five hundred followers.[144] When he found the doors closed, he sent for an ax and himself smashed the gates. The crowd "stormed" the synagogue, but Peña had meanwhile made good his escape over the roof or through a window. The synagogue, probably the most important one in town, was filled with Sabbatai's followers, and remained henceforth the main scene of his strange ceremonials. The liturgy that was performed immediately after the occupation of the synagogue has been described in R. Samson Bacchi's account. Reports concerning Sabbatai's sermon on that occasion differ in details—perhaps they also confuse and combine utterances made on different occasions—but its general tenor seems well established.

After reading from the Torah—from a printed book and not from a Torah scroll—Sabbatai cupped his hands, put them to his mouth, and trumpeted in the direction of the four winds. The kabbalistic purpose of the exercise, like that of blowing the ram's horn on the New Year festival, of which this was an imitation, was to con-

144. The large number is no addition after the event, for the first letter from Smyrna to Hamburg (December, 1665) spoke of "five hundred Jews" accompanying Sabbatai (Sasportas, p. 61).

found Satan and to weaken the power of the *qelippoth*. Then he expounded the kabbalistic reasons for his latest desecration of the Sabbath: "It is time to work for the Lord, [therefore] the Law may be transgressed."[145] By smashing the doors of the synagogue, "many *qelippoth* of the evil power had been broken, and this was a profound mystery."[146] He reviled and insulted the unbelieving rabbis, and five of them in particular. As Lapapa was not present in the synagogue at the time, Sabbatai did not waste much time on him,[147] but the other four, including R. Ḥayyim Benveniste, were compared to the unclean animals mentioned in the Bible. Each ought to feed on the animal corresponding to him, so that he would "eat his own flesh." Benveniste was compared to a camel, the others to a hare, a pig, and a rabbit respectively. Sabbatai also threatened to excommunicate them, and desisted only in deference to the Sabbath day.[148] Not content with reviling the rabbis present, he also heaped abuse on their predecessors. According to Coenen he exclaimed: "What has Jesus done that you ill-treated him thus? I shall see to it that he will be counted among the prophets."[149] The accuracy of the Protestant minister's reporting is, perhaps, open to doubt on this point. Yet we know for certain that Jesus was very much in Sabbatai's mind: he imitated some of the actions of Jesus, and indulged in speculations regarding the latter's "restoration" (*tiqqun*) (see above, pp. 284–86). He was fascinated by the problem of the relation of the soul of Jesus to that of the true messiah, that is, himself. Something to that effect may well have been uttered on that occasion, and Sabbatai would not have been the first Jewish sectarian founder to acknowledge Jesus as a true prophet. Abu Issa in the seventh century had done the same.[150] Perhaps Sabbatai had mentioned Jesus and said something about the *tiqqun* of his soul, in the style of Nathan's disquisitions. His words, startling enough as they were, were then misreported and reached Coenen a year later (or possibly soon after the event?) in a popular and garbled version. We need not be surprised at Coenen's raptures

145. A well-known rabbinic, homiletical interpretation of Ps. 119:126.

146. Frances (p. 110), on the authority of letters from Smyrna. The trumpeting through cupped hands is also mentioned by Coenen, p. 36.

147. Leyb b. Ozer (Emden, p. 8) is the only author to mention this detail.

148. Emden, p. 8; the original source is Coenen, p. 37.

149. Coenen, pp. 35–36.

150. Graetz, *Geschichte der Juden* (3rd edn.), vol. V, pp. 403–6, 417–18.

over Sabbatai's utterance, or at his regret that the rest of the sermon was not on an equally high level.

Sabbatai next spoke of the messiah of the House of Joseph about whom, it seems, he had been frequently interrogated. If the Davidic messiah had come, where then was his precursor who was destined to die in the messianic wars? Sabbatai replied with one of his characteristic inventions: the Messiah b. Joseph had already come in the person of a certain R. Abraham Zalman, and had died a martyr's death in the 1648 massacres in Poland. Sabbatai "paid him great honor as he recited for him the prayer for the defunct, and all the people marveled thereat."[151] We learn from this report that Sabbatai recited the *hashkaba* (requiem prayer) for the Messiah b. Joseph, of whose existence nothing had been known until then. There was logic in the workings of Sabbatai's mind. We know that his experience of his messianic calling was connected with the terrible events of 1648. Small wonder that in his feverish imagination the Messiah b. Joseph, instead of leading the armies of Israel against Armilus and Edom, died as a victim of the Chmielnicki massacres. The eschatological battles between Israel and the nations, described in the apocalyptic legends, had become an internecine war among the gentiles themselves. This changed emphasis[152] in the idea of the dying messiah has a grandeur of its own: it is the people as such who have made atonement for their sins. The person of the Messiah b. Joseph remains hidden and anonymous, for his dignity and his sacrifice are those of Israel as a whole.

At the end of his sermon, Sabbatai went up to the Ark, took a Torah scroll in his arms, and sang his favorite song, the Spanish *romanza* "Meliselda." This ancient Castilian love song was very popular among the Spanish exiles in Turkey. For Sabbatai the story of the lover who lay with the emperor's beautiful daughter became a mystical allegory of himself. He was "like a bridegroom coming out of his chamber, the husband of the beloved Torah." The Torah was none other than the divine Shekhinah herself: the symbolism had already been implicit in the mystical marriage to the Torah, which he

151. Sasportas (p. 61, on the authority of the first letters from Smyrna) is the only author to mention this detail.

152. Sasportas (p. 89) immediately seized on this point: it was unheard of that the Messiah b. Joseph should be killed in the wars between the gentiles. He would fall in battle at the head of the armies of Israel!

celebrated many years ago in Salonika (see above, p. 159). Now she is Meliselda:

To the mountain I ascended
To the river I descended
Meliselda I met there,
The king's daughter bright and fair.
There I saw the shining lass
As she came up from the bath.
Her arched brow dark as the night
Her face a gleaming sword of light
Her lips like corals red and bright,
Her flesh as milk, so fair and white.[153]

Sabbatai's enthusiasm increased as he expounded the mystical significance of the song, quoting from the description of the beloved in the Song of Songs as well as from the Psalms, until he finally revealed himself in clear and unequivocal terms as the Anointed of the God of Jacob, and the Redeemer of Israel. Carried away by his enthusiasm, he fixed the date of redemption for the Fifteenth of Sivan, 5426. Precise announcements of this kind were unusual for Sabbatai, but his choice of a date was not fortuitous. It was the anniversary of the "first sprouting of the kingdom," that is, of his public self-revelation in Gaza, the Fifteenth or Seventeenth of Sivan, 1665. Though we cannot be sure who determined this early date for the final redemption, Sabbatai or his prophet, there is much to be said in support of the correspondent from Smyrna who wrote that its origin was a prophecy of Nathan.

153. Coenen quotes only part of the *romanza*, in his own Dutch translation which he endeavored to make "as accurate as possible." The Spanish text is extant in two versions (M. Attias, *Romancero Sefardi*, 2nd edn. [1961], pp. 82–83), of which the second (Attias, no. 13a) was preserved by the Sabbatian sect in Salonika (the Dönmeh version which Sabbatai used to sing), but his contention can be questioned in the light of the fact that Coenen's Dutch text is much closer to the first version. An interesting Hebrew version of the song has been discovered among the MSS. originally in the possession of the Dönmeh of Salonika and was published by A. Amarillo, *Sefunoth*, V (1961), 245. The title reads "From the Book of Hymns of R. Abraham Yakhini, concerning AMIRAH, and AMIRAH was wont to sing it to the tune of Meliselda." The twelve stanzas end each with the identical refrain, which contains the words *meliṣ ʾel da* ("the advocate with God is this"—namely Sabbatai)—an obvious mystical word play on Meliselda. The erotic imagery of the Hebrew version is unoriginal, and is drawn from the Song of Songs. The first letters of the stanzas form the name Abraham (Yakhini).

We know that after composing his letter to Raphael Joseph, Nathan came to consider the possibility of an earlier advent of redemption than originally predicted. If he informed Sabbatai of his change of mind on this point, Sabbatai's choice of this particular date would be understandable. Unfortunately Nathan's letters to Sabbatai have not survived (with one exception). Sasportas' account of Sabbatai's sermon suggests that he followed Nathan's forecast of the sequence of events, and merely foreshortened the temporal perspective of the first stages. "In a few days he would take away the kingdom from the Turk, who would become a servant unto tribute, and more such strange things as never came to pass. But the rabble listened to his words as if they were the voice of God, and never considered whether he conformed to the criteria laid down by [the prophet] Isaiah,"[154] that is, whether he "smelled with the fear of the Lord," etc.[155]

Sabbatai was sure of himself during those days. Immediately after the Sabbath he seems to have dispatched R. Abraham Shebili to Constantinople to make preparations for his arrival. According to the earliest reports from believers in Smyrna, the same messenger was also charged with a message to the sultan, but this part of his mission is never mentioned again.[156] Sabbatai's feverish activity immediately after his self-revelation was running true to type. His enthusiasm was genuine, but it spent itself on trifles.

Benveniste, who was present in the synagogue during the stormy scene, then asked Sabbatai by what sign he could prove his mission. At this manifestation of doubt Sabbatai flew into a towering rage. He laid Benveniste under excommunication until he would beg for pardon, and once more threatened to feed him the flesh of camels. Finally he called on some of those present to testify to their faith by uttering the Ineffable Name. The obstinacy with which he insisted

154. Sasportas, p. 85, and the "Notes from Italy," *Zion,* X (1945), 65, where the specification of the date is attributed to Nathan. The other sources do not specify 15 Sivan, and refer in a general way only to Sabbatai's prediction of immediate conquests. The prediction was clearly in the mind of Serrarius, whose wording in his letter of February 26, 1666 (C. Roth, *Anglo-Jewish Letters,* p. 71) almost reads like a translation from the Hebrew original as quoted by Sasportas.

155. Cf. B. Sanhedrin 93b, for the rabbinic interpretation of Isa. 11:3.

156. Sasportas (p. 16) is the only author to mention this detail, but his information, based on the first letters from Smyrna, is beyond doubt correct. I have not been able so far to identify R. Abraham Shebili.

on this sacrilegious demonstration suggests that he regarded it as a symbol and earnest of the new age that had dawned. The dramatic proceedings at the synagogue made a deep impression on the bystanders, a number of whom converted then and there. The several eyewitness reports add up to a fantastic, yet more or less concrete and convincing, picture. Sabbatai moved in a dizzy whirl of illuminate exaltation, abolishing ancient and hallowed laws, instituting new customs, excommunicating rabbis and appointing kings. The world seemed to be out of joint, although to Sabbatai, in his paroxysm of messianic frenzy, it undoubtedly appeared as the world set right.

A striking and very revealing sign of the messianic transformation of the old order, and of the substitution of a messianic Judaism for the traditional and imperfect one, was Sabbatai's innovation of calling women to the reading of the Torah. Sabbatai evidently envisaged a change in the status of women. There can be little doubt about that, since Coenen, who did not know of this particular innovation, reports other details pointing in the same direction. Coenen's somewhat jejune explanation was that Sabbatai's feminist inventions were artful stratagems to win the women over to his side.[157] But in the social situation of those days, feminine support would hardly have advanced Sabbatai's cause. Moreover, stratagem was hardly required, for such support was assured by the prevailing emotionalism and mass hysteria. The truth of the matter is that Sabbatai, in whose life the love or favor of women never played any ascertainable role, dreamed of a radical reform of the status of women. Perhaps Sarah, his beautiful wife, demanded freedom to satisfy her sensual desires, but we should be wary of attributing too much to her influence. In fact, only the two satirical poems of the brothers Frances hold her responsible for inciting Sabbatai to usurp the messianic title, and the charge is demonstrably false, although it cut much favor with modern belletrists and dramatists. Yet the two Frances brothers may dimly have sensed the power of what the kabbalists called the "female principle" behind the workings of Sabbatai's imagination. We know enough of the latter, and of the forces moving it, not to need Sarah as an explanation of his feminist reforms. Sabbatai began to offend, openly and deliberately, against traditional roles of behavior between the sexes. In the homes of his friends he met his two divorced wives, and sat next to

157. Coenen, p. 32.

them in friendly conversation. Reports in Italy mentioned that he flouted all norms of decency by commanding a banquet to be held at which men and women danced together, while he himself retired to another room together with his first wife.[158] Emanuel Frances did not fail to pillory this misconduct in one of his verses:

Is he the Lord's anointed or a traitor,
A wicked sinner and a fornicator?
In public he the Sabbath desecrates
And of the synagogue he breaks the gates.
To pronounce the Name Ineffable he dares,
And with profanity he impiously swears.
Forbidden women he embraces;
As first the one, and then the other he caresses.
The foolish people, gaping as spellbound,
Affirm: This is a mystery profound.[159]

There is something genuine about Sabbatai's revolutionary attitude in this matter. Coenen reports instructive details of Sabbatai's conversations with women. He liked to quote to them Psalm 45:10 (A.V., 45:9): "King's daughters were among thy honorable women, upon thy right hand did stand the queen in gold of Ophir,"[160] and he promised to free them of the curse of Eve: "Woe unto you, miserable women, who for Eve's sin must bring forth your children in sorrow, and are subject to your husbands, and all that you do depends on their consent. Blessed are you, for I have come to make you free and happy like your husbands; for I have come to take away Adam's sin."[161] These were revolutionary words indeed for a Jew of Smyrna in the year 1665. A new *Lebensgefühl* and utopian vision of the equality of the sexes seem to have taken root in Sabbatai's heart—perhaps even as early as 1658, when the idea of the freedom of the spiritual law first began to take shape in his mind. Perhaps, at this point, we should also seek the key to his marriage with a woman of ill repute,

158. Sasportas, p. 80; Frances, pp. 124–26. The charge (*ibid.,* p. 135) that he was wont to sing "unspeakably" erotic songs seems to be an exaggeration resulting from Sabbatai's predilection for the *romanza* of Meliselda.

159. Frances, p. 125.

160. No doubt Sabbatai quoted this verse in connection with his mystical exegesis of Meliselda, the "king's daughter."

161. Coenen, p. 33.

and not vice versa. He may have been attracted by the audacity of Sarah, the reputed harlot, because he cherished the dream of the reparation of Adam's sin and of the consequent restoration of woman to her original freedom. The notion that Adam's sin would be repaired by the messiah was current in Lurianic writings. The early kabbalists had described the messiah as a reincarnation of Adam's soul.[162] In spite of the commonplace premise, Sabbatai seems to have been the first to draw the conclusion in terms of the emancipation of women. But he lacked the capacity to give this ideal of emancipation definite form and contents. His ideal, which found such noble expression in the sentence reported—albeit with a disparaging intention—by Coenen, remained vague and ephemeral.

A wave of enthusiasm swept over Smyrna, and R. Ḥayyim Benveniste, too, was carried away by it. Personal motives, such as bitterness over the outcome of the conflict with Lapapa, may also have played a part. Sabbatai, also, was inconstant in his human relations; he would excommunicate one day and shower with favors on the next. It is said that when he was asked why he so violently abused and publicly insulted an eminent and blameless rabbi, he replied—to everyone's surprise—that he had meant to praise and not, God forbid, to revile Benveniste. The remarks about feeding him the flesh of camels had a profound kabbalistic significance, since the Hebrew word for "camel" (*gml*) was the same as that for "dealing (*gml*) kindly," and "he bestoweth (*gml*) lovingkindness upon a man in accordance with his work." This was a complete about-face, and Sabbatai now began to sing the praise of Benveniste. Benveniste joined the camp of the believers on the following day, and proclaimed with a loud voice: "Brethren, he is the true messiah; he and no other"![163] Henceforth this formula, which originated perhaps in the inspired utterances of the Sabbatian prophets, constantly recurs in Sabbatian literature. Since many people in Smyrna prophesied in this style, it seems probable that the formula was not coined by Benveniste. The title "true messiah" was, as we know, a long-time favorite with Sabbatai because its numerical value equaled that of his name.

On the same Sunday, the Fifth of Tebeth, Sabbatai expelled R. Aaron Lapapa from his office, that is, he caused the elders to dis-

162. The letters of the Hebrew word ADaM are formed of the initials of *A*dam, *D*avid, *M*essiah; see above, p. 304.

163. Coenen, p. 38.

miss Lapapa and to tear up the agreement regarding the division of duties between the two chief rabbis that had been signed in the presence of R. Eskapha. In the account by the emissary from Casale we read that on Sunday the rabbis summoned Sabbatai Ṣevi to account for his public desecration of the Sabbath, and that Sabbatai "answered them angrily, saying that he well knew what he was doing." If R. Samson Bacchi's chronology is correct, then this summons was Lapapa's last official action; perhaps it was also the one that caused his dismissal. Much obscurity still surrounds the dismissal of Lapapa, and the appointment, on the next day, of Benveniste to the office of sole chief rabbi. What made Benveniste behave as he did? Was it the impulsion of a mounting enthusiasm, or the persuasiveness of a clever go-between? The author of the anonymous responsum from Smyrna claims, in his very circumstantial account of the affair, that the matter was arranged "by the counsel of Ahitophel [cf. I Sam. 15–17] for he [the anonymous "Ahitophel"] was familiar with him [Sabbatai Ṣevi] and went to him in the dead of night. And as he believed that he [Sabbatai] was the anointed of the God of Jacob who might do as he pleased, he arranged that matter. But heaven is my witness that my hand has not been in this trespass. After some time a talebearer revealed their secret . . . , but with the help of the jealous and revengeful God, the schemer beheld that his counsel did not succeed. So he went home and hanged himself."[164] The anonymous writer, supporter of the Sabbatian cause, thus knew who the schemer was that "arranged that matter" by visiting Sabbatai in the dead of night. Coenen evidently exaggerated with his statement that all the rabbis of Smyrna opposed Sabbatai. Here we have a rabbi, favorably disposed toward Benveniste and knowing of the bitterness of his heart, successfully pleading with the messiah. Sabbatai's about-face the next morning was thus due to an "Ahitophelian" plot, and not to a sudden change of heart on his part or Benveniste's. And the anonymous Ahitophel, who could maneuver the messiah's fickle moods with such skill, was not the only rabbi to side with Sabbatai. The anonymous writer to whom we owe the account contritely confesses his own share in the affair: "For God knoweth that . . . I did not do it for either profit or honor, but in the innocence of my heart, believing with a perfect faith that the time of redemption had come

164. *Qobeṣ ʿal Yad*, IX, p. 7 (separate pagination).

and that the Lord had visited his people."[165] As for Benveniste, we know next to nothing of his part in the events, which seem to have happened all within twenty-four hours, though the exact chronology is obscure.[166] Did his change of heart precede or follow Lapapa's dismissal? And how much of it was due to spontaneous emotion, how much to cold calculation? Whatever his conscious or unconscious motives, Benveniste remained a steadfast believer, as appears from one of his written responsa.

Coenen was told that Sabbatai had proclaimed himself messiah on the Sixth of Tebeth, that is, on a Monday, December 14, 1665. Yet Coenen's story leaves no doubt that the proclamation was merely the climax of the dramatic scene that had begun with the forcible occupation of the synagogue on the Sabbath, the Fourth of Tebeth. On the other hand, Coenen's reference to the Sixth of Tebeth suggests that this, too, was a significant date. Perhaps two events which took place on different days were later confused by chroniclers: first, the public homage to the newly proclaimed king, and second, the induction of Rabbi Benveniste in his new dignity. The events of the Sixth of Tebeth are also described in the anonymous responsum from Smyrna: "Of a sudden it was announced by royal proclamation that everybody should repair to the Portuguese Synagogue to kiss the hands of the chief rabbi . . . for the spirit was upon him and he was like

165. *Ibid.,* p. 6.

166. Leyb b. Ozer follows Coenen's account, supplementing it by additional information gathered from travelers coming from the Orient. Some of his informants had also been to Smyrna. In spite of its popular and semilegendary character, Leyb's story occasionally contains authentic details. According to Leyb's version, Sabbatai explained to his followers that his burst of invective was meant for Benveniste's good, and that it had been understood in that sense by Benveniste, who was "a great rabbi" and who would "convert to the faith within two (months) [days]." These remarks were reported to Benveniste, and Sabbatai's flattery, combined with fear of the believers' terrorism, caused Benveniste to change his mind and to exclaim, "Know ye that I have long been mistaken, but now I confess that I have sinned" (Emden, p. 8). If Leyb's story is true, it confirms the impression that go-betweens had a part in bringing the two parties together. The reasons given by Leyb for Benveniste's change of mind are no compliment to his character, and a similar judgment seems to be implied by R. Samson Bacchi. No doubt Benveniste was widely condemned later for his about-face, but it is possible that there was more to it than mere flattery and fear, and that a genuine conversion to the messianic faith may have occurred.

the prophet Samuel. They that thirsted for the salvation of the Lord sped thither with haste, but even the unbelievers went . . . and kissed Rabbi Benveniste's hand, for fear of the punishment which the rabble would wreak on those who rebelled against the Lord's anointed. And from this day on R. Aaron [Lapapa], may the Lord preserve him, lived ostracized and retired in a corner of his house and dared not go out, not even to the synagogue, because people would insult, revile, and abuse him for being an infidel. But he heard his reproach and made no answer."[167] The agreement regulating the division of duties between the two chief rabbis was taken from the archives and torn to bits.

We learn from this patently reliable account that two days after proclaiming himself king, Sabbatai could issue decrees of this kind without encountering active opposition. Coenen knew of the appointment of a new chief rabbi, but had not heard of the ceremony of kissing the hand—the Sephardi way of paying respect. On the other hand, Coenen mentions a ceremony of Sabbatai's "assumption of kingship" which took place on the same day. Coenen's information is supplemented by the detailed account of the rabbi of Casale.

Monday has, for liturgical purposes, the character of a minor fast. On this particular Monday, Sabbatai may have repeated some of his earlier proclamations. "He, who had many times been ejected from the synagogue and decried as a fool and heretic, now returned to the same synagogue and aroused the people to repentance, prayer, and charity."[168] The fact that he declared this Monday to be his holy Sabbath[169] indicates that the day was significant to Sabbatai personally, and not only in connection with Benveniste. We are familiar with Sabbatai's fondness for changing liturgical dates. Declaring the Monday to be a Sabbath is similar to the celebration, in 1658, of the three pilgrimage festivals in one week. In Gallipoli, in 1666, he

167. Bernfeld, p. 4. Samson Bacchi seems to have in mind Sunday rather than Monday, for he speaks of a great rejoicing on "the day following" the occupation of the synagogue. Coenen distinguishes between the deposition of Lapapa (on the day after the occupation of the synagogue) and the appointment of Benveniste as sole chief rabbi (on the following day). His chronology agrees with that of the anonymous responsum, and indirectly confirms the date 6 Tebeth. On the other hand, Coenen seems to contradict himself when dating the homage to Sabbatai after Benveniste's investiture.

168. Coenen, p. 14.

169. Samson Bacchi, quoted above, p. 397.

repeated the same ceremony and proclaimed a Monday to be Sabbath. The meaning of this particular Sabbath is unknown, but so are the complexities of Sabbatai's psychology in general. Two possibilities suggest themselves. After his public desecration of the Sabbath, Sabbatai may have felt the need to institute a new Sabbath. But we must also consider the possible impact of another surprising incident: Sabbatai's visit to the cadi of Smyrna, from which he returned unscathed.

The visit to the cadi is only briefly mentioned by the rabbi of Casale who does, however, give a precise date: the Sunday following the dramatic Sabbath in the Portuguese Synagogue. Coenen's description is more circumstantial, and the incident is mentioned in all the letters written at the time from Smyrna. Though the two events were soon transfigured by legend, there was a certain logic in their madness. Perhaps the course of events can be reconstructed as follows: Sabbatai had publicly proclaimed himself as messianic king, divided the whole world among his followers, and appointed viceroys for Rome and Constantinople. His enthusiasm next drove him to a spectacular demonstration before the Turkish authorities. Summoned to appear before the rabbis of Smyrna, he left the court in a violent rage and, apparently, forced the dismissal of Lapapa. By that time he may already have known of Benveniste's adherence, which was to exert such a mighty influence on the public.[170] Acting in a welter of confused emotions, Sabbatai may have been impelled to his next step by manic exaltation as well as by vengeful spite. Coenen says that he went to the cadi suddenly and in great mental agitation. When his intention became known, a large crowd assembled, as usual, to accompany him. Marching at the head of the crowd, Sabbatai intoned Psalm 118:16: "The right hand of the Lord is exalted, the right hand of the Lord doeth valiantly," the people singing the responses until they arrived at the cadi's court. This verse from the Psalms is mentioned in other sources, too, as one of Sabbatai's favorite songs during his illuminate ecstasies. Witnesses, such as, for example, the emissaries and visitors who saw him in Gallipoli, describe the radiance of his countenance as he chanted this verse; others (for example, R. Israel Ḥazzan of Kastoria) tell how he used to repeat the verse over and over again when he came to it in the course of the recitation of the Hallel Psalms. Sabbatai's enthusiastic elation was genuine but ephemeral. Admitted

170. Coenen (p. 39) says that Sabbatai and his party were greatly encouraged by Benveniste's unexpected about-face.

to the cadi's presence, together with his brother Elijah who acted as his interpreter,[171] Sabbatai was at first confused and speechless but then picked himself up and—in the words of the rabbi of Casale—"had his say," which consisted in slandering three of his chief opponents and accusing them of *lèse majesté*. The cadi let him go because, Coenen says, he considered him a fool or a madman; moreover he had already been bribed by some Jewish notables not to harm Sabbatai. Apparently those accused of being unbelievers also had to pay considerable sums, and "the Kadee, according to the custom of the Turks swallowed money on both sides, and afterwards remitted them to the determination of their own justice."[172] As Sabbatai left the cadi's house, his followers again chanted, "The right hand of the Lord is exalted." The fact that Sabbatai was not immediately put under arrest as a rebel was regarded as a mighty sign, and perhaps contributed to the proclamation of the new Sabbath.

Was the visit to the cadi really Sabbatai's own initiative—a spontaneous demonstration compounded of enthusiasm and spite? For all we know some Turks—or, for that matter, some Jews—may have complained to the cadi about the disturbance of the public peace occasioned by the messianic unrest which, in fact, could easily be construed as a rebellion against the sultan's majesty. The leniency of the Turkish authorities is surprising indeed. They allowed the agitation to grow and propagate itself without interfering in any way. Bribes from all sides seem to be the most satisfactory explanation. An Armenian document written the same year reports that the authorities had consulted on the matter and that some had proposed to write to Constantinople for instructions, whereas others had dismissed the whole affair as unimportant and trifling, contenting themselves with squeezing bribes from both parties.[173] According to a Sabbatian source it was the unbelievers who informed against Sabbatai after he had

171. Sabbatai could not yet converse freely in Turkish at the time. Coenen's testimony on this point is definite and decisive. When brought before the sultan, Sabbatai again required an interpreter. He mastered the Turkish language only after his apostasy.

172. Rycaut, p. 205.

173. Galanté, pp. 85, 98. Bribes are also mentioned by de la Croix (p. 325); for the rest his detailed account of the incidents with the cadi and with Lapapa cannot even qualify as popular legend; it is pure fiction. According to Rycaut (p. 205) the believers complained about Lapapa to the cadi, who, however, took bribes from both sides.

broken into the synagogue; but when the cadi, who had summoned him, beheld Sabbatai, "he was seized by trembling, and rendered him great honor. He sent for the men who had slandered him, but they were afraid and fled into hiding."[174]

In the last version it is thus not Sabbatai who does the slandering, but the unbelievers. No doubt the believers themselves did not relish the idea of their messiah in the role of an informer. Coenen tells us that when Sabbatai was asked by his friends how he could falsely accuse fellow Jews before the Turkish authorities, he replied that he was the "king" against whom they had committed *lèse majesté*. In any event, the incident was apt to cast a slur on Sabbatai's character, and there were many who reproached him, saying that he had taken an internal Jewish quarrel to the gentile courts out of sheer spite. The believers had a simple method of dealing with accusations of this kind: they transformed the visit into a miracle story. There had been no discussions and, of course, no informing. What happened was this: when Sabbatai entered the cadi's room he found it empty. He seated himself in the cadi's chair, and did not rise as the latter came into the room. He even stepped on the cadi's cloak. The cadi did not dare to open his mouth, but when Sabbatai began to speak, a flame of fire issued from his mouth and caught the cadi's beard, almost burning the whole room. A pillar of fire appeared between Sabbatai and the cadi, until the latter exclaimed, "Take him away from here, for fear and trembling have fallen upon me. This is no flesh and blood, but an angel of God."[175]

174. Baruch of Arezzo (Freimann, p. 49), inserting his own explanation into Samson Bacchi's report.

175. Coenen, p. 30, and similarly Rycaut, p. 207, who, however, does not seem to be clear about the incident. The miracle stories vary from one letter to another, but they already appear in the very first news letters from Smyrna. One such letter reports that on December 18 (10 Tebeth) Sabbatai paraded in the streets like a king. The Turks complained to the cadi, who referred this "political" affair to the pasha of Smyrna. The latter decided to "Massacre all the Jews, and to that purpose gave order to his Captain to be ready for the next morning: But that very night appeared to them the Prophet Elias in a fiery Colomn, saying to him, *Take heed of doing any harm to the Jews*" (Wilenski, p. 168). In a letter sent to Leghorn in December, 1665 (Aeshcoly, pp. 226–27), the miraculous encroaches even more on the factual: the cadi and the pasha become one person, the Turks take the matter to the chief preacher of the city, and the incident is dated December 25–26, i.e., just before Sabbatai's departure.

As a matter of fact, reports about the messianic unrest in town had been sent to Constantinople, but the reply, that is, the order to arrest Sabbatai, arrived only after the latter had already left Smyrna for the capital.[176]

The precise date and details of the public homage by the community of Smyrna to their king are still doubtful, but the margin of error is not very great. The event took place either on Monday evening (the eve of the Seventh of Tebeth) or on Tuesday morning, the Seventh of Tebeth, if not on Sunday, the Fifth of Tebeth.

According to one source the ceremony took place in the Portuguese Synagogue,[177] according to others it was in Sabbatai's house.[178] On the first day the men, and on the next day the women, came forward and offered money to be used for charitable purposes in honor of the messiah; each received a blessing.[179] One letter states that the money was used to ransom Jewish prisoners who had been sent to the galleys.[180] Both Coenen and the anonymous responsum report that the unbelievers, fearing violence, also came forward to kiss the hands of Sabbatai and of R. Ḥayyim Benveniste. The rabbis of Smyrna had apparently all succumbed to the pressure, and Lapapa showed considerable courage in staying away.[181] A reign of terror began in the Jewish community. Faith and terrorism combined are powerful social factors and can remove many inhibitions. Henceforth the believers lorded it over the community, and the messiah found himself in a position of unchallenged authority.

176. No official Turkish documents bearing on Sabbatai Ṣevi have so far come to light, nor is there any likelihood of their being discovered in the future. Prof. Uriel Heydt has found that the volumes containing the government decrees for the period October 1665–April 1678 are missing from the state archives in Istanbul (see *Tarbiz,* XXV [1956], 337).

177. Coenen, p. 16; the men did homage on 7 Tebeth, the women on the 8th. Bacchi does not specify the place of the ceremony, but his account suggests the synagogue.

178. Leyb b. Ozer (Emden, p. 6). Leyb as well as Samson Bacchi (p. 17) mention the kissing of Sabatai's feet as part of the ceremony, but Coenen (p. 16) speaks of kissing the hands only.

179. Our source says *mi sheberakh,* which is the formula of blessing used in the regular services of the synagogue. This again suggests that the ceremony took place in the synagogue.

180. *Hollandtze Merkurius,* January, 1666, p. 3 (where, however, the ceremony of public homage is not explicitly mentioned); see also Coenen, p. 17.

181. Letter from Smyrna, quoted by Sasportas, p. 61.

Sabbatai's feverish paroxysm drove him from one provocative demonstration to another. His next surprise involved his wife. It seems that, exactly as he had done with his first two wives, he himself had a hand in spreading the rumor that he had never touched his third wife, Sarah. The rumor may well have been true. One Christian author[182] suggested that Sabbatai was impotent, and ironically added that Sarah seemed to have married a priest of Cybele. On the other hand, Sarah had the reputation of a harlot, although, it is true, no scandals were told of her from the time of her marriage until she lapsed into licentiousness in Smyrna. On the Seventh of Tebeth, at the height of the royal celebrations, Sabbatai announced that he and Sarah had had independent revelations to the effect that their union was now required for the messianic fulfillment. The union was duly consummated that night, and the "indubitable" evidence of Sarah's virginity presented to the rejoicing crowd. Coenen, who does not hide his contempt for the miserable farce, also states that in the morning Sabbatai announced in the synagogue that Sarah had conceived a son who, however, would not live long.[183] The strange performance was possibly staged specifically in order to silence the unpleasant rumors about Sarah. Even so, much still remains obscure. Did Sabbatai really believe that he could throw dust into the eyes of the public? After all, Sarah's antecedents were so well known that some believers in Constantinople even compared the messiah's marriage to a harlot to the marriage of the prophet Hosea to Gomer, the "wife of fornications." Moreover, her licentious behavior in Smyrna was no secret. But whatever Sabbatai's motives—which are, perhaps, for psychoanalysts rather than historians to discover—it is a fact that in October, 1666, or (by a later pregnancy) in the summer of 1667, Sarah bore him a son who, in fact, died in adolescence. Coenen and the writers following him erred in pronouncing all references to Sabbatai's children a product of the imagination of believing simpletons. This particular prophecy was fulfilled, and the evidence for the existence of the child, Ishmael Mordecai, is incontestable.[184]

Immediately afterward, the fast of the Tenth of Tebeth, which in that year fell on a Friday (December 18), was abolished by royal

182. J. B. de Rocoles (1683), at the beginning of the chapter.

183. Coenen, p. 15.

184. See Scholem, in *Schocken Volume,* pp. 172–73, and below, chs. 7 and 8, for further details on his son.

proclamation. All fasts commemorating the destruction of the Temple and Israel's exile were to be discontinued, and "the sorrow of the fast turned into the rejoicing of gladness" (Sasportas). These fasts were rabbinic ordinances and their abrogation was thus, formally at least, less serious than the solemn eating of forbidden fat, accompanied by a benediction, which Sabbatai had commanded to some of his followers. Yet the new proclamation had profound symbolic significance. Nathan's penitential instructions imposed many and severe fasts, but these were ascetic exercises born of messianic enthusiasm and not of sorrow. The traditional fasts were no longer acceptable precisely because they expressed grief and mourning. But the regular fasts of Monday and Thursday, which are exercises of penitence rather than of mourning, were retained, according to Coenen's explicit testimony.[185] The abolition of the fast provoked a last flicker of resistance. R. Solomon Algazi and several of his colleagues refused to obey the new instruction, and were almost lynched by the mob. Three rabbis, including Algazi, fled from Smyrna; the others capitulated. Lapapa's name is not even mentioned in connection with the incident. Since his deposition he lived in hiding in the house of his friend R. Judah Murcia;[186] he no longer counted. The believers triumphantly wrote to Hamburg that "the whole people followed the messiah, with the exception of eleven or twelve men"[187] (including Lapapa)—surely

185. Coenen, p. 32.

186. The report from Smyrna published in the *Hollandtze Merkurius,* January, 1666, p. 3, mentions the reign of terror in the city and states that the "chief of the unbelievers had to flee to Sardes [apparently meaning Magnesia] and his house was sacked." The reference seems to be to Lapapa who had come from Magnesia to Smyrna half a year before. The rumor about his flight was perhaps deliberately spread by his friends, to divert public attention from his actual hideout in the city. De la Croix (p. 336), who mentions Lapapa's flight to Magnesia, may possibly quote actual rumors, although the rest of his story (p. 342) is sheer fiction.

187. Letters from Smyrna, summarized by Sasportas (pp. 61, 86) and Frances (p. 110). Coenen says nothing of the abolition of the fast of 10 Tebeth, but mentions the flight of three unnamed rabbis (p. 39). Sasportas reports that the first letter received in Hamburg did mention the abolition of the fast; subsequent letters also mentioned the opposition of a small minority led by R. Solomon Algazi. Sasportas is not very particular about the sequence in which he quotes letters and reports events, and the earliest letters from Smyrna, which could help us in establishing a correct chronology, were not included by him in his *Ṣiṣath Nobel Ṣevi.* Nevertheless, the general chronology that emerges from

an insignificant minority in a community which should be estimated at several thousand souls.

Although the opposition was temporarily paralyzed, it was not broken, and soon after Sabbatai's departure from Smyrna it again raised its head. The fugitive rabbis returned and led the counterattack. Lapapa, it is true, was no longer associate chief rabbi, but he and Algazi were still members of the rabbinic court. They and five other men composed a memorandum on Sabbatai's unorthodox behavior in Smyrna and sent it to Constantinople, probably in February, before or shortly after Sabbatai's arrival in the capital. The writers complained about his behavior in Smyrna only, and evidently had, as yet, no idea of what was going on in Constantinople. Unfortunately, their letter is lost, but the reply of the believing rabbis in the capital (made weightier by the addition of a few forged signatures)[188] has been preserved. R. Abraham Yakhini, whose signature comes in the fourth place, almost certainly had a hand in drawing up the reply, which displays an intimate knowledge of the Smyrna scene, a knowledge which R. Yomtob ibn Yaqar, R. Moses Benveniste, and old R. Isaac Anakawa could not possibly possess, but which could be supplied by Yakhini who had been to Smyrna. Several months after Sabbatai's apostasy, the rabbis of Constantinople wrote another letter to Smyrna in which they made obscure references to an earlier letter, perhaps none other than the one under discussion. The later missive does not disclaim responsibility for the earlier letter by calling it a forgery, but, on the contrary, apologizes for it: "And if in the past [that is, at the height of the movement] a letter written by the reverend rabbis and signed by several notables was sent from here, the reason was that it was believed here that there were troubles in Smyrna, every day anew, which cost much money to both parties and which would have caused grave harm had they continued."[189] The sequel refers

his account agrees with the one adopted here: Lapapa was deposed because he refused to do homage and to kiss the messiah's hand; the decision to abolish the fast was opposed by Algazi; when the abolition was forced through, Algazi fled from the city.

188. The suggestion that the signatures were forged is made by Sasportas (p. 133), albeit very cautiously. His suspicion is confirmed by a comparison of the letter with that sent a fortnight later to Jerusalem by the same rabbis; see also below, pp. 611 ff.

189. Coenen's Dutch summary (p. 112) of the Hebrew letter.

to certain forged letters which "strengthened this erroneous impression." Altogether the extremely cautious wording suggests that the rabbis of Constantinople had indeed written the kind of compromising letter that later, after the apostasy, needed a lot of explaining away. There is, of course, no uncertainty that the earlier letter referred to is the one mentioned above; the reference may well be to some other letter to Smyrna, supporting the party of the believers.

In any event, the letter in which Yakhini had a part definitely attests the existence of organized opposition in Smyrna, and actually identifies some of the original protesters. In the eyes of the believers in Constantinople, it was the infidels in Smyrna who resorted to terror, and not the other way around. Yakhini accuses the rabbis of Smyrna of associating their signatures with those of "men who do not know the Lord, men of violence and strife and contention, who cannot even read the Bible, as is well known here. . . . and in particular the tails of firebrands Abraham Boton, Mordecai b. Ezra [and] Isaac b. Maimon. They [the rabbis] should not have associated themselves with them. . . ."[190] The author of the reply was evidently initiated into the mystery of the messiah's "strange actions," for he takes the Smyrna rabbis to task for having dared to criticize "a unique saint . . . [and] to condemn him for certain wondrous deeds which in the eyes of the spectator may seem strange. . . . How did you fail to consider that he knows the proper place and order of these things? . . . Praise be to God who gave us a heart to understand these matters, that which really took place and the inventions which they [the authors of the memorandum from Smyrna] added in order to incite the public. . . . They spoke false words concerning an angel and a holy one, a prince of the Torah." The attempt to gloss over the serious nature of Sabbatai's "strange actions" is obvious. After complaining about the terrorism and violence of the infidels, the writers turn the tables and proceed to assert their right to persecute and silence the unbelievers. With the specific exception of the two leading infidel rabbis, "we excommunicate all other signatories . . . and all the curse that is written in the Book of the Law shall lie upon them, until their

190. Sasportas, pp. 133–34; Baruch of Arezzo (Freimann, pp. 53–54, where, however, the names of the infidels are corrupt). The names are those of well-known and respected families, and the claim that the opponents were "illiterates" seems very odd.

uncircumcised heart be humbled and they seek God, lest they continue to speak iniquity. We are in duty bound to pursue even unto excommunication them that speak grievously against the righteous, for if we hold our peace then sin will overtake us, and what shall we do when God riseth up [to judgment]. Therefore, they that believe not should lay their hand upon their mouth, and not multiply proud speech." The argument is characteristic of the reasoning of believers everywhere during the high tide of the movement in 1665–66; the messiah's disconcerting personality was largely ignored, and the violent repression of the infidels theologically justified.

VI

It was, however, some weeks before the unbelievers had recovered sufficiently to counterattack. Meanwhile Smyrna was in a festive mood, and the believers moved in a dizzy whirl of legends, miracles, and revelations. Abraham Yakhini, who was in Smyrna at the time, well summed up the mood of the period when, a few years later, he spoke of "those blessed days." The transition from mere factual reality to the transfigured reality of the heart, that is, to legend, was rapid. Collective enthusiasm quickly surrounded events with a halo. Tales of the appearance of a pillar of fire and similar miraculous signs became indubitable facts. The people of Smyrna saw miracles and heard prophecies, providing the best possible illustration of Rénan's remark about the infectious character of visions. It is enough for one member of a group sharing the same beliefs to claim to have seen or heard a supernatural manifestation, and the others too will see and hear it. Hardly had the report arrived from Aleppo that Elijah had appeared in the Old Synagogue there, and Elijah walked the streets of Smyrna. Dozens, even hundreds, had seen him: he was the anonymous beggar asking for alms, as well as the invisible guest at every banquet. Solomon Cremona, one of the wealthiest Jews in Smyrna, had invited friends to a great feast. One of the guests, his gaze falling on the shining brass plates hanging on the wall, started from his seat and, bowing deeply, exclaimed: "Arise brethren and behold the prophet Elijah"—and all rose, bowed, and beheld Elijah. Sabbatai encouraged these fancies. Invited to a circumcision ceremony in the house of Abraham Gutiere, Sabbatai stayed the proceedings for a while. "After a good half hour Sabbatai ordered them to proceed," explaining that he had "retarded the performance . . . [because] Elias had not as yet taken his Seat,[191] whom as soon as he saw placed, he ordered them to proceed."[192] In Amsterdam alone "more than thirty letters" were received, announcing this particular appearance of Elijah.[193]

"Everybody talked about having seen a pillar of fire. To one it had appeared at noontime; to another at night; a third one had seen the moon like red fire; to a fourth the heavens had been opened and he beheld a fiery gate in which there stood a man in the likeness of Rabbi Ṣevi with a crown on his head; a fifth had seen a star falling from heaven into the sea and rising again heavenward, and much more of this kind. . . . Miracles became the daily bread of these poor wretches, who even ceased to wonder about these strange tales."[194] The Sabbatian preachers applied the prophecy of Joel (3:3–4) to their own days: "And I will show wonders in the heavens and in the earth, blood, and fire, and pillars of smoke. The sun shall be turned into darkness, and the moon into blood, before the great and terrible day of the Lord come." But Joel had prophesied more than cosmic signs: "I will pour out My spirit upon all flesh, and your sons and your daughters shall prophesy, your old men shall dream dreams, your young men shall see visions" (Joel 3:1) and indeed, as the hearts opened, mass prophecy came to Smyrna.

The phenomenon of mass prophecy is by no means rare in the history of religious movements that are borne by popular enthusiasm. Christian sects, from the second-century Montanists to the eighteenth-century Methodists, furnish many examples. Twenty years after the Sabbatian awakening, in 1685, an apocalyptic movement arose among the French Protestants who struggled against the abolition of their liberties and the attempts to bring them by force into the Catholic Church. Mass prophecy, by children in particular, was one of the principal features of the movement, and the eyewitness reports of the

191. The prophet Elijah is said to be present at every circumcision ceremony, and a special seat of honor is reserved for him.

192. Coenen, pp. 66, 73; Rycaut, p. 212. According to Rycaut, Gutière was "a kinsman of Sabbatai."

193. Thus a letter from Amsterdam, mentioning the arrival of thirty letters from Smyrna on March 13, 1666 (Aeshcoly, p. 228). Many people in the Sephardi community of Amsterdam had close relatives in Smyrna.

194. Coenen, p. 31.

prophetic ecstasies among the Camisards in the Cévennes mountains, on the one hand, and the Sabbatian enthusiasts in Smyrna, on the other, are strikingly similar. There was little of the passionate warning and of the urgent sense of individual mission, so characteristic of classical, "apostolic" prophecy, in the incoherent stammering of a mass ecstasy generated by oppression, revolt, and emotional high tension among the lower classes. The prophets spewed forth ancient words and phrases that had become clichés, though here and there an individual expression of noble spirituality could be heard.

A Dutch merchant writing early in April, 1666, soon after the excitement had passed its peak, thus described the scene: "At that time [winter, 1665–66] there appeared— some say by the workings of the devil—more than two hundred prophets and prophetesses upon whom there fell a mighty trembling so that they swooned. In this state they exclaimed that Sabbatai Ṣevi was the messiah and king of Israel who would lead his people safely to the Holy Land, and that ships of Tarshish, that is, with Dutch crews, would come to transport them. Thereafter their spirits returned unto them, but they remembered nothing of what they had spoken, much to the amazement of our Christians who see and hear this every day. Even little children of four years and less recited psalms in Hebrew."[195]

The first to prophesy in Smyrna were apparently the two emissaries from Jerusalem and Aleppo, Moses Galanté and Daniel Pinto; Pinto's name occurs in a list of prophets who prophesied in Smyrna. One of the first prophetesses was Sarah, Sabbatai's wife.[196] This was one of the few instances of her active participation in the movement, and it undoubtedly made an impression. Coenen heard from Dutch merchants who had witnessed the prophecy on the Ninth of Tebeth that the spirit that descended on the first prophetess also moved the daughters of the arch-infidel Ḥayyim Peña, and that Peña was so

195. *Hollandtze Merkurius,* January, 1666 [actually published 1667], p. 3, and similarly in German, with slight variations only, in the *Diarium Europaeum,* XVI (1688), 510; the editors of the *Diarium* may actually have had the original letter before them. The number of the prophets in Smyrna is also given by Sasportas (p. 60).

196. Baruch of Arezzo (Freimann, p. 49), who also mentions Ḥayyim Peña's sister-in-law (the wife of Jacob Peña and possibly Sabbatai's sister), but not his daughters. The "daughters of the infidels that prophesy" are also mentioned in letters from Smyrna.

much impressed by this miracle happening in his own house that he converted to the faith. On returning to his home on Thursday, the Eighth of Tebeth (a day of considerable excitement and commotion, in view of the change of the forthcoming fast day to a festival), he found his daughters seized by a trembling and dizziness, and foaming at the mouth in the usual prophetic manner. In his presence they began to prophesy: "The *Ḥakham* Sabbatai Ṣevi sitteth on an exalted throne in heaven, with a crown on his head, crown, crown, crown. . . ."[197] Coenen himself points out the analogy with similar phenomena among the first English Quakers, and suggests that these prophecies were the work of the devil who was smiting the stiff-necked people with even greater blindness. The fullest account is given by Baruch of Arezzo: "And this is an account of the prophecy as it befell in those days. A deep sleep fell upon them, and they fell to the ground as the dead in whom there is no more spirit. After about half an hour a spirit would sound from their mouth, though their lips did not move, and they would utter [scriptural] verses of praise and consolation, and all would say 'Sabbatai Ṣevi, the anointed of the God of Jacob.' Thereafter they would arise without remembering what they had done or said. In Smyrna more than a hundred and fifty prophets prophesied." Baruch of Arezzo actually quotes the text of one such prophecy, which not only perfectly illustrates the many other general descriptions, but also conveys something of the psychological quality of the outburst: short staccato sentences, mixing biblical phrases with expressions of immediate experience, and thrown out in an unconscious paroxysm. On the Fourth of Shebat, when Sabbatai was already on his way to Constantinople, Abraham b. Jacob Jessurun "prophesied" in Smyrna:

"Lord I have heard thy speech. The Lord reigneth, the Lord has reigned, the Lord shall reign forevermore. Hear, O Israel, the Lord our God,

197. Coenen, p. 41. 9 Tebeth as the date of Peña's conversion, and 6 Tebeth as the date of Benveniste's appointment as chief rabbi, provide the pivot for a correct chronology of the events in Smyrna. Coenen's account suggests that the reconciliation between Sabbatai and Peña took place before the prophesying of the daughters: during a friendly discussion between the two, Sabbatai is said to have told Peña that his daughters, who were in mourning over the recent death of their mother, should put on their best clothes; as soon as they did they began to prophesy. Perhaps the reconciliation took place as early as 6 Tebeth, when Benveniste joined the Sabbatian camp.

the Lord is one. Blessed be His name, whose glorious kingdom is forevermore. Our king Sabbatai Ṣevi has been crowned with the crown. A solemn ban has been laid in heaven on them that believe not. The Lord keepeth Israel. Our prayers have been heard. A song of degrees, Out of the depths have I cried unto thee, O Lord. Great joy. Blessed is he who liveth. They have brought the crown to Our Lord, the king. Woe unto him that believeth not, he is in the ban. Blessed is he who liveth at this time. A song of degrees, Blessed is everyone that feareth the Lord. There will be a great rejoicing. Hear, O Lord, and have mercy upon me. They have given him the crown. His kingdom is an everlasting kingdom. The king Sabbatai Ṣevi sitteth on the throne of his kingdom. Hear O Lord. Precious in the sight of the Lord are the Jews. Rejoice in the Lord, O ye righteous. Give thanks unto the Lord, for He is good. God is true, Moses is true and his Law is true, Sabbatai Ṣevi is true. Great rejoicing. Thou openest thine hand. The Lord is God. The king Sabbatai Ṣevi sitteth on his throne. Hear O Israel. A song of degrees, When the Lord turned again the captivity of Zion. A great rejoicing for the Jews. The Lord is God. Blessed is the man that feareth the Lord. How great are His signs and how mighty are His wonders. When the Lord turned again the captivity of Zion. A great rejoicing. O give thanks unto the Lord, O give thanks unto the God of heaven. Woe unto him that believeth not. Our Lord the king reigneth. Unto thee O Lord belongeth righteousness. Great rejoicing. A song of degrees, When the Lord turned again the captivity of Zion. They have fallen before the Jews. The star of our kingdom has risen. O give thanks unto the Lord, for His mercy endureth forever. O Lord be merciful unto me and raise me up. I called upon the Lord in distress. Blessed be he that cometh in the name of the Lord. The Lord hear thee in the day of trouble. O give thanks unto the Lord, for He is good (*three times*). The Lord strong and mighty forever. The king sitteth on the throne of mercy. The Lord of Hosts sitteth on the throne of His kingdom. The Lord shall fight for you. The Lord is the king of glory. The Lord strong and mighty, may His kingdom be exalted. True, true, true. Save, O Lord, according to thy mercy. Rejoicing to the Jews. Save me according to thy mercy (*three times*). Give thanks unto the Lord, for He is good. Blessed be His name, whose glorious kingdom is forevermore. Hear O Israel. For thou wilt light my candle. Great is the Lord, and greatly to be praised. There is no longer any evil *yeṣer* [lust]. O Lord, hear my prayer. Give thanks unto the

Lord, for He is good. . . ." And all these things he spoke four or five times.[198]

The new prophecy, as even a cursory reading of the foregoing example shows, was devoid of originality. The prophetic utterance was a mere jumble of well-known phrases and quotations from the Bible and the prayer book, repeated over and over again. The only visionary element is the reference to Sabbatai's crown and his sitting on the throne of his kingdom.[199] Only one sentence, toward the end of the prophecy, has a theological significance: the phrase "there is no longer any evil *yeṣer*" evidently reflects the teaching of Nathan's letters. The sparks of the Shekhinah had been extricated from the realm of the "shells" and had returned to their sphere of pristine purity. If this doctrine could be uttered in a prophetic fit by an unlettered man, then surely the messiah's strange behavior would be accepted without protest by the enthusiastic masses.

The emissary from Casale saw people acting under "all manner of compulsion" in the mass prophecy, meaning, no doubt, the rolling and twitching reminiscent of an epileptic fit. It was this pathologically compulsive character that Sasportas emphasized in his analysis of the detailed reports arriving from Smyrna. One letter stated that a Christian slave-girl "had beheld what the sages of Israel did not see, and she confirmed the prophecy of the [other] women and children."[200] Another report quoted a prophecy by a woman who had seen Sabbatai raised on his throne above the stars and ruling over heaven and earth. Sasportas diagnosed these utterances as "idiocy or epilepsy or madness," which made the prophets "behold Sabbatai's image graven in the seventh heaven, and all the host of heaven proclaiming, 'Render majesty and glory to your Lord.' . . . and they mistake rubbish and

198. Baruch of Arezzo (Freimann, pp. 49–50). Texts of similar prophecies were received in Amsterdam; e.g., the letter from Smyrna, received on March 10, 1666, which contained the prophecies—mainly in Hebrew and consisting of parts of scriptural verses—of several women. One girl prophesied in Spanish (Aeshcoly, p. 227). This letter was also known to Sasportas, pp. 148, 162.

199. Coenen (p. 32) wondered why nobody ever spoke of the messiah as "lowly and riding upon an ass."

200. Sasportas, p. 148. The same case is described in the letter published by Aeshcoly, p. 227: when a priest was called in to exorcize her, the girl insulted him in the presence of Christians and Turks, and declared that Sabbati Ṣevi was the messiah.

straw for prophecy."[201] His explanation was that "their lust and desire [for the gift of prophecy] aroused their imagination until they beheld visions that were occasionally true, but were mostly false; possibly the spirit also rested upon them accidentally, speaking [through them] and announcing various things, as does one who is possessed by a demon."[202] Sasportas insisted that only ignorant and unlettered people, and not the scholars and genuinely pious men, prophesied.[203] He carefully ignored such prophets as Moses Galanté and Daniel Pinto in Smyrna and Moses Suriel in Constantinople.

The prophetic enthusiasm spread from Smyrna to other communities in Asia Minor,[204] the Aegean islands,[205] and Greece, but nowhere did it articulate itself in orderly, literary form, or produce new kabbalistic insights, namely, "mysteries." The awakening let loose a flood of emotion without clear contents and it was easy for critics to point out that the prophetic revelations "revealed" nothing at all. In fact, their language and form are reminiscent of the earliest suras of the Quran, which are, likewise, ecstatic exclamations rather than a well-ordered prophetic argument. But Sasportas was definitely wrong in dismissing the whole phenomenon as the hysteria of ignorant fools. Among the prophets were men renowned for scholarship and piety, and their prophesying was surely more alarming—from Sasportas' point of view—than that of the unlettered enthusiasts.

Trade and commerce in the city came to a standstill.[206] Smyrna

201. Sasportas, p. 96.

202. *Ibid.*, p. 147.

203. *Ibid.*, p. 96.

204. *Ibid.*, pp. 156 (letter of R. Hosea Nantawa from Alexandria) and 182. Leyb b. Ozer's account (Emden, p. 10) exaggerates as usual: women prophesied in Zoharic Aramaic (probably a confusion with Moses Suriel's prophecy; see below, pp. 436–38), and there were "hundreds of prophets" in Adrianople.

205. Rhodes and Chios. The daughter of a certain Caimo (Ḥayyim) b. Aaron prophesied in Corfu in 1666; see H. Mizraḥi's (Hebrew) article, "Evidence of Messianic Agitation on Corfu, from a Christian Source" in *Sefunoth*, III–IV (1960), 537–40, from Andrea Marmora's *Historia di Corfu* (Venice, 1672).

206. The French *Relation*, p. 17. Litigation was suspended or neglected. In 1668 a broker, Sabbatai ha-Levi, explained to the rabbinic court of Smyrna that he had not lodged his claims two years earlier, "because everybody and everything was confused in connection with the well-known disturbances" (Benveniste's responsa *Baᶜey Ḥayyey*, ad *Ḥoshen Mishpat*, no. 175).

was in a festive mood of mounting exaltation and rejoicing. Banqueting, dancing, and festive processions alternated with the penitential exercises prescribed by Nathan. Even in the cold winter months there were many who would repair to the sea to perform ritual immersions, while others submitted to the penance of flogging.[207] At night torchlight processions would move through the city to cries of "Long live the messianic king" or "Long live Sabbatai Ṣevi."[208] Psalm 21:1, "The king shall joy in thy strength, O Lord, And in thy salvation how greatly shall he rejoice," was recited in the synagogues three times daily, at the morning, afternoon, and evening services. The psalm had been given a Sabbatian interpretation in Gaza, not so much because of the messianic significance of its contents, but primarily because of the *gematria* by which the numerical value of "and in thy salvation" equaled that of Sabbatai Ṣevi. In some synagogues the psalm, inscribed on a wooden board decorated with floral designs and surmounted by a crown with the legend "THE CROWN OF SABBATAI ṢEVI" was displayed on the wall.[209] The traditional prayer for the ruler of the land, recited on the Sabbath and holidays, was abolished, and the text adapted so as to apply to the new king of Israel:

He who giveth salvation unto kings and dominion unto princes, whose kingdom is an everlasting kingdom, who delivered his servant David from the destructive sword, who makes a way in the sea and a path in the mighty waters, may he bless, preserve, guard and exalt ever more our Lord and our Messiah, the Anointed of the God of Jacob, the Celestial Lion and Celestial Stag,[210] the Messiah of Righteousness, the King of kings, the sultan Sabbatai Ṣevi. May the supreme King of kings [that is, God] preserve him and grant him life. May the supreme King of kings exalt his star and his kingdom, and inspire the hearts of rulers

207. Coenen, pp. 58–59.

208. Coenen (p. 34) emphasizes the extraordinary character of the proceedings, since normally only "Franks," i.e., Europeans, were permitted to walk the streets at night with torches. The permissive attitude of the Turkish police (who were probably bribed) was considered another miracle by the believers. See also *Hollandtze Merkurius,* January, 1666, p. 3. De la Croix (p. 315) reports cries of *"Vive Sultan Ṣevi."*

209. Coenen, p. 63.

210. Rabbinic idioms. Aramaic, *tavya,* "stag," the equivalent of Hebrew, *Ṣevi.*

and princes with good will toward him and us and all Israel, and let us say, Amen.[211]

This prayer was recited from the Sabbath following the invasion of the synagogue, the Eleventh of Tebeth, if not earlier. On this Sabbath, too, Sabbatai exhibited his fondness for bizarre demonstrations. At first he regretted the desecration of the previous Sabbath, and he announced a general fast to atone for "the desecration of the past Sabbath." In the middle of the day, however, he changed his mind and commanded that everybody should eat and drink, since God had forgiven them.[212]

Several accounts state that hundreds of visitors came from other cities to offer gifts to the messiah; some even speak of delegations from far-away countries. But the accounts are all based on rumors and not on eyewitness reports, and most of them are simply the result of confusion with later events in Gallipoli.[213] In fact, there was hardly time for pilgrims to arrive and for embassies to be dispatched. No Sabbatian tidings had been spread from Smyrna before the beginning of the great messianic outbreak in the middle of December, 1665, and the actual messianic fever lasted no more than three weeks. Only twelve days passed from the Tenth of Tebeth, when Sabbatai made himself master of the Jewish community, to his departure for Constantinople. No visitors from other cities are mentioned by either Coenen

211. The prayer is given by Coenen in a Dutch translation. The Hebrew text printed by Rosanes and claimed by him to be the form used in Smyrna is really derived from Leyb b. Ozer (Emden, p. 8), who, of course, gives the Amsterdam version of the prayer, parts of which were recited to him by his informants.

212. This detail is mentioned only by Frances (p. 110).

213. Coenen (p. 32) merely says that Sabbatai and his wife accepted gifts from the many people that desired their favor. Rycaut, on the other hand, states (p. 207) that Sabbatai "could have commanded all the Wealth of Smyrna, but he was too subtle to accept their money, lest he should render his design suspected by any acts of covetousness." Leyb b. Ozer (Emden, p. 8) expanded Coenen's brief reference to gifts into a long and obviously impossible story about multitudes of believers bearing gifts and waiting—some of them for three or four weeks, i.e., longer than Sabbatai's manifest "messianic residence" in the city—to be admitted to the royal presence. Emden's statement (p. 28)—allegedly translated from Coenen—regarding the many embassies bringing precious gifts from far and near, nowhere occurs in the Dutch original. De la Croix's account (p. 308) too attributes to Smyrna what actually took place later in Constantinople and Gallipoli.

or the earliest news letters. No doubt inquirers or believers from the neighboring communities (Magnesia, Thiraea, Rhodes) would hasten to Smyrna, and some might even have come as far as Brussa and Constantinople, but the latter would probably have set out long before, in response to letters from Gaza and Aleppo which announced that the messiah was repairing to his native city. That is how Abraham Yakhini came to Smyrna, and the same may have been the case with others. Though their number cannot have been large, the visitors were of some consequence, being, in the main, earnest scholars and rabbis who attached themselves to Sabbatai's entourage. Some of them also accompanied the messiah from Smyrna to Constantinople. There is no evidence that Samuel Primo, subsequently Sabbatai's secretary, traveled with him from Aleppo to Smyrna; he may not have joined Sabbatai until Smyrna, or possibly not until Constantinople.[214] The absence of his name from the list of kings is surely significant, unless the omission is due to the forgetfulness of the compiler. Coenen's informant had forgotten the names of other kings, too.

The group of scholars and rabbis that collected around Sabbatai, though consisting in the main of believers from Smyrna, also included some foreign rabbis. Yakhini refers to them as the "brotherhood of his faithful servants" and mentions among their number a Polish rabbi who had come to Smyrna on his way to Safed. This R. Elijah, a scholar steeped in the traditions of his Polish masters, had converted to the "faith" and had become an enthusiastic Sabbatian missionary and preacher. "He served Our Lord, his majesty be exalted, and aroused Israel to repentance . . . proclaiming the faith in every city. . . . and Our Lord greatly loved him in those blessed days."[215]

Sabbatai rewarded his leading believers by conferring on them royal titles. The emissary of Casale (quoted above, p. 422) states that on the Sabbath on which Sabbatai proclaimed himself messiah, he distributed the kingdoms of the earth among some of the faithful present. According to Coenen the royal appointments took place before Sabbatai's departure for the capital. Both accounts may be correct,

214. De la Croix (p. 300) is the only author to say that Sabbatai arrived in Smyrna accompanied by two rabbis (from Jerusalem! p. 343) who had forsaken their families in order to follow him. De la Croix may have thought of the rabbis Moses Galanté and Daniel Pinto (both from Aleppo), but his information on the whole period is confused and unreliable.

215. See the paragraph on R. Elijah in Yakhini's letter of 1673 to Nathan (*RÉJ*, XXVI [1893], 215).

since not all the appointees were living in Smyrna, and the list includes some of Sabbatai's supporters in Palestine and Egypt. Announcement was made not only of their future dominions, but also of the "roots" of their souls, since each was supposed to be a spark or reincarnation of one of the ancient Israelite kings from David to Zerubbabel. Coenen says that the titles were taken very seriously in Smyrna, and that the dignitaries were addressed by their new names: King Jehoshaphat, King Zedekiah, etc. Kings and viceroys were appointed, and the names of the ancient kings of Judah and Israel distributed among the new holders of the royal office. Some of them were afraid that the promise might be revoked or forgotten, and obtained handwritten letters patent from the messiah. One of the new kings, Abraham Rubio, was a poor man who lived on alms, but he refused to sell his kingdom even when offered a large sum.

Coenen obtained from his Jewish informants the following list of the kings appointed by Sabbatai Ṣevi:[216]

Isaac Silveira (King David), one of Sabbatai's earliest disciples.[217]

Abraham Yakhini (King Solomon), the famous preacher from Constantinople. He remained a steadfast believer all his life and was greatly esteemed by Sabbatai.[218]

Solomon Laniado (king of Zoba), the rabbi of Aleppo (in Hebrew, ʾ*Aram Zoba*). His letter written in 1669 shows that he persevered in his faith even after the apostasy.[219] He was probably made king of the district of Aleppo where he lived.

216. See Coenen, pp. 43–45, 78. Only Coenen's list can rank as a primary source. Graetz mentions Rycaut's *History,* but no such list occurs in the 1st edn. of that work (London, 1680). Perhaps the list was added in the French translation (used by Graetz), from John Evelyn's *History* (1st edn. 1669, p. 64). Evelyn had copied the list either from Coenen or from an appendix to Rycaut's report which he pirated and printed under his own name. The corruptions in the spellings of the names suggest that his source was Coenen's Dutch book.

217. Died 11 Heshvan 5442 (1681); his epitaph contains the honorifics "pious and humble" (see Freimann, p. 142, and R. Elijah Kohen's *Yado bakol* [Smyrna, 1867], fol. 231a).

218. Died 1682. An account (possibly legendary) of the strange mystical rite by which Sabbatai persuaded Yakhini to "accept the faith in the messianic king" is given in a Sabbatian commentary on Gen. 12–17; see Y. R. Molkho in *Sefunoth,* III–IV (1960), 441. Evelyn's list omits Yakhini's name, but has two kings named Solomon Laniado.

219. See *Zion,* VII (1942), 174, 190–93. He was still alive in 1714 (see *SS,* p. 348, n. 3).

Joseph Kohen (King Uzziah), as yet unidentified.[220]

Moses Galanté (King Jehoshaphat), the rabbi from Jerusalem who came to Smyrna via Aleppo and accompanied Sabbatai to Constantinople.

Daniel Pinto (King Hezekiah), the rabbi from Aleppo. Together with his colleague Galanté, he was one of the first prophets in Smyrna.

Abraham Ḥandali (King Jotham), a steadfast believer even after the apostasy. He remained in contact with Sabbatai Ṣevi and Yakhini as late as 1673.[221]

An Ashkenazi rabbi called "the Preacher" (King Zedekiah), the Polish preacher R. Elijah.[222]

Abraham Leon (King Ahaz), one of the wealthiest Jews in Smyrna and an elder of the community. According to Coenen he was sent in 1667 by the rabbis of Smyrna to meet Nathan and persuade him not to come to the city.[223]

Ephraim Arditti (King Joram), a wealthy member of the Smyrna community.[224]

Shalom Cremona (King Ahab), a wealthy man whose "heart rejoiced exceedingly at the manifestation of the new messiah" and in whose house Elijah appeared during a banquet.[225]

220. Evelyn gave the name as Moses Kohen—an error which in its turn bred further errors, e.g., the suggestion of identity with R. Moses Kohen of Adrianople, one of his later followers in that town (see Tishby, n. 206, to Sasportas).

221. He was living at the time in Constantinople. He is mentioned as a believer, in Yakhini's letter of that year; the printed text (*RÉJ,* XXVI, p. 213) corrupts the name to Mandal. Ḥandali is the name of a well-known family of rabbis. A R. Joshua b. Joseph Ḥandali is mentioned among the rabbis of Jerusalem in Sabbatai's time (Frumkin, vol. II, p. 32), and other scholars of that name lived in Salonika.

222. R. Elijah is mentioned in Yakhini's letter, and fits the indications in Coenen's list remarkably well. Evelyn misunderstood the Dutch word *berisper* ("reprover," Coenen's translation of the Hebrew *mokhiah,* that is, a preacher who calls the people to repentance) and hence produced a rabbi with the fantastic name Mokhiah Gasper. Elijah was a favorite with Sabbatai, and accompanied him to Constantinople; Baruch of Arezzo (Freimann, p. 50) refers to him only by his title King Zedekiah.

223. Coenen, p. 134. He is mentioned several times, from 1648 to 1671, in Beneviste's responsa *Baᶜey Ḥayyey* (e.g., II, 52; IV, 35).

224. He is mentioned in the responsa of Benveniste (II, 50) and of R. Solomon ha-Levi (*Leb Shelomo,* no. 26). In 1677 Abraham Leon and Arditti signed, on behalf of the elders of the community, a document in the notebook of an emissary from Safed (see J. M. Toledano, *Sarid u-Falit,* fasc. 1, p. 50).

225. Coenen's spelling Carmona (p. 66) is copied by Evelyn. Rycaut has Solomon Cremona.

Mattathias Ashkenazi (King Asa), R. Mattathias Bloch Ashkenazi, whom Sabbatai met in 1665 in Jerusalem. He remained a staunch believer even after the apostasy, when he became rabbi of Mosul.[226] He was not in Smyrna at the time, but had proceeded from Gaza to Egypt.

Meir Alcaire (King Rehoboam), of Constantinople, brother-in-law of Sabbatai's wealthy follower Solomon Galamidi.[227]

Jacob Loxas (King Amon), as yet unidentified.

Mordecai Jessurun (King Jehoiakim), that is, Mordecai b. Isaac Jessurun, a wealthy merchant in Smyrna. He is mentioned, together with Abraham Leon, in two responsa of 1671 by Ḥayyim Benveniste.[228]

Ḥayyim Peña (King Jeroboam), the wealthy infidel who became a believer. The appearance of his name on the list suggests that not all appointments were made on the Sabbath of the invasion of the Portuguese Synagogue, since Peña's conversion took place a few days later.[229]

Joseph Karillo (King Abiah), R. Joseph Karillo of Brussa. A query which he submitted to Benveniste in 1651 is printed in the collection of the latter's responsa.[230] Like Yakhini, he came to Smyrna after having heard the messianic rumors. He followed Sabbatai wherever he went, and in 1671 apostatized in the steps of his master. He was a leading member of the apostate group, and Sabbatai's trusted friend in Adrianople.[231]

226. See G. Scholem in *Zion*, VII (1942), 175–78, 193–95, and A. Yaᶜari in *Kiryath Sepher*, XXXVI (1961), 525–34.

227. See Cardozo's autobiographical letter in *Sefunoth*, III–IV (1960), 230.

228. *Baᶜey Ḥayyey*, IV, nos. 35 and 68.

229. On the other hand, it could be argued that Peña's appointment was meant as an insult, since Jeroboam figures in Jewish tradition as an arch-sinner and rebel against the House of David. After his conversion, Peña would have kept his new name by way of mystical *tiqqun* of Jeroboam's soul that was reincarnated in him. But the explanation seems far-fetched. Cremona, an early and enthusiastic follower, was straightway appointed to be "King Ahab."

230. *Baᶜey Ḥayyey*, I (supplements to *Eben ha-ᶜEzer*, no. 20).

231. Sasportas, p. 206; Israel Ḥazzan's commentary on Psalms (*Schocken Volume*, pp. 166, 206); Cardozo's treatises (in *Z. H. Chajes Memorial Volume* [1933], p. 345, and A. H. Weiss, *Beth ha-Midrash* [1865], p. 65). A letter written toward the end of his life by Sabbatai Ṣevi to "my dearly beloved companion and friend" Karillo is published in Freimann, p. 68. A report on his apostasy is in *Sefunoth* V (1961), 259. His descendants belonged to the Dönmeh group in Salonika.

Nehemiah Conorte (King Zerubbabel), unknown. Perhaps Coenen or his printer dropped a letter and the name should be read Conforti, in which case Nehemiah could be a relative of David Conforti of Salonika, the author of the historical work *Qore ha-Doroth.*

Joseph del Caire (King Joash), almost certainly Raphael Joseph the *chelebi,* of Cairo.

Eliakim Haber (King Amaziah), unknown. Probably from Smyrna.

Abraham Rubio (King Josiah), the aforementioned pious beggar who refused to sell his kingdom.

The list is headed by Sabbatai's two brothers, Elijah Ṣevi, "king of kings" over all the kings of Israel, and Joseph Ṣevi, "king of kings" over all the kings of Judah. Their vice-regents were Elijah Azar and Joseph Perniq of Smyrna, otherwise unknown.

The list is incomplete. The names of many biblical kings of Israel are missing, and so is the name of one of Sabbatai's kings, who is mentioned in several sources, as well as by Coenen himself in another context (see below). Moreover, the geographical areas of their dominions are not indicated, except for five kingdoms which are specified. The whole world was divided between Sabbatai's brothers, each a "king of kings," and the division seems to reflect his "geopolitical" notions. The two halves correspond to Rome (that is, possibly the Holy Roman Empire, the chief enemy of the Ottoman Empire) and Turkey (that is, the Muslim world). That much we know from the report of the emissary from Casale. Laniado was made king of Aleppo, and Yakhini, according to a report preserved by Sasportas, became king of Constantinople and its environs. The account quoted by Sasportas also provides interesting information regarding the prophecy of Yakhini and Galanté: "It is said [of R. Abraham Yakhini] that the Master [that is, Sabbatai Ṣevi] laid his hand on him and thereby put upon him his spirit of prophecy. Thereupon something resembling a brilliant star grew on his forehead—and it seems to me that it was the planet Saturn[232]—and it is said that he [Yakhini] too then prophesied regarding the new kingdom, and confirmed it. And it is said that the king rewarded him for this by appointing him ruler of Constantinople, so that the Rabbi Yakhini was vouchsafed [the twofold honors of] prophecy and kingship. Also as regards R. Moses Galanté, his witness cannot be trusted, for he was subservient to him [Sabbatai]

232. In Hebrew *shabbethay* (i.e., Sabbatai).

and tried to attain the rays of his majesty and the spirit began to move him but nothing came of it [that is, his prophecy did not get to a real start]."[233]

Several sources state that a well-known Jewish physician in Smyrna was appointed king of Portugal, but the spellings of the name are so corrupt that it can no longer be identified with certainty. The author of the French *Relation* was told that this physician was a Portuguese marrano who had spent the greater part of his life in Bordeaux. "Many of his relatives still are there, attempting to conceal their Jewish religion; and he firmly believed that he would soon be ruling over Portugal, because the messiah promised it to him when he made him king, shortly before leaving Smyrna."[234] This testimony confirms the account of the emissary of Casale which stated that the kingdoms distributed by Sabbatai corresponded to actual countries.

The distribution of the kingdoms was, as far as we know, Sabbatai's last messianic act in Smyrna. From his departure from Palestine until his arrival in Constantinople, his behavior had been as consistent as his uneven character would allow: he was sure of his calling, and believed that some supernatural intervention would bring his messianic mission to fruition. When, in August, 1665, he refused to remain in Aleppo, he already knew that Smyrna would be no more than an intermediary station. After he had gained the upper hand in his own city—as if to give the lie to the ancient proverb—he felt that there was no point in lingering there. He had repeatedly spoken of going to the capital, and his utterances on the subject are referred to in all the news letters from Smyrna. Nevertheless, a distinct lessening

233. Sasportas, pp. 165–66. His account, based on letters (now lost) from Smyrna and Constantinople, implies that Yakhini was in Smyrna at the time, and that he was made a king after being "ordained" to the prophecy by Sabbatai. The Italian letter, *JJS,* XII, p. 51, calls him "Dottor Morano, nativo di Portogallo."

234. *Relation*, p. 29. The Italian version is longer and might contain the better text. Coenen (p. 78) says that his services were much in demand by Christians. He may be identical with the Dr. Barut who was mentioned by Coenen, p. 93. When Nathan paid a visit to Smyrna after Sabbatai's apostasy, he hid in the doctor's house. According to Sasportas (p. 200) his name was Cardozo, but this seems to be a confusion with Abraham Miguel Cardozo, who was a physician too, but who was not in Smyrna at the time. On the other hand, the name may well be correct, since members of the Cardozo family were residing in Smyrna; one of them may have been a physician. (A responsum of Benveniste is addressed to R. Moses Cardozo of Smyrna, *Baʿey Ḥayyey*, IV, no. 24; cf. below, ch. 7. n. 95).

of his tension is noticeable toward the end of his stay. The illumination did not last longer than two weeks. Sabbatai did not, it is true, relapse into passivity and melancholia, but his behavior lacked the expansive energy and the provocative violence exhibited during Hanukkah and the succeeding days.[235]

We do not know whether Sabbatai was expelled from Smyrna by the local Turkish authorities, who, according to one source, gave him three days to leave,[236] or whether he departed solely on his own initiative and in accordance with his original intentions. The messianic expectations current among the Jews were very well known to the Turks, and Sabbatai's departure in a small saic, accompanied by only a few followers, has been explained as an attempt on his part to avoid irritating the Turkish authorities.[237] He sailed on December 30, 1665, accompanied by three or four rabbis who also appear in the list of kings[238]—we know of Moses Galanté, Daniel Pinto, and R. Elijah,

235. No use has been made in the foregoing of Rycaut's account. Rycaut was absent from Smyrna at the time of the events, and after his return from Europe gathered his information (orally and in writing) from Coenen. His dependence on Coenen is apparent even in his misunderstandings of the latter. His chronology is hopelessly confused; e.g., he took from Coenen a letter written by Nathan after the apostasy, but antedated it by a whole year (December, 1665). The letter abolishing the fast of 9 Ab, is turned into a proclamation issued in Smyrna (Rycaut, p. 205). The same letter is then quoted once more at great length, with the result that what is really one document appears as two. Occasionally Rycaut preserves a detail that is not found in Coenen and which, nevertheless, is no imaginative fiction or error. At the beginning of the chapter (p. 201), Rycaut hints that his story of Sabbatai Ṣevi had already been published by someone else—evidently an allusion to John Evelyn's *History of the Three Late Famous Impostors.* As the latter was published in the same year as Coenen's book (1669), Rycaut must have known Coenen's original account (i.e., the collection of letters sent to the Levant Trade Company in Holland) which was completed in the summer of 1667. Rycaut probably used Coenen's private copies of his letters, and then sent his own report in 1668 to friends in England, where it was pirated by Evelyn.

236. *Hollandtze Merkurius,* January, 1666, p. 3. No order for his arrest had yet been received.

237. Rycaut, p. 207.

238. There is agreement on the date in the local sources (Coenen, p. 46, and the letters from Smyrna written shortly after Sabbatai's departure). The letter mentioned by Sasportas (p. 74) already reports the miracles that attended the voyage. Sasportas and Emanuel Frances (*Haggadah* for the 9th of Ab, ed. Haberman [1940], p. 201) say that he was accompanied by three followers;

the preacher from Poland. Sabbatai's wife stayed behind in Smyrna, and probably joined her husband in the capital after his arrest.[239] Other followers of Sabbatai Ṣevi are said to have traveled to Constantinople overland.[240]

VII

Meanwhile Sabbatai's arrival was expected in Constantinople with mounting tension. The sensational news from Smyrna had divided the community, and the number of unbelievers was far from negligible. Those who doubted the optimistic tidings, and expected no quick transfer of the sultan's power to Sabbatai Ṣevi, could not but fear the worst for the House of Israel. Revolts were not infrequent in the Ottoman Empire, and when they failed they were dealt with thor-

---

Baruch of Arezzo (Freimann, p. 50) mentions four: King Jehoshaphat (Moses Galanté), King Zedekiah (R. Elijah the Preacher), "and two of the kings of Israel." The letter which Sasportas reproduced in very abbreviated form, is contained in full in the news letter from Flanders, published by Aeshcoly. The *"2 Prophètes de Halepo,"* said there (p. 227) to have accompanied Sabbatai, are identical with the "two rabbis from Jerusalem" mentioned by de la Croix (p. 343) who, of course, refers to Galanté and Pinto, but is partly mistaken about their city of origin. The English pamphlet *A New Letter concerning the Jews* gives a wrong date ("5th or 6th of January"), but knows that "the King with his four Prophets took Ship to go to *Constantinople,* without any Mariner, (as some say) or pilote. He being aboard the Ship, was taken up in a fiery Colomn, and went so swift, that the King commanded to take some Port because he was to arrive at *Constantinople* not before the 17th of *Shebet* (or January 21)" (Wilenski, p. 168). Leyb b. Ozer had heard reports that Sabbatai was also accompanied by his brother Joseph Ṣevi (Emden, p. 11), but this seems unlikely.

239. *Hollandtze Merkurius,* January, 1666, p. 134. According to this report, Sarah did not arrive until summer, and Sabbatai thus spent the greater part of his imprisonment without her.

240. Rycaut, p. 208. The author of *A Brief Relation of Several Remarkable Passages of the Jews* (p. 8) wrote in February, 1666, that according to letters received in London and Amsterdam, the Jews of Smyrna had dispatched four rabbis overland to Constantinople, to observe and report on the developments there. As the journey over the land route did not take more than ten days, these emissaries must have arrived long before Sabbatai and should have had ample time to prepare the Jews of Constantinople to meet their king—if the report is true.

oughly and ruthlessly. The leaders of the Jewish community in Constantinople knew that the authorities would hold them responsible for the conduct of the Jewish population. Their lives were at stake with Sabbatai's success or failure, since any messianic movement, even if it relied on miracles and the mystical power of hymns rather than on military prowess, was tantamount to an open rebellion. Concern for the community as well as for their own fate of necessity forced them to take some sort of action, as did also the Turkish authorities who had received information, from diverse sources, regarding the revolutionary agitation among the Jews. The reports describing the steps taken by either side are not, therefore, contradictory.

The believers later accused the leaders of the infidel party of having informed against the messiah, and some of our sources lend support to the charge. According to one report, a messenger of the rabbinate of Constantinople carried a letter to Sabbatai, warning him to watch his words and actions, lest he bring disaster on all the Jews of Turkey. Sabbatai replied that the rabbis need not worry, but should exhort the people to repent.[241] Another report states that before Sabbatai's arrival in the capital, the leaders of the congregation "went to the Great Vizier, which is the viceroy, and told him: Be it known to you that one of our nation is coming here and pretends to be the messiah. But we do not believe in him. You will know what to do"; as a result of this treachery Sabbatai was arrested.[242] This version was current in Smyrna, and R. Samson Bacchi quotes it to explain Sabbatai's imprisonment.[243] The Armenian account, which was composed soon after the apostasy and which gives a detailed report of events in the capital, similarly mentions the fears of the rabbis of Constantinople without, however, ascribing Sabbatai's arrest to Jewish intervention.[244] One rabbi preached a violent sermon against Sabbatai

241. The detail is contained in a report received in Italy as early as the end of December, 1665 (See *Vessillo Israelitico,* LV [1907], 330) and whose correctness there is no reason to doubt.

242. Baruch of Arezzo (Freimann, p. 50); see also below, p. 445.

243. Carpi, p. 17.

244. Galanté, p. 86. The two Armenian writers mingle fact and fiction in their accounts of the events in Smyrna. Both agree on one curious detail: Sabbatai was offered three virgins to serve him; he kept them for some time and then sent them away unharmed. The report should, perhaps, be connected with Cuenque's statement (Emden, p. 41) about the seventy beautiful virgins that attended on Sabbatai in Gallipoli.

in his private synagogue, and roundly condemned the alleged messiah's behavior and insidious propaganda.

Whatever opposition there was, it was powerless against the irresistible waves of messianic enthusiasm. Letters arrived bringing increasingly fantastic news of the mighty and miraculous deeds of the king and his prophet, and raising the messianic fever to even higher pitch. There may be truth in the report that the contents of the letters were so fantastic that the rabbis suspected a forgery, and in the course of their investigation discovered a "factory" which produced these news letters and sold them at a good price. Those responsible for the forgeries were severely punished,[245] but the flow of miraculous reports continued, and the historian has no means of distinguishing between the products of the overheated imagination of enthusiastic believers, and the fabrications of unscrupulous journalistic profiteers. Seventeenth-century Jewry, too, had its smart journalists, and their forged letters are reminiscent in many ways of the fantastic Christian pamphlets printed in Europe in the same year.

The messianic tidings aroused the enthusiasm not only of the masses but also of many members of the ruling classes. The Catholic priest who witnessed the events in Constantinople spoke of "transports of joy such as one can never understand unless one has seen it."[246] Even before Sabbatai's arrival, a number of enthusiasts had left Constantinople for Jerusalem—some quietly, others publicly and with much ado—in order to be present at the messiah's entry into the Holy City. The Jews of the capital prepared to meet their king, and indulged in provocative and dangerous talk. "All their conversation turned on the war and the imminent establishment of the kingdom of Israel, on the fall of the Crescent and of all the royal crowns in Christendom."[247] Their days and nights were spent expecting the great event in their synagogues and homes.

Prophets and preachers strengthened the hearts by proving from the Scriptures and the Zohar that the time of redemption had come. The chief prophet in Constantinople was a young rabbi from Brussa, the first prophet after Nathan to utter genuine revelations and mystical sermons, instead of the usual ecstatic ejaculations of biblical phrases.

245. De la Croix, p. 296.

246. *Relation*, p. 17: *"transports d'une joye qu'on ne comprendra pas si on ne l'a veüe."*

247. *Ibid.*

Details about him are preserved in several sources, and his name is given, in various spellings, as Moses Serviel or Suriel.[248]

Leyb b. Ozer, drawing on reliable accounts by visitors to Gallipoli in 1666, states that R. Moses considered himself a reincarnation of R. Simon bar Yoḥay.

He composed a new Zohar in those days, though I cannot say where this Zohar can be found. He could tell anyone the good deeds which he had performed that day, the sins of which he had repented and those of which he had not, and he gave to everyone penances for their sins, and this is truly wonderful. . . . Every night notables and rabbis would gather to him and hear from his mouth the mighty deeds of the Lord. They would sit with him and sing hymns of praise to Sabbatai Ṣevi, to the accompaniment of musical instruments. Then this R. Moses would begin to dance like a young lad, until he fell down as one who has an epileptic attack, from which God preserve us. He would twitch for a while and then begin to speak. Then they covered him with a veil, and he spoke clearly [. . . in Zoharic Aramaic], revealing infinite mysteries, all in the language of the Zohar, although nothing of what he said is written in the Zohar. Two scribes would sit at his side and take down everything he said. The burden [of his prophecy] was that Sabbatai is our king and messiah, our righteous redeemer, he and none other. When he had finished [his discourse] he arose, washed his face and his hands, and bowed to the divine presence. Thus he did four times every day, [that is] every six hours, day and night. . . . And this R. Moses told people the root of their souls; and all his prophecies, regarding the past as well as the future, were found to be true. And I have spoken to some of the greatest rabbis who testified that this

248. Moses Serviel (Coenen, p. 54, and—following him—Leyb b. Ozer); Moses Serupel (*Hollandtze Merkurius*, January, 1666, p. 135); Moyse Suriel (de la Croix, p. 357). The surname Suriel (Surviel) occurs in the index of names in the 1st edn. of *Midrash Talpioth*, but in the text itself (fol. 10d) the name of the scholar is Abr. Saraval. So far I have found only one reference to Moses Suriel in the writings of contemporary kabbalists. It occurs in the section on the 9th of Ab, in R. Israel Yaffe of Shklov's *ʾOr Yisraʾel* (1702). The eschatological remark by "the rabbi Moses Sarval in Constantinople" quoted there (fol. 151b), presents a comment on a Zoharic passage and fixes the end of the exile for the year 427, i.e., 1667. (The printed text, in an attempt to conceal the Sabbatian bias of the book, deliberately "misprints" 457, i.e., 1697.) Zevi Harkavy's "whitewashing" of this book (*Le-ḥeqer mishpaḥoth* [Jerusalem, 1943], p. 21) is pointless.

prophet R. Moses had told them the sins of their youth which they had, in fact, committed, and had given them a penance.[249]

The prophet's fame spread far and wide, and his charisma was considered as miraculous as Nathan's to which, indeed, it bore a striking resemblance.[250]

The description given by de la Croix on the authority of his Jewish informant, a former Sabbatian believer, is essentially similar though less sympathetic.

They brought a young man from Brussa, called Moses Suriel, a great kabbalist. In order to camouflage his game, he first wanted [that is, pretended] to exercise the spirits of the prophets that had prophesied, but they answered him that as a punishment for his unbelief in their prophecy, a soul higher and mightier than all others would enter his body and soul, and would announce amazing things. His words brought about many conversions, and made a great name for him. On the following morning the young man was seized by a prophetic furor (*fureur Pithonienne*) at the sound of musical instruments. He fell to the ground foaming at his mouth, and a voice issued from him with such rapidity that the scribes could hardly follow. When his spirit returned to him after this simulated ecstasy, they showed him the text of what he had said in his trance, but he pretended not to understand his own words because of the excellence of their style and the depth of their wisdom. He began every day at the same hour, which attracted many spectators and turned many people to Sabbatai Ṣevi, for all his utterances ended with the words: "Repent ye, for our salvation is at hand, and ye shall behold Sabbatai Ṣevi, the Messiah, the son of David and our righteous Redeemer, crowned on earth even as we have seen him crowned in heaven with the triple crown . . . corresponding to the three patriarchs Abraham, Isaac, and Jacob." . . . Moses Suriel acquired such a reputation among the Jews that every day his house was filled with people, and he instructed them and gave them rules of virtue [that is, penances].[251]

249. Thus the account in Leyb b. Ozer's original (Yiddish) text (MS. Shazar, fols. 28b ff.); the Hebrew version (Emden, p. 10) omits important details. The Yiddish text also states that Suriel came from Brussa.

250. Even his ecstatic dance and subsequent swoon are paralleled by Nathan's similar performance at the *Shabu^coth* vigil in Gaza; cf. above, p. 217.

251. This is probably the meaning of the French phrase *"il leur faisoit des leçons et leur donnait des règles de vertu."*

By way of confirming his message he pointed to a comet that had appeared in those days, and explained that the same sign had appeared in the sky at the time of the exodus from Egypt, and that now Jacob's dream was fulfilled and the angels of God descended from heaven and incarnated themselves in human bodies, and the earth was full of the knowledge of the Lord as the waters cover the sea."[252]

The remarkable agreement of the two completely independent accounts leaves no doubt as to their essential veracity.

The new prophecy found a wide echo and many imitators. Even if Leyb b. Ozer's informants, speaking of many hundreds of prophets, were guilty of exaggeration, there can be no doubt that Moses Suriel established a new pattern of prophetic homiletics and inspired kabbalistical composition. The kabbalistic mysteries were no longer revealed by *maggidim* (see above, p. 82) but by supernal spirits and by angels incarnate in human bodies. The idea that they should reveal a "new Zohar" was not devoid of an inner logic. The mysteries pertaining to last things were to be revealed at the end of days; it was fitting, therefore, that R. Simon bar Yoḥay should now reveal the Zohar of the messianic era. If the Torah were to be divested of its material clothing and reveal itself in its essential, messianic spirituality, then it was only natural that it should be accompanied by a messianic Zohar. Ideas which Nathan did not formulate until after the apostasy, but which lay implicit in his original doctrines, were clearly expressed by the prophets who were inspired by his example. There is probably little exaggeration in the words of the witnesses whom R. Jacob Emden remembered[253] as having declared that "more than ten thousand leaves of kabbalistic mysteries" were written under such prophetic inspiration.

The kabbalists were divided among themselves with regard to the manifestations of Elijah and the prophetic phenomena of the winter of 1665–66. Their wavering and doubts are reflected in a remarkable document from the Yemen. The Sabbatian apocalypse *Gey Ḥizzayon* (*Valley of Vision*, cf. Isa. 22:1), written in 1666 in Sanaᶜa, the capital of the Yemen, and indebted for its facts as well as for most of its legendary material to letters received from

252. De la Croix, pp. 357–59.

253. Emden, p. 9 (in his annotations to Leyb b. Ozer's text). He had also heard that "illiterate men and women quoted the Zohar and expounded it in profound kabbalistic manner."

Egypt, repeatedly refers to the new prophecy with varying degrees of appreciation. One passage reads:

Verily there is a spirit in Israel, and the breath of the Almighty awakens them,[254] the sparks of prophecy are beginning [to appear] in the children who prophesied regarding the messianic king. The spirit is also in the mouth of the gentiles who say, "Your king has come," and Israel are making themselves strong in [the performance of] the commandments, saying, "This is a sign unto us, that the praise of the Matron [Israel] is uttered even by her rivals. It is an acceptable time to pray for divine mercy. . . . Let us therefore make a little chamber on the wall[255] and let us strengthen the wall [of penitence], for . . . there lieth Leviathan and his consort, God and His Shekhinah, [the *sefiroth*] *Tif᾽ereth* and *Malkhuth*, *nefesh*, and *neshamah*. Then he called the well-known prince [of demons] Samael, and brought him against his will, surrounded him with terrors [and compelled him] to cry with a loud voice and to proclaim throughout the world, "Make room for Israel, that the Redeemer come."

Samael, the prince of evil, is described here as being forced to announce the messianic kingdom. However, it is not he that inspired the prophecy of the little children, but the "breath of the Almighty." A surprising explanation of the nature of the new prophecy is offered a few pages later. Since God compels Samael, the accuser of Israel, to become its defender, the latter inspires prophecies that are mistaken for revelations by the prophet Elijah. But far from being false prophecies, they are evidence of a change in the character of Samael! It seems as if the letters received in the Yemen had hinted that the believers in the Sabbatian gospel were free to elaborate their own interpretations of the phenomena. The apocalypse continues:

In the messianic future, when the time has come, it will not be the bringer of glad tidings [namely, Elijah] who will plead for Israel, but Samael . . . for he has some hold on Holiness. . . . Therefore he will hiss for the demons of the sea and the demons of the wilderness to appear and to announce tidings of gladness and comfort, by means of both well-known people and little children to whom these demons appear and make them—great scholars, men and women—announce the advent of the messiah. And the man or woman who prophesies, thinks that it is by [the inspiration of] Elijah; but it is not so, for Elijah does not

254. A play on Job 32:8.
255. A play on II Kings 4:10.

appear to everyone. [He is really inspired by Samael] and a spirit clothes him, or a spark of the Holy Spirit. However, if supernal mysteries are revealed to him, or he publicly preaches and expounds profound matters, he whom it befalleth thus undoubtedly experiences the manifestation of Elijah (by way of sensation, or intellection, or dream). . . . But with those who have not reached this level it is a matter of "the wild beasts of the desert meeting with the wolves," [cf. Isa. 34:14] that is, the demons of the sea and of the wilderness for whom their prince has hissed in the power of Samael.[256]

The writer evidently oscillates in his evaluation of the prophecies. Some, he asserts, were inspired by demons carrying out, against their will, a holy purpose, in the power of the holy spark that burns even in them. Other revelations were inspired by Elijah, and this author's wording suggests that accounts of the activity of prophets of the type of Moses Suriel had reached the Yemen. Very possibly the author of *Gey Ḥizzayon* considered himself as one of this latter group.

The main elements of the Sabbatian preaching which spread to all congregations were calls to repentance, expressions of gratitude for being vouchsafed to behold what previous generations had longed for in vain, and eschatological computations attempting to find indications of the years 1665–67, and of the names of Sabbatai and Nathan, in the Scriptures. None of the many sermons preached at that time will be found in the homiletic literature printed subsequently. The homilies, which several preachers collected during the year 1666, later prudently disappeared. However, some sermons, or parts of them, have survived, either indirectly, by quotations in the polemical writings of the unbelievers, or, more rarely, in their original form. One such collection of sermons, Moses Abudiente's *Fin de los Dias,* actually survived to our day in print, in spite of its having been banned by the elders of the Sephardi community in Hamburg. Some samples of Sabbatian homiletics have been preserved—surprisingly enough—in letters addressed to French noblemen by correspondents who collected information on contemporary events for their subscribers. The French news letters contain a long sermon,[257] preached toward the end of

256. *Qobeṣ ᶜal Yad,* IV, New Series (1947), 115, 120.

257. An almost identical sermon occurs in Abudiente's *Fin de los Dias.* Perhaps Abudiente—and not some preacher in Smyrna or Constantinople—was the author of this piece, which he may have sent from Hamburg to his many friends in Amsterdam.

1665 or at the beginning of 1666, as well as a shorter one, preached almost certainly in Constantinople before Sabbatai's arrival there.

The longer sermon is based on the seventy weeks of the Book of Daniel: "Seventy weeks are decreed upon thy people and upon thy holy city, to finish transgression, and to make an end of sins, and to make reconciliation for iniquity, and to bring in everlasting righteousness, and to seal up vision and prophecy, and to anoint the most holy" (Dan. 9:24). The verse is expounded as follows:

According to the laws of the number seven, which is preferred by God above all other numbers, and its mysteries and combinations, it will be understood that our redemption, at the end of days, will take place in accordance with the mystery of the sevens. And Scripture says [Deut. 29:28]: "The secret things are unto the Lord our God," because these mysteries were hidden in the counsel of God, sealed in his treasuries from the six days of creation until now, the time of our redemption. Now, by the glad tidings, it is easy to understand the mystery of the seventy weeks which the angel had revealed to Daniel, but until this day nobody could penetrate and understand it. This is the mystery of the "time and times and half a time" which is mentioned there [Dan. 7:25], and everything is in the mystery of the number seven. Seven times seventy are four hundred and ninety ("a time"); and seventy times seventy are four thousand and nine hundred ("and times"); and half of seventy is thirty-five ("half a time"), which makes five thousand four hundred and twenty-five, that is the past year when God made his spirit rest on the mighty man, the man of God, Nathan Ashkenazi the prophet of Gaza, and the messiah, the son of David, Our Lord Sabbatai Ṣevi, was anointed, for his name [. . . contains many kabbalistic allusions to the "week"]. . . . And that which was "decreed upon thy people, etc. to finish transgression and to make an end of sins" is now fulfilled, for our holy prophet from Gaza has roused us to a great and mighty repentance in all the congregations of Israel, and all sins have undoubtedly been wiped away by the merits of the fasts, alms, mighty devotions, and penitential exercises—in fact, of all that you can observe in yourselves and in all the congregations of Israel—as well as by the merit of the old man that appeared in the sepulcher of Zachariah, announcing that the slaying of the prophet had been forgiven and the sin atoned for, to bring everlasting righteousness in order that the Lord God may be known by all creatures. This is meant by the end of the verse "to seal up vision and prophecy, and to anoint the most holy," that is to say, to confirm the prophecies that foretold our redemption, and that there is a prophet in our midst (which we consider a manifest and well-known fact);[258] "and to anoint the most holy"—all this has been fulfilled in our messiah, the anointed of the God of Jacob. In his excellence and holiness he is deserving of the title king and of the messianic crown, the son of David and king of Israel, his glory be exalted and his kingdom lifted up and raised. Happy the people whose lot is thus, happy the people whose God is the Lord.[259]

The homily well illustrates the mood of both the preachers and their audiences. The forms of thought and expression of these sermons are thoroughly traditional, and devoid of the revolutionary audacity implicit in the very fact of a revival of prophecy (and explicit in the strange behavior of the messiah).

Prophecy aside, other strange things happened in Constantinople. A letter from Smyrna, written shortly after Sabbatai's departure, graphically conveys the atmosphere reigning in the capital. The letter, which was received in Amsterdam in March, 1666, reported that "two days after his departure [from Smyrna], two emissaries arrived from the congregations of Constantinople, carrying letters of credence, written on gilded parchment and wrapped in gold brocade adorned with diamonds, by which all the Jews acknowledge him as their king, placing their lives and their strength in his hand, and entreating him to speed his journey because the Grand Turk was eager to see him. The reason for this will be explained by the bearers of this letter, the deputies of the synagogues. . . ."[260]

258. The wording in Abudiente (*Fin de los Dias,* pp. 79–80), is even more explicit: "to seal up vision and prophecy—since [prophetic] vision and the prophets were sealed up and hidden away; but now, from the year 5425 [1665], the seal has been taken away and [these things] are manifest to all, and we have a vision and a true prophet, as has become widely known during that year."

259. The text was published by Aeshcoly, pp. 223–26. Unfortunately Aeshcoly's Hebrew translation from the French (*ibid.,* pp. 232–33) does not recapture the style of the undoubtedly Hebrew original. Aeshcoly thought he had proved that the sermon was originally written in Spanish or another European language, but he was unaware of the existence of Abudiente's *Fin de los Dias* in which the author explicitly states that he had first composed his sermons in Hebrew and then translated them into Spanish.

260. Aeshcoly, pp. 227–29. It is unfortunate that no other MSS. of this text are known, particularly as the French translation in the news letter from Flanders shows signs of haste and negligence.

This is the first definite and reliable reference to emissaries carrying letters of homage to the messianic king. Similar deputations from other cities may have arrived before, but no evidence has survived. We may assume that descriptions of the magnificent letters of homage were sent to other congregations besides Amsterdam, and probably stimulated the dispatch of more deputations and letters. The embassy from Constantinople was almost certainly prompted by the reports from Smyrna regarding the events of the Fourth through the Eighth of Tebeth, and by the mounting enthusiasm which they generated. The letter also states that before his departure, Sabbatai had authorized R. Ḥayyim Benveniste to open all letters addressed to him. That is why the contents of the document from Constantinople was known in Smyrna. So far everything sounds credible enough. However, the emissaries' account of the circumstances of their dispatch soon transports us into the world of legend. The capital was given over to penitence, sackcloth, almsgiving, and devotions, when Elijah appeared to the chief rabbi, led him out of the city, and showed him an army of foot soldiers and horsemen, their flags flying. He said to him: "These are the hosts of Israel," and promised to show him their king and chief. Thereupon he [that is, the chief rabbi] beheld in a vision the Lord Sabbatai Ṣevi descending from Heaven, sitting on a golden throne studded with sapphires and diamonds, and it was revealed to him that the words of Daniel (12:12), "Blessed is he that waiteth, and cometh to the thousand three hundred and five times thirty days," referred to Sabbatai Ṣevi and Nathan. "Go and tell the Jews that redemption has come, and that they should celebrate a festival." R. Gamaliel thereupon recounted his experience in the synagogues. The hero of the story, whose name occurs twice more in Sabbatian sources, is either R. Moses ibn Jamil, one of the leading rabbis of Constantinople, or—more probably—R. Abraham Gamaliel,[261] a Sabbatian believer who later apostatized in the footsteps of the messiah. If the latter identification is correct, then we must assume that the visionary experience of the lesser-known figure was later ascribed to the "chief rabbi." The sequel of the story is pure legend: the rejoicing of the Jews angered the Turks, and the sultan,

261. Gamaliel is named together with Karillo in Cardozo's polemic against the apostates (*Sefunoth,* V [1961], 259. The Polish emissaries (in their account of their visit to Gallipoli, Emden p. 15) and de la Croix (p. 364) mention him as Sabbatai's messenger from Gallipoli to Constantinople.

at the instigation of an Armenian informer, ordered the Jewish leaders to produce Sabbatai within one week; otherwise they would all be massacred. Sundry miracles and celestial warnings caused the sultan to revoke his order, but he requested the Jews to transmit his invitation to the messiah, promising him a royal welcome.[262] The tale may have been brought by the messengers from Constantinople, or it may have originated in Smyrna, where the local legend of Sabbatai's meeting with the cadi was simply adapted and transferred to the sultan.

The peculiar atmosphere of feverish expectation that reigned in the Jewish quarter of the capital during the last months of 1665 was a psychological and social reality. There was, however, another no less decisive reality. After some as yet unexplained hesitation, the Turkish authorities decided to act. There is no reason to reject the story of the arrival in Smyrna of a Jewish embassy from Constantinople; but at the same time there also arrived other messengers, carrying orders to arrest the king of the Jews as a suspect rebel. As the messengers arrived too late for an arrest, orders were issued to lie in wait for Sabbatai's boat near the straits of the Dardanelles, and to bring him as a prisoner to the port.

There are good reasons to believe that Sabbatai's arrest was not solely due to the initiative of the Turkish government, alarmed by the messianic unrest among the Jewish population and by reports received from the local authorities in Smyrna and elsewhere. The Jewish opponents and unbelievers seem to have had a hand in the matter. The suspicion is borne out by the Hebrew sources, some of which

262. The version in *A New Letter concerning the Jews* (Wilenski, pp. 168–69) is similar to that in the French news letter from Flanders, but the story of R. Gamaliel is lacking. The news letter from Flanders also quotes a report from Lièges in Belgium, dated December 14, 1665, and telling of Sabbatai's miracles and the sultan's invitation (p. 220). If the report is derived from letters from Smyrna, then the date cannot be correct; events taking place in the middle, viz. the second half, of December could not possibly have been known in Belgium on the 14th of the month. Perhaps the original report referred to events in Palestine, and the Belgian correspondent confused things and wrote *le messie est arrivé et estoit à Smyrne,* where his source had merely said that the messiah originally came from Smyrna or was going there. In any event most of the prodigies told in the Belgian letter without specific mention of dates and places are actually legends of Sabbatai's miracles in Palestine. The story about the sultan's messengers is an exception, but this detail may very well be independent of the story of the sultan's invitation as told in the letter of March 18 (*ibid.,* p. 228).

appear to be reliable even if some others are not. To the latter class belongs the account in the "Relation of Sabbatai Ṣevi" by Emanuel Frances: "Sabbatai left Smyrna for Constantinople, but before he arrived there, the elders sent messengers unto him, saying, 'Go away from us, and come not into the city to make us stink in the eyes of the inhabitants of the land,' but Sabbatai would not hearken unto them. And the elders were much afraid, and they went to the Great Vizier and said, 'A madman has come to us, vaunting himself to be the messianic king. Therefore, by thy grace, command that he be imprisoned or exiled, for we wash our hands of him. And Sabbatai was put in irons by the vizier's orders."[263] It is extremely unlikely that the Jewish leaders could send messengers to meet Sabbatai at sea, and as Sabbatai was arrested immediately, there was no opportunity for negotiations between him and the elders of the community. Leyb b. Ozer, it is true, reports that Sabbatai enjoyed a brief period of freedom in Constantinople before being arrested, but all the evidence is against his account. Some kind of Jewish intervention is explicitly attested by the emissary from Casale, who says that the elders "secretly went after him to the vizier, and at their request he was imprisoned."[264] Sasportas, who did not know R. Samson Bacchi's report, surmised as much.[265] The expression "went after him" is obscure. If it means that the elders "shadowed" Sabbatai, the implication being that he was free for a while, then Samson Bacchi's testimony on this point must be dismissed as worthless. But perhaps the wording should not be pressed unduly, and all it means is that the elders had secretly addressed themselves to the vizier before Sabbatai's arrival.

However that may be, the Turks were well aware of the feelings that agitated the Jewish population. The street urchins in Smyrna, who had heard the Jews discussing "believers" and "infidels," gratefully picked up what they decided must be a new Jewish term of abuse, and shouted *"kopher"* (Hebrew for "heretic," "unbeliever") at every Jewish passerby.[266] Christian witnesses in Constantinople tell

263. Frances, p. 135. The whole account *ibid.*, pp. 134–35, abounds in misrepresentations and distortions.

264. Carpi, p. 17; see also above, p. 434. The idiom "went after him" is not Hebrew but reflects the Italian usage (which resembles the English) in Bacchi's mother tongue.

265. Sasportas, p. 86: "Perhaps the rabbis and lay leaders arranged this together."

266. Coenen, p. 64.

a similar story. As Sabbatai's arrival was delayed by rough seas and winter storms, the fever of expectation rose to even greater heights, and the Jews greeted one another in the streets with the eager question, "Has he come?" Whenever a Jew passed by, the Turkish street urchins would jeer at him, *"Gheldemi?"* ("Has he come?").[267] The Armenian source also says that satirical songs about the messiah were sung in the streets.[268]

Sabbatai's arrival in Constantinople was delayed beyond all expectation. The voyage lasted thirty-six days instead of the usual ten to fourteen, and in the telling it was inevitably accompanied by no end of miracles. Some of these miracles almost certainly originated in the aforementioned workshop for the wholesale production of forged news letters; others may well have been spread by *bona fide* enthusiasts.[269]

A letter written in Constantinople during the days of expectation preceding Sabbatai's arrival speaks of a penitential awakening as well as of apparitions of the prophet Elijah, "whom many have seen."[270] Many believers had given up their business and had left, or were about to leave, for Gaza and Jerusalem. The Catholic author of the French *Relation* noted the unquestioning faith of the masses in the miracles that would take place immediately after Sabbatai's arrival, as well as the threats which they addressed to the gentiles. "They threatened us with dire disaster if we failed to join them as soon as possible, and of our own good and free will walked in front of the king who would rule over them, acknowledging his kingdom and sub-

267. *Relation,* p. 19; similarly also the Armenian song quoted by Galanté, p. 86.

268. Galanté, p. 99.

269. Of the two stories told by de la Croix (p. 345), the one may go back to a genuinely Sabbatian source. Sabbatai is said to have stilled the tempest by ordering his companions to recite Ps. 116 up to vs. 28, which he then recited himself, whereupon the sea ceased from her raging. As Ps. 116 has 19 verses only, it may be conjectured that the original story referred either to Ps. 107 (vs. 29: "He maketh the storm a calm, so that the waves thereof are still") or to Ps. 118. In the latter case, Sabbatai would have recited his favorite verse (Ps. 118:16): "The right hand of the Lord is exalted" etc. See also the similar reports mentioned by Sasportas, pp. 74–75, and Sasportas' comments, p. 86.

270. The letter is lost, but a summary has been preserved; see *Zion,* X (1945), 63.

mitting to the religion and the laws which he would establish in the world."[271]

There is an abundance of information concerning Sabbatai's arrest. All kinds of stories were told by Jews as well as gentiles, and reports are conflicting as regards most details. Nevertheless, local tradition in Constantinople seems to have preserved the main outline of events, and a fairly accurate picture emerges from the wealth of details.[272] It is also possible to establish an exact chronology.[273] Sabbatai's caïque was met by two boats (according to some sources by the two officers who had first gone to Smyrna to arrest him) in the sea of Marmara, after having passed the straits of the Dardanelles, and was escorted to port. According to another version he was arrested as his boat entered a small harbor near Gallipoli to escape the violent storm.[274] De la Croix's rather overdramatized account says that Sab-

271. *Relation,* p. 18.

272. Whereas Coenen is our chief source of information as regards Smyrna, other and more authoritative informants are available regarding the events in Constantinople. Details of Sabbatai's imprisonment are given in the French *Relation* (pp. 17–21), the Italian letter in *JJS,* XII, 43–47, and by de la Croix (pp. 345–55), whose information on this point is derived from good sources and is confirmed by the Armenian texts discovered by Galanté (an Armenian poem by Jeremiah Cumargian, Galanté, pp. 86–88, and a prose account by the priest Arakal, Galanté, pp. 98–100). To these should be added Rycaut, pp. 208–9; the report—written in the middle of March—of the Venetian Ambassador Giambattista Ballarino to the doge of Venice; Sasportas, pp. 75 and 86 (based on letters received in Hamburg). Other letters from Constantinople complete the picture by providing the legends and popular expectations current at the time, especially the letter of March 7, 1666, printed in a German broadsheet, *Neues von dem erhöheten Josvehel Cam* etc., published in the summer of 1666, perhaps in Augsburg.

273. Coenen (p. 46) and Sasportas (p. 86) speak of thirty-nine days having passed from Sabbatai's departure from Smyrna to his arrest; elsewhere (p. 75) Sasportas speaks of thirty-six days. Both numbers are correct as Sabbatai was arrested at sea, three days before his arrival in Constantinople. The Armenian source specifies that the arrest took place on a Sunday, but antedates his arrival at Marmara by one week (January 28 instead of February 4). The Italian letter from Constantinople gives February 6 as the date of his arrival; cf. *JJS,* XII, 45.

274. The Armenian account says that Sabbatai had heard (at one of the ports which he entered to avoid the storm?) of the order to arrest him and meant to escape to Salonika, but was captured at sea. The letter from Aleppo written on February 20, 1666, states that he was arrested in Gallipoli and was taken to Constantinople (*Kiryath Sepher,* XXXIII, 537).

batai was found studying the Law with twenty other Jews when he was arrested.[275] This happened before the Sabbath. On Monday, the Third of Adar I (February 8, 1666), he was brought ashore in chains.[276] On that occasion he was hit by the Turkish guards, who also charged with truncheons into the crowd of Jews that had come out in little craft to meet the messiah and who now wanted to accompany him. The Jews fled to their houses in panic, where they stayed for three days for fear of more violence from the Turkish and Christian populace. They proclaimed a fast, and waited for the signs and miracles that were to happen. The French priest recorded in his *Relation* a conversation which he had had the very same evening with a Jewish acquaintance. They were returning to the city on the same boat, and the Jewish merchant expressed his certainty that the ten plagues of Egypt would soon be visited on the gentiles. He urged the priest to repent before it was too late, and was almost beaten up by the other Christians on board the ship.[277]

It is not clear whether the sultan, Mehemed IV, was in Constantinople or Adrianople at the time,[278] but his Great Vizier, Ahmed Köprülü, one of Turkey's greatest statesmen, was in the capital and in charge of affairs. He (and not his deputy as suggested by some accounts) had given the order for Sabbatai's arrest, and he continued

275. This detail, like others in de la Croix's colorful account, is highly improbable. According to de la Croix, Sabbatai was riding on horseback when the Turks found him after he had landed at Gallipoli. The Turkish guard took him to Kutchuk Chekmeze, three miles from the capital. There the horses were exchanged for a boat, while the Turkish mob prepared to lynch Sabbatai; a believer who had got wind of the preparations obtained permission from the kaimakam to take the prisoner to Constantinople by sea. Sasportas too (p. 86) states that Sabbatai, after arriving in Marmara, kept himself in hiding (in Gallipoli?), and studied the Law until arrested by the Turks. The dialogues, speeches, and picturesque details reported by de la Croix are pure fiction (e.g., the incident with the Turkish guard who smote him on his cheek, but the "crafty" Sabbatai turned to him the other cheek also).

276. Coenen, p. 47; de la Croix, p. 346; Sasportas, p. 86, and more particularly Ballarino's letter to the doge (*RÉJ,* XXXIV [1897], 308). The believers answered jibes about their messiah being in chains with a reference to Scripture (Song of Songs 7:6: "the king is held captive in the tresses thereof") being fulfilled.

277. *Relation,* p. 19.

278. My late colleague Uriel Heydt examined the records of the sultan's movements and found some evidence, in the Turkish historian Rashid, that Mehemed IV left the capital only on April 12, 1666, for Crete.

to deal with the case himself. Köprülü was known for his moderation, and was not given to unnecessary bloodshed. He had evidently considered the strange case of a messiah who claimed the kingdom for himself without making any military preparations. Perhaps the extraordinary phenomenon of a "rebellion" that involved no armed threat whatever appealed to his sense of moderation and caution—rare qualities in those days, particularly in matters of high treason. Sabbatai had forfeited his life anyway as a rebel and troublemaker. This, at least, is what Ballarino, the Venetian ambassador, reported to his government on March 18, that is, six weeks after the arrest, in a letter which constitutes a valuable source of information as to what was known and rumored in diplomatic circles in Constantinople. The ambassador wrote to the doge that the Great Vizier was compelled to intervene, after the penitential awakening had reached the point where it caused many of the poor to sell their few belongings and neglect their families in order to follow their false prophet.

Clearly it was not so much the boldness of the Jewish talk about the coming of the messianic kingdom which alarmed the Turkish authorities as the disruption of normal life and the cessation of business activities in the Jewish community which controlled so much of Turkey's commerce. The conspicuous preparations of many believers for their voyage to the Holy Land must not only have provoked hostility and suspicion on the part of the government, but may easily have led to serious clashes between the Jews and the Turkish population. Travelers in Turkey in the seventeenth century all noted the fact that trade, and foreign trade in particular, was almost exclusively in the hands of the Jews, who also monopolized the contacts with the European traders in the country. A messianic movement would have immediate repercussions on the non-Jewish environment. The departure of a great number of believers for Palestine, leaving behind many destitute families, created a serious social problem. There was more than the virtue of charity in the decision of the community of Aleppo to establish a special charitable fund for the poor; it was sound practical commonsense to conceal such social upheavals as far as possible from the watchful eye of the authorities. In Constantinople the movement assumed such proportions that the almsbox was no longer sufficient for the needs, and communal life was seriously affected. It is not unlikely that these aspects of the movement played a part in prompting the government to take action.

Within three days of his arrest,[279] Sabbatai was brought before the Divan, presided over by the Great Vizier himself.[280] Accounts of the proceedings at the Divan are conflicting. The Venetian ambassador reported that Sabbatai's intelligent and sensible deportment won the heart of the Great Vizier and saved his life. What actually happened remains a mystery. Everybody, with the exception of the Jews, had been convinced that Sabbatai would be executed without further ado. The fact that he was sent to prison instead was nothing short of miraculous. The Jews were quick to proffer explanations of their own. According to Ballarino, Sabbatai spoke such perfect and elegant Arabic that the vizier, a great lover and connoisseur of the language and its literature, took a liking to him.[281] Since we know that Sabbatai's knowledge of the Turkish language was, at best, very poor (see above, p. 410), it seems extremely unlikely that he had a perfect command of Arabic. The French *Relation* is marred by contempt of the Jews, and its jeering account of the proceedings is hardly credible. Sabbatai is said to have scoffed at the foolish Jews who wanted to impose on him a messianic office for which he did not care. On

279. And not immediately on coming ashore, as stated by de la Croix. A comparison of de la Croix's account with Ballarino's brings the unreliability of the former into greater relief. De la Croix (pp. 350–55) constantly refers to the kaimakam, the deputy Great Vizier, instead of the Great Vizier. As a matter of fact there was no kaimakam at the time; the next kaimakam, Kara Mustapha, was only appointed with the sultan's and the vizier's departure for Crete on April 12, 1666. De la Croix's report is a highly dramatized account after the fact, whereas Ballarino's letter was written while the events described were taking place. Sasportas correctly speaks of the Great Vizier. The reliable information in the letter from Aleppo (n. 278) states that Sabbatai was brought before the vizier on 3 Adar I. The German broadsheet (see n. 272) quotes a story, written eleven days earlier than Ballarino's report, according to which the sultan and the Great Vizier had gone hunting for some days and there was indeed a kaimakam acting who took the decision to imprison Sabbatai because his landing had caused great unrest among both Jews and janissaries. But the entirely legendary character of the continuation of this story throws suspicion on its beginning too. There is no record of an acting Great Vizier for these days.

280. Also the French *Relation* (p. 20) and the letter from Smyrna in the *Hollandtze Merkurius,* January, 1666, p. 4, confirm that Sabbatai's case was brought to the Divan.

281. Ballarino, *ibid.* Baruch of Arezzo also mentions Sabbatai's performance in Arabic (see below, n. 286). The exact opposite is said by Leyb b. Ozer, who quotes Sabbatian sources: Sabbatai communicated with the vizier through his brother Joseph Ṣevi, who had accompanied him from Smyrna.

the other hand, the French priest mentions a detail which also occurs in the Jewish sources used by Sasportas. On being asked who he was, Sabbatai described himself as a scholar from Jerusalem,[282] traveling to collect alms for the poor of the Holy Land. Also present at the hearing was "the judge of Smyrna who had come especially to testify against him and against the rebellious Jews, and who had taken much money from the Jews [when Sabbatai was brought before him in Smyrna].[283] When the cadi asked him: "Did you not call yourself the messianic king, and the Jews followed you and were fined a great sum?' Sabbatai answered: 'I said nothing.' " There may be some truth in this account, but it is far from explaining the surprising leniency and patience of the vizier. Perhaps Sabbatai's natural charm and the fascination of his personality impressed the vizier—as they later impressed the sultan—and saved his life at a critical moment.[284]

At first Sabbatai was kept in what some accounts describe as "the most loathsome and darkest Dungeon in the Town,"[285] but after a while he was transferred to "fairly comfortable" quarters. The Venetian ambassador also knew that Sabbatai was

> under the supervision of the kasem bashi [the jailer], who permitted him to speak freely with the Jews that wanted to visit him. He [Sabbatai] confirmed the fasts and the severe penitential exercises. He himself kept regular fasts of three days, at the end of which he caused torches of light[286] to appear by his [kabbalistic] conjuration in the whole prison.

282. *Relation,* p. 20.

283. See above, pp. 409–11. The presence of the cadi of Smyrna at the hearing is mentioned only by Sasportas (p. 75).

284. Ballarino too stresses Sabbatai's comely appearance: *Hebreo di assai bella apparenza.*

285. Rycaut, p. 208.

286. Light phenomena are also mentioned by other writers. De la Croix (p. 356) had heard that the lights above Sabbatai's head turned into stars and olive plants. Baruch of Arezzo (Freimann, p. 50) relates that after two days and one night in prison, Sabbatai "had a great illumination, and his face was shining like a torch." Baruch evidently interpreted the reported miracle in terms of his knowledge of Sabbatai's "states of light," and his account should therefore be understood as a rationalization of the legend of the light shining in the prison, rather than as evidence of a new illumination which—according to Ballarino—occurred only after Sabbatai's examination in the Divan. There are other similarities between the accounts of Ballarino and Baruch of Arezzo. According to the latter, Sabbatai asked the vizier to choose the language of their conversation. The vizier spoke in four or five languages—in all of which Sabbatai made

After some time he was allowed, albeit under strong guard, to go to the sea for his ritual immersions. The Jews dared not walk the streets, because of the abuse with which the gentiles, and the Turks in particular, reviled them. The chiefs of the community assembled therefore, and went to the vizier [to obtain assurances] for walking in the streets without molestation. This they finally obtained, though at a cost of 60,000 reales [lion's thalers], plus another 40,000 reales for permission to visit Sabbatai at any time. This sum was levied from each according to his capacity. The vizier even offered to release him for another 100,000 reales. They all consented in their hearts to this new offering, and they went to announce it to the prisoner.

But Sabbatai refused. He became very excited and forbade them to spend as much as a penny on liberating him. He would not resort to such means, "since in a few days great things would happen. And the masses of the Jews were greatly elated by the hopes which were thus aroused."[287]

All this took place before March 18, the date of Ballarino's report. This diplomatic letter enables us to check the reliability of certain other reports, and to distinguish facts from accretions that were added in the telling. We learn that the leaders of the community, far from conspiring against Sabbatai, did not shrink from great sacrifices to obtain permission for accompanying him in procession to his ritual baths in the sea, visiting him in prison, and even ransoming him. Sabbatai's refusal to obtain his release by means of bribes greatly enhanced his reputation and further increased the "desire of redemption of this stiff-necked nation." This detail, for which Ballarino is our only source, may well be true. It may serve as an apt illustration not only of Sabbatai's adroitness in "impressing the masses by a noble gesture,"[288] but also of his extreme self-confidence. It was, no doubt, a barren kind of self-confidence, which produced nothing but passivity

---

reply—and finally settled on Arabic. Sabbatai's mastery of the language gave him "such pleasure, that he did not want to kill him, although he was guilty of a capital offense" (p. 51). Either Baruch of Arezzo, who lived in Venice, had heard of Ballarino's letter (the Venetian senators may have talked about it to their Jewish acquaintances), or else he obtained his knowledge from Sabbatian letters containing similar information as that given to Ballarino.

287. *RÉJ,* XXXIV, pp. 307–8.

288. David Kaufmann, in *Allgemeine Zeitung des Judentums* (1898), p. 365, in his discussion of Ballarino's report.

and a fatalistic trust in God's mighty miracles. During the weeks of his imprisonment in Constantinople, Sabbatai did nothing whatever, and no "strange actions" are reported.[289] He again led the life of a pious ascetic, preaching repentance and setting an example of penitential fervor without even the shadow of a claim of any special privileges for himself. Evidently his spirit was in a trough between two tidal waves of illumination. There were none of the riotous antinomian outbursts that had occurred in Smyrna. The rabbis of the capital who visited him in prison, possibly to examine him, found an affable and dignified ascetic who bore his sufferings with love and an air of nobility, rather than a sinner who set himself above the laws of the Torah and tradition. Sabbatai showed no surprise at his imprisonment. Though he had extricated himself from the prison of the *qelippoth,* they still had an occasional hold on him (see above, p. 310). His actual sojourn in the prison house of the "prince of Ishmael" was nothing but a concrete symbolic expression of that captivity of the soul which he had experienced in his spiritual struggles. There is no rebelling against fate and against the symbols that express the essence of one's life. If he was destined to suffer captivity in the hands of the demons and the *qelippoth,* then it was only natural that his fate express itself also in external, material reality. But the filth and squalor of his "loathsome and dark dungeon" failed to touch his personality, which impressed his visitors by its quiet dignity.

The Jews of Constantinople heaved a sigh of relief when they learned that Sabbatai had been imprisoned and not killed, but the rift between the two parties deepened. Some of the leading rabbis undoubtedly sided with Sabbatai Ṣevi, among them R. Abraham Anakawa,[290] who, according to Coenen, was highly respected even by the Turkish authorities. Anakawa visited Sabbatai several times in prison, where he and others "attended . . . before him, with their eyes cast down, their bodies bending forward, and hands cross'd before them" in an attitude of reverence and homage before the anointed of the God of Jacob.

The reports that reached Europe from Constantinople reflected the conflicting trends in the community. The critical and sober letters

289. At least during the first stage of his imprisonment.

290. Rycaut (p. 208), who paraphrases Coenen (p. 47). Coenen spells the name Anaquagia, Rycaut spells it Anacago.

that came to the eyes of Sasportas were evidently written by doubters or outright "infidels." They emphasized that Sabbatai had not come to Constantinople of his free will, but admitted that in spite of the arrest and the hearing before the vizier

> the believers continued to go to him in large crowds, openly rejoicing and praying with him. They wrote letters telling of the great miracles which he wrought in prison, such as curing a dying person by giving him something to eat, the appearance of pillars of fire and clouds, and the greatness which the vizier accorded to him. But they did not tell the truth, for seven days after his arrest he was put in chains and brought to an even narrower dungeon, so that he himself begged of the Jews to intercede for him with the vizier's *chelebi*[291] [and ask the latter] to plead for him and obtain his transfer to any other place, for he could no longer suffer [his present place of confinement]. After they had bribed the vizier, they suggested to him that it would be advisable to remove Sabbatai from the city, where he could not stir up the people with his follies. This they did, and on the Twelfth of Nisan [April 18, 1666] he was sent to the fortress of Gallipoli and confined there.[292] Some of the leading members of the community realized that if Sabbatai could not save himself, he certainly could not save others; they repented of their faith and held him for a fool. But the majority of the crowd were not disturbed by his imprisonment; indeed, their faith increased because they said that the messiah had predicted that he would suffer much on behalf of Israel, in order to lighten the messianic woes.[293]

The letters referred to by Sasportas were probably written in February, and thus supplement Ballarino's report of March 18, which touches only very briefly on the earliest happenings in January. It appears that Sabbatai at first had to endure a very harsh imprisonment, and that the high bribe of 60,000 plus 40,000 reales (lion's thalers)—four reales had the equivalent value of one gold ducat—was paid in order to secure his removal to more comfortable quarters. Whether it was Sabbatai who requested this transaction (as asserted by his opponents), or whether the believers took the initiative, the

291. I.e., probably the vizier's Jewish banker and financial adviser. Rosanes (IV, p. 68) states that the vizier's banker was a certain Judah b. Mordecai ha-Kohen; he seems to have been a "believer."

292. For the date, see below, n. 311.

293. Sasportas, p. 75.

account quoted by Sasportas leaves no doubt that some of the Jewish leaders supported him. The enormous bribe was certainly not raised by Sabbatai's opponents.[294]

One of the rabbis who accompanied Sabbatai to Constantinople returned to Smyrna in March, 1666, and on April 5 wrote a letter to Amsterdam which provides valuable insight into the mentality of the believers. Inevitably facts were slightly twisted when viewed with the eyes of faith, and freely embellished by fond imaginings and hopes. The identity of the writer is unknown, but an English summary of his letters has survived.[295] We learn that the king of the Jews,

> by Order of the Grand Signiour is Conveighed to a Castle at Gallipolie about 30 Leagues distant from Constantinople because the Grand Signiour and prime Visior were to go for Adrianople to get forward there warlicke preparations against the Tartars, to the end the said King during there absence might be secured against any affronts or attempts of the Tumu[l]tuating Multitude, and this the rather because the City was so full of strangers which flocked from all parts to see him and to speake with him and that the great Turke hath allowed him in this seeming place of restraint 50 Aspers every day being a pension he useth to allow his Chiefest Commandery, and that the Turke in

294. Some of Ballarino's information is also given, together with much legendary nonsense, in the Dutch letter of April 2, 1665 published in the *Hollandtze Merkurius* January, 1666. The letter reports (*ibid.*, p. 72) that Sabbatai's sentence had already been decided upon in advance: his tongue was to be cut off, he was to ride through the city on a donkey, and thereafter to be hanged and quartered. A bribe of one hundred thousand reales succeeded in mitigating the sentence. Another hundred thousand reales were promised if he were set free; nevertheless he was sentenced to imprisonment for life. The detail about two distinct bribes is reminiscent of Ballarino's account, but in general the chronology and details of the Dutch letter are confused and unreliable. There is no escaping the fact, emphasized by Ballarino but suppressed by the Dutch correspondent and by Sasportas, that for one reason or another the vizier had taken a liking to Sabbatai. The Dutch correspondent seems to have known that the sultan was still in the capital, and hence made him (and not the vizier) preside over the hearing at the Divan, as against the other sources.

295. The letter from Smyrna was used by Serrarius, an English summary of whose letters was sent by Thomas Chappell to his friend James Fitton in Chester: "Before I had finished what I intended there came to my Hand from a friend some letters from Mr Peter Serarius in Holland, Touching the Jewes." The original of Chappell's letter, which was written on May 12, 1666, is preserved at the Public Record Office in London (S.P. 29-162-85).

removing him there eyed nothing but the security of his person and the peace of his great City Constantinople. The King since his Arivall hath assured the Jews that the Redemption of Israel is at hand, and that as soone as the Prophet Nathan shall be arrived, who is expected every houre that the same shall by great wonders and miracles be proclaimed and make known to all the world. *The Jews have received a letter of the fifth of April from one at Smyrna who accompanied the King to Constantinople,* relating that when he came away from thence things were in this posture Viz. that the King was in a Certaine Palace of the Grand Signiour, where he had with him severall Rabbines and Israelites and the Books of their Law, and the free exercise of all their Ceremonies that any Jew might freely come to visit him, and that the Great Turke had sent him word that he might goe abroad in Publick wheresoever it pleased him, whose Answer was he would not do so untill he was assured from God that the tyme was come in which he should publickly manifest himselfe, that a piller of fire surrounded with severall Starres was seen hovering over the place where he was, of his appearing in the Turkes Bed Chamber, and in short sayth the letter a confirmation of what we had last Post, and over and above this that Severall who were sent from the Visier to strangle him fell down dead in his presence.

From the last incident it was but one step to the further miracle of resurrecting the dead Turks.

The two manuals received from Gaza, for daily and nightly devotions respectively, were printed by the believers at the press of Abraham Franco in Constantinople. The "*tiqqun* for the night, which hath been brought from the GLORIOUS Land,[296] suitable for recitation after midnight for the benefit of our souls, to behold the beauty of the Lord, and to inquire in his temple. In the year 426 [1666 C.E.]" was printed at the expense of Judah b. Joseph Obadia[297] and in it the prophet's name is not mentioned even once. The other volume,[298] possibly the second to be printed, was an "Order of the *tiqqun* for the day, arranged for daily recitation and brought from the GLORI-

296. Cf. Dan. 11:6; lit., "the land of *ṣevi*" (Hebrew, *ṣevi* = also "glory"). All the capitalized words contain allusions to Sabbatai Ṣevi, Nathan, and the year 1666.

297. A copy of the book (47 leaves in very small format) is at the Bodleian Library, Oxford (Oppenh. 12° 364).

298. 56 leaves in very small format, also at the Bodleian Library (Oppenh. 12° 363).

OUS Land, from the mouth of the light of Israel, who hath GIVEN[299] us eternal life, to behold the beauty of the Lord, speedily in our days, Amen. Constantinople, in the year 'and the kingdom SHALL BE[300] the Lord's' " (cf. Obad. 21). The printer's foreword confirms that "our heart rejoices in thy SALVATION"[301] and quotes the verse "and I shall dwell in THE MIDST[302] of the children of Israel." The fact that Nathan's devotional manuals were printed in the capital—though we do not know whether before or after Sabbatai's arrival—indicates that the Jewish authorities did not hinder the activities of the believers.

A third text of a similar character was published by Abraham Franco's press, of which only one copy is extant (in the writer's collection). This is a collection of penances, from Lurianic sources, which was edited by Solomon b. David Gabbai in 1666, who, in his introduction, hints at the messianic movement which has caused him to publish the book: "Perhaps God is about to proclaim freedom for the remnant of Israel, and the kingdom shall be the Lord's and thine days of mourning are over." Although the little book is perfectly orthodox in content, this apparently was sufficient to have got it suppressed when the movement had come to grief.[303]

At the behest of the prophet Elijah, the believers also introduced new customs, that is, they insisted on the strict observance of certain ancient practices that had fallen into neglect.

Elias . . . habited like a Turk . . . injoyned the observation of the neglected Ceremonies and particularly the Zesit, Numbers 15,38 *Speak unto the children of Israel, and bid them that they make them fringes in the borders of their garments throughout their generations, and that they put upon the fringe of each border a cord of blue.* Also the Peotz, Leviticus 19,27 *Ye shall not round the corners of your heads, neither shalt thou mar the corners of thy beard.* This apparition of Elias being published, and as soon believed, every one began to obey the vision by fringing their garments; and for their heads, though always shaved according to the Turkish and Eastern fashion. . . . Yet to begin again to renew, as far as possible, the ancient Ceremonies, every one nourished

299. In Hebrew, *nathan.*

300. Numerical value 426, the year of printing, 1666.

301. By *gematria* equals "Sabbatai Ṣevi."

302. Numerical value 426.

303. Only later, the missing title page turned up, proving that the book was actually published in 1666, and not earlier. Cf. Scholem, *Kiryath Sepher,* XXX, 414–16.

a lock of hair on each side, which was visible beneath their Caps, which soon after began to become a sign of distinction between the believers and the Koparims [that is, *kopherim,* infidels]. . . .[304]

The Jews of Turkey, while growing beards, used to shave their heads, but now the custom of the Polish Jews of letting side-locks grow at "the corners of your head"[305] was reintroduced as a Sabbatian innovation. It was noised "that the People of the Jews who came from the river Sabatyon [that is, the 'Sons of Moses'] . . . shall take vengeance of those who are guilty of these omissions" and who thus lack the distinguishing marks of the true believer.[306] This renewal of a traditional custom illustrates the absence of antinomian tendencies. The enthusiasm of the believers in Constantinople was not fired by the abolition of ceremonial traditions, but, on the contrary, by the renewed and strict observance of hitherto neglected practices.

The almost complete cessation of trade and business had a curious result. According to the English consul in Smyrna, many believers were so "mad and distracted" with preparing for the messianic events that they neglected to pay their debts. The English merchants at Galata, "not knowing the way to receive their money, partly for their interest, and partly for curiosity, thought fit to visit this Sabbatai" in his prison, and to ask him "to signifie to those his subjects his

304. Rycaut, p. 212; also Coenen, p. 68, and the French *Relation,* p. 16. The French priest attests that the innovation was strictly observed in Galata and Constantinople, particularly in the case of children. In Italy the exhortation to wear the fringed scapular was attributed to Nathan (see *Zion,* X [1945], 64). As the "Notes from Italy" refers to a letter written in Üsküb in December, 1665, it is not impossible that the innovation really originated in Gaza and only manifested itself in such spectacular fashion in Constantinople. In that case, Nathan's warning "he who is not properly clothed with the *breastplate of repentance* will suffer great tribulations" (Haberman, p. 211; cf. also above, p. 291) may be a concrete reference to the fringed scapular, rather than a general metaphor.

305. There is no definite information regarding the origin of the custom of growing long side-locks. Judging from medieval iconography this "characteristic" Yemenite and Ashkenazi feature was known since the late Middle Ages; cf. the article "Juden" in the *Lexikon der christlichen Ikonographie*, II (1970). The Sabbatian innovation consisted in the reintroduction of a tradition well established in German and Polish Jewry. As regards the growing of side-locks in kabbalistic circles, cf. S. Schechter, *Studies in Judaism*, II, p. 298 (on the Brotherhood of Isaac Luria), and J. M. Toledano, *ᵓOṣar Genazim*, p. 50 (quoting a text from the year 1577).

306. Rycaut, p. 212.

pleasure to have satisfaction given." Sabbatai thereupon "with much affection, took pen and paper, and wrote to this effect":

To you of the Nation of the Jews, who expect the appearance of the Messiah and the salvation of Israel, Peace without end, Whereas we are informed That you . . . are indebted to several of the English Nation, It seemeth right to us to enorder you to make satisfaction to these your just debts: which if you refuse to do, and not obey herein; know you that you are not to enter with us into our Joy and Dominions.[307]

Sabbatai remained in prison in Constantinople for more than two months. The vizier Ahmed Köprülü was busy preparing his army and fleet for the expedition to Crete and the conquest of the island from the Venetians. He wished to prevent further excitement and agitation among the Jews and therefore ordered Sabbatai to be removed to the fortress of Gallipoli, on the European side of the straits of the Dardanelles.[308] The order was carried out on April 19, 1666, the day preceding the Passover festival. "On approaching the fortress, it being the eve of the Passover, he sacrificed a Passover lamb[309] and roasted it with its fat.[310] He made his company, as well as some of the Jews living in the fortress, eat of it, and they believed that his actions were by the word of God."[311] R. Moses ibn Ḥabib also heard

307. *Ibid.*, p. 208.

308. All sources agree that Sabbatai was detained in the fortress on the Gallipoli peninsula, and Rosanes is definitely wrong in situating his prison on the Asian side of the Dardanelles, known as Kum-Kalé. Rosanes refers to Rycaut in support of his contention, but Rycaut explicitly says the exact opposite: ". . . changed his prison to the Dardanelli, otherwise called the castle of Abydos, being on the Europe side of the Hellespont, opposite to Sestos, place famous in Greek poetry." Also de la Croix (p. 355) speaks of the "new fortress of the Dardanelles, on the European side."

309. A transgression of the prohibition to perform sacrifices outside Jerusalem.

310. A transgression of a severe biblical prohibition; see above, p. 242.

311. Sasportas (p. 2), who also gives the date as 12 Nisan (*ibid.*, p. 75). But 12 Nisan fell on a Sabbath, and it is not very likely that Sabbatai was transferred to Gallipoli on that day (unless he was moved in the evening, after the termination of the Sabbath). Coenen (p. 48) gives the date as 3 Nisan—probably a slip of the pen or misprint for 13 Nisan. The date is supported by de la Croix's remark (p. 354) that Sabbatai's imprisonment in Constantinople lasted for two months and that his jailer grew rich from the admission fee of one real (about one dollar) which he charged every Jewish visitor. Leyb

that the eating of the forbidden fat at this illegal Passover sacrifice was accompanied—as on previous occasions—by the benediction "Blessed art thou, O God, who permittest that which is forbidden."[312] Sabbatai's strange appetite for bizarre rituals reasserted itself at the moment of his removal from the capital; the rabbis who accompanied the prisoner with royal honors humbly accepted the mystical significance of this kabbalistic *tiqqun*.

There is general agreement in the sources that the prisoner was transferred by order of the vizier;[313] this does not exclude some kind of intervention by Jewish leaders who wished to see Sabbatai removed for one reason or another from the capital.[314] The fortress of Abydos was used as a prison for important political prisoners. By means of bribes, the believers soon converted Sabbatai's detention into an "honorable confinement," and his prison was soon known as *Migdal ᶜOz*, the "Tower of Strength," with an obvious reference to Proverbs 18:10: "The name of the Lord is a tower of strength; the righteous runneth into it and is safe."

Sabbatai's residence in Gallipoli opened a new chapter in the history of the movement. But before proceeding with our account of Sabbatai's career, it may be useful, at this stage, to turn our attention to the impact of the messianic tidings on the far-flung Jewish Diaspora.

---

b. Ozer's account is worthless: Sabbatai moved about freely in the capital until 3 Nisan (the date is obviously derived from Coenen), when he went to the vizier together with his brother, who had accompanied him from Smyrna (MS. Shazar, fols. 29b–30a). Generally speaking, Leyb b. Ozer filled the lacunae in Coenen's account with legendary information supplied by former believers in whom some of the old fires were, apparently, still burning.

312. Emden, p. 53.

313. Only in de la Croix's account (pp. 354–55) the kaimakam and not the vizier is in charge. The dialogue between the kaimakam and the provost of the prison, in which the latter describes how his prisoner's presence had turned a squalid jail into a fragrant paradise, is, of course, pure fiction, like all the other dialogues in this work.

314. Sasportas' suggestion (p. 2) that the Jewish elders wanted to get the dangerous messianic agitator out of the way, may be an *ex post facto* explanation. There is evidence that many—if not the majority—of the leaders of the community believed in, or at least sympathized with, Sabbatai; they may have desired his removal to Abydos for his own safety and comfort.

5

THE MOVEMENT IN EUROPE (1666)

I

THE SABBATIAN MOVEMENT spread rapidly once the Jews of Palestine and Egypt had begun to announce the glad tidings to their friends and relatives in the Diaspora. The excitement produced by their letters was tremendous, and the similarity of the reactions everywhere indicates that the basic causes of the response must not be sought in particular local conditions. No doubt local factors played a role in some communities or even in some countries—as we know they did in Smyrna—but they cannot be considered as decisive. The effects of the massacres of 1648 on the state of mind of the Polish and Russian Jews are well attested and should certainly not be underestimated, yet the general receptivity to the good news cannot be ascribed solely to massacres and persecution. The messianic wave swept no less over communities that had had no immediate experience of oppression and bloodshed than over those which had. As a matter of fact, the communities that enjoyed most freedom took the lead in the messianic revival and its propagation. Jewish sources mention—and many Christian sources bitterly complain about—the freedom enjoyed by the Jews of Salonika, Leghorn, and Amsterdam, where the rulers, for various economic reasons, wished to attract a Jewish population. The Duke of Tuscany granted extraordinary privileges to the Jews of Leghorn when he decided to turn his new city into a major port that would compete with Venice and Genoa. The prosperity of the Jews of Amsterdam is well-known, yet their messianic enthusiasm yielded in nothing to that of other communities. Opponents of the movement such as Sasportas had every reason to complain about the role played by these leading communities, and Amsterdam in particular was accused not only of failing to repress the messianic frenzy, but of actually inflaming it even more.

Social and religious factors were inextricably combined in the genesis of the messianic outbreak. Setting aside the "explanations" of historical materialism, which do not explain anything, and even without invoking internal class struggles in the Jewish communities, it is obvious that Jewish messianism, particularly in its later manifestations, fulfilled a definite social function. In the peculiar conditions of Jewish existence, messianism was the expression not so much of internal Jewish struggles—class or otherwise—as of the abnormal situation of a pariah nation. The sense of insecurity and permanent danger to life and property, affected the upper classes no less than the lower; in fact, the former often had more to fear. The relationship between messianism and poverty was anything but unequivocal. It is true that any radical change in the situation of the Jewish people would inevitably affect the interests of the ruling classes, and this surely explains in part the responsiveness to the messianic ideas. On the other hand, there can be no doubt of the popular appeal of the more catastrophic and revolutionary aspect of apocalyptic messianism, and of its influence on the masses. Poverty and deprivation breed utopian hopes, but it was the situation of the nation as a whole which provided the relevant background. The messianic aspects of the national myth could, in their turn, become social factors of prime importance, as was illustrated by the career of Lurianic kabbalism and the manner in which it established itself as the mystical theology of precisely those circles that carried the religious and social responsibility for Jewry. But although the Lurianic doctrine of *tiqqun* expressed a social situation, the latter was not its "real," covert content. The real content was essentially religious. It takes a great deal of modern naïveté to believe that every expectation of a transformation of human existence is "essentially" social because it has social aspects and implications.

The world-view of the generations with which we are concerned here was not yet impoverished to that extent, and their experience still had room for a spiritual dimension that was more than the direct or indirect reflection of social reality. It was the interlocking of the various elements in the historical actuality of the Sabbatian movement which accounts for much of its explosive charge.

The attitude of the rich had been a matter of interest also to Jewish and Christian contemporaries of the movement. A careful examination of the sources reveals an utter absence of class-conditioned uniformity. Many members of the financial elite took a leading part in the messianic propaganda, with genuine enthusiasm and not because of fear of terrorist pressure. Testimonies from Italy, Holland, and the Germano-Austrian Empire agree on this point. On the other hand, many of the wealthier class appreciated the comforts of their position and distrusted messianic changes. Not a few of them must have been caught in the dilemma of national-religious inclination *versus* economic self-interest; Jacob Tausk's poem (see below, p. 538) provides a striking illustration of this conflict. Martin Meyer, a Christian with little sympathy for the Jews, in 1668 thus summarized his impressions regarding this matter: "Also the rich and the wealthy rejoiced in these hopes, but in their hearts they feared for their wealth, which they would not be able to take with them and which they would have to leave in Christian hands if things come to the point when they would have to leave their exile."[1] Jokes and puns on the subject made the rounds. Hottinger preserved a story told about a Jew of Amsterdam whose wealth was estimated at a hundred tons of gold. When he was approached with the request to contribute to the cause of the messiah and his prophet, he replied that "he was more interested in great profits than in great prophets."[2] His was probably not the only case, and the conflict between the call of the Holy Land, on the one hand, and the attraction of established wealth and comfort, on the other, surely did not begin with the modern Zionist movement. But these incontrovertible facts should be viewed in proper focus together with other, equally incontrovertible facts. There is little

1. *Diarium Europaeum,* XVI (1668), 514–15.

2. MS. Hottinger 30 (Zurich), fol. 357b. The story, which Hottinger recorded at the height of the movement, evidently inspired Martin Meyer's statement (see n. 1) that the rich Jews were not very enthusiastic about the messiah *"und hielten mehr von den alten Profiten als von den neuen Propheten."*

chance of tackling the complexities of the Sabbatian movement with the naïve simplicity of dialectical materialism.[3] Messianism can function as a powerful progressive and revolutionary force, especially when its content undergoes reformulation in the experience of great visionary minds, but it can also act as a regressive and inhibiting factor when its dynamism has yielded before the petrified patterns of ancient popular myth.

Several factors contributed to the success of the message from Gaza:

1. The messianic call came from the Holy Land. If the awakening had started somewhere in the Diaspora, its impact would probably have been less powerful. The distance of Palestine from the main centers of Jewish life at that time, and the numerical and material insignificance of the community there, merely enhanced its spiritual prestige. There were few or no social tensions among the handful of Jews in Palestine, hardly more than a few thousand souls. Many of them were rabbinic scholars and were poor—at times the two terms tended to be synonymous. Only a few provided for their own livelihood; the greater part were supported by their families abroad or by the Jewish community at large. The revival emanated from the center that stood for pure spirituality at its most intense. A messiah could hardly choose a better place than Palestine for his appearance, for there he occupied the one Archimedean point from which the Diaspora could be challenged. A message from Jerusalem would be received in Persia or the Yemen with a matter-of-course respect which it could not have commanded had it arrived from Poland or Italy. The prestige of the Holy Land increased even more after the new kabbalah, which emanated from Safed, had conquered Jewry, and kabbalists from all lands had settled there in quest of spiritual perfection.

2. The messianic manifestation was accompanied by a renewal of prophecy. The first reports concerning the "anointed of the God of Jacob" also announced that his mission had been confirmed by a prophet whose truthfulness was vouched for by the rabbi of Gaza and other scholars. In fact, the original emphasis was on the prophet, for it was his testimony that established the messiah's mission, and

3. As e.g., in the very poor and disappointing chapter "Messianism and Social Strata" in M. Lahav's (Hebrew) book *The Sociology of the Jewish Diaspora in the Light of Marxism* (1951), pp. 170–74.

not vice versa. The dating found in some books and letters—"in the first year of the renewal of prophecy and the kingdom"[4]—is significant in that respect. The conspicuous figure of the brilliant young scholar and severe ascetic-turned-prophet helped to obscure the more dubious facets of the messiah's personality, which, indeed, played little or no role in the consciousness of the believers, let alone of the masses, until after the apostasy.

3. The message contained a curious combination of traditional, popular apocalyptic and of hints at its reinterpretation in the light of Lurianic kabbalism. The former element predominates in the messianic literature addressed to the masses, who were not particularly exercised by the problems that preoccupied the kabbalists. Their world was one of messianic legend and apocalyptic wars. The early propaganda addressed to them essentially adhered to the traditional pattern in its general character, though deviating from it in most details. The ancient beliefs were not relinquished, but their elements were rearranged (for example, in the widely circulating letter of Nathan) and new details were added. The letters and traditions dating from 1666 confirm the decisive significance of this particular point: the messiah of the masses was that of the ancient eschatological midrashim which, originating in circles of apocalyptic visionaries, had become popular property in the Middle Ages. The popular messianic expectations were definitely "political" in character, though the means by which redemption would be worked were supernatural. The military dreams of apocalyptic were retained but split into two parts: there would be an immediate conquest without battle, and a messianic war much later. Popular imagination also promptly introduced the lost tribes, upon whom devolved all the warlike functions which the Diaspora Jews knew themselves unable to fulfill. The Sabbatian propaganda made no attempt to minimize the importance of this mythology which combined ancient and new legends or, rather, retained enough of the old to enable it to absorb many new elements.

The important thing about this popular myth is its orthodox character. Revolutionary as it was regarding the nations of the world and

4. This form of dating occurs in several books printed in Amsterdam in 1666, as well as in letters, e.g., by Isaac Nahar, writing from Amsterdam in February, 1666 (Sasportas, p. 57); Raphael Supino, writing from Leghorn in April, 1666 (Sasportas, p. 70); and the letter of March, 1666, from Vienna (*Zion*, X [1945], 144).

their rulers, its conception of the future Jewish life was thoroughly conservative. Possibly some voices sounded a more antinomian note during the height of the movement,[5] but they must have been drowned by the voice of the great majority which saw in the messianic world a guarantee for the strictest observance of the Law. The mass of simple "believers" held no theories about a mystical change in the status of the Torah; when they said "fulfillment of the Law" they meant what they said, and for them fulfillment was no paradoxical euphemism for abolition. However, at the same time the messianic propaganda also addressed a considerable class of kabbalistic scholars to whom it presented a system of ambiguous symbols, interpreting the Sabbatian gospel in terms of Zoharic and Lurianic esotericism. Nathan and his friends spoke the language of the kabbalists. Hence they were understood, and their teaching was accepted without their audience even stopping to ask themselves whether Nathan's symbolism, or its implications, were really orthodox. The readers were satisfied by the similarity of the Sabbatian symbolism to their traditional terminology, and the apparent continuity enabled the new and revolutionary elements to exist undetected under the cover of the old kabbalism. The appeal of the message to the kabbalists was of decisive significance, since they were the most active and alert religious group. The double response of the broad masses and of the kabbalistic elite imparted a powerful impetus to the movement.

4. The prophet's call to repentance, as reiterated and developed in his letters and tracts, played a decisive role in determining the public response to the messianic message. The call, welling up from the depths of the prophet's heart, was an act of faith and not a tactical gambit, but its effect was to reduce considerably the possibilities of opposition. The exhortation to repent appealed to the noblest longings in every Jewish heart, but this time it was coupled to the very specific purpose of shortening the messianic woes and hastening the advent of redemption. But whatever the motives of the penitential enthusiasm, what orthodox rabbi could possibly object to the eagerness with which a whole people responded to the call to repent? Even the most determined opponent of the prophet and the messiah could hardly condemn the one demand which they made in public; on the contrary, he could only desire: "O that there were such an heart in them for

5. The charge was made by some of the "infidel" opponents; see below, pp. 489, 582.

ever" (Deut. 5:26). Many months of intense propaganda for extreme mortifications and penitential exercises passed before the first messianic commands were issued for a general, public transgression of the Law (the abolition of the fast of the Ninth of Ab), and even these commands did not reach the Jewish centers outside Turkey until much later. Meanwhile the rabbis had to debate within their consciences not only the question of their own "faith" or unbelief, but whether they were justified in obstructing a great penitential awakening. Cautioning words on their part inevitably provoked the unanswerable reply: if you cannot believe, at least do not keep the people from repenting. Considerations of this kind must have caused many doubters to refrain from active opposition.

5. When the rising messianic tide began to engulf the whole people, there was, as yet, no differentiation among the several elements taking part in it. Conservative minds could unhesitatingly accept the message which seemed to promise them the fulfillment of traditional eschatological expectations; their presence in the movement made for an unquestioned feeling of unbroken and matter-of-course continuity. They did not analyze details, nor realize the seeds of crisis that were hidden in the very nature of the messianic awakening. As far as the content of and the values governing their lives were concerned, they conceived of the messianic world as a direct continuation of the world they knew. Outwardly everything would change, but the inner reality would remain the same—or, to be more precise, would be perfected. There was little difference in this respect between the great masses, on the one hand, and the rabbis and the more conservative kabbalists, on the other. However, there was also another kind of "believer": utopianists with a sense of crisis and with an avidity for the new age, who would shed no tears for the passing away of the old state of things. For the time being the all-embracing, national character of the awakening obscured the contrasts in the emotional make-up of its participants, and the diffuse light that shone for all believers was not yet refracted into distinct colors by the prism of apostasy and crisis.

The five considerations detailed above apply equally to the Jewries of the east and of the west throughout the fateful year 1665–66. The differentiation of the various parts of the Diaspora was only beginning, and Jewish society was, as yet, more or less the same everywhere. Jews were reading and meditating on the same literature—from the Bible to the Lurianic writings—and the similarities of social climate and of religious and national consciousness in all parts of the Diaspora were bound to produce similar results. What these were like is described with remarkable agreement by both Jewish and non-Jewish sources. Local variations certainly existed, but they did not affect the over-all picture of the movement. There were extremists and moderates, enthusiasts who proudly challenged the gentiles and believers who repressed the gladness of the kingdom in their hearts. But such differences were matters of personal temperament and had little significance for the public physiognomy of the movement, which was characterized by participation of the masses, intense penitential ardor and excessive mortifications accompanied by public outbursts and demonstrations of rejoicing, cessation of normal business and commerce, feverish correspondence between the Jewish communities and dissemination of imaginary news, and not infrequently also the sale of property and similar concrete preparations for departure to the Holy Land.

The absence of organized missionary activity is surprising. The glad tidings were spread almost exclusively by letter and by rumor. Several rabbis from Palestine, and subsequently from other countries too, joined Sabbatai Ṣevi and accompanied him on his travels, but there was no traffic in the opposite direction, from Sabbatai Ṣevi to the Jewish communities. Contrary to the exaggerated reports by later writers, there is no evidence of apostles going forth to announce the good news to the dispersion of Israel. Two propagandists are said to have been "sent forth" from Palestine, but it is doubtful whether they were really charged with a formal mission: Mattathias Bloch Ashkenazi went to Egypt, where he remained until after the apostasy in 1666, and Sabbatai Raphael (see below, pp. 782 ff.) traveled—apparently even earlier—to Italy. No other missionaries to any other country are known, and already Sasportas wondered why the rabbis of Palestine, who were wont to send emissaries abroad at short intervals to collect alms and for other purposes, were so remiss in announcing the good news.[6] According to one report, Sabbatai intended, during his residence in Constantinople, to send messengers proclaiming his glory to all countries, but nothing came of it,[7] and there is no record in the more reliable sources of the dispatch of ambassadors

6. Sasportas, pp. 23, 84.
7. Coenen, p. 53.

by the messiah. As a matter of fact, there was no need of messengers by that time. In the spring and summer of 1666, visitors were thronging the "Tower of Strength" in order to behold the face of the messiah, and they returned home with wonderful accounts of what their eyes had seen. They were the real, albeit unofficial, missionaries of the messianic faith.

Another curious feature is the apparent contradiction—due, perhaps, to individual differences in temperament—between the publicity of the messianic proclamations, on the one hand, and the exhortations to secrecy, lest the gentiles wreak vengeance on Israel, on the other. Sabbatai himself acted his part in the public limelight, in Gaza, Aleppo, and Smyrna; elsewhere too the Sabbatians made no secret of their joy and their expectations. On the other hand, many communities enjoined strict silence, and some even threatened publicity-mongers with excommunication. It is not difficult to understand the prudent discretion of the elders of the communities who, pending definite confirmation of the news, feared anti-Jewish riots and wished to conceal the messianic agitation from their gentile neighbors; but even many Sabbatian writers adopted an esoteric and allusive style.[8] Definite reports of the appearance of a prophet in Gaza and of the "anointing" of the messiah began to arrive in Europe in October–November, 1665; before that date only fantastic rumors about the lost tribes had circulated (see above, pp. 332 ff.). The news generally traveled via Italy (Venice and Leghorn in particular) to Germany, Holland, England, and the rest of the continent. To Poland there was an additional route from Turkey via the Balkans. Information reaching what today are Bulgaria and Yugoslavia was immediately relayed further north. Certain cities were centers for the transmission of news, for example, Vienna and, especially, Amsterdam. Italy and Holland, on the one hand, and Turkey, on the other, were connected not only by close commercial ties, but also by many family relations. In fact, it was to the family relations that the intense trade was largely due. Those expelled from Spain, and the descendants of escaping marranos in particular, were dispersed in many countries. Even members of the same family would be scattered, some settling in Holland or Hamburg, others in Italy or Turkey. Practically every Sephardic family in Europe had relatives in Smyrna or Salonika, who would keep them

8. Sasportas (p. 141), drew attention to this contradiction.

posted of the great awakening. Ashkenazic Jews too had family relations, albeit to a much lesser extent, in the Orient and especially in the Holy Land. The spate of news arriving from diverse quarters at almost the same time added to the excitement. Every mail brought dozens of letters, and every recipient of such a letter could report a detail that was not in the news received by his neighbor. The extant collections of letters faithfully reflect the composite nature of this mosaic of news. Three lines from a letter received from Venice, five from a letter from Leghorn, some brief reports passed on from one or more of the small cities in Italy, and a few lines from a letter from Vienna or Paris would be combined into one letter and dispatched from Amsterdam to London, Poland, or Germany. Most of these letters are lost, but a sufficient number have survived to give us an idea of what happened.

To the Jewish sources of information were soon added Christian news reports. These were, of course, dependent on Jewish sources for their news from the East, but added to them exaggerations and distortions of their own. The impression which the movement made on the gentiles in its turn impressed the Jews, who soon took to quoting from the Christian sources. The pamphlets that began to appear in some Christian countries were avidly read by the Jews, and forwarded to their brethren elsewhere. A Jew writing in Casale in Italy would quote from pamphlets printed in Amsterdam or London. Aaron Sarphati in Amsterdam would hasten to inform his brother-in-law in Hamburg of the reports current among the Christians;[9] and another believer—probably the rabbi of the Sephardic congregation in Hamburg—preached a sermon on Isaiah 27:13 ("And it shall come to pass in that day, that the great trumpet shall be blown; . . . "), in which he explained that the "great trumpet" referred to the many pamphlets and news letters "than which there is no greater trumpet," not a bad description of the power of the press.[10] Newspapers in the modern sense of the word did not yet exist at the time, and *Zeitung* in contemporary usage signified a broadsheet or a small pamphlet, generally of about six to eight pages, reporting (that is, discussing) topical subjects. The pamphlets with which we are concerned here were written either by men who (like Serrarius) were genuinely interested in the movement and who faithfully reproduced the information

9. Sasportas, p. 29.
10. *Ibid.*, p. 47.

which they had obtained, or by newsmongers who did not hesitate to add details or even to contribute whole stories from their imagination. Sasportas[11] bitterly complained about the Christian writers who exaggerated the reports and then printed and spread them in order to mislead the Jews and make them a laughingstock. A German theologian angrily reports that many Christians were not only "reading the pamphlets to the Jews, adding to them inventions of their own so as to add sin to iniquity," but actually justified their deceit by arguing that it was a meritorious deed to trick the Jews, in accordance with the rule of "an eye for an eye."[12] The Christian news letters no doubt played their part, albeit a minor one, in spreading the movement. Christian reactions were mixed. For some Christians the movement was an object of derision and further proof of the blindness with which this stiff-necked people was smitten. Others were alarmed and irritated by the signs of confidence and pride displayed by the despised Jews, and wondered where all this would lead to. In any event, the penitential enthusiasm could not fail to make a profound impression everywhere, and some Protestant sectarians hastened to point to the Jews as edifying contrasts to the Christians, who were sunk in worldly pleasures and pursuits. Others, again, were prepared to regard Sabbatai as a "glorious instrument of the Lord," and entertained no doubts as to the imminent redemption of Israel.[13]

It is necessary to distinguish between accounts that were written after the event and early testimonies that had not yet undergone editorial treatment of one kind or another. We must also distinguish between inside, that is, Sabbatian, and outside reporting. The later accounts tended to exaggerate the unanimity of the messianic enthusiasm, and to obscure the bitter quarrels and differences of opinion between believers and infidels. The Christian pamphlets were mostly unaware of the existence of infidels, since their knowledge of happenings in the Jewish world did not go beyond the more visible manifestations and public expressions of fervent belief. Jewish sources, too, occasionally failed to mention the existence of infidels, in order

11. In letters written in the period from autumn, 1665, through winter, 1666; see pp. 17, 47, 81.

12. Buchenroeder, *Eilende Messias Juden-Post,* at the beginning of ch. 7.

13. Statement made by a German or a Dutch merchant in July, 1666, quoted by Josef Kastein, p. 289. I have so far not been able to trace Kastein's source.

to preserve the simplified and idealized image of the early movement free from the taint of discord and contention. The early sources bear witness to facts which later popular legend, as represented by the "history" of Leyb b. Ozer, for example, preferred to pass over in silence. The legend was developed to a large degree by people who had themselves been believers until Sabbatai's apostasy. Though they rejected the messiah, they did not repudiate the awakening in which they had taken part and which still appeared to them transfigured in a glorious light of piety and holiness. Hence also the evident sympathy and even enthusiasm with which, many years later, the popular accounts described the awakening. Perhaps it was also easier to do so at a distance, for much of what is told in the later accounts is true and borne out by the evidence; they merely had to forget the negative and unpleasant parts of the story. Folk memory tends to simplify history by selective telling, rather than to complicate it by analysis. For the rabbis the messianic outburst was a shameful disaster which they wished to hush up; on the folk level it remained one of the greatest and noblest awakenings which Israel had ever experienced in its exile, the tragic ending notwithstanding.

Two texts, one from a Sephardic source, the other Ashkenazic, may illustrate this point. In 1673, seven years after the events, R. Jacob b. Boton in Salonika composed a responsum regarding the legality of certain witnesses to a marriage contract. The men concerned had been known as transgressors and were, therefore, inadmissible as witnesses according to rabbinic law. The decision hinged on the question whether or not the witnesses had, at some time, formally repented and thus ceased to be "sinners." At this point the author's sober legal argument becomes a passionate outburst:

Even if I were sure that these witnesses were utter sinners who have transgressed all the prohibitions of the Law and disqualified themselves as witnesses, yet [I would argue that] if this happened before the great repentance in the year 426 [The printed text reads 427, obviously a misprint.] then undoubtedly all their sins have been forgiven as a consequence of that great repentance, the like of which has never been seen before, and they have regained their status quo ante. For at that time everyone repented of his evil ways and returned [unto God] with his whole heart, confessing their sins and undergoing flagellation for every trespass and practicing innumerable fasts and mortifications. . . . And this repentance took place . . . wherever Jews dwelt. . . . O that there were such an heart in them forever! But if you hold against us the sins which we committed [at the height of the penitential movement] in connection with the eating and drinking on the fast of the Ninth of Ab, then you have practically disqualified all Jews, . . . because the whole people without exception erred in this matter. . . . But God is righteous and merciful. . . . "the good Lord pardon every one" (II Chron. 30:18) and we have nothing to do with the secrets of God. If, however, these witnesses committed the sins as a result of which they are disqualified, *after* the great repentance, then they cannot be reinstated until their repentance is confirmed by witnesses in court.[14]

The responsum was addressed to R. Ḥayyim Benveniste who, as we know, had supported Sabbatai Ṣevi in Smyrna. The fact that such a passionate argument occurs in a legal document adds to its significance. The witnesses can be considered admissible if their sins were committed before 1666, since every Jew in Turkey could be presumed to have taken part in the great penitential awakening of that year. There is deep emotion in the author's words as he remembers those days, and he seems to express a widely held opinion when he suggests that the events were, at least in part, of a supernatural character and that "we have nothing to do with the secrets of God." The awakening had been holy and pure, and the people's belief in the messianic tidings and their obedience to the abolition of the fast of the Ninth of Ab should not be held against them.

Leyb b. Ozer's description of the penitential awakening in Europe is based on information which he had gathered from travelers and visitors:

The prophet Nathan prophesied, and Sabbatai Ṣevi preached that whoever did not mend his ways would not behold the comforting of Zion and Jerusalem, and that they would be to shame and to everlasting contempt. And there was a repentance, the like of which has never been since the world was created and unto this day . . . in Turkey, and from there it spread to all the dispersions of Israel . . . and it is impossible to describe it and it will not be believed, though it be told.

First of all, there were many people everywhere who fasted the

14. ᶜ*Eduth be-Yaᶜaqob* (Salonika, 1720), fol. 42a.

whole week and immersed themselves every day. Those who could not do this fasted two or three consecutive days [every week], and women and children fasted at least every Monday and Thursday. They would arise at midnight and recite the Midnight Devotions, and at dawn would immerse themselves, reciting the great confession of sins while standing in the ritual bath, which was so crowded that it was almost impossible to enter there. They devoted the whole day to good works, and recited the daily devotions as arranged at that time. At night men would lie down naked in the snow, and roll in it for half an hour or at least a quarter of an hour. Then they would take thorns and nettles and scourge themselves until their bodies were covered with blisters, and every day they would take a scourging with a hard lash. . . . They gave more alms than can be told, and nobody would touch a coin that had a cross on it such as the German thaler. . . . A knife or cup with a cross on it was broken to pieces or made anew. They sold their houses and property for almost nothing, for they firmly believed that they would soon go to Palestine and therefore sold everything at half price, so as to leave nothing behind.

There were wealthy youths who married poor orphan girls without dowry for the sake of Heaven. No young man wanted to remain a bachelor, and each one married the first and best woman he could find, for the rabbis quoted the Talmud (B. Yebamoth 63): "the son of David will not come before the souls in the *guf* [the celestial storehouse of souls] are disposed of." . . . There was no distinction between rich and poor, . . . and nobody was really poor because people wanted nothing but their immediate needs, and those who had nothing received their wants from those who had. Everyone desired to take a scholar into his house in order to study the Law with him day and night, and the rich would offer them lodging in their houses and provide for them. In brief, there was not one wicked Jew or sinner at the time, since everybody repented in his heart, and no such repentance has ever been seen or heard of before. They neglected all other business and spent their time in the synagogues in deep meditation and repentance. Some caused boiling wax to drip down their naked bodies for an hour or more, others again wrapped their naked flesh in nettles and put on heavy clothes in order to increase the mortification of the flesh. In larger communities the supply of nettles from the neighborhood was insufficient, and they had to be obtained from afar and at great cost. . . .

No Jew attended to business. The shops were closed, and the artisans plied penance and fasts instead of their trade. People tried to sell their goods and belongings at any price they could get, and kept themselves in readiness for the moment when the messiah and the prophet Elijah would appear and announce the end, so as to be able to proceed [to the Holy Land] without delay. No Jew was allowed—under threat of excommunication—to buy from his fellow Jew. This repentance took place in the year 5426 of the Creation of the world. And let no one say that I have exaggerated in my description, for you should know that what I have written is not even a half of what has been reported, by not one but by hundreds of trustworthy witnesses who have told most wondrous things of the repentance that was wrought in our parts [that is, Germany, Holland, etc.]. But in Turkey they did ten times more, because there they were especially exhorted to repent and they beheld miracles with their own eyes, whereas in these countries we received this [that is, messianic tidings] by letters only.[15]

The two quotations faithfully reflect the image of the great awakening as it lived in the memory of the people. The image is true enough as far as it goes, and the details recorded did, in fact, occur in hundreds and thousands of cases. However, the accounts omit the violent conflict between the two camps, and the bitter struggles between what was, in many communities, a vast majority, on the one hand, and a small but obstinate minority, on the other. There is undoubtedly an apologetic intention in this silence regarding the anti-Sabbatians: if all, without exception, erred, then nobody was wrong and nobody could be accused. There may have been instances, particularly in smaller communities and villages, where the movement embraced the whole Jewish population. But in the great centers the situation was more complex, and the documents bear eloquent witness to the strife of the parties.

Sasportas, the spokesman of the handful of stubborn "infidels," admits that the believers were in the majority and the infidels a tiny minority.[16] As regards the relative strength of the parties, Sasportas is very guarded in his language and only three years later, in 1669, he expressed himself more clearly, but by then he may have been exaggerating in the opposite direction. In his later letters he admits that the "rabble" had the upper hand, and that in every community

15. MS. Shazar, fols. 23–24.
16. Sasportas, p. 123.

there had been some rabbis who supported the movement and others who kept quiet "for fear of the rabble." Some rabbis, in his words, "courageously supported me. . . . Also some of the more intelligent lay people everywhere arose to help us at great risk to their lives, but the great mass considered them as infidels." In a letter to R. Jacob Saᶜadun in Morocco, Sasportas mentions that "everywhere opinions were divided, and even among the unlettered crowd some believed in him and others held it to be sheer folly."[17] Even stronger language is used—again several years after the event—in a responsum by R. Jacob b. Joseph Lindos of Egypt regarding the sale of a house in Djerba (Tunisia) at the height of the messianic agitation. The author asserts at the end of the responsum that "the [Sabbatian] beliefs, in spite of their publicity, were not shared by all except for simpletons and fools . . . or crooks who traveled from one city to another in order to cheat and rob people. But to those whose hearts had been touched by God [that is, the more intelligent] it was obvious that everything was vanity and lies, vanity and the work of errors."[18] However, this version of the general reaction is exceptional and seems to reflect the writer's strong feelings on the subject rather than the actual facts. The responsa of Lindos' colleagues concerning the same case suggest the contrary. R. Nathan b. Zeraḥya Guta, who was in Egypt at the time, wrote that it was a well-known fact "that the majority firmly believed in this matter . . . and the minority, though qualitatively superior, could not turn the public away from this opinion, since [thereby] they would have exposed themselves to great danger from our fellow Jews—and I speak from experience."[19] This was also the opinion of his colleague R. Moses Saragossi.

17. *Ibid.*, pp. 1, 355. The wording of the letters written in 1666 is more cautious. We know that Sasportas subsequently "edited" and rephrased his earlier utterances so as to make them appear more definite and aggressive; see below, pp. 568–69, 576.

18. Quoted from *Shebaḥ Neᶜurim* by Samuel b. Ḥabib of Cairo (MS. Oxford 845). Saragossi's responsum has been dated 1674 (see *Zion*, VII [1942], 179), but the responsa of Isaac de Boton of Jerusalem and Nathan Guta of Cairo suggest that the case of the Djerba property was discussed by the rabbinic authorities in 1667–68. See also M. Benayahu, *Sinai*, XLVI (1958–59), 33–53 (and particularly pp. 34–36), who has published all the relevant correspondence.

19. The last phrase shows that Guta was in Egypt at the time and not in Jerusalem where the infidels were in the majority (at least during the first months of the movement).

These general conclusions are confirmed by the concrete details that are known from the various countries in which the movement flourished. One question, however, remains. The years following the great awakening offer no evidence at all of a previous sale of property on a large scale. If the many reports to the effect that the Jews had disposed wholesale of their belongings were true, then their economic situation afterward ought to have been desperate. There is no indication that this was, in fact, the case. The known instances of the sale of property, and of litigation as a result of such sales, are not necessarily characteristic of the behavior of the public in general. The number of such transactions was probably greatly exaggerated in retrospect. Many believers presumably prepared to wind up their affairs, but postponed definitive action until they would receive the decisive sign.[20] No sign came and everything returned to normal. But the fact that the Jews could stand the severe financial strain resulting from the suspension of all business and from the raising of sufficient funds to maintain the masses of penitents and the poor throws an unexpected light on their economic strength. They emerged from the crisis severely damaged,[21] no doubt; but even if their economic situation had deteriorated in consequence of the events, it was not ruined.

II ITALY

The reports arriving first from Egypt, then from Smyrna and the Balkans, caused profound agitation in Italy. The kind of news that reached Italy is illustrated by the summary made by Emanuel Frances[22] as well as by copies of, and quotations from, letters and

20. This also seems to be the implication of Bossuet's account of the Sabbatian movement (*Discours sur l'Histoire Universelle,* pt. II, ch. 22): "Il n'y a point d'imposture si grossiere qui ne les séduise. De nos jours, un imposteur s'est dit le Christ en Orient: tous le Juifs commençoient a s'attrouper autour de luy; nous les avon veûs en Italie, en Hollande, en Allemagne et à Mets, *se préparer à tout vendre* et à tout quitter pour le suivre. Ils s'imaginoient déjà qu'ils alloient devenir les maistres du monde, quand ils apprirent que leur Christ s'estoit fait Turc et avoit abandonné la loy de Moïse."

21. Cf. R. Moses Zacuto's letter written in the summer of 1668 (*Zion,* XIII [1948], 56) and the detailed evidence adduced in the course of this chapter.

22. Published by Haberman, *Qobeṣ ʿal Yad,* III, New Series (1940), under the title "Selections from Letters concerning the Sabbatian Movement." In a MS. in the British Museum (Margolliouth 1077), they are entitled "Several letters in Praise of Sabbatai and Nathan of Gaza."

news reports that have been preserved. Copies of the news reports from the East circulated in all congregations, and it was not long before the first reactions manifested themselves. The movement did not begin at the bottom, among the lower classes, for we find a goodly number of rabbis and lay leaders heading the revival. In the greater communities, such as Leghorn, Venice, Florence, Ancona, Mantua, and Casale, the majority of the scholars were believers, and as the most prominent feature of the messianic tidings was the call to repentance, even the more cautious and hesitant rabbis—and there were many of them, particularly in Venice—could not but support a movement that promised a religious revival and a reformation of morals. Nathan's manuals of devotions, of which two editions appeared in Mantua,[23] were appointed to be used in the synagogues. The aloofness of the printing houses in Venice is surprising.[24] They may have refrained so as not to irritate the government of the republic, or—more probably—because the "Scholars of the Great Academy," who were also the rabbinic licensing authority for the printing of Jewish books, could not agree on the matter.

Italian Jewry had been profoundly affected by the kabbalistic movement of the preceding century. Italy had been the first European country to be reached by the kabbalistic propaganda emanating from Safed in the sixteenth century, and in many communities brotherhoods were formed for the purpose of practicing special ascetic and liturgical devotions. These brotherhoods played an important role in the life of the Jewish communities in the period preceding the messianic stir, and their copious liturgical literature bears witness to the profound influence of the new kabbalah.[25] The messianic tidings appeared as a continuation of the original, more pietistic revival. The leading exponents of Palestinian kabbalism, R. Benjamin ha-Levi of Safed and Jerusalem, and R. Nathan Shapira of Jerusalem, had spent much

23. The first in April, 1666 (a single copy in the library of G. Scholem), and the other in October, 1666, i.e., after Sabbatai's apostasy, but before the news had reached Italy.

24. Schulwass, *Rome and Jerusalem* (Hebrew), (1944), p. 119, who states that the *tiqqun* was printed in Venice, was misled by false bibliographical references to a (nonexistent) *Tiqqun Shabbethay Ṣevi.* Such a title is unthinkable in Hebrew, and the original reference was obviously to one of the editions containing a picture of Sabbatai, as Wolf, *Bibl. Hebr.*, III, p. 1225, supposed.

25. Cf. Schulwass, *op. cit.*, pp. 110–14.

time in Italy. The former did not return to Palestine until 1660–63, and the latter died in Reggio in the spring of 1664,[26] about two years before the messianic awakening. Both had exerted great influence, through their many friends and disciples, on the religious life of the more kabbalistically minded. R. Benjamin ha-Levi supported the movement from Palestine, and wrote to his Mantuan friends, members of the patrician Norsa and Sullam families, about "our redemption by our king Sabbatai Ṣevi."[27] R. Nathan Shapira had preached before his death a series of what may perhaps be described as "proto-Sabbatian" sermons, since Mortara, who had examined a manuscript of these homilies, concluded from them that their author "shared the fantastic illusions of some of his contemporaries regarding the imminent advent of redemption."[28]

In Siena newborn children were being given the name Sabbatai as early as December, 1665, "for in all the provinces of Israel reports were heard regarding imminent redemption by the rabbi Sabbatai Ṣevi."[29] A *mohel* (circumciser) in some northern Italian community has left a copybook containing a list of the children he introduced into the Covenant of Abraham. He began it "in the first year of the

26. The date of his death has been a matter of some doubt; cf. the detailed discussion in *SS*, I, pp. 392–93, n. 4. Meanwhile the exact date has been established by a short poem—which is none other than Nathan Shapira's epitaph—published by M. Benayahu in *Sinai,* XXXV (1954), 58.

27. Baruch of Arezzo (Freimann, p. 59).

28. Mortara, *Mazkereth Ḥakhmey ʾItalyah,* (1886), p. 63, on Nathan Shapira's twenty-four homilies. Similar homilies can also be found in MS. Brit. Mus., Margoliouth 847–49.

29. From the notes of a circumciser, quoted by D. Kaufmann, *RÉJ,* XXXIV (1897), 305. The same circumciser also mentions that in April, 1666, Isaac Nunez Lombroso, a notable from one of the Sephardic families which settled in Reggio, had named his son Sabbatai. Schulwass (*op. cit.,* p. 117) apparently refers to this case, but wrongly connects it with Siena. Schulwass' book is the first attempt to assemble all the information from Italy; some of his quotations, however, are irrelevant as they do not refer to the Sabbatian movement at all, while many more testimonies should be added. Unfortunately, Schulwass repeats the erroneous, or at any rate unproved, view that Moses Pinheiro taught Sabbatian doctrines in Leghorn even before 1665 (*op. cit.,* p. 116), and also maintains that Abraham Cardozo was in contact with Pinheiro as early as 1650. The latter assertion is based on a misunderstanding of the sources. Cardozo's discussions with Pinheiro took place in 1675, after his return to Leghorn; it was then that Pinheiro told Cardozo what Sabbatai had taught his friends and disciples as far back as 1650.

coming of our messiah."[30] In the smaller communities all sorts of rumors were rife about the appearance of strange and wondrous men. From the very beginning opinions were divided as to the measure of publicity that should be allowed these reports. Some believers proclaimed the good news without any inhibitions, but in many instances the rabbis and elders prohibited open propaganda, on pain of excommunication, lest "the Philistines" (that is, the gentiles) wreak vengeance upon Israel, which they might easily do until the fullness of redemption had become manifest. Hence many believers refrained from mentioning Sabbatai's name in writing, or used initials and similar devices. Much valuable information can be gleaned from a notebook that has fortunately been preserved.[31] The writer, a Jew living near Venice, was traveling in northern Italy toward the end of 1665 and during the first months of 1666. He found the Jewish congregations in a state of messianic excitement, which he evidently shared, and he apparently reported home everything he saw and learned on his travels. He recorded rumors which he had heard, and copied documents which he had occasion to see; for example, a copy of Nathan's letter to the *chelebi* Raphael Joseph. (The latter had forwarded the text of the letter to his brother Solomon Joseph in Leghorn, whence copies were sent to the other Italian communities). His firsthand account of his impressions and experiences, in addition to confirming information provided by other sources, also constitutes an important primary source. Written in a mixture of Hebrew and Italian, and in a fresh and lively style, the notebook reflects the spontaneousness and immediacy of its composition. It contains the earliest extant description of the movement in Venice and Leghorn, and provides a particuiary vivid and detailed account of the atmosphere in Casale, the largest Jewish congregation in Piedmont. The diarist faithfully chronicles the rumors, which had arrived from England even before the similar reports from the Orient, concerning the lost tribes. The army of the Jews was preparing an onslaught on the Ashkenazim (the Russians, Poles, Germans?), and the Temple was being miracu-

30. Cf. Harry Rabinowicz, *The Jewish Library Treasures of England and America* (1962), p. 79. The copybook is in the library of the Jewish Theological Seminary, New York.

31. MS. in the library of the Jewish Theological Seminary, New York. I have published the unknown parts of the notebook in *Zion,* X (1945), 55–66. Quotations are from this article, unless stated otherwise.

lously rebuilt by invisible hands. The writer expected that "soon we shall leave for the Holy Land in rejoicing and in good health."

Even the Christians, we are told, had taken notice of the messianic agitation, and the Venetian authorities had demanded explanations of the Jewish elders. When these feigned total ignorance, the magistrates told them that they knew full well that the Jews had received news which they wished to conceal. The penitential awakening had already begun in Venice: "the sinners, and the many illiterates who could not even read the *Shema*ᶜ prayer . . . and the bastards are diligently studying with three rabbis who teach them without payment." Christians were said to have converted to Judaism: according to reports from Ferrara, the Inquisition had arrested four Frenchmen who had declared that the only true religion was that of Moses. A report from Rome said that "a chief of the Church [a cardinal?] had told the Jews, 'Rejoice, for your messiah has come.' " Other sources too report excitement in ecclesiastical circles in Rome. Serrarius had heard that "in Rome it was generally concluded that now the Antichrist was to come forth,"[32] while Coenen mentions a rumor to the effect that the Roman Catholic monks in Jerusalem had notified the pope of Sabbatai's appearance and that the pope had sent envoys to investigate the matter.[33] At the end of January, 1666, rumors were current in Leghorn telling of two Jesuits who had confirmed the tidings from abroad and strengthened the faith of the Jews.

On February 16, 1666, the traveler wrote to his family from Casale:[34]

Praise be to God that I can announce to you glad tidings which arrived here yesterday. . . . There is no end to the confirmations of that which [is reported to have] happened, and they all write that time is too scarce to describe all the miracles and signs that occur all the time. I pray

32. Wilenski, p. 172. Possibly Serrarius' pamphlet is the source of the report quoted by Schudt, *Jüdische Denckwürdigkeiten,* IV, p. 238, from a Dutch writer, W. Goerze, to the effect that Sabbatai's appearance had caused a great trembling even in the Vatican. The news letter from Flanders too (Aeshcoly, p. 221) says: "Rome tremble, & les Cardinaux, & tous les Évêques."

33. Coenen, p. 132. Coenen may have heard the rumor from Jews in Smyrna, or read it in one of the pamphlets he had received from Europe. Leyb b. Ozer (Emden, p. 14) inflated the report to a full-blown Sabbatian legend, and Schulwass (p. 118) mistook Leyb's story for a fact.

34. The Italian text of the letter in *Zion,* X (1945), 61–66.

you to announce to the whole holy congregation that they should settle all their affairs as soon as possible. Let this hint suffice that they should cease from all trade, since there is hope that our redemption may come sooner than we expected. Four hundred families are waiting in Frankfurt, all ready for the journey, and many others of the same neighborhood have already left. I never wished to write untruths; but as I behold that from all sides they confirm the miracle, I must tell you about it. All this [news] arrived last night and caused such a great rejoicing that many wept for excess of joy. Immediately all copies of the roles of the comedy which they had intended to perform were torn up, since this is not a time for vanities but for the study of the Law and for good works. New devotions will be introduced today, and I shall send you a copy of it for the Sabbath. Other reports are expected; I hope that they will be comforting and I shall notify you of them. I regret that I have to leave here, because I believe that great things will happen in this congregation. Everyone must seek the welfare of his fellow man if we want to share in this blessedness. Nobody here enters any claims against anyone, but the most important thing is to restore all dishonest gain.

The picture is vivid indeed. Preparations for a Purim play or carnival comedy are called off because it is not a time for vanities such as theatrical performances. In particular the exhortation to restore all ill-gotten gains seems to have made a great impression on this traveler. The same admonition was also made by preachers elsewhere.[35] The failure of the people to take the social morality implied in the call to repentance seriously enough was later put forward by a Sabbatian believer as a partial explanation of the debacle, "for throughout Italy not one case has been reported of a man saying to his fellow: here are a hundred *scudi* which I dishonestly took from you. . . ."[36]

The crusade against worldly amusement such as carnivals and the like began as early as the end of 1665: "Letters from Ancona report the arrival, last Thursday, in Senegaglia, of a messenger dressed like a pilgrim," who announced that he had come from Alexandria and that he was on his way from Venice to Rome. He showed the rabbis

35. Writing to Sasportas from Leghorn, R. Joseph ha-Levi complained about the difficulty which the masses had in accepting the demand to restore all dishonest gains (Sasportas, p. 170).

36. Baruch of Arezzo (Freimann, p. 62).

a case filled with letters, among which a bundle of letters wrapped in parchment and sealed with three seals, addressed to the community of Rome, and a similar bundle addressed to the community of Leghorn. He said that he was under orders to proceed to Rome first. Nobody knows whether he also delivered letters in Venice, but we assume that he did, although nothing is known of it since they forbade anyone to write or talk about it, for they are sorely afraid of the Philistines. But it is known that they are practicing penances and rules, the like of which would not have been believed before. Among their new rules are prohibitions to recite the blessing over the cup at the beginning and the end of the Sabbath over any but ritually permitted wine, and to go to the *comedie* and *maschiere* and the like. They also took upon themselves to live chastely, and in that city [Venice?] these are great things. The messenger also said, "Blessed are you Jews . . . , the Jews in Jerusalem have made a Jewish king whose name, as is well known, is Rabbi X [!]." When they asked him whether he needed anything, provisions or money, for his journey, . . . he replied that he had everything, and he departed. Hence there is great rejoicing in this city [Ancona?] and they expect good news from Rome.

The abstention of the Italian Jews from worldly amusements such as theaters and masks was soon imitated by the Jews of Amsterdam who likewise "refrained not only from actual sins but also from all vanities."[37] Reciprocal influence is in evidence everywhere. News reports from Amsterdam were immediately spread in Italy and, conversely, the Dutch Jews would invoke the authority of rumors and devotional practices coming from Italy. Early in 1666 (Christian?) merchants arriving in Leghorn from Amsterdam publicly sold books and pamphlets "relating all these things and announcing our redemption"—surely an interesting testimony regarding the dissemination of this kind of Christian literature. The same entry in the notebook also mentions a report that a hundred and twenty-five boats had sailed from Holland, carrying Jews to the Holy Land. The fortuitousness of the diarist's account suggests that the atmosphere in other Italian communities must have been very similar.

The sources are remarkably silent about Rome, which is mentioned only in passing. Reports by Christian correspondents must

37. The Polish correspondent writing from Amsterdam concerning the Jews of Italy (Balaban, p. 41).

surely have reached this center of Christendom; those which happen to have survived abound in the most fantastic exaggerations. A Roman monk, informing a friend of the recent "assembly of the Jews to their new messiah" writes that he had received letters from Jerusalem which described not only the exuberant joy of the Jews but also the appearance of the messiah. The latter was a comely youth whose parents were living in Jerusalem. At the age of twelve he was anointed by the prophet Nathan, and now he had already conquered the Holy Land, where all the tribes would assemble.[38] These and similar reports from Rome indicate that at the end of 1665 no genuine information had reached Christian circles there, and no value at all should therefore be attached to the statements of Christian correspondents in Holland to the effect that fear and trembling had seized the Church in Rome. Nevertheless, stories of this kind circulated also among Jews. Letters from Rome were received in Casale, apprising the Jews that the sultan had promised to rebuild the Temple. One rabbi and several members of the congregation had been arrested in Rome "because of the impudence which they displayed as a result of this news." This significant remark may well contain an explanation of the curious silence of the Roman Jews. It was obviously dangerous to exhibit messianic assurance and "insolence" in the capital of Catholic Christendom. No doubt the day of reckoning was drawing nigh, but their very special situation imposed very special responsibilities on the leaders of Roman Jewry. There seems to have been some unpleasantness resulting in arrests, but it is only toward the end of the summer

38. The substance of the letter is contained in a MS. in the Museum Czartoryskich in Cracow (MS. 1656, fol. 490). Prof. Sofia Amaizanóva kindly transcribed the passage for me: "Extractum ex litteris Roma religiosi cuiusdam ad amicum continentem Hebraeam aggregationem cum novo Messia qui in presenti plurimos sibi habet adhaerentes et magna perpetrat miracula. 26. Novembris 1665. Ecce litteras accipio Hierosolimae in quibus tumultus inter Hebraeos et laetitia propter adventura die expectati Messiae non sat declarari potest et describunt nempe speratum Messiam sequente stylo: Juvenis forma egregius, Sabeta nomine, XII [*sic!*] anno aetatis suae unctus a propheta Nathan quem penes redebinet [retinebatur? redivivit?]. Huius pater et mater Hierosolyman habitant. Idem sub regimine suam multam dicitur gentem habere, civitates et terram promissam sibi subiugendi causa et ibidem legum more imperandi quo omnes Hebraeorum tribus convocentur. Hunc itaque clare patet extremi iudicii diem tandem in limine esse quoniam fere ubique tumultus bella, armorum strepitus, haereses et pseudoprophetae consurgunt quae inter cetera etiam infallibile signum extremi iudicii est."

of 1666 that there is again definite news from Rome. The rabbi of Rome, R. Joshua Menaggen, seems to have been particularly hesitant. Judging from his correspondence with R. Samuel Aboab of Venice, he did not take kindly to the innovations propagated by the believers (for example, the abolition of fasts), possibly under the influence of a young adventurer from Sabbatai's circle in Jerusalem who arrived in Rome late in the summer of 1666 at the earliest, and was expelled by the elders and the rabbis "who beheld his stupidity and folly."[39] So far no information about the movement has been forthcoming from the Vatican archives.

In Leghorn, a new and rising Jewish center that in 1660 numbered about twelve hundred Jews,[40] the awakening was general, and the facts here as elsewhere belie the claim that the "rabble" rallied to the movement and then terrorized the rest of the community into compliance. The city was an important commercial center, and the Jews who had settled there and received considerable "liberties" (that is, privileges) were certainly no paupers. The poor probably formed a small minority only. A large part of the Near Eastern and Mediterranean trade, including that with North Africa and Turkey, was in the hands of the Jews. Prominent among the latter was the marrano element, and it is the marranos who everywhere appear among the leading supporters of the movement. Sasportas and other anti-Sabbatians assiduously overlooked this fact—for obvious reasons. It was, after all, so much easier to denounce the "rabble," whereas an admission of the part played by the wealthy and respected group of former marranos would have been very awkward. Yet the fact remains that in the great centers of former marranos (Salonika, Leghorn, Amsterdam, Hamburg, to name only the most important), the Sabbatian gospel was eagerly received; it evidently struck a chord in the hearts of those who had themselves, or whose parents had, been through the misery of a life of forced hypocrisy and dissimulation in Spain and Portugal. There was not a little of the desire to atone for their Christian past in the messianic enthusiasm of the marranos, for although their conscious attitude was anti-Christian, the Sabbatian

39. Sasportas (p. 271), who undoubtedly obtained his information from one of the Roman rabbis. There is no support in Sasportas' words for the contention of some modern authors that Sabbatai Raphael and Mattathias Bloch had previously been associated in Egypt.

40. See *Vessillo Israelitico,* LIX, p. 425.

awakening provided them with a Jewish and hence "legitimate" equivalent of the devout messianic fervor which they had known in their Spanish youth. Not only were merchants and laymen swept by the wave of enthusiasm, but also most of the rabbis and scholars who had themselves had no marrano past. The combination of these two social elements considerably strengthened the movement in Leghorn. Only R. Joseph ha-Levi, the preacher of the community, steadfastly persevered in his denial from beginning to end, but his warnings went unheeded. He relentlessly preached that true repentance consisted in forsaking sin and in right behavior toward one's fellow man, rather than in ascetic feats of mortification. Some of his letters to Sasportas have been preserved, and they bear eloquent witness to his perspicacity and strength of character.

R. Joseph complained of his isolation. Apart from a few enlightened members of the community—among them the poet Emanuel Frances who later moved to Venice—most rabbinic scholars as well as the members of the rabbinate had embraced the faith. R. Moses Pinheiro, Sabbatai's friend and colleague during their student days in Smyrna, had been living for many years in Leghorn, where his father had settled after 1650, possibly in connection with the disbanding of the little group around Sabbatai.[41] There he led a devout and ascetic life, and enjoyed the respect of the whole community. In spite of the absence of corroborating evidence, the possibility cannot be ruled out that Pinheiro remained in contact with Sabbatai throughout all these years. He never, it is true, indicated that he had believed in Sabbatai's messiahship during those early years.[42] With the arrival of the messianic tidings, all eyes were turned on the pious kabbalist. In Pinheiro's case, too, Nathan's prophecy was more effective than many years' companionship with Sabbatai. Pinheiro, together with Raphael Supino, a highly respected scholar and a close friend of Sasportas, became the spokesmen of the believing party. Both reproved

41. Cf. above, p. 144. In 1650 Moses Pinheiro was still a young man. According to Sasportas (p. 4) young Pinheiro and his father were followers of Sabbatai in Smyrna, and Moses was expelled from the city by the rabbis, but there is no evidence that they moved to Leghorn for that reason. Sasportas derived this information from R. Joseph ha-Levi's highly polemical letter, written after Sabbatai's apostasy, and there is no guarantee that the details are correct.

42. Sasportas merely asserts that "his master had revealed to him the messianic secret"—which is undoubtedly correct—but does not claim that Pinheiro also believed in it.

Joseph ha-Levi for his lack of faith. Pinheiro moreover could describe to his fellow citizens in glowing terms Sabbatai's personality as it appeared to him now, in messianic transfiguration. His great reputation for piety, and the fact that he was the only one to know Sabbatai personally, lent weight to his testimony. He probably also communicated with Sabbatai and the group of believers surrounding him. He may also have planned a pilgrimage to the Master, but he did not, in fact, leave Italy until summer, 1666.[43]

Letters continued to arrive in Leghorn from Alexandria, Palestine, Aleppo, and other communities in Asia, and the penitential awakening, fanned by the prophet's letters and devotional manuals, grew in strength. Writing a year later, R. Joseph ha-Levi (whose style increased in harshness after Sabbatai's apostasy had become known) described the revival in these words:

And as many went astray in these parts and commanded me to preach about the ways of penitence, I spoke out in public . . . and exhorted them to perfect repentance, [reminding them] that they were wrong in thinking that repentance was a matter of fasting and penitential devotions, when it really meant to give back what they had swallowed [that is, ill-gotten gain] and that which they had dishonestly taken from their fellow men, to do away with all hatred among themselves, to abstain from gentile wine[44] and from shaving off the side-locks [but cf. above, p. 458] and from associating with strange [that is, gentile] and pagan [that is, Christian] women and the like. . . . This displeased the great mass of the people, especially the matter of returning dishonest profits, . . . for they firmly relied on the messages they had received from many quarters, to the effect that he who believed was assured of salvation . . . and he [namely, the prophet of Gaza] had written that an unbeliever, though he had Torah and good works, could not

43. The few indications in Sasportas' account do not permit the conclusion that Pinheiro immediately set out on his voyage but, rather, the opposite. Pinheiro "went to Constantinople to see him, but on his arrival in Smyrna [on his way to the capital, or after meeting Sabbatai?] he learned that he had apostatized" (p. 4). This proves that until the summer Pinheiro remained in Italy and devoted himself to Sabbatian propaganda. The same is also suggested by Joseph ha-Levi's letter (Sasportas, p. 256).

44. Neglect of the strict rabbinic prohibition against drinking wine produced, or as much as touched, by gentiles has always been held to indicate a relaxation of the standards of rabbinic orthodoxy.

be saved. . . . *This heresy was believed by everybody as if it were the Law of Moses.* And I openly preached against it and said that lack of faith [in the messiah] did not matter, and that the main thing was Torah and good works.[45]

Joseph ha-Levi also claims to have used hard words against Pinheiro, "who adhered to this faith more than anyone else." In another letter he admits serious opposition from the believers: "And I looked and there was none to help [Isa. 63:5], . . . for not only the ignorant crowd, but the scholars too [were against me] and [it is best] not to expatiate on this." The latter remark is very characteristic in its naïvely obvious desire to misrepresent the nature of the movement by shifting the onus onto one social class and being silent about the part played by the other classes and by the rabbis in particular.[46] There was an open conflict. The believers tried to get rid of the unpopular preacher and wrote letters, complaining that in his sermons on prophecy, he obstructed the repentance and weakened the faith of believers by casting doubts on Nathan's mission.[47] His struggle was fruitless, and when R. Isaac Nahar (or Naar), a leading believer from Amsterdam and a former friend of Sasportas, arrived in Leghorn on his way to Sabbatai Ṣevi, the people asked him to stay. He immediately became a popular favorite and remained in Leghorn throughout the spring and summer of 1666, "for every believer was loved and honored by the people." He "assembled groups and preached to them," and the people wanted to appoint him as second preacher; "and they gave him a certain stipend to preach in public on occasion, and all believers followed him."[48] When Pinheiro left for the Orient, the leaders and

45. Sasportas, p. 170.

46. All quotations are from Joseph ha-Levi's second letter, written after Sabbatai's apostasy (Sasportas, p. 256).

47. Sasportas, p. 171. Ha-Levi's claim that the wealthier members of the community congratulated him on his sermon is belied by the contents of the letter.

48. Sasportas, p. 57 (where it is said that he was promised an annual stipend of 200 grossos for his preaching) and p. 256. There is so much personal animosity in Sasportas' account of Isaac Nahar's journey and the offers made to him in Leghorn, that I doubt its trustworthiness. Sasportas, who negotiated at the time with the elders of the community about his appointment to the rabbinate of Leghorn, accuses Nahar of having gone to Leghorn with the treacherous intention of obtaining the rabbinate for himself.

rabbis of the community handed him an address of homage to Sabbatai, and Raphael Supino composed a poem which was written in gilded letters and apparently inserted in the letter that Pinheiro received from the elders.[49]

Joseph ha-Levi's statement that the new faith was considered as if it were "the Law of Moses" is no polemical exaggeration, but an exact description. The expression occurs in the writings of the believers themselves. Raphael Supino[50] mentions a letter received in Leghorn at the beginning of the revival in which the rabbis of Alexandria "were saying deep things concerning this faith, like the Law of Moses." The phrase occurs not only in a letter of the rabbi of Alexandria, R. Hosea Nantawa, who wrote that "to deny this [that is, Sabbatai's messiahship] is like denying the Law of Moses and the resurrection of the dead,"[51] but in other documents too. Joseph ha-Levi mentions a letter to Leghorn "from one of the chief believers, David Yiṣḥaki," according to whom it was necessary to believe in Sabbatai no less than in the unity of God and in His Law.[52] David Yiṣḥaki, who had received this doctrine from Nantawa,[53] was an eminent scholar[54] and an old friend of Joseph ha-Levi, with whom he had studied in Salonika under R. Elijah Guartil.[55] He had gone to Jerusalem and there

49. Sasportas, p. 256. According to Joseph ha-Levi, Supino wrote several poems in honor of the messiah. In this particular poem Supino is said to have requested Sabbatai to appoint him as a commander in his army. Ha-Levi's account is that of an embittered opponent.

50. Sasportas, p. 72.

51. *Ibid.,* p. 156. The letter was written toward the end of summer, 1666. The writer pretends to quote Nathan, but the prophet of Gaza nowhere uses this extreme formulation. The identification of the unbelievers with the "mixed multitude" of course goes back to Nathan.

52. Sasportas, p. 187.

53. This is evident from the opening of the sentence (Sasportas, p. 187): "And how could you [R. Nantawa] compare the faith to the Law of Moses, as you affirmed to one of the chief believers, David Yiṣḥaki, who then wrote it to Leghorn." If Nantawa "affirmed" it orally, then it means that Yiṣḥaki was in Alexandria at the time and wrote his letter from there. However the precise dates of Yiṣḥaki's movements in 1665–66 are unknown, and it is possible that he was in Jerusalem where he received a written communication from Nantawa; see also *Zion,* VI (1941), 86.

54. Conforti, fol. 51a. Conforti knew Yiṣḥaki personally.

55. Conforti, fol. 44b. Rabbi Guartil (or Gawartil) died in 1634; hence David Yiṣḥaki was born some time around 1615.

married the daughter of the celebrated kabbalist R. Abraham Azulay of Hebron, and was greatly respected as a rabbinic judge. He was in Alexandria when the first news of the messianic awakening reached Europe, but we do not know whether he remained there for the rest of the summer, or whether he returned to Jerusalem to strengthen the group of believers there. His words on the importance of the faith are about the most extreme to be found in texts dating from the first year, but they no doubt reflect the view held by many believers.

The conflict in Leghorn continued to grow. Isaac Castro, a leading member of the community with family relations in Egypt, asked R. Hosea Nantawa for guidance on the subject. Nantawa, who had studied in Jerusalem before Sabbatai arrived there and who, as we have seen, was a fervent believer, replied with a formal epistle addressed to the whole congregation. Written toward the end of the summer, 1666, it was meant to answer the many bewildered questions that were asked after Sabbatai's imprisonment in Gallipoli. Nantawa emphasized the supreme value of the "holy faith" and exhorted his readers to embrace it wholeheartedly, explaining that the messiah's imprisonment was "necessary, so that Scripture [Song of Songs 7:6] be fulfilled, 'The king is held captive in the tresses thereof,' until the fullness of time come. His imprisonment is more apparent than real, since he is dressed in royal apparel . . . like unto a king on his throne, and the Turks and the uncircumcised in Constantinople all go to see him, and when they behold him they fall upon their faces. . . . And this matter of his imprisonment is predicted in the prophecy of Zerubbabel, where it is said that the leaders and sages of Israel will deny the messianic king and revile him and smite him, and that he will be held in prison."[56] Sasportas was wrong in accusing Nantawa of inventing nonexistent predictions.[57] Prophecies of this kind could be found in the *Book of Zerubbabel* and in several manuscript works composed before Sabbatai's time, and there was plenty in them which believers could use for their purposes even before the messiah's apostasy.[58] The epistle greatly irritated the infidel party, and several replies to it appeared after Sabbatai's apostasy, among which was a satirical poem by Emanuel Frances.[59]

56. Sasportas, p. 157.
57. *Ibid.*, p. 154.
58. See G. Scholem in *Zion*, VII (1942), 184.
59. Frances, p. 125.

Nantawa's epistle mentioned the prophetic manifestations "in Smyrna, Chios, Rhodes, Germany, Morea [meaning here Greece in general], and Morocco" as well as the activities of the prophet Mattathias Bloch in Egypt. The Jews of Leghorn needed no confirmation from afar, since a prophet had appeared much nearer home. Early in 1666 a prophet arose in Portoferraio on the island of Elba, and Raphael Supino (who seems to have visited the prophet in Elba, unless we assume the latter to have come to Leghorn) thus describes his appearance: "I beheld a young scholar . . . who uttered biblical verses while in a complete swoon and almost without heartbeat. Then he said: 'Sabbatai Ṣevi is our King and Savior, the Teacher of Righteousness, crowned with the supreme crown. And thou shalt reign over the whole earth and over the host of heaven, . . .' and he would repeat [scriptural] verses, . . . prostrating himself and alternately crying and laughing. . . . When he recovers he remembers nothing, and although people may tell lies, they cannot dissemble their heartbeat. In my opinion this [prophecy] is a possession by the souls of departed saints who have entered [the prophet's body] to proclaim the praises of the Lord."[60] Sasportas seems to have had several sources of information concerning the prophet, for he states[61] that the Elba prophet was a tailor by profession and that he still prophesied when Sabbatai Raphael passed through the cities of Italy. The latter spared no words in disparaging this particular prophet to the greater glory of Nathan of Gaza.[62]

Messianic agitation was in evidence in other communities too. Nathan's penitential exercises were introduced everywhere, and R. Isaac Lampronti (1679–1756) preserves the interesting information that "in Ferrara three people died as a result of this fast [an uninterrupted fast of six days and six nights] at the time of the pseudo-messiah Sabbatai Ṣevi. . . . Also in 1666, when reports came from the Orient to the effect that Sabbatai Ṣevi was generally acknowledged as the Messiah, son of David, two people died after fasting four days and

60. Letter of Supino to Sasportas (p. 73). The same prophet is alluded to in an English pamphlet printed in February, 1666: "Our last Letters from *Legorn* and *Smyrna* say, That at *Porto Regio* is risen a new Prophet, who tells them, on such a day the King arrived at *Constantinople;* and that such a day passeth such a thing" (*A Brief Relation of the Jews,* p. 8).

61. Sasportas, p. 93.

62. *Ibid.,* p. 271; see also below, p. 784, on Sabbatai Raphael.

four nights. In other communities several Jews died after fasting three days and three nights only."[63] Kabbalists and preachers discovered allusions by *gematria* to the imminent redemption. Psalm 68:32 could be shown to indicate the years 426–427, while R. Moses Daiena of Carmagnola proved from the Pentateuch that the beginning of the year 426 was the predestined time of salvation.[64]

Raphael Supino was surely not the only believer to compose poems in honor of the messiah, though most of these compositions were made to disappear later. Jacob Frances of Mantua wrote a long poem disguised as praise of Sabbatai, in order to be able to answer it in another poem destroying all the words of praise, one by one, and heaping scorn on the messiah.[65] Of the Sabbatian poems, we possess the full text of a hymn composed by the rabbi of Ancona, R. Mahallallel Halleluyah, for use in his congregation. R. Halleluyah was sixty-five years old at the time, and well known throughout northern Italy as a rabbinic scholar and poet. Being a kabbalist himself and having many devotees of the kabbalah in his congregation, it is not surprising that his *Book of Hymns and Prayers* (*Sefer Halleluyah*) contains many kabbalistic items. Ancona was a major Adriatic port, and as such had many excellent trade relations, and consequently also the advantage of firsthand information from the Orient.[66] The rabbi and the majority of his congregation became fervent believers, and many of them remained such—albeit in a more subdued tone—even after Sabbatai's apostasy. R. Halleluyah's hymnal contains two completely different versions of his song in praise of the

63. Lampronti's information is buried in his Talmudic encyclopaedia *Paḥad Yiṣḥaq*, s.v. *Ta^canith* ("Fast"), fol. 84b. After quoting Elijah de Vidas' remarks (*Reshith Ḥokhmah*, pt. II, ch. 6) regarding the supernatural aid granted to those who mortify themselves in a manner which, "as the physicians say, constitutes a danger to life according to the ways of nature," Lampronti adds, "but I am afraid that they commit a sin [in thus mortifying themselves] by endangering their lives" and then proceeds to give the aforementioned examples.

64. *Zion*, X (1945), 59.

65. Frances, p. 103. The poem was undoubtedly written before Sabbatai's apostasy. Many more anti-Sabbatian poems by him are now to be found in Peninah Naveh, *The Collected Poems of Jacob Frances* (Jerusalem, 1969).

66. Two members of the Community, Judah Ḥayyim and David Coutinho, received a lengthy report concerning Sabbatai Ṣevi and Nathan from the rabbis of Aleppo, Solomon Laniado and Nathan b. Mordecai, as has been described in chs. 3 and 4.

messiah. The one was written during the heyday of the movement in Italy, the other after the apostasy. The fact that R. Halleluyah had no qualms about including both versions in his hymnal indicates that the worshipers for whose use it was intended had none either. The first poem is dedicated, in the author's own handwriting, to "The King, our Messiah, Who is in the City of Smyrna . . . the great Rabbi, our Master SABBATAI ṢEVI. . . ."[67]

Also in other north Italian cities (for example, Verona, Mantua, and Turin) the movement was in the ascendant and the believers dominated the scene. If no trace of messianic enthusiasm can be found in the communal records, this is not so much due to the loss of documents as to the fact that great care was taken to keep out of the official records anything that might supply ammunition to enemies outside (for example, the gentile authorities). However, an echo of the events seems to have found its way into the record book of the community of Mantua, which has been preserved in its entirety. Every year the names of the new members of the *Waᶜad ha-Gadol*, that is, the Board of Elders, the governing body of the Jewish community of Mantua—which, at the time, was second in importance only to Venice—were entered in the book. In December, 1665 (at the time when the glad tidings were arriving from Gaza and Egypt), one of the leading kabbalists and rabbis in the community, R. Solomon Formiggini, embellished the list of names of the newly elected members with an unusual and significant rhetorical flourish: "Moreover the elders were appointed by ballot as usual, and the following were elected. . . . May the Lord our God be with them and with us; may they be vouchsafed to share in the ingathering of the dispersed of Israel, speedily in our days. Amen. [The names:] Samson Jonah, Abraham Provençale, Azriel Finzi."[68] A delegation from northern Italy left at the end of the summer of 1666 in order to pay homage to Sabbatai Ṣevi, and one of the three members was a Mantuan. For some obscure reason the

67. On different versions of the poem, see S. Bernstein, *HUCA*, VII (1930), 510–15. The later version was given in 1668 to Nathan when he visited Ancona, cf. Scholem, *H. A. Wolfson Jubilee Volume* (1965), p. 229, of the Hebrew Volume.

68. A microfilm of the original record book of the Mantua community has been made by Dr. S. Simonsohn of Tel Aviv, and I am indebted to him for tracing the reference.

delegation went to Smyrna first, and there Coenen heard from the Mantuan, whose name he gives as Jorino (?), about the reports that had reached not only the Jews but also the gentiles at Mantua from their correspondents in Turkey. A German merchant living in the Orient had written to a Mantuan nobleman that he had seen Sabbatai Ṣevi in Smyrna and that the latter was a learned man who spoke several languages.[69]

The movement was very strong in Verona, where many believers persevered in the faith even after the apostasy,[70] though there were also prominent infidels such as the well-known Dr. Isaac Cardozo, the elder brother of the Sabbatian enthusiast Abraham Cardozo in Tripoli.[71] The Jews of Turin could flatter themselves about receiving the messianic tidings from "official" sources, since the chief elder of the community, Abraham Nuñez, was kept informed by the Prince of Savoy and Piedmont of the reports and rumors forwarded to him by his diplomatic representatives.[72] The accounts given in Smyrna by members of the north Italian delegation confirm that some of the Italian rulers communicated to their Jews the contents of letters they had received from non-Jewish sources. These reports exercised a considerable influence on the Jewish public, to whom they appeared as impartial confirmation of the tidings they had received from their brethren. The spark that was kindled at the time in the heart of young Abraham Rovigo, the son of a wealthy and highly respected family in Modena, was to burn in him for a lifetime of fervent and devout faith. In Ferrara, too, Pelatiah Yaghel Monselese, of a well-known family, is attested as a fervent "fighter" (*propugnator*) for the movement.[73]

The mood of enthusiasm and expectation that was rife in many communities is well conveyed in the two letters of homage which the

69. Coenen, pp. 131–32; Leyb b. Ozer (Emden, p. 14) gives a garbled version of the same story. Coenen certainly heard this report in Smyrna from a Mantuan envoy, whose identity is not yet ascertained; perhaps Coenen misspelled the name. It is extremely unlikely that Coenen confused Mantua and Leghorn (as suggested by Carpi, p. 20, who holds the reference to be to Pinheiro).

70. Sasportas, p. 247.

71. On Cardozo, see below, pp. 645 f.

72. *Zion,* X (1945), 61, and Coenen, p. 131.

73. Bartolocci, *Bibliotheca Hebraica,* IV, p. 112. Later he became disenchanted and wanted to embrace Christianity.

congregation of Casale sent to Sabbatai Ṣevi by its two envoys, R. Samson Bacchi of Casale and R. Ḥayyim Segré of Vercelli.[74] In these letters "the poor sheep of the congregation of Casale Monferrato in Italy, who are far away from the Holy Land and upon whom the splendor of the glory of your exalted and excellent Majesty has not shone directly, but only indirectly, as through the eye of a needle, by various reports . . . which all agree that God has visited his people." Paying homage to the messiah, they affirm that since "the voice was heard for the first time and your fame went out through all the provinces, we have not transgressed the commandments of the prophet of Gaza regarding penitential exercises and liturgies, and we have been mindful to praise your exalted and holy Majesty every day." They apologize for not coming themselves, as they ought to, but "we feared for our lives from the government—and this hint will suffice," and therefore they dispatched a faithful messenger who would bring to them the messiah's commandments. The envoys also carried credentials to be presented to Nathan of Gaza "the man of God, who beholds visions of the Almighty as in a bright glass, and the light is with him, he that bringeth good tidings and announceth peace," praising God for vouchsafing "unto us a voice and speech, and giving us a true prophet whose inspiration is true, and we confess and believe that his word is faithful and his promise steadfast. . . . Wherefore we of the congregation of Casale have bestirred ourselves to dispatch, on behalf of the whole community, two envoys. May they be graciously received by His Majesty and also benefit from the light of the Holy Spirit that is in you, so that [on their return] they may instruct us in [your] exoteric as well as esoteric teaching . . . to lead us to perfection."[75]

74. Bacchi subsequently became rabbi of Casale and one of the leading kabbalists of Italy. The two were in their thirties when they were charged with the mission to Sabbatai. Bacchi died in 1691. Segré was seventy years old in 1700 and died soon afterward (according to his work *Binyan ᵓAb*, MS. Jerusalem 8°2024).

75. The three letters in Carpi, pp. 20–24, and in MS. Jerusalem 8° 1466, fols. 261b–263a. The signatures are missing from the extant copies and hence we cannot know whether they were all sent by the same authority. The letter to Sabbatai makes mention of one "faithful messenger" (in the singular), i.e., Samson Bacchi, but the letter to Nathan also refers to "his companion" Ḥayyim Segré. The letter to Nathan, which has been preserved as by a miracle, is mentioned by Coenen, pp. 127–28, in his account of his talk with the two Italian envoys.

The peaceful idyll of near unanimity in these communities contrasts strongly with the violent and tempestuous clash of opinions in Venice, one of the major cultural centers in the Jewish world at the time. The Jewish community entertained close contacts with the Levant and Palestine, and practically all travelers between East and West passed, sooner or later, through the city. Marrano refugees from the Inquisition concentrated in Venice and Leghorn, where a strong government would not brook any high-handed action on the part of the Inquisition and where crypto-Jews could openly return to the faith of their fathers. (According to canon law apostasy from Christianity was a capital offense which the Inquisition never failed to prosecute.)

All contemporary Jewish trends met, combined, or collided in the ghetto of Venice. R. Moses Zacuto, at the age of about fifty-five and at the height of his activity, propagated the kabbalah and the kind of ascetic piety that it fostered. The rabbis and scholars of the city met in the *yeshibah,* "Great Academy," the activities of which kept Talmudic knowledge alive among the Jews even though the printing of the Talmud was forbidden in Italy. The members of the Academy constituted a well-organized, "orthodox" body, and they, together with the lay leaders of the community (the "Small Committee"), conducted all public affairs. There was much rivalry and constant friction between the powerful lay leaders and the proud, and sometimes rather arrogant, rabbis, who would not yield an inch of what they considered their dignity and their rights; but both groups were united in their desire to maintain a strong and conservative aristocratic authority over the community.

The message of imminent redemption produced tremendous excitement.[76] The lower classes reacted with an enthusiasm that was shared by some of the rabbinic scholars, while others hesitated and even publicly proclaimed their unbelief. The response was by no means uniform, and Baruch of Arezzo's account, though it may well reflect the truth as seen by a believer, certainly does not tell the whole truth. "The vast majority believed that God had visited His people to give them bread, that is, the bread of salvation. The sages and lay leaders decided, in joint session, to proclaim a great repentance the like of which has never been seen before in this city,"[77] which was known for its gay life. While encouraging the penitential fervor, the leaders

76. Sasportas, p. 58.
77. Freimann, p. 51.

also spared no effort to prevent excesses or deviations from the path of tradition. The head of the Academy and chief rabbi of Venice, R. Samuel Aboab, was a shrewd and cautious scholar, and not prone to emotional transports. His warning voice endeavored to curb the heady enthusiasm of the public, and there is reason to think that he never believed any of the glad tidings—neither Sabbatai's messiahship nor the miraculous events to which all the letters, and those arriving from the East in particular, testified. But he was prudent in his utterances and never expressed a definitely negative opinion. In reply to queries he insisted that the penitential revival should not be suppressed. Undoubtedly he considered the latter a very positive aspect of the movement and possibly he, like other rabbis, hoped that the great repentance would ultimately bear fruit of blessing to Israel, even if the immediate messianic expectations were not fulfilled.

Aboab's first reaction to the news has fortunately been preserved. On receiving the first letters, the rabbi of Verona, R. Saul Merari, wrote to Aboab and asked his advice. Aboab's brief reply accords well with his attitude throughout the high tide of the movement. He agreed with his correspondent that the news might provoke anti-Jewish riots, and advised discretion and restraint. No mention should be made of these matters in public, particularly with a view to the natural excitability of most people, lest the bitter experiences of former messianic movements repeat themselves. He, like all quiet opponents of the movement, quoted the warnings of earlier authorities against messianic enthusiasm—for example, Solomon b. Adret's responsum of 1295 regarding the prophet of Avila, or Maimonides' *Epistle to Yemen* in connection with a messianic agitator there in the twelfth century. However, "a penitential revival is good at any time, but the essential service [of God] is in the individual heart, walking humbly with God, examining one's conscience, and ridding oneself of all sins that delay the messianic advent." Aboab's counsel is to keep strict silence and to follow the advice of Lamentations 3:26: "It is good that a man should both hope and quietly wait for the salvation of the Lord."[78] This attitude agrees well with the report, already mentioned, that the Venetian authorities had summoned the elders of the community (the "Small Committee") and questioned them, but that the latter

78. Aboab's letter (written at the end of 1665) was published by M. Benayahu, from MS. Montefiore 257, in ʾ*Ereṣ Yisraʾel*, IV (1956), 200 (published by the Israel Archeological Society).

feigned total ignorance, or at least claimed that they had no reliable information. Even after receiving the letters of Sasportas denouncing the movement, Aboab persisted in his attitude of prudence and public-minded diplomacy. He was well aware that Sasportas, unencumbered by actual responsibility for the moral and spiritual welfare of a community, could permit himself as strong language as he liked; he, Aboab, felt the full weight of public responsibility. He encouraged Sasportas and hinted at his own doubts and misgivings, but he refused to join in the hue and cry. He was unwilling to organize an anti-Sabbatian movement, possibly because he felt that any provocation of the high-strung masses might easily lead to a serious schism. He and his colleagues counseled prudence "until these things clarify themselves"; and in any event they felt that they ought to encourage the public "to persist in their repentance."[79]

Aboab's letter of February 18 reveals considerable diplomatic skill. He agreed that the inflammatory news letters and pamphlets should be carefully and critically examined, especially as they contained some very disconcerting details.[80] He deplored the believers' habit of speaking of the messiah as if he were no different from them, "which is not as the prophets of truth and righteousness described him." He was also perturbed by the rashness of the believers (among whom there were many prominent rabbis), but he declared himself unwilling to oppose the general penitential awakening. In fact, he and his colleagues felt that it would be positively sinful to dampen the penitential ardor of the people, "for even if the [messianic] reports will not be confirmed, yet the power of whole-hearted repentance may hasten the advent of redemption." Aboab also informed Sasportas that the rabbis of Venice had enjoined strict silence on the believers: the messianic rumors should not be discussed in public or in the presence of gentiles.[81] In the climate of feverish messianic enthusiasm this admonition was, of course, purely academic. In his correspondence with Italian colleagues, Aboab adopted the same attitude. When R. Abraham Michael Malakh of Mantua asked his opinion of the reports arriving in the spring of 1666, Aboab answered (early in the summer

79. Sasportas, p. 60.

80. *Ibid.*, p. 58. The reference probably is to the startling reports from Smyrna, which cannot have arrived in Venice much earlier than at the time of the writing of Aboab's letter.

81. *Ibid.*, pp. 59–60.

of the same year): "As regards the rumors which are loudly noised about and the reports which captivate the hearts of the people, we know no more about them than Your Reverence."[82]

From the very beginning the rabbis of Venice were puzzled by the mysterious silence of the rabbis of Palestine and of Constantinople. Venice was the center for the transfer of alms collected for the Holy Land, and most emissaries sent from there made it their first stopping place. It was not without reason that people everywhere turned to the rabbinate of Venice for reliable information, but it was in vain. The excellent overseas connections of the Venetians were as good as nonexistent during the messianic crisis. It was not as a result of reliable information—which he did not possess—but on account of his critical shrewdness and his unemotional temperament that Aboab behaved as he did. We had occasion in a previous chapter to speculate on the possible reasons of the Jerusalem rabbinate for keeping silence and thereby adding to the dangerous confusion. But whatever these reasons were, Aboab and his colleagues could not have had the slightest inkling of them. Aboab's letter to Sasportas, in which he expressed his astonishment at the silence of those who ought to know, was written shortly after the arrival in Venice of R. Lemmlein (Lemmel), an emissary of the Ashkenazic community in Jerusalem. His bag of official correspondence to the "Commissioner for Jerusalem" (the functionary responsible for the distribution of alms to the Jews in the Holy Land and in whose hands all the contacts with Palestine were concentrated) did not contain a single reference to the momentous events. The "Commissioner for Jerusalem" at the time was R. Solomon Ḥay Saraval, a prominent Venetian rabbi and descendant of an ancient family. He was the obvious person to question regarding the messianic rumors, but, as his correspondence with the rabbi of Prague amply shows, in Venice too the movement fed on legendary reports rather than on authentic information. When R. Lemmlein arrived in Venice at the end of January, 1666, the city was athirst for news, yet for two more months the movement had nothing else to go on but the imaginative news letters discussed in an earlier chapter. As it happened these were quite enough to assure the growth of the movement. Even

82. The letter was published by M. Benayahu (see reference above, n. 78), p. 197. Benayahu points out that in the same week Aboab also wrote to Benveniste in Smyrna, without as much as hinting in it at the dramatic events in which Benveniste played so central a part.

the new emissary from Jerusalem had his place in the formation of the legend. As early as February 3 news of his arrival was received in Casale; the report added that as Saraval was out of town, Lemmlein had immediately proceeded to the province of Feriul where he met Saraval, who thereupon wrote to the Academy at Venice, informing them that he would soon return to the city with glad tidings at which the whole Diaspora would rejoice.[83] However, Saraval's letter to the rabbi of Prague, written about a month later, describes the emissary from Jerusalem as exhibiting more restraint and prudence. The most sanguine letters kept arriving from Egypt, but when "I cross-examined the emissary R. Lemmel . . . [I] found that he had no definite and reliable information, though it seems that this R. Nathan is truly a holy man and a prophet who can predict the future. He told the people of Jerusalem that if Israel were worthy, then the high place of the gentiles would collapse on a Sunday, and if they did not have sufficient merits, then only a hundred and two stones would fall from the building. And indeed they witnessed how on that day the stones fell, but not the building. It is probably because of this that they and the Jews in neighboring countries have begun to practice penances, as is done now in all parts of the Jewish Diaspora." This was all the information that Lemmlein could offer to Saraval, apart from the brief note by R. Israel Isserles which he brought in his mailbag (see above, p. 360). Saraval, on his part, implored the rabbi of Prague to communicate to him without delay any reliable and definite information that he might possess, adding that he had already written to the rabbis of Jerusalem and adjured them to let him know immediately and "in detail everything concerning these reports, whether good or bad, . . . but the whole and full truth. I also asked them to reply immediately, even if it meant dispatching a special courier, as I would pay for it. I also sent a polite letter to this R. Nathan, asking many questions of him."[84]

Saraval's letters to Palestine were thus dispatched before he wrote to Prague on March 1, 1666. It is evident, therefore, that the rabbis of Venice did their best to obtain accurate information. Obviously they could not know that Jerusalem had decided on silence. Unfortunately we do not possess the text of the letters to Jerusalem, but their

83. *Zion,* X (1945), 59–60.
84. Sasportas, pp. 122–23.

counterpart, a letter addressed to the rabbinate of Constantinople and sent not by ordinary mail but by special courier[85] has been preserved. The letter, which was written in the middle of March, after receipt of reports of events in Smyrna and elsewhere but before the news of Sabbatai's arrest in Constantinople had reached Venice, well describes the clash of opinions within the community. "Everywhere you can see groups of people vociferously and noisily discussing the stream of news regarding our redemption. Some are firm believers, whereas others have doubts and reservations. It therefore seems best to us to inquire of the truth from those who know it . . . particularly as everybody is in great trouble and confusion, and the consequences may be grave. . . ." The Venetian rabbis wanted to know "whether it is a day of glad tidings . . . or whether the rumors have no foundation. . . . And even if the matter is doubtful, let us know whither your opinion inclines, for the eyes of Israel are upon you to enlighten them with the whole and full truth of the matter." The letter was signed by the heads of the Academy, R. Jacob ha-Levi, R. Moses Treves, R. Moses Zacuto, R. Joseph Valensi and R. Solomon Ḥay Saraval. The document bespeaks reasonableness and sound good sense, as well as the confusion and hesitation of the writers who may not all have held the same views on the subject, though the line of division is not clear. In any event, the principal of the Academy, R. Samuel Aboab, did not sign the letter, and from his correspondence with Sasportas we know that he did not believe in the message. Perhaps his colleagues adopted a more favorable attitude, but even the believers among the Venetian rabbis would on no account tolerate the Sabbatian innovations that were being introduced in sundry groups.

As Nathan's letters became more widely known, believers abolished the Midnight Devotions, and some kabbalists wondered whether the Lurianic meditations at prayer should be continued. The leading kabbalist in Italy, R. Moses Zacuto,[86] was formally asked by his disciple R. Samson Bacchi of Casale Monferrato to give guidance on the subject. The Jews of Casale, including their rabbi, were fervent believers, and in their enthusiasm they and the community of Mantua dispatched a joint delegation, as mentioned above (cf. p. 493). Zacuto's

85. According to the testimony of Aboab (Sasportas, p. 107) and Baruch of Arezzo (Freimann, p. 51).

86. On Moses Zacuto's origin and early years, see I. Melkman, in *Sefunoth,* IX (1964), 127–32.

reply to Bacchi[87] throws light on the writer's attitude to the movement at its height and disposes for good of earlier presentations of Zacuto either as the leading and most active believer in Venice, or—at the other extreme—as an unbeliever undefiled by any trace of Sabbatianism.[88] As a matter of fact, Zacuto did believe in the tidings and felt "that the present time was a time of grace"; yet he was moderate in his views and did not take a leading part in the movement. His reactions to Nathan's instructions to discontinue the Lurianic meditations was surprising indeed: by doubting the authenticity of the letter and declaring it to be a forgery, he repudiated its authority without rejecting the messianic message as such. He thus could "believe" while remaining indistinguishable in liturgical practice from the infidels. Zacuto's letter, written in February or March, implies dissent from the more radical faith of some of his colleagues. Regarding the Lurianic meditations he writes to Samson Bacchi: "For about two months I have carefully studied the letter alleged to have been sent by R. Nathan to a personage in Egypt. At first I was bewildered, but after considering the matter I decided—and this for many reasons—not to depart from my former custom." First of all, Nathan had not yet been generally recognized and established as a true prophet. And what guarantee was there that the letter was really his? "After all, many things have been spread in his name, for example, the date of the arrival of the lost tribes, and later it was learned that he had set no date for the event. Many more foolish things of this kind are daily noised about. . . . Wherefore I conclude: the Lurianic kabbalah is certain, whereas R. Nathan's instructions are doubtful, . . . all the more since the holy man of God, R. Sabbatai Ṣevi, who has been in Smyrna for a while and who now is in Constantinople, never, to our knowledge, mentioned this subject." Zacuto also pointed out certain contradictions in Nathan's argument. Nathan's own devotions were based on Lurianic premises, and since he himself had declared that the light of the Holy Ancient One would ultimately be revealed by Sabbatai Ṣevi, he had practically admitted that the *tiqqun* was not, as yet, completed. "I therefore continue the customary Lurianic practices, though with one difference. I no longer recite the

87. Published by G. Scholem, from MS. Jerusalem 8° 1466, in *Zion,* XII (1947), 49–51. Zacuto's letter was dispatched to other countries, too. The copy sent to Solomon Fernandes Diaz in Salonika has survived in MS. Ben-Zvi Institute 2262, pp. 61–62.

88. See the article referred to in n. 87.

lamentations, nor do I sit on the ground during the Midnight Devotion, since I consider the present time to be undoubtedly a time of grace. I have heard from reliable informants that in Constantinople they did not recite the *qinoth* and penitential prayers on the [fast of the] Tenth of Tebeth—not to speak of what happened in Smyrna where they did not fast at all—and I am most uneasy about this." In conclusion he assured R. Samson Bacchi that this was the first time he had expressed himself to anyone on the subject, "for I differ with some of the rabbis here, and cannot agree to their attitude in this matter, particularly as they are not kabbalists."

The reasonable tone and balanced argument of the letter prove Zacuto to have been anything but the "foolishly credulous kabbalist" and chief Sabbatian agitator that some historians have made him. The distinction between believers and unbelievers was not all that simple and clear-cut, and the kabbalists too, as we have seen, were divided on the issue. Moses Zacuto took no part in determining the policy of the Venetian community. He was ready to accept the reports concerning the messiah at their face value, but saw no reason for departing from traditional practice and for introducing religious "reforms." The one change which he permitted himself at the Midnight Devotions "because the time was one of grace" is sufficient proof that his cautious conservatism was not merely a disguise for unbelief. But his positive response to the messianic tidings did not affect his criticism of Nathan. Sasportas too used the method of declaring unwelcome documents to be forgeries. Zacuto, however, wanted to believe; therefore, he did not utter his doubts in public and even now confided them to his correspondent in strict secrecy. His faith was essentially that of a doubter, and it is not surprising that he forsook it immediately after Sabbatai's apostasy.[89]

A far more negative approach to the question of continuing or abolishing the Midnight Devotions is exhibited in a letter of the Palestinian emissary R. Sabbatai Bar, who seems to have been traveling in Italy at the time (spring, 1666). Replying to a query by an unidentified community, whether the Midnight Devotions should still be recited now that the good news was proclaimed and "from the uttermost part of the earth we have heard songs," young and old had prophesied, and the lost tribes were marching on Jerusalem; wherefore it was, perhaps, no longer "a time to weep and to mourn, but rather a time

89. According to R. Gabriel Pontremoli, who heard this report from "reliable informants" (*Zion,* XII [1947], p. 48).

to laugh and to dance" (cf. Eccles. 3:4). R. Sabbatai Bar advanced the standard arguments of any conservative kabbalist.[90] So far there had been rumors only and no proofs, and nothing had changed as yet. "Our mouth will be filled with laughter when the Lord shall have done great things for us" (cf. Ps. 126:2–3), but meanwhile he has not yet done so. Rabbi Bar quotes the words of Maimonides to the effect that if a king arises who compels Israel to observe the Law of the Lord, gathers them all to Jerusalem and rebuilds the Temple, then he may be presumed to be the messiah (cf. above, p. 13). In fact, Jewish tradition requires that the Messiah prove himself by appropriate signs. "So far we have seen none of the signs. Why then should we cease to mourn for the exile of the Shekhinah" or introduce any other changes?

Whereas in Venice itself there was no outburst of prophecy, we have the record of a prophetess in Corfu, which was then part of the Venetian republic and in close relation with the metropolis. A member of the Corfu gentry, Andrea Marmora, has left a description of the phenomenon which, though written in the usual anti-Jewish style and making no mention of the Sabbatian movement as such, leaves no doubt as to the true circumstances of the event which took place in 1666. There were five hundred Jewish families in Corfu and the messianic excitement gripped the major part of the community, including the rabbis and the elders. When the daughter of the merchant Ḥayyim b. Aaron, a native of Venice who had settled in Corfu, started prophesying—her pronouncements accompanied by convulsions and contortions—the rabbis were afraid of riots if the news spread to the gentiles. They had her committed to the house of her father, and "everybody was running to the house to revere her and bringing her presents." The writer depicts the episode as a conspiracy between father and daughter for material gain, an explanation refuted by his own account.[91] The Sabbatian enthusiasm continued in Corfu for several years.

90. *Be᾽er ᶜEseq* (Venice, 1674), responsum no. 29.

91. Cf. Andrea Marmora, *Della Historia di Corfu Libri otto* (Venice, 1672), and H. Mizraḥi, *Sefunoth,* III–IV (1960), 537–40. Mizraḥi draws attention to the fact that when, in 1902, the book was translated into Greek by a descendant of the author and published in Corfu, the whole story was censored and omitted, apparently out of consideration for the sensitivities of the Jewish community in Corfu.

There was thus no uniformity in the reaction of the Italian rabbis, and each one could explain the messianic reports in a way that suited his views. In spite of their counsels of prudence, the Venetian rabbis were unable to bridge the widening gulf between the two parties. The minority of "infidels" voiced their protests on every occasion, while the believers adopted the liturgical innovations suggested in the letters from abroad. No doubt they also insisted on the solemn recitation of the prayer for the king of Israel (see above, p. 424), and quarrels in the synagogue must have been frequent, particularly on the Sabbath. One unbeliever was beaten up and severely wounded on the Sabbath, and when Moses Naḥmias made the pilgrimage to Gallipoli he was instructed by the believing party to inquire whether or not it was permitted to shed the blood of unbelievers who spoke contemptuously of the messiah. Sabbatai replied that this was permitted.

The aforementioned letters and queries were all written in February or March, 1666, and several months passed before the replies to them reached their destinations. In the meantime, legends and rumors spread unchecked. Not until July was an official reply received from Constantinople.[92] The letter was composed by the believing party in the rabbinate, and Sasportas may well have been right in his assertion that some of the "signatories" never saw the document, since "at that time they forged documents and wrote lies." Some of the signatories indeed protested later against the forgery and declared that "it is an utter lie that we ever signed this letter," but their protest was made only after Sabbatai's apostasy. In fact, the protesting rabbis as much as admitted that at first they had kept quiet instead of publicly repudiating their signatures, though the Venetian rabbis had been unhappy at seeing their names on the pro-Sabbatian document.[93]

The letter, dated May 25, 1666, was written in a highly allusive and enigmatic style, which, however, was transparent enough to its recipients. The rabbis of Constantinople desired to reply to the query of their colleagues of Venice concerning a certain merchandise which R. Israel, the son of R. Abraham, of Jerusalem, at present in Con-

92. The late date is surprising. Aboab was in correspondence with Benveniste concerning both private and business matters, yet there is no reference or even query regarding the messianic events in his letters; cf. Aboab's letter to Benveniste of May, 1666, published by M. Benayahu in *Sinai,* XXXIV (1945), 201.

93. Coenen, p. 112; cf. also below, ch. 7.

stantinople, had bought and about which dissension had arisen in his family, some saying that the merchandise was worthless and the transaction sinful. The rabbis of Constantinople aver that they had carefully investigated the matter and found the merchandise to be perfect. Commercial experts had judged that the merchandise would yield great profit, "but it will be necessary to wait until the time of the Great Fair next year when, with God's help, it will be sold at a high price, under the benevolent Providence of the Cause of All Causes and the Origin of All Origins.[94] All this we carefully investigated, and the truth is with the aforementioned R. Israel, as we assured ourselves beyond peradventure. And it is incumbent upon you the priests [that is, the rabbis of Venice] to act accordingly. And God grant peace to the quarreling parties that they mind their deeds and no longer doubt this matter, for R. Israel is established before God." There follow the signatures of Ḥananiah b. Yakar, Moses ibn Shanji, Caleb b. Samuel, Moses b. Abraham Galanté, Abraham Yakhini (whose signature is preceded by several words, the initial letters of which yield the name Sabbatai Ṣevi), and Nissim b. Ḥayyim Egozi.[95]

If the report is correct that the Venetian rabbis dispatched a special envoy to Constantinople, then it is strange that he received the document without making further personal inquiries with the rabbis whose names appeared as signatories. Perhaps he merely brought a letter from Venice to Constantinople, and the reply of the rabbis there was sent by ordinary post. This may also account for the code language of the answer. In any event, the rabbis of Venice received, not the detailed information they had asked for, but the credo of fervent believers. Copies of the letter were sent by the believers to all parts of Europe, and the rabbis of Amsterdam quoted it as an official document.[96]

94. This phrase occurs in the writings of Abraham Yakhini even before 1666, e.g., in his letter regarding the patriarch Abraham, to the Dutch scholar Warner (MS. Leiden, Warner 72). Warner died before the beginning of the Sabbatian movement.

95. Sasportas, pp. 110–11; Baruch of Arezzo (Freimann, pp. 51–52). The signatures differ in the extant copies of the letter. Moses b. Abraham Galanté, known from other sources as a member of the Constantinople rabbinate, is not identical with his namesake from Jerusalem who prophesied in Aleppo (see above, p. 257).

96. Sasportas, p. 107; see also below, p. 581, on Sasportas' reaction to this letter. I have not made any use of another "document" quoted by several authors

Fortunately we also possess an account of the events that followed in Venice on the reception of the letter from Constantinople. R. Isaac b. Jacob de Levita (born ca. 1623), a grandson of R. Leone da Modena (1571–1648) and one of the less prominent but all the more sensitive rabbis in Venice, composed an autobiographical tract recounting all the slights and indignities which he considered himself to have suffered. This brief writing also contains a chapter on the messianic commotion, without, however, specifying either Sabbatai's name or the precise nature of the disturbance.[97] R. Isaac claims to have been a consistent opponent of the movement from beginning to end, but his preaching "for the last eight months" (that is, since November, 1665) went unheeded.

According to Isaac de Levita the Small Committee summoned the rabbis to a meeting, on Friday the Twenty-eighth (read Twenty-ninth) of Sivan (July 2, 1666), at which "a letter from Constantinople" was read. The meeting (to which the peeved R. Isaac was not invited "as usual") led to violent altercations and quarrels, but arrived at no decision. The elders, led by Simon Parenzo, wished to keep the letter a secret, but two or three rabbis (of the believing party?) tried to force its publication. Probably the controversy raged

(e.g. Schulwass, p. 117): the letter allegedly sent from Constantinople to R. Isaac Iseron in Venice, and signed "by seventeen rabbis, recounting the miracles and portents which Sabbatai Ṣevi performed in the sight of all Israel, so that they may believe in him that will speedily redeem Israel," was never written; it came into existence merely as a result of Leyb b. Ozer's usual confusions and misunderstandings. Coenen (p. 111) mentions the name of Isaac Iseron as one of the rabbis of Smyrna, and Leyb b. Ozer confused a letter addressed to the latter with the aforementioned letter from Constantinople to Venice. The imagination of Leyb's informants had added more signatories, and the result was the letter that appears in his memoir (Emden, p. 14); see also below, pp. 699, 712. The name Iserun is a corruption of Jessurun.

97. *Medabber Tahpukhoth*, ed. L. Blau, in *ha-Ṣopheh me-ʾEreṣ Hagar*, II–III (1912–13). The title is from Prov. 2:12. The chapter on the Sabbatian disturbances and the writer's part in them (III, pp. 84–90) bears the lachrymose heading "An apology for what occurred in Venice in the year 426, when every rabbi was deprived of his rabbinic dignity, a confusion the like of which has never been before, and concerning the accusations of the rabbinic council against me." Strangely enough the learned editor of the memoir failed to notice that the chapter dealt with the Sabbatian movement. The autograph copy of the book has been discovered recently in Milano, cf. N. Alony and E. Kupfer in *ʾAresheth*, IV (Jerusalem, 1966), 256. It is much better than the corrupt copy edited by Blau.

not only about Yakhini's letter from Constantinople, but also about the instruction to abolish the fast of the Seventeenth of Tammuz, which the believers wanted to have proclaimed in good time. The sense of the meeting was to impose restraint and silence on the excited public, but two questions may well have been involved here. The one concerned careless talk to gentiles, the other a formal affirmation of the obligation to observe the fast. A quarrel of competence ensued between elders and rabbis, the former maintaining that rabbinic authority extended to purely religious affairs only, but that matters pertaining to the public welfare were *ultra vires* as far as the rabbis were concerned. The rabbis thereupon decided for themselves and issued a proclamation "in the name of the *yeshibah*" on the eve of the Second of Tammuz (July 4, 1666), at the time of the closing of the gates of the ghetto. If this proclamation is identical with the "resolution" invoked three months later by Aboab, when refusing to answer queries regarding Sabbatai Ṣevi, then it must have enjoined secrecy and silence not only toward gentiles but also within the Jewish fold. The authors of the proclamation seem to have believed that an interdict on all discussions of the subject might prevent the increasingly acute danger of a schism, but their hope was founded on poor psychology. Three months later Aboab admitted that the public could not possibly abide by the prohibition. The believers who were not members of the rabbinic circle continued to write to their friends and to spread all sorts of rumors and miracle stories.

The proclamation of the rabbis provoked a storm in the ghetto of Venice. The Small Committee, upset by the usurpation of authority on the part of the rabbis, issued a proclamation of their own in which they declared the former proclamation (of whose contents Isaac de Levita does not breathe a word) invalid, and prohibited—on pain of excommunication and a fine of two hundred ducats—calling anyone by the title "our master." The latter title is usually prefixed to the name of an ordained rabbi when calling him to the liturgical reading of the scriptural lesson in the synagogue service. Evidently the clash between believers and infidels got caught up in the traditional feud between lay leaders and the rabbinate. That much, at least, appears from Isaac de Levita's account, which is otherwise concerned more with his private grievances than with the great public events surrounding them. The shameful happenings, we are told, were due to a certain wicked man, and it seems that the fasts of the Seventeenth of Tammuz and the Ninth of Ab were suspended in Venice. R. Isaac, at any rate, makes a point of emphasizing: "I wept for Tammuz even as I wept for Ab," mourning in particular for "the fall of the Torah and of them that brought it about [the Small Committee?] as also for the rabbis who failed to exercise sufficient foresight." Rabbinic dignity was soon restored, the original proclamation remained in force, and the two authoritative bodies patched up their quarrel. However, the incident illustrates the latent tensions which could explode, at the slighest provocation, into a major conflict. The testimonies of Moses Zacuto and Isaac de Levita show that there were many shades and degrees of adherence to the movement, and that the lines of demarcation were anything but definite and clear-cut. Their criticisms of their colleagues, moreover, prove that the attitudes of the rabbinic groups were not merely the result of intimidation by the enthusiastic crowd. The truth was far from the subsequent presentation by apologists.

The events referred to by Isaac de Levita are echoed by another letter, written toward the end of summer. The Jews of Rome were in an even more precarious position than the communities elsewhere. They lived in immediate proximity to the Holy See, and after some initial brushes between Jews and Christians, the believers kept complete silence (see above, pp. 484–85). There is no evidence to support the view that the Sabbatian prophet Sabbatai Raphael was active in Rome at this early period; he seems to have arrived toward the end of the summer (August or September, 1666). The rabbi of Rome, R. Joshua Menaggen, wrote to Aboab in August, 1666, for accurate information. His query may have been prompted by the brief but intense activity of the Sabbatian missionary, though Aboab's reply suggests that certain vexatious events had occurred in Rome in the wake of Sabbatai Raphael's visit. Aboab's reply, written in September, 1666 (before the news of Sabbatai's apostasy had reached Venice) has recently come to light[98] and helps to explain the paucity of direct reports from Venice in the months preceding the apostasy. Apparently the rabbis considered themselves bound by their solemn resolution, enjoining silence on anything connected with Sabbatai Ṣevi. In the circumstances they certainly would not pass on the flood of news reports arriving in Venice from Gallipoli. The ban on any public mention of the affair may also have been responsible for the fact that

98. Published by M. Benayahu in *ʾEreṣ Yisraʾel*, IV (1956), 201.

not one edition of Nathan's devotional manuals was published in Venice, the Jewish printing center of Italy.[99] Even outside Venice believers hesitated for some months, and between March and September, 1666, no such tract was printed in Italy. Not until September was Nathan's tract reprinted in Mantua under the title *Tiqqun ha-Middoth*.

In his reply R. Samuel Aboab apologizes to the rabbi of Rome, explaining that a resolution passed three months earlier in Venice had prevented him from giving the desired information, "but silence is a remedy for everything." The danger threatening from the gentiles as well as the fear of a renewed outbreak of internecine strife in the Jewish camp rendered it advisable to avoid "stumbling into the trap of the tongue." Since the passing of the resolution, he had left unanswered the many letters addressed to Venice from far and near. Instead of a full reply, Aboab sent the rabbi of Rome a copy of his letter of February, 1666, to Sasportas, adding that the reports from Constantinople and Palestine, received since that date, contained nothing reliable or materially affecting the issue. If anything, this implies that the letters from Jerusalem had failed to answer the questions addressed thither. Aboab also hinted to his colleague in Rome that the resolution had restored a measure of domestic peace in Venice, and that a new statement from him might "again kindle the flame of dissension in our congregation." Opinions were divided also in the rabbinic camp. Hence the safest course lay in a tolerant reserve: time would in due course reveal the truth of the matter. Meanwhile, the rabbis should guide the people gently in the paths of penitence, but otherwise let everyone believe or disbelieve the messianic tidings—provided, of course, that there was no deviation from rabbinic tradition and "full acceptance of the yoke of [God's] kingdom [that is] of the commandments, both biblical and rabbinic."

Another letter from Constantinople to Venice seems to have made a profound impression on both parties by its insolent radicalism,

99. The testimony of the convert Friedrich Peter Wessel, *Der geistlich todte Jude* (Copenhagen, 1721), p. 17, is based on his memories of what his parents told him about the movement in Germany. He says: "I well remember that [they] told me about the repentence and how they [the Jews] issued new books called *Tikkun Sabbetai Zewi* which were printed in Venice." This is obviously a mixup. No *Tikkun* was published under that name, but in later memories they may well have been spoken about as the *tiqqun* of Sabbatai Ṣevi. Venice was substituted for Amsterdam; see above, p. 478.

though no testimonies as to the reactions of the leaders of the Venetian community have survived. The letter, written by Samuel Primo, Sabbatai's secretary in Gallipoli[100] and signed by him "at the behest of the messianic King," gave orders regarding the punishment of infidels guilty of the crime of *lèse majesté*. Sasportas accused Primo of disseminating, over the seal of his "king," the most heinous blasphemies.[101] Particularly disturbing for pious and devout Jews was the fact that these blasphemies (for example, the ascription of divine attributes to Sabbatai) were not Primo's but the messiah's own. Yet Primo's literary contribution is unmistakable. He was no mean scholar, and his style combined rabbinic idiom with a ravishingly sonorous, high-flown, and majestic "royal" strain, the like of which had not been heard in Israel for a long time. The "royal edicts" must have thrilled every reader to the core.

Primo's letter reflects Sabbatai's mood at the time. It was he who had promulgated the new law and who wished to congratulate the believers in Venice on extirpating all wickedness and pursuing even unto destruction every man that spoke evil of the messiah, "slaying him even on the Sabbath day." Primo announced the verdict of "Our Lord the King, to the effect that there is no greater sanctification of the Sabbath than that performed by those people [who beat up an infidel in the synagogue on the Sabbath]," and called upon believers to proclaim this royal rescript in the streets and market places. While the leaders of the community wanted nothing but silence, the believers were exhorted "and ye shall rejoice, that is, ye shall make others rejoice together with you. For whithersoever the King's com-

100. The date of Primo's joining the group of believers in Constantinople is unknown. There is no evidence that he acted as Sabbatai's secretary prior to his imprisonment in Gallipoli, or that he accompanied Sabbatai on his journey from Palestine to Smyrna. Perhaps he never went to Smyrna but proceeded from Jerusalem straight to Constantinople (possibly stopping at his native city, Brussa, to preach the Sabbatian message there?). The proclamation abolishing the fast of 10 Tebeth, quoted by Z. Rubashov (Shazar) in his Hebrew article "The Messiah's Secretary" (*Ha-Shiloaḥ,* XXIX [1913], 37, and reprinted as a separate pamphlet, 1970) is based on Rycaut (p. 206), whose text has no reference at all to 10 Tebeth but seems rather to be a summary of the letter abolishing the fast of 17 Tammuz.

101. Sasportas, p. 165. The letter was written at the end of the summer, and there is no evidence that letters signed by Primo were sent out before Sabbatai's imprisonment in Gallipoli.

mand and his faith come, ye shall proclaim the tidings of salvation and comfort, and hold fast to the stronghold of repentance. . . . Behold, Our Lord the King will give to you all riches and honor and glory, and especially to the righteous [believers] who smote that man that rebelled against the Lord of the universe [that is, Sabbatai], and who thereby properly observed the [true] Sabbath which is Our Lord and King." The messiah being the true Sabbath, any act done in defense of his honor was the true Sabbath observance. Primo summed up the spiritual and political aspects of the messianic faith with the exhortation, "Rejoice in your King, your Savior and the Redeemer of your souls and your bodies in heaven and on earth, Who will resurrect your dead and save you from subjugation to the kingdoms and from the punishment of hell. These things are beyond the power of the mouth to utter, for none can fathom the *SHin Daleth Yod* [that is, Shadday, one of the names of God] which is Our Lord [that is, Sabbatai Ṣevi]."[102]

Primo's letter is instructive in more than one way. None of its readers could be unaware of the fact that the king, ignoring with a royal gesture his actual situation as a prisoner, was sending forth imperious messages from his prisonhouse, which had become the messiah's "Tower of Strength." The messianic vision embraced both the spiritual and the political aspects of existence. A psychologically significant feature of the letter is the blurring of past and future. Events such as the resurrection, which would only take place in the course of the redeemer's future ministry, are referred to as if they were happening in the present. The process by which the vision of the future is converted into a present psychological reality is an almost inevitable concomitant of movements of this kind, but Primo's letter enables us to observe it actually happening. The borderlines of reality become blurred, and the call to a messianic revival opens up new dimensions of existence in the experience of the believers. There was no more need to wait and hope for redemption, since it had become a living reality in the believers' hearts. Legendary reports of miracles and portents helped to build up an "inner" universe that was independent of "external" historical actuality.

The letter, moreover, contained an unmistakable invitation to terrorism. The problem had, in fact, become inevitable from the

102. Baruch of Arezzo (Freimann, pp. 55–56) and Sasportas (pp. 128–29).

moment that the great utopian dream of the redemption of Israel and the world appeared on the verge of realization. What were the enthusiasts to do with those who wished to sabotage the great awakening? A new and dangerous "pneumatic" authority reared its head and threatened traditional religious authority. The danger was clearly perceived by the few sober opponents of the movement (cf. the letter of R. Joseph ha-Levi of Leghorn, above, p. 488, and below, p. 759). If the real Sabbath observance consisted in honoring Sabbatai Ṣevi, the true Sabbath, then allegory had taken the place of plain understanding, and no traditional commandment or prohibition was safe from spiritual and figurative reinterpretation. The fact that the allegory was "mystical" merely increased its revolutionary potentialities. Hitherto the rabbis had led Jewry in the authority of the Law, which they understood and interpreted according to their tradition and their lights, and made them bear the "yoke of the kingdom of Heaven." Now that the kingdom of the messiah-Shadday was at hand—in fact, was an actual reality in the hearts of the believers—rabbinic authority gave way to that of the heralds of the new order. The question of authority inevitably led to that of the use of force, namely, terrorism, and a proper appreciation of the intrinsic relationship of the two may help us toward a better understanding of more than one chapter in Jewish history. If disbelief in Sabbatai, whose kingdom, it is true, was merely beginning to grow but was not, as yet, fully manifest, was tantamount to rebellion against the messiah's majesty, then the corollary was obvious. In fact, Primo's letter (to which Sabbatai added a few lines in his own handwriting) served formal notice of the existence of a new messianic authority superior to the traditional one.

It should now become evident that the events in Smyrna, described in a previous chapter, were by no means exceptional or freak irregularities. They were rooted in Sabbatai's psychology no less than in the immanent causality of an eschatological vision turning into reality. Primo's letter was not unique in encouraging terrorism, and there is plenty of evidence to show that informing had become a very serious plague. Leyb b. Ozer's statement that "it is absolutely certain that there was no informer among the Jews in those days" belongs to the realm of idealizing legend. "It was good that there were no informers in Israel who would betray to the authorities what was going on and what was being said about the princes and kings, otherwise not one Jew would have escaped [the vengeance of the gentiles]. For even the lowliest Jew boasted how he would lord it over the gentiles and what he would do to those in authority, for every one lived in complete certainty as if the Messiah had already come and they had established their rule and thrown off the yoke of the gentiles."[103] As a matter of fact, both infidels and believers fought with all the weapons at their disposal, including intimidation and informing. Early in 1666 the following problem was submitted to R. Ḥayyim Benveniste by the elders of the community of Smyrna: two men had been quarreling, and one had shouted in Turkish, in the presence of a mixed audience, "You are all rebels against the sultan and guilty of a capital crime." Should the man be excommunicated and declared an outlaw? Benveniste, who had been appointed chief rabbi of Smyrna by Sabbatai Ṣevi, replied that as an informer this man should either be handed over, under some pretext, to the gentiles for capital punishment, or else be mutilated in lieu of death (for example, by plucking out an eye, cutting his tongue, etc.). In any event, it was unthinkable to let him go unpunished, as this would encourage traitors and informers.[104] Benveniste's ruling was no academic exercise. Coenen reports that in the summer of 1666 one of the leaders of the infidel party, a prominent and scholarly member of the community, lodged a formal statement with the cadi to the effect that he did not recognize Sabbatai Ṣevi and had no part in the movement. The believers thereupon produced false witnesses who accused the man of the most heinous crimes. The cadi, who suspected a plot, pretended to sentence the accused to the galleys, ordered his beard to be shaved, and deported him—not to the galleys but to the house of a high Turkish official in another city where the man remained until the storm had blown over.[105]

103. Emden, p. 9, and MS. Shazar, fol. 30b.

104. Benveniste, *Baᶜey Ḥayyey*, III, no. 228. S. Verses has drawn attention to this responsum in an article in *Yavneh*, III (1942), 107–8. It is worthy of note that Benveniste had no scruples about including this unequivocally Sabbatian responsum in his collection of responsa which he edited much later for publication. Another case of informing is discussed *ibid.*, no. 229. The details are not clear, but the date (1666) suggests a Sabbatian background. The responsum mentions that the elders had resolved to spend any amount necessary [i.e., on bribes] in order to avert the danger which the informer had brought upon them.

105. Coenen, pp. 75–77. According to Rycaut (pp. 210–11), the believers secured the conviction of the infidel by bribing the cadi. Leyb b. Ozer (Emden, p. 10) transfers the incident to Constantinople where the Great Vizier himself

The incident proves that the believers treated active opponents as outlaws. Passive infidels were terrorized into compliance and some of them feigned conversion to the Sabbatian faith.[106] One of the few obstinate infidels, expecting an attack by the mob on his house, actually carried all his valuables to the safety of Coenen's house.[107] Another case of terrorism, involving the delivering up of a group of infidels into the hands of their Turkish torturers occurred elsewhere in Asia Minor. The incident resembles in some respects the expulsion from office of Lapapa, but by now antagonisms had greatly increased in violence and believers were no longer content with the mere expulsion of their opponents from office. In one community, apparently near Magnesia, the lay elder was an ardent follower of Sabbatai Ṣevi, while the rabbi was an infidel. "And when he heard that [the rabbi] reviled and blasphemed the messiah on account of his actions by which he led a great number of the people astray, he became his enemy and sought his hurt. . . . And of a sudden he delivered the rabbi and some of his supporters into the hands of the ruler [that is, the local Turkish authorities] who executed judgment against them and smote them deadly blows and put them in prison. He hurt their feet with fetters and caused much loss of money, yet for all this his anger was not turned away from the aforementioned rabbi until he forced the congregation to remove him from office and to sign a document [wherein they undertook] not to reinstate him as rabbi within the next three years."[108]

The doctrines expressed in Primo's letter illustrate the increasingly intransigent mood in the Sabbatian camp, and the intensity of their belief in Sabbatai Ṣevi as the King of Israel and the Lord's Anointed. However, in spite of encouragement from Nathan, Samuel Primo, and Sabbatai himself, terror and intimidation did not gain mastery over Italian Jewry. The lay leaders and rabbis of Venice never lost their authority over the masses, though it must have hung precariously

---

is said to have passed judgment. The story was evidently told by many informants and was much enriched in the telling. Nevertheless Leyb b. Ozer's account, in spite of its glaring contradictions, well conveys the atmosphere of terror spread by the believers.

106. Coenen, p. 77.

107. *Ibid.*

108. Benveniste's responsum to an inquiry, dated autumn 1667 (*Baᶜey Ḥayyey*, no. 206).

in the balance more than once. Messianic letters in the form of royal edicts did not begin to arrive before early summer; until then Sabbatian propaganda consisted mainly of Nathan's penitential tracts whose ascetic and devotional character effectively obscured their revolutionary implications.

The two brothers Jacob and Emanuel b. David Frances[109] were living at the time in Florence and Leghorn respectively. The idea of composing satirical poems lampooning the Sabbatian movement and its leaders seems to have occurred first to the elder brother, Jacob (1615–67), of Florence. Soon the two brothers were exchanging satirical poems, and as the movement reached its climax Emanuel suggested that they publish their joint efforts under the title *Ṣevi Muddaḥ* (*The Chased Roe;* cf. Isa. 13:14).[110] The poems provided a running commentary on the letters and legends arriving from the Orient, and pilloried Nathan's teachings and Sabbatai's "madness" in biting sarcasms. Jacob Frances also refers to the hostility of the believers and their attempts to harass him on account of his infidelity.[111] To rumors emanating from Vienna that Sabbatai had been crowned by the sultan in Constantinople, Emanuel riposted with a caustic sonnet[112] in which he made skillful use of all the possibilities of punning on the Hebrew word *ṣevi,* which frequently occurs in the Bible in the senses of "splendor" and of "roe" or "hart." The news of Sabbatai's arrest was emphasized and exploited to the full by the two brothers, while the believers tried to play it down as best they could. Jacob Frances, like R. Joseph ha-Levi, accused the Sabbatian leaders of making light of the Law and of rabbinic tradition, but the vehemence of his criticism poses some problems. Are his indignant references to the breaking of the Law and the desecration of the Talmud and religion poetic exaggerations, provoked by the abolition of fast days and some of

109. The Frances family, of Mantua, seems to have been of Portuguese marrano descent, as the brothers wrote the explanatory notes to their Hebrew poems in Portuguese.

110. Jacob Frances wrote many more poems of an anti-Sabbatian character. They have now been published by Peninah Naveh, *The Collected Poems of Jacob Frances* (Jerusalem, 1969), pp. 440–551, and form an important addition to our knowledge of the polemics between the two camps. It is a pity that their Hebrew style, full of biblical and Talmudic allusions and puns, makes it impossible to render its particular flavor in translation. In the Hebrew edn. (*SS*) some examples have been given.

111. Frances, p. 107.

112. *Ibid.,* p. 124.

Sabbatai's other performances in Smyrna, or were they aimed at antinomian tendencies among the Italian believers? Are the sarcasms about "so-called kabbalists"[113] directed at the kabbalist circle round Sabbatai or at the kabbalist rabbis in Leghorn and other Italian communities? Whatever the correct answer, there is no doubt that the tension between traditionalists, on the one hand, and the enthusiasts for whom all things were now being made new, on the other, found forceful expression in their satirical poems.

Jacob Frances was an exceptional character for his time. He was an orthodox Jew and a Talmudic scholar, but of a markedly rationalist bend. Even before he became known as an obstinate and uncompromising opponent of Sabbatian enthusiasm, he had already achieved notoriety as a disbeliever in the kabbalah. He was born in Mantua, where he also lived for many years after having attended the rabbinic *yeshibah* in Venice. The great eighteenth-century apologist of the authenticity of kabbalistic tradition, R. Abiad Sar Shalom Bazila of Mantua (1680–1743), mentions a certain person "who did not believe in our esoteric tradition and who used to say that the kabbalists 'have walked after vanity and have become vain.' He also denied the [authenticity of the] Zohar and taught that the book was forged and not written by R. Simon bar Yoḥay . . . and every day he would let loose the bridle of his tongue against the scholars in our city [Mantua] because they study the kabbalah."[114] In 1661 Frances published a broadsheet containing a satirical poem against the kabbalah, and the rabbis of Mantua, headed by the kabbalist Solomon Formiggini, ordered a proclamation against him to be read in all synagogues and all copies of the broadsheet to be seized and destroyed.[115] An officiating rabbinic scholar but no rabbi, Frances was a merchant of independent means and, unlike the Venetian rabbi Leone da Modena a generation earlier, he made no efforts to hide his critical views. He evaded further persecution by the Mantuan rabbis by moving to Florence, where he resided during the Sabbatian outbreak. He died in the summer of 1667. His rationalism (which is sufficient explanation for his uncompromising rejection of Sabbatian messianism) also rendered him unfit and ineffective as a rallying point of the "infidel" opposition. In an age in which theology and devotional life breathed

113. *Ibid.*, p. 115.

114. ᵓ*Emunath Ḥakhamim* (Mantua, 1730), ch. 22 (fol. 31a).

115. The poem is reprinted in P. Naveh's collection, pp. 401–12.

the spirit of kabbalism, a radical critic of the kabbalah was an undesirable ally. Many a rabbi of the anti-Sabbatian party—including Sasportas, who was a kabbalist too—must have felt that the support of Frances' brilliant polemical pen was more of a liability than an asset.[116] But Frances, for his part, needed no allies. The messianic news reports and legends were easy game for his incisive wit. Whether or not the satirical poems which Jacob exchanged with his younger brother in Leghorn circulated immediately as they were written, the brothers' opposition to the movement was notorious and brought upon them much vexation and persecution.[117] They were even attacked in their houses. Jacob Frances summoned the rabbis to sound the alarm "lest the Lord's people sin," and accused the shepherds, that is, the rabbis, of neglecting their duty. But his was a lone voice, and the few opponents of the movement in Italy did not band together in a concerted effort to stem the tide.

III AMSTERDAM

Most of the messianic reports from the East passed through Italy, and so it was over the Italian communities that the wave of enthusiasm swept first in its westward spread to Europe. However, as regards its role in Sabbatian history, the Jewish community of Amsterdam may well compete with Italy for the first place. In any event, the movement owed much of its drive to the powerful influence of the two centers. Circumstances in Amsterdam were indeed uniquely propitious for the success of the Sabbatian message. Amsterdam Jewry, which was by far the greater part of the Jewry of the Low Countries, was made up of two elements, each—for its own reasons—particularly responsive to the messianic tidings. The Sephardi (Portuguese) community, founded by marranos from Spain and Portugal, counted many members who had themselves escaped the Inquisition. In the Ashkenazi community the memory of the Cossack massacres of 1648 was still very much alive, particularly as many of the survivors (including Sabbatai's wife and her brother) had found refuge in Amsterdam. The relative freedom enjoyed by the Jews in Amsterdam further con-

116. Emanuel Frances' defense of his brother Jacob (*Wikuaḥ Libni ve-Shimᶜi*, Cracow, 1893) cannot be taken seriously, and the distinction between "true" and "false" kabbalists is hardly more than an apologetic device; cf. Ezra Fleischer's review of P. Naveh's book in *Kiryath Sepher*, XLV (1970), 186. The *Dispute*, which was written in 1668, does not contain a single reference to the Sabbatian movement.

117. Cf. the poem in *Ṣevi Muddaḥ*, p. 116.

tributed to their responsiveness. They had indeed found a haven of safety in the Dutch republic, but they were still close enough to the tempests and catastrophes of the immediate past to make the messianic call meaningful. Their sense of safety—unique in that age—enabled them to react freely and without the inhibiting fear of "What will the gentiles say?" In Turkey the movement was tantamount to rebellion. In Catholic countries, such as Poland and Italy, the danger of provoking the antagonism of the Church and the secular Christian authorities, forced responsible leadership to impose restraint; even so, the voice of prudence was often drowned by the roar of popular enthusiasm. In Amsterdam there was no need for dissimulation and disguise, and the community may therefore be taken as a fair index of what the rest of Jewry really felt. Sasportas was well aware of this when, in 1668, he flung this reproach in the face of the community: "The eyes of all Israel were upon you when this error began, and if you had rejected the reports, or [at least] not accepted them as certainties, the other communities would not have fallen into error, for they followed your example."[118] Sasportas' rebuke was addressed to the descendants of the Spanish and Portuguese marrano refugees, whose wealth and dazzling, albeit short-lived, splendor had made them—rightly or wrongly—the Jewish aristocracy of Europe, rather than to the Ashkenazi community, which was still considered inferior. The glory of the Amsterdam Sephardim soon declined, and survived as legend rather than as fact; but in the fateful year 1666 it was still at its height. Their prestige was an important factor in the Sabbatian movement, and was by itself enough to condemn every opposition to failure. If the Jews of Amsterdam, enjoying comparative ease and safety, responded thus openly to the messianic tidings, we may easily guess the feelings of their persecuted and harrassed brethren in Germany and Poland. The problem of the Sabbatian "reign of terror" and the allegation that the believers intimidated the communities has been discussed before. It is a remarkable fact that in Amsterdam and Salonika, where the Jews enjoyed more liberties than anywhere else, there was almost no terror. With a few exceptions, the elders, lay leaders, and rabbis marched at the head of the believers and there is no evidence of tension between prudent leadership, on the one hand, and mass enthusiasm, on the other. Their almost unanimous shouts of triumph were audible far and wide.

118. Sasportas, p. 285; also *id.* in his responsa *ʾOhel Yaʿaqob*, no. 48 (fol. 54d).

The memoir of Leyb b. Ozer, the notary of the Ashkenazi community at the end of the seventeenth century, conveys something of the atmosphere prevailing in Amsterdam, although his description generally glosses over the conflicts in the community. As we know from Sasportas, instances of intimidation occurred even here. Abraham de Souza, one of the wealthiest merchant princes of Amsterdam, "was an unbeliever from beginning to end and boldly risked his life [by appearing] before the people who detested him and his family. Nevertheless, he was firm in his [un]belief." He corresponded with the infidels in other communities, who sent him reports and documents which he, in his turn, forwarded to Sasportas in Hamburg. "And he suffered indescribable abuse and harassment because of this, and but for the grace of God which protected him they would have killed him, for many a time they were lying in wait to get hold of him."[119] Leyb b. Ozer mentions yet another infidel who created a stir in the community: "A Sephardi merchant called Alatino denied all the reports and letters, and said in public, 'You are mad! Where are the signs? Where are the tidings which the prophet Elijah is himself to bring? Where is the celestial Temple [that is to descend on Jerusalem]? Where are the [eschatological] wars which are foretold? Why have we not heard of the Messiah b. Joseph who is to fall in battle?' But everyone was cursing him and saying, 'Surely he shall not behold the face of the messiah.' One day as he had returned from the Bourse in order to have his meal, between the washing of the hands and the breaking of the bread he fell down and died suddenly. When this became known to the Jews, and to the gentiles too, a great fear and trembling fell upon them."[120]

However, such instances of militant unbelief were exceptional in Amsterdam, where by far the great majority of the congregation (and not merely the "rabble") were seized by messianic enthusiasm. Nevertheless, controversy continued. Writing in the middle of 1666, R. Isaac Aboab, himself a believer, assured Sasportas that he and his colleagues in the rabbinate were careful not to injure his honor or disparage his name, but as for the mass of the people "they are set on mischief against whoever opposes their faith . . . regarding our messiah. And all day long there is quarrel and contention between the parties in the market places and in the streets, for [the unbelievers]

119. Sasportas, p. 260. 120. Emden, p. 7.

taunt and insult them until their wrath is kindled beyond repair."[121] Aboab complained about Sasportas' partisans who hastened to bring his letters to everybody's notice, including the "ignorant crowd," and thereby caused much strife and offense. Aboab's letter enables us to make some corrections in Leyb b. Ozer's idyllic picture.

The first definite reports from the Orient arrived in November, 1665,[122] together with the text of Nathan's letter to Raphael Joseph. "And there was a great commotion in the city of Amsterdam, so that it was a very great trembling. They rejoiced exceedingly, with timbrels and with dances, in all the streets. The scrolls of the Law were taken out of the Ark [for ceremonial processional] with their beautiful ornaments, without considering the possible danger from the jealousy and hatred of the gentiles. On the contrary, they publicly proclaimed [the news] and informed the gentiles of all the reports."[123] Before long the first pamphlets on the movement appeared in Holland, and both Jews and gentiles wrote letters to all and sundry. One of the most assiduous letter-writers was Peter Serrarius, who passed the news on to England and other countries. But from the start the Christian correspondents confused the names as well as the persons of the main actors in the drama. The unfamiliar name "Ṣevi" became "Levi," and before long Christian writers referred to the prophet as "Nathan Levi." This form of the name recurs in all Christian writings on the movement, and was thence taken over by some later Jewish writers.[124]

The rabbis and scholars of the Sephardic community accepted the reports without hesitation, apparently on the strength of certain

121. Sasportas, p. 106.

122. The testimony of Serrarius (see also Wilenski, p. 170) that letters from Jerusalem and Gaza concerning Nathan's prophecy arrived in Amsterdam, via Leghorn and Venice, on November 27 agrees with the information and dates of Sasportas, as well as with the fact that the same news was received one week later in Hamburg (from Amsterdam).

123. Sasportas, p. 17.

124. Serrarius refers to the messiah several times as Sabothas Levi; the spelling is surely not just a misprint. The report in the *Hollandtze Merkurius,* January, 1666, p. 2, speaks of "Caeram Sevy alias Nathan Levie"; cf. also *ibid.,* "der Joodtze Messias Nathan Levi." The name never occurs in any of the letters from the Orient. The translation of Ḥayyim Joseph's letter to his brother the *chelebi* (see Serrarius' letter, Wilenski, p. 171, and above, p. 375 and notes) which was made from a Hebrew original, makes no mention of Nathan Levi, but only of "our prophet," "the prophet," or "the prophet Nathan of Gaza." Coenen too never mentions names other than those found in the Hebrew sources.

letters from Cairo which are no longer extant, but which seem to have contained official confirmation of Nathan's status as prophet. R. Isaac Nahar argued that since the prophet had been duly accredited by a rabbinic court (that is, at Cairo), no further doubts must be entertained on that score.[125] The believing party was headed by none other than the chief rabbi, Isaac Aboab da Fonseca (1605–93), whose correspondence with Sasportas has been preserved in great part. His kabbalistic interests were evident from his Hebrew translation of Herrera's[126] *House of God* and *Gate of Heaven,* which was published in 1655 and widely used. Aboab welcomed the popular devotional revival and defended it against Sasportas; there was nothing in it, he maintained, that was in any way repugnant to "the Law and our tradition," that is, to rabbinic Judaism.[127] A consideration of the ruinous consequences of a possible failure never presented itself to the naïve faith of the Amsterdam rabbis. "And if Your Reverence fears the disastrous results 'if the thing follow not, nor come to pass' [Deut. 18:22] [wrote Isaac Nahar to Sasportas] no Jew will despair of redemption because of that, for they are faithful believers, the descendants of faithful believers. And [meanwhile] it is good that they repent." Sasportas, in a letter of December, 1665,[128] angrily dismissed this view as "foolish piety."

The most respected and prominent men in the community supported Aboab in the propagation of the faith. There was the preacher R. Aaron Sarphati, originally from Morocco and an old friend of Sasportas, who now sent passionate confessions of "faith" to his doubting colleague. There was R. Moses Raphael d'Aguilar of whom his friend Sasportas complained that he considered himself "wiser than Daniel." There was also the physician and rabbi, Dr. Isaac Nahar,[129] a former fellow student of Spinoza in the *Talmud Toraḥ* of Amsterdam.

Their letters to their friend Sasportas exhibit interesting individual differences in temperament. Whereas Aboab and Nahar wrote

125. Sasportas, p. 25; see also R. Isaac Nahar's letter of December, 1665, *ibid.,* p. 24, who refers *expressis verbis* to semiofficial letters from Cairo.

126. Abraham Kohen Herrera of Florence (ca. 1570–1635 or 1639) was a former marrano, and the only kabbalist to write in Spanish. He died in Amsterdam, where he had been active in spreading the Lurianic doctrine.

127. Sasportas, p. 24. 128. *Ibid.,* pp. 25, 44.

129. The material relating to him has been assembled by M. Benayahu in *ʾEreṣ Yisraʾel,* IV (1956), 202. He received his medical diploma in Leiden, 1665.

cordially and argued their case in a reasonable way, Sarphati's letter to Hamburg after learning of the aspersions cast by his friend on Nathan's letter, was a violent eruption: "Praised be the Lord Who has given unto His people Israel the prophet Nathan, a prophet of truth and righteousness, and the beauty of his splendor, our messiah of righteousness. Blessed are we . . . who have been vouchsafed to behold what R. Simon bar Yoḥay . . . [and many other generations] did not see until this day." There was no doubt but the scepter would soon be restored to Judah. Sasportas, who had scoffed at Nathan's prophecies, was warned: "What will you say when you shall hear in three or four weeks from now . . . that the Grand Turk has placed the royal crown on his [the messiah's] head and given him the whole land of Judah and Jerusalem?" The kingdom of Israel was about to be restored, and Sarphati, as preacher of his congregation, had chosen as his subject for the previous Sabbath sermon the verse—taken from a widely quoted poem by Judah ha-Levi—"the salvation of the Lord comes in the twinkling of an eye."[130] In the meantime Israel should repent and pray. Sarphati's letter concludes: "Behold it is midnight already, and I have to rise at the first dawn of morning to pray and to make supplication to our God, and so do all the Holy Congregation whose fervor is beyond description. If you beheld it with your eyes you would agree that this is the Lord's doing. For they spend all day and all night in the synagogue as on the Day of Atonement, and on the Sabbath they offered more than ten thousand silver florins.[131] More benches had to be added to our *yeshibah* [for the many penitents and worshipers] and [if you were here] you would behold the world upside down. For [at] all the houses where they used to play at dice and lotteries, they have of themselves stopped it, without [waiting for] an order from the heads of the congregation, and all day and night they put the Law of the Lord to their hearts[132] . . . and all their conversation is in our holy Law. Verily

130. Sarphati's letter to Sasportas, pp. 26–29. Sarphati's letter is also mentioned by Aboab, in a letter of January, 1666: "R. Aaron Sarphati has already bestirred himself and replied to your reverence"; hence Sarphati must have written before 15 Tebeth 5426, i.e., in December, 1665. The sermon was probably preached on the Sabbath of Hanukkah.

131. See also Baruch Fubini's (see below, n. 155) letter from Amsterdam to Italy: on *Rosh Ḥodesh* Adar offerings for charity had amounted to 3,000 ducats (*Zion,* X [1945], 66).

132. The same detail is also mentioned in a letter to Italy, *ibid.*

the Lord sent a word into Jacob. Therefore hearken unto me Jacob [Sasportas], do thus my brother and thou shalt be saved." Sarphati also advised his friend to burn his letters, lest later they bring "iniquity to remembrance" and discredit him, and "lest it happen to you as with R. Jacob Ḥagiz who is still under censure because he did not believe."[133]

The penitential revival received a powerful stimulus from Nathan's liturgical handbook for the daily and nightly devotions. The first manuscript copies of these devotional manuals arrived toward the end of December, 1665, and were immediately sent to press. From January to the end of the summer, 1666, the printing presses poured forth a large number of constantly revised editions of these devotional and penitential liturgies. The number of editions suggests that they were published to satisfy not only the needs of Amsterdam but of other European communities as well, some of which (for example, Frankfurt and Prague) subsequently printed their own editions. Also, Serrarius, writing from Amsterdam on February 26, 1666, mentions the subject: "Behold the title of a book of Prayers, written and prescribed by *Nathan* the Prophet for all the Jews; which takes much among the Jews, and hath some esteem among Christians. I have begun to translate it."[134] The Jewish printing houses in Amsterdam (Joseph Attias, David de Castro Tartas, the Ashkenazi printer Uri Feibush b. Aaron ha-Levi) competed in producing better and more complete versions of the prayer book, all in very small format. The first Hebrew editions contained selections from the Bible and nothing else: "The Order of daily prayers to prepare every man, that he may order his steps in the way which is right and straight before God, and may turn himself to the Lord; that he may have compassion upon us; and we may behold the delight of the Lord and view and behold his Temple. In the year Behold I will *save* [Hebrew, *moshiᶜa;* see Zech. 8:7. The numerical value of the Hebrew word is 426 (1665–66)] my people." As time went by all kinds of additions were made. Some

133. Sasportas, p. 29. The source of this, possibly incorrect, detail probably was a letter written by believers in Palestine.

134. *A New Letter concerning the Jews,* p. 6; also in Roth [1938], p. 71. The Sabbatian *Letters,* ed. Haberman, p. 211, state that the *tiqqun* for the devotions at day and at night had been dispatched from Gaza "at the beginning of the month Marḥeshwan 426"; it cannot, therefore, have arrived in Amsterdam before December, 1665.

editions specify "In the year *moshi^ca;* the first year."[135] Nathan's name is not mentioned on the title pages of the Hebrew editions, though I have found "the Haham Nathan Esqenasi" in the title of one Spanish edition.[136] Some editions carried additional prayers, confessions of sins, and hymns by the local rabbis, especially Isaac Aboab and Solomon Oliveira. Almost all editions open with a glowing preface (by Oliveira?), announcing in rhapsodic language that the Lord our God had entrusted the work of redemption to "the Crown of Glory" (Hebrew, *ᶜatereth ṣevi*, that is, Sabbatai Ṣevi; the expression is derived from Isa. 28:5). Unlike the prayer and confession of sins by "the President of the Court and Head of the Academy in this glorious city," Isaac Aboab, which are composed in the traditional style of ascetic and devotional writers, and devoid of any direct reference to their immediate occasion, Oliveira's contributions are rhymed and also more explicit. Oliveira, who was a well-known poet, or rather rhymester, composed a special confession of sins for the afternoon service preceding the eve of the First of Adar I, which was subsequently included in some of the editions of the *tiqqun* that appeared during the summer of 1666. He also composed a "prayer of supplication, containing details regarding the Redemption," and poems that are rhymed versions of several psalms, especially Psalm 126, "when the Lord turned again the captivity of Zion."[137] The haste with which these editions were produced is illustrated by a postscript to one of them, appended, by way of apology, by the printer (or proofreader): "It is true that I have printed this *tiqqun* before, but because of the exceeding haste and the great number of my people who were urging me, 'Finish your work that we may read in it day and night as *commanded by our prophet, the man of God that is in Gaza*,' the misfortunes of every printing befell also me and there are a few errors in the text. Wherefore I decided to print it once more, leading on slowly according as the work in hand and the proofreaders are able to endure [The idiom is imitated from Gen. 33:14], so that this glorious labor is now

135. Thus on the title page of one of the edns. published by David de Castro Tartas.

136. "Tikkun della Noche," in the library of the Hebrew Union College, Cincinnati; see Pl. IV.

137. This poem, which is undoubtedly by Oliveira, was also printed by Freimann, p. 115.

achieved with the utmost perfection as regards letter-type, paper, and ink."[138]

At least three editions have full-page copperplate engravings facing the title page. In two of the three editions (the one by a Sephardi, the other by an Ashkenazi printer), the page is occupied by two engravings (see plate III). The upper half represents Sabbatai Ṣevi as a king seated on his throne, with four old men on each side who seem to be chanting hymns in his honor. The six steps leading to the throne are flanked by lions. The throne is evidently that of King Solomon as described in the Haggadic midrashim. Sabbatai holds a scepter in his hand; and a large crown, inscribed *ᶜatereth ṣevi* ("Crown of Glory"; see Isa. 28:5) is held suspended over his head by four angels. The steps are inscribed with Jeremiah 33:15: "In those days and at that time will I cause the Branch of righteousness to grow up unto David; and he shall execute judgment and righteousness in the land." The lower picture shows twelve bearded men, together with an oversized thirteenth—evidently the Twelve Tribes and the messiah—seated at a round table and studying from a book. Behind them a large multitude of men and women, and at the bottom of the picture the legend (Josh. 1:8): "Thou shalt meditate therein day and night." The engraving in the third edition (published by Joseph Attias) contains three pictures, in the center of which is a shield inscribed: "*Tiqqun* for recitation at day and night." The upper picture represents the giving of the Law at Mount Sinai. The middle shows five men on each side of the shield, engaged in learned discussion. The lower picture resembles that in the middle, but one of the rabbis on the left is shown with his hat falling off, while a hand protruding from the wall is pouring on him water or oil. Another pair of hands is holding a laurel wreath above his head, probably about to crown him. Five rabbis and a cherublike boy are looking up from their books and gazing in astonishment at the man—probably the messiah.

This edition, like many others, ends with a thoroughly messianic prayer, to be said after recitation of the *tiqqun:* "Let the horn of thy servant David flourish, and grant rekindling of light unto the son of Jesse thine anointed, and let his majesty be raised and his kingdom be exalted above the whole world. His name shall be continued as long as the sun . . . and Israel return to their folds, and the palace

138. Fol. 4b of the unnumbered pages that follow, in Attias' last edn., after fol. 82.

remain after the manner thereof [Jer. 30:18]. Even the first dominion, the kingdom shall come to the daughter of Jerusalem [Mic. 4:8] and a king shall reign and prosper, . . . and shall execute judgment and righteousness in the land [Jer. 23:5]. . . . For Thy salvation we wait, O Lord. O do not put us to shame in our hope, O Lord our God. O Lord show us Thy mercy, and grant us Thy salvation" [Ps. 85:8].[139]

In addition to six or seven Hebrew editions,[140] at least three or four Spanish and Portuguese versions were printed in Amsterdam.[141] The translations were evidently made for the benefit of the women and of more recent marrano arrivals who would have difficulty in reciting their devotions in Hebrew. In keeping with the distinctly penitential character of the great awakening, other anthologies of diverse penitential prayers selected from earlier ascetic and kabbalistic literature[142] (and hence without specifically Sabbatian qualities) were printed in both Hebrew and Spanish, for example, the *Enseña a Pecadores* (*Instruction to Sinners*). In Poland and Italy, too, messianic fervor did not long remain content with Nathan's devotional exercises. The writings of the German Hasidim and the Safed kabbalists, for example, were searched for guidance and prescriptions of penances, and it is surely no accident that lists of ascetic rules drawn up by the kabbalists of Safed should have survived in Sabbatian manuscripts.[143] When a humble rhymester in Amsterdam indited a poem in honor of Sabbatai Ṣevi, the printer subjoined to it a new edition of the "Penitential Exercises of R. Isaac Luria" and thus combined rejoicing and penance.

139. Edn. Attias, fol. 66b.

140. Because of the considerable curiosity value of the "portraits," several copies of these edns. have escaped the destruction ordered by the communal authorities after the debacle of the movement. Their owners simply hid them, some of them even inscribing their names, such as the Amsterdam bookseller Nathan b. Moses from Frankfurt; cf. the copy described in the Catalogue of the Sassoon Collection of Hebrew books, 1st portion, put on sale by Sotheby & Co., London, 30 June, 1970, p. 63 (no. 146). Copies of these edns. are sold today at exorbitant prices.

141. I have, so far, come across one Portuguese and three Spanish edns., apparently all from the printing houses of David de Castro Tartas and Joseph Attias.

142. E.g., from Isaiah Horovitz's *Sheney Luḥoth ha-Berith,* and from Isaac Luria's *Confession of Sins,* which had been translated into Spanish by Manasseh b. Israel and published in 1623.

143. Thus the "rules" of R. Abraham Galanté and R. Abraham ha-Levi, published by S. Schechter (*Studies in Judaism,* Second Series, pp. 294–99), have been preserved only in the thoroughly Sabbatian MS. Halberstamm 40.

Momentous events such as the inception of redemption clearly required a new calendar reckoning. Also, the Maccabees had expressed what their victory meant to them by inscribing their coins "Year 1 of the Deliverance of Israel," and Bar Kokhba's coins were similarly dated, for example, "Year 1 of the Freedom of Israel." The same procedure was adopted, as we have seen (see above, p. 262) by believers in Palestine and Egypt. In "the first year of the restoration of Prophecy and of the Kingdom" an edition of the Pentateuch —the first edition of the Torah in the messianic era—and one of the weekly *Haftaroth* were published in Amsterdam. The title pages are adorned with Sabbatian illustrations; for example, the title page of the *Haftaroth* shows a large crown and a diadem, on which are inscribed the words ^{c}*atereth ṣevi*, and underneath it the legend: "Sabbatai Ṣevi, King of Israel and the Anointed of the God of Jacob." Below this comes the ordinary title: "The order of the *Haftaroth* for the whole year," etc.[144] Messianic fervor was manifest not only in the title pages of new editions but even in the changes made in earlier printings. Naphtali Bacharach's ^{c}*Emeq ha-Melekh* (Amsterdam, 1648) was, as we have seen (see above, pp. 68 ff.), not only the most comprehensive compendium of Lurianic kabbalah in its time, but also a testimony of acute eschatological expectation. In fact, the author expected the redemption (see p. 89) in the year 1648, which happened to be the year of publication of his work. In 1666, when the hope of Israel appeared to be on the point of realization, the printer brought out all his unsold copies, after having provided them with a new title page, in what purported to be a new edition dated "In the year Israel is SAVED [the numerical value of the Hebrew word *nosha*^{c} is 426 (1665–66)] by the Lord."[145] As late as autumn, 1666, just before the news of Sabbatai's apostasy reached Amsterdam, there appeared a purely halakhic work dealing with the laws of marriage and divorce,[146] whose title page gave the date of publication as "The year the MESSIAH THE SON OF DAVID [numerical value in Hebrew, 427] has come."

144. See A. M. Haberman, *A History of the Hebrew Book* (Hebrew), p. 104, for details about this publication and for a reproduction of the title page. The book was printed by Castro Tartas.

145. The "messianic" edition of ^{c}*Emeq ha-Melekh* is ignored in all bibliographies, but one copy has come into my possession; see G. Scholem, *Kiryath Sepher*, XXX (1955), 413, where a reproduction of the title page is to be found.

146. *Naḥalath Shib^{c}ah*, by R. Samuel b. David ha-Levi. See below, p. 589.

The activities of the printing houses were but one aspect, as well as a reflection, of the general enthusiasm. The most prominent "believer" in the city was Abraham Pereira, a descendant of a family of marranos in Madrid and one of the wealthiest industrialists and merchant princes in Holland. Pereira was much given to works of piety and devotion, and in 1659 he founded and endowed the *yeshibah* "*Ḥesed le-ʾAbraham*" in Hebron. As the scholars of the Hebron *yeshibah* were ardent "believers" and sent enthusiastic letters to their patron, inviting him to join them at this hour of grace, Pereira had firsthand information from Palestine. He supported the movement with all his power and prestige, and he and Dr. Isaac Nahar decided to journey to the Holy Land to await the messiah's final and triumphant manifestation at the *yeshibah* which Pereira had founded in Hebron. They left Amsterdam about the middle of March,[147] some days before the Purim festival, but tarried more than a year in Italy—Nahar in Leghorn and Pereira in Venice—whence they returned to Amsterdam.[148] A Christian news letter reported that "Abraham Perena [!], a rich Jew of this Town, parted on Monday last[149] with his family for Jerusalem, after he

147. An account of their adventures during their journey through Westhphalia, Germany, and the Rhineland is given in Pereira's *Espejo de la Vanidad del Mundo* (Amsterdam, 1671), pp. 96–98. Purim, 1666, they were in Aremberg, in Westphalia.

148. On Abraham Pereira, see *ha-Karmel*, VI (1866–67), pp. 294–96; M. B. Amzalak, *Abraham Israel Pereyra* (Lisbon, 1927); and A. Yaᶜari's article on Pereira's *yeshibah* in Hebron in the Hebrew quarterly *Yerushalayim*, IV (1952), 185. Yaᶜari misunderstood some of the statements in his sources (which all refer to Pereira's voyage to Palestine in 1666) and wrongly assumed another voyage to Gaza, in 1673, for the purpose of meeting the prophet. This alleged voyage is said to have been interrupted in Venice "for unknown reasons," but here again Yaᶜari misinterpreted Sasportas (p. 363), who clearly refers to the year 1666. Dr. Isaac Nahar mentioned his imminent departure for the Holy Land "during the next month" in a letter of February, 1666 (Sasportas, p. 57).

149. Wilenski (*ibid.*, p. 167, n. 50) wrongly takes this to refer to a departure from Paris because of the superscription over the preceding paragraph: "From Paris, February 19, 1666." But the new paragraph and its continuation were clearly taken from a letter written by a Christian in Amsterdam (Serrarius?). This is also borne out by the reference (*ibid.*, p. 168) to the great rejoicing "on the tenth of *March*," after the receipt of new reports from the East—an event which is known from other sources too. The paragraph mentioning Pereira was not written in February, but in the middle or latter half of March. "Monday last" may refer to March 15, 1666.

had taken his leave of our Magistrate, and acknowledged his thankfulness for the favour he and his Nation in their dispersion had received here etc. It's said he offered to sell a Countrey-house of his worth Three thousand pound *Sterling*, at much loss, and on this Condition, That the Buyer should not pay one farthing till he be convinced in his own Conscience, That the *Jews* have a King."[150]

Before departing for the Holy Land, Pereira published, in Spanish, a substantial volume of moral, devotional, and ascetic counsel *La Certeza del Camino* (*The Certainty of the Way*). The work was certainly written before 1666,[151] but its publication at this particular date cannot have been accidental, and it was probably meant to encourage the Sabbatian revival among the marranos no less than to "atone for the author's sins." Sasportas tells us that after he had written his first anti-Sabbatian letters, Pereira protested and asked him to desist from denying Nathan's prophecy and from publishing declarations that would destroy the faith and penitential fervor of the simple folk, and he adds: "and other wealthy notables wrote to me in the same vein."[152] The author of the French *Relation* reports, with his usual venom, that several rich Jews had written to Sabbatai "in order to curry his favor and to assure themselves of a place when the principal offices in his kingdom were distributed," adding by way of illustration a detail which may well refer to Pereira and one of his friends: "Two of the richest Jews of Holland wrote to him [that is, Sabbatai] in a recent letter from Venice—where they have already arrived—and notified him that they had sold all their houses and lands, and that they hastened to come unto him from the far ends of the earth to receive his blessings and his orders, and to lay their wealth of several millions (*plusieurs millions*) at his feet, so that he could freely dispose of it."[153] This detail agrees well with another report in the same source, according to which two Dutch merchants had sent Sabbatai a notification signed by a notary public and attesting the expenditure of one hundred thousand lion's thalers for dowering poor brides and for other charitable works.[154] The Jewish merchants in Amsterdam also wrote to Italy to inform their friends there of the latest reports.[155]

150. *Ap.* Wilenski, pp. 167–68.

151. It contains no trace of Sabbatian beliefs.

152. Sasportas, p. 49.

153. *Relation,* pp. 24–25; the Italian letter in *JJS,* XII, p. 48.

154. *Ibid.*, p. 34.

155. Cf. e.g., the news reports sent by Isaac Baruch Fubini to his family, "A Notebook [or, Notes] from Italy" in *Zion,* X (1945), 65–66 (where the

Preparations also seem to have been made, in the first spurt of enthusiasm, to remove the bones of the dead from their graves and to carry them to the Holy Land. R. Samuel Aboab of Venice had heard rumors to that effect and expressed astonishment that "the graves of them that sleep in the dust have been disturbed [contrary to Jewish Law] so as to remove the bones of the dead from their graves."[156] Moreover, it was only fitting that in a great seaport town where many of the wealthy Jews were shipowners, attention should be given to more practical problems of the mass exodus. Unlike the Jews of Russia or Greece, believers in Amsterdam thought of regular means of transport rather than of a miraculous translation to the Holy Land on the clouds of heaven.[157] The main difficulty seemed to be the maritime war between England and Holland, which would make any Dutch vessel welcome spoil for British raiders. The Public Record Office in London preserves a petition presented on February 5, 1666, to the king of England by a Jew of Amsterdam, Jean d'Illan, requesting a pass for a Dutch ship. "Since I behold that God in his mercy has begun to gather in his scattered people and has raised up a prophet for us, therefore I and several of my Jewish brethren, together with fifty poor families desire to hire a ship to bring us to Jerusalem. And in order that this may be accomplished without being captured or molested on the high sea, we humbly petition Your Majesty to grant

---

spelling of the name was erroneous and must be corrected), and the mention (*ibid.*, p. 66) of a letter by the wealthy merchant Moreno "who is in possession of many news reports." The name "Fubini" which occurs three times in the Italian notebook, is that of a well-known family in Turin. The English pamphlet (Wilenski, p. 167) misspells Pereira's name as Perena. In the first edn. I had read the name as "Fucchini," but Dr. Cecil Roth suggests (in a private communication) that the name should be read "Fubini"—a Piedmontese name that was fairly common among Jews in Turin and its environs. "Fubini," however, is said to be traveling with his family via Marseilles to Italy.

156. Sasportas, p. 59. Aboab's letter is dated 13 Adar (February 18), hence the events referred to must have occurred in January or earlier.

157. Curiously enough, the problem of transport had already been brought up in 1649, in a petition by "Johanna Cartenright, widow, and her son Ebenezer Cartwright [*sic*], now inhabitants of the city of Amsterdam" to the English government, in favor of the readmission of Jews to England. They write: "And this nation of England, with the inhabitants of the Netherlands, shall be the first and readiest to transport Israel's sons and daughters in their ships to the Land promised to their forefathers . . . for an everlasting Inheritance." See *The Petition of the Jewes,* a unique pamphlet described in *Hebraica from Denmark,* a catalogue of an exhibition in New York, 1969, no. 29.

us a pass for one Dutch ship which is to sail from here . . . without let, search, or molestation by vessels of His Majesty's fleet, and after arriving in Jerusalem we shall pray for His Majesty's success."[158] Jeronimo Nuñez da Costa (also known by his Jewish name Moses Curiel), one of the wealthiest Jews in Amsterdam and agent of the king of Portugal in the Low Countries—he also acted as agent for Charles II during the latter's exile in Holland—invited one of his friends to join him on the voyage, "since he had many ships."[159] As early as December, 1665, the Polish correspondent in Amsterdam had heard "from a good friend who entertains friendly relations with the rabbis" that the wealthy Jews were selling their houses and their property, neglecting their business, and getting ready for the voyage. "Two ships are to sail [from here], one to Jaffa and another to Gaza."[160] In the summer of 1666 a Yiddish rhymester still exhorted his rich co-religionists to deal kindly with the poor and to provide for their transportation to the Holy Land (see below, p. 538). An English newsgatherer reported on March 15 that the Jews were making haste with their preparations for leaving Amsterdam.[161]

On February 5, 1666, letters arrived from Smyrna that caused great excitement.[162] The report of the abolition of the fast of the Tenth of Tebeth and its conversion into a day of rejoicing, by royal decree and with the alleged consent of the rabbis, was accepted without hesitation or qualms; in fact, it merely served to confirm the authenticity of the messianic message. Enthusiasm mounted as news of the mass prophecy arrived, after considerable delay, on March 10, and

158. Public Record Office, S.P. 29-147-33, fol. 65. The petition is written in French. C. Roth, *History of the Jews in England* (1941), p. 175, gives the Portuguese form of the petitioner's name as João d'Ilhão.

159. "A Notebook from Italy," *Zion* X (1945), 66, where, however, the name is corrupted to Jerolimo Nuñez of Constantina. On Nuñez da Costa see Roth (1941), p. 169, and the *Catalogus Herdenkingstentoonstelling Portug.-Israelit. Synagoge* (Amsterdam, 1950), p. 27.

160. Balaban, p. 42.

161. Muddiman's letter, in "Calendar of State Papers," Domestic Series 1665–66, vol CLI, no. 23, p. 300. The letter also contains the curious information that the messiah of whom the Jews entertained at present such great expectations had originally been "an ordinary fellow and the son of a baker."

162. Isaac Nahar's reproachful letter, of the same date, to Sasportas closes with the words "Friday, the day of glad tidings" (Sasportas, p. 49). The date corresponds to 30 Shebat, *Rosh Ḥodesh* Adar 1.

was read in public.[163] "This time the throng was so great when the mail arrived in Amsterdam, that people were almost crushed in their eagerness to hear the most recent news."[164] On the following day a solemn service was held in the specially illuminated synagogue and the festival psalms (called the *Hallel*) were recited.[165]

Sabbatian innovations were introduced into the synagogue service at Amsterdam—for example, the daily recitation of Psalm 21 and of the prayer for the King's Majesty (see above, p. 424).[166] Each of the two rabbis, Oliveira and Aboab, composed a special, expanded version of this prayer to replace the shorter text that had, apparently, come from the Orient. This is one of the longer versions:

He who giveth salvation unto kings and dominion unto princes; whose kingdom is an everlasting kingdom, who delivereth his servant David from the hurtful sword, who maketh a way in the sea and a path in the mighty waters, the great, mighty, and revered God, who giveth strength in the terrible might of His arm, who doeth great things and whose right hand is glorious in power: Art [thou] not it which hath dried the sea, the waters of the great deep, that hath made the depths of the sea a way for the ransomed to pass over? The king who alone is exalted, the everlasting God, who giveth great salvation to His king and showeth lovingkindness to His anointed, may He bless, preserve, guard, help, assist, prosper, magnify, raise and highly exalt Our Lord the Great King Sabbatai Ṣevi, the Anointed of the Lord, the Messiah son of David, the Messiah King, the Messiah Redeemer, the Messiah Savior, our Messiah of Righteousness, the Anointed of the God of Jacob.

163. Aeshcoly, p. 226–27. The correspondent, writing on March 18, 1666, refers to an earlier letter written "last week," immediately after receipt of the original news from Smyrna.

164. Leyb b. Ozer, MS. Shazar, fol. 13a.

165. According to a Dutch broadsheet (*Afbeelding* etc.) published at the end of March or early in April. The writer reports that there were firm believers in the community, as well as doubters and such as had not yet made up their minds, "but there is great rejoicing among them, . . . as was clearly proved on March 11–12, 1666, in the Synagogue in Amsterdam." The broadsheet also published for the first time the purely imaginary portrait of Sabbatai, which was then copied in the French *Relation* (see above, ch. 2, n. 233). A copy of the broadsheet is in the *Bibliotheca Rosenthaliana* of the University Library at Amsterdam.

166. Normally the prayer for the governing authorities is said on Sabbath and festival days only.

May the supreme King of kings in His mercy and with His mighty arm forever exalt his majesty and magnify his kingdom everlastingly in his strength. May his enemies be clothed with shame, but upon him his crown shall flourish. And they that wait upon the Lord shall renew their strength, and the redeemed of the Lord shall return and come with singing unto Zion; and everlasting joy shall be upon their head; they shall obtain gladness and joy, and sorrow and mourning shall flee away. And all the kingdoms of the earth shall know that thou alone, O Lord, art king. Thine, O Lord, is the greatness, and the power, and the glory, and the victory, and the majesty. May we be vouchsafed to behold the face of our King, Messiah, and Savior, and may we live to behold our glorious Temple, and may in us be fulfilled that which is written, "For ye shall go out with joy and be led forth with peace; the mountains and the hills shall break forth before you into singing, and all the trees of the field shall clap their hands." And it is further said, "For ye shall not go out with haste, nor go by flight; for the Lord will go before you, and the God of Israel will be your reward." May this be the divine will, and let us say: Amen.[167]

The Portuguese community in Amsterdam had always followed the custom of all congregations in the Diaspora, according to which the priestly blessing was given on the major festivals only. To mark the beginning of redemption and in anticipation of the messianic liturgy, the priestly blessing was now to be given every Sabbath. The innovation later led to a violent controversy between Sasportas and the rabbis of Amsterdam. The latter wished to maintain the practice even after the debacle, since, formally at least, it was a return to an unobjectionable custom mentioned in ancient sources. Sasportas argued—without success—that nevertheless the recent renewal of the custom had been "conceived in sin" and that it should, therefore, be discontinued.[168]

The two cantors of the community, Jacob de Farro and Emanuel Benattar, were ardent believers. De Farro, to whose family there attached a traditional assumption that they might be of priestly descent,

167. Freimann, p. 114, from a MS. in Amsterdam. The other version (*ibid.*, pp. 113–14) was based on letters bearing Sabbatai's signature and containing his favorite titles. The information regarding the authors of these prayers (Freimann's notes, *ibid.*) was copied, without acknowledgment, from J. S. da Silva Rosa, the librarian of the ᶜ*Eṣ Ḥayyim* Library in Amsterdam, who drew on oral traditions in the Portuguese community.

168. See Sasportas, pp. 211 ff.

inquired of Nathan, who informed him in the summer of 1666 that he was no priest. De Farro, who had until then scrupulously observed the special prohibitions applying to priests, thereupon demonstratively "defiled himself by contact with dead bodies, to show that he was a [nonpriestly] Israelite," for which act he was severely reprimanded by the elders.[169] In their messianic enthusiasm the two cantors permitted themselves departures from the traditional text of the liturgy, and were punished by the elders who, though themselves believers, held that no premature changes should be made in the text of the traditional prayers.[170] One of them, when singing the *yigdal* hymn at the end of the Sabbath eve service, had loudly declaimed: "He hath sent our anointed at the end of days" (instead of "He will send"); the other had said at the *habdalah* service at the conclusion of the Sabbath: "The prophet Elijah hath come to us with the Messiah son of David" (instead of "Elijah, . . . O come to us speedily, etc."). Former opponents of the kabbalah, such as the physician and philologist Dr. Benjamin Mussafia who enjoyed great prestige also among Christian scholars, converted to the "faith" and became very active in the movement. Sasportas, who considered himself an expert kabbalist, ironically inquired of them in February, 1666, whether they had now adopted the kabbalistic teachings which they had previously despised.[171]

The messiah's imprisonment in no way affected the electrified atmosphere in the city or dampened the spirits. Letters arrived from Constantinople, bringing the most fantastic news, which was eagerly spread by word of mouth and even by an occasional pamphlet. Sabbatai, it was told, had resurrected the dead and passed through the locked and barred doors of his prison, which opened of themselves. The iron chains with which his hands and feet were fettered had broken of themselves. In fact, his imprisonment was of his own free

169. *Ibid.*, p. 138. A similar story is told of Abraham de Pinto (*ibid.*, p. 137) who had been informed by Nathan that he was of the tribe of Benjamin and not of Aaron. On de Pinto see M. Benayahu in *ᶜEreṣ Yisraᶜel*, IV (1956), 204.

170. Sasportas (p. 237), reports the incident without mentioning the two cantors by name. The names are given by da Silva Rosa in his short article in the Dutch weekly *De Vrydagavond* (trial issue of January 11, 1926, p. 6).

171. Sasportas, pp. 56–57. Sasportas "doctored" the original text of his letter, the autograph of which has been preserved. His "edited" version is meant to convey an impression of biting sarcasm, whereas in actual fact the letter was written in the brief period when Sasportas was going through a crisis of doubt and uncertainty; see below, pp. 575–78.

will.[172] Rumors that Sabbatai had been killed while being arrested (or immediately afterward) circulated in Amsterdam, but were soon contradicted. Considering the long time which letters from the Orient normally took to arrive, the speed with which the news of Sabbatai's removal to Gallipoli traveled to Amsterdam is truly surprising. Serrarius reported the matter in great detail to his English correspondents as early as May, 1666. In the same letter he also mentioned that "the Jews [of Amsterdam] have received a letter of the fifth of Aprill [about two weeks before Sabbatai's removal to Gallipoli] from a person at Smyrna who accompanied the king to Constantinople" (see above, p. 455, for the text of the letter). How a letter from Symrna could reach Amsterdam in less than four weeks is something of a riddle, but the contents runs true to type and faithfully reflects the admixture of truth and fiction current among the believers in Constantinople in February, 1666. If the letter was actually written by a prominent eyewitness, it is not surprising that it was accorded implicit credence. In any event its testimony confirmed the illusion that Sabbatai enjoyed almost complete freedom.

The rabbis of the Sabbatian party in Constantinople continued to dispatch letters in all directions. Especially the cryptic letter in which they apprised believers of the "great fair" to be held in the year 427, where "R. Israel, the son of Abraham" would sell his merchandise (see above, p. 505), gladdened the hearts of Rabbi Aboab and his colleagues. During the summer months copies of Sabbatai's own letters were received, as well as copies of a special letter of encouragement from the prophet in Gaza. A missive of June 1, by seven prominent rabbis in Constantinople, was received in Amsterdam on July 23. The contents of this highly optimistic letter were summarized by a Christian correspondent:

Everything seems to be going as well as can be, and they have no doubts but their deliverance will take place very soon. The king is in Gallipoli, enjoying great freedom, the doors of the palace are open to all, and the king publicly celebrated the Passover and holds divine service there in the presence of four hundred people. They told me, on the authority of the king and the prophet, that the gathering of Israel to their land will take place in the year 427, which begins next September. All this greatly encourages the Jews here [in Amsterdam] in a wondrous manner,

172. Leyb b. Ozer (MS. Shazar, fol. 50a-b).

and causes them to persevere in their penances, all the more so as these counsels came to them from their chiefest rabbis in Constantinople who had written in answer to the questions which the rabbis of Venice had asked them as to what they thought of the matter.[173]

The believers in Constantinople had probably sent to Amsterdam a copy of the letter of Yakhini and his colleagues, together with a covering letter giving additional information.[174] Reports arriving during August and September[175] fanned the expectation that Nathan would soon join Sabbatai in order to set in motion the series of events that would lead to the ingathering of the exiles. The letters from Constantinople, and especially the "official" missive to the rabbis of Venice, impressed even the unbelievers in Amsterdam, some of whom began to "obey the instructions contained therein."[176]

173. MS. in the Hottinger Collection (Zurich), vol. XXX, fol. 349. The account (by Serrarius?) is written in French (one of Serrarius' two main languages), but a Latin version of the same text is given in the same MS., fol. 347b.

174. The letter to Amsterdam is dated June 1, one week after the famous letter concerning "R. Israel, the son of Abraham." The Amsterdam version of the latter epistle bears the signatures of seven rabbis, whereas all other sources mention six or even less signatories. According to Sasportas (p. 107), the famous letter from Constantinople arrived in the week July 10–17, i.e., one week before the date given in the French document.

175. MS. Hottinger, fol. 349b: "R. Solomon and others that have great credit here [in Amsterdam] testify that Nathan is a true prophet if ever there was one in Israel (*si jamais il y a eu Prophète en Israel*)." The emphasis on the credit given "here" to the witnesses suggests that they were well-known in Amsterdam, though no longer resident there but writing from the East. Perhaps "R. Solomon" is none other than R. Shalom b. Joseph, the schoolmaster from Amsterdam who had gone to Palestine, whence he wrote to his former compatriots, strengthening their faith in the messiah. The suggestion gains in verisimilitude in the light of the parallel Latin text (fol. 347b) where the sentence about R. Solomon, etc., is omitted altogether. The summary of the letters from Constantinople is followed by a report that "letters from Jerusalem and Alexandria of the 6th of June arrived here on August 18, announcing the departure of Nathan from Gaza to Jerusalem at the behest of God, and that he had been charged to make known unto all the will of God." Very possibly the French and the Latin versions represent different summaries of the same letters from Palestine and Egypt, the one quoting R. Shalom's intimations regarding Nathan's future moves, the other quoting an account in which Nathan's intention had been converted into a fact.

176. Sasportas, p. 106.

In July, 1666, a booklet was published in Amsterdam which contained, in addition to the "Penitential Exercises according to Isaac Luria," a Yiddish poem *Ein schön neu Lied fun Moschiach*[177] by one Jacob Tausk of Prague, apparently a poor schoolteacher in Amsterdam who thus hoped to gladden the hearts of "some devout Jews, women and children, young lads and maidens—and even rabbis may read it." The poem, which was sold out immediately and which appeared in at least two printings in 1666,[178] is an invaluable record of the attitudes and feelings of the simple and devout "common people" among the Ashkenazi Jews. Devoid of any literary pretensions, the poem has a peculiar charm due to its naïve and simple faith, The poet or, rather, rhymester, was a simple soul, and his childlike faith was far removed both from kabbalistic sophistication and from the mystical rebellion which some heresy-hunters found in the movement. The poem may not tell us much about Sabbatai Ṣevi, but it does tell us, clearly and plainly, a great deal about what the ordinary everyday Jew, who believed in him, thought and felt. For more than a millennium and a half, the poet says, we have endured the sufferings of exile, but our hope and our tribulation have not been in vain. Now at last we shall go to the Holy Land "and there dwell in peace. We shall do no work, but only study the Law and serve the Lord." His messianic vision kept strictly within the bounds of traditional piety, and did not envisage any deviation from the familiar pattern of the Jewish religion. Sabbatai Ṣevi is *ein frummer Held* ("a pious hero"). The past and the future merged in the writer's imagination. The Temple has already been rebuilt (past tense!) by God.

> Grosse Freid in Amsterdam hob ich viel gehert und auch gesehn
> Wie gute Brief gekummen sein, was Freid war do geshehn.
> Wie die Portugiesen hoben die Sifrey Taure ausgenumme,
> Darkegen getanzt un geshprunge.[179]

The poem mentions letters that had arrived early in June, bringing good news and telling of the miracles wrought by the messiah as he

177. "A Comely New Poem concerning the Messiah." The transliterations in the quotations from the poem are not philologically correct, but represent an approximation to German.

178. See Max Weinreich, pp. 219–52, who also reprinted the poem. So far only one copy, in the Bodleian Library, Oxford, is known.

179. "I have heard and seen great joy in Amsterdam/ As good letters arrived, how great was the rejoicing./ How the Portuguese [Jews] took the scrolls of the Law out [of the Holy Ark]/ and danced and jumped around them."

was arrested.[180] "Our brethren clearly write that the messiah will come this year," while "our brethren from Safed" advised us to prepare ourselves to bring sacrifices (in the Temple of Jerusalem) before the year was out. Above all, it was necessary to repent, give alms, and lay aside all hatred in order to come to Jerusalem *mit guten Harzen* ("with a good heart").[181]

An audible overtone of social protest seems to vibrate in the submissive, yet nonetheless menacing, exhortations addressed to the rich: do not miss the chance of taking the poor with you as you go to Palestine. Woe unto the rich that do not heed the messianic call: they will perish on the dunghills.

Neiert unzer Gott allejn, waz iz mer zu gleichen
Er nemmt for sich die Tefille fun arme Lait so woll as fun die Reichen
Die Reiche treiben mit ihr Geld eitel Lust un Fraid
Un achten nit kein arme Lait.

Haben unzer Newiim geshrieben aus ihren Land zu die reiche Leiten,
Sie zollen arme Lait wohl teilen mit, dass zie auch mit kummen beizeiten.
Wenn zie die arme Lait nit welln heren
Wern zie unter wegen ihr Gelt mit Sorg verzehren.

Meint ein Teil reiche Lait: zie wern in Erez Jisroel nit hoben zu leben
Wenn zie arme Lait wern mechabbed sein un Zdokeh geben.
Man wert zie dort halten zischt der hecher!
Sie sollen nur brengen schejne Kiddush-Becher.

Kibbudim wert man die zelbigen Reichen antun, wenn zie wern nach
Erez Jisroel kummen,
Die da hoben Guts getan an arme Lait, un hoben zie mitgenummen.
Manche Reiche halten die Ge'ulle gar for nisht,
Die werden hipegern auf den Mist.[182]

180. E.g., the splendor that shone from him in his prison (stanza 36); the prison doors opened miraculously before him (stanza 28); angels attended him (stanza 37); he refused to leave the prison (*ibid.*).

181. Stanzas 35 and 39.

182. "There is none like our God who hears the prayers of poor and rich alike. The rich spend their money on delights and pleasures, and heed not the poor. Our [new!] prophets have written from their country to the rich, that they should deal kindly with the poor so that they too may voyage in time. But if they do not hearken to the poor, then they shall consume their money in sorrow. There are some rich people who think they will not have wherewith to live in Palestine if they honor the poor and give them alms. However, they will be esteemed there all the more highly! They should only bring beautiful

It is the voice of the people, coming from the bottom of the heart, that speaks in this diatribe against the rich. The poet does not envisage the disappearance of the rich as a class, and he even promises them great honors in the Holy Land; yet his suppressed hostility and anger burst forth in the last two lines of the stanzas devoted to them. These lines also provide additional testimony to the division of opinion among the wealthy Jews regarding the messianic tidings.

Others in Amsterdam besides Jacob Tausk were inspired to poetic compositions by the good news. The Spanish poems in honor of the messiah by the most prominent marrano poet in Amsterdam, Daniel Levi de Barrios (1625–1701) have, unfortunately, not survived,[183] but a Sabbatian hymn has been preserved among the poetic compositions of R. Solomon d'Oliveira. The poem, which opens and concludes with an invocation to the prophet Elijah (see above, p. 525) is entitled: "A hymn for the conclusion of the Sabbath, containing allusions to the name of the prophet and his city, as well as to the name and title of the King and his native city, and to the coming of the tribes."[184]

In the summer of 1666 it became known in Amsterdam that many communities had dispatched embassies, or at least letters of homage, to Sabbatai Ṣevi. The practice had spread from Turkey to other countries, and instances are known from Persia, Italy, Poland, Germany, France, and Holland. So far no evidence has been found to show that either the elders of the congregation or the members of the *yeshibah ᶜEs Ḥayyim* (most of whom were ardent believers)[185] had taken any formal and official steps. On the other hand, the "humble addresses" by several other Sephardi *yeshiboth* (academies) have been preserved. In one case we even possess the original document which was never delivered to Sabbatai; apparently the envoys heard of the messiah's apostasy while still on their

---

[silver] cups for the Kiddush blessing. Such rich people as have dealt kindly with the poor and taken them on the voyage, will be greatly honored when they come to Palestine. [But] there are some rich people who think nothing of redemption; they will perish here on a dung heap" (stanzas 43–46).

183. According to Sasportas (p. 364), de Barrios also kept a book on which he recorded the visions that he had in the years 1666–75; see also below, pp. 893 ff.

184. Freimann, pp. 116–17.

185. A letter by Aboab, writing on behalf of the members of *ᶜEṣ Ḥayyim* and taking Sasportas to task for his hostile propaganda, which undermined the faith in the messiah, is reproduced by Sasportas (pp. 105–7).

way, and they returned home, crestfallen and abashed, with the letter in their hands. The letters were written in September. The signatories in Amsterdam could not know that in Turkey the movement had already entered upon a severe crisis, and they dispatched their addresses to R. Isaac Nahar in Leghorn, who was to present them to Sabbatai Ṣevi. The first letter was signed by the chief rabbi, Isaac Aboab, together with the members of the *yeshibah Torah ᵓOr*, but no copy has so far been found. The physician, Dr. Benjamin Mussafia, who also wished to pay homage to the messiah, was not a little offended at being left out by Aboab, and on the Twenty-fourth of Ellul he and the members of the *yeshibah Kether Torah* wrote another "humble address." In this letter, the original of which is extant, they acknowledged Sabbatai as their king and requested guidance regarding "the way wherein we must walk and the work that we must do," that is, whether to set out immediately in order to throw themselves at the messiah's feet, or to bide their time until the signal was given for the general gathering of the exiles. "And we know not what to do . . . and are waiting for the reply and commandment of Our Lord." The letter was signed by "The servants of the Spanish expulsion which are dwelling in Amsterdam, this day, the Twenty-fourth of Ellul . . ." [September 24, 1666] and the fourteen signatories include Benjamin Mussafia, Aaron Sarphati, Moses Raphael d'Aguilar, Abraham Pimentel, David Shalom d'Azevedo, Moses Nahar (brother of Isaac Nahar), and Solomon de Oliveira.[186] By one of the strange ironies of history, this testimony of faith was signed on the same day that Sabbatai, having apostatized and being in a fit of deep depression, wrote his first letter to his former co-religionists (see below, p. 686).

The senders of this letter were scholars, and some of them were reputed to be "philosophers" and rationalists. Mussafia in particular was severely berated by Sasportas, who scornfully asked: "This physician's philosophy did not avail him at this time, . . . and he made no use of it, but sank deeply into this 'faith.' Where are his arguments and his logic? And where is his sagacity and his system of reducing everything to the laws of nature?"[187] No less illuminat-

186. Sasportas, pp. 126–27; Freimann, pp. 112–13. Photographic reproductions of the document appeared in the monthly *Ost und West*, VI (1906), 273–74; see also the article by M. Gaster, *ibid.*, pp. 267–78.

187. Sasportas, p. 128.

ing is a letter sent by one of the new *yeshiboth* that were founded as a result of the great awakening. Most members of the *yeshibah Yeshuᶜoth Meshiḥo* ("The Salvation of His Anointed") were ordinary people, penitents rather than scholars, and only a few signed their names in Hebrew script. The letter is written in a florid style that abounds in biblical and Talmudic expressions as well as in kabbalistic and messianic allusions gleaned from Nathan's letters and other writings. It was addressed to the "Light of Israel . . . the beauty of the pride of Jacob . . . the King whom our eyes may behold in his beauty . . . Our Lord and Our King . . . the rabbi Sabbatai Ṣevi, may his seed live forever before the Rock who dwelleth on high." The writers crave the pardon of "Our Lord and Our Messiah of Righteousness, the Spirit of Our God—which is the Spirit of Our Messiah Sabbatai Ṣevi—which [hovers] over his people and the sheep of his pasture like an eagle stirring up her nest" for their presumption in addressing "the radiant splendor of his face." But taking heart at the example of "R. Isaac Aboab, the chief rabbi of our congregation in general and of the members of the *yeshibah Torah ᵓOr* in particular, . . . who has gone forth with all his followers to meet the honor of Your exalted glory, we too, the young sheep of the *yeshibah Yeshuᶜoth Meshiḥo*, which bears the name of Our King and Messiah, . . . have decided to seek the peace of the King of Peace. Wherefore we bow down night and day to the Lord Messiah of the God of Jacob, eagerly longing to hear of the mighty deeds of his right hand. The right hand of the Lord is exalted, the right hand of the Lord doth valiantly. . . . May [His Majesty], when he sits on the throne of his kingdom, remember all his servants who make supplication before him . . . though they be despised and lowly. May our supplication rise from the depths and be accepted on the altar of your greatness. . . . May [God] speedily fulfill His word concerning Our Lord . . . to be a crown of glory unto them that are borne [by God] from the belly and who shall be renewed under the shadow of SH D Y [Hebrew, *Shadday*, "the Almighty"; see above, p. 296], for His name is in him. May we, his servants, the young sheep, behold his beauty, and worship the King, the Lord of Hosts, at Mount Zion."[188]

Throughout September and October more letters arrived bringing glad tidings. Also the Ashkenazi rabbis, like their Sephardi con-

188. *Ibid.*, p. 111.

frères, spread the good news to all their acquaintances. R. Yaʾir Ḥayyim Bacharach and his father, who were in Mainz or Worms at the time, were kept informed by R. Isaac Deckingen, the rabbi of the Ashkenazi community, "of the marvelous letters arriving there [that is, in Amsterdam] every day."[189] It was probably from Ashkenazi circles that the Christian scholar Johann Christoph Wagenseil obtained his information. In preparing for their exodus, many Ashkenazi Jews also sold their books and manuscripts, and Wagenseil, who visited Amsterdam at the time, bought some important works on that occasion.[190]

Documentary evidence regarding other parts of Holland is scarce, but it may safely be assumed that the movement which was so powerful in Amsterdam also spread to the lesser communities. In a letter of January, 1667, R. Josiah Pardo, the rabbi of the Sephardi community in Rotterdam, admitted that he too had been a believer until disabused by the report of Sabbatai's apostasy. The many reports, spread and confirmed by the most eminent rabbis, "persuaded me to follow the opinion of the majority, since everybody agreed and none dissented except a few quarrelsome individuals, or such as were affected by the leprosy of heresy, or such as had little faith and believed nothing but what their eyes could see and their hands touch. And every unbeliever was considered to belong to one of these three groups."[191]

Echoes of the movement penetrated even the cloistered seclusion of Baruch Spinoza's study. Since his excommunication in 1656, Spinoza had had no contacts whatever with the Jewish community, but one of his correspondents, Henry Oldenburg, a native of Bremen in Germany, who lived in London where he had become secretary of the Royal Society, showed great interest in the Sabbatian movement. Many letters are extant in which Oldenburg inquires of friends and acquaintances regarding the movement that had arisen among the Jews. Oldenburg was interested mainly in the political aspect of the possibility of a restoration of the Jews. Early in December, 1665,

189. See the summary of the contents of Yaʾir Bacharach's private file on the Sabbatian movement, in A. H. Weiss (1865), p. 92.

190. Thus Wagenseil's own testimony in one of his books, as quoted by Hosmann, *Das schwer zu bekehrende Juden-Hertz,* 2nd edn. (1701), Appendix, p. 104.

191. The letter was discovered by M. Benayahu in the ʿ*Eṣ Ḥayyim* Library at Amsterdam, and published by him in ʾ*Ereṣ Yisraʾel*, IV (1956), 203–4.

immediately after arrival of the first sensational reports, he wrote to Spinoza: "As for politics, there is a rumor everywhere here concerning the return of the Jews, who have been dispersed for more than two thousand years, to their native country. Only a few here believe in this, yet there are many[192] hoping for it. May it please you to communicate to a friend what you have heard regarding this matter, and what you think of it. As for me, I cannot believe this report until it is confirmed by reliable people from the city of Constantinople, which it touches most of all. If the tidings prove to be true, it is sure to bring about an upheaval of everything in the world."[193]

Unfortunately, Spinoza's reply to Oldenburg is lost, though elsewhere[194] he expressed his opinion that a restoration of temporal rule by the Jews should by no means be considered an impossibility. The practice of circumcision, he thought, had preserved (and would continue to do so) the distinct identity of the Jewish people throughout the ages, and therefore, "I am inclined to believe that, with the opportunity afforded, since human affairs are notoriously changeable, they may again recover their kingdom, and God elect them to Himself anew." It matters little, for our purpose, whether Spinoza meant his words regarding a renewed election of Israel by God to be taken literally or as a figure of speech only. In any event Oldenburg seems to have taken a positive view of the messianic movement among the Jews, about which he continued to keep himself informed.[195]

192. Apparently, Christians.

193. Spinoza's *Letters,* no. 33: "qui, verus si fuerit, rerum omnium in Mundo Catastrophen induturus sane videtur." It seems to me that the printed text of the letter to Spinoza contains a misprint. I read, according to the conjecture, *indu[c]turus.*

194. *Tractatus Theologico-Politicus,* at the end of ch. 3.

195. This appears from his letters to various other friends. On March 6, 1666, Oldenburg wrote to Robert Boyle, informing him of the latest news that had arrived from Amsterdam (see *Works of Robert Boyle,* a new edn. [London, 1722], vol. VI, p. 219). No doubt the letter of November 10, 1666, to Joseph Williamson, signed with the initials H.O., is also by Oldenburg (as C. Roth was the first to perceive); see "Calendar of State Papers," Domestic Series, 1665–66, p. 50, where, however, the letter has been placed by mistake under November, 1665. As the letter mentions the first reports concerning Sabbatai's apostasy, the date is obviously November, 1666. The identity of the writer is further confirmed by the sequel of the letter, in which he discusses certain information he had received from the astronomer Hevelius in Danzig. Hevelius was a member of the scientific society of which Oldenburg was secretary.

Among Christian sectarians, chiliasts, and visionary mystics in Holland, interest in the movement was naturally less detached than in the case of Spinoza and Oldenburg. Some of them, like Serrarius, waxed enthusiastic in their praise of the Jews and contrasted the penitential revival among the Jews of Amsterdam with the laxness of the Christians. In the summer of 1666 Jean de Labadie, who had just broken with the Church of Rome, arrived in Holland from Geneva, and in July of that year he spoke to his chiliast circle on the subject of Christ's manifestation on earth. The anonymous correspondent to whom we are indebted for this information associates his account of Labadie's address with the recent news concerning Sabbatai Ṣevi: "Even if there were no other sign of the [impending] judgment on Babylon [that is, the Roman Catholic Church] and of the redemption of Israel, but the fire of dissension and the confusion among Christians, on the one hand, and the zeal for penitence among the Jews, on the other—it should be enough to awaken us."[196] The subject of a renewed election of Israel and rejection of the gentiles seems to have exercised the minds of members of this circle as early as autumn, 1666. The positive attitude of this Christian group contrasts strongly with the disparaging and vituperative polemical tone in which most Christian writers spoke of the messianic movement and of the "blindness of the Jews" in the many pamphlets that began to circulate among the Christian public.[197]

196. The source of information concerning Labadie's circle in Holland is MS. Hottinger (Zurich), vol. XXX, fols. 349a–350a. At that time Labadie had not yet met the visionary Antoinette Bourignon; their acquaintance and close relationship dates from 1667. Nevertheless, even at the time of his arrival Labadie was already open and eager for divine signs and revelations, which he expected in the near future.

197. The authors of these pamphlets seized the opportunity to present not only confused news, derived from the various news letters, about Sabbatai and Nathan, but also to parade their expert knowledge of Jewish matters, including Jewish messianic doctrines and previous pseudo-messiahs. Their missionary interest is obvious, yet they faithfully reflect the atmosphere in which many frank discussions on the subject took place between Jews and Christians. Particularly instructive in this respect is a pamphlet entitled *Den gewaanden Joodsche Messias Sabatha Sebi ontdeckt* ("The pretended Jewish Messiah Sabatha Sebi Exposed"), published in Amsterdam in April, 1666. The anonymous author reports several—almost certainly authentic—discussions with Jews in Amsterdam. In spite of some curious divergences (e.g., the story of Ḥayyim "Pegnia" [i.e., Peña] becomes an account of the resurrection of a dead man performed by

IV GERMANY

From Amsterdam the good news spread in all directions. We have already remarked upon the peculiar composition of the Jewish community in Amsterdam and its strong component of former marranos. The latter continued to entertain relations, both secret and open, with their relatives in Spain and Portugal, and word of the thrilling messianic tidings must have reached the latter very soon. Echoes of the Sabbatian ferment among the New Christians were discovered by H. C. Lea, the historian of the Spanish Inquisition, among the documents of the Inquisition. Until 1666 the laws restricting emigration of New Christians had not been strictly enforced. The appearance of Sabbatai Ṣevi, however, caused alarm in the Suprema (the Supreme Council) of the Inquisition, lest some marranos might attempt to join their messiah in the East. Instructions were issued to all Spanish ports to detain under some pretext any suspect travelers endeavoring to embark, to seize and examine their property, and to report to the Suprema.[198] Nevertheless, according to an eyewitness in Constantinople, "many Jews arrived from countries where they had lived in secret" (that is, as marranos); the Jesuit author of the *Relation* actually specifies that they came "from Spain."[199]

But whereas the rumors that reached the Iberian marranos were probably vague and confused, the news that was passed on to England was abundant and detailed. In autumn, 1665, the Great Plague devastated London, and the small Jewish community suffered heavily.[200] Sasportas, who in 1664 had become the first rabbi

---

Nathan, and the incident is transferred from Smyrna to Cairo; *ibid.,* p. 7) the legends are generally rendered more or less as they were told to the author. He had also heard that there were two people in Amsterdam who had been present at Sabbatai's wedding (probably one of Sabbatai's early marriages in Smyrna, mentioned *ibid.,* p. 7). The author mentions a conversation with a certain R. Benjamin L. concerning the mass prophecy in Smyrna. At the end of the pamphlet the Jew is said to have invited his Christian discussion partner to visit him at his home on April 12 (*ibid.,* p. 14). The pamphlet was therefore printed immediately after the receipt of the first reports from Constantinople.

198. H. C. Lea, *A History of the Inquisition of Spain,* III (1907), 303–4.

199. *Relation,* p. 24. An earlier version of this account, which was written one month before the French text and published under the title *Lettera mandata da Constantinopoli,* makes no mention of marranos; however, it explicitly states that people had come also from Spain and Portugal, which means the same thing.

200. Roth (1941), p. 174.

עטרת צבי
בימים ההםובעתההיא
אצמיח לדוד צמחצדקה
ועשה משפט וצדקה בארץ
תקון
והגית בו יומם ולילה

Sabbatai Șevi as messiah, sitting on the kingly throne, under a celestial crown held by angels and bearing the inscription "Crown of Șevi." Below: the Ten Tribes studying the Torah with the messiah. From an etching after the title page of one of the editions of Nathan's *Tiqqun Qeri'ah* (Amsterdam, 1666)

TICVN

DE LA NOCHE;

Y DE EL DIA

ORDENADO

Para la ſaluacion

Por el S. H. R.

NATAN

SQVENAZI.

(l'Anno 5426.)

Title page of *Ticun de la Noche,* a Spanish translation of Nathan's *Tiqqun* for the nightly devotions (Amsterdam, 5426 = C.E. 1666)

Den Nieuwen Iooden Koningh. *Den Propheet der Iooden.*

Afbeelding, van den gewaenden, nieuwen Joodſchen Koning

SABETHA SEBI,

Met zijn byhebbende Profeet, opgeſtaen in den jare 1665, etc. zoo vele daer van tot noch toe bekent is, of van de Joden geſeit wort, uit de nauwkeurigſte brieven, en ſchriften opgeteekent.

Sijn naem en afkomſt. DEſen *Sabetha Sebi*, is gebooren in *Aſia*, in de vermaarde koopſtad *Smirna*, van ſlechte doch vroome Ouders, beide als noch in leven, als mede verſcheide Broeders en Suſters hebbende; van de ouderdom ontrent veertig jaren.

Gedaente. Hy is gheen moy man, maar rouw van aangheſicht, het hair een weinigh gekrolt, kloeck en dickachtige geſtalte, hebbende op ſtaande knevels, en aen de kin een weinig baerts.

Leven. Heeft wel in verſcheide geweſten des weerelds geweeſt, maer meeſt zijn tijd in zijn Vaderlijke Stad door gebracht, met het onderſoeken der *Schriften*, *Talmud*, en oude *Rabynen*. Levende zoo ſtrickt na de Wet *Moſes*, dat onberiſpelijk is geweeſt; van God meenigmael vermaent, als een beſonder heilig Man, wat groots van hem ſtont te zullen werden: hy ſpreeckt meeſt alle Talen, hebbende geleert by eenen R. *Gagas*.

Gevolg. Sijn voornaemſte gevolgh, beſtaet uit den Profeet *Nathan*, van afkomſte uit de Stad *Gaza*, een hoogh geleert Man, rechtvaerdigh, oprecht en ſeer ootmoedigh, begaeft met den Geeſt. Voorts vier of ſes van de deftigſte Rabijnen.

Aenhang. De aenhang van deſe *Sabetha*, en Profeet *Nathan Levi*, is ſeer groot. In het Land van *Sus*, zijn 8000 Troupen, ider der zelve van 100 tot 1000 mannen gerekent. In *Barbarien*, in de Woeſtyne van *Theophileta*; zijn ongevaer hondert duyſent Jooden, om dezen als haren Koning en Profeet te volghen, en op te trekken. Ontelbaer is het ghetal van deze Iſraëliten die dagelijks in die quartieren aen komen.

Mirakelen door hem, of den Profeet gedaen Aen het Graf van *Zacharias*, die de Joden tuſſchen den Tempel en den Autaer gedood, en waer in zy groote zonden begaen hebben, gekomen zijnde; was een oudt Man (*Zacharias* zelfs) daer uit voortgekomen, met een kom vol waters in zijn hand, waer in de Jooden haer gewaſſchen, en met een van die zonden gereinight zijn. Uit de Graf-ſteeden der oude Rabynen, over honderden van jaren gheſtorven, hoordemen levendighe ſtemmen; Hy ontdeckt de ſecreten eens menſchen hert; doet vier van den Hemel dalen, gelijck op den dagh van ſijn vertreck van *Smirna*, en meermalen is geſchiedt: als oock ter zelver tijd, des Turkſen Overſten hand, die hem meinde te vatten, verdorven, en op ſijn ootmoedige beede weer tot ſigh zelven gekomen. De plaetſe van *Ieruſalem* beſchijnt een geduurig licht; de fondamenten der muuren geven ſigh op; en die van den Tempel, zijn alreede eenige voeten gerezen, zo datmen bequamelijk de vertrekken, daer in kan onder kennen. En ontallijck veel wonderen meer, die al was de geheele werelt papier, alle de wateren inkt, alle boomen pennen, niet magtig zijn te beſchrijven.

Waer de zelve nu is. Den 31 December 1665. is dezelve met een Schip oft Barque, vergezelſchapt met eenige weinige perſoonen, met een goede wind, van *Smirna* na *Conſtantinopolen* gezeylt; om daer van den Turkſen Sultan te vorderen de Kroon van *Paleſtina*, en de erffelijke Landen der Jooden, en daer op zal terſtont de optocht der Stammen, alreede verzamelt, derwaerts aen volgen.

Gevoelen der Jooden hier van. De Joodſche Natie in de deelen van *Aſien* is allenthalven in ghevoelen, dit bovenſtaende, en noch veel meer, waerachtig te zijn. Houden dezen Koning, en Profeet, te wezen haren herſteller des Rijks, en kort om, haren beloofden *Meſsias*, die hare zonden oock zal dragen en weg nemen. In andere quartieren des Werelts, zijn de Joden, door ſchrijvens daer van, verzeekert, zommige vaſt en zommige klein geloovig; eenige zeggen ront uit het is den *Meſsias*, andere willen haer oordeel noch een maendt op ſchorten, immers is een algemeene vreugd onder haer, hier over, 'twelk zy, op den 11 en 12 Meert 1666, in hare Synagoge tot *Amſterdam*, met het aanſteken van lichten, ſingen van Pſalmen, ſlaande op de Verloſſinge Iſraëls, en anders, opentlijk vertoont hebben.

Gevoelen van andere Turken, en Chriſtenen, houden den zelven meerendeel voor een bedrieger, Turkſen oft Joodſen Quaker: en het geheele werk, een verleidinge, oft voor teeken van den Jongſten Dag; hoewel voor beide zeltzame dingen zijn vertoont, zeggen, hem, eenen anderen *Machumeth*, *Simon Magus* oft Tovenaer te wezen, en daer over alreede, op ſijne reize van *Smirna* na *Conſtantinopolen* van de Turcken geſtranguleert, oft op de Galeye voor Slaaf ghebannen. Eenighe ſchorten haar oordeel noch tot nader beſcheit op: ons aengaende, wy zeggen, met den ouden Leeraer *Hieronimus*, *De Iooden verwachten een gulde en met koſtelijke ſteenen verçierden Ieruſalem: en dat de Offerhanden en het Ryck des Heeren Meſsiæ op aerde herſtelt ſullen werden; welke dingen, alhoewel wy niet en volgen, lykewel en konnen wy-ſe niet verdoemen: alzoo veele Kerkelyke perſonen en Martelaren ook zoo geſprooken hebben.* *In Jer 19 10. Ed. Baſ fol 377*

E Y N D E.

Fictitious portraits of the "new king of the Jews" and his prophet Nathan, at the head of a Dutch broadsheet giving a résumé of the events (some of them legendary) until March, 1666 (Holland, spring, 1666)

Fictitious news and picture of the arrest and supposed execution of Sabbatai Ṣevi (identified here with Josvahel Cam), showing several legendary episodes from Nathan's and Sabbatai's career: (1–2) Miracles performed by the prophet (Nathan) as testimony of the coming of the Jewish messiah. (3) Sabbatai crowned king of the Jews. (4) Sabbatai presented by the prophet to the sultan. (5) Sabbatai arrested. (6) His throat cut by the Turks. (7) Disemboweling of his body. (8) Hanging upside down, to the lamentation of the Jews of Constantinople. German broadsheet: *Verwunderlicher Anfang und schmählicher Aussgang des unlängst neuentstandenen Juden Propheten Nathan Levi und des . . . jüdischen Messiae Sabezae, folgends aber Josvahel Cam genannt . . .* (probably Augsburg, summer, 1666)

Neubelebter König/oder Printz der Jüden. Das ist/

Etwas Neues/ von dem erhöheten Josvehel Cam/ wie sel-
iger nacher Constantinopel kommen/ daselbst anfangs gefangen gesetzt/ aber endlich wider von dem Groß-Tür-
cken erlediget und zu hohen Ehren erhaben worden/solches durch gewisse Hand aus Constantinopel den 7. Martii/Anno 1666.
Wie auch aus Schmirna und andern Orten gewaltig Confirmirct wird.

Geliebter Leser! was neulich in unter-
schiedlichen Zeitungen von des Jüdischen Königs schmählicher Hinrich-
tung und Tod ist ausgesprenget wor-
den/ist nunmehr vö glaubwürdige Or-
en verworffen worden; und melden in Gegentheil
ie Brieffe von Constantinopel vom 7. Martii fol-
endes: Der Jüdē König ist zu Constantinopel nun-
iehro ankommen/ allda er den Türckischen Kayser
nd dem Primo Vezier nicht gefunden/in deme selbe
uf der Jagd gewesen/ist von denen daselbst sich auf-
altenden Jüden mit Freuden empfangen worden!
ie Janitscharen aber und andere grosse Herren ha-
en einen gefährlichen Aufruhr erwecket/ in deme
ie überlaut geruffen/man solte die Jüden ohne Un-
erschied und einiges Verschonen ermorden/und zu
od schlagen; und ob wol der Vice Vezier sich hier-
berhefftig entsetzet/und alle Mittel gesucht diesem
rossen Unheil vorzukommen/auch den Jüden Kö-
ig/der sich ungeheissen eingestellet/ und ihm willig
efolgt/in das Gefängnus setzen lassen/haben doch
ie Janitscharen mit ihren Anlauff und Tumult
och immer fortgefahren/biß endlich der Türckische
Kayser und Groß-Vezier so von der Jagd wider zu-
ück gekommen/ solches Unwesen gäntzlich gestil-
t. Wurde also dem Cypier die Verwahrung des
Jüdischen Königes anbefohlen/ der sich aber bey
em Türckischen Kayser so bald beklagt/daß Jhme
nmöglich wäre/ den Jüdischen König in der Gefängnus zubehalten; Jn deme alle Thüren und
Schlösser von sich selbst auffgiengen und zer-
springeten; er auch ohngehindert ein und aus-
gehen könte. Es hat ihn auch gedachter Cypier vielmal auff dem Dach des Hauses beten
sehen/war solches Haus so wol von aussen als
inwendig in schröcklichem und wunderlichem
Feuerglantz umbgeben zusehen/ also/ daß der
Cypier sich nicht dorffte herzumachen/ viel weniger das Hause ansehen. Der Jüden König
hat auch seinem Volck/ als den Jüden lassen
ansagen/ sie solten sich nicht fürchten/ sondern
gutes Muths sein/ dann alles was er gethan/
und noch zuthun in Willens habe/komme von
hoher Hand her/ und sey dem Menschen un-
möglich solches zuverwehren. Jhrer viel dieses Orts halten/ihn und seine Gesellschafft in
hohen Ehren/ als von GOtt gesandte; Sein
Kleid ist von Feuer und giebt einen vortreffli-
chen Glantz von sich. Ferner so wird berichtet/
es habe der Türckische Keyser befohlen/ man
solle Jhn/als der Jüden Köng/ in ein prächtiges Haus oder Zimmer führen/ und daselbst
auff das herrlichste halten; gab Jhm auch eine
grosse Anzahl Volcks zu; also daß Jhme als einem grossen Fürsten begegnet wurde. Endlich
hat Jhm auch der Türckische Kayser den Ti-
tul: Printz der Jüden gegeben/und durch einen
Trommelschlag lassen publiciren/ durch die
gantze Stadt/daß niemand bey Leibes und Lebens Straff einen Juden verstossen/viel weniger beleidigen solte; Der Jüden König soll un-
terschiedliche Nächte nacheinander in des
Gros-Türcken Kammer kommen sein/ wor-
über der Türckische Kayser fast auf den Tod er-
schrocken sey/und sich hefftig entsetzet habe.

Der Bassa von Schmirna hat auch einen
Expressen Currirer von Constantinopel be-
kommen/ welcher vermeldet/ daß/ wie Er
von dannen ziehen wollen/ habe Er den Jüden König mit einem grossen Staat und vielen gemeinen Volck sehen durch die Strassen
gehen/ nicht anders als wann der Türckische
Kayser selbsten/wäre durchgangen. So
viel vor dißmahl/ins künfftig ein mehrers.

Erklärung des Kupffers.

A. Die Rebellirende Janitscharen / über den Ein-
zug des Jüdischen Königs.

B. Der Jüden König / wie er von etlichen Türcken zur Gefängnis geführet wird / darüber viel Jüden
sich kläglich gebärdet haben.

C. Der Jüden König / spatzieret auff dem Dach
der Gefängnis.

D. Der Jüden König / mit einem sonderlichen
Glantz umbgeben/ ist in dem versperten Gefängnis zusehen / davon die Rigel und Schlösser zerbrochen/ zur Er-
den liegen.

E. Der Jüden König betet auff dem Dach/deß Ge-
fängnis/ welcher mit Flammen umbgeben.

F. Der Jüden König/wie er in ein prächtiges Lust-
haus geführet / und ihme grosse Ehr von Türcken und
Jüden erwiesen wird.

G. Der Jüden König kommt bey Nacht/ in des
Gros-Türckischen Kaisers/Schlaff-Gemach.

E N D E.

More news of the elevated Josvahel Cam (Sabbatai), how he came to Constantinople, was at first imprisoned there, but eventually was freed again by the Grand Turk and raised to great honor. According to let-

VII →

ters from Constantinople and Smyrna. The pictures, referring to legendary reports, are described as follows (though the details of D and E have been confused): (A) The janissaries rebelling over the entrance of the Jewish king. (B) The Jewish king taken by some Turks to prison, at which the Jews complained bitterly. (C) The Jewish king goes for a walk on the prison roof. (D) The Jewish king, surrounded by a wonderful aureole, is to be seen in the entrance to his locked prison, with the locks and bolts lying broken on the ground. (E) The Jewish king prays on the roof of the prison, which appears surrounded with flames. (F) The Jewish king is led to a magnificent palace, and is shown every honor by the Turks and Jews. (G) The Jewish king comes at night into the Grand Turk's bedroom. German broadsheet: *Etwas Neues von dem erhöheten Josvehel Cam* (probably Augsburg, summer, 1666). Continuing and correcting broadsheet in Plate VI

Fictitious picture of the expulsion of the Jews from Vienna and other places as they lament their fate and prepare to march to their prophet Nathan. Satirical broadsheet: *Jüdische neue Zeitung vom Marsch aus Wien und anderen Orten . . .* (no place and date, but probably summer, 1666)

VIII

of the newly formed Sephardi community in London, fled from the plague before the first reports of the messianic awakening reached the city. The small congregation, which called itself *Sha^carey Shamayim* ("The Gates of Heaven"), had begun to organize itself in those years in the wake of Manasseh b. Israel's efforts to secure the readmission of the Jews to England. Sasportas was assisted in his work by Raphael Supino, who had accompanied him to London and who subsequently, after his return to Leghorn, became one of the leading believers there. Several of the marranos who were living in London outwardly as Christians joined the nascent congregation, but the London community was as yet of little consequence and is rarely mentioned in the pamphlets and news letters concerning the movement that were printed in London. Some light on the reaction of the London Jews to the messianic tidings comes from an unexpected source. One of the New Christians who had returned to Spain or Portugal told the Inquisition that the Spanish and Portuguese merchants in London who had openly returned to their ancestral faith and joined the Jewish congregation were endeavoring to persuade the other New Christians to declare themselves Jews in order to participate in the joys of the messianic era.[201] We may assume, therefore, that in London, too, the good news was received with enthusiasm. We know, as a matter of fact, that the scribe and slaughterer of the congregation, Benjamin Levi, received letters from believers abroad who informed him of the messianic events.

On the other hand, the many tracts and pamphlets printed in London are evidence of the keen interest exhibited by certain Christian circles, and of their curiosity regarding the strange reports that seemed to confirm their views concerning the impending Day of Judgment. England had just witnessed the appearance of George Fox and other Quaker enthusiasts, whose behavior seemed little different from that reported of the Sabbatian prophets. The similarities between the two movements were not lost upon their contemporaries and may have contributed to the interest with which many Christians in England, and particularly in sectarian circles, followed the messianic movement

201. Roth, *ibid.,* p. 282. The testimony was discovered in the documents of the Inquisition by the historian of Anglo-Jewry, Lucien Woolf (according to C. Roth who heard it from Woolf). The document itself has not been identified, much less published.

among the Jews. Only a few years before, in 1657, there had been a minor messianic outbreak when one of the Quakers, James Nayler, proclaimed himself Messiah and King of Israel, and rode into Bristol amid cries of Hosanna (see above, p. 101). The news of a messianic movement among the Jews gave rise to a rumor that a boat had sailed from Bristol, a center of Quakerism—one source even explicitly stated "from a people called Quakers"—"without any merchandise, [merely] in order to know the truth of the matter."[202] In the first English book on Sabbatai Ṣevi, John Evelyn's *History of the Three Late Famous Impostors* (1669), the biography of James Nayler appears next to that of the Jewish messiah.

The Portuguese Jews in London were informed of the beginning of Nathan's prophecy and of his subsequent activities by letters that came to the scribe and slaughterer of the community, R. Benjamin Levi.[203] By April, 1666, the arrival of such letters in London was known to Raphael Supino, who had come to London with Manasseh b. Israel and later returned to Leghorn, whence he corresponded with Benjamin Levi. After Sasportas' departure at the time of the Great Plague, Levi was the only scholar in the London community, and he probably was a believer as well. Samuel Pepys was informed "of a Jew in town, that in the name of the rest do offer to give any man £10 to be paid £100, if a certain person now at Smyrna be within these two years owned by all the Princes of the East, and particularly the grand Signor as the King of the world . . . and . . . the true Messiah."[204] Actually the betting seems to have started in

202. According to "A Notebook from Italy" (*Zion,* X [1945], 66), reports from Amsterdam in the spring of 1666 specified that the ship had been sent by Quakers. A Polish correspondent (Balaban, p. 42) reported from Amsterdam that "recently a ship sailed from Bristol to Jerusalem [!], carrying many that are curious to behold the wonders of the Lord." Jerusalem was often synonymous with Palestine for Christian writers.

203. The letter summarized by Sasportas (p. 71) seems to give news of Nathan's prophecy rather than of the conquests of the army of the lost tribes (as assumed by Tishby). Benjamin Levi had no connection whatever with the English letters published in London, at about the same time, by Christians (*contra* Roth [1938], p. 72); see also above, ch. 4, n. 31.

204. *Diary,* February 19, 1666. The *Diarium Europaeum* (1668), p. 516, reports the same detail from London, adding that Christians too were laying wagers that Sabbatai would be anointed king in Jerusalem "within these two years."

Hamburg,[205] where the Sephardic Jews were laying ten to one—the same odds that were offered in London—until the *parnasim* ("elders") prohibited this misdemeanor.

The good news also reached the Americas, and more especially the West Indies where many former marranos had settled. They had come from Holland and remained in close contact with their mother congregation.[206] We have, in fact, some additional information that the message of the arrival of the Ten Tribes had reached the American continent. The well-known preacher Increase Mather, in Boston, preached, late in 1665, several sermons "in a time when constant reports from sundry places and lands gave out to the world, that the Israelites were upon their journey towards Jerusalem, from sundry foreign parts in great multitudes, and that they were carryed on with great signs and wonders by a high and mighty hand of extraordinary providence, to the . . . astonishment of all that heard it, and that they had written to others in their Nation, in Europe and America, to encourage and invite them to hasten to them, this seemed to many godly and judicious [people] to be a beginning of that Prophesie [Ezekiel 37:7]."[207] It is interesting that no mention is made here of the messiah and his prophet, but we may safely infer that the invitation of the Jews to their brethren in America (the West Indies?) to join them was connected with the messianic message and not only with the appearance of the lost tribes.

Paris, like London, was not a Jewish center at the time. Very few Jews were permitted to live in the city, and even these only temporarily. Signs of interest in the messianic movement come mainly from Christian sources. Conrart, the permanent secretary of the *Académie Française,* gathered news on the subject, which he obtained from

205. *JJLG,* XI (1916), 12, and Sasportas, p. 75. The date of the report from Hamburg is earlier than that in Pepys' *Diary.*

206. See the letter of Abraham Cardozo (*Zion,* XIX [1954], 14): "his name was known as far as the Spanish Indies."

207. John Davenport of New Haven in his prefatory "epistle to the reader" which preceded Increase Mather's long tract *The Mystery of Israel's Salvation explained and applied* (London, 1669). The epistle is dated 1667. This proves that in New England, too, there were repercussions from the first reports. Mather maintained in his sermons of 1665–66 that the time for the restoration of the Jews had not yet come. (I owe this information to Prof. Jacob R. Marcus, Cincinnati.)

Dutch and Belgian sources and not from the French Jews.[208] French diplomats and ecclesiastics in Constantinople seem to have reported on the movement in their letters, and the *Muse de la Cour* published for the diversion of courtly circles also preserves some echoes of the events.[209]

There was considerable agitation in Avignon, which still formed part of the papal states and was a place where Jews were permitted to reside. Christian sources report that in March, 1666, the Jews prepared themselves for the voyage to Palestine.[210] Manuscript copies are extant of the "Midnight Devotions, arranged by the holy kabbalist R. Abraham Nathan the Prophet," written in Carpentras, in the district of Avignon, by the scribe "Immanuel b. Gad de Milhaud. The text is that of Nathan's "Devotions for the Night"; it was probably sent to France directly from Gaza or Egypt. One of the three extant copies was written on February 26, 1666, another "in the first month" (Nisan?—April, 1666). Milhaud, who was a well-known scribe, probably made copies to order until the printed Amsterdam editions of the prayer book became available in Avignon.[211]

The Jews of Metz and Lorraine behaved like their brethren elsewhere. They contributed a considerable amount toward the cost of the dispatch of a "famous rabbi" from Prague (whose name is nowhere given in the sources) as envoy to Sabbatai Ṣevi. The rich merchants in Metz believed in the messiah[212] no less than their

208. Aeshcoly, p. 218.

209. See N. Szabolcsi, "Témoignages Contemporains Français sur Sabbatai Zevi," in *Semitic Studies in Memory of Immanuel Löw* (1947), pp. 184–88. The gazettes contain nothing of value to the historian of the movement. Most of them are malicious *plaisanteries*.

210. *Diarium Europaeum,* p. 515.

211. The first MS. (February 21, 1666) is no. 683 in the Sassoon Collection (*Catalogue Ohel David,* p. 840); two others were in the collection of the President of Israel, Z. Shazar, who presented me with one of them. The title page of the first MS. differs from that of the other two copies. Of the latter, one mentions Nathan's name, the other does not. The place of writing is nowhere mentioned, but the scribe as well as his place of residence and the names of his customers are well known from other MSS.; see H. Gross, *Gallia Judaica* (1897), p. 345.

212. According to the testimonies of Ancillon and Bossuet, who were both in Metz at the time; their remarks are quoted by A. Cahen, *RÉJ,* VII (1883), 226. Ancillon, who was a Calvinist minister in Metz, mentions the embassy to Sabbatai Ṣevi "on behalf of the Jews of Germany and France" in his memoirs. For Bossuet, see also above, n. 20.

rabbi, R. Jonah Fränkel-Te'omim, one of the foremost Talmudic scholars of his time.[213]

In the German communities the response followed the pattern of Italy and Amsterdam. Of Frankfurt-on-the-Main, which was a major center of messianic ferment, a Christian eyewitness has this to tell: "The Jews eagerly received the vain reports and rumors that came from Vienna, Prague, Amsterdam, and Poland. They truly believed in their deliverance and spoke about it in Christian houses as well as in the ghetto and in the synagogues, where they prayed for it." The Christians were annoyed by the insolence of the Jews, who countered Christian ridicule with the reply "that times would soon change, that they had suffered enough, and that the tables were about to be turned."[214] Letters received in Casale in February, 1666, reported that in Frankfurt four hundred families were ready to set forth on the journey, and that many others from that region had already departed.[215] Two editions of the "Daily Devotions" were printed in Frankfurt "in the year *And The Kingdom SHALL BE* [numerical value in Hebrew: 426 = 1666] *the Lord's*."[216] Despite the absence of explicit documentary confirmation, we may assume that the messianic awakening in Frankfurt was led by the rabbi. Nathan's Devotional Manual would hardly have been printed without the rabbi's approbation. R. Menaḥem Mendel Bass of Cracow, who had officiated as rabbi of Frankfurt since 1664, was very highly regarded in his community and beyond.[217] He was an ardent kabbalist, and in 1647 had approved the publication of Naphtali Ḥayyim Bacharach's *ʿEmeq ha-Melekh*, the first printed work to bring a full-length exposition of the Lurianic kabbalah (that is, Sarug's version of it) before a wider public. In his approbation he spoke in the highest terms of the author, a kabbalist from Frankfurt, and declared the publication most opportune "since we are now [in 1647!] at the messianic end, and although he tarry, yet we wait

213. His approbation to Isaiah Horovitz's *Beth ha-Levi* (Venice, 1666) is dated "in the year [Israel is] SAVED [by the Lord]"; see above, p. 528.

214. *Diarium Europaeum*, p. 515.

215. "Notes from Italy," *Zion*, X (1945), 61–62.

216. One edn. in small octavo and small letters, the other in a somewhat larger format and letter-type. The only extant copies of the two edns. are in the Bodleian Library, Oxford (see Steinschneider, *Cat. Bodl.*, nos. 3038 and 3039).

217. See M. Horovitz, *Frankfurter Rabbinen*, fasc. 2 (1883), pp. 40–49.

for him." He also encouraged the printing of other kabbalistic works. It is not surprising, therefore, that he saw his messianic longing fulfilled when the good news was proclaimed in his old age. He was spared the bitterness of disappointment: he died in September, 1666, before the news of Sabbatai's apostasy could reach him. Whether, on a local level, the great plague that ravaged the Frankfurt ghetto in 1666 functioned as a contributory factor is indeed doubtful. The messianic enthusiasm was already at its height when the plague broke out.

Throughout Germany the penitential revival embraced the rabbinic scholars as well as the masses. In Mainz a group of thirteen people formed around R. Yaʾir Bacharach of Worms "in order to study under his direction every day, on account of the glad tidings," and signed a document establishing their brotherhood.[218]

An interesting eyewitness report from Westphalia throws much light on the atmosphere prevailing in the smaller communities and villages. R. Judah Leyb b. Moses of Zelykhov, who was officiating at the time as cantor in the little community of Abterode, tells us that in the year 1665–66 R. Wolf Segal, the rabbi of Witzenhausen in Hesse and famed for his scholarship and saintliness, had come to Abterode on his travels and tarried there for a while because he found many scholars in the community. "And there was a great repentance in all Israel" during that year, "and the aforementioned saintly rabbi taught penitence to all them that came to him . . . so as to merit the redemption which we were waiting and hoping for at that time, because the year was a time of grace as we could see with our eyes, . . . and even sinners repented with all their heart, . . . and the joy increased every day." One day R. Wolf told him with a frown on his face that the time of grace had passed because of the sin of Israel in not properly responding "Amen" to the benediction "Who spreadest the tabernacle of peace" (in the Sabbath eve service), and to the benediction "Who restorest thy divine presence unto Zion" (in the daily *ʿamidah*[218a]), and added: "I am exceedingly troubled because of the two Amens that were sinfully neglected by our community." R. Judah Leyb did not dare to interrogate the rabbi further, "because my heart melted like wax before the fire when I heard this. For all, without exception, applied themselves to a perfect penitence the like of which had never been

218. A. H. Weiss, *Beth ha-Midrash* (1865), p. 92; D. Kaufmann, *J. Ch. Bachrach* (1894), p. 49.

218a. Consisting of eighteen benedictions.

heard of before . . . in order to merit the redemption of the Lord, as is known to all contemporaries of the event who are still alive. And all were confident that God would lead us out of bondage to freedom in that same year. . . . And my spirit was depressed as I gathered from his words that because of the aforementioned sin the matter and the time of grace would be reversed. And so indeed it happened . . . and our dance was turned into mourning. Surely this celestial decree had been revealed in a dream to the rabbi. At the time—and until now—I never revealed this to any man, for fear of discouraging the heart of the children of Israel in their penitence."[219]

However, the penitential revival with its romantic and legendary halo is only one side of the picture. There was also an economic side to the matter, and the importance of this factor is clearly brought out by documents in German archives. In some parts of central and southern Germany rumors were rife among the peasantry and among debtors to the Jews that the latter were about to sell everything and "to follow some prophet." Many Jews had, indeed, begun to make preparations for their departure and to collect their debts, and thereby provoked much irritation and hostility in the villages and small towns. The convert Friedrich Albert Christiani, who at the time was cantor in the small Jewish community of Bruchsal (northern Baden), tells about the great agitation among the Jews in all places (*weit und breit*). "In many places they made preparations for their departure, wanted to sell their household effects and were satisfied if their debtors paid only half of their debts[220] in order to provide for their journey." Details are known from Franconia and Baden in particular: debtors refused payment since their Jewish creditors would anyhow be leaving the country before long, and the lord of one manor near Nuremberg forbade his peasants to pay and actually distrained their debts. Neither principal nor interest were paid, and even payments for goods received were suspended. In Ansbach stones were thrown at Jewish houses and Jews were insulted, attacked, and prevented by violence from collecting their debts. The Jews turned to the authorities (that is, to the many "independent" lords and barons who ruled over their territories) for help, arguing that with their debtors defaulting they

219. *Shirey Yehudah* (Amsterdam, 1696), fols. 4–5. D. Kaufmann (*loc. cit.*, n. 218, above) was the first to draw attention to this important testimony.

220. F. A. Christiani, *Der Juden Glaube und Aberglaube* (Leipzig, 1705), p. 66. and also in the preface.

could no longer meet their many obligations in rates and taxes to their Christian overlords. Several rulers of these tiny states in fact issued orders to protect the Jews (and the state treasury) from the dangerous consequences of this "vain intelligence." On February 22, 1666, the ruler (*Markgraf*) of Ansbach issued a printed proclamation, which was probably affixed in all the villages in his territories, assuring the Jews of his protection and commanding all officials to assist them in the collection of their debts and protect them in case of riots. At the same time the Jews were strictly forbidden to transfer their property, or themselves to leave the country without special permission.[221]

221. A copy of the edict was preserved in the archives of the Jewish community of Ansbach, now in "The General Archives for Jewish History" in Jerusalem, where I discovered the document (vol. IV of the Ansbach archives). The text, in the original spelling, reads:

VOn GOttes Gnaden/Albrecht/Marggraf zu Brandenburg/zu Magdeburg/in Preussen/[etc]... Demnach uns die gesambte Judenschafft in disem unserm Land und Fuerstenthumb klagend zu erkennen gegeben/wasmassen denenselben von dem gemeinen Volck allerhand Beschwerde und Ungelegenheiten ineme zugezogen werden/dass Sie und die Ihrigen nicht allein mit schimpflichen Worten uñ Schmaehungen hart tractirt/und ihnen bey Naechtlicher Weil/auff offenen Gassen/in die Fenster unnd Laeden mit Steinen geworffen/sondern auch sie bey ihren Debitorn an einbringung ihrer Schulden/und unserer Herrschafftlichen Schuldigkeiten/gehindert werden/und sie dato eines unnd andern Orts sich weing Huelff zu getroesten gehabt/dahero uns Dieselbe umb gnaedigsten Schutz unnd Handhabung unterthaenigst gebetten.

Als befehlen Wir/Krafft diss unser zu Maenniglichs Wissenschaft in Truck gegebenen unnd besigelten Patents, allen unsern Ober: und andern Beambten/Verwaeltern/Caestnern/Voegten/Richtern/Schultheisen/Burgermeister/Rath un Gerichten/in Staetten/auff dem Land/und ins Gemein allen unsern Dienern und Unterthanen/und wollen/dass hinfüro niemand sich an ihnen Juden/und deren Angehoerigen/es seyen Eltern/Kinder/oder Gesind/an orten und enden/wo sie sich in unserm Schutz enthalten/oder sonsten im raisen durchkomen/bey vermeydung hoher unaussbleiblicher straf/weder mit worten noch wercken vergreiffe/desswegen sie dann von ihnen unsern Amptleuthen unnd Bedienten darwider/von Ampts wegen/jedesmahls gehoerig zu mainteniren/und wider die Verbrecher mit allem Ernst zu verfahren/auch ihnen Juden auff gebuehrend Anruffen/zu ihren rechtmessig zu erfordern habenden Schulden/und deren Einbringung/wie solche unter den Contrahenten jedesmahls bedingt und verglichen unnd es den armen Leuthen erschwinglich/schleunig verhelffen/nicht weniger gegen die Benachbarte auff bedirffen mit Vorschrifften unnd in andere dienliche Wege an hand gehen sollen: da hingegen sie Juden sich hinwider aller bescheidenheit zu gebrauchen/und weder durch unbillliche Beschwehr: oder Ubernehmung in jhrem Handel und Wandel/noch auff andere unziemliche Weiss/Ursach zu geben/ dass man wider sie/der Gebuehr nach/verfahrn muesse:

The ruling princes evidently realized that many of their Jewish subjects intended to go to Palestine, but, unlike the peasant population, they did not view such an exodus of their Jews with favor. Other Bavarian authorities issued similar proclamations and orders, and even urged the Free City of Nuremberg not to obstruct the Jews lawfully collecting their debts. The picture was more or less the same everywhere in those parts. The Jews of Schneitach in the district of Rothenberg were repeatedly subjected to violence; in March, 1666, they obtained special letters of protection from the Bavarian authorities. The evidence suggests concerted action by the representatives of the various Jewish communities, and a favorable response by the gentile authorities. The steps taken by the Jews sufficiently prove that far from proclaiming their messianic hopes, they actually concealed them as best they could. The economic and the national-religious motives evidently clashed with each other. In their relations with magistrates and rulers the Jews manifested none of the messianic "insolence" of which contemporary pamphlets and broadsheets accused them. They endeavored to sell their houses and property, but were taken by surprise at the reaction of the populace.[222]

Massen auch von allen unsern Beampten darauff zu sehen/dass weder sie Juden von jhrer Haab/und Vermoegen/etwas auss dem Land verschleichen/noch vor jhre Personen/ohne von Uns erlangte gnaedigste Erlaubnuss/jhren Abzug nehmen moegen.

Wornach sich Maenniglich zu achten/Signatum unter Unserem hievor gedruckten Fuerstlichen Cantzley Secret-Innsigel/Onoltzbach/den 22. Februarij Anno 1666.

At about the same time, a preacher in the same principality of Ansbach-Bayreuth published a sermon, given on Ash Wednesday, 1666, discussing the current rumors concerning the return of the Ten Tribes; see Johann Rephun, *Jüdischer Heer-Zug* etc. (Culmbach, 1666). A copy of the very rare pamphlet is in the Hottinger Collection in Zurich, vol. XXX.

222. See M. Weinberg, *Geschichte der Juden in der Oberpfalz,* III (Bezirk Rothenberg; 1909), 49–50; *id.* "Das Messiasjahr 1666," in *Bayrische Israelitische Gemeinde Zeitung* (1928), no. 1, pp. 2–3. The author used documents whose tenor is similar to that of the edict quoted in the previous note, but unfortunately did not print their full text. Reference to agitation among the Jews on May 21, 1666, because of their alleged messiah, is made in the village chronicle of Hüffenhart, North Baden; see K. Darmstädter *Israelitisches Wochenblatt für die Schweiz* of April 5, 1957, p. 41. The Jew Koppel who owned rural property in the village, made a contract with the mayor about its sale, as "he planned to go with all his domestics" to receive the face of the messiah. The contract is still extant.

No Jews were allowed to reside in Nuremberg, but the nearby city of Fürth had an important Jewish congregation which served as a spiritual center for the Jewish population of the surrounding rural areas. In the year 1664 the scribe R. Isaac Seckendorf made manuscript copies, which are still extant, of the Lurianic writings. When Nathan's penitential devotions arrived two years later, Seckendorf, who also acted as principal of the *Beth Midrash* which a wealthy member of the community had founded a short time before, copied them too.[223] The beautifully written manuscript and its solemn superscription, "Penitential Devotions from Gaza, sought out and set in order by the holy man, the lamp of light, Rabbi Nathan Ashkenazi the Prophet . . . of truth and righteousness," suggest that the copy was made when messianic enthusiasm was at its height and the prophet's name held in high regard by the kabbalists of the *Beth Midrash* in Fürth.

The messianic reports that made the rounds both orally and in printed German pamphlets, inspired a Lutheran minister at Heldburg near Nuremberg to write a booklet proving the vanity of the Jewish hopes and, incidentally, giving some very lively accounts of what was going on: "The Jews are brimful of the hope of the messiah, running from one village to another and rushing in the streets from one house to another, in order to hear, with their ears pricked up, further news of the messiah. Some [Christian] youths have the impudence to blow trumpets at night in the vicinity of the Jews' houses, so as to strengthen their belief in the [imminent] blowing of the messiah's trumpet."[224]

223. MS. Oxford (Neubauer 1794). The same MS. also contains an erroneous and misleading note by R. Phineas Katzenellenbogen, whose father was rabbi of Fürth early in the 18th century (the note has been published by L. Löwenstein in *JJLG*, VIII, pp. 199–200). According to this note, the copy of Nathan's manual was brought from Italy by R. Abraham Rovigo, who had come to Fürth in order to print there the work *ᵓEshel ᵓAbraham* of his disciple Mordecai Ashkenazi; but the assertion has no foundation whatever. The script of the manual is the same as that of the Lurianic treatises copied by Seckendorf in 1664, and the two texts were almost certainly copies at more or less the same time and not at an interval of thirty-seven years. The kabbalist scribe in Fürth evidently regarded Nathan as a true prophet, and it is greatly to be regretted that his existence was unknown to Jacob Wassermann when he wrote the short story "Sabbatai Zewi, ein Vorspiel," (1897) as a prologue to his first novel *Die Juden von Zirndorf*, dealing with the Sabbatian movement in Fürth and the surrounding villages. (For a different interpretation of Katzenellenbogen's note, see Tishby's detailed discussion in *Sefunoth*, III (1960), 80–83.)

224. M. Buchenroeder (1666), at the beginning of ch. 8.

Early in 1666 several pamphlets appeared in Germany (especially in the southern parts) whose authors dealt in rather highhanded fashion with the current news—adding, omitting, and changing at their pleasure. The central figure in these accounts was the newly risen prophet, but many writers associated the recent reports with the earlier pamphlets of 1642 (see above, p. 155), as is evident from the Christian name under which Sabbatai Ṣevi appears several times. According to the German pamplets, the prophet "Nathan Levi" had anointed as king, not far from Jerusalem, a certain youth whose name had hitherto been "Sobeza" (that is, Sabbatai), but whom the prophet had renamed Iosua Helcam (also Iusvahelcam). The king had sent an envoy to claim all his dominions from the sultan, promising to appoint the latter, at a later date, as messianic viceroy. The envoy who brought the message to Constantinople was put to death, etc., etc.[225] Another pamphlet combined rumors about the armies of the lost tribes and their conquest of Mecca with the reports of the imaginary exploits of the prophet Nathan Levi. The illustrated pamphlet also informed its readers that after being anointed, the king, now renamed Iosua Helcam, led a large army into Arabia. The author's special interest centered on the flags of the three camps of the messiah's army.[226]

225. See the broadsheet printed at Augsburg on March 2, 1666 (Bibl. no. 62) and reprinted by M. Stern, *Magazin f.d. Wissenschaft des Judentums,* XV (1888), 101–4. The account contains detailed, albeit exaggerated and distorted, reports up to Sabbatai's arrival in Smyrna (e.g., about the rioting of some four hundred poor followers of the messiah against the rich who had refused to pay him taxes), but the sequel is sheer imagination: the messiah had marched on Constantinople, and the vizier, at the head of an army of thirty thousand men, had met him in battle. The messiah was defeated and taken as a prisoner to the sultan. At first he persevered in his pretense, but under torture admitted his fraud. The prophet Nathan fled with about a thousand men, and thousands of others were left dead on the battlefield. The messiah was brought to judgment, flogged, and his tongue cut off; and finally he was flayed and hanged upside down. (This was the manner of execution practiced in Germany on Jewish criminals!) His skin was stuffed with straw and exposed to the public, much to the shame and discomfiture of the Jews of Constantinople.

226. A copy of the pamphlet, entitled *Warhafftes Conterfey . . . des Propheten Nathan Levi* (Bibl. no. 71), is preserved in the Hottinger Collection (Zurich), vol. XXX, fol. 287; a short description is given by L. Geiger in *Zeitschrift f. Geschichte d. Juden in Deutschland,* V (1892), 101–2. This pamphlet, which was based on an earlier German broadsheet (Bibl. no. 72), in its turn served as the source of the Latin account contained in a letter sent to a Hun-

The same editors also published another broadsheet which is, in fact, a greatly enlarged and nicely ornamented portrait of the commander-in-chief of the Ten Tribes. Sabbatai's name has completely vanished, and the portrait is said to be of "Iosua Helcam, whom Nathan Levi, their new prophet, has chosen as chief general (*Obristen-General*) over them that are called the Ten Tribes of Israel."[227] The name Iosua Helcam was derived, in part, from a broadsheet of 1642, but had been further "Christianized," since it can only refer to Jesus ("Iosua"), the God ("Hel" = Hebrew *ʾel*, "God") that rose from the dead ("cam" = Hebrew *qam*, "rose"). The name Iosua, even as a Hebrew form of Jesus, is not surprising and actually befits the messiah's role as a second Joshua, son of Nun, conquering the Holy Land. Yet one cannot help wondering why the authors also adorned the new messiah Joshua—in his most earthly and untheological role of military commander—with a thoroughly Christian theological name. The military portraits of Sabbatai Ṣevi soon found their way to the Jews and were carried aloft through the streets in the great messianic processions in Poland.

Polemicists mainly criticized the stories of the lost tribes and the miracles told in the earlier letters about Nathan. The picture drawn in the pamphlets of the general reaction of the German Jews agrees with what we know from other sources. The tendency to liquidate all property seems to have been strongest immediately after receipt of the first reports, early in 1666. As time went by, people became more cautious and preferred to wait and see which course the events would take. According to the aforementioned illustrated broadsheet,

---

garian nobleman (publ. by M. Dercsényi in *Goldziher Memorial Volume* [1948], pp. 400–11). The editor of the Latin text failed to notice its dependence on the German source; the Latin version lacks only the large illustration found in the German original. The mottoes inscribed on the flags (*Goldziher Volume,* p. 406) are worthy of their author's imagination: (1) *Non curo ventura fati;* (2) *Mortis imago;* (3) *Nil fortius.* Also the German pamphlet gives these mottoes in Latin. Apocalyptic imagination seems always to have been fascinated by the question of the inscriptions on the eschatological flags, as appears from "The War of the Children of Light and the Children of Darkness" found among the Dead Sea Scrolls.

227. Of this broadsheet too, a copy is to be found in the Hottinger Collection (vol. XXX, fol. 289); see the reproduction in our plate II, and cf. plate VI.

most Jews in Germany were preparing themselves for the final hour of the messianic call, "just as some of the wealthy Jews in Amsterdam have done, who sold their land and their houses at two-thirds or three-quarters of their value, so as to be ready for the departure to the Holy Land."

Also from other parts of the German Empire, for example, from Austria, Bohemia, and Moravia, occasional bits of information have survived. The Jews of Vienna and Prague, in particular, were known for their active participation in the movement. Vienna and Prague were major centers of commerce as well as of rabbinic learning, and many of their scholars were ardent kabbalists. Vienna was near the Turkish border (Hungary was still under Turkish rule) and all the mail routes of central Europe met there; hence it also was the most natural center for the dissemination of Sabbatian news and propaganda. Many of the most fantastic tales were spread by letters from Vienna. The Protestant quietist mystic J. G. Gichtel recounts in his letters that during his sojourn in Vienna in 1666, the Jews of that city endeavored to draw him to their faith in the manifestation of the messiah Sabbatai Ṣevi.[228] Nothing is known of the attitude adopted by the leader of the kabbalist conventicle, R. Jacob Temerles, who died in April, 1666, just as the high tide of dramatic news from Smyrna and Constantinople came flooding in. His epitaph makes no allusion to the messianic hour, but no conclusions can be drawn from such an *argumentum ex silentio*, since none of the numerous known inscriptions on tombstones from the year 1666 in the cemeteries of Frankfurt, Vienna, Hamburg, and Prague make any reference to the advent of redemption, though earlier tombstones speak eloquently of messianic expectations. In 1664 the rabbi of Holleschau in Moravia, the renowned Talmudic scholar R. Sabbatai Kohen, author of the standard commentary *Sifthey Kohen* on parts of Joseph Karo's code *Shulḥan ᶜArukh*, died, and his epitaph[229] gives the date of his demise as "the year MESSIAH SON OF DAVID" (numerical value in Hebrew, 424). For some reason, as yet unexplained, the messianic testimonies on the tombstones

228. Cf. A. von Harless, *Jakob Boehme und die Alchemysten* (2nd edn., 1882), p. 143, on the basis of Gichtel's theosophical correspondence (1722), vol. VI, p. 3295.

229. The text is quoted in several books. I saw a photograph of the tombstone on a picture postcard printed in Holischau.

ceased as the fullness of time was proclaimed. When the Christian scholar Wagenseil visited Vienna in 1661, he met Jews who were ready to swear that the messiah would come within the next few years.[230] It may well have been Wagenseil's Jews who became the enthusiastic believers of 1666.

An anti-Jewish broadsheet was published, possibly in Vienna, which made fun of the great expectations by pretending that the Jews were about to be expelled from Vienna and other places and were turning with their complaints to the prophet Nathan.[231] The upper half contains a picture of the exodus of the Jews from the gate of Vienna; the lower half has two mocking poems about the plight of the Jews complaining to the prophet, one of them in pseudo-Yiddish (13 stanzas).

In general the news came to Vienna from the Turkish Balkans. Nathan's Devotional Manuals, which the Jews of Vienna were reciting "day and night in the synagogue with much noise and crying" had been sent from Sarajevo.[232] In Vienna, too, business came to a standstill and people applied themselves to mortifications and penances. A report of March, 1666, states that "several Jews in Vienna applied to the Imperial Court for permission to depart, because their messiah had arrived."[233] Reports current in Hamburg in June, 1666, said that the Jews of Vienna had dispatched investigators to make inquiries in Constantinople, and that the envoys had returned as believers, confirming the truth of all the news. In July Sasportas indited a long letter, in his most florid and artful style, to R. Gershom Olif Ashkenazi, the rabbi of Vienna (died 1693) and a renowned scholar and ardent Sabbatian believer. Sasportas approached the recipient of his letter gently and with circumspection. There were none of the usual polemical sallies and biting sarcasms, but grave doubts and profound anxiety. He desired reliable information from his colleague in Vienna, but couched his request in language that clearly expressed

230. Kaufmann, *Letzte Vertreibung aus Wien* (1889), p. 29.

231. *Jüdische neue Zeitung vom Marsch aus Wien und anderen Orten* (in large 4°). A copy is in the Hebrew Union College, Cincinnati; see plate VIII.

232. See *Diarium Europaeum,* XVI (1668), 516.

233. MS. Hottinger, vol. XXX, fol. 348a. J. J. Schudt, *Jüdische Merckwürdigkeiten,* vol. II, p. 41, speaks of "the insolence of the Jews of Vienna who, in the emperor's residence, boasted of their king and the new kingdom of Judah in order to insult the Christians."

his misgivings with regard to the alleged facts and their religious implications. He was also unstinting in his praise of the obstinate unbelief of the rabbis of Smyrna. Sasportas' diplomatic skill and his capacity to adapt himself to his correspondents without compromising his views are well illustrated by a comparison of his two letters, written at approximately the same time, to Vienna and Smyrna respectively. To the infidel rabbis at Smyrna, whom he knew to share his views, he permitted himself an outburst of uninhibited fury and vehemence. The letter to Vienna was all sweet reasonableness and persuasive deliberation,[234] and it is much to be regretted that R. Gershom's reply has not been preserved. Sasportas' repeated warnings against deviations from the path of rabbinic tradition were surely out of place in the central and eastern European communities, where the rabbis always seem to have kept a tight rein over their people.[235] There were no antinomian outbursts or demonstrative departures from halakhic tradition. Moses Zacuto, writing in 1668 to R. Meir Isserles, the principal of the *yeshibah* at Vienna, praised the Ashkenazi communities for never having swerved from the path of halakhic rectitude or broken the statutory fasts.[236] The absence of any such irregularities was largely due to the rabbinic leadership, as illustrated by a letter of the rabbi of Prague bearing on that question.

The Jewish community of Prague was the largest and most important in the Hapsburg Empire, and it exerted considerable spiritual influence. According to the account of a former rabbinic student in Prague who had apostatized (see above, pp. 154–55), a messiah appeared in Bohemia about the year 1650 and gained a considerable following until exposed as an impostor. Nothing is said about the identity of the messianic pretender, who has left no other traces in the contemporary records, but it is not impossible that in the wake of the massacres of 1648 and onward, there was some messianic unrest in those parts. When the good tidings arrived toward the end of 1665, they were received eagerly and with great rejoicing by the masses as well as by many educated people. However, R. Aaron Simon Spira, chief rabbi of Prague for almost thirty years, and his colleagues of the rabbinic court, were unbelievers. The chief rabbi had written to

234. Sasportas, pp. 114–20.

235. Such outbursts as have been described in detail in some widely read modern works of fiction are figments of the authors' imagination.

236. *Zion*, XIII (1948), 56.

Venice, but the reply, as we can gather from R. Solomon Ḥay Saraval's letter to Rabbi Spira (see above, p. 500), had not been very helpful. Sasportas had replied as early as December, 1665, to Spira's inquiries and apparently found the latter's response to his satisfaction. Sasportas wrote once more in April or May, 1666, and Spira's reply of June has been preserved.[237] His attitude was characteristic of the unbelievers who would not, or possibly could not, actively combat the rising tide of enthusiasm. "The truth is that I and my colleagues rejoice at the great repentance that was done in our community, . . . though we never ceased from reproving them and disabusing their minds . . . concerning the prophecy and the kingdom which were vouched for by ignorant people. We all, with one consent, are keeping a watchful eye lest there be the slightest detriment to our tradition, or [people] give obedience to such a prophet and to that which is not in accordance with the Jewish religion (*dath ha-yehudim*)." The rabbinic court of Prague also wrote in this sense to all the Bohemian communities, but as regards the faith in Sabbatai Ṣevi they contented themselves with a few vague and evasive phrases, trusting that truth would become manifest in the end "to darken the eyes of them that rebel against their Lord by calling 'Our Lord and King' a man of whom it is not known whether he is . . . of royal blood. . . . But what shall we do . . . for our brethren . . . who are so eager in this their faith? Let us not disturb them, for great is the power of penitence which can turn even willful sins into merits."

The boastful confidence shown by the Jews caused disturbances. During the carnival of 1666 some noblemen in Prague performed a kind of comedy, including a procession through the streets, in which they parodied the joyful expectation of the Jews, who had shut themselves up in their ghetto to prevent more violent attacks.[238] Parody and mockery, however, did not dampen the messianic enthusiasm. In the spring of 1666 Nathan's Devotional Manual was printed in Prague, probably from a copy of one of the Amsterdam editions.[239] The popular response to the messianic tidings found

237. Sasportas, pp. 120–21; Saraval's letter, *ibid.*, p. 122. On Rabbi Spira cf. T. Jacobovits, *Jahrbuch der Gesellschaft für die Geshichte der Juden in der CSR*, IV (1932), 274–90. He headed the community from 1640 until 1679.

238. Hottinger Collection, vol. XXX, fol. 348a.

239. The title page gives as date Exod. 23:20, the numerical value of which amounts to 421 = 1661 C.E., but it is beyond doubt that the booklet (53 fols.

glowing expression in an extraordinary document. The synagogue in Prague known as the *Pinkas Shul* possessed relics of the martyr Solomon Molkho, who was burned at the stake in Mantua in 1534. R. Yomtob Lipman Heller, author of a standard commentary, the *Tosafoth Yomtob*, on the Mishnah and rabbi of Prague until 1625, mentions in one of his works (*Maᶜadanney Melekh ve-Leḥem Ḥamudoth*, Prague, 1628) that he had seen the martyr's *ᵓarbaᶜ kanfoth*,[240] and that it was "yellow like the yolk of an egg." Sabbatian legend soon attached itself to the relic of the martyr, who had himself been a messianic enthusiast and whose apocalyptic speculations were extant in print. In a letter from Vienna dated Friday, the Fifth of Adar II (March 12, 1666), "in the first year of the reign of our messiah," an anonymous writer informed his father-in-law that it was a custom in Prague to expose the garments of Solomon Molkho to reverent view in the synagogue once a year, on *Simḥath Torah*, "except the *ᵓarbaᶜ kanfoth* which was not exhibited because holy [that is, divine] names were embroidered on it with silk. But these names are disarrayed all over [the garment—and therefore did not make any sense]. Once the beadle of the synagogue wanted to copy these names, and he became blind. And once . . . the illustrious R. Lipman [Heller], . . . trusting in his virtue, wished to copy these names; and indeed his saintliness saved him [from worse disaster] and he himself escaped unharmed, but his paper and inkhorn mysteriously vanished. Wherefore he decreed . . . that no man should ever approach to read these holy names or copy them." The letter from Vienna then proceeds to give the "holy names—six Hebrew words and three letters, arranged in three columns.[241] Now, however (the writer continues), letters had been sent from Prague to all communities proclaiming the miracle: word had been received from Aleppo, where the first great mass prophecy had occurred at the beginning of the movement, charging the Jews of Prague to take the garment and to copy the holy names, "for it is an acceptable time . . . and the previously disarrayed names were

---

in large letters) was printed in 1666. Neither the printer's name nor the place of printing are given, but the letter type is that characteristic of Prague. A copy is in Oxford.

240. A kind of small, fringed scapular worn by male Jews in fulfillment of the commandment in Num. 15:38.

241. *Zion*, X (1945), p. 144.

now [found mysteriously] joined together in their proper sequence." The letters and holy names combined to form a kabbalistic formula which declared Sabbatai Ṣevi to be the messiah in 426 (1666).[242] Kabbalistic formulas of this kind, that is, holy names that are given a messianic interpretation, are also known from earlier messianic movements.[243] The popular mind, evidently little impressed by the rabbinic counsels of prudence, had produced its own messianic legend, in which it linked the two great messianic revivals of two centuries by turning Solomon Molkho into a prophet and precursor of Sabbatai Ṣevi. This was the original contribution of Prague to the Sabbatian legend.

Jewish sources provide no information on the movement in the communities of Bohemia and Moravia. However, Martin Meyer, a Christian chronicler who gathered information on the events as they happened, reported serious disturbances from Moravia which "compelled the Prince Dietrichstein, as governor of the province, to intervene and to post official notices in order to quiet the citizens."[244] Nikolsburg, the residence of the prince, had the oldest Jewish community in Moravia, and the proclamation probably referred to disturbances there. No copy of the proclamation has so far been found, but the disturbances were probably similar to those which had occurred in the communities around Nuremberg, for the exhortation to keep the peace was addressed to "the citizens," which term can only signify Christians and never the Jewish population. There are two other facts which may be taken as indicative of the success of the movement in those parts. (1) Moravia was one of the strongholds of Sabbatianism even into the eighteenth century, and it is surely more reasonable to assume that the sectaries were the direct heirs of the great awakening of 1666 than that they converted to the Sabbatian faith at a later date. (2) The Sabbatian innovation of reciting Psalm 21 every day at the conclusion of the morning service was still prac-

242. Two versions of the letter are extant. The Hebrew version is found at the end of the Cambridge MS. of Baruch of Arezzo's memoir; I published it in *Zion,* X (1945), p. 145. Later I discovered that a Latin version had been published as early as 1714 by the Christian scholar Hermann v. d. Hardt, and was reprinted by Wolf, *Bibliotheca Hebraica,* III (1727), 1055. V. d. Hardt had already seen the connection of the letter with Sabbatian propaganda.

243. Cf. J. Mann, *Texts and Studies,* vol. I, p. 39, and S. H. Kook in *Reshumoth,* II, New Series (1946), 162.

244. *Diarium Europaeum,* XVI (1668), 516.

ticed in the eighteenth century in many communities in Moravia and Hungary, "although the origin of the custom had been forgotten and nobody knew whence it came to them."[245]

Although the greater part of Hungary was under Turkish rule until 1686, the Ashkenazi communities there were in close contact with their brethren in Austria, Poland, and Germany. The impact of the messianic tidings on the Jews of Hungary and the Balkan countries in general is described by Rycaut, the English consul in Smyrna, who traveled in 1666 from Constantinople to Buda,[246] where he "perceived a strange transport in the Jews, none of them attending to any business, unless to wind up former Negotiations, and to prepare themselves and Families for a Journey to *Jerusalem;* all their Discourses, their Dreams, and disposal of their affairs tended to no other design" than the messianic consummation. He adds: "It was strange to see, how this fancy took, and how fast the report of *Sabatai,* and his Doctrine, flew through all parts where Jews inhabited."[247] Fifty years later, the Sabbatian theologian and adventurer Nehemiah Ḥayyon wrote that R. Jacob, the father of the great enemy and persecutor of Sabbatians Ṣevi Hirsch ("Ḥakham Ṣevi") Ashkenazi, had been "a great believer" when he was rabbi of Budapest, and had actually caused the death of an infidel who had refused, in the synagogue, to pray for the life of the messiah. "He ruled that this person was a rebel against the royal House of David and declared him outlawed . . . and there are witnesses of this here [in Amsterdam]."[248] Although Ḥayyon is anything but a trustworthy witness, there is nothing inherently improbable in this account, and even the merciless sentence attributed to R. Jacob has a precedent in R. Ḥayyim Benveniste's responsum (see above, p. 514). Many of the Jews living in Hungary were refugees from the Chmielnicki massacres. For them the advent of the messiah was exactly what they had expected. Among

245. Emden's note in his abbreviated edn. of Sasportas (Altona, 1755, fol. 57a); Ezekiel Landau, in a letter to the rabbi of Rechnitz, printed in his responsa *Noda᾿ bi-Yehudah*, pt. I (*Ḥoshen Mishpat*), no. 16. The custom is also attested to for Holland as late as 1789 in a letter of Solomon Dubno to Wolf Heidenheim (see Auerbach's *Geschichte der israelitischen Gemeinde Halberstadt* [1866], p. 181).

246. Later, Budapest. In Jewish sources *Buda* generally appears under its German name *Ofen*.

247. Rycaut, p. 201.

248. Nehemiah Ḥayyon, *Ha-ṣad ṣevi* (1714), in the "Author's Apology" on the first (unnumbered) page.

the information gathered by Martin Meyer in his *Diarium Europaeum* there was also a report from Slovakia to the effect that the Jews had begun to take down the roofs from their houses.

V HAMBURG

Whereas the information reviewed so far was incomplete and often incidental, the record of the movement in Hamburg is as full and detailed as can be desired. Residing in Hamburg at the time was R. Jacob Sasportas, the most uncompromising and relentless enemy of the movement. Standing like an immovable rock in a sea of messianic frenzy, he immortalized himself in Jewish history not only by his fierce and unbending struggle, but also by skillfully creating the image in which he wished to be seen by posterity. This he did by collecting in one volume his correspondence and other documents concerning the movement. This "file," entitled *Ṣiṣath Nobel Ṣevi* ("The Fading Flower of Ṣevi," a pun based on Isa. 28:1) is not only a record of his valiant struggle, but also one of our chief sources for the history of the Sabbatian movement.

Sasportas' rabbinic career was dogged by bad luck, which may well have been a direct result of his difficult character. He was, no doubt, a great Talmudic scholar, trained in the best rabbinic tradition of Sephardic Jewry as well as of his own family. According to his family tree he was a descendant, in the eleventh generation, of the great Naḥmanides (1194–ca. 1270),[249] and he prided himself on his thorough training in "Bible and Talmud, rabbinic codes and kabbalah, logic and [composition in an] elegant style according to the rules of grammar." Sasportas was, indeed, a past master of the "elegant style" known as *meliṣah*,[250] characterized by a flowery and highly artificial, involuted, and allusive use of biblical and Talmudic phrases. Tishby, in the introduction to his edition of *Ṣiṣath Nobel Ṣevi* has given a careful analysis of the character and personality of Sasportas, and his analysis is confirmed by an oil painting made in Amsterdam about 1680. The portrait shows a stern and dour face, looking out with shrewd and unfriendly eyes: the face of a Jewish "Grand Inquisi-

249. Sasportas, p. 169. Naḥmanides' Spanish family name is given in Christian documents as da Porta or (in its Catalan form) Saporta.

250. Cf. also Isaac Aboab's praise of his "elegant style"; Sasportas, pp. 34, 106.

tor."[251] The same basic qualities of harshness, irascibility, arrogance, and fanaticism are much in evidence in his letters on the Sabbatian movement; perhaps they were apparent also before 1666 and may have been responsible for the lack of success of his rabbinic career.[252]

Sasportas was ordained a rabbi in Morocco and held the important and influential rabbinates of Salé and Tlemcen. As a result of a conflict with the Moroccan authorities he had to flee the country when he was about thirty-seven years old (in 1647?), and thereafter never recovered the official standing and publicly acknowledged authority which he had enjoyed before. He lived in Amsterdam for about seventeen years without being appointed to rabbinic office. When in 1693, at the age of eighty-three, he was finally elected *ḥakham,* he did not succeed in maintaining his leadership of the congregation for long.[253] In 1664 he accepted an invitation by the small Sephardic congregation in London which was just beginning to organize itself, but he fled the city a year later, during the Great Plague in the autumn of 1665. He arrived in Hamburg on November 7, and after six weeks in quarantine settled with his family in the city just as the first messianic reports began to arrive. For several years he lived in Hamburg as a private visitor, and although the considerable Sephardi congregation treated him with respect and provided for him and his family, yet he held no office. In the Sabbatian crisis his role was that of an onlooker and a freelance; lacking the authority of actual rabbinic office, he was no formal protagonist in the drama. He coveted the power and status of rabbinic office, and his thwarted ambition merely added to his bitterness and frustration. There is a hollow and unconvincing ring about the constantly reiterated protestations of his dislike of the rabbinate. Sasportas was both learned and shrewd, but his arrogance and unsteadiness in human relations, which are only too evident in his writings, cast a shadow over him. His egotism and excessive self-confidence had manifested themselves long before the Sabbatian controversy and were probably not diminished by his experience of

251. See plate IX. The painting is in the possession of the Israel Museum, Jerusalem.

252. In his review of the Hebrew edn. of the present book, Tishby has taken issue with some of the views expressed here; cf. *Tabiz,* XXVIII (1958–59), 119–23, trying to defend Sasportas. As I am not convinced of the validity of his strictures, I have not changed my presentation.

253. Tishby, in his introduction (p. 23) to Sasportas.

frustration in Amsterdam. He was petulant and touchy, and sensitive about his honor. His colleagues, when writing to him, exercised the utmost caution, for the slightest hint at criticism made him fly into a towering rage. His irascibility and contentiousness show in all his letters, and not merely in his contributions to the Sabbatian controversy.[254]

Sasportas' attitude during the messianic crisis was thus considerably influenced by personal motivations. Moreover, his personal situation as a "private" citizen accounts for some of the differences in reaction between him and the rabbis who bore the burden of authority and of responsibility for their flocks. All this, however, does not detract from the relative courage and considerable foresight exhibited by this embittered and frustrated zealot. Historically, his merits are beyond dispute, even though the modern historian may have to qualify his appreciation of Sasportas' honesty and reliability as a witness. Evidence of Sasportas' tampering with the original text of his own letters—and with some of the most important at that—has come to light in the most unexpected manner. When preparing for publication the text of the unique manuscript of *Ṣiṣath Nobel Ṣevi,* Tishby was also able to use a photostat of what he rightly recognized to be Sasportas' autograph draft, that is, the original notebook in which Sasportas copied his own letters as well as those that he received.[255] The discrepancies between the two texts permit some surprising glimpses into the editorial methods of Sasportas, and afford many examples of his "doctoring" his own letters and changing their original form in a manner that is often tantamount to falsification. Not content with the facts, which show him in his actual role of a warning, perspicacious, and courageous voice in the wilderness, he wished to appear as the lone and fearless fighter in a heroic battle. Whereas in his original letters he had often expressed himself with caution and moderation, the "revised version" exhibits a fiery, aggressive, and vituperative language which, had he really used it in the dangerous situation in which he found himself, would undoubtedly have resulted in his excommunication and his ex-

254. Sasportas was equally unbending in his later quarrel (1681) with the lay leaders of the Leghorn community, the files of which have been published by Is. Tishby. See, for instance, his correspondence with the leaders of the community of Leghorn in 1681; cf. Is. Tishby in *Qobeṣ ᶜal Yad,* IV, New Series (1946), pp. 145–59. Cf. also, Alfredo S. Toaff in *Sefunoth,* IX (1964), 167–91.

255. This autograph was in the library of the Hochschule für die Wissenschaft des Judentums in Berlin, and was lost during World War II.

pulsion from Hamburg. There was a brief period when Sasportas wavered and actually inclined to accept Nathan's prophecy. This brief interlude, which throws much light on the pervasive influence exerted by the letters coming from the Orient on even the most sober and critical minds, was more than Sasportas' vanity could admit, and he carefully obliterated all references to it, thus bearing out his own remark that both parties, believers and infidels alike, had been falsifying documents. Nevertheless, however much the comparison of the original draft of the letters with their edited "heroic" version may detract from Sasportas' integrity as man and historian, it surely adds to our understanding of his personality and of his actual role in the controversy.

Sasportas' letters contain a wealth of information on the state of affairs in the Sephardi community of Hamburg, and invaluable corroborative evidence is furnished by a rare document that has fortunately been preserved. Practically no "official" records (minutes, resolutions, proclamations, etc.) of the Jewish communities regarding the Sabbatian agitation have come down to us. After the dismal failure of the movement, either the records relating to the events of 1665–66 disappeared or the relevant pages were torn out. Little is known, therefore, of the deliberations and formal decisions of the responsible leaders of the communities. The record book of the Sephardi community of Hamburg—written in Portuguese—somehow survived in its original form, that is, without excisions, deletions, and similar marks of self-censorship.[256]

The first letters on the messianic events came from Egypt and were received in Hamburg on November 30, 1665. Each mail brought further news and confirmation, and on December 9 the elders recorded the following solemn resolution:

Praise be to the Lord of the Universe for the news that came from the East, and from Italy, and from other countries, to the effect that He in His grace has given us a prophet in the Holy Land, the rabbi Nathan Ashkenazi, and a messianic king, the rabbi Sabbatai Ṣevi, whom the Lord has chosen to deliver His people from the nations and to exalt His Name that is profaned among the gentiles. And we believe these reports on account of the many signs and miracles performed, according to the letters, by the Prophet and the King. Wherefore we

256. The entries for the years 1665–66 and 1666–67 have been translated into German by A. Cassuto in *JJLG,* vols. X–XI (1913, 1916).

have sung today the Festival Psalms as on the Festival of the Rejoicing of the Law (*Simḥath Torah*). May it be the will of the God of Israel that this news be confirmed and that we be granted the inheritance of our land. May it be the divine will that our eyes shall behold this great salvation.[257]

The entry—and there must have been many similar ones in the record books of other communities—is of considerable interest. Most of the Portuguese Jews in Hamburg were either former marranos themselves, or descendants in the first or second generation of former marranos. They were no scholars but wealthy and sensible merchants. In religious matters they relied on their rabbi, R. Moses Israel, and the few scholars who had settled in their midst. They read the letters pouring in on them, weighed their trustworthiness, and probably consulted with their rabbi; finally they were persuaded of the truthfulness of the reports. (For them too, it should be noted, faith in the prophet was prior to that in the messiah). They were far removed from kabbalistic speculations, and they interpreted the messianic tidings in the ordinary, traditional, politico-national terms.

Sasportas, on the other hand, was a kabbalist. The kabbalah was a powerful factor in the religious life of his native Morocco, and Sasportas, like most of his colleagues, pursued kabbalistic studies. In Amsterdam, whither he had escaped from the wrath of the Moroccan authorities, he taught at the *yeshibah ʾOr ha-Ḥayyim* and in 1653 published, for the benefit of its members, a kabbalistic commentary on the prayer book, composed in 1575 by a Moroccan scholar, R. Moses Albaz. The commentary, *Heykhal ha-Qodesh*, is prefaced by a long kabbalistic dissertation by Sasportas which, incidentally, shows him to be much closer to Cordovero's speculative kabbalah than to the dominant Lurianic system. Looking at Sasportas and Abraham Yakhini, we find two typical rabbinic contemporaries, sharing similar attitudes to the kabbalah, yet each representing an opposite aspect of it. The kabbalah, as has been pointed out in an earlier chapter, fulfilled a double function in the history of the Jewish religion: a conservative function by interpreting traditional forms, and a revolutionary function by releasing the springs of utterly new ideas. Sasportas represented the conservative

257. The record book disappeared during World War II. Some parts of it are now in the Jewish Historical Archive, Jerusalem. *Loc. cit.*, vol. X, p. 292.

aspect. He had no use for innovations and departures from tradition, and even less for their justification in terms of esoteric mysteries. If the kabbalah justified anything, it was the existing tradition as taught and practiced. No sense of crisis haunted the soul of this fiercely orthodox rabbi.

Nathan's letter on the stages of redemption filled his heart with grave misgivings. The fantastic character of its contents provoked immediate resistance and criticism, which he communicated without delay (December, 1665) to his friends in Amsterdam.[258] The kabbalist insisted on the plain and literal fulfillment of the traditional messianic signs, and would not permit any allegorical and esoteric interpretations! Kabbalistic mysteries were no substitute for the plain sense. On receipt of the news that a prophet had arisen, he immediately sought to obtain confirmation of Nathan's authenticity, and when his Amsterdam friends accused him of inconsistency, he wrote back: "I never claimed it [that is, the prophecy regarding Sabbatai Ṣevi] to be impossible as such, for it is indeed possible that the rabbi Sabbatai Ṣevi will be our king and savior. If the prophecy is properly authenticated, I shall accept as true whatever a duly confirmed prophet says."[259] For Sasportas everything hinged on the proper authentication of Nathan's prophetic mission, that is, on the testimony of a recognized rabbinic court, to the effect that Nathan had proved his mission by the requisite signs and miracles. Hence also Sasportas' initial hesitation and final radical negation.

As for Sabbatai Ṣevi,[260] Sasportas soon realized that his character did not conform to the traditional image of the messiah, and early in July, 1666, in his letter of encouragement to the infidel rabbis at Smyrna, he gave this as his final verdict.[261] One of his first actions had been to write to all his acquaintances in Jerusalem (for example, R. Moses Tardiola) for reliable information and also to request them to ask the prophet for his interpretation of an obscure passage in the

258. Sasportas, pp. 18–23, 40–44. Sasportas also says (p. 34) that the rabbis of Venice and Prague replied to his first expressions of doubt and protest—apparently as early as December, 1665—but he does not reproduce their letters.

259. Sasportas, p. 39, according to the original version, which was later "edited" for the book.

260. All honorifics and respectful references to him in Sasportas' original letters were omitted in the "edited" version.

261. *Ibid.*, p. 161.

Zohar, where the paradisical place of the messiah is called "the bird's nest." But none of his friends in Jerusalem replied to his inquiries.

His lack of official status increased his bitterness and sense of frustration. R. Moses Israel, the rabbi of the community and formerly a rabbi in Morocco, sided with the believers, but Sasportas had the satisfaction of being supported by R. David Kohen de Lara, the former rabbi of the community who had retired in March, 1665, because of old age, and of Abraham Nahar, one of the lay elders. Abraham Nahar seems to have wavered at the beginning and even to have written to Nathan asking for spiritual guidance, for he had a note—of not more than one line—from Nathan: "Abraham Nahar [his soul] is from the heels (see above, pp. 303–4) of the messiah. 1,800 fasts. He is from the tribe of Judah." According to Sasportas, who relates this story, Nahar joked about it: "Since by doubting the messiah I am a lost soul . . . how can he say that by [mere] fasting I may save myself?"[262] Nevertheless, Nahar later joined the conventicle *Sha^carey Ṣedeq*, which was founded by the Hamburg believers and was where Moses Abudiente preached his Sabbatian sermons.

Early in January, 1666, further tidings were received of the king and the prophet, as well as of the Sons of Reuben and Gad who were preceding the other tribes. According to Sasportas there was great rejoicing in Hamburg, and even the gentiles came to watch the Jews making music and dancing in the synagogue with the scrolls of the Law. Those who did not believe were insulted "and called infidels, so that my hand waxed feeble and I could not speak out, for *so few followed me that a child might write them. Even they dared not speak loudly, but only in secret* . . . and many a time they wanted to excommunicate the unbelievers." It was only out of respect for Sasportas that the infidels were not molested further.[263] Sasportas was forced to preach a sermon on the subject of redemption, and was so exceedingly cautious and ambiguous that some of his listeners complained that he seemed to doubt the messianic reports while others wrote to Amsterdam that he had spoken in praise of the messiah and the prophet.[264]

262. *Ibid.*, pp. 7, 137. Nathan's note had been forwarded by the former Amsterdam schoolmaster, Shalom b. Joseph.

263. *Ibid.*, p. 47.

264. *Ibid.*, pp. 48–49.

The wealthiest Jew in Hamburg was Isaac Señor de Texeira. His father had been agent in Hamburg for the Queen of Sweden, and Isaac maintained in his house a *yeshibah* for the scholars in the congregation. He too was a believer, and it was in his *yeshibah* that R. Moses Israel preached a sermon on Song of Songs 4:4: "Thy neck is like the tower of David/Builded for an army" [Hebrew, *tal-piyyoth*]—"This is Sabbatai Ṣevi who will rebuild the Temple in the year 470 [Hebrew, *tal,* numerical value 470 = A.D. 1670] according to the prophecies [Hebrew, *piyyoth;* lit., "mouths"] of Nathan."[265] The infidels, on the other hand, liked to quote a warning from the *Sefer Hasidim* of R. Judah the Pious (fl. ca. 1200), to the effect that those who used "holy names" risked their lives and exposed themselves to demonic delusions and deceptive visions concerning the time of redemption.[266] The quotation was obviously aimed at the kabbalistic studies of Sabbatai and Nathan.

Several entries were made into the record book of the congregation during those weeks. In December, 1665, the elders deliberated on the reports appearing in Christian news sheets. Apprehending the possibility of rioting by the Christian mob, it was resolved that no member of the community should speak to gentiles of the news that arrived every week. The rabbi, R. Moses Israel, was charged "to exhort the members of the congregation not to speak of these tidings to anyone who is not a Jew." A fine of five *thalers* was imposed for contraventions of this regulation.[267]

Excitement mounted in February, 1666, especially on receipt of the news of Sabbatai's mighty deeds in Smyrna. The letters from Smyrna were read from the pulpit in the synagogue, and since they were generally addressed to members of the Sephardi congregation, the Ashkenazim used to come to the Portuguese Synagogue in order to hear the good news. The younger people donned their best clothes and wore, in addition, "broad sashes of green silk—the color of Sabbatai Ṣevi."[268] Sasportas describes the scenes at the synagogue with

265. *Ibid.,* p. 48, and particularly p. 95.

266. *Ibid.,* pp. 81, 94, 113. The dictum alluded to is found in *Sefer Hasidim,* edn. Wistinetzky, §212; other edns. §206.

267. *JJLG,* X (1915), 295.

268. *Die Memoiren der Glückel von Hameln,* ed. D. Kaufmann (1896), pp. 80–82. Glückel was a little girl when "people began to talk about Sabbatai Ṣevi" and her memoirs supplement the account of Sasportas.

biting sarcasm: the believers danced with such enthusiasm that everything was thrown into confusion and the rabbi, R. Moses Israel, had to mount the pulpit and call for more comely conduct. Not more than twelve dancers, chosen by lot, were to perform, but this call to order went unheeded in the general enthusiasm and rejoicing.[269] The record book mentions that eight elders were practicing a special dance "to express our joy at the tidings . . . concerning our deliverance," but the dance was not performed because the few infidels started a tumult in the synagogue.[270] The demonstrations of joy were accompanied by penances and mortifications. We hear of believers who throughout the messianic year fasted every day from daybreak to sunset, and underwent severe mortifications; one of them, a schoolmaster of the Ashkenazi congregation, apostatized in despair after the final disillusionment.[271] Sasportas severely castigated the penitential exercises and their disastrous consequences, and in a letter of May, 1666, he wrote to his friend Raphael Supino in Leghorn (a believer!): "What is the use of fasting at day if at night we fill ourselves with the plunder of the poor?"[272]

As a result of the letters from Smyrna which brought the news of Sabbatai's proclamation as king, and of the homage paid to him by the community there, enthusiasm rose to such pitch that on February 25 the president of the Board of Elders called a meeting of all present and past members of the board, and a few ordinary members of the congregation, at which it was resolved to dispatch a delegation from Hamburg "to prostrate themselves, as is fitting, before our king Sabbatai Ṣevi." Among those present was Dr. Baruch Nahmias de Castro (1597–1684), a well-known humanist and a former physician to Queen Christina of Sweden.[273] R. Moses Israel was designated as official ambassador and Samuel Abas as his companion, and their departure was to be within a few days. However, as many members of the congregation took offense at not having been invited to so important a meeting, another meeting was called and all heads of families

269. Sasportas, p. 61; also *ibid.*, p. 47. 270. *JJLG*, XI (1916), 9–10.

271. J. J. Schudt, *Compendium Historiae Judaicae* (1700), p. 518.

272. Sasportas, p. 91; cf. *ibid.*, p. 137, for a similar comment made orally to Abraham Nahar: "Does fasting atone for ill-gotten gain or other injustice toward one's fellow man?"

273. J. Schoeps in *Festschrift für Werner Leibbrand* (1967), pp. 127–28. See also the incident (below, p. 580) showing his firm faith.

invited. But before the meeting could take place, the elders had deliberated once more and weighed some serious objections "on account of the harm that might result for our envoys on the way, from the letters which they are carrying [the letter addressed to the 'King of Israel' might fall into the hands of the gentiles] and [the injury] that might result therefrom for the other congregations of our brethren in Germany; and also because it is estimated that the journey from here to Constantinople will take about three months. Now we hope and hold it for certain that Our King will be in Palestine before the end of that period, and [if the envoys were] to follow him and then bring us his reply, this would take more than a year. Therefore we consider this voyage and the expenses connected with it superfluous."[274] This sober argument should not be mistaken for polite irony or an evasive subterfuge of some skeptics, for it was resolved at the same time to offer all the real estate owned by the wealthy congregation for private sale or, if necessary, for public auction, in order to cancel all debts of the community "and to prepare ourselves for the journey which we soon hope to make with God's help." We thus find that in Hamburg, too, the Jews contemplated the liquidation of their property, though the subsequent entries in the record book suggest that the plan was never carried out.

An interesting episode, which throws much light on the factors operating in the spread of the movement, occurred in the weeks between February 9 and March 10. The doubts and perplexities of Sasportas during that period clearly appear from his letters as copied in his original notebook. As has been pointed out earlier, Sasportas subsequently "rewrote" some of his letters when he conceived the idea of publishing his "file" on the Sabbatian movement. Not content with his actual record of a bewildered skeptic becoming a fierce opponent, he wanted to cast himself in the role of the hero-martyr who fought the movement from its very beginning. Letters which in their original form bespoke questioning doubt and diplomatic prudence were changed into fiercely pugnacious anti-Sabbatian manifestoes.[275] The

274. *JJLG,* XI (1916), 5–6.

275. E.g., a letter to Morocco (1669), written, as it were, by one of Sasportas' disciples, alleges that even when the movement was at its height, the master never uttered Sabbatai's name without adding a curse (Sasportas, p. 352). This is an obvious falsehood, for Sasportas would undoubtedly have been excommunicated if he had shown such suicidal courage. The record book of

two main problems that troubled Sasportas during the first months were the attitude of the Jerusalem rabbinate and the authenticity of Nathan's prophetic mission. He was disturbed by the bewildering silence of the rabbis of Jerusalem who, whether believers or not, could reasonably be expected to send word to all the congregations of Israel.[276] He endeavored—without success—to break their silence, particularly as he knew (from the letters of the believers themselves) that the rabbis of Jerusalem had denied Nathan's mission. When letters arrived saying that the rabbis had "repented" and acknowledged the prophet, Sasportas immediately realized that this report provided implicit evidence of their original disbelief, but no proof at all of their subsequent change of mind.[277] He diligently inquired from acquaintances everywhere whether any reliable, nonpartisan confirmation had been received from a recognized rabbinic authority or court in Palestine, and insisted that unless such confirmation regarding the legitimation of the prophet by signs and miracles was received, there was no obligation to believe in his mission. Meanwhile he was prepared to admit that the facts reported were not per se impossible.

Hence also the decisive importance attached by Sasportas to the testimonies arriving from abroad, and the exceedingly cautious language in which he expressed his doubts. Essentially distrustful of the messianic news, he was careful to ensure himself against the contingency of having one day to eat his words. Should the glad tidings be confirmed, he would always be able to prove that he had never denied, let alone disparaged, the messiah; he had merely demanded conclusive evidence which, happily, had now been furnished. Comparing the original letters with their revised version in which Sasportas appears as a bold and lion-hearted dissenter, one cannot but admire the editorial skill with which he could transform, by a few deft touches, expressions of cautious hesitancy into fierce denunciations. Sasportas was also careful to distinguish between the prophet and the messianic

---

the community (August 9, 1666) decreed severe punishment for them "that speak grievously against our King and our Prophet." Sasportas was courageous enough, and it is all the more pity that the measure of courage and perspicacity which he possessed did not satisfy his vainglory. Examples of Sasportas' "doctoring" his original letters are analyzed by Rivkah Shatz in her review of Tishby's edn. of *Ṣiṣath Nobel Ṣevi* (*Beḥinoth,* X [1956], 51–56).

276. Sasportas, p. 23 (letter of December, 1665), and *ibid.,* p. 84.

277. *Ibid.,* pp. 42, 46 (January, 1666).

missions. Unlike the latter, the former required legitimation by duly attested signs and miracles. It was possible, theoretically, that Nathan was a false prophet and yet Sabbatai might be the Lord's Anointed.[278] Since everything depended upon the proper legitimation of the prophet, any incoming mail might affect his verdict. Most Jews considered the testimony of the new letters as sufficient. Sasportas still waited, but he too had his hour of spiritual trial.

Early in February, 1666, a letter from an as yet unidentified rabbi in Jerusalem was received by the Ashkenazic rabbi of Altona near Hamburg.[279] The letter, whose genuineness is beyond doubt, corroborated the testimony of R. Abraham Gedaliah and the other rabbis of Gaza, which Sasportas had so far dismissed as lacking sufficient confirmation. It also confirmed the abolition of the fast of the Tenth of Tebeth, quoting eyewitnesses and referring to the public character of all the events recounted.[280] Sasportas was greatly impressed, and for some time the relentless infidel (as which he wished to appear later) became an actual believer. Writing on February 9 to Isaac Nahar in Amsterdam, he confessed his change of mind and apologized for his prolonged hesitation. This confession, which has been preserved in Sasportas' autograph notebook, was thoroughly rewritten in due course and turned into an unequivocal denunciation of the messiah.[281] One cannot but marvel at the unabashed thoroughness of Sasportas' forgery, as well as at his good luck. Had the *Ṣiṣath Nobel Ṣevi* been published during his lifetime, his correspondent, Isaac Nahar, could easily have given him the lie by producing the original letter. As it happened, the little interlude soon fell into oblivion, where it would have remained but for the discovery and comparison of the two manuscripts.

In his letter to Nahar, Sasportas admitted that the most recent report removed all doubts, but argued that he had been entitled to

278. Cf. in particular Sasportas' letter (p. 41) to Isaac Nahar. The original readings are given in Tishby's footnotes to Sasportas' heavily edited text. The historian's gratitude must go out to Tishby, who collected these original readings.

279. Probably R. David Hanau. The references to the writer were added by Sasportas in the "revised" version of his letter to Aaron Sarphati; see Sasportas, p. 38.

280. Sasportas, p. 52 in the original version.

281. *Ibid.*, pp. 50–57. The abbreviated edn. printed by Emden omits even the edited version of the letter, thus leaving no trace at all of this significant episode.

doubt until convinced by satisfactory testimony. Undoubtedly also the learned and saintly rabbis in Smyrna and elsewhere had accepted the faith only after having duly satisfied themselves of the authenticity of the messianic prophecy. Now, however, "their faith is mine too," and were it not for the rigors of the winter season he would set forth immediately to appear before the messiah and the prophet as their humble disciple.[282] The last remark also explains an entry in the congregation's record book to the effect that Sasportas had formally notified the Board of Elders of his intention to depart for Jerusalem, via Italy, after the Purim festival (March 21).[283] Sasportas' decision to go to the Holy Land was thus inspired by messianic motives, and indeed, as soon as he had realized that his reliance on the letter to Altona had been precipitate, he abandoned his plan.[284] His second change of mind was due to the arrival of further letters from Smyrna which indicated that (contrary to his earlier impression) not all the rabbis there had acknowledged Sabbatai Ṣevi or approved of his abolition of the fast of the Tenth of Tebeth. Realizing that even in Smyrna some rabbis were still far from satisfied by the messiah's credentials, Sasportas reverted to his original attitude which, by the middle of

282. *Ibid.*, p. 57. It is evident from Nahar's reply (*ibid.*) that he had indeed received the original version of Sasportas' letter (as preserved in the Berlin MS.), and not by any means the revised text. Rejoicing at the conversion of his friend, Nahar suggested that they meet in Leghorn or elsewhere and travel together to the messiah.

283. *JJLG*, XI (1916), 9. The date of the entry is 4 Adar 2 (March 11), perhaps a scribal error for 4 Adar 1 (February 9), since the letter to Nahar was written on the latter date. On the other hand, Sasportas also mentioned his intention of departing "before Passover" in order to "behold the face of the King and the Prophet," in a letter of March 10 to Raphael Supino (*ibid.*, p. 70). According to the minute book, however, the departure was scheduled "immediately after Purim." Sasportas notified the elders of his intention, in order to solicit their financial assistance. The elders resolved to grant him one hundred thalers toward his travel expenses, provided he took his family with him.

284. His son, Moses Sasportas, who was still a child at the time of the messianic awakening, actually went to Palestine in 1694, but left again, after less than a year, on an urgent mission on behalf of the Sephardi community of Jerusalem. In their letter of appointment, the rabbis of Jerusalem also requested R. Benjamin Kohen of Reggio (a secret Sabbatian believer!) to assist their emissary; see Isaac Rivkind in *Isaiah Wolfsberg Jubilee Volume* (1956), pp. 226–27.

March, hardened to militant opposition.[285] According to his account of the matter, he heard the full and dramatic story only when the report from Smyrna was solemnly read in the synagogue, whereupon he went home weeping in his heart and immediately wrote two letters to Italy in which he once again asked his old questions: Why was there no official and reliable confirmation of the news by a recognized rabbinic court or a similar authority?[286] This time Sasportas was writing as a burned child, for had he himself not given credence, for a while, to reports which subsequently proved untrustworthy? Though we cannot completely trust Sasportas' own account of the sequence and dates of his reactions, yet it is certain that early in March he had reverted to his disbelief. The story has an obvious moral. If a shrewd, sober, and arrogant observer like Sasportas could be carried away, albeit for a short while only, and be persuaded of the truth of the reports, then it is not surprising that the Jewish masses saw no reason to doubt the good news which, all their minor discrepancies and contradictions notwithstanding, agreed on the main point: salvation was at hand. Sasportas canceled his projected pilgrimage to the messiah and the prophet, but other members of the congregation who had relatives in Smyrna (for example, R. Isaac Palache)[287] set forth on the journey, with the apparent aim of visiting Sabbatai Ṣevi in Constantinople.

In March, 1666, the solemn prayer for the king's majesty was introduced into the synagogue service at Hamburg, at first on Sabbath and festival days only, but subsequently also on Mondays and Thursdays.[288] The innovation caused repeated scandal in the synagogue.

285. The letter from Jerusalem to Altona, which had caused Sasportas' temporary conversion, was subsequently referred to by him in the most negative terms in the "edited" version of his letter to Abraham Sarphati. The original version of the letter contained, of course, no such obloquy; see Sasportas, p. 38.

286. Sasportas, p. 64. His letters of March 11 to Samuel Aboab and to Raphael Supino exhibit continuity of attitude and argument with the earlier letters of December and January. Were it not for the letter of February 9 to Isaac Nahar, it would seem incredible that in between there was a brief phase of positive belief.

287. Sasportas, in a letter to R. Isaac ha-Levi (p. 139), refers to him as "our beloved friend." Palache intended to travel via Leghorn, and Sasportas asked him to deliver a letter to R. Isaac ha-Levi there (p. 169).

288. Sasportas, pp. 62, 132. On p. 62 he quotes the full version of the prayer for Sabbatai as recited in Hamburg. See also above, pp. 533–34.

The aged R. David Kohen de Lara who, as former rabbi of the community, could permit himself greater liberties than the visiting stranger Sasportas, openly flouted the messiah and, by way of demonstration, walked out every time the prayer was said. On one occasion, as he wanted to leave the synagogue, he found the doors locked. At first the prayer had been recited after the reading of the Law, but then "they decided to say it before the opening of the Ark, so that nobody could leave [as this would have meant missing the central part of the service, the reading of the Law]. . . . And when he heard the opening of the prayer he tried to walk out, but they held him fast and forced him to listen against his will and there was a great commotion in the synagogue, because his disciples, . . . although they too were smitten with the disease of this faith, yet defended his honor. Thereafter they moved the prayer back to its original place after the reading of the Law. And [Rabbi Kohen de Lara] sometimes walked out, and sometimes simply turned his back." On the Eighth of Tishri (October 7, 1666) it was announced that all members of the congregation were to rise to their feet at the prayer. On the following day, at the Eve of Atonement service, things came to a head when the highly respected physician Dr. Baruch Nahmias de Castro insulted old Rabbi Kohen de Lara and all but assaulted him physically. Also on the Day of Atonement the prayer for "Our Lord, the holy rabbi Sabbatai Ṣevi, may his majesty be exalted and his kingdom magnified," was said several times.[289]

Sasportas was more prudent than Kohen de Lara. Toward the end of May he wrote to Raphael Supino, and the withering sarcasms of his letter reflect the complete and utter certainty at which he had arrived. News had just been received of Sabbatai's arrest, together with accounts of many miracles and assurances that "he freely chose imprisonment . . . in order to lighten the messianic woes [by vicarious suffering]." Enthusiasm in Hamburg rose to new fever pitch, and Sasportas had to admit (in the original, "uncensored" version of the letter) that "they believe so firmly that I postponed dispatching the letter, lest [its contents become known and] the mob lay their hands upon me." He finally sent the letter off in September (that is, about a month before the news of the messiah's apostasy was received in Hamburg), probably after he had heard of Sabbatai's abolition of

289. *Ibid.*, pp. 132–33.

the fast of the Ninth of Ab.[290] By that time the infidels had rallied again in several places, although the stream of confirmatory news pouring in from the East throughout the summer months also turned some infidels into penitent believers.[291] Sasportas' letter to Supino concludes with a passionate repudiation of Sabbatai and Nathan, and a proud confession of faith in the future true messiah; it is signed: "Thus saith the man who was raised up against the 'anointed of God,' Jacob Sasportas."[292] Alas, this withering pun, parodying Sabbatai's favorite signature ("Thus saith the man who was raised up on high, the anointed of the God of Jacob"; see II Sam. 23:1) would be more convincing if it were found at the end of the original version of Sasportas' letter; as it is, the final paragraph seems to have been added when the letter was dispatched in September, 1666.

In any event, Sasportas had already used sharper language in his letter of August, 1666, to the two infidel rabbis in Smyrna. Smyrna was far away, and there would be no hostile repercussions from there. Meanwhile many letters arrived written and signed by Samuel Primo on behalf of the messiah, and they provoked Sasportas even more. The letters themselves are no longer extant, but they seem to have contained references to Sabbatai as "the firstborn of God." At the same time the letter from Constantinople concerning the mysterious merchandise of "R. Israel of Jerusalem" made a tremendous impression in Amsterdam and Hamburg, particularly as it was signed by so many names and no suspicion attached—as yet—to any of the signatures. Even Sasportas seems to have been impressed, and his subsequent claim to have immediately recognized the forgery[293] is belied by the facts. As a matter of fact it was he who forged his own letter to Isaac Aboab in Amsterdam when "editing" it for publication in *Ṣiṣath Nobel Ṣevi.*[294] The original draft, as preserved in Sasportas' autograph, expresses a mood of neutral and as yet uncommitted expectation; although the letter from Constantinople did not "prove" anything, it raised possibilities to the level of probabilities.

There was much discussion, in the summer of 1666, of the question whether or not faith was required in the absence of confirmatory

290. *Ibid.,* p. 80. Tishby (in his footnotes, *ibid.,* p. 81) has shown that the letter was not sent for several months. On Sasportas' dishonest maneuvers to obscure the truth about the dispatch of his letter, see Rivkah Shatz in *Beḥinoth,* no. 10 (1956), p. 56.

291. Sasportas, p. 135.

292. *Ibid.,* p. 100.

293. *Ibid.,* p. 111.

294. *Ibid.,* pp. 107–8.

miracles. One believer, speaking in the Hamburg synagogue, maintained that since Nathan's mission was to preach repentance, no further credentials were necessary. If he were to introduce innovations, or even temporary changes only, into religion, then he would have to legitimize his claims by signs and miracles. Sasportas was furious at such "elementary" theological incompetence,[295] but his lonely protest was not heard.[296] The audacity of the believers caused him concern for the future of rabbinic Judasim. "I fear lest in the future our religion become two religions" he wrote on July 21 to the rabbis of Venice, and in a letter to Vienna he ominously recalled the beginnings of the Christian schism.[297] In September, 1666, he preached a sermon which the believers took to be an outright attack on Sabbatai Ṣevi ("who wants to found a new religion, like Jesus") and which made him the object of renewed outbursts of abuse and vilification.[298]

In this discussion Sasportas gave proof of considerable foresight and perspicacity. If a prophet could demand credence even without satisfying the preliminary conditions and criteria laid down by the Talmud, and claim power to abolish traditional customs, then this opened the door to further departures from the Law and Tradition. The awareness of this danger is not yet evident in the letters written during the first six months of the movement, but it steadily gained in strength during the summer. The letters written shortly before Sabbatai's apostasy became known in Hamburg (at the end of November, 1666) are quite explicit on this point. Although Sasportas still adopted a moderate tone when writing to European rabbis, he poured out his wrath and bitterness with uninhibited vehemence in his letter to the rabbis Lapapa and Algazi in Smyrna (July, 1666), to whom he was as yet a stranger, even as they had been unknown to him until quite recently. Congratulating them on their steadfast unbelief, he apologized for being unable to persecute the believers and especially their chiefs who were leading the people astray. He also reiterated his concern for the future of the Jewish religion: the controversies caused by the Sabbatian movement were pregnant with heresy and schism, and were, in fact, playing into the hands of Christianity.[299]

Of course the charge of heresy, namely, illegitimate deviation from tradition, was beside the point, since every believer could muster suffi-

295. *Ibid.*, pp. 144–46. 296. *Ibid.*, p. 132.
297. *Ibid.*, pp. 113, 115. 298. *Ibid.*, p. 132.
299. *Ibid.*, p. 166.

cient kabbalistic, homiletical, and exegetical arguments to justify any messianic innovation. After all, even Sasportas himself had been ready, for a brief moment, to forget (that is, to explain away) his objections. The arguments of the believers would provoke more counterarguments and produce another vicious circle of mutual accusations. Time and again Sasportas pointed an accusing finger at Sabbatai's "strange actions," but his colleagues were not impressed, and their replies[300] merely showed that believers East and West would resort to the same type of argument. The same logic of paradox would serve to justify the messiah's strange actions before his apostasy, as well as his subsequent apostasy. Sasportas saw the seed of schism and heresy long before the believers themselves suspected it.

In Hamburg, as in Amsterdam, many *yeshiboth* were founded in the course of the great awakening. These *yeshiboth* were brotherhoods founded for the purpose of prayer, penitence, and works of charity. The members of the "holy *yeshibah Sha*ᶜ*arey Ṣedeq*" ("The Gates of Righteousness") in Hamburg were no rabbinic scholars but wealthy merchants of the kind that provided the lay leadership of the community.[301] Moved by "zeal for the Lord and the fear of heaven," the members met "three times a day for prayer . . . and to practice mortifications and fasts, shedding tears and bringing forth works of charity, in faith, concerning our redemption which is shining in all of you, by the grace of heaven." They chose as their head Moses b. Gideon Abudiente (died 1688), a well-known scholar and Hebrew grammarian.[302] A former marrano, Abudiente had escaped in the twenties from Portugal to Amsterdam in order to return to the faith of his fathers, and had been active for many years as a teacher among the Sephardim in and near Hamburg. The minute book of the congregation mentions him as trustee of the *Talmud Torah* for the year 1665–66. He was a fervent believer and preached many sermons on the subject of redemption to the mem-

300. *Ibid.,* p. 131.

301. Of the thirty-one members enumerated on the first page of Abudiente's *Fin de los Dias* (see n. 303, below), the names of eight are known from the minute book of the congregation. All belong to the aforementioned group of wealthy lay leaders: Abraham Chilão, Abr. Benveniste, Abr. Nahar, Abr. Senior de Mattos, David and Isaac Aboab, Jacob Fidanque, Gideon Kohen Lobatto, Daniel and Joshua Benzur (Benṣur), Joseph Bravo, Joseph Jessurun, Joshua Ḥabillo, Samuel Gades, Samson de Lima, Nathaniel and Samson Abudiente.

302. See about him in Kayserling, *MGWJ,* X (1861), 69 ff.

bers of the *yeshibah.* He wrote down his sermons in Hebrew, and collected them in a small volume which he then, in the summer of 1666, after receipt of the news of Sabbatai's imprisonment in Gallipoli, translated into Spanish and had printed in Glückstadt (near Hamburg) without first obtaining, as was customary, the permission of the elders. There was considerable consternation among the elders at this high-handed disregard of their solemn injunction not to bring the messianic movement to the notice of the gentiles.

The volume *The End of Days, announcing the advent of the end of days predicted by all the prophets, and explaining many obscure passages in the Holy Bible* was dedicated to the members of the *yeshibah* on the Tenth of Ab (August 11, 1666).[303] Three weeks later, on the Third of Ellul, the elders decided that the book was likely to "endanger our position among the Christians" and ordered all copies to be confiscated and kept in the strong box of the congregation "until the hoped-for time which God may bring nigh speedily," when the whole edition would be returned to the author.[304] Only one copy of the book has survived.[305] It is the only extant collection of Sabbatian sermons from that period. No doubt similar volumes were written by other preachers during that year, and occasionally an author makes reference to his homilies of that period, but none of this literature has been preserved. Abudiente's volume was published in Spanish and not in Hebrew, and may thus serve as testimony of the audacity of its author's faith.

In the introduction to his work, Abudiente enlarges on the analogy between the first deliverance through Moses and the final deliverance through Sabbatai Ṣevi "in order to dispel all doubts and lack of faith concerning our deliverance," that is, to answer the arguments of critics such as Sasportas. The author explains that his generation was now beholding the beginning of Israel's redemption and freedom, which they had hoped for for 1,598 years, "the greatest bliss that was or ever will be in the world. It will be similar to the exodus from

303. *Fin de los Dias.* Publica ser llegado el fin de los dias pronosticado por todos los Prophetas y explica muchos passos obscuros de la Sacra Biblia. Compuesto en la lengua Sancta y Redusido ala espanola por Mosseh Hijo de Gidhon Abudiente, Dirigido a la muy noble Yeshibha Shahare Zeddek, en 10 de Menachem, anno 5426 en Gluckstadt. 126 [1], pp. 8°.

304. *JJLG,* XI (1916), 27.

305. In the library of the Portuguese Congregation in Amsterdam.

Egypt, but incomparably more noble and pure."[306] All biblical commandments are stated in Scripture once only, except the commandment to remember the exodus from Egypt which is found many times "because it is a sign and type of our future redemption." Also, the first exodus was hampered by many obstacles and diverse "reasons for unbelief, even as in our own days," and "there was no lack of unbelievers (*incredulos*) in Israel." It behooved them to remember this, in order that at the time of the final redemption "which God has now begun to announce to us, we should not be like our fathers . . . a stiff-necked people, but rather, 'It is good that a man should both hope and quietly wait for the salvation of the Lord' [Lam. 3:26], that is to say, in all that concerns the salvation of the Lord, it is better to hope and be quiet than to despair and speak." Apparent obstacles were harbingers of our promised bliss and should strengthen our hope. "The imprisonment of Our Lord Sabbatai Ṣevi, may God help him, which seems to (hasten) [impede] our redemption, [actually] strengthens and establishes it. Psalm 2 hints at the imprisonment of the messiah, who will in the end receive the kingdom on Zion, the holy mountain."[307] Moses too had been imprisoned in Midian for ten years, until God set him free to lead his people out of Egypt.[308] Joseph, another type and symbol of the messiah, was brought out of the dungeon to be ruler of Egypt. The midrash [309] describes the imprisonment and the pain suffered by the messiah before his exaltation to the kingdom, and many more proofs could be adduced to show that "both redeemers of Israel [that is, Moses and Sabbatai] had to be prisoners. . . . The most certain proof that this Holy Lord is our Redeemer and Messiah is his imprisonment.[310] . . . Wherefore strengthen ye the weak hands and confirm the feeble knees [Isa. 35:3] by means of penitence. . . .

306. Abudiente, p. 13.

307. *Ibid.*, pp. 14, 17–19. Ps. 2 as a prediction of the messiah's imprisonment is mentioned once more, pp. 104–5.

308. According to the *Sefer ha-Yashar*, a medieval compilation of legends on the Bible, Moses spent ten years in a dungeon in Midian and was kept alive by his wife, Zipporah, who brought him food. Abudiente quotes the legend from *Yalqut Shimᶜoni* on Isa. 53:8, where, however, I could not find it.

309. *Pesiqta Rabbathi* on Isa. 60.

310. Abudiente p. 20: *La mas gran seguridad que podemos tener de ser este Santo señor nuestro Redemptor y Misiah, es su prison.* This is the first occurrence of the messianic epithet "Señor Santo," which was later applied to the successors of Sabbatai Ṣevi (Baruchia, Jacob Frank).

This strengthening is necessary in order to subdue the unbelief to which the evil inclination is tempting you,[311] . . . for who is strong? He who subdues his evil inclination."[312]

Abudiente's typological exegesis clearly betrays his Christian upbringing among the marranos of Portugal. Although the concrete details of his typology are derived from midrashic literature, the idea of taking an Old Testament figure such as Moses as a type of the messiah seems to be Christian. The paradoxical proof of the messiah's mission by his imprisonment already prefigures the similar, more radical, arguments to be advanced by later Sabbatian theology. Abudiente's preface seems to have been written in August, 1666, as the volume went to press, but the main body of the book was composed earlier. Its purpose was to prove from Scripture that the year 1664–65 was the prophesied end of days. Though it was wrong to attempt "to compute the end" in the period of exile, yet now "that the blissful time has drawn near" it was surely permissible to discuss publicly a subject "which has been hidden by the ancient sages until this day, and was concealed until this generation and locked away in the divine treasuries (*en los divinos archivos*), . . . for the predestined end of days has come. . . . For at the end of days the consideration (*ponderaçion*) of so holy a matter, which has been forbidden until now, will be permitted." The prophets, though they beheld this glorious time, did not understand its meaning (Dan. 8:27: "and I was appalled at the vision, but understood it not"); but now the dark parables and riddles had become clear, and God has "made us participate in the supernatural bliss and glory. He has sent us the holy messianic king, Sabbatai Ṣevi, to redeem us, and the prophet Nathan to make us return unto God. . . . And since it is now permitted to discuss this momentous subject, it is not surprising that even an untalented person like myself . . . should attempt to interpret the most obscure prophecies in Scripture."[313]

Sabbatai's imprisonment is touched on only incidentally in the main part of the book, and the author suggests that it might continue for some time, until the messiah had reached his forty-fifth year.[314] Abudiente expected the final consummation of redemption for the

311. *Ibid.*, p. 21: *para abatir la incredulidad acque el apetito te inclina.*

312. A proverb from the *Mishnah ʾAboth* 4:1.

313. Abudiente, pp. 22–24.

314. *Ibid.*, p. 73, and also p. 104. The calculation is based on Dan. 12:11–12.

year 1668, that is, 1,600 years after the destruction of the Temple. The captivity in Egypt had lasted four hundred years, and therefore the dominion which the four kingdoms had been given over Israel was also fixed for four hundred years each, coming to an end in 1668, when Sabbatai would be forty-five and Nathan twenty-five years old.[315] Curiously enough the year 1665–66 plays no role at all in Abudiente's numerical speculations; his efforts are directed at discovering, by means of *gematria,* allusions to the year 1664–65 in the Book of Daniel, in Zechariah's vision of the golden candlestick (Zech. 4), in the law of the Jubilee Year in Leviticus, in the prophecies of Ezekiel, and in the last chapter of the Song of Songs. It is interesting to note that the discussion of the seventy weeks of Daniel 9[316] is identical with a homily on the same subject copied, in a French version, in Amsterdam before March, 1666.[317] Perhaps a "Discourse on the Seventy Weeks of the Prophet Daniel" sent from Egypt or Palestine and circulating in Amsterdam and Hamburg was incorporated by Abudiente into his work. Alternatively the homily may have been Abudiente's own work; and a first, Hebrew version of it, which he sent to Amsterdam, was translated there into French. A close analysis of the two versions lends support to the latter alternative.[318] Also, the law of the sabbatical year contains Sabbatian mysteries. In the year 5425, which is about the middle of the sixth day of the cosmic week, that which is written Leviticus 25:6 shall be fulfilled: "and the sabbath-produce of the land shall be food for you," that is the spiritual food of redemption. This cosmic Sabbath of messianic rest, which is also indicated in the laws of the Jubilee Year (Lev. 25:10: "and proclaim liberty throughout the land"), is "mystically revealed in the name of our Holy King and Redeemer Sabbatai."[319]

315. *Ibid.,* pp. 30, 74. Abudiente had no precise information regarding Sabbatai's age. In the case of Nathan he was only one year off. Nathan was probably born in 1644 and not (as Abudiente thought) in 1643.

316. *Ibid.,* pp. 75–80.

317. *Ap.* Aeshcoly in *Dinaburg Jubilee Volume,* pp. 223–24.

318. Abudiente's excursus on the qualities of the number 7 is identical with the corresponding passages in the French text (Aeshcoly, pp. 223–24). Some of Abudiente's favorite phrases (e.g., p. 23: *en los divinos archivos*) occur in the French text (e.g., p. 224: *cachée et scellée dans ses divins trésors*) even in places where the corresponding Spanish text does not have them. This strongly suggests that we are dealing with an earlier and a later version by the same author.

319. Abudiente, pp. 95–99.

It is indeed a strange coincidence that the Sephardi congregation of Hamburg has bequeathed to the historian of the Sabbatian movement two such diverse documents as *Ṣiṣath Nobel Ṣevi* by the arch-infidel Sasportas, and *Fin de los Dias* by the ardent believer Abudiente.

The Ashkenazi communities in that part of Germany were affected no less than the Sephardim, and perhaps even more, since there is evidence showing that the messianic enthusiasm persisted among them for a considerable time after the apostasy, when life among the Hamburg Sephardim had long since returned to normal. Glückel von Hameln relates in her celebrated memoirs how her father-in-law had made preparations for the journey, sending all the household furniture as well as provisions to Hamburg so that they might be dispatched to Palestine at a moment's notice, as soon as the sign was given. Three barrels containing provisions were kept in readiness, and only after three years of waiting (of which two were after the apostasy!) was the hope of immediate messianic redemption finally abandoned.[320]

Under the impact of the messianic news, the Ashkenazi congregations of Hamburg and Altona agreed to settle a serious dispute that had arisen between them in 1664 regarding their joint burial-ground in Ottensen. The agreement, which was signed before the Christian magistrates on May 4, 1666, is as dry and formal as any legal document, but nine days later, on May 14, an additional, private instrument was signed which contained a clause, the wording of which is of great interest. The clause provided for a payment by the Hamburg congregation to that of Altona of one hundred and fifty *Reichsthaler*, to be made in three installments. "And if redemption should take place before that date [that is, of the second installment, due in December, 1666] the Hamburg congregation will nevertheless pay the due amount of fifty thalers to the Altona congregation, who will give it for the building of the Temple. . . ."[321]

This remarkable document, signed by the elders of the two Ashkenazi communities, perfectly illustrates the way in which the messianic expectation entered into their practical life and financial arrangements. Another, no less revealing, testimony regarding the

320. Glückel's *Memoirs*, p. 82, and below, p. 756. Also Sasportas, p. 75, mentions letters from Poland being received by the Ashkenazim in Hamburg.

321. The document was published by B. Brilling, in *YIWO-Blätter*, V (1933), 45.

atmosphere that prevailed in the Ashkenazi community, is preserved among the responsa of R. Samuel b. Moses ha-Levi. The incident discussed in the responsum seems to have occurred at about the same time that the compromise agreement was signed by the communities of Hamburg and Altona. The problem submitted to R. Samuel ha-Levi was this: in the year 1666, while everybody was expecting the exile to come to an end "within a year or two at the utmost," several emissaries came to Hamburg from the Holy Land in order to collect alms for the poor there. One glib emissary from Jerusalem coaxed a poor rabbi into promising him an annual donation of two *Reichsthaler* (in rabbinic law such a promise has the binding character of a religious vow). The poor scholar, who certainly could not permit himself such liberality, had evidently assumed that almsgiving would cease before long, in the messianic kingdom, but had "taken this hardship upon himself for a year or two, as is well known that at the time all Israel was giving alms very liberally, . . . especially for the poor of the Holy Land who would still need it for a little while [that is, until the assumption, by the messiah, of his kingdom]." However, the rabbi soon regretted his impulsive vow when he was visited a few days later by another emissary, this time from Safed, who had come to ask him for judgment in some lawsuit which he had against the emissary from Jerusalem. On that occasion the rabbi also heard some unedifying reports about the emissary from Jerusalem. The absolute integrity of the emissary from Safed was vouched for by such men as R. Jonah Fränkel-Te^comim of Metz. The emissary from Safed also produced "testimony and definite proof" against the character of his colleague from Jerusalem, "as unto this day no end has come to things." The local rabbi now regretted his rash promise to the emissary from Jerusalem, and requested Sasportas to absolve him from his vow. The question submitted to R. Samuel ha-Levi[322] was whether the absolution granted by Sasportas was valid or not. The fact that emissaries from Jerusalem engaged in Sabbatian propaganda is of special interest in the light of what we know of the negative attitude of the Jerusalem rabbinate, though, of course, it is

322. Responsa *Naḥalath Shib^cah*, II, no. 81. M. Kushnir (*Musaf Davar*, VI, no. 37, of 21 Iyyar 1929) was the first to draw attention to this responsum and to analyze its historical implications. On the Sabbatian title page of the first part of this work, see above, p. 528.

more than probable that these emissaries had been traveling in Europe for some time and had not been in Palestine when the messianic events took place there in the summer of 1665. The minute book of the Sephardic community (entry of the Fourth of Iyyar) confirms the presence in Hamburg of two emissaries of the Ashkenazic community of Jerusalem, R. Nathan b. Raphael and R. Mordecai Ashkenazi.[323] The emissary from Jerusalem was clearly a believer who had declared that "an end has come to things," while his colleague from Safed denied this with "testimony and definite proof." As it happened, the emissary from Safed took his litigation with his colleague from Jerusalem to the same local rabbi at Altona or Hamburg from whom the Jerusalem representative had extraced a vow. Feeling that his promise had been extracted under false pretenses, the rabbi characteristically enough applied for absolution to Sasportas, who was known as the unbeliever par excellence among the rabbinic authorities. The incident, however, gives the lie to Sasportas' charge that people refrained from giving alms for the Holy Land because of the unbelief of the rabbis there. But believers were rather liberal with their alms, since the poor of the Holy Land "would still need it for a little while."

A rare human document has been preserved in the state archives of Oslo, Norway, regarding one Jacob Segal from Hamburg who was then in prison in Oslo. There exist four letters in Yiddish, written in late summer of 1666, partly by his wife Shaindl Schönchen bath R. Solomon and partly by his friend Nathan b. Aaron Neumark, both in Hamburg. They, too, keep the prisoner posted about the progress of the messianic wave. His wife tells him *Ḥiddushim fun Melekh ha-Moshiaḥ* (news of the messiah): Nathan the prophet is about to arrive with ten rabbis in Constantinople, and after that *soll die geʾulle mefurssem weren* (will redemption be proclaimed; cf. below, p. 631). By next mail she will write more. His friend informs him that many letters about the ingathering of the exiles are arriving and comforts him, saying that he should sleep well awaiting further news, *sollt ir nit leer shlufn.*[324] We do not know for sure whether the poor wretch in Oslo ever got the letters or whether the jailer, unable to read Yiddish, turned them over to the

323. Brilling, *JJLG*, XXI, p. 32; Yaʿari (1951), pp. 159–60.

324. For photostats of these letters I am indebted to Mr. Hollander in Stockholm, who drew my attention to them.

authorities. But from the context it would seem that he actually was allowed to receive such letters.

VI POLAND

By far the greater part of the Jewry of Christian Europe was living, at the time, in Poland. Polish Jewry shared with their brethren elsewhere a common—rabbinic and kabbalistic—eschatological tradition, a basic feeling of insecurity, and a certain popular-religious atmosphere which was the product of more recent developments. In addition to these general conditions which provided the common background of the messianic outburst, the situation in Poland was characterized by certain more specific local factors. Mention has already been made of the 1648 massacres and their impact on Polish Jewry. The year that had been expected to be a messianic date not only had failed to bring redemption, but had actually seen the worst massacres in Jewish history so far. The Chmielnicki rising, which had hit mainly the Jews of southern Poland and the Ukraine, was followed by the war with Sweden and the large-scale massacres in Greater Poland and Lithuania (1655–66). Polish Jewry, which had been flourishing until 1648, was materially ruined and its masses pauperized. The trek to the west that began after 1648 was one symptom of the situation. Those who remained behind under the oppressive conditions of Poland and Russia became even more receptive, in their bewilderment and despair, to the influence of the kabbalah. The continual persecutions, the repeated blood-libels in Poland, the vicious anti-Semitism of the Catholic clergy, and the unceasing bribes and taxes that had to be paid to church and civil authorities, deepened the sense of gloom and oppression, and provided fertile soil for the messianic awakening. The tidings arriving from Palestine, Turkey, and elsewhere were eagerly received, "for we, the Jews in this bitter exile, love to hear good tidings of comfort and salvation, and *especially in Poland* where evil [hatred of the Jews] and [the oppression of] exile are exceedingly great, and every day brings new persecution and harassment."[235]

It was soon known in Poland that Sabbatai had declared the massacres of 1648 to have been the beginning of the era of redemption, and that he had announced in Smyrna that an unknown Jewish

325. Leyb b. Ozer, MS. Shazar, fol. 38b.

martyr, by name of Abraham Zalman, had been the messiah of the tribe of Joseph. Like the thirty-six righteous of Jewish legend, who maintain the world in utter anonymity, the unknown martyr-messiah also had fulfilled his mission in obscurity. It had been the news of the great massacres which had probably inspired Sabbatai's first messianic fantasies (see above, p. 130). Now it was the turn of Polish Jewry to hear the message of comfort and hope, coming to them in their distress and affliction. Nathan's prophecy (in his letter to Raphael Joseph; see above, pp. 270 ff.) that "there will be no slaughter among the uncircumcised, *except in the German lands*" surely held out to them a very special promise of deliverance and revenge. In a later version which the prophet himself "rewrote" in 1666 and sent out to several countries, it is stated that in Poland alone vengeance would be wreaked on the gentiles "to avenge the blood of our martyred brethren."[326] Many Polish preachers interpreted the past events accordingly. R. Jacob b. Solomon of Lobsenz[327] declared the troubles in Poland 1648–56 to have been a "preparation for the coming of Sabbatai Ṣevi," proving his point by a homiletical pun on Zechariah 6:12.

The available evidence regarding the diffusion of the movement in Poland indicates that very little was known about Sabbatai's personality or the actual events connected with him. Legend reigned supreme and nourished the messianic hunger of the masses. Each day produced its new crop of miracle stories. Early in 1666 it was told in Poland, and duly reported to Germany, that the Grand Turk had placed a royal crown on Sabbatai's head and had made him ride on horseback at his right side. "And on the day that he came [to Constantinople], the earth shook and quaked, and he entered the royal court riding on a lion . . . and more of this kind."[328] This sample of popular legend well illustrates the kind of messianic propaganda characteristic of the movement in Poland; it also resounds with the

326. The full text of this later version is preserved in MS. Ben-Zvi Institute 2262, fols. 69–72.

327. In his work *Shem Yaᶜaqob* (which he published in his old age in Frankfurt/Oder, 1716), fol. 26d. See above, p. 93. In 1666 R. Jacob seems to have lived in Zoltawa. For another homiletical interpretation of the numbers 408 and 426 (i.e., the years in which the decisive events occurred, 1648 and 1666), cf. R. Israel of Shklov's *Tifᵓereth Yisraᵓel* (Frankfurt/Oder, 1774), fol. 36a.

328. Sasportas, p. 75.

shouts of triumph with which the downtrodden masses greeted the day of reckoning. In point of fact, the messiah did not see the Grand Turk until the day of his apostasy, but legends emanating from Constantinople and Poland continued to feed the popular appetite for miracles (which, according to Nathan's teaching, the messiah was not even permitted to perform!). It is quite possible that some of the legendary reports communicated to the Polish aristocracy by their correspondents in Amsterdam,[329] also came to the knowledge of the Jews, but in any event they had their own channels of communication and surely heard all the news and rumors that were current, and read all the pamphlets and broadsheets concerning Sabbatai. That this kind of printed propaganda also reached Poland appears from a rescript by the king of Poland (see below, p. 597).

Eschatological preaching went hand in hand with the call to repent. In Cracow, at least two editions were printed of a popular penitential manual in Yiddish.[330] The exercises and devotions recommended in the booklet are not those of Nathan's *tiqqun,* but were selected from earlier ascetic and kabbalistic writings,[331] and published with an approbation by the rabbi of Cracow, R. Aryeh Leyb b. Zechariah Mendel, who also arranged for copies of Nathan's letters to be made and disseminated.[332] These penitential tracts were literally worn out with use and no copy of the first edition has survived. The penitential fervor and messianic enthusiasm of the Russian and Polish

329. Partly published by Balaban (1935), pp. 38–43; passages from these bulletins have been quoted in the present and the preceding chapters.

330. Only one copy of the second edn. of the beautifully printed booklet is extant, in the Bodleian Library, Oxford (12 fols. in 4°). The title *Tiqquney Teshubah/ᵓEreṣ Ṣevi* does not mean that the text was sent from Palestine. The word *Ṣevi*, which is emphasized by a special type and stands in a line by itself, clearly refers to the messiah. The title means "penances practiced in the Land of Ṣevi."

331. *Torath ha-ᵓAsham*, *ᶜEmeq ha-Melekh*, R. Judah the Pious, *Yesod Yosef*, and the Lurianic writings. I doubt the correctness of Balaban's statement (p. 33)—on the authority of Prof. Freimann—that a third such manual in Yiddish was printed in Cracow in the same year. As the only extant copy (in the Municipal Library of Frankfurt) of this alleged edition was burned during World War II, the point cannot be examined. It should be noted, however, that according to Balaban's information, the booklet gave neither place nor date of publication, whereas the two aforementioned Cracow edns. give all the details and even mention the names of the compositors.

332. Dembitzer, *Kelilath Yofi,* vol. I, p. 78.

Jews are also described by a Greek Catholic priest, the archimandrite Johannes Galatowski:[333]

Not long ago, in 1666, the Jewish heresy raised its head in Volhynia, Podolia, in all the provinces of Little Russia, in the Duchy of Lithuania, in the kingdom of Poland and the neighboring countries. They raised on high their horn and their insolent obstinacy, they hoisted the flag of backsliding and insolently blew the trumpet of victory. At that time an impostor called Sabbatai Ṣevi appeared in Smyrna, who called himself the messiah of the Jews and drew them to his side by false miracles. He promised the Jews to bring them out of their exile among the nations, and to restore unto them Jerusalem and the kingdom of Palestine. . . . The foolish Jews rejoiced, and expected that the messiah would take them to Jerusalem on a cloud. Whenever a cloud appeared over some city, they would boast before the Christians and say that the messiah would soon take them to dwell in Palestine and in Jerusalem. At that time they fasted several days in the week because of the messiah, and some fasted the whole week. They gave no food even to their little children, and they immersed themselves in winter under the ice while reciting recently invented prayers. Many Jews died during the winter because of their immersions in the severe cold. They went to their synagogue every day and held services. Even some fools among the Christian masses acted and thought like them.

Nathan's Manual of Devotions ("newly invented prayers") was thus used throughout Poland and Russia. The detail about the expectation of being transported on the clouds of heaven seems to be authentic too. The motif occurs in a midrashic source,[334] where it accounts for the method by which all flesh shall come to worship in the Temple of Jerusalem "from one new moon to another,/And from one sabbath to another" (Isa. 66:23). The midrashic answer, inspired by Isaiah 60:8: "Who are these that fly as a cloud?" was now applied to the problem of Israel's passage to the Holy Land. The belief was current not only in Russia and Poland, but also in Germany and Turkey. A German Jew who later converted writes: "My mother has often said that, being pregnant at the time, she was worried how she

333. *Messias prawdziwy* (1672). The book was published in Polish and Russian; see Balaban, p. 36, and Z. Rubashov (Shazar) in *Yevreyskaya Staryna,* vol. V, pp. 219–21.

334. *Pesiqta Rabbathi,* I (edn. Friedmann, fol. 2a).

Portrait of Rabbi Jacob Sasportas, the adversary of Sabbatai Ṣevi. Oil, by Isaack Luttichuijs (Amsterdam, about 1680–90)

IX

אור

שבתי צבי

ארוננו

שבתי צבי

ישועת משיחו

והיתה

אליהו בכה״ר מיכאל יהודה ליאון זצ״ל

Statement acknowledging the kingship of Sabbatai Ṣevi, written and signed by the members of the yeshibah *Yeshu'oth Meshiḥo* in Amsterdam, dated September 26–28, 1666. The Hebrew text was published in the Hebrew edition of the present work, II, 448–449. Archives of the Portuguese Community in Amsterdam, Library *Eṣ Ḥayyim*

would be able to leave, whereupon my father and grandfather answered her: 'Do not worry, my daughter! God will send a cloud on which all pregnant women will be carried to Jerusalem.' "[335] In a similar vein, Maltios, the Greek Orthodox bishop in Athens, mentions in his account of the messianic movement[336] that the Jews in Greece were wont to look at the clouds and announce that such as these would bring them to Jerusalem; one Jew in Arta actually attempted, one night, to soar up to the clouds but fell from the roof and died. The Sabbatian enthusiasts were not the first to believe in a miraculous journey to the Holy Land on the clouds of heaven. An Arabic account, by an apostate Jew, of a messianic movement in Baghdad in the first half of the twelfth century, makes mention of letters which announced that one night all the Jews would fly to Jerusalem, "and the Jews of Baghdad, who boast of their cleverness and rationalism, believed it. . . . They gave a great part of their property to charity, prepared green garments for themselves, and assembled on the appointed night on the roofs of their houses, where they waited for the angels that would carry them to Jerusalem on their wings." For a long time, that year was referred to as "the year of the flight" by the Jews of Baghdad.[337] The same motif already had occurred in an earlier messianic movement, inspired by a certain Serenus (?). The fragmentary references to this movement, which occurred in the Orient at the beginning of the eighth century, indicate that the Jews expected to fly through the air to Jerusalem.

An illuminating, albeit indirect, testimony to the penitential awakening in Lithuania during the messianic year is preserved in one of the works of the Lithuanian Talmudist, moralist, and kabbalistic preacher, R. Judah Pochovitzer of Pinsk.[338] The author relates how he had been approached by several people "whose hearts had been touched by the fear of God" and who wished to be given penances for certain sins they had committed in their youth. Originally they

335. Fr. P. Wessel, *Der geistlich todte Jude* (Copenhagen, 1721), p. 17.

336. In his *Greek History of the Church,* quoted by Galanté, pp. 108–9. Galanté's far-fetched explanations of the idea of traveling on clouds become superfluous once the midrashic source is recognized.

337. See J. Mann, *Ha-Tequfah,* XXIV (1928), 345–48.

338. Best known as the author of *Kebod Ḥakhamim* and *Dibrey Ḥakhamim.* The incident referred to is mentioned in the latter work, pt. I, *Daʿath Ḥokhmah* (Hamburg, 1692), fol. 23d.

had wished to perform all the mortifications and fasts "prescribed in the [book] *Roqeaḥ* and in the Lurianic writings," but they soon realized that if they did the full penance prescribed for each and every transgression, they would never be able to bear all the rigors and expiate all their sins. In order not to discourage penitent sinners, Pochovitzer advised them to do the penance of mortification three times for each category of sin (instead of doing a full penance for each sinful act), "and the great luminaries, the learned presidents of the rabbinic courts and the heads of the rabbinic academies of the holy congregations in Lithuania assented to my suggestion." Pochovitzer relates the matter without mentioning any date. But why—and when—did ordinary people suddenly desire to do all the penances prescribed in the book *Roqeaḥ* by R. Eleazar of Worms and in the Lurianic writings? This happened precisely in the messianic year 1666 when, as we have seen (see above, p. 593), the penitential exercises prescribed in the early ascetic classics were collected and published by the rabbi of Cracow. Pochovitzer, elsewhere in his work,[339] explicitly mentions the penitential tracts printed in the year 1666. Incidentally, we also learn that the Polish and Lithuanian rabbis were much concerned with the problem of how to guide and encourage the penitential enthusiasm, and for that reason agreed with their colleague's proposal for mitigating the traditional penances.

The Polish preachers exhorted the people to repent and proclaimed the imminent advent of redemption. R. Joseph b. Solomon, preacher in the large and prominent congregation of Posen, collected his homilies of the year 1665–66 on the messianic advent in a volume entitled *Maṣmiaḥ Yeshu*ᶜ*ah* (*Who Causes Salvation to Spring Forth*) and actually referred to this volume as late as 1679.[340]

The new mood of confidence and defiance manifested by the Jews did not fail to provoke anti-Jewish demonstrations and even riots. The Jews menacingly told their Christian neighbors that the day of

339. *Ibid.*, fol. 32c.

340. In his edn. of the Midnight Devotions (*Tiqqun Ḥaṣoth*, Frankfurt/Oder, 1679), fol. 10a (unnumbered), the author gives a messianic interpretation of Ps. 21 (a great favorite with Sabbatian writers!) and adds: "We have discussed this point at length in our homilies, and especially in the homilies of the year 1665–66, . . . cf. my work *Maṣmiaḥ Yeshu*ᶜ*ah*." The latter work is lost; of his edn. of the Midnight Devotions, very few copies are extant. R. Joseph Darshan, as he was called, was widely known as one of the outstanding preachers of his time.

vengeance was at hand,[341] and carried about pictures of Sabbatai Ṣevi and Nathan. The Christian mob seems to have attacked the Jews in several places, for example, in Pinsk (March 21), Vilna (March 28), Lublin (April 27).[342] A rescript of May 5 by King John Casimir forbade the Jews to carry Sabbatai's picture and made the local authorities responsible for keeping the peace:

It has come to our ears for a second time that villainous persons who are contriving schemes and plotting to destroy the Jews in this state, have—with the intention to plunder—launched rumors alleging that the high courts of the kingdom have given permission to all to harry the Jews and to destroy them. As a result there have been riots, oppression, plundering and bloodshed in several places, as is known to all. Now they [meaning the Jews] have also waxed insolent and are spreading, as plain and indubitable truth, a false report from foreign lands, about some messiah, and they prove this to the simple-minded by printed pamphlets and pictures. In some places where Jews are dwelling . . . the results of this folly are already visible, and even greater trouble is approaching, which threatens to bring affliction and distress upon those Jews, since under the pretext of these forgeries there will be occasion to plunder the belongings and the property of the Jews.

The king ordered all printed pictures, pamphlets, and broadsheets to be destroyed.[343] Since the Jews themselves did not print any accounts of Sabbatai Ṣevi, let alone his picture, the order must refer to the illustrated broadsheets and pamphlets published and diffused by reckless Christian news writers in Holland and Germany (and possibly also in Poland?). The Catholic bishop of Przemyśl, Stanislaw Sarnicky, wrote in a Pastoral Letter of June 22 that "as a result of a new superstition that has arisen among them," the Jews were "carrying in public processions in the streets some printed pamphlets that

341. An incident of this kind was also reported to Martin Meyer, the editor of the *Diarium Europaeum* (Vol. XVI [1668], p. 515): The agent of a Christian merchant in Eperjes (Slovakia) was traveling in Poland in March, 1666. The Jewish innkeeper with whom he stayed boasted of the revenge which the Jews would soon be taking on the Christians. "The Christian replied, 'I shall not wait till you strike me,' and he seized him by the head, struck him many times and dragged him about the room."

342. Balaban, p. 43.

343. The royal order was discovered by Balaban (pp. 44–45) in the archives at Lvov.

offend against [the Christian] religion, as well as pictures of their vanities." News of this scandal had reached the bishop from many towns and villages in his diocese in central Galicia.[344] The royal rescript and the episcopal letter both illustrate the popular character of the movement. Some of its outward expressions were peculiar to Poland: apparently the Jews had adapted for their own purposes the Catholic custom of holding processions and pilgrimages. Some of the Christian pamphlets with their strong chiliast flavor (for example, the letters of Peter Serrarius) could easily appear to the bishop as offending against the Christian religion. In fact we have a poem by Waclaw Potocki, a well-known Polish writer of the time, on the "new Jewish messiah" (*Nowy Mesjasz Żydowski*) which gives a vivid picture of the events as reflected in the mind of a Christian observer.[345]

Several Jewish sources throw light on the movement during the spring and summer of 1666. An interesting exchange between two leading rabbinic scholars and kabbalists, R. Ṣevi Hirsh Horovitz, rabbi of the three districts of Zamot (Kaidan, Vizon, and Bierz) and subsequently of Zablodov, and R. Isaac b. Abraham, the rabbi of Vilna and subsequently of Posen, has been preserved among the responsa of the former.[346] The rabbi of Zamot in northern Poland wrote to his colleague in Vilna concerning some purely halakhic matters, but used the opportunity to inquire, in passing, about the "renewal." He would be grateful if his colleague could arrange for copies to be made of all the reports that had reached Vilna, and send them to Zamot; he would gladly pay the copyist's fee. In his reply R. Isaac, who was also known as R. Isaac the Preacher, dealt very fully with the halakhic query, and added, in a final sentence: "As for the renewal, I have nothing to say but that which the rabbi of Jassy [or Iazi, then the capital of the principality of Moldavia] has written to me and which is surely also known to Your Reverence. Mayest thou delight thyself in great peace forever." The tenor of the correspondence suggests a date prior to Sabbatai's apostasy. Jassy was, at the time, in Turkish territory, and reports of Sabbatai's splendid "imprisonment" in the "Tower of Strength," and of the nightly miracles wrought there, would have passed quickly from the Turkish border-city to Poland.

344. Balaban, p. 45.

345. *Ibid.*, p. 37. The poem was first published by Al. Brickner *Ogród fraszek niewyplewionny*, 1907.

346. Prague, 1776, fol. 2c. R. Ṣevi Hirsh Horovitz also wrote a commentary on the Zohar, entitled *ᵓAspaqlaryah ha-Meᵓirah,* published in Fürth, 1776.

Vilna, which in the eighteenth century established a reputation for uncompromising hostility to revivalist emotionalism—it was the center of Talmudic orthodoxy that led the opposition to the Hasidic movement—yielded to none in messianic fervor in the year 1666. Believers from Vilna made the pilgrimage to Gallipoli, among them R. Abraham Kokesh, a Talmudic scholar and a relative of the wife of Leyb b. Ozer. R. Abraham subsequently visited his family in Amsterdam to whom he recounted, with tears of repentance in his eyes, "how he had eaten meat and other dainties with Sabbatai Ṣevi on the Ninth of Ab, and drunk wine with him, while musicians were playing and Turks were dancing before them with their sticks, as is their wont when they make merry." When he asked Sabbatai why he permitted eating on the fast of the Ninth of Ab, the latter explained that the name Sabbatai Ṣevi could be mystically read as an acrostic signifying "On the Day of the Ninth of Ab Sabbatai Ṣevi shall not fast."[347] One of the messianic enthusiasts in Vilna, Heshel Ṣoref, a silversmith, went through a great revival and was to become the chief Sabbatian prophet of the next generation.

At about the same time that the rabbi of Zamot inquired of his colleague in Vilna about the "renewal," a scribe in Cracow wrote a parchment volume containing the *haftaroth* (weekly lessons from the prophets) for the whole liturgical year. The manuscript has been preserved in the R. Moses Isserles Synagogue at Cracow, and its title page, dated the Twenty-fifth of Sivan, 426 (June 29, 1666) gives eloquent expression to the mood of the period. In a short messianic prayer of five lines, the author succeeded in introducing Sabbatai's name five times in acrostic![348]

Of the visitors who made the pilgrimage to Gallipoli to pay homage to the prisoner who held court there, some came in a private capacity, others as official representatives of their communities. Several names are mentioned in a Sabbatian source,[349] but no details are given of their respective missions. On the other hand, a great deal is known of the embassy sent by the community of Lvov

347. Leyb b. Ozer, MS. Shazar, fol. 54a. The text in the shorter version (Emden, p. 26) is corrupt.

348. Facsimiles of the title page in Balaban's Polish work *History of the Jews of Cracow and Casimir,* vol. II (1936), facing p. 64. For the text of the prayer see the original (Hebrew) edn. of this work, p. 500.

349. Baruch of Arezzo (in Freimann, p. 53): R. Eliezer of Krotoshin, R. Mordecai the *Shtadlan,* and R. Jacob Neshner (perhaps Neshwisher, i.e., from Neshwiz in Lithuania?).

(Lemberg). The rabbi of Lvov, R. David ha-Levi, one of the most celebrated Talmudists of his time and best known for his glosses *Turey Zahab* on parts of Joseph Karo's code *Shulḥan ᶜArukh*, was over eighty years old, but two of his closest relatives volunteered to serve as emissaries of the congregation: his son R. Isaiah, also known as R. Isaiah Mokhiah ("the Reprover"),[350] the rabbi of Komarno, and his stepson R. Aryeh Leyb b. Samuel Ṣevi Hirsch,[351] who was to acquire fame later as one of the most brilliant Talmudic scholars of his generation. The two were worthy ambassadors to be sent to the messiah, as both were renowned scholars and descendants of a long line of distinguished rabbis. (Both were grandsons of the celebrated R. Joel Sirkis, author of the commentary *Bayith Ḥadash* on Jacob b. Asher's code *ᵓArbaᶜah Turim*).[352] About the beginning or middle of March they left Lvov for Constantinople—probably on account of reports from Smyrna to the effect that the messiah was intending to proceed to the capital—but they tarried on the way and did not arrive at their destination until July, 1666. The details of their visit, which throw much light on the mentality both of the Polish rabbis and of Sabbatai's entourage, will be discussed in the following chapter. At any event, they left the messiah's presence full of enthusiasm and as fervent believers.

They left Constantinople early in August and returned to Lvov in the second half of September. There they reported "the glory which they had beheld, and the abundance of gold, silver, precious cloth and ornaments, and the royal apparel which he was wearing every day, and the multitudes that were attending on him, and the honor shown him by the gentiles who would not touch any of the Jews that came to visit him. They also brought a letter from the messiah . . . to their aged father, the rabbi David, and the whole of Poland was in agitation and the fame thereof was heard in all those parts, and their faith was greatly strengthened."[353] The tale of the

350. See Sol. Buber, *ᵓAnshey Shem*, p. 127. The title *mokhiaḥ* is mentioned by Baruch of Arezzo, *loc. cit.*

351. He officiated as rabbi in several congregations; from 1701 he was rabbi in Brest-Litovsk (Brisk), where he died in 1718 (see Zunz, *ᶜIr ha-Ṣedeq*, pp. 150–54). When Leyb b. Ozer wrote his memoir of Sabbatai Ṣevi, R. Aryeh Leyb was already rabbi of Brest-Litovsk (MS. Shazar, fol. 38a).

352. This fact is emphasized in a letter, reproduced by Sasportas, p. 70.

353. Sasportas, p. 77.

emissaries is also told by R. Moses Segal of Cracow, writing on October 8, 1666 (the day before the Day of Atonement, and about one month after Sabbatai's apostasy, news of which had not yet reached Poland), to his brother-in-law R. Meir Isserles in Vienna. The writer emphasizes that his account was but "a drop from the ocean, for who can write all the wondrous things which they told,"[354] but his letter leaves no doubt that R. David ha-Levi too, like the other leading rabbis of Poland, firmly believed in the messiah. (In fact, there are no records of differences of opinion concerning the "faith" among the Polish rabbis, though it is well to remember that our documentation as regards personal attitudes is very scanty). R. Isaiah had explained to Sabbatai that his father was too old to travel, and Sabbatai had presented him with a cloak which he was to put upon his father while reciting the words (Ps. 103:5): "Thy youth is renewed like the eagle ['s]." Sabbatai's brief, handwritten note to R. David reads like a proclamation of vengeance, by the messianic king, for the Jewish blood shed like water in Poland: "An offering sent from me to the man of faith [the numerical value of the Hebrew word for "faith," 102, equals that of Ṣevi] the aged and esteemed R. David of the House of Levi, author of *Turey Zahab*. May he still bring forth fruit in old age, and be fat and flourishing [cf. Ps. 92:15]. Soon I shall avenge you and comfort you as one whom his mother comforteth [cf. Isa. 66:13], but how much more numerous and manifold the day of vengeance is in mine heart *and the year of my redeemed is come* [cf. Isa. 63:4; the numerical value of the italicized words equals that of *Sabbatai Ṣevi*]. Thus saith David the son of Jesse, higher than the kings of the earth, who was raised up on high, above all blessing and praise, the Anointed of the God of Jacob, the celestial lion and the celestial stag, Sabbatai Ṣevi."[355] According to Leyb b. Ozer, the two emissaries also made a written report on their embassy;[356] Leyb b. Ozer probably saw this report and used it in his memoir.[357]

354. *Ibid.*, p. 79. 355. *Ibid.*, p. 78. 356. Emden p. 17.

357. In the Yiddish original of Leyb's *Beshreybung fun Shabb. Zewi,* the passages relating to the embassy from Lvov are in Hebrew; this suggests that they were copied from a written source. On the occasion Leyb actually states (MS. Shazar, fol. 34b): "The same rabbis also *described* many things which they had discussed . . . and seen with him." In Leyb's usage "described" (*beshrieben*) always refers to writing; oral description is termed "recounted" (*derzählt*); see also MS. Shazar, fol. 54a.

Also R. Berakhya Berakh of Cracow, the most prominent Polish preacher of his generation, visited Sabbatai Ṣevi (possibly on his way to the Holy Land where he wished to settle in his old age) "and went out from him with a glad heart."[358] He gave a detailed account of his visit in a letter, copies of which circulated in Cracow as well as in Germany.[359]

This completes the survey of our knowledge of the movement in Europe until the end of 1666. The evidence, though less complete than one could wish, is sufficient to indicate the depth and the breadth of the messianic awakening.

358. Leyb b. Ozer (*ap.* Emden, p. 16).

359. R. Yaʾir Ḥayyim Bacharach in Frankfurt/Main had seen a copy and so probably had others elsewhere; see A. H. Weiss (1865), *Beth ha-Midrash*, p. 92. Berakhya Berakh's visit in Gallipoli proves that he cannot have died in 1665, as has often been asserted.

6

THE MOVEMENT IN THE EAST AND THE CENTER AT GALLIPOLI UNTIL SABBATAI'S APOSTASY (1666)

I

THERE IS little doubt that Sabbatai's removal to Gallipoli was due to political considerations. The vizier Ahmed Köprülü wished to avoid internal disturbances, and evidently realized that outbursts of some kind would be inevitable if the messiah, in whom practically all Jews believed, were put to death. His moderation had the effect of confirming the expectations of the believers, whose optimism was further encouraged by the fact that Sabbatai's captivity was much alleviated by bribes as well as by the Turkish custom which allowed a jailer to admit visitors paying an appropriate "entrance fee." The jailers at Gallipoli soon realized that they had a goose that laid golden eggs. Thousands of Jews, especially from the eastern provinces of the Ottoman Empire, flocked to the capital in the early months of 1666 in order to behold the messiah, and their increasing numbers forced up the food prices in Constantinople. During the last weeks of Sabbatai's detention in Constantinople, and especially after his removal to Gallipoli, the number of visitors steadily increased, and believers spared no expense to pay homage to the Lord's Anointed. All local witnesses comment on the flourishing business of the Turkish jailers. Sabbatai seems to have enjoyed freedom of movement within the walls of the fortress. In the pavilion assigned to him as his dwelling, the "Holy Brotherhood" (an elect band of believing rabbis and scholars) and others who had bribed the Turks into permitting them to stay in the fortress or to return thither every day kept him company. All this further strengthened the popular belief in the "freedom" enjoyed, as it were, by the messiah. "Regular pilgrimages were organized from the capital to the Dardanelles . . . and never did the business of the boatsmen flourish more. Day and night long rows of boats plied in both directions. . . . The governor of the fortress collected immense sums from the sale of permits for visiting his prisoner."[1] The Turks set the price of admission "sometimes at five, sometimes at ten Dollars, or more or less, according as they guessed at the abilities and zeal of the Person."[2]

There were instances of brutal ill-usage of the pilgrims. Several sources report that once the chief of the maritime police at Constantinople stopped seven or eight large boats filled with pilgrims on their way to the Dardanelles. The travelers were cruelly beaten and despoiled, and when they complained to the kaimakam, the highest official in town, they were beaten up once more and thrown into prison. They were released only after having paid bribes to several high officials as well as to the gendarmes who had ill-treated them.[3] An Armenian eyewitness says that "the vizier left for the war in Crete. The Jews, men, women and children, in fact everybody, betook themselves to the Straits [of the Dardanelles]. Our city was full of pilgrims from Poland, the Crimea, Persia, and Jerusalem, as well as from Turkey and the Frankish lands."[4] The parallel Armenian chronicle similarly reports that pilgrims came from as far as Moldavia and Poland, Jaffa and Jerusalem and Anatolia, as well as from the nearby capital.[5]

1. *Relation,* p. 22. See also Coenen, p. 48; Sasportas, p. 76; de la Croix, p. 346.

2. Rycaut, p. 209; cf. also *Hollandtze Merkurius,* January, 1666, p. 135.

3. *Relation,* p. 23. The same story, albeit with differences in details, is also told in the Armenian poem quoted by Galanté, pp. 88–89, and in the Armenian chronicle, *ibid.,* p. 101.

4. Galanté, p. 88.

5. *Ibid.,* p. 101.

According to the French Jesuit writer, believers came from all parts of Europe, and even from countries where Jews could not openly practice their religion (he specifically mentions France and Spain).[6] Occasionally, conflicting details are presented even in one and the same account. For instance, the author of the French *Relation* describes the enthusiasm of the believers for whom no sacrifice was too great and who, coming by the thousands, brought the most expensive gifts in jewelry and money, yet asserts two pages later that most of the pilgrims were beggars "who no doubt hoped to find a quick and easy remedy for their poverty in the revolution" that the messiah was soon to bring about.[7]

The miracle stories which quickly spread among the masses conformed to the pattern of the popular legends of the saints. At first some prophets in Constantinople announced that the messiah had never been taken prisoner: when the soldiers arrived to arrest him, he ascended into heaven and the archangel Gabriel, for some mysterious reason which would be revealed soon, assumed Sabbatai's form.[8] Subsequently, each day produced a new crop of legends. A resident of Constantinople was told by believers that Sabbatai left his prison every night and crossed the Dardanelles from Europe into Asia by the power of the divine name; in the morning he returned in the same mysterious fashion and voluntarily re-entered his prison. Others knew that he was surrounded by angelic hosts who revealed to him the mysteries of heaven and of his future kingdom. Accounts circulated of his many and prolonged fasts, and of the liberality with which he shared his wealth with the many poor who came to do homage to him.[9]

6. *Relation,* p. 24.

7. *Ibid;* see also *ibid.,* p. 22; "even the poor women offered their ornaments to the messiah."

8. Sasportas, p. 126. Israel Friedländer (JQR, II, New Series [1912], 507–16) suggested possible Shiᶜite influence on the Turkish Jews to account for this Docetist doctrine, but the explanation seems far-fetched and unnecessary.

9. *Relation,* p. 25. The Jesuit writer comments: "If the rumor of such miracles, attributed to this impostor, could spread at the very place where their falsehood was patent to every beholder, then I am not astonished at the wondrous tales which were told in France and elsewhere, and which their subject never even imagined. . . . For even the Devil never worked anything for him or through him . . . that could be called a miracle" (p. 26). Leyb b. Ozer (*ap.* Emden, p. 14) had heard of letters alleging that Sabbatai had resurrected several dead who had died many years before, and that he had healed lepers.

The majority of the Jews of Constantinople supported Sabbatai. Even Sasportas, who, whenever he could, shifted the guilt onto the "wretched rabble," had to admit that the wealthy Jews of the capital and elsewhere sent Sabbatai royal apparel and sumptuous cloth fabrics, as a result of which "all the Jews coming from the ends of the earth and beholding his splendor and his apparel, and the many gifts arriving all the time, were easily misled into believing that he was the messianic king. . . . The Jews would say [to the governor of the fortress] that they came to visit a holy man of God, whereupon the governor and his men would treat him with respect in his prison. This, in turn, would further confirm the Jews in their mistaken faith in him, for seeing that even the gentiles paid him respect, they concluded that this was the Lord's doing." Indeed, the surprising fact that Sabbatai had not been executed immediately as a rebel was considered conclusive proof of his messianic character.[10] The respectful behavior of the Turks toward Sabbatai was noted in several letters sent from Constantinople to correspondents abroad.[11]

Meanwhile, the gift of prophecy continued powerfully in Constantinople. The example of Moses Suriel, or Saraval, was followed by hundreds of men and women, and the French eyewitness scornfully reported on the strange spectacle of seven to eight hundred women prophesying for several months in the Galata quarter of Constantinople, acting as if possessed and imitating the enthusiastic behavior of such as have received the Spirit. Several women had to be bound and beaten in order to drive out the spirit of folly that had turned their brains and caused them to rave and indulge in disorderly behavior. This happened not only with women but even with infants, who seemed to be possessed.[12] There were also other, in some ways more impressive, cases of prophecy which the Jesuit writer, bent as he was on holding the movement up to ridicule, did not mention. Letters to Egypt spoke of five hundred prophets and prophetesses in the capital during the summer of 1666, "the most recent among them being a very celebrated and old rabbi from *Ashkenaz* (Poland?), R. Mordecai the Pious, who happened to be in Constantinople. He went to see Our Lord at the 'Tower of Strength,' but could hardly look at him because his face was shining

10. Sasportas, p. 76.
11. Cf. Sasportas, p. 157.
12. *Relation,* pp. 23–24.

with [a supernatural] light so that he was almost blinded.[13] yet he saw a crown of fire rising from his head heavenwards. Thereupon he fell on his face, and he went through the streets, crying with all his might, 'He is Our Lord, and there is no other. In truth, he is our King and there is none besides him.'[14] Then the Holy Spirit descended upon him and he became a celebrated prophet. All this has been reported by letter from well-known and esteemed persons in Constantinople."[15] Elsewhere this same R. Mordecai Ashkenazi is said to have discovered a new *gematria* referring to Sabbatai Ṣevi. The Hebrew letters of the phrase "the man who was raised up by God, the anointed of the God of Jacob" (II Sam. 23:1)—a favorite phrase in Sabbatai's and Primo's proclamations—were found to be equivalent to the numerical value of "Sabbatai Ṣevi Yahweh ʾEhyeh."[16] The author of this *gematria* apparently attributed some sort of divinity to Sabbatai. Meir Rofe of Hebron was in Constantinople sometime in 1666 and saw the mass prophecy with his own eyes.[17]

Next to nothing is known of Sabbatai's state of mind and behavior during the first weeks at Gallipoli, and of his reactions to the dramatic events of which he was the center. There are no references or allusions to any further "strange actions" after the ceremony at which Sabbatai ate a kid roasted in ritually forbidden fat as a Passover sacrifice. He had evidently entered on one of his "normal" periods. For aught we know he may have suffered from this fall from enthusiastic grace and interpreted it as the final onslaught of the demonic powers. According to Leyb b. Ozer, letters signed by Sabbatai Ṣevi were received in all countries after his imprisonment in Gallipoli, telling the faithful that except for more acts of penitence, everything was now ready for redemption. Wherefore "everyone should repent, so as not to delay redemption. But although it was now the time of the end, there might be a delay of some months or years. He therefore urgently begged that none should spare himself, but everyone should better his works and pray for the messiah that God in His great mercy

13. I.e., he visited Sabbatai during one of his fits of manic exaltation.

14. An adaptation of a liturgical formula originally referring to God.

15. Report quoted in R. Hosea Nantawa's letter (Sasportas, pp. 156–57).

16. Coenen, pp. 108–9.

17. See his letter, written at the end of 1677, *Sefunoth,* III–IV (1960), 117. They explained, he says, deep passages in the Zohar.

prosper His way, and that His kingdom be made manifest soon, and the spirit of impurity and the *qelippoth* be made to pass away. For soon Scripture will be fulfilled: 'and I will cause the unclean spirit to pass out of the land' [Zech. 13:2]. Meanwhile, the demonic powers have caused his imprisonment so that he cannot act, wherefore none should spare himself in acts of penance."[18] The existence of letters couched in such terms is not corroborated by any other source, but Leyb's account sounds authentic enough. Many other letters from Sabbatai have been lost, and some have been discovered only in recent times and by sheer accident. The original letter may well have been composed by the royal scribe Samuel Primo. We know that Primo composed most of the messiah's letters and proclamations from Gallipoli, to which Sabbatai used to add, in his own handwriting, a line or two in which he gave full rein to his symbolic and metaphorical fancies. These figures of speech, with their more or less veiled hints at the messiah's divinity, seem to have pleased Sabbatai as much as they infuriated the infidels. It must have been some such letter, signed by Sabbatai's "impure hand" and containing titles such as the Firstborn of God, King Solomon, the Celestial Stag, etc., which still was available to R. Abraham Ḥamoy of Aleppo as recently as a hundred years ago.[19] These cryptic hints and messianic titles were surely the fond inventions of Sabbatai's imagination, and suited his temperament better than the majestic and sonorous periods of the royal edicts. The composition of the latter was left to Primo, whose literary style even Sasportas—himself no mean expert at the same craft—grudgingly admired.[20] The final onslaught of the demonic powers and the need to pray for the success of Sabbatai's messianic mission were surely the most obvious themes for a letter addressed to the Jewish Diaspora and intended to explain the messiah's imprisonment. Perhaps they may also be taken as indicative of a certain melancholia: Sabbatai, in accordance with his essentially passive temperament, probably spent his time with his companions searching for an explanation of the re-

18. Leyb b. Ozer (MS. Shazar, fol. 30b). The passage is thoroughly currupted in the abbreviated printed version (Emden, p. 11). D. Kahana, though in possession of the original MS., unfortunately relied for his account on the printed edn.

19. *Beth Din* (Leghorn, 1873), fol. 126b. Ḥamoy (or Ḥamawi) traveled widely and edited many collections of kabbalistic material.

20. Sasportas, p. 150 (in the original autograph version).

cent happenings, rather than thinking of any active steps that he might take.

As a matter of fact there is some evidence that Sabbatai suffered a fit of depression during his first month at Gallipoli, and the evidence incidentally also confirms Leyb's report that letters, written by him or in his behalf, had been received in various Jewish communities. A Christian in Amsterdam who was interested in the movement and had some knowledge of Hebrew (Serrarius?) translated into Latin, for the benefit of a friend in Switzerland, a letter of Sabbatai's that had been received toward the end of August, 1666. The letter seems to have been written very shortly after the experience described in it, that is, in the second half of May, at about the same time that Sabbatai's followers in Constantinople composed their reply to the rabbis of Venice concerning the mysterious merchandise of R. Israel, the son of Abraham, of Jerusalem. The letter says:

Thus speaketh the Great King, Our Lord and holy King, with my greetings, which I want you to announce to all my faithful people, that love me. I shall so act that I may cause them that love me to inherit substance, that is to say, I will fill their treasures with spiritual and material bliss, and they that love me will be filled with good, saith the Lord. And all the people of my faith shall be blessed, men and women, brothers and sisters, sons and daughters; I say that they will be blessed from the mouth of the great God and the mouth of His chosen servant.

Be it known unto you that on the Sabbath "if ye walk in my statutes,"[21] God beheld my severe affliction, and overwhelmed me with great joy from which I perceived not darkly that the expected time of the hope of Israel is very near. What I said here must suffice you [for the present]. Wherefore be strong and of good courage, and may your heart be strong all ye that trust in the Lord and in His Anointed.

Our brethern, when these words shall reach their ears, let them shout with joy, and let them be glad that favor my righteous cause, yea let them say continually, "Let the Lord be magnified which hath pleasure in the prosperity of his servant [cf. Ps. 35:27], and let his great and revered name be praised forever." For my soul which was sorely troubled and afflicted has now been filled with a great splendor and

21. The pentateuchal lesson beginning Lev. 26:3 (*be-Ḥuqqothay*) was read in that year on the Sabbath, 17 Iyyar (May 22, 1666).

exults with joy. May the Most High, for the sake of His truth and His great mercy, grant permanence and increase to this consolation even as I felt it within myself when I read the passage [cf. Lev. 26:9–11]: "and I will turn unto you and I will set my tabernacle among you, and my soul shall not abhor you." Verily with you [Scripture will be fulfilled, Ps. 149:2]: "Let Israel rejoice in him that made him, let the children of Zion be joyful in their king." And in my solitude Scripture will be fulfilled and confirmed [Prov. 18:10]: "The name of the Lord is a strong tower, the righteous runneth into it and is safe." Behold now is the time of love [cf. Ezek. 16:8], therefore be strong and of good courage in the faith, in prayer, in penitence, in fasts, and in many and frequently repeated ritual immersions, for the redemption of Israel is at hand with the help of God. Sabbatai Ṣevi.[22]

22. The Latin text in MS. Hottinger, vol. 30, fol. 374a, reads as follows:

"Apographum epistolae Regis Judaeorum
Amsterdamo huc missae, 24 Aug. 1666

"Sic dixit Rex Magnus, Noster Dominus, Rex Sanctus cum salutationibus meis quas communicabitis toto populo fideli qui me amant ut faciam amicos meos haereditatem possidere, quod est ut repleam thesauros corum felicitate tam spirituali quam corporali, ac ut misericordes mei mea bonitate saturentur, dictum Domini; adeoque sint benedicti omnes meae fidei homines, tam viri quam foeminae, fratres et sorrores, filii ei filiae meae, sint, inquam, benedicti ab ore Magni Dei et ore servi electi sui.

"Notum vobis sit, quod Sabato illo quo legebatur parasa incipiens si ambulaveritis in statutis meis, Deus respexerit afflictionem meam non fictam meque magno gaudio et consolatione cumulaverit ex quo haud obscure percepi, instare illus expectatum spei Israeliticae tempus quod dixissi vobis in praesenti sufficiat. Quapropter roboremini ac estote fortes. Confortetur cor vestrum omnes qui expectatis dominum ac unctum ejus.

"Fratres nostri, cum verba haec ad aures illorum pervenirent, cantabunt praeconia ac prae gaudio exultabunt omnes qui desiderant justitiam ejus, et dicent semper magnificetur Dominus, qui vult pacem servi sui, ac benedictum sit nomen ipsius magnum et gloriosum in secula. Anima enim mea, qua multum afflicta et angustata fuit, magno nunc splendore perficitur, ac prae gaudio subsultat. Faxit Altissumus pro sua veritate ac magna misercordia ut consolatio illa continua sit et multiplicetur quam persensi in me, cum legeretur sectio illa, et respiciam ad vos et dabo tabernaculum meum in medio vestri et ambulabo inter vos and non amplius repudiabit vos anima mea. Sane vobiscum gaudebat Israel cum creatore suo et filii Zion cum rego suo, ac in solitudine mea confirmabitur et verificabitur versus illus turris munitionis, nomen Domini, justus accurrit et fortificatur. En tempus amorum. Verum tamen vos roboremini, ac fortes estote in fide, in precibus, in contritione, in jejuniis, in lavationibus multis ac saepius repetitis; Redemtio enim Israëlitica prope est cum auxilio divino.

"Sabbathai Sebi"

The letter is of extraordinary interest, inasmuch as it reports no actions but an emotion which Sabbatai had experienced while reading the weekly portion of the Pentateuch. However, when viewed as a sequel to the kind of letters mentioned by Leyb b. Ozer, the contents is easily understandable. Sabbatai had as much as admitted in the earlier letters that he felt himself a prisoner of the *qelippoth* against which he had struggled all his life. Now, however, about five weeks after his removal to Gallipoli, his heart was filled again with the radiance of comfort and salvation. The allusions to the anguish of his soul and the subsequent great light admit of two interpretations. They may refer to mental states of depression and renewed illumination, or to his objective situation as a prisoner and his gradually returning hope. To those familiar with Sabbatai's psychic life, the wording inevitably suggests the former interpretation; to the ordinary reader, unaware of its implications, it must have conveyed a different meaning. The letter, in all its simplicity, throws much light on Sabbatai's psychological condition at the time, and certainly should not be dismissed as a mere piece of propaganda, designed to boost the morale of the despondent believers by an appeal to one of the best-known biblical prophecies of bliss. There is a ring of genuine piety in Sabbatai's exhortations to repentance, expressing one of the two conflicting tendencies in his soul. In any event, the other tendency, namely, the impulse toward "strange actions," was in abeyance when he wrote this letter. He demanded of his followers no novel rituals or liturgical celebrations, but perseverance in their penitential fervor.

From May onward, and particularly during June and July, there was much epistolary activity among both believers and doubters. A few days before Sabbatai wrote the aforementioned letter, the rabbis of Constantinople addressed an official query to Amigo, the chief rabbi of Jerusalem. The letter, whose authenticity is beyond suspicion, was signed by three members of the rabbinic court (R. Yomtob b. Ḥananiah ibn Yakar, R. Moses Shanji, and R. Caleb b. Samuel) and several other rabbis. Chronologically it comes between the letter to Smyrna, in which the two infidel rabbis were exhorted to pay respect to Sabbatai Ṣevi, and the one to Venice, in which the faith was solemnly confirmed (see above, pp. 505–6). The former letter preceded the letter to Amigo of Jerusalem by about a fortnight, and at least two of the signatories on both documents are identical. Sasportas contended that some of the signatures on the letter to Smyrna, as also on the subsequent letter to Venice, were forged, but the matter is far from certain (see above, p. 415, n. 188). There are, no doubt, stylistic and other grounds for such a suspicion, but, on the other hand, there is a noticeable restraint in the earlier letter. The signatories speak of Sabbatai in terms of the highest esteem and even defend his "strange actions" in the manner of true believers, yet they refrained from roundly asserting that he was the messiah. Perhaps they were, like many others, profoundly impressed by the penitential awakening, but at the same time wished to steer clear of any statement that might increase discord. It is quite possible, therefore, that the letter is genuine even though some of its signatories may have had doubts or mental reservations. The codicil to the letter, which was signed by a large number of believers, differs noticeably in style and mood from the main part, and bespeaks a more radical attitude.[23]

Whatever the truth about the letter to Smyrna, the letter to Jerusalem is undoubtedly genuine and well illustrates the perplexity of the rabbis of Constantinople. They had only recently learned of Sabbatai's excommunication in Jerusalem, and had subsequently had the opportunity of observing him in their midst. They had found no trace of heresy or antinomianism in the pious ascetic to whom (as well as to Nathan) they referred in terms of the highest respect in their letter to Jerusalem. Sabbatai is even alluded to with a messianic title—*Bar Nafley* (see above, p. 134). They were keenly aware of the danger threatening the Jewish community, "particularly in such close proximity to the seat of the government," and the elders had enjoined strict silence on all: "Blessed is he that waiteth *in his heart*." Unfortunately the enthusiastic masses would not heed these warnings, especially since the "Holy Lamp," the prophet of Gaza, had advised them that they need not fear anything. In carefully guarded language the rabbis of Constantinople avow their perplexity: "So far we have not beheld a single miracle or sign" from the messiah or from the prophet of Gaza, "only the noise of rumors and testimonies at secondhand. . . . Hence we cannot examine the matter properly, wherefore there is no unanimity on the subject but divergence of opinions. . . . This has given rise to contention on all sides . . . and no peace cometh out of this strife." They had resolved, therefore, to request four of the most eminent, learned and trustworthy rabbis to serve as a kind of commission of inquiry. The four rabbis were to travel to Gaza and "discuss" matters with Nathan (that is, examine him),

23. Baruch of Arezzo (*ap.* Freimann, p. 54); Sasportas, p. 134.

"and if they agree that they have seen the signs and miracles [required] . . . according to the principles of our holy Torah and the holy Talmud, let them write to us. But if the matter remain doubtful and uncertain in their eyes, they should notify us in their wisdom . . . in order that we may at least warn the people." The writers proposed as members of the inquiry commission R. Abraham Amigo himself (the addressee of the letter) and one representative of each of the three major communities in the Holy Land: R. Gabriel Esperança of Safed, R. Solomon Alleman of Jerusalem, and R. Ḥayyim Abulafia of Hebron.[24] The rabbis of Constantinople must have known that at least three of the proposed four members were unbelievers, and that Amigo had been the initiator of Sabbatai's excommunication. The wording of their proposal suggests that the writers were not only aware of the attitude already adopted by the rabbis of their choice, but that they actually desired a negative verdict. However, they couched their request in such diplomatic language that even believers could put their signatures to it. To obviate any hesitations for financial reasons, they also notified Amigo that Judah b. Mordecai Kohen, one of the wealthiest Jews in Constantinople, would defray all the expenses of the delegation to Gaza. The rabbis of Jerusalem apparently never replied to this letter. Their silence (see above, p. 363) which, in the circumstance, was pregnant with the most serious consequences, effectively tied the hands of the rabbis at Constantinople and elsewhere. The believers, it goes without saying, felt free to act.

II

The believers lived in a state of high-pitched exaltation throughout the summer of 1666. Sabbatai too emerged from his state of melancholia and exhibited the familiar manic outbursts. One of the rituals instituted by him at this period confirms our suspicion of Christian influences. In a letter to Smyrna he "published the same Indulgence and privilege to every one who should pray at the Tomb of his Mother, as if he had taken on him a Pilgrimage to pray and sacrifice at Jerusalem."[25] The Jews of Smyrna did, in fact, make the pilgrimage "much

24. Sasportas, pp. 123–25. Rosanes, IV, pp. 362–64 has placed Sol. Esperança in Jerusalem, but at the time he was still in Safed, cf. M. Benayahu in *Sinai,* XLIII (1958), 103–4.

25. Rycaut, p. 210, apparently transcribing Coenen, pp. 55, 94, 137.

like the pilgrimages which the Italians make to their holy places to obtain forgiveness of sin," and on that occasion would also drink from a spring near the cemetery, not far from the spot at the seashore where Sabbatai and his early companions used to take their ritual baths. The spring, which had hitherto been known as Santa Veneranda (after a saint of the Greek Orthodox Church), was now called "the Spring of Our Lord."[26] The rabbis of Smyrna issued a prohibition against keeping cats, dogs, and other unclean beasts, as the prophet Elijah would not enter a house in which these could be found. They also ordered that the Hebrew books in every household should be kept open, by way of testimony to the religious character of the house.[27]

There was much coming and going between Smyrna (as well as other communities) and Gallipoli,[28] and one of the "kings" appointed by Sabbatai who accompanied him to Constantinople sent enthusiastic reports to the Jewries abroad after returning (see above, p. 455). Also Sabbatai's elder brother, Elijah Ṣevi, traveled to Gallipoli, and after his return to Smyrna was visited by Coenen. Good-natured and naïve, the minister of the Dutch Reformed congregation in Smyrna hoped to extract information from the messiah's two brothers whom he knew to be agents for a Dutch firm. The visit seems to have taken place some time in August. Elijah Ṣevi evaded Coenen's theological questions by insisting that he was an expert in cloth and linen but not in divinity. He was, however, unstinting in his praise of his saintly brother who, he said, had from his youth devoted himself to the study of the Law and to whom God had revealed his future messianic destiny. When Coenen tried to advance arguments from Scripture, Elijah simply said that all questions would be answered when God made the messiah's mission fully manifest. However, he pointed out to Coenen the miraculous fact that Sabbatai was still alive and was kept at the expense of the Grand Turk; in fact, even some Turks were showing faith in him.[29]

The militant attitude adopted by the believers and Benveniste's ruling on the subject of the proper treatment of infidels have been described in a previous chapter (see above, p. 514). The few obstinate infidels suffered much vexation, and some of them saved themselves

26. Coenen, p. 56. In a very good engraving (around 1660), giving the view of Smyrna as seen from the sea, all these places are pointed out.

27. *Ibid.*, p. 65.

28. *Ibid.*, p. 75.

29. *Ibid.*, pp. 79–81.

from more serious harm by appearing before the rabbi, pretending a change of mind and confessing their faith in the messiah.[30]

Sabbatai's behavior, once the "great illumination"[31] was upon him, was not conducive to bridging the widening gulf between believers and infidels. In July the fast of the Seventeenth of Tammuz was abolished, as had already been done the year before in Gaza.[32] An interesting proclamation which, however, probably refers to the fast of the Ninth of Ab rather than the Seventeenth of Tammuz,[33] was issued at the time to the Jewish communities in Turkey. The Hebrew text, which is no longer extant, was translated into Italian for Rycaut, the British consul in Smyrna, who mistakenly held it to be Sabbatai's first official messianic proclamation.[34] More recently a fuller Armenian translation of the same document has been discovered[35] which enables

30. *Ibid.*, p. 77.

31. The expression is Baruch of Arezzo's (*ap.* Freimann, p. 64).

32. Rosanes (IV, p. 72) quotes a letter of Primo abolishing the fast of Tammuz "because on that day the Divine Presence will rest upon Sabbatai Ṣevi." No such letter exists, least of all in the source (Sasportas, *ap.* Emden, fol. 25a) quoted by him. Rosanes misread and confused many of his sources, which, moreover, he often quoted at secondhand; hence his account of Sabbatai Ṣevi is gravely deficient, see above, ch. 4, n. 102.

33. Sabbatai may have been inspired by the midrashic dictum (*Yalqut Shimᶜoni* ad Lam., §998) that in the messianic age "God will turn the [fast of] 9 Ab into rejoicing."

34. Rycaut, pp. 205–6, gives the Italian translation which was then taken over by Evelyn, p. 62. Coenen makes no mention of the proclamation and merely refers to the letter that contained the detailed liturgical instructions for the celebration of 9 Ab. Rycaut mentions both documents, but confused their chronology. He also antedated Nathan's letter of December, 1666, by a whole year, thereby leading astray all subsequent writers who copied from him or from Evelyn. Rycaut was away from Smyrna at the time, and began to collect documents concerning Sabbatai Ṣevi only after returning to his post (in 1667?). Hence also the many inaccuracies in his account. The authenticity of the proclamation is, however, confirmed by the Armenian source; see n. 35 below.

35. The Armenian exists in two recensions: (*a*) the Armenian chronicle, translated into French by Galanté, p. 102. The same source also mentions the name of the translator (from Greek into Armenian), who is identical with the author of the Armenian poem printed by Galanté; (*b*) an Armenian collection of documents and letters, from the archives of a prominent Armenian family. The text was published by Galanté, *Encore un nouveau recueil de documents concernant l'histoire des Juifs de Turquie* (Istanbul, 1953), p. 19. The second recension avoids some of the more obvious mistakes of the first version and is closer to Rycaut's Italian text. The Hebrew original was evidently written in a stilted and flowery style, leading to variations and misunderstandings in the translations. In addition

us to establish its exact date, though the name of the festival has been corrupted and the text says that Purim [!] had been converted into a feast. It is evident, nevertheless, that the two versions are derived from the same Hebrew original. The following text is based on Rycaut's English translation from the Italian, supplemented where necessary in accordance with the Armenian and Greek versions:

The only-begotten and first-born Son of God Sabbatai Ṣevi, the Anointed of the God of Jacob and Saviour of Israel, to all the Sons of Israel, peace. Since that you are made worthy to see the great day of Deliverance and Salvation unto Israel, which our Forefathers were not vouchsafed, to behold the accomplishment of the Word of God and his Promises by his Prophets and by his beloved son Israel[36]—let your bitter sorrows therefore be turned into Joy, and your fast into Festivals, for you shall weep no more, O my Sons of Israel and no longer suffer the tribulations of days past. For God having given you this unspeakable joy and comfort, rejoice at your prayers with Drums, Organs and Musick, giving thanks to him for fulfilling his promises to our Forefathers from all Ages. Perform your duties every day as you are wont to do and on the day of the new moon.[37] And that day dedicated to affliction and sorrow, convert you unto a day of mirth for my appearance.[38] Let

---

to these Armenian translations, a Greek one has been discovered (September, 1970) in a MS. of St. Catherine's monastery on Mount Sinai, of all places. My colleague A. Wasserstein, to whom I am indebted for this information, found it in a MS. written in 1673, accompanied by the remark: "This letter was translated from the Hebrew into the Romaic [i.e., Greek] tongue in the year 1668, in the month of Januar[y]." The text is basically the same as the one used by the Armenian translator, including the curious mistake *Purim* instead of *Tish*ᶜ*a be-Ab*. A Greek translation was already made in July, 1666, and the date given in the Greek MS. is therefore surprising. The name of the messiah is rendered in the corrupt form Josapai Ṣevi. The MS. does not say whether the new translation was made in Constantinople or elsewhere. See Wasserstein, *Zion,* XXXVII (1972; pub. 1974), pp. 239–43.

36. Here meant as a messianic title; cf. also Sabbatai's signature in some of his letters: "Israel, your father."

37. The Italian text reads "facendo ogni giorno quelle cose che solete fare nelle Calende."

38. The strange reference, at this point, to Purim, in the Armenian (and Greek) versions must be due, as Galanté pointed out, to some mistake in the Armenian translator's Greek source. The Italian text too seems to refer to a specific day and may well have in mind the conversion of 9 Ab into the Sabbatian Feast of Rejoicing. Could Purim stand, perhaps, for the day preceding every new moon, called *Kippur Katan?*

none in your camp engage in any labour, but only in works of gladness and rejoicing.[39] And fear you nothing, for you shall have Dominion over the Nations, and not only over those who are on the surface of the Earth, but over those creatures also which are in the depth of the Sea.[40] All which is for your consolation and rejoicing and life.

The messianic proclamation was rendered into Turkish by the sultan's chief translator.[41] The fact that messages of this kind were promptly translated by the Turkish government offices indicates that the authorities were closely watching the movement.

As the fast days of the Seventeenth of Tammuz and the Ninth of Ab approached, Sabbatai's euphoric enthusiasm mounted, expressing itself, as usual, in changes in the liturgical calendar and the institution of new festivals. Sabbatai's attitude to time was certainly remarkable for a Jew of that age. The harmonious rhythm and solid framework of the traditional liturgical year had ceased to exist for him. From the moment that he knew himself to be the Lord's Anointed, time had assumed a new quality and rhythm. His restless groping toward a new sense of time was not devoid of symbolic significance: it expressed his awareness that the calendar of the messianic age was different from that of the exile. Most probably Sabbatai had never considered the original, biblical character of the Jewish festivals, but had always experienced them in the light of the kabbalistic doctrine of the exile of the Shekhinah. In his consciousness there was no difference between scriptural holidays (for example, Passover or the Day of Atonement), and those instituted by "rabbinic authority" (for example, Hanukkah or the fast of the Seventeenth of Tammuz). With the dawn of the messianic age the nature and order of time had changed too; his curious behavior in Smyrna (see above, p. 408), and again in Gallipoli in the week of the fast of the Seventeenth of Tammuz, was merely an extreme manifestation of this new consciousness of time in his soul. In addition to the hectic sequence of festivals described in our sources, Sabbatai apparently even contemplated further, some time in July or August, "[transferring] the set feasts of the Lord from their appointed time, and [observing] the Day of

39. This sentence is missing in the Italian version.

40. The latter phrase is missing from the first Armenian recension, but is found in the Greek one.

41. See Galanté (p. 103), who also gives the translator's name as Panaghiotis Nicossios.

Atonement [which in the year 5427 fell on a Sabbath (Saturday, October 9, 1666)] on a Thursday in that year."[42] This, of course, would have constituted the climax of Sabbatai's tampering with the liturgical calendar, which had begun in 1658, when he celebrated the three pilgrimage festivals in one week (see above, p. 162).

Sabbatai's deportment at that period impressed all visitors by its noble grandeur and its clearly symbolic significance. Many months previously the prophet Nathan had explained in his treatises that the forces of Stern Judgment would be in the ascendant at the beginning of the messianic age. In kabbalistic symbolism the color of Stern Judgment is red, and indeed the color looms large in Leyb b. Ozer's vivid account of Sabbatai's court. Leyb had been told by many witnesses who had made the pilgrimage to Gallipoli[43] that Sabbatai was

> sitting in his fortress . . . in red garments, and the Torah scroll which he held in his hands was likewise draped in red. . . . Usually the Torah scroll was placed at his right. The walls of the room in which he sat were draped with golden carpets, and the floor was covered with rugs made of gold and silver. It was a princely room. He sat at a table made of silver and covered with gold, and the inkstand on the table was made of gold and jewels. He ate and drank from gold and silver vessels inlaid with jewels. In his right hand he held a golden staff topped by a scarf of [that is, embroidered with] gold, and in his left hand a fan with a silver handle. There were many rooms in the fortress, as in the palace of the Turkish king, and also a tower and a beautiful vineyard. Many guards were round the fortress, but his servant was a learned Jew.[44] All day long he was singing hymns of praise to God, . . . and whoever went in, left him with joy and great consolation. Sabbatai was a peerless kabbalist. He told [his visitors] that the Shekhinah

42. Sasportas (p. 174) quoting R. Joseph ha-Levi who had heard it from believers who had been to Gallipoli in September, 1666.

43. Leyb himself never says Gallipoli but uses *castillo* (in phonetic spelling) or a similar form (e.g., MS. Shazar, fol. 32b; *das Schloss castillo;* cf. also *ibid.*, fol. 54a); the same holds also true for Cuenque (Emden, p. 41). Also Ḥayyim Benveniste, who on several occasions refers to the "congregation of Gallipoli," mentions the name *Castillos* (*Baᶜey Ḥayyey*, no. 171). The plural form also occurs in a letter by A. M. Cardozo, where the messiah's prison is referred to as *migdaloth* ("towers"); see *Sefunoth*, III–IV (1960), 195. Sasportas generally uses Gallipoli, but in a more detailed description (p. 113) he writes, "the place called Seven Towers, where political prisoners were kept." Several rabbis of the congregation of Gallipoli are mentioned in contemporary rabbinic responsa.

44. Perhaps an allusion to R. Samuel Primo or R. Abraham Gamaliel?

was now manifest and had, as it were, risen from her exile; it was now forty years since the Shekhinah had risen . . . and therefore ye need not fast any more on the seventeenth of Tammuz and the Ninth of Ab. For, he said, he had now reached his fortieth year and Scripture was fulfilled: "forty years was I grieved with this generation, and said it is a people that do err in their heart, and they have not known my ways" [Ps. 95:10]."[45]

At a certain hour on the Seventeenth of Tammuz the prophets in the capital announced that the messiah had just broken the fast and was now eating, whereupon everybody began to eat.[46] Expectancy in Constantinople had reached the bursting point. R. Abraham Yakhini, Sabbatai's confidant in the capital, virtually acted as his representative.[47] It was to him that the emissaries from foreign lands repaired first, and his homilies and hymns conveyed the message of the "faith" to the masses. By a fortunate accident his sermon for the Sabbath preceding the Seventeenth of Tammuz has been preserved,[48] and there is little doubt but his rhetorical flourishes—"they shall receive a blessing from the Lord of peace who eat their measure of meat and drink their wine until the path shineth"—were meant to serve notice of the impending abolition of the fast. "A people saved by the Lord with an everlasting salvation, and our enemies shall behold and be put to shame, for our salvation is near in two or three days," meaning, on the Seventeenth of Tammuz, for which day, it appears, spectacular events were expected. One of Yakhini's hymns was clearly composed for a fast that had been turned into a feast, since mention is made of the "mystery of the banquet" and of the messiah who would "reveal to us the mysteries of the Torah."[49] In another poem Yakhini emphasized the connection between the messiah's soul and God; the source of the former was in the mystical origins of the creation of the world.[50]

45. Emden, p. 12. 46. *Ibid.*, p. 13.
47. Sasportas, p. 76. 48. Danon, p. 40.
49. See *Zion*, VII (1942), 181.
50. Danon (p. 47), from an autograph of Yakhini's homilies which had come into his possession. D. Kahana's statement (pt. I, p. 91) that Yakhini composed his *Wawey ha-ᶜAmudim* at that period is without foundation. Yakhini wrote the book shortly before his death, during 1681–82. Yakhini's allusions in the poem are vague and do not permit definite theological conclusions, though I incline to the view that he was acquainted with Nathan's theories concerning the origin of the messiah's soul in the "great abyss," and that the allusions in the hymn are to these doctrines.

A great many poems in honor of the messiah were composed at the time, and a number of them—though scarcely of any literary or theological interest—have survived.[51]

The Seventeenth of Tammuz was celebrated by Sabbatai and his entourage as the "day of the revival of his spirit and his light." The festival had probably been introduced the year before in Gaza and was, therefore, no innovation in 1666. The earliest Sabbatian liturgical calendars, from the end of the seventeenth century, specifically state "the Seventeenth of Tammuz is the first day of AMIRAH's illumination and the revival of his spirit."[52] Concerning the events of that week we are well informed by the reports of the two envoys of the congregation of Lvov.[53] The envoys arrived in Constantinople about the middle of July and proceeded to Gallipoli. They saw Sabbatai twice, but he did not speak much "because of the affliction that had come upon him," meaning, according to Kahana,[54] that the governor of the fortress had, for unknown reasons, issued strict orders not to admit any visitors to the prisoner. The Polish emissaries returned with the other pilgrims to Constantinople, where they had a conversation on the "Mystery of the Faith" with Abraham Yakhini[55] and also visited the prophet Moses Suriel (see above, pp. 436 f.). We may, however, doubt whether the suggested interpretation of the nature of Sabbatai's "affliction" is correct. Perhaps he suffered from one of his attacks of melancholia, and his close attendants wished to hide his pitiful state from the public. We know that during his fits of depression Sabbatai would shut himself up and refuse to see people; this was his manner in Smyrna, in Gaza, and again, at the end of his life, in Dulcigno. Most of the pilgrims, however, stayed in Gallipoli, outside the fortress, and celebrated the appointed festivals. According

51. See M. Güdemann, *MGWJ,* XVII (1868), 117–18. The alphabetic poem published in *RÉJ,* XVIII (1889), 105, was possibly also composed in Constantinople. Several other poems from this time are preserved among the MSS. of the Ben-Zvi Institute.

52. MS. Adler 493, as well as the MS. used by Freimann (p. 96) who, however, produced a corrupted text.

53. See above, p. 601. Their mission is described in three sources: (*a*) Leyb b. Ozer in MS. Shazar (which was used by D. Kahana, pt. I, pp. 91–96); (*b*) Sasportas, pp. 76–80; (*c*) Baruch of Arezzo, *ap.* Freimann, p. 53. In spite of many errors and misunderstandings, (*a*) contains the most accurate and detailed account; (*a*) and (*b*) complement each other, (*a*) is based on a written reported by the envoys themselves; see above, p. 601.

54. See Kahana, *op. cit.,* p. 92.

55. Sasportas, p. 76.

to Sasportas' source more than four thousand men and women had assembled to pay homage to the messiah and "they observed this day[56] more strictly than the [ordinary] holy Sabbath."[57]

The Polish envoys apologized to the prophet for wishing to test him with some questions, but they had been charged to investigate the messianic tidings and bring back a true report. If he could tell them their hidden sins and give them an appropriate *tiqqun,* they would be convinced. Suriel answered: "You clever *Ashkenazim!* So you have come to test me! Come back tomorrow and I shall tell you some of your sins." The following day he did, in fact, tell them the sins of their youth, gave them a *tiqqun,* and also showed them a letter from Sabbatai Ṣevi proving that the latter had had knowledge of their coming even before they had arrived. In this letter Sabbatai also advised them what to do "while I am in this great affliction."[58] Meanwhile the "illumination" had returned to Sabbatai, and two days after the Seventeenth of Tammuz, which had been celebrated with banquets and rejoicing, a new proclamation was issued appointing the following Monday, the Twenty-third of Tammuz (July 26, 1666) as the "festival of lights": every house had to burn seventeen candles of fat and one candle of wax. Leyb b. Ozer describes the events as follows:

"On Monday, the Twenty-third of Tammuz, he decreed a festival. I have spoken to people who were at the time in the synagogue at Castillos [that is, Gallipoli], for they had come by hundreds and thousands to honor Sabbatai Ṣevi. But nobody was allowed to visit him by order of the emperor [*sic*]. There was an indescribable rejoicing in the synagogue. They took all the Torah scrolls out [of the Holy Ark], dancing and singing hymns in honor of Sabbatai Ṣevi. In the *ᶜAmidah* prayer they said[59]: 'this day of

56. I.e., Sabbatai's "Great Sabbath," celebrated on Monday, 23 Tammuz.

57. Sasportas, pp. 76–77; cf. Tishby's note there (n. 6).

58. Kahana, basing himself on Leyb b. Ozer (see above, n. 53), interprets this phrase as meaning "as long as I am not permitted to receive you." But Leyb b. Ozer's account adds "and nobody knew why he said that he was in a great affliction." Kahana understood the sentence to refer to the order to keep Sabbatai incommunicado; to me it seems more probable that it refers to a fit of depression. The incident proves that Sabbatai was all the while in correspondence with his leading supporters in the capital.

59. At the point where, on a holiday, the name of the festival is specifically mentioned.

the festival of lights, the season of our tidings.' . . . He also sent word to the Jews of the Straits that the following day, Wednesday, the Twenty-fifth of Tammuz [*sic*] was to be the Great Sabbath," to be strictly observed on pain of death by stoning. "He later justified this with kabbalistic reasons."[60] The account undoubtedly refers to two distinct festivals, subsumed by Sabbatai under one phrase when he spoke of "my holiday and my Great Sabbath." The precise dates, however, particularly with regard to the days of the week, are uncertain. The tradition represented by Sasportas and the early Sabbatian liturgical calendars[61] contradicts the tradition of the Dönmeh as well as the account of Leyb b. Ozer[62] who, on this point, had excellent sources, to wit, eyewitness reports and the written account of the Polish envoys. There is, at present, no way of deciding the question, but no matter whether the Great Sabbath was kept on a Monday or on a subsequent day (Tuesday or Wednesday), the outline of events is sufficiently clear.[63]

The symbolic meaning of the seventeen candles was not revealed to the visitors, and Leyb b. Ozer explicitly states that he had never heard a reason for it. Is the number connected, perhaps, with the period of mourning that had come to an end with the celebration of the Seventeenth of Tammuz? On the other hand, the mystical significance of the Great Sabbath was explained by Sabbatai to several scholars who had asked him about it.[64]

The Polish emissaries returned to Gallipoli after the Seventeenth of Tammuz and were showered with honors. Evidently Sabbatai's court officials were aware of the importance of the congregation of Lvov and of the authority of the two envoys.[65] On returning to the inn after their audience with Sabbatai, they both fell seriously ill, but neither medicines nor even bread were obtain-

60. MS. Shazar, fol. 34a. The abbreviated version *ap*. Emden (p. 14) omits many important details and corrects the date to 24 Tammuz.

61. The festival on Sunday the 22nd; the Sabbath on Monday the 23rd.

62. The festival on the 23rd, the Sabbath on the 24th or 25th of Tammuz.

63. For a discussion of the chronological problem see Tishby's note in his edn. of Sasportas (p. 78, n. 1) and G. Scholem, *SS,* p. 520, n. 2. Cf. also the text of Sabbatai's letter published by A. Amarillo in *Sefunoth,* V (1961), 250.

64. Emden, pp. 14–15; *SS,* p. 521.

65. Kahana's account of the visit is marred by prejudice. There is not the least evidence to show that Primo immediately recognized that the Polish envoys were "naïve and almost foolish" (pt. I, p. 94).

able as everything had been sold out. However, on the Sabbath (the Twenty-first of Tammuz) Sabbatai sent one of the rabbis of his court "with a jar of wine, a dish of candies, two lemons and a few lumps of sugar." The messenger informed them that "Our Lord" could not send them anything else, as there was practically no food left in his house, but that he was praying for their recovery on the following morning. The next day they were in perfect health again. This probably happened after the proclamation of the great festival, when all the food was bought up in the market. The exact date of their audience with Sabbatai is uncertain, however. It may have taken place on Sunday, the Twenty-second of Tammuz, that is, before the Festival of Lights and the Great Sabbath, or afterward, on Wednesday or Thursday of the same week.[66] In any event Leyb's description of the visit, based on the emissaries' own report to their father, R. David, is one of the most revealing documents we possess regarding Sabbatai's personality. His majestic deportment accompanied by ecstatic outbursts aroused a genuine enthusiasm in the hearts of all visitors. In the case of the envoys from Poland there was the additional factor of the recent sufferings of Polish Jewry. The earliest and widely read chronicle of the massacres of 1648–49, R. Moses of Shebreshin's *Ṣuq ha-ᶜIttim* (*The Troublous Times*)[67] lay open on Sabbatai's table "all day long," and the Polish visitors were no doubt suitably impressed.

As they entered they bent their knees and prostrated themselves before him. Sabbatai asked them, "Were you here during my festival and the Great Sabbath?" and they answered, "Yes, Our Lord." He then asked, "And did you have any doubts [because I changed the Law]?" and they said, "God forbid." . . .[68] They wanted to tell him of the tribulations and massacres suffered by the Polish Jews, but Sabbatai said "You need not tell me. Behold the book *Ṣuq ha-ᶜIttim* . . . is open here with me all day long."[69] He added, "Why do you think I am dressed in red and my Torah

66. See *SS,* p. 521, n. 3, on this question.

67. One edn. of which had appeared in Constantinople.

68. This detail is told at the end of Leyb's account of the visit and not at the beginning. The incident must have occurred *after* the Great Sabbath, but it is not certain that the conversation really took place during the visit described in the first part of Leyb's narrative, and the account perhaps implies two visits.

69. The words "all day long," which occur in the original MS., are omitted in the text given by Emden (p. 15) and by Kahana (p. 94).

scroll is draped with red? Because the day of vengeance is in my heart, and the year of my redeemed is come" [see above, p. 602]. The envoys said, "Our Lord, for many years, and quite recently again, sacrifices and holocausts have been made because of our sins [that is, there have been many massacres of Jews], and the sacrifice of Isaac has been repeated over and over again in Poland." He replied, "I will make mine arrows drunk with blood" [Deut. 32:42]. He revealed to them many kabbalistic mysteries, and then began to sing hymns and songs [arranged] according to the alphabet. When he came to the letter *zayin* he cried out, "Remember [Hebrew, *zekhor*] mine affliction and mine anguish" [Lam. 3:19] and wept bitterly. Then he bade them sit at his side and, taking R. Isaiah by the hand, asked him, "Are you the son of the [author of the commentary] *Turey Zahab?*" and he answered, "Yes, Our Lord." Next he asked R. Aryeh Leyb, "And you are the son of the same author's present wife?" and he answered, "Yes, Our Lord." Then he inquired after the health of their father, and they answered, "Our Lord! Our father is an old man of eighty years, and his hands and feet are very weak. As we passed through Constantinople we met an old man who told us that he had had a bad fall and almost died of it, but that Our Lord had sent him a morsel of food to cure him, commanding him to arise and walk on the next morning; and so indeed it happened. May Our Lord give us something to cure [our father]." Thereupon he gave them a piece of sugar, saying, "He shall eat this and be healed forthwith." Then he took a silk coat, and also took off a valuable woolen garment that he was wearing, and said to R. Aryeh Leyb, "Take this coat and put it on your father, reciting the verse [Ps. 103:5] 'Thy youth is renewed like the eagle['s]." R. Isaiah said, "Our Lord! I am his son and as such have precedence [in this sacred duty]," but Sabbatai answered him in Yiddish, "*Schweig*," and, taking out a scarf embroidered with gold, told R. Isaiah, "Take this and wrap it round your father's neck on my behalf, and it will be for him unto greatness and honor and glory." He also said, "The coat which R. Leyb will put on your father is not such a great thing because it is for the body only, but you shall do something that will be for your father's honor." He bade them sit at his side, but they replied, "Our Lord! It is sufficient for us to lick the dust of Our Lord; we must not approach the Holiness." He said, "But I want you to sit with me," and so they sat with him. A bowl filled with fruit was brought in and he said to them, "Recite the benediction," but they replied, "How can we eat? This would be to fulfill Scripture [Exod. 24:11]: and they saw God, and did eat and drink, for now it seems to us that we are in the celestial paradise." Sabbatai took two gold coins, gave one to each and said, "When my kingdom will be manifest, you shall appear before me for a remembrance." Then Sabbatai took a scarf embroidered with gold and said to R. Isaiah, "Bow your head," and when he had done so he wrapped it round his neck and said, "I make you kings in this world; you shall be kings and princes before me. . . ." Then he took a scarf from the neck of one of the rabbis present, a certain R. Gamaliel [see above, p. 443], and told them each to hold one end of the scarf. When they had done so, Sabbatai stood facing them and began to dance, singing melodiously the whole Psalm 118, up to verse 20: "This is the gate of the Lord, The righteous shall enter into it,"[70] and after every verse he repeated [as a refrain] ten times, with his eyes raised heavenward, verse 17: "I shall not die, but live." But he pronounced the last word not *we-ʾeḥyeh* ("I shall live") but *wa-ʾaḥayyeh* ("I shall resuscitate"), which is to say, I shall resurrect the dead. And he continued with a loud and mighty voice: "The right hand of the Lord is exalted, the right hand of the Lord doeth valiantly—for I have already done valiantly." Thus he continued to sing and to dance for about half an hour, and the envoys could barely contain their joy. Then Sabbatai ordered everybody to leave the room, and when he was alone with the two emissaries he said, "I adjure you not to divulge to anyone, not even to your aged father R. David ha-Levi, that which I am now going to reveal to you," and he revealed to them great kabbalistic mysteries. They said to him, "Our Lord and King! May it please you to let us be servants at your gates," but Sabbatai answered, "This is not necessary. Go in peace and bring glad tidings to your brethren." They asked him for a written message to their fellow Jews in Poland, and he wrote a letter to their father R. David ha-Levi [see above, pp. 601-2] and signed "on the tenth day of the revival of my spirit and my light . . . in [the week of] the pentateuchal lesson 'and they journeyed from Rithmah, and pitched in Rimmon-Perez' [Num. 33:19]." When they asked him why Our Lord used this verse [to designate the weekly pericope], he replied . . . [with a kabbalistic explanation in which he said, among other things, that as the messiah he was a descendant of Perez].[71]

The account well illustrates the magnetism of Sabbatai's personality and his marvelous capacity for entering into the feelings of people and striking responsive chords in their hearts. He did not hesitate

70. Sabbatai interpreted this verse as referring to himself, because the first letters of the second part from the word *ṣevi: Ṣevi* is the gate to God.

71. Kahana, pp. 94-96, quoting from the original MS.; cf. the abbreviated version, *ap.* Emden, pp. 15–16.

to dance in front of his visitors when he felt moved to do so during their conversation on the fate of Polish Jewry. At the same time his behavior exhibited some of the traits usually associated with that of eighteenth- or nineteenth-century Hasidic rabbis: he would present his believers with a scarf, a morsel of food, or some other object which, by his very touch, had become a kind of holy relic.[72] We know that Sabbatai continued this practice long after his apostasy, for example, when called to cure a sick believer in Adrianople.[73] The narrative shows that the "Hasidic" style so often said to be specifically characteristic of Russian and Polish Jewry was perfectly possible a hundred years earlier in a completely different environment. Perhaps Sabbatai's gestures and behavior toward his believers were not even original with him; perhaps the apparent originality of Sabbatai's behavior is merely the result of our ignorance, due to the complete lack of literary testimonies regarding the relationship between kabbalistic saints and their admirers in the Sephardic Orient. Sabbatai's personal contribution seems to have consisted in his royal bearing, and it was no doubt the mixture of the traditional behavior of the holy man with the majestic deportment of the "son of David" that conquered hearts. His musical gift, too, contributed much to the impression he made, especially during his imprisonment. Leyb's account (on the authority of eyewitnesses) of the musicians playing "day and night" at the Tower of Strength illustrates not only Sabbatai's euphoric mood at the time, but also the blurring of the difference between a prison house and a banqueting hall. No wonder many pilgrims believed that the messiah's imprisonment was but a symbolic, outward manifestation. There are other examples of leaders who continued to rule their followers even from their prison, but the peculiar circumstances made the unique situation at Gallipoli seem almost unreal. When the visitors realized that they beheld reality and no dream, this could only strengthen their faith even more.

In addition to the brief missive addressed to R. David ha-Levi ("soon I shall avenge and comfort you"), the Polish envoys also received from Sabbatai a kabbalistic tract containing "many mysteries from the Zohar and other kabbalistic works, all relating to him and showing that everything had to occur as it did."[74] This testimony con-

72. Many such stories were told in Germany, too, of a charismatic rabbi, the so-called Ba^cal Shem of Michelstadt (R. Seckel Löb Wormser, 1769–1847).

73. Rosanes, vol. IV, p. 232.

74. Emden, p. 16.

firms R. Israel Ḥazzan's claim that he had seen numerical speculations (*gematria*) of Sabbatai Ṣevi concerning himself. The tract presented to the Polish emissaries had been written by a scribe and signed by Sabbatai's own hand. The signature may have been intended as evidence of Sabbatai's authorship of the tract, or perhaps merely as a mark of the royal approval of the messianic mysteries expounded in it by the kabbalists at his court. The tract, which is lost, would undoubtedly have illuminated many obscure details in Sabbatai's biography, as it was evidently conceived as a kabbalistic *apologia* for the messiah's career.[75] Copies of the tract were probably given also to other important visitors who desired to be enlightened with regard to the messiah's strange actions. The fact that "certified" copies were made of the tract is highly significant, for it indicates a definite attempt at propaganda. Also R. Berakhya Berakh of Cracow had sent, along with his letter reporting on his visit to Gallipoli, "a multitude of kabbalistic interpretations of Scripture, indicating the year and the name of the messiah." This text, of which many copies were sent from Cracow to Germany, may well have been identical with the one given by Sabbatai Ṣevi to the Polish emissaries.[76]

The two envoys left the Tower of Strength on Sunday, August 1, which was immediately after the Sabbath following their last meeting with Sabbatai Ṣevi. Their sojourn at Constantinople and Gallipoli thus coincided with the two tempestuous weeks of Sabbatai's renewed illumination. During their visit, at the conclusion of the Great Sab-

75. At about the same time Nathan composed a similar *apologia* (*Treatise on the Dragons*) in which he expounded the mystical significance of the messiah's imprisonment.

76. Many years later the visits of the Polish rabbis were still remembered by an eyewitness, the Polish kabbalist R. Meir of Tarnigrad, who told R. Abraham Rovigo (see Rovigo's *Sabbatian Diary*, MS. Sonne at the Ben-Zvi Institute, Jerusalem, fol. 49b) that he had been "with AMIRAH when the three Polish envoys arrived, the venerable and aged author of *Zera*ᶜ *Berakh* [i.e., Berakhya], and the two sons of the author of *Turey Zahab*, and the great preacher R. Jacob Ratner." (On R. Jacob Ratner of Cracow see H. D. Friedberg, *Luḥoth Zikkaron* [1904], p. 27.) R. Meir of Tarnigrad "had witnessed all these things, and how AMIRAH told them not to fear anything . . . and that he tore up a tree and burned it, saying that thus he would burn and destroy the *qelippoth* and the gentiles." This testimony confirms the story told by R. Abraham Kokesh of Vilna (see above, p. 190). It is, of course, possible that several distinct events merged into one in Meir of Tarnigrad's memory and were subsequently told as if they had occurred together on one day.

bath, letters signed by Sabbatai Ṣevi were dispatched to all Turkish congregations, commanding them to abolish the fast of the Ninth of Ab, the day of the destruction of the Temple, and to make it a great festival. Whether Sabbatai was really born on that day in 1626, or whether he "adapted" his birthday to the most fitting date, there is no doubt that the day was fraught with messianic symbolism. Of course the ancient rabbinic legend did not mean to foretell the birth of the future Messiah on a Ninth of Ab; what it said was that the Messiah had been born on the very day of the destruction of the Temple. Rabbinic Haggadah had, in this way, bridged the chasm between catastrophe and salvation. If Sabbatai was really born on the Ninth of Ab, this fact would naturally have functioned not only as symbolic confirmation of his calling, but also as a further stimulus which, combined with his penchant for liturgical innovations, would find expression in the conversion of the darkest day in Jewish historical consciousness into a festival: "And ye shall make it a day of great banqueting and great rejoicing, with choice food and delicious drinks, and with many candles and lights, and with many melodies and songs, for it is the birthday of your king Sabbatai Ṣevi, highest among the kings of the earth. And concerning [the prohibition of] work, observe it like a full holiday, with your best clothes and the festival liturgy." Detailed liturgical instructions for the new "Festival of Consolation" were provided, including a Kiddush (the festive blessing over the cup) for the Ninth of Ab which was adapted from the normal festival Kiddush: "And thou hast given us in love, O Lord Our God, appointed times for gladness, festivals and seasons for joy, this day of the Feast of Consolation, the season of the birth of our anointed king Sabbatai Ṣevi, thy servant and thy firstborn."[77] In addition to the festival psalms, Sabbatai commanded certain other psalms to be recited, for example, Psalms 89 and 126, and especially Psalm 45, which he had sung in front of the women of Smyrna: "Thou art fairer than the children of men; /Grace is poured upon thy lips. . . . /Kings' daughters are among thy favourites; /At thy right hand doth stand the queen. . . ." For the Sabbatian believers all these were obvious mystical allusions to the Shekhinah and her redemption.[77a]

77. The prayer is preserved in the sources mentioned below (n. 78) as well as in the prayer book of the Dönmeh (see Scholem [1942], p. 25) where, however, the day is called the "Feast of Rejoicing" (and not of "consolation") and elements from the liturgy of the Day of Atonement are incorporated into the text.

77a. On Ps. 45, see also below, p. 639.

The text of the letters to Smyrna and Sofia, announcing the abolition of the fast of the Ninth of Ab, has been preserved.[78] From Sofia copies of the letter were sent by special couriers to the other Balkan communities as far as Ofen (Buda). The messianic decree, which reached all the Balkan countries and most of the communities in Asia Minor in time for the Ninth of Ab, made a tremendous impression. The festival was celebrated with exuberant joy, much to the grief of the few steadfast souls who refused to follow the "new religion."[79]

In Constantinople serious clashes occurred between believers and infidels. While Abraham Yakhini, his enthusiasm fired by the messianic decree, was composing a commentary on Psalm 45—the psalm appointed to be read on the festival of the Ninth of Ab—expounding its hidden Sabbatian meaning,[80] the unbelieving minority seems to have attempted something like organized resistance. Several members of the Armenian community had inquired from Jewish acquaintances concerning Sabbatai's messiahship. They were told, among other things, that eighty Jewish notables had publicly protested against Sabbatai's messianic pretensions and the abolition of the fast. Sabbatai was an epileptic and an impostor who had not performed a single miracle; in fact he had been imprisoned after attempting to run away. The believers were furious and stoned the infidels. According to this Armenian source, there were repeated quarrels between the two parties, but "the mass of the poor adhered to him with great love, and even the notables were full of hope and sent to do homage to him. Many who went thither disguised themselves as Armenians in order to escape the jeers and insults of the Turks."[81]

A more idealized account of the reaction in Constantinople is given in a Sabbatian legend current at the time: in their perplexity the rabbis of the capital had prayerfully resolved to seek divine guidance and, having written "Festival" and "Fast" on two slips of paper,

78. Coenen's version (pp. 49–50) is corrupt, but a correct text is given by Baruch of Arezzo (pp. 57–58), and by Sasportas (pp. 129–30); see also the letter published by A. Amarillo, *Sefunoth,* V (1961), pp. 250–51. De la Croix's account (pp. 361–64) shows that his information concerning the letter was secondhand and incorrect.

79. Thus Sasportas, p. 131.

80. Danon, p. 45. Danon had seen Yakhini's autograph (5 fols.), but failed to recognize the circumstances of its composition and its connection with 9 Ab.

81. Galanté, pp. 90, 103.

had the lot drawn by an innocent child. Three times the child drew the answer "Festival." Other rabbis sought guidance by the method of "dream questions," and they too received the answer that the Ninth of Ab was to be a major festival.[82] Sasportas also, on receiving news of the abolition of the fast in Smyrna, resorted to this standard kabbalistic method of obtaining guidance: as could be expected, the reply which he received in his dream was curt and unequivocal: "They shall be driven forth from among men" (Job 30:5).[83] Sasportas' argument that the rabbis of the capital could not possibly have condoned the abolition of the fast is not very convincing, and the mass of believers were certainly nearer the truth when they claimed that "if it was abolished in Constantinople, it must have been with the consent of the rabbis there."[84] Whatever the identity of the eighty anonymous notables who protested against the messiah's command, their opposition cannot have been very effective in a Jewish community that numbered tens of thousands. De la Croix too was told that the abolition of the fast had been strictly obeyed in the capital.

The messianic edict cannot have reached Palestine and Egypt in time for the Ninth of Ab. We must assume, therefore, that in those parts the initiative was taken by Nathan of Gaza and his companions, for example, Mattathias Bloch in Egypt. A responsum by an anonymous rabbi in Jerusalem makes reference, in the late eighties, to the abolition of the fast and shows, incidentally, that the number of believers there had increased during 1666: "The [fast of the] Ninth of Ab was abolished, and by order of the king they were not to fast but to celebrate with banquets and rejoicing, exactly as on the Feast of Purim. However, this was not the case everywhere, but [mainly] throughout the cities of Turkey, except Jerusalem where the community [that is, the communal authorities] did not abolish the fast, yet most members of the community did not keep the fast."[85] The value of this testimony is enhanced by the fact that the writer was no believer himself and does not hide his regret at what he has to report. Evidently the minority of believers in 1665 had become a majority by the summer of 1666. The leaders of the community re-

82. Baruch of Arezzo, pp. 56–57.

83. Sasportas, p. 79.

84. *Ibid.*, p. 151; see also de la Croix, p. 364.

85. From a fragmentary responsum, preserved in MS. Adler 3354, fol. 3a; see Scholem, in ᵓ*Ereṣ Yisraᵓel*, IV (1956), 189.

fused to abolish the fast in spite of instructions from the prophet of Gaza, whereas the majority of the members, ignoring their local authorities, celebrated the messiah's birthday.

The abolition of the fast of the Ninth of Ab constituted the climax of the movement in the Orient. Another and more momentous climax was generally expected to take place in the same summer and to trigger off the train of decisive messianic events. However, the great event—namely, a renewed meeting between the messiah and his prophet—failed to materialize. Early in June reports from Alexandria had stated that Nathan had left for the capital "according to the command of the Lord," and a letter from Constantinople (written probably in July) said that Nathan was expected there together with twelve companions representing the Twelve Tribes of Israel.[86] In reality there was no substance at all to these rumors. Nathan did not leave Gaza until after he had learned of the messiah's apostasy. Plans for a meeting with Sabbatai may have been discussed in Gaza more than once, but if so we do not know what prevented their realization. It was general knowledge in Constantinople that Nathan had written to Sabbatai, prophesying the latter's accession to the messianic kingdom in autumn, 1666, as provided in the original timetable.[87] Sabbatai's wife arrived from Smyrna before the Ninth of Ab, and the governor of the fortress permitted her to join her husband.[88] The "Queen of Palestine" was received with due honors by the Jews of the capital, and she took an active part in the messianic propaganda and in the discussions with the local rabbis. The purpose of her coming, she said, was for the preparations for the messiah's birthday and coronation.[89] Unexpected propagandists also appeared on the scene:

86. MS. Hottinger, vol. 30, fols. 347b and 349b. The second letter was received in Amsterdam on September 24, 1666. Reports of Nathan's departure from Gaza before Sabbatai's apostasy had also come to the ears of Abraham Miguel Cardozo, who relied on them in his long letter to the rabbinic court of Smyrna, but there can be no doubt that the information was erroneous. The same rumor is mentioned in the letters from Hamburg to the prisoner in Oslo.

87. De la Croix, p. 356.

88. *Ibid.* Coenen (p. 32) also calls her "the Queen."

89. *Hollandtze Merkurius,* August, 1666, p. 134. It is difficult to reconcile this statement with the report, in several other sources, that Sarah gave birth to a son immediately after the apostasy, for in that case she must have been in the seventh or eighth month of her pregnancy when she arrived in Gallipoli. More reliable evidence, however, suggests that she gave birth several months after the apostasy.

several dervishes prophesied the fall of the Turkish empire and the return of the kingdom to the Jews. Although de la Croix's imaginative accounts often belong to the realm of fiction, this particular detail seems to be confirmed by a letter sent to Amsterdam in July, 1666.[90] R. Tobias Kohen also reports that there were Muslims who believed in Sabbatai and that the Turkish authorities were alarmed at this.

It seems that Sabbatai had for a while considered dispatching three emissaries to Europe to announce the glad tidings of the abolition of the fast.[91] As a matter of fact, this would have seemed the most obvious thing to do, and it is something of a mystery why he gave up the idea. It is most unlikely that Sabbatai was afraid of exposing his messengers to the cross-examination of the European rabbis. After all, hundreds and thousands had made the pilgrimage to Gallipoli and had been thoroughly questioned after their return home, with results that redounded to the greater glory of the messiah. The clue to the abandonment of the original decision must surely be sought in the complexities of Sabbatai's psychology with its impulsive actions and sudden inhibitions, rather than in completely erroneous notions about carefully laid plans and strategems.

There is, however, another possibility to be considered. Coenen may have been wrong in stating that the messengers were never dispatched. Perhaps the three emissaries left for Europe, but only one of them arrived. Several sources mention three messengers from Jerusalem that were taken captive by Maltese ships; two remained in the hands of the Knights of Malta and one was brought to Leghorn.

90. MS. Hottinger, vol. 30, fol. 349: "l'on escrit de Constantinople que Darvisers estimez leur saints hommes ne font difficulté de dire en public que l'Empire d'Ottomans s'en va expirer et que le Royaume doibt retourner aux Juifs. On attend le prophete Nathan à Constantinople en compagnie de 12 Chachamim duquel R. Schelomo et autres hommes de bon credit ici rendent témoignage d'estre vrayement Prophete de Dieu si jamail il y a eu Prophete en Israel." According to de la Croix's lengthy account (pp. 365–69), the dervish preacher had been hired by Sabbatai to preach in the streets to the Turks. He was severely beaten up and arraigned before the cadi on a charge of heresy. The cadi sent him to the madhouse ("le Dervisch fut conduit au Timar-hané, l'hôpital de fols"), but the physicians who examined him demanded his release. He was finally released as a fool to whom no attention should be paid, but the Jews of the capital were much edified by his prophecies.

91. Coenen, p. 53.

Unfortunately, the evidence is very confused[92] and pending the discovery of further documents no conclusions can be drawn from it.

III

Compared to the plentiful sources regarding developments in Smyrna, Constantinople, and Gallipoli (as well as in the European communities), accounts of the movement in the rest of the Turkish Empire—and in the Islamic world in general—are scarce. For many areas in Turkey and Asia we have little more than incidental scraps of information, though these too help to fill in the over-all picture and to confirm the impression of a mighty eruption of messianic enthusiasm.

The paucity of information is particularly striking in the case of Salonika where, as the sequel will show, the Sabbatian movement struck its deepest and most permanent roots. Salonika was, at the time, one of the largest, if not the largest, Jewish community in the world. Its Jewish population has been estimated at sixty thousand souls.[93] The testimony of R. Jacob de Boton of Salonika (see above, p. 472) regarding the penitential awakening and the general breach of the fast of the Ninth of Ab in 1666 shows beyond doubt that the rabbis in the city participated in the movement and obeyed the orders from Gallipoli.

A detailed account of the movement in Salonika is provided by Coenen, who probably obtained his information from the many eyewitnesses traveling between Salonika and Smyrna. According to Coenen the Jews of Salonika surpassed all others in their messianic faith and penitential fervor. His account, which was subsequently used by Leyb b. Ozer, also inspired several of the illustrations that appeared in gentile publications on Sabbatai Ṣevi.[94] People would present themselves before a "court" of four rabbis to confess their sins and receive

92. The messengers are said to have been sent from Jerusalem and not from Constantinople. Among these messengers were R. Israel Benjamin and R. Judah Sharaf. The latter remained a believer in Sabbatai until his death (in Leghorn, 1675). For a detailed discussion of the sources see *SS,* pp. 530–32.

93. Baruch of Arezzo, *ap.* Freimann, p. 57.

94. E.g., in the chapter "Greuel der falschen Messien" in Johann Christoph Müller, *Anabaptisticum et Enthusiasticum Pantheon* (Coethen, 1702). The chapter has a separate title page and I have seen copies of the chapter bound as a separate book.

penances. Many penitents buried themselves up to their necks, only their heads sticking out of the ground, and remained thus in prayer for three hours. Others performed symbolic imitations of the four kinds of capital punishment recognized by rabbinic law (stoning, burning, beheading, and strangling). Coenen, like R. Jacob de Boton, emphasizes that beggary disappeared and that all sinners repented. Shops and business houses were closed, and new forms of mortification were continually introduced. It was in Salonika that believers, remembering the rabbinic dictum that the son of David would not come until all souls had entered the bodies destined for them (see above, p. 474), began to marry off young children in order to remove the last obstacle to the messianic advent. According to Coenen, about seven to eight hundred such marriages were performed,[95] resulting in much subsequent unhappiness and misfortune. The question how the community survived the economic crisis brought about by the excess of messianic enthusiasm is not yet satisfactorily answered. The wealthier classes were completely impoverished, and according to the Jesuit author of the French *Relation,* Sabbatai Ṣevi scornfully boasted of having "reduced to beggary" all the rich Jews of Salonika.[96] Throughout the winter and summer of 1666 some four hundred poor lived on public charity. The mortifications practiced by the believers in this major center of Sephardic Jewry also illustrate the extent to which the ascetic exercises of the German Hasidim had become generally diffused. A Sabbatian enthusiast desirous of performing some heroic penance would not simply resort to the mortifications introduced by the sixteenth-century kabbalists in Safed, but would follow the more rigorous prescriptions of the *Roqeaḥ* or the *Sefer Hasidim.* Isaac Roman of Constantinople, an eyewitness, told about people who continued for seven weeks to fast all the six weekdays and died in consequence thereof.[97] Such deaths as a result of mortifications are also mentioned by the rabbis of Smyrna in 1668 (see below, p. 716). The awakening was encouraged by the leading rabbis and preachers, some of whose sermons have been preserved.[98] Salonika was a center of rabbinic learn-

95. If the number is correct, it permits conclusions as to the size of the community.

96. *Relation,* p. 34; Coenen, pp. 59–62.

97. In a statement included in his son's polemical pamphlet against A. M. Cardozo, *Meribath Kadesh,* in Freimann, pp. 7–8. He also complains of men and women sitting together in the synagogues.

98. E.g., R. Aaron Peraḥyah, *Bigdey Kehunah,* sermon nos. 10 and 26.

ing. The members of the rabbinic academies[99] eagerly responded to the messanic message, and many of them persevered in the faith even after the apostasy. On the other hand, Sabbatian tradition also reports doubts in the city regarding the abolition of the fast of the Ninth of Ab, but the story may be apocryphal: "A courier was dispatched to Our Lord . . . to tell him that unless he performed a miracle in his presence, they could not celebrate the festival. Our Lord answered: 'They will celebrate the festival without my performing a miracle—and this will be the real miracle.' "[100]

The other Balkan communities, whether large (for example, Adrianople and Sofia) or small (for example, Arta in Greece; see above, p. 595), seem to have followed the example set by Salonika. Abraham Azaryah Ṣebi, apparently a member of the Greek branch of Sabbatai's family, was active in Thebes in 1666–67.[101] Though we have little detailed information for the year 1666, we know that the messianic movement continued there for many years after the apostasy. The celebration of the Ninth of Ab in Adrianople—the favorite residence of the sultan Muhammad IV—is attested by two sources.[102] Christian eyewitnesses stated that the whole Jewish population adhered to the faith. Adrianople, however, unlike Salonika, exhibited some rabbinic opposition, led by the "great infidel" R. Jacob Danon[103] and by R. Abraham Magresso.[104] The Ashkenazi scholar R. Jacob Striemer of Prague,[105] who lived in Adrianople at the time, was a believer too until the apostasy, "without, however, deviating from

99. E.g., halakhists like R. Solomon Florentin and kabbalists like R. Abraham Pereṣ and R. Isaac Ḥanan; for the two latter see below, pp. 778, 815. Rosanes (vol. IV, p. 124) was unaware of Rabbi Ḥanan's Sabbatian connections.

100. Baruch of Arezzo, *ap.* Freimann, p. 57.

101. M. Benayahu, *Kiryath Sepher,* XXXV (1960), 392.

102. Baruch of Arezzo, *ibid.;* de la Croix, p. 369. De la Croix thought that the celebration was an attempt to draw the attention of the sultan—who was in Adrianople at the time—to the messianic rebellion. This is obviously a poor rationalization.

103. Baruch of Arezzo, *ap.* Freimann, p. 65.

104. Danon (p. 23), who rightly recognized one phrase on Magresso's epitaph (of 1682 or 1687) to allude to his firm stand during the Sabbatian awakening. A halakhic query of Magresso addressed to R. Moses Benveniste in Constantinople is mentioned by Rosanes (vol. IV, p. 127).

105. A brother of the first Hebrew bibliographer, R. Sabbatai Bass, author of *Sifthey Yeshenim.*

pious conduct,"[106] that is, without participating in the Sabbatian breaking of the Law. The Jewry of Sofia, both Ashkenazi and Sephardi, embraced the faith, and it is interesting to note that the letter abolishing the fast of the Ninth of Ab, which was sent from Gallipoli to Europe, was addressed to Sofia and not to Adrianople.[107]

The community of Belgrade dispatched two official emissaries to Sabbatai Ṣevi.[108] The rabbi, Joseph Almosnino, had been a fellow student of Nathan's at the *yeshibah* of R. Jacob Ḥagiz in Jerusalem; now he was a prominent believer, and devoutly copied all the writings of the prophet that reached his city.[109] Concerning the general atmosphere obtaining in the Hungarian and Balkan communities, R. Hirsh b. Jacob, better known as *Ḥakham* Ṣevi, preserved some vivid childhood memories which he related to his son, R. Jacob Emden. *Ḥakham* Ṣevi was born in 1658[110] in Budapest, where he also spent his childhood. He studied in Salonika and served for several years as rabbi of Sarajevo. He remembered that "at that time there were women who said, 'Let us go and slay demons.' They dressed themselves in white linen garments and made strange movements in the air with their hands. Then they would spread out their garments and collect much blood coming from the air as if with their hands . . . they had slaughtered [the demons]. There was one woman who would say,

106. Emden (p. 56), whose father, *Ḥakham* Ṣevi, knew him well in Adrianople.

107. Rosanes (IV, p. 64) reports that the Mashiaḥ family in Sofia had adopted its name at that time in honor of Sabbatai. Very possible the family possessed a definite tradition to that effect, for the mere name as such proves nothing. Mashiaḥ is a frequent name (personal as well as family name) among Sephardim and does not imply Sabbatian connections.

108. According to a letter from Ofen to Vienna, in the late summer of 1666, listed in the catalogue of the MSS. of the Jewish Community of Vienna, no. 141 §11 (*ap.* A. Z. Schwarz, *Die hebr. Handschriften in Oesterreich* [1931], p. 90). The letter, of which I have a photostat, was copied by an Italian Jew, Moses Cases, and is full of corrupt readings.

109. The copy, preserved in MS. Oxford 1777, also contains a "Prayer sent from Gaza by the holy kabbalist R. Nathan Benjamin" (fol. 130b), followed by another prayer in which "the holy rabbi, the Messianic King" ranks equal with R. Simon b. Yoḥay as a kabbalist. This latter prayer was later omitted from the MS. Neubauer noted in his catalogue that the MS. had belonged to Almosnino, but overlooked the fact that the decisive pages were written in Almosnino's own hand.

110. See A. Wagenaar, *Toledoth Yaᶜbes* (Amsterdam, 1868), p. 57.

'Who wants me to give him the smell of Paradise?' and then she would raise her hands heavenward, catch something in the air, and offer an exceedingly fragrant odor to anyone who wanted it." *Ḥakham* Ṣevi also remembered an incident in Sarajevo involving Samuel Almoli, subsequently the father-in-law of the later Sabbatian heresiarch Nehemiah Ḥayyon. Almoli, who was known as "a great sinner," had decided to test an ignorant young ne'er-do-well who had turned prophet. The boy, in fact, told him all his secret faults and sins, but in addition accused him of a certain sin of which Almoli knew himself to be innocent. He thereupon declared, "The hand which is put forth against a true prophet will be dried up [cf. I Kings 13:4], and now let us see," and he hit the boy over the head until blood flowed from his nose, "whereupon the prophecy ceased from him."[111]

These are later reports. We have, however, a contemporary letter from Budapest (Ofen), written in the early summer of 1666 by Moses Kohen to his brother, Solomon Linz, in Vienna. He tells the usual fantastic stories about the events in Constantinople, but there is also a new piece of information, concerning the departure for Palestine: "Our King has given order that nobody should move from his present place to go from abroad to the Holy Land, because all the miracles will occur just in the countries outside of the land. The congregation of Ofen would have to pass directly through the land of Edom [the Christian countries, and not through Turkey], because they are near the slain [that is, they should pass through the places where the great massacres had taken place], and on Hanukkah, 1666 [December!], all the exiles are sure to be ingathered and we will make offerings on the altar of the Lord."[112] This interesting information must have originated in the days of high expectancy in Constantinople. The detail about the route to be taken by the Jews of Hungary shows how much thought was given to such questions. That premature departure was discouraged, and even forbidden, is in line with Nathan's letter of 1665. But here it appears as an order from Sabbatai himself, quite consistent with his remarks to the delegates from Lvov.

The Jewries of Asia were soon aflame with messianic ardor. The reactions of the congregations in Asia Minor, Syria, and Palestine have already been described. Little information exists from Babylonia (Iraq) and Persia, though it is known that Nathan exchanged letters

111. Emden, pp. 9–10.

112. Cf. above, n. 108, about the source.

with correspondents in Baghdad. Writing in 1668, Abraham Cardozo refers to a query that was addressed to Nathan from Baghdad regarding the whereabouts of the messiah of the tribe of Joseph. Nathan replied that "he was with us," but that many "had removed their faith from him" because they could not properly understand the matter.[113] Believers from those parts came in great numbers to behold the messiah, and Leyb b. Ozer several times mentions the many pilgrims, "men and women, who came to him from Persia and Media and Babylonia and Turkey."[114] The faith established itself firmly also among the Jewish mountain-dwellers in Kurdistan, and the communities of Urmia and Rawanduz kept in close contact with their brethren in Aleppo, who forwarded to them Sabbatian news and literature.[115] Among the leading Kurdish Jews at the time were R. Isaac Ḥariri of Rawanduz, and his sons Phineas and Moses, whose kabbalistic writings and Hebrew and Aramaic hymns are extant. They became staunch believers immediately on receipt of the glad tidings, and R. Isaac produced "numerical computations of biblical verses" (that is, messianic interpretations by way of *gematria*) regarding Sabbatai Ṣevi.[116] A whole chapter in his *Berith Menuḥah* is devoted to the person of the messiah, and even the Kaddish doxology was made to yield, by *gematria*, an allusion to Sabbatai.[117] Also in Kurdistan, liturgical changes were introduced "as ordained by Our Messiah," for example, the recitation of Psalm 21 at the morning service.[118] Phineas Ḥariri also mentions a liturgical innovation of which nothing is said in other Sabbatian sources: Sabbatai appointed Psalm 45 (see pp. 404, 628)

113. A. M. Cardozo in a letter printed *ap.* Freimann, p. 92, and Sasportas, p. 296. (The letter was probably written soon after the apostasy.)

114. MS. Shazar, fols. 36a, 38a.

115. Most of the Sabbatian material from Kurdistan dates from the period after the messiah's apostasy; see G. Scholem in *Zion,* VII (1942), 172 ff., and M. Benayahu, "Sabbatian Liturgical Compositions and Other Documents from a Persian MS.," *Sefunoth,* III–IV (1960), 9–38. But the evidence shows that the movement there began much earlier. The two liturgical poems published by M. Benayahu (*loc. cit.,* pp. 21–24) seem to date from the early days of the revival in 1665 or the beginning of 1666, before Sabbatai's apostasy (Benayahu, *loc. cit.,* p. 14). They were clearly meant to be included in services.

116. *Zion,* VII (1942), 176, where I have collected the material relating to the Ḥariri family.

117. *Ibid.,* p. 195.

118. *Ibid.,* pp. 178, 196.

to be recited instead of Psalm 145.[119] R. Phineas makes an incidental but highly interesting remark in connection with the abolition of the four fasts and their renewed observance in Kurdistan. It appears that the letters notifying even the most distant communities of the abolition of the fasts bore Sabbatai's own signature. The messiah, it seems, personally signed all the copies of the proclamation that were made by his secretaries. R. Phineas reports that "we" suspended the fast days "only in the first year, when we received a letter from Our Lord himself." This can hardly refer to Sabbatai's proclamation in the summer of 1666. Do we have to infer that Sabbatai sent letters abolishing the fast of the Tenth of Tebeth from Aleppo or Smyrna toward the end of 1665? As the Jews of Kurdistan again observed all the fasts after the apostasy (while continuing to believe in Sabbatai Ṣevi), the reference cannot be to the year 1667. Two recently published liturgical compositions from Persian Kurdistan provide further evidence of the messianic fervor there. One text, a long poetic introduction to the *Nishmath* prayer, speaks of Sabbatai as destined to offer sacrifice in the Temple of the Lord, possibly implying that the messiah would also minister as high priest, although he was a descendant of the royal House of David and not of the priestly House of Aaron. The other composition, a poetic introduction to the Kaddish doxology, mentions the celebration of the "Feast of Consolation" when "Thou hast turned the fast of our mourning to joy and gladness," and was, therefore, written before the apostasy, in the one year that the fast was not observed.[120] In any event, it appears that the Kurdish communities acted in concert as regards both the abolition and the reinstitution of the fasts.[121] Kurdistan had been the scene of a major messianic uprising in the twelfth century.[122] Thanks to the purely accidental preservation of the Ḥariri documents[123] and the more recently dis-

119. The MS. reading "A Prayer of David" (i.e., Ps. 86) should probably be emended to "A Praise of David" (i.e., Ps. 145), since the latter psalm occupies a prominent place in the daily liturgy, whereas Ps. 86 does not occur in the prayer book. Ps. 45 was seen as a mystical praise of women.

120. See above, n. 115, and M. Benayahu, *loc. cit.*, pp. 22, 24.

121. *Zion,* VII (1942), 196.

122. This uprising inspired Benjamin Disraeli's (unhistorical) novel *The Wondrous Tale of David Alroy.*

123. The author of the book *Toᶜey Ruaḥ* on the false messiahs (MS. Enelow, Jewish Theological Seminary of America, no. 2223) was a scholar from Damascus who traveled, about a hundred years ago, in Kurdistan where he found much

covered liturgical poems, we know that the Kurdish Jews did not lack in messianic enthusiasm in the seventeenth century either. The communities of Arbel, Urmia, Rawanduz, and Amadiyah continued in the faith for many years after the apostasy.

From Persia we have the eyewitness report of the Frenchman Chardin who traveled there in 1666. The Persian Jews left their houses and lived in the fields where, in sackcloth and ashes, they fasted and prayed for the advent of the messiah. When admonished by the provincial governor to think of the taxes they had to pay and to go back to work, they replied, "The tax, our Lord, we shall never pay again, for our Redeemer has come." They reached an agreement with the governor which permitted them to continue to serve God in their present fashion without molestation, but also obliged them, in return, to pay a heavy fine if the messiah did not appear within three months. In fact, after three months they did pay the agreed amount of two hundred *thomans,* equivalent to nine thousand French *livres* at the time.[124] Envoys were sent to Constantinople to inquire about the messianic tidings, and one of them, a certain R. Aaron,[125] returned to Persia with a letter written by a prominent believer in the capital.[126]

The ample documentation assembled in Sasportas' *Ṣiṣath Nobel Ṣevi* throws much light on the movement in North Africa, from Morocco to Egypt. Throughout this wide area, kabbalistic doctrine played a prominent part in the Sabbatian awakening; the combination of messianic enthusiasm and Lurianic theology at the court of the

---

material relating to the Sabbatian movement, some of which he incorporated in his work. His name was Joseph b. Joseph (died 1888 in Baghdad); cf. M. Benayahu in *Kiryath Sepher* XXXV (1960), 387–90. He was born in Jerusalem and traveled widely as a bookseller. His copybooks contained much Sabbatian material from oriental manuscripts. In 1853 he was in Kurdistan.

124. See W. Fischel, "The History of Persian Jews during the Sefevid Dynasty," *Zion,* II (1937), 289.

125. On the identity of this R. Aaron see M. Benayahu, *loc. cit.,* pp. 9–11. He is not identical with R. Aaron the Physician, a Persian scholar who, in 1674 or earlier, wrote a long letter in which he proved with quotations from Maimonides the utter falsity of Sabbatai's pretentions. His account of the vexations suffered by the Persian Jews agrees with that given by the French traveler Chardin; see Benayahu, *loc. cit.,* pp. 25–32. The MS. used by Benayahu is now in the Hebrew Union College, Cincinnati, no. 2001.

126. The fragment was published by Scholem, *Zion,* VII (1942), 175. The style would seem to point to somebody like Abraham Yakhini.

chelebi Raphael Joseph is a case in point. We are particularly well informed of the beginnings and development of the movement in Egypt. There were, apparently, two main centers of messianic propaganda: Raphael Joseph's court in Cairo and the circle around the prophet Nathan in Gaza. There was much coming and going between the two centers, especially by Raphael Joseph's emissaries. Nathan's kabbalistic tracts of 1665 were, as we have seen, most probably addressed to the Cairo circle, whose leading kabbalists, R. Samuel Gandoor and R. Judah Sharaf, were close adherents and associates of Nathan's. Sharaf was also closely associated with members of Sabbatai's immediate entourage. Sabbatai's letter from Safed (see above, p. 186) was addressed to Sharaf and to Raphael Joseph. Sharaf had lived some time in Jerusalem and had been Samuel Primo's teacher.[127] He may no longer have been in Egypt in the autumn of 1665, since he is said to have left Gaza with letters from the prophet to Sabbatai Ṣevi,[128] who was then at Smyrna. We do not know whether he reached Smyrna and (possibly) returned to Gaza, or whether he was made captive on the way by Maltese ships (see above, p. 633). In any event it is not certain whether the signature on the letter of admonition by the rabbis of Constantinople to their colleagues in Smyrna is really Sharaf's.[129] In May, 1666 (about a month after the dispatch of the aforementioned letter of admonition), Sasportas quotes letters written by Sharaf—probably from Gaza—in confirmation of Nathan's prophecy. But apparently Sharaf's endorsement of the prophecy was not convincing enough, for Sasportas concluded his quotation with the ironic question why the writer had not succeeded in dispelling all uncertainty "in Egypt and the surroundings countries where there are still doubters."[130] In any event it appears that Sharaf had written letters *to* Egypt and must, therefore, have been elsewhere at the time. Perhaps he

127. Z. Rubashov (Shazar), "The Scribe of the Messiah," p. 41, suggests that Primo had studied with Sharaf in Egypt, but it may well have been in Jerusalem; there is no conclusive evidence either way. Primo (in his homilies ᵓ*Imrey Shefer*, printed at the end of the responsa *Kehunath* ᶜ*Olam*, Constantinople, 1740) refers to Sharaf as his teacher. Also Abraham Cardozo knew that Primo had been Sharaf's disciple; see G. Scholem in *Z. P. Chajes Memorial Volume* (1933), p. 333. According to Frumkin (pt. II, p. 31), Sharaf had been a disciple of R. Zeraḥya Guta in Jerusalem.

128. Haberman, *Letters,* p. 212.

129. See above, pp. 415–16, and Baruch of Arezzo, p. 55.

130. Sasportas, p. 81.

returned to Egypt only after the apostasy. Ḥayyim Vital's son Samuel was a member of Raphael Joseph's kabbalistic circle, but although he presided over the penitential exercises in 1665–66, there is no definite evidence as to his Sabbatian faith. A record of Samuel Vital's exorcism, on the Twenty-sixth of Tammuz (July 29), 1666, of an evil spirit possessing a man in Cairo,[131] seems to suggest that life in Cairo continued as usual, since no reference is made to the messianic awakening. The spirit is said to have greatly plagued the patient on the Seventeenth of Tammuz, but no mention is made of the fact that the day was celebrated as a feast in that year (or at least that the fast had been abolished). This silence may, perhaps, serve as support for Sasportas' claim (based on a letter to Amsterdam by R. Shalom b. Joseph) that "most of the rabbis in Egypt were still doubting the matter."[132]

Among the opponents of the Sabbatian agitation in Egypt were Palestinian rabbis who had settled there—among them, R. Zeraḥya Guta of Jerusalem and R. Yomtob b. Akiba Ṣahalon of Safed. Sasportas praised these doubters, and especially R. Yomtob Ṣahalon whom he had met when the latter visited Amsterdam on behalf of the community of Safed about 1665,[133] for their piety and wisdom. Apparently both had insisted that Nathan substantiate his prophetic claims by a miracle, but had otherwise remained inactive, evidently preferring to await the outcome of the prophet's predictions. Sasportas, who usually has very hard words for those who remained passive in the face of the messianic propaganda, nevertheless applauded the prudence of these two rabbis. According to Nathan Guta's account (see above, p. 476) the mood of the enthusiasts in Egypt seems to have been such as to render "prudence" on the part of the infidels advisable.

Next in importance to Raphael Joseph's circle in Cairo as a center of the faith was the community of Alexandria whose rabbi, R. Hosea Nantawa, was one of the most extreme and radical enthusiasts. His fervent letter of late summer, 1666, in addition to being a valuable and instructive confession of the Sabbatian faith, also permits us some glimpses of the messianic awakening in Alexandria. At the end

131. Printed at the end of Samuel Vital's *Shaᶜar ha-Gilgulim.*

132. Sasportas, p. 137.

133. Cf. Sasportas, p. 82, and M. Benayahu, in *ᵓEreṣ Yisraᵓel*, III (1954), 246.

of the letter Nantawa signs himself "the servant of them that believe this holy faith,"[134] reminiscent of the papal *servus servorum dei.* One of the few apostles of the original Sabbatian group in Jerusalem and Gaza was active in Alexandria, and Nantawa rejoiced that "God has illumined our eyes, for a certain prophet has arrived here some time ago, a great rabbi in whom the spirit of the Lord speaketh . . . the rabbi Mattathias Bloch Ashkenazi who has erstwhile been with Our Lord, who put some of his honor upon him and laid his hands upon him [cf. Num. 27:20, 23]. Since then the Holy Spirit rests upon him and every day he prophesies great things, all in the Holy Faith. Blessed is he that waiteth, and woe unto him that denies it."[135] We may presume that Bloch arrived in Egypt several months before Nantawa's letter was written, probably not later than April, 1666, and that he zealously preached the faith. No other prophet is known to have been active in Egypt. As Bloch was an ordained rabbi and a rabbinical author, his prophecies (none of which has been preserved) were no doubt more impressive and convincing than the stammering ejaculations of women and children. He was evidently held in high regard by Sabbatai Ṣevi, for his name appears on the list of kings whom the messiah appointed in Smyrna.[136] Raphael Supino, writing to Sasportas in April, 1666, gives some news of events in Egypt but makes no mention of Bloch, although letters from Alexandria were continually arriving in Leghorn and Venice.[137] Travelers coming from Alexandria had told Supino that in that city alone two hundred men were following the penitential instructions of Nathan, who had written to everyone, revealing to them their sins as well as the roots of their souls. Letters from Alexandria reported that people were fasting from Sunday to Friday evening, and that young boys had inspired knowledge of the Talmud and the Zohar. In any event Mattathias Bloch's authority must have been influential enough to secure the abolition of the fast of the Ninth of Ab.[138] Sabbatai's order to abolish the fast

134. Sasportas, p. 157.

135. *Ibid.*, p. 156.

136. Coenen, p. 45; see above, p. 429.

137. Cf. Sasportas, p. 122, regarding a long letter from Egypt written in March, 1666, and *ibid.*, p. 72, the text of a letter concerning the faith, by the rabbis of Alexandria.

138. *Ibid.*, p. 192, in a letter from R. Joseph ha-Levi to R. Hosea Nantawa. The writer had already learned of Sabbatai's apostasy, and gives full vent in his letter to his accumulated hatred of the "believers."

could not have reached Palestine or Egypt in time, and the step must therefore have been taken on the independent initiative of Nathan and his friends. There is no need to assume that the matter had been decided upon long in advance by correspondence between the messiah and his prophet in Gaza. Nathan and Mattathias Bloch had both been in Gaza the previous year when the fast of the Seventeenth of Tammuz was abolished, and there is no reason why they should not have continued along the same lines in 1666. There is no evidence that Bloch's injunction was also obeyed in Cairo.[139] According to Sasportas, Bloch was an old man;[140] and lest anyone misunderstand the adjective "old" and take it in the idiomatic sense of "venerable," Sasportas specifies that he was an "old fool" and an "ass."

Little is known about R. Jacob Palache of Marrakesh in Morocco, who was active in Egypt at that time. The rabbis of Cairo subsequently regarded him as one of the worst Sabbatian agitators. When news of the apostasy became known in Cairo toward the end of 1666, the rabbis solemnly excommunicated Sabbatai Ṣevi together with his three "chief accomplices" Nathan, Mattathias Bloch, and Jacob Palache, "who has caused strife and contention."[141] R. Nathan Guta, a consistent opponent of the movement who had actually been in danger of his life from the enthusiastic crowd (see above, p. 476), was one of the five signatories of the letter of excommunication. There is no evidence regarding the original attitude of the other four. The radical-

139. Emanuel Frances, using the same sources as R. Joseph ha-Levi, states that the fast of 9 Ab was abolished in Alexandria at the behest of the pseudo-prophet R. Mattathias, but makes no mention of other cities in Egypt (*Ṣevi Muddaḥ,* p. 128).

140. Sasportas, p. 182. Contrary to the opinion expressed earlier by me (in *Zion,* VII [1942], 176) and by Is. Tishby (in his note to Sasportas, p. 271), the prophet Bloch cannot have been identical with the man who accompanied Sabbatai Raphael to preach the faith in Italy. Sabbatai Raphael was a young man of twenty-three (or of twenty-seven at the most) when he told Sasportas that he and his companion had come from Palestine to Rome on a Sabbatian mission, and he would certainly not have described the aged rabbi as his "companion."

141. *Ibid.,* p. 198, where, however, his home town is not mentioned. He is referred to, long after the apostasy, as an active Sabbatian by Abraham Cardozo who possibly met him in Tunis "when he [Palache] passed through Tunis on his way to his home town Marrakesh" (Cardozo's letter to R. Samuel de Paz in Leghorn, *ap.* Weiss, *Beth ha-Midrash,* p. 65).

ism of the rabbis of Alexandria, who had raised the faith in Sabbatai Ṣevi to a par with the faith in the unity of God and in His Law, may have exasperated the opponents; it certainly fired the enthusiasm of the believers. As early as November, 1666, Nantawa's letter to the congregation of Leghorn was solemnly read from the pulpit in the Portuguese Synagogue in Hamburg;[142] it was a letter which, as we have seen (see above, p. 490), anticipated much of the specifically sectarian mentality of later Sabbatianism.

There is no dearth of information from Tripoli, where one of the most colorful figures of the Sabbatian movement resided at the time and took up a feverish activity on behalf of the messianic awakening. Abraham Miguel Cardozo (1627–1707)—or Cardoso, as the correct Spanish spelling would be—was, besides Nathan and for twenty-five years after his death, the most important speaker and theologian of seventeenth-century Sabbatianism. The main part of his career comprises the period after Sabbatai's death and shall not detain us here, but it will be useful to recall the earlier stages of his life and activities. His own writings, for all their wealth of autobiographical information, are full of inconsistencies and contradictions, and yet there can be but little doubt about the stages of his development. He was born into a marrano family in Rio Seco in Castile, and as a child learned of his Jewish origin.[143] He grew up in Madrid under the tutelage of his much older brother, Isaac Cardozo (1604–80), one of the outstanding representatives of marrano Jewry and, after his return to Judaism, one of its chief apologists in the Spanish language.[144] The junior brother, too, studied medicine in Salamanca for at least two years, and at the same time—according to his own testimony—took up the study of Catholic theology, obvi-

142. Sasportas, p. 169.

143. C. Bernheimer, "Some new contributions to Abraham Cardoso's Biography," in *JQR*, XVIII, New Series (1927), 112.

144. He wrote *Las Excelencias y Calunias de los Hebreos* (Amsterdam, 1679). The later relations between the brothers were very cool. About the date of his birth, cf. Julio Caro Baroja, *La Sociedad criptojudica en la corte de Felipe IV* (Madrid, 1963), pp. 102–3. When the present work went to press, there appeared the comprehensive and valuable monograph on Isaac Cardoso by Yosef Hayim Yerushalmi, *From Spanish Court to Italian Ghetto* (New York, Columbia University Press, 1971), in which a long chapter (pp. 302–49) is devoted to the relations between the two brothers and to Isaac Cardoso's hostile attitude to Sabbatianism.

ously for polemical reasons.[145] At the age of twenty-one he left Spain, returned to Judaism in Leghorn,[146] and took up the study of Jewish religion in Venice, under great teachers like Abraham Valensi, Samuel Aboab, and Moses Zacuto.[147] He finished his medical studies, probably in Padua, and practiced medicine all his life. Surely he was no Talmudist; even less likely an ordained rabbi, but an eager student of all other branches of Jewish literature and well-versed in midrash and kabbalah. He tells later that he was troubled from the beginning about the identity of the true "God of Israel," and started searching for it in the ancient books, finding nobody to set his mind at rest.[148] He also claimed to have had dreams about the forthcoming messianic redemption, but we do not know how far these statements are to be taken at their face value. He had an extraordinary imagination, as is fully shown by his later writings and activities. He tells of seeing Isaac Luria in his visions since 1658.[149] He returned for some time to Leghorn (about 1659) and from then on led a life of wanderings and peregrinations. He spent some years in Cairo where he might possibly have met Sabbatai Ṣevi, when he first passed through Egypt, on his way to Jerusalem. There he immersed himself in kabbalistic studies.[150] In 1663 or 1664, he settled in Tripoli as a physician to

145. J. Basnage, *Histoire des Juifs,* IX (2nd edn., 1716), p. 793 (not in the 1st edn.) and Cardozo's testimony about the two years he studied theology, in *Zion,* VII (1942), 25. Basnage had also information regarding Cardozo's firm belief in the predictions of Nostradamus which he had read in Salamanca. I suppose Cardozo knew of Nostradamus' Jewish origin and considered him a marrano like himself.

146. Cf. *Sefunoth,* III–IV (1960), 221, and *Zion,* XIX (1953), 15, where he tells of a dream he had in 1649 about the Jews of Venice: the messiah had appeared, but they would not believe in him. Yerushalmi, p. 192, considers it as "practically certain that the two brothers left Spain together." Concerning the sojourn of the two brothers in Venice, cf. Yerushalmi, pp. 195–205.

147. *JQR,* XVIII, New Series (1927), 113. Valensi died in March, 1649, at the age of eighty-five; cf. *MGWJ* (1892), p. 273. It is therefore highly improbable that he could have been among Cardozo's teachers.

148. *JQR,* XVIII, New Series (1927), 114–16.

149. Cf. *Sefunoth,* III–IV (1960), 233, but in another book he gives 1662 as the first time he had a vision of Luria; *Zion,* VII (1942), 17.

150. See Bernheimer's note on the contradictions in Cardozo's statements regarding his travels to Cairo and Tripoli, *JQR, loc. cit.,* p. 114. In later years, he dated the beginning of his kabbalistic writing from 1664; cf. *Essays in Memory of H. P. Chajes* (Vienna, 1933), p. 326 (of the Hebrew section).

Osman Pasha, the bey of Tripoli. Having married shortly after his return to Judaism, he took now a second wife and had numerous progeny, but all his children died long before him.[151] His position in Tripoli was very strong and as a result of the revelations and visions which he was vouchsafed, he was soon recognized by laymen and rabbis alike as a spiritual leader of the community. Most of them steadfastly stood by him, and when he was later attacked and accused of laxity in the performance of Jewish ritual, they paid a most glowing tribute to his good standing as an observant Jew.[152] His letters state that as early as 1664 he had had a revelation to the effect that the messiah would manifest himself in 1665,[153] and it is small wonder that after the arrival of the good tidings from Gaza, he was confirmed by new visions and became an enthusiastic spokesman for the "faith."[154] Prompted by his own enthusiasm, Cardozo seems to have written to Nathan and to other leaders of the movement, and he remained in close contact with them, particularly after Sabbatai's apostasy, which he defended passionately in many letters, in both Spanish and Hebrew.[155] In those years, however, he had not yet founded a school of his own, as he was to do later. Nantawa's remark in September, 1666, concerning the existence of prophets "in the Maghreb" may well refer to Cardozo.

As to other parts of North Africa, our information is scant. A collection of "Penitential Prayers according to the African Rite" in the Günzburg Collection, Moscow (No. 195), contains a hymn in honor of Sabbatai Ṣevi, but there is no way of determining its exact provenance. Regarding Algiers and Tunis we possess general information but no details.[156] Much light, however, is thrown on the messianic agitation in the area by a legal query addressed to R. Nathan Guta by the island community of Djerba off the Tunisian coast.

151. Cf. Bernheimer, *loc. cit.*, p. 127.

152. Cf. MS. Hamburg 312, fols. 14a–15a. The two testimonials are from November, 1668, including one of the rabbinical court of Tripoli.

153. Sasportas, p. 289. 154. *Ibid.*, pp. 290–91.

155. Sasportas (p. 93), writing to Raphael Supino, refers to an earlier communication from the latter in which mention was made of a messianic augury in the form of a visionary appearance of the planet "Sabbatai" (i.e., Saturn). The name of the visionary is not mentioned, but the incident is reminiscent of Cardozo's account of a vision he had in March, 1666; cf. Sasportas, pp. 290–91.

156. Sasportas, p. 209.

"In the year of the rumors and the false alarms" a certain inhabitant of Djerba "who had fallen into the same error as the other children of Israel" decided to go to the Holy Land. As he needed money for the voyage, he mortgaged his house to the community for forty lion's thalers. Before his departure he signed an instrument of sale in order to enable the officers of the community not only to recover their mortgage but also to sell his house together with the property of the community which they would, no doubt, dispose of in the imminent messianic future. In due course the disabused Djerbaite claimed his property back, submitting that (*a*) he had never sold his house to the community but merely mortgaged it, (*b*) the instrument of sale to the community had been meant as a formal device to enable the community to dispose of the house along with the rest of their property, and (*c*) the whole transaction had been based on the assumption that the messianic reports were correct.[157] The case was submitted to several rabbis in Palestine and Egypt. (The plaintiff, it appears, was in Cairo at the time.) The wording of the query as well as of the rabbinic judgments indicates that the officers of the Djerba community indeed expected to sell the whole community property before long "for the hour had come and the end had arrived."[158]

As to Morocco, the grievous loss of a main source must be recorded. Up to the time of the French occupation, a large manuscript was extant in the library of R. Mattathias Serrero of Fez which contained documents concerning Sabbatai Ṣevi, among others the autograph letters of Sabbatai and Nathan sent to the rabbis of Fez. Some years after the occupation the library was plundered and set on fire.[159] We have thus to piece together our information from available sources. In Algiers, Oran, and Morocco the good news encountered no serious opposition. On the contrary, it aroused mighty hopes in the populous Jewries of "Barbary" (as those parts of North Africa were called at the time), where brutal persecutions were the order of the day. In Morocco especially the Jews were in constant danger of their lives, and their situation resembled that of their brethren in Poland. At

157. MS. Oxford 845, fol. 198a; a photocopy of the MS. is at the Ben-Zvi Institute in Jerusalem.

158. Cf. also "New Sabbatian Documents from the Book *Toᶜey Ruaḥ*," *Zion*, VII (1942), 179. See also above, ch. 5, end of section 1.

159. Written communication from R. Joseph Mashash, Haifa, who has held and perused the MS. (December 9, 1965).

the mercy of their rulers' whims, they also suffered greatly in the wars between the various local rulers and in the endemic rebellions. In 1666 the Jews of Salé suffered heavily in the course of such internal warfare, and Moroccan Jewry as a whole was threatened with disaster "because of their excessive enthusiasm in this faith, when the wicked Ghailan arose and decreed against them a decree of slaughter and destruction." The danger was averted by the payment of an enormous bribe.[160] Later in the year Ghailan was put to flight by his opponent, the ruler of Tafilet. Sasportas, who was a native of Morocco and a member of one of the two most aristocratic Jewish families in the country (Sasportas and Toledano), always kept in close touch with Jewish affairs there, frequently exchanging letters with his Moroccan colleagues and especially with the rabbis of Salé, where he himself had been rabbi until he fell in disgrace with the authorities and barely escaped with his life. It was from Salé that the first reports to the effect that the Ten Tribes were marching up from the African desert spread in the summer of 1665 (see above, p. 333). On receiving the glad tidings from Gaza, the rabbis of Salé embraced the messianic faith and led the penitential awakening in Morocco. This provoked the Moroccan authorities to such stern reprisals that (in the words of Sasportas) the rabbis "had to do penance for their penances."[161] One poor but ardent young student immediately set out on foot from Morocco, through Egypt, to Gaza where the prophet Nathan prostrated himself before him because he recognized the visitor's soul as a spark of that of Simon b. Yoḥay.[162]

The Moroccan rabbis may have been favorably disposed toward the movement for another reason too: they all knew and highly esteemed the prophet's father, R. Elisha Ḥayyim Ashkenazi, who had spent many years in their midst as an emissary of the community of Jerusalem. Moreover, it appears from the correspondence between Sasportas and the rabbis of Salé that even Sasportas had at first responded with some enthusiasm to the good news. Sasportas was a past master in the art of deftly covering up the traces of his equivocations, and not beyond "doctoring" earlier statements and letters to suit his vanity (see above, p. 568). In this he was no different from any diplomat writing his memoirs. The

160. Sasportas, p. 152.
161. *Ibid.*, p. 91.
162. *Ibid.*, p. 73, in a letter to Raphael Supino.

rabbis of Salé, including Sasportas' old friend R. Jacob Saᶜadun, were less forgetful. When, after Sabbatai's apostasy, Sasportas self-righteously reminded them that he alone had unwaveringly fought the pernicious faith from beginning to end, they registered polite surprise and reminded him of a letter which he had written in the autumn of 1665 and in which he had testified that many rabbis held the matter to be true. In fact, he had concluded his letter with the assertion "and this will come to pass in the year 1670"[163]—the date given in Nathan's original prophecy in the letter to Raphael Joseph. Unfortunately—though understandably enough—this embarrassing letter was not included in Sasportas' "file for publication," *Ṣiṣath Nobel Ṣevi*. In his reply, Sasportas insisted that he had merely quoted but not endorsed the opinions voiced by others, and that he had been skeptical even then. Lacking the original letter, there is no way of knowing who was untruthful in this case; there are reasons for mistrusting both Sasportas and Saᶜadun. Sasportas' assertion that when he wrote the letter to Morocco he had no knowledge of Nathan's letter to the *chelebi*, and that as soon as he had seen the letter from Gaza on the following day, he had publicly denounced the prophet and his messiah,[164] is patently untrue, as is proved by the reference to the year 1670. Judging by the evidence of some of his other letters (or rather, by a comparison of the original and the "edited" versions of his letters), it seems probable that the letter to Salé was sufficiently ambiguous to encourage the Moroccan rabbis in their faith, while providing, at the same time, enough loopholes for subsequent denials. This impression is strengthened by the curious fact that Sasportas did not write again to Morocco until after the apostasy when, of course, it was easy to assume an air of censorious righteousness. But until then he refrained from further correspondence, probably because his first letter had been too positive in tone.[165]

The movement was firmly entrenched throughout Morocco, from its very beginning in 1665–66. Its strength is indicated by the fact

163. *Ibid.*, p. 328.

164. *Ibid.*, pp. 351–52.

165. In his letter to Salé, Sasportas (p. 352) lists all the missives he had sent to the various communities in the course of his relentless struggle against the Sabbatian movement, but significantly makes no mention of any further letters to Morocco.

that believers continued to be active for some time after the apostasy. Nothing is known regarding the observance of the Ninth of Ab (1666), and perhaps the messiah's instructions had not reached the believers. Cardozo was in close contact with the Moroccan rabbis, and his relations with the latter were strengthened further after he had moved from Tripoli to Tunis.

IV

The messianic tidings also reached South Arabia, where the Yemenite Jews had created a curious and unique spiritual world—or perhaps we should say "ghetto"—of their own. This world was a strange compound of two prima facie incompatible elements: Maimonides and the kabbalah. No apocalyptic movements are known from the Yemen since the twelfth century, when a serious messianic agitation prompted Maimonides to expound his views on eschatology in his *Epistle to the Jews of Yemen* (see above, p. 14). In spite of their isolation, Yemenite Jewry had always been in contact with their Egyptian brethren. Copies of the letters from Gaza received in Egypt toward the end of 1665 were forwarded to the Yemen, where they stimulated the growth of apocalyptic legends. In due course the facts and legends of the messianic awakening were forgotten, and the history of the Sabbatian movement in the Yemen had to be rediscovered by recent research. When Ḥayyim Ḥabshush, one of the pioneers of the Yemenite Jewish "Enlightenment" at the end of the nineteenth century, began to write the history of the Sabbatian movement in his country, he had only vague and garbled oral traditions to draw upon, and the most important contemporary document was unknown to him. Here and there his account[166] contains a reliable detail (for example, that the rabbis had decreed "not to eat boiled meat but only roast, not to drink even at the Passover celebration, and to eat all their food unseasoned, without salt"), but the essentials are all wrong. Ḥabshush believed that the Yemenite Jews were too far away to have been drawn into the movement, and that the reports concerning Sabbatai Ṣevi did not reach them until 1668, two years after the apostasy. As a matter of fact, news would travel from Egypt to Jedda or Hodayda, and

166. M. Kehathi, published the relevant chapter from Ḥabshush's *Dofi ha-Zeman* in his Hebrew article "The Sabbatian Movement in the Yemen" in *Zion* (annual), V (1933), 78–88; see especially pp. 82 ff.

thence to Sanᶜa, in about two months and the author himself mentions a tradition to the effect that the glad tidings "winged their way like an eagle" from Egypt to Yemen. The Yemenite Jews, miserable, oppressed, and cruelly persecuted, immediately responded to the message of comfort and joy. They suspended all business and commerce, spent their money on alms and works of charity, and generally displayed such proud and confident bearing as to provoke the wrath of their rulers—exactly as in Poland and in Morocco. If Ḥabshush's tradition is reliable, the movement triggered off a wave of violent persecution in the course of which the head of Yemenite Jewry, R. Solomon al-Jamal was killed in Sanᶜa by a rioting Arab mob and his dead body mutilated after he had refused to become a Muslim. The tradition is confirmed by another source, according to which the womenfolk donned their best clothes and ornaments, and infected their menfolk with their enthusiasm. Their preparations for a speedy departure for Jerusalem infuriated the Arabs who, upon a sign from their imam, murdered and robbed the departing Jews. "He also ordered the arrest of the chief rabbi, Solomon al-Jamal, who was dressed in festive robes expecting the messiah, and they put him to death with terrible tortures."[167] There was a general expectation of the messiah's advent on Passover, the biblical feast of redemption, which appears as the time of future redemption in several eschatological Haggadoth. Whether 1666 or 1667 was meant is not quite certain. Even at so early a date as 1670, a colophon in a Yemenite prayerbook speaks of "the year of glad tidings [*besurah*] 5427" and laments "the delay of the coming of our messiah because of our sins" which instead of redemption "brought upon us heavy persecutions."[168] But this may

167. Idelsohn, in the Hebrew monthly *Mizraḥ u-Maᶜarav*, I (Jerusalem, 1920), 13. The attempt by the Yemenite scholar Abraham Nadaf to deny any connection between this tradition and the Sabbatian movement (*ibid.*, p. 332) is evidently due to his ignorance of the relevant evidence. His quotations from a Hebrew MS. *History of the Arabs* merely show that in several versions the original date as well as Sabbatai's name were purposely omitted. Ḥabshush's version in *Dofi ha-Zeman* is now confirmed by the important document that has since come to light.

168. This is the colophon of the *Tikhlal* (the Yemenite order of prayers) in the MS. 4°497 of the Jewish National Library.

be explained by the prophecy (see below) that the messiah would come to Yemen at the end of this year (summer, 1667). According to Ḥabshush, however, the letters from Egypt are said to have spoken of 1667 as the year of deliverance. On the other hand, we have firsthand evidence that the excitement broke out in 5426 (1665–66). Several poems joyfully greeting the messianic dawn and giving this date have been preserved. Shalom Shabbazi, the greatest poet of Yemenite Jewry, wrote several fervent pieces in this vein, of which at least one makes very moving reading even today.[169] At least two other poets in Yemen made their bow to the messiah.[170]

The Sabbatian reference of the Yemenite poems and historical traditions is now definitely borne out by the Sabbatian apocalypse *Gey Ḥizzayon* (*The Valley of Vision*) composed in Sanᶜa late in the summer of 1666. This important text, which is extant in several manuscripts and was published in 1949,[171] reflects the impact of the great awakening on the heart and mind of a Yemenite kabbalist. No clear division exists for the author[172] between the supernal kabbalistic sphere of the divine *sefiroth* and the lower sphere of historical events. The two worlds merge into one: the author expounds the mysteries of the messiah's ministry among the supernal *sefiroth* and, in the same breath, explains happenings on earth and predicts future events. His kabbalistic system owes nothing to the

169. This poem is found in the complete *diwan* of Shabbazi's poems, MS. 3274 of the Ben-Zvi Institute, Jerusalem, fol. 3a. He mentions "this year 1666," the sale of the landed property, and the prophecy of Nathan. Other Sabbatian poems by him are quoted by Nadaf (*loc. cit.*, p. 331) who interpreted them as reflecting ordinary messianic expectation rather than Sabbatian adventism. He rightly insists that the word *ṣevi* often refers to God, and its feminine form (*ṣivyah*) to the Shekhinah, but overlooks the fact that in several of Shabbazi's poems the *ṣevi ṣaddiq,* i.e., the messiah, Ṣevi appears to be definitely distinct from God.

170. Cf. the poem, composed in 1666, by Saᶜid Mansur, published in A. Z. Idelsohn's anthology *Shirey Teyman* (Berlin, 1924), pp. 269–70. The messianic poem by Uas b. Saᶜid (see *REJ*, vol. LII, p. 44) may also be a product of the Sabbatian movement.

171. *Qobeṣ ᶜal Yad*, IV, New Series (1949), 105–41. In the introduction to my edn. of the text I have shown that the extant apocalypse must originally have formed part of a larger kabbalistic work.

172. The MSS. are anonymous, and only MS. Enelow notes (in a different hand) on the title page "This is the Book *Gey Ḥizzayon* of the Good Brother Solomon b. Zechariah b. Saᶜadya," but the name may be that of the owner of the book.

Lurianic doctrine of "sparks," "configurations," etc., and operates exclusively with the doctrine of *sefiroth* of the earlier kabbalah. Factual information about the messiah and his activities is immediately combined with esoteric accounts of the sefirotic life, until a fantastic picture emerges in which the messianic events are far removed from the scene of concrete historical realities. This picture, partly inspired by letters from abroad purveying Sabbatian legends and partly the author's own fond invention, is all the more surprising as the author was evidently in possession of reliable information regarding Sabbatai's youth. In fact, for several details of the messiah's early career, the Yemenite apocalypse is our only source, though on the whole the account is utterly fantastic. On one point, however, our author deviates from purely mystical biography: we are told that the messiah began his career, surprisingly enough, as commander-in-chief of the armies of the Roman emperor.[173] The messiah was born in "Rome"[174] but was taken away from his mother at the age of three by the archangel Gabriel, who transferred him to the keeping of the patriarchs in Paradise. (This detail also serves as an explanation of the "odor of Paradise" exuding from Sabbatai and mentioned in several sources; see above, p. 139.) On being returned again to Rome, he lived in perfect silence and anonymity, unknown to himself as well as to others. His food was brought to him by the archangel Michael, and neither women nor music or other luxuries and delicacies held any attraction for him. (An obvious echo of the many accounts of the young Sabbatai's ascetic life.) Only when he saw that a Jew was treated unjustly, would he, like another Moses (cf. Exod. 2:11–12), wreak vengeance on the evildoer.

The subject of the messiah's anonymity seems to have held a curious fascination for our author. For also the messiah of the tribe of Joseph was "growing up somewhere," attended by angels and by the prophet Elijah,[175] until God would reveal to each his calling and ministry. The manifestation of the two messiahs is surrounded by a halo of legend, inspired no doubt by accounts of the miracles that were reported from Palestine in 1665, and especially the mass prophecy of women and children. The author apparently believed that both

173. *Qobeṣ ʿal Yad*, IV, New Series (1949), 124.

174. Which, in Hebrew usage since the Byzantine period, could also mean the Second Rome, Byzantium (i.e., Constantinople).

175. *Qobeṣ ʿal Yad*, IV, New Series (1949), 125.

redeemers had some sort of messianic consciousness, but that neither knew whether he was the son of David or the son of Joseph. There are frequent inconsistencies and contradictions, due to the author's uncertainty regarding the precise nature of Sabbatai's messianic ministry. Thus the messiah of the House of Joseph is said to have manifested himself in the "German lands"[176] where he fought mighty wars,[177] but elsewhere it is suggested that Sabbatai himself was the messiah of the House of Joseph and that his mistaken identification as the son of David was due to demonic action that had somehow succeeded in confusing the mass prophecies.[178] It is the name of the messiah of the House of Joseph that will become widely known in the year "put on strength" (cf. Isa. 51:9), that is, 1665, because he is the warrior hero, whereas the Davidic messiah, who will manifest himself at the same time, "will seclude himself in prayer and spiritual advancement, and fly in the air with [the archangel] Michael." But whereas the son of Joseph acquires his reputation gradually by his conquests, the son of David will reveal himself all of a sudden after the death of the warrior messiah, "and then the messiah of the tribe of Joseph and all that died with him will resurrect, except the gentiles, the sinners, and the apostates."[179] Though there were no saints in Israel worthy of bringing down the divine Presence, yet the messiah "would come through the merits of the little children who have to forgo their childish plays in order to study the Torah."[180]

However, the distinction between the two messiahs is not carried through consistently. At times the author simply speaks of "the messiah," that is, Sabbatai Ṣevi, but then again confuses the issue, for example, by applying to both messiahs a formula[181] which originally occurred in an account of Sabbatai's early beginnings.[182] According to the Yemenite author, the train of messianic events began in the year 1664. In the year "put on strength" (1665) the messiah pro-

176. *Ibid.*, p. 118.

177. An obvious echo of Nathan's prophecy of messianic vengeance in Poland and Russia; see above, p. 273.

178. *Qobeṣ ʿal Yad*, IV, New Series (1949), 118, cf. also pp. 115, 120, 125.

179. *Ibid.*, p. 110.

180. *Ibid.*, p. 113.

181. *Ibid.*, p. 125.

182. *Ibid.*, p. 116. The original letters from which the formula was borrowed are no longer extant.

ceeded to "Rome," that is, Constantinople, where he would remain until 1666, the appointed date for the humiliation and overthrow of the Turkish rule. But until his manifestation in power to wreak vengeance on the sons of the handmaid (that is, the descendants of Ishmael, the son of Hagar), the messiah's face "will be hidden for seven months" and there will be severe trials and great tribulations and plagues. The "hiding of the face" of the messiah and the great trials and tribulations are accounted for in kabbalistic terms, but it is evident that the author had heard of Sabbatai's imprisonment in Gallipoli and of the prophecy of the seven months occurring in Nathan's *Treatise on the Dragons*. At the end of this period, in the year 1667, the messiah would come to the Yemen.[183] The author was thus writing in the year 1666. The messiah's mystical ministry had begun in Galilee in 1648 and had subsequently been exercised partly in the Jewish communities in Germany and elsewhere, and partly in the supernal world of the *sefiroth*.[184] The ingathering of the exiles would take place in 1668, after the messiah's advent in the Yemen. In 1669 not a single Jew would remain behind "on the impure soil" outside Palestine[185] and, conversely, all the gentiles would be driven out of the Holy Land by a prophet who would arise in Gaza and proclaim the messianic king. The two messiahs would appear together in Palestine in 1667, the patriarchs would rise from their tombs in Hebron, and all the palaces and sanctuaries of the gentiles in Hebron and Zion would crumble and be destroyed by a miraculous fire. The events of the year 1667 are foretold with much fantastic detail, including strange meteorological phenomena, the arrival of the sons of Moses who come flying through the air like birds,[186] and the translation of the messiah from "Rome" to the Holy City by the Holy Spirit. Mighty dark clouds will circle the Mount of Zion and when they clear up, houses will be found torn from their foundations and the Western Wall will have been raised to much greater height, even at its base.[187] Utter destruction is prophesied to the sons of Ishmael

183. *Ibid.*, pp. 114, 116. The belief that the final stage of the messianic redemption would begin in the Yemen was shared by other Yemenite writers; cf. the Yemenite apocalypse published in Scholem, *Kitvey Yad be-Kabbalah* (Jerusalem, 1930), pp. 240–42, and in the Hebrew anthology *From Yemen to Zion*, eds. S. Garidi and I. Yeshaya (Tel Aviv, 1938), pp. 174–79.

184. *Ibid.*, p. 123.

185. *Ibid.*, p. 137.

186. *Ibid.*, pp. 124, 126.

187. *Ibid.*, pp. 125–26, 137.

(identified symbolically with Muhammad) who have darkened the light of Israel and brought terrible sufferings upon them in their long and bitter exile. The Muslim peoples were all, without exception, wicked pagans, whereas in Rome[188] a few God-fearing gentiles could be found among the followers of the Christian religion.[189] The author's digression on the subject illustrates a characteristic optical illusion: many Jewish writers have tended, like him, to consider the gentiles in whose midst they lived and under whose rule they smarted as utterly reprobate, while conceding the possibility of rare exceptions (the "pious gentiles") in other and less familiar parts of the Diaspora. This rule has often been overlooked in modern discussions.

The apocalypse mirrors the response of a Jewish community for whom the concrete facts of the Sabbatian movement were of no consequence. They heard the messianic reports and simply wove them into the fabric of their own peculiar hopes and imaginings. Their "mythopoeic" imagination combined hidden processes in the mystic world of the *sefiroth* with legendary accounts of the messiah's biography and their own dream of a day of vengeance and recompense. The combination was characteristic of Yemenite Jewry, for whom Sabbatai and Nathan were symbols of a new messianic myth rather than real persons. The Polish Jews did not expect the messiah to visit them in order to accomplish his mission; it was they who made the pilgrimage to Gallipoli. But in the distant and isolated Yemen the expectation seemed almost natural. In Europe it had been Christian pamphleteers and not the Polish Jews who had invented the fantastic picture of Sabbatai Ṣevi as a general commanding the army of the lost tribes. Strangely enough, the Yemenite apocalypse also emphasizes the military stage in the messiah's career: the messiah grows up in utter anonymity as one of the thirty-six hidden righteous, and completely unaware of his calling. He becomes commander of the army of the sultan and still does not know whether his ministry will be that of the triumphant son of David or of the martyr messiah of the tribe of Joseph who falls in battle. The theological problem of the nature of Sabbatai's ministry in relation to the two messianic types reappeared in subsequent Sabbatian history, but in the first year of the movement the Yemenite author seems to have been the only believer who was dimly conscious of it.

188. Here the reference is to Western Rome, i.e., the Christian world.
189. *Qobeṣ ᶜal Yad*, IV, New Series (1949), 135.

V

The solemn abolition of the fast of the Ninth of Ab, with much pomp and circumstance and amid public enthusiasm, constituted the climax of the movement. At the time this messianic demonstration was generally expected to be followed by another climactic event: the arrival of the prophet Nathan at the messiah's court (see above, p. 631). Instead, events took a dramatic turn that still baffles the historian. The messiah was visited not by Nathan of Gaza but by another prophet, a R. Nehemiah, who (in Sasportas' words) proved to be "the beginning of his undoing."

The role of R. Nehemiah Kohen remains an obscure chapter in the history of Sabbatai Ṣevi. The sudden appearance of the man and the unexpected denouement which it precipitated appealed, understandably enough, to the dramatic instincts of earlier students of the movement. Novelists and historical writers made grateful use of Nehemiah as a *deus ex machina*. The historian, however, who tries to investigate the details of this strange incident is faced with insoluble riddles.

The text of Sabbatai's letter to R. David ha-Levi (as quoted by Sasportas) suggests that the messiah had invited to his court a certain Sabbatian prophet of whose activity in Poland he had been acquainted by the two emissaries from Lvov. Under his signature to the letter, Sabbatai had added in a postscript: "Let the prophet R. Nehemiah speedily come to me with rejoicing and jubilation."[190] However, the postscript is missing in Leyb b. Ozer's version of the letter,[191] which was probably based on a copy of the emissaries' original report. According to Leyb's account, R. Nehemiah came on his own initiative or that of a group of Polish believers. Leyb, who not only had heard much about Nehemiah but also knew him personally during his (Nehemiah's) last days, describes him as a kabbalist without peer. But Leyb's notions of kabbalah were somewhat vague and rather of the popular and folkloric kind, and we shall soon come across a blatant example of his misconceptions in matters kabbalistic. In fact, apart from his role in the Sabbatian movement, Nehemiah is not mentioned in any known sources and there is no reason to assume that before 1666 he had enjoyed a wide reputation as a kabbalist or a prophet.

190. Sasportas, p. 78.

191. Cf. also the original Yiddish version, MS. Shazar, fol. 36a.

Nehemiah is mentioned twice by Sasportas, whose information purports to be based on rumors or letters from Poland. "Sabbatai learned of the existence [in Lvov] . . . of a man who had been prophesying and who was generally regarded as mad. He now sent for him . . . in order to lead people astray by putting into his mouth prophecies concerning his messiahship."[192] In a letter written in 1669, Sasportas tells in somewhat greater detail that Nehemiah was considered a fool in Poland "and at times spoke in a spirit of folly. The fools who were seduced by the false prophets [meaning, the Sabbatian believers] believed that he was a man of the spirit, and when this became known to Sabbatai he sent for him in order to put false words into his mouth as he had done with Nathan of Gaza. When he [Nehemiah] arrived . . . in Gallipoli, he [Sabbatai] advised him to apostatize for a mystical reason. [Nehemiah] did thus, but when he understood [Sabbatai's] evil intentions, he fled and returned to Lvov in Poland where he did a great penance. His apostasy lasted for a few days only."[193] Elsewhere Sasportas specifies that Nehemiah, who had been generally regarded as a madman in Poland, was invited by Sabbatai who then deceived him with "mystical reasons" and persuaded him to apostatize "by way of reparation for his evil deed, so that he [Sabbatai] might prove to the sultan that he had been drawing the Jews toward the Muslim religion."[194]

All this is more than doubtful. There is not a shred of evidence to support Sasportas' assertion that Sabbatai had planned his apostasy in advance or that he had used Nehemiah for this purpose. Both the facts and what we know of Sabbatai's psychology render this kind of crafty and insidious scheming highly improbable. Sasportas' account of the matter is evidently colored by prejudice, and possibly also based on erroneous information.

R. Nehemiah seems to have enjoyed a local reputation in parts of Poland. In any event he was recognized, during his later wanderings in Germany and Holland, by Polish Jews who remembered him from earlier years, and this in spite of the fact that he had changed his name and his costume. However, next to nothing is known of the nature of his reputation and of the kind of "madness" that made him famous. Did he engage in apocalyptic preaching even prior to

192. Sasportas, p. 77.
193. *Ibid.*, p. 345.
194. *Ibid.*, p. 174.

1665, prophesying an imminent messianic advent? Was he a wandering preacher or did he acquire celebrity as a "practical kabbalist"? The latter possibility is suggested by the report of a Jew who had met Nehemiah in Germany in 1677 and to whom Nehemiah said that he had been in Sweden and there "had brought the holy ten *sefiroth* into a place full of impurity."[195] If we can trust Leyb's account, Nehemiah's mind seems to have moved in a kabbalistic climate that was not dissimilar from that of Sabbatai's messianic speculations. The Jew to whom Nehemiah told his story was "a pious man, R. Anshel Haltern" from the district of Münster in western Germany. At the time of the messianic awakening, Anshel had received many letters—also from Nehemiah—concerning the Sabbatian movement.[196] Evidently Nehemiah had expressed himself in 1666 on the messianic tidings, but there is no way of knowing exactly what he said and on what grounds Sabbatai may have considered him as one of his prophets.

Nehemiah's story, as told to Leyb b. Ozer, was that several Polish communities had collected money for his journey to Gallipoli. When the emissaries from Lvov visited Sabbatai Ṣevi, the latter already knew that "R. Nehemiah the prophet was on his way" to him.[197] Even assuming the likelihood that Leyb confused some details and that Sabbatai heard of Nehemiah's impending arrival from the two Polish emissaries (and not the reverse), it nevertheless remains a fact that Nehemiah had left Poland *before* the emissaries saw Sabbatai. They cannot, therefore, have been the bearers of Sabbatai's invitation. In fact, Nehemiah arrived in Gallipoli toward the end of August, that is to say, about a month after the departure of the Polish emissaries. Leyb b. Ozer describes Nehemiah's mission in the following terms: Nehemiah, who was "a great scholar and the greatest kabbalist in Poland," traveled to Turkey in order to see Sabbatai Ṣevi and to get "to the root and substance" of the matter. His expenses were provided for by the Polish communities, who were eager to pay handsomely for the privilege of having the glad tidings examined and confirmed by so eminent a kabbalistic authority. "For we, the Jews in this bitter exile, are eager to hear good tidings of salvation and comfort, more especially in Poland where wickedness and [the misery of] exile abound, and every day brings new disasters and persecutions."[198] The Sabbatian accounts of the meeting of Nehemiah and the messiah are

195. Leyb b. Ozer, *ap.* Emden, p. 26. 196. MS. Shazar, fol. 55a.
197. *Ibid.*, fol. 38b. 198. *Ibid.*

pure legend, but they too suggest that Sabbatai knew of the Polish prophet before the arrival of the emissaries from Lvov.[199] Nehemiah arrived in Gallipoli on September 3 or 4, and remained for three[200] or perhaps only two[201] days. The hours which Nehemiah spent in "secret converse" with Sabbatai were of momentous consequence for the history of the Sabbatian movement.

Leyb b. Ozer, as we have seen, presents Nehemiah as a formidable kabbalist who knew the Zohar and other kabbalistic classics by heart.[202] But strangely enough neither Leyb's nor any other account of the momentous discussion at Gallipoli ascribes a single kabbalistic argument to Nehemiah. Leyb insists that they debated kabbalistic issues, but the assertion is belied by his actual account, for Nehemiah's arguments, as reported by Leyb, are of an extremely simplistic and naïvely fundamentalist kind. Nehemiah appears as the spokesman of popular apocalyptic tradition. The difference between him and Sasportas is merely this, that whereas the latter drew his anti-Sabbatian arguments from Scripture and from the writings of Maimonides, Nehemiah appealed to rabbinic Haggadah and popular apocalyptic, which he interpreted in strictly literal fashion. He took his texts not from the Zohar but from *ʾOthoth Mashiaḥ* (*The Signs of the Messiah*) and the *Book of Zerubbabel*.[203]

199. Baruch of Arezzo, *ap.* Freimann, p. 53: "[Sabbatai] asked them whether there was a prophet in their country, and they said, 'No.' Thereupon he told them: 'Know that there is a prophet, and his name is R. Nehemiah. Tell him to come to me. You shall find him at a certain place' [the legend had already fogotten that Nehemiah was supposed to come from Lvov], and they found him, indeed, at the place indicated by Our Lord. R. Nehemiah received them with the words, 'I know that when you came to Our Lord, you found him . . . in the company of many scholars. In his arm he held a small Torah scroll . . . and there was a large piece of glass to protect those present from the heat radiating from him, for he is like an angel of fire. You also kept at a distance of four cubits, because of the brightness of his light.' "

200. Leyb b. Ozer (*ap.* Emden, p. 17); Joseph ha-Levi of Leghorn (Sasportas, p. 172).

201. According to R. Samson Bacchi of Casale (Carpi, p. 18).

202. Emden, p. 26; Coenen too (p. 81) had heard that he was a prominent scholar.

203. The tract "The Signs of the Messiah" was known to him from the kabbalistic book *Abkat Rokhel*. Cf. Jellinek's *Bet ha-Midrash*, II, 58–63, and a German translation in August Wünsche, *Aus Israels Lehrhallen*, III (Leipzig, 1909), 106–17. The *Book of Zerubbabel* was printed in Constantinople in 1519; cf. Israel Levi, "*L'apocalypse de Zorobabel*," in *RÉJ*, LXVIII, 129–60; LXIX, 108–21; LXX, 57–65, and Judah Eben-Shmuel, *Midreshey Geʾullah* (Jerusalem, 1954), pp. 55–88.

On one point, however, our sources differ, though they all agree that the question of the messiah of the tribe of Joseph was the stumbling block over which the discussion broke down. According to Leyb b. Ozer it was an abstract, theoretical debate, turning on the correct interpretation of the various apocalyptic traditions and what they had to say about the messiah of the tribe of Joseph. The Christian informants, however, writing soon after the event, are unanimous in describing the debate as a battle between two claimants to the messianic office. Nehemiah did not merely argue that the messiah of the House of Joseph had not yet appeared, but actually claimed that he himself was that messiah. Until he, the son of Joseph, had fulfilled his mission, the son of David could not possibly appear, and hence Sabbatai's claims had no foundation.

The difference between the two accounts is considerable. According to the former version Nehemiah was an arch-conservative literalist, insisting with the merciless rationalism of all orthodox fundamentalists on the literal understanding of each and every statement in the texts that he considered authoritative. He therefore examined the details of Sabbatai's career for their correspondence with the predictions in *The Signs of the Messiah* and similar writings. In the absence of such correspondences, Sabbatai was automatically disqualified. His advent had not been preceded by the appearance of the messiah of the tribe of Ephraim, nor by the wars of Gog and Magog in which the son of Joseph would first be victorious but subsequently fall at the gates of Jerusalem. The final tribulation, in the course of which the Jews would be scattered in the wilderness with only a few perfectly righteous surviving, had not yet been visited upon Israel. Even the small remnant would be scattered, each escapee believing himself the only surviving Jew, until Elijah would appear and announce redemption. Only then would the son of David appear, to gather the dispersed from the four corners of the earth, and the great trumpet be blown.[204]

Nothing of the kind had happened so far, and R. Nehemiah, marshaling against Sabbatai the vast and varied tradition of apocalyptic imagination and legend, challenged the latter's messianic pretensions with his own dogged literalism. An utterly fantastic scene ensued: the Anointed of the Lord begins to argue with his challenger. He tries to prove the legitimacy of his claim and the authenticity of his

204. *Ap.* Emden, p. 17. Kahana (I, p. 97) already pointed to the minor apocalyptic midrashim as the source of these ideas.

mission not by manifestations of messianic power but by an appeal to books. Sabbatai had hitherto lived in a visionary world of his own and had succeeded in imposing this private world of his on his followers, for whom every action and gesture of the messiah was a tremendous and inspiring mystery. Suddenly he was jolted out of his private mythology and made to face the popular myth, namely, the national messianic tradition in its most literal form. His personal charm was of no avail against the spokesman of the most fantastic kind of "plain sense." Nehemiah was not susceptible to the charisma of eccentricity, and his mythological literalism was deaf to the exegetical virtuosity of Sabbatai's kabbalistic tropology. In the circumstances the disputation was foredoomed to failure. As the wrangling continued in the presence of Sabbatai's assembled court, "one kabbalistic book after the other was brought in all day long, and they angrily disputed until midnight when they ceased and slept for a few hours. Thereafter they began to argue anew, but none would yield and all proofs adduced by Sabbatai Ṣevi were dismissed by R. Nehemiah, who said that they were vanity and that Sabbatai did not understand the meaning of the kabbalistic books." It is possible, of course, that Sabbatai appealed to kabbalistic texts to justify his interpretation of the apocalyptic midrashim, but Leyb's account certainly does not substantiate the assertion that Nehemiah used kabbalistic arguments. On the contrary, it appears that Nehemiah's main point was the inadmissibility of kabbalistic allegory in interpreting apocalyptic texts. The messianic events had to be a literal fulfillment of the traditional apocalypses, or they were no messianic events. A disputation between Sabbatai Ṣevi and Sasportas would probably have followed very similar lines, with rabbinic texts being substituted for popular apocalypses.

A very different story is told by the Christian writers in Turkey, who had obtained their information from Jewish eyewitnesses:

These two great Rabbins being together, a hot Dispute arose between them. For [Nehemiah] *Cohen* alleged, That according to Scripture and Exposition of the Learned thereupon, there were to be two Messiahs, one called *Ben.* [!] *Ephraim* and the other *Ben.* [!] *David:* the first was to be a Preacher of the Law, poor and despised, and a Servant to the second, and his Fore runner; the other was to be great and rich, to restore the Jews to *Jerusalem*, to sit upon the Throne of *David,* and to perform and act all those Triumphs and Conquests which were expected from *Sabatai. Nehemiah* was contented to be *Ben. Ephraim,* the afflicted and poor Messiah, and *Sabatai* was well enough contented he should be so; but that *Nehemiah* accused him for being too forward in publishing himself as the latter Messiah, before *Ben. Ephraim* had first been known to the World; *Sabatai* took this reprehension so ill, either out of pride and thoughts of his own Infallibility, or that he suspected *Nehemiah* being once admitted for *Ben. Ephraim,* would quickly, being a subtle and learned Person, perswade the World that he was *Ben. David,* would by no means understand or admit of this Doctrine, or of *Ben. Ephraim* for a necessary Officer: and thereupon the Dispute grew so hot, and the Controversie so irreconcileable, as was taken notice of by the Jews, and controverted amongst them as every one fancied; but *Sabatai* being of greater Authority, his Sentence prevailed, and *Nehemiah* was rejected as Schismatical, and an Enemy to the Messiah which afterwards proved the ruine and downfal of this Imposture.[205]

According to this version the argument was not about points of exegesis. Nehemiah's role was that of the prospective martyr messiah of the House of Joseph who had not yet begun his ministry. For the time being he was still a poor and unknown rabbi. But as long as he had not even begun to fulfill his mission and start on the road to messianic martyrdom, Sabbatai had no right to proclaim himself the Davidic redeemer. All chances of a compromise were shipwrecked on the rock of Nehemiah's dogmatic obstinacy. Sabbatai, the Christian sources suggest, would have been ready to compromise and recognize Nehemiah's claim, even though he had previously declared a former disciple of his, a victim of the Chmielnicki massacres in 1648, to have been the messiah of the tribe of Joseph.[206] But no agreement was possible on the relationship of the two messiahs, since Nehemiah insisted that the son of David could not manifest himself until after the messiah of the House of Joseph had fulfilled his mission. Confirma-

205. Rycaut, p. 213; see also Coenen, pp. 81–82 and the two Armenian accounts *ap.* Galanté, pp. 93, 105.

206. On this point Coenen and Leyb b. Ozer are in agreement. But although Coenen was the main source of Leyb's memoir, Leyb did not necessarily depend on him for this particular detail. Leyb had many additional sources for his account of the debate with Nehemiah, chief among them Nehemiah's own story. It is not known whether "R. Abraham Zalman" really existed and, if he did, whether he had ever been one of Sabbatai's early disciples in Smyrna.

tion of this version of the debate is provided by R. Samson Bacchi of Casale, who states that Nehemiah described himself as the "avenger of the blood,"[207] meaning, the messiah of the tribe of Joseph who takes revenge upon the gentiles for the Jewish blood that they have shed.

There seems to be little room for doubt that historical and psychological verisimilitude are in favor of the second version, though certain elements of the first version should be combined with it.[208] The absence, in the former version, of any mention of Nehemiah's messianic claim is easily explained. Nehemiah himself suppressed this inglorious detail when, as an old man, he told his story in 1690, shortly before his death, to Leyb b. Ozer. There is no reason why the informants of Coenen and Rycaut should have invented the story which, as a matter of fact, receives indirect confirmation not only from Sasportas' references to Nehemiah's "madness," but also from an explicit statement by Leyb b. Ozer himself: "It was said that he proclaimed himself as the future messiah of the House of Joseph" during his wanderings in Poland and Germany after 1666. Reporting this rumor, Leyb, in the innocence of his heart, even wondered how Nehemiah *Kohen* ("the priest"), that is, a descendant of the House of Aaron of the tribe of Levi, could possibly be a member of the tribe of Ephraim; he evidently did not realize that logical considerations of this kind were not always relevant in matters of faith. In striking contrast to Sabbatai, Nehemiah was a messianic pretender without imaginative originality. His imagination enabled him to envisage himself as the future martyr messiah of the tribe of Joseph and to apply to himself all the associated traditional expectations in their most rigidly literal form. But he was incapable of an original and personal re-creation or recasting of the apocalyptic traditions. However, once posed by Nehemiah, the problem of the messiah of the House of Joseph became a permanent and often burning issue in the Sabbatian movement.

The acrimonious debate continued "for three days and nights, during which they scarcely ate and drank, and had very little sleep.

207. Carpi, p. 18 (there is a lacuna in line 4).

208. Is. Sonne has proferred the theory that the whole episode of Nehemiah was nothing but a clever maneuver instigated by Sabbatai himself in order to pave the way for his own long-planned apostasy. Nehemiah was sent on a secret mission to Adrianople to bring about the climax. There is no shred of evidence for this construction of a conspiracy, which misjudges Sabbatai's character completely. Cf. Sonne in *Sefunoth,* III–IV (1960), 62–66.

He [Nehemiah] would not admit any of Sabbatai's proofs and arguments. The rabbis [present] were at a loss, but inclined toward Sabbatai."[209] According to Nehemiah's account (as given to Leyb), the altercation culminated in a furious outburst in the course of which Nehemiah accused Sabbatai of plunging Israel into deadly peril by his lies and deceitful pretensions. He even called him an "enticer and renegade" who deserved the death penalty according to Jewish law. The situation having come to a head, Nehemiah suddenly ran away, shouting to the Turkish guards that he wanted to become a Muslim. For a circumcised Jew this required little formality: he merely had to throw away his Jewish headgear and don a Turkish turban. Nehemiah was immediately taken to Adrianople where he denounced Sabbatai for fomenting sedition. Soon afterward he returned to Poland and "greatly repented."[210]

Contemporaries were divided on the subject of this spectacular though brief apostasy. Nehemiah indicated that he had been running for his life, as he had reason to fear violence at the hands of Sabbatai's supporters.[211] On the other hand, he also hinted that his action was prompted by the purest and most laudable motives; in fact, he wanted to save Jewry from disaster.[212] The latter explanation was generally accepted and indeed was quoted (on the authority of reports from Smyrna) by R. Joseph ha-Levi of Leghorn in a letter written in the second half of November, 1666.[213] The explanation would obviously recommend itself to the unbelievers, and Coenen too had heard it from several rabbis in Smyrna.[214] Nehemiah's behavior after his return to Lvov was conspicuous for "strict observance of the Law and exceeding piety." He declined to answer questions regarding Sabbatai Ṣevi and merely said, "Wait for the true Messiah, but not for this one."[215]

209. Emden, p. 17. 210. Sasportas, p. 345.

211. Leyb, *ap.* Emden, p. 17, "they intended to kill R. Nehemiah," and *ibid.,* p. 18, "he was much afraid, . . . for he saw them whispering to one another." These quotations, however, are Emden's paraphrase of Leyb's account which, according to the original MS., merely said, "they would have liked to kill him, but were afraid of the Turkish guards around the fortress."

212. Emden, p. 18; MS. Shazar, fol. 54b.

213. Sasportas, p. 174. This is the first known reference to Nehemiah's apostasy, about ten weeks after the event.

214. Coenen, p. 83.

215. Sasportas, p. 175, on the authority of informants from Poland who had spoken to Nehemiah.

Other and contradictory versions of the sequel to the apostasy were current too, but they imply a degree of inconsistency and fickleness on the part of Nehemiah which seems incompatible with his firmness and consistency in the debate with Sabbatai. In any event, Leyb's version, which no doubt reproduces Nehemiah's own story, does not inspire much confidence. Nehemiah is said to have been brought before the Great Vizier in Constantinople, in whose presence he converted to Islam. The vizier then wrote a letter (whose contents is reproduced by Leyb) to the sultan, recommending that Nehemiah be admitted to the royal presence in order to give a personal account of the events. Nehemiah was duly admitted and told the sultan that Sabbatai was an impostor who tried to sow sedition among the Jews, but that the Jews were innocent.[216] All this is, of course, pure fiction. The vizier was away from Constantinople at the time, making war against Crete, and Nehemiah never saw the sultan but only some court officials.[217] There is no evidence of his journey from Adrianople to Constantinople. The formal declaration of conversion to Islam was made before the cadi of Gallipoli on September 5 or 6.[218] Nehemiah probably went straight from Gallipoli to Adrianople, denounced the Sabbatian "plot," and returned to his native country and religion. In his old age, it appears, he told a more boastful version of his exploits to Leyb b. Ozer.

As a matter of fact his subsequent career too was not free from scandal. Leyb, after recounting Nehemiah's version of the story, significantly adds, "but according to what I have heard,[219] he returned to Poland and said that Sabbatai was truly the messiah, the son of

216. *Ap.* Emden, p. 18.

217. Cf. Rycaut, p. 213: "[Nehemiah] took a Journey to Adrianople, and there informed the Chief Ministers of State and Officers of the Court, who . . . [until then had] heard nothing of all this concourse of people, and Prophecies of Revolt of the Jews. . . . And taking likewise to his Counsel some certain discontented and unbelieving Cochams [rabbis], who being zealous for their Nation . . . took liberty to inform the Chimacam (who was Deputy for the Great Vizier then at Candia [Crete]) that the Jew Prisoner at the Castle was a lewd person [and a rebel]." Rycaut makes no mention of Nehemiah's apostasy.

218. According to Coenen (p. 82), on September 5.

219. Thus the original reading in MS. Shazar. The printed version *ap.* Emden (p. 26), omits the contrastive "*but* according to what I have heard . . . ."

David, who would redeem Israel. He seduced many people in Poland, adhering to the Sabbatian faith and calling himself the future messiah of the House of Joseph. In the end the Polish rabbis excommunicated and expelled him, and he departed from there and wandered through Germany. Some say that there he called himself the messiah of the House of Joseph." Possibly Nehemiah was really excommunicated and expelled from Poland because of his claims to the messiahship of the House of Joseph and not because of any Sabbatian beliefs. A confusion of this kind, however, seems strange even in so confused a writer as Leyb. Perhaps the "believers" spread these rumors about Nehemiah in order to avenge themselves on the traitor who had informed against the messiah.[220] Alternatively, we must assume Nehemiah to have been of a strangely erratic and fickle disposition. It is not impossible that he was genuinely loathed by most Jews (except by inveterate unbelievers such as R. Joseph ha-Levi) for having acted the part of a Judas, and that the "madness" which had been overlooked prior to 1666 was now used as an excuse to persecute him. In any event, it is a fact that henceforth he wandered about, changing his name in an attempt to conceal his identity and avoiding all places where he might be recognized by former acquaintances.

VI

Lacking the relevant documents from the Turkish archives, it is impossible to determine to what extent Nehemiah's action was the immediate cause of the subsequent events. No doubt the Jewish masses considered Nehemiah as the chief villain of the piece, but there are good reasons for believing that other factors had been at work also. Rycaut, it is true, claims that the "chief Ministers of State and Officers of the Court . . . [had] heard nothing . . . [of the] Revolt of the Jews from their obedience to the Grand Signior," but his statement is hardly credible. Even assuming that the central government and the court, which resided at the time in Adrianople, received no direct reports from Gallipoli "by reason of the gain the Turks [that is, the commander and the guards] made of their Prisoner at the Castle on the Hellespont," it is extremely unlikely that the authorities in Constantinople remained unaware of what was going on in the immediate vicinity of the capital. From our Armenian source (see above, p. 617)

220. Cf. the story quoted above, n. 199, which seems to be a Sabbatian invention.

we learn that Sabbatai's "seditious" proclamations regarding the abolition of the fast and the institution of the "Feast of the Nativity of Our King and Messiah" had promptly been translated into Turkish by the chief translator of the sultan, and there is no reason to assume that the translation was not forwarded to the proper quarters. As a matter of fact, the Armenian accounts (of which at least one was composed soon after Sabbatai's apostasy and in any case no later than 1667) mention complaints to the authorities apart from the denunciation by the "rabbi from Poland." The Armenian source confirms Rycaut's account, according to which Nehemiah's testimony to the authorities in Adrianople was brought to the attention of the kaimakam Mustapha Pasha who acted as "Deputy of the Great Vizier then at Crete." But even before Nehemiah's arrival, a certain sheikh Mahmud who lived near the Dardanelles had appeared before the local cadi (in Gallipoli?) together with several Turkish notables and reported on what was going on at the fortress. Their deposition was duly taken down and the sheikh proceeded to Adrianople where he submitted the documents to the kaimakam. The complaint, it seems, was directed against the sirdar (the local commander) who permitted all this commotion for his own profit while the Turkish population suffered from a shortage of food and rising prices, owing to the influx of so many visitors.

The two Armenian accounts as well as Rycaut state that the complaints also included charges of immorality. According to the Armenian poem, Sabbatai "was found to have relations with women,"[221] and the prose account mentions accusations of lewdness and "debauches with women and with favorites."[222] Rycaut states that the rabbis who accompanied Nehemiah to the kaimakam testified that Sabbatai "was a lewd person."[223] These accusations, surprising and strange as they may seem, cannot be dismissed lightly. They were certainly not invented by Rycaut and the Armenian authors, who merely reported the charges actually brought against Sabbatai. It is true that accusations of libertinism and immorality against "heretics" are almost standard procedure in the history of religions. In this par-

221. "Il fut trouvé en rapports avec des femmes" (Galanté, p. 94).

222. *Ibid.*, p. 106. It is difficult, on the basis of Galanté's French translation (*favoris*), to determine whether the Armenian original referred to homosexual relations or to female concubines.

223. Rycaut, p. 213.

ticular case the reproaches may also reflect the unenviable reputation of Sarah, who had joined her husband at the Tower of Strength. Debauchery had not been a characteristic trait of Sabbatai's behavior as long as he was a Jewish rabbi, and—judging from the extant polemical literature—even his enemies never accused him of it during the early period. Rumors of this kind seem to be hinted at in a letter of Sasportas to Raphael Supino (May, 1666), where Sabbatai's misdeeds are said to include "things that cannot even be mentioned, as trustworthy witnesses have reported."[224] A comparison with Sasportas' autograph, however, shows that these words do not occur in the original text but were added later in the "revised" version of the letter.

There are, however, several puzzling testimonies which should discourage us from dismissing the accusation too summarily. We are told that in Smyrna "three virgins were delivered into his hands. He kept them for several days and then returned them, without having touched them."[225] The believers would hardly have offered their daughters unless at the messiah's express command. The fact that Sabbatai did not touch the maidens does not render his conduct any less disconcerting. Similar incidents are reported from the period following his apostasy: Sabbatai took a betrothed girl away from her fiancé and returned her after some time, allegedly without having touched her (see p. 879). Even more puzzling is Abraham Cuenque's idealized account of Sabbatai's residence at the Tower of Strength. This ardent and pious believer tells us how all the rabbis flocked to the messiah in order to submit to him their queries and difficulties in matters of rabbinic law, and that Sabbatai was attended by "seventy beautiful virgins, the daughters of the most illustrious rabbis, all dressed in royal apparel. Sarah was like unto a queen."[226] Cuenque's account may be exaggerated or altogether fictitious. But if this kind of legend was current among pious believers in Palestine, then one cannot help wondering whether it did not have foundation in certain facts. In any case, the description is oddly reminiscent of similar—and anything but legendary or "platonic"—arrangements at the court of Jacob

224. Sasportas, p. 98.

225. Galanté, pp. 85, 97, on the authority of Armenian sources. Cf. also above, ch. 4, n. 244.

226. *Ap.* Emden, p. 41. It is not quite clear whether Moses Ḥagiz's remark (*ibid.*) to the effect that Sabbatai called seven virgins to the reading of the Law refers to a specific occasion or to a regular ritual.

Frank. Cuenque's testimony, given in good and simple faith, should not be lightly set aside, particularly as it admits that the complaints to the Turkish authorities also mentioned "unbearable . . . abominations committed at the king's [meaning, Sabbatai's] court." The pious believer in Hebron thus bears out the statements made by the Armenian writer. For all we know there may have been tendencies in Sabbatai which remained suppressed for a long time by his ascetic way of life, but which erupted sooner or later. Perhaps his behavior was also influenced by his wife and by his own ideas regarding the messianic liberation of women from the yoke of their husbands.

Rumors of libertinism increased considerably after the apostasy and, judging from what the believers themselves said on the subject, not without reason. Perhaps the "abominations" which Sabbatai perpetrated at that time were projected back on the earlier period before his apostasy.[227] As a matter of fact, it is not easy to see why Sabbatai's accusers at Gallipoli and Adrianople should have thought that the Turkish authorities would be particularly scandalized by charges of sexual relations with several women. Nevertheless the various indications cannot simply be dismissed. More recently, important and weighty testimony has come to light, to the effect that Sabbatai prided himself on his ability to have intercourse with virgin women without actually deflowering them.[228] The same source mentions, in addition to this example of erotic perversity, instances of antinomianism such as treading *tefillin* under foot or tearing up a Torah scroll and trampling upon it.[229] This behavior agrees well with the mood exhibited by Sabbatai's benediction "that hast permitted that which is forbidden." I have already suggested (see above, p. 242) that the ritual consumption of forbidden animal fats, preceded by his blasphemous

227. Moses ibn Ḥabib (*ap.* Emden, p. 53) quotes the testimony of a believer who had apostatized but subsequently returned to the Jewish faith. This eyewitness alleged that the accursed Sabbatai "wearing the *tefillin* [phylacteries] on his head, had intercourse with a boy and declared that this was a great [mystical] *tiqqun*." In the absence of more reliable evidence, the testimony of this "penitent" ex-Sabbatian should be treated with reserve. However, the charges brought before the authorities at Gallipoli also included immoral relations with *favoris;* cf. above, n. 222.

228. Is. Tishby in *Sefunoth,* III–IV (1960), 89, quoting from the writings of R. Elijah Mojajon (MS. Günzburg 517).

229. *Ibid.,* pp. 88–91. Similar rituals concerning the desecration of a Torah scroll are testified to by autobiographical stories told by Jacob Frank.

benediction, was essentially a symbolic expression of the abolition of all sexual taboos and prohibitions.

Once formal complaints were lodged, the authorities in Adrianople seem to have acted swiftly. Nehemiah took the turban on September 5 or 6. On September 12 or 13, four messengers arrived from Adrianople to fetch the prisoner.[230] All at once the stir and bustle and joyful exuberance at Gallipoli stopped short. The Jews were chased away with blows. Sabbatai was not even allowed "an hours space to take solemn farewell of his Followers and Adorers";[231] he was put into a carriage and transported under strong escort to where the sultan held court.[232] There, no doubt, consultations had been held in the meantime as to what to do with the prisoner. The ambassador of the Hapsburg emperor in Constantinople reported that the mufti (presumably, the sheikh al-Islam, the highest religious dignitary in

230. No value is to be placed on de la Croix's account (p. 369) of the termination of Sabbatai's imprisonment in Gallipoli. De la Croix had never heard of Nehemiah's visit and thought that the authorities had been prompted to take action by the festivities held on 9 Ab. The sultan's attention having been drawn to the celebrations held by the Jews, he ordered an investigation and severely reprimanded the kaimakam Mustapha Pasha. However, the speeches attributed to the sultan and the kaimakam, as well as certain other details, suggest that the whole scene forms part of the "historical novel" with which de la Croix filled the lacunae in his information.

231. Rycaut, p. 214.

232. According to Coenen (p. 84) this happened on September 12; R. Joseph ha-Levi (Sasportas, p. 172) says 13 Ellul = September 13, and adds that the commotion at Gallipoli was stopped on the day of Nehemiah's apostasy: "on the same day all the Jews were driven away with hard blows, and a report sent to the sultan at Adrianople." Other sources suggest an earlier date, e.g., de la Croix, where Sabbatai is said to have arrived in Adrianople on September 14. Rosanes' account (vol. IV, pp. 428–29) is inexact and faulty; there is no evidence that Sabbatai passed through Constantinople. According to the French *Relation* (p. 29) the mufti and the religious dignitaries had complained to the sultan about the scandal of the Sabbatian agitation, but the account is not borne out by any other source; the Jesuit author had evidently not heard of Nehemiah's visit. The Armenian accounts report (Galanté, pp. 94, 106) that the kaimakam had first sent an officer with orders to hang Sabbatai immediately in Gallipoli, but that soon afterward a second messenger arrived with the counterorder to bring Sabbatai alive to Adrianople "lest they spread the rumor that he [Sabbatai] had ascended to heaven and someone else had been hanged." When Sabbatai passed through the streets of Gallipoli, the believers bribed the escort to be allowed to see the prisoner. These reports may well be based on facts.

Turkey) was consulted and that he advised them to refrain from any action that might cause the Jews to regard Sabbatai as a saint or a martyr.[233] Abraham Miguel Cardozo, writing in 1668, similarly stated that the Muslim religious authorities advised against taking his life "lest they make a new religion."[234] Perhaps the original decision had been to put Sabbatai to death immediately, but as a result of further deliberations it was resolved to bring him alive to Adrianople (cf. above, n. 232).

The prisoner arrived in Adrianople—some 150 miles from Gallipoli—on September 15, and on the following day was brought to the sultan's court.[235] According to a Jewish report, Sabbatai was accompanied by three rabbis who subsequently also followed him into apostasy.[236] There was great excitement among the Jews in Adrianople, many of whom believed that the hour had come when the messiah would take the sultan's crown and place it on his own head. Robert de Dreux, the chaplain at the French embassy in Constantinople, who happened to be in Adrianople at the time, has left us a vivid eyewitness report. In the morning hours he heard, all of a sudden, a great clamor in the street, and looking out the window he beheld crowds of Jews running about and spreading carpets on the pavement. The Jewish innkeeper informed him that they were preparing the roads along which the messiah would pass, as was the duty of subjects toward their sultan. When de Dreux made a mocking remark, the innkeeper's

233. Graetz, vol. X, p. 455, quoting Count Gautier de Leslie.

234. *Ap.* Freimann, p. 90.

235. The date is confirmed by several sources. According to de la Croix (p. 372) Sabbatai arrived on September 14, but Coenen's dates (pp. 84–85) are more reliable. Both Sabbatai Ṣevi (in a letter written after the apostasy; cf. Coenen, p. 86) and the Turkish sources quoted by Galanté (pp. 80–82) state that the audience at the Divan took place on September 16. The Turkish date given in Hammer, *Histoire de l'Empire Ottoman*, XI (1838), 241 (24 Rabiᶜa al-Awwal 1077 = September 24, 1666) must be a mistake. The French *Relation* (p. 30) says that the apostasy took place on September 17.

236. A letter written in Amsterdam on November 23, 1666 (MS. Hottinger, fol. 350a) reports that news had been received from Christian merchants in Smyrna of Sabbatai's apostasy, "but our Jews have received no such news. On the other hand, they have been informed that the King [that is, Sabbatai] left Gallipoli on September 13 and traveled in a carriage (*en carosse*) accompanied by three rabbis. He arrived in Adrianople on September 16 and was received by the Grand Turk with great honors, but nothing was written to them about his having turned Turk."

eldest son told him "there is nothing to scoff at, for before long you will be our slaves by the power of the messiah."[237] Leyb b. Ozer had heard from eyewitnesses that Sabbatai, as he was "led to the sultan's court on Thursday, September 16, was accompanied by many rabbis, and the Jews prayed for him saying the Priestly Blessing [Num. 5:24–26], and accompanied him to the palace. On the way he told them: 'Behold what I have done; I am going to the king [girt] with a green and miserable belt, and I am much distressed about this.' When they heard him thus they were afraid and their spirit melted away; and they said: 'First he said that he was about to take the crown from the sultan's head, and now he is afraid of appearing before him in a green belt.' "[238]

Many and conflicting versions of what happened at this memorable interview are given in the diverse Sabbatian, "infidel," and Christian reports. The Turkish sources, which might have given us the most reliable accounts, unfortunately mention what was to them a negligible incident only briefly and without going into detail. Even so the little information which they give us is highly interesting. We learn that what actually took place was not a formal audience with the sultan (as suggested by the Jewish and Christian accounts), but a meeting of a kind of Privy Council.[239] These "cabinet" meetings were normally watched by the sultan from a latticed alcove (Turk., *kafes*). The sultan, though not formally present, thus saw and heard everything, and could always intervene in the

237. Robert de Dreux, *Voyage en Turquie,* publié et annoté par H. Pernot (Paris 1925), p. 41: "Cette nation . . . reçut une extrême confusion, dans le temps que nous étions à Andrinople, dont je fuis en quelque façon témoin, car étant logé sur la rue et entendant, de grand matin, le bruit de beaucoup de personnes qui passaient, . . . je vis quantité d'hommes qui passaient et qui portaient des bêches, des hoyaux, des pelles et autres instruments à remuer la terre et m'étant informé où ils allaient j'appris qu'ils allaient applanir le chemin pour lequel leur Messie allait arriver. Et parce que je me raillais d'eux le fils ainé du Juif où nous étions logés me dit que je n'avais que faire de rire, parce que dans peu de temps nous allions tous devenir leurs esclaves par la vertu de leur Messie." I am indebted for this reference to my colleague A. J. Duff.

238. MS. Shazar, fol. 40b. Emden (p. 18) introduced exaggerated figures into his Hebrew edn. of Leyb's memoir.

239. The relevant passages from the writings of two contemporary Turkish historians, Abdi Pasha and Mehemed Rashid, have been translated from the original MSS. by Galanté, pp. 80–82. The Turkish text is now available in Ibrahim Gövsa, *Sabatay Sevi* (Istanbul, n. d.), pp. 47–52.

Deß vermeinten Jüdischen Messiæ entdeckter Betrug und Absall.

Wie solches aus Constantinopel von glaubwürdiger Hand / unter dem dato des 10. und 20. Novemb. Anno 1666. nacher Wien/ und von dar an andere Oerter berichtet worden.

DEm günstigen Leser wird zweifels ohne wissend seyn/ was gestalt hiebevor mit zwar ungleichen Bericht/ die Avisen / von dem vermeinten Juden Messia / unterschiedliches spargiret haben / woron das Gewisseste / daß selbiger Zeithero in einen 10. oder 12. Meilwegs von Adrianopel gelegenen Schloß / in Arrest oder Verhafft gehalten worden / umb zu vernehmen/ was aus diesen/durch die gantze Türckey erschollenen Geschrey/und aus diesem Propheten/ von welchen auch viel Türcken etwas halten wollen/ werden möchte. Wehrendes solches Arrests nun haben sich die Juden/ aus Constantinopel und Adrianopel/ wie auch von andern fernen Orten/häuffig bey solchem gefangenen Messia eingefunden / ihme sehr reiche Verehrung an Gold/ Silber / Kleinodien und Geld gethan/ und was sie vor Wunder und Zeichen von ihme gesehen / in dem Land allenthalben sehr gepreiset. Deßwegen dann der Zulauff immer je grösser worden / also daß sich eine zimliche Theurung und Brodmangel dieses Orts ereignet / sich auch selbiger Schloß-Hauptmann oder Commendant einer Rebellion oder Ausstands täglich besorgen müssen; Weßwegen er sich dañ bey der Ottomannischen Porten Raths erholet/ und um eyligste Hülffmittel gebeten. So bald solcher Bericht an der Porten eingeloffen / hat der Türckische Kayser einen Chiausen/nebens etlich tausend Janitscharen abgeordnet/ mit Befehl an den Schloß-Hauptmañ/ gedachten Juden-Messiam schleunigst nach Adrianopel (woselbst der Türckische Kayser/der Zeit residirte) zu liefern. Als die Juden solches mit grosser Bestürtzung vernommen/ erboten sie sich dem Schloß-Hauptmann eine Verehrung von 10000. Reichsthal. zu thun/damit solche Lifferung nicht bey Tag/ sondern bey Nacht geschehen möchte / zu Vermeidung besorgliches Schimpfs und Spotts/ so von dem gemeinen Pöfel / ihrem Propheten geschehen möchte; Aber weil solches wider deß Kaysers Befehl/ also kunten sie nichts erhalten.

Als man nun kaum diesen Lugen-Propheten zu Adrianopel eingebracht hatte / lieff der Pöfel mit grossem Geschrey häuffig zu / wurffen ihn mit faulen Obst/ Melonen und Koth/ daß die Quardi gnug zu thun hatte / selbigen gantz nacher des Kaysers Pallast zu bringen / woselbst der Kayser sein mit Verlangen erwartete / und ihn in Beyseyn deß Obristen Mufti, das ist der vornehmste Priester/ und eines Efendi oder Schrifftgelehrten / und des gantzen Raths/ folgender Gestalt anredete: Weil die Juden dich für ihren Messiam halten/ und du so viel Zeichen und Wunder gethan hast/ so verlangen wir auch ein Wunderzeichen/ oder grosses Werck von dir zu sehen; Widriges falls/ wird der zugegen stehende Scharffrichter ein Wunderzeichen thun / daß du umb ein Kopff wirst kürtzer werden. Der vermeynte Messias antwortete hierauf mit tieffer Reverentz und lächlenden Mund/ daß solches ein falscher Rumor/ und sprach: Ich hab die Zeit meines Lebens kein Wunder gethan / werde auch jetzunder keines wircken mögen / diß zwar laugne ich nicht/ daß ich in meiner Jugend studirt / und in den Jüdischen Ceremonien und Gesetzen mich bester massen geübet. Diesen nun hat meinen Glaubensgenossen/ den Juden / einen falschen Wahn verursachet / daß sie mich für den Messiam gehalten / und angefangen mich zu verehren und beschencken; Weil ich nun gesehen / daß durch diß Mittel ich mich nicht wenig würde bereichern/hab ich sie in solchen Gedancken bleiben lassen/ auch ihnen Rath und Unterricht mitgetheilet/ wie das gemeine Wesen in Flor und Wachsthum möchte gebracht werden/ mich aber selbsten niemal in solchen Selbst-Betrug einführen lassen/ daß ich der Messias wäre/ sintemal der von den Propheten weißgesagte/ und von den Juden erwartende Messias schon längsten kommen ist.

Hierauf antwortete der Käiser: Wohlan eines auß beyden resolvire dich / entweder daß du ein Türck werden / oder diese Viertelstund deinen Kopf verliehren wollest? Er antwortete: Mein Leben hier zu lassen bin ich zwar nicht gesinnet/ sondern vielmehr den Mahumethischen Glauben / als zu welchen ich schon lang ein Verlangen getragen / anzunehmen. So diß dir ein Ernst / sagte der Mufti, so ist nöthig/ daß du mit aufgereckter Hand / nach Türckischem Gebrauch / aydlich bekennest / daß der Messias kommen sey. Als er nun solches gar willfährig gethan / hat der Türckische Kayser befohlen / ihn mit einem Zobel-Beltz zubekleiden/ und für täglichen Unterhalt $1\frac{1}{2}$ Reichsthaler zureichen. Hierauf ist er zu den Obristen Præsidenten geführet worden / mit Befehl ihn Türckisch zu kleiden. Als man ihme nun seine alte Kleider abgethan / hat man darinnen 4. Pfund Piscoten oder zwey gebacken Brod gefunden/ wovon er heimlich gegessen/ und die Juden also geblendet/ und überredet/ er faste eine gantze Wochen über/ und wurde durch einen Engel gestärcket / darinn er sich in beyseyn der thörichten Juden aller Speise enthalten / und inzwischen die Bibel oder Altes Testament gelesen / welches Buch dann mit Gold/ Edelsteinen und Diamanten auf das künstlichst und kostbarste gezieret war; Heimlich aber hat er ihme durch einen vertrauten Diener solches Brod uñ Wasser wie auch andere Speisen heimlich zutragen lassen: Kaum als solcher Abfall geschehen/ ist ein Jüdischer Abgesandter auß Polen mit vielen Geschencken bey ihme ankommen/ als er aber vernommen daß der Messias ein Türck worden / hat er sich gleichfalls zu dem Türckischen Glauben bequemet/ hierauf hat auch dieser Verführer sein Ehweib / und Haußgesind hohlen lassen/ welche dann vermittelst der Geschencke sich alle zum Türcken Glauben begeben haben. Finden sich also die Juden hierüber sehr bestürtzt und schamroth / und müssen sich von jedermänniglich sehr beschimpfen und verhönen lassen / so wol von den Griechen und Armeniern/ als von den Türcken selbsten. Darinn sie sich dann offentlich vernehmen lassen / künfftig nimmermehr / einem so sich für den Messiam ausgeben würde / Glauben beyzumessen/ weilen sie schon so offt und viel betrogen/ auch deßwegen in nicht geringe Gefahr und Unkosten gebracht worden.

1. Hier wird der falsche Messias auf der Post nach Constantinopel geführet.
2. Hier wird er verhönet verspottet und mit faulen Früchten geworffen.
3. Wird vor den Türckischen Kayser gestellt.
4. Hier verläugnet er den Jüdischen und schwert auf den Türckischen Glauben.
5. Hier wird er zu den Obristen Præsidenten geführet.
6. Hier werden ihme seine Kleider außgezogen die Piscotten gefunden / und Türckische Kleider angezogen.
7. Der Polnische Juden-Gesandt wird ein Türck und verschweret seinen Glauben.
8. Hier steht der abgefallene Messias sambt seinen Dienern/ und ist Türckisch bekleidet.
9. Hier ist des Messiæ Ehweib zusehen / so auch eine Türckin worden.

The exposure of the deceit and apostasy of the pretended Jewish messiah, from an authoritative source in Constantinople under the dates November 10 and 20, 1666, via Vienna. The pictures are described as follows: (1) The false messiah is taken by courier to Constantinople. (2) He is mocked and pelted with rotten fruit. (3) He is presented to the Turkish emperor. (4) [The emperor gives him the choice between Islam and death.] Sabbatai denies the Jewish and →

accepts the Turkish faith. (5) He is taken to the Lord President. (6) His clothes are removed, biscuits [with which he had secretly relieved his "miraculous" fasts] are found on him, and he is dressed in Turkish clothes. (7) The emissary from the Jews of Poland turns Turk and renounces his faith. (8) The apostate messiah stands with his servants in Turkish clothes. (9) The messiah's wife, who also becomes a Turk. German broadsheet: *Dess vermeinten jüdischen Messiae entdeckter Betrug und Abfall* (the last of the broadsheets in the series printed probably in Augsburg, beginning of 1667)

proceedings by sending in his orders.[240] The Turkish sources as well as the French *Relation* (which was written only a few weeks after the apostasy) state that this particular meeting was attended by the following: the sheikh al-Islam; the sultan's chief preacher, Mehemed Vani Effendi;[241] the kaimakam of Adrianople, Kuru Mustapha Pasha; and several high government and court officials. Vani Effendi was a very prominent and influential personality, and enjoyed the full confidence of the extremely religious sultan. He showed a great interest in the conversion of the Jews to Islam, and no doubt had a major voice in the deliberations that resulted in the decision to present Sabbatai with the fateful choice. All except the Turkish accounts mention yet another participant at the decisive meeting. This was the sultan's physician, Mustapha Fawzi Hayati Zadé ("the son of the tailor"), an apostate Jew and a well-known personality in his time.[242] Information regarding his original Jewish name is conflicting and untrustworthy. The Hebrew translation of selections from Coenen's account, as printed in Emden's *Torath ha Qenaʾoth*, contains a long and completely fictitious interpolation in which the physician appears not as an apostate but as a devout and pious Jew by name of Moses b. Raphael Abrabanel.[243] In an extant fragment of a Sabbatian manuscript, the physician's name

240. Galanté, *ibid.*, p. 80: "Sa Majesté impériale regardait sans être vue et écoutait par la fenêtre."

241. Rycaut (p. 218) describes him as "Preacher to the Seraglio, or as we may so term him, Chaplain to the Sultan."

242. Rosanes (vol. IV, p. 116) has assembled information regarding Hayati Zadé from Turkish sources. Among Jewish authors only Tobias Kohen (*Maᶜaseh Tobiah*, *ap.* Emden, p. 46) gives the Turkish name ("Mayati Zadé," probably a printer's error duly corrected by Rosanes, p. 430). The Armenian accounts too give the name as Hayati Zadé (Galanté, pp. 95, 106). The full name is given by the Turkish sources quoted by Gövsa, *op. cit.*, p. 51. He was the son of a Jewish tailor (Hebrew, Hayat), whence the Turkish name he received later.

243. The interpolated passage has generally been considered an elaboration of Coenen's account, and its distinct and spurious character has not been recognized. The physician, who is presented as an "unbeliever" but a devout Jew, is said to have had a long talk with the sultan but not to have made any proposals as to how to deal with Sabbatai. The author of the Hebrew version evidently knew of the Turkish custom according to which the sultan himself remained invisible behind a curtain or latticed window, but he states that in Sabbatai's case the sultan departed from the rule and spoke to him personally. The story may have been copied by Emden from some Sephardi Jewish source.

is given as Isaac Zafiri, "a great sage, especially in physick. He was forced by the sultan to apostatize, and this was God's doing in order that he might save the Jewish nation."[244] In Coenen's account, the doctor's name is given as Guidom.[245] An English traveler, Edward Browne, who passed through Larissa[246] in 1669 noted in his diary: "In this Town I also heard some *Turkish* Songs, but especially concerning *Sabatai Sevi*, the famous *Jewish* Impostor, who had made a great noyse in the world, and how *Cussum Basha* so handled him, that he was glad to turn *Turk*. This *Cussum Basha* is a person much honoured by the Turks, and cryed up for his great skill and Practise in Physick."[247] Djerrah ("surgeon") Kasim Pasha was a well-known personality.[248] He was married to the sultan's sister, and at the time of Browne's visit to Larissa he was "*Visier* of *Erzerum* in Asia." In 1671–72 he was kaimakam of Istanbul and deputy for the Great Vizier, and subsequently held other high offices. He was pasha of Temesvar (Hungary) until 1665 and was later transferred to Buda, a very important appointment at the time. We do not know when he took up his new post, but on October 20, 1666, he sent a delegation to Vienna, as was the custom when a new pasha informed the emperor of his appointment; it is quite possible that before he entered his new position he was called to Adrianople

244. MS. Adler 494 (Jewish Theological Seminary of America, New York), fol. 38a. The Sabbatian character of this late 17th-century Sephardic MS. seems beyond doubt; cf. below, p. 685.

245. Leyb b. Ozer's Hebrew transliteration of the name proves his dependence on Coenen. Tobias Kohen (see above, n. 242) gives the name as Didon. Rosanes (vol. IV, p. 77) suggested that Guidom was no name at all but a corrupted form of the sobriquet *Judio* ("Jew") by which the apostate was known, but Coenen's spelling excludes the phonetic reading *Judio*. But Guidom may be a slight phonetic corruption from Cussum. Coenen would have mixed up two physicians, an apostate and a Turk.

246. The sultan's court was at Larissa from September (or October), 1668, until the spring of 1670. There is thus no intrinsic impossibility in the English traveler having heard songs and stories referring to the events of 1666 and mocking the Jewish messiah. Browne would have had no difficulty in finding translators for the Turkish songs he heard.

247. Edwarde Browne, *A Brief account of some Travels in Hungaria . . . Thessaly . . . and Friuli* (London, 1673), p. 58; see Geoffrey L. Lewis and Cecil Roth, "New Light on the Apostasy of Sabbatai Zevi," *JQR*, LIII (1963), 219–25.

248. I am indebted for the details concerning Kasim Pasha and his part in contemporaneous Turkish affairs to my late colleague, U. Heydt, who had made a special study of that period of Turkish history.

for political deliberations. It has been established (cf. A. D. Alderson, *Structure of the Ottoman Dynasty*, Oxford, 1956) that Kasim Pasha married the sultan's sister in December, 1666. But even if he was present at the Privy Council meeting that dealt with Sabbatai Ṣevi, he certainly was not identical with the Jewish apostate physician mentioned by the other Jewish and Christian sources.[249]

The fact that a Jewish apostate was present at the consultation that eventually led to Sabbatai's apostasy could not but appeal to the romantic imagination, and popular as well as scholarly accounts of the proceedings assigned a major role to the Jewish physician. A sober reading of the sources, however, suggests that the proposal to apostatize did not emanate from the doctor. This shrewd politico-religious move was decided upon by the council of high government and court officials (including, perhaps, Kasim Pasha), and the physician was called only after Sabbatai had been brought in and, as usual, had asked for an interpreter.[250] The alternatives that the physician placed before Sabbatai—to be tortured to death or to apostatize—were certainly not of his own devising but had been decided upon at the preceding consultation.

Sasportas refers to an "Epistle of the Congregation of Adrianople," that is, an official letter sent by the rabbis or the elders of the community, in which the crucial scene was described in great detail,[251] and to a similar letter by the rabbis of Smyrna[252] to the effect that Sabbatai apostatized in order to save his life. Though these two letters are no longer extant, their substance is confirmed by Coenen, Rycaut, and the Turkish accounts. The proceedings were no preconcerted game, with Sabbatai going through certain prearranged motions. He

249. As is suggested by Lewis and Roth, *loc. cit.* (n. 247 above).

250. According to Rycaut (p. 214) the "Grand Signior" himself questioned Sabbatai through his interpreter. Coenen (p. 84) and the French *Relation* (p. 31) correctly state that he was addressed "on behalf of the Grand Turk."

251. Sasportas refers to this important document once only (p. 299), but strangely enough does not reproduce the text. Although it is not improbable that such a report was written by the authorities of the Jewish community "on the spot," the fact remains that elsewhere Sasportas explicitly refers to letters from Constantinople, Smyrna, and Egypt as the sources of his information. Perhaps there really was no letter from Adrianople, and Sasportas' reference to it is due to mere confusion. It is vexing to the historian that so many of the most important sources of this story have been lost.

252. Sasportas, *ibid.* The letter is also mentioned several times by Abraham Cardozo; cf. Cardozo's letter in *Zion,* XIX (1954), 21.

was examined by the council and given a fateful choice. On being questioned, Sabbatai denied—as he had done before in similar circumstances—ever having entertained messianic pretensions or having had a share in the messianic agitation among the Jews. In fact, the French Jesuit writer affirms that Sabbatai had said as much on several occasions to Christian interlocutors who had visited him at the Tower of Strength.[253] According to the Turkish accounts, Sabbatai made a long speech, denying all the follies ascribed to him. Finally he was offered the choice between being put to death forthwith or converting to Islam "in which case we shall petition the padisha (that is, the sultan) to have mercy on you."

Sabbatai's messianic pretensions when in the presence of Jews and his emphatic denials vis-à-vis the gentiles present a curious problem. Perhaps his essentially passive character inclined him to avoid the issue with gentile questioners as long as no visible sign from Heaven had vindicated his claims.[254] We have suggested in an earlier chapter that Sabbatai exhibited initiative and action only with regard to his private world of messianic dreams and speculations. Even at the height of the movement his activities (for example, his "strange actions") never went beyond that private world of his. He never attempted to influence the course of "outer," historic events, but passively waited for things to happen. In a sense there may, after all, have been some logic and consistency in his denials: if God had not yet made manifest the kingdom of His anointed, then evidently the time had not yet come and his messianic secret should not be divulged to the gentiles. Sabbatai was no fighter, and, as it happened, his passivity saved his life. He was preordained for a messianic destiny and not for immediate martyrdom. He had suffered much sorrow and affliction, and the Lord had delivered him. Perhaps this new trial appeared to him as just another tribulation through which he had to pass, or a kind of paradoxical climax to the "strange actions" to which he had been impelled

253. *Relation,* p. 30. The author even attributes to Sabbatai the assertion that the messianic rumors may have been started by a hostile *agent provocateur* who thereby hoped to bring about his undoing. According to Sasportas (p. 172) Sabbatai later explicitly mentioned Nathan as the chief instigator.

254. This was also the explanation put forward by several Sabbatian writers. According to Cuenque (*ap.* Emden, p. 41) Sabbatai had said to the sultan's physician that "the hour had not yet come." Emden (*ibid.*) was outraged by such "inconsistency," since he altogether failed to grasp the paradoxical nature of Sabbatai's psychology.

on previous occasions. In his feverish and fitful career of messianic enthusiasm and eschatological "transvaluation of values," Sabbatai had gone a long way toward this last and crowning trial. The last step was no longer inconceivable once the borderline between the possible and the impossible had become blurred, and traditional—and indeed axiomatic—certainties and values had been inverted.

Sabbatai's course of conduct in this crisis invites, and all but enjoins, psychological speculation which, however, will always remain in the realm of sheer conjecture. We cannot even be sure that he had a clear notion of what he was doing. What we can be sure of are certain facts: having been questioned by the council and having denied any messianic pretensions, Sabbatai bought his life at the price of apostasy. The Christian accounts broadly agree on the general outline of the proceedings. Sabbatai was told that as he had fomented rebellion and caused commotion and disturbances, he was to die unless he either proved his messiahship by a miracle right away or consented to embrace Islam. The accounts differ with regard to two points: the nature of the punishment with which he was threatened and the declaration which he made as he adopted the Muslim religion. According to the French Jesuit writer, he was to be beheaded forthwith unless he apostatized; Sabbatai asked to be allowed some time for reflection, but this was not granted.[255] Other accounts report—and there is no reason to disbelieve them—that the miracle required of Sabbatai was to "be stripped naked and set as a mark to his [the sultan's] dextrous Archers; if the arrows passed not through his body, but that his flesh and skin was proof, like Armour, then he would believe him to be the Messiah and the person whom God had designed to those Dominions . . . he pretended. . . . Which if he refused to do, the Stake was ready at the Gate of the Seraglio to impale him."[256] According to Coenen,[257] Sabbatai made a simple declaration signifying his readiness to embrace Islam. A different version is presented by the English consul in Smyrna, who had heard that Sabbatai "replied with much chearfulness, that he was contented to turn Turk, and that it was

255. *Relation*, p. 31.

256. Rycaut, p. 214; see also Coenen, p. 84. The Armenian accounts (Galanté, p. 95) say that diverse other instruments of torture were held in readiness in addition to the archers with their arrows. According to Leyb's purely imaginary account (*ap.* Emden, p. 18) the arrows were to be poisoned.

257. P. 84.

not of force, but of choice, having been a long time desirous of so glorious a possession, he esteemed himself much honoured that he had an opportunity to owne it first in the presence of the Grand Signior."[258] Similar details, including a scornful and angry outburst against the Jewish religion, are also reported in the earliest Jewish account of the apostasy. Writing in November, 1666, R. Joseph ha-Levi quotes reports from Smyrna to the effect that Sabbatai had denied any messianic pretensions: Nathan of Gaza, who was the chief instigator, had anointed him and the Jews had forced the messianic role on him against his will. When the physician, "an apostate who had been forced by the sultan to change his religion many years before,"[259] asked him whether he could perform a miracle, Sabbatai answered that he could not. The physician then told him that his fate was sealed unless he converted to Islam, whereupon Sabbatai fell on his knees, imploring the sultan to accept his conversion "and he threw his [Jewish] hat down and spat on it[260] and reviled the Jewish religion and publicly desecrated the name of Heaven."[261] The joint testimony of the earliest Jewish and Christian reports cannot be easily disregarded even if we dismiss as utterly fictitious the venomous diatribe put into the mouth of the "arch impostor" by the French Jesuit. However, both the French *Relation* and R. Joseph ha-Levi of Leghorn (which is to say, the latter's Jewish informants in Smyrna) agree that Sabbatai slandered and denounced his faithful believers, and their information seems to derive from a common source. Although there are many reasons for doubting the facts in the form in which they are presented, the matter certainly requires further research.[262]

258. Rycaut, p. 214. Similarly also the Armenian account (Galanté, p. 107), where Sabbatai is said to have declared that prolonged study of the Jewish writings had convinced him of the truth of the Muslim religion to which he had secretly adhered for the last twenty years. The venomous anti-Jewish diatribe which the French Jesuit put into Sabbatai's mouth (*Relation,* pp. 32–34) is evidently unhistorical, though there may be some measure of truth in the reference to Sabbatai's discovery "twenty years ago" of the falsity of the Jewish religion. Perhaps Sabbatai really did say something about having departed from the traditional Law for the last twenty years.

259. Cf. the quotation from a Sabbatian source, above, p. 676.

260. Cf. also de la Croix, p. 374: "il jetta à terre le bonnet juif qu'il foula aux pieds."

261. Sasportas, p. 172.

262. The account quoted by Sasportas (p. 173) says that Sabbatai supported his denunciations by submitting letters written to him by the various

All sources are in agreement as to the final denouement: the sultan graciously accepted the convert, permitted him to assume his name, and appointed the onetime Sabbatai and now Mehemed Effendi (or Aziz Mehemed Effendi) to the honorary office of *kapici bashi* (keeper of the palace gates). A royal pension of 150 aspers per day was added to the honorary appointment.[263] A contemporary Turkish report says that Sabbatai "was led, with His Majesty's gracious permission, to the special bath reserved for the servants of the palace where he changed his costume. He was then clothed in robes of honor and presented with a purse full of silver."[264] The French Jesuit states that he also received valuable presents from the high court officials, and two or three purses of money from the sultan, each containing five hundred écus, or lion's silver dollars.[265] The anti-Jewish bias of the Christian writers (which renders their account of Sabbatai's denunciatory speeches somewhat suspect) is also evident in the Jesuit author's assertion that when changing Sabbatai's clothes they found on him three pounds of biscuits with which he secretly nourished himself during his alleged fasts. The biscuits were put there when nobody was watching "by his faithful servant and partner in

---

faithful Jewish communities. However, it is extremely unlikely that at his sudden arrest he quickly provided himself with a file of *pièces justificatives* to be produced at the right moment. This detail casts doubt on the whole story. Similarly, the French Jesuit's violent anti-Semitism casts serious doubts on the reliability of his account of the matter. (As a matter of fact, Sabbatai's long and violently anti-Jewish speech as given in the *Relation* is lacking in the Jesuit Jacob Becherand's first draft, finished on October 21, 1666, and published in Italian; see *Lettera mandata da Constantinopoli a Roma intorno al nuovo Messia* [Siena, 1667], pp. 7–8.) Stories of this kind may easily have originated in the passion and fury of the anti-Sabbatian polemic after the apostasy, though it is not in the least impossible that Sabbatai had said things which his believers later tried to explain away or preferred not to remember altogether.

263. The pension (Turkish, *ulufé*) is mentioned in all accounts of the apostasy. De la Croix (p. 374) mentions fifty écus per month, and similarly the French *Relation* (p. 32) puts the figure at *environ un écu et demy de paye par jour*. According to the late Prof. A. L. Mayer, one lion's dollar (écu) was worth eighty to ninety aspers at the time. This would make one and a half écus correspond to the amount of 150 aspers mentioned by Turkish as well as Hebrew sources (see Sasportas, p. 172). The Italian pamphlet (see above, n. 262), p. 7, quotes the pension as fifteen giulii per day.

264. Galanté, pp. 81–82.

265. *Relation,* p. 32, and already in the earlier, Italian, version, p. 7.

all his impostures, who also apostatized with his master." The story seems to be an obvious falsehood.[266]

A very different account of the whole matter is given by de la Croix. Writing several years after the event, de la Croix asserts that Sabbatai was not examined by the sultan's council, but that the kaimakam dispatched to him an apostate physician who described to Sabbatai in gruesome detail all the agonies which he would be made to undergo: he would be led through the streets of Constantinople with burning torches tied to his body until he was slowly burned to death. The thought of the threatened tortures filled Sabbatai with such terror that he agreed to the doctor's proposals, and on being led before the sultan immediately threw down his Jewish headgear and trampled upon it while an attendant put the white turban on his head.[267] De la Croix's version is not corroborated by any other source, and the details of the physician's speech prove it to be completely fictitious. The author had evidently heard stories, especially from Christian informants, about the apostate physician's part in the affair, and then composed his account with all his talent for belletristic dramatization and his fondness for long, invented speeches in the manner of Thucydides. Graetz, who was repeatedly mistaken in his evaluation of the available sources on Sabbatian history, was greatly taken in by de la Croix and misled to describing the act of apostasy before the sultan as a prearranged sham performance.

On one point, however, de la Croix's account coincides with the Sabbatian version of the event, for the Sabbatians too denied that any question-and-answer session had taken place at the decisive meeting at the Divan. Sabbatai's answers as reported in most sources were most embarrassing indeed for the believers, and they therefore insisted that the messiah "never opened his mouth,"[268] but passively permitted the authorities to do with him as they pleased. According to R. Abraham Cuenque, Sabbatai's only active participation consisted in answering Yes to the sultan's question whether he would be his friend and stay at the palace. As a matter of fact, the Sabbatian version, though primarily intended to sweeten the bitter pill of the messiah's

266. *Ibid.*, pp. 35–36. The Italian version (p. 8) mentions a faithful servant and assistant, but does not say that he too apostatized.

267. De la Croix, pp. 372–74.

268. Cardozo, in his letter to the rabbis of Smyrna; see *Zion*, XIX (1954), p. 13.

apostasy, had the advantage of running true to Sabbatai's temperament. De la Croix's story seems to combine the Sabbatian version current in Constantinople with Christian accounts of a prearranged game between the physician and Sabbatai, the whole combination being presented with the author's characteristic flair for romantic drama.

The Sabbatian manner of presenting the crucial events is well illustrated by Baruch of Arezzo, who tells us that

> whenever he [Sabbatai] passed, on his way [to Adrianople], through a city inhabited by Jews, he would ask the officer [commanding the escort]: "Wait for me as I want to pray in this Synagogue." . . . When it became known among the Turks [that is, Muslims] and the uncircumcised [that is, Christians] in Adrianople that the sultan had sent for Our Lord, they assumed that they would behead him immediately and kill all the Jews, as it was known that the sultan had ordered all the Jews in the city to be killed. Couriers had also been sent [with instructions] to do likewise in Constantinople, and they sharpened their swords and waited for the day when they could do with the Jews as they pleased. But Our Lord arrived in the city two days later than expected, and as he arrived in the evening it was too late to go to him [the sultan]. In the morning he appeared before the sultan, who said to him: "Peace be with thee," and he [Sabbatai] replied in Turkish: "Upon thee, peace." Thereupon a royal attendant came to him bringing a robe which the sultan had worn, and another attendant with one of the sultan's turbans, and they clothed him with these and called him Mehemed, in the name of the sultan. The sultan also gave orders that a large sum be paid to him every day. Thus the rumor got about that he had apostatized, and there was a great deliverance to the Jews. Our Lord made request before the sultan for the Jews to reverse the letters of wrath and anger which he wrote to destroy all the Jews in Constantinople . . . and no Jew suffered any harm because of this.[269]

Though pure fiction uncontaminated by historical fact, the above account is a valuable witness to the mental state of the believers. A poetic version of the event even described Sabbatai sitting down afterward, with the Zohar in his lap and adorned with *tefillin,* "laboring

269. Freimann, p. 58. For other Sabbatian accounts, cf. Sasportas, pp. 247–48.

since then and until now for Israel."[270] The believers were obviously interested in emphasizing Sabbatai's success in warding off danger from Israel. According to Abraham Cuenque,[271] the physician had said to Sabbatai: "Take the turban. If not, no Jew will escape or remain in the whole kingdom of the Turk, and the other kingdoms will see and do likewise."

The question whether Turkish Jewry was really threatened with destruction and, if so, whether Sabbatai had a share in averting the disaster will be discussed in another chapter (see below, pp. 699 ff.). We cannot a priori exclude the possibility of some such development having taken place subsequently. Sabbatian faith and fervor may well have combined two distinct events into one dramatic action. On the other hand, it is perfectly obvious that any legendary fiction would serve the believers' need to "explain" the messiah's scandalous betrayal. But however that may be, there is no doubt that nothing of the kind was as much as mentioned at the council meeting that ended with Sabbatai's apostasy. The fate of Turkish Jewry was not discussed at all, and, having witnessed Sabbatai's conversion, the sultan withdrew to his chambers.

Sabbatai's wife was not present at the crucial interview,[272] but he was permitted afterward to send for her. After her arrival from Gallipoli she apostatized under the patronage of the sultan's mother. If the rumors concerning her early childhood among Christians are more than romantic fiction, then she was already familiar with the experience of outwardly professing another religion. She certainly

270. See M. Attias, *Romancero Sefaradi* (2nd edn, 1961), pp. 177–78: "*šišin ribbón* de *juderia*/ todos iban detrás de él./ Tanto fué su fama buena,/ que en oída ḍel rey;/ que el rey *dés* que lo supo,/ lo mandara a traer./ A la entrada ḍel palacio/ *ş̌eḳina* posó en él;/ a la entrada de la puerta,/ el rey se levantó a él./ Quitó toca ḍe su cabeza/ y el su *samur* tambi̭én;/ hizó *olifé* al día,/ *kapiji* vayan con él./ Le hić̭iera un combite,/ lo mandara a traer; le hićiera poca cuenta/ y poca estima ḍel rey./ Tomó *źohar* en su pecho/ y los *tefilín* tambi̭én;/ de estonces hasta agora,/ trabajando por Israel."
The poem, a Sabbatian-Spanish *romanza,* is found in a collection of Dönmeh hymns which the late I. Ben-Zvi brought from Turkey in 1943. The last lines of the quotation above seem to indicate that the poem was composed in Sabbatai's lifetime. The detail about the Zohar and the phylacteries is also mentioned by Abraham Cuenque.

271. *Ap.* Emden, p. 41.

272. The statements found in several accounts to the effect that she apostatized together with her husband are groundless.

apostatized in obedience to her husband's wish, and possibly with genuine faith in him and his mission. Several of Sabbatai's leading devotees who had joined him in Adrianople followed his example, possibly at his demand. Sarah was henceforth called Fatima Cadin (Lady Fatima).[273] Sabbatai also agreed to take a second wife and to marry one of the queen's maids (or slave girls)—possibly in order to demonstrate his fidelity to his new religion and to put himself beyond suspicion.[274] This marriage was duly denounced by anti-Sabbatian polemicists[275] and glossed over in the Sabbatian accounts, which merely suggest that a proposal of this kind was made to Sabbatai but rejected by him.

Another legendary account of the course of events is preserved in a fragment found in a Sabbatian manuscript:[276] the physician "Isaac Zafiri" had urged Sabbatai to obey the sultan and to embrace Islam, lest he cause the destruction of the nation of the Jews. "When Our Lord heard this he made no answer. The sultan then asked the physician: 'What is it that you are saying in your [that is, the Jewish] language?' The physician answered: 'Sire, [I am persuading him] to do wholeheartedly that which you desire.' Thereupon the sultan with his own hand quickly put the white turban on Our Lord and dressed him in a special royal robe. He gave him a great seraglio for a dwelling and conferred on him a pension of [the number is lacking] aspers [piasters] per day." Later it was reported to the sultan that the new "convert ate nothing but currant bread and almonds, fasted every day and at times three consecutive days and nights. The sultan sent for him and asked him: 'Why do you not eat?' He answered: 'This is my custom since I was a youth.' The sultan then said: 'If this is his habit we must not force him to eat as it might derange him and he will not be able to pray for me and my life.' Next he told him: 'I want to give you my aunt [!] for a wife,' but Our Lord replied:

273. *Relation,* p. 40; de la Croix, p. 377.

274. *Relation,* p. 40: "on dit pourtant qu'elle a esté un peu mortifiée de voir que son mary avoit pris encore une autre femme Turque, cy-devant Demoiselle suivante de la Reyne, ou pour mieux dire une de ses esclaves qu'on a jugé à propos de faire espouser à ce nouveau Mussulman pour l'attacher plus fortement au party; ce qu'il n'a pas fait difficulté d'agréer."

275. Cf. the letter of the Egyptian rabbis *ap.* Sasportas, p. 198, and Sasportas himself, *ibid.,* p. 304.

276. MS. Adler 494, fol. 38a ff.; I have published the text in *ᵓEreṣ Yisraᵓel,* IV (1956), 192–93.

'I already have a wife and she is in Gallipoli.' The sultan immediately dispatched an escort and they brought his wife to the queen, that is, the wife of the Grand Turk, where she was dressed in royal robes and given" [here the fragment ends].

There are no indications as to Sabbatai's state of mind at the time. Statements regarding his high spirits and feverish activity at the beginning of his new life are contradicted by the earliest document from that period. In a brief note to his brother Elijah Ṣevi in Smyrna, Sabbatai wrote: "And now let me alone, for God has made me a Turk. Your brother Mehemed *kapici bashi oturak*.[277] For he spake and it was done; commanded and it stood fast [Ps. 33:9]."[278] The note, which was written on September 24, "the ninth day since my renewal according to His will," suggests profound melancholia.[279] Sabbatai's dejection may have been due to a general feeling of confusion and helplessness, and not necessarily to a recurrence of one of his depressive phases. Although one naturally cannot help wondering whether Sabbatai did not experience a fit of depression at the time of the apostasy, the surmise is not borne out by the extant accounts, with the exception of the Sabbatian sources.[280] R. Elijah Mojajon, one of the more radical Sabbatian theologians, explicitly states that when Sabbatai "took that [that is, the Muslim] robe, he did so without illumination and he had no [spiritual] knowledge of what he was doing."[281] Perhaps a tradition was current among believers to the effect that the messiah was bereft of light, that is, in a depressive phase, when he apostatized. The available evidence, however, does not permit definite conclusions on the subject, nor does it yield any suggestions as to when Sabbatai began to seek mystical explanations and justifications of his action.

277. I.e., an "honorary" kapici bashi and royal pensioner, and not an actual keeper of the palace gates who has to perform certain duties.

278. Coenen (p. 86) copied the original Hebrew wording of the note, which was shown to him.

279. Sabbatai dated the letter by a Hebrew pun. The word *dakh* means 24 [of Ellul] as well as "dejected."

280. See G. Scholem in *Qobeṣ Hoṣaʾath Schocken le-Dibrey Sifruth* (1940), p. 165.

281. Quoted by Is. Tishby, *Sefunoth,* III–IV (1960), 86–87, n. 69, from MS. Günzburg, fol. 24a.

7

AFTER THE APOSTASY

(1667–1668)

I

In order to understand the course of events after Sabbatai's apostasy, we must briefly recapitulate the developments preceding this critical turning-point, and try to realize the state of mind of the Jewish masses when the unexpected news reached them. The decisive circumstance that prevented this unique messianic revival from petering out without leaving more durable traces was, no doubt, the incipient budding of a new kind of "life-feeling." The shock of the messiah's apostasy should normally have been sufficient to shatter completely the structure of faith and hope that had been erected on the tidings announced by the prophet of Gaza, and the Sabbatian episode would have passed like a nightmare, and would have left no noticeable mark on the life and consciousness of the people. Other messianic movements had collapsed in the past without causing serious consequences. Apparently the enthusiasm had not reached down to the roots of their being, and failure, when it came, had not shaken them to the depth of their souls. Recovering from the shock of disappointment they proceeded to the order of the day with traditional formulas of comfort (such as, "the generation was not found worthy"), and the memory of the events lingered in the consciousness of the nation either as a curious freak phenomenon or as dim anguish.

This time, however, things were different. The movement had swept the whole Diaspora into its orbit and had struck deep roots in the soul of the masses. The sheer quantitative magnitude of the revival had become a qualitative factor. Something had happened in the souls of the believers, and these new, inner "facts" were no less decisive than external historical happenings. On the face of it the messianic movement, whose progress we have described in detail, exhibited a traditional character. Its strength had lain in the unexceptional penitential enthusiasm which seemed to guarantee the conformity of the revival with received and acknowledged forms of eschatological expression. The messiah's personal mystery was practically unknown in wider circles, and the little that had penetrated and that seemed to fly in the face of orthodox ideas was easily interpreted as relating to the exceptional nature of his ministry rather than as a new dispensation heralding a revolutionary messianic Law. In the consciousness of the masses there was no expectation of a messianic "transvaluation of all values" as the concrete expression of realized eschatology. Below the threshold of consciousness, however, far-reaching changes were taking place. The intensity and diffusion of the messianic propaganda ultimately produced effects that went far beyond the original intentions of its protagonists.

We should remind ourselves, in this connection, of a significant fact described in a previous chapter: in the minds of the believers imminent redemption and realized redemption came to be confused. Salvation was not merely at hand; it had already begun to be established and to make its inroads upon the old order. The arguments of the doubters to the effect that nothing had really happened so far fell on deaf ears because they took no account of the new emotional reality. The new feeling did not content itself with hopes for political redemption, although the political aspects of traditional messianism and the expectation of Israel's liberation from the yoke of the gentiles and from the degradation of exile were evidently taken for granted. However, the powerful messianic ferment produced psychological byproducts which soon acquired an autonomous life of their own. Many believers were convinced, in their enthusiasm, that the new *aion* had already begun. In fact, they had crossed the threshold into a new world. The kabbalistic doctrine, propounded by the Sabbatian circle, to the effect that the Shekhinah "had risen from the dust" provided theoretical support of this new life-feeling. The contradiction between the profusion of alleged miracles, on the one hand, and the insistence upon pure faith unsupported by outward signs on the other, was more apparent than real. In any event it was of no consequence for the believers who had already drunk deeply of the new wellspring of life-giving water. The emphasis on pure faith in the messiah as a supreme religious value, in spite of temptations and trials, produced an emotional identification with the new, messianic "reality." This emotional identification enabled many believers to persevere even in the face of hard facts. The readiness to enter the messianic kingdom transformed itself into the entry into the kingdom itself. Even before Sabbatai's apostasy the kabbalists' "world of *tiqqun*" had become an emotional reality which nothing in the realm of "outward" events could shake. The believers knew that the world of political and historical reality would soon perish as Sabbatai set out on his marvelous journey to take the crown from the sultan's head. By the time that the discrepancy between the two worlds had become painfully apparent, and Sabbatai's apostasy had shattered the naïve simplicity of the messianic faith, a new historical consciousness had already established itself which could absorb the shocks of external reality. The believers knew that they had been made free by the message of comfort and joy, and would not be discomfited by the "illusions" of the outer world. They too, no doubt, expected the fulfillment of the messianic promises in the outer, political sphere as well; but the kingdom which was already established within them could no longer perish—or could perish only amid severe struggles. New forces had arisen that could not easily be suppressed. Renan's remarks about the first Christian apostles after their hopes of immediate redemption had failed them are in every way applicable to the Sabbatian believers: "Enthusiasm and love know of no hopeless situations. They play with the impossible, and rather than despair, they violate reality."[1]

Sabbatianism as a sectarian and—in varying degrees—heretical movement grew out of the struggle between the new life-feeling and the disappointment of the hopes that had originally given birth to it. Sabbatai's apostasy had revealed the dangerous contradiction between the two levels of redemption, a contradiction which nobody had foreseen in this acute form but which now provided the basis

1. See E. Rénan, *Les Apôtres* (Paris, 1894), p. 2.

for unexpected developments. The orthodox kabbalists had never dreamed of discarding the political elements of messianism. When they added a new, mystical dimension to traditional eschatology and conceived of it as a transformation of the very essence of the cosmos, they meant to say that messianic redemption was more, not less, than liberation from the yoke of the gentiles. Historical reality, far from being abolished, served as a symbol of hidden mystical processes. "The 'ingathering of the exiles' is the ingathering of the [holy] sparks that are imprisoned in exile."[2] The structure of their thought would never have admitted any opposition between the symbol and the reality symbolized. The possibility of such an opposition had never occurred to the kabbalists, though it was implicit in their shift of the messianic emphasis to the hidden and inner spheres of the cosmos. As the messianic gospel suddenly found itself plunged into its gravest crisis, the latent contradiction emerged with full force. The contrast between symbol and reality symbolized, that is, between the outer and the inner reality of redemption, produced a profound and painful dilemma that gave birth to "Sabbatianism" as the sum total of attempts to readjust Jewish consciousness to the new situation.

The great revival of 1666 had prepared the hearts of believers for a new mode of being whose religious dimensions, however, were, in a sense, a continuation rather than a repudiation of what had gone before. The apostasy shattered both the continuity of the eschatological perspective and the simple naïveté of the Sabbatian faith. Every believer saw before him the momentous question of where to hear God's voice: in the cruel verdict of history which, to say the least, unmasked the messianic experience as mere illusion, or in the reality of the faith that had established itself in the depths of his soul. Sectarian Sabbatianism was born when many sections of the people refused to accept the verdict of history, unwilling to admit that their faith had been a vain illusion fondly invented. There was the alternative possibility of faith in an apostate messiah, but it had to be bought at the price of the naïve innocence of the original faith. To believe in an apostate messiah was to build one's hope on foundations of paradox and absurdity, which could only lead to more paradoxes. The unity and consistency of rabbinic Judaism were not affected by the one inevitable paradox inherent in it, as, indeed, in all religion and in human experi-

2. *Sefer ha-Liqqutim,* attributed to Ḥayyim Vital (Jerusalem, 1900), fol. 22c.

ence itself—that of theodicy and the sufferings of the righteous. The universal character of this anguishing paradox in no wise diminished its seriousness, but it rendered it less destructive. No doubt there was a mystery here, but one to which a pure and naïve faith could resign itself in submission and hope. The Sabbatian paradox, however, was not that of a saint who suffers and whose suffering is a mystery hidden with God, but of a saint who sins. A faith based on this destructive paradox has lost its innocence. Its dialectical premise of necessity begets conclusions that are equally marked by the dialectics of paradox.

The various Sabbatian doctrines sought to bridge the gulf between the inner experience and the historic reality that was supposed to symbolize it. They enabled believers to go on living in the growing tension between outer and inner truth by providing them with a theological system whose origin was a profound crisis and whose nature was paradox. The fact that this faith survived for several generations suggests that it expressed a dialectical process within Jewish history.

The Sabbatian believers were not necessarily conscious of the nature of the new life-feeling of which they were the exponents, but there is evidence that at least some of their opponents were not unaware of the revolutionary element that was creeping into the increasingly acrimonious polemic between believers and infidels. The latter seemed to sense the revolt long before it actually took place, and their eyes, sharpened by hostility, foresaw many subsequent developments. Their arguments, it is true, were generally restricted to expressions of anxiety and concern in connection with the believers' transgressions of rabbinic ordinance, though some writers seemed to anticipate the dangerous conclusions implicit in the "faith." Sasportas and Joseph ha-Levi accused the believers of rebelling against the authority of the Talmud and of blaspheming the ancient rabbis by suggesting that the latter did not fully understand the sense of the prohibition of pronouncing the Tetragrammaton.[3] The believers were following strange gods, substituting a new authority for the traditional rabbinic one. Joseph ha-Levi angrily denounced Nathan's advice to his followers to substitute the study of the Zohar and midrash for that of halakhic literature.[4] By substituting the kabbalistic and Haggadic classics for

3. Joseph ha-Levi's letter, *ap.* Sasportas, pp. 171, 186.

4. *Ibid.*, p. 190. Joseph ha-Levi's letter was written in November, 1666, but Nathan's counsel to which it refers was certainly given before the apostasy. Nathan's utterance is also preserved in a Sabbatian source; see Freimann, p. 96.

the traditional halakhic texts (and possibly for the Lurianic kabbalah as well), Nathan may have given expression to his desire to soften the hardened pattern of rabbinic Judaism. Such a desire would agree well with the tendency discernible in his writings of the years 1665–66, including his letters and the *Treatise on the Dragons.* The shift of emphasis from halakhah to Haggadah—which remained characteristic of later Sabbatianism, too—could easily become the prelude to a complete abolition of rabbinic authority and tradition even if originally it was not meant as such. Sasportas had earlier expressed his fear that the religion of Israel might "become two religions" and that the movement might lead to a schism. The abolition of the fasts was merely a portent of graver things to come, and his orthodox instinct sensed future developments which, at the time, had not even begun to take shape.

The new messianic life-feeling was dealt a critical blow by the apostasy. Nobody had foreseen the event, let alone its consequences. Sasportas' boastful claim that he had sounded the alarm and "predicted the apostasy long before it occurred" is not borne out by a closer examination of his letters.[5] Similar claims, albeit for very different reasons, were made by several believers, including Nathan of Gaza.[6] The Sabbatians, of course, had good reason to pretend that the apostasy had been predicted long before. The alleged prediction provided them with an illusion of continuity between the two stages of the movement and took the sting of surprise and scandal out of the unexpected betrayal.

For all the farcical absurdity of the sorry denouement, there was something genuinely tragic about it. A national revival, nourished by the tradition and historical experience of many generations, had, for the first time since the destruction of the Second Temple, aroused

5. Sasportas (p. 352) claims that he had predicted that Sabbatai would finally have no other way out but apostasy. The truth is that early in 1666 Sasportas had asked for celestial guidance and was vouchsafed an answer in a dream. The answer took the form of the vss. Job 30:5 and 27:23. The cryptic reply does not, however, mean what Sasportas later made it to mean (p. 79). As a matter of fact, Sasportas seems to have feared the possibility of an apostasy of the disappointed believers rather than of the messiah (*ibid.*, pp. 47, 166).

6. According to Coenen (p. 96), several informants in Smyrna reported that Sabbatai had prophesied that one day he would take the turban, reveal the mysteries of the Jewish religion to the Turks, and convert the Portuguese Synagogue into a mosque. Coenen himself rightly doubted the veracity of the report.

the entire Jewish people. A unique chance of a mighty renewal seemed to present itself, and the well-nigh unanimous response indicated that the seed had not been sown in vain. The "sprouting of the horn of salvation" was, at last, crowning a long and anguished history of suffering and martyrdom. No doubt the Jewish masses would have eagerly risen to action if there had been anyone to speak the word. As it was, their rediscovered pride and new self-consciousness did not go beyond empty gestures. The leaders of the movement did not think in terms of action. They looked with eyes of faith toward a passive messiah who was himself a prisoner of his psychic rhythm with its ups and downs, and incapable of any thought beyond his own suffering or, to be more exact, beyond the private visions that grew out of his suffering. Of course neither Sabbatai nor his followers should be judged by the standards of modern political action, or condemned because their behavior does not live up to our ideas of revolutionary leadership. But even judging by the standards of his own day, there is something depressing about Sabbatai's passivity. His enthusiasm during his fits of illumination spent itself on fantastic and purely personal eccentricities. Even Nathan's testimony to the effect that Sabbatai considered his agonies as symbolic of the sufferings of Israel cannot alter the fact that his inner life was autistically centered upon himself, a paranoid streak in his psychosis. Sabbatai never freed himself from the narrow circle of his private world even when he offered symbolic interpretations of his personal experiences. Also, in the extremes to which his mental illness led him he remained essentially lonely. The messianic revival bearing his name became a mass movement, but the imprint of the founder's personality was barely noticeable. Then, having reached a climax, the movement found itself suddenly at the brink of the abyss. Small wonder, then, that many believers took the jump. The crisis precipitated by Sabbatai's apostasy was a tragic moment in the history of Israel. But the tragedy also contained the seeds of a new Jewish consciousness.

II

First to announce the news of the apostasy were the Turks; a few days later confirmation also came from Jewish sources in Adrianople. Naturally enough the Jews at first refused to believe the report. The messiah might triumph or—alternatively—die a martyr's death: either eventuality was psychologically acceptable and the reaction to it more or less predictable. But it was simply inconceivable that he should apostatize, and the news came as a bolt from the blue.[7] "Wherever the Jews showed themselves, Christians and Turks would pursue them with ridicule until most of them hid in their houses for several days." The community of Constantinople was so much under the shock of the report that the Jesuit observer wondered "when they will recover from the blow."[8] Confusion reigned everywhere. The infidels were bewildered because Sabbatai was still alive and had not been put to death as a rebel. The believers were perplexed because the messiah had taken neither the sultan's crown nor the crown of martyrdom. From one of Cardozo's letters we know, indeed, that the rabbis of Smyrna argued that if Sabbatai knew himself to be the messiah, it was his holy duty to "sanctify the name of God" by martyrdom.[9] Violent emotions of high hopes crushed and of burning shame agitated the Jewish communities everywhere. "He brought ignominy upon the whole of Jewry by denying his faith and apostatizing, which nobody would ever have expected of him, . . . that a holy man, scholar, and kabbalist like him should suddenly become a renegade from the God of Israel."[10]

As the unbelievable news became confirmed beyond any possible doubt, the first halting attempts were made to justify the inexplicable. There is a surprising similarity between these early attempts at rationalization and the basic themes of later Sabbatian theology. "Some of the believers pretended that the new Muslim still was their true messiah, but that he had to disguise himself for a while for the better success at the execution of his great design."[11] The explanation seemed so utterly ridiculous to the Jesuit observer in Constantinople that he attached no importance at all to this *persuasion frivole*. According to Sasportas "a considerable majority still adheres to their faith" and the evidence suggests that his statement holds true not only of Hamburg but also for most other communities. The belief was current, not only in Turkey but also among the Ashkenazim in Hamburg,

7. *Relation,* p. 36; "ce fut un coup de foudre."

8. *Ibid.*

9. In the version of Cardozo's letter to Smyrna, preserved in MS. Ben-Zvi Institute 2263.

10. Leyb b. Ozer, MS. Shazar, fol. 41a. Leyb adds that one would, rather, have expected Sabbatai to accept the most outrageous tortures "and to permit his limbs to be torn from him one by one."

11. *Relation,* p. 36.

that Sabbatai had not apostatized at all but had ascended to Heaven and only his "shape appeared to them in the likeness of an apostate." Like every Docetist doctrine, this view was clearly based on the assumption that nothing objectionable and ignominous (for example, suffering and death on the cross in the case of Jesus, apostasy in the case of Sabbatai) could be predicated of the messiah. In any event the Ashkenazim in Hamburg would not suffer any ill to be spoken of Sabbatai Ṣevi.[12] These initial and as yet groping attempts to account for what had happened were soon to be succeeded by more systematic doctrinal efforts.

However, in many circles and even among believers, the more usual and, as it were, standard reaction to messianic disappointments asserted itself: the messiah's apostasy plainly and conclusively proved that they had all been mistaken. Everything had been error and delusion, although there were variations in the accounts of the nature of the messianic failure. "Some said the power of evil was rampant at that time and it was thus that he [Sabbatai] could work many things [that is, miracles]. Others said that in the beginning there was in him the power of holiness, but that later the evil powers fastened themselves to him and the devil's work succeeded."[13] The latter version appears in several sources and seems to have been fairly widespread. By introducing demonological notions into the explanation of the events, an alternative evaluation of Sabbatai's person became possible. When Nathan took it over and gave it a new, positive turn, he could even assert that, as Sabbatai had entered the realm of the *qelippoth* in order to reintegrate it into that of holiness, he [Sabbatai] could be called "the king of demons"—indeed, a surprising appellation of the messiah.[14] This mythological explanation was in direct continuity with the kabbalistic view of history. In fact, the notion of the invasion of Sabbatai's soul by the powers of the *qelippah* was merely a special application of generally received Lurianic doctrines. Alongside this

12. Sasportas, p. 175. According to Coenen (pp. 90–91) similar views were held in Constantinople and Smyrna.

13. Leyb b. Ozer, MS. Shazar, fol. 54b. It is worthy of note that this view was shared by the founder of Hasidism, Israel Baᶜal Shem Tob, who is reported to have said "that he [that is, Sabbatai Ṣevi] had a spark of holiness, but Samael [that is, the Prince of Evil] caught him in his net" (*Shibḥey ha-Besht*, ed. Horodezky [1922], p. 81).

14. According to the testimony of R. Elijah Mojajon in MS. Günzburg 517, published by Is. Tishby. *Sefunoth*, III–IV (1960), 87.

view, however, also a more rational-moral explanation was advanced, which finally crystallized in the theory that the whole messianic movement had been founded on deception and intrigue.

Many disappointed believers vented their anger by cursing the apostate messiah,[15] and "many who had erred in loving him now become his enemies," according to Sasportas. The unbelievers wrote squibs and lampoons in which Sabbatai and Nathan were presented as cheats and crooks, and many former believers could not but shamefacedly agree. The brothers Frances, who had been exchanging satirical poems during the high tide of the movement (see above, pp. 516–18), now circulated their squibs throughout Italy. Not content with their original literary output, they also composed a parody in two versions of the Passover Haggadah, in which they gave full rein to their biting sarcasm. The satire is entitled "The order of the night predestined for disaster, that is, the night of the Ninth of Ab which is appointed for a weeping unto all generations, because in it was born the foul and unclean Mehemed Kapici Bashi, formerly called Sabbatai Ṣevi."[16] The authors of the Haggadah render thanks to God for Sabbatai's apostasy, "for if they had killed him, the messiah's followers would have said that he died [a vicarious and atoning death] for his generation."[17] Insult upon insult is heaped upon Sabbatai's name, and in imitation of the Passover Haggadah a list of the ten plagues which he had brought upon Israel is given.[18] The prayers that had been recited in the synagogues for the messianic king were now parodied to become execrations, and one version ends with the invocation "Pour thy wrath upon the followers of the messiah that have not known thee, and that have called upon the name of Sabbatai Ṣevi, for they have devoured Jacob and laid waste his dwelling place."[19] R. Joseph ha-Levi seems to have been the first to state explicitly that the messianic message was a plot hatched by Sabbatai and Nathan.[20] His letter of invective, which was intended as a reply to R. Hosea Nantawa's enthusiastic *credo* of September, 1666 (see above, pp. 489–90), was, it is true, not written until November, but the French

15. *Relation,* p. 36.

16. The two versions of the satire were published by A. M. Haberman in *Qobeṣ ᶜal Yad,* III, New Series (Jerusalem, 1940), 187–206.

17. *Ibid.,* p. 202.

18. *Ibid.,* p. 194.

19. Cf. Ps. 79:6–7, which forms part of the liturgy of the Passover Haggadah.

20. Sasportas, p. 190.

Relation suggests that this view was current in Constantinople as early as October, that is, soon after the apostasy. The explanation recommended itself by its simplicity as well as its polemical piquancy, and consequently gained wide currency. Abraham Cardozo[21] still protests against it as late as 1668: "And as to their assertion that the whole matter was a plot devised by Sabbatai Ṣevi and the prophet Nathan, let the lying lips be put to silence which speak grievous things against the righteous" (cf. Ps. 31:18).

Two attitudes to the now discredited messianic awakening emerged in the camp of the triumphant opponents. There were the contentious polemicists, gleefully taking their revenge on the believers for all the insults and violence that they had suffered at their hands. Emanuel Frances' declaration that "the longer we discourse [on Sabbatai's discomfiture] the more it will be accounted praiseworthy"[22] is not merely an artful adaptation from the Passover Haggadah but reflects the mood of the leading antagonists of the movement. The extremism and extravagance of Nantawa's great confession of the Sabbatian faith, penned only two weeks before the apostasy, had provided Sasportas and ha-Levi with ammunition which they did not fail to exploit to the full. Their letters to Nantawa represent a climax of polemical exacerbation.[23] Inspired by Nathan's apocalypse, the rabbi of Alexandria had gone so far, in his enthusiasm, as to maintain that those who denied Sabbatai and his mission were no true Israelites but the seed of the "mixed multitude." The orthodox rabbis, deeply offended by such application of pneumatic standards of judgment,[24] eagerly took the opportunity to turn the tables on Rabbi Nantawa.

Many lay leaders and rabbis, however, realized that sarcasms and triumphant scorn were not the most effective or advisable method for dealing with the aftermath of so deep and powerful an emotional upheaval. Rather than act on Emanuel Frances' principle that "it was our duty to tell the story,"[25] they considered it their duty to pass over the affair in silence, or at least to treat it with a maximum of discretion and to effect a quiet return to normal life. In choosing this course, the rabbis of Constantinople and Smyrna may have at-

21. In a letter to a believer (and not to his brother, as has been erroneously maintained), *ap.* Freimann, p. 92.

22. Haberman, *loc. cit.*, p. 192.

23. Sasportas, pp. 177–97.

24. Cf. Sasportas, p. 191.

25. In imitation of the Passover Haggadah.

tempted the impossible; at any rate they acted in what seemed to them the most reasonable and responsible fashion. They were probably led to this course of action by two very different considerations. In the first place, Sabbatai was now the sultan's protégé and they could scarcely permit themselves an open attack on a convert to Islam. But they also had to take into account the state of mind prevailing in the Jewish communities. No doubt the majority of rabbis, once they had realized that their hopes were shattered, returned fairly easily to their previous routine. Deeply rooted in the rabbinic tradition and endowed with sufficient intellectual discipline, they were relatively immune against a theology of paradoxes that so evidently ran counter to received notions. An apostate messiah held no attraction for them. Things were different, however, with the great mass of believers. The messianic propaganda, which had not been checked by either the rabbis or the lay leaders, had roused their emotions and faith to such a pitch that rational criticism and appeals to traditional standards would probably have availed little. It seemed safer and wiser to ignore the whole matter as far as possible, and to let time and oblivion heal the wound. Neither condemnation nor apologies, but silence alone would enable the disturbed community to find the way back to normal life. Time and again we find Balak's advice to Balaam (Num. 23:25) quoted in seventeenth- and eighteenth-century sources, for example, by R. Ḥayyim Palache of Smyrna (1788–1863) who writes: "We have a tradition from our holy masters and fathers not to speak either good or evil of the affair of Sabbatai Ṣevi, *neither curse it nor bless it*."[26] In the course of time this counsel of prudence came to be interpreted in a more positive fashion as an exculpation, or at least extenuation, of Sabbatai Ṣevi. Toward the end of the eighteenth century, R. Eleazar Flekeles was told by the famous rabbi of Prague, R. Ezekiel Landau, that whoever used that phrase from Numbers 23:25 had thereby betrayed himself and could be presumed to be a Sabbatian.[27]

26. Ḥayyim Palache, *Kol ha-Ḥayyim* (Smyrna, 1874), fol. 18a; cf. S. Asaf in *Zion*, I (1936), 456, and R. Ḥayyim Elazar Schapira of Munkacz, *Ḥamisha Maʾamaroth* (1922), p. 128. Leyb b. Ozer (*ap.* Emden, p. 25) refers to an agreement to this effect by the Turkish rabbis as a well-known fact.

27. *ʾAhabath Dawid* (Prague, 1800), fol. 19b. The phrase was similarly used in a sense that excluded condemnation among the descendants of R. Menaḥem b. Isaac Ashkenazi of Adrianople. According to a family tradition, R. Menaḥem had been brought as a little child to the apostate, who had blessed him—whereupon he was healed of a severe illness; see Rosanes, IV, p. 232.

The original intention, however, was no doubt to hush up the messianic awakening which was still too strong and too dangerous to render open opposition advisable. The extant sources preserve details of the struggle between the two factions in the camp of the unbelievers.

An important factor, which each side interpreted to its respective advantage, was the extreme reserve manifested by the Turkish authorities. The well-nigh miraculous fact that the Jews were left unharmed although they were guilty of rebellion and *lèse majesté* made a profound impression on all observers, not least on the Jews themselves. The evidence as to what had really happened is contradictory, but it seems that there had been a real danger that was somehow averted. It is not clear whether the whole of Turkish Jewry, or the believers, or only the leaders of the movement were threatened by the wrath of the authorities. Much has been made of a proclamation, that is, a letter, of the rabbis of Constantinople quoted in Leyb's memoir. The document as presented by Leyb is certainly not authentic but "written up" or pieced together from one or more sources.[28] Leyb's methods in treating his sources are familiar, and in this particular instance we are fortunate enough to possess the text of the letter that he used. The letter, written on December 9, 1666, by the rabbis of Constantinople and addressed to R. Isaac Jessurun, one of the wealthiest and most learned Jews in Smyrna,[29] contains the following sentences: "As for Sabbatai Ṣevi, you have received a full report, wherefore we do not wish to expatiate at present on the details of the affair. Let it suffice to say that we and our children should render infinite praise and thanks to God who has saved us from the sword to which our lives would have been forfeited, had it not been for a mediator

28. Emden, p. 20. An examination of Leyb's memoir proves that he used no documents but such as were available to him in printed books, the only exception being the report of the two Polish emissaries (see above, p. 620, n. 53). Most of the documents quoted by Leyb are extracts from letters found in Coenen. The style of the proclamation is sufficient proof that the text was not composed by the rabbis of Constantinople, and no similar text is found elsewhere.

29. Coenen (p. 111) spells Isaac Iseron, and his mistake was copied by others. Leyb b. Ozer (*ap.* Emden, p. 14), misunderstanding Coenen, invented a nonexistent R. Isaac Izran of Venice. Emden, when making his excerpts from Coenen, recognized the real name and correctly emended Jessurun (p. 31). The family was well known in Smyrna; see above, pp. 420–22.

who interceded for us."[30] There are no reasons for doubting the authenticity of this letter,[31] the evidence of which confirms that a grave danger threatened the Jewish community but was averted by the intercession of a "mediator." There is no indication that Sabbatai Ṣevi was the anonymous advocate of the Jews.

Elsewhere Coenen reports that after Sabbatai's apostasy the sultan had given orders to arrest a number of the leading believers in several communities and to bring them to Adrianople where they were to receive (presumably capital) punishment. Couriers were dispatched with lists of the names of the persons to be arrested—which suggests that the authorities possessed detailed information about what was going on in the Jewish communities. Twelve rabbis were to be arrested in Constantinople, and some more in Smyrna.[32] The authorities had already begun to make arrests when new messengers arrived bringing counterorders. The rabbis were given only a reprimand and the Jews were pardoned.[33] Coenen seems to have written this report before he had knowledge of the letter from Constantinople to Isaac Jessurun, which he quotes only in a later chapter. It will be remembered that the chapters of Coenen's book were sent as separate letters to the offices of the Levant Trading Company in The Hague. The two reports occur in two different chapters, the earlier of which mentions two rumors regarding the identity of the intercessor and advocate of the Jews. According to one account the sultan's mother begged for mercy for the Jews, and this version is also confirmed by another source. But "they also tell here [in Smyrna] that it was the false mes-

30. Coenen gives only a Dutch translation: "indien er geen Middelaer geweest was." The original Hebrew was probably in the flowery and allusive epistolary style affected by the rabbis.

31. Leyb's paraphrase is pieced together, as usual, from several elements. The statement that "we have lost not one man, nay not even a penny" is characteristic of the popular view of events about a generation later. No contemporary, aware of the huge losses incurred by the Jews in connection with the messianic movement, would ever have written thus; but no doubt this is what some of Leyb's informants told him, and hence he added this detail in his version of the letter. See also below, p. 702.

32. Leyb's numbers (fifty rabbis altogether, of which twelve were from Constantinople and twelve from Smyrna) probably are his own imaginary addition to Coenen's account, though in this particular instance the number may be correct. If twelve arrests were to be made in the capital, then the total from all Jewish communities might well be around fifty.

33. Coenen, pp. 86–87.

siah himself who influenced the sultan and made him change his mind" by accepting full responsibility for everything that had happened and pleading that the innocent people should not be punished for having been misled by his messianic propaganda.[34] The latter version is contradicted by everything we know about Sabbatai's behavior during his examination in the Divan, and it is therefore probably safe to sssume that the rumor was invented by the believers who wished to represent Sabbatai as the savior of Israel when all appearances indicated that he was a traitor and an informer.

The earliest reports sent by the unbelievers to the Jewish communities abroad did, in fact, suggest that the sultan had decided upon stern reprisals against the Jews as a result of Sabbatai's informing against them. The believers' version seems to have been current as early as October, that is, as soon as the news of the evil decree and its repeal had become known in the wake of the arrest and subsequent release of the rabbis in Constantinople.

Two distinct and successive measures by the authorities are mentioned by R. Joseph ha-Levi of Leghorn. In his first letter written after having received news of the apostasy, R. Joseph reports that Sabbatai had shown to the sultan the letters of homage of the Jewish communities, whereupon the sultan in his anger ordered all the Jews above the age of seven to be put to death and those under seven to be forcibly converted to Islam. "And the books of wrath and anger were written and sealed. But two of the chief men in the kingdom came to the sultan . . . and entreated him to avert his anger and not to destroy a whole people because of one scelerate, the like of which none of his ancestors had ever done; and the sultan's mother, too, took pity . . . and entreated him. And the sultan granted their requests . . . and wrote a letter of pardon. But the apostate's anger was not turned away and he again informed against the rabbis, [saying] that they had incited him. The sultan sent for them in order to put them to death, but he was again entreated in their behalf and he pardoned them."[35] The rabbis of Constantinople (for it was they who were ha-Levi's source of information) thus knew of an official amnesty ("letter of pardon") and of the intervention of the sultan's mother and two of his chief advisers. The substance of the report seems trustworthy, even when discounting the allegations of Sabbatai's base and treacherous behavior. It is not impossible that the arrcsts

34. *Ibid.*, p. 87. 35. Sasportas, p. 173.

as well as other punitive measures had already been decided upon earlier by the Turkish authorities who did not require Sabbatai's informing in order to know who were the leaders of the movement. The government was well aware of what was going on, as evidenced by the translation into Turkish of Sabbatai's proclamation abolishing the fasts.

Summing up the evidence, it appears that Turkish Jewry was in real danger at a certain moment. It seems more than probable that if Sabbatai had chosen martyrdom at the fateful meeting of the Privy Council, his heroism would have had disastrous consequences for the Jewish community or, at any rate, for its leaders. The sultan's advisers counseled wisely when they desisted from useless revenge and instead offered Sabbatai a chance to buy his freedom with his apostasy. The decision to grant a general pardon may have been influenced also by the desire to attract believers to follow Sabbatai's example. According to de la Croix the kaimakam inquired of the sultan what to do with Sabbatai's followers, "and His Majesty replied that it was sufficient that their leader had shown them the way which they should take, and that he wanted to grant them a pardon for this reason."[36] De la Croix, writing only a few years after the event, makes no reference at all to any threatened reprisals and a subsequent amnesty, and compresses several stages into one dramatic action. His account cannot, therefore, be trusted, although it provides further testimony to a "general amnesty" having been granted.

Subsequently, other explanations, ignoring many of the facts and resorting to a purely religious causality, were put forward to account for the nullification of the evil decree. Leyb b. Ozer reports that he had discussed the matter with many rabbis "and they said that it was written in the books that hitherto, whenever men had declared themselves to be messiahs this had brought persecutions upon Israel. But this time no evil at all had befallen the Jews throughout the dispersion, . . . nor had they suffered any financial loss. And they said the reason for this was the great repentance in those days, the like of which had not occurred since the foundation of the earth, and it was through the merits of this repentance that the evil decree was nullified."[37] Discussions of this kind are conceivable only after the

36. De la Croix, p. 374.

37. MS. Shazar, fol. 54b. Leyb's account as summarized by Emden (p. 19) is merely a fanciful elaboration of Coenen. Since, according to Coenen,

actual damage caused by the movement has been forgotten, and popular imagination could behold the past events in a greatly idealizing light. But there was no denying the remarkable fact, which could not but invite all sorts of explanations, of Israel's deliverance from the vengeance of the Turks.

Our sources agree that faith in the messiah remained widespread for some time after the apostasy, although there is no clear evidence as to the relative numbers. Coenen and Rycaut report that most believers, especially in Smyrna and Constantinople, persevered in the faith. According to Rycaut most of them adopted the Docetist explanation: "And yet most of them affirm, That *Sabbatai* is not turned Turk, but his shadow only remains on Earth, and walks with a white head, and in the habit of a Mahometan; but his body and soul are taken into Heaven, there to reside until the time appointed for the accomplishment of these wonders: and this opinion began commonly to take place, as if this people resolved never to be undeceived."[38] On the other hand, the French Jesuit who finished his *Relation* in Constantinople in November, 1666, suggests that most believers confessed their error and cursed the day on which they had believed in the impostor. Echoes of the struggle between the two parties can still be detected in the account of Leyb b. Ozer, who had probably obtained his information from eyewitnesses. According to Leyb, the sultan's amnesty actually intensified the enmity between the parties, since the believers now "compelled them [that is, the infidels] to believe in him [that is, in Sabbatai, who had just "saved" Israel], and there was so much contention and mortal hatred between them that everyone desired to kill his neighbor. But everywhere the rabbis and lay leaders spared no effort, threatening with a ban of excommunication anyone who would lift a hand against his neighbor or curse him, and restoring peace in the synagogues. And they took great pains to arrange this quietly and in secret."[39] According to this version the Jewish authorities attempted to prevent further exacerbation in the communities:

---

the authorities had already begun to make arrests, several days must have elapsed between the issuing of the original orders and their subsequent repeal. In Leyb's account the Jews prepared themselves, immediately after the apostasy, with prayers and fasting against the evil decree which, he alleges, was indeed issued on the following day but immediately revoked.

38. Rycaut, p. 215.

39. MS. Shazar, fol. 42b.

the believers should be left in peace; and time, it was hoped, would open their eyes.

Meanwhile, the Turkish communities were swarming with rumors, some of which had been launched by the believers with the intention of mitigating the shock of the apostasy. Mention has already been made of the Docetist theory. Other rumors tried to account for the apostate's new mode of life by insisting that even in the sultan's palace he did not eat any ritually forbidden food. According to one version, he ate nothing but bread and fruit. According to another version, an angelic messenger exchanged the dishes brought from the sultan's kitchen for celestial food.[40] Among the rumors spread by the unbelievers is one which, curiously enough, refers to territorial ambitions such as were entertained subsequently by Jacob Frank. Sasportas writes that "it has been reported to us from Constantinople that this villain asked the sultan to grant him dominion over some [little] part of his territories and he promised the sultan that the Jews would follow him [thither] and that he could then convert them to Islam. This became known to the rabbis, who forbade, on pain of excommunication, any Jew to visit [Sabbatai] or talk to him. Because there were some who even after his apostasy were seduced by his explanation that for mystical reasons it had to be thus that the messiah enter for a certain period the realm of the *qelippah,* even as David did with Achish, the king of Gath."[41] The analogy with David, "who changed his behavior before Abimelech," the king of the Philistines (Ps. 34:1), was well taken and rings true to style,[42] and Sasportas' report may echo arguments used in the discussions between Sabbatai and his followers during the first months after the apostasy.[43] Sabbatai's request for some territorial dominion and his promise that his believers would follow him thither and adopt Islam are not impossible psychologically; in fact, they would agree well both with his desire to maintain relations with his followers, and with his proclivity for leading a double life under the very eyes of the Turks. But psychological possibilities do not yet make historical certainty and there is, for the time being, nothing to corroborate Sasportas' "territorialist" statement.

40. Coenen, p. 91; cf. also the Sabbatian source quoted above, p. 685.

41. Sasportas, p. 174.

42. The analogy is not used by Nathan in his tracts justifying the apostasy, but Abraham Cardozo mentions it in 1669; see *Zion,* XIX (1954), 21.

43. These discussions, including a speech put into Sabbatai's mouth, are mentioned by de la Croix, p. 375.

The prohibition against visiting Sabbatai and discussing the messianic mystery of his apostasy with his followers is referred to also in Leyb's memoirs. Apparently the arguments of the believers were sufficiently impressive to compel the rabbis of Constantinople to issue a proclamation enjoining on pain of excommunication that "no Jew, young or old, man or woman, utter the name of this man . . . let alone . . . visit his sect or speak to them either good or evil." Those who contravened this order forfeited their lives and would be prosecuted by every means at the disposal of the rabbis.[44] But the genuineness of this proclamation is more than doubtful. Even assuming that Leyb's report has some basis in fact, the wording of the text as he presents it can hardly be genuine. The style differs considerably from that of the authentic letters sent out at the time by the Constantinople rabbinate. A reference to the "sect" of Sabbatai Ṣevi is most unlikely at that date, as the expression came into use only much later. No authentic document dating from 1667 or 1668 threatens believers with death, on the contrary, every effort was made to receive them back into the fold (see below, pp. 715 ff.). On the other hand, a prohibition against visiting Sabbatai and discussing his apostasy ("let not so much as his name proceed out of your mouth")[45] may really have been issued and may represent the historical core of Leyb's spurious proclamation.

III

The rabbis did not succeed in assuaging the agitated spirits, at least not as quickly as they wished. They were, in fact, fighting against odds. Sabbatai, cloistered in his house in Adrianople, remained in touch with his chief adherents, and this fact soon became public knowledge. His new mode of life gave rise to a multitude of theories and explanations, and the air in the Jewish quarters was thick with rumors. As before the apostasy, the believers even now "stuffed their letters . . . with nothing but wonders and miracles wrought by their Messiah,"[46] and circulated their fond inventions to all parts.[47] The

44. Emden, p. 20. 45. Rycaut, p. 216. 46. *Ibid.*

47. A story which spread from Constantinople early in 1667 told how Sabbatai had miraculously escaped the murderous designs of a Turkish pasha who had sent him a poisoned dish of candies (Coenen, pp. 104–5). A very similar story with Nathan and the "pasha of Gaza" as its protagonists had come from Gaza in 1666. Coenen's story was taken over by Leyb b. Ozer (*ap.* Emden, p. 21).

rabbis of Constantinople and Smyrna, including R. Ḥayyim Benveniste, who had been appointed by the messiah as chief rabbi of his native city, turned their backs on the faith and were said greatly to repent of their grievous error. Sasportas seems to have seen a letter by Benveniste expressing his sorrow at what he had done. The Jews of Smyrna "and especially the rabbis now repented with a better repentance than the earlier one [which had led to disaster]."[48] A minority among the rabbis, led by R. Abraham Yakhini, persevered in the faith. The ordinary people were neither shaken by the events nor disturbed by the solemn rabbinic warnings. No single event, not even so contemptible an action as apostasy, could shatter, with one stroke as it were, their "pure faith" in the messiah and his power. To them, there was undoubtedly some great mystery, beyond their limited understanding, about the messiah's present state, which would not last long anyway. The relative strength of the two parties in the various communities was probably changing all the time. Some of those who had lost their faith might return to it as a result of renewed propaganda and vice versa. The important fact is that the movement did not perish at once with the apostasy. Even those who had never thought of Sabbatai in terms of a "holy sinner" were now made to do so by dint of the circumstances that presented them with an apostate messiah. Several rabbis promptly discovered scriptural allusions to the messiah's apostasy, though it was only later that a systematic theory of its mystical significance came to be elaborated. R. Naphtali Ashkenazi (of Smyrna or Constantinople) extracted from Genesis 41:1–2 the prophecy that the Holy King Sabbatai Ṣevi would for some time be called Ishmael Mehemed the Turk, etc.[49]

48. Sasportas, p. 210. On the other hand, Sasportas' statement that Benveniste resigned from the rabbinate because of his association with the messianic heresy (*ibid.*, p. 277) hardly seems correct. The letter by R. Ḥayyim Benveniste to his brother Joshua in Constantinople, printed in the editor's preface to the Palestinian Talmud on the order *Qodashim*, is an obvious forgery as is also the work with which it appeared. (The Palestinian Talmud on *Qodashim* is one of the most notorious forgeries in the history of Hebrew bibliography.) See *Zeitschrift für Hebräische Bibliographie*, XI (1907), 25.

49. The Hebrew wording of this piece of exegesis by the method of *notarikon* is given by Coenen, pp. 107–8. It was probably written or preached in the week *Miqqeṣ*, i.e., the biblical lesson beginning Gen. 41:1, which was read on Hanukkah (December, 1666). I have found this *notarikon*—each word designated by its first letter—in several MSS. from Sabbatian circles.

Rumors were also rife concerning the prophet Nathan. The manifestations of mass prophecy had ceased abruptly as the messiah's apostasy became known, and no better proof is conceivable of the psychological impact made by the news. It is little wonder that in the circumstances all eyes turned toward the prophet of Gaza. The leaders of the communities, too, wondered what Nathan would be doing or saying next. There had been a general expectation, during the summer of 1666, that Nathan would soon arrive in the capital, and there seems to have been correspondence on the subject between him and Sabbatai (see p. 631). Rumors of the prophet's impending arrival persisted after the apostasy. The Jews of Constantinople expected great things to happen on the Twenty-fifth of Kislev, 5427, namely, the beginning of the festival of Hanukkah, in fulfillment of Nathan's prophecy of August, 1665, that redemption would take place "after one year and several months" (see above, p. 272). Nathan was expected to arrive before that date and to work mighty miracles, "and some rabbis believed in this as firmly as if it were one of the articles of faith." When nothing happened in December, 1666, the date was shifted to Passover (April, 1667)[50] and then to September.

We do not know why Nathan tarried in Gaza all summer, in spite of the messiah's pressing invitation. The letters written to Nathan by Sabbatai himself and by several members of his court are no longer extant. There were rumors at the time that Nathan had indeed set out upon his journey at Sabbatai's behest and that the news of the apostasy had reached him in Aleppo. However, all statements to that effect[51] are incorrect. Nathan left Gaza only after learning that Sabbatai had "set the fair miter upon his head,"[52] and journeyed "in the company of more than twenty rabbis from Palestine to behold the face of Our Lord."[53] The infidels explained his departure as a flight from the Turkish authorities who, it was said, intended to arrest him as the chief instigator of the troubles. It was also rumored that Nathan had been specifically excluded from the general amnesty and that messengers had been dispatched to bring him to Adria-

50. Coenen, pp. 91–92.

51. E.g., in a letter of Abraham Cardozo (*Zion,* XIX [1954], 13).

52. This favorite Sabbatian metaphor for Sabbatai's taking the turban is based on Zech. 3:5.

53. Baruch of Arezzo, *ap.* Freimann, p. 58.

54. See Sasportas, pp. 173, 199; the letter of R. Samson Bacchi, *ap.* Carpi, p. 19; the French *Relation,* p. 42.

nople.[54] The unbelievers appear to have been apprehensive lest the Turks might also want Nathan to apostatize in Adrianople. At any rate, the fear of some such possibility may account for the steps taken by the rabbis of Constantinople and Adrianople against Nathan.

As a matter of fact, Nathan did not hide from the Turkish authorities but traveled with a considerable retinue and amid much publicity. Though he himself later alluded to "dangers" that beset him at the time, there is no evidence of any difficulties placed in his way by the authorities. The reason for his departure at precisely that moment is unknown. The news of the apostasy may have caused him to hasten to the messiah, whose invitation he had so far neglected. Perhaps Sabbatai had sent him an urgent message after the apostasy. Abraham Cuenque's account suggests such a second invitation, but the wording of Nathan's letter—possibly the first letter he wrote after the apostasy—is ambiguous. This letter was written in Damascus on November 20, 1666, more than nine weeks after the apostasy. It is not impossible, therefore, that Nathan did not leave Gaza until early in November, after receiving the news from Adrianople.

In his letter from Damascus, Nathan promptly surrounded the apostasy with a smoke screen or, rather, with a halo of kabbalistic mysteries. After addressing Sabbatai in the usual flowery metaphors of his characteristic epistolary style ("Our King and Our Lord, who gathereth our scattered ones, . . . the man who was raised up on high," etc.), Nathan announces that having received "the king's commandment and his decree" he immediately hastened to obey the order, as in duty bound, "and although *we have heard strange reports,* yet our heart is strong as a lion's never to doubt his ways. His works are wonderful and we are holding fast to our faith without doubts, and are ready to give our lives for the holiness of his name. Having arrived here in Damascus, we shall proceed without delay by way of Iskanderun [that is, Alexandrette], as he has commanded us to appear and to behold the light of the face of the living king. And we, the servants of his servants, are licking the dust of his feet, praying to the splendor of his exalted Majesty . . . to sustain us in the strength of his mighty hand. . . . and the sons of wickedness shall no longer afflict us. . . . Thus speaketh the servant of his servants, to be trodden under the soles of his feet, [together with them] that came to appear before him and that sign, here in Damascus, . . . Nathan Benjamin."[55]

From Damascus Nathan also sent a brief letter of encouragement to the rabbis of Aleppo, "to notify your reverences of my safe arrival in Damascus. I shall go to see Our Lord . . . as he has commanded us and the chosen Twelve Tribes [i.e., the twelve scholars appointed by Sabbatai in Gaza as their representatives]. I also want to notify you that *even though you have heard strange things concerning Our Lord,* let not your heart become faint. Be not afraid, but be very strong in your faith, for all his actions are wonderful trials which human reason cannot fathom. . . . But soon all things will become perfectly clear. . . . Blessed is he that waiteth and cometh to the salvation of the true messiah, may his kingdom soon become manifest."[56]

There can be no doubt as to what were the "strange things concerning Our Lord" that Nathan and others had heard. As the apostasy was not mentioned in Sabbatai's pressing invitation to Nathan,[57] the news must have reached Gaza in some other way. In any event, Nathan must have heard the report by the time he set out on his journey, for he already justified the apostasy with mystical arguments to the aged kabbalist R. Benjamin ha-Levi (see above, p. 369), whom he met in Safed on his way from Gaza to Damascus. R. Benjamin accepted Nathan's explanations and wrote enthusiastic letters to his friends in Mantua, informing them that "there were great mysteries in this matter which must not be committed to writing" and that Nathan had proved the matter to be "as clear as day, and few words are sufficient to him that wants to understand."[58] Nathan evidently considered the apostasy a logical, albeit unexpected, sequel to the earlier "strange actions" which had played such a central role in the elaboration of his doctrine of the person and ministry of the messiah. Yet in spite of the significance of Nathan's doctrines for the subsequent development of Sabbatian theology, the immediate currency of the

55. For a long time—till the discovery of the Dönmeh MSS.—this was the only extant letter of Nathan to Sabbatai Ṣevi. The wording suggests that it was signed also by Nathan's travel companions. The text was preserved by Coenen (p. 99), who transliterated the Hebrew original.

56. Coenen, p. 101. The letter proves that Nathan did not visit Aleppo but traveled by some other route from Damascus to the port of Alexandrette.

57. The letter was probably sent before the apostasy; see above, p. 631.

58. Baruch of Arezzo, *ap.* Freimann, p. 59.

mystical explanation of the apostasy was not due solely to him. The notion that the messiah would have "to enter the dominion of the *qelippoth* for some time" appeared spontaneously in several places, for example, in Sabbatai's immediate entourage as well as in Italy, even before Nathan's writings on the subject became known.[59] Considering the fact that mystical paradox had played a major part in previous attempts to account for the messiah's behavior and personality, there is nothing surprising in the spontaneous appearance of identical justifications of the apostasy.

A record of Nathan's passage through Damascus is preserved in a Sabbatian manuscript[60] which tells of the prophet's pilgrimage to the tomb of R. Ḥayyim Vital. After "uniting" his spirit by special meditations to that of the great kabbalist, it was revealed to Nathan that the messiah would have to fall very low "exactly as the feet of the primordial Adam had to descend from the world of *ʾaṣiluth* to the lower worlds (see above, pp. 38 ff.), . . . which almost seems blasphemous." This revelation is indeed characteristic of Nathan's way of thinking and of his habit of developing his Sabbatian paradoxes by way of typological analogies with the relatively more innocent paradoxes of Lurianic kabbalism. A voice was heard from the tomb, making the dark utterance, "Judah [Sabbatai?] will descend, Benjamin [Nathan?] will go up."

News of Nathan's actual and imagined movements circulated in the Jewish communities, whose interest in the prophet's future steps was obviously very great. Several weeks after the apostasy it was known (or perhaps rumored and subsequently confirmed) in Smyrna that the prophet had left Gaza accompanied by many rabbis, but the announcements of his impending arrival proved false time and again.[61] In the camp of the believers there was utter confusion. Smyrna was full of kings, dukes, and other dignitaries of the messiah's kingdom. They had provided themselves with letters-patent confirming their high office, and many of them (including, according to Coenen,

59. Sabbatai's utterances on the subject as well as those of Raphael Supino in Leghorn (quoted by Sasportas, pp. 174, 247) were certainly made before Nathan's views became known.

60. MS. Adler 493 (in the Jewish Theological Seminary, New York), fol. 15b. The MS. dates from the end of the 17th century. The account seems to be based on a letter of Nathan's.

61. Coenen, p. 92.

the president of the Sanhedrin) refused to abandon hope. Others lost heart, like the "viceroy of Judah" appointed by the king of Judah, Sabbatai's brother Joseph Ṣevi, who at the end of October, 1666, sold his vice-regal title for one silver dollar.[62]

Evidence of the agitation in Smyrna and Constantinople is provided by the action which the rabbis of these communities felt compelled to take. On November 29, 1666, Nathan's father, R. Elisha Ashkenazi, arrived in Constantinople[63] on his way from Jerusalem through the Balkans to Budapest and Vienna. The fact that Elisha's unreserved Sabbatian loyalties did not prevent the Ashkenazi community of Jerusalem from dispatching him on an official mission to Europe—for it is unlikely that he traveled in a purely private capacity—raises some interesting questions. Elisha was a staunch supporter of his son's prophetic message and remained an active Sabbatian propagandist even after the apostasy.[64] Father and son were in close contact by correspondence, and Nathan would inform his father of his more important undertakings.[65] Sasportas, who describes Elisha as an unbeliever, was undoubtedly misled by his correspondents.[66] Elisha's arrival encouraged and cheered the believers who promptly notified their brethren in Smyrna of the event. "The rumor has spread in Smyrna that Nathan himself with the rabbis that accompany him has arrrived and that he will immediately proceed to meet that man. There he will prove in the sight of all the greatness of the well-known man and the truth of his [own] prophecy concerning him."[67] This is the first instance of the use of the circumlocution that subsequently gained more and more currency. In due course even the believers took to substituting "the well-known man" for Sabbatai or AMIRAH when writing to one another. Elisha seems to have

62. *Ibid.*, p. 78. According to the list of dignitaries (Coenen, p. 45), his name was Joseph Pernik; he was probably a friend of Joseph Ṣevi and, like the latter, a merchant. Some writers, misunderstanding Coenen, attributed the sale of the title to Joseph Ṣevi himself.

63. He may, therefore, have left Palestine before the news of the apostasy had reached there. In general, the journey by sea took four to five weeks.

64. Two independent sources mention his Sabbatian activity, in Constantinople (Coenen, p. 103) and in Budapest (the MS. quoted by D. Kaufmann, *Letzte Vertreibung*, p. 91).

65. See below, p. 773, Nathan's letter to his father on his mission to Rome.

66. Sasportas, p. 346.

67. Coenen, p. 103.

tarried several weeks in the capital. The reports of his presence there fired enthusiasm in Smyrna to such a degree that on the night of January 13, 1667, the believers held a mass celebration and thanksgiving in one of the synagogues. Meanwhile, news arrived of Nathan himself, and copies of the letters he had written from Damascus were received about three weeks later, early in December, in Constantinople and Smyrna. The letters strengthened the morale of the believers, but also induced the rabbis to take stern measures. A circular letter was sent out to the major communities in Turkey (Aleppo, Brussa, Smyrna, and most probably—though it is not mentioned—Salonika) in an effort to nip the danger in the bud. In a covering letter (December 9, 1666) to R. Isaac Jessurun of Smyrna, the rabbis of Constantinople protest against the continuing fervor of the believers "who hold fast to their folly," and inform their colleagues of the ban of excommunication proclaimed in Constantinople against all Sabbatians. (This is the first instance of a general ban on all believers.) The rabbis admit that "there are many who do not mind the ban and have strengthened themselves in their faith, more especially since rumors have spread that Nathan Ashkenazi of Gaza is on his way to these parts. It was to forestall these rumors and to thwart his [Nathan's] plans that the rabbis wrote to several places."[68]

The letter, signed by nine of the leading rabbis of Constantinople,[69] read as follows:

A voice of noise has come to our ears, that the learned man which was in Gaza, the Rabbi Nathan Benjamin, who is known for the fruit of his lips [that is, his prophecy] has made the world tremble at his dreams and words. At this time we have received advice that this man some dayes since departed from Gaza and took his Journey by the way of Scanderone, intending there to embark for Smyrna or Constantinople. And though it seems a strange thing unto us that he should presume to throw himself into a place of flames and fire: Notwithstanding we ought to fear and suspect it. . . . Wherefore, we undersigned, do adver-

68. Coenen, p. 112; see also above, p. 699.

69. Yomtob b. Ḥananiah ibn Yaqar, Moses Benveniste, Isaac Alnakawa, Joseph Qaṣṣabi, Samuel Acazsina (thus Rycaut's spelling; Coenen spells it Akazlino, which, however, does not faithfully transliterate his own Hebrew spelling; the name is given once [Sasportas, p. 209] as Samuel Kasno), Caleb b. Samuel, Moses Brudo, Eliezer Aluf, Joshua Benveniste.

tise you, That this Man coming within the Compass of your Jurisdiction, you give a stop to his Journey, and not suffer him to proceed further, but presently to return back. For we would have you know that at his Coming he will begin again to move those tumults. . . . And miracles are not wrought every day [that is, another time the Jews may not escape the wrath of the authorities]. God forbid that by his Coming, the People of God should be destroyed in all places where they are, of which he will be the first for his blood is upon his owne head; for in this Conjuncture every little errour or fault is made Capital; you may remember the danger of the first Combustion, and it is very probable that he will be an occasion of greater, which the tong is not able to express with words. Therefore, by virtue of ours, and your own Authority, you are to hinder him from proceeding farther in his Journey, upon the pain of all those Excommunications which our Law can impose, and to force him to return back again, both he and his Company. But if he shall in any manner oppose you, yours is counsel and wisdom to stop him by whatever means and pretext that you find useful for in doing thus it will be well for him and for all Israel . . . for the lives of all the Jews, and his also, depend on this. . . ."[70]

The letter is remarkable for the respectful way in which it refers to Nathan. The same rabbis who, we are told, had just excommunicated all believers in Sabbatai Ṣevi were apparently very careful not to include in the ban "that learned man which was in Gaza, the Rabbi Nathan Benjamin," who, they knew only too well, was actively advocating the Sabbatian faith. They requested the Jewish communities to turn him back wherever he appeared and, above all, to permit no contact between him and the believers. In this way they hoped to prevent a threatening explosion of messianic emotion and consequent disaster, since they knew that they could hardly count on another "amnesty." The letter evinces considerable fear as well as an extreme reluctance to injure Nathan's honor. In the circumstances the rabbis' manner of proceeding gives proof of great prudence and sound commonsense.

70. Rycaut's English version (pp. 217–18), corrected on some points in accordance with the orignal as printed by Coenen (p. 114). The letter was written between December 5 and 9, 1666. Nathan's letter of November 20 announcing his intention to embark at Alexandrette must therefore have arrived in the first days of December.

In their covering letter to R. Isaac Jessurun, the rabbis of Constantinople referred to the material losses suffered by the Jewish community, believers and unbelievers, as a result of the unceasing stream of messianic rumors emanating from Smyrna. They also seized the opportunity to clear up a somewhat awkward point. Letters with the signatures of prominent rabbis and lay leaders endorsing the Sabbatian faith had been sent out by the believers in Constantinople, "as was the case with a letter sent to Venice at which our colleagues [the rabbis of Venice] were not pleased with us [the signatories] when they beheld the signatures of our names but of which we had not apprised them [that is, the signatures were forged], for it is a lie that we signed the letter." This belated protest, some six months after the event, undoubtedly refers to the curious letter concerning the mysterious merchandise of R. Israel, which Abraham Yakhini and his colleagues had sent out (see above, p. 505). The fact that official denial of the forgery (if forgery it was) was not made until after the apostasy, and then only in a letter to R. Isaac Jessurun, does not redound to the credit of the rabbis of Constantinople.

Another letter by the same writers, to Smyrna and probably to other congregations as well, throws further light on the turbulent atmosphere in the Turkish communities during the first months following the apostasy. The seriousness of the situation is attested by the fact that the letter, dated January 30, 1667, was addressed not merely to the rabbis and notables but to "all the people" and was evidently meant to be read from the pulpits in all synagogues:

These our Letters which we sent in your Habitations, are upon occasion of certain Rumors and Tumults come to our ears . . . that there is a sort of men among you, who fortifie themselves in their Errour, and say, Let such an one our King live, and bless him in their publick Synagogues every Sabbath day; and also adjoyn Psalms and Hymns invented in the days of the aforementioned man, with Rules and Devotions which ought not to be done, and yet they still remain obstinate therein. And now behold it is known unto you, how many swelling waters have passed over our souls because of him: for had it not been for the mercies of God which are without end, and the merit of our Forefathers which hath assisted us, the foot of Israel would have slipped. And yet still you continue obstinate in things which do not help but rather do mischief, which God avert. Turn you therefore, for this is not the true way, but restore the Crown to the ancient custom, according to the use of your Forefathers which is the Law, and from thence do not move.

We command you, That with your Authority, under pain of Excommunication and other Penalties, all those Ordinances and Prayers, as well those delivered by the mouth of that man, as those which were injoyned by others for his sake, be all abolished and made void, and to be found no more, and that they never enter more into your hearts; but do according to the ancient Customs of your Forefathers. And every Sabbath say "He that giveth salvation unto kings" [that is, the collect for the sovereign] and bless the Sultan Mahomet; for in his dayes hath great Salvation been wrought for Israel, and become not Rebels to his Kingdom, which God forbid. . . . Wherefore abstain from this man, and let not as much as his name proceed out of your mouths. For if you will not obey us herein, which will be known, who, and what those men are, who refuse to conform unto us, we are resolved to prosecute them as our duty is."[71]

The stern measures of the Jewish authorities were not without, albeit limited, effect. The believers were no longer permitted any organized activity, liturgical or otherwise, or any public demonstration of their faith. In fact, they were driven underground, and "throughout Turkey no believer dared to admit publicly that he was a believer."[72] The outward manifestations of the Sabbatian faith—prayers of thanksgiving, special devotions and new rituals—all vanished, and the old order re-established itself in the Turkish communities. No doubt cases of fanatic believers engaging in secret or semisecret Sabbatian propaganda must have come to the notice of the rabbis, but no actual excommunications are reported during the first year. The main concern of the rabbis appears to have been the restoration of the traditional order of law and observance to the lives of the Jewish masses, and the prevention of enthusiastic outbursts. Their measures were directed at the behavior and rituals of the Sabbatians and not at their faith which, they probably assumed, would gradually die out. Why then

71. Rycaut's English version (pp. 215–16) corrected on some point in accordance with the Hebrew original printed by Coenen (pp. 118–19). The two letters were combined by Leyb b. Ozer into one. Also R. Joseph ha-Levi in Leghorn had heard that believers continued to gather in Sabbatai's house in Smyrna and to recite Nathan's liturgies (Sasportas, p. 255).

72. Leyb b. Ozer, MS. Shazar, fol. 43b.

aggravate a critical situation by waging war on a second front? In the summer of 1667 the rabbis of Constantinople and Smyrna solemnly enjoined, under pain of excommunication, the strict observance of the Ninth of Ab, remembering with a contrite heart how in the previous year "'we went astray like sheep . . . by relying on the staff of broken reed, Nathan of Gaza, . . . whom we took to be a true prophet, . . . but now we know that all was lies and deceit.'"[73]

Exhortations and threats of excommunication were not unnecessary, as we learn from a letter of the rabbinate of Smyrna to the neighboring congregation at Tiré where, it appears, not a few believers had celebrated (albeit in the secrecy of their homes) the Ninth of Ab as a festival. In 1668 the rabbis had to reiterate their stern warnings, addressing them this time not merely to the Turkish communities but to the whole Diaspora. There is much to be learned from their long letter to the congregation of Venice[74] which, incidentally, also shows that the rabbis of Smyrna still adhered to their former policy: strong words behind which there was but half-hearted action. Let the believers conform to the rabbinic standards of behavior and all shall be well. As for their faith—well, they are fools who may believe what they want as long as they keep it to themselves. "Let them adhere to the law of the Lord as our sages taught us, . . . without adding to it or diminishing therefrom. And whoever adds . . . more fasts and mortifications . . . that are not mentioned in the books, is in error and should be rebuked, for we have nothing [to guide us] but the words of the Talmudic sages and the halakhic authorities. . . . A number of persons have perished as a result of these [new] mortifications, as we ourselves have seen.[75] Wherefore you shall proclaim throughout the camp of Israel with severe oaths and anathemas that no one should utter any more words on this affair. All the fools whose hearts still turn to folly to believe in these vain . . . delusions, let them not utter anything." Stern measures were recommended only against those who contravened the ban of silence "and utter speech concerning these delusions."

73. Sasportas, pp. 208–9. R. Solomon b. Benjamin ha-Levi, whose name, among others, is signed on this letter, should not be confused with his namesake who, together with his father, signed letters supporting Sabbatai and Nathan as late as 1667 in Palestine.

74. Sasportas, pp. 268–70. 75. See above, p. 634.

No organized action was taken against the leading believers, however, with the exception of Nathan whose influence the rabbis evidently feared. Even Abraham Yakhini, who continued to preside over the believing party in Constantinople, was not, apparently, anathematized or otherwise molested, for the time being. In fact, the tact and diplomacy with which the responsible leaders attempted to handle an explosive situation bordered on weakness. Whereas in Constantinople some attempts, at least, were made to persecute the believers, there were rabbis in Smyrna who "to this day [April, 1667] acquiesce in the words of the fools, in order to find favor in the eyes of the community, or at least keep silent. And I have been told by trustworthy informants that the rabbis in Smyrna and similarly in other cities have now issued a proclamation enjoining the avoidance of strife and quarrels, and permitting everyone who wants to do so, to believe [in Sabbatai]."[76] That R. Joseph ha-Levi's informants were right, is proved by the letter from the following year, just quoted. It is, then, not surprising that the authorities had only very limited success.

The believers were not impressed by the anathemas which, they argued, were mainly intended to appease the Turkish government. Moreover, they had been pronounced by infidels for whom dire punishment was in store after Nathan's arrival and the manifestation of the messiah.[77] A new but significant social factor also seems to have entered into the relations between believers and infidels after the apostasy. Leyb b. Ozer was told that the ruling group, namely, the rabbis and the wealthy lay leaders, were furious with the believers for endangering their position.[78] Leyb probably refers to the danger of government reprisals against the unabating messianic agitation, though another danger, no less real for not being consciously perceived, threatened the hegemony of the ruling class. The believing camp was composed mainly of "enthusiasts": spiritual, that is "pneumatic," kabbalist rabbis and preachers who had been "awakened" by the messianic message, and their enthusiastic following among the masses. It was a social combination that harbored explosive possibilities, even though the Turkish rabbis seem to have been unaware of them. Joseph ha-Levi and Sasportas were about the only ones who perceived an

76. R. Joseph ha-Levi in a letter of April, 1667 (*ap.* Sasportas, p. 256), based on information from Smyrna dating from November or December, 1666.

77. Leyb b. Ozer, MS. Shazar, fols. 45b and 47b.

78. *Ibid.*, fol. 47a.

"incipient heresy . . . the foundation of a New Law and a different religion, as happened in the days of that man [that is, Jesus]."[79] The Turkish rabbis thought neither of a schism nor of the growth of a dissident or secret sect; the only danger they were aware of was that of a mass apostasy to Islam in the steps of Sabbatai Ṣevi. In actual fact the believers, who could no longer assemble legally and in public, began to meet in secret and to build up a clandestine net of communications. The clandestine conventicles soon assumed a sectarian character. The rabbis shut their eyes as long as there was no open rebellion against their authority. Meanwhile the Sabbatian groups exchanged letters, fantastic rumors, and mutual encouragement, and sang hymns which, unlike the earlier songs of triumph and praise, exhibit a certain melancholy quality:

Oh, my beloved's gone from me
God's chosen one, Sabbatai Ṣevi.
Though fallen low and suffering smart
Yet he is closest to my heart.

. . . .

His faithful servant I remain,
Seek and adore him I would fain
In him I trust, and while I live
May Sabbatai my sins forgive.
My eyes to him in hope I raise:
In his salvation laud and praise.[80]

IV

Nathan's travels in the years 1667 and 1668 illustrate both the success and the failure of the measures taken by the Jewish leadership. Having left Gaza after the messiah's apostasy, Nathan never returned to Palestine but led the life of a fugitive and vagabond until his death in 1680. For a few years he enjoyed a period of comparative rest in one of the Macedonian communities where the leaders, Sabbatian sympathizers, offered him shelter. His movements are more or less known. During the first few months his wanderings were a matter

79. Sasportas, p. 256.

80. The hymn (full text *ap.* Freimann, p. 104) was probably brought to Italy from Turkey. It appears together with the hymn "For Thy Sake and Not for Ours" (cf. Davidson, *Ozar,* vol. III, p. 54) which, according to R. Israel Ḥazzan, was one of Sabbatai's favorites; see *Schocken Volume,* p. 195.

of public interest and concern, and the rabbinic authorities did everything in their power to dog his steps and limit his influence. After 1668 they ignored him completely, probably because they had decided that the man was no longer dangerous. Their evaluation of Nathan's influence is surprising in view of the fact that after 1668 he was a particularly active apostle of the gradually evolving heretical theology of Sabbatianism. His writings exerted a considerable influence, which greatly increased after his death. But while the later neglect of Nathan remains an unsolved riddle, the relentless persecution of which he was the object in 1667 and 1668 was logical and consistent.

It seems that Nathan had originally intended to embark at Alexandrette for Salonika, and thence to travel to Adrianople. Having received news of the strong opposition to him, or for some other reason, he changed his plans and traveled overland through Asia Minor, escorted by thirty-six companions. The party included his father-in-law and other members of his family. It was rumored in Smyrna that Nathan traveled on horseback, girt with a sword, and with the pomp and circumstance befitting a pasha. The journey lasted altogether over two months, and Nathan avoided the larger Jewish communities. His exact itinerary is not known, but toward the end of January, 1667, he arrived in Brussa (now Bursa) where he was received with great rejoicing. The enthusiastic reception given to him by the community of Brussa, whose faith had evidently not been shaken by the apostasy, had immediate repercussions in Smyrna where the believers promptly took heart. Cries went up: "Long live Rabbi Sabbatai Ṣevi, our King and Messiah"; banquets were held and hymns were sung in honor of Sabbatai.[81] Expectations in Smyrna rose at the approach of every traveling party coming from Brussa, but the believers suffered a sudden setback. Several Jews from Brussa complained to the rabbinic authorities in Constantinople of what they rightly considered a blatant contravention of the order to turn Nathan back wherever he appeared. The rabbis of Constantinople thereupon reiterated their instructions and practically forced the rabbis of Brussa to excommunicate Nathan. No Jew in Brussa was allowed to consort with him or even offer him water and bread. Those who had to speak to him were to keep at a distance of three cubits (as in the case of a regular excommunicate). Nathan was told to "keep quiet" and to leave the city, or he would

81. Coenen, pp. 122–23; cf. also the letter of January 30, written by the rabbis of Constantinople (see above, pp. 714–15).

be delivered into the hands of the Turkish authorities. Nathan took fright and left—or rather fled from—Brussa.[82] Only six members of his original party, including his father-in-law and R. Samuel Gandoor, remained with him and accompanied him to Smyrna. Others went to Constantinople, while some remained in Brussa. Several representatives of the "Twelve Tribes of Israel," who had accompanied him, went to Adrianople.

During these months of travel Nathan had time to meditate on the mystery of the apostasy and to discuss it with his companions. His thoughts on the subject crystallized and the hidden meaning of the messiah's apostasy, only hinted at in general terms in his letters of November, 1666, now became more clearly defined. As was to be expected from experts in kabbalistic exegesis and homiletics, a diligent search of the ancient texts promptly yielded a profusion of hidden allusions to the effect that the messiah would have to apostatize. The subsequent theological development exhibits striking analogies with early Christian thought. The disciples of Jesus were dumfounded by the crucifixion, since the death of the messiah was not provided for in their eschatological traditions. In due course the Old Testament Scriptures were made to yield what they never contained: a profound doctrine accounting for the paradox of the savior's atoning death. The Sabbatian believers were under even greater pressure, since the mass of the people and not merely a small band of disciples had followed the messiah. Moreover, the crisis which they had to face was more serious, since an apostate messiah is far more problematical than one who is martyred as a result of his ministry.

Nathan's first doctrinal letter on the subject of the apostasy was probably written before his departure from Brussa.[83] It was addressed to Sabbatai's two brothers in Smyrna, who had asked Nathan for guidance in this matter. Sabbatai was living in Adrianople where he received visitors and dropped dark hints concerning the mysterious purpose of what he had done. It was no longer possible to maintain the Docetist theory that the apostasy was mere illusion, and the believ-

82. Coenen, p. 124; Sasportas, p. 203. Sasportas' account is biased and less reliable than Coenen's. According to Sasportas the rabbis of Brussa were about to deliver Nathan into the hands of the Turks, but the believers warned him and he escaped.

83. According to Epstein (*RÉJ* [1893], p. 218) the letter was written on the island of Chios, but this is incompatible with what we know of Nathan's itinerary.

ers had to face the fact that the messiah had not ascended to Heaven. Nathan was also asked to give proof of the authenticity of his prophecy, but had to admit that "the Word is not with me at present to reveal anything. . . . It is sufficient that the servant be like unto his master [that is, without prophetic illumination]." Like Sabbatai, he was in a passive mood—at least as far as charismatic gifts were concerned—and he resigned himself to the facts. But underneath this resignation (and unlike Sabbatai) his determination and essentially active character asserted themselves, and he unhesitatingly proclaimed his faith: "I lift up mine hand unto the Lord, . . . nor alter that which is gone out of my lips: that without any doubt this is the year of our redemption and our salvation is at hand." The heavenly message of August, 1665, was now reinterpreted to refer to the spring of 1667, "and I trust in God that thus it will be." Dates are subject to change and even celestial intimations are not free from uncertainty, but Sabbatai's messiahship was beyond any doubt. In his letter,[84] Nathan combined whatever notions and texts served his purpose, from the Servant chapters in Deutero-Isaiah to the doctrines of Lurianic kabbalism. However impenetrable the mystery, it was certain that the apostasy represented the crowning event of that phase of the messiah's career during which he had to "do his strange work and bring to pass his strange act" (cf. Isa. 28:21). As time went on, Nathan elaborated this doctrine more systematically and his letters gradually assumed the character of theological tracts. Writing seems to have been the mode of expression most congenial to his natural gifts—ignoring, for the moment, the brief period of inspired prophetic utterance in Gaza. There is nothing to suggest that he excelled as a preacher. Perhaps also his fugitive and restless life during those years was not conducive to successful preaching. He certainly did not declare open revolt against the rabbis who persecuted him. It was meet that "the servant be like unto his master," and he confined himself to expounding his ideas in writing and, occasionally, orally to individuals or small conventicles. His wanderings among the Jewish communities of the Balkans and his doctrinal letters are curiously reminiscent of the missionary activity of Paul of Tarsus.

Nathan left Brussa in the direction of Smyrna, no doubt because the rabbis of Constantinople had ordered him to return and forbidden him to proceed to the capital and to Adrianople. It is equally beyond

84. Sasportas, pp. 200–1.

doubt that Nathan never intended to obey their orders. He merely sought to gain time and evade their supervision. He arrived in Bonerbachi, a village near Smyrna,[85] on Friday evening, March 3.[86] On Sunday, Nathan was visited by a number of believers from Smyrna, but the rabbis, having received the instructions from Constantinople and fearing trouble if Nathan entered the city, sent him a message requesting him not to make any public appearances. (The messenger was Abraham Leon, one of the "kings" appointed by Sabbatai in December, 1665.) According to Coenen, the rabbis feared another outbreak of mass enthusiasm and its disastrous consequences, while many others were certain that no evil could befall them through the man of God and prophet.

Nathan was not the only foreigner in Smyrna at the time. Visitors and emissaries from Italy who had embarked at Venice or Leghorn at the end of the summer had landed in Smyrna at about the time of the apostasy. Among the new arrivals was R. Moses Pinheiro, Sabbatai's friend since their student days in Smyrna and subsequently, at least since 1665, his confidant in Leghorn. Pinheiro heard of the apostasy soon after his arrival and immediately wrote to Sabbatai. In a letter to his friends in Leghorn, Pinheiro reports that he had received a reply from Sabbatai, who was "apparently very ill, . . . but the illness is not too serious and can be healed through apostasy and the light will shine again." R. Joseph ha-Levi of Leghorn, to whom we owe this quotation, added in his report to Sasportas that Sabbatai had this idea from a letter of "his physician, Satan of Gaza."[87] (The punning substitution of Satan for Nathan was gaining currency at that time, as we also learn from R. Tobias Rofe Ashkenazi.) In any event, it appears that in explaining his situation to Pinheiro, Sabbatai quoted a phrase from a letter of Nathan's. The

85. Today Bornova, four miles northeast of Smyrna.

86. Thus Coenen (p. 134), who also gives the corresponding Jewish date (7 Adar). According to the tables in Mahler's *Jüdische Chronologie,* 7 Adar of that year fell on a Thursday. This is by no means the only instance of a discrepancy of one day between Coenen's dates and Mahler's tables. Considering the general trustworthiness of Coenen's reporting (he was practically an eyewitness of many of the events which he recorded) the discrepancy casts doubt on the reliability of Mahler's tables. The dates of Nathan's arrival and departure as given by Rosanes are wrong. Rycaut's account of the visit to Smyrna (pp. 217–18) is copied from Coenen.

87. Sasportas, pp. 251, 256.

idea bears the hallmark of Nathan's paradoxical thinking: whereas Sabbatai's mental sickness had at first been defined in metaphysical terms, his apostasy and present condition were now metaphorically described as an "illness." Sabbatai's letter to Pinheiro once more illustrates his dependence on his "physician" Nathan.

Pinheiro did not continue his journey to Adrianople, and the letter of homage and the hymns of praise which he had brought from the Jews of Leghorn remained undelivered. Nevertheless, he remained steadfast in his faith and eagerly accepted the guidance given in Sabbatai's and Nathan's letters. Also in Smyrna at the time were the emissaries from Casale (see above, pp. 494 f.). On disembarking from the boat they heard from two Jews in the Custom House that the messiah had apostatized. They nevertheless decided to stay for a while in Smyrna, partly in order to learn more about the messianic movement, partly because they did not quite believe the report. At the time of their arrival the news was still fresh, and Sabbatai's brother Elijah Ṣevi still held the Docetist view that the apostasy was an illusion and that the messiah had ascended to Heaven. The emissaries were much impressed by Elijah Ṣevi's explanations and by his announcement of the impending arrival of Nathan, for whom they carried a letter. They therefore remained in Smyrna, waiting for further developments. During their stay they were visited by the Dutch clergyman Coenen, who has left us a detailed account of his long conversation with them.[88] From them Coenen learned many of the rumors and stories that were current among the believers, though he was impressed that by that time the emissaries were already realizing the vanity of their hopes.

After Nathan had arrived, the emissaries from Casale went to see him, but their visit was disappointing. Nathan first tried to evade his visitors, who finally got a chance to deliver to him the letter from the community of Leghorn. Nathan promised to let them have an answer some other time (a promise which he failed to keep) and left them abruptly. In Smyrna, however, the emissaries had a chance to speak to several of Nathan's disciples and to his faithful companion Samuel Gandoor.[89] R. Samson Bacchi's conclusion was that Nathan

88. Coenen, pp. 127–33. They even had knowledge of Balarino's report to the Venetian "Signoria" through the prince of Piedmont.

89. The reference in R. Samson Bacchi's report to "Rabbi Samuel" is undoubtedly to Gandoor and not, as the editor erroneously thought, to Primo. There is no evidence that Primo was in Smyrna at the time.

was a competent kabbalist but a false prophet spreading dangerous doctrines; "may God save us . . . and send us relief and deliverance from another place."[90] Coenen, who was on friendly terms with the emissaries and who heard the story of their visit to Nathan from their own mouths, gives a somewhat different account of the incident. The prophet was in a very despondent mood and would not, at first, receive the visitors. When they had at last gained admission he told them that he was in danger of his life from the Turks and that he could not speak. He also refused to receive the letter from the community of Leghorn with his own hands and asked the rabbi Ḥayyim Abulafia[91] to receive it in his behalf. Though Nathan later unobtrusively entered the city and quietly stayed there for a while, he failed to give the emissaries the reply he had promised them. The Italian rabbis were much annoyed, and confided to Coenen that they hoped their futile voyage would at least serve to disabuse others and bring them back to the faith of their fathers.[92] According to Coenen, they left Smyrna for Italy at the end of March, 1667; according to the Hebrew account based on Samson Bacchi's report, they departed in the middle of March "and arrived in Leghorn together with Rabbi Moses Pinheiro."[93]

Nathan's uncivil behavior toward the Italian rabbis was no doubt caused by the mood of melancholia that had settled on him after his excommunication by the rabbis of Brussa. He wanted no more disputations with unbelievers, and henceforth opened himself only to believers. To them he promised that his prophecies would be fulfilled in September,[94] and even declared that if the year passed without his prophecy being proved true then "he would deliver himself up to the Jews and suffer capital punishment as a false prophet." During his sojourn in Smyrna, Nathan was hiding in the house of a physician, a former Portuguese marrano and a friend of the Ṣevi family whom

90. R. Samson Bacchi's report (Carpi, pp. 19–20).

91. He was one of the believers in Smyrna. In 1673 Abulafia was in Adrianople, together with Sabbatai's brother Elijah Ṣevi, but subsequently returned to Smyrna; see *Sefunoth,* III–IV (1960), 217.

92. Coenen, pp. 135–36.

93. Carpi, p. 20.

94. Coenen (p. 136) says "in the month of Ellul, 5428, which will be at the end of the year 1667" which is impossible; evidently Ellul, 5427, is meant, as also appears from Coenen's words (*ibid.,* p. 139).

Sabbatai had appointed "king of Portugal."[95] Sasportas says that the disabused believers wanted to deliver Nathan to the Turkish authorities, but the doctor helped him to escape through a little hatch-door and Nathan fled to Chios. The story, however, seems very improbable. After Nathan's return from Chios to Smyrna, Coenen went to see him in Elijah Ṣevi's house and found the place full of visitors; evidently nobody thought of keeping Nathan's presence a secret. It appears, therefore, that on his first visit Nathan obeyed the advice to refrain from public appearances, though no threats had been made of traducing him to the authorities.[96]

The prophet, who would hardly speak to a fellow kabbalist of the caliber of R. Samson Bacchi, was not likely to be more encouraging to a visiting Protestant clergyman. But undaunted by the presence of a throng of other visitors and ever ready to discuss theology and religion, Coenen laid his questions before Nathan concerning the latter's prophecy.[97] Nathan, however, would not enter into direct conversation with his visitor. Coenen's questions had to be repeated to the prophet by Nissim Amato, one of the leading believers in Smyrna,[98] and were largely left unanswered. By way of reply, Coenen was merely

95. *Relation,* p. 29. It was through the good offices of this physician that Coenen obtained his first interview with Elijah Ṣevi (Coenen, p. 78). Probably the physician is identical with the "Doctor Barut" mentioned by Coenen, p. 93 (cf. also above, p. 140, n. 87, and p. 431, n. 233 and n. 234) and the name of Cardozo is due to one of Sasportas' not infrequent slips of memory. On one occasion Sasportas (p. 252) ridicules the physicians among the believers and mentions Dr. Benjamin Musaphia and "a certain physician in Smyrna," but there the context leaves no doubt that Abraham Miguel Cardozo is meant and that, consequently, Smyrna is a *lapsus calami* for Tripoli. As one mistake begets another, this may account for the physician in Smyrna being called Cardozo by Sasportas (p. 200).

96. According to Coenen (p. 137) Nathan left for Chios in April, after having made the pilgrimage to the tomb of Sabbatai's mother and having bathed in the sea nearby (see above, p. 613). He was accompanied by two followers or disciples and by three hired Turks. After his return to Smyrna toward the end of the month, he stayed at the house of Elijah Ṣevi.

97. The meeting took place on April 25, 1667. Coenen spoke in Italian and Nathan replied in a mixture of Italian and Spanish, the *lingua franca* of the Levant; see Coenen, p. 138.

98. Nissim Amato's signature still appears with that of other leaders of the community on a document of the year 1677; see J. M. Toledano, *Sarid u-Falit,* p. 50.

reminded of the celestial proclamation of the summer of 1665, which would be fulfilled in September, 1667. Elijah Ṣevi's promise to Coenen to arrange another and more private meeting was merely a polite maneuver to get rid of the unwelcome visitor. Evidently Nathan did not wish to discuss the faith with Jewish doubters and even less with gentiles.

Nathan left Smyrna early in May (the Sixth of Iyyar) in a northerly direction. His destination was Adrianople. The movement in Smyrna persisted for some months, but when the hopes for September had also been disappointed, the number of believers diminished further, and the rabbis who wished to gloss over the whole episode got the upper hand. Coenen's account ends with Nathan's departure from Smyrna, and with it ends our main source of reliable and orderly information on the movement in Sabbatai's native city. The history of the subsequent developments has to be pieced together from the most diverse sources. What is true of Smyrna also applies to the movement as a whole, and the lack of full and systematic information makes itself felt in particular for the period that is not covered by Sasportas' *Ṣiṣath Nobel Ṣevi.*

Nathan knew that his journey took place in defiance of the express order of the rabbis and he consequently avoided the major Jewish communities such as Salonika, where his presence was likely to make a stir. He tarried for a while in Ipsola, a small community on the way to Adrianople, either because the Jewish authorities there would not let him continue his journey or because he expected instructions from Sabbatai. The believers were still strong in this area and seem to have had the support of the majority. In any event, the rabbis of Adrianople knew full well that the masses "still persevered in their deceitful faith."[99] No doubt the immediate proximity to the messiah stimulated the imagination, and all kinds of rumors, some true and others false, were current at the time. Sabbatai was said to be "despised by the Turks and trying to ingratiate himself with them by spending most of the day in the mosque where, however, [according to the credulous believers] he devoted himself to Torah and to kabbalistic meditations."[100] According to the same source, the Jews were strictly forbidden to visit or even approach him.

99. Sasportas, p. 203.

100. R. Samson Bacchi's report (Carpi, p. 19); similarly also Baruch of Arezzo (*ap.* Freimann, p. 63).

Whether the Turkish authorities, like the rabbis of Constantinople, really forbade any contact between the Jews and Mehemed Kapici Bashi is more than doubtful. Sabbatai enjoyed the protection and friendship of Vani Effendi, "chaplain to the sultan" and the outstanding religious personality at the court.[101] Even more, all sources agree that he enjoyed the sympathy of the sultan. Later Sabbatian tradition tells many details of Sabbatai's friendly contacts with Vani Effendi, including the latter's conversion to the "faith."[102] Sabbatai "passed his time devoutly at the Ottoman Court, educated at the Feet of the learned *Gamaliel* of the Turkish Law . . . *Vani* Effendi. . . . To this Master *Sabbatai* was a most docile scholar, and profited, as we may imagine, beyond measure in the Turkish Doctrine" while Vani too learned "something of the Jewish rites" from his new disciple.[103] On the other hand, Sabbatai also maintained relations with his followers, some of whom apostatized in his wake, though, as a rule, he appears to have been content with explaining his action to his believers without demanding that they do likewise. According to R. Israel Ḥazzan, he ordered believers to take the turban only when he was in a fit of manic exaltation.[104] Moreover, it is expressly stated that only those believers who were personally invited by the messiah to apostatize were supposed to do so, but that nobody should embrace Islam on his own initiative.[105] This may account for the fact that most visitors to Sabbatai remained Jews, though there is no definite evidence to show that Israel Ḥazzan's statement which may, perhaps, reflect the situation after 1669, also applies to the first period immediately after the apostasy. It should be borne in mind that Sabbatai may well have promised the Turks a mass conversion of the Jews.

101. *Relation,* pp. 35, 39, and especially Rycaut, pp. 218–19. The facts recounted by Rycaut in a straightforward and objective manner are maliciously slanted by the French Jesuit, who presents Sabbatai as a villain and even puts anti-Semitic speeches into his mouth.

102. In a Dönmeh MS. in the Ben Zvi Institute, Jerusalem, no. 2280; the text has been published by Mr. Molkho in *Sefunoth,* III–IV (1960), p. 505.

103. Rycaut, *loc. cit.;* See also de la Croix, p. 378. An extensive and interesting account of Vani's personality can be found in the diary notes for the year 1675 of John Covel, the physician and friend of the British ambassador in Turkey; see "Extracts from Dr. John Covel's Diary," in J. Th. Bent (ed.), *Early Voyages and Travels in the Levant* (1893), pp. 268–72.

104. See *Schocken Volume*, p. 163.

105. *Ibid.,* p. 176. For more details on this point see below, pp. 857–60.

He was, no doubt, divided and confused in his soul, and the distinctions between truth and falsehood, reality and play-acting became increasingly blurred. His double-faced behavior as a Jew and a Muslim is well attested by several independent sources and is not merely an invention of Sabbatian legend. But we may be sure that at least during his recurring periods of "illumination" his despicable treason appeared to him transfigured by a mystical light, and Nathan's letters helped him to interpret his fate better than he could ever have done by himself.

Sabbatai's meetings with his followers in Adrianople are mentioned in several sources, and his discourses, as quoted by de la Croix, are essentially similar to those reported by Sasportas' correspondents in spite of certain differences in the tropological symbolism. Moses, the first redeemer, foreshadows the messiah. Even as Moses lived as an Egyptian at the court of Pharaoh, so Sabbatai too had to apostatize and live as a Turk in order to redeem his people. The sun had to disappear into darkness before rising again with renewed splendor.[106] According to de la Croix, Sabbatai concealed his double-dealing from the Turks, but the infidels apprised them of it and the sultan and Vani Effendi were exceedingly wroth.[107] It seems more probable, however, that Sabbatai acted with the full knowledge of the Turks, who believed that his contacts with the Jews were designed to gain more converts to Islam. In any event, the believers carefully concealed the fact that they continued to regard Sabbatai as their messiah and that in their view the present situation was a mere interlude before the final downfall of the Turkish Empire. The expectations and the tactics of the believers in Adrianople were similar to Nathan's, for they informed their Polish brethren that the messianic date had to be postponed to Passover (April, 1667).[108] Then, "God's wondrous ways will begin to be revealed, and he [Sabbatai] will reveal himself and come out from his state of occultation."

106. De la Croix, pp. 375–76. According to de la Croix, Sabbatai also said that he was waiting for the prophet Nathan who would bring him the rod with which Moses wrought his miracles; until then, "je suis obligé de me tenir caché." This sounds like a genuine quotation rather than the invention of a Christian writer. The Jews of Constantinople were, of course, spreading many tales about Sabbatai's explanations.

107. *Ibid.*, p. 378.

108. A copy of the letter was sent to Vienna. A summary of its contents is preserved in the Hottinger Collection, vol. 30, fol. 345b.

Many emissaries from the various Jewish, and especially oriental, communities who had arrived in Constantinople after the apostasy proceeded to Adrianople where some of them, in their turn, apostatized. According to Rycaut, "many Jews flocked in, some as far as from *Babylon, Jerusalem,* and other remote places, and casting their Caps on the ground, in the presence of the Grand Signior, voluntarily professed themselves Mahometans."[109] The same incident seems to be referred to, albeit in deliberately obscure language, in a Sabbatian source. "There arrived four emissaries from the land of Cush . . . and when they learned that Our Lord wore this [that is, the Turkish] garb, they too donned this garb [that is, apostatized] and then went to the mosque to kiss the hand of Our Lord, but he would not suffer it. They also said that in their country prophets and prophetesses had arisen. These emissaries brought with them letters from Baghdad, but Our Lord would not make answer to them as he was in a state of occultation. However, to satisfy these emissaries, he gave them a letter confirming that they had found the man about whom their prophets had prophesied."[110] There were, as we shall see, many instances of temporary *ad hoc* apostasies: the "converts" subsequently returned to their home countries as Jews, or fled from Turkey to Italy where they returned to their ancestral religion. The early Sabbatian doctrine of apostasy apparently developed by stages, though with considerable speed.[111]

The many cases of apostasy may account for the excitement caused by the reports of Nathan's imminent arrival in Adrianople. The rabbis decided to send him a message ordering him to put the greatest possible distance between himself and the city, and moreover to recant all his errors and vain inventions.[112] Several of the "noble Lords of Constantinople" (that is, rabbis or lay leaders of the Jewish congregations in the capital) were in Adrianople at the time, and together they dispatched several rabbis to Ipsola where they were to sit as a duly constituted rabbinic court and examine Nathan.[113] Their

109. Rycaut, p. 219.

110. Baruch of Arezzo, *ap.* Freimann, p. 64.

111. See below, pp. 856–65, Israel Ḥazzan's testimony of the doctrine of apostasy of the "Holy Congregation."

112. Sasportas, p. 203.

113. Their report was subsequently published as a broadsheet under the title "A Memorial unto the Children of Israel"; it is also printed at the end of Aboab's responsa *Debar Shemu᾽el.* The names of the three messengers are there given as

report, signed on the Eighth of Sivan, 5427 (May 31, 1667), states that they had found Nathan's arguments "worn thin and patched." In fact Nathan had denied that he was a prophet; he was neither obliged to work a miracle nor capable of doing so. His only prophecy had been the proclamation of Sabbatai's messiahship, which would become manifest after one year and several months. This prophecy would be proved false only if the Twenty-fifth of the month of Ellul passed without any messianic event having taken place. All his other utterances were based on heavenly intimations and *maggidim,* but not on prophecy strictly speaking. The messengers from Adrianople, however, continued to press him for a sign confirming at least his one prophecy, and Nathan finally told them "to wait until the feast of Pentecost, . . . for he had been told by the Holy Spirit that [on that day] the man in Adrianople [Sabbatai Ṣevi] would have a great illumination and that by the virtue of that man he would be able to perform a miracle. They waited . . . but nothing happened, and instead of an illumination a great darkness fell upon him." The messengers thereupon brought heavy pressure to bear on Nathan and demanded that he sign a solemn pledge, (*a*) not to come nearer than a twelve days' journey to Adrianople, (*b*) not to communicate on any account, either directly or indirectly, with "that man in Adrianople," (*c*) not to make any public appearances and not to see anybody except his father-in-law and his servant (R. Samuel Gandoor?), (*d*) to confess that all he had said was lies and falsehood if the messiah did not appear until the Twenty-fifth of Ellul. The pledge was worded in the first-person singular[114] for Nathan to sign, and lest he later contest the genuineness of his signature, R. Samuel Gandoor was also made to sign as a witness. The document was given much publicity, though what the rabbis really expected from their maneuver is doubtful. They must have realized that Nathan would hardly honor a promise which he could claim had been extorted from him under duress. As a matter of fact, Nathan repudiated the document he was made to sign in a vehement

---

the physician David Curiel, Asher b. Abraham Ashkenazi, and R. Judah b. Meshullam. Sasportas (p. 204) mentions four rabbis, reading, instead of the second of the aforementioned, Asher b. Raphael and R. Abraham ha-Levi Ashkenazi. The latter is known as one of the rabbis of Constantinople. Baruch of Arezzo (p. 59) says that four or five rabbis were sent to Ipsola.

114. The full text in Sasportas, p. 205.

letter, the text of which has recently come to light.[115] The heading in the manuscript declares the letter to have been written from Ipsola to the "emissaries" from Constantinople who, by a Hebrew pun, are called the "adversaries" from Constantinople.[116] It seems, however, more probable that the repudiation was written in 1668 as part of his answer to the broadsheet quoted in note 113. It uses the same tactics as his answer to the rabbis of Venice discussed below (p. 767). He maintains that the document was distorted and had a quite different meaning.[117] He cursed the three men who had signed it and called them by the names of three unclean creatures—the hare, the rabbit, and the locust. At any rate, he did not consider himself bound by his signature, and at the first opportunity that presented itself he proceeded to Adrianople and met his messiah.[118]

Nathan did not depart immediately. He tarried for some weeks in Thrace, where "he added to his wickedness by trying to convert others to his faith"—probably not by public preaching but, rather, as in Smyrna, by personal contacts and literary activity. On one occasion, however, he acted in a public and, indeed, demonstrative manner that left no doubts about his unshaken faith in his prophetic mission. Addressing himself to the Thracian communities (or to groups of believers there), he renewed the order abolishing the fast of the Seventeenth of Tammuz and declaring it a feast day.[119] Nathan's continuing influence on the believers, and especially his most recent act of provocation, placed the rabbis of Adrianople in an embarrassing predicament. Realizing that their bans of excommunication availed nothing, they resorted to the curious expedient of negotiating with the hated apostate himself. The rabbis of Constantinople, in their account of the matter, hush up the fact that they had addressed them-

115. The copy from the Dönmeh archives published in *Sefunoth,* V (1961), 270–71, is rather corrupt, including the names of the people involved.

116. He writes *ṣarey* (enemies) instead of *ṣirey* (emissaries).

117. He said, for example, that he had only agreed not to start any direct correspondence with Sabbatai, but that left him free to send a messenger to him, or to answer letters coming from him. There can be little doubt that these statements have a hollow ring.

118. As now appears from the account of Nathan's conversation with Mahallallel Halleluyah of Ancona; see G. Scholem in *H. A. Wolfson Jubilee Volume* (1965), p. 226.

119. The order was sent from Comerjina (Turkish, Gumūlčina), a small community in Thrace; see Sasportas, p. 206.

selves, through a go-between, to Sabbatai Ṣevi, asking him to intervene with his believers. The go-between was Joseph Karillo of Brussa, one of the "kings" appointed by Sabbatai in Smyrna. He had followed the messiah to Adrianople and was, at the time, still a Jew.[120] (He apostatized in 1671; see p. 850.[121]) According to the official report of the rabbis,[122] the Sabbatian believers took the initiative: knowing that if they obeyed Nathan's instructions they were liable to excommunication, they besought the guidance of the messiah, who sent them orders, through Karillo, to observe the fast. The spectacle of the Law being observed because the apostate messiah had countermanded the instructions of his prophet more than justified the indignation of Sasportas, who felt that never before had the Jewish religion fallen so low. Karillo showed Sabbatai's letter to the believers but would not allow the rabbis to see it—perhaps because it contained invectives which it was safer to keep from their eyes. In any event, Karillo was arrested by the Turkish authorities on the demand of the rabbis, and sentenced—we do not know on what grounds or under what pretext—to a fine of four hundred *grosso:* "and now he is in prison. And we have admonished the sect of sinners following this man to disperse." The rabbis, it appears, still distinguished at the time between ordinary believers (such as R. Moses Kohen, in whose house the faithful used to meet) and the "sect of sinners," that is, the few dozen followers who had apostatized with Sabbatai.

In addition to all this, the rabbis of Constantinople had a very strange tale to tell—no doubt with a view to increasing the effect of their anti-Sabbatian propaganda. Sabbatai, they report in their letter, had appeared before them and repented of all he had done. Having heard of Joseph Karillo's arrest, he appeared, panic-stricken, on the following day at the Board Room of the lay leaders of the community (that is, not before the rabbinic court) and "began to excuse himself." The real villain of the piece was the wicked forger Nathan, who had deleted the Redeemer's real name from the *Vision of R. Abraham* and substituted that of Sabbatai. "He thus seduced me and led me astray with lies and deceits, and made me stray from

120. He was still referred to as "R. Karillo."

121. See A. H. Weiss, *Beth ha-Midrash* (1865), p. 65. Karillo's descendants were among the Dönmeh families in Salonika; see *A Sabbatian Hymn Book* (1948), p. 82 (n. 5, on p. 82 of the *Hymn Book,* should be corrected).

122. See Sasportas, pp. 205–6.

the ways of the Lord until I myself began to lead astray the people who still believe in me to this day." He also cursed Abraham Yakhini for his share in the imposture. Graetz was the first to suspect that the rabbis were practicing here some kind of "holy ruse," since the confession was unlike anything we know of Sabbatai's character. Perhaps they thought that if Sabbatai could be used to sabotage Nathan's abolition of the fast, why not put a false confession in his mouth and pretend that he had disavowed the whole movement in general and, in particular, the prophet, who at that moment was the main source of trouble. The confession, composed in the first person and signed: "Thus speaketh the man that hath seen affliction without measure, your very young brother Sabbatai Ṣevi,"[123] was dated "in the week of the pentateuchal lesson 'and his heart fainted for he believed not' "[124] and addressed to:

Our brethren of the House of Israel, be it faithfully known unto you that the bearer of this letter, may God's mercy be with him, is now with me, and I announce to you that having come to think better of it I now realize with utter certainty THAT THERE IS NOTHING WHATEVER ABOUT ME and that whatever has befallen me in this matter, whether through myself or through those that prophesied about me, was nothing but a spirit of utter folly or a spirit of some other kind, and that the world will continue as usual until the true Redeemer arise. Wherefore let everyone be quiet at home and pursue his usual business, and let them not regard vain words but wait for the true salvation, which has not yet come, until Heaven have mercy on us. And God Almighty give you mercy and protect you and all that is yours, and spread the tabernacle of peace upon you, and grant you to behold His salvation and your eyes may see the true king in his beauty. Amen.[125]

123. Perhaps the Hebrew word *me*ʾ*od* ("very") is a scribal error and the text should read: "your young brother Mehemed Sabbatai Ṣevi"; cf. also the signature in Sabbatai's letter published by Z. Rubashov in *Zion* (annual), VI (1934), 54.

124. Gen. 45:26, in the portion *Va-yiggash,* i.e., early January, 1667. This would antedate the retraction four full months.

125. MS. Enelow 2223 (Jewish Theological Seminary, New York), fol. 233a, quoting from a MS. found in Armenia; see *Zion,* VII (1942), 175. In another copy of the same text, preserved in a letter by R. Solomon Bekhor Ḥoṣin of Baghdad, the date is given as "the week of the portion *Va-yiggash,* 429, i.e., early December, 1668 (see *ha-Ṣefirah,* II [1875], 115). According to

The "bearer of this letter" was R. Aaron b. Ḥananiah, one of the emissaries from Persia or Kurdistan who had come to visit Sabbatai in Constantinople but had learned, on arriving there, that the messiah had apostatized. It is significant that the authors of this pretended confession, ostensibly addressed to the whole House of Israel, carefully avoided circulating it in Turkey or in the West and gave it, instead, to the naïve and unsuspecting emissaries from Persia and Kurdistan. The forgery is patent to anyone familiar with Sabbatai's behavior and style in the years after his apostasy. Sabbatai continued to sign himself: "thus speaketh the man who was raised up on high," and throughout 1667 received visitors, accepting their homage although he did not, in most cases, demand that they apostatize. R. Israel Ḥazzan of Kastoria in Macedonia relates how, when he and his friends visited Sabbatai, they would recite the liturgical benediction due to a Jewish king: "who has imparted of His glory to them that fear Him," and Sabbatai showed them biblical references to his person by way of *gematria* which he had written down in his own hand.[126] There is no reliable evidence that even during fits of melancholia or despair he ever cursed or insulted his followers (but see below, p. 842). De la Croix reports one instance of offensive behavior toward his believers (see below, p. 858). This happened on one of the occasions when Sabbatai demanded that his visitors apostatize and his demand was met by a blank refusal.

In their letter to Constantinople, the rabbis of Adrianople also announced that following Sabbatai's confession they had excommunicated Nathan on account of his many lies and on account of his having broken his promise to keep at a twelve days' distance from Adrianople. In fact he had established himself in Comerjina and assembled a following of "vain and light persons" in spite of his oath to abstain from communicating with the local Jews wherever he went, "wherefore we excommunicated him according to the rules of the law."[127] They also requested their colleagues in the capital "to wreak vengeance on these evildoers" without, however, indicating the kind

Sasportas' account, however, the incident occurred in 1667. Either one of the two dates is wrong, or there were two incidents. In the second MS. the name of the Persian emissary is given as Aaron of Merakah. See also M. Benayahu in *Sefunoth,* III-IV (1960), 10.

126. See *Schocken Volume,* p. 164.

127. Sasportas, p. 207. Comerjina is near Adrianople.

of vengeance desired. Did they suggest that the rabbis of Constantinople inform against the believers to the Turkish authorities? It is not quite clear whether the evildoers referred to were the disciples who studied with Nathan (the "vain and light persons" of polemical parlance) or Sabbatian apostates.

In any event, the rabbis of Adrianople were determined to destroy Nathan's reputation by all means fair and less than fair. Their attitude to Nathan had hardened considerably in the few months since the rabbis of Constantinople had sent their pastoral letter charging all communities to prevent "the rabbi Nathan" from joining his messiah. Was the change due merely to exasperation at Nathan's flagrant disregard of his promises in Ipsola, or were the rabbis beginning to realize that the movement was stronger than they had thought and that Nathan had to be cast out even if it meant driving him to apostasy? Similar tactics were employed by the rabbis a century later with regard to Jacob Frank, but the situation in 1667 was very different from that created by the Frankists. Early Sabbatianism, in spite of occasional manifestations of antinomianism, had not yet developed into a radically antinomian movement, and the believers were essentially pious and orthodox Jews who differed from the rest in believing that the messianic redemption had already begun or was about to begin. It is most unlikely that the rabbis were bent on aggravating the crisis by driving Nathan to apostasy, particularly as they must have realized that the prophet's example might inspire his followers to imitate him.

We are still in the dark about Nathan's movements and contacts, especially his contacts with Sabbatai Ṣevi, though we know for certain that he acted in complete disregard of his solemn promises and actually visited Sabbatai in Adrianople. On that occasion Sabbatai charged him with a kabbalistic mission to Rome and even provided him with the necessary means (see below, p. 740, n. 137). Nathan's first station after departing from Thrace was Salonika, where he was sure to find a considerable number of believers. With some of them he established close contacts, and later he sent them his tracts and letters. Nevertheless, the majority of the rabbis were firmly set against Sabbatian preaching, and after his father-in-law, Samuel Lissabona, had fallen ill and died, Nathan was forced to leave the city.[128] Most of the time

128. Sasportas, p. 259; cf. also Tishby's note (Sasportas, p. 203). According to Sasportas the opponents of the movement threatened Nathan with dire vengeance, but there is no evidence to corroborate Sasportas' statement.

Nathan was wandering about the many small communities between Salonika and the Adriatic coast, accompanied only by the faithful Samuel Gandoor. Whereas in the larger communities the majority of the rabbis was for repressing the movement, the smaller communities were much less subject to rabbinic influence and were more easily swayed by a few earnest believers. Occasionally, as in Corfu and Kastoria, the leaders of the community would devoutly accept the prophet's teaching. Nathan himself claimed that his itinerary was prescribed to him by a celestial voice (*maggid*) that always accompanied him: "at its command he journeyed and at its command he pitched."[129] This account of Nathan's peregrinations subsequently became official doctrine among the believers. As we have seen before, these *maggidim,* that is, the souls of departed saints and prophets, were now said to be the source of Nathan's inspiration, with the exception of his first genuinely and fully prophetic experience which came from a higher place.

Meanwhile, the month of Ellul (Sept.), 1667, had passed and the "celestial proclamation" of 1665 had not been fulfilled, Nathan's repeated affirmations notwithstanding. But instead of recanting, Nathan now increasingly emphasized the distinction between two types of inspired utterance which had, so far, been wrongly treated alike. His vision of the divine throne, in the spring of 1665, in which the Lord's voice had announced Israel's redemption through the messiah Sabbatai Ṣevi, was a unique experience of prophecy in the strict sense of the word, the truth of which remained unshaken. The various dates, however, that had been revealed to him by celestial voices, angels, and messengers (including the "heavenly proclamation" heard during the great vision) were of a different kind altogether and subject to change. After September, 1667, other dates were mentioned, though with less categorical certainty, and Nathan's theological labors were directed mainly to expounding the mystical significance and tragic necessity of the messiah's apostasy in the accomplishment of his mission.

Nathan was not the only believer who, at this time, had heavenly inspirations. In the years 1667–68, an otherwise unknown R. Jacob b. Isaac Ṣirojon received revelations from a *maggid* which (probably

129. Baruch of Arezzo, *ap.* Freimann, pp. 59, 63; see also the quotation (Sasportas, p. 331) from Nathan's letters which the emissaries from Jerusalem brought to Salé, in Morocco in 1668.

in his own handwriting) have been preserved in one of the manuscripts from the Dönmeh archives.[130] They are all concerned with the justification of Sabbatai's apostasy and the personal fate awaiting the writer (including possibly his own mystical apostasy?). They are written in pseudo-Zoharic Aramaic.[131] Among them is a revelation dated the day before the final date for redemption given by Nathan, the fateful Twenty-fifth of Ellul, 1667—but no reference is made to the impending events![132] The author was already concerned about economical matters. According to him, Sabbatai (called here *maran,* Our Lord) had declared that those who have little faith in him have worldly possessions because they come from the inferior worlds, whereas concerning the believers, "no money was given to them."[133] This may be an interesting reference to the social composition of the greater part of the Sabbatian following at that time.

In addition to the tracts and letters in which Nathan expounded his rapidly developing doctrines which tended to become more and more extreme, new pseudepigraphical writings made their appearance. They were composed either by Nathan or—more probably—by others. R. Elisha, the prophet's father, testified in the year 1667 that not only the *Vision of R. Abraham* but three more books had been revealed to his son (see above, p. 230). It seems unlikely, however, that the extant pseudo-*Hekhaloth* text is the work of Nathan. The apocalypse in question, written in obvious imitation of the *Hekhaloth* books,[134] is an enlarged version of the *Book of Zerubbabel.* The original text of the latter work was widespread at the time, and the Sabbatians had no difficulties in discovering in it references to the messiah's imprisonment in Gallipoli. After the apostasy, several chapters were added in which Metatron, the "angel of the Presence," revealed to

130. MS. Ben-Zvi Institute 2262, pp. 85–100. The pages have all the indications of an autograph which came into the hand of the collector, R. Abraham Miranda in Salonika who put the MS. together between 1750 and 1760. I do not know whether the author lived in Adrianople, Salonika, or elsewhere in Thrace.

131. To be edited by Rivkah Schatz, in *Sefunoth,* XIV (forthcoming), 220–52 (= *Sefer Yavan,* I).

132. The revelation is dated Tuesday, 24 Ellul, but only in 1667 did this date fall on a Tuesday (September 3, 1667).

133. In a revelation from December, 1667 (Kislev, 5428).

134. See, on these esoteric books from the Talmudic period, G. Scholem, *Major Trends,* ch. 2.

R. Ishmael, the hero of the *Hekhaloth Rabbathi*, the messianic mysteries of which he had already apprised Zerubbabel, the son of Shealtiel. This thoroughly Sabbatian apocalypse was inserted by Sabbatian copyists into the text of *Hekhaloth Rabbathi*, and preserved for posterity through this fortunate circumstance. An unsuspecting rabbi in Jerusalem even published the *Hekhaloth* texts with the Sabbatian interpolations. This amazing apocalypse was undoubtedly composed before 1669 and probably soon after the disappointment of the Twenty-fifth of Ellul, 1667. If it was written by Nathan or by one of his disciples, the most likely date is autumn, 1667.[135] In any event, Nathan, in his later writings, repeatedly refers to Metatron's revelations in the *Book of Zerubbabel* and quotes them as proof of his message: "Behold all this has befallen AMIRAH and not one thing has remained unfulfilled."

Already the original version of the *Book of Zerubbabel* had described the rabbis as disparaging and vilifying the messiah, but the Sabbatian supplement is far more concrete and explicit: the rabbis insult the messiah, calling him a villain and apostate, "whereupon God in his wrath imprisons the messiah for exactly eight years, corresponding to the eight days of circumcision. As a child is not considered a member of the community until the eighth day, when he is circumcised, even so God hides His face from the messiah during the years of his imprisonment. God also tempts Israel to decry the messiah by saying, 'This man erred and led Israel astray. Pharaoh did not imprison Moses as this messenger has been imprisoned.' " This suggests that the hopes of the believers were now pinned on the year 1674, that is, the eighth year after the apostasy.

135. See G. Scholem, *Zion*, VII (1942), 186–87, and Tishby's notes to Sasportas, pp. 333–34. Sasportas, misunderstanding a phrase in R. Jacob Saᶜadun's letter of autumn, 1668, was led to believe that the apocalypse had been written before the apostasy, but a careful reading of the text shows that the messiah's apostasy is its principal theme. The text is printed in S. A. Wertheimer, *Pirqey Hekhaloth* (Jerusalem, 1889), chs. 33 ff. and in Y. Even-Shemuel, *Midreshey Geᵓullah* (1943), pp. 352–70. Even-Shemuel was the first to recognize the Sabbatian character of these chapters. I was subsequently able to confirm his thesis from a Sabbatian MS. (now at the National Library in Jerusalem, no. 381, 8°); cf. my article in *Zion*, *loc. cit.* Another version mentioning the year 1666 is found in MS. Ben-Zvi Institute 2262, pp. 104–5, where it is said to have been copied from Ḥayyim Vital's *ᶜEṣ Ḥayyim* by Solomon Herrera, schoolmaster in the Talmud Torah, Salonika.

The events of 1666—the revelation of the messiah, the controversy over his personality, the penitential revival, the anxiety of the gentiles, the crisis and aftermath of the apostasy—are described in vivid colors in the apocalypse:

Metatron told me that one year before [the manifestation of the messiah] . . . God would send a messenger to Israel. . . . For the messiah has been hidden for many generations and a great slumber has fallen upon them. . . . [But now God] makes the four corners of the world resound, and announces to Israel: "Redemption has come." Thereupon men, women, and children will assemble to pray for God's mercy . . . and all Israel will repent of their sins. And the gentiles too assemble as they behold Israel praying in their synagogues, . . . and they will be afraid and put to shame, and they will say: "Verily there is salvation unto Israel and we have mocked them," and the gentiles too will repent. Then the messiah will plead before God: "Lord of the Universe, let me suffer the worst agonies but let none of the gentiles behold and share the bliss that is laid up for Israel!" Thereupon God takes two iron chains and puts them on the messiah's shoulders, saying to him: "The one is for the sins of this generation, the other is that the gentiles may have no part in salvation." But Israel [seeing the messiah in chains] change their minds and despise the messiah, saying: "Woe unto us that we have followed that madman." Then God will say: "You call him a madman, you shall behold his light." . . . In the first year of his captivity proclamations will be made against him in all Jewish cities, and the rabbis and lay leaders will conspire against him. . . . During the years of his captivity the scholars will be taken away and the believers [!] will pass away. . . . and the generation will be empty [of faith and wisdom] . . . for seven years.[136]

The views expressed in the apocalypse regarding the future of the gentiles argue against Nathan's authorship. Nathan, in his letter to Sabbatai's brother, had declared that the gentiles would be saved through the merits of the messiah's son. According to this apocalypse, however, Sabbatai voluntarily took upon himself further suffering in order to assure the ruin of the gentiles. Nathan, it is true, went to Rome, at Sabbatai's explicit behest (see below, pp. 776 f.), to perform a mystico-magical rite and to bring about the destruction of the city.

136. Chs. 33 and 35 of the *Pirqey Hekhaloth* (referred to above, n. 135), corrected according to the Sabbatian MS.; cf. *Zion,* VII (1942), 186.

But the destruction of the center of iniquity is not necessarily the same as the total ruin of all gentiles. Whether or not Nathan composed the apocalypse, it is evident that the minds of the believers were profoundly agitated during the year 1667, and Nathan was surely not the only one who sought to fathom the mystery of the recent events.

Early in 1668 Nathan arrived on Corfu from Yannina. During his stay on Corfu he no doubt prepared for his mysterious journey to Italy by entering into correspondence with the remaining Italian believers. There is a great deal that is still obscure about this journey. Whatever the exact nature of the kabbalistic mission for which Sabbatai himself is said to have provided the means,[137] Nathan surely knew that the majority of rabbis in Venice were against him. Why then did he head straight for the lion's den—even announcing in advance his intention of doing so—rather than go to communities such as Leghorn or Ancona where he could count on some support? In any event, the few weeks which he spent on Corfu (February–March, 1668) were filled with feverish activity reminiscent of his sojourn in Smyrna. Nathan began to adopt a double-faced behavior, depending on whether he was dealing with believers or with infidels. Sabbatai had exhibited a similar duplicity—impressing his messianic mission on his fellow Jews, but denying it in front of gentiles—but Nathan was the first to practice such double-dealing within the Jewish community. In due course this duplicity became the characteristic hallmark of the Sabbatian movement. To infidels Nathan spoke like a disabused enthusiast; in the trusted circle of believers he spoke his real mind. During that period he wrote several letters expounding the mystery of the apostasy. Sasportas reports that Nathan found "many fools" on Corfu, whom he taught his doctrines and confirmed in their faith. To those who were not of his party he pretended that he intended to do public penance in Venice for his errors, whereas to the believers he confided that he was going to Rome, where the ruin of the gentiles would commence.[138]

137. When the rabbi of Ancona expressed his astonishment at the fact that Nathan and Samuel Gandoor, unlike ordinary emissaries, made no claims on the charity of the communities through which they passed, Nathan replied that all the expenses had been provided for from the savior's own pocket and that Sabbatai had changed them "not to take a penny from any Jew because they were now going on a mission" on behalf of the messiah (*H. A. Wolfson Jubilee Volume,* p. 233).

138. Sasportas, p. 259.

The Sabbatians, however, were not the only ones to indulge in double-dealing. An infidel who posed as a believer succeeded in obtaining from Nathan the text of a letter that was definitely not intended for publication. It is the first document explicitly setting forth the Sabbatian doctrine of the *necessity* of the messiah's apostasy. It was written in January, 1668, and addressed to a believer on the island of Zante, near Corfu, who had inquired regarding "the Lord whom we seek and for whom we wait every day and every hour, . . . the Great Sabbath [that is, Sabbatai] which is the Holy Sabbath. . . ." The letter[139] is of great significance for a better understanding of the means by which the believers justified the apostasy and handled their propaganda, and it deserves to be quoted at least in part:

Know therefore . . . that [it is] he and no other, and besides him there is no Savior of Israel.[140] And although he has put the fair miter [the turban] on his head, his holiness is not profaned, for God has sworn with His right hand and He will not deceive. This is one of God's mysteries, and no one who has any knowledge of the mysteries of the Torah will consider it strange. For although nothing of the kind is indicated in the plain sense of Scripture, yet we have seen that the sayings of the ancient rabbis on these [eschatological] matters are obscure and utterly inexplicable, and we have the testimony of the great luminary Maimonides [who declared] that the rabbinic dicta would become intelligible only after the event.[141] Nevertheless, he who has eyes to see . . . can find [sufficient] proof for these things . . . and not speak falsely against the holiness of the Sabbath [that is, Sabbatai Ṣevi], for whoever inveighs against him no doubt his soul is of the "mixed multitude," as is evident from what is said in the holy book *Raᶜya Mehemna*, which . . . also speaks of the true Redeemer. There it is said[142] that "Thou art wounded because of the guilt of the people [cf. Isa. 53:5] and I suffer great pain as it is said 'and they made his grave with the wicked' [Isa. 53:9], and they do not recognize me and I am accounted in their eyes like the stinking carcass of a dog."

139. *Ibid.*, pp. 260–62; Baruch of Arezzo, pp. 59–61 (with minor variants).

140. Here Nathan repeats the wording employed in his *Vision of R. Abraham* written in 1665.

141. Nathan here twists the words of Maimonides (see above, p. 13) to suit his purpose: since the messianic prophecies will be understood only after the event, therefore their original formulation must have been essentially esoteric.

142. Zohar III, 125b. The speaker is Elijah, addressing Moses. Nathan takes the passage as referring to the fate of the messiah.

This surely refers to what was to happen later. . . . These words certainly do not mean [that the messiah will be despised] because of his sufferings, [but because of his apparent sins].[143] And they of the "mixed multitude" . . . are called wicked [although they may not be actual sinners] . . . because of the poison [of the serpent] that is in their unregenerate souls and which causes them to speak evil of the messiah instead of [at least] keeping quiet and waiting till they saw the end of the matter.[144] This also includes the miserly rich. . . . No doubt the *Raᶜya Mehemna* has revealed that [the messiah] would do strange things and be accounted therefore like a dead dog, as we have, indeed, seen it happening these days with some people who have removed their trust from the Lord. A further definite proof can be found in the *Tiqqunim* [*Tiqqun* 60] where it is said, . . . "good from the inside, but his garment [that is, his outward appearance] is bad—this refers to the lowly one, riding on an ass" [cf. Zech. 9:9]. Here you only need to understand the ordinary, plain sense, . . . for the "bad garment" refers to the turban which he donned. . . . The same text [*Tiqquney Zohar* 60] later uses the expression "bad inside with a good garment." This you can find with many people who wear Jewish dress, which is good [that is, who are observant Jews and have not apostatized], yet they are full of uncleanliness. . . . Elsewhere in the *Tiqqunim*[145] the verse "he was wounded because of our transgressions" is interpreted as meaning "he was profaned,"[146] and he who has understanding knows that none is really profaned but he who has apostatized from the community of Israel. . . . The statement [in the Zohar] that in the last exile the [messiah's] name would become an object of scorn and derision no doubt refers to the fact that he will don the turban. . . . Yet we [the true believers] have learned that the Sabbath has not been

143. The argument is based on an untranslatable pun. Hebrew *srḥ* means "to stink" and (idiomatically) also "to sin."

144. In his repudiation of the Ipsola obligations Nathan says: "All those who hold steadfastly to faith in him are of the fruit of the King Messiah's tree, and those who inveigh against him belong to the 'mixed multitude.' And those who keep quiet and do not vilify him, are not from the same root as the souls of the 'generation of the messiah,' but their wisdom will be judged according to the measure of their generation [according to their behavior]." Cf. *Sefunoth*, V (1961), 270, and *Qobeṣ ᶜal Yad*, XVI (1966), 445.

145. *Tiqqun* 20 (edn. Mantua, fol. 47a). The subject of this passage, too, is Moses and not the messiah.

146. A pun on the Hebrew word *meḥolal*, which could be translated: "has become part of the profane sphere." This pun recurs in most of Nathan's and Cardozo's letters.

profaned because of his donning the turban, . . . but he had to act thus because of the sins of Israel, and his fate was similar to that of Esther who had to eat forbidden food [in King Ahasuerus' palace]. The pious Mordecai realized that "it was not without cause that Esther had been taken [to an unclean place] and, indeed, deliverance came through her."[147] The same will be the case with this one. Our enemies shall see it and be put to shame, . . . but they that wait for him shall taste celestial delights, and their souls shall reach a very high degree. . . . The reason for all this cannot be revealed, let alone committed to writing, except to expert kabbalists, but soon everything will become manifest. . . . Happy is he that waiteth. . . . Wherefore, my brethren and all faithful believers in Israel who stand and wait and tremble at these words, be strong and of good courage, be not affrighted nor dismayed, turn unto the Lord your God with all your heart and all your soul and give thanks unto His great name, for verily we shall behold what our ancestors have not seen. And although people may say that these words of comfort are mere vanity because I am unable, at present, to work a miracle, yet I shall not desist from comforting the downcast that tremble at this word, that ask of me righteous ordinances and desire to draw near unto God, the poor and the needy who are in trouble and distress for the holiness of God's name.[148]

To whom was this letter of comfort and doctrine addressed? The superscription says that it was sent to R. Joseph Ṣevi, but this must be a mistake. Sabbatai's brother Joseph never lived in Zante, and the recipient of the letter was evidently a kabbalist. R. Jacob Saᶜadun of Salé (in Morocco) repeatedly quotes from a letter that Nathan had sent from Corfu "to the rabbi J. Ḥamiṣ,"[149] and his quotations are evidently taken from the letter under discus-

147. A quotation from the *Midrash Rabbah* on Esther, ch. 6.

148. The phraseology and doctrines found in the letter to Zante already occur in a short letter of 1667–68. Writing to the messiah's secretary, Samuel Primo, Nathan affirms that Sabbatai and none other was the messiah: "and besides him there is no savior to Israel." Although the messiah "had put the fair miter on his head, yet his holiness is not profaned." Support for this assertion is adduced from the passage in the *Tiqquney Zohar* which says: "good from the inside, but his garment [i.e., outward appearance] is bad—this refers to the lowly one riding upon an ass." The letter to Primo also reflects Nathan's fugitive and vagabond life, for "I am poor and needy, despised and base, and wandering from place to place in order to perform a general and a special *tiqqun*." Cf. *Sefunoth,* V (1961), 271.

149. Sasportas, pp. 327, 331, 333.

sion. Saᶜadun clearly refers to the kabbalist and physician Joseph Ḥamiṣ,[150] who lived in Venice[151] until at least 1658. In that year he decided to go to the Holy Land, but so far nothing is known of his actual movements and whereabouts for almost ten years. From 1667 until his death[152] (apparently in 1675 or 1676) he lived in Zante, whence he maintained close contacts with the prophet Nathan.[153] Unlike his master and friend, the antikabbalist author and rabbi Leone Modena, Joseph Ḥamiṣ was an ardent follower of the kabbalah, to which he had been drawn by the influence of R. Aaron Berakhya Modena, a disciple of R. Israel Sarug. Ḥamiṣ was on terms of close friendship with the kabbalist Moses Zacuto, who prepared his writings for the press. The opening part of Zacuto's commentary *Yodeᶜey Binah* on the Zohar was actually written by Ḥamiṣ.[154]

150. The identity has now been finally established by Is. Tishby in his Hebrew article "Documents Relating to Nathan of Gaza in the Writings of R. Joseph Ḥamiṣ," *Sefunoth,* I (1957), 117–80. Tishby discovered a considerable collection of kabbalistic homilies by Ḥamiṣ in MS. Oxford 2239, the Sabbatian character of which is concealed so discreetly as almost to escape detection. The author gives himself away, however, by his many enthusiastic references to the prophet Nathan (Tishby, *loc. cit.,* p. 85). For Tishby's discussion of the possible destination of the letter from Corfu, see *ibid.,* pp. 102–3.

151. Several works of Ḥamiṣ were printed in Venice in 1658 (i.e., before his departure) and not in 1663, as has been wrongly believed; see G. Scholem, *Bibliographia Kabbalistica* (1927), p. 175. The correct date also appears on the title page of Ḥamiṣ' *ᵓOr Nogah;* see N. S. Libawitsch, "Extant Fragments from the Writings of the Philosopher, Physician and Kabbalist Joseph Ḥamiṣ" (Jerusalem, 1938), p. 13.

152. During that period Ḥamiṣ composed the homilies referred to above, n. 150.

153. See Tishby, *loc. cit.,* p. 101. Tishby rightly points out that Ḥamiṣ was not a solitary Sabbatian in Zante, but a member of a Sabbatian group that called itself *Rodefey Ṣedeq.* The beginning of a letter (by Nathan?) addressed to this group is preserved in the aforementioned Oxford MS.

154. H. Y. D. Azulay (*Shem ha-Gedolim,* II, s.v. *Yodeᶜey Binah*) reports that he had seen one copy of this book: the beginning and the end of MS., but in the middle about 100 leaves in print. I was fortunate enough to discover a copy of the printed work in the library of the London *Beth Din* (formerly the library of Jews College, as the original collection of R. Solomon Hirschel of London came to be called later). This unfortunately incomplete copy (title page + fols. 144) also contains the part of the commentary composed by Ḥamiṣ. It is possible that no more was printed and the volume was never finished. The title page of Joseph Ḥamiṣ' work *Belil Ḥamiṣ* (Venice, 1624), which belonged to N. S. Libawitsch (see

Ḥamiṣ became an enthusiastic believer in the Sabbatian faith, and in his old age composed a volume of Sabbatian homilies. Israel's sin and repentance were the main themes of his messianic thinking, whereas "the apostasy was but a minor accident, a kind of temporary fall of the messiah and a test for Israel. . . . Since he firmly believed that redemption was imminent, his main problem was whether Israel, having forsaken the messiah, still merited salvation."[155] Contemporary events were viewed in messianic perspective, and the war between Venice and Turkey in particular played an important part in his speculations. This war, identified by Ḥamiṣ with the birthpangs of the messianic age and the war of Gog and Magog, reached its climax in 1668 and the peace treaty of September, 1669, was a bitter disappointment to his eschatological expectations.

According to R. Jacob Saᶜadun, Nathan's letter to Ḥamiṣ was widely known and copies of it circulated everywhere.[156] The name of the addressee as given in Sasportas' version is probably due to confusion on the part of the copyist. Nathan used to write also to Joseph Ṣevi—one such letter, dealing with Nathan's secret mission to Rome, was actually preserved among the papers of Ḥamiṣ—and the scribes who provided copies of the prophet's letters for the Jewish communities in Italy and elsewhere may easily have confused the names of Nathan's two correspondents. The copy of the letter that reached Morocco also contains important details regarding Nathan's activities on Corfu, but these were added after Nathan's departure from the island and did not form part of the original letter to Ḥamiṣ.[157]

---

above, n. 151) and which I had occasion to inspect in 1929, has a biting remark written in the hand of Leone Modena (who saw the book through press) and accusing Ḥamiṣ of abetting fornication by providing gentiles with love charms and amulets. When Libawitsch reprinted *Belil Ḥamiṣ* he omitted Modena's marginal remark. If I am not mistaken the copy is now in the library of the Jewish Theological Seminary in New York.

155. Tishby, *loc. cit.*, p. 108.

156. Sasportas, p. 237. Perhaps Saᶜadun learned this fact from Sasportas who had sent him a copy of the MS. *Ṣiṣath Nobel Ṣevi*. A copy of the letter to Zante got to Jassy in Rumania and thence into the possession of R. Yaᵓir Ḥayyim Bacharach; cf. A. H. Weiss, *Beth ha-Midrash* (1865), p. 92.

157. Sasportas, p. 331. Sasportas seems to have recognized the identity of the addressee and was certainly aware of the fact that he was a staunch believer in Nathan's prophecy. The latter fact is not brought out in Saᶜadun's letter (*ap.* Sasportas, pp. 331, 345).

Nathan's letters began to strike a new and significantly social note. In his exposition of the *Raᶜya Mehemna*, Nathan combined two distinct motifs that were never linked in the original Zoharic text. Eschatology and the messianic mysteries, on the one hand, and the "mixed multitude," on the other, appear as two distinct subjects in the *Raᶜya Mehemna*. The latter were described, in violent and bitter diatribes, as a well-defined social class: the worldly and rich oligarchs who lorded it over the Jewish communities in Spain and on whom the "poor," namely, the rabbinic scholars, were utterly dependent. The contrast between the spiritual poor (that is, in the eyes of the author of the *Raᶜya Mehemna*, the kabbalists) and the worldly rich is described throughout in terms of the social realities in Spain at the end of the thirteenth century.[158] The situation created by the messiah's apostasy invited the use of the same typology. As a matter of fact, Nathan had used it as early as 1665 in his first letters from Gaza—Sabbatai Ṣevi's opponents were of the "mixed multitude"—but at that time the typology had a purely theological significance and did not refer to any particular social class. After all, the mainstay of the incipient movement was none other than the wealthiest Jew in Egypt, the *chelebi* Raphael Joseph. After the apostasy, however, Nathan's attitude to the ruling class of the rich became more negative. It is the "miserly rich" for whom the messiah is like the "stinking carcass of a dog" and who, in fact, have brought about the present impasse by their unbelief. The letter of January, 1668, no doubt reflects Nathan's experiences during the preceding year and crystallizes his reaction to the attitude of the rabbis and the wealthy lay leaders of the major Turkish communities. Speaking in social terms, the addressees of the epistle from Corfu were the same as those of the Sabbatian pseudo-*Hekhaloth* texts (see above, p. 741) in which the rabbis and rich lay leaders are berated for vilifying the messiah. Nathan took his imagery from traditional sources, but in applying it to the messianic events of his days he invested it with an explosive actuality. The Sabbatians began to regard themselves as the body of the kabbalist elect, the truly spiritual, persecuted and oppressed by the worldly rich and by the rabbis who had no understanding of the mysteries of the Torah. They interpreted their struggle in terms of the ty-

158. Y. F. Baer, *A History of the Jews in Christian Spain,* I (1961), 270–77; cf. also above, pp. 11, 228.

pology provided by the *Ra^cya Mehemna*. The rabbis, of course, resented the imputation of unspiritual worldliness that judged according to the flesh only. But as the persecution of the believers intensified, the latter increasingly felt themselves to be the true Israel, harassed by the "mixed multitude" because of their faith, "and were it not for the faith that protects us, then they had swallowed us up alive."[159]

Nathan was said to have wrought mighty deeds on Corfu, but it is impossible to sort out fact from fiction. The prophet's admirers reported that the "princes" (the Venetian authorities on Corfu or the Jewish lay leaders?) sought to bring about his death, but they were all struck dumb and finally showered him with honors. Another report from Corfu, signed by several witnesses, said that on Friday evening, the Twentieth of Adar,[160] Nathan, having taken a ritual bath, went to the synagogue and put his head into the Torah scroll and muttered. When he had finished reading the weekly portion he remained standing for almost a quarter of an hour with his right ear to the Torah shrine and his face transfigured with joy. The following morning (Sabbath) he preached a powerful sermon to the assembled congregation, declaring with a solemn oath that "God Himself has appeared unto me and told me that the rabbi Sabbatai Ṣevi will be the Redeemer, and if this come not to pass I shall have no portion in the God of Israel."[161] Nathan probably referred to his original great vision of the spring of 1665 and not to any new revelation. Early in Nisan (end of March), 1668, Nathan, accompanied by Samuel Gandoor, left Corfu for Venice, where he arrived before Passover.

It was not, however, for the purpose of spreading the Sabbatian message and strengthening faint hearts that Nathan traveled to Italy. He was sent thither on a secret mission by Sabbatai himself, though the timing of his movements was by direct heavenly guidance (*maggid*). Whatever the precise nature of the kabbalistic ritual of *tiqqun* which Nathan was to perform in Rome, he undoubtedly considered it as in some way analogous to the messiah's descent into the realm of the *qelippah*. The messiah's ministry was exercised in the

159. Nathan of Gaza, in the Sabbatian notebook in the library of Columbia University, New York (fol. 15a).

160. The date cannot be correct. 20 Adar (March 16, 1667) was a Wednesday.

161. Sasportas, pp. 331–32.

sphere of Ishmael; the faithful—and perhaps Nathan himself—believed that a similar ministry would have to be exercised by the messiah's apostle in the realm of Edom (that is, Rome). What Nathan (or his master) had in mind was probably a magico-kabbalistic act destined to bring about the ruin of Rome. He certainly did not think of apostatizing to the Christian religion.

A letter from Constantinople preserved in a manuscript collection from Armenia throws much light on the mood prevailing at the time in the camp of the believers—provided my dating of the document is correct. The emissary who brought Sabbatai's spurious confession and recantation from Turkey to Persia (see above, p. 734) seems to have carried also letters and documents emanating from Sabbatian quarters. One such letter, probably written after the messianic dates set by Nathan for 1667 had failed, exhorted believers to wait patiently and in silence

> for the word of the Lord shall not return void, and though it tarry, wait for it, and the prudent shall keep silence until this word cometh to pass, for there are many mysteries and secret and hidden things that have not been revealed, and that which has been revealed . . . the heart must not divulge to the mouth. But he who has *seen with his eyes and heard with his ears* even a small part of them will realize the depth of these things and not doubt the ways of God. . . . May it be God's will that the sins of this generation prevent not [the messianic fulfillment]. Pay no heed to the [calculations of messianic] dates and times, nor to voices and rumors and spirits, and be not disturbed by changes and contrarieties, for His thoughts are not our thoughts and the Lord looketh on the heart [cf. I Sam. 16:7], as is written [Deut. 32:47]: "it is no vain thing for you"—and if it appears vain, then it is so in your eyes only[162] because of our poor understanding. These things are hidden and deep, as King Solomon has indicated several times in the Song of Songs [2:7; 3:5; 8:4] "I adjure you, O daughters of Jerusalem, . . . that ye awaken not, nor stir up love until it please." Scripture also says [Exod. 12:22]: "and none of you shall go out of the door of his house until the morning"—that is, until the dawn [of redemption], for we dwell in the world of the *qelippoth* and of matter, and we cannot overcome them "until it please." Especially in this generation which is devoid of merits, we could hardly survive but for God's

162. Traditional rabbinic interpretation of Deut. 32:47.

grace and the merits of our great saints and the humility of Our Lord, who was ready to sacrifice himself, . . . and of whom it is written [Isa. 53:4]: "Surely our diseases he did bear," and without him the evil decree would surely have overtaken Israel. . . . All these things are true but they require lengthy explanations. Meanwhile, all we can do is to repent, to fast and pray, to witness to the truth, . . . and to assist the Shekhinah . . . and not to do like unto them that say *if it is true and the messiah comes, then we shall return* [to believe in him] *but not otherwise,* for they do not know, neither do they understand. They walk in darkness and by their sins they cause the delay of redemption, for all Israel are responsible for one another.[163]

This letter of encouragement and comfort may have been written by Yakhini. We do not know. At any rate, it shows that the prophecies and heavenly intimations regarding the dates of the messianic events had all proved wrong. "Our Lord was ready to sacrifice himself" and believers should persevere in their faith and penance. The apostasy is explained in simplistic fashion by the sinfulness of the generation and not in terms of a mystico-kabbalistic task. The author directs his polemic at the wait-and-see attitude that was, no doubt, widespread in Turkish Jewry, and argues to the contrary: Israel had been saved from disaster[164] by the messiah, and their lack of faith and their many sins prolonged the exile and delayed the advent of the fullness of redemption. The letter thus presents a complete inversion of the earlier Sabbatian arguments. But while the manner of argumentation changed under the pressure of events, the continuity of the faith remained intact.

V

The immediate effect of the dismaying news of the messiah's apostasy seems to have been more or less identical throughout the European communities, though our information regarding Poland is poor as compared to the full and detailed reports from Italy, Holland, and Germany. Judging by what we know from North Africa—from Morocco to Egypt—and from Kurdistan, the Jews in the Muslim

163. *Toᶜey Ruaḥ* (MS. Enelow, Jewish Theological Seminary, New York, no. 2223), fols. 233b–234a.

164. Probably referring to the danger of a general massacre of the Jewish communities which, according to the Sabbatian accounts, was averted by the messiah; see above, pp. 701–3.

countries reacted no differently from their brethren in Christian Europe. There is, of course, no way of knowing the secret thoughts of the many rabbis who did not express themselves on the subject. The fact that a rabbi remained in office after the apostasy and led a blameless life of orthodox piety does not prove anything one way or another. It is therefore difficult to assess, by means of external criteria alone, the number of scholars and lay leaders who persevered in the faith or were prepared to listen to the oral or literary propaganda of Sabbatian enthusiasts.[165] The responsible leadership was evidently bent on maintaining the traditional pattern of Jewish life, avoiding anything that might add fuel to the fire. In this respect there was little difference between rabbis who dismissed the messianic revival as a complete failure, and those who still entertained some hopes, however faint. All agreed on the immediate task of returning to normal life. This is particularly evident in the Islamic countries where a great many rabbis persevered in the faith, but to all practical intents and purposes enjoined an attitude of patient waiting. Frictions and schisms were thus largely avoided and only a few instances are known where, as for example in Egypt, believers were formally excommunicated.

The letter that the Egyptian rabbis sent out at the end of December, 1666, to the major Jewish communities is, therefore, not representative of the pattern of reaction elsewhere. The Egyptian rabbis hastened to inform their colleagues abroad that they had done what the rabbis of Smyrna and Constantinople, let alone of Adrianople, had not dared to do: they had solemnly excommunicated the traitor who, by his apostasy, had shown his true colors. They had also pronounced the ban over the three most dangerous and active apostles of the faith, Nathan of Gaza, Mattathias Bloch Ashkenazi, and Jacob Palache. The first two had been responsible for the abolition of the fast of the Ninth of Ab in Egypt; the last had been the cause of "strife and dissension" the nature of which is unknown.[166] The ban of excommunication extended to all "who incited and instigated and abetted the evil, . . . wherefore we have resolved to search for their [liturgical and other] rules, devotions, and other writings . . . and to destroy them from the face of the earth . . . and

165. See above, p. 737, about the social composition of the Balkan group of believers.

166. Sasportas, p. 198; cf. also above, p. 644.

to excommunicate everyone who studies or follows them." This is strong language indeed, and the only instance, at this early period, of a general ban on Sabbatian literature. No doubt the proximity of Gaza and the activity at Raphael Joseph's court encouraged the circulation of Sabbatian tracts in Egypt, but even in Amsterdam where Nathan's devotional manuals were printed by the thousands no similar steps were taken although the Egyptian rabbis had urged their colleagues in Amsterdam to be strong and to search diligently for even the minutest shred of Sabbatian literature and "utterly to destroy everything."[167] The doctrinal manuals were, indeed, gradually secreted away, but no drastic measures such as a formal ban appear to have been taken. In Cairo and Alexandria, however, the believers were silenced by the threat of excommunication. At first they too had refused to believe the report of the apostasy. Shortly before the general excommunication, Raphael Joseph had written to Leghorn that whoever said that Sabbatai, "the true messiah, had apostatized was speaking lies and falsehood."[168] The first reaction of the believers in Egypt was thus similar to that of believers everywhere. But the Egyptian rabbis were more radical and violent in the bitterness of their disappointment.

Not all believers, however, were effectively silenced. The "false prophet" Mattathias Bloch Ashkenazi, in spite of his old age, left Egypt for the East, and a year later we find him in Mosul as a member of the rabbinic court. Far from hiding his Sabbatian beliefs, he actually obtained his office by his reputation as a prophet and man of God. Possibly the rabbis of Aleppo also contributed to Bloch's career in Mosul. As late as 1669 R. Solomon Laniado and an emissary from Jerusalem who had just begun his journey to the East[169] testified to their belief in the validity of the Sabbatian explanation of the apostasy: Sabbatai had saved Israel from destruction.[170] If this version of the apostasy was acceptable in so important a community as Aleppo, and

167. Sasportas, p. 199.

168. *Ibid.*, p. 248.

169. The identity of this emissary has been established by M. Benayahu, *Sefunoth*, III–IV (1960), 13. R. Jacob Aryeh, who traveled widely in the East during the years 1669–79, was evidently a member of the group of Sabbatian believers in Jerusalem.

170. In a letter dated 15 Ab 429, i.e., summer, 1669, four years after Sabbatai had passed through Aleppo.

the Sabbatian faith maintained itself there for so long,[171] then it is not surprising that more distant communities in contact with Aleppo would persevere in the faith and even appoint a well-known Sabbatian preacher to rabbinic office. A few years after the apostasy it was still believed in Kurdistan that "to this very day . . . the provinces of Constantinople and Aleppo" celebrate the four fasts as festivals "for their faith is unshaken," though the Kurdish communities themselves observed the fasts.[172] Documents relating to the quarrel between the congregations of Mosul and Amadiya indicate that the movement had not yet died out. People still talked about the imminence of redemption and the coming year of salvation, and Mattathias Bloch would still be referred to in certain circles as "the holy kabbalist . . . the crown of our head whose light—the light of the Shekhinah—is shining upon us."[173] These glowing metaphors highlight the surprising career of the false prophet at whom the Egyptian rabbis had hurled their ban of excommunication. Bloch brought with him copies of Nathan's tracts and letters, from which he quoted liberally in his letters to R. Phineas Ḥariri, the leading kabbalist in those parts.[174] At about the same time (1668), and possibly inspired by Mattathias Bloch's arrival, a prophetic movement occurred in Kurdistan and Persia.[175]

By lucky chance, details of Bloch's subsequent Sabbatian activities are known. In a circular letter he announced that "a chapter of the book of Daniel had been revealed to him that is missing in the [biblical] book."[176] He went from Mosul to Persia and defended Sabbatai's messiahship to the Jewish communities. According to two testimonies

171. In the summer of 1667 Sabbatai Ḥamoy finished a work on ritual law, concluding it with the prayer that the Lord "may grant us understanding of the Law . . . and vouchsafe me to behold the face of Our Lord Sabbatai Ṣevi"; see Z. Rubashov in *Zion* (annual), VI (1934), 54.

172. With the exception of Rawenduz, where in 1667 or 1668 the fasts were celebrated as festivals; cf. *Zion,* VII (1942), 196.

173. See *Zion,* VII (1942), 177. Cf. also the documents assembled in Jacob Mann, *Texts and Studies,* I (1931), 491–519, the correct dates of which I have established in *Zion,* VII, *loc. cit.*

174. On R. Phineas and his father R. Isaac Ḥariri, see above, p. 638.

175. *Zion,* VII (1942), 178. If the date given in *Toᶜey Ruaḥ* is correct, then this is the only prophetic movement during that year of which we have knowledge.

176. The letter and the "vision of Daniel the prophet" are extant in MS. Ben-Zvi Institute 2263, pp. 151–53. He is called "the true messenger R. Mattathias."

he was killed, apparently in or near Isfahan, where his activities had created great trouble.[177] About 1674 a learned physician, Aaron, wrote another circular letter to the Persian communities, refuting in length Sabbatai's messianic claims and warning against those who defend him and spread his message. He attacks his pupil who is presently in these parts (Persia) and expresses the hope that his excecution (which was about to take place or had already taken place) "will atone for our sins," because so many had believed the messianic news.[178] R. Mattathias is probably also the author of the Sabbatian explanation of Proverbs 30:18–20 which the "prophet of peace said from the mouth of his *maggid*."[179]

We are much better informed about the effects of the apostasy on the European communities. The confusion into which European Jewry was thrown by the news lasted for several years and was aggravated not a little by Nathan's appearances in Italy. The news of the apostasy reached Europe early in November, 1666, through several channels, Jewish as well as Christian. At first the report was disbelieved even by some Christians. Henry Oldenburg,[180] writing on November

177. The death of R. Mattathias, "who said: I am the messenger of Sabbatai Ṣevi," is recorded in connection with Isfahan, in Judah b. Eliezer's chronicle *Ḥoboth Jehudah* (written 1686 in Isfahan in Judeo-Persian), MS. Hebrew Union College, Cincinnati, 2007, fol. 113a. I owe this information to Prof. Ezra Spicehandler, who has described the chronicle in studies in *Jewish Bibliography and Booklore,* VIII (1968), 116. The two sources supplement each other.

178. See M. Benayahu, *Sefunoth,* III–IV (1960), 25–32, esp. p. 29. Benayahu rightly assumed that the diatribe was directed against R. Mattathias, whose name is indeed expressly mentioned in the Persian chronicle.

179. Cf. M. Benayahu in *Sefunoth,* III–IV (1960), 33, from the same manuscript that had the letter of R. Aaron, the physician.

180. See above, pp. 543 f. The letter is preserved in the *Calendar of State Papers* for the years 1665–66 (p. 50), but was classified by mistake under 10.11.65 instead of 10.11.66. The initials H.O. with which the letter is signed can only mean Henry Oldenburg, as the sequel of the letter (which I consulted in the original) refers to a letter that the writer had recently received from Hevelius in Danzig and discussing certain scientific questions. We know that Hevelius was a member of the Royal Society at the time when Oldenburg was the Society's secretary. The printed summary gives the impression that the letter referred to the reactions of the London Jews, but a careful reading of the original leaves no doubt that Oldenburg was quoting from a letter that had been received from Amsterdam. The English letter from Amsterdam quoted by Oldenburg bears such close similarity to the French letter from Amsterdam preserved in the Hottinger Collection (vol. 29, fol. 350a) that one cannot but suspect a single author (Serrarius?); see above p. 673, n. 236. The same correspondent reported

10, 1666, reported that according to news received from Amsterdam "the King of the Jews was turned Turk." His correspondent in Amsterdam had informed him that the last letters arriving via Marseilles from Smyrna had reached several Christians here (in Amsterdam) but not the Jews. "Our Jews" did not yet believe the news but hoped that the course of messianic events would continue. It was generally held that Sabbatai's going to the Grand Turk would cost him his life. But since he was received honorably and without harm, they [the Christian or Jewish authors of the letter, in blatant contradiction to what they had written in the preceding line?] concluded that he had turned Turk. A letter dated November 23 quotes two strangely contradictory reports: on the one hand, a letter had been received from Nathan encouraging and reassuring the congregation, who promptly held a special day of prayer, and on the other hand, tidings had arrived of the messiah's apostasy. At about the same time word was also received from the East to the effect that Sabbatai had prophesied as early as the summer of 1666 that sufferings would befall Israel for a period of fourteen or forty days for his sake. Nothing is said in this source[181] of the messiah himself having to suffer.

It was not until early December, 1666, that the news of the apostasy was definitely confirmed and accepted in Amsterdam as an undeniable fact—a fact which the believers interpreted in the light of their faith: Sabbatai still was the king of Israel, and his merits and apparent apostasy had saved Israel from disaster. Even the Christian correspondent in Amsterdam (Serrarius?) seemed to confirm this version.[182] The source of both the confirmation of the fact and

---

on December 1, 1666, that there was no reliable news about Sabbatai Ṣevi except that he was now occupying a high office at the court of the Grand Turk. However, "le bruit qu'il s'est fait Turcq est tenu pour suspect." By the end of November the news of the apostasy was known throughout western Europe. The French gazette *Muse de la Cour* of November 25, 1665, even published a satirical poem on the subject.

181. MS. Hottinger, vol. 30, fol. 350a.

182. *Ibid.:* "touchant l'estat present des Juifs il continue encor assavoir que Sabbathaj Sebi seroit tourné Turcq. Voilà comme escrivent les Chrétiens à l'envie et de mesme les Juifs qui n'ont jamais fait cas de luy. Mais il y apparence que ce Roy esté par cy devant decrié mort mais est trouvé vivant depuis qu'aussi après ce blasme de Turcicme, il se trouvera derechef Juif et Roy des Juifs. Car il est certain que lui et ses compagnons Rabbins ne sont pas seulement en vie mais en honneur auprès de Grand Seigneur et qu'à Adrianopolis nul opprobre n'est arrivé à aucun Juif."

of the interpretation that rendered it acceptable was none other than Dr. Isaac Nahar (see above, p. 529), who was still in Leghorn at the time. R. Isaac Saruk, a member of the *yeshibah* of Amsterdam, apprised his teacher R. Josiah Pardo of Rotterdam of the contents of Nahar's letter as well as of a letter Sasportas had written to his disciple Maimun Ḥiyya in Amsterdam, informing his former student that he had publicly and solemnly excommunicated Sabbatai Ṣevi. The congregation at Hamburg had to approve willy-nilly the anathema, and Sasportas had his revenge on the synagogue that at one time had threatened violence against those who refused to join in the prayer for the messianic king. Isaac Saruk, it appears, persevered in his faith for some time, since he complained to Pardo of the "vain and light persons" in Amsterdam who, encouraged by the evil tidings, opened their mouth against the Lord's Anointed and shook off the yoke of the kingdom of Heaven. Only a few faithful souls continued the devotional practices and the penitential fasts on Mondays and Thursdays.[183] Saruk, though profoundly disturbed, would not repeat, let alone approve, the disparaging denunciations of the opponents. Rabbi Pardo, on the other hand, indicated in his reply that he was forsaking the faith, and suggested to his former student to do likewise and to meditate on the sobering warnings of Maimonides, which would help him "to distinguish between truth and falsehood."[184]

A small group of believers continued to exist in the Sephardic community of Amsterdam and used to meet for several years under the leadership of the *ḥazzan* Immanuel Benattar (Abiatar) and the patronage of the millionaire Abraham Pereira. Abraham Cardozo's literary propaganda, conducted from Tripoli in North Africa, was not without effect even in Amsterdam where he had a brother-in-law, Abraham Baruch Enriquez—probably a believer too. Yet it was not only the Jews who gladly received Cardozo's teachings regarding the mystical significance of the messiah's apostasy. Serrarius, who was active in spreading Sabbatianism among Christians in 1666, supported the cause of the believers until his death in September, 1669. This enthusiastic chiliast found nothing wrong with Cardozo's Sabbatian

183. Saruk's letter was published by M. Benayahu in *ʾEreṣ Yisraʾel*, IV (1956), 202–3. Benayahu (*ibid.*, p. 199) vainly tries to read an anti-Sabbatian meaning into Saruk's first letter. Saruk, it is true, quotes Sasportas' account of the anathema pronounced in Hamburg, but he is far from happy about it. In another letter (*ibid.*, p. 205) he actually describes Sasportas as "quarrelsome."

184. *Ibid.* On Maimonides see above, pp. 12–13.

interpretation of Isaiah 53, or of Psalms 22 and 89,[185] and he firmly believed that the messianic awakening among the Jews was a harbinger of their conversion. As late as 1669, the year of his death, Serrarius still wrote letters to his friends in which he relied heavily on Cardozo's writings.

The hold which the Sabbatian faith had on the Ashkenazi communities of Holland and northern Germany will be illustrated later in this chapter by the detailed analysis of one particular incident. In that particular case only the determined intervention of the Sephardic leaders, who solicited the help of the Christian civil authorities, led to the expulsion of a Sabbatian prophet and trouble-maker. Had they been left to themselves, the Ashkenazi communities would have permitted him to pursue his missionary activity, much to the chagrin of Sasportas. This general picture is confirmed by P. Ragstatt de Weile, who was closely associated with the movement and who became a Christian in 1669. In a book published in 1672, de Weile states that in his own area, that is, Holland and northwest Germany, the Jews still believed in Sabbatai as the true messiah. Believers would justify the apostasy with arguments evidently drawn from the letters of Nathan (and possibly also of Cardozo), and one disciple of Sabbatai is said to have composed "some years ago" a tract on the mystery of the apostasy.[186] R. Abraham b. Moses of Tismenitz in Podolia, who lived at the time as tutor in the house of the wealthy and influential Jewish lay leader Gumpel Weisel in Cleve, wrote, in 1669, a Yiddish continuation of the Hebrew chronicle *Ṣemaḥ David,* which "is permeated by a thoroughly Sabbatian spirit" at its end.[187] It was not only the "poor rabble," as Sasportas would have it, who persevered in the faith. Glückel of Hameln's father-in-law, a pious Jew and shrewd businessman, waited for three years before allowing the casks "packed with linens and with . . . every manner of food that would keep" which he had sent to Hamburg to be opened. "For three years the casks stood ready, and all the while my father-in-law awaited the signal to depart."[188] Evidently the mere fact of the apostasy was not by itself enough to extinguish the faith and quench the hopes.

185. See Wolf, *Bibliotheca Hebraica,* III (1727), 1010. This exceedingly interesting passage in Wolf has so far escaped the notice of scholars.

186. Ragstatt de Weile, *Theatrum lucidum* (Amsterdam, 1672), p. 31.

187. MS. Adler 178; see Adler's handlist, p. 45.

188. *The Memoirs of Glückel of Hameln,* trans. Marvin Lowenthal (1932), pp. 46–47. See also above, pp. 573, 588.

Echoes of the movement are preserved also in non-Jewish literature written after 1666, and the foremost German prose writer of the time actually combined the contemporary messianic awakening with a traditional Christian legend in one of his tales in *Das wunderbarliche Vogelnest.* According to the medieval story, a Christian youth had fallen in love with a Jewish beauty and seduced her by telling her that she would give birth to the messiah. In Grimmelshausen's version the Christian lover pretends to be the prophet Elijah, who appears among men in different guises, and persuades the girl that the messiah would have to be Elijah's son. The rumor soon gives rise to a great popular movement among the Jews, which continues even after the maiden has given birth to a girl, the believers arguing that the messianic child had to look like a girl so as to be safe from the plotting gentiles. This combination of medieval and contemporary themes reflects the peculiar atmosphere engendered by the Sabbatian movement and represents the first belletristic treatment of the subject. Grimmelshausen's tale, written in 1673,[189] precedes by one hundred and forty years the first Hebrew novel on the Sabbatian movement. *The Tale of Dreams: The End of Wonders* (also, *Me᾿ora῾oth Ṣevi*)[190] by an anonymous Galician writer of the Enlightenment period was cast in the form of a historical chronicle and misled many subsequent writers, who mistook it for a genuine historical source.

Our sources indicate that instances of apostasy to Christianity on the part of disabused believers were by no means exceptional. The story printed in the French gazette *Muse de la Cour* of December 12, 1666, to the effect that Jesuit missionaries had baptized over a thousand Jews soon after the news of Sabbatai's apostasy had become known, is an obvious journalistic canard, but there is other and more

189. See F. Aronstein, *Zeitschrift f. d. Geschichte d. Juden in Deutschland,* V (1935), 236–41.

190. 1st edn. Kapust (1814), printed by Israel Yaffe. For unknown reasons this edn. has almost completely disappeared and I have been able to see only two copies. The book was printed again in Lvov about 1830, but the title page gives a false date (1804) and hence the edn. was erroneously thought to be the *editio princeps.* The date 1815 given in H. D. Friedberg's *Bibliography* (III [1954], 762) is also wrong. To my knowledge no student of early *haskalah* literature has dealt with the book or attempt to identify its anonymous author—perhaps because the book was mistaken for a genuine chronicle and not recognized as a novel.

substantial testimony. Several of the apostates published accounts of the circumstances of their conversion, in which they roundly admit their involvement in the movement of 1666. Three more examples may be cited, in addition to the aforementioned Ragstatt de Weile, by way of illustration.

Jacob Melammed from Cornitz [?] in Podolia was a schoolteacher in the Ashkenazi community in Hamburg. During the high-tide of the movement he fasted every day of the week. In 1676 he and his family converted to Christianity, "since the noise which the Jews had made about their Sabbatai Ṣevi, for which we had waited for a whole year with fasts and mortifications, was all lies."[191] Solomon b. Meir of Frankfurt-on-the-Main was baptized in Nordhausen in August, 1673. In the introduction to his pamphlet "A Song of Praise," he states that the Sabbatian affair had aroused in him the first doubts about the Jewish religion. It should be added, however, that this apostate (who actually describes himself as a "former rabbi") makes no mention of Sabbatai's apostasy and even states that according to reports from Constantinople Sabbatai had been burned at the stake.[192] Baruch b. Moses of Prosnitz in Moravia was cantor in the small Jewish community of Bruchsal in Baden in the year 1666. He tells of the excitement that had seized the Jewish communities on hearing the glad tidings, and how, after the disillusionment, he began to re-examine the doctrine of the messiah until he converted to Christianity in 1674.[193]

An echo of the aftermath of the movement can be detected in the records of the Council of the Lithuanian Communities (§612). The council, meeting at Chomsk in 1667, enacted an ordinance strictly

191. See J. J. Schudt, *Jüdische Merckwürdigkeiten,* IV (bk. VI, Second Continuation), 242; also *ibid.*, vol. II, p. 56. Schudt's account is based on the printed confession of the apostate's wife; cf. also above, p. 574.

192. *Danck- und Lob-Gesang . . . zur Bekräfftigung seiner* [*Taufe*] . . . *August 5, 1673, in Nordhausen* (Wittenberg, 1674). As a Christian the author called himself Christophorus Paulus Maier. I found a copy of this pamphlet in the library of the Jewish Theological Seminary in New York. The statement about Sabbatai's death is obviously based on one of the contemporary fantastic broadsheets, such as the one described above, p. 557.

193. See J. J. Schudt, *op. cit.,* II (ch. 27, §32), 56. After his conversion Baruch called himself Friedrich Albert Christiani. His account was printed as a preface to his book *Der Jüden Glaube und Aberglaube* (Leipzig, 1705), pp. 66–67.

prohibiting all recent liturgical innovations, "and we ordain that nothing whatever be changed, not even the tunes." The ordinance suggests that the Sabbatians also introduced new songs and tunes into their liturgy in honor of the messiah.

The news of the apostasy seems to have reached Italy at the end of October, for in the first week of November R. Joseph ha-Levi of Leghorn indited his reply to R. Hosea Nantawa of Alexandria. R. Joseph's letter is one shout of triumph. He was sure that the movement would immediately and utterly collapse, and in the flush of victory he gave full rein to his feelings of accumulated hatred and long-suppressed bitterness.[194] All the words of execration that had remained unsaid in the preceding months now gushed forth in a torrent of righteous anger, vituperation, and sneering sarcasms. His outburst is as revealing of the tension that had accumulated between the parties as were the rhapsodic confessions of faith at the time when the believers still expressed themselves freely. R. Joseph ha-Levi seems to have traveled to Venice in order to obtain permission from the members of the rabbinic Academy, who were no less indignant and furious, to speak on their behalf too. His letter was to be an authoritative disavowal, in the name of traditional Judaism, of all that had happened in the preceding twelve months, and R. Joseph listed item by item all the Sabbatian deviations from the norms of both tradition and commonsense. In his zeal R. Joseph even enumerated perfectly traditional Lurianic customs, such as extreme mortifications and the *tiqqun* of souls, among the wicked innovations which he attributed to Nathan. In addition to his sarcasms and invective, R. Joseph also hurled the charge of heresy at the Sabbatians, "for whoever despises the words of the Talmudic sages is a heretic." The charge, which was here made for the first time, played a decisive role in subsequent stages of the struggle against the movement, though for the time being the rabbis generally preferred to adopt a policy of appeasement. According to R. Joseph, all Sabbatian believers *ipso facto* denied faith in the true Messiah.[195] Only three weeks after unburdening himself of this model barrage of polemical invective did R. Joseph trouble to forward a circumstantial and reasonably correct account of the apostasy to his friend Sasportas.

R. Joseph's hope of a quick collapse of the movement soon proved illusory. Shortly after the arrival of the first reports, the war between

194. *Ap.* Sasportas, pp. 186–97. 195. *Ibid.*, p. 192.

Turkey and Venice over the possession of Crete interrupted all further communications with Turkey. According to R. Joseph no ships from Smyrna and Egypt arrived in Italy for several months, and detailed accounts of the events in the East were not received until February, 1667.[196] For many people the apostasy was merely an unconfirmed rumor, while the believers prepared all kinds of explanations in case the report should be confirmed.

R. Joseph ha-Levi gives an account of the various views that could be heard in Leghorn and Venice. The "believing fools" formed several groups ("sects"), one of which maintained that Sabbatai never apostatized: the mistaken rumor was due to the fact that the sultan had embraced and kissed Sabbatai and placed upon his head a royal crown decked with a green scarf. This view was also spread by the Amsterdam millionaire Abraham Pereira in letters which he wrote from Venice to Leghorn. Similar letters were received in Leghorn from Verona and elsewhere. Others said that perhaps Sabbatai apostatized in order to learn the sultan's secrets of government, in order to prepare himself for his own future task. A third "sect" advanced the kabbalistic argument that the messiah had to enter the realm of the *qelippah* in order to destroy it. The most active advocate of this doctrine was Raphael Supino, while Isaac Nahar held the view of the first group. A fourth group maintained that it was only Sabbatai's shadow that appeared to have apostatized, while a fifth denied the apostasy altogether and claimed that Sabbatai had merely apologized to the sultan for Nathan's activities. "And now these masters of lies are bestirring themselves again and have written that the Grand Turk has made him a commander of his army and has dispatched him with two hundred thousand men to make war in Poland, so as to fulfill the prophecy of Satan [*sic*] Ashkenazi of Gaza who had said that he [the messiah] would revenge the martyrs of Poland."[197] In the process of adaptation, legend had turned Sabbatai from commander of the army of the Ten Tribes into a commander of the Turkish army.

R. Joseph's catalogue of "sects" indicates that several explanations of the apostasy and its significance were current early in 1667, even before the arrival of Nathan's first letters on the subject. Clearly these explanations had no common source but originated spontaneously in several places at the same time. Two important traits of the

196. *Ibid.*, pp. 247, 255. 197. *Ibid.*, pp. 247–48 and also p. 256.

earlier messianic image[198]—that of the military hero marching at the head of his armies to wreak vengeance upon the enemies of Israel, and that of the kabbalist mystic performing a secret mission by descending into the realm of the *qelippoth*—reappear only slightly altered to fit the new circumstances. The leading believers (for example, Abraham Pereira and Isaac Nahar) were not terrified by the paradox of an apostate messiah. Raphael Supino had already used a characteristically "marrano" image in his sermons to the believers in Leghorn: the holy queen Esther too had changed her religion in Ahasuerus' palace in order to bring salvation to Israel. The motif was popular among the marranos in Spain, and it is not surprising that it was taken up by believers in a "marrano" messiah. There were many, and not only the "ignorant fools," who took offense at Joseph ha-Levi's triumphantly aggressive invectives, and ha-Levi had to admit that "in these parts everyone who had believed is loved and esteemed by the people, unlike those that had not believed."[199] R. Joseph's complaint throws an interesting light on the movement. Evidently the people's instinctive sympathy lay with the believers who had been proved wrong, rather than with the shrewd critics. This was a movement of the people, and whether it succeeded or failed, the people did not take kindly to those who had antagonized them and now said, "We told you so."

The believers in Leghorn used to meet regularly in the homes of some of the leading members of the congregations,[200] and had contacts with their brethren in Turkey. One of the most central and active figures in the group was R. Moses Pinheiro, who had returned to Leghorn from Smyrna after Passover, 1667. Pinheiro continued to attract people to the movement even after Isaac Nahar's return to Amsterdam in 1668 and Raphael Supino's disillusionment with the faith. Most of the rabbis who took part in the movement have left us no letters or other written documents, and hence it is almost impossible to decide whether and when a particular believer abandoned the faith. In the circumstances all we can do is to hazard guesses

198. Cf. the Yemenite apocalypse discussed above, p. 654. The military and the mystical images, though apparently contradictory, are not mutually exclusive.

199. Sasportas, p. 256.

200. This holds true of winter and spring, 1667 (Sasportas, *ibid.*), as well as of the time of Nathan's visit.

which may be overturned by the discovery of new documents. Thus, after several years, we again find Raphael Supino in close and friendly relations with Sasportas. This suggests, though it does not prove, that Supino had abandoned the Sabbatian faith, for we know that Sasportas was on friendly terms with other rabbis of whose continued (and secret) Sabbatian allegiance he was completely unaware.

As early as March 16, 1667, letters arrived in Venice from Ragusa and Adrianople which clearly show that there were not a few in those communities who refused to take the apostasy in its "plain" sense and who still considered Sabbatai as a full Jew.[201] It was, in fact, the refusal of so many Jews in Italy to abandon their faith in Sabbatai Ṣevi that prompted Emanuel Frances to collect his own and his brother's satirical poems. Originally the poems had not been intended for publication, and after the apostasy the authors actually felt that it would be better if the whole affair were buried in oblivion. But as it became clear that the believers "still stood upon their watch and held fast to their uncleanliness," Frances decided to hurl his satirical darts at the Sabbatian believers.[202] R. Joseph ha-Levi also wrote a history of Sabbatai Ṣevi and his prophet Nathan, but his account, like his other writings, is lost, while the *Ṣevi Muddaḥ* of the Frances brothers circulated widely in Italy. Yet, although belief in Sabbatai persisted in many circles, the penitential awakening came to a standstill. According to Emanuel Frances only a "tiny minority" of the penitents of the great awakening persevered in their repentance and mended their ways.[203] Nathan's letters justifying the apostasy began to circulate more widely in the summer of 1667 and they were soon followed by similar tracts from other sources, especially the writings of Abraham Cardozo in Tripoli.

Penitential exercises and extreme mortifications having been a characteristic feature of the movement, the rabbis of Venice demanded their cessation. The believers, on the other hand, wished to continue them.[204] The Venetian rabbis also wrote to all the communities, com-

201. One such letter, containing details that are certainly correct, is preserved in the Hottinger Collection, vol. 30, fol. 345.

202. *Ṣevi Muddaḥ*, pp. 101, 135.

203. *Ibid.*, p. 127. The passage does not mean (as Shulwass, *Rome and Jerusalem*, p. 129, misunderstood it) that only a tiny minority forsook the faith after the apostasy.

204. See *Zion*, XIII (1948), 52–54.

manding them to destroy all documents relating to the movement of 1666 and to obliterate all testimony to this shameful episode. This attempt at censorship is mentioned by R. Samuel Aboab in a responsum written about eight years after the event. Aboab states that after the apostasy all the congregations in the Holy Land, Turkey, Germany, Holland, Poland, and Russia admitted that the opponents of the movement had been right, and recognizing their error they "burned all the records and writings in which his name was mentioned, in order that it should not be remembered. . . . And that which we heard from the far-away cities we beheld ourselves in the cities of Italy. . . . They are repented [of their belief in Sabbatai] . . . and confessed, 'Woe unto us, for we have sinned.' Also the rabbis of Constantinople . . . sent orders to the communities near and far . . . [to do away] with everything that had been written about that deceitful affair, . . . that it should be forgotten and mentioned no more."[205]

The large-scale suppression of records and documents relating to the movement was no doubt successful, much to the detriment of historical research. The Italian rabbis were, perhaps, encouraged in their efforts by the example of their Egyptian colleagues. There was plenty for them to suppress. In the autumn of 1666, that is, before the reports of the apostasy were reliably confirmed, R. Moses Borghi published in Mantua a manual of midnight and midday devotions "according to the custom of the remnant of Israel." The little book, which came off the press on December 11, 1666, was merely another edition of Nathan's Midnight Devotions, an earlier edition of which had already been published in Mantua. In fact, the title page expressly describes Borghi's *Tiqqun ha-Middoth* as a "second printing." Perhaps the title was meant to hide the true origin of the publication. Indeed, later bibliographers failed to recognize its Sabbatian origin and mistook it for an ordinary kabbalistic manual of Midnight Devotions. The editor who had, perhaps, already heard early rumors of the

205. *Debar Shemu'el*, fol. 97a. Aboab also mentions a book "recently published" in a gentile tongue and which "to our shame" listed about twenty false messiahs, including the most recent and worst, but it is not certain which work he refers to. The 1st edn. of J. von Lent's book on the false messiahs did not appear until 1683. Perhaps the reference is to Carlo Alfano's Italian pamphlet on Sabbatai Ṣevi, printed (according to Wolf, *Bibliotheca Hebraica*) in Viterbo, 1666 (actually in 1667), but so far I have not been able to examine a copy of this pamphlet.

apostasy, carefully avoided any mention of Nathan and kept his prefatory remarks sufficiently vague. At the end (fols. 53–58) there is an additional prayer for redemption, "sent from Jerusalem," which suggests that in the summer of 1666 there was an active circle of believers in the Holy City—unless "Jerusalem" was deliberately substituted for "Gaza." The prayer lacks any specific Sabbatian features: "O Lord, inscribe us for redemption, and lighten the messianic woes. . . . Hear us when we cry unto Thee," etc. In any event, the publication proves that even at the end of 1666 there were buyers for this kind of devotional publication.

VI

Nathan walked right into the turmoil and tension between the warring parties when he arrived in Venice just before Passover, in March, 1668. Both sides tried to capitalize on his visit, and subsequently circulated their respective versions of it. According to the Sabbatian story, the rabbis were afraid of Nathan and attempted to prevent his entry. There were, however, many believers in the ghetto, among them several who had some influence with the authorities. They complained about the unjust persecution of Nathan to one of the Venetian notables, and the latter's orders secured Nathan's admission to the ghetto.[206] Baruch of Arezzo, on the other hand, states that the rabbis had pronounced a general ban of excommunication on anyone who would receive Nathan into his house or as much as speak to him. Only R. Samuel Aboab, the head of the Academy, went to see Nathan and to inform him that he would not be admitted to the ghetto "lest his presence cause some adversity." Nathan replied that his was a divine errand and that he was on his way "to a certain place on behalf of the whole congregation of Israel." This is a clear reference to his intention to proceed to Rome, though it explains neither his journey to Venice nor the failure of his *maggid* to direct him straight to Rome via the port of Ancona, which was in the papal states and where he could have counted on some support. According to Baruch of Arezzo[207] (a believer himself and possibly also an eyewitness), Nathan offered not to enter the city if his presence was not wanted. On the day before Passover, R. Moses Zacuto visited Nathan and

206. Sasportas, p. 263.
207. *Ap.* Freimann, p. 61.

after a long conversation with him confessed—thus the Sabbatian version—that although he had studied the Zohar for thirty-eight years, his kabbalistic understanding was inferior to Nathan's. Two Venetian magistrates who happened to see Nathan invited him to their palace where he stayed for two days and one night—according to Baruch's chronology the first two days of the feast of Passover!—and subsequently ordered the Jewish community to admit him to the ghetto. Making due allowance for legendary embellishments, the accounts substantially agree.

It is evident that Nathan had planned the visit in advance and informed his followers accordingly. In any event, his followers knew that they could address letters to him in Venice. Two such letters, wishing him success in his enterprise, have been preserved.[208] The writer of the first letter, a certain Moses Abraham, prays for the success of the mission of Nathan and his companion, Samuel Gandoor, and wishes both a happy return to the messiah. He also declares his readiness to go wherever Nathan would send him. The letter was certainly written in 1668. The other letter, written by a certain Samuel Tunia (?), is similar in tone and contents.

Nathan stayed in the ghetto for about a fortnight, during which time he was thoroughly crossexamined by the rabbis who, however, could not prevent the believers from associating with him. One, albeit partial, account of the inquisitorial proceedings is given in the pamphlet "A Memorial unto the Children of Israel" published by the rabbis of Venice and containing, in addition to their own version of the proceedings, the earlier declarations of the rabbinates of Ipsola and Adrianople.[209] On the other hand, we also possess Nathan's account of the proceedings. In a letter to Caleb Kohen, one of the leading believers in Sofia or Corfu, he declared his signature to be null and void, since it had been extorted from him "under duress." Sasportas admits that both in examining Nathan and in publishing the pamphlet the rabbinic Academy had intended "to dispel error" so as to gladden the hearts of the unbelievers who had not been seduced, and to make the believers repent and weep at their folly. In

208. Formerly in the library of the Jewish Community of Vienna (Catalogue Schwarz 141, no. 5).

209. Only a few copies of the pamphlet are extant, but the text was reprinted by R. Samuel Aboab at the end of his responsa *Debar Shemu'el* (Venice, 1702) fols. 263–67.

other words, the rabbis of Venice also preferred a policy of moderation and persuasion to the more radical means of bell, book, and candle.

The long letter of the Venetian rabbis (April 12, 1668) bears eloquent witness to their grave concern for the integrity of the Jewish tradition, which was threatened by the believers. The rabbis congratulated themselves on not having departed from the traditions of the elders and consented to foolish things (referring, probably, to the abolition of the fast days), though they had to admit that their prestige and authority had greatly declined in the eyes of the believers. In fact, the rabbinic authorities had to flatter the masses in order to ensure some obedience. No doubt Aboab, Treves, and Saraval did not easily forget the humiliation they suffered during the high tide of the movement. Now they deplored the fact that Israel had been disgraced in the eyes of the gentiles by their rash belief in vain words that clearly opposed "Scripture, tradition, and reason." As far as that young man Nathan of Gaza was concerned, who had caused such a commotion, they had tried to get rid of him quietly and without scandal, but when this had proved impossible they had no choice but to take such action as would effectively destroy the heresy. Wherefore "before his departure, on Monday the Twelfth of Omer [April 9, 1668], we assembled together, the rabbis of the *yeshibah* and the leaders of the community. We summoned him and he appeared before us, and when we examined him he could not give a satisfactory answer to any question, and shame covered his face and he could hardly speak." He was—they wrote—evidently diseased in his imagination and himself admitted that he had been troubled by an evil spirit and led astray by a spirit of folly to say things which had never been and to declare darkness light and the impure pure. But since he had caused this mischief through a diseased imagination and not through deliberate wickedness, they would not punish him severely. May God forgive "them that could have raised their voice against him in the beginning"—an obvious reference to the rabbis of Palestine whose silence had abetted Nathan's messianic activity—"before we were disgraced in the eyes of all the gentiles." But since others had failed to act, the Venetian rabbis were somewhat at a loss what to do: the matter was "occult and sealed" and nobody could fathom the hidden purposes of Providence. Though they refrained from excommunicating Nathan, they sent their "Memorial unto the Children of Israel" to all congregations in order to discredit the prophet. In this they were undoubtedly successful.

The text, however, of the retraction which Nathan was made to sign is anything but forceful or convincing: "Whereas the rabbis of Venice have ruled that although I said that I have seen the [divine] Chariot as Ezekiel had seen it, and [heard] a prophecy to the effect that Sabbatai Ṣevi is the messiah, yet I was mistaken and there was no substance in the vision, I therefore consented to their words and said my prophecy concerning Sabbatai Ṣevi had no substance. I, Nathan Benjamin." Instead of an expression of repentance and an appeal to the believers to abandon the faith, we merely find a bald statement to the effect that the rabbis denied the prophecy—all right, let them have their way. The weakness of the document was, of course, that it failed to give a full account of the cross-examination and hence it inevitably invited the charge that unfair pressure had been exerted. Indeed, before long Nathan and other Sabbatians impugned the legitimacy of the proceedings. There is an unmistakable note of bitterness in Nathan's account, and it is possible that there may be some truth in his version (see below, n. 212, on Azulay).

Nathan wrote to the believers not to be impressed by the official pamphlets and proclamations, "since there is nothing in them." The rabbis of Venice were worthless men who thought that there were none like them in Israel and who pretended "that they had investigated and examined the matter and found it to be nothing, as if they were masters of the assay." According to Nathan's account, the rabbis had asked him to perform a miracle and he had replied—as always—that it was not in his power to do so, but that he intended to go to a special place (Rome) to perform a mystical *tiqqun* on behalf of Israel. Thereupon they declared his prophecy to be vain and void, "and this is what their investigation amounts to." The rabbis may have exulted at their victory in forcing him to sign the confession, but he had got the better of them, since everyone could see "how I deceived them, to fulfill the verse [Ps. 18:27]: 'With the pure Thou wilt show Thyself pure and with the froward Thou wilt show Thyself froward.' For I merely said thar I consented to . . . what they had ruled—in a matter which is not subject to rulings. They wished to persecute me, . . . but for the grace of God, . . . who destroyed their counsel, they could not even speak one hard word against me."[210] Nathan as much as admits that he was neither intimidated nor bullied into signing. Baruch of Arezzo[211] specifies the nature of Nathan's deceit: in the signature "I, Nathan Benjamin" the Hebrew word *ᵓani* ("I") was written so as to be indistinguishable from *ᵓag*—to be interpreted as the initials of *ᵓanus gamur* ("totally under duress"). What seems to be the fanciful invention of a Sabbatian chronicler is surprisingly corroborated by no less a witness than R. Moses Zacuto.[212]

In Venice and elsewhere Nathan had many followers and supporters who received the official "Memorial" (published in April, 1668) with undisguised hostility and audible protests. One of the Venetian rabbis who had preached an anti-Sabbatian sermon was promptly answered by a scornful circular letter[213] in which the author, Meir of Mestre, an inhabitant of Venice,[214] derided the "examination" of Nathan by the rabbinic court and exhorted the believers to persevere in their penitential exercises. In their official "Memorial," the rabbis of Venice had accused the believers of "calculating the end." R. Meir of Mestre returns the compliment: it is the unbelievers who are calculating the end—albeit in a negative way—by insisting that the present moment could not possibly be the time of the messianic advent. The believers, on the other hand, were ready for redemption at any moment, even "today if ye will hear his voice." Penitence can never do any harm, and woe unto the rabbis who damp the people's penitential ardor. The tenor and contents of the pamphlet indicate that the writer was acting as the mouthpiece of a fairly strong group in Venice.

Among the rabbinic authorities execrated by the author of the pamphlet we also find the name of R. Moses Zacuto, no doubt because the latter had definitely broken with the "faith" after the apostasy. Zacuto, who seems to have been under attack from several quarters, stated his position in a letter written in May, 1668 (that is, about

210. *Ap.* Freimann, p. 63. 211. *Ibid.*

212. As reported by H. Y. D. Azulay; see M. Benayahu in *Sefunoth,* V (1961), 335. On the transmission of this tradition from Zacuto to Azulay see *ibid.,* p. 322. By the time Zacuto noticed the imposture, Nathan had already vanished. The formula used by Nathan is the precise counterpart of the Latin C. F. (*coactus feci*) used under such circumstances.

213. Published by G. Scholem in *Zion,* XIII (1948), 52–54.

214. He was in touch with Leone Modena, as appears from a letter written in 1647; cf. Benayahu in *Sinai,* XXXIV (1945), 187.

a month after Nathan's appearance before the rabbinic court in Venice), to R. Meir Isserles of the *yeshibah* in Vienna. R. Meir had received a copy of the "Memorial" circulated by the Academy of Venice, but desired more detailed information about the proceedings. He therefore wrote to Zacuto, whose reputation as a kabbalist was already well established. In his reply[215] Zacuto stated his views as they had definitely crystallized after the apostasy in sharp and unambiguous language. The believers were utter fools, misleading the people with their deceitful imaginings and keeping up "a strange fire . . . within the congregation of the Lord." They had no respect for the rabbis, and he himself had suffered ignominy at their hands in Rovigo. Zacuto identifies himself with the letters of the Venetian rabbis contained in the "Memorial." The movement had caused threefold harm to Italian Jewry: it had occasioned material losses to the community, it had contributed to the danger of apostasy among the foolish disappointed believers, and it had exposed the Jews to the hostility of their Christian neighbors. Zacuto assured his correspondent that "the rabbi Nathan" had been properly and thoroughly cross-examined, though the official letter of the Venetian rabbis did not give any details lest these come to the knowledge of the gentiles. On this point Zacuto's information, which there is no good reason to doubt, contradicts Nathan's account. Zacuto praises the German communities for having observed the fasts even in the year 1666—unlike, we may infer, the Italian Jews some of whom feasted on the Seventeenth of Tammuz and the Ninth of Ab even in 1667. In spite of his emphatic condemnation of the Sabbatians, Zacuto is moderate as compared to Sasportas and Joseph ha-Levi, and he clearly shared the view of the Turkish rabbis that silence was a better policy than persecution and public controversy.

As a theologian Zacuto was not impressed by the kabbalistic heterodoxies of the Sabbatians. Whether he really complimented Nathan on his knowledge of the Zohar (as affirmed by Baruch of Arezzo) or not is immaterial. Nathan's restless and revolutionary spirit was utterly alien to Zacuto's essentially conservative temperament, though some of Zacuto's favorite disciples became and remained staunch adherents of the Sabbatian movement.

It is evident—minor contradictions in our sources notwithstand-

215. *Zion,* XIII, pp. 55–56.

ing—that Nathan pursued the aim of his journey with remarkable singlemindedness. According to one account[216] he was sent to Leghorn by the Venetian rabbis who, knowing that he had powerful Christian protectors in Venice, did not dare to excommunicate him. In Leghorn, where the Jewish community enjoyed greater freedom, the rabbis would be able to deal with him more severely. Nathan, however, evaded them and went straight to Rome. A Sabbatian (and possibly more exact) account ascribes friendlier intentions to the Venetian authorities: alarmed by signs of Christian interest in Nathan—his arrival had been noted in the gazettes—and fearing that it might lead to his arrest by the Inquisition, the rabbis advised him to travel quietly to Florence.[217]

The details of Nathan's journey are not quite clear, but we know his itinerary. Accompanied by Samuel Gandoor, he sailed from Venice to Finale di Modona and thence traveled overland to Bologna, Florence, and Leghorn. In Leghorn he tarried for about two months[218] and taught the Sabbatian doctrine to a group of devout and enthusiastic believers that had formed around Moses Pinheiro. He did not, however, appear in public and he refrained from open propaganda. Sabbatian preaching was going underground, and the faith was proclaimed in the private homes of believers.

216. Sasportas, p. 267.

217. Baruch of Arezzo clearly gives us firsthand information, since he reports (*ap.* Freimann, p. 62) that he had been sent from Venice with letters to his uncle Samuel Formiggini, requesting the latter to arrange for Nathan's travel from Finale di Modena. The fear, expressed in the letter from Venice, that the "messengers of the pope" might harm Nathan clearly contradicts Sasportas' version. Baruch of Arezzo describes the danger in which Nathan found himself when a Christian crowd assembled at the bank of the river Panaro, shouting "Behold the messiah of the Jews," but the incident is rather obscure. Perhaps research in the Venetian gazettes of that year may throw light on the matter. So far I have been unable to locate the gazettes.

218. Thus Abraham Cardozo, in a letter written in 1669; see *Zion,* XIX (1954), 13. Baruch of Arezzo (*ap.* Freimann, p. 62) is less definite and therefore probably more correct when he simply says that Nathan remained there "for some time." Samuel Catalani's letter explicitly states that by 1 Tammuz (June 10, 1668) Nathan had already left Ancona, thus compressing Nathan's Italian travels into the short period from the middle of April to the middle of June. However, the date given in the extant copy of Catalani's letter is the result of a scribal error. Nathan arrived in Ancona on June 21, and left on the 29th; see below, n. 221.

Accompanied by Moses Capsuto, a wealthy merchant and for many years one of the most active Sabbatians in Italy,[219] Nathan proceeded to Rome, whither he "went in peace and returned in peace. But what he did and spoke there I do not know, and even if I knew I would not breathe a word of it." The latter part of the statement is nearer to the truth, as Baruch of Arezzo surely knew the purpose of Nathan's mystical mission. According to Sasportas, Nathan went to Rome incognito but his presence became known. The Jewish authorities wanted to deal sternly with him, but Nathan disguised himself, shaved his beard and escaped to Leghorn. To his believers in Leghorn he said that he had been to Rome "on a mission from his messiah, and that he had performed his mission by throwing into the river an inscribed scroll—and yet one year and Rome shall be overthrown."[220] A slightly different version is given in the detailed account which R. Samuel Catalani of Ancona sent to his son Raphael Catalani on Corfu. Samuel's letter[221] was written early in July, 1668, and al-

219. His name is repeatedly mentioned in Meir Rofe's correspondence from Leghorn to R. Abraham Rovigo in the years 1674–78 (Brit. Mus., MS. Or. 9165, published by Is. Tishby in *Sefunoth,* III–IV [1960], 71–130). Capsuto acted as a link between the various Sabbatian groups, receiving letters from metropolitan Turkey and the Balkans, and transmitting money for the believers; see the documents published by Tishby in *Sefunoth,* I (1956), 93–95. During the sixties and seventies he lived in Leghorn (see *Sefunoth,* III–IV [1960], p. 95, n. 24). The Moses whose father David Capsuto died in Florence in 1684 (see Freimann, p. 62, n. 4) is, perhaps, not identical with our Moses Capsuto. In Meir Rofe's letter to Rovigo (Tishby, *loc. cit.,* p. 91), David Capsuto of Florence is still referred to as living. The family name was later changed to Cassuto.

220. Sasportas, p. 268. Sasportas probably meant to say that this sentence, halfway between a prophecy and a spell and clearly modeled on Jonah's prophecy in Nineveh, was written on the scroll which Nathan threw into the Tiber. Cf. also Sasportas, p. 259.

221. The letter was discovered by Tishby in the Bodleian, Oxford (no. 2239, fol. 191a); see Tishby's article in *Sefunoth,* I (1956), 113. The date *Rosh Ḥodesh* Tammuz (June 10, 1668) seems to be a scribal error. The correct date, 25 Tammuz, is given in the Milan MS. (see below, n. 230) discovered by Dr. N. A. Alloni in 1960; the chronology derived from Samuel Catalani's letter and adopted in the original Hebrew version of the present work (p. 656) must be corrected accordingly. According to MS. Milan (fol. 1a) Nathan and Gandoor arrived in Ancona on "Thursday, 12 Tammuz 428 (June 21, 1668) . . . and did not reveal themselves to any Jew . . . until R. Jacob b. Sabbatai Kohen recognized them." The date *R.Ḥ.* (*Rosh Ḥodesh*) in R. Joseph Ḥamiṣ' copy of Catalani's letter must be due to either a misreading or a scribal

ready shows evidence of legendary transformation of the events. According to Samuel Catalani, all the Jews of Rome were convinced by Nathan's extraordinary behavior that he acted on a divine commission. He had shaved his head and was very well dressed. He remained in Rome one night only, but spent this night, together with his companion (Moses Capsuto?) in the shelter for destitute wayfarers. As his companion was known as a wealthy merchant, everybody was greatly astonished and people began to wonder whether the stranger was not Nathan of Gaza. The companion told them that the visitor was an Ashkenazi and could not speak [their language]. The two left before dawn and betook themselves to the papal palace (S. Angelo) where they loitered "around and around" for a whole day, Nathan being engaged all the time in mystical meditations. They left an hour before midnight "and traveled a distance of eight days within two days, and arrived here in Ancona. He remained here for eight days, and departed joyful and with a glad heart. And wherever he went no harm befell the Jews and nothing became known to the authorities, although these places are swarming with informers and apostates."

The two accounts, though differing in details, provide a fairly clear picture of Nathan's Roman visit. It was evidently the attention of the papal authorities and not (as Sasportas thought) of the Jewish community that Nathan wanted to escape. His circumambulations "around and around the palace" were a magical rite intended to bring about the destruction of Rome and probably had a twofold symbolic significance. In the first place, Nathan's action was in imitation of his messiah. Like Sabbatai, the prophet too penetrated into the realm of the evil powers (that is, the pope's residence) and performed mystical acts bringing about the destruction of the latter. Unlike the messiah, however, Nathan did not tarry in the embrace of the *qelippah* but hastened away as fast as he could—according to the Sabbatian legend an eight days' journey within two days. Second, Nathan's mystical acts were clearly inspired by the rabbinic legend (B. Sanhedrin 98a) according to which the messiah was sitting like an outcast among the lepers and beggars at the gates of Rome. A similar act of symbolic

error. Tammuz 28 is unlikely (as this day was a Sabbath) and hence we may assume the original reading to have been 25 Tammuz (the respective Hebrew letters being very similar). Catalani's statement that Nathan proceeded straight from Rome to Ancona is contradicted by our other sources, which suggest that he returned for a while to Leghorn.

identification had been performed in 1530 by the messianic enthusiast, visionary, and martyr Solomon Molkho, and described in his autobiographical letter:[222]

I entered the city and left my horse and fine apparel with the innkeeper, and told him that I had a ladylove in these parts whom I loved since days of old and ancient years: my soul was bound to hers, but her parents were hiding her [in a place] where I could speak to her only disguised in the rags of a beggar. I asked him to procure me this disguise . . . and I blackened my face and donned the filthy rags . . . and walked about despised and rejected of men, like a man of sorrows and acquainted with grief. . . . And I went through the streets of the city until I came to the bridge over the Tiber near the pope's fortress, where the beggars and the sick are, and I remained among them like one stricken, smitten of God, for thirty days.

No doubt Molkho's dramatic account was known to Nathan and almost certainly inspired his symbolic action, beginning with a night among the poor and ending on the famous bridge in front of the Castle of S. Angelo. Whether Nathan acted on Sabbatai's instructions (as averred by himself and Sasportas) or on his own initiative, he certainly attached great importance to the mystical *tiqqun* which he performed vicariously for the messiah. To his trusted friends and associates he reported the successful accomplishment of his mission in short letters.[223] To his father Elisha Ḥayyim, who seems to have been in Vienna at the time, he wrote: "Blessed be God to whom thanksgivings are due, who has rendered all good unto me and has granted me strength and help to do his service and to unify his great name and to execute my intention." To Sabbatai's brother Joseph Ṣevi he wrote: "I betook myself to the well-known great city, for this was the purpose of my voyage to Italy." On his return to Leghorn, Nathan composed an "Account of the Mission Accomplished by the Rabbi," copies of which were sent to believers in several places. This strange and obscure apocalyptic letter is written in a curiously artificial and allusive rhymed Aramaic which occasionally defies comprehension, though it is evident that the symbolic language is indebted to some passages in the Tal-

222. Printed under the title *Ḥayyath Qaneh,* Amsterdam (1658?); the account of his mystical disguise, *ibid.,* fols. 3b–4a.

223. The letters were discovered by Tishby in the Bodleian MS. mentioned above, n. 221.

mud.[224] So much, however, is clear from this cryptic letter: Nathan, trusting his soul with God, cast himself from his spiritual heights into the dark abyss and *qelippah* of Rome, where he successfully battled—in the power and the light of the messiah Sabbatai Ṣevi "whose Lamp shineth in the Levant"—against the forces of evil.

Nathan gives no indication why he issued this communiqué concerning his mystical warfare. Perhaps it was meant to encourage the believers: the power of the *qelippah* was not yet completely broken, and many strange and incomprehensible things would have to happen in the course of the struggle, but Sabbatai and Nathan were both fighting the battle, each according to his calling. Sabbatai had entered the sultan's palace and the realm of Ishmael, while Nathan had taken up the struggle against Rome. Let no one despair, for the messiah and his prophet were laboring hard to accomplish the final *tiqqun*. R. Joseph Ḥamiṣ, in an enthusiastic sermon, extolled Nathan's courage in facing "an unprecedented danger, and surely he was protected by angels because he could not otherwise have escaped the mouth of the lion in a natural way. . . . For he had to descend to the depth of the *qelippoth* and to cast himself thither, so as to fulfill [Ps. 91:13]: 'Thou shalt tread upon the lion and the adder, upon the young lion and the serpent shalt thou trample'—as he no doubt did on that occasion."[225] Another *pronunciamento* in the same enigmatic style was sent to Nathan's followers in Venice, probably written by himself. It predicts the fall of "the land of thick darkness" (that is, Rome; cf. Jer. 2:31).[226]

After his return to Leghorn, Nathan continued to strengthen the hearts of his followers, who held a kind of formal counterinquiry into his prophetic credentials. This was meant as a countermove to the inquiry of the Venetian rabbis, and the "proceedings" were circulated among the believers in Italy. R. Moses Pinheiro's testimony (see above,

224. Such as Pesaḥim 36, Baba Kamma 3b, Sanhedrin 7a. The text, as given in *SS,* (pp. 658–59) and based on Sasportas (p. 268), the Sabbatian notebook in the library of Columbia University (fol. 24a) and MS. Oxford 2239, can now be further corrected with the help of the MS. discovered in the Ambrosiana in Milan (see above, n. 221, and below, n. 230). It appears that Nathan himself changed the readings in the copies he left with different people.

225. See the whole sermon in Tishby's article, *Sefunoth,* I (1956), 112–17, particularly p. 114.

226. It was found among Meir of Mestre's papers; cf. the text in *H. A. Wolfson Jubilee Volume* (1965), Hebrew part, pp. 228–29.

p. 205) regarding his conversations with Nathan contains evidence of the bitterness which the prophet harbored against his persecutors, for he "was not in the least afraid of the gentiles, *but* only of the wicked among the Jews."[227] The present failure of the messianic hopes and the delay of redemption were due to the "mixed multitude" and the sinners in Israel (that is, probably, his rabbinic opponents) rather than to the gentiles. There is a significant shift here in Nathan's position. His earliest letters had stated quite clearly that the unbelievers could neither disturb nor delay the inexorable progress of the messianic consummation: the cosmic *tiqqun* had been completed and the unbelievers were merely hurting themselves (see above, p. 272). Now, under the pressure of events, Nathan had to revise his earlier opinions and ponder where he had misinterpreted his original vision. In the hour of crisis and trial he realized that the sinners, that is, unbelievers, were capable of actively obstructing the process of messianic fulfillment.

Nathan may have had good reasons for fearing the hostility of the rabbis. At any rate, after his return from Italy to Turkey he and his followers concealed his whereabouts for a considerable time with such success that he was thought by some to have died or to have been captured by pirates.[228] In Venice too it was rumored that Nathan had fled from Turkey and was leading an errant life.[229] In reality Nathan and Gandoor, having accomplished their mystical mission in Rome, proceeded to Ancona, where they arrived on Thursday, June 21, 1668,[230] and remained until June 29.[231] They concealed their iden-

227. Freimann, p. 95. The italicized word *but* translates the Hebrew ᵓ*ela*ᵓ of the MSS.; Freimann's printed text corrupts ᵓ*ela*ᵓ *lo*ᵓ—the exact opposite.

228. Cardozo's letter to the rabbis of Smyrna suggests that this was, in fact, what the latter believed; hence they must have been unaware of Nathan's actual whereabouts at the end of the summer of 1668. Cf. Zion, XIX (1954), 13.

229. Baruch of Arezzo, *ap.* Freimann, p. 62. Cardozo's letter of summer, 1669, shows that he too did not know where Nathan was at the time. An anti-Sabbatian poem by the Karaite author Daniel b. Moses Melammed of Damascus states that after the apostasy the prophet "fled to a far away place, and nobody knows his whereabouts." The poem was written in 1669; for the full text see S. Poznanski in *MGWJ*, LX (1916), 149–50.

230. See above, n. 221. The MS. in which this date is given was discovered in the Abrosiana in Milan by Dr. N. Alloni. The MS., which is not listed in Bernheimer's catalogue, is marked *x 148 sup.* on the outside, and *MS III.47* on the inside. Its 14 fols., written in a beautiful Italian hand, contain several

tity but were recognized by one Jacob b. Sabbatai Kohen who had seen them earlier this year in Corfu and had brought one of Nathan's "messages of comfort" on his return to Ancona.[232] Thereupon the blind and aged rabbi of the community, R. Mahallallel Halleluyah—himself kabbalist, poet, and ardent believer in Sabbatai Ṣevi—approached them in the synagogue and bade them welcome. The rabbi of Ancona's account of his prolonged conversations with Nathan[233] is not only an important historical source but also a *document humain* of considerable psychological interest. The two kabbalists approached each other with oriental ceremoniousness and with the utmost prudence and circumspection if not suspicion. After some initial beating about the bush, the two gradually opened up to each other, and R. Mahallallel began to probe Nathan on the "faith." To his questions, which exhibit a curious mixture of rationalist and homiletical argument, Nathan replied quietly and methodically, countering halakhic points with legal considerations and theological ones with kabbalistic arguments and *gematria*. We learn, incidentally, of Sabbatai's positive attitude to the Karaites (of whom a number believed in his messiahship) and are also told that Sabbatai had personally charged Nathan with the mysterious mission to Rome and himself met all the expenses.[234] Nathan confided to R. Mahallallel the nature of this mission[235] and expounded to him the mystical allu-

---

Sabbatian documents, some of them hitherto unknown. Fols. 1a–7b contain a detailed account of Nathan's visit to Ancona, almost certainly composed, that is, dictated, by the blind rabbi of Ancona, R. Mahallallel Halleluyah, and written down by a scribe. R. Mahallellel, in the manner of chroniclers, refers to himself in the third person as "the rabbi"; but there can be little doubt about the author's identity. See G. Scholem, "Sabbatian Documents concerning Nathan of Gaza from the Archives of R. Mahallallel Halleluyah of Ancona," in *H. A. Wolfson Jubilee Volume* (1965), Hebrew part, pp. 225–41. Baruch of Arezzo, whose information on the Ancona visit is generally reliable (though he wrongly prolongs its duration to three weeks) says that Nathan held converse "with the blind rabbi" whose name, however, he does not mention.

231. Samuel Catalani's letter, *Sefunoth,* I (1956), p. 113: "he remained here for eight days."

232. The text of this letter in *H. A. Wolfson Jubilee Volume* (1965), pp. 237–38.

233. *Ibid.,* pp. 230–36. 234. *Ibid.,* p. 233.

235. Cf. also Baruch of Arezzo (*ap.* Freimann, p. 62) where *maᶜaseh ha-sheliḥim* should be emended to *maᶜaseh ha-sheliḥuth,* in accordance with the reading in the Sabbatian notebook in the library of Columbia University.

sions in Scripture to Sabbatai's name and ministry. When Nathan embarked the two embraced and kissed, and wept on each other's shoulders. A miraculous breeze sped Nathan's passage from Ancona to the Balkan shore.[236]

According to one source, they disembarked at Ragusa (Dalmatia),[237] but we have an autograph letter written by Nathan from Durazzo (Albania) to his friend David Yiṣḥaki, who was then with Sabbatai in Adrianople. He announced on the Tenth of Ellul (August 17, 1668) that he had finished his mission to Rome "where I have cast myself into the deep of the great abyss."[238] Since the passage from Ancona to Durazzo would not have lasted six weeks, it stands to reason that Nathan and Gandoor stayed for some time in Ragusa and then went down the shore of the Adriatic. From Durazzo, they wandered "the length and breadth" of Greece, guided by a celestial *maggid* until they came to Salonika[239] where (according to a Sabbatian source) Nathan stayed for about six months and taught the Sabbatian gospel.[240]

A collection of Sabbatian notes, written in 1668 in Salonika, has been preserved in the Musayoff Collection in Jerusalem. The anonymous writer asks himself why, "since today, in the year 5428 [1668] the Shekhinah has already risen from the dust," we are still in exile, and he accounts for this because there are, all the time, some sparks left in the realm of the *qelippoth*. The manuscript contains also the first pages of a Sabbatian commentary on the Esther scroll,

236. *H. A. Wolfson Jubilee Volume* (1965), p. 236.

237. Baruch of Arezzo, *ap*. Freimann, p. 63.

238. The letter has been published from the Dönmeh archives; cf. *Sefunoth,* V (1961), 262–63. It has also Gandoor's signature. It is curious that the letter does not mention Sabbatai Ṣevi with whom Yiṣḥaki was visiting. Probably they sent him a separate letter.

239. On their way to Salonika they passed through Patras and Navarino (Baruch of Arezzo, *ibid.*).

240. Cardozo's letter to Samuel de Paz in Leghorn, printed in A. H. Weiss, *Beth ha-Midrash* (1865), p. 66. Our present knowledge of the chronology of Nathan's movements does not allow for any such extended stay, except in the late summer and autumn of 1668, i.e., until his departure for Adrianople and Kastoria. His earlier visit to Salonika, in 1667, was much shorter, and subsequent visits, though not per se impossible, must have been very brief. As hostility to the believers grew, it is unlikely that Nathan would stay for a longer period. M. Benayahu tends to fix this long stay after 1674.

the biblical text that lent itself most readily to Sabbatian typology.[241] Another Sabbatian source[242] lists the names of the rabbis in Salonika who became Nathan's disciples at that period and received from him the new (that is, postapostasy) doctrine. Several of the rabbis mentioned in this list are known as Sabbatian believers from other sources too, and hence the list gains in credibility. The names,[243] it is true, are not of the top-ranking rabbis of Salonika. These, apparently, had left the movement after the apostasy. Nevertheless, Nathan's followers were far from negligible, and many of them are mentioned in other sources as well-known scholars and preachers. The panegyrical terms in which several of them who died at the end of the seventeenth century were eulogized by the then greatest preacher in Salonika, R. Solomon Amarillo, sufficiently attests their reputation.[244] Solomon Florentin and Joseph Filosoff (a son-in-law of the illustrious rabbi Baruch Angel) seem to have been the senior members of the group; they subsequently led the mass apostasy that resulted in the formation of the Dönmeh sect. R. Isaac Ḥanan was one of the more prominent rabbis of Salonika. His homilies[245] are permeated not only by kabbalism in general, but also by specifically Sabbatian ideas as taught at that time by Nathan. Doctrines which the author had heard "from the mouth of the Holy Lamp, Rabbi N." and which can be found in Nathan's writings after the apostasy are quoted several times. There can be no doubt as to the identity of "Rabbi N.," and since a number of these homilies were composed after Nathan's death, the conclusion

241. The MS. (formerly listed as no. 213) belonged to one Jacob Vidal of Salonika.

242. See *Zion,* VI (1941), 128–29. Other MSS. of the list (from the Günzburg Collection) have now become available on microfilm.

243. They are R. Solomon Florentin, R. Joseph Filosoff, R. Joseph Russo, R. Isaac Ḥanan (on his epitaph the name is spelled Ḥanin; he was probably the leading member of the group), R. Abraham Pereṣ, R. Jeremiah, R. Judah Brussa, R. Joseph Konat, R. Raphael Baruch (Florentin's son-in-law), R. Mordecai Kohen Ḥasid, R. Eliezer Kohen, R. Asher Abravanel, R. Sabbatai Immanuel, and R. David Kerimisin.

244. See Solomon Amarillo, *Peney Shelomoh* (Salonika, 1717), fol. 59a (on R. Sabbatai Immanuel, died 1690), fol. 61a (on R. Eliezer Kohen, died 1690), fol. 82d (on R. Asher Abravanel, died 1698). In the years 1668–69 these rabbis can hardly have been above middle age. The epitaphs of five of these pupils have now been published by Isaac Emmanuel, *Precious Stones of the Jews of Salonika* [Hebrew], vol. II (Jerusalem, 1968). Mordecai Kohen died 1699.

245. A collection of them was printed in 1756 under the title *Beney Yiṣḥak.*

imposes itself that Isaac Ḥanan persevered in the faith until his death.[246] His book is one of the rare cases of published Sabbatian literature.

From Salonika, Nathan finally proceeded—in further flagrant disregard of the prohibition which the rabbis had imposed on him—to Adrianople, where he arrived in the spring or summer of 1669. Henceforth, meetings between the two were to take place frequently until Sabbatai's death, even after Nathan had left Adrianople and settled in Kastoria. It is not impossible, however, that after Nathan's return from Rome, he and Sabbatai met already, in the late summer of 1668, in Salonika. Tobias Rofe Ashkenazi, whose little information about the period after the apostasy is generally reliable (though his chronology is confused), states that Sabbatai visited the three major communities, Adrianople, Constantinople, "and sometimes Salonika."[247] A joint visit to Salonika by Sabbatai and Nathan is mentioned in the "testimony" of Moses b. Isaac b. Ḥabib,[248] but the date 425 (1665) is clearly impossible and should, perhaps, read 428 or later. Dönmeh tradition also tells of Sabbatai's sojourn in Salonika, of his sermons there to his believers, and of his friendship with R. Joseph Filosoff, whose daughter he subsequently married.[249]

From Adrianople, where he tarried for an unknown length of time, Nathan moved to Kastoria. There was a considerable Jewish community in Kastoria, consisting mainly of wealthy fur dealers, and Nathan found many believers among both the merchants and the rabbis. One of the more prominent members of the community, Jacob Kohen, had even apostatized in imitation of the messiah, but subsequently repented and moved to a far-away community where his lapse would not be known.[250] This, however, seems to have been an exceptional case, and most believers in Kastoria remained faithful Jews. They offered shelter to Nathan, who arrived in Kastoria for the first time in Sivan, 1669, on his way either to or from Adrianople.[251] During the period of his stay in Adrianople and his sub-

246. Nathan died in 1680. R. Isaac Ḥanan died on December 15, 1684, according to his epitaph. See also *Zion*, VI (1941), 200–1.

247. Emden, p. 46.

248. *Ibid.*, p. 53. The author was a native of Salonika and could have preserved local tradition.

249. Isaac R. Molkho in *Reshumoth*, VI (1936), 538–39.

250. Rosanes, IV, p. 150.

251. Nathan's visit (or visits?) to Adrianople is mentioned by Baruch of Arezzo (p. 63) and is also referred to several times in the commentary on Psalms

sequent residence in Kastoria, Sabbatai traveled much among the Jewish communities in Thrace, Macedonia, and Bulgaria. Wherever he went he found ardent believers, and there is no evidence of any action taken against him by the "infidels." The authority of the "Holy Lamp" (as Nathan came to be called) was generally recognized in those parts, and in Kastoria he was even asked to arbitrate internal disputes.[252] In his many letters to the Balkan communities he expounded the mysteries of the Sabbatian faith and exhorted the believers to persevere in the expectation of the messiah's second manifestation in glory. "A vast collection of these letters was extant in Salonika until the eve of the Second World War."[253] In Kastoria, R. Israel Ḥazzan became Nathan's disciple and served as his amanuensis for three years.[254] The two letters that are all that was formerly published from the Salonika collection (see above, n. 253) were addressed to Kastoria about 1675 and 1677, thus corroborating Nathan's close ties with that community. In 1670 Nathan composed his chief work *Sefer ha-Beri᾿ah* (*The Book of Creation*) in which he expounded his doctrines of the structure of the cosmos, the divine emanation, and the function of the messiah Sabbatai Ṣevi in the cosmic process. The argument of *The Book of Creation* is conceived on a large scale and elaborated in great detail, and the book seems to have been written during a period of uninterrupted residence in one place—probably in Kastoria. *The Book of Creation* became the standard work of Sabbatian kabbalah during

---

by Nathan's disciple and amanuensis R. Israel Ḥazzan. The earliest testimony regarding Nathan's sojourn in Kastoria is contained in a letter, dated 27 Sivan 429, of David Kohen of Patras, discovered among other Sabbatian documents in MS. Oxford 2239; see Is. Tishby in *Sefunoth,* I (1956), 115. Baruch of Arezzo (p. 63) too mentions Nathan's "prolonged" stay in Kastoria.

252. Cf. the document published by S. Asaf in *Zion,* I (1936), 454–55.

253. Oral communication from R. Michael Molho, who had himself seen this collection. After the publication of the Hebrew edn. of this book, this collection was recovered through the good services of Mr. Albert (Abraham) Amarillo, who later donated this most valuable MS. to the Ben-Zvi Institute, where it is now listed as no. 2262. (See my preface to the present edn.). At the time, Molho was allowed to copy and publish two short letters only relating to Kastoria; see *RÉJ,* CIV (1938), 119–21, and also below, p. 900.

254. The printed text of Baruch of Arezzo's memoir (*ap.* Freimann, p. 94) reads "twenty years," but the correct reading is given in the original MS. in the Jewish Theological Seminary in New York.

the next generation, and its doctrines, as well as those contained in Nathan's other writings, played a decisive role in the subsequent development of Sabbatianism, especially in its heretical forms.[255]

VII

Reference has been made on several occasions to the role played by "prophets" in the history of the Sabbatian movement and in the dissemination of its propaganda. Not all prophets were men of stature. Indeed, some of them were men of doubtful integrity, and the career of Sabbatai Raphael may serve as an instructive example. Sabbatai Raphael[256] appeared on the scene immediately after the messiah's apostasy, and—fortunately for the historian—his brief but colorful career has been reported in great detail by Sasportas. Compared to Nathan's spiritual stature, Sabbatai Raphael is a mere dwarf. We do not know whether he was sent on a "mission" by the believers in Palestine or whether he acted as a self-appointed emissary, neither do we know whether he played the part of a prophet everywhere or to the simple and unlettered only.

Sabbatai Raphael, like Sabbatai Ṣevi, came of a wealthy Greco-Jewish family. He spent his childhood in Misithra (also called Mistra)[257] on the Peloponnese peninsula—a medieval city built near the site of ancient Sparta and for some time the capital of the province of Morea and the seat of a great fifteenth-century philosophical school of Platonism. In 1662, at the age of nineteen or twenty-three,[258] he

255. Cf. C. Wirszubski's important (Hebrew) article, "The Sabbatian Theology of Nathan of Gaza," in *Keneseth* (published by Mosad Bialik), VIII (1944), 210–44.

256. In his introduction to *Taᶜalumoth u-Meqoroth ha-Ḥokhmah*, a collection of magico-kabbalistic recipes which he printed in Venice in 1667, he gave his name as "Sabbatai Raphael, the son of Daniel Raphael." This would suggest that Raphael was the family name. On the other hand, his two letters to Sasportas are signed "Sabbatai, the son of R. Raphael" (Sasportas, pp. 274, 276).

257. Sabbatai Raphael's introduction to his kabbalistic tract (see n. 256); Sasportas, p. 273. See also the letter of recommendation by the rabbis of Constantinople, quoted by Sasportas, p. 278.

258. Two documents of the year 1667 give his age as twenty-seven (Sasportas, p. 273) and twenty-four (see J. Meijer in *Liber amicorum Prof. J. Romein* [Amsterdam, 1953], pp. 103–4) respectively. According to the document printed by J. Meijer, Sabbatai Raphael claimed that his mother was from Jerusalem and that both he and his father were natives of Sicily. Since no Jews were permitted to reside in Sicily at the time, this detail must be a mistake

went to Constantinople to continue his rabbinic studies, and was encouraged by R. Moses and R. Joshua Benveniste. He later claimed to have been a *dayyan* (rabbinic judge) in several great congregations,[259] but the truth seems to be that after a very short period of study he went into business and lost his fortune.[260] The rabbis of Constantinople provided him with a letter of recommendation in which they stated that he intended to continue his studies in Jerusalem. He begged his way to the Holy Land, where he probably arrived in 1663 and joined himself to the group around Sabbatai Ṣevi, "who studied with some disciples but did not yet call himself messiah."[261] This, at any rate, is the story he told Sasportas, though nothing is known from any other source about Sabbatai Ṣevi presiding in those years over a group of disciples in Jerusalem. Sasportas described Sabbatai Raphael as "devoid of learning and piety,"[262] and although his judgments on Sabbatian believers are not, as a rule, characterized by objectivity and moderation, his opinion in this case is borne out by the little that is extant of Sabbatai Raphael's writings, whose inflated verboseness and artificial pseudo-Aramaic language do not suggest any profound rabbinic culture.

Sabbatai Raphael claimed to have witnessed not only the prophetic ecstasy of Nathan on *Shabu*ᶜ*oth*, 1665, in Gaza, but also the subsequent doings of the prophet and the messiah in the Holy Land. He afterward left Palestine together "with one companion"—wrongly identified by several writers as Mattathias Bloch Ashkenazi, who was twice Sabbatai Raphael's age—to preach the Sabbatian gospel, and according to Sasportas he considered himself not merely a preacher but a prophet.[263] There is no evidence that he passed through Egypt, where Mattathias Bloch was active at the time, and it is more likely that he traveled straight to Italy, probably in the summer of 1666. In Rome he met with no success, but he later compensated himself for his failure by boasting in Amsterdam that he had spoken to Pope Alexander VII and prophesied his death

---

or a deliberate misstatement. Iohannes Pastritius, in a letter written in 1698 (see Wolf, *Bibliotheca Hebraica,* IV [1733], 971), quotes the statement of an apostate Jew in Rome and a former acquaintance of Sabbatai Raphael to the effect that the latter had been born somewhere "between Adrianople and Philipople." This would not exclude his growing up in Misithra.

259. Sasportas, p. 275. 260. *Ibid.*, pp. 271, 322.

261. *Ibid.*, p. 271. 262. *Ibid.*, p. 322. 263. *Ibid.*, pp. 271, 322.

"within a few days."[264] From Rome he traveled to Venice, where he remained for an unknown length of time. He was in Venice when the discomfiting news of the messiah's apostasy arrived.

In Venice he also published an ancient collection of magico-kabbalistic texts and formulas to which he gave the title *The Mysteries and Sources of Wisdom.*[265] In his introduction to the booklet, Sabbatai Raphael does not lay claim to authorship. In fact, his claim is of a different order altogether: he had tried out the kabbalistic formulas contained in the publication, and as a result the prophet Elijah had appeared to him. "And thus did he appear to me: he had one great eye to the right and two smaller ones to the left." Sabbatai Raphael seems to have repeated this account of Elijah's apparition wherever he went. In Amsterdam he confirmed this version once more, adding that Elijah had come to him when awake (that is, not merely in a dream) in a synagogue in Jerusalem. When asked how he knew the identity of the apparition he explained that Elijah had introduced himself by name.[266] The booklet shows Sabbatai Raphael to have been a typical *Ba^cal Shem*, that is, an itinerant "Master of [mystico-magical] Divine Names" by means of which he could heal the sick. The introduction explicitly states that "I resolved to print it to help me with those that seek cure," that is, as a *vade mecum* for the wandering magic healer. Sabbatai Raphael seems to have been the first in the long series of Sabbatian *Ba^caley Shem* wandering up and down Europe and combining "practical kabbalah" with Sabbatian propaganda.

The date of Sabbatai Raphael's departure from Venice is unknown; he probably left some time after the news of the apostasy

264. *Ibid.*, pp. 271, 273. Tishby (note *ad loc.*) dates Sabbatai Raphael's visit to Rome in April, 1667, since the pope died in May of that year. This chronology is based on the assumption that Sabbatai Raphael arrived in Italy after the apostasy. The evidence, however, suggests the opposite. Sabbatai Raphael was probably still in Italy when Alexander VII died, and promptly invented the story of his interview with the pope for the benefit of those who did not know him and the real chronology of his movements.

265. The title page states that the book was printed in the summer of 1662, but this date is a misprint or a deliberate falsification. In 1662 Sabbatai Raphael was still in Constantinople and had not yet gone to Jerusalem, let alone to Italy. The real date is 1667; see the discussion (*SS*, p. 667, n. 2).

266. J. Meijer, *loc. cit.*, p. 3[illegible]4. The document printed by Meijer was first published by Hillesum in the monthly *Elsevier* (August, 1917), which, however, I have not seen.

had seriously weakened the position of the believers.[267] Sasportas tells a somewhat confused story of a quarrel between Sabbatai Raphael and a tailor of Portoferraio on the island of Elba who had achieved some notoriety as a Sabbatian prophet in 1666 (see above, p. 491). According to Sasportas, the prophet of Elba had exclaimed: "May God punish Sabbatai Raphael for pretending to be a prophet and claiming to be superior to Nathan. For Nathan is a true prophet." It was only because he realized that the tailor's followers were more numerous than his own that Sabbatai Raphael desisted from using violence against the rival prophet and decided to leave Italy for northern Europe. Unfortunately, Sasportas' account[268] contains no indication as to the nature of the quarrel between the two prophets. What indeed were the issues that could possibly cause dissension among the believers before the messiah's apostasy provided ample reasons for discord? Perhaps the quarrel was, in fact, caused by the news of the apostasy. It appears from what Sabbatai Raphael said in Amsterdam that his major doctrinal innovation was the theory that Sabbatai Ṣevi was the messiah of the House of Ephraim (Joseph) who would have to suffer, and perhaps to die, before the son of David appeared. This doctrine, which contradicted Nathan's teaching about the person of Sabbatai Ṣevi, may well account for the clash between the two prophets. If the prophet of Portoferraio adhered to the earlier, "orthodox" doctrine, then Sabbatai Raphael's innovation must have involved the claim to a prophetic authority superior to Nathan's. Sabbatai Raphael soon realized that the majority of believers followed Nathan and the prophet of Elba, and decided that he had better depart from Italy. This must have happened some time in the summer (or late summer) of 1667. The fact that the introduction to the kabbalistic book which he printed at Venice contains no reference to Sabbatai Ṣevi (except, perhaps, a very oblique and veiled one) may well be due to the change in public opinion brought about by the apostasy. Altogether it appears that the rabbis of Venice did not give much scope to Sabbatian prophets.

No details are known of Sabbatai Raphael's "misdeeds" in Frankfurt, where he passed on his way to Amsterdam. David de Mercado, a scholarly Sephardic merchant who lived in Frankfurt at the time, wrote to his friends in Amsterdam bidding them to be on their guard against the visitor. To render his warnings more effective, de Mercado

267. Cf. Sasportas, p. 321.

268. Sasportas, pp. 271, 281.

also quoted Sabbatai Raphael as saying something that was certain to infuriate the Amsterdam Sephardim, to wit, that they were all "the sons of menstruating women."[269] This was indeed a sore point with all marrano descendants, since marrano women in Spain and Portugal were not in a position to take the prescribed monthly ritual bath of purification. Hence all their children were conceived in mortal sin and it was easy to cast aspersions at the ritual purity of their offspring.

Sabbatai Raphael's arrival in Amsterdam, on the eve of the Day of Atonement (September 27, 1667), immediately caused a commotion. Most of the Ashkenazim and some Sephardim still held fast to the faith, and the presence of an "emissary" from the Holy Land could not but raise their hopes. Sabbatai Raphael played a double game: with the believers he acted the part of prophet and apostle, whereas to the "infidels" he complained that the foolish crowd mistook him for a prophet because of his kabbalistic and chiromantic knowledge.[270] The Sephardim dispatched three scholars to examine the visitor "and found that he was [no saint but] a latrine." He preached in the Ashkenazi synagogue, where a gullible audience duly took his confused bogus learning for profound kabbalistic mysteries. He did, however, explicitly claim to be a prophet and to have held converse with Elijah.[271] To believers (and some unbelievers) who questioned him, he replied "in Hebrew, Aramaic, Greek, and Spanish," explaining that Sabbatai was the messiah of the House of Joseph and that the Davidic messiah would appear before long, and implying that he was destined for the latter role.[272] When questioned on behalf of the *Mahamad,* the council of the Sephardic community, he reiterated his claim to the gift of prophecy and prescience.[273]

The assertion that Sabbatai Ṣevi was the messiah of the House of Joseph, which was a novel twist of Sabbatian "ideology," naturally created a sensation. Some Sephardim wanted to use violence against

269. *Ibid.,* p. 271. Sabbatai Raphael, in a letter to Sasportas, denied having made this remark to de Mercado (*ibid.,* p. 275).

270. *Ibid.,* pp. 277, 281, 321.

271. *Ibid.,* p. 271. Sasportas' reference to a tract by Raphael Joseph on "Ritual Slaughtering and Dietary Laws" is due to a slip of memory. In a letter to Morocco (*ibid.,* p. 321) he correctly states that the claim to have seen the prophet Elijah had been made by Sabbatai Raphael in print in a work of practical kabbalah (and not of ritual law).

272. *Ibid.,* p. 273.

273. *Ibid.,* p. 283.

him, but the mass of Ashkenazim were on his side. His activities as a practical kabbalist and purveyor of amulets merely added to the agitation. All kinds of miracles were told of him, and when the Sephardim began to press him too hard he threatened to burn their synagogue by means of kabbalistic incantations. The commotion increased in the few days between the Day of Atonement (September 28) and the Festival of Tabernacles (October 3). The Ashkenazi believers, whose enthusiasm knew no bounds, forced their rabbi, Isaac Deckingen, to lodge the prophet in his house and threatened him with expulsion if he dared to join the opposition led by his Sephardi colleagues. The latter (Aboab, Mussafia, and Moses Raphael de Aguilar) had badly burned their fingers in the great awakening of 1666 and were loathe to encourage any further Sabbatian activity. The endemic tension between Sephardim and Ashkenazim flared up once more as the latter gave shelter and protection to a visitor whom the former wanted to excommunicate. Sabbatai Raphael stayed indoors while the Sephardic rabbis, on October 2, 1667, ordered him to leave the city on October 5 that is, immediately after the first days of the festival, unless "he repented"—that is, probably, recanted his Sabbatian beliefs. This Sabbatai Raphael refused to do and, instigated by his Ashkenazi followers, he lodged a formal complaint with the magistrates of the city to the effect that the Sephardic community were usurping the prerogatives of the magistrates by ordering the expulsion of a distinguished visitor merely because they were jealous of his great learning.[274]

The Sephardim considered this appeal to the magistrates a base treachery and countered by lodging a complaint in their turn. The records of Sabbatai Raphael's examination by the city fathers are preserved in the city archives of Amsterdam. The hostility of the rabbis, Sabbatai Raphael explained to the magistrates, was due to their jealousy of his great learning, since he had studied all the rabbinic books. He denied all other accusations: he had never claimed to be a prophet or a practical kabbalist and healer. He had never said that he had made himself invisible when the papal police tried to arrest him in Rome. But, he insisted, he had seen the prophet Elijah. On October 7, 1667, the magistrates signed an order expelling Sabbatai Raphael from Amsterdam, but granting him a delay of one week

274. *Ibid.*, cf. also *ibid.*, p. 274.

to wind up his affairs provided he refrained from holding meetings or preaching in public.[275]

From Amsterdam, Sabbatai Raphael betook himself to Hamburg, where he arrived by boat in the middle of October. His arrival provided the arch-infidel Sasportas with the opportunity of actually meeting a Sabbatian prophet and apostle in the flesh. He promptly vented his fury on this object of his execration, and he sternly reprimanded the rabbis of Amsterdam for not having brought about the impostor's death or at least imprisoning him. The Amsterdam rabbis, who well knew the intransigent temper of their forbidding colleague, replied politely but sharply by quoting the Talmudic counsel: "Do not judge your fellow man until you have been in his situation."[276] Sabbatai Raphael had been preceded by letters from Amsterdam informing the Hamburg community of all that had happened, though the rabbis and elders refrained—for unknown reasons—from sending an official report to their colleagues in Hamburg.[277] In Hamburg, too, the prophet's arrival caused a communal storm. He was enthusiastically welcomed by the Ashkenazim, who gave him a seat of honor in their synagogue, invited him to their weddings, and acclaimed him as a mighty kabbalist and miracle worker. He always carried about him his book of kabbalistic magic, and one of the elders of the Ashkenazi congregation confirmed that he had seen the prophet miraculously cure a child who had been paralyzed and bedridden for years.[278] Sabbatai Raphael carefully kept aloof from the Sephardim and made no attempt to conceal his hostility toward them.

As a matter of fact the *Mahamad* of the Sephardic community had excommunicated the prophet immediately on his arrival in Altona near Hamburg.[279] In this awkward situation Sabbatai Raphael acted

275. The document published by Hillesum and again by J. Meijer (*loc. cit.*, p. 304) confirms and supplements the accounts of Sasportas (pp. 272–74) and of the Amsterdam rabbis (*ibid.*, p. 283). A copy of the expulsion order was finally obtained by the Hamburg community, though not without their having to surmount considerable administrative difficulties (Sasportas, pp. 287, 288).

276. Sasportas, pp. 281, 283; cf. also p. 287.

277. *Ibid.*, p. 283. 278. *Ibid.*, p. 284.

279. For the relevant entry in the minutes of the congregation, see *JJLG*, XI (1916), 47. The elders consulted with the rabbi, who advised against the "Great Ban of Excommunication," since it would be impossible to enforce Sabbatai Raphael's expulsion without the co-operation of the Ashkenazi community. They therefore pronounced the "Minor Ban," prohibiting members of the congregation to consort with him.

in a most surprising manner, which may throw some light on his character: he wrote a letter, in his usual verbose, inflated, and artificial style, to the arch-enemy Sasportas. If Sabbatai Raphael really was the odious and execrable miscreant Sasportas makes him out to be, why then did he wish to walk right into the lion's den? Perhaps Sasportas did not, after all, describe him correctly, and his passing reference to the "deluded wretch"[280] may be nearer the truth than he intended. Sasportas answered with a letter full of biting sarcasms, and advised him not to appear in public and to leave the city as quickly as possible. In his reply Sabbatai Raphael denied having ever posed as a prophet: he was traveling "to see the world, and not because of the messiah." Sasportas dismissed this defense with a haughty letter and intimated that he would not receive the innocent tourist. However, when Sabbatai Raphael knocked at his door two days later, Sasportas requested leave of the *Mahamad* to speak to the excommunicate whom, to be sure, he immediately recognized to be a "brigand . . . insolent . . . and ignorant." Sabbatai Raphael apparently asked for permission to stay in Hamburg and Sasportas was willing to support his request, provided he abjured the Sabbatian faith. According to Sasportas, Sabbatai Raphael once more confessed his error and expressed his readiness to recant publicly in the synagogue. At the same time letters were arriving from Smyrna, bringing news of Nathan's visit there and of the fasts and mortifications with which Rabbi Benveniste (who—it was rumored—had renounced his rabbinical office) expiated his grievous error. Sasportas promptly held up Benveniste as a model for Sabbatai Raphael's emulation.[281]

Sasportas was not the kind of shepherd who brings back lost sheep by sheer kindness and paternal love. As a matter of fact, one of his reasons for inviting Sabbatai Raphael back to the fold was the fear that the prophet might apostatize to Christianity[282] as, indeed, had happened with other disabused and embittered believers in Germany (see above, p. 758). Meanwhile, Sabbatai Raphael continued to arouse much enthusiasm among the Ashkenazim, gaining followers not only among the beggars and the rabble (as Sasportas would have it) but also among the leaders of the community.[283] His appearance

280. Sasportas, p. 272. 281. *Ibid.*, pp. 275–77, also p. 281.

282. *Ibid.*, p. 283.

283. The minutes of the Sephardic congregation mention the case of Benjamin Wulff, a tobacco merchant, who tried to persuade all the sick and the ill

about a year after the apostasy made a deep impression on the Jews of Hamburg who, so far, had lived on distant and secondhand reports of the messiah and the prophet Nathan. Now, at last, they had among them an eyewitness who could give them the authentic story of the events in which he himself had taken part. On learning that Sabbatai Raphael continued to spread the Sabbatian poison among the Ashkenazim, Sasportas sent a messenger to him who showed him the accounts by the rabbis of Smyrna, Constantinople, and Adrianople of Sabbatai's and Nathan's doings in the summer of 1667. Sabbatai Raphael dismissed the letters as "nonsense" and pretended that they had been written by the beadles of the synagogues and other ignorant men. The rabbis of Constantinople, he declared, were still holding fast to the faith. After all, he really was in the know, unlike all the others who depended on letters, hearsay, and false reports.[284]

Meanwhile, Sabbatai Raphael's reputation as a *Ba^c^al Shem* continued to grow, and the record book of the Sephardic community indignantly reports that several members of the congregation had requested permission to seek cure at his hands. Needless to say, the permission was refused, but powerful support came from the most unexpected quarter. The burgomaster of Hamburg, Peter Lütkens, had been suffering from gout for a long time, and his hands and feet were paralyzed. Sabbatai Raphael promised to cure him and was permitted to stay in the city, much to the chagrin of the Sephardic community who had to see the excommunicate riding out on horseback or in the burgomaster's carriage, and strutting in the streets attired in his exotic dress and accompanied by two servants.[285] Meanwhile, the elders of the Sephardic congregation tried to persuade their Ashkenazi colleagues to excommunicate Sabbatai Raphael also. The disenchantment of the Ashkenazi leaders proceeded apace: at first they held the visitor to be a prophet,

---

to seek cure at the hands of the *Ba^c^al Shem* Sabbatai Raphael. He was put under a ban early in December, 1667; see *JJLG*, XI (1916), 48. Benjamin Wulff later settled in Dessau where he died in 1696. His sister was the great-grandmother of Moses Mendelssohn, as has been shown by Alex. Altmann, *Bulletin des Leo Baeck Instituts*, X (1968), 243–52.

284. Sasportas, pp. 278, 281–82.

285. *Ibid.*, pp. 278–79. An account of the protection extended by the burgomaster to Sabbatai Raphael is also contained in a letter written early in February, 1668, by the *Mahamad* of Hamburg to their colleagues in Amsterdam; see J. Meijer, *loc. cit.*, p. 105.

then a great rabbinic scholar, then a mere doctor, then a fool until, at last, they realized that he was a scoundrel.[286] On more than one occasion he was caught transgressing the Law, and Sasportas also accuses him of adultery and fornication.[287] There was much correspondence between the elders and rabbis of Hamburg, on the one hand, and those of Amsterdam, on the other. The former wanted from Amsterdam the text of the official order of expulsion, but could not obtain it for some weeks until the *Mahamad* of Hamburg formally applied to the *Mahamad* of Amsterdam. In their letter to Amsterdam the Hamburg elders referred to "the deceit of the man of Smyrna and the lies of the man of Gaza who caught the whole dispersion in their nets," and admitted that "all those who had believed in those days could not but feel most unhappy" at present. Recurrences of such vanities ought to be prevented at any cost, and miscreants like Sabbatai Raphael should be given no chance.[288] As the writers of this letter were themselves among those "that had believed in those days," their testimony is of considerable interest.

Upon receipt of the desired document from Amsterdam (February 6, 1668),[289] the elders of the Hamburg congregation hastened to show it to the burgomaster, whose gout had not improved in spite of Sabbatai Raphael's ministrations. Nevertheless, Sabbatai Raphael managed to hold out in Altona until after Passover (April, 1668),[290]

286. Sasportas, p. 279.

287. *Ibid.*, pp. 279, 322. The accusation is rather flimsy and was brought forward only after Sabbatai Raphael had left the city.

288. The original letter, written in Portuguese, is preserved in the archives of the Spanish-Portuguese congregation of Amsterdam.

289. Sasportas had written to the rabbis of Amsterdam for a full report on Sabbatai Raphael as early as the beginning of November, 1667 (Sasportas, p. 282). In his second letter, four weeks later, he also asked for a copy of the order of expulsion (*ibid.*, p. 285), promising the co-operation of the two Hamburg congregations in excommunicating Sabbatai Raphael and circulating the ban of excommunication in print. In February the elders of the Sephardic congregation sent a formal request for a copy of the expulsion order to the Amsterdam *Mahamad* (cf. *ibid.*, p. 288). The certified copy arrived in Hamburg on 24 Shebat (cf. *JJLG,* XI [1916], 58). The rabbis of Amsterdam replied to Sasportas in the week 23–28 Shebat, i.e., after the *Mahamad* had dispatched the requested copy of the expulsion order to Hamburg.

290. The legal domicile of the Ashkenazi community was in Altona which, at the time, was Danish territory. An expulsion order from the Free City of

when he realized that his cause was lost and he fled to Posen in Poland. Sasportas immediately alerted the Polish rabbis, and in particular the famous rabbi of Posen, Isaac b. Abraham. On his way, Sabbatai Raphael passed through many villages and small communities where he was received as a prophet and preached sermons on the messianic redemption. In his *Adress to the Jews* (Dublin, 1716), Abraham Jacobs, a Polish Jew who subsequently came to Ireland and converted to Christianity in 1706, still remembered having heard in his youth the preaching of Sabbatai Raphael.[291] The prophet, it appears, did not wander about incognito (as alleged by Sasportas), but continued his activities in public. Letters from Posen informed Sasportas that Sabbatai Raphael had married in one of the Polish congregations and was considered a prophet. When R. Isaac of Posen dispatched three scholars to examine him and bring him to Posen, Sabbatai Raphael disappeared overnight and fled. According to the report from Poland,[292] Sabbatai Raphael—like Jacob Frank a century later—wore "Turkish garb," but this may mean no more than that, like many other oriental rabbis, he wore eastern costume on his travels in Europe.

Rycaut[293] reports that

> in January 1674[294] appeared another bold Impostor amongst the Jews in Smyrna from the Morea, as it was said, or not known from whence, who in despight of Sabbatai, and his own Governours[295] pretended to be Messiah; but with so inconsiderable and petty a Deluder as this, the Jews thought to make quick work; but being ashamed at first to bring another Messiah on the Stage, by help of money they accused

---

Hamburg would not, therefore, apply to Altona. Nevertheless, the Sephardim seem to have hoped that by preventing Sabbatai Raphael from entering Hamburg, the Ashkenazim would agree to expel him from Altona as well. Sasportas (p. 279) mentions that Sabbatai Raphael was caught transgressing one of the special dietary laws of Passover. This suggests that he did not leave Altona until the end of April.

291. I owe this detail to the kindness of Mr. N. L. Hyman of Haifa (letter of October 18, 1943), who has seen the pamphlet.

292. Sasportas, p. 289.

293. *Op. cit.*, p. 219.

294. Thus the date in Rycaut. Graetz, who did not quote from the English original but from a French translation (*Histoire de l'Empire Ottoman* [The Hague, 1709], p. 208) gave the year, as he found in his source, as 1672; other writers copied from Graetz.

295. Probably meaning the Jewish leaders in Smyrna.

him of Adultery, and procured a sentence from the Kadi, condemning him to the Gallies; in order unto which, and in proof of his good behaviour he remained some time in prison, in which Interim he found means to clear himself of that Crime by open evidence to the contrary, and had for the present escaped out of the power of the Synagogue, had not their Authority and money prevailed more than the Friends or Disciples of this Impostour; whom we will leave in prison. . . .

Graetz[296] assumed that Rycaut's account of the anonymous impostor referred to Sabbatai Raphael, but there is no evidence to support this identification. The fact that the latter messiah was a native of the district of Morea is no reason for identifying the two. There is nothing (except one of Sasportas' polemical sallies) to indicate that Sabbatai Raphael ever claimed to be the messiah, and there were plenty of other messianic pretenders at the time.[297] Pending the discovery of new evidence, there is no way of knowing whether Sabbatai Raphael remained in Poland or returned to Turkey.

VIII

We have described in the foregoing the events and developments taking place during the first years after the apostasy, the reactions of the public to this severe and unexpected blow, the widening rift between believers and infidels, and the changes in the array of forces. We must now return once more to the theological side of the matter. Sabbatai's apostasy, as has been remarked before, proved to be one of the most tragic moments in Jewish history. For a whole year or more the Jewish masses had been stirred in the depths of their soul by the tidings of redemption. An unprecedented emotion had seized all hearts, and the eyes beheld a new and bright world. Redemption was not merely "around the corner." It was right there, and the believers felt themselves standing on the threshold of the new *aion*.

Into this high-strung mood of enthusiasm and expectation, Sabbatai's apostasy burst like a bombshell, taking by surprise the messiah's closest associates as well as the most vehement unbelievers. Neither literary tradition nor the psychology of the ordinary Jew had envisaged the possibility of an apostate messiah, and the resultant bewilderment and perplexity could only breed confusion and ambiguity for many

296. *Geschichte der Juden,* 3rd edn. vol. X, p. 459.

297. Cf. the instance referred to in my article in *Schocken Volume,* p. 174.

years to come. The essential elements of the crisis have been described earlier in this chapter. The paroxysms of exultation and penitence at the climax of the movement had given birth to a thoroughly new life-feeling and to a sense of liberation in which the world of the ghetto melted away. In the perspective of the believers, the spiritual regeneration of the cosmos (the *tiqqun*) and redemption from the misery of exile had merged into one, and the spiritual forces liberated by the mighty emotional surge could no longer be repressed. Their faith in the messiah was nourished not on outward events but on the inward vision of their souls. Why then should the verdict of outward events undo the affirmation of their messianic experience? The signs of redemption had been clearly visible to all who had eyes to see. Should they now be written off as a nightmarish illusion? But if the messiah had not failed, why then did he apostatize and why did the fullness of redemption tarry?

In the face of such questions the gulf between the two aspects of the notion of redemption inevitably widened. Nothing had changed in the political sphere, and neither the messiah nor his followers had been given kingdom and dominion. In kabbalistic theology, however, the mystical element of redemption—the raising of the "holy sparks" imprisoned in the "husks" and the restoration of the cosmos to its spiritual essence—had been considered essential and primary. The two notions which had hitherto been held to be aspects of one and the same reality now fell apart as each began to lead its own, independent life. The drama of redemption was no longer acted out on one stage only or, to put it differently, the two stages were no longer congruent. As the chasm between the two spheres widened, believers had to opt for the one or the other. The choice was ineluctable, and it destroyed the naïve and simple oneness of the original messianic faith.

As we have seen, a considerable part of Jewry did, in fact, prefer the reality of their heart's vision above that of the disenchanting outer reality. Henceforth the Sabbatian movement depended on the paradoxical assumption that the messiah's apostasy was a mystery and—appearances notwithstanding—an essentially positive event. In order to survive, the movement had to develop an ideology that would enable its followers to live amid the tensions between inner and outer realities. It had to provide concepts that would express the fullness of the paradox. In fact, it would have not only to account for the existence of the chasm between the two spheres, but also to depreciate the visible and tangible "outer" reality. Emphasis came increasingly to be placed on the hidden, inner life of faith. This shift of emphasis could, at times, lead to a radical "transvaluation" of traditional values; historical reality became mere illusion, and only the incontestable inner reality was truly real.

This development could not but have far-reaching consequences for historical, meaning rabbinic, Judaism. In theory, of course, it was possible to restrict the paradox that was at the heart of the Sabbatian faith to the person of the messiah, and that, indeed, is what some of the theologians of the movement (for example, Abraham Miguel Cardozo) attempted to do. But religious movements have an inner logic and a dynamism of their own, and the paradox of the messiah's mission almost inevitably led to a revaluation of rabbinic tradition. The believers possessed a new standard by which to measure the traditional realities of the ghetto where, for the time being, the infidels who interpreted the Torah "according to the flesh" still held sway. In due course the believers, that is, the truly "spiritual" Jews, would become critics—some moderate and others radical—of rabbinic Judaism as such. Unlike the criticism of the Enlightenment (in the period of the French Revolution or during the struggle for political emancipation) which was inspired by ideas and circumstances impinging from the outside, the Sabbatian criticism of rabbinic Judaism was an internal phenomenon: it was the criticism of "spirituals" whose paradoxical values no longer fitted into the traditional mold and who sought new modes of expression for their utopian Judaism. Although they were engaged in open conflict with traditional Jewish society, they never thought of denying their historical identity as Jews.

Of course, negation of and opposition to rabbinic Judaism was not all. The Sabbatians also tried to define the positive contents of their new Judaism, that is, a Judaism based on a "realized eschatology." In this they failed, although in the "heretical" developments of their theology they succeeded in suggesting certain answers and drawing certain conclusions which enabled the movement to maintain itself. The failure in formulating a postmessianic Judaism was inevitable, for no positive definition of freedom is possible as long as the freedom referred to remains abstract and is not actually and fully realized. Only he who lives the life of freedom can say what the contents of freedom is. The Sabbatians were living a fiction which they had turned into a psychological reality, and hence their attempts at doctrinal definition were doomed to failure. Although they appeared in the guise of new and positive assertions, these doctrinal endeavors were essentially negations of the old values, and in this respect too the fate of Sabbatianism resembles both that of Christianity and that of the Socialist movement.

The peculiar Sabbatian doctrines developed and crystallized with extraordinary rapidity in the years following the apostasy. Two factors were responsible for this, as for many similar developments in the history of religions: on the one hand, a deeply rooted faith, nourished by a profound and immediate experience the truth of which was independent of rational reflection, and, on the other hand, the ideological need to explain and rationalize the painful contradiction between historical reality and faith. The interaction of these two factors gave birth to Sabbatian theology, whose doctrine of the messiah was defined by the prophet Nathan in the years after the apostasy. It is, of course, easy to see in the Sabbatian doctrines nothing but rationalizations and ludicrous attempts at inventing an ideology that would substitute triumph for failure. Such a view of the matter is undoubtedly correct, but it presents, equally undoubtedly, only one half of the total picture.

When discussing the Sabbatian paradox by means of which cruel disappointment was turned into a positive affirmation of faith, the analogy with early Christianity almost obtrudes itself. The two messianic movements exhibit many similarities which are as instructive as the equally obvious differences. Both movements were the product of the operation of the twin factors faith and rationalization. Both had to provide an ideology accounting for initial disappointment. Their master's death was a blow which the disciples of Jesus could overcome only by cultivating the image of his resurrection and the hope in his triumphant return as lord and judge. While historians should beware of regarding theology as nothing but ideology and the product of rationalizations, there is little doubt that without the additional stress of having to account also for the delay of the Second Coming, the impressive edifice of Catholic theology would never have arisen. Both Christianity and the Sabbatian movement took as their point of departure the ancient Jewish paradox of the Suffering Servant which, however, they stressed with such radicalism that they practically stood it on its head. Both movements gave rise to a mystical faith centered on a definite historical event, and drawing its strength from the paradoxical character of this event.

A savior who dies like a criminal and a redeemer whose mission leads him to apostasy are equally unacceptable to the naïve religious consciousness. Yet the apparent stumbling-block proved to be a source of strength from which both movements drew their religious justification, for both believed in a second manifestation in glory of him whom they had beheld in his degradation. The early Christians believed in the return of the crucified after his ascension to Heaven. The Sabbatians too believed that the redeemer's absence (a moral absence after his apostasy, a physical absence after his death) was temporary only and that he would return before long to achieve his messianic mission. As time passed and disillusionment deepened, the dogmatic formulations became increasingly radical. At first the doctrinal developments bore mainly on the nature and person of the messiah and on the hidden mystery of his suffering. But very soon early Christianity found itself diverging widely from traditional Jewish belief and practice. The same also happened with the Sabbatian movement, and with the same rapidity.

In both instances a new religious value came to the fore. The Sabbatian notion of pure faith, unaccompanied by specific works and requiring no sign or miracle, has its predecessor in Paul's doctrine of faith. Pre-Sabbatian, traditional Judaism had never entertained the idea of a pure faith, dissociated from specific works yet endowed with redemptive power, as a supreme religious value. Messianic faith, however, now changed its character: not faith in imminent redemption but faith in the paradox of the messiah's mission was declared to be the crucial issue. The basic paradox of the new faith inevitably led to further and no less audacious paradoxes.

The new doctrinal developments extended beyond the question of the messiah's mission and of the place of the "law" in the messianic age, to the doctrine of the Godhead, which now took a definitely heretical turn—at least from the point of view of rabbinic Judaism. The two main points of dissimilarity between Christianity and Judaism in this respect are the doctrine of the Trinity and that of the incarnation of the Godhead in the messiah. Judaism, including kabbalistic Judaism, had never admitted these ideas, but now they began to take root in some Sabbatian circles, probably under the influence (direct and indirect) of the analogous Christian doctrines. The many marranos returning to Judaism at that period no doubt acted as a channel by which Christian ideas and doctrines were mediated to Sabbatian theology. In fact, several of the leading believers were former marranos, but the ideas which they introduced into Sabbatianism belonged to the heretical rather than to the orthodox traditions of Christianity. The gnostic character of most Sabbatian systems is surprising indeed. Abraham Cardozo's theological studies may have acquainted him with early gnostic heresies, and, like him, other Sabbatian writers too may have developed, in a specifically Jewish context, gnostic ideas which originally derived from patristic literature. Nevertheless, the significance of extraneous, Christian influences should not be exaggerated. Certain developments are immanent in the very nature and structure of religious phenomena. Sabbatian theology would probably have developed the way it did even without Christian gnosticism and the return of many marranos to their ancestral religion. Lurianic kabbalism, the Sabbatians' original system of reference, was, after all, based on an essentially gnostic set of ideas. Every crisis in the doctrinal formulation of the experience of redemption, let alone in the matter of the eschatological, and even more so, of the pre-eschatological, existence of Israel, was bound to lead to analogous developments in religious speculation.

In both cases the destruction of traditional values in the wake of bitter disillusionment and intense religious awakening led to an outburst of antagonism toward the Law. The experience of the freedom of the children of God gave birth to antinomian doctrines, such as those of Paul, which contained the seeds of even more radical developments as exemplified by some of the more extreme gnostic sects. In the case of the Sabbatian movement, the antinomian element was intensified by Sabbatai Ṣevi's personality and his "strange acts." There was a core of potential antinomianism in the legacy which Sabbatai bequeathed to later Sabbatian doctrine as elaborated by Nathan. In the history of the Sabbatian movement, Nathan's writings played a role similar to that of Paul's letters in the development of Christian doctrine. However cautious Nathan's formulation of certain radical ideas, it encouraged the more violently antinomian tendencies of some Sabbatian circles. Similarities in the historical situations of Christianity and Sabbatianism, and the inner logic of their respective doctrinal notions, led to similar results. Each considered the appearance of its respective messiah as the beginning of a new era and as the foundation of a new reality. Hence they had to adopt a radically different attitude toward the values that had been dominant until then, namely, the

Law of Moses and the halakhic tradition of rabbinic Judaism respectively.

However, the structural similarities must not blind us to the profound differences between early Christianity and Sabbatianism. Each of the two movements has its own historical, religious, and psychological horizon. The Sabbatian awakening was a revolt against the ghetto, taking place within the narrow confines of the ghetto, and bearing the marks of the latter even where it promised to make all things new. Lacking the natural breadth and width of the Judaism that gave birth to Christianity, Sabbatianism constituted an attempt to defend, within the ghetto, a spiritual world that had already broken out of the ghetto walls. In a way, the movement can be said to have played a pioneering role in envisaging a new world which, as yet, it lacked the means of grasping, let alone of adequately conceptualizing. One hundred and twenty years had to pass before this "new World" became sufficiently concrete for the Jews to be susceptible of a more adequate definition. The tangled complexities resulting from the tension between the religious vision of the new world, on the one hand, and the unwillingness to leave the ghetto, on the other, plainly appeared in the subsequent developments of the movement.

Differences in historical background and social realities do not, however, fully account for the tremendous difference between the two religious movements. An even more important factor is the decisive role played by their respective central personalities. Sabbatai Ṣevi, in spite of the undoubted fascination which he exercised on others, lacked greatness both of character and of expression. It was not he who made the messianic movement, but the faith of the masses which, in an explosive discharge of messianic energies accumulated during many generations, swept him to the heights of messiahship. The popular fervor and enthusiasm that turned him into an object of hope for the House of Israel cannot conceal the essential weakness of his otherwise colorful personality. This weakness did not prevent the Jewish masses from acclaiming him as their messiah, especially as rabbinic tradition lacked a vigorous and clear-cut image of the Redeemer (see above, pp. 52 ff.). No doubt traditional Judaism possessed a potent and vital image of redemption, but the person of the Redeemer was all but hidden behind the grandeur of his mission—unlike Christianity, at the heart of which there stands a great personality.

Further, the critical events that precipitated the respective developments of Christianity and Sabbatianism are hardly comparable. Unlike the Sabbatian messiah, the Christian savior had paid the highest price a man can possibly pay. No doubt an apostate messiah constitutes an even greater paradox than a crucified messiah, but the paradox has no constructive value. The doctrine that by betraying his religion the redeemer fulfilled his messianic mission is essentially nihilistic, and once the first step was taken on this slippery road anything became possible. If the most despicable act, than which none could be more execrable to the Jewish mind, could become the doctrinal cornerstone of the Sabbatian faith, then all fences were down and there was nothing at which one would conceivably have to stop. Unlike the passion and death of Jesus, Sabbatai's apostasy, though surrounded with a tragic halo by Sabbatian literature, was essentially destructive of all values. The Sabbatian redeemer who was prepared to surrender passively to the power of impurity and to sink into the abyss of the *qelippah* while continuing to cultivate his dream of accomplishing a messianic mission, actually opened the door to the most nihilistic transvaluation of religious values. It was only natural that Frankism, the most important form of later Sabbatianism, drew the conclusions implicit in the founder's "constitutive act." The efforts of the believers to discover a positive and constructive meaning in what was an essentially negative and destructive act, constitutes their peculiar contribution to the history of religion in general and to the subsequent history of Judaism in particular. Their faith required of them a measure of tension and a struggle with paradox that went beyond anything demanded of the Christian believer.

The personal paradox of the founder (that is, his "strange actions") became generalized into a sacramental pattern for the community of his followers. Sabbatai's "illuminations" bequeathed to the movement a legacy that bore his personal stamp: the faithful would glorify certain "strange actions," or even demand their ritual performance as an expression of their peculiar religious consciousness. But beyond this pattern of paradoxical behavior very little of Sabbatai's personality remained alive in the movement that bore his name. His figure became vague almost to the point of anonymity, and all that remained was the tale of a mythical hero whose resemblances to the actual historical individual were purely coincidental.

In order to maintain the faith in the messiah it was not enough to justify his apostasy: it had to be justified in traditional Jewish terms.

Nevertheless, the resultant doctrine was necessarily novel and even heretical in terms of traditional Judaism. The doctrine of the messiah as expounded by Nathan of Gaza and his disciples during the ten years following the apostasy emphasizes three novel points.[298]

In the first place, it was roundly asserted that redemption was not yet complete. The original, naïve, and overenthusiastic assertions to the effect that the realm of the *qelippoth* was completely vanquished were now said to have been mistaken. Redemption had begun, but had yet to be fully realized and consummated amid pain and suffering—including the anguishing shame of the messiah's apostasy. The Shekhinah had "risen from the dust," but had not yet been fully restored. It was this intermediary stage between the awakening of the Shekhinah and her complete restoration which provided the spiritual and emotional horizon of the Sabbatian movement.

The second doctrinal point is an immediate corollary of the foregoing. The conception of an intermediary stage resulted in a different understanding of the messiah's mission. According to the different forms of Sabbatian theology this mission could be of an active or of a more passive character. The apostasy could be interpreted in purely passive terms as the mysterious passion of the savior who "sitteth alone and keepeth silence, because he hath borne it upon him" (Lam. 3:28), or as an active descent into the abyss of the *qelippoth*. Either way, the messiah no longer served as a symbol of redemption accomplished (as in Lurianic kabbalism), but became an agent fulfilling a decisive and unique mission. All other saints had "raised"

298. The sources for our knowledge of this doctrine are, above all, Nathan's and Cardozo's letters, which were widely copied at the time. The most important of Nathan's letters, to be discussed in the next section of this chapter, is undoubtedly the long circular letter which he wrote about 1673–74. The full text was preserved in the Dönmeh archives and became accessible only after the Hebrew version of the present book was published. It is now available in my edn., *Qobeṣ ʿal Yad*, XVI, New Series (1966), pt. II, pp. 421–56. Parts of it had been known before and were published by Ch. Wirszubski in *Zion*, III (1938), 227–35 (see his discussion of its contents, *ibid.*, pp. 215–27). The full text disproved Wirszubski's and my own former assumption that the letter was written in 1667. Another letter, written early in 1668, has been quoted above, pp. 741–43, and part of another, written after 1668, has been published by me in *ʾEreṣ Yisraʾel*, IV (1956), 191–92. Cardozo's relevant letters, apart from the *Magen Abraham*, to be discussed below, are his letter to the rabbis of Smyrna, *Zion*, XIX (1954), 1–22; the letters to his brother-in-law, in Hebrew (*ap.* Freimann, pp. 87–92) and in Spanish, MS. Oxford, Neubauer 2481.

the holy sparks from the depths of the *qelippah* while keeping themselves aloof from the danger zone. Only the messiah performed the terrible *descensus ad inferos,* "that He may do His work, strange is His work, and bring to pass His act, strange is His act" (Isa. 28:21).

Third, the cosmic struggle between good and evil assumes, in its final stage, a more complicated and paradoxical form. Lurianic kabbalah had taught a way of separating, that is, raising and extracting the holy sparks from the clutches of evil in which they were held. In fact, evil existed by virtue of the vitality which it drew from the sparks of good that it had snatched and held imprisoned. Once these sparks were released and "raised," evil, impotent and lifeless as it is by itself, would automatically collapse. At this point, Sabbatian doctrine introduces a dialectical twist into the Lurianic idea. According to the new, Sabbatian version, it is not enough to extract the sparks of holiness from the realm of impurity. In order to accomplish its mission, the power of holiness—as incarnate in the messiah—has to descend into impurity, and good has to assume the form of evil. This mission is fraught with danger, as it appears to strengthen the power of evil before its final defeat. During Sabbatai's lifetime the doctrinal position was that by entering the realm of the *qelippah,* good had become evil *in appearance* only. But there were more radical possibilities waiting to be explored: only the complete transformation of good into evil would exhaust the full potential of the latter and thereby explode it, as it were, from within. This dialectical liquidation of evil requires not only the disguise of good in the form of evil but total identification with it. It was along such lines that the subsequent theology of the Sabbatian radicals developed.

For the mass of believers the certainty that the messiah's apostasy had a positive religious value was primary; the precise nature and contents of this religious value were a secondary, "ideological" problem. Hence it was possible to entertain two apparently contradictory answers to the question as to what exactly was the significance of Sabbatai's action. According to one reply, the messiah became one of the gentiles in order to save the latter from utter destruction. As has been remarked before, the extreme traditionalism of popular Jewish eschatology was not content with the defeat and submission of the gentiles but exulted in the idea of their ultimate annihilation. The eschatology of Lurianic kabbalism largely, if not entirely, shared this attitude. The Sabbatian doctrine said, surprisingly enough, that the messiah would submit to the dominion of the gentiles in order to save the souls that could be saved and to raise them to himself.

The other reply takes the opposite view. The messiah descended into the realm of the *qelippah* in order to destroy it from within. Only by feigning submission to the *qelippah* could he achieve his purpose of utterly destroying it. This strategem or "holy ruse" can be compared to the action of a worm in a tree that appears healthy from outside but, when split open, is seen to be worm-eaten. "Wherefore it is utterly impossible for any creature to comprehend any of his actions, and whoever says that he understands the ways of the messianic king is completely mistaken."[299] The same text contains another, extremely revealing, simile in the parable of the king (that is, God) whose bride (that is, the Shekhinah) and family (that is, the holy sparks) have been captured by enemies (that is, the *qelippah*), and who sends his trusted servant (that is, the messiah) as a spy into the enemy country to inquire about the captives. This servant has to act with great cunning "and to adopt the dress of the people through whose land he passes, and to behave as they do, lest they notice that he is a spy. . . . Keep this parable in your heart, for it is a foundation to satisfy you regarding several doubts in the matter."[300] Both answers occur side by side in the writings of Nathan and his disciples.

IX

Sabbatai's followers and believers were good Jews. They believed in the holy books. Hence their first reaction—one might almost say reflex—was to search Scripture and tradition for intimations, hints, and indications of the extraordinary and bewildering events. And lo and behold—the Bible, rabbinic Haggadah, and kabbalistic literature turned out to abound in allusions to Sabbatai Ṣevi in general and to the mystery of his apostasy in particular. The Sabbatians were second to none in the art of interpreting, hairsplitting, and twisting texts, for which the Jews forever have had such an uncontested reputation. And though their tropological and kabbalistic exegesis was far removed from the plain sense of their texts, it certainly reflected the plain

299. Cardozo, in his *Magen Abraham* (ed. G. Scholem, in *Qobeṣ ᶜal Yad*, XII [1938], 138). The comparison of Sabbatai Ṣevi to a worm is already found in Nathan's *Treatise on the Dragons* (see G. Scholem, *Beᶜlqvoth Mashiaḥ*, p. 37).

300. *Magen Abraham, loc. cit.*, p. 139.

sense of what moved their hearts. "From biblical verses and fragments of verses, from rabbinic sayings whose implicit possibilities nobody had noticed before, from paradoxical expressions in kabbalistic literature, and from the oddest corners of Jewish literature, they produced material the like of which had never been seen in Jewish theology."[301] The ridicule which some historians have poured over this exegetical "nonsense" bespeaks little understanding of the actual phenomenon, namely, the emergence, out of the blue, of an original Jewish terminology grappling with the contradictions in the life and ministry of the redeemer. As regards their contents, the Sabbatian interpretations were, no doubt, audacious and novel, but their exegetical methods were not much different from those traditionally employed in rabbinic literature. Hence also the success and the power of persuasion of the Sabbatian preaching, which not only appealed to hidden religious emotions but also fascinated the public by the manner in which it filled traditional images and figures of speech with new contents. It represented, in fact, a dialectical explosion within traditional linguistic and conceptual usage.

Paradoxcial explanations of the messiah's fate had already been offered, albeit on a smaller scale, after Sabbatai's imprisonment in Gallipoli. Now the same methods were applied to the much more serious question of the apostasy. Where the ancient texts failed to yield what exegetical ingenuity and ardent faith required of them, they were, on occasion, misquoted or falsified. Readers of Paul's letters can learn a great deal from these later Jewish writings, composed in a very similar psychological situation. The clash between the old and the new, which is so conspicuous a feature in Paul's thinking, manifests itself in a more traditionally Jewish, though no less radical, fashion in the extant letters of Nathan.

To appreciate the Sabbatian literature one has, of course, to take into account the traditional role of the allegorical and typological method. Arguments that are utterly devoid of sense to the modern reader were full of meaning to Sabbatai's contemporaries in the age of the European baroque. Tradition provided them with a vast treasury of living allegory which the Sabbatian writers exploited to the full. For Nathan of Gaza the lives of Abraham, Moses, Pharaoh, Job, David, Esther, and others were images and prefigurations of the mes-

301. Quoting my own formulation in the essay *Miṣwah ha-baʾah ba-ʿaberah*, in *Keneseth*, II (1937), 360; see Scholem, *The Messianic Idea* (1971), p. 96.

siah. Indeed, the biblical heroes were sparks of the messiah's soul. In addition to the scriptural texts, rabbinic and kabbalistic literature provided the homiletical eagerness of believers thirsting for confirmation with an inexhaustible fund of symbols. The magic wand of faith produced water for the thirsty imagination from even the most dry and rocklike texts. According to the ancient rabbis, "Scripture has seventy different meanings," and R. Abraham Yakhini added that one of these seventy meanings always "referred to the messiah AMIRAH. And when he reveals himself, then we shall be able to understand Scripture in this sense."[302] In the work from which this quotation is taken, Yakhini offered over one thousand two hundred Sabbatian interpretations of one verse in the Book of Exodus.

Explanations originally advanced by Nathan to account for Sabbatai's personality and his "strange actions" were enlarged upon and applied to the strange action par excellence. Thus Nathan had asserted that the messiah's soul would have to be liberated from the prison house of the *qelippoth,* where it had to be held captive during the months preceding the final *tiqqun,* before his ultimate self-revelation. With a minor but realistic change, this doctrine was now applied to the situation created by the apostasy: even after his self-revelation the messiah would have to offer himself once more as a captive to the demonic powers.

The biblical heroes also foreshadowed the messiah's apostasy, and every instance of exile, debasement, humiliation, or false pretense (for example, David at the court of Achish, the king of Gath; Moses at the court of Pharaoh; Abraham going down to Egypt; Esther, who did not reveal "her people nor her kindred" at the court of Ahasuerus) could serve as grist to the typological mill of the believers. Nathan had interpreted Job as a prototype of the messiah (see above, pp. 309 f.) even before the apostasy. The Suffering Servant of Isaiah was an obvious figure of Sabbatai Ṣevi: the messiah "was wounded because of our transgressions" (Isa. 53:5), but the Hebrew word *meḥolal* ("wounded") can also be rendered as "profaned." After the apostasy, the "profanation" of the messiah could be interpreted in several ways. Nathan declared that the messiah was profaned by the rabbis because

302. A quotation from Yakhini's *Wawey ha-ᶜAmudim* found in Sabbatian MSS.; see G. Scholem in *Zion,* VII (1942), 181. The quotation seems to be from the introduction to Yakhini's book which is missing in the autograph copy in the Bodleian Library (Neubauer no. 2761).

of "the sins of the world" (that is, the sins of his contemporaries; there is no reference here to original sin).[303] But he and Cardozo had also explained that the prophet referred to the messiah's exodus from the sphere of holiness (that is, Israel) and his entry into the profane sphere of the gentiles.[304] Many other expressions in the Servant chapters could be construed as referring to the messiah's submission to the power of the *qelippah*. This typological interpretation of the Suffering Servant is perfectly accountable in terms of its Jewish background and of the inner logic of Sabbatian homiletics; there is no need to look for specific Christian influences. Allusions to the fate of the apostate messiah and his future glory were also found in the Book of Psalms (see below, pp. 863–66).

The profusion of utterly new and unheard-of interpretations with which all these writings abound may have raised some questions, but the Sabbatians were ready with an explanation: only *after* the apostasy had their eyes been opened to the real meaning of the biblical, rabbinic, and kabbalistic texts. Nathan wrote that the details of the messiah's ministry "were not explicitly revealed in the Talmud, lest people misunderstood them; and in the book Zohar . . . they are stated in a hidden fashion. . . . It is also said there that several books of Haggadah revealing these things would be found at the time of the messiah's advent."[305] Certain Talmudic sayings, such as, "David wished to worship idols" (B. Sanhedrin 107a), or "A transgression performed with good intention is better than a precept performed with evil intention" (B. Nazir 23b) were particular favorites, especially as transgressions for the sake of redemption were required not only of the messiah but, perhaps, also of the believers. On the rabbinic dictum that the messiah cometh "unawares" (lit., "in the absence of mind") Nathan commented, "for the mind cannot accept this, since his behavior appears to go against traditional religion."[306] According to another Talmudic saying (B. Sanhedrin 97a), "the kingdom [namely, the Roman Empire] will be converted to heresy." Nathan quotes R. Joseph Taytatsak, a leading scholar and kabbalist in Salonika in the

303. *Qobeṣ ʿal Yad*, XVI (1966), 428.

304. Nathan, in the letter quoted above, pp. 428–29, and Cardozo, *ap.* Friemann, pp. 88–90.

305. *Qobeṣ ʿal Yad*, XVI (1966), 428. The last sentence may contain a hint as to his own pseudepigraphy.

306. *Ibid.*, p. 426.

first half of the sixteenth century, to the effect that this rabbinic dictum must refer to the kingdom of Heaven and not to Rome, which was heathen anyway.[307] In other words, the kingdom of Heaven itself, as represented by the messiah, would have to turn to heresy and be profaned before the messianic mission could be accomplished.

The sixteenth-century kabbalist R. Abraham Galanté of Safed had written in his commentary on the Zohar that it was impossible to reach the height of perfection unless one had descended first into the realm of evil and risen from there; this, in fact, was the mystical significance of Abraham's descent into Egypt (Gen. 12:10).[308] In Nathan's teaching, the descent of the righteous into the realm of the *qelippah* became a major principle, allegedly derived from the Zohar where, of course, nothing even remotely resembling Nathan's radicalism can be found. The Zohar merely says that the patriarchs journeyed through Egypt and Haran (that is, the realm of the *qelippoth*) and emerged untainted and unharmed. In Nathan's paraphrase, however, the conclusion is that "no one can be called a perfect righteous [*ṣaddiq*] unless he has entered impurity and emerged pure."[309]

Nathan found a striking illustration of his doctrine of the descent of the righteous into the *qelippah* in the utterances of the kabbalists concerning the supplicatory prayer known as "falling on the face." This prayer (Ps. 25 in the Sephardic, Ps. 6 in the Ashkenazic, rite) is recited on weekdays after the main prayer, the *ᶜamidah*, in the morning and afternoon service. Prayer being essentially an elevation of the soul to the highest rungs of the cosmic-spiritual ladder, the worship may be assumed to have reached the highest point at the conclusion of the *ᶜamidah*. At this moment the truly righteous one casts himself from the top of the world of *ᵓaṣiluth* into the abyss of the *qelippoth* in order to snatch the sparks of holiness held captive there.[310] The higher the spiritual ascent during prayer, the deeper the plunge into the *qelippah* during the "falling on the face." In Lurianic practice this exercise is, of course, purely a matter of mystical meditation, though it contains an element of risk and adventure: in his meditative plunge the worshiper

307. *Ibid.*, p. 431.

308. Abraham Galanté, *Zahorey Ḥammah,* commentary on Zohar I, 81b.

309. *Qobeṣ ᶜal Yad*, XVI (1966), 434. Nathan's paraphrase refers to Zohar I, 147b. In the sequel Nathan also refers to Zohar II, 34a.

310. Cf. Ḥayyim Vital, *Sha ᶜar ha-Kawwanoth* (Jerusalem, 1873), fol. 47a.

exposes himself to the dangers threatening from the *qelippah.* In the Sabbatian version, this spiritual adventure serves as an allegorical type of the messiah's apostasy.[311]

A similar paradox exercising considerable attraction on the Sabbatian believers was the image of the hind as applied by the Zohar to Israel's redemption from Egypt (and possibly also to their ultimate messianic redemption). A Talmudic passage (B. Baba Bathra 16b) says that the womb of the hind is so narrow that she cannot, in a natural way, give birth. When she crouches for delivery, God therefore sends a serpent which bites her at the opening of the womb, and she is delivered of her offspring. The Zohar interprets this passage allegorically: the hind is the divine Shekhinah which is hemmed in from all sides and cannot give birth. She places her head between her knees and cries loudly, whereupon God sends a serpent to bite her and open her womb. R. Simon bar Yoḥay ends his Zoharic exposition with the grave warning: "and regarding this matter do not ask and do not tempt the Lord."[312] According to Nathan's disciples, the messiah's apostasy is precisely this serpent's bite without which the birth of redemption cannot proceed. The messiah's transgression of the Law is as painful to Israel as a serpent's sting.[313]

The very strangeness of the messiah's actions is proof of the authenticity of his calling.[314] The fact that the messiah transgresses the Law and leads others into sin is no argument against him, for not only is he entitled to special dispensations (under the rabbinic law regarding "decisions under emergency") but he actually has the power to demote Jews from their holiness and, conversely, to make holiness pass from Israel to other nations. "Wherefore Hosea [2:1; AV 1:10] has said 'that, instead of that which was said unto them: 'Ye are not My people,' it shall be said unto them: 'Ye are the children of the living God.' That is to say that even though he make them pass to another nation [that is, religion] and it would seem that they may no longer be called 'My people,' yet it is precisely by virtue of that

311. Thus Nathan in a letter to Sabbatai Ṣevi's brother (Sasportas, p. 201) and in his subsequent writings (cf. MS. Brit. Mus., Margoliouth 856, fol. 75a). Nathan adds that when a man casts himself into the *qelippoth* there is real danger, but not when he is cast in by God. Cf. also *Qobeṣ ᶜal Yad,* XVI (1966), p. 454.

312. Zohar II, 52b.

313. MS. Kaufmann 255 (Budapest), fol. 17a.

314. Nathan of Gaza, in the letter, *Qobeṣ ᶜal Yad,* XVI (1966), 426.

action that 'it shall be said unto them: Ye are the children of the living God.' "[315] There is thus evidence that Nathan considered the possibility of a mass apostasy at the behest of the messiah. Nathan also suggests a certain analogy between the messiah's apostasy and metempsychosis. An essentially holy soul may be punished, for one reason or another, by transmigration into the body of a gentile man or woman, where it will perforce live a life far removed from the holiness of the Law. Nevertheless, such a soul will not thereby lose the merits it had acquired in its previous existences.[316] In order to save Israel, the messiah deliberately "transmigrates" from his state of holiness to the sphere of the profane, and hence the Talmud very appropriately calls him *bar nafle* ("the fallen one").[317]

The law of the red heifer (Num., ch. 19) is said by Nathan to symbolize the curious situation of the messiah who saves the world by himself transgressing the Law. The ancient rabbis had already noted that the purification ritual involving the ashes of a red heifer was incomprehensible, since in its performance the impure became pure while the pure officiants at the ceremony became impure. According to Nathan this was precisely the incomprehensible mystery of Sabbatai's ministry.[318] Nathan had taught that the soul of the messiah originated in the *tehiru,* namely, that part of the cosmos which since the "breaking of the vessels" awaited its *tiqqun* at the messiah's hands (see above, p. 305). In the writings composed after the apostasy, Nathan explained that the incomprehensible laws of the Torah were similarly rooted in the *tehiru,* and since the law of the red heifer referred to the construction of the spiritual vessel for the messiah's soul, there were of necessity "several contrarieties in it."[319] Nathan did not hesitate to "emend" quotations from Lurianic texts to suit

315. *Ibid.,* p. 433. 316. *Ibid.,* p. 435.

317. Cf. Nathan's tract in the Sabbatian notebook in the library of Columbia University, fol. 9a. See also above, p. 134.

318. *Ibid.,* fol. 18a.

319. MS. Adler 493 (Jewish Theological Seminary, New York), fol. 8b. See also my article on R. Elijah Kohen ha-Ittamari in *A. Marx Jubilee Volume* (New York, 1950), Hebrew part, pp. 459–60. By means of a homiletical pun Nathan connects the red heifer with Ishmael the "wild man" (cf. Gen. 16:12). The numerical value of Ishmael is equal to that of *tehom* ("abyss"); at the beginning of creation the messiah's soul was in the abyss of the *tehiru;* in the messianic phase, after the apostasy, it was in the abyss of Ishmael (MS. Adler 493, fols. 9–10).

his purposes, for example, to prove that certain types of souls might transgress the Law with impunity.[320] Misquotations of this kind are not infrequent in Sabbatian literature and it is not always easy to identify the sources and to assess the extent of the changes made.

To justify the apostasy Nathan also resorted, as we have seen, to the conventional legalistic argument that the messiah was entitled to special dispensations under the relevant provisions of rabbinic law. Yet we may presume his real opinion on the subject to be represented by the far more radical and profound views expounded in his *Zemir ᶜAriṣim* and again in *The Book of Creation.* The doctrine of the two types of Torah deriving from the "Tree of Life" and the "Tree of Knowledge" respectively, as developed in the Zohar (namely, in that part of it entitled *Raᶜya Mehemna*; see above, p. 11), was taken up by Nathan and systematically combined with his cosmological theory of the *tehiru.* The Tree of Life symbolizes the paradisiacal unity of the Torah before its separation into the duality of the Tree of Knowledge. In the eschatologic future the dominion of the Tree of Life would encompass the whole cosmos, and the laws and rules deriving from the Tree of Knowledge, which is the Tree of Death, would pass away.

The soul of the messiah was struggling to free itself from its original abode in the abyss of the *tehiru.* Its metaphysical victories in this struggle were the result of long and heroic labors, and the ordeal left its impress on the savior's personality even after his birth and his assumption of his final ministry. In spite of its origin in the *tehiru,* his soul had succeeded in raising itself to the highest level of communion with the Tree of Life, where it was beyond good and evil. Hence the messiah's relation to the Law was a special and unique one. This doctrine, to be sure, does not square too well with Nathan's other idea that in the course of his mission the messiah had to assume the form of evil and identify with it. If the messiah's soul is beyond the duality and distinctions of good and evil which derive from the Tree of Knowledge, then it does not identify dialectically with evil but, on the contrary, having realized the absolute good, can descend without defiling itself into the abyss of the *qelippah* in

320. *Qobeṣ ᶜal Yad,* XVI (1966), 435; see also Tishby's notes in his *Torath ha-Raᶜ weha-Qelippah be-Kabbalath ha-ᵓAri* (1942), p. 112. The original Lurianic statement (in *ᶜEṣ Ḥayyim, Shaᶜar Qlippath Nogah,* ch. 5) is perfectly orthodox and there is nothing antinomian about it.

order to liberate whatever holiness is imprisoned there. The categories of *forbidden* and *permitted* do not apply to the messiah, "and though his power is broken and he is drawn into the sphere of evil and fallen into their nets, . . . behaving [since the apostasy] according to their manner and their religion, yet this in no wise detracts from him, . . . since by virtue of his adherence to the Tree of Life everything he does is a *tiqqun*. He is like a soul in Paradise, . . . exempt from all the precepts of this world." The breaking of his power and the dimming of his light do not alter his essential nature, and far from being delivered into the hands of the mystery of death "even the broken fragments derive from the mystery of life and remain in their high estate."[321] There is, strictly speaking, no such thing as an apostate messiah who sins against the Law, since his actions cannot be measured by the ordinary yardstick of right and wrong. Nathan's doctrine is one more instance of the well-known tenet that the perfect man cannot sin, all appearances to the contrary notwithstanding. Spiritualist views of this kind often tended toward an explicit antinomianism, and Sabbatianism is no exception to this rule. Nathan's writings (especially his *Zemir ᶜAriṣim*) with their pointed formulations of potentially antinomian conclusions are exemplary in this respect.

The touchstone of all antinomian theories is the delicate subject of sexual morality. The severe and austerely ascetic Sabbatian prophet did not shrink from the most audacious antinomian speculations on this subject: in the perspective of the paradisiac order of things, where the Tree of Life has supplanted the Tree of Knowledge, even the biblical laws of incest—symbolizing the restraints of sexual morality—lose their unconditional validity. The laws of incest were imposed on Adam in this lower world, but in the higher world of *ᵓaṣiluth* "there is no incest."[322] As long as incest taboos are in force here on earth "it is impossible to perform the unifications above"; in the mystical suspension of the prohibitions of incest, man will become "like unto his Creator in the mystery of the Tree of Life."[323]

321. See Nathan's *Treatise on the Menorah* in G. Scholem, *Beᶜ Iqvoth Mashiaḥ*, p. 102. The treatise is part of Nathan's larger work *Zemir ᶜAriṣim*, which is extant in several MSS. (e.g., Brit. Mus., Margoliouth 856).

322. *Tiqquney Zohar* 69, at the beginning.

323. See G. Scholem, *Beᶜ Iqvoth Mashiaḥ*, p. 104, and Wirszubski's article (referred to above, n. 255), p. 239. The Sabbatians found support for their thesis

The *Raᶜya Mehemna*'s doctrine of the Torah and the two Trees assumed an immediate and vital relevance for Nathan's thinking. In the dispensation according to the Tree of Life, the Torah means "the study of the Law without the obligation of keeping its commandments, but solely for [the purpose of] the unification of the supernal lights and the working of spiritual acts" that would bring about the destruction of the "evil side."[324] This definition of the Torah certainly applies to the messiah and to other spiritual *perfecti* who have realized permanent communion with the Tree of Life. The whole people of Israel had once achieved this state of perfection for a brief moment at the giving of the Law on Mount Sinai.[325] By virtue of the supernal light inhering in the Tree of Life, these *perfecti* are capable of saving even evil itself and restoring it to good, whereas souls of a lower order can, at best, extricate and separate the good from the evil.[326] This doctrine is, of course, closely related to Nathan's views on the possibility of a total restoration of the *qelippoth* to holiness and perfection.

Another tenet of classical kabbalah exerted a considerable though less conspicuous influence on the Sabbatian conception of the messianic Torah. This is the doctrine of world cycles (*shemittoth*) as expounded in the thirteenth-century book *Temunah*.[327] According to this historico-cosmological doctrine, the power of the seven lower *sefiroth* manifests itself in seven successive periods of cosmic development lasting seven thousand years each. Every *sefirah*, from *Ḥesed* to *Malkhuth*, builds a complete cosmic structure. At the end of seven such cosmic "weeks" that is, in the fifty-thousandth year (the Great Jubilee), the cosmos would return to its source in the higher *sefirah*,

---

in the Talmudic statement (B. ᶜErubin 100b) that incest and adultery were forbidden only after Eve had been cursed for her sin. R. Elijah b. Kalonymos, a well-known preacher at the end of the 17th century, quotes a saying to this effect from the writings of "the kabbalists," cf. his *ᵓAddereth Eliyahu* (Frankfurt/Oder, [1694], fol. 93c). I suspect that the kabbalists in question were none other than Nathan and his disciples.

324. Scholem, *Beᶜlqvoth Mashiaḥ*, p. 96.

325. Nathan, in his *Sepher ha-Beriᵓah;* see G. Scholem, *loc. cit.*, p. 93.

326. *Ibid.*, p. 97.

327. The best edn. is Lvov, 1892. On the book and its doctrine see G. Scholem, *Ursprung und Anfänge der Kabbalah* (1962), pp. 407–14, and *ibid.*, *On the Kabbalah and Its Symbolism* (New York, 1965), pp. 77–82.

Binah. The absolute and primordial Torah, which is none other than the divine Wisdom and to which alone the dogma of the eternity and immutability of the Torah is applicable, manifests itself in different ways during the successive world cycles. Within any given period, the specific manifestation of the Torah possesses absolute validity, but with the advent of a new cycle, a new and different aspect of the Torah manifests itself. In the language of kabbalistic letter-mysticism: the letters of the Torah, reflecting the divine Wisdom, do not change, but their combinations and meanings change in accordance with the nature of the various periods. The current period, according to the book *Temunah,* is that of the second *sefirah,* Stern Judgment (*Geburah* or *Din*), and hence its nature and "law" is expressed in terms of precepts and prohibitions, pure and impure, holy and profane—in accordance with the present reading of the Torah. In the coming age, however, the Torah will be read in a different manner, and that which is prohibited now will not necessarily be prohibited then. Speculations on the nature of the Torah in the present and the coming *shemittah* periods occupy much space in kabbalistic literature up to the sixteenth century, when they lost favor as a result of the rejection of the doctrine of *shemittoth* by the great kabbalists of Safed, Moses Cordovero and Isaac Luria. Yet there is an undeniable utopian quality which makes for a certain similarity between the *Temunah*'s doctrine of world cycles (which the Safed kabbalists rejected) and the Zoharic doctrine of the two Trees (which they accepted). It is not surprising, therefore, that these doctrines should fuse, in spite of their distinct historical origins, in the hearts of the Sabbatian believers.

Three generations before the Sabbatian outbreak, an orthodox kabbalist and Talmudic scholar, R. Mordecai Yaffe of Lublin, had asserted that the transition from the first to the second *shemittah* had taken place during the giving of the Law on Mount Sinai, that is, *within* the present cosmic order. The end of one cycle and the ushering in of the next one did not, therefore, necessitate a catastrophic destruction of the world.[328] There was no reason why the Sabbatians should not announce a similar transition to a new age with the advent of the messiah. As the messiah was about to usher in this transition, the dominant force, namely, *sefirah,* of the coming *shemittah* was asserting itself already at the end of the preceding cycle.

328. See M. Yaffe's *Lebush ᵓOr Yeqaroth* (Lvov, 1881), pt. II, fol. 8d.

On one point, however, Nathan made a major departure from the traditional doctrine of *shemittoth:* our present cycle of seven thousand years, he held, was created in the power of the *sefirah Ḥesed* (Mercy). We were still living in the first cosmic cycle, and not in the second *shemittah* (that is, that of *Geburah*, Stern Judgment) as taught by the classical doctrine. The coming period of *Geburah* would begin with the advent of the messiah,[329] whose ministry would effect the transition from the one to the other. The *tiqqun* of the divine *sefiroth*, pictured as circles or spheres in the *tehiru*, could be accomplished solely by the "Holy Serpent," that is, the messiah. Unlike the Law of Moses (symbolized by his rod), which is straight, the messiah is curved or "crooked" like a serpent and like the *sefiroth* circles in the *tehiru*. That is why the rod of Moses "became a serpent . . . and Moses fled from it." What had been under the dominion of the "straight ray" of divine light, coming from *En-Sof*, that is, the Mosaic Law, had to be exchanged for a dispensation which would obtain its power from the "circular light." Therefore all matters connected with the messiah who works through the circular light are mysterious and incomprehensible, and not in accordance with the Law of Moses. Moses himself was aware of this, but "he fled from it" and its implications. Moses' Torah was indeed the "Torah of Truth," *torath ᵓemeth*, but Islam is now called in the Sabbatian writings *torath ḥesed*, the Torah of grace, using the ambiguity of the Hebrew word *ḥesed* which means both grace (or lovingkindness) and shame. The messianic Torah—where things which were formerly shameful are now permitted as acts of grace and lovingkindness—is disguised under the cloak of a Torah representing this *aion* and its dominant power, namely, Islam and its holy book, the Quran.[330] By discovering typological analogies of this kind, Nathan could explain why the true Moses, that is, Sabbatai Ṣevi, would have first to abandon the Mosaic Law and accept

329. G. Scholem, *Beᶜ Iqvoth Mashiaḥ*, pp. 120–22 (from Nathan's *Treatise on the Menorah*).

330. *Ibid.*, p. 124, and Nathan's *Treatise on the Merkabah*, MS. Adler 493 (in the Jewish Theological Seminary, New York), fol. 9a. On the preceding folios, the latter manuscript has a long explanation of how those rituals and commandments of the Torah for which no conceivable reason is given will become illuminated and comprehensible in the messianic age, and all this through a new arranagement of the letter of the present Torah. See the quotation in *SS*, pp. 699–700.

the religion of Ishmael, and thereafter to disappear into the supernal lights. The doctrine of the messiah's occultation Nathan had learned from Sabbatai himself.

Nathan and his disciples frequently quoted from the book *Temunah* in support of their doctrines. A good illustration of the use to which they put this thirteenth-century source is provided by the following example. The *Temunah* states that just as the holy souls multiplied at first from one (Adam) to three (the patriarchs) to threescore and ten (the number of souls that came into Egypt with Jacob; see Gen. 46:27) to six hundred thousand (the number of Israelites at the time of the exodus), so they would decrease again at the end of days until, between one *shemittah* and the next, the world would be waste and devoid of life. Nathan's mystical reinterpretation of this text ignores the picture of a decline and final cessation of life, and substitutes for it the notion of unity in communion with the sources of life. "Then all bodies will be united and will become as one body, . . . though previously they were completely separate. . . . And this is due to the wonderful union which souls in Israel have with the supernal *sefiroth*. For the *tiqqun* of the cosmos is not accomplished until all the souls in Israel have achieved their perfect *tiqqun* by becoming all united in one body, which is the messiah."[331] Nathan offers us here a remarkable Sabbatian analogy to Paul's doctrine of the unity of the faithful in the mystical body of Christ. Nathan's argument is based on the exegesis of a kabbalistic text. The fact that his exegesis actually inverted the original meaning of the text did not bother the Sabbatian prophet as long as it showed that all Israel would be united in one body, namely, in the messiah who was identical with Adam. In accomplishing this unity, the present *shemittah* would find its consummation and end.

X

Nathan's ideas regarding the messiah's mission and the meaning of the Torah in the eschatological age found exemplary expression

331. The quotation is taken from a part of Nathan's book on creation published by Ch. Wirszubski in the literary almanac *Qobeṣ Hoṣaʾath Schocken le-Dibrey Sifruth* (Tel-Aviv, 1940), pp. 180–91, particularly, pp. 182–83. Wirszubski was unable to trace the alleged quotation from the book *Peliʾah*, but the actual source is the book *Temunah*. The same passage from the book *Temunah* is also quoted in Cardozo's epistle *Magen Abraham*, p. 136.

in a tract written by Abraham Cardozo in Tripoli, Libya.[332] Copies of some of Nathan's writings had been brought there and aroused Cardozo's interest. He then proceeded to write a defense of the apostasy and composed in 1668 the *ʾIggereth Magen Abraham Meʾereṣ ha-Maʿarab*, the *Epistle Magen Abraham* [shield of Abraham] *from the Maghreb*. Cardozo's authorship about which there has been considerable doubt is now conclusively proved by his own testimony,[333] and the affirmation of one manuscript ascribing it to one of Nathan's pupils in Salonika, Abraham Pereṣ, must be discounted.[334] The tract is evidence of the speed with which extremely radical tendencies asserted themselves in the first years after the apostasy. At about the same time (1668–69), after the renewed contact with Sabbatai, Nathan composed his work *Zemir ʿAriṣim*.[335] Nathan's

332. The text was published by me, from an anonymous manuscript in Oxford, in *Qobeṣ ʿal Yad*, II, New Series (XII), (1938), 121–55, where I ascribed it, albeit with considerable doubt, to Abraham Cardozo. The doctrine of *Magen Abraham* was analyzed by Wirszubski in *Zion*, III (1938), 234–45.

333. The MS. Ben-Zvi Institute 2263, which comes from the archives of the Dönmeh, contains not only (pp. 1–30) the text of the tract, stating that it was brought from the Maghreb to Salonika by one of Cardozo's disciples, but also (pp. 32–53) a later and fuller version of Cardozo's answer to the rabbis of Smyrna, the original version of which I published in *Zion*, XIX (1954), 1–22. In this enlarged version Cardozo expressly quotes the *Magen Abraham* as his own work, a copy of which, he says, he had sent to Smyrna.

334. In the Hebrew edn. of the present work (p. 701), I accepted the testimony of MS. Günzburg 517 in Moscow. How the erroneous ascription to Pereṣ came into being is not clear. Another tract of Sabbatian kabbalah, giving the full name of its author Abraham Pereṣ, is preserved in MS. Halberstam 40, at present in the library of the rabbinical court of London (see above, n. 154). This text was printed anonymously and with the omission of Nathan's name from all quotations, in a collection of commentaries on the Zohar (*Torath Nathan* [Lvov, 1894], pp. 71–75). This tract, based on Nathan's later writings, was certainly written by Pereṣ after the prophet's death. I found several sayings of "the late Abraham Pereṣ" quoted in *Yalqut David* (Dyhernfurth, 1691), fol. 72d. Pereṣ seems to have died as a Jew and apparently did not take part in the mass apostasy of 1683 in Salonika.

335. I have published lengthy extracts from *Zemir ʿAriṣim* (from a MS. where it was styled *Treatise on the Menorah*) in my book *BeʿIqvoth Mashiaḥ* (1944), pp. 88–128. The complete work is extant in several MSS. (e.g., Brit. Mus., Margoliouth 856, fols. 13–76; Oxford, Neubauer 1897; Günzburg 187^3; Kaufmann 536^2; Berlin, Staatsbibliothek 3076, 8°; Jewish Theological Seminary, New York, Enelow Collection 731; Jews College, London (see above, n. 154), 123, fols. 12–40. Evidently the work enjoyed a wide circulation.

and Cardozo's writings complement each other, and the continuous evolution of Nathan's thinking, from the *Treatise on the Dragons* to his later writings, is evident. His earlier views on the essential metaphysical connection of the messiah's soul with the "lower *tehiru*" reappear in a more fully developed form, as if matured and confirmed by the experience of the apostasy. Both Nathan's *Zemir ᶜAriṣim* and Cardozo's *Magen Abraham* exhibit the thoroughly gnostic character of Sabbatian mysticism in all its dynamism and at the turning point where its impetus swung in a heretical direction. Cardozo's tract, however, presents a more systematic and methodical argument, and is free of Nathan's prolixity and his tendency to go off at a tangent and follow the rambling byways of his associations, which makes the reading of his larger treatises rather difficult.

Cardozo shows little interest in concrete historical events and circumstances and concentrates on the theological issues which he expounds in trenchant and radical formulations. He evades the flowery and allusive rabbinic style and writes a straightforward and rather modern Hebrew. He too makes use of the kabbalistic ideas and symbols described in the foregoing pages, but he insists that "we have not arrived at this perfect faith by means of [the homiletical interpretation of] these texts, . . . but because we entered into the depths of the faith by virtue of the roots of our souls as soon as we heard the glad tidings."[336] The author evidently considered himself as one of the pneumatic *perfecti* whose capacities for typological interpretation of the midrash and the Zohar were due to immediate spiritual apprehensions vouchsafed to superior souls. Yet, in spite of his pneumatic claims, his argument is distinguished by consistency and logic.

Cardozo was the first author to state clearly what was subsequently to become a Sabbatian stock argument: God does not "permit the beast of the righteous to sin in error, how much less the righteous themselves,"[337] and he certainly would not allow his saints, let alone his whole people, to fall into such grievous error. The argument is of considerable interest. Cardozo rejects the view, apparently voiced by many disabused believers, that Sabbatai had acted in good faith at the beginning of his career, but had taken to deceit and sin after realizing his error. For if this view were cor-

336. *Magen Abraham,* p. 148.

337. A famous Talmudic saying (cf. B. Ḥullin 7a).

rect, it would show that a life of exemplary saintliness may be rewarded by falling into sin, and thousands of devout penitents and earnest believers would have become victims of lies and deceit. This would be tantamount to denying God's justice and providence.[338] The messiah's soul was from the highest world of *ʾaṣiluth*, and ordinary human beings whose souls came from lower spheres could not possibly comprehend his actions.[339]

The author expounds the deeper meaning of exile and redemption on traditional Lurianic premises. Israel's exile and suffering were ultimately a result of the descent of the supernal lights and the subsequent demotion of the divine Shekhinah. This, in its turn, brought about the fall of Adam in whose soul all other souls were contained. Adam's fall caused the descent of the holy sparks into the abyss of the *qelippoth*. Every generation had to perform the *tiqqun* appropriate to the specific origin of its souls in the body of the First Adam, by means of the appropriate commandments. Hence different periods (Adam, Noah, Israel at Mount Sinai) required different versions of the Torah and its precepts.[340] The original cosmic fall and the subsequent *tiqqun* by means of the Law may be compared to a man who fell into a deep pit. All his limbs (like those of the divine macroanthropos) are badly bruised and require the application of plasters and poultices by an expert physician, who also prescribes a strict diet. As the patient is cured he can dispense with the treatment and the diet which, strictly speaking, go against his nature. "This parable is easily applied to the precepts [of the Law] which are like poultices, as a result of which the lights and all the worlds will surely rise to a very high degree. But this can be accomplished only in the days of the messiah, who alone can perform the *tiqqun* of all the worlds, being himself the First Adam."[341]

At this point of his argument, Cardozo draws an extraordinary conclusion from the Talmudic distinction between two possible times of redemption. Alleging a contradiction in the prophecy of Isaiah (60:22), "I the Lord will hasten it in its time," the Talmud (B. Sanhedrin 98a) explains: "if they are worthy I will hasten it; if not, then [the messiah will come] at the due time." If Israel had lived up to its high calling and performed the *tiqqun*, then redemption would have been hastened. Owing to their remissness, how-

338. *Magen Abraham*, p. 129. 339. *Ibid.*, p. 128.
340. *Ibid.*, p. 132. 341. *Ibid.*, p. 133.

ever, redemption would have to be wrought by God and His messiah at the due and appointed time, "and God no longer requires their [that is, Israel's] study and observance of the Law."[342] The author proves at great length that the appointed time had now arrived, and he impresses on his readers the implications of this fact for a proper understanding of the present status of the Law. For "the present Torah"—that is, traditional, rabbinic *halakhah*—"does not apply to the messianic era" at which time "the Oral Law becomes nugatory." The Oral Law with its six orders and sixty tractates of the Mishnah corresponds to the six days of the week that are subject to the dominion of the Tree of Knowledge wherewith Adam had sinned. The Sabbath, however, is dominated by the Tree of Life, and hence the law of the Mishnah and the Talmud no longer applies, "and whoever wants [to continue] to serve [God] in the present manner . . . destroys the plantations and desecrates the Sabbath," according to the standards of the messianic age.[343] Sabbatian logic led therefore to a radical antinomian conclusion: the precepts of the Law would not only lapse; their observance would become a positively sinful desecration of the messianic Sabbath. The author supports his argument by ample quotations from the *Raᶜya Mehemna* and *Tiqquney Zohar*, and also appeals to a midrashic comment on Psalm 146:7: "The Lord looseth the prisoners." Reading *ᵓissurim* ("prohibitions") for *ᵓasurim* ("prisoners") the verse can be made to mean: "The Lord will loose all prohibitions—including the prohibition of pork."[344] "It is clear from even a superficial reading of these dicta that when the worlds will be cleansed of the dross of the *qelippoth*, then the outer garments [of the Torah] will become superfluous . . . and the Torah will be renewed. . . . But no creature can accomplish this except the messianic king, who is none other than [a reincarnation of] Moses."[345]

As a devout and pious Jew, the author protects himself against the antinomian consequences of his own teaching. He warns his readers not to draw hasty conclusions from his argument or to permit

342. *Ibid.*, pp. 133–34.

343. *Ibid.*, p. 135. This statement is based on one of the most audacious passages in the *Tiqquney Zohar* (*Zohar Ḥadash,* ed. R. Margalioth, fol. 108a).

344. *Ibid.*, p. 145; cf. *Midrash Tehillim* 146, §4, in Buber's edn. and the editor's note *ad loc.*

345. *Ibid.*, p. 146.

themselves even the slightest departure from rabbinic law and custom, for the dispensation of the Tree of Life will be inaugurated only after that of the Tree of Knowledge has been completely fulfilled. But none knoweth the moment of this fulfillment except the messiah.[346] As long as the messiah remains—albeit as a kind of Trojan horse—in the realm of the *qelippoth,* the traditional Law has lost nothing of its validity. The author's position is as clear and definite as can be, and it was probably shared by many other believers. Yet it also shows how thin and precarious was the line that separated a theoretical and potential antinomianism from its practical application.

According to Cardozo, the messiah would play a decisive role in ushering in the new age, since Israel had failed to accomplish the cosmic *tiqqun.* The nature of his ministry, however, would be beyond the comprehension of ordinary mortals, for the messiah's strange actions "are very secret *tiqqunim* to raise the worlds and the sparks of holiness that fell together with him into the great abyss above, at the breaking of the vessels." This fall is symbolically referred to in Exodus 21:33: "if a man shall dig a pit . . . and an ox or an ass fall therein." According to the Zohar,[347] the ox symbolizes the messiah of the House of Joseph, the ass symbolizes the son of David, "lowly and riding on an ass." The contraction of the primordial light and the subsequent breaking of the vessels was like the digging of a pit, "and the messiah, that is Moses, fell into it." Hence also the servitude of Moses at the court of Pharaoh and in the land of Cush. The messiah's actions must be adapted to the nature and character of the particular *qelippah* which he must conquer "and into which he must enter in order to snatch the sparks of holiness as if from a fire."[348] There is a slight difference here between Cardozo and the prophet of Gaza. In the *Treatise on the Dragons* and elsewhere, Nathan asserts that the messiah's soul was in the Great Abyss of the *tehiru* from the very beginning of the *ṣimṣum,* whereas the letter *Magen Abraham* seems to suggest that the messiah "fell" into the abyss at the breaking of the vessels. But perhaps Cardozo did not mean his loose and figurative use of language to be pressed too much.

In order to accomplish his mission, the messiah would have to

346. *Ibid.,* p. 147.

347. Zohar III (*Raᶜya Mehemna*), 279a.

348. *Magen Abraham,* pp. 137–38. The continuation of this passage is quoted above, p. 802.

adopt "crooked" ways. These, as we have seen, were attributed by Nathan to the origin of the messiah's soul in the circles of the *tehiru,* in contrast to the "straight line" of the light of *En-Sof* that penetrated the *tehiru* after the *ṣimṣum.* It is not without reason that the origins and the history of David, the founder of the messianic dynasty, were "crooked" by ordinary human standards: Lot's incest with his daughters (from which descended the ancestress Ruth the Moabite), Judah and Tamar, Boaz and Ruth, the circumstances of David's conception[349] and his lapse with Bathsheba. In fact, the leaders of the opposition against David, such as Doeg the Edomite and Sheba the son of Bichri, far from being mere villains and rascals were (according to Talmudic legend) among the greatest rabbinic authorities of their day and chiefs of the Sanhedrin. Let no one, therefore, rashly cast aspersions at the Lord's Anointed. To understand these mysteries one should search diligently in the ancient books, "for such profound things are not understood by simplistic knowledge."[350] Believers should not be disconcerted by the opposition of so many eminent rabbis, for it was inevitable that there should be two parties at the time of the messiah's advent. Moreover, all the true kabbalists were on the messiah's side.[351] The author no doubt exaggerates when he claims that all kabbalists were in the Sabbatian camp, but his testimony may well reflect the general feeling among the believers. In any event there must have been many kabbalists and believers during the first years after the apostasy who were impressed by the kind of arguments advanced by Nathan and Cardozo.

349. His father, Jesse, came to his wife, mistaking her for one of his handmaids; see above, p. 64, n. 90.

350. *Magen Abraham,* pp. 139–40. Similarly also R. Isaac Ḥanan, another disciple of Nathan in Salonika, in his work *Beney Yiṣḥak* (Salonika, 1756), fols. 55–56.

351. *Magen Abraham,* pp. 147–48.

8

THE LAST YEARS OF SABBATAI ṢEVI (1668–1676)

I

THE PRECEDING ACCOUNT of the immediate effects of the apostasy on the Jewries of Europe and the Orient has somewhat neglected the person of the messiah himself, Sabbatai Ṣevi, *alias* Mehemed Kapici Bashi, whom we left, in the summer of 1667, in Adrianople.

Sabbatai's state of mind after the apostasy has been briefly described in an earlier chapter (see above, p. 686). At first he seemed utterly confused and lost, but as time went on his low spirits gave way to new fits of exaltation, and the familiar rhythm of manic-depressive alternations reasserted itself. During the periods of illumination all his doubts vanished. He was again sure of his calling and his mysterious mission, and his followers were as susceptible as ever to the strange fascination that seemed to radiate from the apostate messiah. His apostasy gradually assumed its definite character as the logical climax of all previous trials, experiences, and "strange actions." Once before, Sabbatai had experienced release from the prison of the *qelippoth,* but now he was their prisoner again and his last trial was the most difficult of all. He sought to plumb the depths of the mystery of his suffering, and his exchange of letters with leading believers who tried to fathom the same mystery no doubt helped him to formulate his own interpretation of his fate.

Sabbatai also remained in contact with Nathan, and the rabbis had good reason to complain that the prophet of Gaza had not kept his word (see above, p. 735). Some followers, for example, Abraham Yakhini, visited Sabbatai and consulted with him, and then returned home without having been asked to apostatize. Others took up residence in or near Adrianople in order to be close to the messiah. Samuel Primo, who had moved to Sofia some time before, nevertheless continued to visit Sabbatai and to receive his teaching. Though some of Sabbatai's visitors apostatized at his behest, there is no evidence at all that Nathan's companions, who had separated from him at Brussa and proceeded to Adrianople (see above, p. 720), did the same. In fact, we do not know the names of the first apostates. When Nathan arrived in Adrianople he found several members of his group, including representatives of the "Twelve Tribes of Israel." A number of leading believers and close associates of Sabbatai had been summoned to Adrianople. When Coenen visited Nathan in Smyrna at the house of Sabbatai's wealthy brother Elijah Ṣevi, he heard that the latter was about to leave for Adrianople. As a matter of fact, Elijah Ṣevi and his eldest son traveled to Adrianople in the summer of 1667, but apostatized only later at Sabbatai's behest, as did many others of the messiah's entourage.[1] Thus came into being the first group of apostates, who used to accompany Sabbatai wherever he went, arousing the attention of Christian observers no less than the anger of many Jews. Elijah Ṣevi, who had advanced meanwhile from a mere merchant "who knew nothing of mystical theology" (see above, p. 614) to the rank of a "great sage," remained with his brother. After Sabbatai's death he fled, and returned to his ancestral religion and even succeeded in re-establishing himself in Smyrna as a respected member of the community.[2] Apparently nobody was interested in stirring up the past or in betraying the lapsed convert to the Turkish authorities. As far as we know, neither of Sabbatai's two brothers subsequently joined the Dönmeh, and no traditions are preserved associating any members of the family with the sect.

1. Coenen, p. 139; Baruch of Arezzo, *ap.* Freimann, p. 63; de la Croix, p. 382; and esp. the chronicle of Jacob Najara, *Sefunoth*, V (1961), pp. 254–62 (see below, pp. 846–51).

2. See R. Solomon ha-Levi's responsa *Leb Shelomoh,* no. 57.

Sabbatai's double-faced behavior is attested by both Sabbatian and other sources. The Sabbatians, of course, had their own reasons for emphasizing this duplicity, since they wished—at least during the first year or so—to foster the view that the apostasy had been mere pretense. As time went on, however, the new Sabbatian doctrine regarding the positive significance of the apostasy was advanced more boldly, and believers ceased to pretend that the messiah had not really transgressed and abolished the Law. According to Tobias Rofe, Sabbatai "behaved like a rabbi as was his wont. Sometimes he prayed and behaved like a Jew, and sometimes like a Muslim, and he did queer things."[3] Christians who saw Sabbatai during those years report the same. It seems probable, therefore, that the stories of Sabbatai Ṣevi sitting with the Quran in one hand and the scroll of the Law in the other, or wearing phylacteries when saying his prayers, should not be dismissed—as the emissaries from Casale and Isaac Sasportas were inclined to do—as foolish prattle.[4] The letters written shortly after the apostasy by believers in Adrianople and Ragusa, and reporting that Sabbatai had observed the Jewish high holidays (September–October, 1666) in traditional liturgical fashion[5] without let or hindrance, may tell the truth.

De la Croix claims to have on more than one occasion seen Sabbatai Ṣevi walking about surrounded by a large company of apostate Jews "who followed him to the synagogues where he preached conversion to Islam with such success that during the five years or so that the mission of this zealot for the religion of Mahomet lasted, the number of Turks [that is, Jewish apostates to Islam] increased every day."[6] Sabbatai's sermons on conversion are also mentioned by the Florentine ambassador, Santi Bani, in a report written on February 28, 1671.[7]

3. *Ap.* Emden, p. 46. Tobias was not a Sabbatian believer and does not use the technical term "strange actions" current among Sabbatians.

4. *Ap.* Carpi, p. 19; Sasportas, p. 248. Cf. also the descriptions quoted by Baruch of Arezzo (*ap.* Freimann, p. 64) and the legends told by A. Cuenque (*ap.* Emden, pp. 41–42). Israel Ḥazzan's testimony about his behavior on many occasions is equally reliable.

5. MS. Hottinger, vol. 30, fol. 345, quoting reports of March 16, 1667, received in Venice from Ragusa and Adrianople.

6. De la Croix, p. 381. A description of one such ceremonial procession including Sabbatai's entourage of apostates is given in Najara's chronicle, *loc. cit.*, p. 258.

7. The text was published in *Vessillo Israelitico,* LIX (1911), 513.

Rycaut describes Sabbatai's behavior during those years as follows:[8]

In this manner Sabatai passed his days in the Turkish-Court, as some time Moses did in that of the Egyptians; and perhaps in imitation of him, cast his eyes often on the Afflictions of his Brethren, of whom, during his life, he continued to profess himself a Deliverer, but with that care and caution of giving scandal to the Turks, that he declared, Unless their Nation became like him, that is renounce the Shadows, and imperfect Elements of the Mosaical Law, which will be compleated by adherence to the Mahometan, and such other Additions as his inspired Wisdom should suggest, he should never be able to prevail with God for them, or conduct them to the holy Land of their Forefathers. Hence-upon many Jews flocked in, some as far as from Babylon, Jerusalem, and other remote places, and casting their Caps on the ground, in presence of the Grand Signior, voluntarily professed themselves Mahometans. Sabatai himself by these Proselytes gaining ground in the esteem of the Turks, had priviledge granted him to visit familiarly his Brethren, which he employed in Circumcising their Children the eighth Day, according to the precept of Moses, preaching his new Doctrines, by which he hath confirmed many in their Faith of his being the Messiah, and startled all with expectation of what these strange ways of Enthusiasm may produce; but none durst publickly owne him, lest they should displease the Turks, and the Jews, and incurr the danger of Excommunication from one, and the Gallows from the other.

Rycaut's account is a faithful description of a sect in the process of formation. All is disguise and dissimulation: Sabbatai and his followers concealed their real beliefs, and the apostate's sermons on conversion were as deceptive as the public denials, by many believers, of their faith in their messiah. Rycaut's description, though not applicable to all believers, is certainly true of a great many of them. Pressure from two sides—from the Turks as well as the Jews—caused the movement to go underground. Sabbatai's group flourished in the twilight in which it began to operate, but a public confession of its beliefs and aims would have spelled disaster. Rycaut also mentions Sabbatai's "new doctrine," and on this point too, as we shall see, his information was correct.

8. Rycaut, p. 219.

Although the aforementioned testimonies refer mainly to the last years of Sabbatai's activity (1669–72), they would be almost equally true of the period immediately following the apostasy. Leyb b. Ozer was told by travelers arriving from Turkey that the disciples and rabbis who had apostatized were trying to persuade the other Jews to follow their example and had, in fact, "drawn unto themselves many sinners." Sabbatai also commanded many of his followers "to appear before him, and he explained to them that everything had been ordained in Heaven, as it was written in the *Pirqey de-Rabbi Eliezer* that the messiah would be swallowed among the Ishmaelites.[9] He explained everything in accordance with his false kabbalah, and had ready answers for everything and thus caused more than three hundred Jews to apostatize in the course of two or three months."[10] Leyb b. Ozer probably confused reports of Sabbatai's conversionary efforts with the subsequent activities of the Dönmeh.[11] There is no evidence that during Sabbatai's lifetime his apostate followers engaged in active proselytizing, and the Sabbatian sources suggest that efforts in this direction were made by Sabbatai alone. Also, the number given by Leyb seems to be exaggerated. A Christian traveler who was in Turkey in the years 1672–73 estimated the number of apostates at two hundred families.[12] If his estimate for 1673 was correct, then the number must have been considerably less in 1667, immediately after the messiah's apostasy.

There were cases, even in the first years, of apostates repenting and returning to the Jewish religion. As early as 1669 Sasportas informed his correspondents in Morocco that several associates of Sabbatai Ṣevi who had apostatized with him and married gentile women in Constantinople had "repented of their error": they had left their

9. This is a Sabbatian misrendering of the text in *Pirqey de-Rabbi Eliezer*, end of ch. 30; see *Pirke de Rabbi Eliezer*, trans. G. Friedlander (1916), p. 222.

10. MS. Shazar, fol. 41a–b.

11. This surmise is confirmed by the sequel of Leyb's account (MS. Shazar, fol. 41a): "they recite the *Shema*ᶜ three times daily in their prayers, but where the Jews say, 'Hear, O Israel,' they say, 'Hear, O Ishmael,' and other similar changes in accordance with their heresy." Leyb heard this from "several trustworthy men," but the report surely refers to the practices of the Dönmeh in his own day.

12. *Journal d'Antoine Galland*, I (Paris, 1881), 194. I assume that Leyb's numbers similarly refer to heads of families and not to individuals.

wives and fled to the principality of Walachia near the Polish border.[13] There must have been many other cases of Sabbatian followers feeling pricks of conscience.

In 1667 a son was born to Sabbatai Ṣevi. The event had been prophesied by Nathan in his letter written early in 1667 when Sabbatai's wife was already with child, and the boy was called Ishmael Mordecai in accordance with Nathan's prophecy ("Mordecai" in honor of Sabbatai's father, Mordecai Ṣevi). But contrary to Nathan's prophecy[14] the child was not born circumcised (as was, according to rabbinic legend, the earlier redeemer, Moses), and Sabbatian sources state that Sabbatai himself circumcised him according to the Jewish rite in the presence of many Turks and held a banquet in honor of the event.[15] If this report is true it would indicate that the prohibition against visiting Sabbatai was not enforced by the Turkish authorities until he was arrested again and banished in 1672. For aught we know there never was any such prohibition, though the emissaries from Casale heard rumors to that effect in Smyrna; if there was, it was probably rescinded after the apostasy. R. Israel Ḥazzan of Kastoria describes his pilgrimage to Sabbatai in 1667: upon being admitted to the presence he pronounced the liturgical benediction prescribed on the occasion of beholding a king in Israel, and Sabbatai showed him writings which he had composed regarding his person and messianic calling.[16] A Christian traveler, on the other hand, was told that Sabbatai had written to the Jews and asked to be left alone;[17] but

13. Sasportas, p. 345; Walachia was not bordering on Poland, and Sasportas must have mixed it up with Moldavia. Cf. also the incident in Kastoria mentioned above, p. 779.

14. In a letter quoted by Sasportas, pp. 200–1.

15. Baruch of Arezzo, *ap.* Freimann, p. 68; de la Croix, p. 377. A conflicting account of Ishmael's circumcision is given in Jacob Najara's chronicle, quoted below, p. 848. There is a slight discrepancy between Baruch of Arezzo's report and that of de la Croix. According to Baruch, Sabbatai "knew his wife after he put the pure miter upon his head, and she conceived and gave birth," whereas de la Croix states that she was already with child at the time of the apostasy. De la Croix's version is borne out by Nathan's letter (Sasportas, p. 201), and Sabbatai's announcement in Smyrna that his wife had conceived and was with child was therefore incorrect. Cuenque's account of Ishmael's birth (*ap.* Emden, p. 42) is somewhat obscure but evidently uses (and expands) the same Sabbatian tradition that also underlies Baruch's report. Symbolically the son was also called Isaac (see *Schocken Volume,* pp. 172–73).

16. See Scholem in *Schocken Volume,* p. 146.

17. Galland, *loc. cit.*

it would be futile to seek consistency and logic in Sabbatai's erratic and impulsive behavior. Perhaps the letters discouraging visitors from coming to him were written at a time when the persecution of the believers in Constantinople by the rabbis had assumed serious proportions.

The sources not only suggest that followers from all countries continued to visit Sabbatai, but also enable us to learn something about the varieties of types and characters among the believers. One is all too easily tempted to assume that the faithful who continued to believe even after the apostasy were recruited mainly from among the emotional and the unstable whose reason was an easy prey to their feelings, but this assumption would certainly be wrong. There were, among the believers, people whom one would normally describe as clever, rational, and having commonsense. Jonas Salvador of Pinerolo, near Turin, is a case in point. Salvador, a merchant and scholar active in Jewish communal affairs, was in Paris for several months early in 1670. There he became friendly with the French scholar and well-known biblical critic, Richard Simon, and it is to Simon's letters that we owe our knowledge of Jonas Salvador. A pious and orthodox Jew, Salvador was interested in the ideas current among the more enlightened French intellectuals and hoped to enlist their support for his own plans. He was much preoccupied with the idea of a return to Palestine and the restoration of political dominion to the Jews. Hence he was greatly impressed by Isaac de la Peyrère's *Du Rappel des Juifs* (1643),[18] of which he had knowledge through Richard Simon, and he refused to believe that an author who spoke so positively about Israel was not of Jewish (marrano) descent. In his conversations with Richard Simon, Salvador showed himself to be a man of sound and critical commonsense, which, however, did not prevent him from admitting to being a Sabbatian as well. Sabbatai's apostasy notwithstanding, "he is convinced—or at least pretends to be convinced—that this messiah who is at present in Adrianople will bring his people under his raised banner to the Holy City, and there the worship of God would be re-established in its purity." Simon men-

18. Cf. H. J. Schoeps, *Philosemitismus im Barock* (1952), pp. 3–17. Surprisingly enough, Peyrère himself does not seem to have taken an active interest in the Sabbatian movement, although R. Simon suggested to him (with tongue in cheek?) that Salvador would provide him with a letter of introduction should he wish to pay a visit to Sabbatai Ṣevi.

tions having seen a letter on this subject which Salvador had written to his daughter, who had been educated at a convent in Turin. Salvador also told Simon that Jews from all countries continued to visit Sabbatai Ṣevi in Adrianople, and his testimony agrees with what we know from other sources. The case of Jonas Salvador shows, at any rate, that, in spite of the negative report of the emissaries from Casale, there still were believers in Piedmont and that these believers were not necessarily unrealistic, fantastic dreamers. A description of the whole Sabbatian camp as a separatist sect which had already at that early date cut itself loose from the wider Jewish community would certainly be erroneous. There were all kinds of Sabbatians, as their literature amply shows, and among them were practical men, active in public affairs and devoid of anything that could be called a "sectarian" mentality. Jonas Salvador was surely not the only believer to talk frankly and openly about his faith.[19]

II

About a year and a half after the apostasy there was renewed commotion in Adrianople around the person of Sabbatai Ṣevi, this time in connection with a "great illumination" that had come upon him during the Passover festival of 1668. Sabbatai who, as we know, had no talents as a writer, seems to have confined himself to giving an oral account of his celestial visions to his close associates, who then put them down in writing. Apparently two such tracts were written in the spring or summer of 1668. One of the two tracts seems now to be lost, though Rosanes saw it in Salonika in 1915 when the Dönmeh permitted him to examine their secret archives. On that occasion Rosanes saw a manuscript which he described as follows: "Revelation—a small tract in two parts, about 30 fols., beginning, 'Know ye[20] that in the year 1668, as Our Lord AMIRAH was at his table celebrating the ritual of the Passover night, there appeared to him twenty-four thousand angels, all saying: Thou art our Lord, thou art our King, thou art our Redeemer.' "[21] The other tract, entitled *Sahadutha de-Mehemenutha* (*Testimony concerning the Faith*), seems to have circu-

19. On Jonas Salvador see *Lettres Choisies de Richard Simon* (Amsterdam, 1730), vol. I, p. 15 and vol. III, p. 13.

20. Rosanes reads "They knew"; I have corrected the reading in accordance with the second MS.

21. Rosanes, IV, p. 475.

lated among the believers, and several copies are extant. The text contains an account, in five chapters, of the visionary encounter between God and Sabbatai Ṣevi on Passover, 1668, a commentary on the first chapter, and a Sabbatian commentary on Psalm 19.[22]

The account, written in a simple, attractive, and at times even beautiful, style, bespeaks a genuine and profound emotion. Its importance resides in the fact that it is the first document emanating from Sabbatai's immediate entourage after the apostasy and permitting us a glimpse into the hearts and minds of the more resolute and enthusiastic believers. Whether the author of the *Testimony* apostatized together with Sabbatai or not is unknown. In any event his account breathes a spirit of firm and resolute faith and of deep Jewish feeling, indicative of a very definite and clear-cut line of thought, possibly reflecting Sabbatai's own attitude at the time. The views and doctrines expressed by the author are very different from those developed by Nathan of Gaza in his tracts and letters of the years 1667–68.[23] Nathan is far more extreme and radical in his interpretation of the apostasy and in his doctrine of the messiah's mission and the mystery of his descent into the realm of the *qelippoth*. His attitude to the gentile nations is consistently hostile: the messiah has entered their world not to save them but to hasten their utter destruction. In 1668 the believers in Adrianople had evidently not yet absorbed the new trend of Nathan's teaching and were unaware of its full implications. They were still exercised by the problems of the messiah's mission to the gentiles and

22. I have published the text in *Beᶜ Iqvoth Mashiaḥ*, pp. 69–77. At the time I considered the possible authorship of Nathan, but this hypothesis can now be ruled out; cf. Tishby's remarks in *Kiryath Sepher*, XXI (1944), 17. Tishby rightly pointed out the wide differences between Nathan's doctrines and those of the author of the *Testimony*. The tract was composed, moreover, at a time when Nathan was far away from Adrianople, in Italy. A very surprising testimony about the author of the piece has come to light in a marginal note to another copy of the tract, in MS. Ben-Zvi Institute 2262, p. 74. The note is in the handwriting of R. Abraham Miranda, the collector of the tracts and documents assembled in this MS. (about 1760). In one of his books, called *Neʾeman Shemuʾel*, he reports that Abraham Yakhini had quoted these chapters as having been composed by R. Solomon Laniado, the well-known rabbi of Aleppo. If this is true—and Yakhini was in a position to know what was going on in the Sabbatian camp—we would have to assume that Laniado made a pilgrimage to Adrianople in 1668.

23. Several of Nathan's writings of the period are still extant; a more detailed analysis of Nathan's revolutionary and heretical Sabbatian theology will be given in the sequel to the present work.

of the attitude which Israel had to adopt toward a redeemer who had become defiled. There must have been many attempts during the first years after the apostasy to explain the disconcerting and depressing events, and no doubt such explanations often took the form of heavenly revelations. Many of these treatises were subsequently lost, though a specimen of this kind of literature has survived in the diary in which an otherwise unknown believer, R. Jacob b. Isaac Ṣirojon, recorded the *maggidic* revelations concerning Sabbatai Ṣevi's apostasy and "strange actions," which he was vouchsafed in the period from the Day of Atonement, September 29, 1667, until the year 1668. These revelations, inspired by the Shekhinah and delivered in the language of the Zohar, consisted mainly of Sabbatian "proofs" in the form of *gematria*.[24]

The author of the *Testimony concerning the Faith* addresses himself to these questions by assuming the part of an onlooker at the heavenly encounter between God and the messiah. His account is therefore couched in the language of an apocalyptic vision rather than that of kabbalistic theology. In fact, the writer would never have divulged these awesome facts but for unmistakable punishment from Heaven. For every chapter that he wished to suppress, he was visited by fire and tortures "worse than a hundred deaths," suffering the penalty with which Scripture threatens "a witness, whether he hath seen or known, if he do not utter it, then he shall bear his iniquity" (Lev. 5:1).[25] The testimony of this "witness" states:

Know ye . . . that in the night of Passover, 1668, God willed to let His Holy Spirit rest on the true redeemer, Our Lord the great and pure and holy King and Messiah Sabbatai Ṣevi . . . to save and redeem Israel at that very moment. But the Redeemer replied: "If thou abidest by the original condition which I stipulated that thou sparest thy children the tribulations of the messianic age . . . then I shall take it upon myself to redeem, but if not I beg thee to wait a while." Then God said to him: "Thou hast more pity on my children than I do. Half the [preordained] tribulations have already been discharged; let them

24. The revelations are preserved in a MS. in the Amarillo Collection, now at the Ben-Zvi Institute at the Hebrew University of Jerusalem (MS. 2262, pp. 85–100). M. Benayahu was the first to have drawn attention to this MS. (*Sefunoth,* V [1961], 307, n. 55). See above, pp. 736–37, and the notes.

25. See G. Scholem, *Be^cIqvoth Mashiaḥ*, p. 72. Unless stated otherwise, all quotations are taken from the text of the *Testimony concerning the Faith.*

take upon themselves the other half and do not suffer thyself." Thereupon he replied: "Lord of the universe! Thou doest all this to save my honor, which has been profaned among some Jews *since the day that I went out into the field to reap the seed that had been sown among the nations.* Behold, since that day I have gathered many sheaves which I have converted and which I have added from the gentiles to Israel. Let my own honor be profaned in order to increase the glory of God and the glory of Israel, for they will all repent with a perfect repentance when they shall behold the thousands and myriads of gentiles joining themselves to Israel." Then he called the patriarchs and said to them: "Know ye not that if the gentiles dared to admit to one another the new and perfect faith which entered their hearts after they knew and probed and proved me . . . and beheld the bright and resplendent light within me, they could annihilate the enemies of Israel [that is—euphemistically—Israel], but each doubts whether the other shares his faith. Israel know not that they are the mockery of the gentiles for not knowing the future felicity that is laid up for them, but they think that they are mocked because they believed in me. However, this is not so, and [the gentiles] merely pretend this to be the reason, for since they are afraid to show one another what is in their hearts they certainly would not show it to the Jews.

God urged him, in the presence of the patriarchs, saying: "Even the reaper of corn cannot gather everything without losing a grain or two from every ear. I am the owner of the field, and the wheat is mine. I do not mind losing a few grains provided that thou harvest the wheat." He answered: "Give me leave," and he called a bird to come and pick a grain. . . . Then [the messiah] killed the bird and took out the grain and sowed it and watered it with the sweat of the heavenly beasts, and it became a mighty tree that brought forth flowers and wonderful fruit. He took the firstlings of the fruit and gave it to God, who smelled it as the smell of the spices of Paradise. Then [the messiah] said: "If one grain can produce much marvelous fruit, how then can I redeem Israel [in such manner] that some souls should be lost."[26]

The messiah then carefully collects every single grain from all the four corners of the earth, and addresses the birds and lions and wild beasts as follows: "I charge you by my faith and knowledge

26. *Ibid.* The "heavenly beasts" mentioned here are those carrying the heavenly chariot, the *merkabah.*

that you render back forthwith everything that you have pecked and taken from the flesh of the children of Israel." As the birds and animals bring back the dismembered body of one that had despaired of redemption in 1648, the messiah recounts to each one of them what he had done: the eagle had picked out his heart, the birds had eaten his flesh, etc. This passage seems to suggest that the *Testimony* is indeed based on Sabbatai's own reports of his visions. R. Israel Ḥazzan of Kastoria, who was very close to Sabbatai in the years 1667 (or 1668)–1672, expounds Job 39:12—"he will bring home thy seed"—as follows: "Not one grain of wheat will be lost. This is why AMIRAH said that even if one person died and the birds ate his flesh he would command them to render it back and make it perfect again. . . . and thus have I heard from his holy mouth: I can gather all the wheat and bring them together in one barn, and not one grain shall be lost. And if perchance a bird swallow a grain, I shall retrieve it from his mouth, . . . for the purpose of the *tiqqun* of his mighty deeds is that not one soul of Israel should be lost."[27]

The view held by Sabbatai and his circle in Adrianople concerning the secret meaning of his apostasy is here clearly expressed: there is a "holy seed" even among the gentiles, and the messiah has to garner it not merely by raising the holy sparks and souls that had "fallen among the thorns" (as taught by Ḥayyim Vital and classical Lurianic kabbalah), but by actually spreading the faith and converting gentiles to Sabbatian Judaism. Christian sources refer in a general way to the fact that gentiles (probably Turks) had come to believe in Sabbatai Ṣevi, but there was nothing to corroborate this assertion. In the *Testimony* we find Sabbatai boasting of his converts, although the thousands of which the vision speaks were probably no more than a few individuals. R. Israel Ḥazzan refers to the "gentile believers" as a well-known fact which did not require further elaboration.[28]

27. See G. Scholem in *Schocken Volume,* p. 168. Unless Israel Ḥazzan himself heard all this in a vision—in which case he is the author of the *Testimony* (but see above, n. 22)—we must assume that Sabbatai told his visitors and believers about his visionary experience. The author of the *Testimony* always refers to Sabbatai in the third person.

28. On the verse "He will not despise their prayer" (Ps. 102:18) Israel Ḥazzan comments: "These are the believers who hold the true faith and who are the root of Israel, for both Jewish and gentile believers were praying for him and swearing by the life of AMIRAH"; see G. Scholem in *Schocken Volume,* p. 180.

The redeemer does not abandon a single grain—neither of the wicked and unbelieving Israelites who will eventually repent, nor of the seed that is sown among the gentiles and which the messiah alone can gather in. And until all are gathered in, he would not consider his preparatory mission as completed and make redemption manifest. Prior to the apostasy nobody ever thought of such a doctrine, while afterward it seems to have arisen in several places at once—though in its most extreme form in Adrianople—as the most obvious explanation of the messiah's voluntary entry into the realm of the *qelippah.* This doctrine lacks the notion, so conspicuous in the writings of Nathan of Gaza, of undermining from within, as it were, the power of the *qelippah,* but it certainly shows that all believers shared the sense of tragedy at the messiah's "going out into the fields." This feeling found its profoundest expression to that date in the doctrine of the Adrianople group. Lurianic kabbalah had developed the sense of high drama in the historic mission of Israel. In its Sabbatian transformation this became the drama of the messiah's mission.

The basic idea that the messiah would not abandon even a single soul recurs throughout the *Testimony.* Chapter 3 in particular deals with a problem that seems to have exercised many believers:[29] What is the worth and merit of Israel's works after she has rejected the messiah? The vision replies with this message:

Know ye, O House of Israel, that a group of new angels that were created in the year 426 [1666] from Israel's acts of penitence are now much grieved, complaining before the divine throne and saying: "Where are the crowns made of the good deeds of Israel which we were wont to bring to God? . . . and now our hands are empty, and but for the few in Israel who vivify us by their faith we would already have ceased to exist. If they too backslide, God forbid, what shall become of us?" While they were still complaining, another group of new angels arrived, bearing in their hands thousands and myriads of good works done by Israel, but when they beheld the first group weeping, they said: "Perhaps all our labor is in vain too?" . . . [Whereupon God sent angels] to bring Our Lord the messianic king Sabbatai Ṣevi . . . to make reply unto them. And God said to him: "Did I not tell thee not to be righteous overmuch? Take this seal wherein are engraved

29. This is also the theme of many of the homilies of the learned kabbalist and Sabbatian believer R. Joseph Ḥamiṣ.

the names of all the children of Israel, . . . and whoever causes pain to these angels, blot him out." Then he said: "Lord of the universe! Why hast thou added the letter *h* [to the name of Abraham, changing his name from Abram to Abraham; see Gen. 17:5]? Is it not in order that all his members may inherit eternal life?[30] And if thou hast had pity on one of Abraham's members, wilt thou not have pity on thousands and myriads of Israel? A scroll of the Law is invalid if one single letter is missing. How then can I blot out so many names of the children of Israel from thy seal, they being like the number of the letters of the Law . . . ?"[31] Then God said unto him: "What wilt thou do with all these weeping angels?". . . and Our Lord too wept with them. . . . Thereupon the patriarchs went to Moses, taking him [Sabbatai Ṣevi] with them and said unto him: "The enemies of Israel [a euphemism for the children of Israel] will perish," . . . [whereupon Moses too interceded; cf. Exod. 31:11–14 and 34:8–9] and God said: "Let iniquity be forgiven in lovingkindness and truth."

The fifth vision is even more explicit. The author evidently does not expect the utter annihilation of the *qelippah* as a result of the extraction of the elements of holiness imprisoned in it, but, on the contrary, anticipates the apotheosis of Sabbatai Ṣevi, who will be exalted above the princes of the seventy nations and mediate between them and God. The emphasis here is on two ideas. In his ultimate manifestation, the messiah, sitting on the throne of God in Jerusalem, will expound all the mysteries of the Torah. There is no hint here of a new messianic Law and nothing is said of the abolition of the commandments. The antinomian elements so characteristic of Nathan's utterances are totally absent.[32] Moreover, those princes of the nations that had persevered in their rebellion, drawing strength from the sin of the unbelievers (who probably were not the heathen denying the unity of God but the Israelites denying the messianic character of Sabbatai Ṣevi) would repent, and all the seventy nations would accept the yoke of his kingdom. Israel will be gathered in Jerusalem and Sabbatai will expound the Torah to both Israel and the

30. The phrasing here is taken from one of the earliest kabbalistic texts, the book *Bahir*.

31. The notion that every letter in the Torah corresponds to one of the "six hundred thousand" souls of Israel is current in Lurianic kabbalah, cf. G. Scholem, *On the Kabbalah and Its Symbolism* (1965), p. 65.

32. Cf. Is. Tishby in *Kiryath Sepher,* XXI (1944), 17.

nations. The messianic mission therefore means salvation for the gentiles too.

It seems evident, therefore, that in 1668 some kind of very definite vision was experienced in Sabbatai's circle. The messiah, despised by most Jews for his apostasy, still beheld himself—or was beheld by others—as highly exalted and sitting either on the throne of God or at His right hand.[33] The latter phrase, however, does not necessarily signify that the messiah is held to be divine. In the fifth chapter, which also contains a commentary on Psalm 19, an explicit warning is sounded in the messianic prayer: "O Lord, my strength and my redeemer (Ps. 19:15)—this means that the messiah enjoins upon the world not to err as the angels erred when[34] they wanted to adore the First Man [because of his Godlikeness], for God is my strength and my redeemer, . . . and He has formed me thus."[35] There is an untranslatable pun here, associating the Hebrew words for "strength" (or "rock") and "form," and our author goes on to say that "God will transform," that is, transfigure, the messiah. However, this transfiguration will take place not in the present world but after the messiah's occultation and ascent to the supernal lights. The polemical intention can hardly be doubted, and is doubly interesting in view of Sabbatai's tendency of toying—though never explicitly—with the idea of his divinity. Moses Pinheiro recounts[36] that during those years Sabbatai used to sign his name *Turco,* but the same Hebrew letters that could be read as "the Turk" could also be read kabbalistically as "the mountain of God." For his wife, he used a similar signature, equally susceptible of an identical esoteric interpretation. Did he mean to imply that the Deity was resting upon him as upon Mount Sinai? Sabbatai had already previously applied to himself the words of the midrash to the effect that the messiah would be called by the name of God, and so had several of his believers. No doubt the midrash could bear an innocuous interpretation as well as a more audaciously

33. The fourth "Testimony" ("Vision") reports a disputation in the presence of God between the souls of Israel and the unbelievers in which reference is made to the messiah sitting at the right hand of the Lord. The image does not necessarily imply Christian influence, since an ancient midrash applies Ps. 110:1 to the messianic king; cf. *Midrash Tehillim* 18 (ed. Buber, fol. 79a).

34. According to rabbinic legend, *Genesis Rabba,* edn. Theodor, p. 63.

35. *Be^cIqvoth Mashiaḥ*, p. 84.

36. *Ap.* Freimann, p. 96. See also Israel Ḥazzan, *ap.* G. Scholem in *Schocken Volume,* p. 169.

radical one, and apparently diverse trends, moderate and extreme, were contending in Adrianople. Israel Ḥazzan's testimony regarding the liturgical practice of the believers in those years is illuminating in this respect: "Every morning and every evening we say: he and no other, he is our God." This confession of faith was probably recited together with the traditional one: "Hear O Israel, the Lord Our God, the Lord is one." This custom, which was established either by Sabbatai Ṣevi himself or by Nathan after he had joined the group of believers in the Balkans, subsequently passed into the prayer book of the Dönmeh.[37] The deification of the messiah thus became a very acute problem.

Sabbatai, exploiting the freedom of movement and of contact which both Turks and Jews granted him, paid several visits to Constantinople where he took counsel with his many faithful believers, headed by Abraham Yakhini.[38] It seems that on these occasions he also established contact with certain Muslim religious groups whose situation in Turkey was similar to his. The Sabbatians were outwardly Muslims, but inwardly were seeking an esoteric and, in a way, concrete Judaism, the precise nature of which was not yet clear to them. Their double-faced existence undoubtedly brought them close to certain dervish orders, like the Bektashi, whose Muslim orthodoxy and loyalty had similarly been suspected throughout their history.[39] They were reputed to be Muslims in outward appearance only, and to practice among themselves libertinism and the "freedom" of children of the spirit. This subject, while of considerable importance in the subsequent history of Sabbatianism, need not concern us at the present stage, but it seems probable enough that Sabbatai somehow found his way to dervish circles. A hundred years ago Dönmeh tradition still knew that Sabbatai was on friendly terms with a Turkish dervish and poet called Nyazi and that he stayed at the latter's monastery during his visits to Constantinople.[40] Although there is a great deal of confusion in the historical traditions of the Dönmeh, there is no reason to doubt this particular detail. Mehemet Nyazi is a historical personality (died 1694) and is known as the head of a dervish order

37. G. Scholem, *loc. cit.*, p. 175; see above, p. 825, n. 11.

38. Yakhini refers to these meetings several times in his autograph MS. *Wawey ha-ᶜAmudim* (MS. Oxford 2761).

39. See John K. Birge, *The Bektashi Order of Dervishes* (London, 1937).

40. See *MGWJ*, XXXIII (1884), 60.

and as the author of mystical poems with a pantheistic flavor. It is not in the least impossible that the two found a common language beyond their respective Jewish and Muslim symbols.

In his commentary on Psalm 143:10, "Teach me to do Thy will; for Thou art my God; Thy spirit is good," Israel Ḥazzan puts the following prayer into the messiah's mouth: "Since I do not as yet know anything of the laws of this religion, therefore I must be taught, . . . for thou art my God, thou and none other. Thy spirit is good, for the way of this nation [the Ishmaelites] is in madness, for they behave madly in the root of the madman [Muhammad], and when they behave madly they bring upon themselves an evil spirit. *But though I am among them I am not of them;* for Thou, O God, Thy spirit is good, but their spirit is evil."[41] This homily seems to suggest that Sabbatai took part in the ecstatic rites of the "mad" dervishes who brought upon themselves an "evil spirit" by means of their dances and invocations of the name of Allah. It is this practice of *dhikr* to which Israel Ḥazzan seems to refer when he applies the words "my throat is dried" (Ps. 69:4) to "them that repeat the name of God so-and-so many times in their prayers according to a number that is known to them."[42]

Sabbatai did not give up his habit of inventing occasional feasts and rituals of his own. According to Israel Ḥazzan, "he once sacrificed a dove, uttering with great devotion 'an offering made by fire, of a sweet savor unto the Lord.' "[43] (He had offered sacrifices twice before—once in Palestine, and again in Constantinople where he sacrificed the Passover Lamb which, according to the Law, must not be offered outside Jerusalem.) Having abolished the rejoicing of the Ninth of Ab in the summer of 1667 (see above, p. 732), he reintroduced this messianic innovation in 1671 when he decreed that all believers should celebrate the festival like the Passover, for a whole week.[44]

41. *Schocken Volume,* p. 182.

42. *Ibid.,* p. 209.

43. *Ibid.,* p. 167.

44. Sabbatai's decree is quoted verbatim in a letter preserved in the Amarillo Collection from the Dönmeh archives; see *Sefunoth,* V (1961), 252. It is also referred to by A. M. Cardozo in an undated letter which he sent from Tripoli to his brother-in-law in Amsterdam (MS. Hamburg 312, fol. 17). Cf. also below, pp. 844 f., for R. Solomon Kohen's letter on the same subject. According to Samuel Gandoor's testimony (see below, p. 883) this celebration was discontinued, on Sabbatai's orders, after 1672.

Attempts by Jewish opponents to persuade the Turkish authorities[45] to take steps against Sabbatai proved unsuccessful. Evidently Sabbatai was still considered a *bona fide* missionary, and the authorities had instructions not to interfere even though he appeared to be guilty of religious innovations that were neither Jewish nor Muslim. This particular celebration, like the three pilgrimage festivals celebrated all in one week in 1658, was not repeated again, but Nathan of Gaza, in a letter to Salonika, found a warrant for "the seven days of the festival of rejoicing" in the *Tiqquney Zohar,* fol. 44 (edn. 1558).[46]

Israel Ḥazzan's commentary on the Psalms preserves some interesting details about Sabbatai's behavior in those years. He continued to sing Spanish *romanzas* ("and the ignorant say that he is singing lewd songs") as well as psalms. Whenever he recited Psalm 118, he would repeat verse 16 ("The right hand of the Lord is exalted") seven times, "and we do likewise, as is befitting." Israel Ḥazzan seems to have observed Sabbatai sunk in kabbalistic meditations: "When AMIRAH practiced solitude with his holy soul, he would unite his soul" to the four supernal worlds of the kabbalistic cosmos, uniting and raising these worlds in the sign of "the son of Jesse liveth" and performing the supreme and holy union in the world of *ʾaṣiluth.* "And I beheld all this. Blessed be the Lord that I was vouchsafed to see his face when he practiced this solitude."[47] Sabbatai always entertained the highest regard for the sultan who, as we know, seems to have had a special liking for him. Israel Ḥazzan knew that "the Grand Turk would enjoy a place of honor before AMIRAH even after the [latter's full] manifestation. . . . and I have heard with my own ears that AMIRAH would not suffer

45. Cardozo, *loc. cit.;* "the kaimakam and the chief of the janissaries," see also the Amarillo Collection (*Sefunoth, loc. cit.*), according to which the cadi and the chief of police (*bustanji bashi*) were called in.

46. See G. Scholem in *Zion,* VII (1942), 188. At the time of the writing of that article, this celebration of 9 Ab was not yet known to me and hence I could not explain Nathan's statement.

47. See *Schocken Volume,* p. 165. Another incident recounted there suggests that Sabbatai and the other apostate believers continued to observe the Jewish laws and practices when they were among themselves, and that Sabbatai expected his followers to inquire about his mystical reasons whenever he acted contrary to traditional Jewish practice. He reprimanded one who failed to question him on a given occasion.

anyone to curse him [that is, the sultan].[48] Another Sabbatian believer, Moses Franco, was told by "the Lady" (*matrona*, probably meaning Sarah) on the authority of Sabbatai himself that the sultan would be rewarded for the kindness shown to Sabbatai by great honor and the *tiqqun* of his soul.[49]

The Adrianople group received considerable reinforcement by Nathan's frequent visits, and they began to prepare for the "second manifestation" of the messiah. This manifestation in power and glory was expected to take place in 1673 or 1674, that is, seven years after the apostasy undertaken for the purpose of "collecting the seed that was sown among the gentiles." The Jewish masses in Adrianople had not yet lost their faith in the messiah[50] and were prepared to trust the rumor that before long the mystical purpose of the apostasy would become fully evident. Meanwhile, the messiah and his prophet should be given the benefit of the doubt. At first "the sect of this man" used to assemble in the house of the wealthy believer Moses Kohen[51] and subsequently in the courtyard of Joseph Karillo, who had not yet donned the turban "in the presence of the Grand Turk" and was highly regarded in the Sabbatian group.[52] Many scholars from among the believers in the various communities visited Sabbatai during those years. R. Meir Rofe from Hebron later gave a considerably toned-down report on the events which will be described below (pp. 846 ff.), and before the decisive document was discovered, his account could be read in a rather idyllic way. He came with three scholars from Brussa, "and they and other great scholars sat with AMIRAH in the presence of the Grand Turk. Finally Sabbatai told them that God was like unto a glorious youth that resembled him." Meir Rofe left

48. *Ibid.*, p. 168.

49. MS. Günzburg 517, fol. 80b.

50. Sasportas, pp. 206–7.

51. See above, p. 732. He is probably not identical with Samuel Primo's son-in-law, the author of the rabbinic work *Kehunath ᶜOlam.* It is unlikely that the latter was already sufficiently old in 1667, and there is no basis for the identification proposed by Rosanes (IV, p. 238).

52. See below, p. 847. Cf. also the account of the visit of the proselyte astrologer to Sabbatai Ṣevi (quoted by G. Scholem, in *Schocken Volume,* p. 166, from a MS. by Israel Ḥazzan): "when our holy company met, together with R. Nathan, in the city of Adrianople, in the courtyard of R. Joseph Karillo."

it all very vague and did not unduly emphasize the fact that some of the most famous apostasies took place on these occasions.[53] From Israel Ḥazzan's testimony we learn that some of these apostasies took place at Sabbatai's express demand during his moments of illumination, when Sabbatai Ṣevi was like a snake, "hitting out at anyone who came his way. And that is why Rabbi Nathan warned us to keep away from AMIRAH as much as possible during his illuminations, for at such moments he wants all present to embrace the religion of Ishmael."[54] Of course the Sabbatian sources do not permit us to judge in what ways the Turkish authorities in Adrianople used gatherings of the believers for their own propaganda aims, and to what extent the psychological processes and behavior of the celebrated apostate suited their own purposes. The mystical atmosphere with all its lights and twilights as described by Israel Ḥazzan is surely only one half of the picture, and there is no way of knowing the nonmystical and more down-to-earth considerations of the Turkish authorities.

We have spoken of Israel Ḥazzan's testimony. But we have a more authoritative witness: Sabbatai Ṣevi himself. In one of Nathan's letters to Kastoria he included a circular letter written by the messiah in one of his more aggressive moods. The letter, written in a mixture of Spanish and Hebrew, shows Sabbatai in his most forbidding manner.[55] He lashes out at the old, traditional Judaism and defends the new ways of Islam which he now embraces with an astonishing enthusiasm—although, to be sure, this too did not last. He writes:

Know ye my brethren, my children, and my friends that I recognized with great clarity that the True [God] whom I alone know for many generations and for whom I have done so much, has willed that I should enter with all my heart into the Islamic religion [*din islam*], the religion of Ishmael, to permit what it permits, and to forbid what it forbids, and to nullify the Torah of Moses until the time of the End. For this is important for the glory of His Godhead and for His revelation that I should induct herein everyone whose soul would agree with me [to

53. Cf. Cardozo's homily *ap.* A. H. Weiss, *Beth ha-Midrash* (1865), p. 65, where mention is also made of Karillo's later apostasy in the presence of the sultan. Cardozo evidently received this report from Meir Rofe when they met in Leghorn in the spring of 1675.

54. *Schocken Volume,* p. 163. This is confirmed by the events told in Najara's chronicle, see n. 72.

55. The letter was published in *Sefunoth,* V (1961), 266–67.

do so] after I would reveal to them the [Mystery of] His Godhead, which is [capable of being] demonstrated with utmost stringency; that is, the supreme rank of His true being and the wondrous glory of the Cause of All Causes. And this is what the psalm says [Ps. 119:126]: [When] it is time to work for God, they nullify Thy Torah,[56] as the Ishmaelites used to say: The Torah of Moses is nullified, as is also esoterically implied in the Talmudic saying [where God is reported to have said to Moses]: May thy strength increase because you broke the tablets of the Covenant.[57] [And this is so] because the Torah of Moses without [the knowledge of] the True One is worth nothing as it is said [II Chron. 15:3]: For a long time Israel is [to be] without the True God and without Torah. Since they do not have the True God, his [Moses'] Torah is no Torah. But *Din Islam ḥaqq ḥaqq* [the religion of Islam is the very Truth].[58] . . . And when Maimonides of blessed memory was formulating the dogma "The Law God gave he never will amend/Nor ever by another Law replace,"[59] he was completely mistaken because he did not know the God of Truth, who is the God of Sabbatai Ṣevi. And do not believe, my brethren, that I did this [becoming a Muslim] on the strength of an illumination so that you become terrified and say: today or tomorrow the illumination will depart from him and he will regret what he had said and will be very sorry for it. This is not so, but I did this on my own, through the great power and strength of the Truth and Faith which no wind in the world and no sages and prophets can cause me to leave my place. . . . Thus speaks the master of Truth and Faith, the Turco and the Meṣurman.

The curious signature *Meṣurman* obviously means one who has become "Egyptianized," that is, brought into the sphere of Miṣrayim, Egypt, which is a symbol for the power and realm of the *qelippah,* the power of evil. Sabbatai likes to play with associations connected with the word "Miṣrayim," such as *meṣrey yam,* "the straits of the sea." He is "in straits," he has become a Turk and an "Egyptian"

56. This audacious explanation of the verse—whose literal sense is a complaint to God that His foes have voided the Law—is already found several times in the Talmud.

57. This is a Talmudic quotation, B. Shabbath 87a.

58. Probably a popular sentence which Sabbatai learned from his Muslim teachers.

59. Sabbatai does not quote the actual formulation by Maimonides but that used in the later poem *Yigdal,* which forms part of the daily services.

for the sake of his mission. We learn here too that people who knew him spoke about his lack of stability of mind and doubted the validity of the acts he committed in the state of illumination.

There is no definite way to determine the date the letter was written, but the context would point to a date before 1670, perhaps about 1668–69. Nathan tells his correspondent that he has written a long letter to Primo explaining the foregoing radical rhetoric which he encloses—but the enclosure has not been preserved. He has added, however, another paragraph telling of a meeting with Sabbatai and of his [Nathan's] hope that Sabbatai may soon reveal the Glory of the Godhead no longer to the few elect only, but to a gathering of the chosen people. He then adds, apparently in continuing his report about the sequence of events, that people had maligned him, whereupon Sabbatai wrote him a letter of bitter remonstrance, dated in the week of October 20–25, 1669, copied by Nathan.[60] Here Sabbatai ordered him and his friend Samuel Gandoor to come to see him. He accuses Nathan of being the cause of his "desecration" (in the eyes of the world?) and of not having correctly understood the Mystery of the Godhead which he would be expounding to him now. He launches into innuendoes about Nathan's literary activity, which are not easily understood, but which appear to express great dissatisfaction with Nathan's kabbalistic writings. "I will pluck the prey, the unripe fig, out of your teeth as you have treaspassed on my ban and have stolen and eaten and have made others eat in your wake, and have clothed yourself in seemingly refined garb which in truth are nothing but rags, and you have done evil to yourself and an injury to my soul."[61] These words suggest much bitterness and dissatisfaction on Sabbatai's part and can be explained only as a protest against Nathan's teachings and writings which were already disseminated among believers. This is remarkable enough in itself, but is confirmed by the astounding but well-authenticated fact that Nathan was not admitted to Sabbatai's later esoteric teachings about the "Mystery of the Godhead," until after he already had composed most of his treatises and tracts.[62] This helps us in understanding the acrimonious

60. There is of course a possibility that the year 5430 mentioned in the copy preserved may have been corrupted and that the letter may belong to a later period, between 1670–72.

61. Cf. *Sefunoth,* V (1961), 268.

62. Cf. the evidence from Cardozo and Ch. Malᶜakh quoted by G. Scholem, *Zion,* XI (1946), 173.

tone of Sabbatai's letter, written by a man who was himself unable to develop his intuitions in a well-reasoned context and to express them in literary fashion according to his own standards. It reveals an ambiguity of feeling toward his prophet which, without the knowledge of this document, we would scarcely have expected.

Exactly how Nathan reacted to such vilification by his master and king is not known, but a long letter of his, a copy of which has been preserved in the Dönmeh archives, gives us a glimpse into his attitude, which was one of complete subservience and submission.[63] Sent to Sabbatai and spread among the believers, it is couched in the most solemn and ceremonial style of rabbinical rhymed prose. Its untranslatable biblical and kabbalistic allusions combine in a most artful way an evocation of the thirty-two "intelligible lights" which, according to classical texts of the kabbalah, emanated from the divine Sophia, with the biblical phrases describing the progress of creation in Genesis, chapter 1. All said and done, it amounts to a declaration of Nathan's absolute and unshakable acceptance of Sabbatai's messiahship and supreme authority. Whether, in fact, it was written as an answer to the aforementioned letter of reprobation, which is quite possible, or was written on some later occasion between 1670–75 is impossible to say. At any rate, friendly relations continued after all between the messiah and his prophet.

There can be little doubt of the fascination that still radiated from the "scorned man" (as Cardozo called him) in Adrianople. He continued to attract a multitude of visitors, some of whom came in order to test him, while others desired to enjoy the beatific vision of the messiah's countenance. A valuable description of such a visit has been preserved in a letter which a rabbi from Volhynia, Solomon Kohen, sent on August 11, 1672, to his brother after his return from Adrianople to Poland in the spring of that year. The author had been a rabbinic judge (*dayyan*) in Budapest for more than twelve years, but had left his office in order to "see the face of Our Lord" in Adrianople.[64] The letter, of which several copies are extant, seems

63. MS. Ben-Zvi Institute 2262, pp. 247–51.

64. According to Rosanes (IV, p. 143) there was a case of Sabbatian apostasy in Budapest: the president of the "Holy Brotherhood" (in charge of burials), a certain Jacob b. Mordecai, became a Muslim in order to speed the coming of redemption, but soon recognized his error and returned to the fold. Rosanes based himself on the collection of responsa *Shaʿar Ephraim* by Ephraim Kohen of

to have circulated widely among Sabbatian believers, especially in Italy, and is also quoted by Baruch of Arezzo.[65] The enthusiastic description seems to reflect the high-pitched atmosphere in Adrianople at the time, and it supplements and confirms Israel Ḥazzan's account:

Thanks be to God that I was vouchsafed there [in Adrianople] to be with the messiah of our righteousness and with the true prophet R. Nathan and with other leading scholars who are still with Our Lord. And I beheld the face of the king in his shining radiance on the great festival of the Ninth of Ab until the Seventeenth of the month [July 16–24, 1671).[66] There we beheld the most awe-inspiring things. . . . For all his deeds are true, and he is without any doubt the true redeemer; we were with him continuously day and night for more than eight weeks. I can testify that when the great light is upon him he has no regular sleep, though he occasionally dozes, and his face shines with a great light. . . . I was also vouchsafed to pray with him several times. And now we hope that soon all things will become clear and evident, and the hidden things will become manifest and they who use their tongue against the righteous will be put to shame, as has happened recently that they made a treacherous plot and spent much money to deliver him to the authorities, [but in the end] they fell down before him with prayers and supplications. . . . "and the righteous shall live by his

---

Vilna, responsum no. 121 (*lege* 122). R. Ephraim Kohen was rabbi of Budapest. But a careful reading of the responsum shows that the case has no connection with the Sabbatian movement. Jacob b. Mordecai apostatized not because of any Sabbatian beliefs, but because he was threatened with cruel tortures (see edn. Lemberg [1887], fol. 78a). On the other hand R. Elisha Ashkenazi, the father of the prophet Nathan, mentions an elder of the congregation in Budapest who was a believer but not an apostate. Elisha Ashkenazi lived for some time after 1667 in Budapest and in Vienna. The above detail is quoted from one of R. Elisha's letters by D. Kaufmann, *Die letzte Vertreibung der Juden aus Wien* (1889), p. 91, These letters were in the possession of a Jewish family in Italy.

65. *Ap.* Freimann, pp. 65–66. The fragment published by Carpi in *Toledoth Shabbetai Ṣevi* (1879), pp. 18–19, is from the same letter. Another copy is extant in MS. Jerusalem 1466, 8°. This MS. was written in Italy in the circle of R. Benjamin Kohen of Reggio, and Solomon Kohen's letter is said there (fol. 114b) to have been brought by the Polish Sabbatian R. Leyb Ziwitover, who had also been to Adrianople.

66. He thus saw Sabbatai in a state of illumination for about ten days. This illumination apparently coincided with the seven-day festival that Sabbatai commanded on all his followers; see above, p. 837, and below, p. 860.

faith."[67] And the blasphemers greatly repented, for they realized that the matter would come to pass very soon and his glory become manifest over all the earth and the eyes of all Israel would behold it. In the synagogue of Our Lord I saw awe-inspiring things which no mouth can utter nor pen write down.[68] I also spoke to the brother of our messiah, a very learned and extremely wealthy man who is several years older than Our Lord, and he told me all that had happened to his brother from his childhood to this very day, and I wrote down everything.[69] . . . I was also privileged to preach in the great Portuguese Synagogue in Adrianople in the presence of R. Nathan and other scholars (who were there with the consent of Our Lord), and later Our Lord himself came because no service was held at Our Lord's because of this sermon for which all came to the Portuguese Synagogue. I also spoke to the heart of the unbelievers. And the learned Dinan [that is, R. Jacob Danon], the principal unbeliever who was present in the synagogue, was perforce afraid of Our Lord because he now repented but did not dare show it to the world, having been the chief blasphemer against God and His anointed. . . . for all those that had sought his undoing had died, and Our Lord was waxing stronger every day, for it was manifest to all the Turks that he was the messiah. . . . My dearly beloved brother, whom I know to be God-fearing, pray fervently that thou mayest share the faith in Our Lord and merit the great goodness [which God has reserved for those that fear him; cf. Ps. 31:20], for the faith in this matter is greater than the whole Torah. . . . this our King and Lord is the true messiah. . . .

The visit to which this letter refers apparently took place in 1671, and its historical and psychological value can hardly be overestimated. The writer was a Polish Talmudist and a member of the rabbinic court of which R. Ephraim Kohen, the author of *Shaᶜarey Ephraim* and one of the leading scholars of his age, was president. But even to this pious and upright scholar it seemed perfectly ac-

67. Hab. 2:4; the initials of the three Hebrew words form the acrostic "ṣevi." The events alluded are those described below, pp. 846 ff.

68. This probably refers to the messiah's "strange actions" during his illuminations or possibly to some of the actions of the congregation of the believers, such as the apostasies recorded in the following pages.

69. Solomon Kohen's was thus the first biographical account of Sabbatai Ṣevi written by a Jew, antedating Baruch of Arezzo's by several years. It has not been preserved for us.

ceptable that "the faith in this matter is greater than the whole Torah." These words were written not in a sudden upsurge of mass hysteria as occurred in 1667 just before Sabbatai's apostasy, but several years later. The letter is a moving testimony to the profound crisis which the messianic movement could precipitate in the soul of a scholarly rabbi. The messianic "faith" was becoming increasingly paradoxical, and those who succumbed to the paradox were not necessarily aware of it.

Full evidence regarding the atmosphere prevailing among the believers in Adrianople as well as Sabbatai's own double-faced behavior (and more especially his efforts to persuade his followers to apostatize) can be found in the chronicle of R. Jacob Najara's visit to the messiah, one of the most extraordinary documents shedding light on Sabbatai's personality. The chronicle is contained in a manuscript from the Dönmeh archives which has recently come to light.[70] Jacob Najara, the rabbi of Gaza, and a colleague from Jerusalem were traveling to Morocco (either on a specifically Sabbatian mission or on behalf of the Jewish communities in the Holy Land), and in the summer of 1672 both were in Tetuán with their Sabbatian faith still unshaken (Freimann, p. 98). On their way to Morocco they passed through Adrianople where they spent several months in 1671, perhaps even a whole year. The chronicle opens with an interesting account of a dream in which Sabbatai, "who had been without illumination for a year and two months," saw himself falling into a deep pit. When he looked up he saw his father and mother standing above and throwing him a rope on which he climbed out of the pit. The chronicle dates this dream, which clearly marks the beginning of a new phase of illumination, on the Seventeenth of Shebat, that is, January 28, 1671. Similarly Nathan, in 1672, refers to the Eighteenth of Shebat as the day of the renewal of Sabbatai's illumination.[71] Throughout 1670, Sabbatai was, therefore, in a normal phase.

70. *Sefunoth,* V (1961), 254–62; cf. also above n. 44. The details given in the chronicle supplement what has been said above about Sabbatai's behavior and contacts, as well as Israel Ḥazzan's testimony regarding Sabbatai's pressure on his followers to apostatize when he was in a state of illumination. The title of the document is "A Chronicle of what came to pass here, in Adrianople, from the day the distinguished scholar R. Jacob Najara arrived."

71. In a letter contained in the same MS.; see *Sefunoth,* V (1961), 263–65. The letter supplements the chronicle in many details.

During Najara's first audience with Sabbatai, the latter explained that most Jews—or at least the elect among the true believers—would have to take the turban. On the day preceding the feast of Purim, Sabbatai, accompanied by "four of Vani Effendi's men" visited his brother, urging him to apostatize immediately and assuring him that never before in all his life had he experienced so powerful an illumination. Sabbatai's brother, together with the brother's son, thereupon went to Vani Effendi's residence where "they took the turban." On the day of Purim, Sabbatai celebrated the festival at the house of Joseph Karillo with the traditional liturgical reading of the Scroll of Esther and banquet. On the next day Sabbatai rode about town on horseback, and on the following Sabbath he held Jewish services both in a private home and in the Portuguese Synagogue. These services were conducted with a great deal of noise and publicity so that the Turks, including some janissaries, could hear them, "but nobody dared open his mouth." In the evening Sabbatai assembled a number of followers who were ready to aspostatize, and on the next morning he brought them—twelve men and five women—to the imperial council chamber where they took the turban. The sultan, who had watched the proceedings from his *kafes* offered the new converts a pension (*ulufé*), but Sabbatai indignantly declared that his followers embraced Islam as a matter of faith alone and that he would not permit anything that might suggest or encourage unworthy motives.

A week later a Jew arriving from Ipsola was promptly persuaded to take the turban, and was told to bring his co-religionists from Ipsola to Adrianople for the same purpose. On the following Sabbath, the messiah appeared with all his apostate followers in the synagogue, silenced the congregation, and led the prayer service himself. Before the reading of the Law he preached a long sermon in which he asserted that the many contradictions in Scripture and rabbinic literature could only be satisfactorily explained in terms of his messianic mysteries. At the end of the sermon he produced a copy of the Quran from which he read some passages (see above, p. 823). A few days later, on the Fourth of Nisan, he dictated letters announcing a general convocation of the leading scholars among his followers in order to persuade them to apostatize at a disputation to be held in the presence of the sultan. In fact, he had as much as said to Vani Effendi that he alone possessed the true Mystery of the Godhead, but that he could divulge this mystery only when all the Jewish scholars whom he had invited were assembled. He also indicated to the sultan and to Vani Effendi that—like a true prophet—he could not predict the outcome of such disputations, as everything depended on the measure of the spirit and illumination that he would be granted from above. For like the true prophets of olden times, "and as was the case with Jesus according to their books," he too was at times inspired and at times not. The letters of convocation were, in the end, sent only to Constantinople, Sofia, and Brussa, and a number of leading believers from these cities repaired to Adrianople. Among them there was R. Meir Rofe of Hebron who was then staying in Constantinople and, some years later, told Cardozo about the meeting. Some of the rabbis were prevented from coming by official business with the Turkish government, among them R. Moses Alfandari and R. Aaron ibn Ḥayyim, of whose connection with the movement after the apostasy no other testimony has come down to us. Originally an invitation to Nathan, who at the time was in Iznemed (Nicomedia), had been planned but was canceled; we do not know why.

On the Fifth of Nisan (March 6, 1671), Sabbatai divorced his wife Sarah, whom he had married seven years earlier (see above, pp. 192), justifying his action by a scriptural proof-text: "six years he [the Hebrew slave!] shall serve and in the seventh he shall go out free" (Exod. 21:2). Sarah, however, did not want to part with the four-year-old boy Ishmael (see above, p. 826). In fact, under Muslim law she was entitled to keep the child until his seventh year, but Vani Effendi persuaded her to send the boy to his father. The arrival of the boy on the Seventh of Nisan was promptly given a mystical interpretation by his father, who also announced that he would circumcise him on the following day so that Scripture should be fulfilled: "three years shall it be as uncircumcised unto you. And in the fourth year all the fruit thereof shall be holy" (Lev. 19:23–24). When Sabbatai sent out the invitations on the Eighth of Nisan, the Turkish notables very naturally assumed that the ceremony would take place on the following day (the Ninth of Nisan, according to the Jewish calendar), but Sabbatai performed the rite on the same day (the Eighth) with Joseph Karillo acting as godfather (*sandaq*). The ceremony took place strictly according to the Jewish rite, though not without some of Sabbatai's characteristic ritual innovations. At the ceremony the boy was given the name Israel, while the ten-year-old son of one of Sabbatai's apostate followers who was circumcised on the same occasion was given the name Ishmael. This contradicts the earlier reports about the circumcision (see p. 826). On the following Sabbath, Sabbatai solemnly read from his Bible Leviticus, chapter 14, beginning with the words "This shall be the law of the leper in the day of his cleansing" (referring, no doubt, to his separation from his impure wife), and Exodus, chapters 19–20 (indicating that the occasion was as significant as the great theophany and the giving of the Ten Commandments on Mount Sinai). The service and the subsequent banquet were held with the windows open for all the Turks to hear. Sabbatai ordered those of his followers who had apostatized to recite aloud the *ᶜalenu* prayer (which contains some derogatory references to other religions that "bow down to vanity and hollowness, and pray to a god that saveth not"), but would not permit them to participate at the subsequent banquet. In the evening he again held a traditional Jewish evening service and then rode about town, accompanied by thirty of his apostate followers and carrying in his hand a copy of the Zohar. On the First of Iyyar (April 11), Sabbatai persuaded several believers from Ipsola to become Muslims.

At this point there is a lacuna in the Najara chronicle, which resumes with an account of the disputation held by Sabbatai with the rabbis whom he had summoned. The proceedings, described in much ceremonial detail, began in the imperial audience hall (the *bash oda*) and in the presence of the sultan, who was seated on his throne (*takht*); Vani Effendi; and other dignitaries. Vani Effendi asked the rabbis (in Arabic) why they had come, and they replied that Sabbatai was highly esteemed among them but that they could not understand his conversion to Islam. Since he had taken the trouble to summon them, they would argue the matter with him and—if convinced by his arguments—would follow his example. Sabbatai and the rest of the company thereupon repaired from the *bash oda* to the Divan, while the sultan retired to the *kafes* (a latticed alcove) from where he could watch the disputation held in Spanish, which soon degenerated into a vociferous debate "as in a Talmudic school." When the palace officials suggested that Elijah Ṣevi request his brother to conduct the discussion in a quieter and more dignified manner in deference to the sultan, who was watching from his *kafes*, Sabbatai exclaimed in Turkish: "Litigants shout in this Divan about a few pennies, so why should I not shout when it is a matter of the words of the living God." In the end he asked each one separately whether he was willing to embrace Islam but all refused and only Abraham Gamaliel from Constantinople and Joseph Karillo apostatized. According to the chronicle, the sultan had given orders to his *jalat* (executioner) to put to death those who would not embrace Islam, but when he heard Sabbatai reassure his audience that there would be no coercion or duress whatever, and that only those ought to take the turban who did so of their own free will, he recalled the *jalat*. Sabbatai apologized to the sultan for the meager result by reminding him that the Jews were a stiff-necked people, and presented to him the two new converts. Sabbatai next wrote a letter to Sofia, summoning Samuel Primo, Aaron Majar, and ten others to Adrianople. He had previously called Najara and canceled the honorary titles of the "Ten Tribes" appointed in Gaza because they no longer represented the new order of things beginning now. Apparently he wanted to appoint new representatives, this time from Sofia where his followers still had the upper hand. On the following day, in high spirits, he renewed his order to Nathan to come and see him. As it happened Nathan had decided of his own accord to visit the messiah, arriving in Adrianople on the Nineteenth of Sivan (May 18) together with Samuel Gandoor and another companion. Before, however, setting out from Rodosto to Adrianople, Nathan had written to Sabbatai, imploring the latter not to demand of him to apostatize. Nathan clearly knew what Sabbatai was wont to impose on his visitors and he was afraid of it.[72]

By the time Nathan arrived in Adrianople, Sabbatai had lapsed again into a despondent mood which lasted until the day of his betrothal to his new wife, the daughter of R. Aaron Majar of Sofia. The Najara chronicle dates the renewal of the illumination on the Twenty-fifth of Sivan (May 24, 1671), the day of the "consummation of the blessed match." The latter expression, however, seems to be a mere figure of speech, and what actually happened was that a marriage agreement was entered into by Sabbatai and Aaron Majar. Nathan's letter of the winter of 1672 to Shemayah de Mayo[73] discusses Sabbatai's divorce and this match in some detail. The new documents throw, for the first time, some light on the state of Sabbatai's marriage, at least after the apostasy. He saw himself as a Hebrew slave who had suffered under Sarah for seven years and considered her a bad

72. See above, p. 840. 73. *Sefunoth,* V (1961), 263–65.

wife who (in a Jewish proverb) is like "leprosy to her husband." Nathan, no great admirer of hers from the start, says that "the poison of the old serpent prevailed in her and she was constantly picking quarrels with him and sought to persecute him with all her might. She tried twice to put poison in his food, and though no harm came to him, she persisted in her insolence, and this was the real reason for the divorce." (In all other sources this episode is always glossed over or alluded to in such enigmatic terms that nobody would have so much as expected it.) On the other hand, Nathan himself told in the same letter that by the end of 1671 Sarah had borne a daughter to Sabbatai. The decision to divorce her must therefore have been made a short time after she had conceived. Now Sabbatai announced his intention of marrying again the daughter of a Jew and not a Turkish woman. His new wife should not formally convert to Islam, though she should dress like a Muslim woman and play the role of an Esther to Ahasuerus (that is, Sabbatai). On hearing of the messiah's intentions, Aaron Majar offered his daughter, but by the time he arrived in Adrianople, Sabbatai was again in a depression and unwilling to talk about a new match. Only after the renewal of his illumination was the new match contracted. Aaron Majar's daughter (who remained in Sofia) was therefore technically Sabbatai's betrothed. The marriage was never consummated, since the girl died in Sofia before she could join Sabbatai in Dulcigno (also, Ulcinj; see below, p. 885). The real reason for the postponement was another one of Sabbatai's impulsive and unpredictable actions. Nathan reports in his letter that soon afterward Sabbatai's illumination ceased again, and that at such times he would hardly remember, let alone understand, what he had done during his manic phases. He had mercy on his divorced wife and "against the advice of all his friends"—as he pointedly says—took her back, whereupon his illumination returned to him. Nevertheless, he did not give up the idea of consummating, at a later date, the marriage with the daughter of Aaron Majar. At any rate a betrothal was contracted on the Twenty-fifth of Sivan, and Sabbatai, who was in a state of illumination, summoned his visitors who had come to Adrianople, "and we beheld him in his beauty and strength, and we all fanned him with a fan in the manner of slaves to their master."[74] Najara gives a most punctilious description of this occasion and Sabbatai's behavior.

74. *Ibid.*, p. 261.

That this peculiar state of mind persisted in Adrianople until the time of Sabbatai's last journey to Constantinople is attested to by an equally revealing document covering the month of February, 1672. This is a letter to Samuel Primo written by an anonymous scholar belonging to the inner circle.[75] He had been with Sabbatai in Gallipoli. Where he was in the interim years is not clear. Now he has come from Smyrna and describes his experiences with Sabbatai between February 4 and March 6, 1672. They are in line with events described by Najara: a constant alternation of manic and depressive states, full of bizarre and provocative demeanor. The writer feels himself "in the garden of Eden" when he is vouchsafed to observe the gradual growth of Sabbatai's "light" and his "complete reversal from the holy side" on the Sabbath—meaning, no doubt, the performance of holy transgressions. But on this very occasion he refuses "to speak anything but the holy tongue, and this too only for the most urgent purposes." Sabbatai goes to a known Dervish convent[76] and later to

75. The letter was copied about 1815 by Abraham Khalfon in Tripoli, Libya, and incorporated in his chronicle *Ma^c^aseh Ṣaddiqim*, MS. Ben-Zvi Institute in Jerusalem, §132. He had before him a collection of Sabbatian material, written in a copybook, which because of its worn condition and blurred script he could not completely transcribe. But the present letter contains only minor lacunae or misreadings. The year 1672 is not expressly mentioned but it can be fixed by the context and one of the dates, showing that the events took place in a leap year. This, combined with the other data, leaves only the Jewish year 5432 (1672). The writer mentions that R. Jacob Ludai was still in Adrianople but the misreading can be easily corrected in Ludri[k], denoting one of the rabbis from Brussa who were summoned by Sabbatai in April, 1671: Jacob Ludrik, Moses Yafeh, and Isaac Sardina (cf. *Sefunoth*, III–IV [1960], 166). He also mentions his sitting with R. Jacob Marga and R. Jacob Ashkenazi discussing at length the proofs for Sabbatai's messiahship from biblical and kabbalistic literature. The name Marga, otherwise unknown, may be explained as a misreading instead of Nagra (= Najara).

76. The letter says: "he went to a place called Izurilak." This is obviously a misspelling (or misreading) of Hizirlik, which—as I am kindly told by Prof. Norman Itzkowitz of Princeton University—is a hilltop northwest of Adrianople. There was a *tekke* (dervish convent) there which was closed by the authorities in 1641–42 when some people complained that it had given refuge to ungodly people. Mehemed IV erected a pavillion there and the place was reopened as a *zariye* (retreat); cf. M. Tayyib Gökbilgin, "The Founders of the City of Edirne" (Turkish), in the *Jubilee Volume Edirne Edirnenin 600* (ed. Fethi Hildönümü [Ankara, 1965]). This is, then additional proof of Sabbatai's close relations with dervish circles. I have been unable to find out whether the place was a Bektashi retreat or not.

the serail, accompanied by the mollah Mustafa and two or three of the rabbis—among them the apostate Moses Harari who later returned to Judaism—and behaves in an odd way, but the guards who reprimand him do not touch him, being soothed by a bagshish of ten tomans. In the serail he behaved publicly in a Jewish manner, "according to Mosaic Law," sat himself on the chair of the Great Vizier and recited from the Hebrew Bible. The writer says he felt constrained to pronounce the benediction prescribed for extraordinary events. In the state of illumination which often goes on for six days, "all creatures appear to him as many flies," but "when God hides Himself from Our Lord, he thinks nothing at all of his rank" and refuses to go out "in order not to see the Jews, low and high alike." He celebrates Purim in high spirits in the Jewish manner, and also sometime later he goes with his brother Elijah, Benjamin Rijwan, and Abraham Alsheikh to the house of a high official, Ali Pasha, with whom he seems to have had friendly relations. There he gives a banquet for which kosher food and wine are brought by the writer and others from the house of R. Moses Kohen, his steadfast follower. It seems that preparations had been made for Sabbatai to go to Constantinople with Benjamin Rijwan—which may point to his being one of the chief apostates—but he did not feel strong enough and the trip was canceled. (It took place four months later.) The writer tells of his being with Sabbatai three hours each day, listening to his prayers and to his talk concerning the "Mystery of the Godhead" and the "God of Sabbatai Ṣevi." The writer does not say whether he himself was called upon to convert to Islam, and probably he, like so many others, remained Jewish. But he tells that on March 3, 1672 (Fourth of Adar *sheni*), Sabbatai "turned completely to the law of *ḥesed,*" that is Islam. The meaning of the remark can be only this: instead of playing a double role he becomes, at least for some time, a devout Muslim who again engages in active missionary work and becomes a defender of Islam, as he had already done some years before when he wrote the circular letter quoted above (p. 840). This explains his later behavior in Constantinople. The writer transmits two sayings of Sabbatai on this occasion: "He said to us: do not worry about this, for this is the will of God and I have to carry out His order. And they [Sabbatai's group] responded by saying: Haven't you told us many times 'I raised and I abased; I abased and I raised'? At the eve and exit of the Sabbath I ate with him in his house, and since yesterday the illumination returned to him anew. I am praying to

God that this joy may manifest itself in the face of the sun, for he said to me: 'I have no satisfaction from anything, and I am not going to forsake the law of *ḥesed* [Islam], for through it there will be my redemption in the face of the sun.' "

These chronicles and letters combine with other testimonies (such as Israel Ḥazzan's) to convey a vivid impression not only of the actual events, but also of the mental universe of the Sabbatian believers. Also R. David Yiṣḥaki, who was subsequently to become president of the rabbinic court in Jerusalem, was still a staunch believer at that time.[77] Like Samuel Primo and Nathan of Gaza, David Yiṣḥaki had left Palestine sometime in 1666 or 1667. He stayed for a while in Adrianople where he learned the "Mystery of the Faith" from Sabbatai's own mouth. When he and R. Benjamin Rijwan were accused of wavering in their faith, they addressed an apology to Sabbatai who sent them a gracious reply,[78] promising them that the salvation of God would soon be made manifest by "His servant whose name is the same as that of his master." Sabbatai's letter is signed: "Thus speaketh your brother in the truth [this is a pun, since the Hebrew word *me'emeth* can also be pronounced to sound like "Mehemed" or "Me'emed"] of the faith of the Lord, the God of Truth, this gate of the Lord into which the righteous shall enter." In other words: Mehemed Sabbatai Ṣevi is the gate of the Lord (cf. Ps. 118:20) and the guarantor of the true faith.

R. David Yiṣḥaki was not the only rabbi from Jerusalem whose faith withstood the crisis of the apostasy. A curious and partly undecipherable cryptograph letter sent to the believers in Jerusalem, Safed, and Hebron in 1669 shows that the "faith" was still alive there even in scholarly rabbinic circles.[79] The letter was probably written in

77. On the part he played in the movement in 1666, see above, p. 245. I have collected the fragmentary testimonies and references in *Zion,* VI (1941), 87–89, and XIII (1948), 59–62.

78. Quoted by Baruch of Arezzo, *ap.* Freimann, p. 64. On Benjamin Rijwan see G. Scholem in *Zion,* VI (1941), 89, and in *Schocken Volume,* p. 166. Benjamin Rejwan was the only person to have seen the physical marks of Sabbatai's messiahship when he once (and quite exceptionally) accompanied the messiah to the bath. As a rule nobody was allowed to accompany Sabbatai to the bath, in accordance with the Talmudic rule that no one may look at the king taking his bath (see B. Sanhedrin 22a).

79. I have published the document in *Zion,* X (1945), 144–45; cf. also

Adrianople, and much of its contents (for example, the reference to an old rabbinic judge in Jerusalem who would become a prophet before his death) defies attempts at interpretation; yet it may serve as evidence of the fact that even two years after the apostasy there still were believers among the rabbis in Jerusalem and that they were in contact with their colleagues in the Balkans.

The existence of a Sabbatian group in Jerusalem in 1669 is also confirmed by the interesting and controversial liturgical work *Ḥemdath Yamim.*[80] In the present context it is the liturgy prescribed for the "minor day of atonement" (that is, the day preceding the beginning of a new month) which is of interest, since this order of service is nothing but a Sabbatian liturgy. It contains a long prayer which the author and the members of his circle apparently used to say at the tombs of the holy men buried in Jerusalem, and hence the Jerusalemite origin of the prayer seems beyond doubt. On the other hand, it is evident that the liturgy originated in Sabbatian circles soon after the apostasy. One of the prayers states that "we are prisoners in captivity 1,601 years since the destruction of our Temple," which, according to traditional chronology, would yield the year 1669. In one prayer, the messiah, who has gone out to save the holy sparks that have fallen into the abyss of the *qelippah*, is apostrophized in the following words:

Arise messianic king, and behold the congregation of the Lord like unto a flock without a shepherd.

---

my remarks, *ibid.*, p. 143. M. Benayahu has tried to interpret the letter as having been written by David Yiṣḥaki, who was then in Egypt; cf. his remarks in *Studies in Mysticism and Religion in Honor of G. Scholem* (1970), Hebrew part, pp. 41–45.

80. It is unnecessary to summarize here the discussions regarding this work and its Sabbatian character. The most recent phase of the controversy, in which A. Yaᶜari, Is. Tishby and G. Scholem have taken part, has succeeded in establishing that the book cannot have been composed in the 17th century. It was written neither by Nathan of Gaza (as alleged by Jacob Emden) nor by Benjamin ha-Levi (as maintained by Yaᶜari). For the purpose of our present argument only the section giving the liturgy for the day preceding the new moon (*Rosh Ḥodesh*) is relevant, as this particular liturgy (edn. Venice [1763], pt. II, fols. 3–14) is clearly based on Sabbatian doctrines as current during the first years after the apostasy. For literature on the controversy regarding *Ḥemdath Yamim* see *SS*, I, p. 727, n. 1.

The prayer is couched in biblical terminology taken mainly from Psalm 89 and from Isaiah, chapter 53. The messiah is bidden to implore his heavenly father:

How long wilt Thou cast off and abhor, wilt Thou be wroth with Thine anointed, wilt Thou make void the covenant of Thy servant, profane his crown by casting it to the ground . . . so that all that pass by the way spoil him and he is a reproach to his neighbors? [How long] wilt Thou set up the right hand of his adversaries, make his enemies rejoice . . . and cast his throne down to the ground? I am today a man of sorrows and acquainted with grief, smitten of God and afflicted, brought as a lamb to the slaughter: . . . What have I achieved by bearing these griefs and sorrows . . . [and] atoning for Thy children, since they are still bound in chains and in the fetters of exile? O Lord, turn not away the face of Thine anointed, and let Thy hand be established with him; and in Thy name shall his horn be exalted and be openly manifest to Israel Thy holy people, to save them that are sunk in the deep abyss, and to bring out of the darkness them that have been lost and polluted among the nations, to perfect the world in the kingdom of the Almighty, and the Lord shall be king over all the earth."

None but Sabbatian believers in the first years after the apostasy would have used this kind of terminology when speaking of the messiah and his mission. There is little, if any, difference between the prayers which R. Israel Ḥazzan in Adrianople puts into the messiah's mouth (see below, pp. 863 ff.) and those with which the anonymous believer, performing his devotions at the holy tombs in Jerusalem, apostrophizes the messiah. The believers in Adrianople and their correspondents, "the men of faith in the Holy City of Jerusalem," are speaking the same language: that of the Sabbatian "men of faith."

III

The group of believers in Adrianople and the visitors from other communities who made their pilgrimages to the messiah gradually developed the attitudes and behavior patterns of an emergent sect, and began to exhibit the characteristic features of what may be described as an incipient "sectarian" feeling and organization. They knew themselves to be the elect of the "true Israel," and their "tropological" homilies, explaining the savior's tragic mystery, bear a striking resemblance to those advanced by the early Christians. In fact, the analogy reveals a psychological substratum that is common to all messianic revivals, no matter how widely they differ in other respects.

Perhaps the most illuminating and deeply moving human document expounding the views held by the Sabbatian believers who were closest to the very source of inspiration (AMIRAH, the holy king, and R. Nathan, the "holy lamp") is provided by Israel Ḥazzan's commentary on several psalms and other biblical texts. Ḥazzan's commentaries illuminate some of the abysses of the messianic faith, and their value for the historian is greatly enhanced by the wholesale destruction of most Sabbatian literature. In fact, next to nothing has survived of the (presumptive) literary output of the first generation of apostates around Sabbatai,[81] and hence the writings of this faithful believer from Kastoria, who was also Nathan's disciple and amanuensis, ought to rank as a theological and historical source of the first importance.[82]

Time and again the author attempts to descend into the tortuous depths of the messiah's soul after the apostasy, and it is there that he finds the key to the desperate cries of the psalmist. The apostasy is more than the messiah's personal problem. It is the cross, as it were, which an elect group within the "holy congregation" of believers has to bear, that is, that group of which the messiah had demanded that they share his terrible trial and *tiqqun*. Israel Ḥazzan does not hide his relief at having been spared this supreme trial, though he leaves no doubt that he too would have been ready to follow in the steps of his messiah if required to do so. It was the good fortune of some not to be present at Sabbatai's moments of illumination when he was "hitting out like a snake" (see above, p. 840), but woe betide those who were commanded by the messiah to apostatize and disobeyed: their refusal would actually prevent the accomplishment of the full redemption. Israel Ḥazzan's wording suggests that voluntary apostasy to Islam was not deemed necessary or meritorious in Sabbatai's circle,

81. The only exceptions are two texts from the first Dönmeh generation, both published by me: (1) "The Sprouting of the Horn of the Son of David," in *Essays in Honor of Abba Hillel Silver* (1963), pp. 368–86 (English); (2) a text from the beginnings of the Dönmeh sect in Salonika (Hebrew), *Sefunoth*, IX (1965), 193–207. They were composed after Nathan's death.

82. All quotations, unless otherwise stated, are taken from my article on R. Israel Ḥazzan in the *Schocken Volume* (pp. 176–94), where I have given the detailed references to the only extant source (and probably, Ḥazzan's own autograph) which is MS. Kaufmann 255 in Budapest.

and that the "holy faith" in the messiah's mission did not entail this extreme consequence. But of those who were specifically invited to take this step it could be said that "none of them that trust in him shall be guilty" (Ps. 34:22)—and hence none of them that "entered the crucible and forsook the Law of Moses in order to bring about the *tiqqun* of the world by taking the turban" would have to atone for their transgression. The author explains the expression in Isaiah 2:2, "and shall be exalted above the hills" (the Hebrew word for "above the hills," can also be [mis]interpreted as meaning "hats" or "turbans"): "They who took the turban at the behest of AMIRAH will be judged according to the righteousness which they dealt with Israel in entering this *tiqqun* for the sake of the Israelite nation."

Apostasy was therefore subject to the messiah's command and was not a matter of the believer's individual desire. Not every believer was required or even permitted to apostatize, "and we have seen people who implored AMIRAH to join him in his *tiqqun* when he took the turban, but he would not permit it except to a few" whom he found worthy to participate in his mission. Whether Israel Ḥazzan's account is reliable evidence or a tendentious rewriting of history is a moot question. This author at any rate wants to suggest that from the very beginning Sabbatai distinguished between several mystical categories of believers and apostates. He quotes the messiah as saying: "Some don the turban for good and others for evil, even as there are some who keep the [Jewish] bonnet for good and others for evil." It was evident to Israel Ḥazzan that some would wear the turban "for good" even after the messiah's manifestation in glory, whereas "I shall allow others to keep to their bonnet [that is, Judaism] for good and shall not bring them to this trial." Nathan of Gaza and Israel Ḥazzan were of this latter kind.

A very different and more depressing picture, however, is painted by de la Croix,[83] who alleges that Sabbatai, in the imperial Divan, accused those who refused to apostatize of having reviled and blasphemed the Muslim religion. The unfortunate victims of Sabbatai's zeal were forced to embrace the despised religion to save themselves from death. Did Sabbatai really sink that low, behaving with a wicked spitefulness that was part of his character and had nothing to do with his manic illumination? Sabbatai had exhibited some of these charac-

83. De la Croix, p. 382, but possibly referring to the events recorded more reliably by R. Jacob Najara (above, p. 850).

ter traits before, in the synagogue of Smyrna, and de la Croix's account cannot simply be dismissed because it casts aspersions on the messiah. As a matter of fact, de la Croix's information regarding Sabbatai's last years is far more reliable than his accounts of the earlier period, as he was in Turkey at the time and had occasion to observe Sabbatai's sermons in the synagogues of Adrianople until his final banishment to Albania. Sabbatai's behavior in those years, much like his original illness, may well have been subject to later theological rewriting. Perhaps Israel Ḥazzan's account represents the view of an honest believer who, in elaborating his theology, falsifies some of the facts of history.

There is, however, one obvious discrepancy between Israel Ḥazzan's account and the evidence from other sources that must not be overlooked: Sabbatai did not confine himself to urging "chosen" individuals to apostatize, but actually preached sermons urging conversion in the synagogues. De la Croix[84] reports that on several occasions he saw Sabbatai preaching "with considerable success—for he never left a synagogue without some Jew throwing away his Jewish bonnet in order to receive the turban from Sabbatai, who then paraded the new convert through the Jewish quarter in order to encourage others by this example." No hint of all this can be found in the writings of Israel Ḥazzan, who seems to have suppressed these awkward facts either because they did not fit his theological bias, or because he did not think that these "external" actions, in which Sabbatai was going, as it were, through the motions of doing things which he did not really mean, were significant. Ḥazzan's silence is reminiscent of that of the eighteenth-century Frankist authors in Poland who never as much as mentioned, in the writings destined for their own circle, the accusation of ritual murder which their leaders had publicly leveled at the Jewish community and its rabbis. The Frankist writers probably held that the blood libel had been advanced under pressure from the Catholic Church and hence was really irrelevant to their own missionary and theological purposes. Similarly, Israel Ḥazzan may have believed that this side of Sabbatai's public missionary activity merely intended to silence the Turks and hence did not require any serious discussion on his part.

Sabbatai's attempts—whether public or private—to persuade his followers to apostatize provoked a most unusual type of criticism within the Sabbatian camp. The believers certainly did not think of

84. *Ibid.*, p. 381.

criticizing any of the messiah's actions. These were, by definition, pure and mystically inspired, and it was taken for granted that the messiah would have to act in a strange manner and to test his followers even to the point of demanding their apostasy. Neverthelesss it behooved the believer to stand the test and to resist the messiah's demand. Criticism was therefore directed at those who succumbed to Sabbatai's pressure. Evidence of this attitude can be found in a letter from Abraham Cardozo to his brother-in-law, written some time in 1672 or 1673. The reports reaching Tripoli had been so discouraging that Cardozo gave up engaging in public polemics (as he had still done in 1669) with the anti-Sabbatians. The news that Sabbatai demanded that his followers take the turban was so obviously and utterly incompatible with any Jewish doctrine that "I would rather not play the fool and therefore prefer to keep silent." It was, in fact, impossible in the circumstances to give to others a satisfactory explanation of the messianic mystery, "and I for one am incapable of producing convincing proof." To justify Sabbatai's behavior by finding recondite allusions to it in Scripture was too reminiscent of the methods of Christian exegesis. Yet, though he had no "proof," Cardozo had an opinion on the matter. "Sabbatai Ṣevi is the messiah, the redeemer and savior; and all the winds in the world and all [his] strange actions cannot quench this light of my knowledge. . . . But from my mouth to your ear I shall explain the mystery of this strange service. . . . [Providence] has decreed a [terrible persecution that would lead to mass] apostasy. The messiah knew of it and caused it to be through him, to afflict our hearts and to aggrieve our spirit with his shame and with the desecration of the Torah and the despair of redemption. And although they that take the turban [because they think they have to follow the messiah] are sinning, yet it is not as bad as if they had apostatized under persecution and avoided martyrdom, for that would have been a real desecration of God's name.[85] In the present case, however, they sin in ignorance, thinking that they bring redemption nearer and that thus it was right to do."[86]

Israel Ḥazzan, unlike Cardozo, was not plagued by any doubts. Writing in 1678 or 1679,[87] he unhesitatingly declares that the true

85. Here Cardozo no doubt alludes to the marranos of Portugal.

86. MS. Hamburg 312, fol. 17a–b. The same letter also mentions the celebration of 9 Ab as a seven-day festival; see above, pp. 837, 844.

87. For the dating of Ḥazzan's tract, see G. Scholem in *Schocken Volume,* p. 161.

mourners in Zion to whom Scripture promised "beauty instead of ashes" (cf. Isa. 61:3) were the Sabbatian apostates who were now anointed with the "oil of gladness" of the messianic king. They are rightly called "mourners" because they have forsaken the Law of Moses, yet thereby they establish God's kingdom even in the realm of the *qelippoth* and hence they are "the planting of the Lord, that He may be glorified."

In accounting for the apellation "men of faith," Ḥazzan incidentally provides some interesting historical information. "When AMIRAH was about to introduce a person to this *tiqqun* [that is, apostasy], he would reveal to him the Mystery of the Godhead." The "Mystery of the Godhead" was the special revelation vouchsafed to Sabbatai, and he passed it on to the elect few. Once Sabbatai divulged the mystery to one of his followers, but the latter refused, at the last moment, to take the turban, whereupon Sabbatai reproached him: "Why did you steal my gods?" (cf. Gen. 31:30), that is, Why did you let me impart to you the mystery reserved for the elect that apostatize? (See also above, pp. 840–41.)

Ḥazzan's story, instructive and illuminating as it is, may exaggerate a partial truth, for we know of several believers who received the "Mystery of the Godhead" without being invited to take the turban, although it was rumored about some of them that they had apostatized.[88] Cardozo mentions[89] that the rabbis who visited Sabbatai in Adrianople received the mystery, and also reports[90] that the pious rabbi Azariah ha-Levi had repeatedly heard from Sabbatai Ṣevi "that the Holy One Blessed Be He, the God of Israel, was a Second Cause clothed in the *sefirah Tif'ereth.*" All sources seem to agree that Sabbatai adjured those who had received the mystery from him not to divulge it to others. According to Israel Ḥazzan the Mystery of the Godhead and apostasy were closely associated not only with regard to the believers who imitated their master, but also in the case of Sabbatai himself: it was only as a result of his apostasy that he was granted permission to reveal the mystery to others. It will be remembered that Moses Pinheiro claimed that Sabbatai had revealed the mystery to him and to his other friends in Smyrna as early as 1650 (see above,

88. Cardozo's letter to Samuel de Paz on the Mystery of the Godhead.
89. *Ibid., Beth ha-Midrash* (1865), p. 65.
90. *Raza de-Razin,* in MS. Deinard 153, Jewish Theological Seminary, New York, fol. 11a. See also below, p. 909.

pp. 120 f.). The truth of the matter is that hardly any trace of such a mystery exists in the sources relating to the years 1665–66 (with the possible exception of the accounts of Sabbatai's discussions with Nathan); all references to it[91] date from the period after the apostasy. There is no unanimity in the sources as to what exactly this mystery consisted of, though all seem to agree that it somehow related to the manifestation of the "God of Israel" in the *sefirah Tif'ereth.* Sometimes it is suggested that the God of Israel is identical with *Tif'ereth*, in which case the mystery hardly goes beyond the explicit doctrine of the Zohar. Sometimes *Tif'ereth* is said to be but a "clothing" for that more interior being which, however, is not identical with *En-Sof* but is a "secondary cause" emanating from it. Israel Ḥazzan, who frequently mentions the "Mystery of the Godhead," never spells out its precise meaning and contents himself with the usual references to *Tif'ereth*, namely, the letter *waw* (that is, the third letter of the Tetragrammaton) as the "God of the Faith of AMIRAH." The formula is too vague to permit a more precise understanding of how the Godhead was thought to manifest itself in the sixth *sefirah*, namely, in the letter *waw* of the Tetragrammaton.

But let us revert to the subject of the apostasy and to the controversies that arose in connection with it. Israel Ḥazzan reports that the believers were divided into two schools of thought. One group held that the messiah had to be obeyed in whatever he said, "even in the matter of the turban"—to which Ḥazzan adds, "and this, in my opinion, is the correct view." The opposite attitude was defended by those believers who had disobeyed Sabbatai and refused to apostatize. "They shall bear their sin," Israel Ḥazzan comments ominously, "for it is possible that because of them the redemption of Israel was delayed." Both parties justified their views by an exegesis of Deuteronomy 30:2. Clearly the radical and moderate trends as well as the arguments advanced by both groups crystallized as soon as the messianic mass movement transformed itself into a "sect" of believers. The radicals would stop at nothing, provided it was commanded by the messiah; the moderates drew the line at what God had commanded, namely, at the Law of Moses as a whole. On one occasion, Israel Ḥazzan divides the believers into three groups:[92] the "young

91. Especially the many detailed references in Cardozo's writings to the believers who have received the mystery from Sabbatai.

92. See the text in *Schocken Volume,* pp. 179–80.

men" full of zeal and ready to submit to all trials; the "old men," who chose what was convenient to them but backed out when the faith became too demanding; and the "babes," who changed from faith to disbelief and back again without any constancy. Apparently the second and third groups were well represented in Israel Ḥazzan's environment in the Balkans.

The typology of kinds of believers is evidently inspired by the author's doctrines regarding the status of the messiah after his apostasy. Ḥazzan's homilies on the Book of Psalms drain to the bottom the cup of suffering and bitterness that goes with the messianic mystery. The apostate messiah is depicted by Ḥazzan with the vitality and urgency of a living paradox. This paradox was the great and central problem, compared to which all other doctrinal issues (for example, the origin and nature of the messiah's soul) were but derivative and relatively "simple." Although Israel Ḥazzan's views were clearly influenced by the writings of Nathan—even where the prophet of Gaza is not explicitly mentioned—yet his homiletical talent imparts to his commentary a highly individual character and interest.

Ḥazzan frequently uses the terms *Torath ᵓEmeth* and *Torath Ḥesed*, "law of truth" and "law of kindness," that is "mercy" (see Prov. 31:26), the former denoting the Law of Moses and the Jewish religion, the latter signifying the Quran and Islam. The use of this pair of concepts derives from Nathan, who mentioned it very often.[93] Ḥazzan says: "The religion of Ishmael is called the law of kindness, and our holy religion is truth, . . . for the Ishmaelites merely have what their ancestors handed down to them; hence . . . their religion is called 'mercy' as it is written [Ps. 26:3] 'for Thy mercy is before mine eyes'—this is the mystery of the turban which is 'before mine eyes'; and yet I do not walk in their words and in their ways but 'I have walked in Thy truth' [Ps. 26:3], which is our holy religion that is called Truth." Both religions are aspects of the one Law—in 1670–80 a very audacious statement indeed.

Psalm 143 is interpreted in this sense, in an at times profoundly moving manner, as the messiah's prayer after his apostasy. By his apostasy he entered into the "religion of mercy," yet he continues to long for the religion of truth. When Sabbatai "chants the law of mercy, or lovingkindness," that is, recites the Quran of the Ishmaelites,

93. See the quotation above, p. 813.

he fulfills Scripture (Prov. 31:26), opening his mouth with wisdom and keeping the law of kindness of his tongue, for he combines two laws. That is also the mystical meaning of Psalm 85:11: "Mercy and truth are met together." The two laws meet in Sabbatai and he consequently has to fulfill both, although to those who "have eyes but cannot see" he appears to have forsaken the law of truth and to transgress its commandments. In fact, only God who searches the reins and the heart can know the truth about the service of the messiah, who therefore prays [Ps. 26:2]: "Examine me, O Lord, and try me," and who desires to be tried by God with the bitter waters like the wife suspected of infidelity (cf. Num. ch. 5). According to the Talmud (B. Sukkah 49b) commenting on Proverbs 31:26, the Torah of lovingkindness is that which is pursued solely for the love of God.

There is nothing of the Christian preference for the law of love in Israel Ḥazzan's usage. It is true that God's throne shall be established in mercy (that is, by the mystical *tiqqun* performed through the law of lovingkindness), yet "he shall sit upon it in truth," for the "true enthronement and the supernal kingdom are only in the Law of Truth" (cf. Isa. 16:5: "and in mercy shall the throne be established and he shall sit upon it in truth"). Nor can Ḥazzan's law of love be identified with the "Law of the world of divine emanation," of which more will be said later. The law of love is an intermediary stage on the road to messianic consummation, but it is not that ultimate revelation of the spirituality of the Torah which will become manifest, in the fullness of time, as the "new law" of the messiah. It is still nothing but a convenient code name for Islam.

The apostasy has a threefold religious significance. It is meant to restore the divine Shekhinah, to save the nations of the world, and to destroy the realm of the *qelippoth*. The Shekhinah is imprisoned by the *qelippah,* but the messiah who cleaves to her and descends for her sake into the realm of the "law of lovingkindness" can restore her, thus illustrating the Talmudic saying (B. Nazir 23b), "a transgression performed with the right intention [that is, for the Sabbatian kabbalist, for the sake of restoring the fallen Shekhinah] is better than a precept performed with the wrong intention." The path of the messiah is that which "no bird of prey knows, and the falcon's eye has not seen it" (Job 28:7), for it is a strange way that no one had ever walked before and for which the messiah has to suffer reproach and ignominy. The messiah took this sore trial upon himself in order to destroy the realm of the *qelippoth,* to "extract the precious from the vile" (Jer. 15:19), that is, to lift the holy sparks that had fallen into the great abyss, "and even to make the *qelippah* itself return in repentance and to restore it to holiness." The doctrine that the messiah is instrumental in redeeming the nations of the world and the *qelippah* itself, and restoring them to the sphere of holiness, may have had a special appeal to Sabbatai and may well have helped to soothe his troubled conscience. On the other hand, there is some evidence to show that this doctrine was not very popular with a good many simple believers who had difficulty in imagining a messianic age in which the *qelippah* would not be annihilated and the gentiles trodden underfoot. Israel Ḥazzan suggests a compromise formula,[94] but his discussion makes it clear that there was much controversy on this issue. Occasionally it is suggested that the messiah's redemptive activity on behalf of the gentiles extends to Ishmael only. Sometimes the doctrine that the messiah chose to enter the *qelippah* of his own free will and in accordance with God's purpose is contradicted by the opposite notion that the satanic powers pursued the messiah until he was caught in their net.

The believer's tortured conscience erupts in Israel Ḥazzan's anguished cry, "Jealousy is cruel as the grave[95]—this is the jealousy which we feel because the light and holiness of Israel has had to enter this trial. It is a very cruel jealousy." No explanations can completely remove the sting of the paradox, and Israel Ḥazzan puts into the messiah's mouth the "prayer of the afflicted" (Ps. 102) as well as all the other psalms in which the sufferer, overwhelmed by anguish, turns to God. It was preordained that the messiah would have to walk crooked byways that are beyond human understanding, and hence the special significance of the psalmist's prayer, "Teach me Thy ways." The symbol of the "crooked Torah" easily links up with Nathan's concept of the "crooked circle" (see p. 813), and hence the messiah prays—according to Israel Ḥazzan—"Sustain my goings in Thy paths (Ps. 17:5)—for although I have walked in crooked circles [the Hebrew word translated as 'path' can also mean 'circle'] yet these are the paths [or circles] of righteousness, as R. Nathan has explained,

94. MS. Kaufmann 255, fol. 120a–b. Here we read also that the believers are the true "Mourners of Zion" (see above, p. 861).

95. Song of Songs 8:6; the Hebrew word for "jealousy" can also mean "zeal" or "violent feelings," cf. Num. 25:11.

and therefore 'let not my footsteps slip' (Ps. 17:5), for many unsuccessfully tried to do the same, but I descended into the depths of the *qelippoth* and yet my footsteps slipped not." Sabbatai Ṣevi will successfully accomplish his mission because his soul is continuously united to the Shekhinah, which in kabbalistic symbolism is also called "righteousness." Hence the messianic prayer ends with the words, "As for me, I will behold Thy face in righteousness" (Ps. 17:5), that is to say, that by his intimate union with "righteousness" the messiah succeeds in collecting and saving all the sparks and holy souls from the prison of the *qelippah.*

Israel Ḥazzan's comments on Psalm 37:7, "Be silent in the Lord," allow us a glimpse into the debate on the correct Sabbatian attitude toward unbelievers. Ḥazzan recommends "silence in the Lord," that is, refraining from all public polemics, disputations, and even apologetic retort. "Even when you hear them scoffing and blaspheming and cursing, . . . do not say anything." The silence enjoined by Israel Ḥazzan is not yet the deceitful hypocritical silence of later Sabbatianism as expounded in its extremest form in Jacob Frank's sayings on *The Burden of Dumah* (Isa. 21:11; the Hebrew word *dumah* can also be translated "silence"). According to Ḥazzan the Sabbatian believer should not deny his faith, but merely keep silent when he hears it reviled. Nevertheless, we seem to be observing here the beginnings of that duplicity which subsequently became the hallmark of Sabbatianism. Israel Ḥazzan emphatically disagrees with the "fools who say that I shall keep the faith in my heart but [outwardly] put a covering on the upper lip and cry, 'Unclean, unclean' [that is, join the chorus of voices reviling Sabbatai Ṣevi; cf. Lev. 13:45)]. They say that they act thus in order that the infidels should not know that they are believers, . . . but this is sheer deceit. . . . Others again . . . with their mouth say that they are great believers [in Sabbatai Ṣevi] in order to deceive the [other] believers." Ḥazzan insists that the heart and the mouth must be congruent in the faith, and he quotes Deuteronomy 30:14, "for the Lord is very nigh unto thee, in thy mouth, and in thy heart, that thou mayest do it."

Here, as in his other allusions to diverse groups and tendencies in the Sabbatian camp, Israel Ḥazzan is providing valuable historical information. Apparently there already were believers who began to dissimulate and conceal their faith, while others—probably in Ḥazzan's own city, Kastoria, and in other communities in Macedonia where the Sabbatians still were in a majority—who were not Sabbatians would pretend that they were. Ḥazzan does not require the Sabbatian believer to step forth and testify, and thereby to risk unnecessary persecution;[96] he merely denounces active dissimulation and deceit. His denunciation, however, does not include the kind of "holy deceit" practiced by Sabbatai Ṣevi and those who apostatized at his behest. This act of deceit was part of the tactics of warfare against the demonic powers of the *qelippah,* and hence of a different order altogether. Israel Ḥazzan's attitude testifies to nobility of character and integrity of mind, though not to rigorous consistency.

The tension and bitterness between the two camps must have been great indeed, and hatred was mutual. In most communities the majority of the rabbis and the lay leadership were "opponents," and Israel Ḥazzan contrasts their "stinking wisdom" with the simplicity and "foolishness" of the believers—probably an admission of the fact that the Sabbatian rank and file was made up of the ignorant and uneducated. The unbelievers were the "mixed multitude" and not the true Israel,[97] and the violent diatribes of the *Raᶜya Mehemna* against the rich lay leaders and the antikabbalist rabbis of his time (see above, p. 228) were now applied to the anti-Sabbatian opposition. The Sabbatians exhibit a characteristically sectarian sense of superiority: they are the true spirituals and gladly describe themselves as fools in contrast to the rabbis, who are full of imaginary wisdom "but there is no spirit in them."[98] Israel Ḥazzan emphasizes that the power of the ruling leadership and the wisdom of the worldly-wise can be misleading indeed and far from the truth of the Lord, "for wisdom and might are His" (Dan. 2:20).

Israel Ḥazzan's tract also provides interesting information on the beliefs current in his circle regarding the sequence of the redemptive process. Although the tract was composed after Sabbatai's death and undoubtedly contains adjustments to the new situation (for example, the idea that there was an intermediate stage between the apostasy

96. The onset of anti-Sabbatian persecution is alluded to several times by Israel Ḥazzan; see G. Scholem in *Schocken Volume,* p. 210, n. 97. Ḥazzan also mentions that the "opponents" invaded the houses of the believers on 9 Ab to find out whether they were secretly eating on the day of fast.

97. Cf. MS. Kaufmann 255, fol. 10b.

98. Abraham Yakhini in a letter to Nathan of Gaza, *RÉJ*, XXVI (1893), 214.

and the ultimate manifestation), we may nevertheless assume that the main outlines of the system were formulated in Sabbatai's lifetime during the late sixties or early seventies. During that period the ultimate manifestation was probably expected soon after the apostasy and we may, therefore, reconstruct the original messianic timetable as follows:

a. Sabbatai is "anointed" as the messianic king. This mystical anointing took place in 1658 (see above, p. 142).
b. The "first manifestation" and the great penintential revival of 1666. This first manifestation, however, at which Sabbatai's kingship was made known to the world, was not the "true [that is, ultimate] manifestation," and therefore the hostile powers could wax strong and necessitate a period of trial.
c. The savior had to "put on alien clothing," and because of the multitude of sins and the increasing power of evil "the redemption that had been sprouting in our days has been postponed."
[*d.* At this point Israel Ḥazzan, writing about two years after Sabbatai's demise, introduces another stage, that of "AMIRAH's occultation." But this stage, like the preceding one, was merely an intermediate period of transition, leading up to]—
e. The ultimate or "true manifestation" when the messiah's kingdom would be finally and definitely established. This final stage is described in a manner that is reminiscent of early Christian ideas about the Parousia, the Second Coming of Christ (see above, p. 95).

The traditional messianic expectations together with their peculiar Sabbatian additions were now transferred (precisely as in Christian millenarianism) to the "ultimate manifestation," when the messiah would consummate what he had begun by taking the turban. "There will be no more need then of weapons of war, but only of songs of praise." Israel Ḥazzan's main concern is with the spiritual significance of this ultimate manifestation rather than with the other changes traditionally expected for the utopian messianic order. His homily on Psalm 19:7 ff. explains that "the law of the Lord is perfect, restoring the soul" because Sabbatai, by this law, would restore all the souls of Israel. The testimony of the Lord is also said to "make wise the simple," because "many are totally ignorant and have nothing save their faith in AMIRAH, but by this faith they shall be great sages and rejoice in the new Torah of the messiah." Of course, those

Sabbatian believers who were kabbalist scholars would not be disadvantaged because of their earlier lack of ignorance but, on the contrary, would also reap indescribable reward. There are also those who had shared the Sabbatian truth, but then "the devil has possessed them." If they lapsed because of ignorance then the verse (Ps. 19:13, AV v. 12) applies to them "who can understand errors" and they may yet be saved. But they that pretended to be believers (that is, in 1666) but subsequently showed their true colors would be cast out, as it is written (Ps. 19:13), "cleanse thou me from those with secret faults" who are even worse than the "cruelly arrogant" who were openly opposing the faith. In this homily Israel Ḥazzan expounds his spiritual aspirations and also settles accounts with the various types of enemies, from the "cruelly arrogant" to the "secret" and dissimulating pseudo-believers. The large number of undecided and bewildered Jews—and there must have been many of them, especially in Turkey—who were neither believers nor opponents, would be reconciled to the messiah by the prophet Elijah.

At the "ultimate holy manifestation" the righteousness of the apostates who had become Muslims together with Sabbatai Ṣevi will become manifest. For the believers the manifestation will be that of the messiah, for the unbelievers that of the serpent (the letters of the Hebrew words for "messiah" and "serpent" having the same numerical value). In the terminology of Lurianic kabbalah, the ultimate manifestation will take place when the configuration called Rachel (which is associated here with the mystery of Sabbatai Ṣevi) will become filled with the supernal knowledge of the Holy King (namely, of *zeᶜir ᵓanpin*). Then only will the new Torah of the messiah be revealed. Like the manna in the wilderness, or the dew that descends from the "Holy Ancient One," the "mystery of our Holy Torah, the Torah of *ᵓaṣiluth*"—the Torah corresponding to the supernal world of Emanation—will be given as a reward to those who have believed with a perfect faith. Without saying so explicitly, Israel Ḥazzan seems to suggest that the Torah of the "wilderness" is that of the "Holy One Blessed Be He" (corresponding to *Tifᵓereth* in the sefirotic system), whereas the new Torah would be that of the "Holy Ancient One." This doctrine is stated explicitly in the Dönmeh hymns.[99] Israel Ḥazzan also identi-

99. See M. Attias, *Songs and Hymns of the Sabbatians* (1948), p. 49, and my note *ibid.*

fies the "true supernal faith" with the "faith of the supernal Holy Ancient One" and explains that when God leads Israel out of the wilderness, that is, out of the Law of Moses, he will reveal the Torah of *ʾaṣiluth* which the messiah would teach them and with which the dead can be resurrected.[100] At any rate it is evident that the term "Torah of *ʾaṣiluth*" does not refer to an extant Sabbatian doctrine as taught by Sabbatai or by Nathan (though this is how the concept was interpreted later by the Dönmeh), but to a thoroughly new revelation to be given at the "ultimate manifestation," rather like the *evangelium aeternum* of the Christian spirituals (see above, pp. 98–99). In his use of the concept of *ʾaṣiluth*, Israel Ḥazzan is clearly indebted to his teacher Nathan of Gaza.[101]

The "wondrous Mystery of the Godhead" which Sabbatai had revealed when (or because) he took the turban, is therefore not to be confused with the Torah of *ʾaṣiluth*. The former is not the whole truth, and its validity is provisional. The full and complete mystery, that is, the Torah of *ʾaṣiluth*, will be revealed only at the messiah's second manifestation, and then it will be revealed not to the elect few but to the whole world.

Israel Ḥazzan's theology is still ignorant of the Sabbatian trinity and never mentions the Zoharic expression "the three knots of the faith" which later Sabbatian literature, especially after 1675, made so much of. Nevertheless, there is a special bond uniting the Holy One Blessed Be He, the Shekhinah, and the "dear son AMIRAH." This is not a bond of identity, and although the Shekhinah and the messiah are frequently called by one and the same name, this homonymy refers to their intimate communion rather than to their identity. Earlier kabbalistic texts too occasionally use the term "messiah" as one of the epithets of the last *sefirah* (*Malkhuth*, Shekhinah), but their usage is a technical-symbolic one and has no connection whatever with ideas of incarnation. Israel Ḥazzan also refers to a mystical union of the messiah with the Shekhinah, which would take place after both have been liberated from their exile and imprisonment in the world of the *qelippah*, and

100. This idea seems to go back to the *Midrash Tehillim* 3. The midrashic notion of the proper sequence of the chapters of the Torah is here replaced by the kabbalistic idea of a Torah of *ʾaṣiluth;* cf. G. Scholem, *On the Symbolism of the Kabbalah*, pp. 37–39, 66–70.

101. Cf. Ch. Wirszubski, "The Sabbatian Theology of Nathan of Gaza," in *Keneseth,* VIII (1944), 238.

have been gathered into the fullness of the divine name. The soul of Sabbatai Ṣevi is associated, from the very beginning of the world, with the Shekhinah. This, however, does not imply the original divinity of the messiah whose *apotheosis* is expected as a final event. The messiah is united *from below* to the last and lowest *sefirah*, until the consummation of the eschatological process when he will ascend to the sphere of *Tif᾿ereth* (namely, that of the configuration *ze῾ir ᾿anpin*). Once the serpent is removed from the world, the messiah will be given a new name and "his light will shine among the supernal *sefiroth* and he will be exalted among them." According to Lurianic kabbalah, however, the *sefirah Malkhuth* too will be exalted then and will ascend to a higher position.[102]

These expressions and figures of speech nevertheless imply something like a deification of the messiah. Such a doctrine was, indeed, gradually taking shape in Nathan's mind, but there can be no doubt that it was originated with Sabbatai Ṣevi himself. It seems to have been based on some of his ecstatic and euphoric experiences when he anticipated some kind of future apotheosis for himself. The ascension of the messiah to the sphere of the divine—obliquely hinted at by Israel Ḥazzan, and explicitly stated by Nathan—refers to his life in his ultimate manifestation and not to an event after his death. As there is no evidence of the occurrence of such notions in Nathan's writings prior to his renewed meeting with Sabbatai, this particular doctrine may, perhaps, have emerged as a compromise. Sabbatai Ṣevi, in his moments of manic illumination, seems to have been convinced of his divinity. His followers, who were under the profound influence of his fascinating personality but who hestitated to go all the way with what seemed to be blasphemous conclusions, probably sought to adapt Sabbatai's claims to an acceptable kabbalistic doctrine. Such a doctrine had already been formulated, before Sabbatai's apostasy, in Nathan's *Treatise on the Dragons*. Israel Ḥazzan expresses himself very cautiously on the subject and avoids explicit mention of the messiah's divinity. Sometime after 1671, however, Nathan wrote a letter to Salonika in which he combined his doctrine of the messiah with his definition of the messiah's ascension "to the rank of perfect God-

102. The idea of the messiah's apotheosis is clearly expressed in Israel Ḥazzan's commentary on Ps. 21, the "royal psalm" which the Sabbatians had prescribed for daily recitation in 1666; cf. *Schocken Volume,* p. 194.

head." Only parts of the letter have survived,[103] but they are enough to show the radical direction in which Nathan's theology was moving. He emphasizes that his own prophetic calling was solely to announce that the messiah had come and to explain his mission and the right faith in him.[104] This faith, his correspondents in Salonika are told, includes the confession that the messiah "will achieve perfect divinity . . . because this is of the essence of messiahship, and if this were not so he would not be a messiah." This is the most extreme formulation of the messiah's divinity written during Sabbatai's lifetime, and it was circulated among only a very small number of believers.

IV

The texts quoted and analyzed in the preceding pages convey much of the atmosphere that characterized the faith and the emergent doctrines in the circle around Sabbatai Ṣevi in the years 1666–72. The believers propagated their views both orally and in writing, while the opposition of the official leadership of the Jewish communities in Turkey gathered strength as the failure of the messianic movement and the feeling of disappointment became increasingly evident. Nathan of Gaza continued to exhort believers to persevere in the faith, and one such letter to a community in Macedonia, written toward the end of January, 1672, has been preserved.[105] Nathan assures his correspondents that the tidings regarding the sprouting of the horn of the son of Jesse were true, firmly founded, established, and right, and that the light of the supernal holy Sabbath (that is, the messiah) would soon shine forth. When the forces of the *qelippah* had taken prisoner the holy souls, they had also captured the soul of the messiah, who was now fallen "into the depth of the great abyss." But although the clothing of his head (that is, the turban) was evil, nonetheless he was "like the body of the Heaven in his purity."

103. The date of the letter can be inferred from the fact that the "Festival of Rejoicing" (i.e., 9 Ab) is mentioned as a celebration lasting seven days; see above, p. 837, n. 44. I have published the text of the letter in *Zion,* VII (1942), 188.

104. Nathan remained consistent in this respect from the beginning of his career to the end. He had written similar words as early as the summer of 1665; cf. *Liqqutey Mikhtavim,* ed. Haberman, p. 209.

105. I have published the text, which is in a bad and corrupt state, from MS. Adler 494 (Jewish Theological Seminary, New York) in *ᶜEreṣ Yisraᵓel,* IV (1956), 191.

Inevitably Sabbatian propaganda increasingly resorted to the more radical and extreme formulations of its theologians, Sabbatai's own letters (such as the one quoted above, p. 840) being known only to the most restricted inner circle. Its dangers to the continuity of Jewish tradition and Jewish life were becoming correspondingly more evident, and the leaders of the Jewish communities, especially in Constantinople and Adrianople, did their best to destroy the "root that beareth gall and wormwood" (cf. Deut. 29:18). The task was not easy even for those leaders who had connections at court, since Sabbatai enjoyed the sultan's special protection. Would it be possible to break the obstinacy of the believers without striking first at their chief? Rabbinic bans of exommunication had no effect on believers who were firmly convinced that dire punishment awaited the rabbis at the messiah's ultimate manifestation.[106] Persecution against the Sabbatians intensified[107] but remained ineffective until the leaders of the community in Constantinople decided to resort to more practical means and to bribe one of the higher officials. There are conflicting versions of what actually happened at the end of 1672, and the utterly imaginary account of de la Croix has been taken at face value by many historians.[108] Little attention has been paid so far to the one reliable account which also provides exact dates. This account can be found in the diary of Antoine Galland, who succeeded de la Croix as secretary of the French ambassador to the Sublime Porte, M. de Nointel. Galland's account is now also confirmed by a Turkish document that has only recently been correctly interpreted.[109] In a way, Galland's account continues the story told above (pp. 852 ff.) in the letter to Samuel Primo in March 1672.

Sabbatai, accompanied by three of his "courtiers" who had apostatized at his behest, arrived in Constantinople shortly before August 23, 1672. There is no reason to believe de la Croix's statement

106. Cf. MS. Shazar, fol. 47b.

107. Nathan of Gaza refers to these persecutions in one of his letters preserved in the Sabbatian notebook in the library of Columbia University, New York. "But for the merits of the faith that protect us, they would have swallowed us alive" (*ibid.*, fol. 15a).

108. Apparently de la Croix was not even in Constantinople when the events occurred, and his account is based on confused and partly false hearsay. See de la Croix, *op. cit.*, p. 383.

109. U. Heydt, "A Turkish Document concerning Sabbatai Ṣevi" (Hebrew), in *Tarbiz*, XXV (1956), 337–39.

to the effect that Sabbatai had fallen into disgrace and his pension from the sultan been cut off, or that the Jews, who were afraid of him, received him with great honor and festivities. Galland reports the exact opposite. Sabbatai *alias* Aziz Mehemed Effendi arrived in Constantinople as an esteemed visitor, and immediately requested the local *sorvaji* to send two janissaries in order to keep away Jewish visitors. Apparently there still were many Jews who, without necessarily being followers and believers, wanted to see him. His request was granted and he moved through the streets of Constantinople in a strange procession, preceded by fifteen of his apostate believers, and followed by fifteen others. He was treated with great respect by all Muslims. To the congregants of the synagogues of Constantinople (Galata, Scutari, Balata) he sent letters requesting them to desist from visiting him. It was also reported that he said his prayers first in Hebrew, together with his apostate followers, and thereafter according to the Muslim rite. The Turks, who knew about this, did not interfere.[110]

Two or three weeks later Sabbatai was arrested. Galland himself records two versions of what was supposed to have happened. On September 12, 1672, he notes in his diary that Sabbatai and a group of his followers had entered a synagogue and conducted Jewish prayers. This was reported to the commander of the janissaries, who immediately ordered the arrest of Sabbatai "together with the Muslims whom he had made Jews and that were with him." The reference to "Muslims whom he had made Jews" (unless it is a *lapsus calami* for "Jews whom he had made Muslims") may perhaps serve as a confirmation of the claim made in the *Testimony of the Faith* (see above, pp. 831 f.) that Sabbatai had also made Turkish converts. The prisoners were put in chains and sent to Adrianople. For the next three months nothing is said anywhere about Sabbatai's fate, but in the middle of December Galland heard an account of what had happened from a reliable informant. According to this report the Jews had laid a trap for Sabbatai, which, however, did not work at first because the two highest officials in Constantinople, including the kaimakam, would not proceed against the sultan's protégé.[111] The

110. *Journal d'Antoine Galland,* II (1881), 194. Cf. also *RÉJ*, XVIII (1889), 106, where Galland's information is reprinted, omitting, however, the all-important dates.

111. The kaimakam at the time was Mustapha Ava. His predecessor, from

matter was then taken up by the bustanji bashi (the commander of the guard of the imperial palaces and parks)[112] who, it appears, had received a sizable bribe. The Turkish document gives the bustanji's name as Othman Pasha the Bosnian. Galland mentions a sum of four thousand piasters (reales), but does not say to whom this very considerable amount—according to the value of money at that time about a thousand gold ducats—was given. Three witnesses were produced to testify against Sabbatai Ṣevi. The nature of the testimony and of the accusation can be inferred from two complementary sources.

In December 1672 the sultan and his Great Vizier Ahmed Köprülü Pasha returned to Adrianople, which they had left in June, 1672, for the war against Poland. This war had ended with the conquest of Kamienicz and the peace treaty of Buczacz by which the province of Podolia became part of the Ottoman Empire. It was the last great Turkish victory in Europe. On their return the sultan and his Great Vizier found Sabbatai imprisoned in Adrianople, and a report from the bustanji bashi to the effect that "several disinterested Muslims had heard him[113] utter blasphemies" and that they were ready to testify "and, if necessary, come to Adrianople." According to Galland (entry of December 15, 1672), the witnesses claimed to have seen Sabbatai "wearing phylacteries and a Jewish bonnet [instead of a turban], surrounded by women, wine, and several leaders [of his sect]."[114] This incident should probably not be confused with the

---

July, 1671–April, 1672, was none other than Kasim Pasha who had been present at the occasion of Sabbatai's apostasy (see above, p. 676). If Sabbatai visited Constantinople during this time as a V.I.P., they may well have met again.

112. The account given by Baruch of Arezzo (*ap.* Freimann, p. 66) is incorrect on this point and interwoven as usual with legendary elements. Baruch wrongly attributes the responsibility for the arrest to the kaimakam of Constantinople, but gives some correct details regarding Sabbatai's "Jewish" behavior. Baruch also states that Sabbatai was arrested and sent to Adrianople while the sultan was away fighting against Poland. This is confirmed by Galland and the Turkish document.

113. U. Heydt correctly interpreted this passage as referring to Sabbatai Ṣevi. The passage is from a letter of the Great Vizier, quoting from the bustanji bashi's first letter to the Central Government; see U. Heydt, *loc. cit.* (above, n. 109), p. 338. The bustanji bashi's part in the affair is also mentioned by Galland in his entry dated December 18, 1672 (vol. I, p. 248).

114. "Leur accusation était d'avoir trouvé Sabbatai Ṣevi avec des téphillines, avec le bonnet à la juive, avec des femmes et du vin chez lui et plusieurs semblables chefs" (Galland, vol. I, p. 243).

prayer service in the synagogue that had led to Sabbatai's arrest. Subsequently the two incidents were combined and, according to de la Croix, the bustanji bashi making the rounds with the guard at night found Sabbatai with a group of followers singing psalms in a house in Courou-Chesmé, a village on the Bosporus. The accusation cannot be dismissed out of hand, and the reference to "women and wine" suggests preparations for a sexual-religious orgy rather than a meeting for the sole purpose of singing psalms.

A French-speaking Jew of Adrianople told Galland that Sabbatai's brother (probably Elijah Ṣevi) had petitioned the sultan to release Sabbatai. He also reported several other details which suggest that Sabbatai was still in favor with Vani Effendi, who demanded his liberation. According to *le sieur Mosé* (Galland's Jewish informant), Sabbatai could easily have obtained this, but he refused to leave the prison; and while Sabbatai's friends endeavored to secure his freedom, the authorities summoned the aforementioned witnesses to Adrianople. As it happens, the order to send the witnesses—a letter from the Great Vizier to Othman Pasha—is the only extant official Turkish document relating to Sabbatai Ṣevi, since all the other documents relating to that period have disappeared from the Turkish archives. The letter does not, of course, tell the background story of Jewish bribes, as a result of which the Great Vizier was now acting in the interests of the Jewish leadership. The vizier does not hide his hostility toward Sabbatai and his desire to bring about his execution. The letter speaks of "the obstinate infidel who came [that is, converted] from the Jews and received the turban, and who is now imprisoned in Adrianople"—Sabbatai is not mentioned by name—and refers to a complaint lodged by Sabbatai: "a complaint of persecution has been lodged with the Imperial Camp by the accursed prisoner who says, 'I am persecuted and treated unjustly.' " The writer then orders the Muslim witnesses who had heard the accused utter the words that would result in his execution to be sent to Adrianople to testify, so that action could be taken in accordance with the provisions of religious law.[115]

The document leaves no doubt that Sabbatai was accused of reviling or denying Islam—either of which meant capital punishment—and that the Great Vizier, who in 1666 had exhibited such extraordinary moderation, was now definitely hostile to Sabbatai and

115. Heydt, *loc. cit.*

ready to cooperate with the Jews in getting rid of the apostate messiah. On January 4, 1673, Galland notes: "I am told that the witnesses [against] Sabbatai Ṣevi have been heard in Adrianople and that four thousand piasters have been paid by the Jews of this city.[116] He was imprisoned in Orta Capi, the prisoners of which are generally held to be condemned [to death]. His execution, however, was postponed till after the month of Ramadan, when the Turks are careful not to shed blood. Even in this state [of a condemned prisoner] Sabbatai obtained permission to visit the bath in order to be clean and pure as prescribed by the religion of the Turks."[117]

The sentence that was passed on Sabbatai Ṣevi after several months of imprisonment came as a surprise to everybody. Galland notes on February 10, 1673: "the Jew Moses tells me that about a month ago [that is, about the middle of January] Sabbatai was banished to the Morea. The Great Vizier would have had him put to death, had it not been for the strong faction at court that supported him (*la forte brigue qu'il avait auprès du Grand-Seigneur*)."[118] Among Sabbatai's supporters were, according to Sabbatian tradition, the sultan's mother and Vani Effendi.[119]

Later accounts state that the bribe was paid by the Jewish leaders in order to have Sabbatai removed to an isolated place in exile. Also, the amount of the bribe was inflated to twelve sackfulls of piasters, totaling fifteen thousand thalers.[120] The truth of the matter is that the Jews wanted Sabbatai's death and sought the help of the Great Vizier and the bustanji bashi to that end. The witnesses were probably hired, and with our knowledge of Sabbatai's attitude toward

116. Referring, most probably, to Adrianople. The payment of these 4,000 piasters would then be in addition to the 4,000 paid in Constantinople. It is possible, however, that Galland refers to one and the same payment, i.e., the bribe paid in Constantinople. Unfortunately the syntax of Galland's sentence admits of either interpretation.

117. Galland, vol. II, p. 4. 118. *Ibid.*, p. 35.

119. Baruch of Arezzo (*ap.* Freimann, p. 66) mixes fact and legendary fiction. The Great Vizier demanded Sabbatai's death as a heretic, but the sultan refused to confirm the sentence and wanted to set him free. Thereupon the vizier demanded that Sabbatai be at least banished. This version seems to me rather doubtful.

120. Leyb b. Ozer (MS. Shazar, fol. 56b). Leyb's account of the events leading up to Sabbatai's exile is confused and devoid of historical value; cf. Emden, p. 25. Yet Rosanes (IV, pp. 88–89) relied heavily on Leyb's account and thereby misled other writers. There is nothing to support the assertion that Sabbatai lived in Constantinople for three years after his apostasy.

Islam, there is no reason to think that he actually uttered the blasphemies attributed to him. On the other hand, there may be some truth in the allegation that he had tried to convert Muslims to his faith. At any rate, it seems that Sabbatian tradition is more reliable on this point than Leyb b. Ozer's memoir, for R. Abraham Yakhini, in one of his homilies, puts the following words into the mouth of the messiah: "The proud have digged pits for me (Ps. 119:85)—this is when they delivered him up to be put to death. . . . For thus says Our Lord, the true messiah: many faithful scholars were with me and I revealed to them the Mystery of your Godhead. . . . Now that I have been exiled by the gentiles because of the slanders of the mixed multitude I pray to thee [in the words of Ps. 119:79], 'Let those that fear thee return unto me.' "[121] Before long Sabbatian legend had metamorphosed the event into a story of miracles that bore no resemblance to historical fact. According to Abraham Cuenque, Sabbatai himself demanded his exile to a distant place, leaving his wife and son at the court of the sultan, who did not want to let him go.[122]

The effect of Sabbatai's banishment on the believers can be gauged from a long letter by R. Abraham Yakhini. The group in Adrianople disbanded, and those of its members who had not apostatized scattered. Samuel Primo went to live for several years in Sofia in Bulgaria where (according to Yakhini) the believers were still in the majority. Nathan wandered as a Sabbatian apostle (and probably as a refugee from the persecution which he encountered) from one place to another, returning from time to time to Kastoria. Yakhini's letter shows that the leading believers remained in close contact, encouraging one another and plying each other with letters, prophecies, visions, and calculations of the date of the "ultimate manifestation." Nathan was still considered by all as the central personality, and his prophetic authority was undisputed.[123] Yakhini gave free rein to his feelings and composed a whole book of poems in praise of Sabbatai.[124]

Yakhini's letter was written several months after Sabbatai's ban-

121. *Wawey ha-ᶜAmudim*, MS. Oxford 2761, fol. 107a.

122. *Ap.* Emden, p. 43. Cuenque conceals the fact of Sabbatai's trial, but represents Sabbatai as the sultan's friend. Even Tobias Rofe (*ibid.*, p. 46) insists that the sultan behaved in a very friendly way toward Sabbatai.

123. See Yakhini's letter, §1, in the text as published by A. Epstein in *RÉJ*, XXVI (1893), 210–15. Epstein misunderstood many details in the document that he published.

124. See *Sefunoth*, V (1961), 155. Only a few of his poems have survived.

ishment—probably in the summer of 1673. The opponents could now afford, after their partial victory, to become even more ruthless, while the believers in Constantinople and elsewhere were becoming a persecuted sect, living in fear of slanderers and informers. Incidentally, the letter provides information about one of the "strange actions" that Sabbatai was wont to perform when in a state of manic illumination. The detail is of considerable significance, since Sabbatian sources, as a rule, contain little specific information, preferring instead to talk in vague euphemisms about the messiah's mystical acts of *tiqqun*. During his last visit to Constantinople, Sabbatai performed such a mystical *tiqqun* with the betrothed of one of his followers and even made her a Muslim. The young man protested to Sabbatai that he had lain with his bride and that she might even be with child from her betrothed—but to no avail. The incident caused a scandal in Constantinople and many believers lost their faith "because they knew not, neither did they understand." At the time Sabbatai Ṣevi wrote to Yakhini, swearing by "the God of his Faith" that he had not as much as touched the girl. After a while it became apparent that the girl was pregnant. The son that was born of necessity had to grow up among the Turks as a son of Sabbatai—although, of course, Sabbatai had never touched the mother and although the child was the exact image of his mother's betrothed, "as is confirmed every day by those who see him." In spite of this comforting similarity, and in spite of the fact "that the fortress of my faith stands fast in my heart," Yakhini is unhappy and bewildered. Perhaps Nathan the prophet would allay his anguish and explain why "Our Lord, the Holy One of Israel" acted in a manner that would inevitably scandalize and alienate many believers. While it was true that the messiah's actions were all pure and holy, and the apocalypse of Zerubbabel had actually predicted that the messiah would give occasion for offense, blasphemy, and revilings,[125] yet why did God permit such terrible transgressions of the Law, which could not but lead people astray and shatter their faith?

125. On this forged apocalypse, see above, pp. 738 ff. Yakhini's opening quotation from the apocalypse was misunderstood by Epstein. The angelic name *mari ᶜaziz* is indeed rare in kabbalistic literature, though it occurs in an ancient magical formula (preserved in MS. Vatican 216, fols. 4b–6b) as *marya aziza* (*ibid.*, fol. 5b). In the present context, however, *mari ᶜaziz* is a Hebraicized form of Sabbatai's Turkish name (as, e.g., given by Galland and later Dönmeh tradition) Aziz Mehemed Effendi. It is the name of the messiah Sabbatai *alias* Aziz Effendi (Turk., *effendi* = Aram., *mari*) which Yakhini attributes to Metatron, the prince of angels.

We learn from Yakhini's letter that Sabbatai had married—in addition to his wife Sarah, who was with him in Adrianople—a woman who was betrothed to another man. The child was therefore legally Sabbatai's.[126] If he had indeed fathered the child of a betrothed woman this was adultery according to Jewish law (cf. Deut. 22:23) and his subsequent denial may serve as a prototype of the sexual license practiced in secret by the more radical groups of later Sabbatians. If Sabbatai did not touch the woman (as he himself asserted and as Yakhini testified—with considerable relief—from the looks of the child), then the incident, being nothing but a provocative and paradoxical demonstration, throws an interesting light on the complexities of Sabbatai's sexual life. Many years before, in Smyrna, Sabbatai had commanded his followers to deliver to him their virgin daughters and a few days later he returned them to their parents without having touched them.[127] Sabbatai's behavior presents a strange mixture of drives and inhibitions, the earliest examples of which can be found in his first two marriages. When he became master over a large number of enthusiastic followers he could indulge his fondness of alternating semierotic and semiascetic rituals. We may here remind ourselves of the charges laid against him in Constantinople (see above, p. 669). Even if there is reason to doubt that Sabbatai reviled and blasphemed the Muslim religion, we can easily imagine him clad in phylacteries, singing psalms and surrounded by women and wine. The picture fits the twilight atmosphere of Sabbatai's erotic mysticism.

Unfortunately, no letters are extant from the opposing camp to correct Yakhini's probably one-sided account. The Jews in Constantinople were presumably in a state of disarray and confusion, and tempers must have been running high. An Ashkenazi rabbi (probably R. Mordecai or R. Jacob Ashkenazi) was excommunicated, and later they insulted "in their wickedness even our master"—which probably means that the ban of excommunication against Nathan was formally renewed. Yakhini reports violent quarrels among the unbelievers in connection with their assessment, though it is not clear whether the reference is to taxes or to the bribe which had to be levied among

126. Epstein thought that the child was the aforementioned Ishmael, but this is impossible as the incident (Epstein calls it an *aventure gallante*) took place six years after the birth of Sabbatai's first son.

127. See above, p. 434, n. 244. I see no reason to doubt the veracity of this version.

the wealthier part of the community. In contrast to the confusion in the camp of the unbelievers, the life of the persecuted believers—like that of the early Christians—is described as an idyll of peace, harmony, and brotherly love.[128] Abraham Yakhini now breaks off his relations with the rabbis who are learned in the Talmud, "but spirit there is none in them," and withdraws into lonely waiting. By now the rabbis also grow more inquisitorial and open the letters of the believers to examine them for heresies. Abraham Cardozo had sent a tract to Sabbatai Ṣevi in which he prophesied the ultimate manifestation for the summer and autumn of 1673. The letter was probably written in Tripoli (and perhaps already in Tunis) where Cardozo lived at the time, but when the bearer came to Gallipoli,[129] the letter was opened. This incident, reported by Yakhini, is the first known case of censorship applied by the rabbis against Sabbatians.[130] Later this was practiced widely. Samuel Primo too is praised by Yakhini for suffering persecution for the sake of the faith,[131] but the allusions are too vague and obscure to permit detailed interpretation.

Yakhini entrusted his letter to R. Elijah Ashkenazi, the Polish preacher who had settled in Safed (see above, p. 428). Yakhini tells us that Elijah Ashkenazi had seen an "awesome dream" in which also Isaac Luria appeared, and as a result of which he recognized "the truth of Our Lord." No reason is given for his departure from Safed, though Yakhini hints that Ashkenazi was traveling in the hope of collecting a dowry for his daughter. When he arrived in Constanti-

128. Yakhini's letter, *loc. cit.* (above, n. 123), §8.

129. Cardozo probably wrote his letter before the news of Sabbatai's banishment had reached him, and hence it was brought to Adrianople. Yakhini heard the story from Abraham Ḥandali, one of the "kings" whom Sabbatai had appointed in Smyrna. Epstein's text (*loc. cit.*, §9) reads "Abraham Mandal," which is either a scribal or a printer's error.

130. Cardozo's letter is not identical with the first of his theological books expatiating on the difference between the "first cause" and the "God of Israel," the doctrine for which he later became widely known as an arch-heretic. This work, *Boqer ᵓAbraham* ("The Morning of Abraham"), which is extant in several manuscripts was written in 1672, and Cardozo sent it to Sabbatai, about whose messiahship the book is completely silent. The MS. Berlin 8°940 of this work (or rather, the work itself) was finished on 2 Kislev 5433 (November 30, 1672). The "long letter" which accompanied the book when it was sent by Cardozo to Adrianople arrived after Sabbatai's banishment to Dulcigno; cf. *Sefunoth* III–IV (1960), 216–17.

131. *Loc. cit.*, §11.

nople—apparently in 1673—he was ostracized by the rabbis because of his faith and decided to go to Sofia where there still was a majority of believers. Yakhini recommends him very warmly to the believers in Sofia. Sabbatai's great love for him "in those blessed days of 1666" should be reason enough for the believers in Sofia to receive the traveler honorably and hospitably.[132]

V

Galland (see above, p. 877) and other foreign diplomats did not specify the place of Sabbatai's exile, but merely reported that he had been "banished to the Morea," which comprised Greece and Albania.[133] Perhaps the Turkish authorities meant to keep the place of his exile a secret so as to avoid further commotion among the Jews. Early in the eighteenth century Leyb b. Ozer still repeated that Sabbatai had been exiled to Bassan (a district in Albania) to a place "where no Jew had ever set foot before,"[134] adding that he had not succeeded in finding out whither exactly he had been sent. According to Leyb, the rabbis in Turkey had threatened with excommunication anyone who mentioned Sabbatai's name, and hence "no good Jew would dare to inquire about this and to incur the penalty of the ban, while the [Sabbatian] believers invented all kinds of lies and confused one another. . . . As a result no Jew in Turkey knows where Sabbatai was and where he died."[135] On this as on other points, Leyb's account abounds in confusion and errors (see below, pp. 920 f.), for there is no doubt that at least during the first years both Jews and Christians knew the place of exile. De la Croix, writing in 1679, says[136] that Sabbatai was imprisoned in the fortress of Dulcigno in the Morea, while according to Tobias Rofe the Turks kept him there to see what he would do next.[137] Sabbatai lived as a political prisoner in banish-

132. *Loc. cit.*, §13–15.

133. Santi Bani, the ambassador of the duke of Tuscany, reported to Florence on January 19, 1673, that the proceedings against Sabbatai had been terminated by the end of December and that he had been banished to a place "where there was none of his nation"; see G. Levi in *Vessillo Israelitico*, LIX (1911), 513–15.

134. *Ap.* Emden, p. 25.

135. MS. Shazar, fol. 53b. In the printed version (*ap.* Emden) Leyb repeatedly mentions his efforts to find out the exact place.

136. *Op. cit.*, p. 384.

137. *Ap.* Emden, p. 46.

ment, that is, not in confinement, and after some time was even permitted to receive occasional visitors.

Dulcigno is at the extreme southern end of what is now Yugoslavia, on the Adriatic, and is today called Ulcinj. Sabbatian tradition preserved the name of the place both in Italian (Dulcigno) and in Turkish (Ülgün). The Turkish form Ülgün was changed by the Sabbatians to Alqum, alluding to Proverbs 30:31: "the king, against whom there is no rising up" (in Hebrew *melekh ᶜalqum*).[138] This verbal association was probably invented by Sabbatai himself, and an autograph letter of 1676 in which he signs as the king over all the kings, and as the anointed of the God of Israel and Judah, specifies "given at Alqum."[139] It stands to reason that his followers would soon have obtained information as to his whereabouts. Abraham Cardozo frequently mentions Alqum as Sabbatai's residence, and there is no reason to doubt that even those believers who would not explicitly mention the place knew of it.[140]

We do not know much about Sabbatai's state of mind after his banishment, though an interesting piece of information is preserved in a letter of Nathan's close associate during those years, R. Samuel Gandoor. Writing in September, 1677, to Moses Capsuto, a Sabbatian believer in Leghorn, Gandoor says, in connection with the fast of the Ninth of Ab, that "Your Honour knows that for the last six years we are observing the fast at his [that is, Sabbatai's] ordinance, . . . but without weeping, lamentations, and dirges."[141] The decree may

138. Samuel Primo, before visiting Sabbatai, wrote that he was about to go to the *melekh alkum;* see *Sefunoth,* V (1961), 274.

139. *Ibid.,* p. 250.

140. Baruch of Arezzo, writing less than ten years after Sabbatai's death (see G. Scholem in *Zion,* XVII [1952], p. 80), says that Sabbatai "was sent to Dulcigno, on the border of the land of Ishmael [i.e., Turkey] and Edom [i.e., the Christian countries, and he dwelt there until his occultation" (*ap.* Freimann, p. 66). A few years later Sabbatian legend is already in full bloom with Abraham Cuenque but, though he does not explicitly mention Dulcigno, Cuenque's description clearly refers to it: "a place far away at the end of the kingdom, where there are no Turks [except, of course, officials and the guards] but only uncircumcised [i.e., Christians]"; cf. *ap.* Emden, p. 43.

141. This letter allows us to date correctly the letter by Nathan as published (but wrongly dated) in *Sefunoth,* V (1961), 253–54. It is almost the same language as Gandoor's letter and explains that, for the time being, the fast of 9 Ab should be honored "in order to associate ourselves with Israel's grief" until everything will be revealed publicly. The letter fits only into the period after 1672.

well have been announced in Adrianople in 1672 and observed until Sabbatai's death, though it is equally possible that it was not issued until 1673 when Sabbatai was already in exile. At any rate we know that in the summer of 1671 the Ninth of Ab was celebrated as a festival for seven or ten days.[142] The compromise solution of observing the fast without, however, reciting the traditional lamentations is an attempt at marking time and clearly reflects the effect on Sabbatai of his exile.

Sabbatai's wife, "the Lady" Sarah, was allowed after some time to join her husband. The permission was given by the Great Vizier, who had received an appropriate bribe from Sabbatai's brother Elijah Ṣevi.[143] In Dulcigno, too, Sabbatai's life exhibited the familiar manic-depressive rhythm. He lived in a private world of his own imaginings, expressing himself in his letters to his followers in an allusive and symbolic style that hovers between the pathetic and the banal.[144] These letters, some of which have survived,[145] are short notes rather than long letters, and contain instructions concerning the observance, which is to say, abolition, of fast days, and an allusion that he might "return" on the Twenty-Fourth of Kislev, 5434 (December 21, 1673). It is not clear whether a return from banishment or a return to Judaism from his life as a Muslim is meant. Perhaps he believed that at that date the period of seven years of imprisonment by the *qelippah*, which had begun in the autumn of 1666, would come to an end, and the messianic mission connected therewith would be accomplished.[146]

142. See above, p. 844, the letter of the rabbi from Budapest, and p. 837.

143. De la Croix, p. 384. Also in Italy the Sabbatian believers knew that the messiah had to go into exile "together with his wife, in order to make reparation for Adam's sin, as it is written (Gen. 3:8), 'and Adam and his wife hid themselves' "; cf. G. Scholem in *Dinaburg Jubilee Volume,* p. 254. Subsequent discoveries enabled me to establish that the texts from which this quotation is taken were composed in the circle of Abraham Rovigo in Modena; cf. Is. Tishby, *In the Paths of Faith and Heresy* (Hebrew), (1964) pp. 81–107, 295–305.

144. Cf. Baruch of Arezzo, *ap.* Freimann, p. 67.

145. *Ibid.,* and also *Sefunoth,* V (1961), 250.

146. This surmise is based on the information given in the list of MSS. in the Günzburg Collection, Moscow, no. 1109 (vol. II, §279). Reference is made there to a Sabbatian MS., at the end of which is one leaf containing the "Holy Mystery of the Godhead" and another leaf beginning with the words "A decree of AMIRAH concerning the fasts [and] that he would return on 24 Kislev 434." No photostatic copy of this MS., which may contain documents

Soon afterward, in 1674, his wife Sarah died, and Sabbatai thought of consummating at last the marriage with the daughter of Aaron Majar of Sofia whom he had betrothed in the summer 1671.[147] The girl died before she could join Sabbatai in Dulcigno, but Sabbatai spoke about resurrecting her before long. Israel Ḥazzan mentions[148] a sealed letter which Sabbatai had sent with a Muslim mollah from Ülgün in Bashan[149] to his father-in-law Aaron Majar. On his way to Sofia, the bearer of the letter also took a message to the group of believers in Kastoria. When Nathan inquired for news about Sabbatai, the mollah told them of "the demise of the Lady and of the resurrection"[150] and that Sabbatai was hewing wood, cutting the big logs himself, and giving the smaller ones "to Our Lord Ishmael."

Ishmael, who was born in 1667 "when the forces of judgment had overcome those of mercy" and "under the turban" (that is, after the apostasy), was seven years old when his mother died. He had been with his father in Adrianople (see above, p. 848) and Israel Ḥazzan knew him personally. Since Nathan had prophesied that through this boy the gentiles would survive and be saved, as God "does not desire the destruction of his creation,"[151] Ishmael was the object of certain soteriological hopes in Sabbataian circles. According to Israel Ḥazzan, "the rank of Our Lord Ishmael will be like that of AMIRAH at the time of his anointing, for [after the ultimate manifestation]

---

relevant to the present subject, are available. The short superscription does not make it clear whether Sabbatai enjoined the observance of the fast (cf. Gandoor's letter, quoted above, p. 883) or whether the reference is to one of his earlier decrees abolishing the fast.

147. See above, p. 851. The exact sequence of events as established by the documents in the Amarillo Collection confirms Tishby's chronology in *Sefunoth,* III–IV (1960), 97, n. 32. Baruch of Arezzo (*ap.* Freimann, p. 66) wrongly dates Sarah's death before the banishment to Albania, whence others concluded that she died in Adrianople. Israel Ḥazzan's testimony as to the year of the death of "the Matrona" is decisive.

148. MS. Kaufmann 225; see *Schocken Volume,* p. 169.

149. The Sabbatians discovered in the name of the district of Bassan an allusion to Ps. 68:22: "The Lord said I will bring again from Bashan," and used "Bassan" for "Albania."

150. This probably refers to a resurrection which he expected to perform rather than to a miracle already performed. Sabbatai's promise "to resurrect his betrothed that died last year in Sofia" is also mentioned in a letter written in the summer of 1675 by Meir Rofe to Abraham Rovigo, *Sefunoth, loc. cit.*

151. Cf. Sasportas, *op. cit.,* p. 201.

AMIRAH will be exalted beyond the comprehension of mortals, but 'his seed shall mighty upon the earth' (Ps. 112:2) and he [that is, Ishmael] will be our Lord. For indeed AMIRAH had called him and told us [in Ishmael's presence]; This is your Lord." Ishmael was evidently still alive when Israel Ḥazzan wrote down these prophecies.[152]

The appointment of Ishmael as "Lord" and as heir to his father's throne may help to explain the custom adopted in the intimate circle of believers of referring to Sabbatai Ṣevi as the "Beloved." Nathan is said to have decreed "to call him [that is, Sabbatai] no longer Our Lord but Our Beloved."[153] This information is confirmed by the series of letters written in Leghorn by R. Meir Rofe of Hebron to R. Abraham Rovigo in Modena,[154] and in which Sabbatai is referred to exclusively by this title (which, incidentally, was also applied by the early Christians to Jesus).

Nothing more is said in our sources of the betrothed woman whom Sabbatai had taken away from her bridegroom in Constantinople, but her child who, according to Yakhini, grew up in Sabbatai's household and was considered by the Turks as his son, may well have been with him in Dulcigno. A child by the Hebrew name Abraham is mentioned by Sabbatai in his letter to his last father-in-law, R. Joseph Filosoff. But aside from Ishmael, Sarah had borne him only one daughter (in 1672).

Filosoff was a highly esteemed scholar in Salonika,[155] and after the death of his betrothed in Sofia, Sabbatai asked Filosoff for his daughter. Joseph Filosoff, who was Nathan's disciple in Sabbatian kabbalah, consented in spite of the grave personal consequences which this new family relationship would entail for him. To the rabbis and lay leaders of the Jewish community who deposed him from the rabbinate and discontinued his salary he answered: "I know what I am

152. See *Schocken Volume,* pp. 172–73.

153. *Ap.* Freimann, p. 96.

154. The quotations from these letters given in the original (Hebrew) edn. of the present work were taken from Meir Rofe's autograph MS. in the Brit. Mus. (Or. 9165). Since then Is. Tishby has published "R. Meir Rofe's letters of 1675–1680 to R. Abraham Rovigo" in *Sefunoth,* III–IV (1960), 73–130.

155. For expressions of the esteem in which Filosoff was held, cf. Michael Wilenski, *Kiryath Sepher,* XV (1939), 491 (quoting R. Joseph David of Salonika), and Rosanes, vol. IV, pp. 15 and 88 (quoting Filosoff's father-in-law, the renowned R. Baruch Angel of Salonika).

doing. The thing proceedeth from the Lord" (cf. Gen. 24:50), and "he sent her, accompanied by his son,[156] and the marriage took place in Dulcigno . . . according to the Jewish rite."[157] Sabbatai considered Joseph Filosoff to be an incarnation of Saul, addressing him in his letters as Saul and referring to his daughter (that is, Sabbatai's wife) as Michal.[158]

The marriage took place in 1675, and the news soon reached Leghorn where Meir Rofe of Hebron was residing at the time. Rofe had left the Holy Land together with Nathan of Gaza in the autumn of 1666, and was a member of Nathan's intimate circle in Adrianople where he also received the "Mystery of the Godhead."[159] Sasportas could not conceal his astonishment that this scholar, "after seeing Sabbatai apostatize, still persevered in his faith, saying that he [Sabbatai] and none other is the Messiah." He exchanged letters with the leading Sabbatians, comforting them and confirming them in their faith. The exact dates of his stay at Leghorn are not known, though he certainly was already there in the summer of 1674,[160] and did not leave before the winter of 1678.[161] While at Leghorn he was appointed by the Jewish community of Hebron as their official emissary,[162] and his pres-

156. This son, Jacob Filosoff (also known as Jacob Qerido) was to become later one of the leaders of the Dönmeh.

157. Baruch of Arezzo, *ap.* Freimann, p. 67; cf. also Moses Ḥagiz's account, *ap.* Emden, p. 43. The marriage is also mentioned by Meir Rofe, *Sefunoth,* III–IV (1960), 96.

158. The daughter of Saul; cf. I Sam. 18:22. In the letter to Filosoff in which Sabbatai asks for the hand of his daughter, Sabbatai writes, "Give me thy daughter Michal for a wife" (MS. Günzburg 517, fol. 81a). At the same time, he was also considered a reincarnation of Mordecai, and his daughter as Esther.

159. Rofe was undoubtedly one of the four unnamed scholars from Hebron whom (according to Cuenque, *ap.* Emden, p. 41) Sabbatai had summoned to Constantinople. On his sojourn in Adrianople, see Sasportas, *op. cit.,* p. 363, and Cardozo's letter, *ap.* Weiss, *Beth ha-Midrash* (1865), p. 64.

160. Sasportas, *op. cit.,* p. 363.

161. That being the date of his last letter from Leghorn to Rovigo.

162. See *Sefunoth,* III–IV (1960), 97. Rofe had been active on behalf of the community of Hebron as early as 1650–52, and was considered as the trustee of their interests. In 1677 he turned homeward and, after having tarried for several months in Egypt, reached Hebron again in the autumn of 1678. (His first letter from Hebron to Modena is dated 15 Kislev 5439, i.e., November 30, 1678.) This disposes of the allegation that Rofe was afraid of returning home; "and some suspect the aforementioned R. Meir of having apostatized with Sabbatai and

tige as a scholar and as a representative of Hebron probably gave him immunity from molestation and contumely although his steadfast Sabbatian faith was well known. He was careful to avoid references to Sabbatai's messiahship in public or in his correspondence with unbelievers,[163] yet his presence in Italy was undoubtedly a source of comfort and strength to the believers there. Writing to Rovigo in the summer of 1675, Rofe reports that the "Beloved" had married the daughter of Rabbi Florentin[164] and that the prophet Nathan and Samuel Primo had gone to him. "Surely it is not without reason that R. Nathan had resolved to visit him [now]," and consequently Rofe was expecting good tidings very soon "and then I shall return to my earlier abode with the Beloved."[165]

Sabbatai had no children from his last marriage, though in a letter to his father-in-law he refers to his wife as the "mother" of his two sons (actually her stepsons). Dönmeh tradition has it that Sabbatai's last wife was called Jochebed,[166] though her husband gave her other, symbolic names. Rovigo's "Sabbatian Notebook"[167] contains a poem by Joseph Filosoff in honor of his daughter's marriage in

---

others, which is proved by the fact that he remained in the Diaspora and did not return home to Hebron, evidently because he was afraid" (Sasportas, *ibid.*). "R. Meir Stern of Hebron" whom Ber Eibeshütz Perlhefter (on the latter see Is. Tishby, "The first Sabbatian *maggid* in Abraham Rovigo's Circle," in *Zion*, XXII [1957], 21–55) met in Rovigo's entourage in Modena (see Perlhefter, *Be᾿er Sheba*ᶜ, MS. Oxford, Catalogue Neubauer no. 1416) is none other than Meir Rofe. On the opinions of other contemporaries on Meir Rofe see M. Benayahu, "The Letters of R. Samuel Aboab" etc., *Yerushalayim*, II, 5 (1955), 153, 179.

163. The letter to Amsterdam (1673 or 1674) in which Rofe reports that after having banished Sabbatai, the sultan "had recalled him and honored him greatly" may have been addressed to Abraham Pereira who was a prominent Sabbatian as well as the maecenas of the *yeshibah* in Hebron.

164. A confusion of the names Florentin and Filosoff.

165. *Sefunoth,* III–IV (1960), 96–97.

166. Cf. Galanté, p. 58, and in a number of Dönmeh songs, e.g., Attias and Scholem, *Shiroth we-Tishbaḥoth* (1948), p. 205. She, too, converted to Islam and took the name ᶜ*Aysha.* Her grave, which still existed fifty years ago, was a place of pilgrimage for the sectarians; cf. I. R. Molkho in *Reshumoth,* VI (Tel Aviv, 1930), 539. It is regrettable that nobody has taken the trouble to copy the Turkish inscription on the stone, which would probably have yielded the date of her death.

167. MS. in the Ben-Zvi Institute at the Hebrew University of Jerusalem, fol. 19b (bequest of Dr. Is. Sonne, formerly Cincinnati).

which she is three times called Esther. The same name also occurs in a short and cryptic letter addressed by Sabbatai Ṣevi to "Saul [that is, Joseph Filosoff], the elect of God, [who is] Mordecai, the son of Jair, the son of Shimei, the son of Kish, a Benjamite"[168] in which reference is made "to my wife Hadassah Mikhal, who is Esther,[169] my sister, my love, my dove, my undefiled [cf. Song of Songs 5:2] and her [*sic*] two sons Ishmael and Abraham." While it is not impossible that Esther and Hadassah are allegorical names too,[170] it is equally possible that her original name was Esther (rather than Jochebed) and that the only allegorical name given to her by Sabbatai was Michal. The letter[171] was written by Sabbatai in the spring of 1676 when he was in a state of illuminate exaltation, and announced his impending visit, accompanied by his family, to Filosoff. It was signed "the Anointed of the God of Israël and Judah"—a signature which recurs in other letters of that period and which may reflect a new development in Sabbatai's theology of the "Mystery of the Godhead."

The first years of Sabbatai's exile were a period of tense waiting for his believers, who expected decisive events at any moment. Abraham Rovigo in Modena was particularly eager in his expectations of good tidings and Meir Rofe had repeatedly to disappoint him: "as regards the Beloved, there is no news. If any good news should arrive, I will let you know." The reports of Sabbatai's marriage raised the messianic hopes in vain. Late in the summer of 1675 Rofe writes that Moses Pinheiro had received a letter in which his correspondent reported that he had spoken "about the Beloved with his brother R. Joseph [Ṣevi], and he told me that there was no news at present but that he daily expected letters from his brother Elijah [Ṣevi] in Adrianople, who had notified him that he would soon have news for him from Our Lord and brother." The "news" probably refers to Sabbatai's marriage.

Rofe's letters to Rovigo illuminate the mood and expectations that were rife in the small circle of believers in Leghorn, and they supplement the information gathered by Sasportas—albeit with the bias of an opponent—during 1674. The letters convey a characteristi-

168. Cf. Esther 2:5; according to rabbinic legend Mordecai was a descendant of Saul.

169. Hadassah and Esther are identical; cf. Esther 2:7.

170. Cf. above, n. 159.

171. Quoted by Baruch of Arezzo, *ap.* Freimann, p. 68.

cally "sectarian" mood, as we also found it in Constantinople,[172] and it developed with remarkable rapidity. The center of sectarian life in Leghorn was the house of Moses Pinheiro, whose grandson, R. Joseph Ergas, was to become one of the leading and most determined anti-Sabbatian fighters some forty years later.[173] Some time in 1674 a young scholar by name of Moses Harari[174] arrived in Leghorn. He had been one of the believers who apostatized in Adrianople, but then escaped to a non-Muslim country in order to return to the Jewish religion without, however, abandoning his Sabbatian faith. In Italy he exhibited the typical double-faced behavior of a clandestine sectarian. To the unbelievers he said that the Sabbatian faith was all lies and falsehood, "but in secret he went to the believers, exhorting them to persevere in their faith and [assuring them] that all he said to the unbelievers was untrue . . . and was merely said for the sake of security." The believers met in Pinheiro's house where Harari expounded to them passages in the Zohar that contained mystical allusions to Sabbatai Ṣevi, and taught "that he who does not believe [in Sabbatai Ṣevi] cannot be called an Israelite." The elders of the Jewish community, who knew that he had already apostatized once, were afraid of excommunicating him lest he apostatize again and become a Christian. Pinheiro and Harari were joined by R. Judah Sharaf, Primo's teacher and one of the earliest believers in Gaza, who spent his last years in Leghorn where he died in 1675. The authority and prestige of this group, renowned as they were for their great learning and ascetic piety, undoubtedly conferred a protective halo on the Sabbatian circle. For a while they were reinforced by the presence of Abraham Cardozo who had come from Tunis to Leghorn in the autumn of 1674, but was forced by the elders of the Jewish community to leave at the end of May, 1675.[175]

172. Cf. the analysis of Yakhini's letter above, pp. 878–80.

173. Curiously enough R. Malachi Kohen of Leghorn (in his preface to Ergas' *Dibrey Yosef,* Leghorn, 1742) praises Pinheiro as a great ascetic and kabbalist, without so much as hinting at Pinheiro's Sabbatian involvements, which were still very strong at the time that R. Emanuel Ergas married his daughter Sarah.

174. He was later to become a rabbi in Aleppo and to acquire a reputation as a master of "practical kabbalah"; see Tishby's note to Sasportas, *op. cit.,* p. 362.

175. Cf. Rofe's letter in *Sefunoth,* III–IV (1960), 95. From Leghorn Cardozo went to Smyrna.

There must have been much coming and going between the Balkans and Italy, and Meir Rofe and Moses Harari were surely not the only travelers bringing the Italian faithful letters and news of Sabbatai Ṣevi and Nathan. A letter written by Abraham Rovigo in 1675 or 1676 to the prophet Nathan in Kastoria throws much light on the inner life, perplexities, and struggles of an earnest Sabbatian, and may serve us as a kind of prototype of a *confessio credentis*. The original letter is lost, but Rovigo's own handwritten copy has survived.[176] Rovigo had entrusted the letter to travelers who had arrived from Kastoria and were about to return thither, and it was clearly written after Rovigo had received—perhaps from Meir Rofe—copies of some of Nathan's Sabbatian writings. In fact, Rovigo's references to "the bearer of this letter" fit Rofe in every respect, and one would be tempted to identify the two were it not for the fact that Rofe settled in Leghorn and did not return to Kastoria.[177] Rovigo clearly exaggerates a little when describing his isolation and loneliness in Modena, far away from the presence of the Lord and of his messiah and even from congenial Sabbatian company, and it is puzzling that he makes no reference at all to the very active Sabbatian group in Leghorn. He is dependent for news and information "on travelers visiting this country and staying at my house," but had the good fortune of seeing some of Nathan's writings, full of his wonderful and awesome wisdom. In particular "the bearer of this letter," arriving from Kastoria, had refreshed the writer's heart with firsthand news of Sabbatai and Nathan, "and thanks be to God that I am a very true believer." Personal circumstances (which the bearer of the letter would explain to Nathan) prevented him from leaving Modena and hastening to the "mountain of the Lord" in the Balkans, yet if Nathan would summon him he would leave everything and spare no expense to obey his command. He begs of Nathan to "reveal to me the root of my soul" and to let him know the appropriate *tiqqun*. He would be very happy if Nathan would deign to answer him ("through the

176. It was published by Is. Sonne in the *Alexander Marx Jubilee Volume* (1953), pp. 89–93. The text of the letter is also given in *SS* (pp. 756–67), where I have corrected some readings on the basis of a photocopy of the Cincinnati MS. which Dr. Sonne had kindly placed at my disposal. A facsimile of the MS. appears in the Hebrew edn. of this work facing p. 770.

177. It is not impossible, however, that the letter was written at a moment when, as a result of the rumors of imminent good tidings in 1675, Rofe expected "every day" to return to the presence of the messiah and the prophet.

same friend") and possibly also give some news about AMIRAH.

Comparing this outpouring of faith, devout abandon, and intense longing with the letters which Rovigo wrote to R. Moses Zacuto, it seems almost impossible that they were written by the same man. Zacuto had been Rovigo's teacher of Lurianic kabbalah, and the letters demonstrate—if such demonstration were needed—the difficulty of drawing valid conclusions from writings addressed by believers to nonbelievers. It was only when writing to fellow believers that the Sabbatians opened their hearts and spoke their minds, a fact which has been conveniently overlooked in the discussions on later Sabbatianism.

Having given up his plans of continuing his voyage to Tunis and Tripoli, and while waiting "every day" to return to the presence of the messiah, Meir Rofe devoted himself to spreading Nathan's writings among the believers. The recipients had to promise not to part with these writings or show them to strangers. The copying, too, had to be done by trusted scribes. Nathan's tracts were thus on the way to becoming "underground literature" as early as 1675.[178] As during the great messianic revival in 1666, rumors were rife of mighty miracles wrought by Sabbatai. Meir Rofe dismisses them as lies and falsehood, and assures Rovigo, "God forbid that I should have concealed them from Your Honor if there had been any truth in them."[179]

Rofe's letters reflect the life and the expectations of the Sabbatian believers in Leghorn and Modena. Their life was one of traditional devotion and ascetic piety. Withdrawn into themselves and experiencing the messianic hope in their hearts, they had neither the antinomian and paradoxical preoccupations of the apostate group, nor any particular desire to debate doctrinal niceties regarding the mystical status of the messiah.[180] Elsewhere, however, the tension of expectation reached new heights and exploded in new manifestations of messianic fervor. Reports received by both unbelievers and believers (and especially in the immediate circle of Sabbatai Ṣevi) indicated that pro-

178. Problems relating to the copying and the transmission of the Sabbatian writings in the possession of Meir Rofe are mentioned several times in his correspondence with Rovigo.

179. *Sefunoth,* III–IV (1960), 105. Similar stories of miracles that were supposed to have occurred toward the end of Sabbatai's life in 1676 are reported by Baruch of Arezzo, *ap.* Freimann, p. 67.

180. R. Joseph Ḥamiṣ of Zante, who until 1675 composed his Sabbatian homilies for his personal reading only, is a similar case, and his faith is marked by ascetic piety.

phetic revelations and other manifestations had occurred in the most diverse and distant places in the years 1674–75 (that is, after Sabbatai's banishment to Dulcigno). Abraham Cardozo's activity during those years, as in fact the whole career of this remarkable former marrano and Sabbatian leader, deserves separate treatment. For our present purpose it may suffice to note that in 1673 he began to send letters to several countries (including one letter to Sabbatai himself; see above, p. 881), confirming the mission of Sabbatai as "the anointed of the God of Jacob"[181] and announcing the beginning of the final denouement for the autumn of 1673. His message produced considerable agitation and divisions in the Jewish communities in Tripoli and Tunis, where Cardozo was at that time.

In Amsterdam, too, Cardozo's message produced a considerable effect on the not insignificant group of believers. We owe our information about this group to the fact that Sasportas happened to live in Amsterdam during those years and added the relevant reports and documents to his "file." Similar reactions may have occurred also in other communities, but there was no Sasportas to chronicle them. Cardozo's letters arrived in Amsterdam before the Ninth of Ab, 1673, and the believers decided to omit the reading of the Book of Lamentations and the recitation of the dirges while, however, observing the fast—just as Nathan and Gandoor had urged their correspondents to behave (see above, p. 883). When the date set by Cardozo had passed, they argued that the termination of the war between Holland and England in February, 1674—undoubtedly an important event in the economic life of the Netherlands—was such a messianic portent. More letters from Cardozo kept arriving, urging believers to be prepared for further events in 1675.

The believers in Amsterdam used to meet in the house of their leader Emanuel Benattar,[182] the *ḥazzan* of the Portuguese Synagogue, and seem to have been unmolested by the Jewish authorities, possibly because they had the very pious and very wealthy Abraham Pereira among their members.[183] The group was joined in 1674 by the well-known marrano writer and poet Daniel Levi de Barrios (1625–1701). De Barrios wrote in Spanish and was highly esteemed among Jews

181. Sasportas, *op. cit.*, p. 361.

182. Cf. above, p. 755; the name is sometimes given as Abiatar (cf. Sasportas, p. 363).

183. Sasportas, *ibid.;* cf. also above, p. 755.

and Christians. He served as an officer in the Spanish army in Belgium even after his public return to Judaism, but subsequently resigned his commission and settled in Amsterdam in order to devote himself to composing poems on biblical subjects which he dedicated to various (including Spanish and Portuguese) noblemen. It is not clear whether he left the army as a result of his religious experiences and Sabbatian visions, or whether these came to him only after he had settled in Amsterdam and made the acquaintance of Sabbatian believers. We owe our knowledge of his Sabbatian contacts to Sasportas, who tells us that after the arrival of Cardozo's messages in 1674, de Barrios "threw away his books [of poetry]. He accepted the rumors, and his imagination waxed powerful . . . to the point that he almost considered himself a prophet, confirming the words of Nathan and Cardozo." There existed a curious friendship between the enthusiastic poet and the stern heresy-hunter. De Barrios, in 1674 or 1675, fasted for several days as a result of a vision which he had had; his wife became very much worried about his state of mind and turned to Sasportas for help. They had a long talk, and de Barrios confided all his "wild exaggerations and vain imaginings" to Sasportas, including such revelations as "the signs of redemption will become manifest before the Ninth of Ab, the messiah Sabbatai Ṣevi will come before the beginning of the Jewish New Year. . . . all the Christians (and especially the ruler of Holland, Prince William of Orange) would become Jews. . . . the king of France was Nebuchadnezzar. . . . and the king of Spain was Hiram, the king of Tyre and such like." De Barrios received his revelations (including the biblical texts that went with them) in Spanish and not in Hebrew, and sought the advice of his friend Sasportas who tried to convince him "that your imaginative faculty has waxed so strong [as a result of] your solitude, that you seem to experience waking revelations."[184] This moderate and friendly tone is very unlike the invective which Sasportas usually poured out when dealing with Sabbatians. In fact, he told de Barrios "that if he wants to believe in Sabbatai let him do so [*sic!*] provided he does not neglect to . . . work on the poems which he has begun. This he promised me to do." Nevertheless, de Barrios continued to act like a prophet, putting up a notice in the synagogue to the effect: "I, Daniel, warn you to repent, for a great punishment will be coming."[185] The book of Sabbatian visions which de Barrios composed

184. Sasportas, *ibid.*, p. 364. 185. *Ibid.*, p. 365.

in 1674 is lost, and he makes no further reference to this episode in his life in the many writings which he composed during the following twenty-five years.[186]

Of much greater proportions was the revival in the Jewish communities of Morocco which, in spite of the many disappointments, still counted a large number of believers. Whereas in Amsterdam the prophetic inspiration was felt by a well-known Spanish marrano who had returned to the ancestral religion, the Moroccan prophet came from a lower social class. He was a "pious but ignorant man," that is, someone who could read the Bible, Haggadic texts, and the writings of the moralists, but was no Talmudic scholar and "unable to read the rabbinic commentators."[187] Thanks to the detailed account and the documents given by Baruch of Arezzo,[188] we are fairly well informed about this episode. The new prophet, Joseph Ben Ṣur, was an unmarried young man in Meknes where, according to Sasportas, the anti-Sabbatian rabbis were the stronger party.[189] Nevertheless, Sabbatian influences were not negligible. Toward the end of his life, R. Elisha Ashkenazi, the father of the prophet Nathan, arrived in Meknes, and his death and burial there in the summer of 1673 made a deep impression on many people.[190] We may assume that wherever he went, Elisha Ashkenazi was asked for news about his illustrious

186. On the significance of de Barrios as historian of the Portuguese congregation in Amsterdam, see W. C. Pieterse, *Daniel Levi de Barrios as a Historian of the Portuguese Jewish Congregation in Amsterdam in His Triumpho de Governo Popular,* 1968. Kenneth Scholberg's article on de Barrios in *JQR* LIII (1962), 120–59, makes no mention of his involvement in the Sabbatian movement.

187. Sasportas, p. 369. Elsewhere it is said that the prophet admitted that he could not even read the Bible.

188. *Ap.* Freimann, pp. 73–76.

189. Sasportas, pp. 324–25. In Meknes, as in other communities near Fez, the fast days were strictly observed.

190. See G. Scholem, *Kitvey Yad be-Kabbalah* (Jerusalem, 1930), p. 104, where the reference to Ashkenazi's death is quoted. The copyist of the MS., Daniel Bahlul, is known from another source (Kabbalistic MS. 91 in the Schocken Library, Jerusalem) to have been an ardent believer who, in addition to writing his own Sabbatian homilies, also copied the revelations of the prophet Joseph Ben Ṣur. Cf. also *Malkey Rabbanan* (Jerusalem, 1931, p. 64a) on the rabbis of Morocco. The Ben Ṣurs were a family of eminent rabbis in Meknes, a fact which raises some doubts about the alleged ignorance of the Moroccan prophet. The most outstanding rabbi of Meknes in the next generation, R. Jacob Ben Ṣur, was "born on the day of the demise" of Elisha Ashkenazi.

son, the prophet of Gaza, and it may have been he who brought with him Nathan's Sabbatian writings which subsequently had such wide circulation in Morocco.

Joseph Ben Ṣur was visited by a celestial *maggid* who announced the coming of the messiah and baptized him with so much water "that he had to change his clothes. Then he was shown Our Lord and King, Sabbatai Ṣevi, in Heaven, and was told: he is the true savior, and R. Nathan Benjamin is a true prophet, and thou art the messiah of the House of Joseph."[191] As we have seen earlier, the non-appearance of a messiah of the House of Joseph who should have preceded the appearance of Sabbatai Ṣevi had worried Sabbatian believers all the time, and many prophetic enthusiasts saw themselves destined for this particular role. On the same occasion the archangel Raphael also revealed to Joseph Ben Ṣur the true order of the alphabet as it was given on Mount Sinai and before it was confused again as a result of Israel's sin when they worshiped the golden calf. This "true order" of the letters was arranged in a manner that it could be read, or at least interpreted, as a Sabbatian prophecy. In the light of this new or, rather, original order of the alphabet, a new understanding of the Torah and its mysteries was possible, and the rabbis of Fez, Salé, and Tetuán came to Meknes and were amazed at the kabbalistic profundities the like of which they had never heard before. The prophet announced that redemption would take place on the eve of Passover, 1675, and the wave of penitence that swept Morocco was said to be "even greater than at the first appearance of Our Lord" in 1665–66. Even rabbis that had spoken evil about Sabbatai repented, "and now they believe in this faith." The patriarch Abraham revealed to the prophet that redemption should actually have taken place in 1665, but was postponed for ten years because Sabbatai had asked God to spare Israel the sufferings and pangs of the messianic coming, and to save the unbelievers from the death to which they had already been condemned. The purpose of the apostasy was that the messiah, being scorned and reviled, would thereby vicariously bear the messianic woes. While dwelling in the *qelippah,* the messiah would draw to himself all the scattered sparks of holiness.[192]

191. Freimann, p. 73. All quotations are taken from Baruch of Arezzo's account, *ibid.,* pp. 73–76. Part of Baruch's account (p. 73) is drawn from a letter that was sent to Leghorn (*ibid.,* p. 75).

192. The Sabbatian author offers an explanation (*ibid.,* p. 74) why the

A kabbalist rabbi who visited the prophet gave a psychologically most valuable account of the meeting in a letter to a friend. Writing on February 5, 1675, to his friend R. Benjamin Duran of Algiers, R. Abraham b. Amram reports that he went to the prophet of Meknes in order to receive answers on some difficult problems of interpretation in the Zohar. The young man, who seemed "humble, God-fearing, and full of virtue" told him that he was so ignorant that he could not read a simple text, let alone explain the mysteries of the Zohar. But when the spirit was upon him he spoke beautifully and most fluently, and revealed mysteries which were too holy to be committed to writing. He also proved by his calculations that the messianic manifestation would take place on Passover. When the visitor insisted on asking questions relating to the Zohar, the prophet replied:

"I do not know who speaks with me, and I neither see nor speak, but my lips are speaking and I hear the voice that proceeds from them." And when I said to him, "Perhaps you can ask [and put my questions to your celestial mentor]," he replied: "all my senses are in abeyance and I do not know whether I am in Heaven or on earth." He cannot even open his eyes for they are weighed down as if by lead. . . . When I asked him whether he was the messiah of the House of Joseph, he replied that this was what he was told. . . . In brief, I went from there with a glad heart, having seen that this was not a matter of an evil spirit or demon. . . . When I asked him for a miracle or sign, he replied: "What is the greater miracle? . . . I could not read even the Bible, and now I discourse on kabbalistic mysteries. I do not even tell you to wait one year or two for the ultimate redemption, but merely two months. You need not ask more."[193]

Stimulated by these prophecies, another Sabbatian believer in Meknes composed his messianic homilies and kabbalistic interpretations, predicting the final redemption for the year 1674. The original messianic year had been 1668—exactly 1,600 years after the destruc-

---

messiah had to descend into the Muslim rather than the Christian *qelippah:* all the holy sparks in Edom (Christendom) were concentrated in Turkey, for the janissaries are chosen from among young Christian boys who are brought up as Turks, and Providence sees to it that only those are chosen who happen to be the bearers of a holy spark. Therefore all the holy sparks of Edom and Ishmael are now "sunk," or concentrated, in the Grand Turk.

193. *Ibid.*, pp. 74–75.

tion of the Temple, according to Jewish chronology—but God in His mercy had added another six years and six months so as to save Israel from the pangs and woes of the messianic coming.[194] When the appointed time had passed and nothing had happened, the prophet explained that this was because of Israel's many sins, but that these sins were now being atoned for vicariously by his [that is, the prophet's] humiliation and sorrow at being considered a liar. A Jew from Salé in Morocco, writing to his brother in Leghorn late in the summer of 1675, reports that "we trust in the Lord that redemption will take place in 1676. All the marranos in the West are engaged in penitential exercises . . . and are preparing festive clothes to be ready to go to Jerusalem." This date also passed, and soon afterward the prophet Joseph Ben Ṣur died.[195] According to Sasportas[196] the believers explained the failure of the prophecy with a curious and novel theory: the messiah of the House of Joseph should have married into the family of the Davidic messiah (that is, he should have married a daughter of Sabbatai Ṣevi). Here the person of the messiah of the House of Joseph is already divested of its traditional meanings and associations, and has become a sort of shadow or viceroy to the Davidic messiah. This notion can be found quite often in later Sabbatian literature.

There was a logic in these outbursts of messianic expectation. They were all based on the assumption of some kind of rhythm in the process of redemption. Periods of seven years or of ten years were equally acceptable units and made sense from a kabbalistic point of view. The only difficulty was how to date the beginning of this period. Did it begin with Sabbatai's manifestation as messiah in 1665, or with his apostasy? Consequently, different dates, ranging from 1672 to 1675, were obtained for the final manifestation. But these were the last convulsions of Sabbatianism as a public phenomenon. Thereafter it went underground also in Holland and Morocco, as it had

194. Cf. above, n. 190, on Daniel b. Juda Bahlul. His autograph MS. was written early in March, 1675.

195. Freimann, p. 76. Baruch of Arezzo (*ibid.*) insists that Joseph Ben Ṣur cannot possibly have been a false prophet, and that it was divine Providence which disposed things that way. The letter from Salé mentions (among other legendary rumors) that the prophet's face was so radiant that visitors could speak to him only through a curtain. This is contradicted by Abraham b. Amram's letter to Algiers.

196. *Op. cit.*, p. 369.

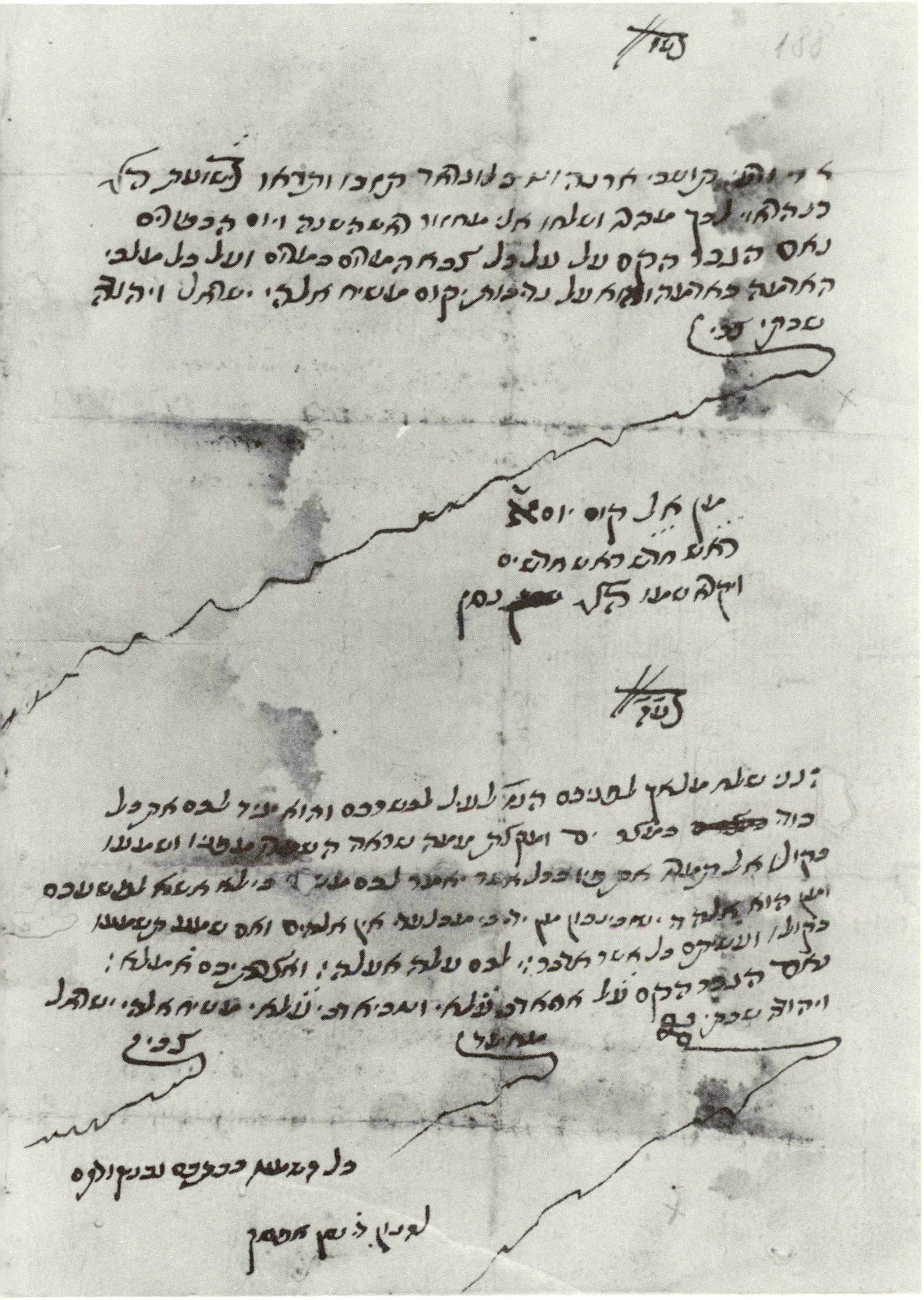

The only autograph letter by Sabbatai Ṣevi, written in August, 1676, to the Jewish community of Berat, Albania, asking for a Hebrew prayerbook for the High Holy Days in September, 1676. MS. 2262, fol. 79, Ben-Zvi Institute, Jerusalem

earlier begun to develop into a clandestine sectarianism in Turkey and Italy.

VI

Most of the time Sabbatai led a solitary life in his Albanian exile. He remained in contact with his faithful in Constantinople, Adrianople, Sofia, Salonika, and Kastoria, but our information is fragmentary and accidental, and hardly permits us to reconstruct the complete picture. His "court rabbis" used to visit him—possibly disguised as Turks. Primo seems to have visited him several times, but at least twice. On the first visit he was accompanied by R. Abraham Gaon (of Sofia?) who marred the visit by some unfriendly acts about whose details Primo keeps silent.[197] On the second visit we have testimonies from both Primo and Nathan. It took place, as was mentioned above (p. 888), in 1675. The small community of Belgrade (or Berat, in Turkish) in Albania had served as a center of communication for some followers of Sabbatai. We have a letter written probably on Nisan 1, [5435?] (March 28, 1675) from Elbassan to R. Isaac Albalag in Belgrade, telling him of the vicissitudes of the journey. Primo regrets having missed Nathan with whom he wished to be together on this occasion. He (Primo) had traveled from Sofia to Üsküb (Skoplje), where he had been taken ill for ten days. At Üsküb he received a special message from Sabbatai inviting him to come because he was in a state of illumination. Next Monday, he says, he would be on his way to see the "king in Alqum," and promises to pass through Belgrade on his way back. He may even have to spend Passover in the comfortable house of the addressee where he promises to show him Sabbatai's letter and other "good tidings." Albalag was a rich member of the community and its foremost lay leader, as we know from other contemporary sources.[198] It is obvious that he shared Primo's Sabbatian convictions and Sabbatai knew that he could turn to him and

197. All this and the following details are based on Primo's autograph letter from Elbassan, published (with a facsimile) from the Dönmeh archives in *Sefunoth,* V (1961), 272–74.

198. See Rosanes, vol. IV, p. 273 (who on p. 245 mixed up the two Belgrades and put Albalag into the Serbian one), and the signature of Albalag as the most prominent member of the community in the notebook kept by Joseph Kohen, an emissary on behalf of Hebron, on June 10, 1676; cf. Jacob M. Toledano, *Sarid u-palait* (1945), p. 47.

his associates without fear of being repudiated, as he did some weeks before his death.

How long Primo actually stayed in Dulcigno is not known. At any rate, we have another letter sent by Nathan to Shemaya de Mayo, a member of the rabbinic court in Kastoria, which probably refers to the same visit: "Five weeks ago I left Sofia in order to travel in these parts, in the hope that I might find grace in the eyes of AMIRAH and be received by him. R. Samuel Primo preceded me by three weeks . . . and he is still standing before the Lord. But when he came, he found him [that is, Sabbatai] in the mystery of the fallen one [that is, in a state of depression]. I waited for a fortnight in Durazzo[199] and sent a messenger to ask permission, but he refused and I had to come hither to Belgrade [that is, Berat][200] to wait until his great light will shine [on me] and I may behold his face."[201]

Some light is thrown on these mysterious visits by Meir Rofe, who seems to have obtained his information either from Nathan and Primo themselves or from one of their confidants, such as Samuel Gandoor. Meir Rofe mentions in one of his letters that visitors came by personal invitation only (as, for example, in the aforementioned case of Samuel Primo). In the summer of 1675 Rofe writes that he postponed his projected voyage to Tunisia because of the arrival of good tidings "and especially the visit of R. Nathan who came to the Beloved *without being called* and this is surely no vain thing . . . and forsooth the time has come that the Lord will remember his people." Evidently Nathan and Primo had heard of the state of renewed illumination and rejoicing coinciding with Sabbatai's marriage, and

199. Baruch of Arezzo (*ap*. Freimann, p. 67) has a story about an emissary of the Ten Tribes who came to Nathan's residence in Kastoria in 1675, bringing a letter to Nathan and Sabbatai. "This emissary then went [from Kastoria] to Dulcigno via Durazzo, and delivered it into the pure hand of Our Lord himself, but its contents are not known." Subsequently it was understood that the letter contained an invitation to the messiah to join the distant tribes (the "Sons of Moses") during his period of occultation. Both Durazzo and Dulcigno were on the shore of the Adriatic.

200. Berat in Albania was also called Arnaut-Belgrade to distinguish it from the better known Belgrade in Yugoslavia. Nathan's letter proves that Sabbatai did not stay at Berat, and that Nathan repaired thither only because he was refused an audience in Dulcigno. Berat had a small Jewish community.

201. The text of the letter is published in *RÉJ*, CIV (1938), 120–21; cf. also my remarks in *Zion*, XVII (1952), 80–81.

they hastened to him without waiting for an invitation. Meanwhile Sabbatai had another fit of depression and would not see Nathan. From a letter by Abraham Cardozo (from Smyrna) to Meir Rofe we learn that Nathan was subsequently admitted, and that he and Primo spent some time with Sabbatai. Cardozo, whose letter tries to conceal the fact of Sabbatai's depression at the time of the visit, reports that "the Beloved had written to his brother [Joseph Ṣevi in Smyrna] that in the winter of 1675 the great light did not cease. His brother was also informed that R. Nathan and R. Samuel Primo visited him and that they were together in great joy and preparing to go to the Grand Turk. May the Lord in his mercy announce to us tidings of salvation and comfort."[202]

This is valuable testimony to the mood of expectation that had once more seized the believers. Another great manifestation was at hand, and the messiah was consulting with his two trusted aides concerning an impending meeting with the sultan. The aforementioned letter to Joseph Filosoff (see above, p. 889) mentioning an imminent departure from Dulcigno, may be connected with the same phase of illumination. The extant documents may thus well complement one another, although there is no way of knowing for certain what was spoken between the messiah and his prophet and his scribe. Whatever the plans and hopes discussed at that time, Sabbatai's enthusiasm and exaltation evaporated, as usual, without leading to any serious action.

One innovation, however—albeit of a doctrinal rather than practical nature—should be attributed to this last period of Sabbatai's life. One of the believers who had been invited to visit him heard from his mouth a fuller version of the "Mystery of the Godhead" and committed it to writing. The text, which fills several pages, is known in Sabbatian literature also under the name *Raza di Mehemnutha*, "The Mystery of the Faith." It is extant in many manuscripts (some of which speak explicitly of "The Mystery of the Faith by AMIRAH")[203] as well as in print. The publication of the text in Nehemiah Ḥayyon's *ᶜOz lᵓElohim* (Berlin, 1713) caused a major uproar at the time. Ḥayyon had changed the title of the

202. MS. Brit. Mus. Or. 9165, fols. 117a and 128a; now *Sefunoth,* V (1961), 98, 103.

203. MSS. are preserved in Moscow (Günzburg Collection), Oxford (Neubauer 1537, 2211), Jewish Theological Seminary, New York (Adler 1653), and elsewhere.

tract to "The Faith of All," but critics were quick to see that it was the work of Sabbatai Ṣevi. R. Ṣevi Ashkenazi (*Ḥakham* Ṣevi) of Amsterdam immediately wrote that "the author is the notorious apostate Sabbatai Ṣevi . . . but [Ḥayyon] was also afraid of publishing it as his own work, since . . . the other Sabbatian believers knew full well that the tract was Sabbatai's and contained the Mystery of the Godhead, which he had invented."[204] R. Joseph Ergas too wrote that this was a tract "which Sabbatai had composed in Alqum [that is, Dulcigno]."[205] Cardozo, however, explicitly states that the tract was not composed by Sabbatai, although it contained his teaching. There is no valid reason for doubting Cardozo's testimony: "When I was in Rodosto [near Constantinople, on the shores of the sea of Marmara] in 1697, a tract came into my hands entitled "The Mystery of the Faith" and written by a certain rabbi in Alqum at the instructions of Sabbatai Ṣevi. Its teaching is shining with wonderful wisdom and true faith, and there is no difference between it and my own teaching regarding the Mystery of the Godhead [except on one major point]."[206] In a letter to his disciples in Smyrna, written shortly after the arrival of Judah Ḥasid's group in Jerusalem (1700), Cardozo again mentions that "in the year (1666) [1696] 'The Mystery of the Faith' came into my hands which a rabbi had given to my disciples in Istanbul. The rabbi said that he had traveled to Alqum disguised as a Turk, staying with Sabbatai for four months and writing down 'The Mystery of the Godhead' as he heard it from his mouth."[207] Cardozo emphasizes that the actual writer of the tract—whom he does not name—had granted permission to his [Cardozo's] disciples to copy the text. Cardozo was aware that the other believers asserted that Sabbatai himself had enjoined strict secrecy on the subject, but he had an explanation for his deviation: the prohibition extended only to the earlier versions of "The Mystery of the God-

204. *Ap.* Freimann, p. 122.

205. In *Tokhaḥath Megullah* (1715), fol. 2b, and *ha-Ṣad Naḥash* (1715), fol. 32a.

206. Cardozo, *Raza de-Razin,* MS. Deinard 153 (Jewish Theological Seminary, New York), fol. 3b. The date given in the MS. is 447 (1687), but should be emended to 457.

207. *Sefunoth,* III–IV (1960), 197. The chronology of Cardozo's letters fits the year 1696 or 1697 rather than 1666, which is a copyist's error, easily explained by the resemblance of the relevant letters.

head." The rabbi who had heard Sabbatai's last and final version in Dulcigno was not under oath to keep the secret and hence, when he realized that Cardozo's teaching was identical with that of the master, divulged the "Mystery" to Cardozo's disciples and permitted them to copy it. The latter version was therefore authoritative "and we must not mind what [Samuel] Primo and others have received on this subject."[208] No matter whether Cardozo's explanation is correct or is merely an instance of wishful thinking, there is no reason to reject his factual account to the effect that the tract was written in Dulcigno. The question, however, remains unanswered: Why did nobody ever hear of the existence of the tract during all those twenty years? There is only one indication that the tract may have been known at an earlier time: in Abraham Rovigo's collection of Sabbatian pieces (Ms. Halberstam 40, in Jews' College, London) there is a copy of the text, in an Italian hand, which might be the oldest one extant. All other pieces in the collection date from before 1695, and there is no indication that Rovigo received it from Cardozo or his circle. It may have been sent from Jerusalem, where the preceding piece (Nathan's *Drush ha-Tanninim*) was copied in October, 1694, but I am not longer altogether sure whether it was written by the same hand. If this were the case, the text would have been known in Jerusalem in 1694, three years before it came into Cardozo's possession.

All earlier accounts of Sabbatai's Mystery of the Godhead do not go beyond short and cryptic sayings (see above, pp. 119–22). Some interpreters identified the mystery with the sixth *sefirah Tif'ereth*, that is, with the third letter (*waw*) of the Tetragrammaton. Cardozo was told by Meir Rofe in Leghorn that Sabbatai never meant to identify the Creator and "God of Israel" with any of the *sefiroth*, and that the mystery referred to a sphere of being above the *sefiroth*, though apparently not the "supernal principle" (that is, *En-Sof* or the First Cause) itself. These and other definitions quoted by Cardozo,[209] while they make sense from a kabbalistic point of view, are nevertheless insufficient to clarify the precise meaning that Sabbatai attached to the "God of my Faith."

208. *Raza de-Razin,* fols. 12b–13a. Cardozo wrote the tract *Raza de-Razin* against Samuel Primo, and hence the latter cannot have been the anonymous scholar to whom Sabbatai dictated "The Mystery of the Faith."

209. *Ap.* A. H. Weiss, *Beth ha-Midrash* (1865), pp. 64–65, 66.

Equally obscure are the testimonies regarding Sabbatai's attitude toward Lurianic kabbalah. Cardozo quotes Sabbatai as frequently saying, "Isaac Luria made a wonderfully beautiful chariot, but did not say who was riding in it,"[210] and asserted that Sabbatai "rejected the Lurianic kabbalah, though he [admitted] its truth, because it caused him confusion and profited him naught in his pursuit and knowledge of God."[211] These testimonies corroborate the conclusion that Sabbatai never had a deeper relationship to Lurianic kabbalah although—like all kabbalists—he studied it. Evidently Sabbatai was looking for something which the Lurianic doctrine of the *tiqqun* of the divine "configurations" (*parṣufim*) did not satisfy. Sabbatai's brother and disciples told Cardozo that he relied mainly on the Talmud and midrashic literature. "He used to kiss the Talmud and the Midrashim, and would say that the Talmudic teachers were his fathers and masters in the doctrine of the Mystery of the Godhead, and that through their words he had been aroused to seek God and through them he had found Him."[212] This agrees with Moses Pinheiro's account of his and Sabbatai's youthful studies of kabbalah (see above, p. 115), for at that time the Zohar and the book *Kanah* were held to be ancient "midrashic" texts.

Sabbatai's distant attitude toward Lurianism is confirmed by the little we know of his basic mystical doctrine. "The Mystery of the Faith," which is essentially an attempt to interpret the *Idra Rabbah* in the Zohar, has few, if any, properly Lurianic elements. The terminology too is Zoharic, and only rarely does the reader catch a Lurianic echo. The rather elaborate and complicated argument is apt to obscure the one really important innovation which Sabbatai introduces by way of (mis)interpreting a passage of Zohar III, 141. Elaborating on Genesis 2:7 "and breathed into his nostrils the soul[213] of life," the *Idra Rabbah* speaks of "the Soul from which all living things above and below depend, and through which they exist." With utter disregard of the syntax of the Zoharic passage, Sabbatai interpreted it as meaning "the soul of all that liveth" (a phrase known to every

210. *Raza de-Razin,* fol. 6a.

211. *Ap.* Weiss, *loc. cit.,* p. 67. I have added the bracketed word following the correct reading in MS. Adler 1653, fol. 202a.

212. Weiss, *loc. cit.,* p. 66.

213. *Neshamah,* which originally meant "breath," acquired in later Hebrew the signification "soul."

Jewish reader from the prayer book) and thereby created a new symbol, denoting a hitherto unknown and hidden aspect in the Godhead. Sabbatai's audacious innovation was to play an important role in subsequent heretical speculations of the Sabbatian theologians.

An analysis of the doctrine of "The Mystery of the Faith" is no easy matter. There are many contradictions (some of them perhaps deliberate), and certain extremely audacious presuppositions are not stated at all (perhaps also deliberately). Aspects of the manifestations of the Godhead which are distinguished in one place are identified elsewhere. Little is said about the two highest grades of all: *En-Sof* and its "will" (which is identified sometimes with the *tehiru* of the Zohar, and at other times with the "Holy Ancient One"). Whatever the subsequent interpretations which this silence invited, it is evident that here *En-Sof* performs no religious function. It is not "God" in the ordinary sense of that term, and nothing more specific is said about it beyond the general statement that everything "proceedeth from the Mystery of *En-Sof*." As a matter of fact, this silence may well conceal Sabbatai's most secret doctrine, for, according to Cardozo, Sabbatai's disciples had to swear an oath not to divulge the doctrine that *En-Sof*, also called the Root of All Roots,[214] "exercises neither providence nor any influence, and is so hidden that it cannot be spoken about."[215] Cardozo thought that the similarity of this doctrine to Epicurus' views on the gods was the reason for Sabbatai's reticence on the subject. The denial of the exercise of providence from *En-Sof* undoubtedly smacked of heresy, and earlier kabbalists had never used such explicit and radical language. The Sabbatians rightly suspected that scandal would be unavoidable once rumors concerning this Mystery of the Faith were afoot—this is precisely what happened a generation later—and undoubtedly the doctrine marked a turning point in Sabbatian speculation. But during Sabbatai's lifetime this doctrine remained unknown to the public, being revealed only to very few of his intimate disciples in Adrianople.

This particularly delicate point is not mentioned at all in "The Mystery of the Faith," though an important testimony concerning the subject will be quoted later in the course of our discussion (see below, p. 912). On the other hand, the text contains an exposition of two aspects of *ᶜatiqa qadisha* ("the Holy Ancient One").

214. A distinction between the two terms was not introduced until later.
215. *Raza de-Razin,* fol. 11a.

The one is "the Holy Ancient and Most Hidden"; the other is "the Holy Ancient One" without further qualification. Occasionally, however, the two are identified, or the higher grade disappears and only "the Holy Ancient One" remains. The latter is the "simple will" of *En-Sof* who "cleft a cleaving," which is the space in which all the worlds were emanated and created. In this *tehiru*, or primordial space, the Holy Ancient One spread a "curtain" on which he drew an infinite number of hidden worlds as well as ten configurations (*parṣufim*). These, in their turn, gave rise to further inner processes in the "curtain" which our tract describes at length in a terminology that is derived from the Zoharic account of the "kings that died" and their restoration (*tiqqun*). The description refers to modes, namely, stages of being that arose in the "will" and which can therefore be said to represent the dialectics of the will. In due course the "configurations" beneath "the Holy Ancient One" received a constant form, especially the very "subtle" configuration *Da^cath* which corresponds to the *sefirah Tif^ɔereth* and which reflects from its light back to the supernal configurations of the Holy Ancient One. In the process of this construction of primordial forms in the "curtain," the "Holy Ancient and Most Hidden of All emanated a soul consisting of both male and female."[216] This is the "Soul of All that Liveth" which is of one substance with the "Holy Ancient One." A "form within form," it organizes itself as a new configuration called "the image of man" and also "the Holy King and His Shekhinah [as well as] the Holy One Blessed Be He and His Shekhinah." On the one hand, it is identical with the Holy Ancient One, namely, the "simple will"—being of one substance with his "soul"—but on the other hand, it is also distinct from him, being brought into being by the soul that emanated from him. It is this configuration that is signified by the Tetragrammaton as well as the other divine names in Scripture,[217] and which is the God of Israel and the God of Revelation who revealed himself to Israel in the giving of the Law. It is the "God of the Faith" of Sabbatai Ṣevi from which, and beneath which, all the other four worlds (*ɔaṣiluth*, *beriɔah*, *yeṣirah*, *casiyyah*) are emanated and derived. All the supernal configurations conceived in the will of the Holy Ancient One are contained in it. All the innumerable hidden worlds drawn in the "curtain" (which is none other

216. Cf. the crucial passage in *cOz lɔElohim*, fol. 54a.
217. *Ibid.*, fol. 58b.

than the "primordial space" (*tehiru* of Zoharic and Lurianic terminology) are governed by this configuration of "the Holy King and His Shekhinah." The author of the tract does not even attempt to explain the manifest contradiction in his doctrine according to which the "God of Israel" rules over the *tehiru*, although He was emanated from the Holy Ancient One in a process related to the existence of the *tehiru* and of the forms and configurations arising in it. The Holy King acts on the lower worlds by assuming the various configurations of *ʾaṣiluth*, more especially the configuration of *zeʿir ʾanpin* (which is identical with the sefirotic stage of *Tifʾereth*). All the worlds (except that of the Holy Ancient One and its configurations) desire and need the "Holy King" which alone is highly exalted above all, even above the "curtain" with which he is connected and which is defined once as the higher part of the *tehiru* and as the *ʾaṣiluth* of *ʾaṣiluth*.[218]

The author's efforts at reading his special doctrinal innovation and interests into the Zoharic text considerably complicate his argument. The three configurations *ʿatiqa*, that is, *ʾarikh ʾanpin*, *zeʿir ʾanpin*, and the *nuqbaʾ* (female partner) of *zeʿir* are already mentioned in the *Idra Rabbah* in the Zohar,[219] which also assumes some kind of identity of *ʿatiqa* and *zeʿir ʾanpin*, in spite of their apparent difference. But the Sabbatian tract introduces the utterly new concept of the "Soul of All that Liveth," and instead of the one configuration of *zeʿir* it speaks of the "Holy King" as being above all the configurations of the realm of *ʾaṣiluth*. According to this novel doctrine there is not just one *zeʿir* and its *nuqbaʾ*, but on every level of the emanation beneath that of the "Ancient One" there recur the configurations of *zeʿir* and its female partner: the supernal *zeʿir* (that is the "Holy King") clothes itself in the lower *zeʿir* of the world of *ʾaṣiluth*. A similar duplication can be found in the Lurianic doctrine of the *Adam Qadmon* which represents a level of being above that of the configurations of the four worlds of *ʾaṣiluth*, *beriʾah*, *yeṣirah*, and *ʿasiyyah*. In "The Mystery of the Faith," however, the emphasis is shifted, probably in deliberate rejection of the Lurianic system. While in Lurianic teaching the decisive center of the Godhead is in the configuration called *zeʿir ʾanpin* of the world of *ʾaṣiluth*, the Sabbatian Mystery of the Faith introduces an intermediate stratum into the Godhead between the *En-Sof*, on the one

218. *Ibid.*, fol. 79a.
219. *See also* G. Scholem, *Major Trends*, pp. 269–70.

hand, and the sphere of the "configurations" (mentioned in the *Idra*, and central to Lurianic kabbalah), on the other. The configuration *ze^cir ᵓanpin* is thus merely the outer veil of a profounder and more interior sphere within the Godhead. This newly discovered sphere is the "Soul of All that Liveth."[220]

The identification of "God," that is, of the configuration *zeᶜir ᵓanpin*, with the "Holy King" permits shifts of emphasis in two directions, according to the predilections of the interpreters. Thus it is quite possible to stress the *impersonal* "Soul of All that Liveth" as the essence of this mystery in a manner that may lead—as, in fact, it did in the following generation—to a mystical pantheism. The "Soul of All that Liveth" is said to fill and unite all worlds, and he that "severeth this Soul from the world and pretends that there is any other soul" will assuredly perish forever.[221] On the other hand, it is equally possible to put the emphasis on the personal character of the "Holy King" in whom the "Soul of All that Liveth" indwells and who is above all the other "configurations" that are in the "curtain."[222] Toward the end of the text, the author gives

220. The teaching of "The Mystery of the Faith" has been thoroughly misunderstood by H. Graetz (*Geschichte der Juden*[3], vol. X, pp. 448–49), who failed to recognize how far it is removed from Lurianic kabbalah proper. Even the doctrine of "configurations" as expounded in the tract is closer to the Zohar than to Lurianism. Graetz's doubts as to the origin of the tract are disposed of by Cardozo's testimony. Graetz completely overlooked the significance of the "Soul of All that Liveth" in the mystical theology of the author, and was misled by Emden into holding the doctrine of incarnation to be the main subject of the tract. According to Emden the doctrine that the "Soul of All" indwells in the Holy King meant that the Deity is incarnate in the messiah. Of course the "Holy King" here does not mean the messiah, and the tract, which deals with the Mystery of the Godhead, does not discuss at all the nature and person of the messiah. Emden interpreted the text in the light of later Sabbatian doctrines, and he and Graetz thereby misled all subsequent historians (Kahana, Rosanes, Kastein). While it is true that Sabbatai occasionally saw himself as an incarnation of the Godhead, he seems to have identified with the Shekhinah rather than with the Holy King. In any case, the problem is completely irrelevant to the text under discussion.

221. The prohibition to "sever the soul from the world" is taken from the *Idra Rabbah* (Zohar III, 141b).

222. *ᶜOz lᵓElohim*, fol. 79a, 81b. The Zohar, of course, knows of no other configuration at this supernal level except that of the Holy Ancient One. The doctrine of "The Mystery of the Faith" regarding the Holy King is clearly a metamorphosis of the Zoharic *zeᶜir ᵓanpin.*

the first hint of some kind of "trinity" in his conception of the Deity: "He [that is, the Holy King and His Shekhinah] alone emanated and created and formed and made everything . . . with His free will, in order that all creatures might behold His greatness, [namely] that He, the Shekhinah of His Might, and the Holy Ancient and Most Hidden One . . . are all one; He is our God and there is no other; in truth our king, there is none else." In general, however, there is little emphasis on this tri-unity, since the unity of the "Soul of All that Liveth" unifies all three aspects, *ᶜatiqa*, *zeᶜir*, and the Shekhinah.

There is no explicit reference in the text to the doctrine of the "indwelling" (*hithlabbeshuth*) of the Holy King, which is the God of Sabbatai's faith, in the *sefirah Tifᵓereth*, but it is not incompatible with the general teaching of "The Mystery of the Faith." For in spite of the author's determination to distinguish (unlike the Zohar) between the Holy King and *zeᶜir ᵓanpin*, the two somehow remain congruent. Whatever the *Idra Rabbah* has to say about *zeᶜir ᵓanpin* is applied in "The Mystery of the Faith" to the Holy King, and since the latter maintains his character as a definite configuration of *zeᶜir ᵓanpin* it is not surprising that the author should consider the latter to be an appropriate "clothing" or dwelling for the attributes of the Holy King.[223] The various definitions of, and allusions to, the Mystery of the Godhead as reported in the several testimonies and quotations are therefore not incompatible with the intentions and tendencies of the text. Cardozo's assertion that the several formulations were irreconcilable may well be a case of special pleading.[224] For all we know there may be no difference at all between the teaching of "The Mystery of the Faith," on the one hand, and, on the other hand, the definition of the "God of Israel" as the "Second Cause indwelling, or clothing itself, in *Tifᵓereth*," which R. Azariah ha-Levi, according to Cardozo, claimed to have "heard hundreds of times from the mouth of Sabbatai Ṣevi,"

223. Whereas the Holy Ancient One is "simple will" and pure mercy without any admixture of "judgment," the Holy King and His Shekhinah are compounded of "mercy" and "judgment" for the purpose of the cosmic *tiqqun; ᶜOz lᵓElohim*, fol. 81b.

224. Cardozo was a theologian with views of his own which he tried to read into the (for him) authoritative "Mystery of the Faith." He had good reason to wish to disqualify certain alternative formulations that went against his grain.

a remark indicating a certain consistency in Sabbatai's later views (see above, p. 861).

There is, however, an undeniable difference between the doctrine expounded in "The Mystery of the Faith" and that formulated by Samuel Primo and presented by him as Sabbatai's teaching. The latter version lacks the specific features of the system analyzed above, such as the doctrine of the "Holy Ancient One" and that of the "Soul of All that Liveth." The text of Primo's version of the "Mystery" is extant in what seems to be Primo's own wording as well as in Cardozo's account of what R. Ḥayyim Mal'akh[225] had heard from Primo in Adrianople. Primo, according to Ḥayyim Mal'akh's report, claimed that Sabbatai had enjoined on him strict secrecy when "he delivered to him the Mystery of the Godhead lastly," that is, toward the end of his life during one of Primo's visits to Dulcigno. The gist of the mystery, as received by Primo and told to Ḥayyim Mal'akh, was this: "There is in the First Cause an infinitely simple will which had from all times been contained in its root [that is, in the root of the First Cause] and which is primeval like it. When this will willed that existents should come into being, it emanated from the Lord, or the owner, of the will like light from its source. As soon as it proceeded from the First Cause, there also proceeded from the simple will the Shekhinah, which is of the nature of Stern Judgment. But the simple will is supernal mercy, and the Lord of the will, that is, the First Cause, is the root of mercy which is the will. The will is the root of judgment, that is, the Shekhinah, which is an effect of the simple will. The Shekhinah is signified by the final H of the Tetragrammaton YHWH, and when she descends into the emanation (*'aṣiluth*), she clothes herself in [the *sefirah*] *Malkhuth*. The simple will, which is the Holy One Blessed Be He, the Holy King, is signified by the [first] three letters YHW of the Tetragrammaton, and it is clothed in [the *sefirah*] *Tif'ereth*. It has the character of the male in relation to the Shekhinah which receives from it, whereas the Shekhinah is like the female in relation to the Holy One Blessed Be He who grants her his influx like a man to his wife."

225. Cardozo, in this passage, calls him Ḥayyim Mal'akh Ashkenazi, though elsewhere he gives his usual name Ḥayyim Mal'akh. The passage referred to is *Raza de-Razin*, fols. 4b–5a. Mal'akh was a famous Polish Sabbatian in the period 1680–1710; see *Encyclopedia Judaica*, XI (1972), cols. 818–19.

This formulation does not correspond, at first sight, with the doctrine of "The Mystery of the Faith," unless we assume that somehow a later, semiphilosophical terminology, deriving from Israel Sarug's disciple Azariah Fano and his work *Yonath ᵓElem*, was substituted for the original Zoharic symbol language. Primo's version of the mystery and the exposition in "The Mystery of the Faith" can be reconciled if we assume that, in the former, *En-Sof* has completely receded into the background, and that Primo's "First Cause" corresponds to the "Holy Ancient One" of the earlier text. This seems to me to be the correct interpretation, and hence it can be argued that the "simple will," contained in the "First Cause" and emanating from it when it willed to create (thus in Primo's version), actually corresponds to the "Holy King." Primo's text, in fact, says so, albeit by way of metaphor only. The will is the Creator and it contains both the male and the female modes or principles, for the First Cause produced the Shekhinah immediately after the procession of the will, and both—the Holy King and his Shekhinah—combine in the Tetragrammaton. It thus appears that the Holy Ancient One, who is called "will" in "The Mystery of the Faith," becomes, in Primo's version, the First Cause in which the will inheres. And Primo explicitly states that this Holy King "is clothed in *Tifᵓereth*.[226] The doctrine of the "Soul of All that Liveth" has completely disappeared from Primo's version. Considering the fact that it was well known in the traditions of the Dönmeh, one wonders why Primo dropped it. If Primo's "First Cause" is the same as the *En-Sof* of "The Mystery of the Faith" then the two statements are really incompatible, all the more so as the "Holy Ancient One" has vanished in Primo's version. Nevertheless—as has been argued above—another interpretation is possible and, indeed, preferable. Primo's version can be reconciled with the doctrine of "The Mystery of the Faith" without resorting to forced interpretations, and there is no necessity to present the two formulations—as Cardozo did—as incompatible. A connection be-

226. *Tifᵓereth*, in this context, means the configuration of *zeᶜir ᵓanpin* in the world of *ᵓaṣiluth*. The many statements to the effect that the God of Sabbatai's faith was *Tifᵓereth* can be construed in the sense of "manifesting," namely, "clothing" himself in *Tifᵓereth;* see above, p. 121. Statements concerning "the God of his faith which is *Tifᵓereth*" can be found not only in Nathan's writings from 1666 on, but also in the commentary on the Psalms written by Israel Ḥazzan toward the end of Sabbatai's life (see above, p. 862).

tween the two divergent terminologies—that speaking of the "Holy Ancient One" and the "Soul of All that Liveth," on the one hand, and that which speaks of the "First Cause," on the other—is also suggested by the tradition according to which Sabbatai revealed to a chosen few that "the Holy One Blessed Be He is a supernal Soul that grew out of the power of the First Cause." This brief statement can bear either of the two possible interpretations of Primo's text. If we assume the "First Cause" to be identical with the Holy Ancient One, then this short sentence is a succinct statement of the doctrine of the "Soul of All that Liveth" which emanates from the Ancient One, namely, the will.

The relationship between the secret doctrine regarding the absence of providence in *En-Sof*, on the one hand, and, on the other hand, the religiously significant God who creates and reveals himself is not explicitly referred to in the versions examined so far. But a relevant passage bearing on this secret "thesis" underlying the Sabbatian Mystery of the Godhead is preserved by Cardozo, who copied from a manuscript by Joseph Karillo the following statement made by Sabbatai Ṣevi himself: "Know that the Cause of All Causes exercises neither influence nor providence in the lower worlds. He brought into being the Supreme Crown (*Kether*) to be God, and the *Tif'ereth* of Israel to be King."[227] This concise formulation agrees with "The Mystery of the Faith" in spite of terminological variations. The *En-Sof* of the one appears here as the "Cause of All Causes";[228] The "Ancient One" of the former is here called *Kether*, the traditional name of the first *sefirah*, and the "Holy King" is now *Tif'ereth.*[229] The deity is thus the union of *Kether* and *Tif'ereth*, namely, the "Soul" and the "King" (with his Shekhinah?). The aforementioned mystical dualism appears here in its most radical form on the authority of Sabbatai himself and preserved by one of the "mystical apostates." The assertion that the "God of his faith" was emanated from a higher principle and that it was, therefore, a

227. MS. in the library of Yale University (New Haven), no. 20, fol. 1a. The MS. is a fragment from an unknown work by Cardozo. The beginning and end are missing. Elsewhere (cf. Weiss, *Beth ha-Midrash,* p. 65) Cardozo mentions a MS. by Karillo which he found in Constantinople. Perhaps the quotation is from this MS.

228. Which is not necessarily identical (as the subsequent development of Sabbatian doctrine illustrates) with the "First Cause."

229. In other words, the language of *sefiroth* has been substituted for the Lurianic terminology of *parṣufim* ("countenances" or "configurations").

Second rather than a First Cause, is based on the "heretical" assumption that the "Cause of All Causes" has no religious significance. As the beginning of the chain of causes, it is a matter of logic or ontology, but not of religious contemplation or worship. The latter are due to a deity which is the "King." It is understandable that this audacious doctrine, taught by the messiah as the true Mystery of the Godhead, was revealed to a few elect only. Very possibly this doctrine was Sabbatai's only original (and heretical) contribution to the mystical theology of the kabbalah. It proved to be of enormous significance for the subsequent development of Sabbatian doctrine.

Whatever the possible explanations of the details of Sabbatai's "Mystery of the Godhead" and of their apparent discrepancies, it appears that Sabbatai's thinking on the subject from his early days in Smyrna to his death in Dulcigno exhibits a remarkable degree of consistency and continuity. His intellectual capacities seem to have been unaffected by his emotional instability and by thirty years of manic-depressive ups and downs. Were it not for the various testimonies relating to his doctrine of the Godhead, one would be tempted to assume that his intellect was as unstable as his pathological personality. As it is, his doctrine of the Godhead appears to have evolved and gradually deepened over the years. Cardozo and Ḥayyim Malʾakh, though representing opposite factions in the Sabbatian camp after the messiah's death, both witness that even Nathan of Gaza learned the true Mystery of the Godhead *after* he had written most of his homilies and tracts, that is, only toward the end of Sabbatai's life.[230]

As has been noted above, "The Mystery of the Faith" deals exclusively with the mystical doctrine of the Godhead and not with the person of the messiah. Hence it does not even touch on the problem of the deification of the messiah or the incarnation of God in the messiah. Israel Ḥazzan of Kastoria, writing soon after Sabbatai's demise, was unaware of the existence of "The Mystery of the Faith,"

230. See G. Scholem in *Zion,* XI (1946), 173. Cuenque (*ap.* Emden, pp. 42–43) gives an utterly imaginary account of the solemn transmission of the Mystery to ten disciples. Having sworn them to secrecy, Sabbatai revealed the Mystery and then dismissed the disciples with the words: "This is the knowledge of God. Henceforth ye shall know whom ye serve and who is your God." The final words may well be authentic. At any rate the story, for all its legendary character, well reflects the sense of numinous awe which the mere mention of the Mystery evoked among the Sabbatians.

which the writer who took it down apparently kept secret for several years. Ḥazzan has therefore nothing to hide on this subject, and never once mentions the trinity of the Holy Ancient One, the Holy King, and His Shekhinah. On the other hand, he frequently refers to another trinity: The Holy One Blessed Be He, His Shekhinah, and the messiah (see above, p. 870). Whether these references imply an allusion to a doctrine of incarnation cannot be determined with any certainty. During his earthly ministry the messiah is closely united to, but not identical with, the "God of his Faith." If Israel Ḥazzan thought that there was more to it than that, he certainly did not reveal it in his writings.

VII

In 1676 Sabbatai experienced one more "great illumination, the like of which had never been before," and again he behaved in a "strange" manner that angered the Turks.[231] In a solemn procession he marched to the quarter of the city in which the Turkish notables and officials were living, and at midnight he ascended the "wall of the tower" (the minaret of the mosque?), singing his songs and hymns. Again nothing happened to him, and later Sabbatian legend embellished this exploit with tales of a miraculous salvation from the sword of his enemies. "Wherefore he decided that the time of redemption had come, and that he was to manifest himself again in the sight of all living." It was on the crest of this new wave of illumination that shortly after Passover, 1676, Sabbatai wrote his last letters and royal proclamations. One such proclamation was addressed to "all the men of faith in Sofia."

The vicissitudes of this latter document are particularly instructive.[232] R. Joseph Kohen, an emissary from Hebron, happened to be in Sofia when Sabbatai's letter arrived and he copied it in his notebook, which fortunately has been preserved.[233] But another copy of

231. The incident is recounted in a Sabbatian source; see Baruch of Arezzo, *ap.* Freimann, pp. 67–68.

232. Some questions connected with this letter have been clarified by Z. Rubashov (Shazar) in *Zion* (annual), VI (1934), 54–58, thirty years before the copy from the Dönmeh papers was discovered.

233. On this notebook see I. M. Toledano, *Sarid u-Falit*, I (1945), 39–52, and A. Yaᶜari, *Sheluḥey ᵓEreṣ Yisraᵓel*, pp. 470–72. This emissary apparently had Sabbatian leanings, for his notebook also contains the copy of another document that throws much light on the prestige which Nathan enjoyed in Kastoria.

the letter which may well be in Sabbatai's own handwriting and is not addressed to any particular community, is extant in one of the manuscripts which have come from the Dönmeh archives and are now in Jerusalem. It has been pasted with great care on strong paper (something not done to any other document in this collection) and at least about 1750–60 must have been considered a genuine autograph of the messiah (see the facsimile in plate XII). It is mentioned as such by R. Abraham Miranda, who put this collection together in Salonika.[234]

According to this letter, "Sabbatai made a serpent of silver and put it upon a pole" (cf. Num. 21:9) on the night of the termination of the Passover festival. Evidently Sabbatai was assuming the role of *Moses redivivus,*[235] and as such addressed his followers:

My brethern and dearly beloved, all men of faith in the city of Sofia, who shall be vouchsafed to behold the salvation of the Lord, and to see eye to eye when the Lord shall bring again Zion [cf. Isa. 52:8]. Behold I send an angel [that is, messenger] before thee [cf. Exod. 23:20] to announce and tell you of all my glory in Egypt[236] and some of what he has seen [cf. Gen. 45:13]. Beware of him and obey his voice, provoke him

234. The main objections to the authenticity of the document as an autograph of Sabbatai Ṣevi are twofold: (1) the leaf contains two letters by Ṣevi of which the first, to judge from its contents, appears to be written later than the second. Only with difficulty could it be argued that both were written at the same time; (2) at the lower end of the leaf there is a remark that all the peculiarities of the spelling are kept as they are. On the other hand, the remark could also be translated as an order: not "are kept" but "are to be kept." The remark itself is clearly by another hand, and could be interpreted as a directive to those who would transmit the letter to other communities. I find it difficult to come to a clearcut decision but I cannot preclude the possibility of the letters being authentic autographs. This text was first published (including a facsimile) in *Sefunoth,* V (1961), 249, and M. Benayahu upheld the authenticity of the autograph; *ibid.,* pp. 237–38. He thinks that Sabbatai just tacked it onto the first letter, written later, as a copy made by himself, and therefore changed and abridged in some places. This might be an explanation of the curious features of the leaf.

235. In Sabbatian literature this identification is taken for granted. The name Ṣevi becomes Moses by AT-BASH inversion of the Hebrew alphabet, a procedure much employed in mystical exegesis. Cf. also above, pp. 235–36, on Sabbatai's seal.

236. He writes *Miṣrayim* in two words *meṣar yam,* a spelling found in several of his missives. It is an allegorical pun based on kabbalistic sources.

not [cf. Exod. 23:21] in anything he says unto you in my name, for I shall not forgive your transgression when God arises to judgment [cf. Ps. 67:9] and the Lord of hosts shall be exalted in judgment [cf. Isa. 5:16],[237] and who is the god that can deliver you out of my hands [cf. Dan. 3:15], for beside me there is no God [cf. Isa. 44:6]. But if thou shalt indeed obey his voice and do all that I speak to you [cf. Exod. 23:22] then I shall indeed go up and fill your treasures [cf. Prov. 8:21]. Thus saith the man who is raised to the heights of the Father,[238] the Celestial Lion and Celestial Stag, the Anointed of the God of Israel and Judah, Sabbatai Mehemed Ṣevi.

This letter, "given at Alqum," is a mosaic of biblical phrases and suggests that the writer was not only in a state of illuminate exaltation but actually attributed to himself some sort of divinity. He is sending a messenger to tell the faithful of his "glory in Egypt" (that is, in his exile), and to deliver his orders. As in 1658, Sabbatai had combined the celebration of Passover and Tabernacles,[239] and the letter, written about six months before his death, echoes some of his earlier favorite themes and quotations. In his youth he had already quoted Isaiah 14:14: "I will ascend above the heights of the clouds; I will be like the Most High," but this time he suggests that he has ascended (or will ascend) "to the heights of the Father." Like his other letters containing allusions to his divinity, this letter was kept by the early believers as a kind of skeleton in the Sabbatian cupboard. Baruch of Arezzo, who possessed a copy of the letter and actually used it when writing his Sabbatian gospel, omitted the telltale date, the quotations from Daniel 3:15 and Isaiah 44:6, and the reference to the ascension to "the heights of the Father." Were it not for the providential copy made by the emissary from Hebron and the copy possibly made by Sabbatai himself, this important document would have fallen a victim to the self-censorship exercised by the believers.[240]

237. These words are written so as to allude to Sabbatai's name Ṣevi.

238. A combination of II Sam. 23:1 and Isa. 14:14, but the expression "ascend to the heights of the clouds" (ᶜ*ab*) has been changed to "father" (ᵓ*ab*). But, the autograph does not contain the two words *bamothey* ᵓ*ab*.

239. The letter is dated "the termination of the Feast of Passover and the Feast of Tabernacles," Monday, 23 Nisan. These words too are missing from the autograph copy.

240. Z. Rubashov, *loc. cit.*, has established that the letter was written on 23 Nisan 1676. The correctness of the date is confirmed by the fact that from 1663 to 1676 the 23rd of Nisan never fell on a Monday.

A few months after his last great illumination, Sabbatai died in Dulcigno on the Day of Atonement, 5437 (September 17, 1676)—two months after his fiftieth birthday and almost exactly ten years after his apostasy on September 16, 1666.

His last letter, possibly preserved in autograph, still presents him in his double role as Jew and Muslim. He writes to his friends in the nearest Jewish community of "Arnaut-Belgrade" (Berat) asking them to hurry and send him a *maḥzor,* the festival prayer book, for the New Year and the Day of Atonement. The letter would appear to have been written in August, 1676. He signs with his usual bombastic self-aggrandizements, ending with "the messiah of the God of Israel and Judah Sabbatai Ṣevi." He does not so much as mention his new name Mehemed, when asking a Jewish community for a prayer book.[241]

About a fortnight before Sabbatai's death, on September 5, 1676, Joseph Karillo and another learned Sabbatian apostate (either Isaac Ḥaber or Abraham Oheb of Sofia) arrived in Dulcigno at the express invitation of Sabbatai brought to them by a Muslim mollah by name of Ali.[242] Karillo's companion gave an account of the meeting with Sabbatai Ṣevi when he saw Cardozo in Constantinople in the spring of 1682. According to this account, Sabbatai took his two visitors to the beach and told them: "Return every man to his house. How long will you hold fast to me? Perhaps until you can see beneath that rock on the coast?"[243] This is a very melancholic utterance indeed, and it suggests that Sabbatai died in a mood of despondency, conscious of his failure. This fact was deliberately obscured in the circle of Nathan. All our sources agree that Sabbatai died on the Day of Atonement,[244] but whereas Sabbatian

241. The letter is published in *Sefunoth,* V (1961), 250.

242. Cf. Cardozo's letter in *Sefunoth,* III–IV (1960), 217, where the name of Karillo's companion is glossed over by a blank space, followed by the honorific *chelebi.* Whether this points to Mustapha Chelebi, later one of the leading members of the Dönmeh group in Salonika, is a matter of conjecture. Sabbatai in his correspondence with the apostates never used their new Turkish names but the old Jewish ones, as is apparent from his letter of invitation to Karillo which is preserved in Baruch of Arezzo's memoir (*ap.* Freimann, p. 68). This was also the custom of the Dönmeh sect whose members, within their own circle, were called by their Jewish proper and family names only.

243. Cardozo, *loc. cit.,* p. 218. According to this account, Sabbatai had talked with his visitors about Cardozo's book *Boqer ʾAbraham.*

244. See my examination of the pertinent sources and traditions in *Zion,* X (1945), 140–42.

tradition insists that he passed away at the time of the *neᶜilah* prayer, Cardozo's informant states that death occurred "early in the morning." The Jewish-Persian chronicle from Isfahan states in 1686, apparently basing itself on anti-Sabbatian sources and letters from Constantinople, that Sabbatai was exiled to Surkan (obviously a corruption of Ulkun), where he was held prisoner in very poor circumstances, mortifications, and tortures (!) until he died "in the fourth hour of the Day of Atonement, 1676."[245] This would conform to Cardozo's information. According to the division of the day, used at the time in Turkey, the hours were reckoned from sunrise. Sabbatai would thus have died between 9:00 and 10:00 A.M. On the other hand, Karillo and his companion had left Dulcigno after Rosh ha-Shanah and before Sabbatai's death on the Day of Atonement, but their statement would seem to agree with Samuel Gandoor's information (see below) that Sabbatai had died "during the day." The hour of the *neᶜilah* prayer at the termination of the Day of Atonement is considered the most solemn and holy moment of the year—indeed, rabbinic legend has it that Moses died at that hour—and hence it is not surprising that Sabbatian tradition moved the time of Sabbatai's death by a few hours.

More than half a year passed after Sabbatai's death before the news reached Italy. It arrived at an unspecified date and in an imprecise manner from Smyrna, telling of his death on the day preceding the Day of Atonement, whereupon Moses Capsuto immediately wrote to Nathan's confidant, Samuel Gandoor, for authoritative confirmation. Obviously, Sabbatai's followers in the Balkans were most reticent to disclose the fact, since the unexpected demise of the messiah must have come as a severe blow to the believers. Their confusion and disarray, as well as the first groping attempts to adjust to the new situation, are reflected in a letter of September 12, 1677, from Meir Rofe to Abraham Rovigo: "And now I will announce to you great news but keep it secret and for God's sake do not divulge it to anyone. A letter arriving from Sofia from R. Samuel Gandoor says that it is true that the Beloved has been asked to the Celestial Academy on the very Day of Atonement. . . . Let thy heart not be faint, and in another letter I shall write to you more about this matter. [Meanwhile] you should ask a question [by means of prophetic dream or maggidic instruction] how his words may come true after this, and

245. MS. Hebrew Union College 2007, fol. 113a.

why and for what reason this has happened, and whether this is a real death. Search this matter diligently and adjure the 'master of the dream' to tell the truth, wheat without chaff [cf. Jer. 23:28] and let me know."[246]

The letter is instructive. We must conclude that the news of the demise was deliberately kept secret, and that it did not become known more widely until the summer of 1677. Rofe's confusion is evident from his desire that his younger friend obtain supernatural information regarding the meaning of this disconcerting event,[247] as well as from the vague suggestion that it might, after all, not be a "real death" but some kind of kabbalistic mystery which "probably even the angels on high cannot grasp." After all, "all matters concerning him are wondrous and mysterious from the beginning to the end, how much more this even." Gandoor and his circle were as strong and steadfast in their faith as ever, but had imposed absolute silence on themselves "not to talk [about this matter], let alone write to distant places. . . . Even our master, the Holy Rabbi, the Holy Lamp [R. Nathan] whose light shines from one end of the world to the other, and from whom this great mystery [of Sabbatai's death] is possibly not hidden, is silent and does not want to speak for the time being. . . . [Sabbatai's] brother Elijah Ṣevi has taken his [that is, Sabbatai's] wife and children to Adrianople."[248]

The Sabbatian legend of the messiah's demise had not yet developed. Samuel Gandoor does not yet say that Elijah Ṣevi or other believers and rabbis had been present at his deathbed. Israel Ḥazzan already tells of the presence of a group of believers, but makes no mention of Sabbatai's brother. According to Israel Ḥaz-

246. *Sefunoth,* III–IV (1960), 111. On the chronology of Rofe's letters, see Tishby's remarks in *Sefunoth,* I (1957), 93.

247. There is reason to assume that already at that date Rovigo had a *maggid* who revealed Sabbatian mysteries. Maggidic revelations and "dream questions" are not two completely distinct phenomena, and a *maggid* may manifest himself in dreams; cf. also Z. Werblowsky, *Joseph Karo* (1962), pp. 41 f. and 76 f. "Dream questions" are very ancient procedure, and there exist many recipes for it; cf. the collection in R. Abraham Ḥamoy's *Lidrosh Elohim* (Leghorn, 1879). A discussion of Rovigo's role in Sabbatian history cannot be undertaken here, as its proper place is in the history of the movement after Sabbatai's death. On Rovigo and the *maggid* that manifested himself in his circle, see Is. Tishby in *Zion,* XXII (1957), 21–55.

248. *Sefunoth,* III–IV (1960), 113–14. Cardozo too mentions that Sabbatai's widow and her servant were taken to Adrianople by Elijah Ṣevi.

zan, Sabbatai lay down to die in a cave which he himself had prepared for that purpose.[249] A few years later Baruch of Arezzo[250] recounts the full-blown legend: Sabbatai called his brother, his wife, and the rabbis who were with him, and announced, "Know ye that I shall pass away on the Day of the Fast of Atonement, at the time of *ne^cilah.* Carry me then to the cave that I have prepared for myself near the sea, and on the third day my brother Elijah shall come to the cave." When Sabbatai's brother came to the cave on the third day, he found the entrance barred by a huge dragon, but he said that his brother had commanded him to come and the dragon let him pass. Once inside, he found the cave empty. "Neither Our Lord nor anything else was in the cave, but it was full of light."

The origin of the legend that was soon to become a central Sabbatian myth was, of course, the embryonic feeling of the believers which Rofe had already expressed to Rovigo: perhaps this was no "real death" at all. Once before, at his apostasy, the messiah had become "hidden" after an initial triumphant manifestation. His passing away may, after all, be a second and even deeper occultation. We do not know what Nathan of Gaza (who, according to Gandoor, "possibly understood the mystery" but preferred to keep silent) thought during the first year. Rovigo's *maggid,* however, was more articulate, and probably expressed the hopes of many believers. In the autumn of 1677, soon after the confirmation of the dismaying news, the *maggid* had replied to his questioners that Sabbatai would return after twelve months and then salvation would become manifest. Meir Rofe criticized the *maggid*[251] for giving unreliable and contradictory messages regarding the Beloved. In fact, more than twelve months had passed, and nothing had happened so far.

The Sabbatian traditions all agree that Sabbatai died in Dulcigno,[252] yet the Jews seem to have tried—with some initial success—to keep this fact a secret, and Leyb b. Ozer was unable, as we have seen, to obtain trustworthy information on the subject (see above, p. 882). At last he was told that Sabbatai died and was buried in Belgrade-Berat in Albania. Sabbatai had been ill there with colic—meaning perhaps *colitis ulcerosa,* intestinal obstruction—for several

249. See *Schocken Volume,* p. 195. 250. *Ap.* Freimann, p. 68.

251. *Sefunoth,* III–IV (1960), 114, 116.

252. Cf. in addition to the sources already mentioned also Cardozo's letter (MS. Adler 2432) which I published in *Zion,* VII (1942), 16.

days, and then died "and was buried on the Day of Atonement. R. Joseph Almosnino, the rabbi of Belgrade [in what is today Yugoslavia] said that he had heard this from a Turk who had attended Sabbatai during his illness and was present at the burial." Leyb already presents a conflation of Sabbatian legend and the version he had heard from *Ḥakham* Ṣevi Ashkenazi in Amsterdam. According to *Ḥakham* Ṣevi, Sabbatai died in Arnaut-Belgrade and was buried on the Day of Atonement. In accordance with his wish he was not buried with the Muslims, but had asked to be laid alone near the water. . . . "There are no Jews at all in those parts." While it is not impossible that Sabbatai died suddenly of an intestinal obstruction, it seems extremely unlikely that shortly before his death he was exiled from Dulcigno (where he certainly was during Passover, 1676) to the one place in Albania that did have a Jewish community at that time.[253] The origin of these conflicting versions is not clear, but the Sabbatian tradition which speaks of Dulcigno appears to be right.[254] There is ample evidence that the unmarked grave in Dulcigno was visited up to the beginning of the twentieth century by Dönmeh pilgrims from Salonika.[255]

The prophet of Gaza remained silent. The man who had fired the believers with his enthusiasm and with the intensity of his faith, was now a prey to bitterness and despondency. He left Kastoria and appears to have stayed most of the time in Sofia. It was probably

253. A list of the elders of the community is given in the notebook of the emissary from Hebron, R. Joseph Kohen (see Toledano, *Sarid u-Falit,* vol. I, p. 47). The community seems to have been wealthy, for its charitable gift to Joseph Kohen was considerable. The itinerary of the emissary from Hebron leaves no doubt that the reference is to Belgrade-Berat in Albania. The community is also mentioned in the notes of Moses Levi, who had preceded Joseph Kohen as emissary of Hebron and whose notes Joseph Kohen copied into his own notebook (*ibid.,* p. 43). Joseph Kohen visited the city early in the summer of 1676, some three months before Sabbatai's death. On that occasion he copied the last letters of Sabbatai that had been received there.

254. On the place of Sabbatai's death and burial see also I. Ben-Zvi (whose conclusion favors Berat) and G. Scholem (who argues for Dulcigno) in *Zion,* XVII (1952), 75–83. The letter to Berat, written some weeks before Sabbatai's death and asking for a prayer book to be sent to him, conclusively disproves Ben-Zvi's hypothesis.

255. Cf. also the articles in the *Allgemeine Zeitung des Judentums,* XLIV (1880), 620, and the Hebrew daily *Davar* (Tel Aviv, 17 Nisan 1965) where a declaration of the "Elders" of Dulcigno–Ulcinj from May, 1962, is quoted, according to which anonymous visitors used to come from far away and put stones and flowers on the grave of an unknown "holy man."

at this period that he addressed his last extant letter to "my brethren and beloved that are in Kastoria." The letter refers to violent quarrels and new persecutions in Kastoria, and evinces a mood of weariness and dejection. Nathan expresses his displeasure at the quarrels rending the community "regarding redemption," and enjoins—on pain of excommunication—strict silence in this controversial matter. "It is good that a man should both hope and quietly wait for the salvation of the Lord" (Lam. 3:26). The letter is signed: "thus speaketh he who seeks and pursues the peace of all Israel, the little child, Wolf of the Wilderness."[256] Apparently both the prophet and the leading believers had come to the conclusion that for the time being it was better "to hope and quietly wait," avoid all argument, propaganda, and controversy, and "keep one's mouth from speaking in this matter, either good or bad." There was no point in quarreling now, and in due course it would become apparent who was right. Nathan's authority was still uncontested and he could issue commands to the believers in Kastoria "on pain of excommunication." Yet what a world of difference between the confident tone of the letter to Shemaya de Mayo (1672) after Nathan's visit to Sabbatai in Adrianople, and the low key of the letter to Kastoria. The symbolism of the signature is obscure. It is the only occasion on which the prophet does not sign Nathan Benjamin but uses metaphorical titles. The little "child" (Hebrew, *ben*) is an obvious pun on Benjamin, and so is the title "wolf" (cf. Gen. 49:50: Benjamin is a raving wolf).

In the years 1678–79 the notion that Sabbatai's death was merely an "occultation" was already gaining ground. The term was probably introduced by Nathan after he had recovered from his initial melancholia.[257] R. Israel Ḥazzan in Kastoria was composing his homilies (see above, pp. 860 ff.), many of which reflect the new situation of

256. *RÉJ*, CIV (1938), 121. The letter is undated, but M. Molho who first published it thought that it was written in 1671–72. From a letter which was actually written in January, 1672 (see above, p. 872), we know that at that time Nathan's mood was one of ardent faith and enthusiastic expectation. The despondency characterizing the present letter seems to fit the time after Sabbatai's death. The letter is signed *zeʾeb ʿaraboth*, after Hab. 1:8.

257. MS. 2262 of the Ben-Zvi Institute contains a mystical (and more than obscure) alphabetic Hebrew poem in Aramaic which "AMIRAH said at the time of his occultation" and which is claimed to have been "copied from a MS. of the prophet of truth and righteousness R. Nathan." It is a Sabbatian imitation of a chapter in the medieval apocalypse called "The Prophecy of the Child."

the believers and the crystallization of the new doctrine. The "opponents" make use of the well-known fact of Sabbatai's death to mock and insult the believers. "Their throat is an open sepulchre" (Ps. 5:10), for with their mouth they gloatingly mention Sabbatai's sepulcher (that is, death and burial) to the discomfiture of the believers. One of the leading opponents[258] had said: "He is dead and buried. What more do you expect of him? Do you still cling to him?" Israel Ḥazzan cannot forget that terrible day when the report of Sabbatai's death arrived in Kastoria and the opponents assembled in the synagogue and mockingly quoted Hosea 10:15: "the king of Israel [is] utterly cut off." The reply to these taunts is the faith that what appears to be death is really an occultation, and that Sabbatai would return for his ultimate manifestation. Psalm 142, the prayer of David "when he was in the cave," is a prophetic anticipation of Sabbatai's occultation.[259]

The Sabbatian doctrine of occultation was not borrowed from other systems but—as happens more often in the history of religions—is the result of similar structures of faith. Elias Bickerman in his study of the ideas of occultation[260] in early Christianity and in the cult of the apotheosis of the Roman emperors, describes the hero of this process as one "who, by the grace of God, is liberated from death at the very moment of death, and is removed to Paradise, Heaven, or a distant land where he continues to live in the body."[261] The Sabbatian doctrine of occultation was formulated by Nathan to whom his celestial "messengers" (or *maggidim*), Joshua and Caleb, revealed in a state of illumination that "AMIRAH was exalted and hidden, body and soul, on the Day of Atonement, at the time of *neᶜilah.* Whoever thinks that he died like all men and his spirit returned to God commits a grave sin. This was revealed by the holy R. Nathan to R. Samuel Primo, R. Samuel Gandoor, and the group of his close friends."[262] Tobias Rofe expressed his aston-

258. Possibly R. Jacob Danon, one of the rabbis in Adrianople whom R. Solomon Katz in a letter called "the great unbeliever." At any rate Israel Ḥazzan seems to refer to a public sermon preached against the Sabbatians.

259. See the sources in *Schocken Volume,* p. 171.

260. The Hebrew terms *hithᶜallemuth, heᶜlem* correspond exactly to the ʾ*αφανισμός* of the Greek legends.

261. E. Bickermann, "Das leere Grab," *ZNW,* XXIII (1924), 285.

262. Sabbatian notebook in the library of Columbia University, New York, fol. 13a. The notebook was written by a disciple of Ḥayyim Malʾakh, who was himself a disciple of Primo.

ishment at the fact that many scholarly and eminent people were persevering in their faith in spite of Sabbatai's death, explaining that what had happened was "mere illusion, for he was still alive, though hidden from the eyes of all living."[263]

The doctrine of occultation lends itself to a more strictly kabbalistic formulation, to wit that Sabbatai had ascended to and been absorbed into the "supernal lights."[264] The legend, however, that was spread by Nathan's disciples was closer to that spirit of popular Haggadah that was present already in Nathan's letter of 1665 to the *chelebi* Raphael Joseph. According to this view, occultation means that "Our Lord has gone to our brethren, the children of Israel, the Ten Tribes that are beyond the river Sambatyon, in order to marry the daughter of Moses. If we are worthy, he will return at once after the wedding celebrations to redeem us; if not, then he will tarry there until we are visited by many tribulations."[265]

It was in this mystico-legendary world which he himself had helped to create that Nathan found refuge during his last years. During those years he lived, as did Primo, in Sofia where the heads of the Jewish community were still followers of Sabbatai. An eyewitness told the Italian Sabbatians that while preaching a sermon in memory of R. Ḥayyim Meborakh, in the Ashkenazi synagogue, he took an oath in public that "Sabbatai Ṣevi was the true messiah and that there would be no other one but he." Nathan lived a pious and ascetic life, and many of his devotional practices were recorded by his erstwhile disciples in Salonika.[266] Some of these are quite remarkable.

263. *Ap.* Emden, p. 46. Similarly there were many who refused to accept the fact that Solomon Molkho was burned at the stake (1532), and they believed that he was still alive.

264. Cf. G. Scholem in *Zion,* VI (1941), 181–87, on the development of this doctrine.

265. Baruch of Arezzo, *ap.* Freimann, p. 68. A rabbi from Greece is also said there to have seen "Our Lord," who informed him "that he was departing that week for Tartary which is the correct route to the river Sambatyon."

266. At least three versions of these have been preserved: one, printed by Freimann (pp. 93–94) with many errors and corruptions from an Italian MS.; the other two in MSS. Günzburg 517 and 672 in Moscow (microfilms in the Institute for Hebrew MSS. at the National and University Library, Jerusalem) fols. 17–20. The latter is a Sephardic MS. originating probably in Salonika or the Balkans. The same MS. (fol. 19a) also tells that when Nathan said his morning prayer a wonderful scent came from his room. Once, when the scent was particularly strong, R. Isaac Ḥanan's brother went up, but was over-

Nathan changed the text of the famous hymn, sung on the eve of Sabbath, in several places in order to give them a more actual messianic ring. He gave great weight to the fourth meal after Sabbath's end and called it "the meal of the king messiah." But most important was his pronouncement that "a man who busies himself with matters pertaining to AMIRAH, *even by telling stories only,* is considered like one who studies the mysteries of the *merkabah.*" This extravagant statement was later taken over by the Hasidim and applied to the telling of tales about the *ṣaddiqim,* their own saints.[267] It has been generally assumed that this was one of the daring innovations introduced by the Hasidim, whereas in fact it was nothing but a restatement of Nathan's saying. In 1679 he was still in Sofia, but in the late summer or autumn of that year he could no longer stay there. Perhaps he also felt that his end was near. A letter addressed to Mordecai Eisenstadt (possibly by Abraham Rovigo) in February, 1680, reports that the prophet Nathan "had left Sofia for Salonika. Before his departure he had preached a sermon and exhorted the community to repent, saying that Sabbatai Ṣevi was surely alive and that he [Nathan] was going to meet him since he [Sabbatai] was now returning from beyond the river Sambatyon. He thus departed from Sofia to Turkey, and the people in Sofia are making great penitence."[268]

The writer of this letter was not aware that at the moment of writing Nathan was no longer alive. He had died on Friday, January 11, 1680, in Üsküb in Macedonia (better known as Skoplje). For many generations the legend was current in the community that

---

powered by the heavenly odor and fainted. Nathan explained to him that the souls from Paradise congregated in his room when he said his morning prayer, but normally wore their celestial garments. On this particular occasion they had come without their garments and hence the odor which they exuded was so powerful.

267. Cf. G. Scholem in *JJS,* XX (1969), 51.

268. The letter (Brit. Mus. Or. 9165, fol. 97b) is not signed, but it seems a reasonable assumption that it was written by Rovigo and copied by one of the members of his circle. The extant copy is written in an Ashkenazi hand and was made by an Ashkenazi Jew, Berl Perlhefter, who, at the time, was an active Sabbatian. See also the reference to these reports in Baruch of Arezzo, *ap.* Freimann, p. 69, and especially, Is. Tishby, *Zion,* XXII (1957), 46. In Rovigo's circle, "revelations" were received after Sabbatai's death that, after all, S. Ṣevi was only the Messiah ben Joseph, and not the true Davidic one.

Nathan had arrived from Kumanovo on a Friday and immediately repaired to the rabbi's house.[269] There he requested that the grave-diggers be immediately sent to prepare his grave, since he was about to die and wished to be buried before the Sabbath. He also predicted that his servant, who was to arrive on Sunday, would die on the same day. "While he was still in the rabbi's house he fell down and died, and the members of the congregation buried him with great honor. Also his servant arrived and died on the appointed day, and he was buried next to Nathan's tomb."[270] A more detailed account of Nathan's departure from Sofia and his death is contained in the longer version of the Sabbatian notes of Benjamin Kohen and Abraham Rovigo.[271] The compiler notes toward the end of 1693 that a visitor from Belgrade had told him "that as a young man he had studied the Talmud with R. Nathan, and that he [Nathan] had been living in his [the informant's] native city, Sofia, for about thirteen years." This confirms that in 1679 Nathan was still in Sofia. The visitor then reports a last ecstatic experience of the prophet. "One night he had a supernatural convulsion and was lying as in a faint when the prophecy came to him. As soon as he had recovered the rabbis came to ask of him what he had to tell." Nathan told them that he had

269. From Abraham Rovigo's notebook we know that the rabbis of Üsküb, Jacob Abulafia and Isaac Yaḥya, were followers of Nathan and possessed copies of his writings; cf. Is. Sonne, "Visitors at the House of R. Abraham Rovigo," *Sefunoth,* V (1961), 295.

270. Rosanes, IV, p. 444. The short story "The Passing Away of R. Nathan" by Ezra Ha-Menaḥem, a native of Skoplje (*Molad*, IV [1950], 103–16), is based on this legend. According to Rosanes it was customary until the beginning of the 20th century to make a pilgrimage to Nathan's tomb on the anniversary of his death, and to celebrate the occasion by reciting the Zohar and holding a banquet. The Dönmeh sect would send representatives to this annual celebration. The legend of the death of the servant is a later addition; its origin has been traced by S. Asaf in *Zion,* I (1936), 455–56. The earlier version of the story was that R. Sabbatai Ventura of Sofia had shown disrespect at Nathan's tomb, whereupon his hand dried up and remained paralyzed until he returned again to the tomb and prayed for forgiveness. When his son Abraham Ventura passed through the city on his travels on behalf of the community of Safed, "a drop fell on him during his first night there and he died: . . . and was buried next to the tomb of R. Nathan." (The story is told by R. Ḥayyim Palache of Smyrna in *Kol ha-Ḥayyim* [Smyrna, 1874], pp. 17–18.)

271. This version is entitled *The Mystery of the Faith of Our Lord*, MS. Günzburg 517 in Moscow. It was compiled by Ḥayyim Segré.

seen a mighty pillar in Heaven, which meant bloodshed and killing. He prophesied that the sultan would wage a great war against the emperor, but would be defeated. At the end of days, however, (which meant "within three or four years") the Turk would wax exceedingly mighty because Samael, the Prince of Evil, would help him, but at the same time also the messiah would manifest himself.[272] The sequel suggests that the prophecy must have occurred shortly before Nathan's departure and death, for "in the same year that the pillar appeared, the Holy Rabbi commanded the people of Sofia to institute vigils every night, except on the Sabbath, . . . for the reading of psalms, Mishnah, and the Zohar. On the last night the meeting took place in the house of the wealthiest Jew in Sofia, and the rabbi [Nathan] asked them to provide for the dowry of a poor girl, saying that this was the last time that he was bothering them as very soon he would enter bitterness. Nobody understood what he meant by this bitterness, but he departed on the same day for Üsküb and immediately on arriving there he fell ill and died." This account gives some indications of the historic background of the legends concerning Nathan's death which subsequently grew in Üsküb.

The tombstone on Nathan's grave was destroyed during the Second World War, but the inscription has been reproduced by Rosanes.[273] It reads: "The house appointed for all living [Job 3:23]. The tombstone for the rest of the divine[ly inspired] rabbi, a watcher and a holy one from heaven [Dan. 4:13]. The Holy Lamp—I have not enlarged on his praises, for unto him silence is praise [cf. Ps. 65:2]—the master and rabbi Abraham Benjamin Nathan Ashkenazi, may his soul rest in Paradise, who was called to the Celestial Academy on Friday, the Eleventh of Shebat in the year 'The punishment of thine iniquity is accomplished [the numerical value of Hebrew, *tam* ("is accomplished") is 440 = 1680], O daughter of Zion' [Lam. 4:22]."[274]

272. This motif underlies the pseudo-Nathan description of the eschatological war compiled during the first years of the Dönmeh sect between 1690 and 1695; cf. *Sefunoth,* IX (1965), 193–207.

273. *Loc. cit.* The photograph of the epitaph at the end of the volume is based on a drawing made in 1917–18 for Rosanes by friends. The text of the inscription proves that Baruch of Arezzo (*ap.* Freimann, p. 69) was not far wrong when he wrote that Nathan died "a year or two" after Sabbatai.

274. Jacob Frank told his pupils in Poland that he, too, had visited Nathan's tomb (sometime during 1752–55) and quoted to them the last line of the epitaph:

"The punishment of thine iniquity is accomplished, O daughter of Zion." These words indeed sum up the message of the tempestuous lives of Sabbatai Ṣevi, the "messiah of the God of Jacob," and Nathan of Gaza, his prophet. They had meant to open the gates of redemption, and succeeded in arousing the whole House of Israel. Yet they did not, and indeed could not, find the way from vision to realization. The furrow which they plowed in the heart of their people was deep, and the seed of their message germinated, albeit in a different manner and in very different circumstances from those envisaged by them, in subsequent phases of Jewish history. The crisis precipitated by the movement which they initiated may well be regarded as one of the decisive turning-points in Jewish history.

There is a sense in which legend expresses more truth than an accurate enumeration of facts, and the legends surrounding a great man often tell us more about him than historical research ever can. The historical truth concerning Sabbatai Ṣevi became obscured even in his lifetime and while his name was still on everybody's lips. Much of this historical truth remains obscure, in spite of our efforts to listen to the testimony of documents, to decipher the stammering symbol-language of the believers, and to penetrate behind the vituperations of the opponents. For the mass of believers as well as for many "infidels," the legend, as it was woven from the time of Sabbatai's first manifestation in Gaza to the years after his death, was the only accessible reality. The legend constituted the power that moved the believers and that cast bewilderment upon the simple people who could not understand the mystery of the tragic debacle. The Sabbatian legend is the historical form in which the person of Sabbatai Ṣevi affected later generations. Although it may have revealed little of the "historical" Sabbatai, it revealed a great deal about the yearnings of a people. A longing for redemption through the mystical power of holiness, combined with a nightmarish awareness of demonic force, invested this legend with a sense of mystery and tragedy, present even in the versions

---

tam ᶜavonekh, bath Zion. But he must have read the month mentioned in the preceding line as Tebeth (roughly equivalent to December), since he said also that Nathan had died in 1679; cf. MS. of Frank's sayings *słowa panskich* (in Polish) in the University Library of Cracow, §39. Frank stated correctly that the tomb was in Skoplje (Üsküb), which was erroneously understood by Graetz as meaning Sofia, thus misleading later writers.

of the non-Sabbatians trying to recount the story of the great messianic revival that shook a whole people.

The Sabbatian legend has come down to us in three "classical" versions. In the two accounts of the believers Abraham Cuenque of Hebron and Baruch of Arezzo, we see Sabbatai in full-blown legendary grandeur only a few years after his death. By its sheer inherent power this legend not only presents the figure of the messiah, but also expresses the yearnings of his followers and the struggles of their faith. With Leyb b. Ozer, the notary of Amsterdam, writing some thirty or forty years after Sabbatai's death, the legend consummates its triumph. For Leyb b. Ozer meant to compose a historical *Beshreybung fun Shabsai Tsevi,* but in fact merely reproduced the current stories. In the telling, the supposedly historical facts crystallized into legend—and a lively, popular legend to boot. And even as the legend is told by a nonbelieving chronicler, some rays of "faith" are shimmering on it. No doubt this faith had been humiliated and discredited. Its hope had been vain and its claims refuted, and yet the question compounded of pride and sadness persisted: Was it not a great opportunity missed, rather than a big lie? A victory of the hostile powers rather than the collapse of a vain thing? The two versions of the legend, that of the two ardent believers and that of the unbelieving Leyb b. Ozer, have much in common, their divergent evaluations of the events notwithstanding. The legend of the great actor and impostor, and the legend of the elect whose mission ended in failure, together form the legend of Sabbatai Ṣevi as it lives in the memory of the Jewish people.

Fantastic engraving of Sabbatai Ṣevi bringing back the Jews to Israel. The heading "Sch[a]lo Sabot[t]oi" seems to mean Schalo[m] Sabbatai (1687, place unknown)

BIBLIOGRAPHY

BIBLIOGRAPHY

A. SOURCES IN HEBREW

I Sources Lost or Suppressed

1 Joseph ha-Levi, preacher in Leghorn, composed in 1667 a book on the Sabbatian movement. The book was in the hands of the poet Emanuel Frances; see *Ṣevi Muddaḥ*, p. 135.

2 Solomon b. Leyb Katz, rabbinic judge in Ofen (Buda), composed in 1671 a biography of Sabbatai Ṣevi on the basis of information he had gathered from Sabbatai's brother Elijah Ṣevi; so Freimann, p. 65.

3 Ya'ir Ḥayyim Bacharach made a collection of documents relating to the Sabbatian movement (1666). Only the table of contents of his collection has been preserved; it is given in A. H. Weiss, *Beth ha-Midrash* (1865), p. 92.

4 Joseph Sambari, "Account of the Events Connected with Sabbatai Ṣevi" (part of his historical work *Dibrey Yosef*, written in 1676; the pages have been removed from the two extant MSS. of the work).

5 "The Book of Revelations Granted to Sabbatai Ṣevi in Adrianople in 1668." The book was still in the hands of the Dönmeh sect in Salonika as late as 1915, but was probably destroyed in the great fire of 1917.

6 A list of documents that were mentioned by Sasportas in his *Ṣiṣath Nobel Ṣevi,* but which were not fully quoted by him in his book and are for the most part lost, is given by Tishby in his edition of Sasportas (see below, No. 10), pp. 375–77.

7 Abraham Yakhini, "A Book of Songs in Praise of Sabbatai Ṣevi," was still extant in Salonika in 1750 and was used by R. Abraham Miranda in MS. Ben-Zvi Institute 2262.

II Extant Sources

8 MS. Epstein, formerly in the library of the Jewish Community in Vienna (Catalogue A. Z. Schwarz, no. 141: "Collection of Documents on the Sabbatian Movement, Brought from Italy in 1887"). The bulk of the MS. is still extant; until 1967 it was preserved in the Jewish Historical Institute in Warsaw.

9 Collection of tracts, letters, and documents from the archives of the Dönmeh sect in Salonika, formerly in the possession of Rabbi Saul Amarillo at the beginning of World War II. Amarillo obtained the MS. from members of the Dönmeh sect at the time of the population exchange between Greece and Turkey. His late son, Abraham Albert Amarillo, presented the whole collection of several MSS. to the Ben-Zvi Institute, Jerusalem. Cited as Amarillo Collection, or Dönmeh Archives.

10 Jacob Sasportas, *Ṣiṣath Nobel Ṣevi,* complete text, based on the MS. copy made by the late Dr. A. Z. Schwarz. Edited, with an introduction, notes, and variant readings by Is. Tishby. Jerusalem, 1954.

Until the publication of the complete text, Sasportas' work was known only from an abbreviated version, *Qiṣṣur Ṣiṣath Nobel Ṣevi:* Amsterdam, 1737; Altona, 1757; Odessa, 1867. This version was prepared by Raphael Meldola, at the request of Sasportas' son, and is about half of the complete text. The first edition was suppressed by the elders of the Sephardic (Portuguese) congregation in Amsterdam as they felt that its contents did not reflect too favorably on the congregation. The book contains mainly Sasportas' correspondence with some of his contemporaries. Sasportas' own letters are given in a "doctored" and tendentiously edited form, but an autograph has survived in which Sasportas kept the draft, or copies, of his original letters.

11 Baruch b. Gershon of Arezzo, *Zikkaron li-Beney Yisrael* ("A Memorial Unto the Children of Israel" and "The Story of Joseph Ben Ṣur"). Printed in A. Freimann, *Inyeney Shabbetai Ṣevi* (1913), pp. 40–78.

12 Leyb b. Ozer, *Beshraybung fun Shabsai Zvi*, author's autograph (in Yiddish) in the possession of the President of Israel, Mr. Zalman Shazar (formerly in the possession of E. Carmoly and D. Kahana). An abbreviated Hebrew version (with many departures from the original) was printed by Jacob Emden in *Torath ha-Qenaʾoth*, pp. 2–26.

13 Abraham Cuenque (or Conque) of Hebron's "Memoir on Sabbatai Ṣevi" (written in Frankfurt in 1690) was printed by Emden, *Torath ha-Qenaʾoth*, pp. 33–45.

14 Jacob Emden (known as Yaʿbeṣ), *Zoth Torath ha-Qenaʾoth* (1st edn. Altona, 1752; 2nd edn. Lvov, 1870). Contains four different accounts of Sabbatai Ṣevi: (*a*) an abbreviated Hebrew version of Leyb b. Ozer's *Beshraybung;* (*b*) a Hebrew rewrite of Coenen's Dutch account, with additions from an unknown source; (*c*) Abraham Cuenque's memoir with critical notes by Moses Ḥagiz; (*d*) Tobias Kohen's account of Sabbatai Ṣevi from his book *Maʿaseh Tovyah* (Venice, 1707). In addition to these Emden also printed the pamphlet *Zikkaron li-Beney Yisraʾel*, originally published by the rabbis of Venice in 1668, against Nathan of Gaza (pp. 47–51), and a "Testimony" (copied from a broadsheet the original of which is no longer extant) in which R. Moses b. Ḥabib of Salonika (about 1700) reports traditions concerning Sabbatai Ṣevi and his followers. Cited as Emden.

15 Jacob and Emanuel Frances, *Ṣevi Muddaḥ* (satirical poems about Sabbatai Ṣevi and Nathan, written in 1666–67 and followed by Emanuel Frances, "The Story of Sabbatai Ṣevi"), published by M. Mortara in *Qobeṣ ʿal Yad* (1885) pp. 101–36. A new critical and more complete edition appeared in *The Poems of Jacob Frances*, edited by Penina Naveh (Jerusalem, 1969), pp. 440–512.

16 Writings concerning Sabbatianism: (*a*) "Haggadah for the Ninth of Ab" (two versions) by Jacob and Emanuel Frances: (*b*) Miscellaneous Letters concerning the Sabbatian Movement (found at the end of the MS. of *Ṣevi Muddaḥ*). Edited

by A. M. Haberman, *Qobeṣ ʿal Yad*, III, New Series (1940), 185–215. Cited as Haberman.

17 "The History of Sabbatai Ṣevi," edited from an ancient MS. by R. Naḥum Brüll. Vilna, 1879. (Extracts from *ʾEleh Toledoth Pareṣ* by Solomon Joseph b. Nathan Carpi, rabbi in Mantua in the first half of the 18th century; contains various documents from the years 1666–67.) Cited as Carpi.

18 *Gey Ḥizzayon*, a Sabbatian apocalypse from Yemen, written in late summer or autumn, 1666. Edited, from two MSS., by G. Scholem, in *Qobeṣ ʿal Yad*, IV, New Series (1946), 103–41.

19 *BeʿIqvoth Mashiaḥ*, a collection of texts from the beginnings of the Sabbatian faith, selected from the writings of R. Abraham Benjamin Nathan b. Elisha Ḥayyim Ashkenazi, known as Nathan of Gaza, and edited from MSS. by G. Scholem. Jerusalem, 1944.

20 Abraham Miguel Cardozo, "The Epistle *Magen Abraham*," edited by G. Scholem, in *Qobeṣ ʿal Yad*, II, New Series (1937), 121–56.

21 Tobias Rofe ha-Kohen, *Maʿaseh Tovyah*. Venice, 1707. (Section *ʿOlam ʿElyon*, ch. 6.) Reprinted by Emden in *Torath ha-Qenaʾoth*, pp. 45–47.

22 Jacob Tausk, *Ein schoen neu Lied fun Moschiach*, Yiddish, in Hebrew letters (Amsterdam, 1666), 24 pp. The poem was published also in German transliteration in Breslau in 1670 and again in 1693 (in Lauban) and in 1733; cf. A. Yaʿari in *Kiryath Sepher*, X (1933–34), 374–76, and D. Weinreb, *ibid.*, XI (1934–35), 131.

23 "*Raza di-Mehemnutha* ("The Mystery of the Faith") by AMIRAH." Printed (anonymously) under the title *Mehemnutha de-khola* in Nehemiah Ḥayyon, *ʿOz lʾElohim*. Berlin, 1713. The tract was not written by Sabbatai Ṣevi himself but at his behest and possibly dictation, by one of his disciples.

24 Nathan of Gaza, "Epistle on Sabbatai Ṣevi and His Apostasy," edited by G. Scholem, in *Qobeṣ ʿal Yad*, VI, New Series, second part (1966), 419–56.

III Editions of Nathan of Gaza's Orders of Penitential Prayers and Devotions, Published in 1666

25 *Sefer Tiqqun ha-Laylah* (nocturnal devotions) "brought from the Holy Land [in Hebrew, 'the Land of Ṣevi'], to be said after

midnight for the benefit of our souls. . . ." Constantinople 5426 (1666) printed at the press of the late R. Abraham b. Solomon Franco by Judah b. Joseph Obadiah. 47 leaves; very small format.

26 *Sefer Seder Tiqqun ha-Yom* "arranged to be said daily, brought from the Holy Land [in Hebrew 'the Land of Ṣevi'] as composed by the light of Israel. . . . Nathan . . . to behold the beauty of the Lord speedily in our days, Amen." Constantinople, "in the year 'and the kingdom shall be the Lord's [= 5426].' Printed at the press of the late R. Abraham b. Solomon Franco." 56 leaves; small format.

27 *Tiqqun liqro᾽ bekhol laylah va-laylah ubekhol yom va-yom*" as it has come to us from the Land of Israel . . . at the press . . . and at the behest of Joseph Athias, Amsterdam." 72 leaves; 8°. Title page has picture of high priest.

28 *Tiqqun liqro᾽ bekhol laylah va-laylah ubekhol yom va-yom*, . . . Amsterdam, "at the press . . . and the behest of Joseph Athias, in the year 'I shall SAVE [= 5426] my people.'" 82 leaves. Frontispiece with copperplate engraving [Israel at Mount Sinai] [with Spanish translation:] *Orden de lo que seá dezir cada dia y noche. Segun vino de Jerusalaim que seá redificada en Nuestra Dias.* 144 pp. (pp. 3–44 *noche*, 45–97 *die*, 97–144 *Perakim*). Colophon: "en casa Joseph Athias en Amsterdam 5426."

29 *Tiqqun* . . . .[as above, No. 28, but after fol. 82 four—and in some copies six—leaves have been added, with the superscription: "Behold, this has just been received from Safed . . . . and we have found that in two or three details it diverges from the printed *tiqqun*"].

30 *Tiqqun Qeri᾽ah lekhol yom* . . . . "in the year 'Behold I shall SAVE [= 5426] my people,' Amsterdam, at the press and behest of David de Castro Tartaz." 59 leaves; 8°. [This edition appeared in January or February, 1666, and is mentioned by Serrarius in a letter written at the end of February. The text of the title page is framed by two columns. The printer's name appears at the bottom in a shield. Above the word *Tiqqun* there is another shield and in it the words "Thou shalt meditate therein day and night." The book contains the devotions for both day and night, and appeared together with a Spanish translation *Orden de lo que se deve leer cada dia y noche.* 5426 (1666). 164 pp.]

31 *Tiqqun Qeri'ah lekhol laylah va-yom* . . . . "printed at the behest of . . . Joshua Sarphati at the press of David de Castro Tartaz. . . . Amsterdam. . . . in the year 'Behold I shall SAVE [= 5426] my people.'" 54 + 32 leaves. [The *selihoth* printed and bound with several copies of this edition are for penitential period beginning with the month of Ellul.]

32 *Tiqqun Qeri'ah lekhol laylah va-yom* . . . . "at the press and behest of Isaac de David Castro Tartaz. Amsterdam, in the year 'Behold I shall SAVE [= 5426] my people.'" 96 leaves. Title page without embellishments and framed with scriptural verses. Frontispiece showing Sabbatai Ṣevi seated on a throne. The changes and additions in the text prove that the edition was printed after No. 31 and—like it—was intended for the penitential period beginning with the month of Ellul.

33 *Tiqqun Qeri'ah leyom va-laylah.* Amsterdam, "at the press of Uri Feyvush b. Aaron ha-Levi. In the year of the SAVIOUR [*Moshi'a* = 5426], the first year." 106 leaves, with illustrated title page, showing King David on his throne and his court facing him. In addition a frontispiece, Sabbatai Ṣevi sitting on a throne. [This edition is very similar to No. 32. Leaves 97–106 contain confessions of sin and prayers for fast days. The picture of Sabbatai Ṣevi is identical with that in No. 32. Of all the editions published in 1666 this is the most lavishly produced. The title pages of Nos. 28, 32, and 33 are reproduced by A. M. Haberman, *Title Pages of Hebrew Books* (Safed, 1969), pp. 54–56.]

34 *Ticun de la noche; y de el dia ordenado para la saluacion por el S. H. R. Natan Squenazi.* [Amsterdam], l'ano 5426. 265 pp. [printed in large letters and in a larger size than any of the other editions].

35 *Tiqqun Qeri'ah lekhol yom* . . . . "in the year 'and the kingdom shall be the Lord's.'" [Frankfurt/Main, 1666] 39 + 12 leaves; large letters.

36 *Tiqqun Qeri'ah lekhol yom* . . . [as above, No. 35, Frankfurt/Main.] 60 + 18 leaves; small letters.

37 "In the name of the Lord, *Tiqqun Qeri'ah lekhol yom* . . . [Prague] 'Behold I send an Angel before thee, to keep thee in the way, and to bring thee into the place which I have prepared.'" [The initial letters of the words of this verse (Exod.

23:20) are marked and add up to the numerical value 426 = 1666. The title page is similar to that of No. 32. The letter type leaves no doubt that the edition was printed in Prague.]

38 *Tiqqun ha-Middoth* "which is the order and *tiqqun* which the remnant of Israel are accustomed to say after midnight and after midday. [published by] R. Moses b. Zion Borghe, Mantua." [Dated second month of Adar 5426]1666]. 51 leaves.

39 *Tiqqun ha-Middoth* [as above, No. 38], Mantua 427. The second printing was finished on 15 Kislev 5427 [December 12, 1666].

B. NON-HEBREW SOURCES

40 Abudiente, Mosseh Gidhon. *Fin de los Dias* publica ser llegado el fin de los Dias pronosticado por todos los Prophetas y explica muchos passos obscuros de la Sacra Biblia, Compuesto En la lengua Sancta y Redusido ala espanola. . . . Dirigido ala muy noble Yeshibha Shahare Zeddek, en 10 de Menachem, anno 5426 en Gluckstadt. [1666.] 126 pp. 8°.

41 Alfano, Carlo. *Il Sabbathai ovvero il finto Messia degli Ebrei*, che nell'anno 1666 dichiarò Maomettano in Constantinopoli. Viterbo, 1667 (?). 12°.

42 Becherand, Jacob. Relazione curiosissima ed insieme verissima del strano successo del preteso Messia degli Ebrei, il quale cagianò tanta commozione in quella Nazione e terminò poi con farsi Turco. Lettera mandata di Constantinopoli a Roma intorno al nuovo Messia degli Ebrei, dal Padre Beccaranda, Gesuita. (No date, 1667), in Venezia ed in Parma, Gozzi. 4 pp. 4°. [Written October 21, 1666. Other editions and translations are anonymous; see below, Nos. 59, 86, 92–94, 138, 180.]

43 Buchenroeder, Michael. *Eilende Messias Juden-Post,* Oder Gründliche Widerlegung des Gedichts von den [!] neuerstandenen Messia der Juden, und seines Propheten Nathans: Wie auch von andern dergleichen sich mehrmahls entbörenden Jüdischen Rebellen. Nürnberg, 1666 [26 unnumbered pages].8°.

44 Coenen, Thomas. *Ydele verwachtinge der Joden* getoont in den Persoon van Sabethai Zevi, haren laetsten vermeynden Messias, ofte historisch verhaal van't gene ten tyde syner opwer-

pinge in 't Ottomannisch Ryck onder de Joden aldaer voorgevallen is, en syn val. Amsterdam, 1669. 140 pp. 8°.

45 De la Croix, Chevalier. *Memoire . . . contenant diverses Relations très curieuses de l'Empire Ottoman.* Vol. II, pp. 259–398: Lettre V. Historie de Sabathai Sevi. Paris, 1684. [Written in 1679.]

46 Essenius, Andreas. *Heilsaem Bericht en Trost aen de Joden,* bysonderlyk aen die gene, welke in deze Vereen. Nederlanden zyn, ter occasie vorn den onlangs vermeinden Messias. Utrecht, 1667. 118 pp. 8°.

47 Evelyn, John. *The History of the three late famous impostors* viz. Padro Ottomane, Mahomed Bei and Sabatai Sevi . . . the supposed Messiah of the Jews. In the *Savoy* (London), 1669. 111 pp. 8° [pp. 41–111: Sabatai Sevi].

48 ———. *Historia de Tribus hujus seculi famosis Impostoribus,* Dass ist Beschreybung der dreyen unlängst beruffenen Betriegere, nehmlich des Padre Ottomanno . . . und Sabatai Sevi, welcher sich für den Messiam der Jüden fälschlich ausgegeben. [Hamburg] 1669. 100 pp. 8° [pp. 35–90: Die Historie von Sabatai Sevi].

49 Galland, Antoine, *Journal d'Antoine Galland pendant son séjour à Constantinople* (1672–1673), publié et annoté par Charles Schefer. 2 vols. Paris, 1881.

50 Hazard, Cornelius. *Kerekelycke Historie van de Sheheele Werelt.* Antwerpen, 1671. Vol. 4, pp. 237–56. [Chs. 19–20: History of Sabatai Sevi. Compiled from Nos. 56 and 59.]

51 [Hottinger, Johann Heinrich.] *Send-Brief* in welchem kurz und begriffentlich enthalten.

I. Das alles was von dem newen Propheten Nathan Levi, und dem auffgeworffenen Koenig der Juden die Zeithero spargiert worden, ungegründet seye.

II. Gleichwol die Juden anlas haben, bey solcher der sachen beschaffenheit, ihrer selbs zu gewahren, und aus ihren eigenen Schriften sich underrichten zulassen. [Zurich?] 1666. 12 fols. 4°.

52 Meyer, Martin. *Continuatio xv Diarii Europaei . . .* oder Täglicher Geschichte Erzehlung Sechzehnder Theil. Frankfurt/Main, 1668. Pp. 508–20.

53 Rephun, Johann. *Jüdischer Heer-Zug,* das ist Einfältige Jüden-

Predigt darinnen gehandelt wird ob die zehen Stämme Israelis das gelobte Land wieder können besitzen und behaupten, denen schwachen Christen zur Stärckung ihres Glaubens am Ascher-Mittwoch (1666). Culmbach, 1666. 16 pp. 8°. [Printed in Bayreuth.]

54 de Rocoles, Jean Baptiste. *Les Imposteurs Insignes,* ou Histoire de plusieurs Hommes de Néant qui ont usurpé la qualité des Empereurs Rois et Princes. Amsterdam, Abraham Wolfgang, 1682 [reprinted: Brussels, 1728]. [A German translation of No. 54 was published anonymously as:]

55 [de Rocoles, J. B.] *Der Erzbetrüger Sabbatai Sevi,* der letzte falsche Messias der Juden. unter Leopold I Regierung. Im Jahre der Welt 5666 [!] und dem 1666sten nach Christi Geburt. Halle, Chr. P. Franken, 1760. 32 pp. 8°.

56 Rycaut, Sir Paul. *The History of the Turkish Empire from 1623–1677.* London, 1680. 2°. [Pp. 200–19: History of Sabatai Sevi.] [Reprinted anonymously as:]

57 ———. *The counterfeit Messiah,* or, False Christ of the Jews at Smyrna, in the Year 1666, written by an English Person of Quality there Resident. In: *Two Journeys to Jerusalem* . . . collected by R. B. [Robert Boulter]. London, 1695. Pp. 125–66.

58 ———. *Die Geschichte von dem großen Betrieger oder Falschen Juden Könige Sabbatai-Sevi von Smyrna,* der sich anno 1666 für einen König der Juden in der Türckey aufgeworffen, nach dem aber den Mahometischen Glauben angenommen und im 1676sten Jahre . . . als ein Türck gestorben. No place (printed in Coethen), 1702, 18 pp. 2°. [Printed as a special supplement to the volume *Anabaptisticum et Enthusiasticum Pantheon,* 1702. German translation from Rycaut, with illustrations.]

ANONYMA

59 *Relation de la veritable Imposture du faux Messie des Juifs.* Nommé Sabbatay Sevi Juif natif de Smyrne, maintenant nommé Achis [=Aziz] Mehemet Aga Turc Portier du Serrail du Grand Seigneur. Escrite de Constantinople le vingt-deuxiesme Nouembre 1666 par un Religieux digne de Foy Fidelle tesmoin de ce qu'il escrit, et envoyée à un de ses amis à Marseille. Avignon, Chez Michel Chastel, 1667. 51 pp. 8°.

60 *A New Letter from Aberdeen in Scotland,* Sent to a Person of Quality, wherein is a more full Account of the Proceedings of the Jewes than has been hitherto published by R. B. [Robert Boulter]. London, printed by A. Maxwell, in the year 1665. 4 pp. 8°.

61 *The Last Letters to the London Merchants and Faithful Ministers* concerning the further Proceedings of the Conversion and Restauration of the Jews. C. Cotton, 1665. 6 pp. 4°.

62 *The Restauration of the Jews:* Or, A true Relation of Their Progress and Proceedings in order to the regaining of their Ancient Kingdom. Being the Substance of several Letters . . . published by R. R., London, printed by A. Maxwell, in the year 1665. 6 pp. 8°. [Reprinted by M. Wilenski in *Zion,* XVII (1952), 160–64; Dutch translation in a broadsheet, see below, No. 85.]

63 *A Brief Relation of several Remarkable Passages of the Jewes,* in their journey out of Persia and Tartaria towards Jerusalem . . . as it was delivered in a Letter written by Dom. Marschalck Lira from Vienna, to the Elector Palatine, very lately sent into England by a worthy man to his good friends in London. No place. Printed in the second Month and hoped for Year of Israels Restoration 1666. 8 pp. 8°.

64 *Gods Love to his people Israel,* Being a true copy of a letter as it was sent to the East-India-Company; Concerning the Jewes: with a more perfect account of them, their Prophet, and the Miracles he has wrought than hath hitherto been Extant. London, Printed by A. Maxwell, in the year 1666. 6 pp. 8°. [Reprinted by M. Wilenski in *Zion,* XVII (1952), 169–72.]

65 *Several New Letters concerning the Jewes:* sent to divers Persons of Quality Here in England: Being A perfect relation of the Miracles wrought by their Prophet, the Magnificence of their King, with the manner of his Entertainment in the Court of the Grand Signior. London, Printed by A. Maxwell for Robert Boulter . . . 1666. 8 pp. 8°.

66 *A New Letter Concerning the Jewes,* written by the French Ambassador, at Constantinople, To his Brother the French Resident at Venice. Being a true Relation of the Proceedings of the Israelites, the wonderful Miracles wrought by their Prophet, with the terrible Judgments that have fallen upon the Turks.

London, Printed by A. Maxwell for Robert Boulter, at the Turks-Head in Cornhil, 1666. 6 pp. 8°.

67 *The Congregating of the Dispersed JEWS,* Certified and Related by Caravans, and Letters, from Morocco, Salea, Sus, Amsterdam and London. Wherein may be observed their reverence to the Sabboth or seventh day . . . their taking of Mekah in their March towards Jerusalem, their Weapons, with many other things worthy of Note. Printed in the year 1666. [One leaf in folio; only copy known, in the collection of Mr. Hofstetter, New York.]

68 *Warhaffte Abbildung dess Newen Jüdischen Propheten Nathan,* So von etliche Seefahrer zu Gaza gesehen und von denen Mitgesellen einem abgezeichnet worden. Anno 1665, den 26 Juli. [First leaf followed by a second title page:] Extract Schreibens auss Sale in Barbareyen de dato 6 August 1665. 10 pp. 4°.

69 *Wahre und nach dem Leben getroffene Contrafectur des jetzigen jüdischen Groß-Propheten* und gesalbten gekrönten König nach Gestalt alter Habit und Auffzug eigentlich entworffen . . . auch das aus dem Hebräischen verteutschte Jüdische Schreiben aus Jerusalem. No place [Augsburg?], 1666. [One leaf in folio, with an engraving and text.]

70 *Ausführliche Relation von dem neuentstandenen Propheten Nathan Levi* und denen zusammenrottierten Juden oder zehen Stämmen Israels etc. wie von ihnen die Stadt Mecka eingenommen und spolieret, theils durch das Kupfer theils durch den Druck. No place and date. [Augsburg? One leaf in folio.]

71 *Wahrhafftes Conterfey oder Abbildung des Jüdisch-vermeinten Wunder-Propheten Nathan Levi,* massen solches von vielen Seefahrenden bey Gaza gesehen und abgezeichnet worden. Nebens ausführlichen Bericht von Alepo, Konstantinopel, Jerusalem und Gaza, was bey etlichen Monaten her mit solchem Propheten sich begeben und zugetragen. . . . Solches wird nebens Bescheinigung des Kupfers . . . deutlich erörtert und bemeldet. No place and date. [One leaf in folio.]

72 *Verwunderlicher Anfang und schmählicher Außgang.* Des unlängst Neuentstandenen Juden Propheten Nathan Levi und des von Ihme creirten und Neuerwehlten Königs oder Jüdischen Messiae Sabezae, folgends aber Joßvahel Cam genaant, welcher die 10. Stämme Israel Auß gantz Europa wider samlen, die

Türcken aussrotten und seinem Volck das Gelobte Land wider außtheilen sollen. . . . Massen solches von Constantinopel, Livorna, Jerusalem, Alepa unterschiedlich avisiret, ferner aber sub dato 2. Marti von Amsterdam auß confirmiret und behaubt worden, massen der Leser solches . . . durch Bescheinigung des Kupfers zu ersehen hat. No place and date. [Augsburg, 1666. One leaf in folio.]

73 [The same engraving and text as No. 72, with some differences in spelling, until Messiae Sabezae; then: erstlich gedruckt zu Augspurg 1666]. No place and date. 3 pp. 8°.

74 *Neubelebter König oder Printz der Jüden.* Das ist, Etwas Neues von dem erhöheten Josvehel Cam, wie selbiger nacher Constantinopel kommen, daselbst anfangs gefangen gesetzt aber endlich wider von dem Gross-Türcken erlediget und zu hohen Ehren erhaben worden, solches durch gewisse Hand aus Constantinopel den 7. Martii Anno 1666. . . . Confirmiret wird. [Engraving and text, one leaf in folio.] No place and date. [Augsburg, 1666.]

75 *Dess vermeinten Jüdischen Messiae entdeckter Betrug und Abfall.* Wie solches aus Constantinopel von glaubwürdiger Hand unter dem dato des 10. und 20. Novemb. Anno 1666, nacher Wien. [Engraving and text, one leaf in folio.] No place and date. [Augsburg, end of 1666 or beginning of 1667.]

[The engraving was incorrectly placed and covers the last line of the caption. It seems, according to the uniformity of the set-up and the decorative ledge surrounding the leaf, that Nos. 70, 71, 72, 74, and 75 form one set of broadsheets published successively in Augsburg as an illustrated chronicle of the events and legends until Sabbatai Ṣevi's apostasy. Possibly to the same set belongs also:]

76 *Wunder über Wunder.* Neue Relation von dem neu entstandenen der Juden vermeinten Messiam Josvaehel Cams, und deß Propheten Nathan Levi und denen zusammem rottirenden Juden von den zehen Stammen Israelis, was sich erst kurtzer Zeit höchst wunderliches zu Jerusalem und Constantinopel hat zugetragen, so theils durch das Kupffer, theils durch den Druck dem geliebten Leser zu Vernehmen gegeben. No place and date. [One leaf in folio, partly corresponding to No. 71; the engravings in symmetric correspondence.]

77 *Wahrhafftige Abildung* [!] *Josuae Helcams,* welchen der Juden neu entstandener Prophet Nathan Levi zum Obristen General über die so genandte 10 Stämme Israeli's erwehlet dessen Conterfey die Seefahrenden von Gaza auf Constantinopel und ferners an andre örter Versendet haben. No place and date [1665–66; one leaf in folio.]

[This is the caption in the print preserved in the Zentralbibliothek, Zurich. In another copy or edition of the print, preserved in Marburg, the leader is called "Des neuen Jüdischen Volcks Oberster Heerführer Nahmens Helkam."]

78 *Jüdische neue Zeitung vom Marsch aus Wien und anderen Orten der jetzigen zwölff Jüdischen Stämmen* . . . Au wey Getzel, Au wey Mauschy, O lader, O lader, der Toderns und das Abrahämge seynd für grossem Leyd auffs Bounym gefallen, welche nun, weil sie aus der Christenheit sollen verbannisiret werden, zu dem Nathan ziehen wollen. No place and date [1666; one leaf, engraving, and two pseudo-Yiddish dirges of the Jews.]

79 *Warhafftiges und recht nach dem Leben gemachtes Contrafait* dess Neuen Jüdischen Propheten welches von einem aus dessen Compagnia Mahlers dieses Contrafait eines Juden zu Alepo nach diesen nach Amsterdam und folgend in Teutschlãd Geschickt worden auf Welchen das Geschlecht der Juden lang gehoffet . . . Natus SCHALO SABOTTOJ 5547. [One leaf, engraving in folio.]

[Reproduced in Alfred Rubens, *A Jewish Iconography* (London, 1954), No. 22, facing p. 112. Possibly a later replica of an older engraving where the text of the caption was not yet corrupt. The year 5547, corresponding to 1787, seems to be equally corrupt. The scene on the prophet's left depicts contemporary letters from Aleppo telling how Sabbatai subdued a gang of robbers.]

80 *Neue Zeitung aus Livorno, den 27. Febr. 1666.* Der Juden vermeynten Messiam betreffend. No place, 1666. 4 pp. 4°.

81 *Leben und Thaten des berufenen Verführers und falschen Messias Sabathai Sevi oder Schabsasvi.* Bey Gelegenheit der Streitigkeiten, so seit einiger Zeit sich unter den Juden hervorgethan haben, aus dem Französischen übersezet, und mit Anmerkungen begleitet von R. R. Frankfurt und Leipzig, 1752. 54 pp. 8°. [Based on No 54.]

82 *Israelita revertens armatus verusne an fictus?* Kurtzer doch gründlicher Bericht von den zehen Stämmen Israel . . . ob sie das israelitische Reich wiederanrichten können. No place, 1666. 20 leaves. 4°.

83 *Seltzamber und Unvermeinter wiewol Umständiger und für Gewiss eingelangter Bericht,* was es mit deme schier Vergessenen nunmehr wider offenbahrn entstandenen Jüdischen König Sabatai Sebi Jetzt und vor eine Beschaffenheit habe. Aus Amsterdam vom 5. August 1666. No place and date [1666; with picture of Nathan.]

84 *Hollandtze Merkurius,* 1666 [printed 1667–68], pp. 2–4, 72–73, 134–35; 1667, p. 33.

85 *Herstelling van de Joden,* ofte Een oprecht verhael van hun voortganck en handeling, omtrent de ordre van hun out Koninckrijk wederom te verkrijgen. Zijnde de inhoudt van verscheydene Brieven, als van Antwerpen, Livorno, Florence. Uyt het Engelsch vertaelt door L. van Bos, op den 17 December 1665. Dordrecht, 1665, Symon Onder de Linde. [One leaf in folio.]

86 *Een seer perfecte Beschryvinge Van 't Leven en Bedrijf, mitsgaders het Turckx [sic] worden, van den gepretendeerden Joodsen Messias.* Overgesonden van een geleert Persoon uyt Galata, in Turckyen. Tot Haarlem, Ghedruckt by Abraham Casteleyn, Stadts Drucker, op do Marckt, in de Blye Druck, 1667. 24 pp. 4°. [A translation of part of the French pamphlet, listed above, No. 59.]

87 *Idolum Judaicum.* Ofte den Ioodschen Messias, zijnde een Beschrijvinge van sijne toekomste, Leven, Staet, ende Regeeringe. Beschreven door eenen ghebooren Iode. Ende nu tot nut der Nederlanders uyt 't Hooghduts, vertaelt door F. S. Amsterdam, 1666. 16 pp. 4°.

88 *Den gewaanden Joodsche Messias Sabatha Sebi ontdeckt:* dat is Een Gespreck russchen een Christen en Jooden. Amsterdam, Samuel Imbrechts, 1666. 15 pp. 8°.

89 *Historis Verhael van den nienwen gemeynden Koning der Joden.* Sabatha Sebi, als mede sijn by hebbende propheet Nathan Levi. Opgestaan in den jare 1666. No place and date, 16 pp. 8°.

90 *Verscheyden uyt-treckingen* van waerachtige Brieven den 10 Mrt.

alhier t'Amsterdam aengekomen, soo uyt Jerusalem en Smyrna, als uyt andere plaetsen, nopende dat groot werck der Wederbrenginge der Joden in haer Landt. Amsterdam, Jozua Rex, 1666. [One leaf in folio.]

91 *Kort en bondigh Verhael*, Hoe datter tot acht malen valsche Joodsche Messiassen geweest zijn. Als ooch wat wondere wercken en Tekenen sy gedaen en uytgerecht hebben, om staend te houden dat sy de rechte Messiassen waren. Gedruckt in 't Jaer der Joden Hoope. No place, 1666.

92 *Lettera mandata da Constantinopoli a Roma* intorno Al nuovo Messia de gli Ebrei. Siena & Bologna, per Giacomo Monti, 1667. 8 pp. 8°. [See No. 42. The first version of the French pamphlet listed above, No. 59. There are also two Portuguese translations, below:]

93 *Copia de huma carta que de Constantinopla se escreueo a Roma,* sobre o fingido Messias dos Iudeus. [Lisbon, 1667.] 14 pp. 4°. [Reprinted in No. 97.]

94 *Segunda Traducçam e verdadeira exposiçam de uma carta mandada de Constantinopla a Roma,* acerca do fingido Messias dos Hebreos. No place and date. [Lisbon, 1667–68]. 6 fols. 4°.

C. BOOKS AND ARTICLES ON SABBATAI ṢEVI AND THE MOVEMENT

95 Aeshcoly, Aaron Zeev. "A Flandrian Newsletter concerning the Sabbatian Movement" (Hebrew). *Dinaburg Jubilee Volume.* Jerusalem, 1949. Pp. 215–36.

96 Amarillo, Abraham. "Sabbatian Documents from the Saul Amarillo Collection" (Hebrew), *Sefunoth,* V (1961), 235–74.

97 Amzalak, Moses B. *Shabbethai Sevi, uma carta em portugues do seculo XVII em que se testemunham factos relativos a sua vida.* Lisbon, 1925. [8], 14 pp.

98 Aronstein, F. "Eine jüdische Novelle von Grimmelshausen." *Zeitschrift für die Geschichte der Juden in Deutschland,* V (1934), 236–41.

99 Asaf, Simha. "Nathan of Gaza in Kastoria" (Hebrew), *Zion,* I (1936), pp. 454–56.

100 Attias, Moshe. "Coplas di Adonenu" (Hebrew), *Sefunoth* III–IV (1960), 525–36.

101 ———. *Romancero Sefaradi.* 2nd edition, Jerusalem, 1961.

102 Attias, M.; Scholem, G.; and Ben-Zvi, I. *Songs and Hymns of the Sabbatians,* edited and translated [into Hebrew] from MS. by . . . , with notes by G. Scholem. Tel Aviv, 1948. [8], 227 pp.

103 Balaban, Majer. "Sabataizm w Polsce." *Księga Jubileuszowa ku czci professora Dr. M. Schorr.* Warsaw, 1935. Pp. 47–90.

104 Benayahu, Meir. "Sources concerning the Printing and Distribution of Hebrew Books in Italy" (Hebrew), Sinai, XXXIV (1945), 156–202.

105 ———. "Reports from Italy and Holland concerning the Beginning of the Sabbatian Movement" (Hebrew), *ʾEreṣ Yiṣraʾel,* IV (1956), 194–205.

106 ———. "Responsa on Sabbatianism in the Collection *Shebaḥ Neʿurim* by Samuel ben Ḥaviv" (Hebrew), *Sinai,* XLVI (1958–59), 33–53.

107 ———. "The 'Holy Brotherhood' of R. Judah Hasid and Their Settlement in Jerusalem" (Hebrew), *Sefunoth,* III–IV (1960), 131–82.

108 ———. "Sabbatian Liturgical Compositions and Other Documents from a Persian MS." (Hebrew), *ibid.,* pp. 7–38.

109 ———. "A Key to the Understanding of Some Documents on the Sabbatian Movement in Jerusalem" (Hebrew). *Studies in Mysticism and Religion Presented to G. G. Scholem.* Jerusalem, 1967. Pp. 35–45.

110 Ben-Zvi, Izhak. "Sabbatai Ṣevi's Burial Place and the Sabbatian Community in Albania" (Hebrew), *Zion,* XVII (1952), 75–78, 174. Reprinted with an addition in his *Studies and Documents* (Jerusalem, 1966), pp. 545–51.

111 Bernfeld, Simon. "On the History of Sabbatai Ṣevi" (Hebrew), *Qobeṣ ʿal Yad,* XV (1899), 1–11.

112 Brilling, Bernhard. "An unbekannter Dokument fun Shabsai Zwis Zeiten" (Yiddish), *YIWO Blaetter,* V (1933), 41–46.

113 Cassuto, Umberto. "Un documento inedito su Shabbethai Zevi," *Il Vessillo Israelitico,* LV (1907), 326–30.

114 Danon, Abraham. *Études Sabbatiennes.* Paris, 1910. 48 pp.

115 Darmstädter, Karl. "Sabbatai Zwi in der Dorfchronik," *Israelitisches Wochenblatt für die Schweiz,* April 5, 1957, p. 41.

116 Dercsényi, Mauricius. "De Pseudopropheta Nathan Ghazati

ignota relatio." *Ignace Goldziher Memorial Volume.* Budapest, 1948. Pp. 399–411.

117 Elmaleh, Abraham. *Sabbatai Ṣevi, His Sects and the Remnants of His Messianic Movement in Our Days* (Hebrew). Jerusalem, 1927. 38 pp.

118 Epstein, Abraham. "Une lettre d'Abraham Ha-Yakhini à Nathan Gazati," *RÉJ,* XXVI (1893), 209–19.

119 Friedländer, Israel. "Jewish Arabic Studies. Shi^citic Elements in Jewish Sectarianism," *JQR*, II, New Series (1912), 481–516.

120 Galanté, Abraham. *Nouveaux Documents sur Sabbetai Ṣevi:* Organisation et us et coutumes de ses adeptes. Istanbul, 1935. 125 pp.

121 ———. "Un document arménien inédit. Sabbetay Sevi dans la legende orientale," *L'Étoile du Levant* (Istanbul), September 10, 1948.

122 Geiger, Ludwig. "Deutsche Schriften über Sabbatai Zevi." *Zeitschrift für die Geschichte der Juden in Deutschland,* V (1892), 100–5.

Geiger, Wolfgang Jacob. *See* No. 187.

123 Goitein, S. D. "On What Day Did Sabbatai Ṣevi Die?" (Hebrew), *Tarbiz,* XXVII (1958), 104.

124 Gövsa, Ibrahim Alâettin. *Sabbatay Sevi,* Izmirli meşhur sahte Mesih hakkinda tarihî ve içtimai tetkik tecrübesi (Turkish). Istanbul, no date [1939–41]. 100 pp.

125 Graetz, Heinrich. *Geschichte der Juden.* Zehnter Band: *Von der Ansiedelung der Marranen in Holland bis zum Beginn der Mendelssohnschen Zeit.* Dritte vermehrte Auflage bearbeitet von M. Brann. Cap. 7, pp. 188–236; Noten no. 3, pp. 428–60; S. Zevi, sein Anhang und seine Lehre.

126 Haberman, A. (ed.). "Collections from Letters concerning the Sabbatian Movement" (Hebrew), *Qobeṣ ^cal Yad,* III, New Series (1940), 207–15.

127 Ha-Menaḥem, Ezra. "The Decease of R. Nathan" (Hebrew), *Molad,* IV (1949), 103–16.

128 Heydt, Uriel. "A Turkish Document concerning Sabbatai Zevi" (Hebrew), *Tarbiz,* XXV (1956), 337–39.

129 Hurwicz, Saul Israel (Ish-Hurwitz, Sh. I.). *Me[>]ayin u-le[>]ayin.* Collection of essays (Hebrew). Berlin, 1914. Pp. 259–86: "On the History of Sabbatai Ṣevi."

130 Hurwitz, Siegmund. "Sabbatai Zevi. Zur Psychologie der häretischen Kabbala," *Studien zur Analytischen Psychologie C. G. Jungs,* II (1955), 239–63.

131 Jost, Isaac Markus. *Geschichte der Israeliten . . . bis auf unsere Tage.* Achter Theil. Berlin, 1828. Pp. 100–34: "Geschichte der Sabbathäer."

132 Kahana (Kogan), David. *History of the Kabbalists, Sabbatians, and Hasidim* (Hebrew). Vol. I, Tel Aviv, 1925 [based on edition Odessa, 1913]. (8), 154 pp.

133 Kastein, Josef. *Sabbatai Zewi: der Messias von Ismir.* Berlin, 1930. 385 pp.

134 ———. *The Messiah of Ismir/Sabbatai Zevi.* Trans. by Huntley Paterson. London, 1931. (4), 346 pp.

135 Kaufmann, David. "Une pièce diplomatique Vénitienne sur Sabbatai Cevi," *RÉJ,* XXXIV (1897), 305–8.

136 Kehathi, Mosheh. "The Sabbatian Movement in the Yemen" (Hebrew), *Zion* (annual), V (1933), 77–88.

137 Kuchuk-Joannesov, Ch. "Armjanskaja letopis o evrejach v Persii XVII-go veka i o messii Sabbatae-Cevi," *Evrejskaja Starina,* X (1918), 60–86.

138 Levi, Giuseppe. "Documenti inediti su Shabbathai Zevi," *Il Vessillo Israelitico,* LIX (1911), 511–16, 588–92. (The text printed on pp. 515 ff. more or less identical with No. 92. The MS. was obviously copied from the printed pamphlet.

139 Levyne, Emmanuel. "À la decouverte d'un manuscript Sabbataiste (à la Bibliothèque de l'Alliance Israélite Universelle)," *Tsedek,* organe de l'Alliance d'Abraham, XI année). No. 78, June–July, 1965. 14 pp. 4° (mimeographed).

140 Lewis, Geoffrey L. and Roth, Cecil. "New Light on the Apostasy of Sabbatai Zevi," *JQR,* LIII (1963), 219–25.

141 Meijer, Jaap. "Sabetai Rephael in Hamburg. Korte bydrage tot de geschiedenis van de Joodse wereld na Sabetai Tswi." *Liber Amicorum Professor Dr. J. Romein.* Amsterdam, 1953. Pp. 103–8.

142 Menéndez Pidal, R. "Un viejo romance cantado por Sabbatai Cevi." *Medieval Studies in Honor of Jeremiah Denis Ford.* Cambridge, Mass., 1948. Pp. 185–90.

143 Mizrahi, Ḥayyim. "Evidence of Messianic Agitation on Corfu (1667) from a Christian Source" (Hebrew), *Sefunoth,* III–IV (1960), 537–40.

144 Molho, Michael. "Deux lettres de Nathan de Gaza," *RÉJ,* CIV (1938), 119–21.

145 Molkho, Isaac Raphael. "On Sabbatai Ṣevi and His Sect" (Hebrew), *Ha^c^olam,* Passover issue, 1947.

146 Molkho, I. R. and Amarillo, A. "Autobiographical Letters of Abraham Cardozo," *Sefunoth,* III–IV (1960), 183–241.

147 de Rie, J. *Wonderlyke Leevens—Loop van Sabatai-Zevi, Valsche Messias der Jooden.* Leyden, 1739. (20+), 122 pp.

148 Rosanes, Solomon. *History of the Jews of Turkey and the Levant, Part IV, from 1640–1730* (Hebrew). Sofia, 1933–34. Pp. 49–92, 401–91.

149 Roth, Cecil. *New Light on the Resettlement.* Vol. XI of *Transactions of the Jewish Historical Society of England.* London, 1929. Pp. 118–26: "Raphael Supino and the Readmission."

150 ———. (ed.). *Anglo-Jewish Letters.* London, 1938. Pp. 67–74.

Rubashov, Z. *See* Shazar.

151 Salomon, H. P. "Midrash, Messianism and Heresy in Two Spanish-Hebrew Hymns," *Studia Rosenthaliana,* IV (Amsterdam, 1970), 169–79.

152 Schoeps, Hans Joachim. *Jüdische Geisteswelt.* Darmstadt, 1953. Pp. 175–87.

153 Scholem, Gershom. "*Miṣvah ha-Ba^ah ba^c^averah:* Toward an Understanding of Sabbatianism" (Hebrew), *Keneseth,* II (1937), 347–92.

154 ———. "Redemption through Sin," in G. Scholem, *The Messianic Idea in Judaism* (New York, 1971), pp. 78–141. (English translation of No. 153.)

155 ———. "Sabbatai Ṣevi and Nathan of Gaza" (Hebrew), *Qobeṣ Hoṣa^ath Schocken le-Dibrey Sifruth* (1940), pp. 150–66.

156 ———. "Studies in the Sabbatian Movement" (Hebrew), *Zion,* VI (1941), 85–100

157 ———. "Barukhya, the Leader of the Sabbatians in Salonika" (Hebrew), *Zion,* VI (1941), 119–47, 181–202.

158 ———. "New Sabbatian Documents from the Book *To^c^ey Ruaḥ* (Hebrew), *Zion,* VII (1942), 172–96.

159 ———. "Notes from Italy on the Sabbatian Movement in 1666" (Hebrew), *Zion,* X (1945), 55–66.

160 ———. "Sabbatian Miscellanea" (Hebrew), *Zion,* X (1945), 140–48.

161 ———. "A Poem by Israel Najara as a Sabbatian Hymn" (Hebrew), *Ignace Goldziher Memorial Volume* (Budapest, 1948), pt. I, pp. 41–44.

162 ———. "Regarding the Attitude of the Rabbis to Sabbatianism" (Hebrew) *Zion,* XIII–XIV (1948–49), 47–62.

163 ———. "Where Did Sabbatai Ṣevi Die?" (Hebrew), *Zion,* XVII (1952), 79–83.

164 ———. "A Commentary on Some Psalms from the Circle of Sabbatai Ṣevi in Adrianople" (Hebrew), *ᶜAley ᶜAyin: Schocken Jubilee Volume* (Jerusalem, 1953), pp. 157–211.

165 ———. "A Letter of Abraham Cardozo to the Rabbis of Smyrna" (Hebrew), *Zion,* XIX (1954), 1–22.

166 ———. *Major Trends in Jewish Mysticism.* 3rd revised edition, New York, 1954. Pp. 287–324, 416–22: Eighth lecture: "Sabbatianism and Mystical Heresy."

167 ———. "And the Riddle Remains" (Hebrew; on the book *Ḥemdath Yamim*), *Beḥinoth,* no. 8 (1955), pp. 79–95, and "Exchange of Letters" with A. Yaᶜri on the above article, *Beḥinoth,* no. 9 (1956), pp. 71–84.

168 ———. "Two MS. Fragments in the Adler Collection Relating to the History of Sabbatianism" (Hebrew), *ᵓEreṣ Yisraᵓel,* IV (1956), 188–94.

169 ———. "A New Document Relating to the Beginning of the Sabbatian Movement" (Hebrew), *Kiryath Sepher,* XXXIII (1958), 532–40.

170 ———. "Documents concerning Nathan of Gaza from the Archives of R. Mahallellel Halleluyah of Ancona" (Hebrew). *H. A. Wolfson Jubilee Volume.* Jerusalem, 1965. Pp. 225–41.

171 ———. "The Crisis of Tradition in Jewish Messianism." *The Messianic Idea in Judaism.* New York, 1971. Pp. 49–77. (German in *Eranos Jahrbuch* 37 [1968], 9–44.)

172 Schönberg, Joseph. "Un mouvement mystico-messianique parmi des juifs de la méditerranée au XVI siècle au point de vue de la médicine." *Actes du VIII. Congrès International d'Histoire des Sciences.* Florence, 1956. Pp. 673–82.

173 Shatz, Rivkah. Review of Tishby's edition of Sasportas. *Ṣiṣath Nobel Ṣevi* (Hebrew), *Beḥinoth,* no. 10 (1956), pp. 50–67.

174 ———. "Visions on the Mystery of the Messiah, an Early Source from a Sabbatian Apostate" (Hebrew), *Sefunoth,* XIII (1973).

175 Shazar, Zalman (Rubashov). "The Messiah's Scribe (on Samuel Primo)" (Hebrew), *ha-Shiloah,* XXIX (1913), 36–47. Reprinted separately, Jerusalem, 1970.

176 ———. "Sabbatai Ṣevi's Servant" (Hebrew), *Tarbiz,* V (1934), pp. 350–57.

177 ———. "Sabbatian Documents from Aleppo" (Hebrew), *Zion* (annual), VI (1934), 54–58.

178 ———. "The Story of Joseph della Reyna in Sabbatian Tradition" (Hebrew). *S. A. Horodezky Jubilee Volume, Eder ha-Yakar.* Tel Aviv, 1947. Pp. 97–118.

179 da Silva Rosa, J. S. "De Indruk van Sabbatai Tsebi, den valschen Messias, te Amsterdam (1666)," *De Vrijdagavond,* Proefnummer, January 11, 1924, pp. 5–6.

180 Simonsohn, Shlomo. "A Christian Report from Constantinople Regarding Shabbethai Sevi (1666)," *JJS,* XII (1961), 33–58.

181 Sonne, Isaiah. "On the History of Sabbatianism in Italy" (Hebrew). *Alexander Marx Jubilee Volume.* New York, 1953. Pp. 89–103.

182 ———. "New Material on Sabbatai Ṣevi from a Notebook of R. Abraham Rovigo," *Sefunoth,* III–IV (1960), 39–69.

183 ———. "Visitors at the House of R. Abraham Rovigo," *Sefunoth,* V (1961), 277–95.

184 Szabolcsi, N. "Témoignages contemporains Français sur Shabbatai Zevi." *Semitic Studies in Memory of Immanuel Löw,* Budapest, 1947. Pp. 184–88.

185 Tadir, Ch. "Messia-otstupnik." In the Russian anthology *Safrut,* edited by L. Jaffe. Berlin, 1922. Pp. 179–92.

186 Talpis, Samuel. *Geklibene Schriften* (Yiddish). Montreal, 1933–35 (?). Pp. 264–81: "Letter from a Turkish Spy: Original Documents Throwing Light on the Sabbatian Movement 1666–1687." (The author mistook Marari's *Letters Writ by a Turkish Spy* [1659–89, vol. VI]—a novel intended solely for the entertainment of its readers—for a historic source and used it as such.)

187 *Theatrum Europaeum.* Zehender Theil. Das ist: Glaubwürdige Beschreibung denckwürdiger Geschichten . . . von 1655 bis in

anno 1671. Alles zusammengetragen und beschrieben von Wolfgang Jacob Geiger. Frankfurt/Main, 1703. Pp. 434–41.

188 Tishby, Isaiah. Review of G. Scholem, *Be^cIqvoth Mashiaḥ* (Hebrew), *Kiryath Sepher*, XXI (1944), 12–17.

189 ———. *Nethivey Emunah u-Minuth* ("Paths of Faith and Heresy; Essays and Studies in Kabbalistic and Sabbatian Literature"). Jerusalem, 1964. 363 pp. (Ten of the twelve studies collected here deal with the Sabbatian movement.)

190 ———. "R. Meir Rofe's Letters of 1675–1680 to R. Abraham Rovigo" (Hebrew), *Sefunoth* III–IV (1960), 71–130.

191 Trivus, S. A. "Massovie psichosi v yevreiskoi istorii—sabbatianstvo" (Russian), *Voschod* (1900), no. 7, pp. 79–101.

192 Vajda, Georges. "Autour de mouvement Sabbataiste," *RÉJ*, VII, New Series (1947), 38–52.

193 ———. "Recherches récentes sur l'ésotérisme juif." II, 7: "Le sabbataisme," *Révue de l'histoire des religions*, CLXV (1964), 48–70.

194 Vulliaud, Paul. "La Legende Messianique de Sabbetai Zébi," *Mercure de France* (47 année), CCLXXI (October 15, 1936), 275–300.

195 Weinreich, M. *Bilder fun der Jiddischer Literaturgeschichte* (Yiddish). Vilna, 1928. Pp. 219–52: "A Jiddisch Lied wegen Shabsai Zvi."

196 Weiss, Eisik Hirsch. *Beth ha-Midrash*. Vienna, 1865. Pp. 63–71, 100–3, 139–42. (A tract by Cardozo, edited by N. Bruell.)

197 Wilensky, Mordecai. "Four English Pamphlets on the Sabbatian Movement," *Zion*, XVII (1952), 157–72.

198 Wirszubski, Ch. "The Sabbatian Ideology Regarding the Messiah's Apostasy, according to Nathan of Gaza and the Epistle *Magen Abraham*" (Hebrew), *Zion*, III (1938), 215–45.

199 ———. "On Spiritual Love. From the Writings of Nathan of Gaza" (Hebrew), *Qobeṣ Hoṣaʾath Schocken le-Dibrey Sifruth* (1940), pp. 180–92.

200 ———. "The Sabbatian Theology of Nathan of Gaza" (Hebrew), *Keneseth* VIII (1944), 210–44.

201 Ya^cari, Abraham. *Emissaries from ʾEreṣ Yisraʾel* (Hebrew). Jerusalem, 1950.

202 ———. *Ta^calumath Sefer:* Who wrote the book *Ḥemdath Yamim?* (Hebrew). Jerusalem, 1954.

203 Zenner, Walter: "The case of the apostate Messiah, a Reconsideration of the 'Failure of Prophecy,'" *Archives de Sociologie des Religions,* XXI (1966), 111–18.

D. OTHER WORKS REFERRED TO

204 Baer, Yitzhak. "The Historical Background of the *Raᶜya Mehemna*" (Hebrew), *Zion,* V (1940), 1–44.
205 ———. *A History of the Jews in Christian Spain,* vol. I. Philadelphia, 1961.
206 Bainton, Roland. *David Joris.* Leipzig, 1937.
207 Benz, Ernst. *Ecclesia Spiritualis.* Stuttgart, 1934.
208 Bietenhard, Hans. *Das tausendjährige Reich.* Bern, 1944.
209 Birge, John K. *The Bektashi Order of Dervishes.* London, 1937.
210 Bloch, Ernst. *Thomas Münzer als Theologe der Revolution.* Berlin, 1921.
211 Bokser, Ben Zion. *From the World of the Cabbalah:* The Philosophy of R. Judah Loew of Prague. New York, 1954.
212 Cassel, Paulus. *Die Offenbarung S. Johannis und das Tier.* Wiesbaden, 1889.
213 Cohn, Norman. *The Pursuit of the Millennium.* London, 1957.
214 Dan, Josef. "The Story of R. Joseph de la Reyna," *Sefunoth,* VI (1962), 313–26.
215 Davies, William B. *The Torah in the Messianic Age.* Philadelphia, 1952.
216 Even-Shemuel (Kaufmann), Jehudah. *Midreshey Geᶜullah:* Jewish Apocalyptic Texts from the End of the Talmudic Period to the Thirteenth Century (Hebrew). 2nd edition, Jerusalem, 1954.
217 Fogelklou, Emilia. *James Nayler, the Rebel Saint.* London, 1931.
218 Froom, L. E. *The Prophetic Faith of Our Fathers.* 4 vols. Washington, 1950–54.
219 Galanté, Abraham. *Encore un nouveau recueil de documents concernant l'histoire des Juifs de Turquie.* Istanbul, 1953.
220 Huck, Johannes. *Joachim von Floris und die joachitische Literatur.* Freiburg i B., 1938.
221 Jones, Rufus M. *Studies in Mystical Religion.* London, 1909.
222 Knox, Ronald. *Enthusiasm.* Oxford, 1950.

223 Mann, Jakob. "Messianic Movements at the Time of the First Crusade" (Hebrew), *ha-Tequfah,* XXIII (1925), 243–61; XXIV (1928), 335–58.

224 Marx, Alexander. "Le faux messie Ascher Laemmlein," *RÉJ,* LXI (1911), 135–38.

225 Nigg, Walter. *Das ewige Reich.* Zurich, 1944.

226 Schechter, Solomon. "Safed in the 16th Century," *Studies in Judaism,* 2nd Series (1908), pp. 202–328.

227 Schoeps, H. J. *Philosemitismus im Barock.* Tübingen, 1952.

228 Scholem, G. "The Kabbalist R. Abraham b. Eliezer ha-Levi" (Hebrew), *Kiryath Sepher,* II (1925), 101–41, 269–73; VII (1931), 149–65, 440–56.

229 ———. "The Story of R. Joseph della Reyna" (Hebrew), *Zion* (annual), V (1933), 123–30.

230 ———. "The Declaration of Solidarity of Luria's Disciples" (Hebrew), *Zion* (quarterly), V (1939–40), 133–60.

231 ———. "Was Israel Sarug a Disciple of Luria?" (Hebrew), *Zion* (quarterly), V (1939–40), 214–43.

232 ———. "Homily on Redemption by R. Solomon Turiel" (Hebrew), *Sefunoth,* I (1956), 62–79.

233 ———. "Schechina: das passiv-weibliche Moment in der Gottheit." *Von der mystischen Gestalt der Gottheit.* Zurich, 1962. Pp. 135–91, 290–96.

234 ———. "Seelenwanderung und Sympathie der Seelen." *Von der mystischen Gestalt der Gottheit.* Zurich, 1962. Pp. 193–247, 297–306.

235 ———. "Tradition and New Creation in the Ritual of the Kabbalists." *On the Kabbalah and Its Symbolism.* New York, 1965. Pp. 118–57.

236 ———. "Toward an Understanding of the Messianic Idea in Judaism." *The Messianic Idea in Judaism and Other Essays.* New York, 1971. Pp. 1–36.

237 Tamar, David. "The Messianic Expectations for 1575 in Italy" (Hebrew), *Sefunoth,* II (1958), 61–88.

238 Tishby, Isaiah. *The Doctrine of Evil and the "Qelippah" in Lurianic Kabbalah* (Hebrew). Jerusalem, 1942.

239 Werblowsky, R. J. Zwi. *Joseph Karo, Lawyer and Mystic.* Oxford, 1962.

INDEX

INDEX

In subentries, N = Nathan of Gaza and SS = Sabbatai Ṣevi. R. = Rabbi.